038637

THE OXFORD HANDBOOK OF

MILTON

THE OXFORD HANDBOOK OF

MILTON

Edited by

NICHOLAS McDOWELL

and

NIGEL SMITH

OXFORD
UNIVERSITY PRESS

OXFORD

UNIVERSITY PRESS

Great Clarendon Street, Oxford OX2 6DP

Oxford University Press is a department of the University of Oxford.
It furthers the University's objective of excellence in research, scholarship,
and education by publishing worldwide in

Oxford New York

Auckland Cape Town Dar es Salaam Hong Kong Karachi
Kuala Lumpur Madrid Melbourne Mexico City Nairobi
New Delhi Shanghai Taipei Toronto

With offices in

Argentina Austria Brazil Chile Czech Republic France Greece
Guatemala Hungary Italy Japan Poland Portugal Singapore
South Korea Switzerland Thailand Turkey Ukraine Vietnam

Oxford is a registered trade mark of Oxford University Press
in the UK and in certain other countries

Published in the United States
by Oxford University Press Inc., New York

© Oxford University Press 2009

The moral rights of the authors have been asserted
Database right Oxford University Press (maker)

First published 2009

All rights reserved. No part of this publication may be reproduced,
stored in a retrieval system, or transmitted, in any form or by any means,
without the prior permission in writing of Oxford University Press,
or as expressly permitted by law, or under terms agreed with the appropriate
reprographics rights organization. Enquiries concerning reproduction
outside the scope of the above should be sent to the Rights Department,
Oxford University Press, at the address above

You must not circulate this book in any other binding or cover
and you must impose the same condition on any acquirer

British Library Cataloguing in Publication Data

Data available

Library of Congress Cataloging in Publication Data
Library of Congress Control Number: 2009935889

Typeset by SPI Publisher Services, Pondicherry, India
Printed in Great Britain
on acid-free paper by
CPI Antony Rowe, Chippenham, Wiltshire

ISBN 978–0–19–921088–6

1 3 5 7 9 10 8 6 4 2

PREFACE

....

9 December 2008 saw the 400th anniversary of John Milton's birth. It also saw the publication of the first instalment of Oxford's *Complete Works of John Milton*—the 1671 Poems, edited by Laura Lunger Knoppers. A further ten volumes will appear over the next few years. The Oxford *Works* will be the first complete works since the Columbia edition of the 1930s. While the project is still very much ongoing, the editors of these volumes are already excavating new contexts for Milton's life and work and proposing new interpretations of both the poetry and prose. As well as throwing fresh light on all aspects of Milton's writing, the Oxford *Works* will have to take account of the huge increase in Milton scholarship over the last fifty years. The rise of critical interest in Milton's political and religious prose is perhaps the most striking aspect of Milton studies in recent times, a consequence in great part of the increasingly fluid relations between literary and historical disciplines. The Oxford *Works* looks set both to embody the interest in Milton's political and religious contexts in the last generation and to inaugurate a new phase in Milton studies through closer integration of the poetry and prose, in particular some of the prose that has been neglected due to the relative rarity, inaccessibility, and age of edited texts.

The *Oxford Handbook of Milton* similarly seeks to incorporate developments in what can broadly be termed historical criticism over the last twenty years and to place both the poetry and the prose in a more continuous, unfolding biographical and historical context. Consequently this volume is unusual in the amount of space it gives to discussions of the prose while still aiming to offer wide-ranging, diverse interpretations of the poetry, open to the full range of Milton's aesthetic accomplishment in verse. It is divided into eight sections—three on the poetry, three on the prose, arranged in broadly chronological sequence, while the opening essays explore what we know about Milton's biography and what it tells us, and the concluding essays offer perspectives on Milton's massive influence on eighteenth-century and Romantic writers. Several of the volume editors of the *Works* have also contributed essays to the *Handbook,* and they have been encouraged to elaborate on their current research in ways that may not be suitable to the formal strictures of an edition. Topics which are currently attracting the most interest in Milton scholarship are thus to the fore in the essays collected here: liberty, encompassing republicanism, national identity, and gender relations; theology, encompassing heresy, toleration, and biblical interpretation; and the history of the book, encompassing issues of editing, publishing, and readership.

But while the space given to discussion of the prose in what follows tends to necessitate engagement with historical context, the contributors, who are based in seven countries and range from veteran Miltonists to relatively new names, were invited with the intention of capturing something of the diversity of critical approaches to the Miltonic canon. Some of the essays on the poetry display the unparalleled virtues of close reading, of exhaustive attention to minute matters of language, form, and rhythm. Yet the rewards of close reading need not be derived only from the verse: essays here illuminate the literary power and intricacy of the prose, in Latin as well as English. Few, however, would deny that the reason why Milton still matters four hundred years on is above all *Paradise Lost*, and that fact is registered in the eight essays devoted to the epic here. *Samson Agonistes* has become the most controversial of Milton's works in the light of world events in the last decade and so is given more room in this *Handbook* than it has found in earlier, less capacious collections.

Of course even thirty-eight essays cannot do justice to the variety and richness of Milton's life, mind, and art. If all thirty-eight essays had been devoted to *Paradise Lost*, we could still not hope to claim anything like 'comprehensive' coverage of the poem; and while we have essays on topics stretching from the Latin verse to the Commonplace Book to the use of *Paradise Lost* in eighteenth-century gardening manuals, we would like to have found space for greater consideration of, say, Milton's Italian verse, or of the influence of the polemical prose on leading figures of the American and French Revolutions. While we hope that readers find much in the essays below with which they can consent, some will probably discover an approach with which they disagree. It will quickly become evident that the contributors disagree among themselves about how we should read and regard Milton. But that is the point of offering, for instance, four different critical perspectives on *Samson Agonistes*. The *Handbook* has been assembled in the spirit of the Miltonic vision of heretical reading in *Areopagitica*: 'perfection consists in this, that out of many moderate varieties and brotherly dissimilitudes that are not vastly disproportional arises the goodly and graceful symmetry that commends the whole pile and structure'.

Chapter 4 first appeared in *Metaphrastes. Or Gained in Translation: Essays and Translations in Honour of Robert H. Jordan* (Belfast Byzantine Texts and Translations, 9; Belfast, 2004); we are grateful to the publisher for permission to reproduce it here. Chapter 26 appeared in *Review of English Studies*, 59 (2008); we are grateful to the editors for permission to reproduce this article.

The editors are indebted to Andrew McNeillie for commissioning us to edit this collection and more generally for his commitment to publishing on Milton, and to Jacqueline Baker for her patience and support during the lengthy process of compiling such a large book. Nicholas McDowell would also especially like to thank the Leverhulme Trust for the award of a 2007 Philip Leverhulme Prize, which granted precious time to work on the volume.

N. McD. and N. S.

December 2008

CONTENTS

List of Illustrations   xi
Note on the Text and List of Abbreviations   xii
Notes on Contributors   xiii
Milton's Life: Some Significant Dates   xviii

PART I: LIVES

1. 'Ere half my days': Milton's Life, 1608–1640   3
   EDWARD JONES

2. John Milton: The Later Life (1641–1674)   26
   NICHOLAS VON MALTZAHN

PART II: SHORTER POEMS

3. The 'adorning of my native tongue': Latin Poetry and Linguistic
   Metamorphosis   51
   ESTELLE HAAN

4. Milton's Early English Poems: The Nativity Ode, 'L'Allegro',
   'Il Penseroso'   66
   GORDON TESKEY

5. 'A thousand fantasies': The Lady and the *Maske*   89
   ANN BAYNES COIRO

6. 'Lycidas' and the Influence of Anxiety   112
   NICHOLAS MCDOWELL

7. The Troubled, Quiet Endings of Milton's English Sonnets   136
   JOHN LEONARD

PART III: CIVIL WAR PROSE, 1641–1645

8. The Anti-Episcopal Tracts: Republican Puritanism and the
   Truth in Poetry   155
   NIGEL SMITH

9. 'A Law in this matter to himself': Contextualizing Milton's
   Divorce Tracts   174
   SHARON ACHINSTEIN

10. Whose Liberty? The Rhetoric of Milton's Divorce Tracts   186
    DIANE PURKISS

11. Milton, *Areopagitica*, and the Parliamentary Cause   200
    ANN HUGHES

12. *Areopagitica* and Liberty   218
    BLAIR HOXBY

PART IV: REGICIDE, REPUBLICAN, AND RESTORATION PROSE, 1649–1673

13. 'The strangest piece of reason': Milton's *Tenure of Kings and Magistrates*   241
    STEPHEN M. FALLON

14. Milton's Regicide Tracts and the Uses of Shakespeare   252
    NICHOLAS McDOWELL

15. John Milton, European: The Rhetoric of Milton's Defences   272
    JOAD RAYMOND

16. *Defensio Prima* and the Latin Poets   291
    ESTELLE HAAN

17. 'Nothing nobler then a free Commonwealth': Milton's Later
    Vernacular Republican Tracts   305
    N. H. KEEBLE

18. Disestablishment, Toleration, the New Testament Nation: Milton's
    Late Religious Tracts   325
    ELIZABETH SAUER

19. Milton and National Identity   342
    PAUL STEVENS

PART V: WRITINGS ON EDUCATION, HISTORY, THEOLOGY

20. The Genres of Milton's Commonplace Book   367
    WILLIAM POOLE

21. Milton, the Hartlib Circle, and the Education of the Aristocracy   382
    TIMOTHY RAYLOR

22. Conquest and Slavery in Milton's *History of Britain*   407
    MARTIN DZELZAINIS

23. *De Doctrina Christiana*: An England that Might Have Been   424
    GORDON CAMPBELL and THOMAS N. CORNS

PART VI: *PARADISE LOST*

24. Writing Epic: *Paradise Lost*   439
    CHARLES MARTINDALE

25. 'A mind of most exceptional energy': Verse Rhythm in *Paradise Lost*   462
    JOHN CREASER

26. Editing Milton: The Case against Modernization   480
    STEPHEN B. DOBRANSKI

27. The 'World' of *Paradise Lost*   496
    KAREN L. EDWARDS

28. *Paradise Lost* and Heresy   510
    NIGEL SMITH

29. God   525
    STUART CURRAN

30. Eve, *Paradise Lost*, and Female Interpretation   534
    SUSAN WISEMAN

31. The Politics of *Paradise Lost*   547
    MARTIN DZELZAINIS

PART VII: 1671 POEMS: *PARADISE REGAINED* AND *SAMSON AGONISTES*

32. 'Englands Case': Contexts of the 1671 Poems   571
    LAURA LUNGER KNOPPERS

33. *Paradise Regained* and the Memory of *Paradise Lost*   589
    JOHN ROGERS

34. *Samson Agonistes* and 'Single Rebellion'   613
    R. W. SERJEANTSON

35. *Samson Agonistes*: The Force of Justice and the Violence of Idolatry   632
    REGINA M. SCHWARTZ

36. *Samson Agonistes* and Milton's Sensible Ethics   649
    ELIZABETH D. HARVEY

PART VIII: ASPECTS OF INFLUENCE

37. Milton Epic and Bucolic: Empire and Readings of
    Paradise Lost, 1667–1837   669
    ANNE-JULIA ZWIERLEIN

38. Miltonic Romanticism   687
    JOSEPH WITTREICH

Index   705

LIST OF ILLUSTRATIONS

1. Early reader's index for *Paradise Regain'd* (1671). Courtesy of the
   Rare Book and Manuscript Library of the University of Illinois at
   Urbana-Champaign   573

2. Early reader's index for *Samson Agonistes* (1671). Courtesy of the
   Rare Book and Manuscript Library of the University of Illinois at
   Urbana-Champaign   574

Note on the Text and List of Abbreviations

The place of publication is London unless otherwise stated. All biblical references are to the Authorized Version (AV) unless otherwise stated. All references to Milton's poetry are to *Complete Shorter Poems*, ed. John Carey, 2nd edn. (Harlow, 1997) (*CSP*) and *Paradise Lost*, ed. Alastair Fowler, 2nd edn. (Harlow, 1998) (*FPL*), unless otherwise stated. All references to Milton's vernacular prose are to the *Complete Prose Works of John Milton*, ed. D. M. Wolfe et al., 8 vols. (New Haven, 1953–82) (*CPW*), unless otherwise stated. Milton's Latin prose is sometimes cited from *The Works of John Milton*, ed. Frank Allen Patterson et al. (New York, 1931–8) (*CW*). Full references are always given within each individual essay other than for the texts whose abbreviations are listed here.

BL	British Library
Campbell, *Chronology*	Gordon Campbell, *A Milton Chronology* (Harlow, 1997)
CPB	Commonplace Book
Darbishire	*The Early Lives of Milton*, ed. Helen Darbishire (1932)
French, *Records*	*Life Records of John Milton*, ed. J. M. French, 5 vols. (New Brunswick, N.J., 1949–58)
Lewalski, *Life*	Barbara Lewalski, *The Life of John Milton: A Critical Biography* (Oxford, 2000)
ODNB	*Oxford Dictionary of National Biography*
Parker	William R. Parker, *Milton: A Biography*, 2nd edn., rev. Gordon Campbell, 2 vols. (Oxford, 1996)
PL	*Paradise Lost*
PR	*Paradise Regained*
SA	*Samson Agonistes*

Notes on Contributors

Sharon Achinstein is Reader in Renaissance Literature, Oxford University, and a Fellow of St Edmund Hall, Oxford. She is the author of *Milton and the Revolutionary Reader* (1994) and *Literature and Dissent in Milton's England* (2003), and the co-editor of *Milton and Toleration* (Oxford University Press, 2007). She is editing the divorce tracts for Volume 5 of the Oxford *Complete Works of John Milton*.

Gordon Campbell is Professor of Renaissance Studies, University of Leicester. His publications include *A Milton Chronology* (1997), *Milton and the Manuscript of De Doctrina Christiana* (with Thomas N. Corns, John K. Hale, and Fiona Tweedie; Oxford University Press, 2007), and, with Thomas N. Corns, *John Milton: Life, Work, and Thought* (Oxford University Press, 2008). With Thomas N. Corns, he is general editor of the Oxford *Complete Works of John Milton*.

Ann Baynes Coiro is Associate Professor of English, Rutgers University. She is the author of *Robert Herrick's "Hesperides" and the Epigram Book Tradition* (1988) and is currently writing a book on Milton and drama. She won the Milton Society of America's James Holly Hanford Award for her article 'Fable and Old Song: *Samson Agonistes* and the Idea of a Poetic Career' in *Milton Studies* (1998).

Thomas N. Corns is Professor of English, University of Wales, Bangor. His books include *The Development of Milton's Prose Style* (Clarendon Press, 1982), *Milton's Language* (1990), *Regaining* Paradise Lost (1994), and, with Gordon Campbell, *John Milton: Life, Work, and Thought* (Oxford University Press, 2008). His edited work includes *A Companion to Milton* (2001). He is, with Gordon Campbell, general editor of the Oxford *Complete Works of John Milton*.

John Creaser is Emeritus Professor, Royal Holloway, University of London (where he was formerly Hildred Carlile Professor of English Literature) and Emeritus Fellow, Mansfield College, Oxford (where he was formerly English Fellow and Vice-Principal). He has edited plays by Jonson and Middleton, and written extensively on Milton, Jonson, and other seventeenth-century poets.

Stuart Curran is Vartan Gregorian Professor of English, University of Pennsylvania. He is the author of *Poetic Form and British Romanticism* (Oxford University Press, 1990) and the editor of *The Cambridge Companion to British Romanticism* (1993) and *The Poems of Charlotte Smith* (Oxford University Press, 1993). He is editing four volumes of the Johns Hopkins University Press edition of Shelley, in progress.

Stephen B. Dobranski is Associate Professor of Early Modern Literature and Textual Studies, Georgia State University. He is the author of *Milton, Authorship, and the Book Trade* (1999) and co-edited, with John Rumrich, *Milton and Heresy* (1998). Most recently, he has completed *A Variorum Commentary on the Poems of John Milton: 'Samson Agonistes'* (2009) and is editing *Milton in Context* (2009).

Martin Dzelzainis is Professor of Early Modern Literature and Thought, Royal Holloway, University of London. His publications include editions of Milton's *Political Writings* (1991) and of Marvell's *The Rehearsall Transpros'd* for Volume 1 of *The Prose Works of Andrew Marvell* (2003). He is a General Editor of the forthcoming Oxford edition of *The Works of Edward Hyde, Earl of Clarendon*, and is editing the *History of Britain* for Volume 10 of the Oxford *Complete Works of John Milton*.

Karen L. Edwards is Senior Lecturer in English, University of Exeter. She is the author of *Milton and the Natural World: Poetry and Science in 'Paradise Lost'* (1999) and *Milton's Reformed Animals: An Early Modern Bestiary* (published as a series of special issues of *Milton Quarterly*, 2005–9).

Stephen M. Fallon is Cavanaugh Professor in the Humanities, University of Notre Dame. He is the author of *Milton among the Philosophers: Poetry and Materialism in 'Paradise Lost'* (1991) and *Milton's Peculiar Grace: Self-Representation and Authority* (2007). He has edited, with William Kerrigan and John Rumrich, *The Complete Poetry and Essential Prose of John Milton* (2007).

Estelle Haan (Sheehan) is Professor of English and Neo-Latin studies, Queen's University, Belfast. She is the author of *From Academia to Amicitia: Milton's Latin Writings and the Italian Academies* (1998) and *Andrew Marvell's Latin Poetry: From Text to Context* (2003). She is editing Milton's Latin poetry for Volume 3 of the Oxford *Complete Works of John Milton*.

Elizabeth D. Harvey is Professor of English, University of Toronto. She is the author of *Ventriloquized Voices: Feminist Theory and Renaissance Texts* (1992), editor of *Soliciting Interpretation: Literary Theory and Seventeenth-Century English Poetry* (1990) and *Sensible Flesh: On Touch in Early Modern Culture* (2002), and co-editor of *Luce Irigaray and Premodern Culture* (2004).

Blair Hoxby is Associate Professor of English, Stanford University. He is the author of *Mammon's Music: Literature and Economics in the Age of Milton* (2001) and *Spectacles of the Gods: Tragedy and Tragic Opera, 1550–1780* (forthcoming). His essay 'Milton's Steps in Time' (1998) won the Monroe Kirk Spears award for the best publication in *Studies in English Literature, 1500–1900*.

Ann Hughes is Professor of Early Modern History, University of Keele. Her publications include *Gangraena and the Struggle for the English Revolution* (Oxford University Press, 2004), a study of the Presbyterian Thomas Edwards, 'shallow Edwards' in Milton's sonnet on the 'New Forcers of Conscience under the Long Parliament'. She is a co-editor of the forthcoming Oxford edition of the *Works of Gerrard Winstanley*.

Edward Jones is Associate Professor of English, Oklahoma State University. His publications include *Milton's Sonnets: An Annotated Bibliography, 1900–1992* (1994) and he has been editor of *Milton Quarterly* since 2005. He is co-editor of Volume 11 of the Oxford *Complete Works of John Milton*, for which he is editing the letters of State.

N. H. Keeble is Professor of English Studies and Senior Deputy Principal, University of Stirling. His publications include *Richard Baxter: Puritan Man of Letters* (Oxford University Press, 1982), *The Literary Culture of Nonconformity in Later Seventeenth-Century England* (1987), and *The Restoration: England in the 1660s* (1992). He is the editor of *The Cambridge Companion to Writing of the English Revolution* (2001) and is editing Milton's later vernacular republican tracts for Volume 6 of the Oxford *Complete Works of John Milton*.

Laura Lunger Knoppers is Professor of English, Pennsylvania State University. She is the author of *Historicizing Milton: Spectacle, Power, and Poetry in Restoration England* (1994) and *Constructing Cromwell: Ceremony, Portrait, and Print, 1645–1661* (2000). She is the editor of *Puritanism and its Discontents* (2003) and co-editor of *Milton in Popular Culture* (2006). She has edited *Paradise Regained* and *Samson Agonistes* for Volume 2 of the Oxford *Complete Works of John Milton* (2008).

John Leonard is Professor of English, University of Western Ontario. He is the author of *Naming in Paradise: Milton and the Language of Adam and Eve* (Oxford University Press, 1990) and has edited the Penguin editions of *Milton's Complete Poems* (1998) and *Paradise Lost* (2000). He is writing the introduction to *Paradise Lost* for the *Milton Variorum Commentary*.

Nicholas McDowell is Associate Professor of English, University of Exeter. He is the author of *The English Radical Imagination: Culture, Religion, and Revolution, 1630–1660* (Oxford University Press, 2003) and *Poetry and Allegiance in the English Civil Wars: Marvell and the Cause of Wit* (Oxford University Press, 2008). He is editing the 1649 prose for Volume 6 of the Oxford *Complete Works of John Milton*.

Charles Martindale is Professor of Latin, University of Bristol. He is the author of *John Milton and the Transformation of Ancient Epic* (1986), *Redeeming the Text: Latin Poetry and the Hermeneutics of Reception* (1993), and *Latin Poetry and the Judgement of Taste: An Essay in Aesthetics* (Oxford University Press, 2005). Among his edited work is, with A. B. Taylor, *Shakespeare and the Classics* (2004).

William Poole is Fellow and Tutor in English, New College, Oxford. He is the author of *Milton and the Idea of the Fall* (2005) and has edited Francis Lodwick's *A Description of a Country not Named* (2007). His *The World-Makers: Changing Conceptions of the Earth in the Scientific Revolution* is forthcoming and he is editing the Commonplace Book for Volume 9 of the Oxford *Complete Works of John Milton*.

Diane Purkiss is Fellow and Tutor in English, Keble College, Oxford. Her publications include *Literature, Gender and Politics during the English Civil War* (2005) and

The English Civil War: A People's History (2006), and, as co-editor with Clare Brant, *Women, Texts and Histories 1575–1760* (1992).

Timothy Raylor is Professor of English, Carleton College, Minnesota. He is the author of *Cavaliers, Clubs, and Literary Culture* (1994) and a co-editor of *Culture and Cultivation in Early Modern England* (1992) and *Samuel Hartlib and Universal Reformation* (1994). He is editing *Of Education* for Volume 9 of the Oxford *Complete Works of John Milton*.

Joad Raymond is Professor of English, University of East Anglia. He is the author of *The Invention of the Newspaper: English Newsbooks, 1641–49* (Oxford University Press, 1996), *Pamphlets and Pamphleteering in Early Modern Britain* (2003), and *Milton's Angels* (Oxford University Press, forthcoming). He is editing the 'Defences' for Volume 7 of the Oxford *Complete Works of John Milton*.

John Rogers is Professor of English, Yale University. He is the author of *The Matter of Revolution: Poetry, Science, and Politics in the Age of Milton* (1996), for which he won the Modern Language Association Prize for a First Book, and of the forthcoming *Milton's Passion*.

Elizabeth Sauer is Professor of English, Brock University. She is the author of *'Paper Contestations' and Textual Communities in England, 1640–1675* (2005) and *Barbarous Dissonance and Images of Voice in Milton's Epics* (1996). Her edited and co-edited books include *Milton and the Imperial Vision* (1999), *Milton and the Climates of Reading* (2006), and *Milton and Toleration* (Oxford University Press, 2007).

Regina M. Schwartz is Professor of English, Northwestern University. She is the author of *Remembering and Repeating: Biblical Creation in Paradise Lost* (1988), *The Curse of Cain: The Violent Legacy of Monotheism* (1997), and *Sacramentality at the Dawn of Secularism: When God Left the World* (2007). She is the editor of *The Book and the Text: The Bible and Literary Theory* (1990).

R. W. Serjeantson is a Fellow of Trinity College, Cambridge. His publications include *Generall Learning: A Seventeenth-Century Treatise on the Formation of the General Scholar, by Meric Casaubon* (Cambridge, 1999) and a range of essays in early modern intellectual history. He is currently editing Volume 3 of the *Oxford Francis Bacon* for the Clarendon Press.

Nigel Smith is Professor of English, Princeton University. He is the author of *Perfection Proclaimed: Language and Literature in English Radical Religion, 1640–1660* (Oxford University Press, 1989), *Literature and Revolution in England, 1640–1660* (1994), and *Is Milton Better than Shakespeare?* (2008), and has edited the Ranter tracts (1983), George Fox's *Journal* (1998), and the *Poems* of Andrew Marvell (2003) for the Longman Annotated English Poets series. He is volume editor of Volume 9 of the Oxford *Complete Works of John Milton*.

Paul Stevens is Professor and Canada Research Chair in English Literature at the University of Toronto. He is the author of *Imagination and the Presence of*

Shakespeare in 'Paradise Lost' (1985). His most recent publications include *Early Modern Nationalism and Milton's England* (co-edited with David Loewenstein, 2008) and *Milton in America* (co-edited special issue of *University of Toronto Quarterly*, 2008).

Gordon Teskey is Professor of English, Harvard University. He is the author of *Allegory and Violence* (1996) and *Delirious Milton: the Fate of the Poet in Modernity* (2006), and the editor of the Norton Critical Edition of *Paradise Lost* (2004).

Nicholas von Maltzahn is Professor of English, University of Ottawa. He is the author of *Milton's 'History of Britain': Republican Historiography in the English Revolution* (Oxford University Press, 1991) and *An Andrew Marvell Chronology* (2005), and editor of Andrew Marvell's *An Account of the Growth of Popery* for Volume 2 of the *Prose Works of Andrew Marvell* (2003). He is editing the tracts on church government and toleration for Volume 4 of the Oxford *Complete Works of John Milton*.

Susan Wiseman is Professsor of Seventeenth-Century Literature, Birkbeck College, University of London. She is the author of *Drama and Politics in the English Civil War* (1998) and *Conspiracy and Virtue: Women, Writing, and Politics in Seventeenth-Century England* (Oxford University Press, 2006), and a co-editor of *Women, Writing, History: 1640–1740* (1992).

Joseph Wittreich is Distinguished Professor, the Graduate School of the City University of New York. His books on Milton include *Angel of Apocalypse: Blake's Idea of Milton* (1975), *Visionary Poetics: Milton's Tradition and his Legacy* (1979), *Interpreting "Samson Agonistes"* (1986), *Feminist Milton* (1987), *Shifting Contexts: Reinterpreting "Samson Agonistes"* (2003), and *Why Milton Matters* (2006).

Anne-Julia Zwierlein is Professor of English Literary and Cultural Studies, the University of Regensburg. She is the author of *Majestick Milton: British Imperial Expansion and Transformations of Paradise Lost, 1667–1837* (2001) and co-editor of *Plotting Early Modern London: New Essays on Jacobean City Comedy* (2004).

Milton's Life: Some Significant Dates

....

1608 9 December. Born to John Milton and his wife Sara, at The Spreadeagle, Bread St., London.

1615 24 November. Brother Christopher born.

1620 Enters St Paul's School, under Alexander Gill. Also tutored at home, possibly earlier, by Thomas Young.

1625 12 February. Admitted to Christ's College, Cambridge, under William Chappell.
      27 March James VI and I dies; Charles I accedes to the English throne.

1626 Possibly rusticated temporarily. Returns to Cambridge under Nathaniel Tovey.
      ?November. Writes epigrams on Gunpowder Plot.

1627 June 11. Lends his future father-in-law, Richard Powell, £500.

1629 16 March. Takes BA.

1632 'On Shakespeare' published, anonymously.
      3 July. Takes MA.
      Retires to family home at Hammersmith to study.

1634 29 September. *A Maske* ('Comus') performed during the installation of Thomas Egerton, the Lord President of Wales, at Ludlow Castle.

1637 Moves with parents to Horton, Buckinghamshire.
      A Maske published, anonymously.
      3 April. Mother Sara dies.
      10 August. Edward King is drowned.
      September. Considers entering Inns of Court.

1638 'Lycidas' is published in the memorial volume for Edward King, *Justa Edouardo King Naufrago*.

May. Begins tour of western Europe, passing through France, then Florence, Siena, Lucca, Rome, Bologna, Ferrara, Verona, Venice, Milan, and Naples, and returning by way of Geneva.
27 August. Charles Diodati buried.

1639   Charles I invades Scotland.
July. Returns home.

1640   Moves to St Bride's Churchyard. Begins to teach nephews Edward and John Phillips, and some aristocratic children. The Long Parliament convened.
? *Epitaphium Damonis* published.
June 30. Takes Richard Powell's lands in Wheatley for nonpayment of debt.

1641   May. *Of Reformation* published.
?June. *Of Prelatical Episcopacy* published.
July. *Animadversions* published.

1642   February. *The Reason for Church Government* published.
May. *Apology against a Pamphlet* ['for Smectymnuus'] published. Marries Mary Powell.
?July. Mary Powell returns to her family home near Oxford.
August. The Civil War begins.
October. Christopher Milton enlists with Royalists at Reading.
23 October. Battle of Edgehill.

1643   1 August. *Doctrine and Discipline of Divorce* published.

1644   2 February. Second edition of *Doctrine and Discipline* published.
5 June. *Of Education* published.
2 July. Battle of Marston Moor.
6 August. *The Judgement of Martin Bucer concerning Divorce* published.
23 November. *Areopagitica* published.
28 December. Summoned before House of Lords.

1645   4 March. *Tetrachordon* and *Colasterion* published.
?September. Moves to larger house at Barbican.
6 October. *Poems of Mr. John Milton, Both English and Latin . . . 1645* registered for publication.
Makes plans to marry the daughter of a Dr Davis. Mary Powell returns.
14 June. Battle of Naseby.

1646   2 January. *Poems . . . 1645* published.
29 July. Daughter Anne born.

1647   March. Father John dies.
        21 April. Moves to a smaller house in High Holborn, near Lincoln's Inn Fields.

1648   25 October. Daughter Mary born.

1649   30 January. Execution of King Charles I.
        13 February. *The Tenure of Kings and Magistrates* published.
        March. Invited to become Secretary for the Foreign Tongues by Council of
        State.
        15 March. Appointed Secretary at £288 per year; ordered to answer *Eikon
        Basilike*.
        11 May. Salmasius's *Defensio Regia* appears.
        16 May. *Observations* upon the *Articles of Peace* published.
        6 October. *Eikonoklastes* published.
        19 November. Given lodgings for official work in Scotland Yard.

1650   Ordered by Council of State to answer Salmasius.

1651   24 February. *Defensio pro populo Anglicano* published.
        16 March. Son John born.
        Milton family moves to a house in Petty France, Westminster.

1652   February. Becomes totally blind towards the end of the month.
        2 May. Daughter Deborah born.
        5 May. Wife Mary dies, probably from complications following childbirth.
        ?16 June. Son John dies.
        August. Following several earlier attacks on the *Defensio*, including Filmer's,
        Pierre du Moulin's *Regii Sanguinis Clamor* published, in reply to Milton's
        Defensio; Milton ordered to reply by the Council of State.

1653   20 February. Writes a letter recommending that Andrew Marvell become his
        assistant.
        3 September. Salmasius dies.

1654   30 May. *Defensio Secunda* published.

1655   Allowed to use amanuensis to take dictation for him in Secretaryship. Resumes
        private scholarship, prepares Latin dictionary and Greek lexicon; possibly
        works on *De Doctrina Christiana* and *Paradise Lost*. Salary reduced from £288
        to £150, but made pension for life.
        8 August. *Defensio Pro Se* published.

1656   12 November. Marries Katherine Woodcock.

1657   19 October. Daughter Katherine born.

1658   3 February. Katherine Woodcock dies.
17 March. Daughter Katherine dies.
?May. Edits and publishes manuscript of Sir Walter Raleigh's *Cabinet Council.*
3 September. Oliver Cromwell dies.

1659   ?16 February. *A Treatise of Civil Power* published.
22 April. Richard Cromwell dissolves Parliament.
7 May. Republic restored.
August. *The Likeliest Means to Remove Hirelings out of the Church* published.
20 October. Writes *Letter to a Friend, Concerning the Ruptures of the Common-wealth* (not published until 1659).

1660   3 March. *Ready and Easy Way to Establish a Free Commonwealth* published in its first edition.
April. *Brief Notes upon a Sermon* published.
May. Goes into hiding to avoid retaliation for supporting regicide.
29 May. Accession of Charles II.
16 June. Parliament looks into the possibility of having Milton arrested.
27 August. *Defensio pro populo Anglicano* and *Eikonoklastes* publicly burned.
29 August. Not excluded from Act of Indemnity.
?September. Takes a house in Holborn, near Red Lion Fields; soon moves again to Jewin St.
?October. Arrested and imprisoned.
15 December. Released by order of Parliament. On 17 December Marvell protests in Parliament about the exorbitance of Milton's jail fees (£150).

1662   Begins tutoring Thomas Ellwood.
19 May. Act of Uniformity.
?June. Sonnet to Sir Henry Vane published. Vane executed 14 June.

1663   24 February. Marries Elizabeth Minshull. Moves from Jewin Street to 'a House in the *artillery*-walk leading to *Bunhill Fields*'. On bad terms with his daughters; new wife allegedly had the two eldest daughters apprenticed as lacemakers.

1665   Ellwood secures a house for Milton in Chalfont St Giles, Buckinghamshire, to escape from the plague in London.

1667   ?August. *Paradise Lost* published in ten books.

1668   *Paradise Lost* reissued with a new title page, the arguments, and other prelim-inary matter.

1669   June. *Accidence Commenced Grammar* published.

1670   *History of Britain* published.

1671   *Paradise Regain'd* and *Samson Agonistes* published together.

1672   ?May. *Art of Logic* published.

1673   ?May. *Of True Religion* published.
       ?November. *Poems, &c. upon Several Occasions . . . 1673* published.

1674   L'Estrange refuses licence for Milton's Letters of State.
       May. *Epistolae Familiares* and *Prolusiones* published.
       ?2 July. Second edition of *Paradise Lost* in twelve books published.
       Between 8 and 10 November. Dies in Bunhill house.

PART I

LIVES

CHAPTER 1

'ERE HALF MY DAYS': MILTON'S LIFE, 1608–1640

EDWARD JONES

THE life story of John Milton, recounted five times within thirty years of his death and over a hundred times since 1700, is remarkable both for the interest it has elicited and the relatively small amount of corroborated evidence upon which it is based.[1] That it is exceptionally well documented for its time (which it is) does not ensure the accuracy of its details, many of which rest upon the porous foundation of recollections from friends, relatives, acquaintances, and enemies. Milton's earliest biographers left to their successors the formidable tasks of verifying contemporary memory and local legends through means other than personal testimony. The pioneering effort of David Masson in the nineteenth century set a high standard. His multivolume account of Milton and his times and its attention to documentary evidence were emulated in the twentieth century by J. Milton French, who produced a fivevolume set of life records, and William Riley Parker, whose two-volume biography

---

[1] The phrase 'early biographers' traditionally refers to five 17th-c. sources: John Aubrey, *Minutes of the Life of Mr. John Milton* (*c.*1681–2), Bodleian MS Aubrey 8; Cyriack Skinner, *The Life of Mr. John Milton*, MS Wood D4, fos. 140–4; Anthony à Wood, *Athenae Oxonienses, Fasti*, 1, cols. 880–4 (1691–2); Edward Phillips, *The Life of Mr. John Milton*, in *Letters of State, Written by Mr. John Milton* (1694); and John Toland, *The Life of John Milton*, in *A Complete Collection of the Historical, Political, and Miscellaneous Works of John Milton*, 3 vols. (Amsterdam and London, 1698), but it has also been used to include 18th-c. commentaries by the Richardsons, Fenton, Johnson, and Warton. Modern biography typically dates from Masson.

includes an archival-based biographical commentary of almost 600 pages.[2] The accomplishments of these works combined with their attention to seventeenth-century sources have given Milton biography its day in the sun. Since the publication of Parker's volumes in 1968, scholars have habitually turned to his findings and/or consulted Masson and French to solve biographical puzzles that have periodically surfaced. This trend continued through the mid-1990s when Gordon Campbell's updating of Parker's research revealed the need to search more thoroughly the documentary canvas. The ultimate result of that revision, *A Milton Chronology*, not only uncovered new material and corrected previous findings, but issued an important caution—that French and Parker conducted much of their work through correspondence and thus reported some of it without looking at original documents.[3]

The ensuing account of Milton's first thirty-two years underscores the need to be aware of the current state of Milton biography by discussing material which, in some instances, has received no attention from previous commentators. At the same time, this half-life will not be entirely new, as it should not be, although it will juxtapose well-known with little-known facts outside the well-trodden biographical path in order to point to unexplored areas of inquiry. Since the evidence for Milton's early life, particularly his childhood and adolescence, will virtually be non-existent (other than christenings and burials found in parish registers and overseer accounts recording apprenticeships and indentures, records for pre-adults were not typically kept), other ways of contextualizing this period, most notably through the professional career of his father, will be central. The belief that evidence remains to be found, a sentiment shared by all who have conducted first-hand study of Milton documents, will also inform this narrative, at once indebted to previous efforts and mindful of its own vulnerability to error in offering corrections to past work. The most memorable parts of Milton's life story often lack verification other than hearsay testimony, and biographers, scrupulous and otherwise, tend to focus upon events which depict him as an individual of talent and shortcomings. The following account will not gain much advantage in this regard. None of the contexts explored in Milton's first three decades conjures up the image of a blind poet composing aloud his distinctive epic to amanuenses. Nor do they offer the chance to discuss his three marriages, a colourful first to a woman half his age who leaves him after a month, reconciles with him three years later, and eventually bears him four children; and two subsequent marriages to women he never sees. In their place unarresting but not uninteresting records from the church, the English legal system, and the state will be brought forward to

---

[2] David Masson, *The Life of John Milton: Narrated in Connexion with the Political, Ecclesiastical, and Literary History of his Time* (1859–80; repr. New York, 1946), 6 vols. plus Index (1894); rev. edn. of vol. i (1881); vol. ii (1894); French, *Records*; Parker.

[3] Campbell, *Chronology*, p. ix. For an overview of how documentary material can shape Milton's biography, see Campbell's 'The Life Records', in Thomas N. Corns (ed.), *A Companion to Milton* (Oxford, 2001), 483–98. An update of some of Campbell's findings appears in Edward Jones, 'Select Chronology: "Speak of things at hand/Useful"', in Angelica Duran (ed.), *A Concise Companion to Milton* (Oxford, 2007), 217–34.

complement, correct, or, at the very least, gauge the viability of testimonial evidence that has held sway since the seventeenth century. The ultimate focus will rest on Milton in context, directly or obliquely linked to a location, either performing a particular action or being exposed to a set of events. Sustained contextualization of this kind has arguably not been accorded a sufficient place in Milton's biographical history; if applied, biographical details long considered lost can be recovered or discovered. For the purposes of this Handbook, Milton's early life has been divided into three parts: his years prior to entering the University of Cambridge (1608–24), his seven years of formal education (1625–32), and the post-university period of 'studious retirement' (1632–40) which encompasses his years at Hammersmith and Horton, his Continental tour, and the initial eighteen months of living on his own in London.

FAMILY ENVIRONMENT AND EARLY EDUCATION (1608–1624)

The undeniable fact regarding Milton's youth is that there is no documentary evidence directly concerned with him apart from the entry in the All Hallows, Bread Street, baptism register establishing his christening on 20 December 1608. Biographers rely on Milton himself for the day and time of his birth (6.30 on the morning of 9 December 1608), information he recorded in his family Bible over three decades later.[4] Comments made to John Aubrey by Milton's widow Elizabeth Minshull and his nephew Edward Phillips do not inspire confidence. She could not remember the date of her husband's birth; he assigned it to 1606. Aubrey made a note to ask Milton's brother Christopher for verification, but it is not clear that he ever obtained it.[5] Dates Milton supplies for other members of his family have also withstood scrutiny, though in some instances (the birth dates of his two nephews) he approximates months instead of specific days. The inconsistency that marks testimony from his widow, brother, and nephew, however, speaks to how the power of contemporary recall can overshadow the void of evidence that often underlies Milton's life story. The void is sometimes considerable: aside from Milton's christening in the year of his birth only one other piece of evidence bearing his name is extant prior to his entrance into Cambridge University in 1625. The occasion—the marriage settlement between his sister Anne and Edward Phillips on 27 November 1623—provides his earliest and his mother's only extant signature.[6] Both serve as

---

[4] The surviving Bible is in the British Library (Add. MS 32310); the parish registers for All Hallows, Bread Street are in the Guildhall Library (GLMS 5031).

[5] Bodleian MS Aubrey 8.

[6] The document can be found in the Pierpont Morgan Library in New York (MS MA 953).

witnesses. In all likelihood, some records of Milton's early education at St Paul's probably were created and would have been available if not for the Great Fire of 1666. Such an absence, given Milton's reputation as one of the most learned men of his age, amounts to a considerable and frustrating loss. The speculative industry of later biographers in an effort to fill that gap, albeit often admirable, cannot compensate.[7]

The two records we do have for Milton's first fifteen years, if understood in their respective contexts, nonetheless shed considerable light on his early life. Additional entries from the All Hallows parish registers reveal a starting point from which to date and keep in view the family's Bread Street residency (an infant child was buried on 12 May 1601), the number of children from the marriage of John Milton and Sara Jeffrey (six, though their daughter Anne's existence is determined through other records), how many survive infancy (three), and the presence of Milton's maternal grandmother as a member of the family until her death in 1611.[8] The second record—Milton's signature on his sister's marriage settlement—also turns out to be more revealing than it seems at first glance. For the marriage marks the beginning of the family's expansion and furnishes additional ways for scholars to monitor the lives of its members. Anne Milton's marriage to Edward Phillips establishes the family's first presence in Westminster in the parish of St Martin-in-the-Fields. Over the next decade upwards of fifty records will be created regarding her family, some of which provide significant insight into the activities of her parents and brothers in Bread Street.[9] Only in the last few years have Milton biographers such as John Shawcross begun to consider how the orbit of the Milton extended family impacts our understanding of his life, not just his early childhood and pre-university years but its entirety.[10] Milton's signature on a contract is befitting in another way because a significant number of his extant life records survive in the English legal system, most in the equity court of Chancery. In fact, while literary scholars have expended great effort to establish dates for Milton's juvenilia, the likelihood of discovering unassailable proof of Milton writing is far less than finding the young Milton taking part (as he does with his sister's marriage contract) in a business-related affair in the interests of his family.

It was J. Milton French who paved the road to such an approach in the first half of the twentieth century, and besides Gordon Campbell, few have travelled down it.[11]

---

[7] The two most often cited efforts are those by Donald Lemen Clark, *John Milton at St. Paul's School* (New York, 1948), and Harris F. Fletcher's *The Intellectual Development of John Milton* (Urbana, Ill., 1956), 2 vols. See also ch. 1 in James Holly Hanford, *John Milton, Englishman* (New York, 1949).

[8] The parish registers of All Hallows, Bread Street were published by the Harleian Society, 43 (1913). The Milton family entries appear on pp. 17, 18, 169, 174, and 175.

[9] Housed in the City of Westminster Archives, the parish chest records for St Martin's include the baptism and burial registers, churchwarden accounts (F3), overseer accounts (F350–8), miscellaneous collections for plague assistance (F3355) and bridge repairs (F3346), and a poor rate ledger (F1011). The Phillips family appears in all of them. Records resulting from Anne Milton Phillips's second marriage to Thomas Agar appear in a few.

[10] See *The Arms of the Family: The Significance of John Milton's Relatives and Associates* (Lexington, Ky., 2004).

[11] *Milton in Chancery: New Chapters in the Lives of the Poet and his Father* (New York, 1939); Campbell, *Chronology*.

French uncovered a substantial cache of evidence regarding the environment in which Milton resided for the first sixteen years of his life. As a scrivener, John Milton senior's livelihood required extensive documentation, and it is that documentation which records his growing prosperity during the first decades of the seventeenth century. Conducting his business out of the family home, Milton senior eventually brought both of his sons into direct contact with it: Christopher will provide legal service for his father in the 1630s, while his elder brother will co-sign a document to purchase property with his father on 25 May 1627, in the same parish in which his sister resided. A little more than two weeks later, as a result of a business arrangement between his father and Richard Powell, Milton begins a seventeen-year financial relationship with his future father-in-law. There may be an element of coincidence in all of this, but it does appear that by following the Milton family money, one has an opportunity to keep the members of the family in clearer view.[12] As these contexts pertain to Milton's early biography, unexamined paths emerge: John Milton senior's professional career furnishes a steady supply of evidence which originated in the family home to which his eldest son was exposed. These records, considered with a knowledge of Milton's shrewd engagement with legal and financial affairs in his adult years, had an impact, arguably a lasting and positive one. The business dealings of the father, however, also provide a key to the family whereabouts in the 1620s; the nominal home remains at Bread Street, but property purchases suggest alternative locations for the family during the periodic outbreaks of the plague during the 1620s and 1630s. A defining element is the coordination between the financial affairs of the father and the widening family sphere. Rather than consider Anne Milton's marriage to Edward Phillips as a departure from the family home, biographers gain advantage by seeing the event as an expansion of the family's financial options. The increased links between Bread Street and Westminster keep both families in clearer view and account for later events in this early period of Milton's own life.

Prior to beginning his university studies at Cambridge, Milton's life has rarely been cast in a financial light. Standard assessments have been more concerned with establishing the future writer of *Paradise Lost* and defender of the Commonwealth in the context of the aspiring artist and child prodigy. There is no harm, of course, in following such paths, but one must grant that little uncontested evidence exists upon which to build such a case. A few matters have undoubtedly helped such a cause, and since they have rarely been overlooked in accounts of Milton's early years, they deserve notice. The first is the portrait of Milton as a 10-year-old boy discovered in the possession of his widow when John Aubrey interviewed her. While neither the circumstances for its creation nor the artist responsible has been definitively settled, the portrait provides for those so inclined an opportunity to begin the profile of Milton as a studious, sober, Protestant youth, often ambiguously labelled Puritan, a writer in formation. Aubrey's comment that Milton's 'schoolmaster was a puritan in Essex, who cut his hair short' has led to an identification of Thomas Young, a Scots

---

[12] All of these matters are conveniently listed in Campbell, *Chronology*.

clergyman, as one of Milton's early tutors, though later letters Milton writes to Young put that identification on more solid ground. There is evidence of Young's being beneficed near Ware before assuming the post of chaplain to the Merchant Adventurers in Hamburg in 1620, and thus the schoolmaster in Essex could be him.[13] The portrayal of Milton as a studious youth has been bolstered by his widow's claim to Aubrey that at ten years of age her husband 'was then a poet' and enhanced by recourse to Milton's comments in *The Reason of Church-Government* (1642) that from his first years he received instruction by 'sundry masters and teachers both at home and at the schools', and in the *Second Defence* that he was in the habit of studying till midnight 'from the age of twelve'. Extant evidence rarely noted but that coheres with such a picture includes a set of floor plans of the Milton Bread Street home created as a result of a survey taken in October 1617.[14] The living quarters of the family were ample enough to accommodate a private study area, though designations of the family living space are general rather than specific. The plans do not allow one to assign a particular room to the boy Milton with any confidence. That has not precluded colourful biographical accounts, one of the more entertaining depicting the youthful Milton loitering in front of his Bread Street chamber while Ben Jonson and Shakespeare passed by on their way to the nearby Mermaid tavern.[15]

Undoubtedly the greatest losses from the earliest period of Milton's life are his school records. Only through the Cambridge admissions register do we know he attended St Paul's School and studied under its high master Alexander Gil the elder.[16] The evidence for when he began and ended his studies is mixed and conflicted. The earliest date is 1615, but any time during the next six years is possible. Similarly, since he begins his university training in Cambridge in the early part of 1625, his attendance at St Paul's most likely concluded by the end of 1624, though it could have ceased even earlier in the year. A far greater source of frustration is the absence of any records regarding his curriculum. While scholarly reconstructions of what he was taught have attempted to be faithful to contemporary educational plans, in the end the particulars of Milton's early education remain a subject of guesswork. As for his writing from this period, there is an epigram ('Philosophus ad Regem'), a fable in imitation of Mantuan ('Apologus de Rustico et Hero'), and a prose theme on early rising. Perhaps fittingly, they all appear in a manuscript in a handwriting that does

---

[13] Few modern biographers, including Masson, fail to discuss the portrait. Its attribution to Cornelius Janssen relies upon highly questionable evidence. For an authoritative account of Milton portraiture, see Leo Miller, *Milton's Portraits: An Impartial Inquiry into their Authentication*, a special issue of *Milton Quarterly*, 10 (1976), 1–43. For a recent overview of Thomas Young, see the entry by Edward Jones in *ODNB*. For evidence of Young's connection to Essex see *The Court and Times of James I*, ed. Thomas Birch, 2 vols. (London, 1849), ii. 240–1.

[14] Eton College Library, MS Records 16. Eton College acquired the Bread Street property in 1449 from the Hospital of St James. Sir Baptist Hicks was the Miltons' landlord. See Noel Blakiston, 'Milton's Birthplace', *London Topographical Record*, 9, no. 80 (1947), 6–12.

[15] Masson's fanciful reconstruction (i. 46) is one of the more memorable.

[16] Christ's College Admissions Book, Cambridge University.

not altogether resemble that found in his supplication for his BA and his signature in the University Subscription Book, both from 1629.[17]

MILTON AND CAMBRIDGE UNIVERSITY
(1625–1632)

The minor pensioner who appears with six other undergraduates in front of the Cambridge University Registrar, James Tabor, and formally matriculates on 9 April 1625, performs his first act of conformity to the University regulations.[18] Several more will take place during the course of the next seven years that leave a trail of evidence somewhat at odds with a long-held view of Milton as an outsider, malcontent, and non-participant in university life. Indeed John Hale's recent study of Milton's Latin 'Exercises' and 'Voluntaries' in prose and verse offers an extended account of just the opposite.[19] Milton not only fulfils university requirements but takes prominent roles in some of them. Participation, of course, is not the same thing as approval or endorsement and because most assignments were degree requirements, one can retain Milton's retrospective disapproval of the Cambridge curriculum. Yet the conflict between conformity and disapproval suggests that the matter requires more deliberation than past biographers have accorded it. A way of negotiating the mixed evidence for Milton's disenchantment with his university training and at the same time his conformity to its regulations, however, is available. It entails new evidence Milton creates during his university years, records that continue to emerge from his father's professional affairs as well as others that result from his sister's marriage to Edward Phillips. Keeping three locations in view—Cambridge, Bread Street, and Westminster—allows a different accounting of Milton's university years.

To cover the most familiar ground first—evidence of Milton's presence in Cambridge—there are, in addition to the 1625 admissions and matriculations records already mentioned, but a handful of records attesting to his presence over the next several years. While there are no grounds for questioning Milton's attendance at the university, there is considerable room for exaggerating his presence given the few records that undeniably locate him there. For example, no incontrovertible records for 1626 exist, but evidence of Milton not being in Cambridge during parts of this year does. On 26 March 1627, he writes the first of his two extant letters to Thomas Young, though the date contains conflicting information from Milton himself. Similarly, there is mixed dating for Milton's letters to Alexander Gil the younger

---

[17] The manuscript is now housed in the Harry Ranson Humanities Research Center in Austin, Texas. It is designated as Pre-1700 Manuscript 127.

[18] Cambridge University Matriculation Book, unnumbered pages.

[19] *Milton's Cambridge Latin: Performing in the Genres, 1625–1632* (Tempe, Ariz., 2005).

from Cambridge (20 May 1628 or 20 May 1630 for one and either 2 July 1628 or 2 July 1631 for a second),[20] and the most recent commentary on an 'Oration, Prolusion 6', and the English poem 'At a Vacation Exercise' assigns Milton's reading of them to members of Christ's College to July 1631, three years later than the widely accepted date of July 1628.[21] On 21 July 1628 Milton writes his second letter to Thomas Young (*Epistolarum Familiarum*, 4), and in 1629, sometime between 13 January and 27 March, Milton supplicates for his BA. Later in the year, he signs the three articles of religion required for him to receive his degree in the University Subscription Book. On 20 April 1631, Milton notes that his 'Epitaph on the Marchioness of Winchester' was sent 'from the banks of the Came', and during the Lent term beginning on 13 January 1632, and ending on 23 March 1632, he once again supplicates and signs the Subscription Book in order to graduate MA on 3 July 1632. This handful of records leaves a patchy account of a seven-year period that also includes vacations between terms. During some, Milton may have elected to stay in Cambridge (not at all uncommon); during others, he may have returned to his parents' home in London; still others may have involved an alternative residence, perhaps in Westminster, perhaps in Hammersmith. Finally, there were periods during these years when the university was closed because of the plague. The ability to establish Milton's whereabouts during his university years is neither easy nor unimportant.

If Milton's whereabouts are not always clear, neither are many of the composition dates for poems he writes while a university student. Fortunately, there are some, primarily those commemorating the deaths of figures associated with the university in one capacity or another, which pose little difficulty. Poems in memory of Lancelot Andrewes (Elegy III), Richard Ridding (Elegy II), Nicholas Felton ('In Obitum Praesulis Eliensis'), and John Gostlin ('In Obitum Procancellarii Medici'), and a series of poems on the Gunpowder Plot can all be assigned with some confidence to the later part of 1626 (September to November) if they are viewed as commemorative responses to occasional events. Lacking controversy but by no means definitively settled is Milton's composition of his 'Nativity Ode', frequently assigned to 25 December 1629. Neither the date nor the place where Milton wrote the poem is as clear as some critics believe. Some of the remaining work is easier to approximate than fix: Sonnet 1, 'Song: On May Morning', and Elegy V, on the grounds of similarity, to either May 1629 or May 1630; 'Naturam non Pati Senium' and 'De Idea Platonica' to June 1631; 'On Shakespeare' to 1630 on the basis of Milton's date inserted in the 1645 *Poems* but in old-style dating this could mean any time before 25

---

[20] William Riley Parker addresses the problem with the date of this letter in 'Milton and Thomas Young, 1620–28', *Modern Language Notes*, 53 (1938), 399–407. For Gill's first letter see Eugenia Chifas, 'Milton's Letter to Gill, May 20, 1628', *Modern Language Notes*, 62 (1947), 37–9. For the second, see John T. Shawcross, 'The Dating of Certain Poems, Letters, and Prolusions Written by Milton', *English Language Notes*, 2 (1965), 261–6.

[21] For convincing arguments for the later date, see Gordon Campbell, 'Milton and the Water Supply of Cambridge', in B. Sokolova and E. Pancheva (eds.), *Essays for Alexander Shurbanov* (Sofia, 2001), 38–43; repr. in revised form in *South African Journal of Medieval and Renaissance Studies*, 15 (2006 for 2005), 121–6, and John T. Shawcross, *Rethinking Milton Studies* (Newark, Del., 2005), 182 n. 1.

March 1631. There are others that continue to elude. Notwithstanding metrical arguments in support of a view that they were written in the summer of 1631, 'L'Allegro' and 'Il Penseroso' could be assigned to any period in the 1630s, and 'The Passion', while possibly a follow-up effort to the Nativity Ode, cannot with certainty be assigned to the Good Friday of 1630 or 1631. Whatever motives Milton may have had in mind when retrospectively dating his poems for the 1645 volume, they are not always helpful. His chosen Latin phrase *anno aetatis* is undoubtedly persuasive in some instances, but it sets approximations rather than specific dates, and in one instance (the Gostlin poem) is incorrect.[22]

To the mixed evidence for establishing Milton's presence in Cambridge and the dating of his writing during these years can be added an account of what is simultaneously taking place in the larger Milton household. The events are not free of ambiguity, but they provide a sense of matters Milton was mindful of and sometimes contended with during his student years. A look at his sister's family proves instructive. The parish chest documents from St Martin-in-the-Fields for the years 1622–31 report Anne Milton Phillips and Edward Phillips the parents of three children. They initially reside in the Waterside ward, relocate to Greene's Lane in 1626, and move again in the following year to the Landside area (locations which turn out to be notable in regard to the Miltons' suburban residence). While the records show the couple's financial standing steadily improving, they also report hardship. Among these, Milton commentators have most often noted the death of the Phillips's second child Anne, whom most assume to be the subject of her uncle's 'On the Death of a Fair Infant', one of the few early compositions which does not appear in the 1645 *Poems*. Was the omission a matter of family propriety or its author's unease with its accomplishment? Its inclusion in the 1673 *Poems* appears to suggest the former, and evidence in the St Martin's records can support such reasoning.

By 1645, the St Martin-in-the-Fields parish records have reported that the first three children of Edward and Anne Phillips have died, John on 15 March 1629, Anne on 22 January 1628, and Elizabeth on 19 February 1631. As he collects his poetry for the volume, does Milton deem the Fair Infant poem inappropriate for singling out one of his sister's children rather than all three? Does the poem's consolation have a hollow ring to it because of the deaths of at least four children by 1645 (a child from Anne's second marriage to Thomas Agar dies in 1641)? This line of reasoning gains greater force if Milton's sister Anne is still alive in 1645 (although most believe she is not).[23] In 1645 Anne would have three surviving children, two sons, Edward and John Phillips from her first marriage, and a daughter Anne from her second marriage to Thomas Agar. It is this second marriage which may be the sticking point for Milton. It takes place within five months of Edward Phillips's death in August 1631, and it involves a second husband and close friend taking on responsibilities of the deceased

---

[22] Gostlin's death in Oct. 1626 conflicts with Milton's *anno aetatis* 16 (a designation he adds to the poem for the 1645 volume). Milton in Oct. 1626 was in his seventeenth year.

[23] An exception may be Ralph Hone, 'New Light on the Milton-Phillips Family Relationship', *Huntington Library Quarterly*, 22 (1958), 63–75.

husband before marrying the widow. Milton's silence regarding his sister (he never mentions her existence in any of his writing) is notable not only because he has an opportunity to put himself in a good light (he raises her two sons even though their stepfather is still alive), but also because he routinely promotes admirable conduct of this kind throughout his prose writings. Something lingers in this matter which does not sound altogether right, and while the parish chest records do not reveal its exact nature, they point towards an irregularity that the family would most likely rather leave unsaid. Interweaving one set of family records with another does not necessarily furnish answers in this instance, but it exposes matters very plausibly at stake—here the matter of Milton's relationship with his sister and a decision involving one of his poems.

A final set of documents for this period, those created through the ongoing business affairs of Milton's father, can further clarify some of the issues involving Milton's time at Cambridge, in particular his absence or presence there. Among his university experiences, one of the most notable concerns his clash with his initial tutor William Chappell, a clash which resulted in Milton being suspended for a term. For some commentators, this event furnishes unquestionable proof of Milton's overall disaffection with Cambridge.[24] The timing of the event—that is, its place in the larger context of Milton's undergraduate programme—is important because of its potential to determine whether Milton elected to complete the degree (if he was already far enough along) or abandon it (because he was at a relatively early stage). Most likely, the incident took place around the midpoint of Milton's programme in April 1627. Support for this date comes from two business transactions Milton conducts with his father in London on 25 May and 11 June 1627, dates which fall during Easter term, when Milton would be expected to be in residence.[25] The nature of the falling out and the allegations that ensued have been equally exploited by admirers and naysayers. Dr Johnson, for one, believed Milton unpopular in his College and 'the last student in either university that suffered the public indignity of corporal correction', while Bishop John Bramhall informed his son in 1654 that Milton deserved not only to be expelled from the University but banished from the society of men.[26] Leo Miller, on the other hand, does not minimize the seriousness of Milton's quarrel with Chappell, but he also does not exaggerate the aftermath, when Milton is assigned to another tutor and carries on, seemingly without further incident.[27] Should the source of Milton's unflattering remarks about the university in his later writing be attributed to his quarrel with Chappell? Before doing so, one should keep in mind that if his rustication is assigned to the spring of 1627, the description of him on an indenture he signs on 25 May in London reads 'John Milton the younger of the University of Cambridge'. Such a description, if composed while

---

[24] Masson and Parker are part of a long list. See also Hanford, *John Milton*, ch. 2.

[25] Housed in the National Archives, the documents are respectively C54/2715/20 and C152/61. The statue staple for the second document recorded the same day (LC 4/56) mentions Milton.

[26] Johnson, *Lives of the English Poets*, ed. George Birkbeck Hill, 3 vols. (Oxford, 1905), i. 140; French, *Records*, iii. 374–5.

[27] 'Milton's Clash with Chappell: A Suggested Reconstruction', *Milton Quarterly*, 14 (1980), 77–87.

he is under suspension, does not indicate nor imply that his status is about to change. As for remarks Milton makes in other correspondence composed while a university student (to Diodati and Gil), is it at all unusual for a degree candidate to express discontent or frustration while completing an academic programme? Milton's disaffection for Cambridge may in the end be genuine, but an assessment must acknowledge that during his university years very little shows up on the protest side of the evidentiary ledger.

Documentary evidence attesting to the improving fortunes and growing status of Milton's father while his son attended university offers another vantage point from which to consider Milton's Cambridge years, particularly how the father in London is preparing the soil that his son will cultivate upon graduation. The senior Milton's standing and wealth were improving as far back as 1615, when he was first appointed to the Stationers' Company, and in the next year, when his musical contributions were included as part of the *Tristitiae Remedium*. These events were followed by appointments in 1620 as a trustee to the Blackfriars Playhouse (not to be understood as an honour but as part of a business transaction), in 1625 as a Steward in the Stationers' Company, and in 1627 as a Warden to the Scriveners' Company.[28] His business transactions during the 1620s, which involve Sir Richard Molyneux (later Viscount Maryborough), Sir Peter Temple, Sir John Lenthall, Sir George Peckham, Sir Francis Leigh, the nephew of John Egerton, Earl of Bridgewater, Sir Fulke Greville, Sir Kenelm Digby, Lord Strange, and Sir John Suckling, make clear his access to the aristocratic, political, and artistic worlds of seventeenth-century London. While these associations have not gone unnoticed, they have yet to receive a full accounting in relation to the advantages accorded the scrivener's unknown son in the early 1630s—a place in Shakespeare's Second Folio and invitations to write court entertainments for the Countess of Derby and the Earl of Bridgewater. Nor will the answers that could result from such a study be unproblematic. Few scholars have ventured in this direction because to do so will require letting go of the label of the young Milton as a radical in waiting.[29] As this account suggests, if there is a characteristic that marks the family profile throughout the first three decades of the seventeenth century, it is largely of a conformist nature. Such a description is buoyed not only by a son who abides by university regulations and graduates by declaring allegiance to the Crown and church, but also by extended family members employed by the Crown (a son-in-law Edward Phillips, to be followed by a second son-in-law Thomas Agar). By the early 1630s, it appears that this pattern has not changed, and that the senior Milton's associations have in due course extended to members of the aristocracy, the Bridgewater and Derby families, from whom his son will most benefit.

---

[28] Most of these events and the business transactions listed in the following sentence appear in French's *Records* but have been verified and corrected in some instances by Campbell, *Chronology*.

[29] A discussion of the radical-in-waiting view appears in Barbara Lewalski, 'How Radical was the Young Milton?', in Stephen B. Dobranski and John P. Rumrich (eds.), *Milton and Heresy* (Cambridge, 1999), 49–72. Less confident is Thomas Corns, 'Milton before "Lycidas"', in Graham Parry and Joad Raymond (eds.), *Milton and the Terms of Liberty* (Cambridge, 2002), 23–36.

HAMMERSMITH, HORTON, AND THE ALLURE OF CONTROVERSY (1632–1640)

Outside the City (1630–1635)

It took over 250 years for biographers to discover that upon completing his MA, Milton did not relocate from Cambridge to a family home in Horton. It took an additional forty years to find out why the Milton family took up residence eight miles outside the City of London in Hammersmith during the latter part of 1630 or the first months of 1631.[30] The most compelling reasons appear practical. By 1630, two of the youngest members of Milton's extended family had died in the parish of St Martin-in-the-Fields; their father Edward Phillips and a third child would die in the following year. The very parish in which Milton senior had purchased property to which his family could retreat during outbreaks of the plague was turning out to be more perilous than safe. In the wake of another outbreak in 1630, the search for another location became imperative. Jeremy Maule's discovery in 1996 of poor rate documents for the parish of All Saints, Fulham, Hammersmith side, covering the years 1631, 1632, and 1633, supplements Chancery depositions locating John Milton senior in this parish by September 1632 and extending through January 1635. The poor rate documents date the Miltons' residence back to early 1631 and raise the possibility that the scrivener served as a churchwarden.[31] A further look into the Hammersmith period uncovers details that buttress suggestions already made regarding the conservative nature of the Milton family in the early years of Milton's life. In 1629, William Laud as Bishop of London had consecrated a chapel of ease in Hammersmith, and in negotiations with the parishioners who petitioned for this chapel (named St Paul) on the basis of its inconvenient distance from the mother church in Fulham, Laud disallowed their request to appoint a minister. Extant documents reveal Laud's concern to prevent disruptive preachers and lecturers from securing the living.[32] Attending a Laudian chapel of ease in the early 1630s does not suggest religious subversion was a decisive factor governing the family move.

While Milton's time in Hammersmith was most likely limited prior to his permanent departure from Cambridge in July 1632, thereafter it appears that his residency was continuous and what has long been considered the conducive rural environment of Horton may in fact have more likely been the suburban outpost of Hammersmith,

---

[30] In 1949 Charles Bernau found chancery depositions by Milton's father in which he listed Hammersmith as his address.

[31] By signing the audit of the parish account books for 1632 (Hammersmith and Fulham Record Office, PAF/1/21/fo. 92^v), Milton's father had to be either a justice of the peace or a churchwarden. Evidence favours the latter, but it has yet to surface.

[32] A transcript of the correspondence between Laud and the parishioners appears in MS DD/818/56 in the Hammersmith and Fulham Record Office.

where the family associations with the aristocracy become overt. Milton writes *Arcades*, which is performed in honour of the Dowager Countess of Derby at Harefield, and he collaborates with Henry Lawes to produce *A Maske Presented at Ludlow Castle* in 1634 for the family of the Earl of Bridgewater. To these years can also be assigned with varying degrees of certainty 'At a Solemn Music', 'Upon the Circumcision', 'On Time', and Sonnet 7, a poem which expresses the first signs of Milton's anxiety over poetic productivity and accomplishment, and the companion poems 'L'Allegro' and 'Il Penseroso'. The frequent visits to London remarked upon in the *Second Defence* were more likely negotiated from the closer suburb of Hammersmith than Horton, where potential bans on travel due to plague would impede frequency and access (see below). The Milton of Hammersmith, if judged by his writing output, may be characterized as invigorated, even energetic, qualities not so easily attributed to his time at Horton.

What is known about the Hammersmith period, and there remains more to know, verifies its importance in the family's history. In the early 1630s, Milton's father begins his gradual withdrawal from business and his preparation for retirement, signalled initially in 1634 by his decision to pay a fine to the Scriveners' Company in lieu of serving as Company Master. His decision to allow his partner Thomas Bower to conduct business in Bread Street while he resided elsewhere appears calculated to reduce personal court appearances and be sufficiently distanced from creditors. Indeed the most logical explanation for the further remove to Horton appears to be these same reasons, and supporting evidence for such a view may be found in the handling of the Cotton–Milton suit, which begins in 1636 and is not resolved until 1638.[33] An event that impacts the family's residence in Hammersmith early on and which has not been given a full hearing is the death in August 1631 of Edward Phillips. The ramifications of this death affect several members of the family and afford a look into decisions made in its aftermath. John Milton senior, first of all, witnessed Phillips's will three weeks before his demise, and therefore would be aware that his daughter, who was once again pregnant, would most likely relocate to her parents' home in Hammersmith with her year-old son Edward upon the death of her husband.[34] Anne's brothers, John and Christopher, were probably already residing in Hammersmith and in late August would return to Westminster for Phillips's burial. After the burial, the entire family, including Anne and her young son, more than likely returned to Hammersmith and resided there through September and the first week of October, when John and Christopher would return to Cambridge for the beginning of Michaelmas term (10 October). Milton's entry in his Bible for the birth of John Phillips 'about October' could reflect his approximate recall of the time of year in terms of the university calendar around which his current life was organized. Anne Milton Phillips's time in Hammersmith in any event would be brief; the parish records from St Martin speak to the presence of her new family by 1632, her marriage

---

[33] A convincing account of this matter is now to be found in Gordon Campbell and Thomas Corns, *John Milton: Life, Work, and Thought* (Oxford, 2008).
[34] The scrivener with his apprentice Henry Rothwell witnessed the will on 1 Aug. (PROB 11/160/99).

to Thomas Agar taking place in the parish of St Dunstan in the East on 5 January 1632.[35] Unfortunately, the missing link in these matters is the Hammersmith registers, which do not survive; if they had, they would in all likelihood establish the birthplaces and christenings of John and Edward Phillips. For Edward to be born in Hammersmith his grandparents would have had to take up residence by August 1630, a date well within the realm of possibility. While admittedly juxtaposing records from different locations cannot furnish definitive answers in this case, the process does allow plausible solutions to emerge.

A Further Remove (1636–1638)

If some light can shine on Milton's Hammersmith years through the shuffling of parish chest records, there will need to be a greater number of them to illuminate the Horton period, a stretch of time in Milton's life which seems to resist attempts to understand it. The shred of evidence indicating the family relocation in May 1636 disappeared in the twentieth century, and nothing has been found to collaborate or validate the date the family changed residences.[36] Initially, the reason for the change was most plausibly to ease Milton's father into full retirement and disentangle him from the messy business of court appearances, law suits, and legal proceedings. To the Horton years, David Masson devoted a hundred pages, not aware that some of his material actually applied to Hammersmith.[37] Masson's sustained effort to collect all he could about this village, its layout, and its inhabitants has not removed the shroud of mystery that hovers over the family's time there, but it did provide suggestions which have led to a few recent discoveries. For the most part, Horton remains the place where Milton's mother died and her son wrote 'Lycidas'. Attempts to grant it more importance beyond these two events have usually failed because of an emphasis upon local testimony and legend rather than documentary evidence.[38] There are opportunities for such a view to change, but such change will depend in part upon the two biographical events which have generated the most interest in the village.

For the first six days of April 1637, three documents attest to the Milton family's presence in Horton, what must be considered an abundance of riches in comparison to what is available for the rest of the time the family lives in the village. On 1 April

---

[35] For an account of the marriage and circumstances pertaining to it, see Rose Clavering and John Shawcross, 'Anne Milton and the Milton Residences', *Journal of English and Germanic Philology*, 59 (1960), 680–90. A parish record for St Martin-in-the-Fields (F3346) displays Phillips's name crossed out and Agar's inserted above it.

[36] In the late 19th c. Hyde Clarke apparently saw a notation that Milton's father was discharged at his own request as Assistant to the Company of Scriveners because of his 'removal to inhabit in the country' (*Athenaeum*, 2746 (12 June 1880), 760–1).

[37] Masson, i. 552–663.

[38] Masson indulges to a degree in 'Local Memories of Milton', *Good Words*, 34 (1893), 41–4; so does G. W. J. Gyll, a 19th-c. family historian, whose chapter on Horton in his *History of the Parish of Wraysbury, Ankerwycke Priory, and Magna Carta Island; with the History of Horton, and the Town of Colnbrook, Bucks* (1862) runs to seventy-three pages.

Christopher Milton submits an affidavit on his father's behalf claiming Milton senior to be too infirm to attend court in Westminster. Two days later his wife Sara dies, and Edward Goodall, the rector of the parish, enters the date of her death into the parish register, a date which will appear as well on her gravestone, which can still be read on a blue marble slab found in the chancel of the parish church. On 6 April Goodall conducts the burial service and records the burial date in the parish register. Commentators have attributed various degrees of significance to this event in Milton's life, but none believes the cause of death to be anything but old age, a view corroborated by the absence of a designation of the plague next to her entry in the parish burial register. Such an indicator is given to others who succumbed to it in Horton during 1636 and 1637.[39] These facts have been long known (although not reported in this sequence), but they have not been evaluated in relation to a writ issued for Milton's father and witnessed by Thomas Agar concerning an ongoing court case with Sir Thomas Cotton about three weeks before Sara Milton's death (10 March). The presence of Agar in this document links the extended family in London and Westminster to Horton and suggests that Anne Agar (if she is in fact still alive), the surviving children from her first marriage (Edward and John Phillips), and two daughters from her second marriage (Mary and Anne Agar) may have already started to gather in anticipation of Sara Milton's death. By the beginning of April, we have proof of the presence of Christopher Milton through the affidavit, and a week after Sara Milton is buried, John Agar, Thomas's brother, who witnesses the scrivener's answer to the writ of 10 March.[40] The family assembly thus appears still in place by mid-April and supports the view that the extended family functions as a viable and valuable source of information concerning events taking place within it. Furthermore, the presence of Agar and his two stepsons may explain how we first found out that Milton lived in this out-of-the-way village. Edward Phillips is the lone early biographer to mention Milton's time there, and he does so with precision: 'at *Horton* near *Colebrook* in *Barkshire*'.[41] Was it the family gathering that the 7-year-old recalled? It is the only piece of evidence linking Phillips to the village.

The other well-reported event from the Horton years is the composition of 'Lycidas', for some, Milton's greatest poetic achievement excepting *Paradise Lost* and one that most believe secures his literary accomplishment on its own. Of its many heralded passages, those expressing its author's denunciation of English church practices in the 1630s have been often cited as proof of Milton's radical leanings. Whether the poem reveals a reformist sensibility, marks a vocational shift away from the church and towards a calling as a poet-prophet, or registers a culminating

---

[39] The 1 Apr. affidavit can be found in the National Archives (Req 1/141, fo. 218). The death and burial notices of Sara Milton are in the parish registers of St Michael, Horton (PR 107/1/1) as are indications by Edward Goodall concerning those parishioners who died of the plague in Horton and Colnbrook in 1636 and 1637. The registers are housed in the Centre for Buckinghamshire Studies in Aylesbury.

[40] The document appears in the British Library (Cottonian Charters 1/5/1) and in the National Archives in the records of the Court of Requests (Reg 2/260).

[41] Horton and Colnbrook are located in southern Buckinghamshire very close to but not in Berkshire or Middlesex. Phillips's error is understandable considering the small distance separating the counties.

expression of protest against a church which has disappointed the poet for over a decade, hard evidence in support of any of these claims has been hard to come by.[42] One document recently uncovered from August 1637 provides a possibility for Miltonic dissent. As a consequence of a jurisdictional dispute between Archbishop Laud and Bishop John Williams of Lincoln, Williams ordered an inspection of the parish churches of Buckinghamshire and in the report for the Horton church of St Michael, John Milton senior is cited for a violation of policy regarding his church seat.[43] Not surprisingly, the scrivener answers the charge and conforms to the church court request by February 1638, but can we conclude that his son agreed with such a decision? Have events in recent months, the second mutilation of William Prynne in June, and the introduction of the Laudian prayer book in Edinburgh in July, prompted Milton to question compliance? The answer is of less importance to the father's situation than it is to the matter of Milton's church career. Does this incident resolve the matter in August rather than in November, when the manuscript of 'Lycidas' appears to settle it definitively? The headnote which Milton adds in 1645, however interesting, does not really help.

If the disaffection with the church voiced in 'Lycidas' indeed captures part of Milton's frame of mind during the Horton period, evidence from local records offers a picture somewhat at odds with the bucolic accounts of the Bucks countryside and its ability to inspire the emerging poet. There are problems in Horton during the years of the Milton family residence and of a sufficient number to offset what has long been assumed to be an environment of advantage. It is best to start with the well known. The knowledge that Milton's time at Horton was less than half of what was once assumed (a little more than two years as opposed to almost six) raises questions about its designation as an impressive period of self-education. In Parker's view Horton should be understood 'as a place of tireless and purposeful study'.[44] James Holly Hanford's account of Milton's reading dates the earliest entries in Milton's Commonplace Book to the Horton residence and contends Milton's plan was systematic and extensive.[45] The changed dates for the Horton period pose no problems for maintaining Hanford's view since by May 1636, the most likely time the Miltons relocate from Hammersmith, Milton's self-education programme was a few months shy of its fourth year (if it is dated from his departure from Cambridge in July 1632). And in Horton, it turns out, the Cambridge-educated parish rector Edward Goodall has access to a theological library located inside a nearby parish

---

[42] Commentary on 'Lycidas' has generated scores of articles addressing such concerns and more. For a representative list, see P. J. Klemp, *The Essential Milton: An Annotated Bibliography of Major Modern Studies* (Boston, 1989), 156–71. C. A. Patrides (ed.), *Milton's 'Lycidas': The Tradition and the Poem*, 2nd edn. (1961; Columbia, Mo., 1983); Scott Elledge, *Milton's 'Lycidas': Edited to Serve as an Introduction to Criticism* (New York, 1966); Clay Hunt, *'Lycidas' and the Italian Critics* (New Haven, 1979); J. Martin Evans, *The Road from Horton: Looking Backwards in 'Lycidas'* (Victoria, B.C., 1983); and David S. Berkeley, *Inwrought with Figures Dim: A Reading of Milton's 'Lycidas'* (The Hague, 1974) attest to the poem's coverage in 20th-c. criticism.

[43] For an account of this event see Edward Jones, '"Church-outed by the Prelats": Milton and the 1637 Inspection of the Horton Parish Church', *Journal of English and Germanic Philology*, 102 (2003), 42–58.

[44] Parker, ii. 798.

[45] 'The Chronology of Milton's Private Studies', *PMLA* 36 (1921), 251–314.

church two miles from the Milton home. Volumes in the Kedermister library in Langley Marish (which still exists) address several of the subjects we know Milton was investigating during this period, and entries he makes in his Commonplace Book help identify some subjects.[46] Thus access to materials, the matter which will prove of greatest importance to the Horton residency, does not appear at first to be an issue. Did Milton use the collection? While unassailable evidence linking Milton with the library remains to be found, collateral evidence, including local travel restrictions because of the plague and the declining health of at least one and possibly both parents in 1636 and 1637, creates circumstances which would make Milton's use of it plausible and convenient. Equally compelling and still unexamined is the possibility that Milton may have used this collection in 1639 and 1640 as well to prepare a response to Cardinal Bellarmine's *Disputationes De Controversiis Christianae Fidei Adversus Huius Temporis Haereticos*, which he eventually abandoned in favour of writing the anti-episcopal tracts in 1641–2.[47] Cast in the most positive light, as the Horton period has traditionally been, a rural environment of few distractions with a local theological library within easy reach would almost seem to guarantee nothing but success for Milton's plans.

In making his case that the Horton period of studious retirement was an important, successful phase of Milton's life, David Masson unknowingly noted some of the specific problems that pertain more tellingly to the second (Horton) as opposed to the first (Hammersmith) rural residence the family inhabits in the 1630s. Foremost is the plague, to which Masson draws attention. He also notes that in the first two and a half years (i.e. the Hammersmith residency) there is more evidence and productivity than can be found for the remaining years (i.e. Horton).[48] Productivity in this case refers to writing as opposed to reading, and records support Masson's conclusions. Aside from Milton's revision of the *Maske* and 'Lycidas' (no slight accomplishments no matter how one understands productivity), there is no poetry that can be confidently assigned to the Horton years ('Ad Patrem' is a possibility, but its composition date can be assigned to a number of months extending over several years beyond the Horton residence).

Was the threat of plague an ongoing distraction from 1635 to 1638, and was Milton's need to care for his parents another? Neither can easily be removed from consideration. In 1636 there was a serious enough outbreak of plague in London for Charles to agree to a petition from debtors in the Fleet Street prison to be set free.[49] Such

---

[46] An account of the library, its relationship to Milton's Commonplace Book, and Milton's possible use of it appears in Edward Jones, '"Filling in a Blank in the Canvas": Milton, Horton, and the Kedermister Library', *Review of English Studies*, 53 (2002), 31–60.

[47] The possibility that Milton may have been preparing a response to Bellarmine upon his return from his tour of the Continent was first raised by Gordon Campbell in 'Milton's *Index Theologicus* and Bellarmine's *Disputationes De Controversiis Christianae Fidei Adversus Huius Temporis Haereticos*', *Milton Quarterly*, 11 (1977), 12–16. The connection to the Kedermister library has not been explored.

[48] Masson, *Life*, i. 562.

[49] See J. G. Jenkins, 'Paper and Plague', *The Paper Maker and the British Paper Trade Journal* (June 1964), 60.

outbreaks encouraged all who were able to retreat to rural locations, but special concerns were raised over the king, his court, and the residences of Theobalds and Windsor. The proximity of Windsor Castle to Horton (approximately five miles) subjected the village to government measures enacted by the Privy Council to ensure the safety of the royal family. Restrictions for the area within ten miles of Windsor, put into place in June 1636, included the closing of the paper mills in Horton and Wraysbury by September because of the fear that rags from London used in the paper-producing process were a main source of infection. The paper mill at Horton had already been suspected as the cause for an outbreak in the parish: victims are recorded in the burial registers for 1636 and 1637.[50] These circumstances in a village as small as Horton would appear unavoidable for not just the members of the Milton household but for all inhabitants. They pose an undeniable challenge to descriptions and depictions of Milton walking through fields, sitting on the banks of the Colne, and writing poetry under trees. In the ensuing squabble that resulted from the refusal of local inhabitants to contribute to the support of unemployed mill workers, hostility was expressed through a petition to the Privy Council which cited not just the incessant noise from the mills to which the inhabitants were subjected day and night, but 'the noisome smells of infected rags', the destruction of arable land, and the damming up of rivers.[51] Conditions in Horton were obviously not as Edenic as some have reported them.

Faced with the challenges of his physical environment, Milton may have retreated more readily into his academic pursuits, but to do so he would need access to books. Assuming he used the Kedermister library, that collection could have supplied at least temporary help. Greater resources were clearly elsewhere, and unlimited access to London looks questionable because of the restrictions in place during 1636 and 1637. With his mother's health seemingly an issue in 1637, the opportunities for uninterrupted study also appear compromised, at least in part. Rather than declaring Milton's Horton period unproductive, it may be more accurate to acknowledge the salutary achievements of his revision of the *Maske* and the composition of 'Lycidas', given the circumstances under which they were completed. As for the description of Horton as 'a tireless and purposeful place of study', there would appear to be sufficient justification to substitute frustrating and fatiguing for tireless and purposeful.

There is an additional document produced during the Horton period which furnishes a final perspective on events in Horton and a transition to an account of Milton's fifteen-month Continental tour, which began in May 1638. On 23 November 1637 Milton writes a letter to Charles Diodati while in London (*Epistolarum Familiarum 7*). Earlier in the day he more than likely attended the funeral of his brother-in-law's father Thomas Agar, who was buried in the chancel of the Milton family's

---

[50] See *Privy Council Order Books* (PC 46 and 47); *Calendar of State Papers Domestic*, 331, no. 126, and the Horton Parish Registers (above, n. 39).

[51] *Calendar of State Papers Domestic*, 344: 373 and 396: 347.

former church of All Hallows on Bread Street.[52] The letter affords another opportunity to link documents which appear at first glance to be unconnected. The Miltons should, by all accounts, be in Horton not London. But the parish chest record reveals a reason for the extended family to gather, and the bringing together of Thomas Agar, Christopher Milton, and John Milton may very well account for why Milton speaks to Diodati of his plans of relocating to the Inns of Court: 'there is a pleasant and shady walk; for that dwelling will be more satisfactory, both for companionship, if I wish to remain at home, and as a more suitable headquarters, if I choose to venture forth. Where I am now, as you know, I live in obscurity and cramped quarters.'[53] Leaving aside for the moment Milton's unfavourable description of his situation in Horton, the desire to leave the family home where he is presumably living alone with his father and move to the very location where his brother resides raises many possibilities—a desire for the freedom his brother enjoys, a desire to be free of the responsibility of caring for his father, a desire for the companionship a city life could bring as opposed to the isolation of a rural village. These all speak to Milton's state of mind in late 1637. But is the actual plan of moving to the Inns of Court nothing more than an idea put into his head because of possible interactions with his brother and brother-in-law earlier in the day? Why would the 29-year-old Milton, who had never lived away from his family except during university terms, suddenly see the Inns of Court as an opportunity for freedom? Christopher entered the Inner Temple in 1632. If Milton's negative comments regarding his situation in Horton are considered along with Christopher Milton's living arrangements in London, there are grounds for recognizing the larger issue of change that will be underscored by the decision to leave England for the Continent. The seed for such an idea is present in the letter.

By implication, Milton's letter to Diodati also addresses a significant, long-held assumption that he would never leave for the Continent without arranging for the care of his father. In the months ahead, it will turn out, Milton will leave his father, and he will leave him without arranging for the care most have assumed was in place through his brother's marriage to Thomasine Webber sometime before Milton's departure in May 1638. By virtue of that marriage, the care of Milton senior would be primarily in the hands of Thomasine while her husband lived in London during term. Thus Milton would be free to go. However, the recent discovery of Christopher's marriage to Thomasine on 13 September 1638, months after his brother's departure, makes clear that some other arrangement must have been in place in Horton.[54] Perhaps befitting this obscure period of Milton's life, finding an answer produces yet another question.

---

[52] GLMS 5031 (the parish registers of All Hallows, Bread Street). The entry appears on p. 188 in the published registers by the Harleian Society.

[53] *CPW*, i. 327. The Yale editors number this letter 8 as opposed to 7, the number it is assigned in the 1674 edition and the Columbia *Works*.

[54] The entry appears in the marriage register (1559–1698) for the parish of St Andrew Holborn (GLMS 6668/1).

Departure and Return (1638–1640)

Milton's preparations for his tour of the Continent are handled through channels he and his family have used before: aristocrats in royal favour. Milton's brief encounter with the Provost of Eton, Sir Henry Wotton, provides advice and contacts. Some will be used, others ignored. Wotton's letter, which speaks well of Milton's masque, will be saved and published in the 1645 *Poems*.[55] The letter also reveals that Milton's work was not immune to coterie manuscript culture: Wotton has read a scribal copy before receiving Milton's presentation copy enclosed with his letter. Even with the evidence of Milton's potentially radical leaning found in 'Lycidas', this point is worth remembering. Most likely through Henry Lawes, Milton's masque is circulating among at least some associated with the Caroline court in the late 1630s. It is Lawes as well who secures Milton the necessary documents so that he can leave the country.[56]

How one understands Milton's experiences abroad depends in part on how one accounts for his post-Cambridge experiences and decisions leading up to it. Has Milton by 1638 completed those parts of a self-designed plan that is now to proceed logically to the tour? In other words, is the tour the conclusion to a finishing procedure through which an educated man reared in one culture relocates for a set period of time into cosmopolitan settings in order to refine skills and reveal talent? Comments in the *Second Defence* concerning Milton's meeting the 'learned Hugo Grotius' and enjoying 'the accomplished society of Lucas Holstenius and many other learned and superior men' support the view that the tour involved more than a 'curiosity ... to see foreign countries, and above all, Italy'.[57] While there has been some success charting Milton's journey, in part because he supplies an account in the *Second Defence*, a daily, even weekly, itinerary cannot be sustained. Moreover, the unwary have too quickly given authoritative weight to Milton's account, one which approximates dates and times, sometimes confuses names of people, and leaves off (as it should) material that will not serve the greater purposes of the prose tract since those purposes are only partially autobiographical. The centrepiece of the tour for Milton was Italy, and an accounting of his experiences there can give the best sense of what it meant to him and correspondingly what it may signify for us.

Of the approximately fifteen months that Milton was abroad, six were spent in Italy. Some of that time presumably involved exposure to the sculpture, painting, and architecture of Italian masters (Michelangelo, Leonardo, Raphael, et al.) though Milton's personal letters, poetry, or prose tracts never directly mention anything he may have seen. In the *Second Defence*, he appears intent upon underscoring the positive reception he received from European intellectuals and men of international

---

[55] The original is lost. The manuscript in the British Library (Add. MS 28637) is an 18th-c. copy derived from the original.

[56] Lawes sends a letter (BL Add. MS 36354) and a passport, which in Milton's time functioned as an exit visa (i.e. giving one permission to leave the country). How Milton financed his fifteen months abroad is not certain, but his sale of land in St Martin-in-the-Fields to Sir Matthew Lyster within a month of his departure (15 Apr. 1638) would appear to be one resource.

[57] John Milton, *Defensio Secunda*, as translated in *CW*, viii. 121.

renown such as Hugo Grotius, Lukas Holste, Giovanni Battista Manso, and Cardinal Francesco Barberini. He also gives recognition to a number of young Italian intellectuals: Jacopo Gaddi, Carlo Dati, Valerio Chimentelli, Agostino Coltellini, Pietro Frescobaldi, Giovanni Salzilli, Benedetto Buonmattei, and Antonio Francini. To some (Dati and Buonmattei) he writes personal letters; to others (Frescobaldi, Francini, and Chimentelli) he makes reference in the *Second Defence*. To still others (Coltellini and Dati), Milton notes that he met them on each of his two visits to Florence. A significant amount of surviving evidence from the tour uncovers Milton's participation in the activities of two Italian academies, the Apatisti and the Svogliati. Not only did he attend meetings but more than likely applied for membership.[58] The finishing-school dimension of the tour can be glimpsed through the acclaim Milton receives for his skill in composing Italian verse and his facility with Spanish (acknowledged in poetical tributes by Francini and Dati). The camaraderie Milton enjoyed with Italian intellectuals can be compared to his later relationships with former students and like-minded acquaintances, but there does appear to be a difference. The formidable great man who interacted with men of learning throughout his life has not left the generous sentiments expressed to the young Italians anywhere else.

Milton's account of his tour has allowed scholars to establish his general whereabouts and on occasion confirm a daily activity. He has dinner at the English College in Rome, attends the premiere of an Italian comic opera featuring a libretto written by Cardinal Giulio Rospigliosi (the future Pope Clement IX), and has a private audience with Cardinal Francesco Barberini, at the time a prominent clergyman in Rome and chief adviser to Pope Urban VIII.[59] Given Milton's distrust of and animosity towards Catholics, his obvious enjoyment of other features of life in Italy speaks to the difficulty of establishing an all-encompassing notion of his religious views. Part of Milton's time was no doubt spent disputing with Catholics (as he makes sure to note in the *Second Defence*); part was spent attending the academies; part was spent writing verse for presentation to those academies, and part was spent buying books. Much time as well was taken up travelling from one location to the other, the difficulty of such travel no doubt fraught with expected and unexpected delay. The tour, based upon Milton's account, was clearly positive, and if the moral imperative he cites for cutting it short sounds convincing only in part (he turns back but does not exactly rush back to England), that explanation gives a verifiable ring to the subject of reform, an idea by 1654 and the publication of the *Second Defence* with which he is firmly associated.

While the England to which Milton returned in July 1639 was far more politically unstable than it was when he left, so too had his family undergone change. The death of an infant son of Christopher Milton and Thomasine Webber in Horton in March

---

[58] Milton's visits to the Svogliati Academy are recorded in the minutes of their meetings. See Campbell, *Chronology*, 61–6. See also A. M. Cinquemani, *Glad to Go for a Feast: Milton, Buonmattei, and the Florentine Academici* (New York, 1998).

[59] For documentary evidence concerning the tour see Campbell, *Chronology*, 59–67.

1639 reveals that Thomasine was already with child by the time she married Christopher in September 1638. How much of an impact this event had on the family harmony is hard to determine because it involved not just the care of the senior Milton but the issue of pre-marital relations. Presumably Thomasine would not relocate to Horton until her condition would draw the notice of others. Milton may have heard of this event for the first time when he took up residence with the family in Horton upon his immediate return.[60] How long he stayed is not easy to determine, but his nephew believes it was not long before he removed to St Bride's Churchyard in London for a brief period before finally relocating to Aldersgate Street in 1641. The eighteen-month period of Milton's life from July 1639 to December 1640 has not received the attention it deserves, especially when one considers two important events that take place during this time. The first involves the care of Milton's two nephews Edward and John Phillips, the latter becoming his sole responsibility by 1640 with Edward coming for day instruction. This development still awaits a satisfactory account, which will no doubt be based upon the discovery and understanding of the fate of Milton's sister Anne. There is an assumption that something must have happened to her, and that she died either while Milton was abroad or after his return.[61] This account has suggested the mystery started earlier. If we combine her mysterious disappearance with the potential problems resulting from Christopher's marriage, the family picture appears murky and Edward Phillips, the lone authority for this time period, would be too young to figure it out. Even writing later, if he happened to have the full story, he understandably will not relate it. But the silence about Anne Milton stands out as odd—perhaps only less so from her brother than her son.

What has been discovered recently is that Anne's second husband Thomas Agar lived in Shoe Lane from 1638 to 1641 and possibly longer, either before 1638 or after 1641.[62] In any event in 1639 and 1640, the distance from his home to Milton's Fleet Street residence in the parish of St Bride's, in the lodging of a tailor named Robert Russell, was not far. The day visits of Edward could be managed easily and allow Agar to maintain his position in Chancery. Indeed this appears to be the most plausible reason for such an arrangement. That Christopher married in Agar's parish of St Andrew Holborn further suggests that communication and interaction among the siblings and their families were of a greater extent than commentators have assumed. The recent discovery of the death of Agar's daughter Mary in Shoe Lane in May 1641 only adds to the uncertainty.[63] If, with her death, Agar had only a daughter Anne

---

[60] The Miltons would reside in Horton until at least the end of 1640. Christopher Milton and his father appear in the 1641 churchwarden accounts for the parish of St Laurence in Reading (D/P 97/5/3, p. 131) and relocation in Mar. 1641 is plausible.

[61] The lack of information regarding Anne Milton has limited the ability of scholars to gauge the nature of her brother's relationships with his two nephews throughout the 1640s, 1650s, and 1660s.

[62] The 1638 Settlement of Tithes locates Agar in the parish of St Andrew, Holborn. See *The Inhabitants of London in 1638*, ed. T. C. Dale (London, 1931). The death of his daughter in Apr. 1641 establishes that his residency was at least in its fourth year if he moved to the parish at the beginning of 1638.

[63] Burial Register 1623–1642, St Andrew Holborn (GLMS 6673/2).

living with him, why is his unmarried brother-in-law raising his two stepsons? The family developments in the 1639–40 period may have altered some of Milton's activities in ways we have yet to discover.

The second item of concern related to 1639–40 has to do with the ongoing progress of Milton's self-education programme. Commentators have been unable to determine the vexed matter of Milton's Commonplace Book—did he take it with him and use it while abroad or is it a record solely of reading and note-taking while in the familiar locales of London and surrounding areas? Evidence that the plan continued appears in the Trinity Manuscript, which has sections devoted to several outlines for compositions dated around 1640. There is also Edward Phillips's remark that around this time he had already read Satan's address to the sun, evidence that his uncle had already begun writing what would eventually become *Paradise Lost*. A less noted example of Milton's ongoing study plan could have involved volumes in the Kedermister library, which, as we have seen, Milton may have used in preparing a response to Cardinal Bellarmine in 1639 and 1640. Although that response was eventually put aside in favour of Milton's anti-episcopal tracts, the location of the family home and resources in the vicinity of Horton make such a possibility plausible. Even with the less than ideal physical conditions in Horton already described, one can also see coherence between the rural village environment and the pastoral setting of Milton's major poem of this period, *Epitaphium Damonis*. The poem's overall mood of loss explicitly addresses a central event in this part of Milton's life—the death of his friend Charles Diodati—but could the occasion also allow for ruminations concerning losses in the immediate family, his sister Anne, nephews, and possibly his mother? Milton's poetic reaction to death, no doubt more personal here than in 'Lycidas', gives another vantage point from which to gauge a host of experiences he is encountering at this time, some addressed overtly in the poem, others potentially hidden behind the scenes, tucked away in the layers of the ode. As a time period when Milton is establishing his own life outside the family home, the years 1639–40 do not allow the family to go away. Indeed the responsibilities of the nephews are clear evidence that independence will only come within rather than apart from the family orbit.

CHAPTER 2

JOHN MILTON: THE LATER LIFE (1641–1674)

NICHOLAS VON MALTZAHN

MILTON is the first English author for whom we have so much in the way of biography. He himself emphasizes his identity in his writings, whether in the *ethos* arguments elaborating his virtue in his prose tracts, or in the self-descriptive invocations that punctuate *Paradise Lost*. To those works' claims his contemporaries responded, so that in addition to the rich and varied writings from Milton's hand and the unusual wealth of his life-records, we have much contemporary report as well as a number of early 'lives' with which to enlarge our sense of the man and his achievement.[1] Moreover, disputes have long raged over the course and very meaning of the English Revolution in which Milton played a part. The resulting historical research has in its volume and detail much helped Miltonists in their scrutiny of his life and times. This broader perspective applies because early in 1641, soon after the calling of what would prove the revolutionary Long Parliament, the 32-year-old Milton embarked on a career in public controversy. That became a lasting engagement whether in his writing as a citizen in the 1640s; as a public servant under the Rump Parliament (1649–53) and Cromwellian Protectorate (1653–8); as a more independent pamphleteer again in the fresh season of political opportunity Milton discovered in the turmoil of 1659–60; or as a subject under the restored monarchy after 1660, when he completed *Paradise Lost*, *Samson Agonistes*, and *Paradise Regained*, and published

---

[1] See Darbishire; French, *Records*; John T. Shawcross, *Milton: A Bibliography, 1624–1700* (1984).

further of his works including a fresh tract *Of True Religion* (1673), before his death in November 1674. Astonishing as Milton's major poems are, they have fostered a curiosity about the life of the author who could so transform English poetry.

For posterity, the composition and publication of *Paradise Lost* (1667, 2nd edn., 1674) is the defining event of Milton's life. For his contemporaries, more notable was Milton's publication of the *Defensio* (1651) and related justifications of the execution of Charles I, which contentious achievement was such that 'He was much more admired abrode then at home'.[2] In his lifetime, his epic and his political interventions were seen as closely related. 'Milton holds to his old Principle', groused one early reader of *Paradise Lost*, who had long suspected Milton of being 'too full of the Devill'.[3] But those who esteemed the epic soon found ways to separate it from Milton's controversial prose, and in two generations the distinction contributed to the success of Joseph Addison's influential *Spectator* essays (1712), which aestheticized *Paradise Lost* in terms that lastingly elevated the sublime epic above the seventeenth-century religious and political convulsions that had so involved Milton. Later writers hostile to Milton's politics might allow their resentment to inform their critical evaluations of his poetry, notably Samuel Johnson in his 'Life of Milton' and T. S. Eliot in his essays on the poet. Others, especially the Romantics, their heirs, and late twentieth-century scholarship, were kinder to Milton's free-thinking in religion and politics alike, and readier to relate his controversial writing to *Paradise Lost*.

Does Milton's biography yield a more coherent understanding of his works, even as it may emphasize their complexity? Early in the twenty-first century, the critical debate remains poised between those who integrate Milton's arguments early and late across the broad range of genres in which he wrote and those who disintegrate his works, emphasizing the inconsistencies and discontinuities in his varied productions. The 'lumpers' have learned to concede how Milton might, in saying the same thing in different circumstances, mean different things at different times. The 'splitters' have learned with postmodernism to emphasize that Milton's inconsistencies may be born of his participation in different debates, genres, or discourses rather than just from his own confusions. Milton's often polemical writing invites re-situation in the controversies in which he was engaged. Moreover, circumstance might invite his economizing with the truth, conspicuously so in his tactic of proposing Alexander More the author of *Regii Sanguinis Clamor* (1652), which occasioned his elaborate attack on that luckless factotum in *Defensio Secunda* (1654).[4] Such were the cross-currents of the English Revolution that the rapidly shifting contexts often inflect the meaning of Milton's claims. Biography may help explain even works long canonized as monuments of English literature.

---

[2] John Aubrey, further inflected by Anthony Wood, in Darbishire, 7, 48.

[3] Nicholas von Maltzahn, 'Laureate, Republican, Calvinist: An Early Response to Milton and *Paradise Lost* (1667)', *Milton Studies*, 29 (1992), 181–98 at 183, 189–90.

[4] For Milton's likely hand in the 'Leiden' letter identifying More as the author of the *Clamor*, to which letter Milton then referred as if sounder evidence, see Blair Worden, *Literature and Politics in Cromwellian England: John Milton, Andrew Marvell, Marchamont Nedham* (Oxford, 2007), 39–42, 208–13.

I

Who was the poet Milton who in 1641 enlisted in what proved the English Revolution? A Londoner through and through, his learning and religion made him a European too, if more especially a citizen of that Protestant Europe now in retreat before the Roman Catholic Continental powers. Greater London was already a metropolis of some 400,000 people, a rapidly growing political and commercial centre that had long sprawled beyond the old city walls, and that dwarfed other towns in England.[5] A member of the emerging urban elite, Milton after his years of education at home, at St Paul's School, at Christ's College, Cambridge, and abroad, was now a bachelor schoolmaster, newly established in a large and quiet house off affluent Aldersgate Street—'a pretty Garden-House . . . at the end of an Entry'—with his 10- and 9-year-old nephews Edward and John Phillips, the first of the small number of pupils he taught in the 1640s (Darbishire, 62; French, *Records*, ii. 29–30). North of St Paul's and just outside the city walls, the Aldersgate Street lodgings suggest Milton's commitment to a life of teaching in London even as he completed to his own satisfaction 'the full circle of my private studies' (*CPW*, i. 807). There he remained for almost five years, when he moved into a house in the nearby Barbican, after which, with his father's death in 1647, he moved into smaller quarters in High Holborn (backing onto Lincoln's Inn Fields), some distance west. The latter seems to mark Milton's fresh ambitions after his inheritance, moving from teaching back to study and then into public life (*CPW*, ii. 762). Later in his life, after his years living in Westminster as a state servant, and some time in hiding and in gaol at the Restoration, he returned to live north of Aldersgate, now a little east in Jewin Street in the parish of St Giles Cripplegate, in which church his father had been buried from their Barbican house in 1647, with Milton buried there too in 1674. As one of his first biographers noted, all his houses backed onto gardens: the pleasure in green spaces evident in Milton's early Ovidian poetry, in his delight in 'retired Leisure, / That in trim gardens takes his pleasure' (*Il Penseroso*, ll. 49–50) and in his garden metaphors elsewhere (the parable of the gardeners, for example, in *Animadversions* (i. 717)), seems connected to his revelling in the fecund Garden of *Paradise Lost*. Milton was not the first or last city-dweller who 'lov'd the Country, but was little There' (Darbishire, 204). During the months of the Great Plague (1665) he retreated from the infected city to rural Buckinghamshire. But he remained a Londoner to the end, despite offers from abroad of 'great preferments', and in his last years moved only to a smaller 'House in the Artillery-walk leading to Bunhill Fields', not far from these former dwellings (Darbishire, 7, 75).

The business of Milton's later life also kept him in London. Whatever the remuneration of taking in pupils, some of whom were well-to-do, Milton's main source of income originated in investments his father had made. 'Ease and leasure', he

---

[5] For its peculiarly rapid growth during Milton's early life see Roger Finlay, *Population and Metropolis: The Demography of London 1580–1750* (Cambridge, 1981), 51 and *passim*.

acknowledged, had been given him for his 'retired thoughts out of the sweat of other men' (*CPW*, i. 804). But his father's success as a businessman was one in which Milton increasingly participated, with mortgages, rentals, and the like yielding an income that in some part survived even the terrifying change in his fortunes at the Restoration. His 'disciple' Cyriack Skinner, in stressing Milton's virtue, perhaps misleadingly followed Milton when he emphasized that it was his frugality or 'Oeconomy' which allowed him to live on his inheritance (Darbishire, 32). Later biographers too have sometimes proven unwilling to emphasize Milton's business life.[6] It was active investments as much as thrift that allowed Milton in the 1650s to save £2,000 out of his public service salary of almost £300 a year, 'which being lodg'd in the Excise, and that Bank failing upon the Restoration, he utterly lost' (Darbishire, 32). His only real estate in the Restoration was the family house leased in Bread Street, which was lost in the Fire of 1666, but evidence of other investments continues to surface.[7] Like his father, Milton preferred lending money on land rather than himself having real estate, which was much more vulnerable to taxation than other forms of wealth. In his pamphlets, Milton laments the burdensome cost as much as the power of the late Renaissance state. The expense of centralized power he identified perhaps too closely with kingship itself and with the subjects' loss of liberty (Darbishire, 186; *CPW*, vii. 446, 450). But he disliked taxation from any quarter, a resentment against state impositions that he memorably expresses as late as *Samson Agonistes* (*CPW*, iv. 627).[8] Milton's lifelong familiarity with business shows in his frequent use of commercial metaphors, even in expressing his ambitions as a religious writer (i. 810).

In London too Milton found conversations and friendships second only to his delight in his Florentine encounters of 1638. Milton had a lasting talent for friendship, not least with women and younger men. Conversation animated these relationships; he was horrified to miss it in his first marriage, which failed almost before it began. He made dialogue central to his anthropology, as when his solitary Adam, conversing with God, makes his heartfelt plea for a better partner than the animals of Eden: 'I by conversing cannot these erect / From prone, nor in their ways complacence find' (8. 432–3). Such exchange shapes Milton's ideal of companionate marriage, his conception of liberty civil and religious, the very plot and conduct of *Paradise Lost*. Conversation plainly met his own emotional needs, early and late, as well as answering a long-standing humanist expectation that conversation might offer a privileged space of intellectual and personal liberty in a world too full of religious and political constraints. His friends plainly enjoyed his flair as a learned freethinker in a period of polarizing debate, when extremes, however much they stimulated different views, might also inhibit them. 'Of a very cheerful humour', reported one of Milton's

---

[6] But compare J. Milton French, *Milton in Chancery* (New York, 1939).

[7] Most recently of a loan outstanding in the 1660s to one 'Gr.' (Bodleian, MS Aubrey 13, fos. 89ʳ, 92); see Nicholas von Maltzahn, 'Making Use of the Jews: Milton and Philosemitism', in Douglas A. Brooks (ed.), *Milton and the Jews* (Cambridge, 2008), 57–82 (72).

[8] Blair Hoxby, *Mammon's Music: Literature and Economics in the Age of Milton* (New Haven, 2002), 207–16.

contemporaries, the poet was 'Extreme pleasant in his conversation, & at dinner, supper &c: But Satyricall' (Darbishire, 6). Glimpses of this conviviality emerge, whether early in the 1640s when he enjoyed a party every 'three Weeks or a Month' with some fashionable young lawyers in the neighbourhood, or later when he speaks of the social pleasure of wine by a winter fireside and in Horatian fashion asks a sometime pupil 'what neat repast shall feast us, light and choice' (Darbishire, 62; Sonnet XVII, 'Lawrence, of virtuous father virtuous son'). Milton's severity with his own students, as they themselves attested, was matched by the familiarity and freedom of his talk with them (Darbishire, 12). The 'honest liberty of free speech' he valued early and late (*CPW*, i. 804). But this conversation was a stricter pleasure than that 'company dancing and merriment' for which his first wife hankered, cut off by the times from her large royalist family in Oxfordshire, to which she soon fled home (Darbishire, 14). Milton was no friend to the recreations including 'mixt dancing' (*CPW*, i. 589) fostered by the royal 'Book of Sports', reissued in 1633. A different culture prevailed in London where, the musical son of a very musical father, Milton skilfully played organ and also bass viol, sang well, and instructed his nephews as singers.

Citizen and gentleman? Milton wore a sword 'and was skill'd in using it' (Darbishire, 32). But this betokened civic virtue, that of the militia man rather than any feudal subject. Military exercise invigorated Milton's programme of education, which with humanist pedagogy much disciplined young citizens in body and mind:

The exercise which I commend first, is the exact use of their weapon; to guard and to strike safely with edge, or point; this will keep them healthy, nimble, strong, and well in breath, is also the likeliest meanes to make them grow large, and tall, and to inspire them with a gallant and fearless courage, which being temper'd with seasonable lectures and precepts to them of true fortitude, and patience, will turn into a native and heroick valour, and make them hate the cowardise of doing wrong. (*CPW*, ii. 409)

The severities then normal to grammar learning seem to have been borne by his pupils without rancour, even when one nephew later recalled how he and his brother were 'often-times' beaten and cried (Darbishire, 14). Milton's embittered mother-in-law attributed all to his 'harsh and choleric' character (Parker, 398). But at that date learning was in many ways written on the body. Milton himself seems to have been whipped by one of his university tutors (Darbishire, 10). Discipline he often extols, since 'God even to a strictnesse requires the improvement of these his intrusted gifts' (*CPW*, i. 801). Hence Milton set a formidable example of 'hard Study and a spare diet' (Darbishire, 62). Another biographer styles him 'a Spare man', meaning that he was either thin or frugal, with other reports confirming both attributes. 'His harmonicall and ingeniose soule dwelt in beautifull & well proportioned body', we are also told; 'His deportment was sweet and affable; and his Gate erect & Manly, bespeaking Courage and undauntedness' (Darbishire, 3, 4, 32).

Milton was 'very healthy' until late in life when he suffered from gout. His blindness was a long time coming, perhaps owing to glaucoma, and complete by 1652 (Parker, 988, 1238). He was proud that it did not change the look of his eyes.

There are no great portraits of Milton as an adult, but his distinctive oval face, thickening in later life, with long brown hair and blue or 'gray' eyes is further attested by his early biographers. Even in his blindness he seems to have worn some sword, 'with a small Silver-Hilt', if not in the last years of his life. By then he was reduced to using 'a Swing for Exercise' (Darbishire, 203–4).

II

Milton's pen was of course mightier than his sword. His later literary career features a succession of great pulses of activity: two in close succession in 1641–2 and 1643–5; another in 1649–51, when he was finally slowed by his going entirely blind; and then more sporadic work before a fresh burst in 1658–63, which saw the composition of *Paradise Lost* as well as a number of tracts on religious liberty and constitutional reform (1659–60), and likely *Samson Agonistes* too (perhaps 1663–5).[9] A final flurry of publication in 1670 and after seems to reflect his finding a market now for works of yesteryear (the *History of Britain*, for example), but *Paradise Regained* and *Of True Religion* are obviously late and self-conscious reflections on matters of lasting concern to Milton. He himself, early and late, comments on his seasons of delaying preparation and the extraordinary force of his powers as a writer when at last engaged. 'They also serve who only stand and wait', he consoled himself after his blindness in Sonnet XVI; with his epic, he saw himself as 'long choosing, and beginning late'; his Samson too has been read biographically as describing his propensity for belated but then supreme effort. His vocational uncertainty had found intermittent reassurance from his evident skill as a poet. But Milton clearly saw his chiefly literary achievements to the age of 32 as lagging behind expectations, his own and others'.

Whatever his professions of modesty, Milton plainly thrilled to the opportunity that came his way in 1641 now to put the 'wearisome labours and studious watchings' (*CPW*, i. 869) of his youth to work in the public sphere. To defend his life and property ('vitam & fortunas') as he puts it in a later report to a Florentine friend, he had to leave his study and to use his 'left hand . . . in the cool element of prose' (ii. 764; i. 808). When enlisted by a group of English Presbyterians, one of whom, Thomas Young, had once been the favourite of his private tutors (see Parker, 707–8, and the essay by Edward Jones above), he gladly followed their lead in supporting the Root and Branch Petition for reforms of the national church. Those reforms had been presented to parliament in December 1640 and became an important part of parliamentary pressure on the crown in 1641. Milton's own 'lively zeale'

---

[9] Dating *Samson Agonistes* is no certain matter: lacking external evidence, I incline to the date after *Paradise Lost* suggested by the strongest contextual reading, that offered by Worden, *Literature and Politics*, 358–83.

was to animate his eloquence, in part to show that literary sophistication was not the preserve of episcopacy (*CPW*, i. 869, 873–4).

At issue was the radical reorientation of the church owing to 'the elect people of God' (*CPW*, i. 861). Might an end be brought to its government by bishops? Their hierarchy and excessive ceremony seemed too great a compromise with the Roman Catholic past and thus an impediment to true religion. Against them Milton directed a barrage of complaints and mockery. But he may have had in view also some other radical changes in government that the twenty-six bishops' membership of the House of Lords forestalled (i. 860–1). They had been appointed by the Crown and were not soon to be found voting against it (i. 852). The question remains how far Milton saw that the transformation he sought of the church—in particular, the selection of bishops not by the Crown but by the laity according to the example of the primitive church, and the ordination of ministers not by bishops (also i. 544, 600, 873)—might well prove a transformation of the state.

Here again Milton seems less unworldly than has sometimes been assumed. His animus was sharpened by his perception that he had been 'Church-outed by the Prelats' (i. 823). For Milton meant from the outset to separate church and state, certainly for the well-being of the church but also of the state. Not for him the more moderate reforms, the 'modified episcopacy' promoted by the widely admired Bishop Ussher, though Milton had to concede the 'learning' of such 'profound Clerks' even as he questioned the uses to which it was put (i. 763, 748). That compromise with the Crown, meant to consolidate constitutional gains in the preceding months, was not Milton's objective, as is reflected in his own preliminary effort in controversy.[10] He seems to have written an anonymous historical appendix to one such Presbyterian tract in February or March 1641, which supplies a hostile summary of the history of English bishops (i. 961–75) and this just as the sequestered Archbishop Laud's fortunes took a turn for the worse.[11] But Milton soon followed this with a more major restatement of the Presbyterians' claims in *Of Reformation* (May 1641), which were made more nearly his own in the four further anti-prelatical pamphlets he wrote in the next year. Not until the fourth of these anti-prelatical pamphlets, *The Reason of Church-Government* (written late in 1641) does Milton climactically declare himself more fully as its author and thus announces ownership of his positions, which by then prove to be moving rather beyond those of the Presbyterians of the day. With them he had made common cause, joining them in forcing reform. Whether he had in view quite their reforms is less certain, and soon his path would diverge from theirs.

The law of unforeseen consequences governs much of Milton's maturity, with many of his victories proving pyrrhic. When he himself sought in his *Defensio*

---

[10] Aristocratic leaders found the compromise advantageous as they promoted their own objectives in transforming the court at Whitehall; see John Adamson, *The Noble Revolt: The Overthrow of Charles I* (2007), 170 and *passim*; Hugh Trevor-Roper, *Catholics, Anglicans and Puritans: 17th-Century Essays* (Chicago, 1988), 149 ff.

[11] David Hoover and Thomas N. Corns, 'The Authorship of the Postscript', *Milton Quarterly*, 38 (2004), 59–75.

Secunda to provide a well-shaped autobiographical narrative, its elisions and un-certainties mark the strain of determining just what providential logic informed his life and times. And worse was to follow. But 1641 offered a bright moment of ecclesiastical and political possibility; the world might seem all before him and where to choose his place as national poet and reformer. He knew himself committed to godly reform, rather than the machinations of any 'modern politician', designed as those were 'to keep up the floting carcas of a crazie, and diseased Monarchy' (*CPW*, i. 571, 572). So his Puritan resentment of 'the many benefice-gaping mouth of a . . . canary-sucking, and swan-eating Prelate' was not just a plea for spiritual discipline in the church. Nor was his resentment of the Church Fathers' writings as 'hard', 'crabbed', and 'abstruse' (i. 568, 626) simply part of his dislike for 'all the heaped names of Angells, and Martyrs, Councells, and Fathers', the 'pride of flesh' yielding those 'jangling opinions' that episcopal writers proposed (i. 652, 704, 684), or 'the unweildy volumes of tradition' (i. 827), 'the scragged and thorny lectures of monkish and miserable sophistry' (i. 854) with which they bedevilled the universities. Attacking the bishops' 'secular high Office', his opposition to them on religious grounds extends beyond Root and Branch reform towards no very monarchical Christian 'commonwealth', Milton's daring impulse perhaps inviting the warning 'No Bishop, No King' (i. 538, 554–7, 582, 640).

The parliament that had met in November 1640 animated 'the people with great courage & expectation' of reform, as Milton later recalled (*CPW*, v. 443). The long period of Charles I's personal rule had now truly ended. Having perhaps overstepped the mark in *Of Reformation*, Milton might then retreat to a more modest insistence on church discipline as separate from the state (i. 575–6), training his attack on bishops once more, while leaving the Crown be, in order better to set them at odds (i. 576–7, 770–1). Thus he could emphasize the threat the priest presented to the king, not least through popular unrest against what might be styled clerical exactions and pretensions (especially i. 593–5, 638, 793, 850–60). But the insistence that kingship had its foundation in justice might be at once a commonplace and also a demanding claim for a different standard of royal conduct (i. 584), as was Milton's insistence that monarchy 'is made up of two parts, the Liberty of the subject, and the supremacie of the King' (i. 592) and his renewed claim that a king (or the King?) might be a Samson, who 'laid down his head among the strumpet flatteries of Prelats' and thus lost his strength (i. 858–60, 859). It remains unclear just how soon the anticlerical Milton determined that 'new Presbyter is but old Priest writ large', as he observed *c*.1646 ('On the New Forcers of Conscience under the Long Parliament'). 1641 was no time for Milton to dwell on differences between Presbyterians Scottish and English, for which nations' unity he can pray, nor to linger over his own differences with either (i. 596–7, 798–800). But his emphasis on toleration presages the independent direction of his career as a controversialist (i. 787–8).

Reformation demanded 'the struggl of contrarieties', those 'wars of Truth' that Milton believed fundamental to our discovery of God's purpose (*CPW*, i. 795; ii. 562). He might express dislike for the 'troubl'd sea of noises and hoars dispute' (i. 821). But the loss of government controls on the press, even as the volume of printing remained limited owing to the monopoly of the Stationers' Company, had led to the dominion in the print marketplace of pamphlet controversies. In this great proliferation of titles, the combination of press freedom and constraint shortened the average publication and anything over a sheet or two (eight or sixteen pages in quarto format) became harder to place. So there were few substantial publications that in thoroughness, system, and elaboration resembled the works Milton had spent the previous decade and more studying. But what style to adventure in this market? Here Milton was far from the Florentine literary societies where he had flourished a few years before. Even so he persisted in demonstrating his authority through an elaborate rhetoric and wide-ranging cultural reference. Moreover, when he himself then came under attack, he resorted to an ever more exalted ethos argument, making great claims for his education and probity. His shifting strategies show as the rich idiom in *Of Reformation* yields to the pared-down discipline in *Of Prelaticall Episcopacy*; with the more laborious *Animadversions*, generically restricted to shorter answers until some longer flights near the end, then leading to the much more fully reasoned *Reason of Church-Government*; with a fuller self-defence in his final *Apology* (i. 884–93). But Milton's self-conception here does not soon change. It seems to be his own voice that he imagines amid the hymns of saints and angels in the apocalyptic peroration to *Of Reformation*, with more of the same in *Animadversions* (i. 616, 706); his 'singing robes' are still to hand in *Reason of Church-Government*, where he contrasts his own writing with that of 'libidinous and ignorant poetasters' (i. 808, 818). Against the less worthy 'projectors' who 'bescraull their Pamflets every day', Milton maintains his sense that his eloquence is evidence of his spiritual election (i. 753, 821–2).

III

But it was not just the times that were turning to increasing gall, when worsening confrontation after the season of hope in 1641 led to war between royal and parliamentary armies in the summer of 1642. Even as Milton had decried those whose public professions were betrayed by their own deficiency 'in the regulating of their own family' (*CPW*, i. 754), his own virginity cult ended in a sudden and disastrous marriage that summer. What began as a business trip to some Oxfordshire gentry to collect on a mortgage, ended in his marriage to the Powells' eldest daughter, Mary. He was 32, she 17. The extended wedding party continued in London for some days before her family left Mary to her marriage. A month or so later Mary's friends, 'possibly incited by her own desire' as Milton's knowing nephew suggests, successfully imposed on him to yield her back to Oxfordshire for the rest of the summer. Meant to return at the end of September, she did not come back for almost four years, with Milton's pleas in the interim said to have met with a brusque response

(Darbishire, 63–5). 'In the full vigor of his Manhood', as one of Milton's pupils recalled, Milton 'could ill bear the disappointment hee mett with by her obstinate absenting' (Darbishire, 23; Parker, 881–2).

Even as Milton endured this domestic crisis, the king had raised his standard in the north in August; the great Battle of Edgehill between royal and parliamentary forces followed in October; the royal army threatened London in November, when Milton in a sonnet pleaded the respect owed poets by men of war ('Captain or colonel'). In Oxfordshire the royalist Powells were now divided from Milton by the opposed lines of the rival armies—he himself seems later to allude to the problem (compare *CPW*, iv. 625)—and it was not until well after the victory of the parliamentary side, with these in-laws' affairs in disarray, and Milton rumoured to be planning a new marriage to a Miss Davis, 'a very Handsome and Witty Gentlewoman', that the Powells changed tack. Was Milton gratified or dismayed by Mary's coming back to London and 'making submission and begging pardon on her knees before him'? He had been 'as it were a single man again' and had developed a taste for women 'of great Wit and Ingenuity'. Most of Milton's biographers have taken a kind view of the excitement of reunion that issued in their first child within the year after. But even now it was only 'at length concluded' that Mary, 'one whom he thought to have never seen more', would first stay with Milton's brother's widowed mother-in-law—this in no very adjacent dwelling over by The Strand—before moving in once more with Milton (Darbishire, 64–67). Even after reconciling with Mary and the birth of their first child, Milton still characterized his marriage as an unprofitable tie, in terms that elicited from his correspondent some learned and sympathetic comment on Venus forcing 'beneath her brazen yoke bodies and hearts ill-mated' (*CPW*, ii. 762, 766, 768).

More recent studies have done much to explain how Milton's ardent ideal of friendship, especially as embodied in his earlier relation with Charles Diodati, informed his high expectations of companionate marriage.[12] He sought no 'mute and spiritles mate' (*CPW*, ii. 251). At the same time, Milton extols his own mother's example of charity (iv. 612) and also the unnamed, virtuous virgin—at once like the biblical Mary (Martha's sister) and like Ruth, whom he celebrates in Sonnet IX ('Lady that in the prime'). Mary Powell may well have baulked at the challenge before her. Reading between the lines in the divorce tracts, Annabel Patterson describes some revulsion on Milton's part at sexual experience, a wounded reaction to frustrated physicality consistent with his dark expectations elsewhere of heresy begetting 'heresie with a certain monstrous haste of pregnancy in her birth, at once borne and giving birth' (i. 781) or his gruesome allegory of Satan, Sin, and Death late in *Paradise Lost*, Book 2.[13] Failing divorce, mortality in London was high and one way to lose a wife

---

[12] Gregory Chaplin, '"One Flesh, One Heart, One Soul": Renaissance Friendship and Miltonic Marriage', *Modern Philology*, 99 (2001), 266–92; Thomas H. Luxon, *Single Imperfection: Milton, Marriage and Friendship* (Pittsburgh, Pa., 2005). Compare William Haller, *Liberty and Reformation in the Puritan Revolution* (New York, 1955), 78–99.

[13] Annabel Patterson, 'Milton, Marriage and Divorce', in Thomas N. Corns (ed.), *A Companion to Milton* (Oxford, 2001), 279–93.

was to 'be fruitful and multiply', to risk her in childbirth. With a maternal death rate well over one in fifty births, it was in 'travaile' especially that the loss of a wife might be feared.[14] Milton's children followed in 1646 (Anne), 1648 (Mary), 1651 (John), and 1652 (Deborah). The mother Mary died a few days after the last birth. Six weeks later Milton's baby son also died owing to 'the ill usage or bad constitution of an ill-chosen nurse' (Darbishire, 71).

Milton did not remarry until 1656, when he enjoyed what seems to have been a happy union with Katherine Woodcock, twenty years his junior. Eleven months later a daughter Katherine was born (19 October 1657). The mother died early in 1658, their infant daughter a month after. Katherine Woodcock is surely the wife of Sonnet XIX, insofar as that projection refers to a person, whom the blind poet dreams of seeing now after her death, free 'from spot of childbed taint' and 'vested all in white, pure as her mind' ('pure' too as in her name, from the Greek *katharos*), only to awaken into a day that her absence renders doubly night. In 1663 Milton married his third wife, Elizabeth Minshull, thirty years his junior, who long survived him (d. 1727). A shrewd eighteenth-century biographer, Jonathan Richardson, observes that Milton would never marry a widow, which emotional preference denied him access to what was a profitable marriage market and to any more seasoned sexuality (Darbishire, 205). *Paradise Lost* shows an eventual delight in the happier carnality he may himself have experienced in later marriage(s). But the rancor of Adam and Eve's arguments after the Fall, and the harrowing exchange between Samson and Dalila in *Samson Agonistes*, argue Milton's bitter experience of marital dissatisfactions, in the former case issuing in reconciliation, in the latter in renewed separation. Milton's poetry, which Samuel Johnson accuses of a 'want of human interest', is in this regard at least arresting (Johnson himself had reason to repress thoughts of marital failure).[15]

As Johnson also observed, Milton 'was naturally a thinker for himself' (i. 294–5). His education in controversy combined now with his profound reappraisal of marriage to lead Milton towards an extraordinary reinvention of himself as a public intellectual. (We might look to Wallace Stevens as a comparable instance of marital failure without divorce issuing in a radical reconception of self.) Milton had learned much from a year of writing and controversial engagements. He also gained now from reflection on his own situation. He was soon to complete the journey from being an orator on behalf of others to becoming an orator for himself.

---

[14]   R. Schofield, 'Did Mothers Really Die?', in L. Bonfield, R. M. Smith, and K. Wrightson (eds.), *The World We Have Gained* (Oxford, 1986), 233, 248, 251–2, 254 (in addition to the special danger of the first birth, the rate of maternity deaths from infectious disease was peculiarly high in London); William Whately, *A Care-cloth: Or a Treatise of the Cumbers and Troubles of Marriage* (1624), 50.

[15]   Johnson, *Lives of the Poets*, ed. Roger Lonsdale, 4 vols. (Oxford, 2006), i. 290.

IV

The second phase of Milton's career in controversy features a rhetoric no less majestic than the first. But the independence and reach of his arguments become much greater. For now he was no longer speaking the language of the times, as he had done in his pamphlets for Root and Branch reforms of the church or even state. His next contributions, favouring divorce and pre-press licensing, display an intellectual inventiveness new to his prose. The effect is startling.

Especially in the *Doctrine and Discipline of Divorce* and *Areopagitica*, Milton articulated positions new to what was no very extensive contemporary debate. In the course of doing so, he pressed the logic of others' arguments and his own to the point of no return. Did others cite natural law in arguing the parliamentary cause? Milton could do so in seeking to legalize divorce and advocating the freedom of the press. If those others, Presbyterians mostly, refused to follow Milton so far, he might round on them: 'I did but prompt the age to quit their clogs' (Sonnet XII, 'On the Detraction which followed upon my Writing Certain Treatises'). If they wished an argument from authority, he might turn to that great reformer Martin Bucer, who had held a like position permitting divorce (*The Judgement of Martin Bucer, Concerning Divorce*, 1644). Did Trinitarian writers quote anti-Trinitarian writings at length in order to refute such heresies? Milton in poring through the heavy tomes of Johann Gerhard discovered the heretics had the better case.[16] Likewise, the customary opprobrium for the ancient bishop Dionysius Alexandrinus owing to his innovative theological opinions might strike Milton as quite unwarranted (*CPW*, ii. 511–12). Clerical arrogations of power had not just afflicted the church itself, of course. One area after another of human endeavour seemed to cry out for emancipation from the dead hand of Custom, which Milton had long discerned as 'but agednesse of Error' (i. 561).

Notable in the divorce tracts, moreover, is Milton's readiness to reconceive his relation to the Bible.[17] Now he was telling no twice-told tale in which the proof-texts might be flopped out, one after another. Instead he engages in a much more inquiring reading of passages from the Old Testament and New. He finds such welcome liberty on this point in the older law that he presses to discover the same in the new. Aggressively contextualizing Jesus' apparent injunctions against divorce, he promotes a Mosaic rather than Pauline perspective on the reason essential to God's laws and to be sought in human ones. Adventurous as his arguments are, Milton's rhetorical flair also shows in this impassioned address to the Long Parliament. Reaction in that quarter against his views induced from Milton no retreat. Instead he republished the *Doctrine and Discipline of Divorce* in a 'much augmented' second edition (1643, 1644 title page), with *The Judgement of Martin Bucer*,

---

[16] Martin Dzelzainis, 'Milton and Antitrinitarianism', in Sharon Achinstein and Elizabeth Sauer (eds.), *Milton and Toleration* (Oxford, 2007), 171–85 at 184–5.

[17] See Jason Rosenblatt, *Torah and Law in* Paradise Lost (Princeton, 1994).

Tetrachordon, and *Colasterion* supporting its positions and defying his detractors. Of those there were a number; he had put his name to work written in English on 'a Subject so new to this age' (*CPW*, ii. 724) and those times rent by political and religious divisions. This was Milton's first fuller experience of fame or infamy. In the main, his chiefly Presbyterian critics lamented Milton as but an instance of sectarian excess; they could lump him with other exponents of free love since antinomians had long been associated, sometimes with cause, with sexual licence. These charges Milton might brush aside, even as he responded at length to the more substantial counter-arguments of a 'nameless' 'Confuter', whose longer *Answer to ... the Doctrine and Discipline of Divorce* (licensed in November 1644) was not so easily dismissed. Milton's harsh reply in *Colasterion* mocked his antagonist, bringing that menial 'mechanic' or 'Serving-man' under his punitive correction. Milton pleaded again for divorce as the only answer to the 'perpetual defraudments of truest conjugal society ... injuries and vexations as importunat as fire'. Those afflictions were a far cry from the 'rationall burning' of the soul's 'inbred desire of joyning to it self in conjugall fellowship a fit conversing soul' (ii. 724, 726, 731, 251).

Milton's Presbyterian critics were in the ascendant because the fortunes of war had forced parliament to seek the Scots' support in 1643. By 1644, Milton's earlier sense of a common cause with English Presbyterians had given way to a deep resentment of their effort, in conjunction with Scots Presbyterians, to enforce their system of church government in an English national church. Just as bad were the compromises with the Crown this seemed to invite. Now it became clear to Milton that there were 'new forcers of conscience' afoot. How bitter a fate to escape bishops only now to succumb to their Presbyterian counterparts! They were gathered at Westminster in an assembly that threatened to confuse church and state in a lasting settlement of a Presbyterian national church. Thus to promote religion by 'bodilie compulsion' rather than 'evangelic perswasion' much offended Milton. Vital to true Christianity was the freedom of believers to engage in conscientious discussion, unconstrained by the dead hand of authority.

Vital to true citizenship was the freedom to advise parliament. That freedom too, Milton feared, was now again to be abrogated. In 1641 the pre-publication licensing of books had lapsed with abolition of Star Chamber, that momentous loss of royal prerogative. The pressure of events in 1643—chiefly successive royalist victories, not finally checked until Cromwell's decisive victory at Marston Moor in July 1644—led parliament to revive such licensing in June 1643 with a view to gaining control over the unruly London press. Milton viewed this as a disastrous mistake. His chosen career in education had already brought him into a circle of reformers, many of them Continental refugees from the Thirty Years War and Counter-Reformation constraints on the freedom of religious and scientific inquiry. With these reformers, Milton foresaw a brave new world of intellectual exchange. His treatise *Of Education* (June 1644), addressed to one of their leading figures, Samuel Hartlib, is much more than a reading list, however impressive the great series of classical authors whom pupils are to read in Latin and Greek. Milton here offers the Hartlib circle and parliament his humanist blueprint for national revival at a time when the outcome of the Civil War still hung in the balance. Critics have noted his freedom in imagining educational, social, and even constitutional change in its pages, if sometimes between the lines, and also his emphasis on military training.[18]

If the education of youth demanded bold reform, the ongoing education of citizens demanded Milton's still more ardent rejection now of pre-publication licensing of the press. By the time he wrote *Areopagitica* (1644), the military successes of parliament invited a more expansive consideration of the national interest. Again styling the tract a speech, Milton Athenianizes the Long Parliament, as if to wrench it away from the baleful influence of the Presbyterians in the House and in the Westminster Assembly now meeting. Their arrogations of power Milton later excoriated in the Digression to his *History of Britain*, in some topical sonnets, and in his anti-monarchical tracts. More generally, he had long lamented the English 'weaknesse and want of better instruction' in religion and politics (*CPW*, i. 796–7), a lasting concern that he continued to voice (see especially v. 451). Constraints internal to the London-centred book trade, governed as it was by the monopolistic Stationers' Company, did bother Milton (ii. 570). But the interference of church or state in selecting what might be printed enraged him. Satirizing pre-publication licensing as a relic of Roman Catholic abuses, Milton instead affirms English national liberty. However quiet the reception of the work in his own day—there are a few allusions to it and even those not uniformly admiring—its exalted description of press freedom in the next centuries gained for *Areopagitica* the most lasting renown of any of Milton's prose.

But what had become of Milton the poet, who already as a youth had agreed with the assurance of his mentors that his work was such as 'aftertimes . . . should not willingly let it die' (*CPW*, i. 810)? Even as he entered the lists as a public intellectual, his poetic production seems to have sunk from the achievement of *A Masque Presented at Ludlow Castle* (performed in 1634, published in 1637) and 'Lycidas' (November 1637) to his superb and varied but more incidental sonnets of the early 1640s. There is ample evidence, however, that his ambitions for his poetry were undiminished all the while. His rough book, now at Trinity College, Cambridge, includes after its draft of 'Lycidas' an extensive list of biblical and British historical subjects for poetic dramas, with some of them, notably an 'Adam unparadiz'd', being sketched more fully. Conspicuous here is the pressure towards narration that leads to ever fuller prologues, prelude to the larger narration when Milton returned to this subject in his epic. Milton's commonplace book, now at the British Library, also shows him alert to how his wide readings might lend themselves to a poet's hand; in his *History of Britain* he would a few years later relate the legendary British prehistory 'be it for nothing else but in favour of our English Poets, and Rhetoricians, who by thir Art will know, how to use them judiciously' (v. 3). Years later he reflected on his having been 'long choosing' his epic 'and beginning late' (*Paradise Lost*, 9. 26). The

---

[18] Nigel Smith, *Literature and Revolution in England, 1640–1660* (New Haven and London, 1994), 155–6; David Norbrook, *Writing the English Republic: Poetry, Rhetoric and Politcs, 1627–1660* (Cambridge, 1999) 131; Martin Dzelzainis, 'Republicanism', in Corns (ed.), *A Companion to Milton*, 294–308 at 300–4.

promises to perform as a national poet that he made in *The Reason of Church-Government* were not soon fulfilled, at least not in verse.

Perhaps conscious of the delay, in 1645 Milton published a book of English and Latin poems with a strongly retrospective cast. Pride and modesty vie in its presentation. The octavo volume includes commendatory notices and poems from distinguished admirers at home and abroad. But both within the book and in comment on it, Milton resorts to modesty topoi, not least in the presentation of some of the Latin works, and by extension the collection as a whole, as something of a miscellany, belonging to the genre of *silva*. Where Statius in his preface to *Silvae* had vaunted his rapid improvisation in such poems ('subito calore'), Milton too can emphasize the impromptu flair of many of his compositions. Here it is the rapidity as much as the 'earliness of his own proficiency' that Milton commends 'to the notice of posterity' (to borrow Samuel Johnson's phrase). For whatever the Horatian persuasion that we should write and rewrite patiently, poets might also delight in displaying their sudden fecundity, whether as personal achievement, or as the working of a Muse that could be associated with the Holy Spirit and hence salvation, in a Christianizing of *furor poeticus*. Hence *silva* could help translate works from a literary system dominated by occasion and patronage to one in which the aesthetic is a more autonomous category.

The generic expectations of *silva* also accorded with poets' self-deprecation about the youthful endeavours they were nonetheless publishing. There was a long tradition of excusing less finished work as an acceptable part of a sylvan woodpile. Milton himself makes this self-deprecatory move repeatedly. He insistently dates his youthful productions, and indicates their origins in school and college. His early poem 'The Passion' is presented still incomplete with a note claiming that 'This Subject the Author finding to be above the yeers he had, when he wrote it, and nothing satisfi'd with what was begun, left it unfinisht'. The poem remains incomplete; the apologetic note remains the same as late as the second edition of 1673. There too, Milton in its last lines attributes most of 'Lycidas' to an uncouth swain. In his 1645 *Poems* and again in 1673 he disavows the Ovidian elegies of his youth, even as he publishes them ('Haec ego mente olim laeva'). And in sending *Poems* 1645 to the Bodleian Library he deprecates the whole volume as if poetry 'juvenilis olim'—boyish and of yesteryear—despite so much of it being the work of his adulthood ('Ad Joannem Rousium', line 5). The bookseller for *Poems* (1645) was Humphrey Moseley, who was now busy purveying the poetry of the 1630s to a nostalgic readership. Almost all of Milton's poetry in the volume pre-dates 1641. Modern criticism has been swift to discover harbingers of Milton the revolutionary in this work. He himself seems to have viewed this work as something of a throwback to a culture now superseded by more turbulent times. His 'left hand' had adjusted to the new possibilities in prose controversy. But reinventing his poetics in response to the new realities was no easy matter, even for Milton. Writing his Florentine friend Carlo Dati in April 1647, he laments the 'lack of any safe retreat for literary leisure among so many civil battles, so much slaughter, flight, and pillaging of goods' (*CPW*, ii. 764).

V

Milton's letter to Dati reveals a dark view of his circumstances as a writer in a nation torn by unrest. That view shapes much of his work in the crisis of the English Revolution that followed in 1648 and 1649, as the king sought compromise with what Milton viewed as the backsliding Presbyterians, only for Army radicalism then to purge parliament further to force the trial that led to the king's execution at Whitehall, on that memorable day 30 January 1648/9. In April 1648 Milton translates the penitential Psalms and that summer, when another civil war broke out, he responds in a sonnet addressed to Lord Fairfax, general of the parliamentary army, with pleas for peace and better fiscal management. Now too he began writing histories to instruct his countrymen in their failings. He seems first to have tried his hand at an 'epitome' of what was to be known about Russia, *The Brief History of Moscovia* (published only posthumously), perhaps in part owing to his interest in the climatic explanation for the difficulty of governing northern nations. This looks like a run-up to his much larger *History of Britain*, which he says he began writing at the king's death (*CPW*, iv. 627–8). Rapidly surveying the early history of England, he seems to have advanced his narrative to Saxon times before taking up employment as Latin secretary to the revolutionary Council of State (20 March 1648/9). Especially in the Digression later omitted from the published *History*, where Milton compares the faltering English in the 1640s with their faltering ancient counterparts after the Roman departure from Britain, his jeremiad denounces the compromising Presbyterians and more generally a nation that might fail its leaders' 'fortitude and Heroick vertue' in service to liberty, whether of church or state. Like misgivings animate his other tracts of 1649, *The Tenure of Kings and Magistrates* and *Eikonoklastes*, where the evils of Charles's reign are found to be perpetuated by Presbyterians in the 1640s (iii. 191–7, 221–2, 251–2, 437–8, 490).

After the Army's purge of the Presbyterians in parliament and then the execution of Charles I, Milton's scorn could be directed against the failed government of the 1640s, with the bold endorsement by contrast of the revolutionary parliamentary government that now sought to legitimize itself, eventually as a republic. Begun during the trial of the king in January and published soon after, *The Tenure of Kings and Magistrates* justifies the individual right of resistance to tyranny, arguing that rebellion against tyrants is due obedience to God. Here Milton's radical position recalls that of his friends and fellow-revolutionaries John Bradshaw (the judge in the king's trial), John Sadler, and perhaps Luke Robinson, who had been Milton's contemporary at Christ's College.[19] The *Tenure* and such acquaintance recommended him to the new government. His role as Latin secretary required his translation of Continental correspondence and diplomatic documents for much of the next decade, in which secretarial service he was bound in close service first of all

---

[19] Parker, 353; Campbell, *Chronology*, 96, 105; Sheffield University, Hartlib Papers, 49/9/5B and 17B; Worden, *Literature and Politics*, 45–7.

to the Council of State.[20] His duties also soon included defending the new government retreat from its many critics. Ordered to help proceedings against the royalist journalist Marchamont Nedham, Milton in time became the versatile Nedham's friend. Ordered to help proceedings against the Presbyterian pamphleteer Clement Walker, harsh critic of Milton and his *Tenure*, Milton could contribute to the case against Walker, who died in the Tower two years later (Campbell, *Chronology*, 103). Milton soon moved into government lodgings at Whitehall, which allowed his close attendance to the Council of State's needs, and entered upon the state service that occupied him for the next decade. Late in 1651, he moved to other lodgings in Westminster, backing onto St James Park, where he lived until the Restoration. He remained close to the workings of government even after his final blindness in 1652 and it is often Continental diplomats whose reports and diaries reveal most about Milton's day-to-day life in this period—most of all in the writings of the Oldenburg emissary Hermann Mylius.

A common theme in his writings of 1649–51 is Milton's anger that the Presbyterians, who had once been such valuable allies against the state church, had now long shown themselves intent on arrogating power in a fresh confusion of church and state (*CPW*, iii. 490). Milton's government service soon invited his harsh *Observations* on the Irish Presbyterians' refusal to accede to the new regime. Next came his extended rebuttal of the *Eikon Basilike*, which purported to be the king's own meditations on his situation on the eve of his trial and execution. To this 'image of the king', a runaway success that drew on wide revulsion at the regicide, Milton responded with his image-breaker *Eikonoklastes*, impugning royal claims at every turn and any pretensions to sacerdotal kingship. But as a state servant he now in a second edition of his *Tenure* muted its radicalism: where the first edition had quoted more radical Presbyterian authorities of yesteryear against the backsliding Presbyterians of the 1640s, the second edition adds further Protestant authorities who insisted on the 'inferior' magistrate's mediating role in executing justice on a ruler.[21] He was shifting to the less radical, constitutionalist arguments that would expand the pages of his Latin *Defensio* of the English people against a French polemicist, Claude Saumaise or 'Salmasius', himself something of a Presbyterian. Salmasius's royalist *Defensio regia* appeared from Continental and English presses in 1650; it was dedicated to the would-be Charles II, who rewarded the author with £100. Milton accused Salmasius of basely writing for hire, but he himself on his yearly salary of £288 was not disinterested in performing the Council's order of 8 January 1650 to answer the attack. He published his *Defensio pro populo Anglicano* a year later; it was much republished thereafter in London and on the Continent.

The *Defensio* contributed most to Milton's fame in his lifetime. Here he returned to something like his role as an orator in the anti-prelatical tracts, assembling a range of arguments, some of them rather jostling with each other, in favour of his brief. It won a wide readership at home and especially abroad. Even the many who

[20] Leo Miller, *Milton and the Oldenburg Safeguard* (New York, 1985); Robert Thomas Fallon, *Milton in Government* (University Park, Pa., 1993).

[21] Milton, *Political Writings*, ed. Martin Dzelzainis (Cambridge, 1991), pp. xi–xiv.

disparaged Milton's politics, early and late, often enough conceded the majesty of his Latin prose. He himself set great store by his humanist accomplishment in this work, which he contrasted with Salmasius's barbarities, the more laughable in such a 'grammarian'. Counter-attacks soon followed, book-burnings too, and further defences, including Milton's of his nation and of himself (*Defensio secunda*, published in 1654; *Pro se defensio*, 1655; with a significantly revised edition of the *Defensio* itself in 1658). Milton's lack of scruple has been observed in this polemical land of no holds barred. The skilful Latinity of the *Defensio* is trained on the violent destruction of Salmasius's credibility as much as on any affirmation of the varied arguments Milton presents on behalf of the regicide and the revolutionary government. *Ad hominem* attacks were the stock-in-trade of such controversialists. Especially in his *Defensio secunda*, Milton was swift to make the most of the sexual misdeeds of his presumed antagonist (another Continental Calvinist minister, Alexander More), even though he soon had assurances of what he already knew, that More had not written the offending *Regii sanguinis clamor* ('The Cry of the Royal Blood', 1652) which had so impugned Milton.

After going entirely blind in 1652, Milton worked more slowly and seems at first to have depended heavily on materials from 1650–1 he had already assembled in the course of composing the *Defensio* and in the aftermath of its publication. He benefited from the arrival in London of a younger man with whom he developed a lasting friendship, Andrew Marvell, an accomplished linguist whom even Milton might admire and for whom he soon wrote an impressive letter of reference.[22] The *Defensio secunda* revealingly responds to the political cross-currents that troubled the Rump Parliament well before Cromwell's dissolution of that assembly in April 1653, even as it also eventually reacts to that event and to the Lord General's fuller usurpation of power in December 1653. Milton has justly been characterized as hopeful here, but not an optimist: 'Whatever arguments Milton might find for or against the rule of Cromwell, he had always to remember the alternatives: the rule of the Stuarts, the dominance of the Presbyterians, the joint sway of those forces.'[23] Moreover, these elaborate defences of the English people's actions in sentencing the king to death might in time prove a comment on any less revolutionary commitments in the successive regimes of Oliver Cromwell.[24]

At issue for Milton were the lasting concerns he voiced in his sonnets to Sir Henry Vane and to Cromwell himself, these in 1652 when a fresh settlement of religion was sought. The sonnet to Vane made it into that statesman's papers, from which, after the Restoration, it was published when Vane was judicially murdered. How to separate 'spiritual power and civil'? Milton's long hopes for a Protestant toleration seemed in the 1650s still to be clouded by the Presbyterians 'Threatening to bind our souls with secular chains'. Like other independently minded Protestants, he had once

---

[22] Nicholas von Maltzahn, *An Andrew Marvell Chronology* (Basingstoke, 2005), 37–8, 41.

[23] Worden, *Literature and Politics*, 293; see also 262–88.

[24] Martin Dzelzainis, 'Milton and the Protectorate in 1658', in David Armitage, Armand Himy, and Quentin Skinner (eds.), *Milton and Republicanism* (Cambridge, 1995), 181–205; Worden, *Literature and Politics*, 294–7, 308–9, 323–5, 335–7.

allied himself with Presbyterians only to find the cost unexpectedly high.[25] Resuming his *History* in the mid-1650s, Milton found in Saxon chronicles occasion for dark reflections on modern English rulers.[26] Later in the Protectorate, his misgivings about the government he served seem only to have intensified: 'I stay nearly always at home—and willingly', he writes to one petitioner late in 1657, and his claim now that he has no friends in high places may not just be tactical (*CPW*, vii. 507). After Cromwell's death in 1658, moreover, Milton renewed his service as a pamphleteer, styling the Protectorate a 'scandalous night of interruption' and venturing fresh prescriptions for the better division of church and state in a *Treatise of Civil power* and *Considerations Touching The likeliest means to remove Hirelings out of the Church* (*CPW*, vii. 274).[27] His publications of 1659–60, when he comes to work with Vane's publisher Livewell Chapman, show his deep commitment to the terms of his earlier sonnet to Vane. He now also penned fresh political proposals and privately declared the need not for a historian of England's troubles but for 'one who can happily end them' (20 December 1659: *CPW*, vii. 515).

VI

Milton's compositions from 1658 to 1665 often suggest some grand simplification of his purpose as an author. In this last great spate, he composed long-planned *Paradise Lost*, and also the twin tracts of 1659, the two editions of *The Readie and Easie Way* (1660), some more polemic (*Brief Notes* and another unpublished tract in 1660), and likely *Samson Agonistes* (*c*.1663–5?). These were dictated amidst huge political upheavals, in which Milton's life was threatened. The Restoration left this apologist for the execution of Charles I now a subject of Charles II. In 1660, Milton's regicide tracts were banned by public decree and burnt by the hangman. Milton was ordered arrested but escaped the death penalty. He was imprisoned that autumn, released in December, then went into a hiding complete enough that as late as June 1666 a Continental correspondent presumed him dead (*CPW*, viii. 1–4). Only in 1667 did he belatedly resurface with the publication of his epic. Then ensued a not unprolific 'retired silence'—the term is his friend Marvell's, defending Milton from fresh attack in 1673—in the succession of his publications until his death late in 1674.[28] But after

---

[25] Nicholas von Maltzahn, 'Milton, Marvell and Toleration', in Achinstein and Sauer (eds.), *Milton and Toleration*, 86–104 at 99–103; Hugh Trevor-Roper, 'Religious Origins of the Enlightenment', in *Religion, the Reformation and Social Change*, 2nd edn. (London, 1972), 193–236.

[26] Nicholas von Maltzahn, *Milton's History of Britain: Republican Historiography in the English Revolution* (Oxford, 1991), 169–74.

[27] See also Worden, *Literature and Politics*, 41–3, 341–3.

[28] *Prose Works of Andrew Marvell*, ed. Annabel Patterson, Martin Dzelzainis, Nicholas von Maltzahn, and Neil Keeble, 2 vols. (New Haven, 2003), i. 418.

1665 his fresh compositions seem much more sporadic, with most of what he brought to press being the work of yesteryear: a Latin primer, *Accedence Commenc't Grammar*, brought to the press at the same time as *Paradise Lost* and appearing from the same bookseller in 1669; his *History of Britain*, ending at the Norman Conquest (1670); and a Latin *Artis Logicae* (1672).[29] Only *Paradise Regained*, the tract *Of True Religion* (1673), and his translation of a Latin *Declaration, or Letters Patents of the Election of this present King of Poland* (1674, a pointed endorsement of elective kingship) are certainly of a late date.

Paradise Lost is of course the grandest expression of Milton's renewed pleasure in his own powers, or of the direct involvement of something like the Holy Spirit, as he understood his success. That epic at last met his self-expectations, having been long meditated if now begun late. Edward Phillips discloses that Milton had already in the 1640s written at least some of Satan's Mount Niphates speech in Book 4, and the expanding outlines of 'Adam unparadiz'd' in the Trinity Manuscript suggest an early attempt at such a drama. But Phillips's biography implies that his uncle composed the epic itself between 1658 and 1663. A return to the work in 1658 may be detected in some perhaps topical details in Book 1: the Satan–Leviathan simile (ll. 200–8) may play on the 58-foot London whale that June; the comparison of Satan's spear to a Norwegian mast (ll. 292–4) may recall parliamentary debate over strategic supplies from the Baltic that winter 1658–9; the reference to a royal setback at 'Fontarabbia' (ll. 586–7) may speak to Charles II's visit to the north of Spain after the failed royalist uprising of August 1659 (Campbell, *Chronology*, 185). The epic, especially in its characterization of Satan and the fallen angels, reflects Milton's familiarity with interregnal politics and political oratory, not least in that early *pièce de résistance*, the Consult in Hell in Book 2. That Milton delayed until 1667 the publication of an epic perhaps already complete in 1663 probably followed from his greater confidence at the later date about his own safety and the reception of his work, not least after the national calamities of the Great Plague (1665), the Fire of London (1666), and the dismaying success of the Dutch late in the Second Anglo–Dutch War (1667). These events issued in a significant change in national mood, resulting in political compromises favourable to Milton's re-emergence and also to his hopes for toleration.[30]

That Milton turned to *Paradise Lost* late in the 1650s is also suggested by evidence from the incompletely revised manuscript of his *De Doctrina Christiana*. That he shifted from a systematic to narrative theology marked his deepening commitment to a biblical reasoning intent on not overdetermining the meaning of Scripture.[31] The simpler idiom of his tracts in this period also bears emphasis. Though still capable of conspicuous rhetorical tours de force, Milton now comes to venture a less spectacular idiom in these exercises in persuasion. His oratorical commissions had

---

[29] London, Stationers' Company, Court Book D, fo. 127ᵛ.

[30] Nicholas von Maltzahn, 'The First Reception of *Paradise Lost* (1667)', *Review of English Studies*, 47 (1996), 479–99.

[31] Gordon Campbell et al., 'The Provenance of De Doctrina Christiana', *Milton Quarterly*, 31 (1997), 67–117; Phillip J. Donnelly, *Milton's Biblical Reasoning: Narrative and Protesant Toleration* (Cambridge, 2009).

perhaps become less fulfilling with the passage of the years, however exalted his Ciceronian description of his earlier defence of the English people (*CPW*, iv. 684–6). Would that people ever live up to his service to them? His political hopes may have been raised after Cromwell's death (3 September 1658), when Richard Cromwell's succession did not long delay the revival of republican expectations and the desire for some better religious settlement. Milton continued his political engagements: several sketches for constitutional reform in 1659 prepare for the fuller published prescriptions of *The Readie and Easie Way to Establish a Free Commonwealth* (2 edns., 1660). That republican advice emphasizes the role of the worthy few in a distribution of power that secures their good government from a retrograde populace too slow to become citizens, too eager again to abject themselves to a monarchy.

Milton had long pondered 'how my light is spent' (Sonnet XVI, 'When I consider') and when his beloved second wife Katherine died (3 February 1658), followed soon by their infant daughter, also Katherine (19 October 1657–17 March 1658), he had fresh cause to contemplate his condition and commitments. His relation to his daughters from his first marriage became a vexed one, with eventual expressions of unkindness reported from both sides (Campbell, *Chronology*, 199). His financial affairs were further complicated by the Restoration and the prudent retreat from public life that required, the blind man enjoying no very settled arrangements in the last fifteen years of his life in London. We may seek to read his political and domestic woes into *Paradise Lost*, but those also energized Milton's insistence on an 'answerable style' (9. 20) raising his epic beyond the encumbrance of any particular failures personal or national.

The intensity of enlightenment that *Paradise Lost* conveys at every turn—in its sudden foregrounding of the fallen Satan, and also its fascinated imagining of the days of Creation; in its bold evocations of God the Father and his Son, and also its lively assertion of paradisal sexuality; in its tender sense of evolving marital relations before the Fall, and its rebuke of tyranny in the age of Nimrod—is not soon explained by biography or anything else. Milton now somehow came to write more freely within his biblicist discipline than ever before. That biblicism he had long tested with his habits of free-thinking—we learn in the 1650s of his having to hand a manuscript of the scandalous 'Heptaplomeres', for example, where seven wise men converse peaceably about their faiths only to arrive at natural religion—and shared with the friends, pupils, and visitors who persisted in associating with him even when the Restoration left him infamous. His often demanding reconception of religion, of politics, of social relations, of genre, eventually extended to his review of his own achievements. Modern students of Milton's last works have discovered in him some abatement of his lordliness. Did readers of *Paradise Lost* too much seize on the virtuosity of its imitations of classical epic? Or did the regeneration of Milton's Samson stagger too uncertainly through the violent night of Old Testament law?[32]

---

[32] See respectively Nicholas von Maltzahn, 'Milton: Nation and Reception', in Paul Stevens and David Loewenstein (eds.), *Early Modern Nationalism and Milton's England* (Toronto, 2008); Feisal G. Mohamed, 'Confronting Religious Violence: Milton's *Samson Agonistes*', *PMLA* 120 (2005), 327–40.

Milton in his briefer epic *Paradise Regained* offers a corrective in biblical poetics and New Testament charity.[33] Had Milton's sacred vehemence too much unsettled the basis for Christian fellowship even in affirming it? Milton in *Of True Religion* at last ventures a defence of Protestant toleration written not in blood but in milk.[34]

The second edition of *Paradise Lost* appeared in 1674. How much was required to bridge between literary fashions of the day and this intransigent prophetic masterpiece appears from the bravura commendatory poem Andrew Marvell supplied for this fresh publication. The effect is most dramatic in the conclusion of the poem, where it proposes that 'Thy verse created like thy theme sublime, / In number, weight, and measure, needs not rhyme'. This comments not only on style, however. The trope has been understood as a recollection of Wisdom 11: 20, but the other biblical text behind it is the writing on the wall at Belshazzar's feast, interpreted by the prophet Daniel:

MENE; God hath numbered thy kingdom, and finished it.
TEKEL; Thou art weighed in the balances, and art found wanting.
PERES; Thy kingdom is divided, and given to the Medes and Persians. (Daniel 5: 25–8)

This might be a restorative text for a revolutionary of Milton's stamp: the idolatrous king and his profligate court denounced by Daniel on the eve of their destruction. But it was Milton who fell sick that summer. He was 'chearfull even in his Gowtefitts', when he sang, though he is also reported to have thought his blindness tolerable compared to that painful disease. Complications of that illness killed him 'in the 9th or 10th of Novemb. 1674', when he died 'with so little pain or Emotion, that the time of his expiring was not perceiv'd by those in the room'. He 'had a very decent interment, according to his Quality, in the Church of St. Giles Cripplegate, being attended from His house [in Bunhill] to the Church by several Gentlemen then in Town, his principal well-wishers and admirers', and 'not without a friendly concourse of the Vulgar' (Darbishire, 5, 33, 76, 193). His death found wide notice at the time, at home and abroad, with his notoriety as a controversialist as first outweighing his fame as a poet.

---

[33] Phillip Donnelly, '*Paradise Regained* as Rule of Charity: Religious Toleration and the End of Typology', *Milton Studies*, 43 (2004), 171–97.

[34] Paul Stevens, 'Intolerance and the Virtues of Sacred Vehemence', in Achinstein and Sauer (eds.), *Milton and Toleration*, 243–67.

PART II

SHORTER POEMS

CHAPTER 3

THE 'ADORNING OF MY NATIVE TONGUE': LATIN POETRY AND LINGUISTIC METAMORPHOSIS

ESTELLE HAAN

It were as wise to cast a violet into a crucible that you might discover the formal principle of its colour and odour, as seek to transfuse from one language into another the creations of a poet.

Shelley, *A Defence of Poetry*

Thus proclaimed Shelley in a famous caveat about the perils of translation.[1] A whole host of literary examples spanning several centuries and as many languages could be cited as a means of determining the truth or otherwise of this statement. But something of its rather blinkered nature emerges once it is acknowledged that translation in itself may possess an ability to recreate. It is an ability, it will be argued, that manifests itself on several levels, whereby the very nature and process of

---

[1] *Percy Bysshe Shelley: Selected Poetry and Prose*, ed. Alasdair D. F. Macrae (London and New York, 1991), 209.

'transfusing' an original creation from one language into another can in fact function as a liberating process—liberating from at least two different perspectives. Firstly, it enhances the dissemination and consequently the reception of a text by rendering it accessible to a wider readership; secondly, it can simultaneously result in the enrichment of the language into which that text has been transfused. Contrary to Shelley's viewpoint, then, surely there is much to be 'gained in translation' in linguistic as well as in methodological terms? Or, as Walter Benjamin puts it: 'Translation is so far removed from being the sterile equation of two dead languages that of all literary forms it is the one charged with the special mission of watching over the maturing process of the original language and the birth pangs of its own.'[2]

This discussion will concern itself both with an 'original' language (Latin), and with the 'maturing process' of two further languages: one, a pseudo-original, as it were (neo-Latin); the other, a seventeenth-century English vernacular. It will do so by focusing on one case in point—that of John Milton, for whom, it will be argued, 'translation' in a variety of guises helped to engender differing forms of linguistic metamorphosis: the 'birth pangs' of innovative neo-Latin and vernacular tongues. It will interpret 'translation' in its broadest sense, not merely as a rendering from one language into another, but also and essentially as appropriation, invention, and linguistic experimentation: from neo-Latin (Mantuan) into neo-Latin (Milton); from classical Latin (Horace) into the vernacular (Milton); from neo-Latin (Milton) into the vernacular (Milton), as a Renaissance poet eventually 'translates' himself in a variety of ways. It will emerge, moreover, that 'translation', as exemplified by Milton, is inextricably linked to Renaissance debate on the relative merits of Latin and the vernacular (the *Questione della lingua*), to pedagogical theory and practice (as manifested in such exercises as the 'double translation system', the 'turning of verses', and the 'metaphrase'), and especially to that peculiarly distinctive form of bilingualism so integral to Milton's poetic practice.

And it is with that bilingualism, and what would appear to be its associated paradoxes, that this discussion commences. While Milton has been regarded (and quite justifiably so) as a polyglot, his poetic corpus proclaims what is for the most part an irrefutable bilingualism.[3] At first glance his comparative use of Latin and the vernacular is not without several tensions. I enumerate here what could be termed (in a reinvention of William Empson's famous dictum) 'seven types of ambiguity', or,

---

[2] Walter Benjamin, 'The Task of the Translator', in *Illuminations*, trans. H. Zohn, ed. H. Arendt (1970), 69–82 at 73. For further discussion see Charles Martindale, *Redeeming The Text: Latin Poetry and the Hermeneutics of Reception* (Cambridge, 1993), 75–7.

[3] See e.g. John K. Hale, *Milton's Languages: The Impact of Multilingualism on Style* (Cambridge, 1997). Hale describes Milton as 'a humanist who wrote poems in four languages (Latin, Greek and Italian as well as his mother-tongue) . . . a lifelong polyglot whose writings evince knowledge of three Semitic languages and further modern languages' (p. 1). As noted below, the 1645 volume, *Poems of Mr John Milton: Both English and Latin*, is presented as a bilingual volume. Furthermore, almost half of Milton's prose writings are in Latin.

more accurately, seven types of linguistic ambiguity attending Milton's respective usages of Latin and the vernacular.[4]

1. A prolific author of Latin verse during his Cambridge years, Milton is nonetheless conspicuous by his absence from bilingual anthologies endlessly produced by Cambridge University on the occasions of royal births, marriages, or deaths.[5]
2. When he does make that sole contribution to such (famously in his pastoral poem 'Lycidas', mourning the death of Edward King, a Latin poet) he writes it not in Latin, but in English, producing a piece that functions as the resounding climax of the vernacular section of a bipartite Cambridge volume, the *Iusta Edouardo King* (1638).[6]
3. While the publication of *A Maske Presented at Ludlow Castle* (1637) and 'Lycidas' (1638) indicates ambitions to be acclaimed as an English poet, later in 1638 in the course of his Italian journey it was as a neo-Latin poet that Milton promoted himself among foreign litterati. Here the benefits of Latin as a universal language are self-evident. Hence it is for his recitation of Latin verse that he is acclaimed in the minutes of a Florentine academy.[7] Likewise it was Latin poetry that he composed during that sojourn and presented to Italian academicians.[8]
4. Hand in hand with such self-promotion, however, is Milton's associated announcement that it was at this time that he began to contemplate writing a great English epic, stating that his so-called decision in favour of the vernacular

---

[4] See Empson, *Seven Types of Ambiguity* (New York, 1947; rev. edn. 1966), 1: 'I propose to use the word in an extended sense, and shall think relevant to my subject any verbal nuance, however slight, which gives room for alternative reactions to the same piece of language.' The present discussion 'extends' this even further to embrace the level of reader response, or 'alternative reactions' to Milton's languages themselves, and to his apparently fluctuating choice between various linguistic media.

[5] Datable to Milton's Cambridge period are seven Latin elegies, several occasional pieces on university academics, a miniature Latin epic poem on the Gunpowder Plot (and five associated Latin epigrams), and two quasi-philosophical pieces on the decay of nature and the Aristotle/Plato controversy respectively.

[6] On King as a Latin poet, see the excellent edition and discussion by Nigel Postlethwaite and Gordon Campbell: 'Edward King, Milton's *Lycidas*: Poems and Documents', *Milton Quarterly*, 28 (1994), 77–111. Part I of the *Iusta* consists of twenty Latin and three Greek poems, Part II of thirteen English poems. Milton's 'Lycidas' is the last and the longest. See *Iusta Edouardo King: A Facsimile Edition of the Memorial Volume in which Milton's Lycidas First Appeared*, ed. Edward Le Comte (Norwood, 1978). Hale interestingly suggests that Milton may have derived from the *Iusta* the idea for his own bilingual 1645 volume (*Milton's Languages*, 21).

[7] That Milton recited his Latin poetry before the Florentine Accademia degli Svogliati is attested by its minutes of 6/16 Sept. 1638, which single him out for his reading of 'a very erudite Latin hexameter poem': 'furono lett'alcune compositioni et particolarmente il Giovanni Miltone Inglese lesse una poesia Latina di versi esametri multo erudita' (Biblioteca Nazionale Centrale, Florence, MSS Magliabecchiana, MSS Cl. IX, cod. 60, fo. 48). The minutes of 7/17 Mar. 1639 include Milton among those who read 'some noble Latin verses': 'nell'Accademia si trovarono li signori . . . Miltonio . . . Furon . . . letti alcuni nobili versi latini' (ibid., fo. 52). For a full discussion, see Estelle Haan, *From Academia to Amicitia: Milton's Latin Writings and the Italian Academies* (Transactions of the American Philosophical Society, 88/6; Philadelphia, 1998), 10–28. Milton's skill as a Latinist is highlighted in the written encomia he received in his honour from academicians in Florence, Rome, and Naples. See Haan, *From Academia to Amicitia*, 38–52, 82–5, 130–6.

[8] See e.g. 'Ad Salsillum', 'Mansus', and the three Latin epigrams in honour of Leonora Baroni. For fuller discussion, see Haan, *From Academia to Amicitia, passim.*

over Latin[9] was governed very much by the precedent of such Italian poets as Ariosto.[10]

5. In what is by now a characteristic paradox Milton announces that decision almost in the same breath as his boast about the 'written encomiums' which he received (and those for his Latin poems) from Italian academicians.[11] And the ambiguities do not end here.

6. Upon his return to England in 1639, he composed a pastoral poem, the *Epitaphium Damonis*, lamenting the premature death of his close boyhood friend Charles Diodati. But here he does what he did not do in the case of 'Lycidas': composes it in Latin. And once again there is an implicit irony.

7. It is in this Latin pastoral (ll. 168–78) that he announces what would appear to be his decision to abandon Latin verse altogether, and to assume the vernacular henceforth.[12] While it is certainly true that after 1639 Milton composed only one further Latin poem, 'Ad Ioannem Rousium' (a piece sent to the Bodleian Librarian to accompany a replacement of a lost copy of his 1645 volume of poetry), the precise nature of that decision is something to which this discussion will have reason to return.[13]

Do these apparent paradoxes, these seven types of linguistic ambiguity, as I have termed them, necessarily imply a tension between Latin and the vernacular in terms of

[9] However, Milton's 'decision' in favour of his native language is anticipated in such an early work as 'At A Vacation Exercise', significantly entitled 'Part Latin, Part English'. After a Latin section consisting of an *Oratio* and a *Prolusio*, Milton somewhat self-consciously asserts: 'The Latin Speeches ended, the English thus began.' He proceeds (ll. 1–10) to salute the English language, assuming an apologetic tone as he invokes its assistance, and begs pardon for his neglect. He recalls the mispronunciations he uttered as a child, and humbly speaks of his inability to do full justice to his native tongue. The implication is that it is English rather than Latin which is inbred in him.

[10] 'For which cause, and not only for that I knew it would be hard to arrive at the second rank among the Latines, I apply'd my selfe to that resolution which Ariosto follow'd against the perswasions of Bembo, to fix all the industry and art I could unite to the adorning of my native tongue; not to make verbal curiosities the end, that were a toylsom vanity, but to be an interpreter and relater of the best and sagest things among mine own Citizens throughout this Iland in the mother dialect. That what the greatest and choycest wits of Athens, Rome, or modern Italy, and those Hebrews of old did for their country, I in my proportion with this over and above of being a Christian, might doe for mine: not caring to be once nam'd abroad, though perhaps I could attaine to that, but content with these British Ilands as my world' (*Reason of Church-Government*, in *CW*, iii. 236–7). It is likely too that Milton was influenced in no small degree by his witnessing or participating in debates in the Italian academies on the relative merits of Latin and the vernacular. On Milton's interest in the Italian vernacular as expressed during his Florentine periods, cf. his Latin letter to Benedetto Buonmattei (31 Aug./10 Sept. 1638), in which he asks him to include in his forthcoming work on the Tuscan dialect a guide to pronunciation for foreigners (*CW*, xii. 34). See Haan, *From Academia to Amicitia*, 17–18.

[11] 'But much latelier in the privat Academies of Italy . . . some trifles which I had in memory, compos'd at under twenty or thereabout (for the manner is, that every one must give some proof of his wit and reading there), met with acceptance above what was lookt for, and other things which I had shifted in scarsity of books and conveniences to patch up amongst them, were receiv'd with written Encomiums, which the Italian is not forward to bestow on men of this side the Alps' (*Reason of Church-Government*, in *CW*, iii. 235–6).

[12] Hale, *Milton's Languages*, 57–61.

[13] See Stella P. Revard, 'Ad Ioannem Rousium: Elegiac Wit and Pindaric Mode', *Milton Studies*, 19 (1984), 205–26, reworked in her *Milton and the Tangles of Neaera's Hair* (Columbia, Mo., 1997), 237–63; Estelle Haan, 'Milton's Ad Ioannem Rousium and the 1645 Volume', *Notes and Queries*, 51 (2004), 356–60.

Milton's methodology and poetic career? Did all roads lead to that decision enunciated in a somewhat grandiloquently self-conscious pronouncement? Or might not the obvious felicity with which he shifts between the two languages suggest something rather different? Perhaps Latin and the vernacular were not always 'conscious' alternatives or mutually exclusive media, but rather, to appropriate a famous Miltonic image, parts of a linguistic 'two-handed engine', so to speak ('Lycidas', l. 130). This possibility is actually corroborated by the fact that the published Milton, the author of the 1645 volume, presented himself as a bilingual poet. This is evident in the title page: *Poems of Mr. John Milton, Both English and Latin*, and in the clear-cut division of the volume into two distinct sections (with separate pagination) of English and Latin poetry respectively.[14] As Hale remarks, 'we see that the book is actually two books'.[15] Significantly, like the languages themselves, they are bound together.

One approach to the linguistic versatility exhibited by Milton's bilingualism, this felicitous ability to shift or to choose between Latin and the vernacular, might be to regard it as a consequence, at least in part, of Renaissance pedagogical theory and practice. According to John Aubrey, Milton was already a poet when he had his portrait painted at the age of 10.[16] While the precise truth of such a viewpoint is open to question, it is clear that his linguistic experimentation would have had its inception while he was a student at St Paul's School, London. And in many ways such experimentation was inevitable. 'Translations' into and out of a variety of languages formed a central part of the core educational system of the day. In Renaissance England, as Ann Moss has shown, translation functioned as 'the "natural" medium through which pupils learn[ed] to manipulate the phraseology of "rhetorically" contrived Latin'.[17] That Latin be taught through the medium of translation was one of the precepts of the Renaissance educator John Brinsley. According to this system the tutor would recite a Latin poem to his pupils, who would translate it into English as it was being dictated in Latin.[18] It was a system which, as Moss observes, was 'aimed quite explicitly at bringing the English language within the scope of the verbal competence inculcated by classroom method'.[19] There was no shortage of types of translation. Such indeed were seen as a means of

---

[14] Among useful surveys of the volume are Louis L. Martz, *Poet of Exile: A Study of Milton's Poetry* (New Haven, 1980), 31–59; C. W. R. D. Moseley, *The Poetic Birth: Milton's Poems of 1645* (Aldershot, 1991), 79–85; John K. Hale, 'Milton's Self-Presentation in Poems . . . 1645', *Milton Quarterly*, 25 (1991), 37–48.

[15] Hale, 'Milton's Self-Presentation', 37. Hale proceeds to point out that while bilingual volumes by diverse hands abounded, 'volumes of verse by one author, assembled for a book by the poet, were still rare in the England of 1645' (p. 38).

[16] John Aubrey, in Darbishire, 2.

[17] Ann Moss, *Printed Commonplace-Books and the Structuring of Renaissance Thought* (Oxford, 1996), 216.

[18] John Brinsley, *Ludus Literarius or The Grammar School*, ed. E. T. Campagnac (Liverpool and London, 1917), 193: 'Take *Flores Poetarum*, and in every Common place make choise of Ovid's verses, or if you find any other which be pleasant and easie . . . Cause also as many as you would have to learne together to set downe the English as you dictate [the Latin verses].'

[19] Moss, *Printed Commonplace-Books*, 216. For further discussion of links between bilingualism and Renaissance pedagogy, see Estelle Haan, *Andrew Marvell's Latin Poetry: From Text to Context* (Collection Latomus, 275; Brussels, 2003), 66–72.

enhancing the very language(s) into which the pupil was 'translating', whether that language be neo-Latin, Greek, Hebrew, or English, to name but a few. And classical precedent was not lacking: Cicero had recommended translation from Greek into Latin as a way of enhancing the pupil's command of his own language, as well as a means of enriching the Latin language itself, while Quintilian announced that in the very act of translating Greek into Latin 'we may use the very best words since all that we use are our own'.[20] As Donald Clark succinctly puts it: 'Milton had to become a little Roman boy of sorts before he could make Latin translations from the Greek classics as he did from the beginning of the Fifth Form'.[21] In seventeenth-century London, even more so than in classical Rome, translation might function as a means of enriching other languages. How then might this have worked in practice?

One exercise expected of the grammar school pupil was that of the 'double translation system'. According to this practice, recommended by such Renaissance educators as Roger Ascham, the pupil would translate a Latin piece into English; then, without looking at the original, translate his own English into Latin, finally comparing what was now his own neo-Latin version with the original.[22] Clark speculates that 'Milton must have done a great deal of translating as well as keeping up of paper books at school—translation from Latin into English, from English into Latin, from Greek into English and into Latin, from Hebrew into English and into Latin'.[23] If he did (as undoubtedly he must have) these do not survive.

Nonetheless evidence of the precise methodology of the 'double translation system' does survive, and is most eloquently exemplified by Milton's friend and contemporary Andrew Marvell, albeit from the other side of the desk, so to speak. For Marvell, as for Milton, bilingualism and pedagogy were inextricably intertwined. It was probably while acting as tutor to Mary Fairfax at Nun Appleton House that Marvell produced his parallel neo-Latin and vernacular poems: 'Ros'/'On a Drop of Dew'; 'Hortus'/'The Garden'. In so doing he may well have been composing his own 'originals', so to speak, his pseudo-classical models, which he then seems to have reworked into English verse, perhaps as a means of illustrating the system to his young pupil. The literary repercussions of this methodology should not be under-estimated. Marvell, through 'translating' his own neo-Latin into an experimental vernacular, simultaneously enhanced that vernacular by quasi-baroque wordplay manifested in a whole series of puns, macaronic and otherwise, appropriated from one language and poem into its vernacular equivalent.[24] The very language, rhetoric, form, and subject matter of Marvell's celebrated English poems would be altogether

---

[20] Cicero, *De Oratore* 1. 155; Quintilian, *De Institutione Oratoria*, 10. 5. 2.

[21] D. L. Clark, *John Milton at St Paul's School* (New York, 1948; repr. Hamden, Conn., 1964), 172.

[22] Thus Roger Ascham, *The Scholemaster*, ed. E. Arber (1870), 26, advises as to how Cicero should be double translated: 'The childe must take a paper booke, and sitting in some place, where no man shall prompt him, by him self, let him translate into Englishe his former lesson. Then shewing it to his master, let the master take from him his Latin booke, and pausing an houre, at the least, then let the childe translate his own Englishe into Latin againe, in an other paper booke. When the childe bringeth it, turned into Latin, the master must compare it with *Tullies* book, and lay them both together.' See also Clark, *John Milton at St Paul's School*, 172–3.

[23] Clark, *John Milton at St Paul's School*, 177.

[24] See Haan, *Andrew Marvell's Latin Poetry*, 57–94, 64–72, 77–87.

very different were it not for the fact that he had composed these works in Latin first. Gordon Campbell compares this practice to that of Samuel Beckett, who 'disciplined his dramatic prose by writing his plays in French and then translating them into English'.[25] For Marvell then the double translation system was surely much more than 'translating'. Regarded in the light of Shelley's dictum, the appropriation of one's own neo-Latin into an experimental vernacular could serve perhaps as a means of both discovering that original 'violet' and actually enhancing the poem and indeed the language into which it was 'translated'.

Can the same be said to be true of translation from neo-Latin into neo-Latin? Or to approach this from the perspective of Clark: did not Milton have to become a little neo-Latin boy as well as a little Roman one? The answer is a resounding affirmative. In his *Apology Against a Pamphlet* (1642) Milton describes the ease and pleasure that attended his schoolboy 'imitations' of Latin elegiac poetry, a likely allusion to his very act of composing neo-Latin verse at St Paul's School.[26] Indeed a key aim of the Renaissance educational system was to equip its subjects with the necessary tools for Latin verse composition. One way in which it did so was through a practice known as the 'turning of verses'. This exercise, recommended and illustrated by Brinsley, required the pupil to rework a Latin poem into a Latin equivalent, substituting alternative words or phrases while preserving the metre and form of the original or applying the subject matter to another, frequently contemporary, topic.[27] This practice is exemplified by both Marvell and Milton. Marvell's university *parodia* on Horace, *Odes* 1. 2, published in a Cambridge anthology (1637) celebrating the birth of Princess Anne, reworks Horace's grim prediction of divine retribution for civil war into a depiction of the bitter consequences of plague in seventeenth-century Cambridge.[28] A more succinct example is provided by Milton's 'Apologus de Rustico et Hero', which in all probability dates to his St Paul's period. Here, as I have illustrated elsewhere, he reworks a neo-Latin fable by Mantuan (on a farmer's loss of an apple-tree as a consequence of his rash transplantation of the same).[29] As Milton describes that 'transposition' (*transtulit*, l. 4) of an apple-tree from its native soil, he does so by 'transposing' the very language of Mantuan's poem, making the Latin his own. By

---

[25] *Andrew Marvell*, ed. Gordon Campbell (1997), p. xii.

[26] He alludes to 'the smooth Elegiack Poets, whereof the Schooles are not scarce. Whom both for the pleasing sound of their numerous writing, which in imitation I found most easie; and most agreeable to nature's part in me, and for their matter which what it is, there be few who know not, I was so allur'd to read, that no recreation came to me better welcome' (*CW*, iii. 302).

[27] Brinsley states: 'Cause them to turne the verses of their Lecture into other verses, either to the same purpose, which is easiest for young beginners, or turne to some other purpose, to express some other matter; yet ever to keep the very phrase of the poet, there or in other places, only transposing the words or phrase, or changing some word or phrase, or the numbers or persons or applying them to matters which are familiar' (*Ludus Literarius*, 194). Clark notes that 'the exercise depends in part on the relative indifference of Latin elegiac verse to word order so long as the metre is kept regular' (*John Milton at St Paul's School*, 181).

[28] See Haan, *Andrew Marvell's Latin Poetry*, 19–56.

[29] See Estelle Haan, 'Mantuan, Milton, and the Fruit of that Forbidden Tree', *Medievalia et Humanistica*, 35 (1998), 75–92, which argues that Milton's poem is an exercise in the 'turning of verses' (contrary to Harris F. Fletcher's reading of the same as exemplifying the 'double translation' system in 'Milton's *Apologus* and its Mantuan Model', *Journal of English and Germanic Philology*, 55 (1956), 230–3).

substituting words and phases, while preserving the metre and sense of the fable, he excels in two ways: first, by fulfilling the prerequisites of the set exercise; second, by moving beyond his 'original' through careful choice of nouns or adjectives, and linguistic and syntactical innovation. Thus hissing sibilants convey the enticing juices of the apple; cleverly juxtaposed phrases reach a climax in the decay of the tree; there is a pun on *malus-i* (f.) 'apple' and *malum-i* (n.) 'evil', while the tragic sense of loss experienced by the master is heightened and personalized. Indeed in this, as in other instances, Milton's methodology anticipates that implemented in his mature vernacular epic: in the laments uttered by Adam and Eve, having eating of the forbidden fruit, and in their consequential 'transplantation', as it were, from the Garden of Eden, their 'native soil'.[30]

What then of classical Latin into the vernacular? Certainly Milton's most obvious example of such is his 'translation' of Horace, *Odes* 1. 5, to which we now turn:

Horace, *Odes* 1. 5	John Milton
	Rendered almost word for word without Rhyme according to the Latin Measure, as near as the Language will permit

Quis multa gracilis te puer in rosa	What slender Youth bedew'd with liquid odours
perfusus liquidis urget odoribus	Courts thee on Roses in some pleasant Cave,
grato, Pyrrha, sub antro?	Pyrrha for whom bindst thou
cui flavam religas comam	In wreaths thy golden Hair,
5 simplex munditiis? Heu quotiens fidem	Plain in thy neatness; O how oft shall he 5
mutatosque deos flebit et aspera	On Faith and changed Gods complain: and Seas
nigris aequora ventis	Rough with black winds and storms
emirabitur insolens,	Unwonted shall admire:
qui nunc te fruitur credulus aurea,	Who now enjoys thee credulous, all Gold,
10 qui semper vacuam, semper amabilem	Who alwayes vacant alwayes amiable 10
sperat, nescius aurae	Hopes thee; of flattering gales
fallacis; miseri, quibus	Unmindful. Hapless they
intemptata nites; me tabula sacer	To whom thou untry'd seem'st fair. Me in my vow'd
votiva paries indicat uvida	Picture the sacred wall declares t'have hung
15 suspendisse potenti	My dank and dropping weeds 15
vestimenta maris deo.[31]	To the stern God of Sea.

---

[30] Compare Michael to Adam at *Paradise Lost* 11. 259–62: 'But longer in this Paradise to dwell / Permits not; to remove thee I am come, / And send thee from the garden forth to till / The ground whence thou wast taken, fitter soil', or Eve's lament at 11. 269–70: 'Must I thus leave thee, Paradise? Thus leave / Thee, native soil!'

[31] The text of both the Latin and the English is that printed in *Poems &c Upon Several Occasions by Mr John Milton: Both English and Latin &c Composed at Several Times* (1673). I have modernized punctuation.

The date of the poem is unknown, with suggestions ranging from 1624 to as late as 1655. Fletcher, Hughes, and Carey regard it as either a school or university exercise, while Clark leaves the question open.[32] By contrast Shawcross and others have argued at length for a later date; while Gordon Campbell has cautiously described the piece as 'wholly undatable'.[33] True as this may be, there are, however, several indications that might support the argument that this is a school or university exercise. Like the *Apologus de Rustico et Hero*, it was published only in 1673 (with the Latin text subjoined), at a time when the elderly Milton seems to have been gathering together his life's work (including his school exercises) for publication. But more striking is the fact that the methodology exemplified by the piece closely approximates that of the 'metaphrase', one of the key exercises practised in Renaissance schools.

In his Preface to Ovid's *Epistles*, published in 1680, John Dryden discusses three different types of 'translation': 'metaphrase', 'paraphrase', and 'imitation'. He defines 'metaphrase' as 'turning an author word by word, and line by line, from one language into another'.[34] In terms of Renaissance pedagogy metaphrase was a rigorously effective means of instilling into a pupil sensitivity to metre and form, to the inflected syntax of the Latin language, and not least to ways in which such could be replicated via creative experimentation in a vernacular translation. For Ascham 'Metaphrasis is to take some notable place out of a good poet and turn the same sense into meter or into other words in prose.'[35] In some respects, then, it was seen as the vernacular equivalent of the 'turning of verses', and demanded of its subject a mental alertness, the ability to substitute words for words, phrases for phrases, while still retaining the structure of the original.[36] But there was, of course, one important distinction: the result was an English version of a Latin original, but one which might seek to recreate that original through the use of Latinate vocabulary, word order, and syntax.

---

[32] Harris F. Fletcher, *The Intellectual Development of John Milton*, 2 vols. (Urbana, Ill., 1956–61), i. 238; Merritt Y. Hughes, *Milton: The Minor Poems* (New York, 1947), p. li; *CSP*, 99, suggests late 1629; Clark, *John Milton at St Paul's School*, 178.

[33] J. T. Shawcross, 'Of Chronology and the Dates of Milton's Translation from Horace and the New Forcers of Conscience', *Studies in English Literature*, 3 (1963), 77–84, argues for a late date, noting that the Latin text supplied in the 1673 volume of Milton's poetry seems not to have been published before 1636 (p. 80). See also D. P. Harding, *The Club of Hercules: Studies in the Classical Background of Paradise Lost* (Urbana, Ill., 1962), 128–34, who detects the development of Milton's mature style, while *The Riverside Milton*, ed. Roy Flannagan (Boston, 1998), 260, dates it 1646–8. There is, however, no reason to assume (as Shawcross and others do) that the Latin text published by Milton in 1673 is necessarily the text he used at the time of composing his English version. For a convincing rejection of Shawcross's reasons, see *A Variorum Commentary on the Poems of John Milton*, gen. ed. Merritt Y. Hughes, 6 vols. (New York, 1970–), ii: *The Minor English Poems*, ed. A. S. P. Woodhouse and Douglas Bush, 502–5: 'If the style does not resemble that of the early Milton, it does not much resemble that of the later poet either; in fact it is unique' (p. 504). Campell, *Chronology*, 214.

[34] *The Works of John Dryden*, ed. E. N. Hooker and H. T. Swedenberg, Jr., 20 vols. (Berkeley and London, 1956–2000), i. 114.

[35] Ascham, *The Scholemaster*, 93.

[36] See ibid. 109–10: 'This exercise may bring much profit to ripe heads and staid judgements because in traveling in it the mind must needs be very attentive and busily occupied in turning and tossing itself many ways and conferrying with great pleasure the variety of worthy wits and judgements together.'

In terms of its reception through the centuries, it might be remarked that Horace's *Odes* 1. 5, with its interconnected themes of love, credulity, betrayal, and retirement from love, is one of the most, if not *the* most, translated of Latin lyrics.[37] Such may also have been the case in the Renaissance classroom. One way into Milton's 'translation' is via the headnote he provided, in which, as Clark remarks, he seems to show 'a very schoolboy pride'.[38] It is a pride, it could be argued, that is closely linked to pedagogical practice, and to Milton's experience and perceptions of the same, both as schoolboy and (by the time he was publishing the version in 1673) as erstwhile schoolmaster.[39] In the following discussion pedagogical methodology (and Milton's consciousness of the same) will be used to support and augment Charles Martindale's reading of the poem as metaphrase.[40]

At the outset it is important to remember that Milton's provision of headnotes to many of his poems frequently acted as a means of self-advertisement, and for the most part as a way of boasting about his youthfulness at the time of composition. For example, in the 1645 volume he takes pains to indicate the date or his precise age at the time of his early compositions, and he does so in the instances of both English and Latin.[41] Indeed very frequently his age in Latin becomes part of the heading of a poem.[42] As such Milton's headnotes may in themselves act as a means of guiding reader response or at the very least as a form of careful signposting for his audience.

What aspects of his 'translation', then, does Milton highlight? First, he points out that his version is verbally close to the original: it is 'rendered almost word for word'. As remarked above, this was perhaps the chief characteristic of the Renaissance metaphrase. Hence Milton is, by implication, revealing himself as master of that art, so to speak, as excelling in this methodology. Second, he announces that his

---

[37] See e.g. Ronald Storrs, *Ad Pyrrham: A Polyglot Collection of Translations of Horace's Ode to Pyrrha (Book 1, Ode 5)* (1959). For studies of the Ode, see among others, E. A. Fredricksmeyer, 'Horace's Ode to Pyrrha (*Carm.* 1.5)', *Classical Philology*, 60 (1965), 180–5; V. Pöschl, 'Die Pyrrhaode des Horaz (c. 1.5)', in M. Renard and R. Schilling (eds.), *Hommages à J. Bayet* (Collection Latomus, 70; Brussels, 1964), 579–86; M. C. J. Putnam, 'Horace, *Carm.* 1.5: Love and Death', *Classical Philology*, 65 (1970), 251–4; K. Quinn, 'Horace as a Love Poet: A Reading of *Odes* 1.5', *Arion*, 2 (1963), 59–77; J. C. Brown, 'The Verbal Art of Horace's *Ode to Pyrrha*', *Transactions of the American Philological Association*, 111 (1981), 17–22; David Coffta, 'Programme and Persona in Horace, *Odes* 1.5', *Eranos*, 96 (1998), 26–31; D. W. Thomson Vessey, 'Pyrrha's Grotto and the Farewell to Love: A Study of Horace, *Odes* 1.5', in W. S. Anderson (ed.), *Why Horace? A Collection of Interpretive Essays* (Wauconda, Ill., 1999), 20–30.

[38] *John Milton at St Paul's School*, 178.

[39] See in general A. F. Leach, *Milton as Schoolboy and Schoolmaster* (Proceedings of the British Academy, 3; 1908; repr. 1976).

[40] Charles Martindale, 'Unlocking the Word-Hoard: In Praise of Metaphrase', *Comparative Criticism*, 6 (1984), 47–72, reworked in his *Redeeming the Text*, 75–100.

[41] 'On the Morning of Christ's Nativity, Compos'd 1629'; 'A Paraphrase on Psalm 114, This and the following Psalm were done by the Author at fifteen yeers old'; 'On Shakespeare, 1630'; *A Maske Presented at Ludlow Castle, 1634*; 'Lycidas . . . 1637'.

[42] 'Elegia Secunda, Anno aetatis 17'; 'Elegia Tertia, Anno aetatis 17'; 'Elegia Quarta, Anno aetatis 18'; 'Elegia Quinta, Anno aetatis 20'; 'Elegia Septima, Anno aetatis undevigesimo'; 'Anno aetatis 16: In Obitum Procancellarii Medici'; 'In Quintum Novembris, Anno aetatis 17'; 'Anno aetatis 17: In Obitum Praesulis Eliensis'. The title page of the second (Latin) section of the 1645 volume has the following heading: 'Ioannis Miltoni Londiniensis Poemata Quorum Pleraque Intra Annum Aetatis Vigesimum Conscripsit'.

version does not rhyme. Rhyming translations were criticized by Roger Ascham, especially if the inclusion of such was likely to hamper the rendering.[43] In fact rhyme and the metaphrase were virtually incompatible. Third, he draws attention to the fact that his poem seeks (on a visual level perhaps)[44] to mirror 'the Latin measure' of the original—'measure' here encompassing metre, but also perhaps the stanzaic structure of the whole.[45] The ability of English verse to reproduce the metre of a classical original is discussed by Ascham, who contrasts the respective clumsiness and felicity of English poetry in rendering hexameter and iambic verse.[46] Indeed Milton's poem proper may (in the number and shape of its stanzas: two iambic pentameters followed by two iambic trimeters) attempt to mirror Horace's metre (third Asclepiad) and line-length.[47] Fourth, he conveys the fact that his poem approximates a Latin original in the English language—or at least 'as near as the Language will permit'. The headnote as a whole, and the latter phrase in particular, is strikingly similar to Brinsley's precepts concerning translation: 'In all such translating either English or Latine this is carefully to be observed; ever to consider well the scope and drift of the Author and the circumstances of the place; and to labour to express lively, not only the matter, but also the force of each phrase, *so near as the propriety of the tongue will permit*.'[48] If Milton's headnote alerts us to ways in which his poem fulfils the necessary prerequisites of the metaphrase, it also, at least by implication, emphasizes the essentially Latinate English of the poem proper. This works on both a verbal and a syntactical level: verbally, in terms of his choice of nouns and adjectives, and the preference for English words with Latin roots as a means of rendering their Horatian equivalent: thus 'liquid odours' (l. 1) / *liquidis... odoribus* (l. 2); 'admire' (l. 8) / *emirabitur* (l. 8); 'credulous' (l. 9) / *credulus* (l. 9); 'vacant' (l. 10) / *vacuam* (l. 10); 'amiable' (l. 10) / *amabilem* (l. 10).[49] Through such Latinisms Milton's metaphrase transposes the 'turning of verses' to the dimension of a Latinate vernacular, its linguistic alterity mirroring 'the alterity of Horace's lyric manner'.[50] But if it looks back to Horace, it also looks ahead to the mature vernacular Milton, the poet of

---

[43] Ascham, *The Scholemaster*, 145–6, in criticizing rhyming, musters the support of Quintilian: 'Quintilian in his learned Chapter *de Compositione*...doth justly inveigh against all rhyming; if there be any, who be angry with me, for misliking of rhyming may be angry...with Quintilian also for the same thing.' Cf. his criticism of 'that barbarous and rude rhyming' (p. 145). Contrast his praise of the Earl of Surrey and of Gonsalvo Periz, who 'avoided the fault of rhyming' in their translations of Virgil, *Georgics*, 4, and Homer's *Odyssey* respectively (p. 147).

[44] For a possible parallel in terms of an English poem's attempt to replicate (on a visual level) Horatian stanzaic structure, compare Marvell's 'An Horatian Ode Upon Cromwell's Return From Ireland'. See Haan, *Andrew Marvell's Latin Poetry*, 53–5.

[45] Contrast Hale, *Milton's Languages*, 71: 'even if "measure" refers only to the metre'.

[46] Ascham, *The Scholemaster*, 146: 'Athough *Carmen Exametrum* doth rather trot and hobble than run smoothly in our English tongue yet I am sure our English tongue will receive *Carmen Iambicum* as naturally as either Greek or Latin.'

[47] Cf. Martindale, 'In Praise of Metaphrase', 54.

[48] Brinsley, *Ludus Literarius*, 156–7. Italics are mine.

[49] Archie Burnett, 'The Fifth Ode of Horace, *Lib*. I, and Milton's Style', *Milton Quarterly*, 16 (1982), 68–72, remarks on the high frequency of adjectives in Milton's version.

[50] Martindale, *Redeeming the Text*, 79.

Paradise Lost, an epic permeated by precisely such Latinisms, by English words used in a Latinate sense.[51]

The poem's Latinity operates on a syntactical level also as Milton replicates the inflected word-order of the ancient language by postponing verbs until the end of clauses ('complain' (l. 6), 'admire' (l. 8), 'hopes thee' (l. 11)).[52] He uses enjambment as a means of enabling his vernacular version (like its Horatian equivalent) to cut across stanzaic division. As in Horace, he holds back the *simplex munditiis* phrase to enable it to open the second stanza, and he replicates the repetition of *qui...qui* (ll. 9–10) in 'who...who' (ll. 9–10) and of *semper...semper* (l. 10) in 'always... always' (l. 10). His emphatically positioned 'me' at the beginning of the final clause (l. 13) balances its precise Latin equivalent *me* (l. 13), thereby achieving complete verbal assimilation, and he reproduces the archaism of the accusative and infinitive construction: *me.../...indicat.../suspendisse* (13–15) in 'me.../...declares t'have hung' (ll. 13–14).

One question remains to be answered: is anything 'lost in translation' in terms of Milton's metaphrastic rendering? Martindale, while regarding the poem as 'astonishingly innovatory, both linguistically and rhythmically', concedes that 'Milton does not really capture the elegance that rather unexpectedly goes with the dense and difficult textures of the original.'[53] This is a judgement that is certainly open to question. Scholars have criticized the poem for its overly puritanical tone. For example, the difficult phrase *simplex munditiis* is rendered by the unsatisfactory 'plain in thy neatness'.[54] But perhaps in such an instance a wholly adequate rendering is impossible. Is this 'as near as the language will permit?'[55] Is this as near as any language will permit? Likewise it might be observed that in Milton's version the sexual undertones of the Horatian *te.../...urget* (ll. 1–2) are not only suppressed but actually countered in the politely refined 'courts thee' (l. 2). But perhaps criticism of the poem's supposedly 'puritanical' nature may be answered, if not countered, by remarking that such Renaissance educational theorists as Brinsley had actually recommended the avoidance of 'words which are insolent'.[56] I would suggest that Roy Flannagan's viewpoint is nearer to the truth:

[51] A few examples will suffice: 'abject' (from *abicio -ere* [to cast down]): 'so thick bestrewn / Abject and lost lay these, covering the flood' (1. 311–12); 'reluctant' (from *reluctor -ari* [to struggle]): 'till supplanted down he fell / A monstrous serpent on his belly prone / Reluctant but in vain' (10. 513–15); 'involved' (from *involvo- ere* [to roll/wrap around]): 'Satan involved in rising mist' (9. 75).

[52] On the 'hopes thee...' construction, Hale, *Milton's Languages*, 71, remarks: '[Milton's] English, forced into the Latin word-order, cannot make clear who is "credulous" and who is "amiable" nor what "vacant" means. What inflection can clarify readily, English fails to: the syntax crumples into nonsense.'

[53] Martindale, *Redeeming the Text*, 79; 'In Praise of Metaphrase', 56.

[54] R. G. M. Nisbet and Margaret Hubbard, *A Commentary on Horace Odes Book I* (Oxford, 1970), 75, state '*munditiis* does not make an oxymoron with *simplex* but points in the same direction'. For Martindale, this rendition 'seems too puritanical' ('In Praise of Metaphrase', 56). He speculates, however, that 'perhaps there was a seventeenth-century (sub-Puritan) usage of the word neat that meant something like "chic"'.

[55] Nisbet and Hubbard, *A Commentary on Horace Odes Book I*, 76, remark of the phrase: 'in the present context an adequate English translation seems impossible'.

[56] Brinsley, *Ludus Literarius*, 164.

For anyone who has struggled to translate the sophisticated and intricate poetry of Horace into English, Milton's translation is a marvel: it is concise, precise, definitive; it is faithful to the original; and it creates its own integrity as an English poem. The English is not in Milton's poetic style, because its style deeply honors Horace's in Latin; it is an exercise on how to write poetry in either language.[57]

Read in this light, this 'exercise on how to write poetry' seems to transcend the level of mere pedagogy. As such it is symptomatic of Milton's poetic methodology.

In *Epitaphium Damonis*, ll. 168–171, Milton announces what would seem at first glance to be his contemplated abandonment of Latin in favour of English. This is depicted through the symbol of the *fistula*, or shepherd's pipe, which will either be hung up for good and forgotten, or else, having undergone a metamorphosis of sorts, it will utter a British theme in the vernacular:

> O mihi tum si vita supersit,
> tu procul annosa pendebis fistula pinu
> multum oblita mihi, aut patriis mutata camoenis
> Brittonicum strides.[58]

Do these lines really bid farewell to the Latin language? Admittedly, Milton, in aiming to be a national poet, must move outside the Latin world of the poem and assume the vernacular (just as the poem itself has to break through the confines of a pagan, pastoral genre in order to describe the apotheosis of Diodati in a Christian Heaven). But what sort of vernacular? Is it not the case that his vernacular is in fact a Latin that has undergone a linguistic metamorphosis (*patriis mutata camoenis*), or rather (as though mirroring the rebirth of Diodati in Heaven) a linguistic apotheosis. If so, Milton's English is thus a Latinate English in a very unique way. It is, in those words of the 1645 volume, 'Both English and Latin'.

It has been argued of Joachim Du Bellay (1522–60) that he translated his own Latin lines into the vernacular.[59] While the present discussion makes no such claim for Milton, it concludes by reverting to 'translation' as the manifold intersections between languages, and by positing just some instances of the frequently complex interplay between Milton's neo-Latin and English poetry.[60] Perhaps Milton's poetic

---

[57] *Riverside Milton*, 260.

[58] *Ep. Dam.*, ll. 168–71. Lines 170–1 have received various interpretations. Walter MacKellar, *The Latin Poems of John Milton* (New Haven, 1930), 169, translates *patriis mutata camoenis* as 'forsaking your [the pipe's] native songs', and explains in a note (p. 347) 'its paternal Muses, i.e. Latin'. I would disagree with this interpretation. It is much more likely that the phrase means *Milton's* native Muses, i.e. the English language. The lines are well translated by Mary Campbell in *John Milton: The Complete Poems*, ed. Gordon Campbell (London and New York, 1980), 543: 'unless, changed, you will utter a British theme in native songs'. Douglas Bush, in *A Variorum Commentary on the Poems of John Milton*, i: *The Latin and Greek Poems* (New York, 1970), 316–17, notes that Ovid (*Epistulae Ex Ponto* 4. 13. 33) uses *patria . . . Camena* for his native language in contrast with Getic.

[59] See Geneviève Demerson, 'Joachim Du Bellay: Traducteur de lui-même', in G. Castor and T. Cave (eds.), *Neo-Latin and the Vernacular in Renaissance France* (Oxford, 1984), 113–28.

[60] It is complex in the sense that this interplay would seem to move beyond that verbal and psychological patterning illustrated by such scholars as Le Comte. See in general E. S. Le Comte, *Yet Once More: Verbal and Psychological Pattern in Milton* (New York, 1953).

practice as a whole can (in a quasi-revisionist version of Marvell's 'double translation' methodology?) exemplify different ways of 'translating' his own neo-Latin into an experimental vernacular. Several examples will suffice.

1. The nightingale of 'Elegia Quinta' ('iam Philomela tuos foliis adoperta novellis / instituis modulos, dum silet omne nemus' (ll. 25–6)) finds a parallel in the opening lines of the first English Sonnet: 'O nightingale, that on yon bloomy spray / warblest at eve, when all the woods are still.' (ll. 1–2).

2. The 'pendulus orbis' of 'Elegia Prima' (l. 76) or 'pendulum telluris orbem' of 'In Obitum Procancellarii Medici' (l. 3) become 'this pendent world' and 'pendulous round Earth' of *Paradise Lost* (2. 1052; 4. 1000).

3. In 'Naturam Non Pati Senium' the collapse of the universe is envisaged in a simile of Vulcan's fall ('qualis in Aegaeam proles Iunonia Lemnon / deturbata sacro cecidit de limine caeli' (ll. 23–4).[61] This receives a much fuller treatment in *Paradise Lost*, in the depiction of Mulciber ('and how he fell / From Heav'n . . . On Lemnos th'Aegaean Isle' (1.740–6)).

4. Aspects of 'In Quintum Novembris' recur in a transmuted form in *Paradise Lost*: Satan as the 'fraudumque magister' (l. 17) / 'artificer of fraud' (4. 121); as the exile from heaven ('aethereo vagus exul Olympo' (l. 8)) / [evicted] 'from the ethereal sky' (1. 45); as the sower of hatred ('unanimes odium struit inter amicos' (l. 13) / 'these acts of hateful strife' (6. 264)); as the disturber of peace ('regnaque olivifera vertit florentia pace' (l. 15) / 'how hast thou disturb'd / Heav'ns blessed peace' (6. 266–7)); as the flying demon, whose pitchy wings oppress the air ('et piceis liquido natat aere pennis' (l. 45) / 'Then with expanded wings he steers his flight / Aloft, incumbent on the dusky air / That felt unusual weight (ll. 225–7)).[62] Satan's address to a sleeping pope ('dormis nate? Etiamne tuos sopor opprimit artus / immemor O fidei, pecorumque oblite tuorum' (ll. 92–3)) is closely mirrored in his attempts to waken Beelzebub: 'Sleepst thou Companion dear? What sleep can close / Thy eye-lids? and remembrest what Decree' (5. 673–4). And King James, described as 'sedebat / in solio, occultique doli securus et hostis' (ll. 5–6), becomes God the Father 'till then as one secure / Sat on his throne' (ll. 638–9). But God is a supreme power who laughs from Heaven at the vain attempts of conspirators ('vanaque perversae ridet conamina turbae' (l. 168) / 'He from heaven's height / All these our motions vain, sees and derides (2. 190–1) / 'Mighty Father, thou thy foes / Justly hast in derision, and secure / Laughst at their vain designs and tumults vain' (5.735–7)).

This discussion commenced with a Shellean violet. It concludes with Miltonic (or perhaps Horatian?) roses: with the 'translation' of *Odes* 1. 5 into a prelapsarian Eden. It is an Eden which possesses its own 'multa in rosa' (l. 1) ('flowers of all hue, and without thorn the rose' (4. 256) / 'And on their naked limbs the

[61] See also 'Elegia Septima', ll. 81–2: 'sic dolet amissum proles Iunonia caelum, / inter Lemniacos praecipitata focos'.

[62] See Macon Cheek, 'Milton's "*In Quintum Novembris*": An Epic Foreshadowing', *Studies in Philology*, 54 (1957), 172–84.

flowery roof / Showered roses, which the morn repaired' (4. 772–3));[63] its
'liquidis…odoribus' (l. 2) ('odorous sweets' (4. 166); 'odorous gums' (4. 248);
'each odorous bushy shrub' (4. 696)); its 'grato…antro' (l. 3) ('umbrageous grots
and caves / of cool recess' (4. 257–8));[64] its golden-haired female ('flavam religas
comam' (l. 4)), her tresses now unbound, as Eve 'her unadorned golden tresses wore /
Dishevelled, but in wanton ringlets waved' (4. 305–6), while 'half her swelling breast /
Naked met his under the flowing gold / Of her loose tresses hid' (4. 495–7). And if the
Horatian *simplex munditiis* (l. 5) has been transmuted into 'simplicity and spotless
innocence' (4. 318), it is a state that will not endure. A young lover's credulity
(*credulus* (l. 9)), his lack of knowledge (*nescius* (l. 11)) of future betrayal, have become
for two lovers an essentially transient present in which prelapsarian ignorance is bliss:

> Ah gentle pair, ye little think how nigh
> Your change approaches, when all these delights
> Will vanish and deliver ye to woe,
> More woe, the more your taste is now of joy (4. 366–9)[65]
>
> Sleep on
> Blest pair; and O yet happiest if ye seek
> No happier state, and know to know no more (4. 773–5)[66]

---

[63] Cf. 'A sylvan scene' (l. 140), 'herself a fairer flower' (l. 270), 'the soft downy bank damasked with
flowers' (l. 334), 'underfoot the violet, / crocus, and hyacinth with rich inlay / broidered the ground' (ll.
700–2).

[64] Cf. 'under a tuft of shade' (l. 325), 'blissful bower' (l. 690), 'inmost bower' (l. 738).

[65] Cf. 'close the serpent sly / Insinuating…/…of his fatal guile / Gave proof unheeded' (ll. 347–50).

[66] Cf. 'Can it be sin to know, / Can it be death? And do they only stand / By ignorance, is that their
happy state' (517–19).

CHAPTER 4

MILTON'S EARLY ENGLISH POEMS: THE NATIVITY ODE, 'L'ALLEGRO', 'IL PENSEROSO'

GORDON TESKEY

SOMETIME at or just before dawn on Christmas morning 1629, two and a half weeks after his twenty-first birthday, John Milton began composing one of the greatest poems in the English language and his first work of genius: 'On the Morning of Christ's Nativity'. He was probably home from Cambridge, on the upper floor of his family house, which was situated on the high ground of Ludgate Hill in what was then west London, on Bread Street, near St Paul's Cathedral. At that hour, and on that particular morning, there would have been very few lights and very few sounds—no torches or candles, no carters' cries or street vendors' songs. Despite the air pollution, which was already a serious problem, the stars would have been visible and bright, especially from the hill. Milton would have had a view to the east, for the city fell away in that direction onto lower ground towards London Bridge, and the sky would have been visible. He was waiting for dawn, which seemed, as it always does when we are watching for it, to hesitate before it arrives. The stars seemed reluctant to leave and the first light of dawn hadn't touched the horizon to the east or the dark overhead. Perhaps he began at the beginning, and said to himself, 'This is the month, and this the happy morn'.

Some days later, when he was still working on the poem, or at least polishing it, Milton described this scene in a Latin verse epistle addressed to his friend Charles Diodati:

I am singing of the peace-bearing king of heavenly origin, of the happy ages prophesied in Scripture, of the infant God born in a poor stable who with his Father dwells in the kingdom of Heaven, of the new star born under the cosmic vault, of the hosts of angels singing in the air, and of the pagan gods surprised in their various shrines and banished to Hell. I gave this gift to Christ for his birthday. The first light of dawn brought it to me. ('Elegia Sexta', ll. 81–8)

The Minor Poems between the Nativity Ode and 'Lycidas'

Milton had been writing poetry from the age of 15, mostly (so far as we can tell from what he wished to preserve) in languages other than English. Before 'On the Morning of Christ's Nativity' he had written one poem in Greek, six poems in Italian, and fully nineteen poems in Latin ranging in length from four-line epigrams to a mini-epic of 226 lines. He wrote only seven poems in English before the Nativity Ode, and three of those seven are translations: two psalm adaptations, which were composed when he was 15, and a word-for-word rendering of a brief ode by Horace, ending with the fine phrase, 'To the stern god of sea'. Of the four remaining compositions in English only two—'On the Death of a Fair Infant Dying of a Cough' and 'At a Vacation Exercise in the College'—give any indication of great poetic powers waiting to be released. We hear them in inconspicuous places, for example, in the concentrated thought and tightly packed monosyllables of such lines from the Fair Infant elegy as 'To slake his wrath whom sin hath made our foe' (l. 66) and in the strong metre and sublime thought of the Vacation Exercise, where the poet describes the kind of poetry he would write in the future: 'Such where the deep transported mind may soar / Above the wheeling poles' (ll. 33–4).

After the Nativity Ode, by contrast, in the seven years leading up to 'Lycidas', Milton wrote only two significant poems in Latin, of 90 and 120 lines respectively: the Sixth Elegy, from which I have already quoted, and 'Ad Patrem', addressed, as the title indicates, to the poet's father. (I exclude the verse postscript to the elegies in the 1645 *Poems*, 'Haec ego mente . . . ', which is of uncertain date and of little artistic interest, and the unpublished couplet—one line of which has been lost—inscribed in the poet's copy of Ariosto.) He did return again to Psalm 114, the one that celebrates the exodus of the Israelites from Egypt and the journey to the Promised Land, translating it this time from the original Hebrew into Doric Greek. He wrote no further poems in Italian.

Each of the two, impressive Latin poems Milton wrote between 'On the Morning of Christ's Nativity' and 'Lycidas' is concerned with *vocation*, with what one is called to in life, a not insignificant question for a man in his twenties. But in both it is clear Milton has already made up his mind: he has been called to be a poet who will serve God by making poetry in God's service and praise and, as he would later put it, 'to breed and cherish in a great nation the seeds of virtue and public civility' (*CPW*, i. 816–17). He would, however, wait until some clear inspiration came to him: 'They also serve who only stand and wait' (Sonnet XVI, l. 14). In the mean time, he would work on his craft, preparing himself—whenever the time came, should it ever come—to be the perfect instrument of God's word. And he would do so in English.

For in the same period Milton composed fully twelve poems in English. These include the major compositions, 'L'Allegro' and 'Il Penseroso' ('The Lively Man' and 'The Reflective Man'), and *A Maske presented at Ludlow Castle, 1634*, or, as it has been known since the eighteenth century, *Comus*. At 1,022 lines (a little short of the typical length of a Greek tragedy), *Comus* is five times longer than the longest poem Milton had written before, the Latin mini-epic, 'In Quintum Novembris'. The other major poem of this period, major despite its brevity, is Sonnet VII, 'How Soon Hath Time', in which the poet beautifully expresses his readiness to serve God—and his readiness to be indefinitely ready to serve God—while betraying as well his anxiety at having produced so little by his twenty-fourth birthday (that is, upon completing his 'three-and-twentieth year'):

> Yet be it less or more, or soon or slow,
> It shall be still in strictest measure even
> To that same lot, however mean or high,
> Toward which time leads me, and the will of Heav'n.
> All is, if I have grace to use it so,
> As ever in my great Task-Master's eye. (ll. 9–14)

As for the rest of the English poems between 'Ode on the Morning of Christ's Nativity' and 'Lycidas', they contain many fine things but are not in the same rank as 'L'Allegro' and 'Il Penseroso', Sonnet VII, and *Comus*. They include Milton's first publication, 'On Shakespeare', which appeared anonymously in the second folio of Shakespeare's *Works*, with its famous closing line, 'That kings for such a tomb would wish to die' (l. 16). There are two jesting elegies on the death at 86 years of age of the University Carrier, Thomas Hobson, whom Death had been unable to catch for some years because of Hobson's being continually in motion with his cart between Cambridge University and the Bull Tavern in London. At last, disguised as a chamberlain, Death caught up with his man, 'Showed him his room where he must lodge that night, / Pulled off his boots, and took away the light' (ll. 15–16). There is an elegant and, at moments, genuinely touching elegy, in trochaic tetrameter, 'An Epitaph on the Marchioness of Winchester', a beautiful, brief masque (109 lines), 'Arcades' (pronounced 'ár-ca-deez'), in which a local wood god, or genius of the wood, nearly steals the show, which is mostly dancing. The genius of the wood describes the music made by the whirling cosmic spheres which 'keep unsteady Nature to her law', governing the motions of creatures in this lower world, 'After the heav'nly tune, which none can hear / Of human mould with gross unpurgèd ear' (ll. 72–3). To capture some of this heavenly tune in his own art Milton would have to 'purge' or cleanse his ears, so far as possible, of the effects of original sin. He would have to follow the ascetic life that he had prescribed in the Sixth Elegy for the poet who would sing of higher things, abstaining from sexual pleasure, dining on vegetables, and drinking (from a simple, beechwood bowl) clear water drawn from the running stream.

Lastly there is 'The Passion', a self-confessed failure, but with some fine things in it. This poem aims at continuing in the vein of the Nativity Ode, as do the three devotional poems, 'At a Solemn Music', 'On Time', and 'Upon the Circumcision'. All three devotional poems experiment with the syncopating effect of short, six-syllable lines, or trimeters, interspersed among the decasyllabic ones, an effect masterfully deployed fourteen times in 'Lycidas', and used in alternating lines of the apotropaic proemia to 'L'Allegro' and 'Il Penseroso'. Of the three devotional poems, 'Upon the Circumcision', being associated with the Feast of the Circumcision on 1 January, is the most obviously connected with the idea behind the Nativity Ode: to celebrate in verse the major feasts of the Christian year. In its opening lines Milton calls on the angels he described in the Nativity Ode singing in the air to 'the shepherds on the lawn':

> Ye flaming powers and wingèd warriors bright,
> That erst with music and triumphant song
> First heard by happy watchful shepherds' ear,
> So sweetly sung your joy the clouds along
> Through the soft silence of the listening night,
> Now mourn.
>
>   . . .
>
> He who with all Heav'n's heraldry whilere
> Entered the world, now bleeds to give us ease.
> Alas, how soon our sin
>   Sore doth begin
>   His infancy to seize! (ll. 1–14)

These competent, thoughtful, uninspired lines stand in marked contrast with the poem to which they refer, seeking to recapture its magic. Whatever the exact dates of the devotional poems, they show Milton caught in a predicament not unfamiliar to young poets of genius. The great work he had done—'On the Morning of Christ's Nativity'—was proof that he could do great work again. But the brilliant achievement was also an obstacle, tempting him to repeat what had already been done supremely well and needed no repetition. But what else was there to do? The success of the Nativity Ode would compel Milton to think about poetry in a new way.

'ON THE MORNING OF CHRIST'S NATIVITY'

Strictly speaking, the Nativity Ode is a 'Hymn', or *hymnos*, the song of praise which in ancient Greek literature is addressed to a god. An *ode*, for which the model is the odes of Pindar, is addressed to a mortal, usually a victorious athlete, who achieves something so splendid he is raised, for a moment, to the condition of the gods, and must be warned against the supposition that he is divine. But by Milton's day, in the Protestant churches, hymns were associated with songs sung in unison by the congregation at Christian worship and the ode (Gr. *aeidein*, 'to sing') was any poem of praise. The subject of Milton's nativity poem is the Incarnation of the Son, who 'laid aside' his majesty in Heaven to live in a mortal, human body ('a darksome house of mortal clay', l. 14), and to be born into our world as we were born into it, as a helpless infant. The poem is therefore at once a hymn to a god and an ode to a hero, although he is a hero rather like the infant Heracles, to whom Milton alludes near the end: 'Our babe to show his godhead true / Can in his swaddling bands control the damnèd crew' (ll. 227–8). The infant Heracles strangled in his cradle the two great serpents the goddess Hera sent to kill him. Since Milton refers to the longer portion of the poem as 'The Hymn', it is less confusing (if not wholly satisfactory) to refer to the whole as an *ode*.

The Nativity Ode is composed of a four-stanza introduction in modified 'rime roiall' and twenty-seven stanzas of 'The Hymn'. The rime roiall stanza is seven decasyllabic lines rhyming ababbcc. But, unusually, the final line of the stanza has twelve syllables instead of ten, forming what some would call an *alexandrine*, after the typical, twelve-syllable French poetic line. But for Milton and his audience the twelve-syllable line would recall the final line of the stanza of Spenser's *Faerie Queene*, which is better referred to as a *hexameter*—having six feet, or (normally) twelve syllables. The effect of the elongated termination is to make each stanza a more pronouncedly integral unit, nor is that separating effect confined to the introductory stanzas. Milton continues it throughout, giving the poem an articulate stateliness of movement from one spectacle to the next, like floats in a parade, an effect that would be lost if each stanza flowed seamlessly into the next. This is so even in the transition from stanza 16 to stanza 17, which is grammatically dependent on its predecessor: 'With such a horrid clang / As on Mount Sinai rang' (ll. 157–8). Because the reader is by this time accustomed to the rhythm of the stanzas with their longer terminal lines, the subordinate preposition beginning stanza 17 at once recalls the integral character of each stanza and sublimely transgresses it at the moment when the trumpet of the apocalypse is sounded.

The four stanzas of the introduction divide neatly in two: two stanzas on the occasion and subject of the poem, two stanzas on the poet's desire to offer his poem as an actual gift to the Christ Child. The opening stanza gives us the occasion:

> This is the month, and this the happy morn
> Wherein the Son of Heav'n's eternal King,
> Of wedded maid and virgin mother born,
> Our great redemption from above did bring,
> For so the holy sages once did sing:
>   That he our deadly forfeit should release,
> And with his Father work us a perpetual peace.

As the prophets of the Old Testament foretold, the Son of God would come down to earth 'from above' and dwell among us as a man. By dying on the cross—a specification the poet reserves for dramatic effect until line 152—Jesus will release us all from the consequences of original sin, our 'deadly forfeit'.

The subject of the poem being thus abstractly stated, in the second two stanzas of the introduction the poet brings us into the present moment, invoking the 'Heav'nly Muse' to give him a gift for the 'infant God' and setting the scene for us in the present time, shortly before dawn, when the stars are still out and the sky is not yet imprinted by the fiery hooves of the horses drawing the chariot of the sun: 'Now while the heav'n by the sun's team untrod, / Hath took no print of the approaching light, / And all the spangled host keep watch in squadrons bright' (ll. 19–21). In the following stanza, immediately after this breathless pause, startlingly, the poet collapses the separation of the present from the past. He looks to the east and descries the three kings of Scripture, hastening to Jesus' cradle with their gifts. Still more startlingly, he urges his muse to get to the stable before them:

> See how from far upon the eastern road
> The star-led wizards haste with odours sweet!
> O run, prevent them with thy humble ode
> And lay it lowly at his blessèd feet.
> Have thou the honour first thy Lord to greet,
>   And join thy voice unto the angel choir
> From out his secret altar, touched with hallowed fire. (ll. 22–8)

The twenty-seven stanzas of 'the hymn' are more complicated metrically than the four stanzas of the introduction. Each stanza is eight lines long, rhyming aabccbdd. The first two rhyming couplets—aa and cc—are six-syllable lines, or trimeters: 'It was the winter wild, / While the Heaven-born child' (ll. 29–30) and 'Nature in awe to him / Had doffed her gaudy trim' (ll. 32–3). The third and final couplet is composed of an eight-syllable tetrameter rhymed with the concluding, twelve-syllable hexameter: 'It was no season then for her / To wanton with the sun, her lusty paramour' (ll. 35–6). But the three rhyming couplets of the stanza are divided, as two fence-posts divide three sections of fence, by two rhyming decasyllabic, iambic pentameter lines: 'All meanly wrapped in the rude manger lies' and 'With her great master so to sympathize' (ll. 31, 34). Put all together, the stanza looks and sounds like this:

> It was the winter wild,
> While the Heaven-born child
>   All meanly wrapped in the rude manger lies.

> Nature in awe to him
> Had doffed her gaudy trim,
>   With her great Master so to sympathize:
> It was no season then for her
> To wanton with the sun, her lusty paramour. (ll 29–36)

Although there are no marked internal divisions to 'The Hymn', it is rhetorically divided into four sections of twelve, six, and eight stanzas plus a single-stanza conclusion. The first section is subdividable into (a) the response of Creation to the entrance of the Creator into what He has created and (b) the shepherds' vision of the angels singing in the air. In the opening seven stanzas Nature is abashed at the coming of her Creator, who stills her fears by sending to earth the goddess of Peace, who with her wand 'strikes a universal peace through sea and land' (l. 52). That peace, extending to human conflicts as well as to nature, is beautifully described in two stanzas (IV and V), followed by another two stanzas (VI and VII), in which the stars do not want to leave the sky, because they would lose the sight of the coming of their Lord into the world, and the sun does not want to rise, because he is ashamed to be compared with the 'Son': 'He saw a greater sun appear / Than his bright throne or burning axle-tree could bear' (ll. 83–4). In a moment of sharp anticipation, time stands still.

The shepherds are then introduced, still before dawn, seated on the ground and 'simply chatting in a rustic row' (ll. 86–7). Suddenly, they are overwhelmed by music that takes their souls in rapture. The music lasts for a while before the shepherds see its source, long enough for Nature to suppose the apocalypse is coming and her existence is nearly over. But then, 'At last' (l. 109), the angels 'Are seen':

> The helmèd cherubim
> And sworded seraphim
>   Are seen in glittering ranks with wings displayed,
> Harping in loud and solemn choir
> With unexpressive [i.e. inexpressibly beautiful] notes to Heaven's
>   new-born heir. (ll. 112–16)

The twelfth stanza is transitional to the next movement and is one of the finest things in the poem. The speaker guesses that the angelic song referred to in the Gospel according to Luke is the same music that was sung by the angels as God made the world. It helps to recall that the 'Creator great' of this stanza is the Son. He is the same person as the babe in the manger, who is now incarnate in the world he has made:

> Such music (as 'tis said)
> Before was never made,
>   But when of old the sons of morning sung,
> While the Creator great
> His constellations set,
>   And the well-balanced world on hinges hung,

> And cast the dark foundations deep,
> And bid the welt'ring waves their oozy channel keep. (ll. 117–24)

We note how Milton here succeeds in giving stature to the infant Jesus, for he was never much interested in the images of helplessness that are central to the Christian imaginary: the babe in its mother's arms and the man on the cross. The babe who will be laid to rest at the poem's conclusion is here, near its centre, the God who 'cast the dark foundations' of the world. Since I have mentioned the special beauty of this stanza, I would note that its individual lines imitate the articulate integrity of the stanzas: each line is strongly end-stopped and the beauty of the stanza is actually increased when we lengthen the time of the pause between lines.

The second section, stanzas XIII to XVII, begins as an apostrophe to the cosmic spheres, asking them to make their music an accompaniment to the angelic song: 'with your ninefold harmony / Make up full consort to the angelic symphony' (ll. 131–2). Something very interesting, and classically Miltonic, happens at this moment. The speaker of the poem indulges in a fantasy that is given considerable scope before it is crushed, an effect not unlike the fantasies of 'L'Allegro' or the brilliant floral catalogue of 'Lycidas', which ends, 'For so to interpose a little ease, / Let our frail thoughts dally with false surmise' (ll. 152–3). 'If such holy song / Enwrap our fancy long', the speaker says, 'Time will run back and fetch the age of gold' (ll. 133–5). By the power of this music, original sin will melt away from our nature, as it will from Nature too: 'Hell itself will pass away'; Truth, Justice, and Mercy will return to the earth; and the heavenly Jerusalem of Revelation will descend so close to the earth that it will appear possible to enter into it now: 'And Heaven as at some festival / Will open wide the gates of her high palace hall' (ll. 147–8).

Stanza XVI contains the turning point of the poem. In it, the fantasy of an early access to heavenly bliss is crushed. We are awakened to the stern reality of the Atonement, of Jesus' having to die for our sins, an atonement that can be achieved only 'on the bitter cross':

> But wisest Fate says no,
> This must not yet be so,
>   The babe lies yet in smiling infancy,
> That on the bitter cross
> Must redeem our loss,
>   So both himself and us to glorify.
> Yet first to those ychained in sleep,
> The wakeful trump of doom must thunder through the deep. (ll. 149–56)

In a dexterous reordering of apocalyptic temporality the poet reaches forward in imagination to the apocalypse itself, putting it, so to speak, in its place. He reaches backwards also to the 'horrid clang' (l. 157) of the giving of the Law on Mount Sinai (the Law that Jesus will complete). And he then resituates us in the time of the event that is the occasion of his poem. At the end of time, in the imponderably distant future, 'at last', we shall be saved. Only then may 'our bliss', as he calls it, be 'Full and perfect'. But far off as that time is, he adds, it 'now begins' (ll. 165–7), because of the Incarnation of the Son. Despite all the horrors that are to follow Christ's death, our bliss begins now.

Why? Because from this point forward Satan will not be free to range in the world, attracting worship to himself:

> for from this happy day
> The old dragon under ground
> In straiter limits bound,
>   Not half so far casts his usurpèd sway,
> And wroth to see his kingdom fail,
> Swinges the scaly horror of his folded tail. (ll. 167–72)

Stanzas XIX to XXVI, beginning 'The oracles are dumb' (l. 173), give a spectacular panorama of the pagan gods—Apollo, the Greek wood gods, the Latin lars and lemurs, the obscene Peor and the numerous Baalim of the Canaanites, Ashtaroth (another plural) and Ammon, the dying god Adonis, grisly Moloch, on whose altar babies were roasted, and the animal gods of Egypt: 'the flocking shadows pale / Troop to the infernal jail' (ll. 232–3). These are all banished from their haunts around the Mediterranean—in Greece, Italy, the Near East, and Egypt—and perhaps even in England: 'And the yellow-skirted fays / Fly after the night-steeds, leaving their moon-loved maze' (ll. 235–6).

The final stanza beautifully recalls the beginning (l. 22), reminding us that we are hearing a performance, a song, by commanding us once again to 'see': 'But see the virgin blest / Hath laid her babe to rest: / Time is our tedious song should here have ending' (ll. 237–9). The song should end so that this infant can sleep, and we should be quiet, too. The final tableau inhabits this disciplined silence. The star that the wise men had followed, and that shines now over the stable of Jesus, has become a handmaid holding a lamp at night, ready to perform any task for her master. Below her, all around the stable, angels in bright armour are seated according to their ranks, guarding the infant King from harm:

> Heav'n's youngest teemèd star
> Hath fixed her polished car,
>   Her sleeping Lord with handmaid lamp attending.
> And all about the courtly stable
> Bright-harnessed angels sit in order serviceable. (ll. 240–4)

It is a typically Miltonic, quiet ending, but the martial note struck by those bright-harnessed angels is typical of Milton, too. His Christianity will not be fugitive and cloistered, retiring and contemplative. It will be a militant Christianity, ready to sally out and fight in the world.

'L'ALLEGRO' AND 'IL PENSEROSO'

The paired poems 'L'Allegro' and 'Il Penseroso' are unique in English literature. Yet the representation of opposite possibilities in the self is common enough in poetry, and Milton had already done something like it in Elegy Six, 'Ad Carolum Diodatum', when he introduced the two contrasting kinds of poets: the bibulous poet of eros, whose songs are beloved of Bacchus, the god of wine ('carmina Bacchus amat', l. 14), and the abstemious *vates*, from whose secret breast and lips sounds the voice of Jove himself ('Spirat et occultum pectus et ora Iovem', l. 78). William Blake's *Songs of Innocence and Experience* constitute perhaps the deepest example of the oppositional and analytic impulse in the poetic imagination—although all Blake's prophecies are inspired by the muse of contraries. Analysis of the self into distinct voices articulating the poet's 'inner quarrel', as Helen Vendler calls it, is a creative principle in Yeats from the early poem 'The Two Trees'—the one bearing trembling flowers and fruit, the other 'the ravens of unresting thought'—to the late, discursive poems expressing ambivalent political and personal judgements.[1] The inner quarrel is formally evident in Yeats's 'Dialogue of Self and Soul', inspired by Marvell's two dialogue poems—'Dialogue between the Resolved Soul and Created Pleasure' and 'Dialogue between Soul and Body'. Indeed, almost all Marvell's poems up to the 'Horatian Ode'—for example, 'To His Coy Mistress' and 'The Mower against Gardens'—express one side of a debate in which the other is implied: 'Half the world shall be thy slave', says Pleasure to the Soul, 'the other half thy friend' (ll. 65–6).

Contradiction, literally 'saying the opposites', is fundamental to the way poetry thinks—metaphor itself is a kind of contradiction—and when Yeats's soul enjoins his self to 'Fix every wandering thought upon / The quarter where all thought is done', he, the soul, would silence verse itself ('Dialogue of Self and Soul', ll. 6–7). For verse, the 'turning' of words, effectuates the delirious movement of poetry between opposite ideas and opposite moods: on the one hand, revulsion at 'the frogspawn of a blind man's ditch' (l. 59); on the other hand, the acceptance (and, no doubt, the detachment) by which we win the strength to say, 'everything we look upon is blest' (l. 72).

But separating the elements of the dialogue into two distinct personae speaking two distinct poems, each persona, or 'mask' (*per* + *sonare*, 'to sound through'), holding the other in horror and contempt, is unique. I refer especially to those symmetrically opposed introductions, the apotropaic proemia wherein the opposing character is formally banished—'Hence, loathèd Melancholy!', 'Hence, vain, deluding joys!' Nor do we find in other poems built on explicitly oppositional terms, such as the poems I have mentioned by Marvell, Blake, and Yeats, what we do find in Milton's 'L'Allegro' and 'Il Penseroso': the feeling of a magic incantation. More broadly, the poems are distinguished for their elaborate artifice, their mythopoeic

---

[1] Vendler, *Our Secret Discipline: Yeats and Lyric Form* (Cambridge, Mass., 2007), 160.

learnedness, their psychological range, as they are for the stunning clarity of the many genre scenes they offer, and for the profound suggestiveness of what is said in them about the power of art. Assuming 'L'Allegro' to have been written first, it is wonderful to contemplate how Milton managed to preserve and reproduce the original inspiration in its opposite mood, while adhering so faithfully to the structure of the earlier poem.

It is uncertain when Milton composed 'L'Allegro' and 'Il Penseroso'. Most scholars believe they were written after he took his MA degree at Cambridge and was embarked on some five years of private study, first at Hammersmith and then at Horton. Other scholars think it possible the poems were written while Milton was still at Cambridge. The delineation of 'characters', originally an ancient literary form, was in Milton's day, just before the rise of the novel, an emerging fashion, although Milton's elegant, playful poems bear little resemblance to the prose character studies of the period. Instead, they reflect a preoccupation with what it means to be a 'persona' in a fully individuated way, rather than a social person bound to others by the ties of family or class, or even by the need to make a living: 'retirèd Leisure' is in Melancholy's train, and an active aesthetic leisure is, so to speak, the condition of the possibility of Mirth.

Milton was a mature man in his twenties when he wrote these poems, but they reflect a younger state of mind—that of what we would now call 'the young adult'— when one can seriously put to oneself the question: 'what kind of a self shall I choose to be?', as if such a choice can be made. (To an extent it can, and to a greater extent it cannot, as one discovers when one is no longer a teenager.) That is why each poem ends with the sort of contractual bargain teenagers at one time or another will imagine they can strike with their fates: 'These delights, if thou canst give, / Mirth with thee, I mean to live'; 'These pleasures Melancholy give, / And I with thee will choose to live.' Such propositions reflect the naive but unavoidable question (unavoidable when you are 16): 'What mood shall I be in, for the rest of my life?'

The Lively Man and the Reflective Man are recognizable in our own jargon as 'extroverted' and 'introverted' personality types. But because the poems concentrate on the self apart from the ties of family and society, the extroversion of L'Allegro is a 'turning-outwards' towards others that remains a private experience, the experience of observing others at work and at play and especially (when the poem concludes), the experience of music, music made without any musicians we can see. So it is too, *mutatis mutandis*, with Il Penseroso, the Reflective Man, whose introversion is made easier by his preferring night to day, the forest to the open fields, and, to the lecture hall or the sociable, university quadrangle, his lonely study in a tower. The Reflective Man's introversion does not, however, resolve itself into a hard core like Milton's heart in Sonnet VI, which 'arms itself within itself, a perfect diamond' ('[il] mio cuor...S'arma di sè, d'intero diamante', l. 8). Instead, the Reflective Man's self is perfected in the ecstatic dissolution it experiences through music:

> There let the pealing organ blow
> To the full-voiced choir below

> In service high and anthems clear,
> As may with sweetness through mine ear
> Dissolve me into ecstasies. (ll. 161–5)

When we consider the representations of music that come near the end of both 'L'Allegro' and 'Il Penseroso', each evoking Orpheus, the archetypal musician and poet, the poems seem to be less about the opposition of two distinct personae than they are about the emotional possibilities of art, from the 'wanton heed and giddy cunning' ('L'Allegro', l. 141) of intensely subjective aesthetic experience to the 'service high and anthems clear' of Christian worship, which is directed to the absolutely other.

'L'Allegro'

'L'Allegro' begins with a proem (something said before one sets out on the *oime* or path of song) intended to drive off its threatening opposite, Melancholy, a monster born in the underworld, by the river Styx. In the realm of primitive magic and Hesiodic daemons, to know the true name and genealogy of something is to control it. How and by whom was Melancholy conceived? By an ugly copulation of the triple-headed hound of Hell, Cerberus, with a vestigially personified Midnight, a Midnight having none of the particularity of Spenser's half-blind, wicked, scheming, crook-backed crone. Since Melancholy is no longer in Hell, but in the world, threatening the mood of the Lively Man, the *allegrezza* of L'Allegro, it must be banished before the speaker may safely invoke its opposite, Euphrosyne or Mirth, lest open war break out between the two: the apotropaic is a necessary part of invocation. The monster is banished, however, not to the Hell in which it was born but to an unknown ('un-couth') cave in the land of the Cimmerians, a strange, remote people who live in perpetual twilight in the wilderness ('desert') at the edge of the world. The monster Melancholy is banished, that is, to the periphery, and what is banished to the periphery will of course return—as a 'pensive nun'. The apotropaic proemium is a temporary gesture, a clearing of space for contemplative reflection on the mirthful-ness that understands itself (mistakenly? provisionally?) to be opposed to contempla-tive reflection:

> Hence, loathèd Melancholy,
>   Of Cerberus and blackest Midnight born,
> In Stygian cave forlorn,
>   'Mongst horrid shapes and shrieks and sights unholy.
> Find out some uncouth cell,
>   Where brooding Darkness spreads his jealous wings,
> And the night-raven sings.
>   There, under ebon shades and low-browed rocks,
> As ragged as thy locks,
>   In dark Cimmerian desert ever dwell. (ll. 1–10)

The complicated rhyme-scheme (abbacddeec) and alternating line lengths show the influence of Italian lyric poetry, now thoroughly absorbed (Milton wrote no more poems in Italian after Sonnet VI, even when he was in Italy), and of Spenser's Italianate 'Epithalamion'. As in Spenser, a mood of enchantment is created by the suspended rhymes, which chime in upon us unexpectedly, notably the 'c' rhyme on 'cell', which remains unmated with 'dwell' until the last word of the introduction: 'In dark Cimmerian desert ever dwell'. The surprise of that final rhyme is increased by our having already heard and been satisfied by the internal rhyme, *desert / ever*. The enchanting effect is enhanced by the syncopated rhythms of the shorter lines, for example, the line 'as ragged as thy locks', which follows the ponderous, open vowels of the preceding verse: 'There, under ebon shades and low-browed rocks / As ragged as thy locks'. The phonic slowness in both lines is overlaid by the rhythmical rapidity of the second, shorter line.

By 'a mood of enchantment' I do not mean just an aesthetic effect. I mean the feeling that we are in the presence of real, incantatory power that has the force of a magic spell, banishing a malign spirit from our presence. The apotropaic magic may then be assumed when the poet changes to the more regular, tetrameter metre that governs the rest of the poem and immediately accelerates it, a trick Milton picked up from the opening of the second act of *A Midsummer Night's Dream*, where the fairies are introduced in exotic measures, indicating their existence on a different plane of reality; but as their discussion proceeds the verse modulates insensibly into regular iambic pentameter couplets. In this poem, the change occurs abruptly with Milton's favourite telltale word, *but*. With that *but*, he turns on his heel from the vicious genealogy of Melancholy to the propitious one of Mirth:

> But come thou goddess fair and free,
> In Heav'n yclept Euphrosyne ['yew-fró-zin-ee']
> And by men, heart-easing Mirth,
> Whom lovely Venus at a birth
> With two sister graces more [presumably as attendants]
> To ivy-crownèd Bacchus bore. (ll. 11–16)

When she wakes the speaker at dawn, Mirth is instructed to bring with her a lengthy train of attendants, among whom is 'the mountain nymph, sweet Liberty':

> Haste thee nymph, and bring with thee
> Jest and youthful Jollity
> . . .
> And in thy right hand lead with thee
> The Mountain nymph, sweet Liberty
> . . .
> And at my window bid good morrow
> . . .
> While the cock with lively din
> Scatters the rear of darkness thin. (ll. 25–6, 35–6, 46, 49–50)

Liberty is a mountain nymph because in Milton's view inhabitants of the mountains live harder lives and are sternly independent, like the ancient Hebrews, or the Greeks, in contrast with peoples who live on coastal plains or in great river valleys, like the ancient Philistines on the Canaanite, Mediterranean plain, or the Egyptians and Babylonians beside the Nile and the Euphrates, who being given to their pleasures are easy prey to tyrants. But here, in 'L'Allegro', *liberty* means little more than freedom from the hard physical labour of the kind the ploughman, the shepherd, the milkmaid, and the mower must do, although the ploughman whistles as he works and the milkmaid sings (ll. 63–8).

With the wonderful, martial image of the cock crow 'scattering the rear of darkness thin', as if darkness were a retreating army, the poet draws the curtain back from the 'landscape' (l. 70)—a new, fashionable term imported from Holland, where landscape painting had just begun—which is disclosed beneath the rising sun, 'Robed in flames and amber light' (l. 61). It is the landscape through which the Lively Man will briskly walk, his eye catching its 'pleasures' (l. 69) one by one. Note that the things listed are not objective things but subjective pleasures. They include fields darkly furrowed from being newly turned; boles of huge elms rising from the hedges bordering those fields; green hills under the rosy clouds; ruddy, burned-over grasslands beside the grey fallows; late-summer meadows spangled with daisies; shallow, rushing brooks flowing into wide, slow-moving rivers; and, in the distance, 'Mountains on whose barren breast / The laboring clouds do often rest' (ll. 73–4). That this is an autumn or late summer landscape is confirmed when Phyllis and Thestylis bind the sheaves. Or, if the hay is still drying in a great, conical heap in the field—'the tanned haycock in the mead' (l. 90)—Thestylis and Phyllis resort thither, for what purpose we remain uninformed, and one suspects this epicoene speaker does not care. So there are people in this landscape, busy with their work and with their pleasures: the hunter who sounds his horn, the ploughman, the milkmaid, the mower pausing to sharpen his scythe, Thestylis and Phyllis on their way to the haycock, and the shepherd in the dale, under a hawthorn's ragged bark, anxiously counting his sheep at first light.

The speaker's objective presence is so vague that he at first lacks any clear grammatical subject, being introduced into the landscape by the participial phrases 'Oft list'ning how the hounds and horn' (l. 53) and 'Sometime walking not unseen' (l. 57). He can wander on the periphery of life and, though he is 'not unseen', he is not much remarked. Yet he sees much. He sees the simple country folk not only when they are outdoors making music, sawing on their 'jocund rebecks' (l. 94) and dancing 'in the chequered shade' (l. 96)—a fine image of the pleasure we take in the afternoon light that falls through the overhanging boughs—but also when they are at supper in their cottages and when they spin their fairy tales by the cheerful hearth, over 'the spicy nut-brown ale' (l. 100). He doesn't take his eyes off them until they are in bed, lulled to sleep by the 'whispering winds' of the evening (l. 116).

Country people go to bed early and rise with the dawn. So once they have turned in, the Lively Man appears to be instantly transported to the city, merely by the recollection of its pleasures: 'Towered cities please us then, / And the busy haunts of men' (ll. 117–18). These pleasures seem to be as much literary as they are social, bringing before the speaker's eyes knights and ladies in their halls or on the tilting yard, or at ceremonies graced with revelry and pageants (ll. 119–24). The dreamlike character of this urban interlude in a medieval past is made explicit in verses that take us back into the country: 'Such sights as youthful poets dream / On summer eves, by haunted stream' (ll. 129–30). *Haunted* stream? We seem to be being reminded of the magic spell under which the poem is supposed to unfold, although the literary quality of the spell is suggested not only by the reference to the youthful poet but by the one contemporary urban pleasure Milton names:

> Then to the well-trod stage anon,
> If Jonson's learned sock be on,
> Or sweetest Shakespeare, fancy's child,
> Warble his native wood-notes wild. (ll. 131–4)

For a brief moment, lasting through these four, rapid lines, we are in a real, public world, that of the London stage in the 1630s: Milton could have attended such plays. He had written an epitaph for Shakespeare, which was published with the second folio, and Ben Jonson was still alive in London when Milton wrote these lines. No longer are we in the imaginary world of the speaker's fantasies, its warm cottages and nut-brown ale as unfamiliar to him as 'Fairy Mab' and the 'drudging goblin', Robin Goodfellow (ll. 102, 105), of whom he had only read in books, among them, incidentally, Ben Jonson's masques. The 'well-trod stage' belongs to a material world, but one in which Jonson's learning and Shakespeare's imagination are more real than anything else.

Even so, the Lively Man's Shakespeare is not writing, or mounting a play: he is 'warbling', that is, singing. The singing is still in our ears when the speaker is 'lapped', that is, submerged in and caressed by 'Lydian airs' (l. 136), the music of the effeminate and sensual east. After a brief opening into the objective world of the theatre, and of social discussion about theatre, subjectivity overwhelms us again. Or it overwhelms the speaker as his soul is pierced (l. 138) by music that is 'Married to immortal verse' (l. 137)—there's Shakespeare again—but that is soon a force of its own, making the self 'wanton' and 'giddy' with its counterpoint:

> Married to immortal verse
> Such as the meeting soul may pierce
> In notes with many a winding bout
> Of linked sweetness long drawn out,
> With wanton heed and giddy cunning,
> The melting voice through mazes running,
> Untwisting all the chains that tie
> The hidden soul of harmony. (ll. 137–144)

What kind of music is this? It sounds to us like the music of extreme subjectivity, music that we will love not for its Apollonian structure but for the ecstasy it induces in our souls, deliciously lost in that larger, hidden soul of harmony. But this is not, after all, a drug, an opiate that will lap at the hard core of the inner self with its warm, soothing waves. It is what it was in the beginning: an incantation, a magic spell. Formerly, this spell had the power to drive Melancholy off to the edge of the world and force it to inhabit, for a time, the Cimmerian land. The incantation then had the power to call the Spirit of Mirth from whatever place she inhabits, bringing with her 'Quips and cranks and wanton wiles, / Nods and becks and wreathed smiles' (ll. 27–8), a well-stocked repertory of cheerful social tics, and also a parade of very minor Greek and Roman gods, from the spirit of youth, Hebe, to 'Sport that wrinkled Care derides / And Laughter'—in the classic pose of that god whom the Romans took seriously indeed—'holding both his sides' (l. 32).

Now the power of the incantation, transmitted through music, reaches past these minor deities far into the underworld, to Elysium, where Orpheus raises his head from its pillow of somniferous blooms to better hear those strains. The music penetrates as far into the underworld as to the Elysian fields, but not, it would seem, to the throne of Pluto. *Had* the strains penetrated that far they would have 'quite' (that is, 'entirely') set free the wife that Orpheus had all but won back from Hell, losing her again, at the last moment, when he unwisely turned to look at her:

> That Orpheus' self may heave his head
> From golden slumber on a bed
> Of heaped Elysian flowers, and hear
> Such strains as would have won the ear
> Of Pluto to have quite quite set free
> His half-regained Eurydice. (ll. 145–50)

On this splendid note, by which the original sense of the poem as an incantation is recaptured, the speaker abruptly concludes with his impossible proposal: 'These delights, if thou canst give, / Mirth with thee, I mean to live.' What delights is he speaking of? That of seeing Orpheus heaving his head from off those Elysian flowers (the head the maenads severed from its body)? Or of watching Corydon and Thyrsis dine on herbs and country messes and drink their nut-brown ale? These are not delights but their shadows: fantasies. Still, they are the fantasies of which poems are made.

'Il Penseroso'

'Il Penseroso' follows the same structure as 'L'Allegro' and was probably, as I have said, composed later. If this is so, then what is remarkable about 'Il Penseroso' in the first instance is the unlikelihood of its peculiar achievement, which is to have imitated the form of the earlier poem with content diametrically opposed—and to have done so with undiminished inspiration.

'Il Penseroso' opens with an apotropaic proem in the same form as that of 'L'Allegro', although this one has no genealogy to parallel the birth of Melancholy from Cerberus and Midnight: 'vain deluding joys', in the plural, are banished. The enemy lineage, that of the goddess of Mirth, and indeed the goddess herself, remain disdainfully unacknowledged. All that the speaker will acknowledge is a crowd of light-weight, 'deluding joys', the children of who knows whom. As the regular, tetrameter measure of the body of the poem begins, the speaker hails the goddess Melancholy and tells us she is black like two legendary black beauties, Prince Memnon's sister and Cassiopea, who became a constellation. We then learn her ancient and staid genealogy: she was born of Vesta, the Roman goddess of the hearth (and hence of the household), and Saturn, the father of the Olympian gods, including Jove, who overthrew him. By reaching back before the Olympian gods of Greek and Roman mythology Milton is emphasizing the extreme antiquity of Melancholy's line, making her fundamental to the metaphysical order of the world: she is 'higher far descended' (l. 22), he says, when comparing her with Memnon's sister and Cassiopea. The remark is aimed at the parents of Mirth, who are the lightest of the Olympians, Venus and Bacchus. Melancholy is invoked as a 'pensive nun'—though nuns had not been seen in England for a hundred years—who is 'devout and pure, / Sober, steadfast, and demure' (ll. 31–2), and she is described rapt in such 'holy passion' that she forgets herself and seems a marble statue (ll. 41–2). That is how Milton had earlier imagined the readers of Shakespeare, as marble figures on a tomb, immobilized by thought: 'Then thou our fancy of itself bereaving, / Dost make us marble with too much conceiving' ('On Shakespeare', ll. 13–14). Milton has fetched back the image here, and improved it.

Attending Melancholy is a long train of vestigial personifications favouring reflection: Peace, Quiet, Fasting, Leisure (for reflection requires leisure, that is, wealth), and Contemplation, the climax of the series, followed by Silence. The word *contemplation* implies inclusive visual inspection and modelling within a cleared mental space, like that of the Roman temple, which is, as of course Milton knew, etymologically present in the word. Contemplation is represented here as prophetic vision, in particular the prophetic vision of Ezekiel, a notion of the prophetic that is far beyond that with which the poem concludes: 'something like prophetic strain' (l. 174).

The following figure of Silence is 'hist' along for the sake of contemplation unless the nightingale sings, which instantly puts us back in the forest. It is like Milton to emphasize, first, the visual character of reflective thinking as inclusive inspection and then, as a musician and a poet, to correct that visual bias by introducing the nightingale, Philomel, smoothing with her song 'the rugged brow of night' (l. 58; compare *Comus*, ll. 250–1, where the Lady's song smoothed 'the raven down / Of darkness till it smiled'). With masterly art, Milton contrasts the alacrity of the measure of 'L'Allegro' with wonderful effects of spaciousness and distance in 'Il Penseroso', as when the moon at her height is 'Like one that hath been led astray / Through the heaven's wide pathless way' (ll. 69–70). (Note how the double rhyme, *hath ... astray / path ... way*, opens up twice from a short 'a' to a long: everything is sonorously lengthened.)

Another such splendid moment is when the speaker, who often wanders in the forest at night, hears across a body of water, from a neighbouring town, the distant curfew bell, calling its citizens (but not the speaker) indoors, enjoining them to cover their fires and go to bed for the night. Milton has caught how the sound of a bell is louder when it crosses water while still seeming to come from afar. We are not sure the curfew bell is objectively 'far off', if *objectively* can mean anything in this connection; it is *subjectively* far off, it sounds so:

> Oft on a plat of rising ground,
> I hear the far-off curfew sound,
> Over some wide-watered shore,
> Swinging slow with sullen roar. (ll. 73–6)

Roar had a wider sense in Milton's day than it does in ours, and could refer to any loud, sustained noise, like the roar of a crowd, but the splendid phrase *sullen roar* is typical of the greater degree of phenomenological distortion in this poem, as compared with its predecessor. We do well to remember that the speaker's is a mind that, altering, alters all, as moonlight breaking through a cloud alters not only the external forms but the very moods that irradiate from things we see in the night. The curfew bell is not peaceful and calm: it is sullen, and it roars.

Almost immediately, we are in a room beside a dying fire in the very town we have just seen from a distance, across water, and it is curfew time again, as the bellman drowsily blesses the doors of each house: this is a small country town, not London. The rapid change of scene, for which the pretext is bad weather ('Or if the air will not permit', l. 77), is the poet's way of showing us that to be reflective is continually to change one's point of view, to bring about that phenomenological distortion. For we are situated in this room only long enough to hear the bellman's drowsy charm and also to hear that last, poignant vestige of Mirth, the lonely cricket on the hearth (l. 82).

As in 'L'Allegro,' we are transported from the rustic cottage to a more exalted scene, although not, on this occasion, the 'towered cities' of 'L'Allegro' (l. 117) but a solitary 'high lonely tower' (l. 86), where our reflective speaker studies. Instead of studying by poring over his books, he calls up the learned spirits at home, out of office hours:

> Or let my lamp at midnight hour
> Be seen in some high lonely tower,
> Where I might oft outwatch the Bear
> With thrice-great Hermes, or unsphere
> The spirit of Plato to unfold
> What worlds or what vast regions hold
> Th'immortal mind that hath forsook
> Her mansion in this fleshly nook. (ll. 85–92)

The tower may remind us of the towers of 'L'Allegro', 'Bosomed high in tufted trees' (l. 78), but this tower is solitary: it is not part of a college, or a monastery, still less of a court. It is more like the Martello tower of *Ulysses*, the place of impotent reflection on the ineluctable modality of all visible—which is to say, phenomenal—things.

Here, however, we see the first signs of exuberance in The Reflective Man, for he presents himself not with his back bent and his spectacles on, poring over the hefty tomes of Hermes Trismegistus and Plato, but as boldly calling down their spirits from the heavenly spheres and questioning them. He likewise presents himself as watching, not reading, the tragedies of ancient Greece and of later ages, presented by 'gorgeous Tragedy' herself (l. 97). He calls on Melancholy again ('But, O sad virgin')—lest we forget the poem is addressed to her—wishing she could also give him access to legendary authors who do not exist in books, Musaeus, and Orpheus, whose lament for Eurydice 'Drew iron tears down Pluto's cheek, / And made Hell grant what love did seek' (ll. 107–8).[2] The speaker wishes that Melancholy might call up Chaucer as well, to finish the *Squire's Tale*, the most mysterious of the *Canterbury Tales*, and that he, the speaker, might also hear—though from what source is unclear ('great bards beside')—more medieval tales of magic and romance: 'Of forests and enchantments drear, / Where more is meant than meets the ear' (ll. 119–20).[3]

After these night scenes, Milton imagines the speaker in the morning, as he has imagined his Lively Man being wakened at dawn by the spirit of Mirth at his window. Now he is greeted by Morn herself, in civil suit, as befits the speaker's mood, and bringing gusts of wind and showers. His morning walk is brief, however, and has none of the brio of 'L'Allegro'. He is soon in the woods again, and in silence, except for the droning of bees and the murmuring of the brook. These sounds put him to sleep so that he may be visited by a strange, mysterious dream. Not the least of what is strange about the dream is its hovering, like a hummingbird, over a pool so still it reflects the sky and also the wings of this dream, so that the dream greets its own reflection: 'And let some strange, mysterious dream, / Wave at his wings in airy stream' (ll. 147–8).

This is the strangest and most difficult moment in 'Il Penseroso'. It is nearly unintelligible. In its own form, the dream waves at its own wings reflected in the stream. But the dream also has a content, an illusion that is its own moving tableau ('lively portraiture', l. 149), which we never see. This tableau, the dream-content, bears no resemblance whatever to the hovering spirit that has brought the illusion and laid it softly on the sleeper's eyelids. When the sleeper wakes from this dream, whatever it was, he has no reason, like Caliban, to cry to dream again, for he is now in a supernatural world, one in which Nordic, fairy spirits, or a Latin *genius loci*, make music that surrounds him in the woods:

> And as I wake, sweet music breathe
> Above, about, or underneath,
> Sent by some spirit to mortals good,
> Or the unseen genius of the wood. (ll. 151–4)

Here the poem might end with the couplet, 'These pleasures Melancholy give, / And I with thee will choose to live' (ll. 175–6), making 'Il Penseroso' only four lines longer

---

[2] Milton would have known the Greek, Hellenistic poem by 'Musaeus', entitled 'Hero and Leander', but would not for a moment have thought that text to have been composed by the shadowy, legendary poet of that name.

[3] *Drear* is a shortened form of *dreary*, which for Milton meant 'dismal' and even 'menacing'. He may have known the word's descent from Old English *dreorig*, 'bloody, gory'.

than 'L'Allegro' and keeping symmetry with the earlier poem. It would be an ending very close in spirit to the forest scenes of Marvell's 'Upon Appleton House', with their spooky evocation of a speaker communing with the spirits of nature and slowly, inadvertently, disclosing to us a mind overstepping the boundaries of normal, common sense, and of educated common sense—a mind hermetically enclosing itself in its fancy. Marvell's speaker is a little like that hovering dream, waving at the reflection of its own, gorgeous wings. Marvell studied 'Il Penseroso' with care and much of his poetry—not just its metre—is indebted to it. If any poet of the seventeenth century was willing to portray through his speakers the reflective man in the fully reflective sense of that waving dream in 'Il Penseroso', it was Marvell.

But Marvell would have been as disinclined to what follows as Milton was impelled to it: a pulling back from this scene of imaginative excess with a churching of its visionary offspring:

> But let my due feet never fail
> To walk the studious cloister's pale
> And love the high embowèd roof
> With antique pillars' massy proof
> And storied windows richly dight,
> Casting a dim religious light. (ll. 155–60)

I noted earlier how fond Milton is of making a transition at a critical moment by a strongly adversative 'But' at the beginning of a line. With such a 'But' both 'L'Allegro' and 'Il Penseroso' modulate in the eleventh line from their apotropaic proemia to the main body of the poems: 'But come thou goddesss fair and free'; 'But hail thou goddess, sage and holy'. That is the last time the word 'But' is used thus in 'L'Allegro', which introduces scene transitions with the smoother, less wrenching words, *Oft*, *There*, and *That* (1 time each), *Then* (2 times), *Or* (4 times), and the paratactic *And*, which is used for this purpose eleven times, and on one occasion in three lines in succession: 'And the milkmaid singeth blithe, / And the mower whets his scythe, / And every shepherd tells his tale' (ll. 65–7). *But* is used in 'Il Penseroso' for a strong transition three times before the peripety. (The *But* beginning line 125 is grammatical rather than rhetorical.)

This peripatetic *but*, however, 'But let my due feet never fail', is much more strongly marked rhetorically than the two that are in the middle of the poem. I paraphrase: 'Bring Peace and Quiet, *but* most of all, bring Contemplation', and 'Let me see gorgeous tragedies, *but* most of all let me see and hear Musaeus and Orpheus'. But this final *but* takes the Reflective Man into church and there dissolves him in the music of the pealing organ and the choir. Extreme subjectivity is always seeking its own dissolution in ecstatic union with an other it has tried to deny. And when it stages such scenes it always reconstitutes itself again as an observer: 'Dissolve me into ecstasies, / And bring all Heaven before mine eyes' (ll. 165–6). There should not be any eyes left before which to bring all heaven.

Once again, we might expect the poem to end here with its concluding couplet: 'These pleasures Melancholy give, / And I with thee will choose to live' (ll. 175–6).

What could be better? It seems the perfect place to end, with the glorious vision of Heaven, like the vision of Heaven in the Nativity Ode, but a vision that is timely here and not falsely anticipatory. For ending here would have suggested, as Milton did in the sixth Elegy, that there are higher things than the poetry of merriment. But Milton seems deliberately to avoid what he normally does as unselfconsciously as breathing, which is to put things in hierarchical relation to one another. Ending the poem with Heaven before our eyes would have radically subordinated the earlier poem, 'L'Allegro', and all the delights of Mirth, an aim not inconsistent with Milton's character. But it would also have subordinated all the pleasures of 'Il Penseroso' except this last pleasure, if it is a pleasure, Heaven. 'These pleasures' would have referred to the *all* of 'all Heaven' (l. 166).

Milton was a Christian poet, and at this time he was seeking how to be a Christian poet, but he was not a Christian poet of the transcendental, otherworldly kind, like Roman Catholic poets of the Counter-Reformation. He was a poet of this world, being more inclined to enlarge the boundaries of Heaven to include this world than to leave this world behind for another. He was also a poet of decorum, which he would call 'the grand masterpiece to observe' (*CPW*, ii. 405). Decorum—the organizing of all parts of a poem into a consistent and harmonious whole—demanded two things at the conclusion of 'Il Penseroso': (1) that the two poems, 'L'Allegro' and 'Il Penseroso', remain equally matched as moral possibilities; and (2) that the speakers of the two poems remain distinct personalities that will not be confused either with each other or, more important, with the poet. We have seen already how the poems would not remain equally matched as moral possibilities if 'Il Penseroso' ended in an apotheosis. In such a case we would also lose sight of the speaker, Il Penseroso, who would dissolve not into heavenly ecstasies but into Milton, his author, rendering the final couplet discordant and perhaps requiring its abandonment.

Milton does not wish us to suppose he is striking any such bargain as these poems strike in their final couplets. Unlike the Lively Man, the Reflective Man has to be brought back into view for us, solidified and placed at a distance, so that he becomes for us a picture—a 'lively portraiture'—as he does even to himself, imagining himself in 'weary age' (l. 167), as a hermit in a 'mossy cell'. He has learned the secret correspondences and cosmic affinities between the stars and the plants, a more modest version of the knowledge he had sought in his tower, which was to trace all the patterns of 'true consent' (l. 95) between the daemons in the terrestrial elements of fire, air, water, and earth and the planets and stars overhead.

The Reflective Man has not changed essentially from the narcissist we saw in his tower—rather, who saw himself in his tower. But he has grown more subtle. He hopes to attain, from the 'old experience' that has made him thus, 'something like' (much virtue in that *like*) 'prophetic strain' (ll. 173–4). What is meant here by the word *prophet*? We are tempted at this moment to identify the speaker of 'Il Penseroso' with Milton, supposing *prophet* to mean 'something like' Hebrew *nabi* and to denote the Old Testament prophets—courageous, visionary speakers of the word of God. It is more likely, however, that the Greek sense of the word *prophet* is meant, a 'speaker forth' of the hidden will of the gods. A Hebrew prophet, as the story of Jonah teaches, does not have a choice whether to speak: he is compelled to do so, despite the bitter consequences. Milton in the prose identifies his own circumstances with this compulsion. The Greek *prophetes*, as we meet him in Homer, notably at the outset of the *Iliad*, in the figure of Chryses, also speaks with reluctance. He asks Achilles for assurances that what he says, should it offend a great king—Agamemnon is present—will not lead to his being punished. Even so, the Greek prophet is very far from being an unwilling speaker through whom the gods *insist* on speaking. He is a searcher of the jealously guarded secrets of the gods, which are wrenched from the organs of sacrificed animals and decoded in the flight of birds.

That is something like the 'prophetic strain' foreseen at the end of 'Il Penseroso', a knowledge to be arrived at by going up an inclined slope from knowledge of the natural world to knowledge of the will of the gods. We call that inclined slope *experience* and, when we have ascended some distance, *old experience*: 'Till old experience do attain / To something like prophetic strain' (ll. 173–4).

I never liked those verses much: they seemed to me to jar with the following, concluding couplet, 'These pleasures Melancholy give, / And I with thee will choose to live' (ll. 175–6), and especially with the word *pleasures*. It may be a pleasure to read Plato and Hermes Trismegistus, or to hear the far-off curfew bell and the song of the nightingale. It is even a pleasure—although more than pleasure is intended by it—to hear 'service high and anthems clear' (l. 163). But is it a pleasure to prophesy? Like the 'high service' with its music, there is something more to prophecy than subjective pleasure; indeed, prophecy has nothing whatever to do with subjective pleasure. Prophecy is for something beyond the self and its pleasures or its sorrows. Prophecy is a social act, and it is just at this boundary between personal pleasure and social action that the horizon of the Reflective Man's intelligence is seen.

COMUS

The speakers of 'L'Allegro' and 'Il Penseroso' confront life as a series of choices between different moods and the pleasures and delights that these bring. They wander through their landscapes observing, listening, delighting, reflecting, and choosing. Their interactions with others are limited. Life for them is not concern for or with others, whether these others are social, erotic, or familial. The Lively Man walks 'Not unseen' (l. 57), but as I mentioned before, he is, for all we can tell, unseen himself, or unremarked. The Reflective Man walks 'unseen' (l. 65)—except by himself—and he instinctively seeks places of resort 'Where no profaner eye may look' (l. 140). Each faces a choice: shall I live with Mirth? Shall I live with Melancholy? The answer to the question is in each case provisional but clear: if the 'delights' I have enumerated are given me, I will live with Mirth. If the 'pleasures' I have enumerated are given me, I will live with Melancholy.

But life isn't like that. We have to deal with others most of the time, and the choices we face are neither so simple as those faced by the Lively Man and by the Reflective Man, nor so unthreatening. In life we face dangerous choices and many—not all—such dangerous choices have to do with temptation. Temptation confronts one with the choice whether to accept or to refuse something offered. *What* is offered suddenly becomes less important than who is doing the offering and what bond will be forged with the offerer, should the offer be accepted. The 'delights' and 'pleasures' enumerated so beautifully in 'L'Allegro' and 'Il Penseroso' are more important than the goddesses who offer them, Mirth and Melancholy. But in real human experience the offerer of 'delights' and 'pleasures' is always more significant than they are. Whether one accepts or refuses the offer is a test of one's ability to see through the screen of what is offered to the character of whomever is doing the offering. In real life, as opposed to the narcissistic fantasy worlds of 'L'Allegro' and 'Il Penseroso', every gift is a bond with the giver. This is the moral insight that would be lodged at the centre of Milton's greatest works, *Paradise Lost, Paradise Regained*, and *Samson Agonistes*. It is an insight that gives imaginative as well as moral force to the central theme of Milton's career: *temptation*, a word that he understood (from its Greek and Latin equivalents) to mean 'testing'. Milton addresses this theme for the first time in *Comus*.

CHAPTER 5

....

'A THOUSAND FANTASIES': THE LADY AND THE *MASKE*

....

ANN BAYNES COIRO

WHEN Milton announced himself to the world as an important writer in 1645, he put *A Maske presented at Ludlow Castle* in the middle of his authorial identity, like a hinge. On one side were most of the poems he had written to that point, beginning with the Nativity Ode and ending with 'Lycidas'. On the other side were his Latin poems, indicating his learning and his place in the European artistic community. In the middle of the volume is the *Maske*, with its own title page and laudatory front matter, clearly marking it in the publishing conventions of the time as Milton's dramatic work. This piece is stubbornly an oddity in a narrative of Milton as reforming prophet, a genius above his age, but it is also a central event in Milton's career. It is not only the culmination of the poetry he had written to that point—mythological, peopled with striking characters and deeply interested in music and expressive verse forms—but also a pivotal artistic experience that influenced all of Milton's subsequent work. *A Maske presented at Ludlow Castle* walks a fine line through dark woods—a work with suspect associations, but a work that draws out Milton's creativity like a joyful spring. To a significant degree it is Milton's debt to English dramatic inventiveness—including the women-centred theatrical culture of the court in the 1630s—that gives *A Maske* its multivocal and unpredictable energy.

Yet an essay about Milton's *A Maske presented at Ludlow Castle* in sympathetic relationship to other seventeenth-century masques is an essay at odds with literary history. Retrospective narratives of Milton in the 1630s often imagine him as his later self, transported back in time, a reforming Puritan out of tune with the self-deluding fantasies of Charles's court productions. That Milton wrote in such a courtly form has thus worried critics, especially given the masque's vaguely Catholic associations under Henrietta Maria's influence. Most scholarship has therefore carefully distanced Milton's *Maske* from contemporary examples of the genre the title announces. The standard reading is that *A Maske* is the youthful work of a Puritan humanist who used his commission to correct the excesses and corrupt values of the court masque.[1] It is my contention, however, that Milton means not so much to correct as to *outdo* contemporary masques by pushing the genre's inherent tendencies to new dramatic and social limits. Crucial to Milton's overgoing of the court form is his utilization of its explosive innovation, a woman actor. Twenty-five years old when he wrote the masque and very ambitious, Milton was not only aware of but also building upon the cultural ferment that was being acted out on the court stage in the early 1630s.[2] While he did have strong anti-Catholic feelings, that did not preclude his attraction to the musical and literary culture of Catholic Europe. It is surely important, for example, that immediately after the stringent Puritan William Prynne condemned theatre as feminizing and women performers as 'notorious whores' in *Histriomastix* (1634) Milton wrote and subsequently published a theatrical piece with a major role for a female performer. Because we have been reluctant to see Milton as part of the 1630s, we have not fully appreciated the subtlety, power, and daring of the Lady's part.

There is no denying, however, that writing a masque was a tricky assignment. Milton's ambition was to rival Shakespeare's 'live-long monument' ('On Shakespeare', l. 8) and to be, like Spenser, a 'sage and serious' teacher (*CPW*, ii. 516). Milton also wished to excel in the cultural form most prominent in his twenties, a form that itself had influenced Shakespeare and that borrowed widely from Spenser. Indeed, *A Maske*'s context in Caroline masque culture reveals not only its innovation, but

---

[1] Important arguments based on the idea of the masque as reformed are: Maryann Cale McGuire, *Milton's Puritan Masque* (Athens, Ga., 1983); David Norbrook, 'The Reformation of the Masque', in David Lindley (ed.) *The Court Masque* (Manchester, 1984), 94–110; Cedric C. Brown, *John Milton's Aristocratic Entertainments* (Cambridge, 1985); and Barbara Lewalski, 'Milton's Comus and the Politics of Masquing', in David Bevington and Peter Holbrook (eds.), *The Politics of the Stuart Court Masque* (Cambridge, 1998), 296–320. But see Heather Dubrow, 'The Masquing of Genre in Comus', *Milton Studies*, 44 (2005), 62–83, who argues Comus is only 'a draft for a reformed masque, not its polished realization' (p. 79) and my 'Anonymous Milton, or *A Maske* Masked', *English Literary History*, 71 (2004), 609–29.

[2] G. F. Sensabaugh ('The Milieu of Comus', *Studies in Philology*, 41 (1944), 238–49) does note the importance of Henrietta Maria and the cult of love and honour, but argues from an assumption that Milton would have loathed everything about the court and that everything about the court was wicked. Norbrook pays fruitful attention to other Caroline masques ('The Reformation of the Masque') as does John Demaray in *Milton and the Masque Tradition: The Early Poems, 'Arcades.' and Comus* (Cambridge, Mass., 1968).

also its conventionality.[3] The work falls into two parts: a long, highly developed dramatic section and a more standard masque frame. While the frame brings the masque to an elegant but decidedly patriarchal conclusion, the body of the work is startlingly feminist. It is easy to assume that Milton's masque of chastity played out in tension with decadent lust reflects his own uniquely high-minded stance in a world of courtly dissolution. Almost the opposite is true. *A Maske* has strong affinities with Henrietta Maria's cult of chaste female power and works in a fusion of genres particularly sympathetic to elite women performers—masque and pastoral.[4] Moreover, Milton appropriates the court's provocative innovation of using women to represent women. But *A Maske*'s amalgam of court masque and English drama, of theatrical performance and dramatic poem, of idealistic beliefs and the realities of human life, and of feminism and paternalism is unstable. Even its commonly accepted title, *Comus*, is anachronistic and contradictory.[5] In 1634 and ever after, *A Maske presented at Ludlow Castle* has proven difficult to control completely.

I

In the early seventeenth century the masque form entailed complicated scenery and stage devices, gorgeous and sometimes provocative costumes, music which in its variety marked the moods and action of the masque, dances both carnivalesque and highly ordered, and silent role-playing by powerful men and women. Ben Jonson's debate with Inigo Jones about the proper pre-eminence of the poet's words over theatrical spectacle defines central tenets of masque scholarship. In the 1630s, however, significant generic shifts amplified the kaleidoscope of sound and sight inherent in this spectacular form by adding more fully dramatic and proto-operatic elements. Elaborated antimasques proliferated, for example, influenced by the French *ballet de cour*, and music became increasing central.[6] In the romantic, Neoplatonic atmosphere of Charles and Henrietta Maria's court, masques were borrowing from and influenced by pastoral drama, tragicomedy, and romance, often with heavily

---

[3] For an analysis of *A Maske*'s conventional elements see Peter Walls, '*Comus*: The Court Masque Questioned', in John Caldwell, Edward Olleson, and Susan Wollenberg (eds.), *The Well-Enchanting Skill: Music, Poetry, and Drama in the Culture of the Renaissance* (Oxford, 1990), 107–13.

[4] See the 'Introduction' in *Three Seventeenth-Century Plays on Women and Performance*, ed. Hero Chalmers, Julie Sanders, and Sophie Tomlinson (Manchester and New York, 2006), 1–11. Leah S. Marcus poses the question: 'What happens if we take seriously the [masque] . . . as a poem particularly attentive to women?' in 'John Milton's *Comus*', in Thomas N. Corns (ed.), *A Companion to Milton* (Oxford, 2003), 232–45.

[5] I will refer to the work by the title Milton gave it, *A Maske presented at Ludlow Castle*. *Comus* is the title of a series of adaptations of the work made in the 18th c.

[6] For a masterful discussion of the influence of French fashion on the English masque see Barbara Ravelhofer, *The Early Stuart Masque: Dance, Costume, and Music* (Oxford, 2006), 15–120.

Spenserian overtones. Certainly, however, the most striking development was the appearance of women as speaking actors and singers in court performances. In 1626 Henrietta Maria and her attendants acted in *Artenice*, a French pastoral. In January 1633, again to the bemusement and unease of the English, the queen and her ladies acted in an English pastoral romance written expressly for them, Walter Montague's *The Shepherd's Paradise*.[7] History remembers William Prynne's punishment for what the court took to be his incendiary attack on the queen for performing in Montague's pastoral. But queens had had a long-standing interest in masques, and, even before Henrietta Maria, the masque was a woman's form—a gateway for public performance that could be used not only for political commentary but to recode the social roles of women.[8]

We gain a new perspective on Milton's career by considering the nature of court productions between 1629 when he wrote his first great poem, the Nativity Ode, a work itself full of the imagery and lexicon of court masques, and 1634 when he wrote his *Maske*. In fact, it is impossible fully to understand any one masque—even Milton's—without understanding the ways in which masques were in ongoing dialogue, referring to and countering each other, borrowing costumes, sets, and tropes in a coded and highly charged language of performance. In the early 1630s the literal and metaphoric role of women was a central subject of this performative conversation. Milton did not write for the queen or the court, but he seized on the court's chaste, heroic feminine ideal and developed it into his own vision of heroic Protestant chastity. In doing so, he wrestled with problems his immediate contemporaries faced as well—an increasing self-consciousness about employing classical mythology and its sexual freight, the Catholic associations of the queen's theatrical innovations, and the ramifying possibilities of women as actors.

In 1634 three gifted writers wrote revisionary masques—a poet, a playwright, and a young writer deeply drawn to drama who eventually became one of England's greatest poets. Thomas Carew, James Shirley, and John Milton each treated the masque form to varying degrees of parody, extravagant celebration, and dramatic innovation.[9] A writer who valued decorum highly, Milton respected the contours and the conventions of a genre even as he irrevocably stamped it with his own voice. His masque is an attempt to suffuse the form with a Shakespearean playfulness and depth

---

[7] For the performance of *Artenice* at Somerset House in Feb. 1626, Henrietta Maria and her French attendants played all the roles including, in a nice reversal of English theatrical practice, men in beards. See Sophie Tomlinson, 'She That Plays the King: Henrietta Maria and the Threat of the Actress in Caroline Culture', in Gordon McMullan and Jonathan Hope (eds.), *The Politics of Tragicomedy: Shakespeare and After* (London and New York, 1992), 189–207, and Karen Britland, *Drama at the Courts of Queen Henrietta Maria* (Cambridge, 2006), 35–52. On the theatrical culture of Henrietta Maria's court more generally see also Sophie Tomlinson, *Women on Stage in Stuart Drama* (Cambridge, 2005) and Erica Veevers, *Images of Love and Religion: Queen Henrietta Maria and Court Entertainments* (Cambridge, 1989).

[8] See Clare McManus, *Women on the Renaissance Stage: Anna of Denmark and Female Masquing in the Stuart Court 1590–1619* (Manchester and New York, 2002).

[9] Mindele Anne Treip demonstrates a number of points of connection between Carew, Shirley, and Milton's masque in '*Comus* and the Stuart Masque Connection, 1632–34', *ANQ* 2/3, (1989), 83–9.

rather than to mock the form satirically. Not so Milton's contemporaries. James Shirley's *The Triumph of Peace* and Thomas Carew's *Coelum Britannicum* are outrageous amplifications of the masque that recognize its weaknesses (sycophancy, self-deluding isolation, and an over-reliance on spectacle, for example) and push these weaknesses hilariously and disturbingly into the open. On the heels of Prynne's antitheatrical *Histriomastix*, they are more self-conscious still about the fashionable conceit of women as chaste heroines at the centre of the universe. Shirley and Carew are impatient as well with pastoral and mythological conventions, but by self-consciously using the fashionable code they can laugh with impunity. Milton scholars assume that their poet stands apart from his generation and that *A Maske* is therefore a criticism of this courtly form. It is truer to say that Milton was deeply attracted to the Caroline masque and that his version is an attempt to elevate the form in the face of contemporary deconstruction and mockery.

Milton's *Maske* has often been linked not with Caroline examples, however, but with a particular Jacobean masque, *Pleasure Reconciled to Virtue* (1618), because Ben Jonson utilized Comus as its jolly drunkard antimasque figure. *Pleasure Reconciled to Virtue* offers many suggestive connections with Milton's work.[10] But there are pointed differences as well. In Milton's version, for example, the magic resides not in a father and his heir, but in the daughter of the house. By convention she should be a silent, allegorical ideal, but her dramatic reality as an imaginative, adventurous girl breaks through any attempt to impose a personified mask upon her. Jonson's Comus masque, on the other hand, has no woman character at all—neither a professional male actor playing a woman in the antimasque nor an aristocratic woman as a silent symbol in the triumphant masque scene.[11]

At least as useful in understanding Milton's masque is Aurelian Townshend's revolutionary *Tempe Restored*, performed at court in 1632. Connections between Townshend's and Milton's masques have long been acknowledged.[12] Because the King's Musick was responsible for staging court masques, Milton's collaborator on the Ludlow masque, Henry Lawes, would have played a role and may have composed

[10] Like *A Maske*, *Pleasure Reconciled to Virtue* was, for example, meant to praise a father by extolling his offspring and to argue for high moral standards as compatible with courtly festivity. For verbal echoes, see *Ben Jonson*, ed. C. H. Herford, Percy Simpson, and Evelyn Simpson, 11 vols. (Oxford, 1925–63), vii. 473–92, x. 573–90. Also see Enid Welsford, *The Court Masque: A Study in the Relationship between Poetry and the Revels* (Cambridge, 1927), 307, 314–18. As useful as Jonson's Comus masque in contextualizing Milton's are the two court masques Jonson wrote for the king and queen in 1631, *Chloridia* and *Love's Triumph through Callipolis*, each dishing Platonic love with a heavy hand. Jonson also wrote two Platonic love entertainments to be presented to the royal couple at William Cavendish's residences in Midlands in 1633 and 1634. His involvement in the theatrical culture of the 1630s is further witnessed by the pastoral play he left unfinished at his death, *The Sad Shepherd, or A Tale of Robin Hood*.

[11] Compare Jonson's masque, commissioned by the king to honour Charles, Prince of Wales, with the assertion of female power in *Tethy's Festival*, the masque Anna of Denmark had Samuel Daniel write to celebrate Prince Henry's investiture as Prince of Wales in 1610.

[12] John Demaray argues that in many ways '*Comus*' is 'a sequel to *Tempe Restored*', and the work thus figures large in his account in *Milton and the Masque Tradition*, esp. 78–96 (83). See also Sophie Tomlinson's subtle and brilliant discussion of both works in *Women on Stage in Stuart Drama*, 52–5, 71–8.

the music.[13] Lady Katherine Egerton appeared as one of Divine Beauty's 'stars' and her younger sister, Lady Alice Egerton, as one of Harmony's fourteen 'Influences'. At Ludlow Castle two years later, when the Attendant Spirit asks 'who knows not Circe / The daughter of the Sun?' (ll. 50–1), it was a gesture to the family involvement in *Tempe Restored*. Although it is unlikely that the scenery would have been transported all the way to Wales, it has been plausibly suggested that Lawes reused *Tempe Restored*'s antimasque costumes for Comus's crew in Ludlow.[14] Milton also builds on the work's conceit. The argument of *Tempe Restored* is that Circe, Comus's mother, has seduced a young man 'who awhile lived with her in all sensual delights'(l. 2).[15] But she grows jealous and so makes him drink from her 'enchanted cup' and touches him with 'her golden wand', transforming him into a lion (ll. 3–4). All is eventually set right by Divine Beauty (aka Henrietta Maria), who 'vouchsafe[s] to stoop / And move to earth' (ll. 206–7). What is extraordinary about this masque is, first, that it has a much more fully developed dramatic narrative than most. And—remarkably—Circe was played by a woman, Madame Coniack. Her participation is part of the work's complexity. When Pallas, played as usual by a cross-dressed man, mocks her, Circe volleys back with a rejoinder that marks theatrical history: 'Man-maid, begone!' (l. 268).[16] Circe's tartly amusing dismissal dramatically underscores the astonishing innovation of an actual *woman* playing a complex, speaking woman. Retrospectively, the joke is even better if, as is entirely possible, Pallas was sung by the most famous countertenor of the time, Henry Lawes, for whose androgynous voice Milton would write the role of the Attendant Spirit.[17]

A fully realized dramatic person, Townshend's Circe is an unusual masque character in ways beyond (although probably also because of) her actor's sex. Circe is a woman disappointed in love, a sensual seductress and a defiant queen who watches her own antimasque while enthroned in her 'sumptuous palace' (l. 92)—an

[13] Little music survives from court masques, although it is clear that they required a great deal. Ian Spink argues that Henry Lawes is the likely composer for *Tempe Restored* (*Henry Lawes: Cavalier Songwriter* (Oxford, 2000), 52–3). In any case, Lawes would have performed in Townshend's masque. See also David Lindley, 'The Politics of Music in the Masque,' in *The Politics of the Stuart Court Masque*, 273–95.

[14] See Demaray, *Milton and the Masque Tradition*, 101.

[15] Aurelian Townshend, *Tempe Restored*, in, *Court Masques: Jacobean and Caroline Entertainments, 1605–1640*, ed. David Lindley (Oxford, 1995), 155–65. Further reference to Townshend will be to this edition.

[16] Sophie Tomlinson and Melinda Gough believe that Madame Coniack, a Frenchwoman and professional singer, played Circe. For them the compelling evidence is Thomas Randolph's extremely popular poem entitled in print 'Upon a very deformed Gentlewoman, but of a voice incomparably sweet'. The poem had an extensive manuscript life with various titles, including 'Upon the French Woman . . . that sings in masques at Court' and 'On a ffrench woeman, one of the Queenes Chapple'. They assume Mistresse Shepherd, the other woman performer listed, is a professional musician as well. See Tomlinson, *Women on Stage in Stuart Drama*, 52–4 and Melinda Gough, '"Not as Myself": The Queen's Voice in *Tempe Restored*', *Modern Philology*, 101 (2003), 48–67, 52. Karen Britland disagrees, arguing that Madame Coniack was actually Elizabeth Coignet, one of Henrietta Maria's French ladies-in-waiting and that Mistress Shepherd was a child and dwarf (*Drama at the Courts*, 91–8).

[17] Tomlinson remarks on the comic potential of Circe revealing 'this masculine Pallas as a fraud', an 'ambiguously gendered transvestite actor and singer' (*Women on Stage in Stuart Drama*, 57).

unsettling metatheatrical conceit since Henrietta Maria and Charles both participated in *Tempe Restored*. Her passionate songs are the product not of evil but of a
heart tormented by love. The allegorical key that accompanied the published text
makes Circe's mixed nature clear: she is 'of extraordinary beauty, and sweetness
of . . . voice' and she 'signifies desire in general, the which hath power on all living
creatures, and being mixed of the divine and sensible, hath diverse effects, leading
some to virtue and others to vice' (ll. 303–4, 298–300). In his *Maske*, Milton splits the
role of Circe: Comus, her son, inherits her cup, her wand, her herd of beast-people,
and her dangerous influence. But the Lady inherits Circe's womanly strength and her
voice.

John Fletcher's *The Faithful Shepherdess* is one of Milton's favourite plays and
reading it can feel like a phantasmagoric encounter with Milton's *Maske*. His close
verbal and structural recall of Fletcher's Jacobean play has normally been regarded as
nostalgia on Milton's part. Yet *The Faithful Shepherdess* was, in fact, a central
theatrical event only months before the Ludlow performance. The first production
of *The Faithful Shepherdess* in 1608–9 had been a failure.[18] But the queen's revival of
the play in 1633 as a kind of sequel to her own controversial project, *The Shepherds
Paradise*, made perfect sense when tastes had changed, and Spenserian pastoral had
become compelling dramatic material. Almost every character in Milton's *Maske* has
a prototype in Fletcher's pastoral.[19] The play has two faithful shepherdesses, for
example—one dedicated to perpetual virginity and one a virgin destined for marriage—eerily reminiscent of Sabrina and the Lady. On the other hand, *The Faithful
Shepherdess* stages explicit and repeated violence against the marriageable virgin.
Although Milton's taste in 1634 is typical of his cultural moment in many ways, his
sexual ethics require a sublimation of the violence of Fletcher's pastoral. Overt
violence against women becomes in Milton's work a topic of constant conversation.
But the moment when Comus begins his menacingly physical move towards the Lady
is the moment when Milton's pastoral drama pivots away from its dramatic complexity and falls back into masque spectacle.

Also performed in 1634 was James Shirley's *The Triumph of Peace*, the most
extravagantly expensive masque ever staged.[20] Overseen by Bulstrode Whitelock

---

[18] As early as 1791 Thomas Warton noted a number of parallels in his edition and in 1801 H. J. Todd
even more. In the front matter of the print edition that appeared soon after, George Chapman
praised Fletcher's experiment in pastoral tragicomedy as 'both a Poeme and a play' in an attempt to
explain its rejection by the vulgar who could not appreciate the 'holy lawes of homely pastorall'
(*The Faithful Shepherdess: A Critical Edition*, ed. Florence Ada Kirk (New York and London, 1987), 8–9).
Ben Jonson correctly predicted that Fletcher's 'murdered poem . . . shall rise / A glorified work to time'
(ll. 14–15). 'To the Worthy Author M John Fletcher', in *The Complete Poems*, ed. George Parfitt
(Harmondsworth, 1975), 257.

[19] Like Thomas Randolph's *Amyntas*, a pastoral play performed at court in 1631 which was also a
significant source for Milton, *The Faithful Shepherdess* has many characters and intertwined plots. For
Randolph, see Coiro, 'Anonymous Milton, or, *A Maske* Masked'.

[20] It cost a staggering £21,000. See Stephen Orgel and Roy Strong, *Inigo Jones: The Theatre of the Stuart
Court*, 2 vols. (London, 1973), ii. 544. Bulstrode Whitlocke commissioned William Lawes, Henry's
brother, and Simon Ives to write the music. Henry participated as a singer and musician. Whitlocke
himself also composed some of the music. It became his signature tune and was played in his honour

(another Puritan who, like Milton, loved theatre and music), Shirley's masque was ostensibly an ingratiating apology by the Inns of Court for the insult one of its members, William Prynne of Lincoln's Inn, had inflicted on the queen and her court theatricals.[21] Packed with characters, jokes, music, and spectacle, Shirley's masque is a wide-tracking shot of the world of Milton's young manhood. Some of its personified characters—Fancy, Jollity, Laughter—seem to walk and talk right out of Milton's 'L'Allegro' and 'Il Penseroso'. But *The Triumph of Peace* takes a self-mocking line on allegorical, mythological culture. Rather than gods and goddesses as stand-ins for kings and queens, in Shirley's citizen masque gods and goddesses are perilously close to being inhabitants of a farce. Moreover, Shirley simply blows the doors off the Banqueting House, opening the form and its privileged audience to the inhabitants of the City. *The Triumph of Peace* ended at court, but it first made the streets of London its stage and the inhabitants of London part of its antimasque repertory, audaciously framing court ritual with the ambitious, ingenious, and raucous city.[22] Nevertheless, although *The Triumph of Peace* is one of the boldest and most inventive theatrical events of the early modern period, it does not touch the third rail of women actors. The queen and her ladies (and the king and his attendants, including the two Egerton boys) appear beautifully costumed and decorously silent.

Milton's collaborator on *A Maske presented at Ludlow Castle*, Henry Lawes, probably wrote the music for and certainly participated in Thomas Carew's *Coelum Britannicum* and so did the two Egerton boys, only months before their roles in Milton's masques (*Coelum Britannicum* was performed on 18 February 18 1634).[23] Carew's brilliant masque takes an edgy, self-mocking line on classical mythology and on chaste behaviour, an ironic distance that puts in perspective how deeply Milton's imagination is infused with classical myths and how sincere is his commitment to the kind of chastity Carew is ostensibly lauding. As with Townshend's *Tempe Restored*, there are a significant number of practical, verbal, and conceptual connections between Carew's masque and Milton's, but there are also fundamental differences. If we bracket Milton's *Maske* as a hybrid innovation, Carew's masque is arguably the greatest realization of the form; it is also an incisive mockery of Caroline pretensions

---

every time he came to the Blackfriars Theatre. See Martin Butler, *Theatre and Crisis, 1632–1642* (Cambridge, 1984), 92.

[21] Its first performance on 3 Feb. 1634 ended at Whitehall; a great success, it was repeated ten days later at the Merchant Taylors' Hall (there were also three editions printed in 1634). Immediately after the second performance of *The Triumph of Peace* Prynne was brutally and ostentatiously punished for his alleged criticism in *Histriomastix* of Henrietta Maria and her ladies.

[22] Shirley may have scripted the crowds as unintentional antimasquers, but the crowds loved *The Triumph of Peace* (Butler, *Theatre and Crisis*, 94).

[23] The Egerton boys appeared in *Coelum Britannicum* among the 'ancient heroes' 'appareled after the old British fashion'; they probably wore those costumes again in *A Maske presented at Ludlow Castle*. See Demaray, *Milton and the Masque Tradition*, 101, and Ravelhofer, *The Early Stuart Masque*, 146–7. The 'sky-robes spun out of Iris' woof' that the Attendant Spirit takes off to disguise himself as Thyrsis may have been the same blue robes Lawes wore as a constellation in *The Triumph of Peace* and as Eternity in *Coelum Britannicum* (Willa McClung Evans, *Henry Lawes, Musician and Friend of Poets* (New York, 1941), 85–8; Spink, *Henry Lawes*, 54–5).

to honour and divinity.[24] Rather than moving the form towards drama, Carew emphasizes spectacle and exaggeration; he literalizes the court code to a degree that dances close to satire. Milton's masque, on the other hand, is a gorgeous unfolding of the form, an exploration of its dramatic range and a daring, if finally interrupted, exploration of women's heroism.

The conceit of *Coelum Britannicum* is that Jove is ashamed of his wanton ways after seeing the loving marriage of Charles and Henrietta Maria. The whole sky is to be depopulated of its old mythological connections and peopled instead with 'ancient' and 'modern' 'heroes of these famous isles' (ll. 806, 809).[25] When Comus claims 'We that are of purer fire / Imitate the starry quire' (ll. 111–12), Milton is probably glancing critically at *Coelum Britannicum*. But Milton does not come close to the acid mockery Carew himself supplies in the person of Momus, who describes himself as a combination of 'old Peter Aretine' and 'Frank Rabalais' (ll. 148, 50). From beginning to end, Momus is sarcastic about women. He is dismissive of 'the martyr-dom of those strumpets', the women punished for the gods' interest in them and dismissive as well of the 'total reformation' of 'the hierarchy' of men and women where 'conjugal affection' reigns and Jove is restricted to 'religiously kissing' his wife's 'two-leaved book' (ll. 189, 234–6, 182). Like his aural twin Comus, Momus is an antimasque figure who joins the main masque and, in fact, becomes, with Mercury, its co-presenter. Inside the conventions of the court masque, then, Carew can be safely critical of the queen and her ideals. Never banished, Momus saunters off stage when he gets bored, 'and bid nobody farewell' (l. 791).

The points of intersection between *Coelum Britannicum* and *A Maske* demonstrate the difference between the sceptical courtier and the romantic humanist. Whereas Carew banishes the gods with irreverent glee, Milton clings to the enchanting stories. The Attendant Spirit cautions against making light of the warnings encoded in classical mythology:

> . . .'tis not vain or fabulous,
> (Though so esteemed by shallow ignorance)
> What the sage poets taught by the heavenly Muse,
> Storied of old in high immortal verse
> Of dire chimeras and enchanted isles,
> And rifted rocks whose entrance leads to hell,
> For such there be, but unbelief is blind. (512–18)

---

[24] *Coelum Britannicum* was the King's dramatic offering in return for the Queen's production of *The Faithful Shepherdess* earlier in 1634. It appeared less than two weeks after the smashing success of Shirley's *Triumph of Peace*. Orgel and Strong call it 'unquestionably the greatest of the Stuart masques, poetically superior to all but the best of Jonson, and in its range and variety utterly unique' (i. 66). Kevin Sharpe claims that it 'may be read as a literary text more satisfying perhaps than any other Stuart masque. Not only is it the longest, it speaks with many of the varied voices of literature—the dramatic as well as the poetic, the voice of question as well as statement, a tone of irony as well as celebration' (*Criticism and Compliment: The Politics of Literature in the England of Charles I* (Cambridge, 1987), 191).

[25] *Court Masques*, ed. Lindley, 166–93. References to *Coelum Britannicum* will be to this edition.

Milton wants the deeply resonant possibilities of Christian humanism available to him so that he can write a Caroline masque that can invoke 'the heavenly Muse' (l. 514). Carew's masque, on the other hand, strips away the delusion that a masque is anything but 'show'.[26] In his own fashion, Carew is arguably as socially reform-minded as Milton is in 1634. In *Coelum Britannicum*, however, Carew works in a form he mocks, perhaps even disdains. Less than a year earlier he had written to Townshend a hauntingly convoluted elegy-refusing elegy on the death of Gustavus Adolphus.[27] He and Townshend live in a world where 'the Masculine stile' has been conquered by 'the Queene of Beautie' and so 'Tourneyes, Masques, Theaters, better become / Our *Halcyon* dayes; what though the German Drum / Bellow for freedome and revenge, the noyse / Concernes not us, nor should divert our joyes' (ll. 71, 83, 95–8). Carew, an intelligent and accomplished poet who would generously repay more critical attention that he now receives, has an uncanny ability to shadow praise with cutting irony.

Milton, on the other hand, thought the masque genre was an appropriate vehicle to celebrate morality. He wanted to preserve the magic and idealism of the form, while deepening it into a psychological, complicatingly human drama. *A Maske presented at Ludlow Castle* is the crucial nexus of Milton's two great English influences—Spenser's pastoral romance and Shakespeare's richly human drama. And it is in real dialogue with the European Baroque culture of song, female subjecthood, and performance that flourished at the English court in the 1630s. This rich amalgam opens up into the future of Milton's work.

II

The most fascinating feature of the masque—both as an occasional theatrical piece and as a canonical poem—is the Lady. In 1634, John Milton asked an adolescent girl to play a full-scale dramatic role in front of a public audience.[28] The strangeness of

---

[26] 'A Rapture', l. 12. The speaker asserts that 'the servile rout / Of baser subjects onely, bend in vaine / To the vast Idoll', the 'Masquer' Honour (*Poems of Thomas Carew*, ed. Rhodes Dunlap (Oxford, 1949), 49, ll. 4–6). Further references to Carew's poetry will be to this edition.

[27] Gustavus Adolphus was killed on 6 Nov. 1632. 'In answer to an Elegiacall Letter Upon the death of the King of Sweden from Aurelian Townshend, inviting me to write on that subject' was written only months before *Coelum Britannicum*, Carew's only masque.

[28] The Records of Early English Drama (REED) project is radically revising our understanding of provincial drama (see Barbara Palmer, 'Early Modern Mobility: Players, Payments, and Patron', *Shakespeare Quarterly*, 56 (2005), 259–308). And it is becoming clearer that aristocratic women enjoyed a much greater degree of freedom to write and participate in private dramatic productions than was formerly believed. However, the production of Milton's *Maske* at Ludlow was a state occasion. The Countess of Bridgewater is notably absent from the masque, and most of the roles would have been played by professional actors and singers. The Lady's part is therefore remarkable, pushing to its far outer limits the incipient move towards women's theatrical involvement.

the Lady's part is all the more remarkable when we consider the nature of that role: a frightened, brave sister who makes a crucial mistake but who is strong and forthright when she realizes she has walked into an explicitly sexual trap. That Comus's trap places her in an unsettlingly compromised position makes Alice Egerton's dramatization of the Lady more remarkable still. Critics who believe that the Castlehaven scandal lies behind the masque argue that part of its purpose was to show Alice's staunch purity, a kind of ritual cleansing of the family taint.[29] On the face of it, this seems a bizarre strategy, but it is typical of the yin-yang magic of the masque genre. A 15-year-old girl can be presented as a pure commodity on the aristocratic marriage market through a courtly form designed to erase any background of disharmony. And this form had been recently feminized to a striking degree. Milton's masque is not so much a critique of court culture, then, as an appropriation and amplification. Its brilliant and teasingly autobiographical innovation, the Lady, has sisters in the cult of chaste, heroic women current at court—but she is much bolder. Perhaps this is because she also has sisters in Shakespeare's comedies and romances: *As You Like It*'s Rosalind in the woods, Portia's tough-mindedness in *The Merchant of Venice*, or Miranda's innocence faced with a wider world in *The Tempest*.

To get a clearer sense of Milton's gender innovations in his masque, it helps to consider a theatrical work he had written some months earlier, the 'entertainment' for a great lady, Alice, the Countess Dowager of Derby (Alice Egerton's grandmother).[30] Milton's *Arcades* is deeply nostalgic for the Elizabethan world of the Countess's young womanhood. He bestows on the Countess Dowager a version of Spenserian magic, but for a prolific matriarch rather than a virgin queen. Alice sits enthroned and brightly lit, her 'sudden blaze of majesty' (l. 2) the visual centre of the work. Among the 'nymphs, and shepherds' (l. 1) who approach her while singing Milton's lovely words are a number of her offspring, almost certainly including the Egerton children. Everyone's role was conventional.[31] The aristocratic family members sang and danced to celebrate their honoured elder. No woman spoke and sang alone (although such participation was not taboo in private family entertainments), and Alice, Countess Dowager was praised in traditional terms as 'a goddess bright', 'a rural queen' (ll. 18, 94).[32] Playfully echoing Marlowe, the last song invites all involved to 'Bring your flocks, and live with us' in this new Arcadia (l. 103).

---

[29] See Barbara Breasted's influential article suggesting that Bridgewater had asked Milton to write the masque as a kind of family absolution because the Countess of Bridgewater's brother-in-law had recently been tried and executed for prostituting his wife and stepdaughter, Alice Egerton's cousin ('*Comus* and the Castlehaven Scandal', *Milton Studies*, 3 (1971), 201–24).

[30] The work was performed at Harefield, the Countess Dowager's Middlesex estate. The date of the performance is unknown, and some scholars have argued for a date as early as 1629. More likely it was performed sometime between the summer of 1632 and the Countess Dowager's seventy-fifth birthday in May 1634. See Carey's headnote to *Arcades* in *CSP*, 161, for a summary of this scholarship.

[31] The surviving text preserved in Milton's Trinity manuscript and published in the 1645 *Poems* is only 'Part of' the entertainment, and it is not entirely clear how the work would have been staged, how large the cast of singers and dancers was, or who exactly was meant to sing the first and last songs.

[32] Based on the brief notes Milton published along with the Harefield entertainment excerpts, the first of *Arcades*'s three songs seems to have been sung by the 'noble persons of her family' as they dance

The imaginative centre of *Arcades* is not, however, the Countess Dowager but the Genius of the Woods, a role almost certainly played by Henry Lawes.[33] The Genius, like Orpheus, controls the natural world in this magical place and can hear the music of the spheres through the night. Since *Arcades* is an entertainment, not a drama, there is no conflict, not even dialogue. The only plot is the movement towards the celebrated old lady. To create the conflict and ambiguity of the Ludlow masque, Milton would split the Genius into several characters. Most obviously, the Genius is an early version of the Attendant Spirit. The local Genius is also an imaginative precursor of Sabrina, who, in turn, foreshadows the climactic *deus* of Milton's 1637 pastoral elegy 'Lycidas', 'the genius of the shore' who 'shalt be good / To all that wander in that perilous flood' at the edge of the world (ll. 183–5). In *Arcades* the Genius is a spirit of the night: 'when drowsiness / Hath locked up mortal sense, then listen I / To the celestial sirens' harmony' (ll. 61–3); in *A Maske*, Milton darkens him into the nocturnal host, Comus. But the most important difference between *Arcades* and *A Maske* is that in *A Maske* Milton displaces the artist figure from the masque's gravitational centre. The silent woman towards whom *Arcades* processes is replaced by a fully involved woman who provides the dramatic conflict.

The piece performed on 29 September at Ludlow Castle would have been instantly recognizable to the sophisticated family who commissioned it. A divine messenger figure, a conventional masque character, presents it. Like the worlds of other masques, the forests, castles, and skies of Milton's piece are peopled with classical gods, such as Jove and Neptune. The antimasque has men and women with animal heads dancing in a forest. The event was as spectacular as possible without the facilities available at court: there were wonderful costumes, rigging for flying (at least Milton wrote his script in hopes that there would be), three sets, and a dramatic use of lighting. The performance ended with singing and dancing that joined audience and performers in celebration, and the children of the commissioning aristocrat were central and admirable figures. Bridgewater probably also got more than he expected, given *A Maske presented at Ludlow Castle*'s formal innovations. It is important,

---

towards her throne. The second song is sung by the Genius of the Wood. The final song, which carefully echoes the first, may also have been sung together by the family participants. Milton's privileging of a truly English 'queen' could be a reprimand to Henrietta Maria, but it is nevertheless an argument that female power resides in a family—the basis of Henrietta Maria's own real and symbolic authority. Cedric Brown points out that the Countess Dowager's first husband was traditionally considered the King of Mann, so that her honorific as queen made particular sense (*Milton's Aristocratic Entertainments*, 15).

[33] The two major Lawes scholars, Willa McClung Evans (*Henry Lawes, Musician and Friend of Poets*, 64–6) and Ian Spink (*Henry Lawes: Cavalier Songwriter*, 56), argue that Lawes played the Genius. There is not, however, absolute proof. Demaray therefore leaves Lawes's role a 'matter of speculation' (*Milton and the Masque Tradition*, 49). Cedric Brown also demurs (*Milton's Aristocratic Entertainments*, 53–4). The circumstantial evidence that Lawes played the role of the Genius of the Woods is, however, significant. Lawes had been the Egerton family's music teacher for years, and he was involved in getting Milton the commission to write both *Arcades* and *A Maske presented at Ludlow Castle*. The role of the Genius is very similar to the role of the Attendant Spirit—a master of ceremonies who is both a musician and a family retainer. The title page of Milton's 1645 *Poems* announces that 'The Songs were set to Musick by Mr. Henry Lawes', an assertion which would include *Arcades*'s three songs.

however, to be clear about the nature and extent of Milton's generic changes. For a number of years it has been argued that the work's reforming agenda is what constitutes Milton's innovation. Yet advocating moral reform in 1634 is neither startlingly original nor the sole province of Puritans. Moreover, readings that insist too strongly on Milton's morality obscure the masque's sensuousness and eroticism and oversimplify the choices left to audience and reader.[34] Milton's work is innovative because it pushes the masque form emphatically towards its dramatic potential, with complex characters and unresolved conflicts. To a greater degree than any previous masque, moreover, it recognizes not only the theatrical but also the readerly potential of the form.

The three verse paragraphs of the Attendant Spirit's prologue exemplify the experimental, multiform nature of *A Maske*. Each paragraph repeats the plot (the Spirit has been sent to guard those favoured by Jove from a dangerous tempter), and each uses the mythological language conventional in masques. But the three iterations are in different registers and become increasingly worldly, bodily, and dramatic. In the first lines, the story and the language tilt towards serious Protestant theology. The Spirit describes his home 'Before the starry threshold of Jove's court' where 'immortal shapes / Of bright aerial spirits live ensphered' (ll. 1–3). He puts on the 'rank vapours of this sin-worn mould' because Jove sent him to aid those—and only those—'that by due steps aspire / To lay their just hands on that golden key / That opes the palace of eternity' (ll. 17, 12–14). In this more high-minded part of the Spirit's speech he promises to lead the Egerton children towards their heavenly reward 'Above the smoke and stir of this dim spot, / Which men call earth' (ll. 5–6). When the Spirit resolves 'But to my task' (l. 18) his speech shifts to more conventional masque language—gorgeous, mythological, and over the top. Neptune, it seems, is in charge of everything between Jove's heaven and the empire of 'nether Jove', the underworld (l. 20). He has generously given his 'tributary gods' 'leave to wear their sapphire crowns, / And wield their little tridents' over the islands 'That like to rich, and various gems inlay / The unadorned bosom of the deep' (ll. 24, 26–7, 22–3). All this sounds fabulously impressive but carries a generous latitude of meaning. Because twenty years of Stuart court masques had utilized such language, the masque-knowledgeable audience at Ludlow would probably have taken Neptune to be Charles by default. Considered carefully, however, the royal compliment gets hazy. Is it Charles who is the lord of all the world's oceans and islands? Or is Neptune another guise for God? At the other extreme, is the king simply one of Neptune's 'blue-haired deities' to whom he has 'quarter[ed]' 'This isle' (ll. 29, 27)? And is Charles therefore no more than an equal of Bridgewater, the 'noble peer of mickle trust, and power' (l. 31) who has this particular 'tract that fronts the falling sun . . . in his charge' (ll. 30, 32)? Because Milton uses conventional panegyric language, readers for centuries have been unclear about how to assign allegorical meaning—or even whether there is any allegorical intent.

---

[34] A notable exception is Stephen Orgel, 'The Case for Comus', *Representations*, 81 (2003), 31–45.

The Attendant Spirit then calls us to attention: 'listen why, for I will tell you now / What never yet was heard in tale or song / From old, or modern bard in hall, or bower' (ll. 43–5). So begins the Ovidian myth-making and metamorphoses at the heart of the masque. This final phase of the Attendant Spirit's prologue is playfully suggestive and erotic. We are coyly invited to imagine the sexual liaison of Circe and Bacchus and its result: 'This nymph that gazed upon his clustering locks, / With Ivy berries wreathed, and his blithe youth, / Had by him, ere he parted thence, a son' (ll. 54–6)—Comus, the masque's antihero. Now 'ripe, and frolic of his full-grown age' Comus is somewhere in 'this ominous wood', the scenic backdrop to the Attendant Spirit's prologue (ll. 59, 61). He is accompanied by his crew whom he has tricked by tempting their 'fond intemperate thirst', as the Spirit rather priggishly says, although they seem simply to have been thirsty from being in the sun (l. 67). Their 'human countenance' has been transformed 'Into some brutish form of wolf, or bear, / Or ounce, or tiger, hog, or bearded goat' (ll. 68–71). The wonderful thing is that Comus's victims, like Bottom, believe they are now more 'comely than before' and forget 'all their friends, and native home . . . To roll with pleasure in a sensual sty' (ll. 75, 76–7). The opening speech of Milton's *Maske* is, in other words, a steady progression into dramatic complexity and away from the relatively simple binaries characteristic of the antimasque–masque structure. The Attendant Spirit begins a process of disguise and metamorphosis that melts him into this Ovidian world where the line between masque and antimasque dissolves. He will drop his masquing 'sky-robes spun out of Iris' woof' and become an actor, to all appearances 'a swain / That to the service of this house belongs' (ll. 83, 84–5).[35] As the Attendant Spirit disappears to change himself, Comus appears in his place with a 'smooth-dittied song' (l. 86) as accomplished in its own way as those of the singing swain the Spirit has left to become; the crew of dancing beasts in the forest was probably the same troupe that played the country dancers that bring the masque to a happy conclusion, and Lawes could have played both the Attendant Spirit and Comus. Without denying Milton's high moral standards, we can acknowledge the elements of play, doubling, and open-ended interpretative difficulty that make the work sensuous as well as chaste, suffused with a heat that Sabrina's cool hands cannot diminish.

To a degree more subtle and profound than any queen-centred masque, Milton's work balances crucially and yet uneasily on the character of the Lady. She is a virgin, destined to be a wife; Philomel and Orpheus; true sister to both the idealistically confident Elder Brother and the realistically frightened Younger Brother; reprimand to court values and indebted to the chaste female ideals fostered by court masques; a strong feminist heroine and a silent patriarchal token. Her centrality radiates out to the masque's other characters, who can be read as refractions of her. At a general level, the masque is densely populated with female allegorical figures, representing both evil and good. More specifically, Comus, the aggressive male principle, is

---

[35] These are both things Lawes would actually have worn. As a singer and in a number of masques he wore blue robes. And as a member of the King's Musick he wore the livery of a servant, like all members of a household.

explicitly feminine ('Much like his father but his mother more' (l. 57)), and he and his crew worship bacchantic female deities, Cotytto and Hecate. The virgin Sabrina, the only other woman in the play, is a redemptive but also, sadly, a deadening version of the Lady. And both the Attendant Spirit and Comus are strongly connected to the Lady through music. Even the Brothers are, in spite of their macho bravado, understood by their sister as feminized or feminine. The Lady implores Echo to tell her of 'a gentle pair / That likest thy Narcissus are' and describes to Comus how 'their unrazored lips' are 'As smooth as Hebe's' (ll. 235–6, 289). The two Egerton sons play endearingly young boy-men who are engaged in a running argument with each other about what it means to be a beautiful virgin girl in general and the character of their sister in particular. As they talk they not only reveal a great deal about themselves but also demonstrate two sides of their sister's personality. The Elder Brother is confident and idealistic, a fitting attitude for the Bridgewater heir. He refuses to dwell on imagined possibilities: 'What need a man forestall his date of grief, / And run to meet what he would most avoid?' (ll. 361–2). He relies on the classical myths of Diana and Minerva as proof of chastity's power, and he believes that nothing but actual danger 'Could stir the constant mood of [the Lady's] calm thoughts' (l. 370). Deploying the work's overarching trope of light and dark, he asserts that 'Virtue could see to do what Virtue would / By her own radiant light, though sun and moon / Were in the flat sea sunk' (ll. 372–4). About this sunny confidence the Elder Brother is only partly right. We have already met the Lady, and when she first appears on stage she is deeply frightened by dangers she imagines in the dark. She talks herself down from her fear and embraces the confident position of the Elder Brother, but, unlike the brash boy, her confidence is a struggle won, not a given.

The Younger Brother, on the other hand, is a realist and a worrier, and his nervousness about her plight is similar to his sister's first impulse. In the face of his brother's high-minded confidence in the power of virginity, the Younger Brother politely insists that a beautiful girl alone in the woods could get badly hurt. Although Milton critics normally assume the idealistic Elder Brother to be the winner in the argument with the Younger Brother, *A Maske* does not support such a simple conclusion. Indeed, the Elder Brother can look dangerously silly next to his brother's concerns. First of all, the boys should rightly feel a degree of culpability since they left their sister alone and then lost their way.[36] The Attendant Spirit in his guise as Thyrsis is clearly worried about the Lady's safety when he finds the two, but the Elder Brother makes no apologies and admits to no wrongdoing. Thyrsis goes into disturbing detail about the lurking Comus, 'Deep skilled in all his mother's witcheries' (l. 522). The Spirit describes his unalloyed shock and fear when he first realized the girl was alone: 'Amazed I stood, harrowed with grief and fear, / And O poor hapless nightingale thought I, / How sweet thou sing'st, how near the deadly snare!' (ll. 564–6). The Younger Brother, who had given into his big brother's lofty argument about virginity

---

[36] In his *Life* of Milton Samuel Johnson criticizes Milton's masque for its lack of human warmth, citing the long philosophical exchange between two boys who have just lost their sister. Johnson ignores, however, the considerable tension between the brothers over how upset they should be. See *Lives of the English Poets*, ed. George Birkbeck Hill, 3 vols. (Oxford, 1905), i. 168–9.

with the (perhaps faintly mocking) line, 'How charming is divine philosophy!' (l. 475), is newly invigorated by Thyrsis's story and reprimands his brother:

> O night and shades,
> How are ye joined with hell in triple knot
> Against the unarmed weakness of one virgin
> Alone, and helpless! Is this the confidence
> You gave me brother? (ll. 579–83)

Nevertheless, the Elder Brother refuses to back down: 'not a period / Shall be unsaid . . . this I hold firm, / Virtue may be assailed, but never hurt, / Surprised by unjust force, but not enthralled' (ll. 584–5, 587–9). As the masque's enigmatic prologue and epilogue suggest, however, Virtue is only unassailable if it has help from outside agents, but such assisted virtue is not what this confident boy intends. He tries to trounce his brother's uprising by claiming grandly that in the face of Virtue 'evil on itself shall back recoil, / And mix no more with goodness' (ll. 592–3). A Maske will prove him quite wrong. When the Brothers finally burst in to rescue the Lady they bungle the plan and allow Comus to escape. As a result, he is never captured but lurks—backstage at Ludlow Castle; in the forests of Wales; in the world.

For the Elder Brother virginity is a principle and a shining aura, but the Younger Brother frankly insists on his sister's real sexual presence. Again both Brothers articulate aspects of the Lady, for she herself struggles to understand how she can be both ideal and real, mind and body. The ways in which the Lady's humanity suffuses abstraction is Milton's most brilliant innovation in the masque form. Crucially, for example, the Lady possesses and projects an erotic imaginative power that thrums under A Maske and adds dramatic tension to the idea of chastity. Yet, although critics have noted her decision to move towards 'the sound / Of riot, and ill-managed merriment' (ll. 170–1) and have speculated over the reasons why she is frozen in Comus's 'enchanted chair' (stage directions after l. 657) that is 'Smeared with gums of glutinous heat' (l. 916), many critics have nevertheless found her determined chastity priggish. Such a judgement is anachronistic: the cult of chaste virtue defined the Caroline years. And a patronizing view of the Lady as a frigid naysayer ignores how complicated her position is, given the clearly sexual role she is intended to play in life. Like Maria in Marvell's 'Upon Appleton House', A Maske's Lady will preside one day over her own home; even Comus recognizes in her song 'such a sacred, and home-felt delight, / Such sober certainty of waking bliss' (ll. 262–3). Overcoming his brief attraction to daytime and domesticity, Comus sets out to seduce her away from her marital destiny and into courtly mores. She is too beautiful for a wifely life, he argues:

> It is for homely features to keep home,
> They had their name thence; course complexions
> And cheeks of sorry grain will serve to ply
> The sampler, and to tease the housewife's wool. (ll. 747–50)

But the Lady briskly counters with a vision of nature as a careful mother:

> Imposter do not charge most innocent Nature,
> As if she would her children should be riotous
> With her abundance she good cateress
> Means her provision only to the good. (ll. 761–4)

Comus and the Lady are arguing about two different ways of life and two different destinations—the court or home—but both are sexual.

Milton's idea of marriage would mature into the fully erotic joy of *Paradise Lost*'s Eden. Already *A Maske*'s marriageable virgin is both beautiful (possessed of 'vermeil-tinctured lip' and 'tresses like the morn' (ll. 751–2)) and sexual. Indeed, what trial would she undergo (and trial is at the heart of Milton's poetics) if virginity were a simple, predetermined condition? Her younger brother states the case more clearly than he may realize when he worries about her, cold and alone: 'What if in wild amazement, and affright, / Or while we speak within the direful grasp / Of savage hunger, or of savage heat?' (ll. 355–7). The Lady has no personal knowledge of savage lusts, as the brother's words momentarily suggest, but she has in her 'memory' 'a thousand fantasies', including the mythological stories that permeate the masque (ll. 205, 204). The work is flooded with personifications from classical myths and from Milton's imagination—among them, Venus, Echo, Aurora, grey-hooded Even, Cotytto and Hecate, Advice, strict Age & sour Severity, Faith, Hope & Chastity—offering the Lady a whole imaginative palate. Nevertheless, the Attendant Spirit's lushly mythological epilogue makes clear that sanctioned sexual union must be the Lady's promised end. He flies off to Hesperides where 'the spruce and jocund Spring' revels with the 'Graces, and the rosy-bosomed Hours', lines that Milton closely repeats in his description of the gorgeously sexual Eden of unfallen marriage (ll. 984–5).[37] The Attendant Spirit's final allusion before he says farewell is predictive. He goes where Cupid

> Holds his dear Psyche sweet entranced
> After her wandering labours long,
> Till free consent the gods among
> Make her his eternal bride,
> And from her fair unspotted side
> Two blissful twins are to be born,
> Youth and Joy; so Jove hath sworn. (ll. 1004–10)

Like Spenser's Britomart, the Lady's chastity is the fitting prologue to marriage. Alone and frightened she had called on Echo. But Echo, a wasted virgin, was the

---

[37]
> The birds their choir apply; airs, vernal airs,
> Breathing the smell of field and grove, attune
> The trembling leaves, while universal Pan
> Knit with the Graces and the Hours in dance
> Led on the eternal spring. (iv. 264–8)

wrong choice and, in fact, the Lady's Echo song betrayed her to Comus and his bodily excesses. The Lady must find the middle way between loneliness and revelry. Fittingly, therefore, as Comus's true opponent, she boldly appropriates the role of Orpheus.[38] But what *she* dares Milton does not, at least not yet. His Lady proves the unsolved problem that fractures Milton's masque.

Music is the source of both the Attendant Spirit's and Comus's power. Like *Arcades's* Genius of the Woods, the Attendant Spirit's music can modulate the natural world; an emissary from the spheres, his 'artful strains', have, with Orphic charms, 'oft delayed / The huddling brook to hear his madrigal, / And sweetened every musk-rose of the dale' (ll. 493–5). Comus's music, on the other hand, is the dark underside of Orphic power—orgiastic, bodily, and hypnotic. At the centre between these poles is the music of the Lady. It is appropriate, therefore, that the Lady's Echo song impels the dramatic action of the masque. In ways evocative of Circe and Harmony in *Tempe Restored*, the Lady's artful union of voice and verse sets good and evil in motion. The Attendant Spirit is listening to the music of Comus and his crew, 'barbarous dissonance' (l. 549), when 'an unusual stop of sudden silence' (l. 551) allows him to hear the Lady, whose song, like Orpheus's, has authority over nature and even over death:

> a soft and solemn-breathing sound
> Rose like a steam of rich distilled perfumes,
> And stole upon the air, that even Silence
> Was took ere she was ware, and wished she might
> Deny her nature, and be never more
> Still to be so displaced. I was all ear,
> And took in strains that might create a soul
> Under the ribs of death. (ll. 554–9)

But the Lady's terrible danger lies in the inherent vulnerability of her Orphic gift, for her voice is audible only when the 'barbarous dissonance' is stilled. Milton will remember the Lady when he writes *Paradise Lost*. At the epic's turning centre, the narrator associates himself with Orpheus and asks for protection against the very danger in which the Lady is profoundly entangled:

> But drive far off the barbarous dissonance
> Of Bacchus and his revellers, the race
> Of that wild rout that tore the Thracian bard
> In Rhodopè, where woods and rocks had ears

---

[38] Thoughtful analyses of the connection between the Lady and Orpheus include Angus Fletcher, *The Transcendental Masque: An Essay on Comus* (Ithaca and London, 1971), 198–203, Christopher Kendrick, 'Milton and Sexuality: A Symptomatic Reading of *Comus*', in Mary Nyquist and Margaret W. Ferguson (eds.), *Re-Membering Milton: Essays on Texts and Translations* (New York and London, 1988), 43–73, and William Shullenberger, 'Milton's Lady and Lady Milton: Chastity, Prophecy, and Gender in *A Maske Presented at Ludlow Castle*', in Claude J. Summers and Ted-Larry Pebworth (eds.), *Fault Lines and Controversies in the Study of Seventeenth-Century English Literature* (Columbia, Mo., 2002), 213–14.

> To rapture, till the savage clamour drowned
> Both harp and voice. (vii. 32–7)

The drama of *A Maske presented at Ludlow Castle* is cancelled by critics who deny the real threat and the conflict facing the Lady. Granted great power she is also granted real temptation and formidable enemies.

When Comus hears the Echo song he recognizes her power as similar to his mother Circe's and the 'Sirens three' (l. 252). Their singing could 'take the prisoned soul, / And lap it in Elysium' using music to reverse Orpheus' life-giving power (ll. 255–6). Yet Comus understands that the Lady's song has a power that extends beyond Circean metamorphoses:

> Can any mortal mixture of earth's mould
> Breathe such divine enchanting ravishment?
> Sure something holy lodges in that breast,
> And with these raptures moves the vocal air
> To testify his hidden residence;
> How sweetly did they float upon the wings
> Of silence, through the empty-vaulted night
> At every fall smoothing the raven down
> Of darkness till it smiled. (ll. 243–51)

But Comus does not understand the Lady's full complexity. There is 'something holy' (l. 245) in the Lady, but she is neither a witch nor an angel; indeed she is a 'mortal mixture of earth's mould' (l. 243). Yet critics too have a tendency to move Milton's meaning towards the ideal and divine. In this instance that might mean comparing the Lady to Milton's ecstatic 'At a Solemn Music', written some time between *Arcades* and *A Maske*, a lyric which appeals to 'Blest pair of sirens, pledges of heaven's joy, / Sphere-borne harmonious sisters, Voice, and Verse' (ll. 1–2) and the happy part of Orpheus' story:

> Wed your divine sounds, and mixed power employ
> Dead things with inbreathed sense able to pierce,
> And to our high-raised phantasy present,
> That undisturbed song of pure concent. (ll. 3–6)

Connecting 'At a Solemn Music' and its salvatory Orpheus with the Lady is only a partial comparison, however. While the Lady's music shares in the divine, it is human and secular, sung by a real girl. The Echo song the good and evil daemons hear is the inseparable concord of Milton's words, Henry Lawes's music—and Alice Egerton's performance.

In order to appreciate fully the significance of *A Maske*'s singer we need to balance the heavenly allegorical creatures of 'At a Solemn Music' with Milton's other celebration of music in the 1630s. Travelling in Italy in 1638 and 1639 (he received his visa through the intercession of Henry Lawes), Milton heard Leonora Baroni sing and wrote three Latin poems in praise of her.[39] Milton may never have heard Alice Egerton perform the role he wrote for her (he was probably not in Wales for the performance).[40] But when he did hear a woman's public performance, the poems he wrote in response are a tribute to Italy, to poetry and music, and to the artistry of women. The first, 'Ad Leonoram Romae canentem', demonstrates the extraordinary claims he makes:

> . . . tua praesentem vox sonat ipsa Deum.
> Aut Deus, aut vacui certe mens tertia coeli
>   Per tua secreto guttura serpit agens;
> Serpit agens, facilisque docet mortalia corda
>   Sensim immortali assuescere posse sono.
> Quod si cuncta quidem Deus est, percunctaque fusus,
>   In te una loquitur, caetera mutus habet. (ll. 4–10)

(the sound of your voice makes it clear that God is present, or, if not God, at any rate a third mind which has left heaven and creeps warbling along, hidden within your throat. Warbling he creeps and graciously teaches mortal hearts how to grow accustomed, little by little, to immortal sound. If God is in all things, and omnipresent, nevertheless he speaks in you alone, and possesses all other creatures in silence.)[41]

The narrator of *Paradise Lost* famously decrees that woman exists at a remove from God: 'He for God only, she for God in him' (iv. 299). But Milton's speaker says precisely the opposite here in late 1638 or early 1639. Milton's attitudes towards women later in his career are elusive—perhaps they changed profoundly. Whatever conclusion we reach about Milton's later feminism, however, it is important to recognize the moving power he attributes to women in the 1630s. Indeed, especially considering Milton's nickname at Cambridge, many readers have connected the *Maske*'s Lady with Milton himself.[42] To make the connection between Milton and the Lady is to remember not only the work's brilliance and daring but its intense ambivalence. Once she realizes she has been tricked, the Lady deploys part of her strength to reject Comus, but she is tempted to do more, explicitly recognizing her own Orphic gift:

> should I try, the uncontrolled worth
> Of this pure cause would kindle my rapt spirits
> To such a flame of sacred vehemence,
> That dumb things would be moved to sympathize,

[39] Lewalski, *Life*, 75, 569.

[40] Milton was not a family servant and would not have been part of the long journey to Wales with the Egertons (for details of the Egerton family in the months before the performance see Brown, Milton's *Aristocratic Entertainments*, 26–40). Moreover, the changes made for the masque's performance seem likely to be the work of Lawes (his role, for example, is more prominent). Still, Orgel's delicious suggestion that Milton could have written the role of Comus for himself is appealing ('The Case for Comus', 38).

[41] Carey's translation in *CSP*, 257–8.

[42] See e.g. Shullenberger, 'Milton's Lady and Lady Milton', 204–26, and Paul Stevens, 'Discontinuities in Milton's Early Public Self-Representation', *Huntington Library Quarterly*, 51 (1988), 260–80.

> And the brute Earth would lend her nerves, and shake,
> Till all thy magic structures reared so high,
> Were shattered into heaps o'er thy false head. (ll. 792–8)

Against her training as a chaste and silent woman, the Lady speaks, willing—perhaps foolishly or intemperately but surely bravely—to pay the consequence:

> I had not thought to have unlocked my lips
> In this unhallowed air, but that this juggler
> Would think to charm my judgement, as mine eyes
> Obtruding false rules pranked in reason's garb. (ll. 755–8)

Milton repeatedly uses Orpheus to explore his own fears about the consequences of being a poet, and critics have connected Orpheus' fate at the hands of crazed women with Milton's misogyny. We should not forget, however, that one of his most fully realized alter egos is an Orphic woman facing down a bacchic male figure.

Nor is the Lady a passive or implicit feminist. When she speaks, she speaks in defence of women. In the poem Milton placed first in his sequence of English poetry in 1645 he himself portrayed Nature as 'guilty' because she is sexual; in the Nativity Ode, Nature uses her 'speeches fair' to woo the air:

> To hide her guilty front with innocent snow,
> And on her naked shame,
> Pollute with sinful blame,
> The saintly veil of maiden white to throw,
> Confounded that her maker's eyes
> Should look so near upon her foul deformities. (ll. 37, 38–44)

In the 1645 *Poems'* last English work, on the other hand, a woman speaks for herself and her kind, redeeming Nature—sexual still, but a good mother not a wanton. Whereas in the Nativity Ode the sun is a 'lusty paramour' (l. 36), in *A Maske* the Lady praises 'the sun-clad power of chastity' (l. 781), a disturbingly realistic admission that night is a dangerous time.[43]

Onstage on 29 September 1634, the Lady spoke in darkest night lit by the light of torches held by 'a rout of monsters, headed like sundry sorts of wild beasts' (Milton's stage direction between ll. 92 and 93). Here at the masque's crisis the dramatic confrontation between Orpheus and wild bacchantes, between light and dark, virgin and wanton is left unresolved. The Lady will never speak again. Comus and his beasts escape unscathed. And Milton's masque becomes something much more conventional and respectable. One of the most recognizably genre-specific pieces of stage business in *A Maske* is Sabrina rising up from under the stage in some kind of 'sliding chariot' (l. 891).[44] Sabrina is an ideal masquing character, perfectly suited to the

---

[43] Carey notes that this line is probably also a reference to 'a woman clothed with the sun' in Rev. 12: 1.
[44] In the Trinity manuscript Milton had first written lines that made the machinery obvious:

> My sliding chariot stayes,
> Thick set with Agat, and the azurne sheen

genre's purposes and to the formal properties of Milton's masque. Her back story is set in Wales, making her salvatory presence an apt compliment to the new Lord President.[45] She is a virgin who chose drowning over violation. As the tutelary genius of the Severn River, Sabrina is an elegant concluding reprise of the masque's opening images of water and Neptune's 'blue-haired deities' (l. 29). In many ways Sabrina is the Lady's opposed reflection, a pairing that would have been striking in performance if Sabrina was also played by a woman and all the more striking if the role was sung by a man.[46] Sabrina speaks in rhymed verse, often octosyllabic verse like Comus—the Lady in dramatic blank verse. Sabrina is dead—the Lady alive. Sabrina is mythological—the Lady a historical reality. Critics have reasonably seen Sabrina as baptismal, her touch a ritual blessing:

> Thrice upon thy finger's tip,
> Thrice upon thy rubied lip,
> Next this marble venomed seat
> Smeared with gums of glutinous heat
> I touch with chaste palms moist and cold. (ll. 913–7)

And the basis of Sabrina's power is her choice of death rather than the loss of her virginity. In sharp contrast, the Lady's fundamental premiss in her argument with Comus is that purity of mind cannot be touched by the body's violation:

> Fool do not boast,
> Thou canst not touch the freedom of my mind
> With all thy charms, although this corporal rind
> Thou hast immanacled, while heaven sees good. (ll. 662–5)

Given the Lady's strong statement, Sabrina's charms, which seem to have nothing at all to do with the freedom of the Lady's mind or, indeed, with heaven, seem pretty but mechanical. Sabrina's sacramental ritual brings the masque to its conclusion with an easy solution to the Lady's dilemma. But this magical, ritualistic ending is at odds with the strong feminist body of Milton's masque. Moreover, her magical charms do not represent the future direction of Milton's artistic or intellectual work; the Lady's

> Of turkis blew, & emrauld greene
> that my rich wheeles inlayes.

He struck out the last of these lines and substituted: 'that in the channell straies' (see *CSP*, 226).

45 Political resistance has been read into the masque's Welsh setting, albeit in sometimes contradictory ways. See e.g. Richard Halpern, 'Puritanism and Maenadism in *A Mask*', in Margaret W. Ferguson, Maureen Quilligan, and Nancy J. Vickers (eds.), *Rewriting the Renaissance: The Discourse of Sexual Difference in Early Modern Europe* (Chicago, 1986), 88–105; Michael Wilding, 'Milton's *A Masque Presented at Ludlow Castle, 1634*: Theatre and Politics on the Border', *Milton Quarterly*, 21 (1987), 35–51; and Philip Schwyzer, 'Purity and Danger on the West Bank of the Severn: The Cultural Geography of *A Masque Presented at Ludlow Castle, 1634*', *Representations*, 60 (1997), 22–48. It is important to remember, however, that Milton is not a local poet and probably had never been to Wales. He certainly takes advantage of stereotypical assumptions about the wild, magical forests of Wales. But the Welsh gestures are confined to the flattering and conventional opening and conclusion.

46 Demaray speculated that one of Alice Egerton's older sisters sang the role (*Milton and the Masque Tradition*, 77). Brown finds this unlikely (*Milton's Aristocratic Entertainments*, 35–6).

unleashed, Orphic rhetoric does. Sabrina reverses the spell binding the Lady, but she releases her into silence. The Lady's vibrant human character, the *Maske*'s greatest innovation, fades back into silent symbolism. But not before we see the future of Milton's work—a woman tempting and tempted, flawed but with power to change everything. She is not perfect, but human, not an allegory, but a dramatic character.

The Attendant Spirit's farewell to his audience toggles between religious morality and a suggestion of permissiveness:

> Mortals that would follow me,
> Love Virtue, she alone is free,
> She can teach ye how to climb
> Higher than the sphery chime;
> Or if Virtue feeble were,
> Heaven itself would stoop to her. (ll. 1017–22)

The queen as Divine Beauty in *Tempe Restored* had 'stoop[ed]' from the heavenly spheres to help undo the trouble caused by Comus's mother, Circe (l. 206).[47] Milton shifts the masquing stage business and vocabulary 'higher' (l. 1020), but he also tempers the praise. His Lady walks the earth, and throughout the body of the masque she faces real struggle. In the end, the Lady is rescued and silently escorted to her father. And in the very last words of the Attendant Spirit's epilogue Milton recalls the hierarchical (and faintly sexual) language of masques, closing the work with a stutter of hesitation: 'Or if Virtue feeble were, / Heaven itself would stoop to her.' Critics have assumed that this strange couplet is evidence of Milton's Christianization of the masque, but like the ending of many of Milton's works, this final subjunctive complicates rather than clarifies meaning. One way or another, the masque's reversion to a conventional *deus ex machina* (Sabrina or, if necessary, Heaven) only underscores retrospectively the boldness of Milton's most original creation in *A Maske*, a real woman acting nobly in the world. Unlike many of his contemporary male writers who palpably bristled at female dominance and mourned the loss of 'the Masculine Stile', Milton responded with powerful creative intensity to the centrality of women in Caroline theatrical culture. The actresses to come—Eve, Mary, Dalila—fully realize the dramatic complexity *A Maske* begins to probe. But their source, like so much of Milton's later work, is here in the 1630s.

---

[47] Brown notes this borrowing as well (*Milton's Aristocratic Entertainments*, 3).

CHAPTER 6

'LYCIDAS' AND THE INFLUENCE OF ANXIETY

NICHOLAS McDOWELL

'Or if Virtue feeble were, / Heaven itself would stoop to her.' Milton must have been pleased with the lines that he gave to the Attendant Spirit to conclude *A Maske presented at Ludlow Castle*. On 10 June 1639, nearly five years after the *Maske* was performed, he wrote them in the visitors' album of Camillo Cerdogni in Geneva, along with a motto adapted from Horace's *Epistulae*: 'Caelum non animum muto dum trans mare curro' ('I change my sky but not my mind when I cross the sea').[1] The Neapolitan Protestant Cerdogni was a religious refugee: the line from Horace marks Milton's own recent, arduous journey across the Pennine Alps and proclaims him morally and spiritually untainted by his travels in the heartland of Catholicism. As he was to insist later in the *Defensio Secunda*: 'in all these places, where so much licence exists, I lived free and untouched by the slightest sin or reproach, reflecting constantly that although I might hide from the gaze of men, I could not elude the sight of God' (*CPW*, iv/i. 620). Such strident declarations as this and the Horatian motto seem to confirm Stephen Fallon's recent argument that Milton refuses to acknowledge the possibility of sinfulness in his self-representations—whether in private autograph books in 1639 or published Latin polemic in 1654.[2] The claim of

---

[1] French, *Records*, i. 149. Cerdogni's *album amicorum* is now in the Houghton Library of Harvard University (MS Sumner 84, Lobby XI. 3. 43). See Horace, *Epistulae*, 1. 11. 27: 'caelum, non animum mutant, qui trans mare currunt'.

[2] Fallon, *Milton's Peculiar Grace: Self-Representation and Authority* (Ithaca, N.Y., 2007).

elect self-sufficiency sits uneasily, though, with the lines from the *Maske*, which imply that if Milton's spiritual and moral virtue had been under threat in Italy an external agent of grace would anyway have intervened, as the Attendant Spirit, assisted by the nymph Sabrina ('a virgin pure'), intervenes to save the Lady from Comus and from what the Elizabethan anti-theatricalist Philip Stubbes liked to call 'devirgination' (a process Stubbes believed to be accelerated by attending dramatic entertainments).[3] Perhaps Milton rather has the Genevan rescue of Cerdogni's Protestant virtue in mind. Yet Milton's self-identification with the Lady of the *Maske* would be appropriate in that it would encourage us to take literally his later insistence that he was 'untouched' by Italian and Catholic 'licence'. His virginity, in other words, remained intact.

Milton's early preoccupation with the preservation of his chastity was bound up with his sense of poetic vocation.[4] In Elegy VI, a Latin verse letter addressed to his St Paul's friend Charles Diodati just after Christmas, 1629, he makes a distinction between the sociable, festive, sensually indulgent life of the poet of love elegy and the obscure, frugal, self-denying existence required of the prophetic poet or *vates*. 'Song loves Bacchus, and Bacchus loves songs', Milton knowingly informs Diodati, and he goes on to display his mastery of the elegiac form that he has outgrown by describing a dance where 'girls' eyes and girls' fingers playing will make Thalia dart into your breast and take command of it' (ll. 14, 47–8). Thalia is the muse of lyric poetry in Horace's Hymn to Apollo (*Odes*, 4. 6) but the classical spirit presiding over this elegiac tradition is Ovid, who could not write good verse during his exile on the Black Sea because 'they did not have banquets or cultivate the vine there' (ll. 19–20), and from whom Milton takes his invocation of the 'Thracian lyre' (l. 37; *Amores*, 2. 11. 32) and of Erato, muse of love poetry (l. 51; *Ars Amatoria*, 2. 16). But while poets like Diodati who stick to experimenting with love elegy 'can get drunk on old wine as often as they like', the poet who writes about wars and heroes and 'a heaven ruled over by Jove' must 'drink soberly from a pure spring', 'his youth must be chaste and free from crime, his morals strict and his hand unstained' (ll. 53–4, 62–4). We hardly associate Milton with clerical ceremony, given the virulent anticlericalism of the prose and the satirical sonnets of the 1640s, but here the poet of epic song is compared to the 'priest' (*sacerdos*) who, 'bathed in holy water and gleaming in . . . holy sacrament', is in direct contact with the divine. Milton does not explicitly identify himself with this type of the priestly poet, whose 'innermost heart and mouth are both full of Jove', but he turns directly to discussion of his recently composed 'On the Morning of Christ's Nativity', which 'the first light of the dawn brought' to him (ll. 65–6, 78).

---

[3] Stubbes, *The Anatomie of Abuses* (1583), ed. F. J. Furnivall (1877–9), 145.

[4] Arguments for whether Milton took a vow of celibacy in the 1630s and then changed his mind, at some stage, before marriage to Mary Powell in 1642 are surveyed and engaged by John Leonard, 'Milton's Vow of Celibacy: A Reconsideration of the Evidence', in P. G. Stanwood (ed.), *Of Poetry and Politics: New Essays on Milton and his World* (Binghamton, N.Y., 1995), 187–201. As will become apparent, I agree with Leonard that there is no clear evidence Milton ever subscribed to a doctrine of celibacy, as opposed to one of *pre-marital* virginity.

While Elegy VI is playful and coy, the palinode that Milton appended to his Ovidian elegies in the Latin book of the 1645 *Poems*, the *Poemata*, is apparently self-recriminating—indeed for Fallon it may be the only moment in the Miltonic canon in which personal experience of sin is candidly admitted.[5] 'Haec ego mente' denounces the elegies, composed at Cambridge in 1626–9, as 'trifling memorials of my levity, which, with a warped mind and base spirit, I once raised'. Milton's self-directed iconoclasm resolves in a morbid satisfaction in the stopping of his lyrical heart: 'seduced' by the superficial attractions of such verse at university, Milton assures his readers that now 'my heart is frozen solid, packed around with thick ice' (ll. 1–2, 8). F. W. Bateson found these lines distasteful in the extreme, calling them 'perhaps the most repellent product of that social vacuum to which Milton confined himself in the reaction against Cambridge'.[6] In fact only four of the seven elegies could be said to treat Ovidian amatory themes: the second and third are funeral elegies and the fourth is a verse epistle to Milton's former tutor Thomas Young. Presumably in the *Poemata* Milton placed the most sensual of his Ovidian poems, Elegy VII—in which the speaker admits his 'whole being was aflame' after Cupid made him fall instantly in love with a girl he saw fleetingly in a crowd in London, and which is full of references to the force and ubiquity of sexual desire in Ovid's *Metamorphoses*—after the verse letter to Diodati because it provides a greater justification for 'Haec ego mente', even though Elegy VII was written earlier (it is headed 'in his nineteenth year'). This section of the *Poemata* is entitled 'Elegiarum Liber Primus', but the recantation makes it clear there will not be a second book of Ovidian elegies—this is a career path that the future *vates* has rejected.[7] Milton's careful insertion of his age above the more Ovidian of the elegies in the *Poemata* is a reminder that the recantation of love elegy as a youthful indiscretion is a conventional gesture of the poet who has left behind childish things as he progresses up the hierarchy of poetic genres, along the lines of the Virgilian *cursus*, from lyric through to epic.

The example of Virgil, regarded as 'sage, prophet, or magus'—his fourth eclogue was widely interpreted as a prophecy of the birth of Christ—as well as the great poet of imperial epic, gave Renaissance poets 'a normative shape to vocation'. The epigraph from Virgil's seventh eclogue on the title page of the 1645 *Poems*—'Baccare frontem / Cingite, ne vati noceat mala lingua futuro' ('Bind on your brow fragrant plants, so no evil tongue may harm the *vates* who is to be')—and the placing of the pastoral elegies 'Lycidas' and *Epitaphium Damonis* (written in Virgilian hexameters) as the final lyrics in the English and Latin books of the volume signal Milton's sense of his rising place on the *cursus*. 'It was natural for Milton so to edit his Latin poems in 1645', argues John Hale, 'as to make a Virgilian gravitation appear' in the movement from the 'Elegiarum Liber' to the 'Sylvae' of the second half of the *Poemata*. The

---

[5] Fallon, *Milton's Peculiar Grace*, 77–8.
[6] F. W. Bateson, *English Poetry: A Critical Introduction* (1950), 161.
[7] Stella Revard, *Milton and the Tangles of Neaera's Hair: The Making of the 1645 Poems* (Columbia, Mo. and London, 1997), 9.

recantation is seen by Hale as signalling the 'closing . . . of the whole Ovidian experimentation'. But how should we then interpret the tone of 'Haec ego mente'? While Bateson finds a vehemence in Milton's attitude towards his former, Ovidian self that seems more than conventional, others have considered the palinode to display 'a touch of mock-heroic banter'.[8] Much depends on whether it was written in the early 1630s, around the same time as the elegies, or specifically for the 1645 volume: *olim* ('memorials') suggests the later date while the language of the recantation is certainly close to the polemical prose, specifically the complaint in *The Reason of Church-Government* (1642) about the 'corruption and bane' that 'our youth and gentry . . . suck in dayly from the writings and interludes of libidinous and ignorant Poetasters, who having scars ever heard of that which is the main consistence of a true poem . . . doe for the most part lap up vitious principles in sweet pils to be swallow'd down, and make the taste of vertuous documents harsh and sowr' (*CPW*, i. 818–19). There is an echo here of the admission in the recantation that Milton was 'seduced' by elegiac poetry and that 'my ignorant youth was a vicious teacher' (l. 4). Milton tells us in the recantation that he aspired only to Ovidian elegy until 'the shady Academy offered me its Socratic streams and taught me to unloose the yoke to which I had submitted' (ll. 5–6); in *An Apology Against a Pamphlet* (1642) he tells us that in his youth he was 'allured' by 'the smooth Elegiack Poets, whereof the Schools are not scarce', until eventually 'the ceaseless round of study and reading led me to the shady places of philosophy, but chiefly to the divine volumes of *Plato*, and his equal *Xenophon*'. Greek philosophy released the young Milton from his enslavement to Ovidian erotics: 'Whereof if I should tell yet what I learnt, of chastity and love, I meane that which is truly so, whose charming cup is only vertue which she bears in her hand to those who are worthy. The rest are cheated with a thick intoxicating potion which a certaine Sorceresse the abuser of loves name carries about' (*CPW*, i. 890). The allusion to Circe's cup in Homer recalls Elegy VI, in which love elegy is played in 'Circe's Hall, where men are made monsters' (ll. 72–3); Comus, of course, is the offspring of Bacchus and Circe, 'Whose charmed cup / Whoever tasted, lost his upright shape, / And downward fell into a grovelling swine' (ll. 51–3).

If the concluding lines of the *Maske* retained peculiar resonance for Milton when he congratulated himself on the imperviousness of his chastity in 1639, it was perhaps because their echo of Marlowe's *Hero and Leander* (1593; first published 1598)

---

[8] John K. Hale, *Milton's Languages: The Impact of Multilingualism on Style* (Cambridge, 1997), 41, 212 n. 21; Louis Martz, *Poet of Exile: A Study of Milton's Poetry* (New Haven and London, 1980), 39. The classic essay on Milton's self-consciously Virgilian self-representation in the 1645 *Poems* is Martz, 'The Rising Poet', in J. H. Summers (ed.), *The Lyric and Dramatic Milton* (New York, 1965), 3–33. But compare Colin Burrow's emphasis on the less assured poet that can also be found in the volume in 'Poems 1645: The Future Poet', in Dennis Danielson (ed.), *The Cambridge Companion to Milton*, 2nd edn. (Cambridge, 1999), 54–69. I assume in this essay that Milton was fully involved in the design of the 1645 *Poems*, although that assumption has been subject to debate. For helpful discussion of the issue and a persuasive argument in favour of 'authorial control over the volume', see Leah Marcus, *Unediting the Renaissance: Shakespeare, Marlowe, Milton* (1996), 177–227 at 219.

reminded him of his repudiation of the career of the Ovidian poet, whether neo-Latin or vernacular:

> And hands so pure, so innocent, nay such
> As might have made heaven stoop to have a touch,
> Did she uphold to Venus, and again
> Vowed spotless chastity, but all in vain.

Heaven may be found stooping often enough in religious writing of the time—in George Wither's *Hallelujah* angels 'Have been pleased from heaven to stoop . . . From evil spirits us to guard', although this was not published until 1641—but what tells in favour of an allusion to Marlowe is the context of virginity under threat.[9] Hero's situation here is the inverted image of the Lady's at the end of the *Maske*. Hero has just been subjected to Leander's (conventional) rhetorical assault on her attachment to virginity ('The richest corn dies, if it be not reaped; Beauty alone is lost, too warily kept' (ll. 327–8)), just as the Lady has faced Comus's *carpe diem* arguments:

> List Lady be not coy, and be not cozened
> With that same vaunted name virginity,
> Beauty is nature's coin, must not be hoarded,
> But must be current, and the good thereof
> Consists in mutual and partaken bliss,
> Unsavoury in the enjoyment of itself
> If you let slip time, like a neglected rose
> It withers on the stalk with languished head. (*Maske*, ll. 736–43)

Leander's strenuous efforts at persuasion may be required by convention but they are also superfluous: 'Wherewith she yielded, that was won before' (l. 330). That Hero's own desire undoes her vows of chastity only makes transparent the contradiction inherent in her status as 'Venus' nun'. As Leander points out, it is by surrendering herself to her desire that Hero will 'most resemble Venus' nun' (l. 319). While Hero comically and vainly invokes the pagan goddess of desire for assistance in maintaining her chastity, the Christian God of grace, on whose behalf the Attendant Spirit works, comes to the physical assistance of the Lady, who has displayed her true virtue in championing the 'sage / And serious doctrine of virginity' against the blandishments of Comus (ll. 785–6). Milton would later refer to 'our sage and serious Poet Spenser' (*CPW*, ii. 516): a Spenserian ideal of resolved chastity is opposed to the moral weakness indulged by Marlowe's erotic narrative when the Lady dismissively tells Comus to 'Enjoy your dear wit, and gay rhetoric / That hath so well been taught her dazzling fence' (ll. 789–90), echoing Hero's light-hearted rejoinder to Leander, 'Who taught thee rhetoric to deceive a maid?' (l. 338) The Lady is impervious to Comus's tropes of seduction (even if she still needs to be rescued); Hero was already

---

[9] *The Collected Poems of Christopher Marlowe*, ed. Patrick Cheney and Brian J. Striar (Oxford, 2006), ll. 365–8. All references to Marlowe's poems are to this edition. Wither, *Hallelujah, or Britain's Second Remembrancer*, ed. Edward Farr (1857), 266.

won before Leander started speaking: 'Ay me, such words I should abhor, / And yet I like them for the orator' (ll. 339–40).

Marlowe may have derived his story mainly from the fifth-century Greek grammarian Musaeus but his poem is under the spell of Ovid, whose *Amores* he was the first to translate in full into English, probably while still at Cambridge, and two of whose *Heroides* are verse epistles addressed by Hero and Leander to each other. It was through the *Heroides*, a standard text on which students practised their imitative skills in humanist Europe, that most English readers first encountered the tale of Hero and Leander. Robert Stapylton observes in the preface to his 1647 translation of Musaeus that 'in imitation of [Ovid's] Epistles, the most eminent Poets of all Climates have (in their native languages) written upon this subject so many Paraphrases and Essays'.[10] *Heroides* 18 and 19 derive their pathos from the reader's knowledge of the tragic end to the story—Leander will drown swimming across the Hellespont in an effort to spend another night with Hero, who will throw herself into the sea in grief. While the opening line of Marlowe's poem admits the Hellespont is 'guiltie of true love's blood'—the pun on 'blood' as youthful desire, a sense frequent in Shakespeare, yokes burning passion with early death—Marlowe notoriously does not go on to depict the fatal consequences of Leander's uncontrolled sexual desire.[11] The narrative ends—most critics now like to think intentionally rather than accidentally, despite the first printer's insertion of *desunt nonulla* at the end of the text—with the unsettling image of Leander's triumph in his acquisition of Hero's virginity: 'And her all naked to his sight displayed, / Whence his admiring eyes more pleasure took / Than Dis, on heaps of gold fixing his look' (ll. 808–10). Marlowe eschews the dramatic irony and tragic pathos of the *Heroides* for the more materialistic Ovid of the *Amores*, insistently defining desire in terms of material lack and physical appetite and developing a narrator who espouses an Epicurean naturalism: 'It lies not in our power to love, or hate, / For will in us is overruled by fate' (ll. 167–8). It was left to George Chapman to conclude the story and 'censure the delights, / That being enjoyed ask judgement' in the 'Continuation' that was published with Marlowe's poem in 1598.[12]

Marlowe's debate between Hero and Leander about the value of virginity seems to be remembered by Milton as a pagan counterpoint to the dramatic action of the *Maske*; as an example of moral weakness and female licence against which to contrast the Christian virtue and intact virginity of the Lady. Much scholarly ink has been spilt on Milton's attitudes towards Spenser, Shakespeare, and, to a lesser extent, Jonson, and on how Milton regarded and positioned himself in relation to the different examples they embodied of the poet and of the literary career. Milton never mentions Marlowe and the two are rarely yoked outside comparisons of

[10] *Musaeus, on the loves of Hero and Leander with annotations upon the originall. / By Sir Robert Stapylton Knight, gentleman of the Privie Chamber to the Prince*, sig. A3ᵛ.

[11] See e.g. *Love's Labour's Lost*, V. ii. 73–4: 'The blood of youth burns not with such excess / As gravity's revolt to wantonness.'

[12] Chapman's 'Continuation of *Hero and Leander*', in *Collected Poems of Christopher Marlowe*, ed. Cheney and Striar, 'Third Sestiad', ll. 8–9.

Milton's Satan with the tragic heroes of Marlovian drama. Yet Marlowe the lyric and narrative poet is a presence, and a challenging one, in early Milton. The most obvious references to Marlowe the poet are in 'L'Allegro' and 'Il Penseroso', and they again come, as in the *Maske*, in the concluding lines. 'These delights, if thou canst give, / Mirth with thee I mean to live' ('L'Allegro', ll. 151–2) echoes the conclusion of Marlowe's much answered and imitated 'The Passionate Shepherd to his Love' as it was printed in 1600 in *England's Helicon* ('If these delights thy mind may move, / Then live with me, and be my love' (ll. 23–4)); except in Marlowe's poem the speaker offers his love 'all the pleasures' of a pastoral and wholly sensual life while in 'L'Allegro' the speaker will live with Mirth on the condition that she can give *him* such pleasures. Marlowe's pastoral love elegy is again present in the concluding couplet of 'Il Penseroso' ('These pleasures Melancholy give, / And I with thee will choose to live' (ll. 175–6)) but the echo now seems potentially ironic. Melancholy is a 'sage and holy goddess', inspiring 'great bards' who 'In sage and solemn tunes have sung, / Of tourneys and of trophies hung'—surely a reference to the 'sage and serious' Spenser (ll. 11, 116–17). The speaker hails Melancholy as the 'pensive nun, devout and pure, / Sober, steadfast, and demure', and looks to a life of virginal retirement in 'the studious cloister's pale' and 'the peaceful hermitage' (ll. 31–2, 156, 168).

While we have to be careful about assuming the sincerity with which Milton advocates Catholic celibacy—just before the appearance of the nun Milton invents a genealogy for Melancholy from the incestuous union of Saturn and Vesta, raising the spectre of anti-Catholic sexual satire—the attraction of cloistered devotional life for the Milton of 'Il Penseroso' appears to lie in its isolation from pastoral sexuality as much as the 'ecstasies' of ceremonial praise. Generations of students may have debated whether there is a hierarchical relation written into 'L'Allegro' and 'Il Penseroso' but if we accept the conventional dating of around 1631 and read the companion poems in the light of Elegy VI it becomes more likely that Milton privileges the 'prophetic strain' (there is a pun on 'strain', indicating the arduous moral effort required of the would-be *vates*) over the 'linked sweetness' of 'soft Lydian airs' that 'lap' over the passive listener ('Il Penseroso', l. 174; 'L'Allegro', ll. 136, 140). In his satirical *Skialetheia* (1598) Edward Guilpin had applied Plato's attack in the *Republic* (3. 398–9) on the effeminizing Lydian mode to the poetic fashions of late Elizabethan England: 'Fie on those *Lydian* tunes which blunt our sprights / And turne our gallants into Hermaphrodites . . . whimpering Sonnets, puling Elegies, / Slaunder the Muses; make the world despise, / Admired poesie' (sig. B8ʳ). Tellingly, Comus is given the language of 'L'Allegro': compare 'Come, and trip it as ye go / On the light fantastic toe' ('L'Allegro', ll. 34–5) with 'Come, knit hands and beat the ground / In a light fantastic round' (*A Maske*, ll. 143–4). The address to Mirth in 'L'Allegro' first invokes the memory of the 'Passionate Shepherd'—'Mirth, admit me of thy crew / To live with her, and live with thee, / In unreproved pleasures free' (ll. 38–40)—and its original *carpe diem* context is restored by Comus.

As John Carey puts it, the 'choice Milton explained to Diodati in Elegy VI between the epic-orientated recluse and the love-poet, painting from life, is rephrased in the twin poems.'[13] But we should note that Milton is not presenting anybody else with a choice: he has no qualms in Elegy VI about recommending that his dearest friend Diodati continue to give himself to wine and love poetry. For while elegy is associated in the verse letter with 'the sirens' song' and 'Circe's hall', strict resistance to sensual temptation is the burden only of the elect poet of sacred and epic song. Stella Revard rightly warns against the assumption that the companion poems are prescriptive, demanding a moral choice from readers in favour of Melancholy; their subject is rather the 'the difference between poetic inspiration in the elegiac as opposed to the epic poet'. This difference for the *vates futurus* must, however, be self-descriptive; and it must be one of moral and spiritual, as well as generic, degree. As Revard argues, 'Milton is not writing odes to mistresses but to deities, and in so doing he redefines for the poet the "come live with me" formula of Marlowe and his followers.' The glaring absence of erotic pleasure in 'L'Allegro' can only remind us of the uses to which this sort of lyric language is usually put. What Carey calls the 'stream of excited sensory responses' that runs through Elegy VI and overflows 'L'Allegro' is associated with a form of poetry, but also a lifestyle and a set of values, that the poet who would cultivate the 'prophetic strain' must subordinate or move beyond.[14]

The echoes of Marlowe in the final lines of three of the major early works suggest that when Milton thought of Marlowe's verse in the early 1630s, he thought of pastoral, *carpe diem* poetics and the expression of an Epicurean, materialist philosophy of pleasure. Milton incorporates Marlovian motifs into his own poetry only to relegate their pagan economy for a distinctively Christian emphasis on sexual restraint and purity. The incorporation and subordination of Marlowe's vernacular Ovidianism sorts with Milton's own experimentation with and renunciation of neo-Latin Ovidian elegy, first playfully in Elegy VI and then with a newly intense moral revulsion in the recantation attached to the elegies in the *Poemata*. Marlowe's association with Epicurean values was of course not confined to his works: his brief life was, and still is, the most infamously ungodly of the major English poets. Milton would have known something of the various godly accounts of Marlowe's violent death as a divinely appropriate punishment for his libertine life. Thomas Beard, Oliver Cromwell's schoolmaster in Huntingdon, presented Marlowe's fate as a prime example, and one close to home, of God's judgement on 'a Play-maker, and a Poet of scurrilitie'.[15] Beard seems to have invented the claim that during the brawl in Deptford it was Marlowe's own dagger that killed him (Beard always enjoys the poetic justice of his sinners' accidental yet providential responsibility for their own demise). The claim is repeated by Edmund Rudierde, who in his chapter on 'Epicures and Atheists' in *The Thunderbolt of God's Wrath Against Hard Hearted and Stiff Necked Atheists* (1618) also emphasizes Marlowe's learned origins as 'a Cambridge Scholler' but is more concerned to turn the episode into a warning specifically to 'ye braine-sicke and prophane Poets and Players, that bewitch idle eares with foolish

---

13 John Carey, *Milton* (London, 1969), 38.
14 Revard, *Milton and the Tangles of Neaera's Hair*, 123; Carey, *Milton*, 29.
15 *The Theatre of God's Judgements* (1597), ch. 23, p. 149.

vanities' (ch. 22, p. 29). Francis Meres, while pointing the reader in the direction of Beard's book, is the first explicitly to connect Marlowe's demise with his sexual affairs: 'stabbed to death by a bawdy serving man, a rivall of his in his lewde love'.[16]

In his extraordinary but characteristic defence of his sexual morality through an account of his reading in *An Apology Against a Pamphlet*, Milton tells us that after his misguided youthful experiments at Cambridge with the fashionable style of 'the smooth Elegiack Poets', he was initially shown a different poetic path, prior to his cleansing immersion in Platonic philosophy, by 'the two famous renowners of *Beatrice* and *Laura*, who never write but honour of them to whom they devote their verse, displaying sublime and pure thoughts, without transgression'. It was Dante and Petrarch who confirmed Milton 'in this opinion, that he who would not be frustrate of his hope to write well hereafter in laudable things, ought himself to be a true poem; that is, a composition of the best and most honourablest things' (*CPW*, i. 889). The life of Marlowe was hardly such a composition. But had he written 'laudable things'? For Beard and the godly moralists, Marlowe's wretched end was divinely just desert for his Epicurean life and prophane wit. But poets tended to think differently about the poetry. Michael Drayton's Marlowe is not gross but 'neat' and ethereal, 'Had in him those brave translunary things / That the first Poets had, his raptures were / All ayre and fire'. Milton's nephew Edward Phillips, who lived with and was tutored by his uncle throughout the 1640s, calls Marlowe 'a kind of second Shakespeare . . . because in his begun poem *Hero and Leander*, he seems to have a resemblance of that clear and unsophisticated Wit, which is natural to that incomparable Poet'.[17] Milton does say in the *Apology* that if he found a talented writer 'speaking unworthy things of themselves or unchaste', then 'their art I still applauded, but the men I deplored'; and the claim that the true poet 'ought himself to be a true poem' is not, it is true, quite the same thing as saying that the good poet must be a good man, leaving open at least the possibility of an aestheticized rather than a simply moral life—although the whole point of this section of the *Apology* is to vindicate Milton's impeccable chastity, and elsewhere in the work he insists that 'how he should be truly eloquent who is not withal a good man, I know not' (i. 874).

Marlowe was dead at 29, within six years of taking his Cambridge MA, and, if his life was remembered as infamous, he had achieved lasting fame as a poet. When in November 1637 Milton came to write a funeral elegy for his Cambridge contemporary Edward King, drowned in the Irish Sea three months earlier, Milton was about to turn 29 and it was just approaching six years since he had taken his MA, a period that he had devoted to intensive private study in Hammersmith and then Horton and that he would later represent as one of 'wearisome labours and studious watchings wherein [he] spent and tired out almost a whole youth', but also one of necessary intellectual preparation for the vatic career (*CPW*, i. 869). While Milton evidently

[16] *Palladis Tamia, Wits Treasury* (1598), 287.

[17] 'To My Most Dearly Loved Friend Henry Reynolds Esquire, Of Poets and Poesy' (1627), in *Works of Michael Drayton*, ed. J. William Hebel, 3 vols. (Oxford, 1931–41), iii. 226–31, ll. 105–8; Phillips, *Theatrum Poetarum* (1675), pt. 2, 'The Modern Poets', 24–5.

had connections in the cultural worlds of Caroline England, he was still little known as a poet (both the poem on Shakespeare in the second Folio and the text of the *Maske* had been published anonymously, in 1632 and 1637 respectively), or, indeed, as anything else—a fact about which his (Latin) letter to Diodati of 23 November seems to register a growing anxiety. Milton bemoans the 'obscurity' of his life in Horton and (again) discloses his dreams of 'an immortality of fame' achieved through a poetic career, though his 'Pegasus still raises himself on very tender wings' (i. 327).

The other elegies in *Justa Edouardo King naufrago* repeatedly emphasize King's classical learning and his status as a poet: 'One whome the Muses courted: rigg'd and fraught / With Arts and Tongues too fully, when he sought / To crosse the seas, was overwhelm'd'.[18] Milton too acknowledges that King 'knew / Himself to sing, and build the lofty rhyme' (ll. 10–11). 'Lycidas' is, famously, a poem which is constantly allusive to other poems, mostly but not exclusively to classical, neo-Latin, and vernacular pastoral. 'Forcing upon the mind the question of where meaning is to be anchored, such allusions', as Joseph Wittreich observes, 'point not to "Lycidas"'s sources but to its context, which, in the broadest sense is literature; yet literature, in turn, yields up less general but still generalized contexts for reading [Milton's poem]. These literary backdrops serve as an antidote to the obscurity of "Lycidas".'[19] It would seem appropriate that when Milton turned to contemplate King's death in the 'perilous flood' (l. 185) and the questions it raised for him concerning mortality, prematurity, and the unfulfilled poetic career, these 'literary backdrops' should include the most famous classical episode of the drowning of a beautiful young man, and Marlowe's famous poem about that episode, *Hero and Leander*—a poem written by a Cambridge scholar of rather more literary accomplishment than King but who had also been violently killed, and at the very age at which Milton was writing.

Milton recalls Marlowe the poet in the first of the poem's digressions, in lines usually received as the most intensely personal in 'Lycidas':

> Alas! What boots it with uncessant care
> To tend the homely slighted shepherd's trade,
> And strictly meditate the thankless Muse,
> Were it not better done as others use,
> To sport with Amaryllis in the shade,
> Or with the tangles of Neaera's hair?
> Fame is the spur that the clear spirit doth raise
> (That last infirmity of noble mind)
> To scorn delights, and live laborious days;
> But the fair guerdon when we hope to find,
> And think to burst out into sudden blaze,
> Comes the blind Fury with th'abhorred shears,
> And slits the thin-spun life. (ll. 64–76)

---

[18] Samson Briggs, 'When common souls break from their courser clay', in the English book of *Justa Edouardo King naufrago* (Cambridge, 1638), 'Obsequies to the memorie of Mr Edward King', 14–15, ll. 13–16.

[19] *Visionary Poetics: Milton's Tradition and his Legacy* (San Marino, Calif., 1979), 89.

Given the amount of critical energy that has been devoted to studying the sources and elaborating the imagery of 'Lycidas', it is surprising that no edition, including the *Variorum*, relates lines 75–6 to the mythopoeic digression which concludes the first 'sestiad' of *Hero and Leander*. Marlowe's dislikeable narrator asks us to give him our full attention as he explains the origins of the enmity between the Fates and Cupid. Mercury was once enflamed with desire for a beautiful 'country maid'. As 'All women are ambitious naturally', this maid demanded that Mercury steal her a 'draught of flowing nectar' from Jove's cup before she would submit (ll. 428, 432). The lust-driven Mercury agreed and was expelled from heaven by Jove for his transgression. Cupid, sympathetic to Mercury and his desire, then wounded 'those on whom heaven, earth, and hell relies, / I mean the adamantine Destinies'—the three sisters who turn, according to Plato, the adamant spindle of Necessity around which the universe is wrapped (ll. 443–4; *Republic*, 10. 616–17). In thrall to their desire for Mercury, the Fates offered him

> the deadly fatal knife
> That shears the slender threads of human life;
> At his fair feathered feet the engines laid,
> Which th'earth from ugly Chaos' den upweighed. (ll. 447–50)

As all editors point out, Milton's 'blind Fury' who holds the shears which cut the thread of life is not a Fury at all but Atropos, one of the three Fates; and neither Atropos nor the Furies are blind. In 'Lycidas' the blindness of Fortuna and the bloodlust of the Furies, born in Greek myth from the blood that fell to the earth when Cronus castrated his father Uranus, are merged with the figure of Atropos and her whirling (perhaps castrating) shears to conjure a terrifying image of unstoppable and seemingly indiscriminate violence. It is hardly a slip on Milton's part, as Atropos is a recurring figure in the early poetry. In his 'Epitaph for the Marchioness of Winchester' (1631) Milton writes of how, when Jane Pulet died soon after giving birth to a stillborn child, 'Atropos for Lucina came / And with remorseless cruelty / Spoiled both fruit and tree' (ll. 28–30). In *Arcades*, the pastoral fragment written around 1633 as part of an 'entertainment presented to the Countess Dowager of Derby', the 'Genius of the Wood' refers to 'those that hold the vital shears, / And turn the adamantine spindle round, / On which the fate of gods and men is wound' (ll. 65–7). Milton no doubt recalls in 'abhorred shears' his own 'vital shears' in *Arcades*. There are also plenty of references to Atropos and her deadly knife in the period. In *The Last Part of the Mirour for Magistrates* (1578) Dame Elianor Cobham wishes that 'the Parcas had untwynde / My vital stringes, or Atropos with knife, / Had cut the lyne of my most wrtched lyfe' (fo. 38ʳ), and later Henry, Duke of Buckingham, asks: 'But what may boote to stay the sisters three? / When Atropos perforce will cut the thred?' (fo. 139ʳ). In *Englands Parnassus* (1600), we find 'cruell Atropos... With cursed knife cutting the twist in twaine' (l. 57). But the image in *Arcades* is static and unthreatening, and other examples of the early modern Atropos in action lack the alliterative slice of Marlowe's 'shears the slender threads of human life', echoed in the 'shears... slits' of 'Lycidas', while Marlowe's 'slender threads' are compressed into

Milton's 'thin-spun'. The 'engines' of fate that are offered to Mercury in Marlowe may provide another perspective on the notorious crux later in 'Lycidas' when St Peter invokes the terror of apocalypse in his diatribe against clerical corruption: 'That two-handed engine at the door, / Stands ready to smite once, and smite no more' (ll. 130–1). The apocalyptic judgement on the bad pastors is deserved, of course, whereas the 'blind Fury' seems to act without reason or meaning; the distinction is one to which we shall return.

Marlowe's Mercury refuses the 'deadly fatal knife', with which, presumably, he could kill Jove, but asks the Fates 'that Jove, usurper of his father's seat, / Might presently be banisht into hell, / And aged Saturn in Olympus dwell'. The request is granted and 'Murder, rape, warre, lust, and trechery, / Were with Jove clos'd in Stigian empery'. But this renewed golden age is short-lived, for Mercury

> did despise
> The love of th' everlasting Destinies.
> They seeing it, both Love and him abhor'd.
> And Jupiter unto his place restored. (ll. 461–4)

The shears in 'Lycidas' are perhaps not simply 'abhorred' by those whose lives they cut short but also embody the abhorrence of Marlowe's Fates for those, whether humans or gods, who think they can spurn their power. This myth of Mercury and the country maid is Marlowe's invention. Why does he include it? Warren Boutcher has shown how Marlowe imitates the structure of the Spanish poet Juan Boscán's version of Musaeus, *Leandro* (1543), which takes the form of a triptych with a digressive centrepiece, and how English readers of the late sixteenth century who used Boscán as a study in eloquence were particularly interested in his mythopoeic digression explaining why Aeolus, god of the winds, would not hear Leander's prayers. Boutcher concludes that humanist readers like Marlowe—and, we might add, Milton—were trained to pay particular attention to and to emulate set-piece moments of rhetorical elaboration and digression in a poem, whether classical, neo-classical, or vernacular.[20] In terms of content we might see Marlowe's digression as 'illustrating the dangers in *voluptas*, the potentially destructive element that it con-tains. In this view, Mercury, under the influence of his love for the shepherdess, acts foolishly, irresponsibly.' The narrative can then be read as 'a recapitulation of the entire poem in a different key', except that Marlowe's poem does not go on to show the destructive consequences of extra-marital sexual desire, or at least only hints in the ambiguous final lines at the deleterious psychological and social effects for Hero of that desire fulfilled.[21] If the drowning of Edward King makes Milton remember

---

[20] Warren Boutcher, '"Who taught thee Rhetoricke to deceive a maid?": Christopher Marlowe's *Hero and Leander*, Juan Boscán's *Leandro*, and Renaissance Vernacular Humanism', *Comparative Literature*, 52 (2000), 11–52.

[21] Richard Neuse, 'Atheism and Some Functions of Myth in Marlowe's *Hero and Leander*', *Modern Language Quarterly*, 31 (1970), 424–39 at 435, 433.

Leander and Marlowe's poem about Leander, in the first digression of his pastoral funeral elegy Milton looks to Marlowe's erotic pastoral digression and its exemplary potential rather than the unfinished main narrative, with its refusal of narrative and moral closure.

A provenance for lines 75–6 of 'Lycidas' in Marlowe's invented myth would be fitting given Milton's anxiety at this point about the obscurity of the scholar-poet who devotes his life to the cultivation of learning and virtue: 'Alas! What boots it with uncessant care / To tend the homely slighted shepherd's trade / And strictly meditate the thankless Muse [?]'. For the narrator's digression in Hero and Leander becomes as much an explanation of the lowliness of scholars as of the pain of lovers. Mercury is the Roman Hermes, god of orators and wits, learning and scholarship, and symbolic of the 'mercurial' human intellect, an identity that Marlowe emphasizes by using the names Mercury and Hermes interchangeably. There are long-term consequences from the sexual behaviour of Mercury/Hermes for the status of the 'Muses' sons' in society:

> And but that Learning, in despite of Fate,
> Will mount aloft, and enter heaven gate,
> And to the seat of Jove itself advance,
> Hermes had slept in hell with Ignorance.
> Yet as a punishment they added this,
> That he and Poverty should always kiss.
> And to this day is every scholar poor;
> Gross gold from then runs headlong to the boor.
> Likewise the angry Sisters, thus deluded,
> To venge themselves on Hermes, have concluded
> That Midas' brood shall sit in Honour's chair,
> To which the Muses' sons are only heir:
> And fruitful wits that in aspiring are
> Shall discontent run into regions far. (ll. 465–78)

If Learning finally takes its rightful place in heaven, 'in despite of Fate', the scholar-poet still languishes in an earthly condition of material deprivation and social exclusion, his virtue unrecognized by the powerful:

> And few great lords in virtuous deeds shall joy,
> But be surprised with every garish toy,
> And still enrich the lofty servile clown,
> Who with encroaching guile keeps learning down. (ll. 479–82)

Marlowe's digression begins as an erotic pastoral narrative and ends as a mythic explanation of society's disregard for wit, learning, and poetry: of why the 'shepherd's trade' is 'slighted'. Marlowe's complaint against a society in which true humanist virtue goes unrecognized and unrewarded was evidently well known in Elizabethan Cambridge and extracted from the erotic narrative of which it was a part: there are clear paraphrases in the opening and closing scenes of the Cambridge play The Pilgrimage to Parnassus (1598): 'yea, Midas brood fore eare must honoured

be, / Wile Phoebus followers live in Miserie'.[22] The unjust subordination of 'the
Muses' sons' in Marlowe, a consequence of Mercury's rejection of the love of the
Fates, has a parallel in Milton's invocation of the helplessness of the Muse's first and
most powerful son, Orpheus, before the frustrated desires of the Thracian Bacchantes
whose sexual invitations he had rejected:

> Had ye been there—for what could that have done?
> What could the Muse herself that Orpheus bore,
> The Muse herself for her enchanting son
> Whom universal nature did lament,
> When by the rout that made the hideous roar,
> His gory visage down the stream was sent,
> Down the swift Hebrus to the Lesbian shore? (ll. 56–63)

In Elegy VI Orpheus is cited as an archetype of the poet as both priest and prophet,
sacerdos and *vates*; such sacred figures must, as we have seen, lead a life of chastity and
the strictest morals: 'In this way, so it is said, wise Tiresias lived after the loss of his
sight, and Theban Linus, and Calchas, when he fled from his doomed home, and old
Orpheus, when he tamed wild beasts among lonely caves' (ll. 67–70). The adjectives
'old' and 'lonely' show Milton to be thinking of Orpheus after he lost his wife
Eurydice to the underworld and 'Alone through Arctic ice, through the snows of
Tanais, over / Frost-bound Riphaean plateaux / He ranged, bewailing his lost
Eurydice and the wasted / Bounty of Death'.[23] In the apology for poetry and the
poetic vocation that Milton offered to his father in the Latin verse epistle 'Ad Patrem',
which now tends to be dated to the Horton period of the mid-1630s, Orpheus again
appears as the archetype of poetic power who 'held streams spellbound and gave ears
to the oak-trees and moved lifeless phantoms to tears' (ll. 53–5). This divinely
powerful and noble figure is essentially the Virgilian Orpheus of the *Georgics*; the
Orpheus of 'Lycidas' is the pathetic Ovidian Orpheus whose music is drowned out by
'Bacchic howlings' and whose 'words had no effect' on the scorned women: 'Dead to
all reverence, they tore him apart and, through those lips to which rocks had listened,
which wild beasts had understood, his last breath slipped away and vanished in the
wind.'[24]

These Ovidian images of the live dismemberment of the archetypal poet by the
forces of uncontrolled passion, an enactment of the Dionysian sacrificial ritual of
sparagmos, 'struck at the heart of Milton's sense of himself and his vocation' and
reappear throughout the Miltonic canon.[25] The dismembering shears of the 'blind
Fury' similarly scatter King's bones perhaps 'beyond the stormy Hebrides', denying
him the formal burial rites for which Milton's poem compensates (ll. 155–6). As a
Fellow of Christ's who was preparing to enter the clergy, King had, like Milton,
turned away from the world of active sexuality, at least temporarily before marriage,

---

[22] See *The Three Parnassus Plays*, ed. J. B. Leishman (London, 1949), ll. 61–4, 76, 1554–7, 1560–6.
[23] Virgil, *Georgics*, trans. C. Day Lewis (Oxford, 1999), 126.
[24] Ovid, *Metamorphoses*, trans. Mary Innes (Harmondsworth, 1955), 246–7.
[25] Michael Lieb, *Milton and the Culture of Violence* (Ithaca and London, 1994), 38–82 at 42.

to live in the world of scholarship and devotion; the frenzied sundering of the body of Orpheus raises the terrifying possibility that, while the restraint of pre- and extra-marital desire may be essential to grant intellectual and even prophetic insight, it might so enrage the Fates that they strike down a man before he is able to exercise that insight. At the least King's drowning seems to undermine the providential notion of early death as a deserved punishment for a depraved life, exemplified in poetry by Leander's drowning as cosmic retribution for his illicit sexual pleasure in Chapman's continuation of *Hero and Leander*, and in life by Marlowe's violent demise as a deserved end to a debauched life in Thomas Beard and other godly moralists. The thought that those who subordinate sexuality to the higher calling of service to the sacred Muse are as likely to die young as those who indulge their desires forces the poet to ask: 'Were it not better done as others use, / To sport with Amaryllis in the shade, / Or with the tangles of Neaera's hair?' Amaryllis and Neaera are very common names for a mistress in classical and Renaissance pastoral, appearing in Virgil, Theocritus, and Horace as well as neo-Latin poets such as Johannes Secundus and George Buchanan.[26] The 'amatory dimension' of 'Lycidas', as Michael Lieb terms it, understandably tends to be overlooked, though at the beginning of the poem Milton's shepherd plucks the myrtle leaves, the emblem of Venus, as well as the laurel of Apollo and the ivy of Bacchus; while Milton makes 'prolonged and unusually specific allusion' to Virgil's tenth eclogue (itself derived from the first *Idyl* of Theocritus), in which the shepherd-poet Gallus laments his betrayal by the unfaithful Lycoris as he nears death from a broken heart.[27] Elegy VI suggests how the type of poetic career was for Milton connected in an essential way with the lifestyle of the poet, and by invoking Amaryllis and Neaera he raises the question not only of the alternative, sexually active lifestyle that he might have led and might still lead, but of the alternative career path that he might have followed as a poet of amatory lyric.

This identification of the sexual morality of the poet and the generic ambition of his poetry was to be made vehemently in the polemical contexts of *The Reason of Church-Government*, when Milton evidently felt confident enough in his future career as the nation's epicist to declare in print that he would

covnant with any knowing reader, that for some few years I may go on trust with him toward the payment of what I am now indebted, as being a work not to be rays'd from the heat of youth, or the vapours of wine, like that which flows at wast from the pen of some vulgar Amorist, or the trencher fury of a riming parasite, nor to be obtained by the Invocation of Dame Memory and her Siren daughters, but by devout prayer to that eternall Spirit who can enrich with all utterance and knowledge, and sends out his Seraphim with the hallow'd fire of his Altar to touch and purify the lips of whome he pleases; to this must be added industrious and select reading, steddy observation, insight into all seemly and generous arts and affaires. (i. 820–1)

---

[26] Revard, *Milton and the Tangles of Neaera's Hair*, 182.

[27] Michael Lieb, *The Sinews of Ulysses: Form and Convention in Milton's Works* (Pittsburgh, Pa., 1989), 67; J. Martin Evans, *The Miltonic Moment* (Lexington, Ky., 1998), 80.

The elegiac poet and the priestly, prophetic poet are opposed in the manner of Elegy VI but in the revolted language of 'Haec ego mente': 'vulgar Amorist' seems to invoke specifically writing in the style of the *Amores*. Epic gravity is opposed to elegiac and lyric flippancy, but the generic hierarchy is also a moral one. As in the invocation of the 'heavenly Muse' in the 'Nativity Ode', where the poet calls for his mouth to be touched by 'hallowed fire' from the angelic altar (l. 28), Milton presents himself as a type of Isaiah, whose prophetic speech is released by a fiery coal placed against his lips by one of the seraphim (Isaiah 6: 6–7). Milton's lips are purified by holy fire but the elegiac poet, the 'Vulgar Amorist', whose desire is directed towards the body, is unable to control his bodily discharges and so is implicitly feminized in terms of contemporary stereotypes of woman as 'leaky vessel'. The wine drunk by the elegiac poet flows 'at wast' back out through his pen—'at wast' punningly reduces the verse to waste product which is produced from the waist, to both urine and, with a recollection of Shakespeare's 'expense of spirit in a waste of shame' in sonnet 129, seminal fluid. Conversely Miltonic texts maintain (like Milton's chaste, sealed-up body) integrity and individuality, preserving 'as in a violl the purest efficacie and extraction of that living intellect that bred them', as *Areopagitica* (1644) would later put it (ii. 492).

The sense in Elegy VI of the generic and moral inferiority of love elegy has intensified in the anti-prelatical prose into visceral hatred for the baseness and corruption of its practitioners, the 'vulgar Amorists'. The literary and moral judgement has become a political and religious one: Milton has seen the writers of Ovidian verse who seduced him into experimenting with the form at Cambridge turn into the 'riming parasites' of Laudian and court society, with their 'trencher fury' or wholly materialistic, patronage-led poetic ambitions. We can begin to see how the first 'digression' of 'Lycidas', in which Milton considers and discounts the attractions of the Ovidian career, and the second, St Peter's attack on the corrupt clergy, are thematically as well as structurally linked. As J. M. French put it many years ago: 'Amaryllis has metamorphosed into ecclesiastical sinecure but the principle is the same.'[28]

In the first digression, however, the anxiety provoked by King's apparently undeserved death initially forces a reconsideration of the temptation to ease, both poetic and bodily, signified by the names Amaryllis and Neaera. It is the prospect of fame, the poet then maintains, which girds him 'To scorn delights, and live laborious days'. 'Delights' and 'live' invoke once more the conclusion of Marlowe's 'Passionate Shepherd': 'If these delights thy mind may move, / then live with me, and be my love.' Fame is 'the spur that clear spirit doth raise'—in the light of the pun on 'wast' in the prose, there seems also to be Shakespearean play on the clearness or purity of the chaste poet's 'spirit', raised or aroused by the prospect of fame. In Shakespeare the sexual pun is materializing and reductive; and while Milton reverses the pun, so that material fluid is sublimed to the spirit of poetic inspiration, its use nonetheless

---

[28] J. M. French, 'The Digressions in Milton's "Lycidas"', *Studies in Philology*, 50 (1953), 485–90 at 488.

threatens to reduce the pursuit of earthly poetic fame to a substitute for sexual pleasure. It is at this point, after the invocation of Amaryllis and Neaera, that Milton remembers the 'deadly fatal knife' of *Hero and Leander*. The figure of Marlowe and his supposedly Epicurean life and death upsets the equation between the scorn of sensual delight and the attainment of 'an immortality of fame', the desire for which apparently impelled, at least in part, the years of 'studious retirement' after leaving Cambridge.[29] Of course the art of 'Lycidas' is to give the impression of agonized internal struggle and debate occurring in the moment of writing; but, in the manner of the Puritan conversion narrative that 'Lycidas' sometimes obscurely resembles, these passages are retrospectively written from a position of assured grace: Milton's mind is already made up.[30]

This may be why Milton thinks specifically of the Mercury digression in *Hero and Leander*: the sentence of social inferiority pronounced on the Muses' sons in Marlowe's narrative is finally a consequence of the unruly *voluptas* both of Mercury and the Fates. It may also explain why Milton so insistently alludes to Virgil's tenth eclogue, despite the apparent incongruity of its amatory subject matter. Virgil's Gallus concludes his deathbed lament by affirming the ultimate sovereignty of profane love: 'In hell, and earth, and seas, and heaven above, / Love conquers all; and we must yield to Love'. In contemporary commentary, however, this eclogue was read as 'a warning, not an affirmation'.[31] According to the Jacobean schoolmaster John Brinsley, when Virgil asks, 'What lawns or woods withheld you from his aid, / Ye nymphs, when Gallus was to love betrayed [?]' (ll. 13–14), echoed in Milton's 'Where were ye Nymphs when the remorseless deep / Closed o'er the head of your loved Lycidas?' (ll. 50–1), he 'accuseth the Muses that they were so careless of Gallus, to let him so to leave his studies and to perish in such unbeseeming love'. Gallus could have found relief from his love sickness, according to Brinsley's marginal commentary, 'by giving his mind to the studie of Poetrie'.[32] Brinsley takes this reading from Continental Reformation authorities that Milton would more likely have known, Petrus Ramus and Philip Melancthon.[33] While ostensibly questioning in the first digression of 'Lycidas' the point of the life devoted to chaste virtue and promiscuous learning—the life he had been leading since leaving Cambridge—Milton incorporates poetic models that oppose, or were read as opposing, the pursuit of learning and poetry to the distracting and destructive power of erotic desire.

---

[29] The phrase is from Milton's letter to an unknown friend (1633), in *CPW*, i. 319.

[30] The analogy with the fractured representation of identity in the conversion narrative, written retrospectively after the subject has reached a (greater) state of psychic unity through experience of grace, and often written in a form of semi-dialogue with God and the reader/audience, is a helpful corrective to the reading of Stanley Fish, who regards the various digressive voices in the poem to leave it finally without a 'unified consciousness' ('"Lycidas": A Poem Finally Anonymous', in C. A. Patrides (ed.), *Lycidas: The Tradition and the Poem*, 2 edn. (Columbia, Mo., 1983)).

[31] Evans, *Miltonic Moment*, 81; *Works of Virgil*, trans. John Dryden (London and New York, 1903), 483–6, ll. 98–9. All references to the *Eclogues* are to Dryden's translation unless otherwise noted.

[32] Brinsley, *Virgils Eclogues* (1620), 95, 98.

[33] See Ramus, *P. Virgilii Maronis Bucolica* (Paris, 1555); Melanchthon, *Argumenta . . . in Eclogas Virgilii* (1568).

In Virgil's tenth eclogue Phoebus Apollo, Roman god of poetry and music (and prophecy), interrupts Gallus' lament to scold him for making the false Lycoris his only care when she cares nothing for him. In 'Lycidas' it turns out that Apollo has been listening to the poet's lament about the 'thankless Muse' and interrupts line 76 to dispel the image of the 'blind Fury' and her 'abhorred shears':

> But not the praise,
> Phoebus replied, and touched my trembling ears;
> Fame is no plant that grows on mortal soil,
> Nor in the glistering foil
> Set off to the world, nor in broad rumour lies,
> But lives and spread aloft by those pure eyes,
> And perfect witness of all judging-Jove;
> As he pronounces on each deed,
> Of so much fame in Heaven expect thy meed. (ll. 76–84)

Apollo's intervention would seem designed to allay the anxiety raised by the thought that King's violent early death shows his chaste and 'clear' life, his strain in the cause of learning, to have been for nothing; but perhaps also any anxiety raised by the memory of Marlowe, and of the lasting poetic fame Marlowe had obtained in a short and supposedly godless existence. The poet looks forward to judgement in the afterlife and is reassured by Apollo that the virtuous life, no matter if it ends early and bloodily and obscure, will receive eternal reward. The conclusion of the first digression thus anticipates the Christian apotheosis of Lycidas, beginning 'Weep no more, woeful shepherds weep no more' (l. 165). The darker side of pagan ritual had earlier overshadowed the poem in the images of *sparagmos*, applied to Orpheus, Lycidas, and, potentially, the poet himself; Milton looks now to the true sacrifice of Christ, which has purchased eternal life for the virtuous and chaste King:

> So Lycidas sunk low, but mounted high,
> Throught the dear might of him that walked the waves:
> Where other groves, and other streams along,
> With nectar pure his oozy locks he laves,
> And hears the unexpressive nuptial song,
> In the blest kingdoms meek of joy and love.
> There entertain him all the saints above,
> In solemn troops, and sweet societies
> That sing, and singing in their glory move,
> And wipe the tears for ever from his eyes. (ll. 172–81)

A series of allusions to Revelation emphasize the release both from mourning and from the cyclic movements of pagan naturalism into the linear narrative of apocalypse. '[O]ther groves, and other streams' alludes to the tree of life (7: 17) and 'living fountains of waters' (12: 2), while the 'unexpressive nuptial song' invokes the 'marriage of the Lamb' (19: 1–7). King's earthly virtue has been rewarded with marriage to Christ, with whom he shall reside eternally in the heavenly paradise where there 'shall be no more death, neither sorrow, nor crying, neither shall there be any more pain' (21: 4).[34] 'Lycidas' begins 'Yet once more', with the poet locked in a cycle of recurrence that is finally broken by 'Weep no more', echoing not only Revelation but the description of apocalyptic judgement by St Paul in the Epistle to the Hebrews, 12: 25–7:

> For if they escaped not who refuse him that spake on earth, much more shall we not escape, if we turn away from him that speaketh from heaven: Whose voice then shook the earth: but now he hath promised, saying, Yet once more I shake not the earth only, but also heaven. And this word, Yet once more, signifieth the removing of those things that are shaken.

This context of the apocalyptic judgement of earthly behaviour developed by the allusions to the New Testament is anticipated by the second digression, the interjection by St Peter warning the corrupt bishops, the 'Blind mouths', of the 'two-handed engine at the door'. While there may be an echo here of the 'engines' or 'fatal knife' that Marlowe's Fates lay at the feet of Mercury, and so of the 'abhorred shears' of the 'blind Fury' in Milton's first digression, the instruments of the pagan Fates have now become (most likely) the two-edged sword of Revelation (1: 16, 19: 15), commonly associated with the Word of God.[35] The Epicurean randomness of King's death in the first digression, which causes the poet such (apparent) anxiety, has been qualified in the digressions and finally replaced in the apotheosis passage by the Christian economy of eternal reward and punishment—an economy entirely absent from Marlowe's version of the Hero and Leander myth, which instead plays out the psychological drama of consensually surrendered virginity.

The movement which 'Lycidas' works through from pagan and pastoral cycles of death and rebirth to apocalyptic linearity informs the remarkable final eight lines, and their sudden introduction of a third-person narrator into what the reader has assumed to be a first-person poem:

> Thus sang the uncouth swain to the oaks and rills,
> While the still morn went out with sandals grey,
> He touched the tender stops of various quills,
> With eager thought warbling his Doric lay:
> And now the sun had stretched out all the hills,
> And now was dropped into the western bay;
> At last he rose, and twitched his mantle blue.
> Tomorrow to fresh woods, and pastures new. (ll. 186–93)

---

[34] As John Leonard argues, there is no need to equate King's apotheosis with celibacy rather than chastity: the 'unexpressive nuptial song' more likely refers to Rev. 19, in which St John hears the voice of 'all [God's] servants . . . saying "Alleluia"', than 14: 1–4, in which 144,000 men who 'were not defiled with women' are 'redeemed from the earth' ('Milton's Vow of Celibacy', 191–3). Milton anyway emphasizes in the *Apology* that defilement in Rev. 14 'doubtlesse means fornication: for marriage must not be called a defilement' (i. 893).

[35] For various elaborate interpretations of the 'two-handed engine', see *CSP*, 242–3.

The celestial rebirth of Lycidas finds a parallel in the sense here of the poet leaving behind the lyric self who sang the pastoral elegy; but if the movement of the poem becomes abruptly teleologic, the process is as much Virgilian as apocalyptic in the renewed echoes of Virgil's tenth and final eclogue and its own concluding lines:

> My muses, here your sacred raptures end:
> The verse was what I owed my suffering friend.
>
> . . .
>
> Now let us rise; for hoarseness oft invades
> The singer's voice, who sings beneath the shades.
> From juniper unwholesome dews distil,
> That blast the sooty corn, the withering herbage kill:
> Away, my goats, away! For you have browsed your fill. (ll. 100–1, 110–14)

The debt to the conclusion of Virgil's last eclogue is combined with the adoption of *ottava rima*, the stanzaic form of the great Italian epic romances, Ariosto's *Orlando furioso* and Tasso's *Gerusalemme liberata*, and of their English translations by John Harington and Edward Fairfax—a regularity always threatened but never quite obtained earlier in 'Lycidas', which in its metrical swells and billows seems to take literally John Cleveland's insistence in *Justa Edouardo King naufrago* that 'The sea's too rough for verse; who rhymes upon't / With Xerxes strives to fetter th'Hellespont'. (The reference is to the Persian king who built a bridge across the Hellespont and had the sea whipped and fetters thrown into it to symbolize his mastery over nature; was it Cleveland, Milton's contemporary at Christ's, who sparked the memory of *Hero and Leander*?) The metrical disruptions of the poem prior to the final eight lines are variations on the complex patterns of the Italian *canzone*, which Milton had been practising both in Italian ('Canzone') and English ('At a Solemn Music').[36] When placed in the context of the self-consciously 'Virgilian gravitation' of the 1645 *Poems*, the final eight lines look forward in their sudden regularity to Milton's next step on the Virgilian *cursus*—he tells us in 1642 that he followed Ariosto's example in resolving to be 'an interpreter and relater of the best and sagest things among mine own citizens throughout this island in the mother dialect'—and perhaps also, as Thomas Newton was the first to suggest in 1752, to Milton's departure six months after he wrote 'Lycidas' from the cloistered 'obscurity' of Horton for the tour of Italy, home of so many of the great poets whose fame he intends to rival, and where he will put his sexual virtue, now reaffirmed after the internal dialogue of 'Lycidas', to Spenserian test against popish sensual temptation (*CPW*, i. 810–11).[37] The rewritten Marlovian lines from the *Maske* scribbled in Cerdogni's *album amicorum* express

---

[36] Cleveland, 'I like not tears in tune', in 'Obsequies to the memorie of Mr Edward King', 9–10, ll. 11–12; F. T. Prince, *The Italian Element in Milton's Verse* (Oxford, 1954), 71–88.

[37] *Paradise Regain'd: A Poem, in Four Books. To which is added Samson Agonistes: and Poems upon Severall Occasions*, ed. Thomas Newton, 2nd edn. (1753), 209. For a strong argument against such biographical readings of the end of 'Lycidas', see Christopher Ricks, '*Poems (1645)*', in Christopher Ricks (ed.), *Penguin History of Literature*, ii: *English Poetry and Prose, 1540–1674*, rev. edn. (1970; Harmondsworth, 1993), 245–75 at 254–5.

Milton's satisfaction at having come through the test and shown his virtue to be, even more soundly than the Lady's chastity, 'clad in complete steel' (*Maske*, l. 420).

The fusing of apocalyptic historical process and the poet's Virgilian literary progress in the conclusion to 'Lycidas' underlines, retrospectively, the inadequacy of Apollo's resolution of the first digression, at least for Milton. Apollo's plucking of the poet's ears to remind him that true fame is only found in heaven alludes to Virgil's sixth eclogue, in which Apollo rather advises the poet against moving too hastily from pastoral to heroic and epic verse (ll. 3–4). The allusion thus works against Apollo's insistence in 'Lycidas' on the meaninglessness of earthly poetic fame to reaffirm instead Milton's decision to dedicate the previous five years to intellectual and spiritual preparation for the career of national epicist. The years of living within 'the studious cloister's pale' have been essential to attaining the 'prophetic strain' invoked at the end of 'Il Penseroso', in the final line before the rewritten couplet from Marlowe's 'Passionate Shepherd to his Love'. As the poet observes in 'Lycidas' after Apollo has finished: 'That strain I heard was of a higher mood'; the 'higher mood' or 'mode' is a matter of genre as well as tone and theme, as in the description of the fallen angels on the move in *Paradise Lost*, i. 549–52: 'anon they move / In perfect phalanx to the Dorian mode / Of flutes and soft recorders; such as raised / To height of noblest temper heroes old'. The 'uncouth swain' sings a 'Dorick lay' or pastoral tune at the end of 'Lycidas', but the poet looks forward to the graver 'Dorian mode' of heroic verse. There is a recollection of the opening of 'E. K.''s preface to *The Shepheardes Calender* (1579), announcing Spenser as

this our new Poete, who for that he is uncouthe (as said Chaucer) is unkist, and unknown to most men, is regarded but of few. But I doubt not, so soone as his name shall come into the knowledg of men, and his worthines be sounded in the tromp of fame, but that he shall be not only kiste, but also beloved of all, embraced of the most, and wondred at of the best. (sig. ii^r)

Carey notes 'seven or eight echoes of Spenser' in 'Lycidas', all but one of which are from *The Shepheardes Calender* (*CSP*, 239). Spenser provided Milton with a native, Protestant example of a poet who had followed a Virgilian route from pastoral to vernacular Christian epic, securing the 'fair guerdon' (a distinctively Spenserian phrase) of earthly poetic fame.[38]

It has been argued at length that Marlowe consciously adopted the model of Ovid's 'counter-Virgilian' literary career (love elegy, tragedy, erotic 'minor epic') in reaction to and critique of Spenser's Virgilian pretensions to the title of England's national and imperial poet.[39] Whether or not we are convinced by this—there is little evidence of any early modern notion of a specifically Ovidian *cursus*—Milton's incorporation and subordination of an Ovidian and Marlovian ethos in several of the major early poems, and in the process of presenting himself as an evolving national poet in the

---

[38] See *The Faerie Queene*, ed. Thomas P. Roche (Harmondsworth, 1987), I. x. 59: 'That glorie does to them for guerdon graunt'.

[39] Patrick Cheney, *Marlowe's Counterfeit Possession: Ovid, Spenser, and Counter-Nationhood* (Toronto, 1997).

mode of Virgil and Spenser in the 1645 *Poems* as a whole, lends some credence to the notion that English poets thought about their career paths in the opposing terms of Ovidian and Virgilian, and indeed Marlovian and Spenserian.[40] Given the finally Spenserian allegiance of 'Lycidas', the second 'digression', St Peter's attack on clerical corruption, is not really the disruption of pastoral generic decorum that the poet suggests when he refers to St Peter as the 'dread voice' that shrinks the streams of pastoral lyricism (l. 132). As Thomas Warton first recognized in his eighteenth-century commentary, the anticlerical complaint of 'Lycidas' is indebted to the example of the May eclogue in *The Shepheardes Calender*, in which the zealous shepherd Piers attacks his rival Palinode, the 'false shepherd ... under whom', as Milton himself puts it in *Animadversions* (1641), 'the poet lively personates our prelates, whose whole life is a recantation of their pastoral vow, and whose profession to forsake the world, as they use the matter, bogs them deeper into the world: those our admired Spenser inveighs against, not without some presage of these reforming times' (*CPW*, i. 722).[41]

The Virgilian and Spenserian career model 'foregrounds the poet's public role in the multi-sphered life of the nation'.[42] In this respect St Peter's attack on clerical corruption embodies the birth pains of Milton's career as national poet. That career path would hardly have been apparent to Cambridge readers of 'Lycidas' by 'J. M.' in 1638; they would have been more likely to recognize the allusion to the digression on the lowliness of scholars in Marlowe's *Hero and Leander*, which, as we have seen, had become a favourite touchstone of Cambridge literary culture. But 'Lycidas' was turned into an explicit 'presage of these reforming times' in the headnote added in 1645, presumably (but not certainly) by Milton (although his authorship is suggested by its retention in the 1673 *Poems*), which claims 'Lycidas' as evidence both of the poet's burgeoning prophetic powers and as a response to a public as much as a personal moment: 'And by occasion foretells the ruin of our corrupted clergy then in their height.' 'Amaryllis has metamorphosed into ecclesiastical sinecure but the principle is the same': 'Church-outed by the Prelats', Milton would reject a clerical career in a corrupt church as he rejected a Cavalier literary career writing *carpe diem* lyrics (*CPW*, i. 822–3). *Hero and Leander* would become a favourite among defeated royalists, though its psychological exploration of sexuality was exaggerated and travestied in reaction to the perceived domination of Puritan moralism.[43]

---

[40] See e.g. the discussion of Spenser's occasional adoption of Ovidian rather than Virgilian models of poetic authority, depending on the vagaries of his relationship to the court, in Syrithe Pugh, *Spenser and Ovid* (Aldershot, 2005). For an account of the late Milton's positive view of Ovid in *Paradise Lost*, or at least of the *Metamorphoses*, see Charles Martindale, 'Paradise Metamorphosed: Ovid in Milton', *Comparative Literature*, 37 (1985), 301–33.

[41] John N. King, *Milton and Religious Controversy: Satire and Polemic in Paradise Lost* (Cambridge, 2000), 25.

[42] Patrick Cheney, '"Joy on, joy on": European Career Paths', in Patrick Cheney (ed.), *European Literary Careers: The Author from Antiquity to the Renaissance* (Toronto, 2002), 3–23 at 9.

[43] Roy Booth, 'Hero's Afterlife: Hero and Leander and "lewd unmannerly verse" in the Late Seventeenth Century', *Early Modern Literary Studies*, 12/3 (2007), 4.1–24 <http://purl.oclc.org/emls/12-3/booth2.htm>.

Yet when Milton returned to England in July 1639, he also returned to the mode of (neo-Latin) pastoral funeral elegy to commemorate the early death of Diodati in *Epitaphium Damonis*, and it is with this poem that he chooses to close the *Poemata*. Writing in the language in which he and Diodati had always communicated and in which he tends to be at his most open, Milton engages more directly, and notably more confidently after his successful navigation of the dangers of Italy, with the themes of moral reward and Virgilian ambition that he had broached obliquely in 'Lycidas'. The heavenly apotheosis of Damon/Diodati is a consequence of, and implicitly compensation for, his sexual purity:

Because the blush of modesty and a youth without stain [*et sine labe juventus*] were your choice, and because you never tasted the delight of the marriage bed [*quod nulla tori libata voluptas*], see—virginal honours are reserved for you! Your radiant head circled with a gleaming crown, the joyful, shady branches of leafy palm in your hands, you will take part for ever in the immortal marriage-rite, where singing is heard and the lyre rages in the midst of the ecstatic dances, and where the festal orgies rave in Bacchic frenzy under the thyrsus of Zion. (ll. 212–19)

'[B]lush of modesty' (*purpureus pudor*) is taken from the third elegy of the first book of Ovid's *Amores*, in which the speaker vows fidelity to his mistress and suggests (quite disingenuously, as we soon discover as we read on) that the reasons she should respond include, as Marlowe has it in the first and rather free English translation: 'My spotless life, which but to gods gives place, / Naked simplicity, and modest grace' (ll. 13–14). In *Epitaphium Damonis* the very physical terms of classical love elegy dissolve into the allegorical language of Revelation ('a great multitude . . . stood before the throne, and before the Lamb, clothed with white robes, and palms in their hands' (7: 9)) enacting linguistically the Christianizing of a pagan sexual abandon that, it transpires, was anyway never more for Diodati than a literary motif: 'purpureus pudor' is snatched from its context and made a motor of ascent to the celestial marriage feast with Christ promised in Revelation. '[E]t sine labe juventus' recalls, surely very deliberately, 'et sine labe manus' from the character of the *vates* in Elegy VI. The distinction made in Elegy VI between Milton the epic, priestly poet and Diodati the elegiac, promiscuous poet is collapsed as Milton and Diodati are revealed as equally untainted by earthly sexuality (though the latter's purity is only apparent in death). Diodati's transient lyric feasts are translated to the eternity of the heavens precisely because he has not 'tasted the delight (*voluptas*) of the marriage bed'. *Torus*, the term Carey renders as 'marriage bed', is in fact used frequently by Ovid in the *Amores* to refer simply to the bed or couch in which sex, of a more or less illicit nature, takes place, as in the opening lines of one of Marlowe's most successfully erotic renderings of the *Amores*, the fifth elegy of the first book: 'In summer's heat and mid-time of the day / To rest my limbes upon a bed I lay' ('Aestus erat, mediamque dies exegerat horam; / adposui medio membra levanda toro'). Diodati finds eternal reward for containing his attraction to Ovidian eroticism to poetic topoi.

Epitaphium Damonis recalls Elegy VI in first displaying Milton's mastery and then renunciation of a neo-Latin lyric genre. The poet announces his intention to turn to heroic verse on a national theme:

Give place, woods. 'Go home, unfed lambs, your shepherd has no time for you now.' I shall tell of Trojan keels ploughing the sea off the Kentish coast . . . I shall tell of Igraine, pregnant with Arthur as a result of fatal deception: I shall tell of the lying features which misled her, and of the borrowing of Gorlois's armour, Merlin's trick. O, if I have any time left to live, you, my pastoral pipe, will hang far away on the branch of some old tree, utterly forgotten by me, or else, transformed by my native muses, you will rasp out a British tune. (ll. 161–71)

'Give place, woods' alludes once more to Gallus' farewell to pastoral life in Virgil's tenth eclogue, while the image of the pastoral pipe or *fistula* is taken from Corydon's renunciation of pastoral verse in the seventh eclogue: 'The prise of artful numbers I resign, / And hang my pipe upon the sacred pine' (ll. 33–4). Milton's vision of an Arthurian subject for his future epic makes clear the immediate vernacular model of Spenser and his Virgilian progress to *The Faerie Queene* (1590–1610). The envisaged shift here is linguistic as well as generic: in the moment of his most consummate Latin poem, Milton declares not only his renunciation of pastoral lyric (explicitly, whereas in 'Lycidas' the anticipated development remains implicit, signalled by allusion) but of Latin as a poetic language. *Epitaphium Damonis* follows Elegy VI and 'Lycidas' in its use of classical poetic tradition—pastoral, love elegy—'not merely as a passive container for the poem but as an active metaphor'.[44] Ovidian erotic languages, whether in Latin or the vernacular, and encompassing Marlovian language in the companion poems, the *Maske*, and 'Lycidas', become in the context of the 1645 *Poems* an active metaphor—political as well as literary, at least by 1645— through which Milton seeks to convey his transcendence of these languages and their foreclosed pagan vision.

[44] R. W. Condee, 'The Latin Poetry of John Milton', in J. W. Binns (ed.), *The Latin Poetry of English Poets* (London and Boston, 1974), 58–92 at 82.

CHAPTER 7

THE TROUBLED, QUIET ENDINGS OF MILTON'S ENGLISH SONNETS

JOHN LEONARD

WORDSWORTH thought that Milton used the sonnet as 'a trumpet, whence he blew / Soul-animating strains'.[1] It is true that Milton begins some sonnets with a clarion call ('Fairfax, whose name', 'Cromwell, our chief', 'Avenge O Lord', etc.), and Wordsworth recreates this effect when he trumpets a soul-animating strain in Milton's honour: 'Milton! thou shouldst be living at this hour'.[2] But we should not imagine that Milton's sonnets, even the political ones, are all blaring brass. Yes, they have epic grandeur, but they also have fragile notes, especially in the sestets. Milton's sonnets, like his long poems, are renowned for their 'quiet' endings, and it is these that I propose to examine. The word 'quiet' is in some ways misleading, for the endings of Milton's sonnets have excited much noisy chatter. Critics disagree even as to their basic meaning. Discussion is usually focused on the last two or three lines. Everyone agrees that Milton's sonnets end on a note of calm, but few people seem to experience it. Critics *worry* at the endings—pulling and prodding at them in an effort to make them make sense. Some complain that they are enigmatic, elliptical, or opaque. Others praise them for their 'ambiguity'. A key figure in the latter critical tradition

---

[1] 'Scorn not the sonnet', in *Poetical Works of William Wordsworth*, ed. E. de Selincourt and Helen Darbishire, 2nd edn., 5 vols. (Oxford, 1952–63), iii. 21.

[2] 'London 1802', in *Poetical Works*, iii. 116.

is Stanley Fish, whose essay 'Interpreting the *Variorum*' has had great influence.[3] But Fish (unlike many who cite him) never uses the word 'ambiguous' when discussing Milton's sonnets, and he concludes his essay by declining to credit Milton with any intended poetic effects. I am indebted to Fish, and shall return to him at the end of this essay when I discuss Milton's sonnet to Edward Lawrence and its famous crux concerning the word 'spare'. But Fish's interests differ from mine. His thesis is that critics make the meanings they think they discover. My aim is to explore the endings of Milton's sonnets and the tensions they create (in themselves and us) by their opposed impulses towards opacity and tranquility.

I do not claim that every sonnet by Milton ends in difficulty. Some close with a simple *diminuendo*: 'Dante shall give fame leave to set thee higher / Than his Casella, whom he wooed to sing / Met in the milder shades of Purgatory' (Sonnet XIII, 'To Mr H. Lawes', ll. 12–14). There has been some disagreement as to whether 'milder' there means 'milder than hell' or 'milder than other parts of Purgatory', but this debate has itself been so mild that I shall have nothing more to say about it. I shall concentrate on sonnets that have provoked sharp disagreement. My question is: how do these poems manage to end so quietly while causing so much trouble? Critics have not ignored this question, but they have tended to ask it of individual poems in isolation from each other. The difficulties have consequently been seen as merely local, and there has been an (often tacit) assumption that it is the critic's task to remove them. I hope to show that difficulty is an integral part of the Miltonic sonnet, and contributes in no small measure to its special character.

F. T. Prince demonstrated some fifty years ago that the Italian poets Giovanni Della Casa and Torquato Tasso exerted a major influence on both the style and subject matter of Milton's sonnets. Most important for my purpose is the Italian technique of *asprezza*. 'The word *asprezza*, "roughness",' Prince writes, 'represents one of Tasso's overriding principles.' Tasso celebrates *asprezza* in his *Discorsi del poema eroico*, where he argues that it is essential to the epic poet's grandeur, and in his lecture on Della Casa's Sonnet LIX, where he identifies *asprezza* as that poet's distinguishing virtue—a virtue to which Tasso's *Sonetti eroici* also aspire. Prince defines *asprezza* as 'difficulty': 'all the devices of language and versification described by Tasso are intended to produce a certain difficulty, even an obscurity, in the sense, and an equivalent difficulty, even a roughness, in the sound'.[4] Tasso had likened such effects to walking over hard terrain. They 'are like one who stumbles, walking through rough paths: but this roughness suggests I know not what magnificence and grandeur'.[5] It is a pity, after these splendid comments, that Prince does not say more about *asprezza* in Milton's English sonnets. His tantalizingly brief chapter 'Milton's Sonnets' devotes

---

[3] Stanley Fish, 'Interpreting the *Variorum*', *Critical Inquiry*, 2 (1976), 465–85, repr. as ch. 6 of *Is There a Text in this Class?* (Cambridge, Mass., 1980), 147–73.

[4] F. T. Prince, *The Italian Element in Milton's Verse* (Oxford, 1954), 38.

[5] Tasso, *Discorsi del poema eroico* (1594), Book 5, trans. in Prince, 39. The Italian words that Prince renders 'rough' and 'roughness' are *aspre* and *asprezza*.

significant space to only one sonnet (IX) in English. Prince has added greatly to our understanding of Milton's sonnets by identifying *asprezza* as one of their key features, but his emphasis on 'roughness' and 'difficulty' tells only half the story. I hope to complement his argument by exploring some of the ways in which Milton's sonnets move through difficulty to calm. Yes, these poems make us stumble, but they also have a way of guiding our feet.

Let us start, then, with Sonnet VII. Here, as so often, debate has centred on the last two lines. The sonnet closes on a note of restful calm, but critics have gone to extraordinary lengths to stir things up. The challenge has been to wrest some kind of positive affirmation out of a conclusion that sounds resigned or resigning:

> How soon hath time the subtle thief of youth,
>   Stol'n on his wing my three and twentieth year!
>   My hasting dayes fly on with full career,
>   But my late spring no bud or blossom sheweth.
> Perhaps my semblance might deceive the truth,
>   That I to manhood am arrived so near,
>   And inward ripeness doth much less appear,
>   That some more timely-happy spirits endueth.
> Yet be it less or more, or soon or slow,
>   It shall be still in strictest measure even,
>   To that same lot, however mean or high,
> Toward which time leads me, and the will of heaven;
>   All is, if I have grace to use it so,
>   As ever in my great task-master's eye.

In 1870 R. C. Browne paved the way for all subsequent commentators by resorting to aggressive paraphrase. He intuited an antithesis between 'It shall be' (l. 10) and 'All is' (l. 13). Milton 'had said, "It shall be"; now he corrects himself—"nay, all my life is so already, if I have grace to use it as in God's sight" '.[6] Kester Svendsen agrees that 'All is' is the key, but he refers the phrase forward, not back: 'All that matters is whether I have grace to use my ripeness in accordance with the will of God as one ever in his sight.'[7] A. S. P. Woodhouse reinforces this reading by reorienting 'so' ('All is, if I have grace to use it so'), so it too faces forward, and he is undeterred by the awkward detail that 'so' is immediately followed by a comma: 'And as to the punctuation, can we...be sure that a comma did not intrude itself after *so* in 1645 and escape detection...? A colon would clarify the probable meaning: "All <that matters> is: whether I have grace to use it so, as ever <conscious of being> in my great Task-master's <enjoining> eye." '[8] All three critics agree that Sonnet VII ends with the heartening affirmation that Milton can and probably will achieve great things if he

---

6 *English Poems by John Milton*, ed. R. C. Browne, 2 vols. (1870; repr. Oxford, 1906), i. 265.

7 Kester Svendsen, 'Milton's "On His Having Arrived at the Age of Twenty-Three"', *Explicator* 7/7 (May 1949), item 53.

8 *A Variorum Commentary on Poems of John Milton*, gen. ed. Merritt Y. Hughes, 6 vols. (New York, 1970–). See vol. ii, *The Minor English Poems*, ed. A. S. P. Woodhouse and Douglas Bush, Pt. 2, 372.

behaves himself and remains 'ever' vigilant. The appeal of this line of interpretation is that it chimes with the common perception of Milton as an egocentric poet with a strong sense of vocation. 'The present life, and the right use of every moment of it', avers E. M. W. Tillyard,

were Milton's principal concern. Now, a belief that every moment is critical, that every action is irrevocable and determining, must heighten the pressure at which life is lived. Life will have nothing of routine in it, but will consist of one gala performance, never to be repeated. A man holding such beliefs will be in the temper to do heroic deeds.[9]

For Browne, Svendsen, and Woodhouse, 'As ever in my great task-master's eye' exalts just such a heroic temper, affirming the momentous importance of 'every moment'. Not everyone seeks to 'heighten the pressure' in this way. Donald C. Dorian suggests a quasi-substantive use of 'ever' as 'eternity' and paraphrases 'All time is, if I have grace to use it so, as eternity in God's sight'.[10] This reading at least aims at a quiet ending, but it too introduces difficulties. It strains grammar by forcing an adverb to work as a noun. All the readings we have so far considered make sense, but all are forced to press their sense upon us by exerting maladroit pressure on particular words (*is*, *so*, *ever*).

My own view is that the ending of Sonnet VII works to release pressure, not heighten it. To appreciate this sense of release we need to look more closely at the preceding pressures. There is a small but significant difference between the printed and manuscript versions of this poem. I have cited Carey's edition, which prints a comma after 'even' at the end of line 10. This comma appears in the printed editions of 1645 and 1673, but not in the Trinity manuscript. Most modern editions print the comma, but it is worth considering how the meaning changes if we leave it out. Editors generally agree that 'even' means 'level with, neither higher nor lower' (*OED*, 5a). This meaning is present with or without the comma, but if we omit the comma an additional sense emerges. As E. A. J. Honigmann notes, 'The comma suggests "It shall be always in strictest measure evenly-paced, proceeding to that same lot"; the MS suggests "... in strictest measure, even to that same lot".'[11] The (now archaic) idiom 'even to' was coined in the sixteenth century in imitation of Latin *usque ad* ('all the way to'). Shakespeare uses it in his sonnets, most memorably in CXVI, when he avers that love 'bears it out even to the edge of doom' (l. 12). Milton also has frequent recourse to the phrase, both in his early poems ('even to nakedness', 'even to ecstasy') and his epics ('even to the deep', 'Even to my mouth', 'even to the death').[12] The case we are now considering is different in that a line break separates

[9] E. M. W. Tillyard, *Milton* (1930), 290.

[10] Donald C. Dorian, 'Milton's "On His Having Arrived at the Age of Twenty-Three"', *Explicator* 8/2 (Nov. 1949), item 10.

[11] E. A. J. Honigmann, *Milton's Sonnets* (1966), 99.

[12] 'Upon the Circumcision', l. 20; *A Maske*, l. 624; *PL*, iii. 586 and v. 83; *PR*, i. 264. Other instances could be cited.

'even' from 'To', but this only heightens the tension. It is as if the onward rush of 'even to' were interrupted by an abrupt edge (the edge of doom):

> Into this wild abyss the wary fiend
> Stood on the brink of hell and looked awhile,
> Pondering his voyage; for no narrow frith
> He had to cross. (*PL*, ii. 917–20)

Milton in Sonnet VII also stands 'Pondering his voyage', and the pointing of line 10 has implications for his state of mind. If we keep the comma, he hesitates 'on the brink', looking warily. If we let the line run on, the implication is that Milton too will run on 'even / To that same lot, however mean or high'.

The question arises as to which version an editor should choose. In my 1998 Penguin edition I chose to omit the comma, and I stand by that decision, even though I think Milton put it there. I would not say of this comma (as Woodhouse says of the one in line 13) that it crept in by accident. I suspect that Milton added it in 1645 because time had now stolen his seven-and-thirtieth year. A bold *usque ad* suits a promising young man of twenty-three or twenty-four, but it cannot be uttered without incongruity by a man in his late thirties who continues to live on promises. The 1645 volume is a significant achievement, but it is not what the younger poet had had in mind when he wrote 'even / To', so his older self adds a comma, still steering right onward, but now on a more even keel.

Both versions 'heighten the pressure', but they do so in different ways. With the comma, line 10 is taut and restrained; without it, it surges eagerly forward, slipping the leash of 'strictest measure'. In either case the last three lines dissolve into a long, breathy sigh:

> It shall be still in strictest measure even[,]
> To that same lot, however mean or high,
> Toward which time leads me, and the will of heaven;
> All is, if I have grace to use it so,
> As ever in my great task-master's eye. (ll. 10–15)

The effect is achieved partly by the slant rhyme of 'even' and 'heaven', partly by the intervening aspirates, and partly by the languid grammar and syntax of line 12, where 'heaven' assumes the nominative case with lordly ease. Most effective is the sequence 'even . . . heaven . . . ever', with its gradual relaxing and opening of vowels and consonants. Yes, the final line suggests that God is 'ever' watchful, so Milton had better watch his step, but it also suggests the absurdity of trying to impress God with a 'gala performance'. Read quietly, the lines just relax and let go: 'All is . . . As ever'. We destroy this quiet if we import tortuous syntax and fretful urgings.

Sonnet XI ('A book was writ of late called *Tetrachordon*') also moves through difficulty to calm resignation, but here the effect is different since frustration is tempered with wry humour. Milton's sardonic eye has been on ill-educated readers who, browsing the booksellers' shops in St Paul's Churchyard, pick up his divorce pamphlet *Tetrachordon*—and fail to understand even the title:

> Cries the stall-reader, Bless us! what a word on
>   A title-page is this! And some in file
>   Stand spelling false, while one might walk to Mile-
> End Green. Why is it harder sirs than Gordon,
> Colkitto, or Macdonnel, or Galasp?
>   Those rugged names to our like mouths grow sleek
>   That would have made Quintilian stare and gasp,
> Thy age, like ours, O soul of Sir John Cheke,
>   Hated not learning worse than toad or asp;
>   When thou taught'st Cambridge, and King Edward Greek. (ll. 5–14)

The humour is delicious, but we too 'stand spelling false' as soon as we try to decipher those last five lines. Is Milton's age like or unlike that of Sir John Cheke? Was Sir John's age propitious or antagonistic to learning? And how does Quintilian fit in? Is his imagined gasp provoked by Scottish names alone (as editors inform us, citing *Institutio Oratoria*, 1. 5. 8, on 'barbarisms') or might it extend to all foreign words—even (*horribile dictu*) Greek ones like *Tetrachordon*? The lines are not impenetrable, but they present difficulties—and they do so in a way that is strangely understated and quiet.

Let us start with the age of Sir John Cheke, English humanist and tutor to Edward VI. Masson took 'like ours' to mean 'your age did not hate learning *as ours does*'.[13] The difficulty with this is that it effectively glosses 'like' as 'unlike'. Smart therefore gave the opposite reading and paraphrased 'Many men in that age, which has been thought so propitious to such studies, hated not learning worse than toad or asp, — but as much as they hated either'.[14] Where Masson contrasts Cheke's learned age with Milton's crass one, Smart draws a parallel between Cheke and Milton: two lonely scholars guarding the fort of learning against the barbarian hordes. Both readings have won support. Schultz supports Smart by citing sixteenth- and seventeenth-century authors (including Cheke) who bemoaned the decay of learning in Cheke's age; French supports Masson by citing *Tetrachordon*, which praises the reign of Edward VI as 'the purest and sincerest that ever shon yet on the reformation of this Iland'.[15] Nardo offers more support to Masson when she remarks how the sonnet's ending 'lifts the reader above the noisy pamphlet warfare of a dull age by invoking an earlier one of great learning and zealous reform'.[16] That rings true. The sonnet's conclusion would have little point if it did not make some kind of contrast. Here, as in the conclusion to Sonnet VIII ('Captain or colonel'), the sestet withdraws from the bustle and noise of Civil War London to a quieter, more cultured time. But even as he yearns for this ideal past when scholars were appreciated and understood, Milton manages to make himself *mis*understood. Quintilian would have stared and

---

[13] *The Poetical Works of John Milton*, ed. David Masson, 3 vols. (1890), iii. 283.

[14] *The Sonnets of Milton*, ed. J. S. Smart (Oxford, 1921), 63.

[15] Howard Schultz, 'A Book Was Writ of Late . . .', *Modern Language Notes*, 69 (1954), 495–7; J. Milton French, 'A Comment on "A Book Was Writ of Late"', *Modern Language Notes*, 70 (1955), 404–5. The passage French cites from *Tetrachordon* tells strongly for his side in this debate. See *CPW*, ii. 716.

[16] Anna K. Nardo, *Milton's Sonnets and the Ideal Community* (Lincoln, Nebr. and London, 1979), 81.

gasped, for he was an ardent champion of perspicuity who had insisted that the orator's aim was not merely 'to make understanding possible, but to make misunderstanding impossible'.[17] Milton falls short of Quintilian's standards when he writes 'like' but means 'unlike'.

So why does he do it? Some might conclude that he was inept, but we must consider the possibility that he knew what he was up to. 'Like' appears twice in Sonnet XI, and both occurrences make us stumble. Just two lines before 'Thy age, like ours' there is a parallel problem in 'Those rugged names to our like mouths grow sleek'. Why *like* mouths? The whole point about the Scottish names (all commentators agree) is that they are uncouth. As Smart notes: 'The Civil War had made Englishmen acquainted with many Scottish names, both of Cavaliers and Covenanters, which seemed strange and harsh' (pp. 61–2). The harshness is still more evident in the cancelled draft of this line in the Trinity manuscript, which first read 'barbarous', then 'rough hewn', and finally 'rugged'. If Scottish names are so barbarous, why say that English mouths are 'like' them? Woodhouse tries to get around the problem by reading 'like' as an adverb: '*to our like mouths*, i.e. in our utterance, which has grown likewise *rugged*'.[18] The appeal of this (for English readers) is that it implies that English mouths were sleek until broad and barbarous Scots contaminated them. But Milton's lines do not say this. In Milton's version, it is Scottish names, not English mouths, that 'grow sleek', and there is no indication that the mouths were ever anything other than 'rugged'. We should at least entertain the possibility that Milton meant what he said. We should not overestimate the esteem in which he held English mouths. In *Of Education*, written just a few years before this sonnet, Milton had declared: 'we Englishmen being farre northerly, doe not open our mouthes in the cold air, wide enough to grace a Southern tongue; but are observ'd by all other nations to speak exceeding close and inward' (*CPW*, ii. 383). It may be that the Scots, being even more 'northerly', are even less inclined to open wide, but the English would still be well advised to keep their mouths shut when 'other nations' debate the topic of sleek and rugged utterances.

I have dwelt on 'sleek' and 'rugged' in Sonnet XI because the endings of Milton's sonnets have their own way of turning gnarled ruggedness into sleek resolution. I again invoke F. T. Prince and *asprezza*. Prince never specifically mentions Sonnet XI in his chapter 'Milton's Sonnets', but it is no doubt this poem (and its companion Sonnet XII, as well as the tailed sonnet 'On the New Forcers') that he is thinking of when he remarks that Milton's sonnets sometimes verge 'upon the mock-heroic', turning 'the stiff difficulty of the verse, the *asprezza* of the "magnificent" style, to a mocking purpose' (p. 103). In Sonnet XI this 'stiff difficulty' asserts itself in the calculated stumbling of the repeated 'like' and in the rough sound both of the

---

[17] 'Quare non, ut intelligere possit, sed, ne omnino possit non intelligere, curandum' (*Institutio Oratoria*, 8. 2. 24), from Quintilian, *Institutiones Oratoriae*, ed. Daniel Pareus (1641), 360.

[18] *A Variorum Commentary*, ii/2, 391.

Scottish names and of *Tetrachordon* itself, which Milton (with endearing self-parody) tacitly acknowledges to be just as hard, though no harder ('Why is it harder sirs') than the names it is 'like'.

Sonnet XII also moves through difficulty to calm, but here the going is rougher, for the emotional terrain is one of anger, not bemusement. The topic is once again the public reception of Milton's divorce pamphlets:

> I did but prompt the age to quit their clogs
>   By the known rules of ancient liberty,
>   When straight a barbarous noise environs me
>   Of owls and cuckoos, asses, apes and dogs.
> As when those hinds that were transformed to frogs
>   Railed at Latona's twin-born progeny
>   Which after held the sun and moon in fee.
>   But this is got by casting pearl to hogs;
> That bawl for freedom in their senseless mood,
>   And still revolt when truth would set them free.
>   Licence they mean when they cry liberty:
> For who loves that, must first be wise and good;
>   But from that mark how far they rove we see
>   For all this waste of wealth, and loss of blood.

Most commentators take 'For all' in the final line to mean 'in spite of', but Lee Cox has argued that 'for' means 'in consequence of' (*OED* 22).[19] If the majority view is correct, Milton is voicing the complaint (shared by many Parliamentary soldiers) that the Civil War has failed to achieve the ends for which it was fought. If Cox is right, Milton's complaint is not that the war has lost its purpose but that it has happened. The debate about 'For' has implications for another question about Sonnet XII: 'Who meant "licence" when they cried "liberty"?' Nathaniel Henry in 1951 made that question the title of an essay that still has influence today.[20] According to Henry, Sonnet XII is aimed not against the Presbyterian detractors of Milton's divorce tracts but against the ignorant enthusiasts who embraced Milton's views all too eagerly. Few have accepted Henry's view that the sectaries are Milton's sole target, but many have been persuaded that Sonnet XII collapses the distinction between declared foes and false friends. Even Christopher Hill, who wants to ally Milton with the radical sects, concedes that Sonnet XII is 'double-edged'.[21]

My own view is that Sonnet XII can and should be sharpened away from ambiguity. A key word is 'revolt' ('still revolt when truth would set them free'). Those who identify the sects as Milton's target point out that it was they, not the Presbyterians,

---

[19] Lee Sheridan Cox, 'Milton's "I Did but Prompt", ll. 13–14', *English Language Notes*, 3 (Dec. 1965), 102–4.

[20] Nathaniel H. Henry, 'Who Meant Licence when They Cried Liberty?', *Modern Language Notes*, 67 (1957), 509–13.

[21] Christopher Hill, *Milton and the English Revolution* (London, 1977), 160. Nardo shares Hill's view that Milton targets both 'Presbyterians' and 'the Independent lunatic fringe' (p. 73).

who *revolted*. This interpretation assumes that 'revolt' has its modern sense 'rise against a constituted authority' (*OED* 1). Milton may glance at this sense to hint that the Presbyterians are the true rebels, but I submit that in Sonnet XII 'revolt' has the opposite sense: 'to draw back *from* a course of action . . . to return to one's allegiance' (*OED* 2b). This sense is now obsolete, but both meanings were current in Milton's lifetime. The English language is rich in words that mean the opposite of themselves, and such words were especially charged during the Civil War. The first English dictionary, Robert Cawdrey's *A Table Alphabetical* (1604), defines 'reuolt' as 'forsake one, to goe to another his enemie'. This definition accommodates both semantic extremes, since people of all political persuasions are capable of forsaking or being forsaken. But political divisions had widened between 1604 and 1645, and by the time Milton wrote Sonnet XII the opposed senses of 'revolt' scowled at each other over an unbridgeable gulf. Milton when he wrote this poem did not know that only one of the two senses would survive. We must therefore make an imaginative effort to hear the sense 'backslide'. Milton in his prose uses 'revolt' in just this sense to condemn the weak-willed for failing to take political reforms far enough. In *The Tenure of Kings and Magistrates* he chides the Presbyterians for their pusillanimous unwillingness to call Charles Stuart to account. Having 'born armes against thir King, devested him, disannointed him, nay curs'd him all over in their Pulpits and Pamphlets . . . beyond what is possible or honest to retreat from', these false revolutionaries now 'turne revolters from those principles' (*CPW*, iii. 191). In *The Readie and Easie Way*, Milton chides the newly royalist Presbyterians for 'revolting from the conscience of deeds welldon both in church and state'. 'By thus relapsing', he continues, they 'verifie all the bitter predictions of our triumphing enemies' (*CPW*, vii. 422). In these instances 'revolt' is synonymous with 'retreat' and 'relapse'. I submit that that is also the meaning in Sonnet XII, where it is Milton's detractors, not his admirers, who 'bawl for freedom in their senseless mood, / And still revolt when truth would set them free'. Milton has offered the detractors the freedom they have bawled for, but still they 'revolt'—by bending the supple knee.

I first made this argument about 'revolt' in 1996.[22] I still think it holds up, but I am now willing to admit that Sonnet XII forces us to negotiate difficulties before we arrive at the correct conclusion. Milton has a clear target, and he hits it, but he takes the *risk* of friendly fire, and this is troubling—especially in a poem that condemns poor marksmanship ('from that mark how far they rove we see'). Even if we insist (as I do) that it is critics' misprision, not Milton's confusion, that has turned Sonnet XII on its head, critics like Henry could still retort that Milton has asked for the trouble he has got. He has asked for it. But he has also prepared for it in the structure of this greatly innovative poem. Consider the rhymes. Uniquely among Milton's sonnets, Sonnet XII has just three. The rhyme scheme (abbaabbacbbcbc) is unusually confining, for the b rhyme ends no fewer than seven of the fourteen lines. It is a surprise when it pops up in the sestet, and it does so in the very line we have been considering,

---

22 John Leonard, 'Revolting as Backsliding in Milton's "Sonnet XII"', *Notes and Queries*, 24/3 (Sept. 1996), 269–73.

'And still revolt when truth would set them free'. The line does what it describes, for in the very moment when the known rules of ancient liberty permit an Italian sonnet the expressive freedom of a new rhyme, this sonnet 'revolts' (backslides) into an old one—and the first word it fetters is 'free'. The next line—'Licence they mean when they cry liberty'—then drives the point home by repeating the rhyme, the sense, and even the word that had first introduced the b rhyme at the end of line 2. 'Liberty' is forced to rhyme with itself. This is not clumsiness. Nothing could more effectively convey the detractors' slavishness than to have them shackle and enervate the noble words they utter. Nor should we miss the suggestive rhyme of 'free' with 'fee'. To 'hold in fee' is a legal term meaning 'hold as one's absolute and rightful possession' (*OED* 2b). The phrase is happy insofar as it refers to Apollo and Diana, but it is also ominous, for a 'fee' in English law is an estate held feudally of the crown, and a recollection of feudal relationships cannot but complicate a poem that yearns to be 'free'. This is one of but two instances of 'fee' (in this sense) in all of Milton's writings. The other occurs in *Colasterion* (one of the pamphlets this sonnet defends) where Milton mocks his adversary, 'a cock-braind Solliciter', for deploying the term 'Fee simple', which Milton contemptuously dismisses as 'gibbrish' (*CPW*, ii. 756). I submit that some memory of this moment in *Colasterion* colours the phrase 'held . . . in fee' in Sonnet XII. The irony is not at the expense of Milton's 'twin-born progeny' *Tetrachordon* and *Colasterion*, but at the expense of the detractors whose bawling mouths turn even words like 'liberty' and 'free' into 'gibbrish'. The c rhyme is also suggestive, for while it comes three times ('mood', 'good', 'blood'), no two instances sound the same. This rhyme is for the eye only—unlike the relentless b rhyme, which keeps harping on the same note. To my ears, this contrast is mimetic of the detractors' roving. They aim at the right mark (liberty), but their bad marksmanship turns 'good' into 'blood'. To return to Cox's reading of the last line: I have no doubt that 'For all' means 'in spite of', not 'in consequence of', but Cox's misreading is still strangely true to this sonnet's sense of waste. Milton does not condemn the war, but he warns that it is in danger of becoming pointless. It ought to bring freedom, but backsliding revolters are robbing it of meaning by reimposing the fetters of the familiar. Some might think my close reading overly ingenious, but it accords with the imagination of a poet for whom sonnets, no less than pamphlets, were 'woven close, both matter, form and style'.

I do not mean to exaggerate the complexity of Milton's sonnets. Sometimes a troubled, quiet ending can be achieved by simple means. In Sonnet XIV ('When faith and love which parted from thee never') one word is enough to add unexpected depth and resonance. The word is 'speak' (l. 12), but there is some textual uncertainty as to whether the correct form should be 'speak' or 'spake':

> When faith and love which parted from thee never,
>   Had ripened thy just soul to dwell with God,
>   Meekly thou didst resign this earthy load
>   Of death, called life; which us from life doth sever,
> Thy works and alms and all thy good endeavour
>   Stayed not behind, nor in the grave were trod;

> But as faith pointed with her golden rod,
>   Followed thee up to joy and bliss for ever.
> Love led them on, and faith who knew them best
>   Thy handmaids, clad them o'er with purple beams
>   And azure wings, that up they flew so dressed,
> And speak the truth of thee on glorious themes
>   Before the judge, who thenceforth bid thee rest
>   And drink thy fill of pure immortal streams.

'Speak' accords with the 1673 printed edition, but all three drafts in the Trinity manuscript read 'spake', and many modern editors have adopted that version because it continues an unbroken sequence of past tenses from the preceding eleven lines. Carey nevertheless prints 'speak', and Woodhouse defends 'speak' on the grounds that line 12 signals a change from temporality to eternity: 'The reason for the change to *speak* (1673) is clear: what has gone before has happened, is concluded, while the speaking, the fame in heaven, continues.'[23] A. E. B. Coldiron supports this conclusion by suggesting that Milton changed 'spake' to 'speak' after he became a mortalist. When Milton first wrote the poem, shortly after Catharine Thomason's death in December 1646, he may have believed that her soul ascended to heaven at the moment of death, but by 1673 he believed that soul and body would be resurrected together at the Last Judgment. Coldiron suggests that the sudden shift of tenses moves the whole poem outside earthly time: 'the 1673 edition's change of "spake" to "speak" (12) makes perfect sense, and in fact becomes a felicitous one-word key to seeing apotheosis as part of an Augustinian eternal present'.[24] As with the comma after 'even' in Sonnet VII, a good case can be made for either the printed or the manuscript version, since each is right for its own moment in Milton's career. 'Speak' nevertheless has both a special advantage and a special disadvantage. It makes the poem's conclusion both quieter and more troubled. 'Speak' is quieter than 'spake' because it is less confident in telling us how it all happened, but it also forces us to make awkward adjustments. These extend to 'bid' in the next line. In the original version, 'bid' is the sonnet's culminating verb in the past tense and indicative mood.[25] In the revised version, 'bid' is no longer a simple past indicative indicating what God did. It is hard to tell just what part of speech 'bid' now is. If pressed, I would argue that it is a subjunctive expressing the wish that God *may* 'thenceforth bid thee rest', but I admit that other parsings are possible. The grammatical uncertainty makes us stumble, but it also creates a strange sense of peace that was absent from the manuscript version.

The next sonnets to lend themselves to my argument are XV ('Avenge O Lord') and XVI ('When I consider'), but I shall pass them over, since Fish has already examined

---

[23] *A Variorum Commentary*, ii/2, 409.

[24] A. E. B. Coldiron, 'Milton *in parvo*: Mortalism and Genre Transformation in Sonnet 14', *Milton Quarterly*, 28 (1994), 1–10 at 7.

[25] 'Bade' was the more usual form for the past tense, but Milton usually employs the alternative form 'bid'. Compare 'bid spare / The house of Pindarus' (Sonnet VIII, l. 10).

both with enviable acumen. Instead, I shall turn to Sonnet XVII and the famous crux concerning the meaning of 'spare' in line 13:

> Lawrence of virtuous father virtuous son,
>> Now that the fields are dank, and ways are mire,
>> Where shall we sometimes meet, and by the fire
>> Help waste a sullen day; what may be won
> From the hard season gaining: time will run
>> On smoother, till Favonius reinspire
>> The frozen earth; and clothe in fresh attire
>> The lily and rose, that neither sowed nor spun.
> What neat repast shall feast us, light and choice,
>> Of Attic taste, with wine, whence we may rise
>> To hear the lute well touched, or artful voice
> Warble immortal notes and Tuscan air?
>> He who of those delights can judge, and spare
>> To interpose them oft, is not unwise.

Is Milton advising his young friend to 'refrain' from frequent delights or to 'afford [time]' for them? The question first arose in 1859, when Thomas Keightley cast his vote for 'afford' with this note: 'spare, sc. time'. In 1882 Masson replied: 'interpreted by Mr. Keightley to mean "spare time to interpose them oft": but surely rather the opposite—"refrain from interposing them oft"'. For the next eighty years editors lined up on one side or the other. Smart in 1921 agreed with Masson; Honigmann in 1966 agreed with Keightley; Hughes in 1937 agreed with Masson, then in 1957 defected to Keightley; Woodhouse and Bush in 1972 disagreed with each other. After discussing the issue in a page-long note, Woodhouse concludes: 'it is plain that all the honours rest with Masson'. Bush's equally long addendum then interposes: 'In spite of the array of scholarly names, the case for "forbear to" may be thought much weaker, and the case for "spare time for" much stronger, than Woodhouse found them.'[26] Fish has famously cited 'this curious performance' as proof that 'evidence brought to bear in the course of formalist analyses . . . will always point in as many directions as there are interpreters; that is, not only will it prove something, it will prove anything'.[27] Fish is now often credited with discovering the ambiguity of 'spare' in Sonnet XVII, but Carey had anticipated him in his 1968 edition ('spare] The word is ambiguous') and he sticks to this view in his 1997 edition: 'The idea that the sonnet would be improved if the ambiguity were resolved seems questionable.'

Carey and Fish have persuaded most Miltonists to decide not to decide. But they have not persuaded everyone. In 1995 Niall Rudd chided Carey and Fish for having 'given up the struggle'. As Rudd sees it, critics have a responsibility to make their minds up, and Carey's word 'ambiguous' abdicates this responsibility. 'In earlier times', Rudd laments, 'such a conclusion would have been reached with regret, and Milton might have been criticized for an expression which left itself open to

---

[26] *A Variorum Commentary*, ii/2, 475.
[27] Fish, 'Interpreting the *Variorum*', 467; *Is There a Text in This Class?*, 150.

contradictory interpretations. But not now.'[28] Whatever one thinks of Rudd's nostalgia for 'earlier times', his tenacity is refreshing after editorial glosses like this: '*spare / To interpose*. Ambiguous—either refrain from or find time for.'[29] The problem with this kind of note is that it trots out the word 'ambiguous' in a flat-footed way that forecloses debate even as it claims to open it. William Empson, our greatest critic on ambiguity, would not have approved. He foresaw the danger and warned against it. 'An ambiguity', Empson writes in the final chapter of *Seven Types of Ambiguity*,

is not satisfying in itself, nor is it, considered as a device on its own, a thing to be attempted; it must in each case arise from, and be justified by, the peculiar requirements of the situation. On the other hand, it is a thing which the more interesting and valuable situations are more likely to justify. Thus the practice of 'trying not to be ambiguous' has a great deal to be said for it, and I suppose was followed by most of the poets I have considered. It is likely to lead to results more direct, more communicable, and hence more durable; it is a necessary safeguard against being ambiguous without proper occasion, and it leads to more serious ambiguities when such occasions arise.[30]

The key question is whether 'spare' in Sonnet XVII is a 'serious' ambiguity, 'justified' by 'proper occasion' and the 'requirements of the situation'. Rudd argues forcefully that it is not and that the whole debate has been 'an avoidable controversy' foisted on us by the lazy and wishful. I do not share this view, and in the remaining space I shall argue against it, but I hold Rudd's essay in high esteem and I applaud both his vigilance and his critical principles. Serious ambiguities should earn their keep.

Rudd comes down unequivocally on the side of 'refrain'. He makes a strong case, stronger than anyone before him, though the force of his argument depends not on new evidence but on his insistence that we should honestly confront the evidence already placed before us. He begins with grammar. Other critics, including Smart and Woodhouse, had deployed this argument, but they had done so in a muttered way (Woodhouse in a parenthesis). Rudd growls an ominous challenge: 'if...the advocates of "spare" = "afford time" wish to command any attention, they must adduce examples of "spare" used in that sense *with the infinitive*, and *without* any noun like "time." So far they have not done so' (p. 110). The point is strong, and I candidly confess that I have for the past twelve years been on the lookout for just such an example (even one would suffice), but have yet to find it. English usage (as is clear from even a cursory glance at *OED* 'spare' v. 6c) provides many instances of 'spare' with the infinitive in the sense 'forbear', but I have yet to encounter even one clear and unequivocal instance of 'spare' meaning 'afford' where the infinitive is not preceded by a noun such as 'time'. Bush had tried to get around this problem by arguing that Milton transcends the pedantry of mere grammarians. 'The absence of any "known precedent"', Bush assures us, 'is not fatal, since Milton's use of words and

---

[28] Niall Rudd, 'Milton, Sonnet XX—an Avoidable Controversy', *Hermathena*, 158 (1995), 109–15 at 109.

[29] *John Milton: A Critical Edition of the Major Works*, ed. Stephen Orgel and Jonathan Goldberg (Oxford, 1991), 783.

[30] William Empson, *Seven Types of Ambiguity* (1930), 235.

idioms is notoriously bold, and his usages cannot be limited by examples in the *OED*.[31] Rudd will have none of that. He counters that the lexical innovation perceived by Bush would be more than just 'bold'. 'In this case', he argues, the innovation would be 'quite unique (there are no previous, and no subsequent, examples); it would also contradict a well-established usage. In spite of Humpty Dumpty's famous principle, a critic has no right to invent a meaning, and then foist it onto a passage which clearly says something quite different' (p. 110). Rudd is on strong ground here, and his position is only strengthened by Bush's lordly disdain. But the case might not be quite so straightforward as he imagines. Most critics who champion 'afford' do not see Milton as boldly inventing a new meaning. Their claim is that the word 'time' is understood. When a word is grammatically 'understood', it is not as if it is not there, but as if it is. A form as tightly woven as the sonnet has frequent recourse to suggestive omissions. Compare: 'But you shall shine more bright in these conténts / Than unswept stone, besmeared with sluttish time'.[32] Here we must supply 'in' between 'Than' and 'unswept' if the compliment is not to be nugatory. If we fail to understand 'in', Shakespeare's lines draw a less than flattering comparison between the youth and a grimy old monument. Milton's sonnet is different in that it makes good sense without the unspoken word, but it is possible to infer unspoken words—and we do not violate grammar when we do so.

So do we have cause to infer 'time' in Sonnet XVII? I would answer in the negative, were it not for one thing: the pregnant white space interposed between 'spare' and 'To'. To judge this effect properly ('He who of those delights can judge, and spare / To interpose them oft, is not unwise'), we should try to imagine how different the lines would be if 'spare' were moved forward to the next line: 'he who of those delights can judge, / And spare to interpose them oft, is wise'. This hypothetical version settles immediately into grim self-denial. Milton's version reaches out for other possibilities even if it fails to apprehend them. I hesitate to call this effect 'ambiguous', since I do not see the issue as one of interpretative choice. If pressed, I would concede that Rudd's reading prevails, but it matters that it must exert itself to prevail. Let me illustrate the point with a cheeky parallel—'cheeky' because Rudd might justly retort that the lines I am about to quote work for his argument, not against it. They do. But it matters that they have to work. Sonnet XVII is not the only place in Milton's poetry where 'spare' and 'interpose' come together. There is a parallel instance in *Paradise Lost*, when Sin rushes between the bellicose antagonists Satan and Death. Satan then exclaims:

> So strange thy outcry, and thy words so strange
> Thou interposest, that my sudden hand
> Prevented spares to tell thee yet by deeds
> What it intends, till first I know of thee,
> What thing thou art. (ii. 737–40)

---

[31] *A Variorum Commentary*, ii/2, 475.
[32] Sonnet LV in *Shakespeare's Sonnets*, ed. Stephen Booth (New Haven and London, 1977), 48.

'Spares' here means 'forbears', but the interposition of 'tell' ('spares to tell thee') briefly awakens the other sense 'afford' to suggest that Satan will spare a moment for words, not deeds. His very next words ('yet by deeds') correct this impression by equating the telling with the doing, and we must make a quick adjustment to register the fact that Satan forbears (not affords) 'to tell' in this aggressive, physical sense. The momentary uncertainty is nevertheless suggestive. The effect would be different had Satan said 'spares to strike thee'. The sequence 'spares to tell thee yet by deeds' conveys the conflicting impulses that drive and restrain Satan's 'sudden hand'. 'Spares' also plays on 'shows mercy' to hint at Satan's power (Sin lives on his forbearance), and this threatening note continues in 'intends', which plays on the Latin sense 'stretch out' to hint at the potential reach of Satan's arm. Satan's utterance has its own long reach and he keeps us as well as Sin in suspense as to what he 'intends'. This moment has not been a textual crux, for the various senses of 'spare' eventually coalesce. But the sense 'afford' is activated, however fleetingly, and its activation has implications for Sonnet XVII.

Rudd's argument does not rest solely on grammar. He also reminds us that the sonnet's last two lines echo one of the *Disticha Catonis* ('Maxims of Cato'), familiar to Milton since his school days:

> Interpone tuis interdum gaudia curis,
> ut possis animo quemvis sufferere laborem.[33]
>
> ('Interpose delights sometimes amidst your cares,
> so you may bear any task with spirit.')

J. A. W. Bennett in 1963 first pointed out the parallel with Milton.[34] He did not enter the debate about 'spare', but J. C. Maxwell, replying to his letter in the *Times Literary Supplement*, concluded that 'one incidental result of Mr. Bennett's discovery . . . ought to be the final disappearance of the old belief that "spare to interpose" can mean "refrain from interposing"'.[35] V. Scholderer then replied that the Latin actually supports 'refrain', since *interdum* 'can only mean "occasionally" or "now and then"'.[36] Rudd agrees, and chides Maxwell for his 'careless error' in understanding *interdum* as *saepe* ('often'). But this argument cuts both ways. If Maxwell leans on the evidence by pushing *interdum* in the direction of *saepe*, Rudd also leans on it by pushing in the direction of *raro* ('seldom'). He even leans with italics: 'Interpose pleasures *occasionally* among your serious concerns' (p. 111). This is not playing fair. We need only shift those italics to appreciate the difference they make ('Interpose *pleasures* occasionally', etc.). 'Occasionally' (with or without italics) is in any case not the only possible rendering of *interdum*. Scholderer was selective when he claimed that *interdum* 'can only mean "occasionally" or "now and then"'.

---

[33] *Catonis Disticha* 3. 6, in *Minor Latin Poets*, trans. J. Wight Duff and Arnold M. Duff (1961). The present translation is my own, as I cannot stomach the Loeb translators' rendering of *Interpone* as 'sandwich'.

[34] J. A. W. Bennett, 'Milton's "Cato"', *Times Literary Supplement*, 5 Apr. 1963, p. 233.

[35] J. C. Maxwell, 'Milton's "Cato"', ibid., 26 Apr. 1963, p. 314.

[36] V. Scholderer, 'Milton's "Cato"', ibid., 10 May 1963, p. 341.

Lewis and Short offer three meanings, not two: 'sometimes, occasionally, now and then'.[37] Rudd and Scholderer ignore 'sometimes' (even when Rudd chides Maxwell for straying 'from *Lewis and Short*'), but we should not ignore it, for it opens up the middle ground. I shall return in a moment to 'sometimes'. Rudd goes on to tell us that Maxwell answered Scholderer 'with an evasive and disingenuous letter which did him no credit' (p. 111). This is unjust to Maxwell, whose reply to Scholderer is both creditable and credible. He begins by acknowledging the distinction between *inter-dum* and *saepe* (he denies having confused them), then goes on to make the crucial point that the lines from 'Cato' were 'a familiar dictum' that Milton's contemporaries and predecessors read as an invitation, not a warning.[38] If 'Cato' is relevant to Milton (and both sides agree he is), it matters how Milton's predecessors read him. Did they infer the cautionary admonition that Rudd infers? Here Rudd has his own way of being 'evasive'. He thinks he has disposed of Maxwell by exposing his alleged misunderstanding of *interdum*, but he does not address Maxwell's central point, which is that Milton's predecessors read 'Cato' in the way that Maxwell reads Milton. Rudd does not ignore these predecessors. He lists them in a footnote. But he does not engage with them. The one medieval translation of 'Cato' he cites does not help his case: 'Sumtyme among thi bysynesse / Melle solace, gamen and ioyowsnesse.' Rudd presumably infers a warning from 'Sumtyme'. I admit that 'Sumtyme' falls short of 'often', but it is still far on the hither side of a finger-wagging '*occasionally*'. The medieval translator uses three words ('solace, gamen and ioyowsnesse') to render the one word *gaudia*, and even manages to smuggle 'mery' into the second half of the translation (not quoted by Rudd): 'That thou may the lyghtlyker / With mery thouht thi travayll ber'.[39] To my ears, 'Sumtyme' sounds neutral—like Milton's 'sometimes' when he asks Lawrence 'where shall we sometimes meet[?]' (3). I submit that *interdum* clinches the case for neither side.

Rudd's essay is a valuable contribution and we should be grateful for it. He convinces me that there are good arguments for 'refrain'. But he does not convince me that 'refrain' has all the good arguments, and he does not convince me that the debate about 'spare' was 'avoidable'. I think the debate was both inevitable and desirable. I do not claim that it is irresolvable. On balance, I think that Rudd wins more points than he loses. But even if we acknowledge that he gets the better of the argument, Milton (not wayward critics) has solicited the argument. The sheer length of the controversy is evidence that the problem it addresses is real. Rudd's opening sentence encourages the notion that the debate about 'spare' has arisen only recently ('For two hundred years ... there is no evidence ... that the sonnet caused any perplexity'), but a debate that goes back to 1859 is venerable,

---

[37] Charlton T. Lewis and Charles Short, *A Latin Dictionary* (Oxford, 1879), 979.

[38] Maxwell, 'Milton's "Cato"', 357.

[39] Rudd cites the first half of this medieval translation in n. 9 (p. 115) at the end of a list of medieval references taken from Glending Olson, *Literature as Recreation in the Later Middle Ages* (Ithaca and London, 1982), 94. It is only fair to add that some of Olson's other analogues, especially Roger Bacon, do recommend a tempering of pleasure with restraint (p. 100). It may be that Rudd has chosen the wrong medieval example to support his case.

not faddish. Nor should we forget that the first critic to raise the issue reached the conclusion opposite to Rudd's. Both sides in this debate have deep roots.

But my main reason for thinking the problem real is that it chimes with parallel problems in Milton's other sonnets. Previous commentators have addressed this problem in isolation from the other sonnets and so failed to see how it accords with a frequent Miltonic practice. I see 'spare' in Sonnet XVII as another instance of *asprezza*—a difficulty that forces us to stumble along rough paths, yet for that very reason achieves a strange sense of calm, creating, in Tasso's words, 'I know not what magnificence and grandeur'.

> Hard are the ways of truth, and rough to walk,
> Smooth on the tongue discoursed, pleasing to the ear,
> And tunable as sylvan pipe or song;
> What wonder then if I delight to hear. (*Paradise Regained*, i. 478–81)

Satan's tribute to Jesus is also the perfect tribute to Milton's sonnets. 'Rough to walk', the endings of these poems are nonetheless 'tunable as sylvan pipe'. In a lesser poet, the semantic difficulties would be exasperating, and their resolution exhausting or claustrophobic. Milton's sonnets are frequently rough and sinewy, but their touch is light and choice as they warble immortal notes and Tuscan air.

PART III

CIVIL WAR PROSE, 1641–1645

THE ANTI-EPISCOPAL TRACTS: REPUBLICAN PURITANISM AND THE TRUTH IN POETRY

NIGEL SMITH

I

Milton's five tracts against the idea of bishops in the Church of England (published between May 1641 and April 1642) argue one essential point: that there is no justification for the position of bishop (as opposed to minister) in the blueprint for Christian churches to be found in the New Testament, and in the Pauline epistles in particular. Milton used the term 'prelate', a cleric of high rank and authority, often, but not as much as he did 'bishop'. In the context of the dispute between the bishops—and especially William Laud, Archbishop of Canterbury, with his conception of authoritarian episcopal rule—and the supporters of Puritanism in the Church and in

Parliament, Milton was writing in broad and not detailed defence of Presbyterianism, a non-episcopal system of church government based on a hierarchy of committees formed jointly by divines and laymen, and in favour of the relatively non-ceremonial worship and non-hierarchal church government that we associate with Puritanism. He writes in line with the 'Root and Branch' position (so called from a petition presented to Parliament on 11 December 1640, which he later claimed to have signed (*CPW*, i. 878)). In it was a demand for an abolition of episcopacy as opposed to a limitation of its powers, and the removal of the liturgy of the established church: the Book of Common Prayer. It may be that he was invited to write the first of these defences, *Of Reformation*, by a former tutor from Cambridge, Thomas Young, the most prominent of a group of divines who made a single author by joining their initials to form 'Smectymnuus'.[1] Before that Milton had apparently written the 'Postscript' to *An Answer to a Booke Entituled, An Humble Remonstrance* (20 March 1641), a list of immoral and corrupt aspects of episcopal behaviour in England since the founder of the See of Canterbury, Augustine. The 'Postscript' bears distinct affinities with *Of Reformation* and *Of Prelatical Episcopacy*, and uses the histories of Speed, Holinshed, and Stow with remarkable accuracy.[2] To the extent that Milton identifies with the positions he argues, and insofar as he was known as the author of his tracts (only *The Reason of Church-Government* was signed), he was undoubtedly adopting a Puritan position, which enjoyed powerful support in the House of Commons between November 1640 and October 1641. To deny Milton this association, as some have recently done, is, to say the least, unpersuasive.[3] The debate was embattled, and no one should be under the illusion that Puritanism was the obvious popular position: petitions in favour of episcopacy were a feature of early 1640s protest, even though observers were struck by the force of hostility towards episcopacy in a variety of forms, from provincial petitions to sermons and speeches in Parliament.[4]

Milton was certainly writing in favour of what was a moderate form of Puritan church government, however extreme he appeared to his opponents. Despite the widespread discussion of separatism and sectarianism in contemporary pamphlets, Milton goes nowhere near these positions. Neither is the Presbyterianism he defends the most authoritarian, or concerned with the details of church governance, of the kind that would inspire the Independents (early Congregationalists) to break ranks in the middle of the decade, and Milton in spirit with them. Yet against Calvin (and following Beza, whom he claims has a better understanding of what Calvin really meant), he maintains that Greek *presbyterion* means a number of ministers, and not a single person (*CPW*, i. 707; Calvin did have room for bishops in his vision of church

---

[1] The Presbyterian divines Stephen Marshall, Edmund Calamy, Thomas Young, Matthew Newcomen, William Spurstowe.

[2] See the preface and notes by Don M. Wolfe to 'A Postscript' in Appendix B, *CPW*, i. 961–5.

[3] Catherine Gimelli Martin, 'The Non-Puritan Ethics, Metaphysics, and Aesthetics of Milton's Spenserian Masque', *Milton Quarterly*, 37 (2003), 215–44. Gordon Campbell and Thomas N. Corns, *John Milton: Life, Work, and Thought* (Oxford, 2008), 95, now see a gradual departure from Laudianism beginning in 1637.

[4] Judith Maltby, *Prayer Book and People in Elizabethan and Early Stuart England* (Cambridge, 1998), 88–9, 94, 96, 247; Anthony Fletcher, *The Outbreak of the English Civil War* (1981), 98, 107–8.

government). Moreover, and above all, 'it is the inward calling of God that makes a Minister, and his own painfull study and diligence that manures and improves his ministeriall gifts', rather than an external act, such as the practice of laying on of hands by bishops on ordinands when they were made ministers, a practice inherited from apostolic times, and which can only be counted, says Milton, as inferior to inward ministerial calling (*CPW*, i. 715). The disputes between Presbyterians and Independents of the mid-1640s and later, and the accusation that Presbyterianism produced its own severe regulatory and persecutory system (as Milton put it in his sonnet 'On the New Forcers of Conscience under the Long Parliament' in August 1646, 'New *Presbyter* is but old *Priest* writ large'), were yet to come.[5]

Did Milton comprehensively revile bishops? At the age of 17 in 1626 he had written poetry in praise of bishops ('In Obitum Praesulis Eliensis' and 'Elegia tertia'; but the following year he had written Latin verse in praise of Thomas Young), while the bishops he appears at first to vilify are those who are distinctly in his view enemies of the king: the Arminians, and in particular William Laud, by 1641 Archbishop of Canterbury and a distinct influence on royal policy. Or was episcopacy in Milton's view generally 'tending to the destruction of Monarchy' (*CPW*, i. 576)? Later on in *The Reason of Church-Government* he imagines the bishops wishing to bring down the king with themselves in a general ruin, likening their action to the cruelty of the Roman Emperor Tiberius. The phrase touted by James I, 'No bishop, no king', is, Milton claims, an invention of the bishops. 'A King' (Charles I obviously comes to mind) is likened to Samson, the bishops the Philistines who have shackled his virtuous powers. Resistance to them will come when he, the king, revises his view of himself. That is, when he 'nourish again his puissant hair, the golden beames of Law and Right; and they sternly shook, thunder with ruin upon the heads of those his evil counsellors', but ominously, 'not without great affliction to himselfe' (i. 859). 'Sternly shook' evokes St Peter shaking his mitred locks in Milton's 'Lycidas', l. 112, as he denounces the bishops. Milton's later republicanism is, at least at first glance, absent in these early 1640s tracts: 'What more banefull to *Monarchy* then Popular Commotion, for the dissolution of *Monarchy* slides aptest into a *Democraty*' (i. 592). Milton's later portrayal of the heroic Israelite in *Samson Agonistes* is usually read as a poem hostile to worldly monarchy as well as episcopacy, but the Samson depicted here in *The Reason of Church-Government is* a monarch. It is the bishops who damage the godly monarch, unless he refuses their bad advice and curtails their power.

Apparently then, Milton upholds monarchy. Yet it might be said that to invoke 'No bishop, no king' in the context of the events of 1640–2 was spectacularly daring and an

---

[5] John K. Graham, ' "Independent" and "Presbyterian": A Study of Religious and Political Language and the Politics of Words during the English Civil War, c. 1640–1646' (Ph.D. diss., Washington University, 1978); Ann Hughes, *Gangraena and the Struggle for the English Revolution* (Oxford, 2004); for the subtlety of Presbyterian thinking, see John Coffey, *Politics, Religion, and the British Revolutions: The Mind of Samuel Rutherford* (Cambridge, 1997); see also Robert S. Paul, *The Assembly of the Lord: Politics and Religion in the Westminster Assembly and the "Grand Debate"* (Edinburgh, 1985). On Presbyterian severity, see Andrew Marvell's 'To his noble Friend, Mr. Richard Lovelace'.

attack upon the monarchy. Charles I had invaded Scotland in 1639 in order to impose the Book of Common Prayer there. It was called the Bishops' War. Was Milton in fact advocating at the very least a very different kind of monarchy from the one that existed at this time, as the Samson image has been seen to imply?[6] Might not a monarch who had become a tyrant be interested in using authoritarian and corrupt church government to his own ends? How close was he even at this stage to imagining the removal of this particular monarch, especially when tyranny is imagined 'groveling upon the fatall block' (i. 924)?[7] Already in his Commonplace Book, in entries compiled in 1639–40, Milton had noted the strictly limited nature of kingship, of the importance of rule under the law as opposed to absolute power, of government with the consent of the people (citing Sir Thomas Smith's *De Republica Anglorum* (1583) and Francesco Guicciardini's *Historia d'Italia* (1537–40)), and that monarchs ought to be elected (*CPW*, i. 442–3). In another quotation taken from Machiavelli's *Art of War* (1519–20) made, it is thought, in 1640–2, Milton noted passages arguing that a commonwealth was preferable to a monarchy (*CPW*, i. 421).[8] We shall return to this theme later in the discussion.

II

Milton's views on church government in these early 1640s tracts are grounded in a profound belief in Scripture-reading for all, and a return to Scripture for church precepts. In long passages dealing with accounts of the early history of the church, Milton urges a return for all believers to the simple truths of the Bible, and the Pauline Epistles in the New Testament in particular:

And that this indeed God hath done for us in the Gospel we shall see with open eyes, not under a vaile. We may passe over the history of the Acts and other places, turning only to those Epistles of *S. Paul* to *Timothy* and *Titus*: where the spirituall eye may discerne more goodly and gracefully erected then all the magnificence of Temple or Tabernacle, such a heavenly structure of evangelick discipline so diffusive of knowledge and charity to the prosperous increase and growth of the Church, that it cannot be wonder'd if that elegant and artfull symmetry of the promised new temple in *Ezechiel*, and all those sumptuous things under the Law were made to signifie the inward beauty and splendor of the Christian Church thus govern'd. (*CPW*, i. 758)

A reliance upon church history and tradition, regularly cited by defenders of episcopacy, is rendered decidedly dubious: 'hee that shall bind himselfe to make Antiquity his rule, if hee read but part, besides the difficulty of choyce, his rule is

---

   [6] See the essay by Nicholas von Maltzahn, Ch. 2 above.

   [7] David Wootton, 'From Rebellion to Revolution: The Crisis of the Winter of 1642/3 and the Origins of Civil War Radicalism', *English Historical Review*, 105 (1990), 654–69. See also David Norbrook, *Writing the English Republic: Poetry, Rhetoric and Politics, 1627–1660* (Cambridge, 1999), 113.

   [8] The 'heightening of Milton's antimonarchist and republican sentiments' at this point is stressed in Lewalski, *Life*, 127.

deficient and utterly unsatisfying' (i. 699). Milton regards the church as progressively corrupted through time by power-hungry bishops and post-scriptural impositions; testimony in support of episcopacy in church historical writing is either unreliable or in error. The history of the councils in the early church is therefore a sad history of one power abuse after another until the rise of the Popes in the Middle Ages, which is even worse.[9] Milton's task, especially in *Of Prelatical Episcopacy*, is to inculcate the proper analytical reading of church history in his readers.

Along with the attack on episcopacy come a series of other concerns raised as Milton tackled first the bishops and then the controversial attacks in published pamphlets he encountered in response to *Of Reformation*.[10] That interest which has been regarded as the most significant is Milton's treatment of the role of poetry and the poet, often taken to be commentary on his chief preoccupation during the 1630s and a record of his ongoing intentions as he began to think about writing a great epic poem: the origins of *Paradise Lost*. Some passages may properly be treated as autobiography, others as the equivalent of a conversion narrative. They have been seen as a developing meditation on human agency, connecting poetry, prophecy, ethical persuasion, moral virtue, intense self-justification, and national redemption.[11] Another developing theme as Milton cut his teeth in the world of controversial exchange was his growing knowledge of the tools of secular political analysis, even though his attention was directed to ecclesial subjects. The final sections of *The Reason of Church-Government* are concerned to show that episcopacy is incompatible with the organization of the state, and his terms of reference are not restricted to monarchy.

Above all, the anti-episcopal tracts are exercises in discursive zeal: in righteous anger raised against the prelates. As a principle of controversial engagement, this has been described as 'kerygmatic' discourse, rooted in preaching or proclaiming.[12] Milton develops an effective register of denunciation, matching tones of abuse and outrage with vocabulary and phrasing ranging from formal academic dispute to colloquial dismissal. Later on, in *An Apology against a Pamphlet*, he offers a theory of vituperative writing that reconciles vehemence with elegance. The terrain of different kinds of writing in the Puritan–Anglican dispute is complex, and righteous anger was by no means the sole preserve of the Puritans. Mockery and rough, jesting terms, both of which Milton deploys in some places, were undoubtedly associated with Martin Marprelate, the pseudonym of the Elizabethan pro-Presbyterian satirist (now thought to be Job Throckmorton), and his later imitators:

---

[9] Andrew Marvell learned much from Milton when constructing his own history of church councils: see Andrew Marvell, *Prose Works*, ed. Annabel Patterson et al., 2 vols. (New Haven, 2003), ii. 159. But see p. 167 below for Milton's positive assessment of councils elsewhere in his works.

[10] 'Peloni Almoni', *A Compendious Discourse, Proving Episcopacy to be of Apostolicall and Consequently of Divine Institution* (31 May 1641); anon., *A Modest Confutation of a Slanderous and Scurrilous Libell* (? Mar. 1642).

[11] See Stephen M. Fallon, *Milton's Peculiar Grace: Self-Representation and Authority* (Ithaca, N.Y., 2007), ch. 4.

[12] Thomas Kranidas, *Milton and the Rhetoric of Zeal* (Pittsburgh, Pa., 2005), 117, 156, 159. 'Kerygmatic' is not used in English until 1929 according to *OED*.

Remon. What a death it is to thinke of the sport and advantage these watchful enemies, these opposite spectators will be sure to make of our sinner and shame.

Answ. This is but to fling and struggle under the inevitable net of God, that now begins to inviron you around.

Remon. No one Clergie in the whole Christian world yeelds so many eminent schollers, learned preachers, grave, holy and accomplish'd Divines as this Church of *England* doth at this day.

Answ. Ha, ha, ha. (*CPW*, i. 726.)[13]

Writing like Marprelate might have been seen as the particular preserve of lay Puritans; Marprelate had offended many of his natural supporters, especially among the clergy, by using *ad hominem* attack. Milton's vituperation is in marked contrast to the meekness of the ministers who penned the Smectymnuus tracts, or the calm but firm reasoning of his first opponent Bishop Joseph Hall's *Humble Remonstrance*, if not the invective of his other enemy, the unidentified 'Modest Confuter'.[14]

It is worth considering in detail the elements that make up this zealous dialect. Startling though it is, none of it is far removed from the language being used to condemn the bishops in Parliament. Archbishop Laud, for instance, was called by a prominent Parliamentarian the 'Sty of all pestilential Filth'.[15] There is a heavy investment in colourful imagery that does the work of embodying the larger metaphors governing the argument. Here is the body of the church imagined as the soul wrecked by disease in that she is ruined by the bishops: 'her pineons now broken, and flagging, shifted off from her selfe, the labour of high soaring any more, forgot her heavenly flight, and left the dull, and droyling carcas to plod on in the old rode, and drudging Trade of outward conformity' (*CPW*, i. 522). The intention is to suggest the physical grossness to which the body of the church has been brought, so fittingly the words name physical embodiment. Decay, deliquescence even, is suggested by the adjectives. Elsewhere such words function as most effective contrasts. Rather like Milton's characters of Comus or Satan they are fascinating in their danger or repulsiveness: 'by cloaking their Servile crouching to all *Religious* Presentments, somtimes lawfull, sometimes Idolatrous, under the name of humility, and terming the Py-bald frippery, and ostentation of Ceremony's, decency' (ibid.). In a few places, this form of conceiving takes off into remarkable extended inventiveness:

---

[13] See Leland H. Carlson, *Martin Marprelate, Gentleman, Satirist, Member of Parliament, Puritan* (San Marino, Calif., 1981); *The Martin Marprelate Tracts: A Modernized and Annotated Edition*, ed. Joseph L. Black (Cambridge, 2008); for Marprelate's influence in the 1640s, see Nigel Smith, 'Richard Overton's Marpriest Tracts: Towards a History of Leveller Style', *Prose Studies*, 9 (1986), 39–66. See further John N. King, *Milton and Religious Controversy: Satire and Polemic in* Paradise Lost (Cambridge, 2000).

[14] Here I maintain the distinction I made in *Literature and Revolution in England, 1640–1660* (New Haven and London, 1994), 41, that has been challenged by Thomas Kranidas, *Milton and the Rhetoric of Zeal*, 235–6 n. 36. Hall's rhetoric and his relation with Milton is further explored by Jameela Lares, *Milton and the Preaching Arts* (Pittsburgh, Pa., 2001), 109–26.

[15] Speech by Harbottle Grimston in the House of Commons, in John Rushworth, *Historical Collections of Private Passages of State*, 8 vols., 1st edn. (1659), iv. 122.

A certaine man of large possessions, had a faire Garden, and kept therein an honest and laborious servant, whose skill and profession was to set or sow all wholsome herbs, and delightfull flowers, according to every season, and what ever else was to be done in a well-husbanded nursery of plants and fruits; now, when the time was come that he should cut his hedges, prune his trees, looke to his tender slips, and pluck up the weeds that hinder'd their growth, he gets him up by breake of day, and makes account to dow what was needfull in his garden, and who would thinke that any other should know better than he how the dayes work was to be spent? (i. 716)

There is a fluidity of syntax here that matches the inventive flux of *Comus*. No one touched Milton for this kind of prose, although it certainly meant that his appeal as a pamphleteer was limited.[16]

The same strategy is directed in *Animadversions* with much more personal animus towards Bishop Joseph Hall, and especially his attack on the postscript to Smectym- nuus, attributed, as we have seen, to Milton: '*that which he will not be sincerely, traines on the easie Christian insensibly within the close ambushment of worst errors, and with a slye shuffle of counterfeit principles chopping and changing till hee have glean'd all the good ones out of their minds*' (*CPW*, i. 663) Milton called this style a '*grim laughter*', designed at once to teach and confute in the quickest way: to stop a rotting of the soul. This is why, he says, anger and laughter were linked human qualities. Taking the battle to Hall can mean meeting Hall's learning with his own:

Remember how they mangle our Brittish names abroad; what trespasse were it, if wee in requital should as much neglect theirs? And our learned *Chaucer* did not stick to doe so, writing *Semyramus* for *Semiramis, Amphiorax* for *Amphiaraus*, K. *Sejes* for K. *Ceyx* the husband of *Alcyone*, with many other names strangely metamorphis'd from true *Orthography,* if he had made any account of that in these kind of words. (i. 667)

Thus scatology ('you doe well to be the Sewer of your owne messe' (i. 667); 'Wipe your fat corpulencies out of our light' (i.732)) is juxtaposed with reference to respectable authorities on the issue of censorship, such as Sir Francis Bacon, who is taken to be more against the bishops than was actually the case (i. 668). Disrespect is never far away from the reader's attention: 'indeed our *Liturgie* hath run up and downe the world like an English gallopping Nun, proffering her selfe, but wee heare of none yet that bids money for her' (i. 680) In this register there is also reference to particular images of the world beyond the text and the controversy, such as Hall reminding Milton of a conjuror or juggler at Stourbridge Fair, the large fair that took place near Cambridge (i. 692).

One source for this kind of rhetoric is literature itself, as we might expect from a dedicated poet. *Of Reformation* (May 1641) is like a poem in prose. It is constructed like a Spenserian allegory of the evils of the Roman church utilizing the governing image of the church as a body in need of a cure by being purged. We are given a history of the Church with England's special place in it—a quintessentially Protestant narrative—but Milton drives history with allegorical incarnations that whirl into sensual overload in long Ciceronian sentences:

---

[16] Thomas N. Corns, *The Development of Milton's Prose Style* (Oxford, 1982), 64–5.

But to dwell no longer in characterizing the *Depravities* of the Church, and how they sprung, and how they tooke increase; when I recall to mind at last, after so many darke Ages, wherein the huge overshadowing train of *Error* had almost swept all the Starres out of the Firmament of the Church; how the bright and blissful *Reformation* (by Divine Power) strook through the black and settled night of *Ignorance* and *Antichristian Tyranny*, me thinks a soveraigne and reviving joy must needs rush into the bosome of him that reads or heares; and the sweet Odour of the returning *Gospell* imbath his Soule with the fragrancy of Heaven. Then was the sacred BIBLE sought out of the dusty corners where profane Falsehood and Neglect had thrown it, the *Schooles* opened, *Divine* and *Humane Learning* rak'd out of the *embers of forgotten Tongues*, the *Princes* and *Cities* trooping apace to the new erected Banner of *Salvation*; the *Martyrs*, with the unresistable *might* of *Weaknesse*, shaking the *Powers* of *Darknesse*, and scorning the *fiery rage* of the old *red Dragon*. (*CPW*, i. 524–5)

At the same time, speaking against corruption involves a desecration of figures hitherto thought beyond reproach. It is with surprise that we see the Christian martyrs suffer Milton's ire in this tract, just as in *Animadversions* he will not allow the Remonstrant, Bishop Hall, any ground in his claim that episcopacy is dignified by the fact that some bishops became martyrs (i. 734–5). The author navigates across the body of history, ancient wisdom, and Christian scholarship to meet error head on and refute it in the name of truth. What appeared white is now black. And thus bishops degenerate in the body of faith, so that they become offensive even to God:

And it is still Episcopacie that before all our eyes worsens and sluggs the most learned, and seeming religious of our *Ministers*, who no sooner advanct to it, but like a seething pot set to cool, sensibly exhale and reek out the greatest part of that zeale, and those Gifts which were formerly in them, settling in a skinny congealment of ease and sloth at the top: and if they keep their Learning by some potent sway of Nature, 'tis a rare chance; but their *devotion* most commonly comes to that queasy temper of luke-warmeness, that gives a Vomit to GOD himselfe. (i. 536–7)

Here Episcopal degeneracy induces a fit of puking in God Himself.[17] What an outrageous statement, almost a parody itself of the terms of strong Puritan disapproval! As Lana Cable puts it: Milton's 'instinct for forceful expression of conviction leads him indiscriminately to accept forcefulness as a test of validity: if it *feels strong*, it must be *True*'.[18]

III

As we have seen, the argument of *Of Reformation* seeks to purify the body of Christ and his Church; its method is a near-frenzied list of accumulated error, a good deal of it denounced in the texts of Milton's favourite authors, such as the poets Dante,

---

[17] For other uses of purgation by vomit in the Episcopacy controversy, see British Library, MS Harl. 163, fo. 625ʳ; Fletcher, *The Outbreak of the English Civil War*, 100.

[18] Lana Cable, *Carnal Rhetoric: Milton's Iconoclasm and the Poetics of Desire* (Durham, N.C., 1995), 74.

Petrarch, Chaucer, and texts Milton believed to be by Chaucer and Gower. By contrast Milton's image of ideal perfection is the commonwealth as much as the church:

To be plainer Sir, how to soder, how to stop a leak, how to keep up the floting carcas of a crazie, and diseased Monarchy, or State betwixt wind, and water, swimming still upon her own dead lees, that now is the deep designe of a politician. Alas Sir! a Commonwealth ought to be but as one huge Christian personage, one mighty growth, and stature of an honest man, as big, and compact in virtue as in body; for looke what the grounds, and causes are of single happines to one man, the same yee shall find them to a whole state, as *Aristotle* both in his ethicks, and politiks, from the principles of reason layes down by consequence therfore, that which is good, and agreeable to monarchy, will appeare soonest to be so, by being good, and agreeable to the true wel-fare of every Christian, and that which can be justly prov'd hurtfull, and offensive to every true Christian, wilbe evinc't to be alike hurtful to monarchy: for God forbid, that we should separate and distinguish the end, and good of a monarch, from the end and good of the monarchy, or of that, from Christianity. (*CPW*, i. 572–3)

The perfected body is both image and reality, and the result of the vision of the inspired poet. Imagining how things ought to be is the province of this visionary form of personification. On the one hand, it enables Milton to argue with enormous rhetorical and polemical force (in this case for the integrity of a Christian monarchy and commonwealth) and on the other, it is a means for analysing the elements that actually make up social and individual wholes: the very matter of bodies, and how they relate to one another.

In *Of Reformation*, Milton presents the poet's ability to 'give a personal form to what they please' (that is, to engage in personification and allegory) as a special form of perceptiveness, and the heroic English the fit object of 'the *Heroick Song* of all POSTERITY' (i. 585, 597). In the preface to the second part of *The Reason of Church-Government*, Milton described his writings as the work of Reformation, the poet being the national redeemer, distilling the best wisdom from ancient Israel, Greece, Rome, and modern Italy for the benefit of 'mine own Citizens throughout this Iland in the mother dialect' (i. 812). In other words, Milton deviates from his argument to provide a theory for the reforming literary poet, and openly confesses that he had been intended for ordination, but could not subscribe to 'tyranny' in the church: submission to the authority of the King as the supreme governor in the church, the Prayer-Book, and the Thirty-Nine Articles. It may indeed be harsh and unpleasant prophecy, but at least the poet must speak, unlike the bishops, who behave like covetous monopolizers, keeping to themselves that which they should make public.[19] Poetry has a function that can replace preaching in pulpits, although it should additionally also delight (i. 819–20). Poets who make the wrong choice of decorum are as guilty of a moral lapse as those who neglect virtuous subject matter, even though Milton confesses that he wasted time before he saw his true worth as a prophetic poet (804–6). Poetry should take its place, Milton says (again looking back

---

[19] The analogy between bishops and merchants also echoes Parliamentary attacks on the monopolizers who benefited directly from the sale of crown monopolies (i. 802, 804).

to the public culture of the ancient city states), in an array of public exercises that sharpen bodies and minds in the causes of justice, temperance, and fortitude, and military preparedness. This amounts to an astonishing attack on one of the fundamental tenets of the art of poetry since ancient times, and one that was deeply embedded in the humanist tradition. Not only was poetry, hitherto regarded as an aspect of youthful ardour, amorousness, or drunkenness, to be put aside. Milton associates amorous verse of this kind with the (to the Puritan) slack legislation of the Book of Sports.[20] Moreover, the role of the art of memory as the chief means of inventing the subject matter of poetry was to be spurned. Instead, true poetry is driven by direct divine inspiration: 'nor to be obtain'd by the invocation of Dame Memory and her *siren* daughters, but by devout prayer to that eternall Spirit who can enrich with all utterance and knowledge, and sends out his Seraphim with the hallow'd fire of his Altar to touch and purify the lips of whom he pleases' (i. 820–1). In this frenzy, the poet, 'soaring in the high region of his fancies with his garland and singing robes about him', is not entirely divorced from the prose writer, the two roles being famously described by Milton as respectively the right- and left-handed tasks of a single person (i. 808). The poet as much as the prose controversialist needs to invest great time in reading: 'industrious and select reading, steddy observation, insight into all seemly and generous arts and affaires' (i. 821). Milton confesses his epic intentions and his understanding of the functions of epic and other poetic genres, and where the Bible furnishes as many examples as classical literature of outstanding generic execution. If he writes from 'below in the cool element of prose', we cannot mistake the energy and zeal invested in the poet's task: the engine for purging corruption.

Liturgy, associated in Puritan eyes not merely with the Book of Common Prayer of the established church, but also the Catholic Mass, is that which kills the true musical, divinely appointed proportions that exist between human and divine worlds, and which the true poet can reflect. Its erroneous accretions are accompanied by tautologies and 'impertinences', such as the call for protection from the sun and the moon for women after childbirth (*CPW*, i. 939). Liturgy thus denies the truest poetry. As the church and the state are kinds of architecture, so the individual soul has an architecture that is poetry and not liturgy. The duty to defend the church in such poetry has in fact replaced the time that might have been spent with pious, mortifying exercises:

Dare not now to say, or doe any thing better then thy former sloth and infancy, or if thou darst, thou dost impudently to make a thrifty purchase of boldnesse to thy selfe out of the painfull merits of other men: what before was thy sin, is now thy duty to be, abject, and worthlesse. These and such like lessons as these, I know would have been my Matins duly, and

---

[20] The Book of Sports was a declaration of James I issued in 1617 (and reissued in 1633 when it was closely associated with Archbishop Laud), listing the sports that were permitted on Sundays and other holy days. The declaration rebuked Puritans and was much resented by them. See Leah Marcus, *The Politics of Mirth: Jonson, Herrick, Milton, Marvell, and the Defense of Old Holiday Pastimes* (Chicago, 1986).

my Even-song. But now by this litle diligence, mark what a privilege I have gain'd; with good men and Saints to clame my right of lamenting the tribulations of the Church, if she should suffer, when others that have ventur'd nothing for her sake, have not the honour to be admitted mourners. (i. 805–6)

Instead Milton's vision in *An Apology for a Pamphlet* fuses insight into reformation through poetry and poetics and the disciplinary fashioning of Athenian tradition, expounded in pulpits, at public poetry readings, and in theatres:

But because the spirit of man cannot demean it selfe lively in this body without some recreating intermission of labour, and serious things, it were happy for the Common wealth, if our Magistrates, as in those famous governments of old, would take into their care, not only the deciding of our contentious Law cases and brauls, but the managing of our publick sports, and festival pastimes, that they might be, not such as were autoriz'd a while since, the provocations of drunkennesse and lust, but such as may inure and harden our bodies by martial exercises to all warlike skil and performance, and may civilize, adorn and make discreet our minds by the learned and affable meeting of frequent Academies, and the procurement of wise and artfull recitations sweetned with eloquent and gracefull inticements to the love and practice of justice, temperance and fortitude, instructing and bettering the Nation at all opportunities, that the call of wisdom and vertu may be heard every where. (*CPW*, i. 818–19)

In *Animadversions*, the authority of tradition (as opposed to Scripture-reading) is represented as an illusorily frightening giant, who cannot hurt, is vulnerable to the droppings of every passing bird, and who might be torn into pieces, even at the risk of danger to those who do the tearing (i. 699). In this way, Milton's poetics of liberty, insofar as it makes its readers see more clearly the nature of their oppression, is beginning to do its work of persuasion.

The Modest Confuter alleges that Milton's tracts amount to a piece of comedy ('a mime thrust forth') between the solemn exchanges of the bishops and Smectymnuus. To which Milton replies that the Confuter is not well informed on ancient literature and ignores the fact that comedy was the bedtime reading of Plato; by the Confuter's standards Plato's dialogues may be regarded as mimes (*CPW*, i. 879–80). These observations come during Milton's defence of his satire and rejection of the charge that he libels (an interchangeable term for satire at this time).[21] Milton strongly states that complaint to the state is justified when there is an abuse (otherwise how could Wycliff and Luther have had their say?), and can be no insult to the honour of the state. *An Apology* builds into Milton's forensic defence of his career at university and afterwards as entirely honourable, against the slurs of the Confuter. It reads as a high Italianate humanist apology, with Milton showing how his talents and education have equipped him with a fullness of appreciation for beauty and taste. In the Confuter he says these qualities are entirely wanting. Just as poetic heroes must be virtuous so poets must compass a moral completeness and chastity:

---

[21] See Benne K. Faber, 'The Poetics of Subversion and Conservatism: Popular Satire, c.1640–c.1649' (D.Phil. thesis, Oxford University, 1992); Andrew McRae, *Literature, Satire and the Early Stuart State* (Cambridge, 2006), 2, 26–8.

he who would not be frustrate of his hope to write well hereafter in laudable things, ought him selfe to bee a true Poem, that is, a composition, and patterne of the best and honourablest things; not presuming to sing high praises of heroick men, or famous Cities, unlesse he have in himselfe the experience and the practice of all that which is praise-worthy. (i. 890)

Yet when it comes to zealous denunciation, plainness and laughter are both perfectly acceptable strategies.

IV

I want now to return to the issue of Milton's political allegiances in these tracts. Monarchs freed from the influence of bishops might still be legitimate rulers for Milton, but republican political theory is nonetheless present in these early tracts. There are allusions to and citations of the sceptical histories of the church such as those of Edwin Sandys and Paolo Sarpi that exposed Roman Catholic and especially Jesuit worldly politics which themselves defied testimonies of true faith. From these works republican theory would in part later grow.[22] The entire second book of *Of Reformation* is concerned with 'the art of policie', and in some of his letters from the late 1630s, Milton is evidently immersed in the civic spirit still alive in the Italian city states, despite the rise of seigneurial rule.[23] Republican Machiavelli, whom Milton read at this time, is a defender of religiously virtuous and religiously knowledgeable citizens, not an apostle of atheism. In Maurizio Viroli's view, it is only convincing that republicanism took on in mid-seventeenth-century England if we take into account the religious dimension.[24] While this cannot be said to be true for every republican (e.g. Henry Marten), it makes sense in respect of Milton; in *Of Reformation* there is an analysis of the constitution of the Hebrew republic in terms that anticipate the republican theorizing of the 1650s:

The ancient Republick of the Jews is evident to have run through all the changes of civil estate, if we survey the Story from the giving of the law to the *Herods*; yet did one manner of priestly government serve without inconvenience to all these temporal mutations; it served the mild Aristocracie of elective Dukes, and heads of Tribes joyned with them; the dictatorship of the Judges, the easie or hardhanded Monarchy's, the domestick or forrein tyrannies. (*CPW,* i. 574–5)

---

[22] *CPW,* i. 553, 581. See Nigel Smith, 'Milton and the Index', in Donald R. Dickson and Holly Faith Nelson (eds.), *Of Paradise and Light: Essays on Henry Vaughan and John Milton in Honor of Alan Rudrum* (Newark, Del., 2004), 101–22; Noel Malcolm, *De Dominis (1560–1624): Venetian, Anglican, Ecumenist and Relapsed Heretic* (1984), 36–8, 81–2.

[23] See especially the letter to Benedetto Buonmattei, 1638, *CPW,* i. 328–32.

[24] Maurizio Viroli, 'Machiavelli and the Republican Idea of Politics', in G. Bock, Q. Skinner, and M. Viroli (eds.), *Machiavelli and Republicanism* (Cambridge, 1990), 156–7.

The human (and hence unscriptural) invention of bishops is regarded as a divine punishment and likened to God's giving the Israelites a king (i. 781), while the positive role of church councils in resolving issues of schism (so Milton chooses to argue in *The Reason of Church-Government*) is likened to the Romans' decision to abandon their dictatorship (i. 791). The Roman censors become the touchstones for judging the degree to which temporal powers may interfere with religious practice (i. 832–3).[25] In *Of Reformation* the English constitutional notion of the three estates is replaced by the Polybian idea of the balanced constitution, where the people give the Parliament final determination of affairs, even though they are all 'under' a free monarch (one not subject to clerical pressure).[26] This notion was anticipated in earlier Puritan discussions of the relationship between religious and political constitutions. In defending Presbyterianism against established church apology in the late sixteenth century, Thomas Cartwright had argued that believers and elders mapped onto people and Parliament, with Christ being the king figure. That itself raises the status of Jesus as earthly as well as heavenly monarch, a position with evident millenarian and apocalyptic connotations. Those connotations survive in *Of Reformation* but the significant issue is that the comparison of the English polity and religion on the one hand and ancient political theory on the other was well established in the debate on church government when Milton came to attack the bishops. Which is to say that the major apologist for Presbyterianism in the later sixteenth century, Cartwright, argued strongly for the presence of the classical mixed constitution as an appropriate analogy for church government: Christ was the monarch of the church, the aristocracy were the elders, and the people, who had some say (such as in the election of ministers), the democracy. It was also implicit in Presbyterian theory that the godly would be the secular office holders, while the influence of the godly oligarchy in political affairs would also be considerable.[27] To the Episcopal conformists such mixed government seemed inherently unstable, as opposed to the singular and sovereign monarchy enjoyed by the English. Hooker did acknowledge the mixed polity, but with the bishops as the 'glue' and 'ligament' tying together the different limbs of the body politic—the different estates. A detailed account of Milton's knowledge of this body of writing remains to be written. Cartwright did not indulge in reference to classical political writing to the degree that Milton does, and the Presbyterians wanted a theocracy, which is contrary to Milton's lay preferences, so some explanation of Milton's development is in this respect still needed.[28]

[25] In 'Human Nature in Republican Tradition and *Paradise Lost*', *Early Modern Literary Studies*, 10 (2004), 1–44, William Walker is at pains to point out the antipathy of ancient pagan and Christian values. Here we have instances of Milton bringing the two together, and making the ancient pagan seemingly support and define the meaning of Christian values.

[26] See Norbrook, *Writing the English Republic*, 113.

[27] See Peter Lake, *Anglicans and Puritans? Presbyterianism and English Conformist Thought from Whitgift to Hooker* (1988), 59; see also 55–6, 62–3, 69 n. 121, 130, 136–7, 201–2, 210–11, 218–9, 236 n. 154. See also A. F. Scott Pearson, *Thomas Cartwright and Elizabethan Puritanism 1535–1603* (Cambridge, 1925; repr. Gloucester, Mass., 1966), chs. 2 and 3.

[28] Thomas Cartwright, *Replye to an ansvvere made of M. Doctor VVhitgifte Agaynste the admonition to the Parliament* (Hemel Hampstead, 1573); see further Janel Mueller, 'Embodying Glory: The Apocalyptic

Part of that explanation is provided by Milton's openness to contemporary apology: one of his compositional procedures was to echo, either restating or reframing, recently published works. In this respect, the argument has been made for the presence of Henry Parker's *The Case of Shipmoney* (1640) in *Of Reformation*, specifically in its promotion of the English Parliament's role as the assembly of a republic, a kind of government that Parker saw as the coming thing in Europe.[29]

The passage in the penultimate chapter of *The Reason of Church-Government* that ends with a consideration of the importance of spiritual self-governance in a person and its relationship with a church community begins with likening this to the respect paid in ancient pagan culture by people to their elders: 'certain it is that whereas Terror is thought such a great stickler in a Commonwealth, honourable shame is a farre greater, and has more reason' (*CPW*, i. 841). Where Jonathan Scott argues for the religious character of English republicanism through the category of virtue and sees Milton's Platonism as crucial in this respect and in its determination of his view of republican citizenship, this formulation might easily be reversed: it is ancient republicanism that is shaping the character of Milton's Christian religion and civic vision.[30]

The decided absence of conventional piety is notable in this context. There is no mention of repentance and conversion, the entire 'morphology' of soul-saving that was so typical of Puritan discourse, and no sense of humiliation and human depravity that is so very present even among the Laudians—take both Laud and Lancelot Andrewes for instance. Bishop Hall's sermons, insofar as they contain dedicatory epistles to Jesus, are ridiculed for their inappropriately directed piety (*CPW*, i. 877). This is ironic because Hall is one writer who does engage his Presbyterian opponents on the level of constitutions, comparing secular and sacred: witness his *Defence of the Humble Remonstrance* (1641) and his questioning of the identity and function of the Athenian Areopagus in Smectymnuus's argument (pp. 2–3), a point picked up by Milton in *Animadversions*. One exception to this trend comes towards the end of *The Reason of Church-Government* where Milton imagines the gentle and communal discipline enjoyed in properly ordered Presbyterian congregations (so he frames it) that should bring believers to a proper place of self-knowledge, assurance, and happiness within the church. Instead, 'Contrition, humiliation, confession, the very sighs of a repentant spirit are there sold by the penny' at the behest of the pecuniary demands of the prelates (i. 849).

Milton shows a clear sense of political theory in the Aristotelian tradition, and maintains that sovereignty, whatever the dominant character of the constitution (monarchy or not), is ultimately popular, in line with a major component of

---

Strain in Milton's *Of Reformation*', in David Loewenstein and James Grantham Turner (eds.), *Politics, Poetics, and Hermeneutics in Milton's Prose* (Cambridge, 1990), 9–40.

[29] Janel Mueller, 'Contextualising Milton's Nascent Republicanism', in P. G. Stanwood (ed.), *Of Poetry and Politics: New Essays on Milton and his World* (Binghamton, N.Y., 1995), 263–82; for other responses to republican government in the early 1640s, see Smith, *Literature and Revolution*, 98–106.

[30] Jonathan Scott, *Commonwealth Principles: Republican Writing of the English Revolution* (Cambridge, 2004), 172.

Parliamentary apology.[31] He also firmly maintains that church officers should not meddle in affairs of state. While he does not suggest the converse (that magistrates should not interfere in church matters), and would implicitly concede Erastian arguments in the mid-1640s (that the state should decide church policy), he is very close to suggesting an absolute separation of church and state. In *Of Reformation*, the improper interweaving of church and secular power was seen to begin with the first Christian Roman emperor, Constantine, a departure from a mainstream Protestant tradition that saw Constantine as a hero. Because the Gospel, the teaching of the New Testament, supplants the Law, the Ten Commandments, there can be no foundation for episcopacy in a political or moral tradition of church hierarchy stretching back to ancient Israel (and the priesthood of Aaron therein), as Bishops Lancelot Andrewes and James Usher had tried to argue (*CPW*, i. 761–8). For all that, Milton is very ready, almost in a converse way, to make analogous arguments from different spheres, once again lending support to the sense that Milton's notion of church government is underwritten by classical, anti-tyrannical political theory. Thus, in *The Reason Church-Government*, the need for discipline in the church is found in ready comparisons with the well-disciplined armies of Persia and Rome, as recounted in Xenophon and Scipio Africanus, and through the actions of great lawgivers: not merely Moses, but also Minos, Lycurgus, Solon, and Numa, all famous figures of authority in the ancient political world (i. 751, 753–4, 779; see also *An Apology*, *CPW*, i. 868). Prose controversy is imagined as a classical military exercise: 'in skirmish to change the compact order, and instead of outward actions to bring inmost thoughts into front' (i. 888). Prelacy is a tyranny in the ancient sense: there is a hint of a reference to Charles I as tyrant in a passage that precedes an image of church tyranny as the bastard child of custom (i. 853).[32]

V

Milton hints at freedom of speech in *The Reason of Church-Government*, so it is clear that the ideas that will emerge in *Areopagitica* were already forming in 1642: 'For me I have determin'd to lay up as the best treasure, and solace of a good old age, if God voutsafe it me, the honest liberty of free speech from my youth, where I shall think it available in so dear a concernment as the Churches good' (*CPW*, i. 804).[33] This comes after a passage in which Milton states that 'sects and errors it seems God suffers to be

---

[31] See John Sanderson, '*But the people's creatures': The Philosophical Basis of the English Civil War* (Manchester, 1989), 15–21.

[32] Quentin Skinner, 'John Milton and the Politics of Slavery', in Graham Parry and Joad Raymond (eds.), *Milton and the Terms of Liberty* (Cambridge, 2002), 1–22.

[33] For the idea of free speech in early modern England, see David Colclough, *Freedom of Speech in Early Stuart England* (Cambridge, 2005).

for the glory of good men' (i. 795), a notable shift in position from *Of Reformation*. In *An Apology against a Pamphlet* Milton notes how the anti-episcopal writers were often imprisoned and so could not respond to prelatical defences: the public sphere was not evenly balanced (i. 907). Even then 'a more free permission of writing *at some times* might be profitable' (my italics). Many of the images that do crucial work in *Areopagitica* appear in a more usual and less vital form in the attacks on the bishops. In *Animadversions*, the double face of Janus is merely an image of the deceit of the episcopalians: how they pretend caution when in fact they are guilty of extreme and unwelcome innovation in the church (i. 679), rather than a linchpin in Milton's explanation of the equivocal working of opinion in the public sphere. Joseph Hall is regarded by Milton as a much inferior writer of utopias than either More or Bacon, but in *Areopagitica* the very idea of utopia, as exemplified in More's *Utopia* and Bacon's *New Atlantis*, will be attacked (i. 881–2). Scenes from the city of London and its various sites of industriousness are invoked in *An Apology against a Pamphlet* but the theory of civil labour advanced in *Areopagitica* remains to be realized.[34] '*Areipokalia* [lack of taste] . . . together with envie is the common disease of those who censure books that are not for their reading' anticipates the elitism of *Areopagitica* but without the theory of liberty in free reading that balances it. 'Reason' as a central element of church discipline is a major aspect of Milton's ecclesiology in these tracts, but there is also the personal and explicitly Stoic 'reason, which they call *Hegemonicon*, . . . the common Mercury conducting without error those that give themselves obediently to be led accordingly': an anticipation of the choosing good from evil that will become so central to Milton's theology and his politics of liberty in the mid-1640s (i. 905).

Through the writing of the divorce tracts to *Areopagitica*, Milton still declined to confess repentance or to address matters of personal piety. Reason as but choosing emerges as a classical, pagan description of rationality however much it is also closely linked to a description of Adamic rationality. To it might be added the appropriation of Platonic notions of shame and esteem, 'whereby men bear an inward reverence toward their own persons'—which itself anticipates the treatment of shame as an aspect of innocence in *Paradise Lost* (*CPW*, i. 841). Indeed, censorship (understood as an aspect of governance) is argued against in *The Reason of Church-Government* on the grounds of likeness between God and man and with probable allusions to texts that would later inspire the English Socinians, as they articulated their own heretical view of the relationship between God and man, making God seem (so the orthodox claimed) like a man: 'But in the Gospel, which is the straitest and the dearest cov'nant can be made between God and man, wee being now his adopted sons, and nothing fitter for us to think on, then to be like him, united to him, and as he pleases to express it, to have fellowship with him, it is all necessity that we should expect this

---

[34] See Marshall Grossman, 'The Fruits of One's Labor in Miltonic Practice and Marxian Theory', *English Literary History*, 59 (1992), 77–105; Blair Hoxby, *Mammon's Music: Literature and Economics in the Age of Milton* (New Haven, 2002), 38–54.

blest efficacy of healing our inward man to be minister'd to us in a more familiar and effectual method then ever before' (*CPW*, i. 837).

Milton's central component for being a Protestant is quite simply the freedom to read the Bible. No form of church government can interrupt this freedom without it becoming a tyranny. So a private person refines himself by reading the Bible and hearing edifying sermons based on the proper and uncorrupted interpretation of the Word (although there is not much said about this in respect of worship itself). Yet Milton's entire imagination of the church as a body of believers starts not with the individual but with the constitutional imagining of the church: 'Nor is there any sociable perfection in this life civill or sacred that can be above discipline, but she is that which with her musicall cords preserves and holds all the parts thereof together' (*CPW*, i. 751). It is indeed a configuration that makes more sense when lined up with Debra Shuger's reading of Hooker as an Aristotelian.[35] Milton's approach is quite different from other contemporary voices from across the Puritan diaspora (for instance Katherine Chidley's *The iustification of the independant churches of Christ* (1641) proposes separation on grounds of spiritual purity for believer and congregation alike). The second book of *Of Reformation*, which might readily be titled 'Of a Christian Commonwealth', appends a praise of Aristotle and his version of rationality to a famous Miltonic image of the commonwealth just before it condemns the un-biblical character of Roman Catholic (and specifically Jesuit) reason of state theorists. The strong statement that follows is that the political order must follow biblical precepts but the fact remains that Milton's articulation of the Christian life dwells upon externals—patterns and shapes of social collectives— rather than matters of individual piety, even as he stresses the significance of inward moving both for believers and ministers. The invocation of the wen tale (where the bishops are the stomach) and the comparison of ideal Christian behaviour to self- sacrificing Roman heroism (as recounted in Livy), add further weight to this perspective:

If you require a further answer, it will not misbecome a Christian to bee either more magnanimous, or more devout then *Scipio* was, who in stead of other answer to the frivolous accusations of *Petilius* the *Tribune*; *This day Romans* (saith he) *I fought with* Hanibal *prosperously*; *let us all goe and thank the gods that gave us so great a victory.* (i. 703–4)

This seem'd so farre from the Apostles to think much of, as if hereby their dignity were impair'd, that, as we may gather by those Epistles of *Peter* and *John*, which are likely to be latest written, when the Church grew to a setling, like those heroick patricians of Rome (if we may use such comparison) hasting to lay downe their dictatorship, they rejoys't to call themselves and to be as fellow Elders among their brethren. Knowing that their high office was but as the scaffolding of the Church yet unbuilt, and would be but a troublesome disfigurement, so soone as the building was finisht. (i. 791)

---

[35] Debora Shuger, '"Society Supernatural": The Imagined Community of Hooker's Laws', in Claire McEachern and Debora Shuger (eds.), *Religion and Culture in Renaissance England* (Cambridge, 1997), 116–41.

In context, Milton's anti-episcopal tracts are notable in a number of ways. First of all, the real enemies of his position were the High Churchers, or, as they are often called, the Arminians.[36] Two (out of three) of Milton's named adversaries, Joseph Hall and James Usher, were moderates, and had been favoured by, or in Hall's case, identified with, Puritanism earlier in the century. Usher proposed a plan that combined Presbyterian and Episcopal church government. Milton tackled Hall because Hall engaged with Milton. Neither Hall nor Usher showed any sign of deviating from believing in Calvinist predestination to the free will theology of the Arminians, however much the episcopal remainder (the followers of Archbishop Laud) defended the office of bishop and the justification of ceremonies, both of which positions Milton strongly attacked. By 1644 at the latest Milton would declare himself a believer in free will in respect of salvation and the significance of human free will. Although a minority of extreme Puritans in the early 1640s also believed in free will, interest in it was more usually associated with the Laudians, and the broader intellectual penumbra to which they belonged. Two figures matter here in particular and were associated with Milton: Sir Henry Wotton, James I's ambassador to Venice and Provost of Eton College, and John Hales, assistant to the 1611 Bible translators, attendant at the Synod of Dort (where the dispute between European Calvinists and Arminians took place), and Vice-Provost of Eton. Both men were at the forefront of English encounters with the new theological fashions of the times, both Arminianism and (Hales in particular) Socinianism—modern anti-Trinitarianism. Milton was under the patronage of the former (the first printed edition of *Comus* was dedicated to him) and he knew the latter: Horton, where Milton spent time in the 1630s, was close to Eton. Clearly, the commitment to a broad Puritanism in the anti-episcopal tracts, a position on church government which looks Presbyterian, but which does not discount Independency, must have been made at the expense of connections and positions that he had reached earlier. Not surprisingly, some of the more unusual elements in the make-up of the anti-episcopal tracts (which are often represented more fully in the Commonplace Book) come from these earlier affiliations, such as the references to Paolo Sarpi's writings (*CPW*, i. 396–8, 402, 406–7, 424, 451, 467, 500–2).

The anti-episcopal tracts were an opportunity for the younger poet in his thirty-third year (the beginning of maturity by one contemporary measure) to engage in public controversy. It was a chance to make poetics do the work of theological argument, and in this respect Milton flexes his muscles in some impressive and delightful ways. It also allowed Milton to declare himself in prose for the Puritan cause. He committed himself. He also defined the prophetic poet with a richness of reference to ancient, medieval, and contemporary European tradition, and related these literary traditions to the Bible and biblical scholarship. As Milton defines the nature of the true church by careful reference to the New Testament, so also a rootedness in the teachings of ancient political and civic thought becomes apparent,

---

[36] For the history of the English Arminians, see Nicholas Tyacke, *Anti-Calvinists: The Rise of English Arminianism, c. 1590–1640* (Oxford, 1987).

and it is not merely a neutral indebtedness to Aristotelian constitutional categories. Milton's case against the bishops and his tract constitute neither the 'language of republicanism' (Pocock), nor 'moral republicanism' (Worden), both features which became prominent in Milton's later writing, but in fact a kind of republican Puritanism, and a spiritual demos.[37]

---

[37] See J. G. A. Pocock, *The Machiavellian Moment: Florentine Political Thought and the Atlantic Republican Tradition* (Princeton, 1975), 395, 414, 476, 507; Blair Worden's assessments of Milton's republicanism have been expressed in several places; the latest and most comprehensive statement is *Literature and Politics in Cromwellian England: John Milton, Andrew Marvell, Marchamont Nedham* (Oxford, 2007), chs. 2, 7–16.

CHAPTER 9

'A LAW IN THIS MATTER TO HIMSELF': CONTEXTUALIZING MILTON'S DIVORCE TRACTS

SHARON ACHINSTEIN

THE divorce tracts, which consist of four prose pamphlets published between August 1643 and March 1645, represent a significant and underappreciated development in Milton's theorizing of liberty. Critical approaches to the tracts have often taken it for granted that they emerge out of the author's disappointments in his first marriage to Mary Powell. There are, however, concerns larger than personal ones. Domestic themes spill out into the public sphere of political theory, as Milton develops his vision of an individual through his opposition to enslavement and compulsion. In the context of a civil war, and of sharpening divides in the political landscape, even among former colleagues, Milton's arguments raise issues not only of family harmony, but also of political commitment. Once we explore what Milton's arguments about marriage and divorce meant—and were taken to mean—in the context of their production and reception, we can see how resonant they are for understanding the climates of division and discord in the England of the 1640s. This chapter explores the emotional and political breakthroughs and sunderings visible in, and prompted by, these works. For they are works of breaking faith. Filled with bitterness and hatred, they argue for the dissolution of contract. In *Paradise Lost* Eve is brought to Adam to answer his desire for a companion, for 'collateral love, and dearest amity' (viii. 426); in the divorce tracts we see intimacy has turned bitter, with images of two souls 'ensnared inevitably to kindle one another, but with a hatred irreconcilable' (*CPW*, ii. 280). 'Hate is', Milton asserts in *Doctrine and Discipline of Divorce*, 'of all things the mightiest divider, nay, is division it self' (ii. 345). Roiling passions, and his attempts to master them, animate his great poetry. Wrath in *Paradise Lost*, as in the ancient epics, gives the sign of the war in heaven: 'In dusky wreaths, reluctant flames, the sign / Of wrath awak't' (vi. 58–9). Satan's 'obdurate pride and steadfast hate' (i. 558) recalls the motive of Virgil's *Aeneid*, 'Juno's unrelenting hate'; enmity serves to impel the genre of epic.[1] Wrath, the sundering of bonds, is Milton's subject in his divorce tracts. In the *Doctrine and Discipline of Divorce* Milton is working out how to manage hateful disagreement, how to overturn the contractual obligation that is marriage once it becomes hateful. Yet the contemporary response to these works shows equally how much the conditions of thought, writing, and argument resonated with Milton's sundering mode. Milton's tracts became the centre of a storm of anti-sectarianism, and were held up for ridicule as a harbinger of anarchy.[2] Milton's divorce tracts, written as they were out of a domestic failure, thus also engaged the stricken political realm.

POLITICAL SUNDERINGS

The dismantling of episcopacy and the abolition of the Church of England in 1641–2 heralded a new era in the history of marriage. To contrive a new religious doctrine and plan of worship for the nation, Parliament called the Westminster Assembly, comprised of Members of Parliament along with selected English and Scottish ministers. This group of men first met on 1 July 1643; the *Doctrine and Discipline of Divorce* was published one month later, and its very title echoes the Protestation sworn by each member each day, an oath swearing to 'maintain nothing in point of doctrine but what I believe to be most agreeable to the Word of God; nor in point of discipline'. Milton's earliest entries into print had aligned him with the Presbyterians. In the divorce tracts and *Areopagitica* (1644), Milton gives evidence of his embrace of more radical theological positions. These works hail his birth as an Independent, who rejects the Presbyterian vision of national church government and imposed religious orthodoxy as he had earlier rejected that of Catholicism and

---

[1] *The Poems of John Dryden*, ed. James Kinsley, 4 vols. (Oxford, 1958), iii, l. 2.
[2] See the essays by Diane Purkiss and Ann Hughes, Chs. 10 and 11 below.

Laudianism.[3] The question of when Milton 'broke' with the Presbyterians may, however, be a falsely construed one. There were differences between the Scottish and the Continental and the native English varieties of Presbyterianism. Indeed, in the early moments of the Westminster Assembly, it may have been the case that Independents were upholding the ideals of a distinctively English Presbyterianism, laying greater emphasis on independent church organization, and resisting the Scottish model.[4] In 1645, for instance, John Bastwick called the Assembly's proposals 'Presbyterian Government Independent' as opposed to the Scottish 'Presbyterian Government Dependant'.[5] In his anti-prelatical tracts Milton was flying neither the 'Presbyterian' nor the 'Independent' flag because, like many who would later segregate into these groups, he saw a common purpose in their desire for a further reformation through Parliament and then in the Assembly.[6] Although Milton later offered indictments of the Assembly in his sonnet 'On the New Forcers of Conscience Under the Long Parliament' (1646?) and the 'Digression' to the History of Britain, probably written in 1648–9, in his 1643–4 tracts he was attempting to influence opinion within that body: the second edition of the tract, appearing on 2 February 1644, was addressed 'To the Parliament of England, with the Assembly'. A better account of Milton's precise and changing relations to the Westminster Assembly is therefore called for in order to assess Milton's development as a political thinker at this time.

This chapter, in recontextualizing Milton's divorce writings, places his analysis of irremediable difference, both on a personal and political level, in relation to the practical political work of the day. This means looking to the polemical and divided conditions that were newly shocking and arousing passions in Milton's contemporaries. Institutions—the church, Parliament, marriage—were under scrutiny during the early period of the English Revolution. Since the Reformation, marriage had been de-sacralized; but it was still the unacknowledged basis of much social and political order. Gender relations were particularly unstable at this time and the question of marriage had yet to be settled in the civic realm.[7] The place

---

[3] See Jason Rosenblatt, 'Milton, Natural Law, and Toleration', in Sharon Achinstein and Elizabeth Sauer (eds.), Milton and Toleration (Oxford, 2007), and William Haller, 'Before Areopagitica', Publications of the Modern Language Association, 42 (1927), 875–900.

[4] C. G. Bolam, Jeremy Goring, H. L. Short, and Roger Thomas, The English Presbyterians: From Elizabethan Puritanism to Modern Unitarianism (London, 1968), 40. See also Tom Webster, Godly Clergy: The Caroline Puritan Movement, 1620–1643 (Cambridge, 1997), 38–9; J. H. Hexter, 'The Problem of the Presbyterian Independents', American Historical Review, 44 (1938), 29–49, though the focus is on 1647–53.

[5] John Bastwick, Independency not God's Ordinance (1645) t.p., 7–8.

[6] See Sharon Achinstein, 'John Milton and the Communities of Resistance, 1641–42', in Anthony Johnson and Roger Sell (eds.), Religion and Writing in England 1558–1689: Studies in Community-Making and Cultural Memory (Aldershot, forthcoming); and George Yule, Puritans in Politics, 1640–1647 (Sutton Courtenay, 1981).

[7] See Gordon Schochet, Patriarchalism and Political Thought: The Authoritarian Family and Political Speculation in Seventeenth-Century England (New York, 1975) and Susan Amussen, An Ordered Society: Gender and Class in Early Modern England (Oxford, 1988) on ideologies; and Laura Gowing, Domestic Dangers: Women, Words, and Sex in Early Modern London (Oxford, 1999), on worsening gender relations in the courts.

where this matter was to be decided was the Westminster Assembly, charged with making recommendations to Parliament on marriage and divorce. In the negotiations between the Westminster Assembly and Parliament in 1644, marriage was defined and laws regarding marriage and divorce were drawn up.[8] This story has not yet been told by historians of Parliament or the Westminster Assembly, and is an important context for Milton's writings. Milton stood for the kinds of radicalism of religious and personal belief that some conservative reformers wanted to anathematize in the period when the unity of reform was crumbling. He raised fundamental questions in his tracts concerning the meaning of human obligations, asking in what sense human contracts were indissoluble. This matter was of grave concern in the context of Civil War political obligations as well as in the analysis Milton gives of irreconcilable personal differences.

Profound differences over church organization were made public in 1643–4, over the course of hammering out doctrine and practice in the Westminster Assembly. Yet those splits were not inevitable nor thought irremediable: much time in the Assembly was spent figuring out how to accommodate variance of opinion and theology, though there were also those outside the Assembly, like the Presbyterian cleric Thomas Edwards, using scare tactics to stigmatize differences of opinion. There were debates in the Assembly about how much discussion could be permitted, given the need for expediency. In preaching on the Parliamentary fast day of 17 May 1644, Stephen Marshall likened the work of the Assembly 'to the work of repeairing & building [God's] house', but lamented that 'it pleaseth God that we have many a sad breach'.[9] That building metaphor was common among the preachers in the Assembly; in *Areopagitica* Milton also develops imagery of political reform as building ('Let us therefore be more considerat builders, more wise in spirituall architecture' (ii. 555)). Unlike Parliament, the Assembly did not hold votes, but worked to hammer out consensus. In their discussions, members argued about ecclesiology and discipline; but they also debated the conduct of debate itself. There were those in the Assembly, unlike Marshall, who denied that disagreements

---

[8] See discussion and revision in Commons (see e.g. 6 Dec. 1644, *Commons Journal*, iii. 715, where Commons requests specific changes), both in the issue of the *Directory of Worship* (1644) and in the *Confession of Faith* (1647–8). Revisions evident in the manuscript drafts of 1644 Westminster Assembly proposals submitted to Parliament are found in Bodleian MS Tanner 61 (Speaker of the House of Commons Lenthall's papers) fos. 162^r, 210$^{r–v}$, 211^r; and Bodleian MS Nalson 22 (on marriage in particular fos. 22$^{r–v}$, 118$^{r–v}$, 119^r). On the history of the Westminster Assembly, see William Maxwell Hetherington, *History of the Westminster Assembly of Divines* (Edinburgh, 1843); *Minutes of the Sessions of the Westminster Assembly of Divines, Nov. 1644 to March 1649*, ed. Alexander Mitchell and John Struthers (1874; repr. Edmonton, 1991); W. Beveridge, *A Short History of the Westminster Assembly* (Edinburgh, 1904); R. S. Paul, *The Assembly of the Lord* (1985).

[9] Chad Van Dixhoorn, 'Reforming the Reformation: Theological Doctrine at the Westminster Assembly, 1643–1652' (Ph.D. thesis, University of Cambridge, 2004), Appendix B (hereafter cited as 'WA minutes'), iv. 93: 17 May 1644. Excellent critical literature has, however, focused only on splits over toleration, for example John Coffey 'Puritanism and Liberty Revisited: The Case for Toleration in the English Revolution', *Historical Journal*, 41 (1998), 961–85.

should be disenabling. The Independent minister Jeremiah Burroughs had a motto over his study door: 'Opinionum varietas et opinantium unitas non sunt asystata' (variety of opinions and the unity of the people who hold those opinions are not irreconcilable). The Scottish Presbyterian Robert Baillie was repeatedly driven to frustrated outbursts because of this procedural need for consensus. These procedures allowed minority voices to hold disproportionate power as the Independents took their campaign to the London media, making use of the newly active polemical press.[10]

Baillie, one of the canniest clerics in analysing the situation and in fomenting propaganda to suit his ends, lamented the splits emerging in the Assembly. As he wrote in a private letter in December 1643, he endeavoured to

eschew a publick rupture with the Independents, till we were more able for them, as yet Presbyterie to this people [the English] is conceaved to be a strange monster. It was our good therefore to go on hand in hand, so far as we did agree, against the common enemie; hopeing that in our differences, when we behooved to come to them, God would give us light.[11]

Soon after (1 January 1644), Baillie reported: 'If we carie not the independents with us, there will be ground laid for a verie troublesome schisme.'[12] Still, when on 18 February 1644, a copy of the Independents' manifesto the *Apologetical Narration* (1644) was presented to each member of the Assembly, Baillie was still working for concord: 'We mind yet againe', he writes on 18 February, 'to assay the Independents in a privie conference, if we can draw them to a reasonable accommodation.'[13] And yet, this is the period in which he publicly preaches his sermon entitled 'Satan the Leader in chief to all who resist the Reparation of Sion' (28 February 1644), in which he disparaged the lengthy debate in the Assembly, saying the Reformation in Edward's or Elizabeth's time would have been crushed, if every 'Dissenter, over and over, had made to the full, against every part of every Proposition, all the contradiction, his wit, his learning, his eloquence, was able to furnish him'. Rather, his listeners should look to speeding up the work, or else it will be 'more then a week of yeers, before we can begin to lay so much as the Foundation of our Building'.[14] The Marriage Directory negotiations replicated this growing discord over variance of opinion no less than of worship.

[10] See Jason Peacey, *Politicians and Pamphleteers: Propaganda during the English Civil Wars and Interregnum* (Aldershot, 2004), 36–50; Sharon Achinstein, *Milton and the Revolutionary Reader* (Princeton, 1994), 102–35.

[11] Robert Baillie, *Letters and Journals of Robert Baillie*, 3 vols. (Edinburgh, 1841), ii. 117 (no precise date for this entry).

[12] Ibid. 122.

[13] Ibid. 140.

[14] Robert Baillie, *Satan the Leader in chief to all who resist the Reparation of Sion* (1644), preached 28 Feb. 1644, sig. A4^v.

PRIVATE AND PUBLIC IN MILTON'S
DIVORCE TRACTS

There is an uneasy relation between Milton's divorce writings and the rest of his political canon. Some scholarship has taken Milton's occasion for writing these tracts as a personal one made public. William Riley Parker sums up this perspective: 'to objectify personal feeling was a necessity with Milton'.[15] Yet it is not necessary to see Milton as a political outlier, writing predominantly out of personal misery. Ernest Sirluck powerfully asserts that Milton 'has completely integrated the case for divorce with that for Parliamentary supremacy: they are twin consequences of a single principle' (CPW, ii. 157).[16] Milton later claimed in the Second Defence to have fought for the 'three varieties of liberty without which civilized life is scarcely possible, namely ecclesiastical liberty, domestic or personal liberty, and civil liberty' (CPW, iv. 624); 'Cum itaque tres omnino animadverterem libertatis esse species, quae nisi adsint, vita ulla transigi commodè vix possit, Ecclesiasticam, domesticam seu privatam, atque civilem' (Angli Pro Populo anglicano Defensio Secunda (1654), 90). Critics have tended to see these three varieties of liberty as separate categories, and have prioritized 'liberty' over 'the settling of a fit life' ('vita ulla transigi commodè vix posssit' may be translated as 'without which a settling of a fit life is scarcely possible'). Yet it is important to remember that the ethical, the domestic, and the personal were all significant components of the 'settling of a fit life' which was the *ultimate* aim of all his work on liberty: in Paradise Lost Milton seeks a 'fit audience' (vii. 31). In the divorce tracts, Milton worked on a definition of, or means to achieve, that commodious, or 'fit', life.

Unhappiness within his own marriage is only part of the story of the controversy. Milton had been taking notes in his Commonplace Book on the subjects of marriage and divorce years before his own marriage and its breakdown (CPW, i. 393–403, 406–10, 411–14). There, he had considered the dangers of marriage to foreign wives; worried about marriages of those of varying faiths ('dangerous' (p. 399)); and in his outlines of tragedies had thought about subjects where marital discord played a major role. Tragedies on biblical subjects included not simply several versions of the Christ story, but also stories of Tamar, wrongly accused by her father-in-law and lover Judah (Genesis 38), as well as tales of dangerous, idolatrous, and usurping wives: Jezebel, the wife of Ahab, and their daughter, Athaliah (1 and 2 Kings). The tragic plot featuring Dinah must have been very promising and was given an outline of characters: Dinah's rape by a foreign prince is avenged by her family, who slay all the males of the city (Genesis 34).

[15] W. R. Parker, *Milton's Contemporary Reputation* (Columbus, Ohio, 1940), 237.
[16] Yet see Sharon Achinstein, 'Cold War Milton', *University of Toronto Quarterly*, 77 (2008), 801–36, on the liberal and progressivist political biases of the Yale edition.

In his divorce tracts, as well as in these outlines for tragedies and in his notes in the Commonplace Book, Milton was ever aware of the political significance of marriage, and of its value as a contract that mirrored other social contracts. As he did in arguing against the imposition of uniformity by the Church, and as he did in protesting against the effects of reliance on custom, Milton makes one's individual experience the basis of his ethics, what he calls the 'radical and innocent affections of nature, as is not within the diocese of Law to tamper with' (*CPW*, ii. 345). This is a passage added to the second edition of the *Doctrine and Discipline of Divorce* of 1644, based on a reading of the Dutch intellectual Hugo Grotius (1583–1645) on the distinction between Law and Charity. In the original 1643 passage this account of charity is, however, starker in its insistence on the stubbornness of natural instinct and the unchangeableness of individual personality. In that first edition of the work, Milton had written that for the Magistrate 'to interpose his jurisdictive power upon the inward and irremediable disposition of man, to command love and *sympathy*, to forbid dislike against the guiltles instinct of nature, is not within the province of any law to reach' (1643 edn., 44–5; *CPW*, ii. 346).[17] (This is in the context of an argument about how law ought to stay out of the personal, but the language is intriguingly pessimistic in its invocation of the 'irremediable disposition of man'.) The authorities should stay out of one's intimate affairs because the workings of domestic passions are beyond human control, not blameworthy, but 'guiltles' natural instinct. Milton must have been troubled by his means of conducting his argument here: the changes for the revised edition reveal his attempts to find a workable means of expressing the problem he wishes to address. In 1643, the text continues: 'For if natures resistless sway in love or hate be once compell'd it grows careles of it self, vitious, useles to friend, unserviceable and spiritles to the Common-wealth' (45; ii. 347). The argument at first is about compulsion and about the foundations of a commonwealth in the happy subject. But Milton also addresses the experience of human feeling, and confronts its stubborn particularity, its resistance to state or other mandated control. The moral outlook Milton engenders regarding unhappy marriage is radical, not simply because he wants to take divorce out of the church courts: 'For ev'n the freedom and eminence of mans creation gives him to be a Law in this matter to himself, beeing the head of the other sex which was made for him' (*CPW*, ii. 347). Milton steps back from the inflammatory antinomian implication here by offering a practical ceremony: divorce should take place in the presence of a minister or elders, where the afflicted party confesses his faith. In 1644, the potentially dangerous, libertine 'law unto himself' is further buttressed by an allusion to Aristotle's *Ethics* (10. 10) that sets up a distinction between public and private law.

Milton's original impetus—personal, grieving, indignant, as well as politically motivated and engaged—became transformed by events that unfolded around him after the second edition of the *Doctrine and Discipline of Divorce* had appeared. The Westminster Assembly left the sections on marriage among the last to be completed

---

[17] Milton continues, 'and were indeed an uncommodious rudeness, not a just power' (1643 edn., 45).

for the Directory, and they created a surprising depth of theological dispute. On 13 August, the English divine Herbert Palmer, a member of the Westminster Assembly and long an opponent of Laudian church reform who had defended the war against the King, preached a sermon against Milton's vision of divorce before Parliament. The Assembly minutes record that marriage was to be the topic to be taken up on the following day, 14 August 1644 (WA minutes, v. 230). A moderate English Presbyterian minister who often softened the harder edges of the Scottish Presbyterians, Palmer was charged with the mission of reporting to the larger Assembly on the subcommittee's recommendations for reform in the wording of the Directory for Marriage. He was thus an active player in writing the marriage and divorce recommendations that would be sent up to Parliament. The diaries and records of speeches in the Assembly reveal that discussion focused on rethinking the nature of the marital bond, and whether it was to be officiated by the ministry; they also touched on larger political concerns about sovereignty and magistracy. Reading the minutes in the light of Milton's writings on divorce, one feels the excitement of entering new territory. Rather than assuming divorce for Milton was a personal matter gone public, one can see the thoroughly political nature of the debate—in fact one of the most exciting political debates before the Putney debates of 1647.

Marriage, it turns out, was important to matters of democracy, church government, magistracy, the nature of secular institutions, and freedom of debate; and that importance was made clear in the debates in the Westminster Assembly, where one issue was whether marriage was to be considered a civil or a religious procedure. The Edinburgh minister Alexander Henderson rejected the notion of marriage as only a civil bond, and gave a speech on the matter on 21 November 1644: 'I doubt it is not a mere carnall contract; it is the covenant of God. Civill contract may be dissolved with consent of the partyes' (WA minutes, vi. 7). After Henderson's speech, Thomas Wilson responded with a marriage contract–civil contract analogy: 'It may be a civill contract, though called the covenant of God: soe is magistracy' (vi. 8). The Independent Thomas Goodwin denied this comparison: magistracy is commanded as an oath of worship 'but the business about which he swares [in marriage] is not of that nature' (ibid.). The Scottish covenanter Samuel Rutherford, who would be singled out by Milton for contempt in his 'Forcers' sonnet, aimed for compromise.[18] He claimed marriage was to be a part of worship, even though the former part of the Directory had axed it as a sacrament: 'ther is some divine thing in civill contracts as in magistacy, so something more than that is merely civill in mariadge' (ibid.). Goodwin responded that this matter be given 'great consideration ... because many stumble at the poynt of mariadge because appropriated to a ministry, & by the law noe man may be married lawfully but by a minister' (ibid.). Goodwin now turned to the Hebrew Bible for precedent, as would Milton in preferring Mosaic over

---

[18] For background on these Westminster Assembly ministers see *Letters of Samuel Rutherford*, ed. A. A. Bonar, 3rd edn. (1891); J. Coffey, *Politics, Religion and the British Revolutions: The Mind of Samuel Rutherford* (Cambridge, 1997); and his *John Goodwin and the Puritan Revolution: Religion and Intellectual Change in Seventeenth-Century England* (Woodbridge, Suffolk, 2006).

Christian divorce law: 'In the Ould Testament mariadge was not apropriated to a priest, but as in the case of Ruth, to the elders of the citty' (p. 9). His next comment must have touched off some kind of disturbance in the Assembly because the minutes record that the body had to be 'called to order'. Goodwin went on to say 'that ther is something divine in maradge must needs be acknowledged, & as in the maradge of the heathen, I doe not know but that that is a type of Christ and his church' (ibid.). This debate touches at the heart of the matter of sacramentality— both of marriage and of kingship. The quarrel over marriage had obvious resonances for the conflict between Parliament and the king, redounding on matters of faith, loyalty, and justification for rebellion. If marriage, like political obedience, was based solely upon a civil contract, then it was manageable by civil authority and not by God. Desacralizing divorce meant no less than desacralizing kingship, and the two issues metaphorically implicated each other.

There was then a discussion (minuted but not recorded) of whether marriage was a vow or a promise. The Parliamentary representative Lord Philip Herbert, Earl of Pembroke, who believed in subordination of ecclesiastical to secular power, and who almost never spoke, weighed in on this occasion: 'I will not medle with the learned part. Beg to take care of the manner of doing of it; it is of great consequence. I would be sorry if any child of mine should be marryed but by a minister' (p. 9). The discussion continued over several days, with questions centring on the interpretation of the biblical injunctions to marry and about the legitimacy of the dissolution of marriage. Rutherford insisted that Christ had commanded that 'uncleanness may dissolve, [but] ther will not be a warrant in that text for separation of maradge' (vi. 10); while another Scottish minister thought that the discussion was digressing: 'here are questions that are not very necessary' (ibid.). Still, the divines sought a definition of marriage that could encompass its purpose so as to limit causes for its dissolution: the English minister Henry Wilkinson asked that marriage be defined as 'a remedy of God for preservation of chastity. Desire ther may be some strong bonds expressed to bind us unto chastity' (ibid.). The next day debate continued (unrecorded as to specifics) on such topics as whether marriage was 'ordained in the state of Innocency' (p. 12) and consideration of how Adam and Eve were joined together; further days brought discussion of degrees of consanguinity permitted in marriage, and about the formal ceremonies required. On 3 December, a report was drawn up to be sent to both Houses for consideration.

Consensus seemed impossible to reach on the topic of marriage and divorce. And, because of the intimate and personal feeling no less than because of the political resonances, tempers ran high. Robert Baillie reported on 1 December 1644 that

after two days tough debate, and great appearance of irreconcileable difference, thanks to God we have gotten the Independents satisfied, and ane unanimous consent of all the Assemblie, that marriage shall be celebrate only by the minister, and that in the church, after our [the Scottish kirk's] fashion...In the Assemblie we have stuck longer than we expected on marriage: but I hope tomorrow we will end it. (*Letters and Journals*, ii. 243–4)

On 6 December, however, he reported sadly that 'many sharpe debates' were still taking place on the marriage issue (ii. 245). Baillie's language is strikingly Miltonic here: expressing 'irreconcileable difference', he summons fears of disunity leading to anarchy. At this very moment, when the work of the Assembly was reaching its first achievement, there were now open and deep differences over the constitution of the state church, and awareness that in the discussion of marriage the nature and bond of magistracy were being called into question.

MILTON AND THE GENESIS OF SECTARIAN SCHISM

This discussion helps to explain the larger, both more local and more philosophical, significance of Milton's analogy between marriage contract and the contract of civil obedience to the magistrate. As Milton added to the preface of his second edition: 'He who marries, intends as little to conspire his own ruine, as he that swears Allegiance: and as a whole people is in proportion to an ill Government, so is one man to an ill mariage' (CPW, ii. 229). The relationship between a bond of marriage and a bond of state was dangerously close, and to argue for the sundering of wedlock was also to evoke arguments about the right to resist.[19] Those fulminating most harshly against Milton the divorcer were those wishing to anathematize sectarian activity, who wished to tarnish the moderate Independents as libertine radicals. Baillie, who had worked long and hard in the Assembly to persuade the Independents to come over to his side, was typical in the energy he then devoted to this smear campaign. Baillie placed Milton on divorce among the alleged 'Tenets of the Independents', which include sending marriage 'from the church to the townhouse, making its solemnization the dutie of the magistrate ... not to mention Mr Milton, who in a large Treatise hath pleaded for a full liberty for any man to put away his wife, whensoever he pleaseth'.[20] Baillie later wrote, as the movement for Presbyterian reform declined in 1646–7, that 'the Sectaries having done with the Church, proceed to the overthrow of the State'. Baillie mentions 'M[r] Miltons doctrine of dismissing wives so oft as men please', naming the Doctrine and Discipline of Divorce. Baillie, citing only Thomas Edwards's Gangraena

---

[19] On the analogy between marriage contract and civil contract, see Mary Lyndon Shanley, 'Marriage Contract and Social Contract in Seventeenth-Century English Political Thought', Western Political Quarterly, 32 (1979), 79–91; on the crisis in metaphors of contract in magistracy, see Victoria Kahn, Wayward Contracts: The Crisis of Political Obligation in Seventeenth-Century England, 1640–1674 (Princeton, 2004).

[20] Robert Baillie, Dissuasive from the Errours of the Time (1645), 116.

(3 parts, 1646) as a source, claimed Milton advocated 'the dissolution of all unequall Marriages'.[21]

In writing on divorce, Milton, knowingly or not, played right into the hands of these anti-tolerationist clerics. While Parliament was deciding upon the Directory, the Westminster Assembly's majority Presbyterians were promoting an all-out assault on the separatists. Milton himself was summoned to appear before Lords on 28 December 1644 to be examined for his role in the 'frequent Printing of scandalous books'.[22] The Stationers' Company, pushed by the Presbyterian polemicists, was seeking to clamp down on the published campaign of dissent, and Milton—nominated for investigation at the precise time that the Assembly's recommendations on marriage and divorce were under consideration by Parliament—came to be a symbol of dangerous dissent. The Stationers' Company was enlisted to silence a significant voice articulating a radical theory of contract and marriage, just at a crucial moment where his ideas might have some political resonance, and might hold up the conclusion of the Directory of Worship. In the window between Parliament's receipt of the Assembly's advice and debates (4 December 1644) and the final approval of the emended Directory (18 March 1645) came Milton's last two pamphlets on the divorce issue, *Tetrachordon* and *Colasterion* (4 March 1645). That *Tetrachordon* was dedicated to Parliament alone indicates he now considered that body as appropriate for considering his proposals, having given up on the Assembly.

In these contemporary debates the key issues created ruptures in the political landscape going far beyond the topic of divorce. The debates were especially resonant because at the very moment that the Assembly was debating marriage, the major schism became evident in those advocating reform, between the Independents and Presbyterians. The split among reforming groups can be seen as well in the discussion of the nature of the marriage relation, and in the political questions raised by the debate: was marriage a civil contract only; did it compare to the bond between people and sovereign, and was it an oath, a promise, or a vow? All these questions relate to issues driving political division in the period of England's Civil War. Milton's advocacy of human volition and emphasis on the importance of individual feelings forge the basis of his vision of the political subject. Indeed, he makes the point in the *Doctrine and Discipline of Divorce* that people fly to radical beliefs and sects because of the constraints of uniformity, what he calls an 'ill grounded strictnes' (ii. 279). Rather than leading to anarchy, the expression of individual volition will lead to greater harmony and humanity; as Milton reworks the Presbyterian building metaphor, he insists that irregularity is a kind of perfection: '[N]ay rather the perfection consists in this, that out of many moderat varieties and brotherly dissimilitudes that are not vastly disproportional arises the goodly and the gracefull symmetry that commends the whole pile and structure' (ii. 555). In his divorce tracts, Milton

---

[21] Robert Baillie, *Anabaptism* (1647), sig. AA2, 100. And compare Samuel Rutherford, *A Survey of the Spiritual Antichrist* (1648), which has a whole chapter on David George (Joris), the 16th-c. Dutch Anabaptist and polygamist.

[22] *Lords Journals*, vii. 116 (28 Dec. 1644).

engages with the Westminster Assembly's Presbyterian attack on religious toleration that was coming to a head in 1643 and 1644 to defend a toleration of individual feeling and passion, organizing marriage into a secular framework. Such a policy will actually lead to a decrease in sectarianism: 'many they shall reclaime from obscure and giddy sects, many regain from dissolute and brutish license' (ii. 355). The remedy to civil and personal discord was liberty, within and without marriage. The postscript added to the last of Milton's divorce tracts, *Colasterion*, combines a defence of secularized divorce with advocacy of freedom of speech that echoes *Areopagitica*. As Milton saw it, this reformation was 'a time of free speaking, free writing', and he warned his readers of a demeaning censorship, 'a permission to the Presse', and of the 'danger of new fetters and captivity after all our hopes and labours lost' (ii. 479). The freedom to debate, to touch upon sensitive and central matters of sovereignty and contract, and the freedom to dissolve a hateful marriage here form an interlocking chain in the early years of the revolutionary struggle.

CHAPTER 10

....

WHOSE LIBERTY? THE RHETORIC OF MILTON'S DIVORCE TRACTS

....

DIANE PURKISS

ON 1 August 1643, a pamphlet called the *Doctrine and Discipline of Divorce* appeared on the London bookstalls, anonymous and unlicensed, advocating an ideal of marriage in which the wife existed to be the husband's companion. This ideal depended on the shocking proposition that marriages should be dissolved not solely on grounds of adultery, but on grounds of incompatibility, or simple misery. Milton sought to reverse the priorities of current divorce law by privileging the mind over the body, companionship over sexual matters: 'And with all generous persons married thus it is, that where the Mind and Person pleases aptly, there some unaccomplishment of the Body's delight may be better born with, than when the Mind hangs off in an unclosing disproportion, though the Body be as it ought; for there all corporal delight will soon become unsavoury and contemptible' (*CPW*, ii. 246). Milton tries to show that divorce is consonant with the Gospels, particularly Matthew 19: 3–9, where Christ is direct and specific in his prohibition on divorce on any grounds except fornication. Despite this awkward fact, for Milton, the telos of marriage is not procreation or the prevention of sexual sin, but 'the apt and cheerful conversation of man with woman, to comfort and refresh him against the evils of solitary life' (ii. 235). From the bookseller's point of view the publication was a success; the entire edition of twelve hundred or so copies was sold within five months. But it quickly became the subject of vehement criticism, in particular from the Presbyterians in Parliament and the Westminster Assembly, the authorities to whom Milton addressed the heavily revised second edition of 1 February 1644, to which he did put his name. Milton tried to repair the damage by a series of further works: the *Judgment of Martin Bucer* (6 August 1644), which sought to ground his ideas, branded as dangerous and heretical innovations, in the work of a respected Reformation theologian; then *Tetrachordon* and *Colasterion*, both issued on 4 March 1645, in which he sought to refute his critics. But his ideas never found acceptance among his contemporaries, and in this sense the publications were a failure which hurt and angered him.

The pamphlets necessarily concern gender roles, and their arguments depend on an ideology and a metaphoric subtext which are both profoundly gendered. We can begin to unravel the complex issues surrounding women and also children in the divorce tracts with the quotation on the title page of the *Tetrachordon*. Milton cites Euripides's *Medea* (in the Greek):

> If thou bring strange wisdom unto dullards
> Useless thou shalt be counted and not wise
> And, if thy fame outshine those heretofore
> Held wise; thou shalt be odious in men's eyes.[1]

Milton is using the quotation humanistically and aphoristically, as an argument from authority that supports his vision of the world that scorns him.[2] But it is also an excerpt from a play in which a marriage breaks spectacularly and in violence, a play in which an abandoned woman becomes articulate. No story could be more relevant to Milton's mission, but that very relevance is double edged in reminding us of his exclusion of the wishes or thoughts of anyone but adult males from his arguments about marriage and divorce. Medea herself says:

And if we manage this well and our husband lives with us and bears the yoke of marriage lightly, then life is enviable. But if not, death would be welcome. As for a man, when he has had enough of life at home, he can stop his heart's sickness by going out—to see one of his friends or contemporaries. But we are forced to look to one soul alone.[3]

This sorts with Milton's purpose *only* if he identifies himself with Medea, as he does implicitly in the epigraph. But Medea is also famous as a woman whose husband, Jason, has deserted her for a younger and prettier woman once she has outlived her usefulness. So she is also that which Milton's text cannot encounter or meet, its shadow. The lines he cites identify themselves as distinctive because they come from a

---

[1] *Medea*, trans. Arthur S. Way (1912), ll. 298–391.

[2] For an excellent discussion of Medea's significance that nonetheless reads her differently from the way I suggest here, see Sharon Achinstein, 'Politics as Passion in Milton's Divorce Tracts', in Ann Baynes Coiro and Thomas Fulton (eds.), *Rethinking Historicism: Essays in Honour of Annabel Patterson* (forthcoming). I am grateful to Sharon Achinstein for showing me her illuminating work.

[3] Euripides, *Medea and Other Plays*, trans. and ed. James Morwood, with an introduction by Edith Hall (Oxford, 1997), 7, ll. 241–9.

wise woman, a σοφη. In a modern version the lines read: 'If you present stupid people with a wisdom that is new, you will strike them as useless and idiotic. Then again, if you are considered superior to those who think they are subtly clever, you will be thought offensive in the city. I myself do not escape this ill feeling. I am clever . . . .'[4] Termed by David Norbrook a 'somewhat risky' model for an author who wishes to appeal to a godly audience, Medea is also the voice the divorce tracts repress: the voice of a knowledgeable woman, coupled with the cries of children who become victims of a broken marriage.[5] The title-page reference to *Medea* is in fact emblematic of issues the divorce tracts evade, and of which Milton was accused of evading by contemporary opponents.

Milton's divorce tracts tend to receive an eager critical welcome as crucial in the formation of his progressive views about individual liberty: their publication brackets *Areopagitica*, whose clarion calls for freedom of speech were a response to the condemnation of Milton's arguments about divorce as heretical and libertine.[6] Every aspect of the divorce tracts consequently becomes read through Milton's supposed emergent liberalism. The editors of the tracts for the Yale *Complete Prose Works* see Milton's ingeniousness in altering and misrepresenting sources such as Martin Bucer to fit his argument as a sign of 'literary independence', that 'at no time is he a slave to the letter'. Arnold Williams hails as 'an example of Milton's independent translation from the Greek' the preference in *Tetrachordon* for 'wives, be subject to your husbands' over the Authorized Version's 'wives, submit yourselves to your own husbands' (*CPW*, ii. 589 n. 11). Subjection suggests a natural, permanent, and even constitutional state of being and order, and brings to bear an entire political rhetoric on the role and status of the wife. Significantly, Milton was to use both words within three lines in the ambiguous description of Eve's curling hair in *Paradise Lost*:

> As the vine curls her tendrils, which implied
> Subjection, but required with gentle sway,
> And by her yielded, by him best received,
> Yielded with coy submission, modest pride,
> And sweet reluctant amorous delay. (iv. 307–11)

Yet if Milton's divorce pamphlets are really central to the formation of his doctrine of liberty, then his freedom of translation indicates how this doctrine excludes women in the same fashion that women are excluded from the right to divorce. Milton's divorce tracts raise a variety of gender issues in acute form: autobiography and the relevance of Milton's own experience of broken marriage; the ideology of gender relations in seventeenth-century discourse on marriage, and the workings of gender within the texts' metaphoric architecture. Most criticism has focused on the

---

4 *Medea and Other Plays*, 9.
5 'Euripides, Milton, and *Christian Doctrine*', *Milton Quarterly*, 29 (1995), 37–41.
6 See the essay by Sharon Achinstein above, Ch. 9, on 20th-c. liberal readings of the divorce tracts; and the essay by Ann Hughes, Ch. 11 below, on the relationship of *Areopagitica* to the hostile reception of the divorce tracts.

first issue, with some attention given to the third, and that sporadic. Less attention has been paid to how the divorce tracts intersect with the discourses of marital ideology, and much of what has been done focuses on high theology and neglects other, more popular influences.[7] Where marital conduct books have been considered, they have often been treated sentimentally as advocating equality.[8] We should also consider the texts' intended pragmatic consequences—the political and legal outcomes the prose is intended to effect (i.e. easier divorce on grounds of incompatibility). Scholars have not accepted the invitation held out by Milton's contemporary opponents to consider the potential impact of his words on lives. An exclusive focus on metaphoricity can be a means to take refuge in the text and to ignore the question of how its arguments might affect the lives of real women and real children.[9]

The contemporary ideology of godly femininity governs and determines what Milton counts as the kind of behaviour that might be called 'wilful' or 'unclosing'. Crucial for an understanding of the way godly marital ideology and Miltonic metaphor intertwine is a passage in which Milton seeks to mark signifiers of wifely incompatibility. These are marked in two ways: first, they belong exclusively to the wife through invocation of marital conduct discourse, and secondly they are a synecdoche of the 'unclosing' disproportion which allows for divorce:

I find that *Grotius* on this place hath observ'd . . . [that it] be a divorsive fornication, if the wife attempted either against the knowledge, or obstinately against the will of her husband, such things as gave open suspicion of adulterizing; as the wilfull haunting of feasts, and invitations with men not of her neer kindred, the lying forth of her house without probable cause, the frequenting of Theaters against her husbands mind, her endeavour to prevent, or destroy conception . . . He shews also that fornication is tak'n in Scripture for such a continual headstrong behaviour, as tends to plain contempt of the husband . . . This therfore may be enough to inform us that divorsive adultery is not limited by our Saviour to the utmost act . . . but may be extended also to divers obvious actions, which either plainly lead to

---

[7] For important biographical interpretations, see Annabel Patterson, '"No meer amatorious novel"?', in David Loewenstein and James Grantham Turner (eds.), *Politics, Poetics, and Hermeneutics in Milton's Prose* (Cambridge, 1990), 85–101; Stephen Fallon, 'The Spur of Self-Concernment: Milton in his Divorce Tracts', *Milton Studies* (2000), 220–42. For theological and Reformation contexts, see James Grantham Turner, *One Flesh: Paradisal Marriage and Sexual Relations in the Age of Milton* (Oxford, 1987), and, more recently, Turner, 'The Aesthetics of Divorce: "Masculinism", Idolatry, and Poetic Authority in *Tetrachordon* and *Paradise Lost*', in Catherine Gimelli Martin (ed.), *Milton and Gender* (Cambridge, 2004), 34–52.

[8] William Haller and Margaret Haller, 'The Puritan Art of Love', *Huntington Library Quarterly*, 5 (1941–2), 236–72; John G. Halkett, *Milton and the Idea of Matrimony: A Study of the Divorce Tracts and Paradise Lost* (New Haven and London, 1970). But see Sylvia Brown, 'Godly Household Government from Perkins to Milton: The Rhetoric and Politics of *Oeconomia*, 1600–1645' (Ph.D. diss., Princeton University, 1994).

[9] Lana Cable, Mary Nyquist, and Patricia Parker are among the few Miltonists to offer sustained feminist readings of Milton's gender ideology: see Cable, 'Coupling Logic and Milton's Doctrine of Divorce', *Milton Studies*, 15 (1981), 143–59; Nyquist, 'The Genesis of Gendered Subjectivity in the Divorce Tracts and in *Paradise Lost*', in Margaret W. Ferguson and Mary Nyquist (eds.), *Re-Membering Milton: Essays on the Texts and Traditions* (1988), 99–127; Parker, *Literary Fat Ladies: Rhetoric, Gender, Property* (1987); see also Susanne Woods, 'How Free Are Milton's Women?', in Julia M. Walker (ed.), *Milton and the Idea of Woman* (Urbana, Ill., 1988), 15–22; Catherine Gimelli Martin, 'Dalila, Misogyny, and Milton's Christian Liberty of Divorce', in ead. (ed.), *Milton and Gender*, 53–76.

adultery, or give such presumtion wherby sensible men may suspect the deed to be already don. (*Doctrine and Discipline of Divorce, CPW*, ii. 334–7)

What governs this passage is the wife's domestic role as scripted in the godly ideology of marriage. He is to get goods; she is to gather them together, and save them. According to John Dod and Robert Cleaver in *A Godly Forme of Householde Governmente* (1614):

The dutie of the husband is to travell abroad, to seeke living, and the wives dutie is to keepe the house. The dutie of the Husband is to get money, and provision; and of the wives, not vainely to spend it. The dutie of the Husband is to deale with many men; and of the Wives to talke with few. (sig. L4^r)

The metaphor of saving operates in relation to the reproductive body. The woman's whole purpose is to retain that which does not belong to her, forming and acculturating it without changing its essential nature. Note too how in Milton adulterous freedom of the body, its extrusion from the household, is equated with contraception and abortion, with lack of care to preserve and guard the husband's seed and its products. Like money, seed is the husband's property, and must be preserved inside the wife, privately. Her role is opposed not only to her husband's, but also to that of the 'bad' woman, the one who goes out of doors to consume, who puts her money and her body into free circulation.[10] The man is allowed to spend; the woman must keep his money and goods inside. Given the obvious sexual connotations of such dictums, it is not surprising that adherence to this code of behaviour came to have sexual significance. Or rather, sexuality and suspicions of sexual infidelity came to be metaphors for the threat posed to masculine identity by female emergence into the public world: 'We call the wife huswife, that is housewife, not streetwife, one that gaddeth up and downe' (*A Godly Form of Householde Governmente*, sig. H3^v). Street-wife implies prostitute. In just the same way, Milton sees female entry into public spheres of consumption as a form of adultery. While it has been suggested by Natasha Korda that some discourses of household government could be enabling or empowering for women, this discourse on which Milton draws is less about household prowess than about the need for femininity to affirm rather than to question masculinity.[11]

   Thomas Luxon has recently argued that Milton was attempting in the divorce tracts the redefinition of Protestant marriage as a heterosexual version of classical friendship, originally a homoerotic cultural practice, but without assigning to marriage the equality which characterized such relations. This classical ideal had been exemplified for Milton in his friendship with Charles Diodati, and Luxon brilliantly shows how that friendship may have been largely a literary construction, conducted

---

[10] On the representation in early modern drama of women outside the household as 'leaky vessels', incontinent sexually and economically, who require the imposition of bodily discipline by men, see Gail Kern Paster, *The Body Embarrassed: Drama and the Disciplines of Shame in Early Modern England* (Ithaca, N.Y., 1993).

[11] Natasha Korda, *Shakespeare's Domestic Economies: Gender and Property in Early Modern England* (Philadelphia, 2002), 15–52.

through epistolary and poetic correspondence.[12] The argument is ingenious but risks imparting a dignity to Milton's model of marriage which it may not entirely warrant. When Milton refers to the value of the wife in terms of her 'resembling unliknes, and most unlike resemblance', for example, she is seen also as a holiday for the husband from the rigours of masculinity:

There is a peculiar comfort in the maried state besides the genial bed, which no other society affords. No mortall nature can endure either in the actions of Religion, or study of wisdome, without somtime slackning the cords of intense thought and labour: which lest we should think faulty, God himself conceals us not his own recreations before the world was built . . . We cannot therefore alwayes be contemplative, or pragmaticall abroad, but have need of som delightfull intermissions, wherin the enlarg'd soul may leav off a while her severe schooling; and like a glad youth in wandring vacancy, may keep her hollidaies to joy and harmles pastime: which as she cannot well doe without company, so in no company so well as where the different sexe in most resembling unlikenes, and most unlike resemblance cannot but please best and be pleas'd in the aptitude of that variety. (*Tetrachordon*, in *CPW*, ii. 596–7)

Men require women to be different in order to give them relief from the cares imposed on them by the public world which only they can inhabit, but they also require sameness rather than the domestic menace of contradiction. Mary Astell, a witty commentator on Milton ('not *Milton* himself wou'd cry up Liberty to poor *Female Slaves*, or plead for the Lawfulness of Resisting a Private Tyranny') summed up the ideology expressed here with searing clarity:

For under many sounding Compliments, Words that have nothing in them, this is [the man's] true meaning, he wants one to manage his Family, an House-keeper, a necessary Evil, one whose Interest it will be not to wrong him, and in whom therefore he can put greater confidence than in any he can hire for Money. One who may breed his Children, taking all the care and trouble of their Education, to preserve his Name and Family. One whose Beauty, Wit, or good Humour and agreeable Conversation, will entertain him at Home when he has been contradicted and disappointed abroad; who will do him that Justice the ill-natur'd World denies him, that is, in any one's Language but his own, sooth his Pride and Flatter his Vanity, by having always so much good Sense as to be on his side, to conclude him in the right, when others are so Ignorant, or so rude as to deny it.[13]

Critics determined to think sympathetically of Milton's marital plight would do well to reflect on this passage, for he is complaining about being denied the regime described by Astell.

Thus it is that the notion of 'one flesh' in the divorce tracts is haunted by the possibility that the union will be characterized by difference rather than reflective affirmation, a dread figured in images of physical torture and horror:

'they must be one flesh'; which, when all conjecturing is done, will be found to import no more but to make legitimate and good the carnal act, which else might seem to have somthing of pollution in it; and infers thus much over, that the fit union of their souls be such as may

---

[12] *Single Imperfection: Milton, Marriage and Friendship* (Pittsburgh, Pa., 2005), esp. 23–55.
[13] *Some Reflections Upon Marriage* (1700), 56, 35–6.

even incorporate them to love and amity: but that can never be where no correspondence is of the mind; nay instead of being one flesh, they will be rather two carcases chain'd unnaturally together; or, as it may happen, a living soul bound to a dead corpse, a punishment too like that inflicted by the Tyrant Mezentius, so little worthy to be received as that remedy of loneliness which God meant us. (*Doctrine and Discipline, CPW,* ii. 326)

Theological insistence that marriage makes all couples one flesh is misguided because if it is true, it risks a kind of grotesque *memento mori.* The purpose of becoming one flesh is, Milton thinks, to 'make legitimate' the carnal act, and he insists that the act is meaningful only if there is 'correspondence' of the mind, which means both reflection and communication, or 'conversation'.[14] Such communication is proof of life; without it what is left is the binding together of bodies even in death, or (worse still) a living soul permanently attached to a dead body. The apparent absence of gender division here gives way to an opposition of male/female along the lines of the soul/body binary; earlier Milton assumes this Platonic binary when he laments how a man who 'spent his youth unblamably, and layd up his chiefest earthly comforts in the enjoyment of a contented marriage' can then 'find himself bound fast to an uncomplying discord of nature, or, as it oft happens, to an image of earth and fleam [phlegm]' (ii. 254).[15]

In the invocation of the Etruscan tyrant Mezentius, Milton again offers an account of a classical story as interesting for its larger context as for its immediate relevance to his argument. In the *Aeneid* Mezentius' tyrannical acts of torture are described by Evander:

> mortua quin etiam iungebat corpora uiuis
> componens manibusque manus atque oribus ora,
> tormenti genus, et sanie taboque fluentis
> complexu in misero longa sic morte necabat. (viii. 485–8)

In Dryden's translation of 1697, the sexualized terms 'coupled' and 'embraces' emphasize the sexual analogy, and amplify the implication of the Latin *manibus* and *oribus ora*:

> The living and the dead at his command
> Were coupled, face to face, and hand to hand,
> Till, chok'd with stench, in loath'd embraces tied,
> The ling'ring wretches pin'd away and died.[16]

The Miltonic analogy cannot help but consign fleshly mortality to the erring wife, to whom the living husband is unforgivably shackled. Her flesh reproduces itself in him, dragging him into death with her in an allegory of the Fall of Man itself. The

---

[14] On the centrality of Milton's definition of 'conversation', a euphemism for sex in the period, to his efforts to revise conceptions of the purpose of marriage, see Luxon, *Single Imperfection,* 57–93.

[15] On dualistic conceptions of the body and soul, but also signs of Milton's emergent monism, in the divorce tracts, see Stephen Fallon, 'The Metaphysics of Milton's Divorce Tracts', in Loewenstein and Turner (eds.), *Politics, Poetics and Hermeneutics in Milton's Prose,* 69–84.

[16] *The Poems of John Dryden,* ed. James Kinsley, 4 vols. (Oxford, 1958), iii. 1279, ll. 636–9.

quasi-erotic imagery makes the idea of 'one flesh' seem itself a perversion. And yet in Virgil's narrative, Mezentius is also figured as participating in a different kind of doubling, a less problematic and more promising kind. During the Etruscan revolt, Mezentius' son Lausus is killed by Aeneas while trying to save his father. Ashamed he has dishonoured the young man's name, Mezentius' final request before he kills himself is to be buried with his son. This harmonious doubling offers an orderly conclusion to the chaos of Mezentian tyranny; while in the context of Milton's underlying marriage model of classical friendship the episode invokes an aspect of Greek homosocial and homoerotic bonding crucial to Platonism, which was the notion that the *eromenos* was as a son to his lover, the *erastes* growing in likeness to him as he grew to full manhood.[17] Mezentius' tyranny also connects the private misery of incompatibility with a public sphere of repressive government. For Milton, the image of the tyrant insisting on the shackling of the lovers is crucial to his argument, for it casts marital law as the tyrannical confinement of the free spirit to a decaying body. This punishment is also symbolic, representing the tyrant's link with death as tyrannical law. The tyrant's effeminacy—Mezentius on the battlefield 'sought to save himself by flight' (iii. 1349, l. 1127)—becomes the occasion for his dethroning, and remains unmitigated by his son's masculine sacrifice—'Shouts of applause ran ringing through the field, / To see the son the vanquished father shield' (iii. 1349, ll. 1134–5). Also, and of more moment to Milton, the Mezentius story highlights the tyrant's power to feminize the subject, and hence raises the spectre of the wife's power to feminize the husband.

Milton's connection between freedom to divorce and the political liberty of the male subject is more explicit in a series of careful references to Henry VIII:

Hence it is that the law forbidding Divorce, never attains to any good end of such Prohibition, but rather multiplies evil . . . The Parlament also and Clergy of England were not ignorant of this, when they consented that Harry the 8th might put away his Queen Anne of Cleve, whom he could not like after he had been wedded half a year; unless it were that, contrary to the Proverb, they made a necessity of that which might have been a virtue in them to do: for even the freedom and eminence of Man's creation gives him to be a Law in this matter to himself, being the head of the other sex which was made for him. (*Doctrine and Discipline*, *CPW*, ii. 346–7)

Implying that the Parliament was a little frightened of Henry, Milton also implies that Henry is a model for Protestant men, standing no nonsense from the tyranny of custom. Yet Milton is also anxious that Henry's image is not quite the right one; it requires and receives tweaking:

Such uncomely exigencies it befel no less a Majesty than Henry the VIII to be reduc'd to, who finding just reason in his conscience to forgo his brother's Wife, after many indignities of being deluded, and made a boy of by those his two Cardinal Judges, was constrain'd at last, for

---

[17] See e.g. Kenneth Dover, *Greek Homosexuality* (London, 1978); S. Sara Monoson, 'Citizen as Erastes: Erotic Imagery and the Idea of Reciprocity in the Periclean Funeral Oration', *Political Theory*, 22 (1994), 253–76.

want of other proof, that she had been carnally known by Prince Arthur, even to uncover the nakedness of that virtuous Lady, and to recite openly the obscene evidence of his Brother's Chamberlain. Yet it pleas'd God to make him see all the Tyranny of Rome, by discovering this which they exercis'd over Divorce, and to make him the beginner of a Reformation to this whole Kingdom, by first asserting into his familiary Power the Right of just Divorce. (347–8)

In this passage Milton carefully marks off female sexuality as unsuitable for the public sphere occupied by Henry in his fight against tyranny, while defining that sphere as a space where man is free to divorce without recourse to law. Tyranny, then, is the menace that household affairs might be governed by an authority that deposes the *paterfamilias* as head of the private realm. That tyranny is associated with the always-feminized Church of Rome, and elsewhere I have argued that this anxiety about the loss of masculinity by the head of a household living under tyranny governs Milton's political responses to absolutism.[18] Using the feminine figure of the Roman church as again a means of defining the sanctity of this masculine space in *Tetrachordon*, Milton amplifies his argument

Which if we consider, this papal and unjust restriction of Divorce need not be so dear to us, since the plausible restraining of that was in a manner the first loosening of Antichrist, and as it were, the substance of his eldest horn. Nor do we less remarkably owe the first means of his fall here in England, to the contemning of that restraint by Henry the 8th, whose Divorce he opposed. (ii. 706)

Here the king's liberty to divorce becomes representative of national liberty from the Antichrist. Henry's divorce, ostensibly something of an embarrassment to the Church of England, becomes an asset because it signifies that the liberty of the kingdom and that of the man within the household are one and the same.

Henry's key motivation in his divorce, his quest for a legitimate son, is not mentioned. The absence or suppression of discussion of children in the tracts is explicable in terms of Milton's redefinition of the purpose of marriage as companionship rather than merely reproduction. Yet the divorce tracts are preoccupied with metaphors of fatherhood, motherhood, and reproductivity.[19] Those who reflexively brand all new ideas as dangerous behave, Milton tells Parliament and the Westminster Assembly in the address which prefaces the revised edition of the *Doctrine and Discipline of Divorce*, 'as if the Womb of teeming Truth were to be clos'd up, if she presume to bring forth aught that sorts not with their unchew'd notions and suspicions'. Truth is a fertile female body, but the mother of Truth is the (male) author:

For Truth is as impossible to be soil'd by any outward touch, as the Sun beam. Though this ill hap wait on her nativity, that shee never comes into the world, but like a Bastard, to the

---

[18] Diane Purkiss, *Literature, Gender, and Politics during the English Civil War* (Cambridge, 2005), 186–209.

[19] Sara van den Berg, 'Women, Children, and the Rhetoric of Milton's Divorce Tracts', *Early Modern Literary Studies*, 10/1 (May, 2004), 4. 1–13: <http://purl.oclc.org/emls/10-1/bergmilt.htm>; Purkiss, *Literature, Gender and Politics*, 194–5.

ignominy of him that brought her forth: till Time the Midwife rather then the mother of Truth, have washt and salted the Infant, declar'd her legitimat, and Churcht the father of his young *Minerva*, from the needlesse causes of his purgation. (*CPW*, ii. 224–5)

Here, Milton substitutes the father for the mother. It is the mother who is 'churched' when a clergyman gives public thanks for the safe delivery of her child.[20] And Milton further insists on the male appropriation of the power of motherhood through the rewriting of the popular proverb that Truth is the daughter of Time. Time is not the mother of Truth; she is a midwife. Truth's mother is the male author. Midwifery is identified not as the profession which helps the mother give birth, but as needed only because of practices required by those who would impede truth. The consequence of all this is to argue that the legitimating function, properly belonging to 'him that brought her forth', to the maternal father, is wrongly appropriated by a state authority or by a reading public which requires an empty ritual to recognize Truth for what it is. By figuring Truth as the male author's self-replication, Milton is able to figure public or state repudiation of Truth in terms of male fears of midwifery and the female control of childbearing. The figuration of Truth as the daughter of the male writer does not have the effect of elevating 'real' women. Foregrounding the merely symbolic value of Truth through the reference to Minerva, who springs fully formed from the head of Jupiter (as Sin springs from the head of Satan in the only allegorical episode of *Paradise Lost* (x. 751–60)), excludes women from any partici-pation in her genesis.[21] Milton is able to separate Truth entirely from the maternal body. The correctly generated text becomes a reliable substitute for the vagaries of natural reproduction. But this displacement might point to a Miltonic lack which must be repressed, along with the children of Jason, Mezentius, and Henry VIII.

At the time of writing the divorce tracts, Milton himself had no son; his first son, also John, was finally born to him in March 1651. In fact, in 1643/4 he had no children; his daughter Anne was born on 29 July 1646, and proved problematic in almost the way Milton apparently dreaded: she was not exactly a young Minerva, due to her lifelong lameness and defective speech. Of course Milton could not know that this was to be her fate and his, but so many children were disappointments in an era of untreated disability and illness that Anne's life must remind us of how many of them Milton had encountered. Generally, too, the mother's sins were blamed for any birth defects.[22] Milton hoped instead for simpler methods of self-replication in the form of a Truth embodied in the written and printed word. It is ironic, then, that the first edition of the *Doctrine and Discipline of Divorce* was sent fatherless into the world, without a name; the title page of the revised edition, however, proclaims it the work of 'J. M.' and the prefatory epistle is signed. It might be said that Milton then sought to look for respectable father-figures for ideas charged with illegitimacy in Martin Bucer and other learned Reformation patriarchs. The theme of

---

[20] Sara Mendalson and Patricia Crawford, *Women in Early Modern England* (Oxford, 1998), 153–4.
[21] For discussion of the gender dynamics of the Sin and Death episode, see Purkiss, *Literature, Gender and Politics*, 201–9.
[22] Mendalson and Crawford, *Women in Early Modern England*, 151.

textual legitimacy is brought to the fore by the polemical strategy of *Colasterion*, in which the anonymity of the attack on Milton is made to signify not only the illegitimacy of his opponent's arguments but of the opponent himself, who is relentlessly charged with social and educational lowliness as well as moral degeneracy. The tract to which Milton responds in *Colasterion* was the most substantial of the attacks on his ideas, and in fact it explicitly raises the problem of the children of a divorce. *An Answere to a book intituled, The doctrine and discipline of divorce, or, A plea for ladies and gentlewomen, and all other maried women against divorce wherein both sexes are vindicated from all bonadge* [sic] *of canon law, and other mistakes whatsoever* appeared on 14 November 1644. I quote the title in full because from it alone we learn that *An Answere* declares itself the champion of wives and mothers. Licensed and given a laudatory preface by the cleric Joseph Caryl, a moderate member of the Westminster Assembly, it does not so much grapple with Milton's argument as put forward a different ideology of marriage altogether, an ideology which skirts his claims for marriage as a perfect mirroring in favour of an idea of marriage as a pragmatic series of adaptations.

The author explains the current causes of divorce as impotence and gross immorality, telling stories that whittle away at Milton's rhetorical equation between such sexual betrayals and spiritual incompatibility. *An Answere*'s account of incompatibility is more gender-neutral than Milton's: 'that disagreement of minde or disposition between husband and wife, yea though it shewes it selfe in much sharpnesse each to other, is not by the law of God allowed of for a just cause of divorce, neither ought to be allowed of by the lawes of man' (p. 4). With a lower ideal of marital compatibility, *An Answere* is brisk, even brusque, about the issues over which Milton agonizes: 'through the p[e]evishness or ill dispositions of their natures, their troubles should increase to multitudes above what is ordinarie betwixt maried persons, yet ought they not to part and to marrie to others, because some sort and measure of troubles and discontent in mariage are inavoidable; and therefore where one is by mariage bound by so many bonds, he ought not to break the bonds to ease himself of disquietnesse and trouble' (p. 8). Like modern feminist critics, the author reads the *Doctrine and Discipline of Divorce* as a plea for the man to be able to put away his wife, and responds in the same terms. For the author of the *Answere* the couple are substantially one flesh, and so the man cannot put away his wife any more than he can put away himself: 'In the next place, if the Husband ought to love his Wife as himself, then may he not for discontent or disagreement put her away, no more then for some discontent or disquietnesse in himselfe, he may separate his soule from his body' (p. 8). This subverts the opposition between the (feminized) body and the (masculine) soul that Milton has been constructing. With this work done, the author can turn his attention to the problems that Milton's reforms might create for women, and significantly for their children:

who sees not, how many thousands of lustfull and libidinous men would be parting from their Wives every week and marying others: and upon this, who should keep the children of these divorcers which somtimes they would leave in their Wives bellies? how shall they come by their Portions, of whom, or where? and how shall the Wife be endowed of her Husbands estates? Nay, commonly, to what reproach would the woman be left to, as being one left who was not fit for any ones company? and so who would venture upon her againe[?] And so by this means through her just cause of discouragement, she would probably hazard her self upon some dishonest and disgracefull course, with a hundred more the like inconveniencies. (p. 9)

Generations of Milton critics may have disregarded *An Answere* as shallow, but it grasps and addresses the way the asymmetrically gendered world created by Milton himself cannot support the approach he advocates.[23] It is precisely because they are 'weaker' that women require the protection of the law. Patriarchy is difficult to dismantle piece by piece because reform risks disadvantaging those already most disempowered. The fear that reform will free men at women's expense is made visible in *An Answere*'s retrograde response. Conversely, of course, a liberal feminist might well ask whether protectiveness increases the 'weakness' which it offers to shield, as Wollstonecraft was to conclude some hundred or more years later.

For Milton's most loquacious opponent, Milton's gestures at inclusiveness—'restored to the good of both sexes', as the title page of the *Doctrine and Discipline of Divorce* has it—were not adequate to the occasion. It was evident to his respondent that he was not interested in the possibility that the restrictive marriage laws existed to protect women and children from exploitation and abandonment. Especially telling is the author's espousal of the cause of the children of the marriage, a topic evaded or repressed in Milton in favour of images of the text as the only entirely legitimate, because unmothered, offspring of the father. The references to Medea, Mezentius, and Henry VIII at once invoke and omit the fate of children. It was evident to his critic that Milton had not given any sustained thought to the lot of children under the reforms he proposed—according to *Tetrachordon*, 'if ther be children, while they are fewest, they may follow either parent, as shall bee agreed, or judg'd, from the house of hatred and discord' (ii. 631)—and the problem is hardly resolved by Milton's vehement reply in *Colasterion*, which if anything intensifies it through the continual emphasis on bastardy and the paternity of both text and author. The only time the word 'child' occurs in *Colasterion* is as a disparaging epithet applied to his opponent's 'childishness'. But modernity is unlikely to embrace *An Answere* because its refutation of Milton turns out to be grounded in what it sees as a steeper gradient of sexual difference:

that solace and peace which is contrary to discord and variance (in which sense you seem to take it) is not the main end of mariage or conjugall society, is very plain and apparent: nor yet the solace and content in the gifts of the minde of one another only, for then would it have been every wayes as much, yea more content and solace to *Adam*; and so consequently to every man, to have had another man made to him of his Rib instead of *Eve*: this is apparent by

---

[23] Parker, i. 276–80; Lewalski, *Life*, 179–80, 599 nn. 95–100, who concedes that the 'strongest arguments' of the critique are those in favour of the rights of wives and children. The text is rarely discussed.

experiences, which shews, that man ordinarily exceeds woman in naturall gifts of minde, and in delectablensse of converse. (p. 12)

Milton's vision of transmuting the classical and humanist same-sex model of friendship into marriage is dismissed. His expectations of women are simply too high for nature. The use of bodily terms of generation to express mental states is seen as absurdly mistaken:

And for your other phrase of *a great violence to the reverent secret of nature by sowing the furrow of mans nativitie, with the seed of two incoherent and incombining dispositions.* This frothie discourse, were it not s[u]gred over with a little neat language, would appear so immeritous and undeserving, so contrary to all humane learning, yea, truth and common experience it self, that all that reade it must needs count it worthie to be burnt by the Hangman. For who ever thought before you, that the reverent secret of Nature, or the furrow of mans nativitie (so there was lawfull mariage preceded) might not be sowed by the seeds of such as are of different or uncombining disposition, if any such there be, without violence or foul incongruitie? If any think otherwise as you it seems doe; give advice that a Petition may be drawn, to have a Committee in every Countie of the Kingdome who shall carefully see to, and severely restraine the mariage of any two Men or Maids who differ in constitution, complexion, hair, countenance, or in disposition, lest this reverent secret of Nature be defiled and violated. (p. 40)

This polemical strategy of ridiculing Milton's metaphoric language as inappropriate for other than bodily states exposes Milton's argument to depend upon successfully blaming bodily adultery upon incompatibility of mind.

While the author takes the side of women against the 'many thousands of lustfull and libidinous men would be parting from their Wives every week and marrying others', he also seeks to identify Milton with unruly women: 'And whereas you say, *It is not the outward continance of mariage which keeps the covenant of mariage whole, but whosoever doth most according to peace and love, whether in mariage or divorce, he breaks mariage least.* We answer: this is a wilde, mad, and frantick divinitie, just like to the opinions of the Maids of Algate' (p. 36). This links Milton with the women described in Laura Gowing's work as gathered for gossip and scolding around the Aldgate Pump, boundary marker of the East End.[24] It anticipates the discrediting of Milton's arguments through their association with the unruliness of the female preacher Mrs Attaway. The case of Mrs Attaway (we do not know her first name) gives us some evidence of the practical results of Milton's teaching for women and for children. In his voluminous denunciation of sectarianism, *Gangraena: or a Catalogue and Discovery of many of the Errours, Heresies, Blasphemies and pernicious Practices of the Sectaries of this time, vented and acted in England in these four last years* (3 pts., 1646), the Presbyterian cleric Thomas Edwards reports that among 'other passages' in her illegal sermons Mrs Attaway spoke of the *Doctrine and Discipline of Divorce*, saying: 'she for her part would look more into it, for she had an unsanctified

---

24 ' "The freedom of the streets": Women and Social Space, 1560–1640', in Paul Griffiths and Mark S. R. Jenner (eds.), *Londinopolis: Essays in the Cultural and Social History of Early Modern London* (Manchester, 2000), 130–53.

husband, that did not walk in the way of *Sion*, nor speak the language of *Canaan*'. Mrs Attaway walked out on her husband, announcing in a letter 'You have been for me rather a disturber of my body and soul than a meet help for me'. The conclusion of the episode leaves Milton as the cause of the abandonment of children: Edwards was informed by two 'godly understanding' men that Attaway had deserted her children of 6 and 7, conveyed 'away' all her goods of 'worth', and 'run away with another womans husband, with whom she had bin to familiar along time'. This man was William Jenney, who had listened to Attaway's preaching and was 'a preacher too'. It was 'commonly reported' that they had gone 'beyond seas'. Edwards added that: ''tis given out she met with a Prophet here in *London*, who hath revealed to her and others that they must go to Jerusalem, and repair Jerusalem, and for that end Mrs *Attaway* hath gotten money of some persons, ten pounds of one yong maid, and other money of others towards the building up of Jerusalem' (pt. i, appendix, 120–1).

For Edwards, Mrs Attaway as a reader of the *Doctrine and Discipline of Divorce* embodies its doctrine and represents its lack of discipline. Milton's divorce laws are the ruin of husbands and children, and with them the social order. For Edwards, too much is sacrificed to the construction of the free and independent male subject. Like the author of *An Answere*, he advocates an identity defined by its social relations. Yet, if we are to believe Edwards, Mrs Attaway's story offers a rebuke to a too-careful reading of the rhetoric of gender in the divorce tracts. It seems that *she* was able to appropriate the carefully delimited authority of the male subject, and to act upon it.[25] The episode may have provoked Milton's bitter satirical sonnet 'On the Detraction which followed upon my Writing Certain Treatises' (1646), in which he laments the reception of the divorce tracts:

> But this is got by casting pearl to hogs;
> That bawl for freedom in their senseless mood,
> And still revolt when truth would set them free.
> Licence they mean when they cry liberty. (ll. 8–11)[26]

Later, in the *Second Defence*, Milton expressed regret that he had not kept his ideas on divorce in Latin, thereby making them inaccessible to the classically uneducated— and so to women (*CPW*, iv. 610). Milton was upset and angry about a misreading that brought him into reflective apposition not with compliant difference, but with unruly mimicry. And we do not know, nor can we ever know, what Mrs Attaway's children thought.

---

[25] See the discussion in Susan Wiseman, *Conspiracy and Virtue: Women, Writing, and Politics in Seventeenth-Century England* (Oxford, 2006), 54–8: 'For Edwards "Mistris Attoway" was an example of the way female reading and interpretation outside the structures of the national church endangered state and family' (p. 56).

[26] On Edwards's reliability, see Ann Hughes, *Gangraena and the Struggle for the English Revolution* (Oxford, 2004), 45. The argument that Milton's sonnet is aimed at sectarian radicals is made by Nathaniel H. Henry, 'Who Meant Licence when They Cried Liberty?', *Modern Language Notes*, 66 (1951), 509–13; but see also John Leonard, 'Revolting as Back-Sliding in Milton's Sonnet XII', *Notes and Queries*, 43 (1996), 269–73, which argues that Milton is more concerned with the Presbyterians.

CHAPTER 11

....

MILTON, *AREOPAGITICA,* AND THE PARLIAMENTARY CAUSE

....

ANN HUGHES

ONE of the most obvious aspects of *Areopagitica*, its presentation as an address to the Parliament, is also one of the most illuminating:

For he who freely magnifies what hath been nobly done, and fears not to declare as freely what might be done better, gives ye the best cov'nant of his fidelity; and that his loyalest affection and his hopes waits on your proceedings. His highest praising is not flattery, and his plainest advice is a kinde of praising: for though I should affirme and hold by argument, that it would fare better with truth, with learning, and the Commonwealth, if one of your publist Orders, which I should name, were call'd in, yet at the same time it could not but much redound to the lustre of your milde and equall Government, when as private persons are hereby animated to thinke ye better pleas'd with publick advice, then other statists have been delighted heretofore with publicke flattery. And men will then see what difference there is between the magnanimity of a triennial Parlament, and that jealous hautinesse of Prelates and cabin Counsellers. (*CPW*, ii. 488)

Milton's language is more stately than that of most pamphleteers, and, despite his disclaimers, the passage is obvious flattery, but the framing of *Areopagitica* as a call to the Parliament to be true to its own principles (as Milton himself defines them) is a characteristic move within 1640s parliamentarian discourse. As many commentators on *Areopagitica* have suggested, this pamphlet arguing for open debate on public affairs elicited little direct response, and had little discernible influence.[1] Indeed, Milton's appeal for active controversy—for 'knowing good by evil'—and his rejection of 'a fugitive, cloistered virtue' occur in a tract that may, paradoxically, have been produced mainly for circulation to friends and contacts. Several surviving copies are presentation ones, and most include manuscript corrections that may be in Milton's own hand.[2] However, this chapter is less concerned with the impact Milton's tract had on political and religious debates in the 1640s; rather it seeks to demonstrate how closely Milton engaged with parliamentarian dilemmas, and how *Areopagitica* illuminates the tensions within parliamentarianism. Milton's self-presentation as an adviser to the state, his construction of his 'authorial persona' in Dobranski's term, as well as four centuries of critical appreciation, encourage us to regard him as a unique or a distinctive presence, but it is rewarding to place him within a wider, shared context.[3] The complexities and ambiguities in Milton's text, the ways in which 'possibilities and limitations are simultaneously indicated', have many parallels within parliamentarian debate, while his association of regulation of printing with a more general Presbyterian drive towards thorough-going, authoritarian reformation placed him decisively on one side of emerging fissures in the parliamentary cause.[4] Finally, Milton's determination to resist alarmist Presbyterian rhetoric about 'sects and schisms' (in which his own divorce tracts played a minor role) prefigured a bitterer struggle over church government and 'toleration' that consumed parliamentarians in 1645–7.

I

The 'publisht order' rejected in *Areopagitica* was the Ordinance 'for the Regulating of Printing', passed by the Houses of Parliament on 14 June 1643. The preamble presented the Ordinance as an uncontroversial means of reasserting a necessary control:

---

[1] Important exceptions include Sirluck's commentary in *CPW*, which points to the influence of Milton's account of the origins of censorship, and David Norbrook, '*Areopagitica*, Censorship and the Early Modern Public Sphere', in Richard Burt (ed.), *The Administration of Aesthetics: Censorship, Political Criticism and the Public Sphere* (Minneapolis and London, 1994), 3–33.

[2] *CPW*, ii. 514–15; French, *Records*, ii. 114–15. In addition to the copies discussed by French, the copies in the William Andrews Clark Memorial Library, and the Huntington Library, Los Angeles, have manuscript corrections. The best-known presentation copy is the gift to the London bookseller George Thomason, among his magnificent pamphlet collection in the British Library.

[3] See Stephen B. Dobranski, *Milton, Authorship and the Book Trade* (Cambridge, 1999).

[4] Nigel Smith, '*Areopagitica*: Voicing Contexts', in David Loewenstein and James Grantham Turner (eds.), *Politics, Poetics and Hermeneutics in Milton's Prose* (Cambridge, 1990), 103–22 at 116.

Whereas divers good orders have been lately made by both Houses of Parliament, for suppressing the great late abuses and frequent disorders in Printing many false, forged, scandalous, seditious, libelous, and unlicensed Papers, Pamphlets, and Books to the great defamation of Religion and Government. Which Orders . . . have taken little or no effect.[5]

For Milton, however, this restoration of pre-publication licensing was unworthy of the English Parliament, which was adopting measures unknown to the republics of Athens or Rome and other civilized societies. These inventions of the Catholic Church, 'from the most Antichristian Councel, and the most tyrannous Inquisition that ever inquir'd' had been, predictably, taken up by the English prelates and their chaplains, who were 'bewitcht' and 'besotted' into

The gay imitation of a lordly Imprimatur, one from Lambeth House, another from the West end of Pauls, so apishly Romanizing, that the word of command still was set downe in Latine; as if the learned Grammaticall pen that wrote it, would cast no ink without Latine: or perhaps, as they thought, because no vulgar tongue was worthy to expresse the pure conceit of an Imprimatur. (CPW, ii. 504–5)

Before the Civil War, divinity books required a licence of approval from a designated chaplain of the Bishop of London or Archbishop of Canterbury, before being 'entered' in the register of the Stationers' Company; similar arrangements operated for other types of print. This system relied on the prerogative power of the king rather than on parliamentary statute, and was enforced chiefly through the Court of Star Chamber. Hence Milton's dismay that control of printing was re-established, 'all this the Parliament yet sitting', under pressure, he alleged, from the selfish monopolists of the Company of Stationers, and from self-serving, authoritarian Presbyterian clergy. It was in hindsight significant that the printing ordinance was agreed only two days after an ordinance was passed to summon 'learned, godly and judicious divines' to settle the 'liturgy, government and discipline of the church'.[6] The Westminster Assembly set to work to establish a compulsory, reformed national church with an effective disciplinary structure in place of the episcopal government that had collapsed in 1640–1. In the event, it proved impossible to implement and enforce a fully Presbyterian system, but when Milton was writing Areopagitica in the summer of 1644 his fears (expressed in phrases that were later to find their way into a well-known poem) were entirely plausible: 'It cannot but be guest what is intended by some but a second tyranny over learning; and will soon put it out of controversie that Bishops and Presbyters are the same to us both name and thing' (ii. 559).[7]

Areopagitica was not published until late 1644: George Thomason's copy is dated 24 November; the copy at Yale has 23 November. The summer and autumn of 1644, rather than the summer of 1643, provide the most relevant context. In these months Milton's own circumstances, however exaggerated in his account, illustrate more

---

[5] *Acts and Ordinances of the Interregnum*, ed. C. H. Firth and R. S. Rait (1911), 180; also available online at <http://www.british-history.ac.uk>.

[6] Ibid. 184.

[7] Compare the sonnet 'On the New Forcers of Conscience Under the Long Parliament', dated by *CSP* to Aug. 1646, which ends 'New Presbyter is but old Priest writ large'.

general divisions over control of the press, church government, and religious liberty. Milton's *Doctrine and Discipline of Divorce* featured prominently in Presbyterian arguments for speedy settlement of the church. The publication of such dangerously heterodox ideas starkly revealed the need for church discipline and press regulation. A sermon preached before the House of Commons by Assemblyman Herbert Palmer on 13 August 1644, attacked Milton among others. The published version bemoaned the general spread of 'errors and strange opinions', particularly among the godly themselves, 'the better party among us'. Opposition to infant baptism and 'exercising Ministeriall acts without any calling' were blamed on specious appeals to liberty of conscience ('toleration', in Palmer's terms). Was 'all pretence of Conscience' to be a 'plea for Toleration and Liberty'? Surely Parliament could not allow people to refuse oaths on grounds of conscience or to deny contributions to 'your Just and Necessary Defence'? Surely '[i]f any plead conscience for the Lawfulnesse of Polygamy (or for divorce for other causes then Christ and his Apostles mention; of which a wicked booke is abroad and uncensured, though deserving to be burnt, whose Author has been so impudent as to set his Name to it, and dedicate it to your Selves), or for Liberty to marry incestuously, will you grant a Toleration for all this?' A few days later, the Stationers' Company petitioned the House of Commons over inadequate regulation of printing, prompting an inquiry into the 'Authors, Printers and Publishers, of the Pamphlets against the Immortality of the Soul, and concerning Divorce'.[8]

In poems and pamphlets, Milton expressed indignation and, less plausibly, surprise at the reaction to his divorce tracts:

> I did but prompt the age to quit their clogs
> By the known rules of ancient liberty,
> When straight a barbarous noise environs me
> Of owls and cuckoos, asses, apes and dogs.
> (Sonnet XII. On the Detraction which followed upon
> my Writing Certain Treatises, ll. 1–4)

Milton complained about attacks both in Parliament, and in print:

It was my hap at length lighting on a certain parcel of *Queries*, that seek and finde not, to finde not seeking, at the taile of *Anabaptistical, Antinomian, Heretical, Atheistical epithets, a jolly slander, call'd Divorce at pleasure*: I stood a while and wonder'd, what wee might doe to a mans heart, or what anatomie use, to finde in it sincerity . . . For what book hath hee ever met with, as his complaint is, *Printed in the City*, maintaining either in the title, or in the whole pursuance, *Divorce at Pleasure?*[9]

---

[8] Herbert Palmer, *The Glasse of Gods Providence towards his Faithfull Ones* (1644), 26–7, 31, 33, 56–7; *Commons Journals*, iii. 606. Palmer's work was not entered in the Stationers' Register until 7 Nov., and so probably not published before *Areopagitica*. Palmer's reference is probably to the second edition of the *Doctrine and Discipline*, published in Feb. 1644. This had a dedication to the Parliament signed by Milton (French, *Records*, ii. 109). Thomason's copy of the second edition of the *Doctrine and Discipline* is B.L. E 31 (5).

[9] *Colasterion: A Reply to a Nameless Answer against the Doctrine and Discipline of Divorce* (1645), 'by the former author, J.M.' (*CPW*, ii. 722–3).

This reference was to *Twelve Considerable Serious Questions*, by William Prynne, who had himself suffered mutilation for defying Laudian censorship, but was by 1644 a convinced enemy of religious liberty. Prynne asked whether 'Independent Government' was not 'a floud-Gate to let in an inundation of all manner of Heresies, Errors, Sects, Religions, distructive opinions, Libertinisme and lawlessnesse'? He condemned: 'The late, dangerous increase of many *Anabaptisticall, Antinomian, Heretical, Atheisticall opinions, as of the soules mortality, divorce at pleasure,* etc lately broached, preached, printed in this famous City, which I hope our grand Councell will speedily and carefully suppresse' (6–7). Prynne's tract inaugurated a common Presbyterian strategy of placing Milton, as author of the divorce tracts, within a longer roll-call of threatening ideas, an 'egregious example of libertine heterodoxy' in Thomas N. Corns's terms.[10] Like the Stationers, Prynne linked Milton's works with *Mans Mortalitie*, a startlingly radical attack on conventional distinctions between the soul and the body, and on orthodox understandings of heaven and hell, by the future Leveller Richard Overton, published at the start of 1644.[11] Prynne also condemned 'Master Williams in his late dangerous Licentious Booke' for its 'detestable' argument for complete liberty of conscience, and this pamphlet, Roger Williams, *The Bloody Tenent of Persecution* (July 1644), was commonly associated with Milton's tracts in polemics against 'toleration' and 'libertinism'.[12]

From its earliest meetings the Presbyterian majority in the Westminster Assembly shared the fears of Prynne and other polemicists that *de facto* religious liberty and unregulated printing encouraged the spread of dangerous heresy. The Assembly pressed the Parliament for action against 'Antinomianism' and other 'corrupt doctrines', and against the rising number of gathered and separatist congregations, especially in London. In December 1643, prompted by the Presbyterian clergy of the city of London, the Assembly issued a declaration against the further gathering of churches, but its own divisions over church government were immediately revealed when the congregational or 'Independent' sympathizers among its members issued the *Apologeticall Narration*, an appeal for liberty of conscience outside a Presbyterian establishment. This manifesto provoked Presbyterians but also disappointed more radical opinion, for the 'Apologists' were at pains to stress their own respectability, doctrinal orthodoxy, and opposition to separatism.[13] Dissatisfaction with the *Apologeticall Narration* prompted another future Leveller, William Walwyn, to write *The Compassionate Samaritane*, published in summer 1644 and often compared to *Areopagitica*. Walwyn's tract, like Milton's, was presented to the Parliament, or more

---

[10] Thomas N. Corns, 'John Milton, Roger Williams, and the Limits of Toleration', in Sharon Achinstein and Elizabeth Sauer (eds.), *Milton and Toleration* (Oxford, 2007), 72–85 at 83.

[11] For the high profile and complex implications of Overton's work see Nicholas McDowell, 'Latin Drama and Leveller Ideas: Pedagogy and Power in the Writings of Richard Overton', *Seventeenth Century*, 18 (2003), 230–51.

[12] For an illuminating comparison between Milton and Williams see Corns, 'John Milton, Roger Williams, and the Limits of Toleration'.

[13] For these developments see Ann Hughes, *Gangraena and the Struggle for the English Revolution* (Oxford, 2004), 44–5, 156–7.

specifically to the House of Commons, 'without boldnesse and without feare: for I am well assured that as it is mine and every mans duty to furnish you with what we conceive will advance the Common good . . . so likewise it is your duty to heare and put in execution whatsoever to Your owne judgements shall appeare conducing to those good ends and purposes'.[14] Like Milton, Walwyn condemned the printing ordinance, asking Parliament to 'consider whether more was not gained by that Ordinance then you intended'; and like Milton he blamed the Presbyterians for it. The 'Presbyter as 'tis conceived will bee more violent, as slaves usually are when they become masters' and England would have 'instead of a Lord Bishop, a ruling Presbyter' (pp. 18, 20).

Divisions over church government and the regulation of the press were heightened by Parliament's changing military fortunes in the summer of 1644. The comprehensive victory at Marston Moor in July provoked angry debate over whether the Presbyterian Scots army or the 'Independent' forces of the Eastern Association deserved most of the credit.[15] The humiliating surrender of the parliamentary infantry at Lostwithiel in September, followed by a frustrating failure to defeat the king at Newbury in late October, prompted even bitterer disputes. A majority in Parliament sought to minimize division by establishing a committee to discuss 'accommodation' between Presbyterians and Independents. Others drew different conclusions. The London minister John Goodwin, whose gathered congregation was at the heart of radical politics in the city, preached on the occasion of the 'late disaster' at Lostwithiel that Parliament was being punished for its failures to secure religious liberty. Like Milton, Goodwin insisted that 'error cannot be healed or suppressed but by the manifestation of the truth'.[16] The Presbyterian Edmund Calamy denounced such views in the Westminster Assembly and declared that 'the Assembly hath not endeavoured after uniformity as they ought to have done'. In the autumn of 1644, the Assembly continued to bombard Parliament with evidence of shocking error. They denounced John Bachelor, one of the press licensors nominated in 1643, for licensing *Mans Mortalitie* and warned of the 'mischiefs that will arise from . . . the divulging the dangerous opinions of Antinomianism and Anabaptism'.[17] Milton 'the divorcer' was caught up in these alarms; Milton, the defender of 'liberty' was provoked to respond in *Areopagitica*.

[14] William Walwyn, *The Compassionate Samaritane* (1644), sig. A3^{r-v}; see also Joad Raymond, *Pamphlets and Pamphleteering in Early Modern Britain* (Cambridge, 2003), 259–60.

[15] Hughes, *Gangraena*, 42–3.

[16] Ibid. 158; David Loewenstein, 'Toleration and the Specter of Heresy in Milton's England', in Achinstein and Sauer (eds.), *Milton and Toleration*, 45–71; John Coffey, *John Goodwin and the Puritan Revolution: Religion and Intellectual Change in Seventeenth-Century England* (Woodbridge, Suffolk, 2006); John Goodwin, *Theomachia* (1644), quoted in *CPW*, ii. 112.

[17] Bodleian Library, Tanner MS 61, fo. 162, quoted in Hughes, *Gangraena and the Struggle for the English Revolution*, 158.

II

How had the regulation of printing become such a troubling matter for parliamentarians in 1643–4? To answer this question we need to go back to the dramatic changes in political communication in general, and in printing in particular, at the start of the decade. Since the mid-sixteenth century, cheaper printed genres—short religious tracts, practical handbooks, sensationalist news pamphlets, stories of romance and adventure—had been issued in greater numbers, with particularly significant leaps in the 1590s and the 1620s. But the changes of the early 1640s were of a different order. In 1641 over 2,000 items were published, in 1642 4,000, some six or seven times the average for each year in the 1630s. This was not a result of any significant expansion in the overall capacity of England's print trade, rather the product of a portentous shift from long, expensive books to smaller, cheaper, topical works of one or two 'sheets' (the equivalent of eight to sixteen quarto pages). In 1640, Milton's friend the London bookseller George Thomason took the momentous decision, itself a marker of the unprecedented context, to collect the newsbooks and pamphlets pouring from the press; by 1661 he had amassed 22,000 items.[18] The pre-war licensing regime was ill-equipped to cope with this transformation, but, in any case, Parliament's assault on the Laudian establishment had the unintended consequence of dismantling this regime. Consequently, as Michael Mendle has shown, 'in a three to four month spell in the winter of 1640–41, an imposing edifice of control over printed political communication utterly collapsed'. The machinery which had taken a century to establish disappeared in weeks; even if the system was more 'ramshackle and dilapidated' than either its advocates intended or its high-profile victims alleged, this was a dramatic change.[19]

Much of the cheap print of the early 1640s might be regarded as frivolous or scurrilous, but many vulgar tracts had a serious political and religious message. Sexual innuendo, accusations of cannibalism, mock trials, ghosts, and portents were all used to attack Charles's personal rule, and his chief advisers, Laud and Strafford. Newsbooks proliferated after November 1641, and printed petitions, oaths, sermons, declarations, and remonstrances delivered more sober political and religious messages. The fundamental divisions over power in the kingdom, and over the nature of the true church, gave pamphlets and pamphleteers an urgent purpose. Milton was of course a participant on the serious wing of these debates, in the

---

[18] Raymond, *Pamphlets and Pamphleteering*, 160–6, for the developments of 1640–1. See also Tessa Watt, *Cheap Print and Popular Piety 1550–1640* (Cambridge, 1991); John Barnard and D. F. McKenzie (eds.), with the assistance of Maureen Bell, *The Cambridge History of the Book in Britain*, iv: *1557–1695* (Cambridge, 2002), for the broader context.

[19] Michael Mendle, 'De facto Freedom, de facto Authority: Press and Parliament, 1640–1643', *Historical Journal*, 38 (1995), 307–32 at 309. For balanced accounts of the effectiveness of the Laudian regime see Anthony Milton, 'Licensing, Censorship and Religious Orthodoxy in Early Stuart England', *Historical Journal*, 41 (1998), 625–51; C. S. Clegg, 'Censorship and the Courts of Star Chamber in England to 1640', *Journal of Modern European History*, 3 (2005), 50–80.

'Smectymnuan' controversy over the validity of the episcopacy, and, in his own estimation at least, in the divorce tracts. Milton's decision to become a pamphleteer was, as Raymond insists, 'part of a watershed in the history of print and of political culture in Britain'.[20] *Areopagitica* demonstrates a working author's detailed knowledge of the pains and pleasures of writing, and the mechanics of book production, as when Milton highlights the inconvenience of leaving presses at a standstill while an author sought the licensor's approval for late revisions to his text. *Areopagitica* is concerned with the new print, 'the disorderly, vociferous, and sometimes radical tracts hawked on the streets', rather than exclusive, learned books.[21]

As Milton recognized, Parliament's own actions had contributed enormously to these dramatic changes: 'If it be desir'd to know the immediat cause of all this free writing and free speaking, there cannot be assigned a truer then your own mild, and free, and humane government; it is the liberty, Lords and Commons, which your own valorous and happy counsels have puchast us.' Parliament could not now make the people 'lesse eagerly pursuing of the truth, unless ye first make yourselves, that made us so, lesse the lovers, lesse the founders of true liberty' (*CPW*, ii. 559). The transformations in print culture owed much to the complexities of the parliamentary cause. Parliament was not simply an aristocratic assembly seeking the removal of evil counsellors and the redress of specific grievances. It put itself at the head of a godly struggle for true religion, and the House of Commons, in particular, claimed to be the 'representative of the people', defending that people's rights and liberties. In these guises, Parliament had to communicate with and arouse a broad constituency. Parliamentarians were thus torn between the dangers and the opportunities afforded by print, between 'authoritarian' and 'libertarian' impulses.[22] Print was an essential means of mobilizing potential support, and from its earliest days, Parliament distinguished its own stance from that of the Laudian 'censors' who had suppressed good books, but from the beginning also it was conscious of the risks of unregulated, uncontrollable printing.

From December 1640, Parliament routinely authorized the printing of the sermons preached at its monthly fasts, contributing to a vast expansion in clerical publishing, on which Milton commented sardonically in *Areopagitica*. He alleged that the clergy supported restrictions on the press to protect their own lazy outpourings: 'the multitude of Sermons ready printed and pil'd up, on every text that is not difficult'. Surely all the lectures and sermons 'printed, vented in such numbers and such volumes as have now well nigh made all other books unsalable' had nothing to fear from short, unlicensed, pamphlets?[23] The most significant move by the Commons,

---

[20] Joad Raymond, 'The Literature of Controversy', in Thomas N. Corns (ed.), *A Companion to Milton* (Oxford, 2001), 191–210 at 209.

[21] Joad Raymond, 'Milton', in Barnard and McKenzie (eds.), *Cambridge History of the Book*, 376–87 at 377. See also Dobranski, *Milton, Authorship and the Book Trade*, 104–6, 119–22.

[22] Mendle, 'De facto Freedom', 317.

[23] *Commons Journals*, ii. 48 (10 Dec. 1640) for the first order for the printing of fast sermons; *CPW*, ii. 546–7, 537.

and an illuminating example, is the printing of the 'Protestation' Oath of May 1641. The oath, imposed at the height of alarm over the king's 'Army' plot against the Parliament, bound its takers to the defence of true religion, the privileges of Parliament, and the royal prerogative. First taken by MPs, it was then required of all adult males and 11,000 copies were printed to send throughout the country. The circulation of the Protestation inaugurated Parliament's commitment to the political use of print, as the means through which it became established as an alternative government, as well as a tool of its propaganda. Parliament's publications made up 17 per cent of all works printed in 1642, 15 per cent in 1644, 23 per cent in 1645.[24] A later milestone was the controversial and contested decision by the House of Commons to print its 'Grand Remonstrance' against Charles's misgovernment. The Remonstrance passed the House on 22 November, but only on 15 December, in an ill-tempered debate, was its printing agreed. Edward Dering, MP, increasingly alarmed at the course of events protested: 'Mr Speaker, when I first heard of a Remonstrance, I presently imagined that like faithful councillors, we should hold up a glass unto his Majesty...I did not dream that we should remonstrate downward, tell stories to the people, and talk of the King as of a third person.'[25] It was in the same weeks of crisis that the first, regular, printed newsbooks covering domestic events were established in London.[26] Where fundamental divisions were expressed through printed propaganda, neither king nor Parliament had much choice over the resort to the press. On 12 March 1642, the Commons voted to print an answer to a message from the king: 'the King's Message being printed, and not the Declaration, it might much reflect upon the Parliament' (*Commons Journals*, ii. 477). By 1646 Parliament had published two large volumes of its own most important printed declarations, including, in a sign of confidence in readers' judgement, many of the King's parallel orders and responses. These 'Books of Declarations' were to be deployed in unpredicted ways by radical parliamentarians in the later 1640s.[27]

Parliament thus from 1641 appealed to the 'people' directly through printed instructions, ordinances, and declarations, and specifically through print that invited reflection and action. Other crucial parliamentarian modes, such as oath-taking and petitioning, interacted with, and were dependent on print. Print recorded oath-taking and enabled further commitment, as with the Protestation; petitions were printed as records of allegiance, to counter to royalist initiatives, and, again, to inspire emulation. Through rival printed declarations and petitions, men and

---

[24] *Commons Journals*, ii. 135; *Printing for Parliament, 1641–1700*, ed. Sheila Lambert, List and Index Society, Special Series, vol. 20 (1984), 1. After the king's attempt on the 'five members', the Protestation was reprinted with a declaration 'touching the late breach of our privileges' and the order to take it renewed: *Commons Journals*, ii. 389.

[25] John Rushworth, *Historical Collections* (1721), iv. 425.

[26] *Commons Journals*, ii. 322, 344; Raymond, *Pamphlets and Pamphleteering*, 151.

[27] *An Exact Collection of All Remonstrances, Declarations, Votes, Orders, Ordinances...and other Remarkable Passages* (1643); *Orders, Ordinances and Declarations of both Houses of Parliament* (1646).

women were informed and invited to reflect on the nature of parliamentarianism. Hence Milton and Walwyn could call Parliament to account, demanding that it live up to the expectations raised. Hence too, the Levellers and their precursors in 1645–7 developed a critique of 'parliamentary tyranny' through deploying Parliament's own rhetoric. John Lilburne quoted from Parliament's 'Book of Declarations' almost as much as from the Bible.[28]

Print was especially potent within a political culture where reading skills were spreading and cheap print was more widely available. Printed communication was new and exciting for people who had skills their parents lacked. Fluent technical skills were confined to a minority determined by social status, gender, and geography. It has been estimated, for example, that 65 per cent of men but only 20 per cent of women in mid-seventeenth-century Bristol could sign their names; the figures would have been higher in Milton's London, but throughout England, perhaps one in seven people were fully literate. But statistics based on individual 'sign' literacy underestimate the extent to which print could influence this partially literate society. In the first place, reading was taught before writing so people from humbler backgrounds who had had some schooling might be able to read even if they could not write their names. Furthermore, individual silent reading was not the most important way of apprehending the printed word in revolutionary England, where collective reading and discussion was more typical; all English communities included people who could read to and with their less skilled neighbours.[29]

Laudian censorship, 'inhibiting the Printing of divers orthodox and good Books', was an early target of the Long Parliament, and a major plank of the prosecution case against Archbishop Laud in 1644 (*Commons Journals*, ii. 79). Prynne, who played a major role in Laud's prosecution, was, as we have seen, a high-profile victim of Laudian repression who nonetheless saw nothing inconsistent in advocating parliamentarian regulation of printing. Both Walwyn and Milton, on the other hand, regarded the parliamentary supporters of the printing ordinance as hypocrites. Walwyn noted that when the bishops had protested at the printed assaults on them, Parliament had insisted 'there was no remedy, forasmuch as the Presse was to be open and free for all in time of Parliament' (*Compassionate Samaritane*, sig. A4ʳ). Milton similarly noted that many Presbyterians who now called for licensing

---

[28] David Zaret, *Origins of Democratic Culture: Printing, Petitions and the Public Sphere in Early-Modern England* (Princeton, 2000); John Walter, 'Confessional Politics in Pre-Civil War Essex: Prayer Books, Profanation and Petitions', *Historical Journal*, 44 (2001), 677–701; David Wootton, 'From Rebellion to Revolution: The Crisis of the Winter of 1642/3 and the Origins of Civil War Radicalism', *English Historical Review*, 105 (1990), 654–69; Andrew Sharp, 'John Lilburne and the Long Parliament's *Book of Declarations*: A Radical's Exploitation of the Words of Authorities', *History of Political Thought*, 9 (1988), 19–44.

[29] Jonathan Barry, 'Literacy and Literature in Popular Culture: Reading and Writing in Historical Perspective', in Tim Harris (ed.), *Popular Culture in England c. 1500–1850* (Basingstoke, 1995); David Cressy, *Literacy and the Social Order: Reading and Writing in Tudor and Stuart England* (Cambridge, 1980); Margaret Spufford, 'First Steps in Literacy: The Reading and Writing Experiences of the Humblest Seventeenth-Century Spiritual Autobiographers', *Social History*, 4 (1979), 407–35.

had themselves 'by their unlicen't books to the contempt of an Imprimatur first broke that triple ice clung about our hearts', and that

while the Bishops were to be baited down, then all the Presses might be open; it was the people's birthright and priviledge in time of Parlament, it was the breaking forth of light. But now the Bishops abrogated and voided out of the Church, as if our Reformation sought no more, but to make room for others into their seats under another name . . . liberty of Printing must be enthralled again. (*CPW*, ii. 568, 541)

Milton's contemptuous 'But some will say, What though the Inventors were bad, the thing for all that may be good?' in fact exactly summed up parliament's attitude to regulation of printing (p. 507). A Remonstrance from the Stationers' Company to the Parliament in April 1643 insisted 'it is not meere Printing, but well-ordered Printing, that merits so much favour and respect' and went on to praise the Inquisition condemned by Milton: 'We must in this give Papists their due; for as well where the Inquisition predominates, as not, regulation is more strict by far, then it is amongst Protestants; we are not so wise in our Generation, nor take so much care to preserve the true Religion, as they do the false.'[30] From early 1641, parliament, often in cooperation with the Stationers' Company, and spurred on by orthodox Presbyterian clergy, had sought to control the press. Parliament regularly summoned printers who had published unauthorized versions of approved texts (such as the Protestation) and condemned 'scandalous' material. Lord Digby's speech in favour of Strafford, for example, was declared scandalous and burnt by the common hangman in May 1641.[31] In May 1641 a group of London Presbyterians petitioned Parliament in support of the Stationers' demand for closer regulation of printing, and the Stationers continued to act as the agents of the authorities in suppressing illegal printing. They were required to seize all copies of Digby's pro-Strafford speech in May 1641 and authorized to search for illegal printing under an order of 26 August 1642, which prefigured the June 1643 ordinance. This laid down that no book 'false or scandalous to the Proceedings of the Houses of Parliament' was to be printed, and that all parliamentary printing had to be officially approved and entered in the Stationers' register.[32] Other measures that look forward to the ordinance and back to the 1630s include the requirement in January 1642 that printers could not print anything without the 'name and consent of the author' and the powers, reminiscent of Star Chamber, given to the Committee of Examinations in March 1643 to search for and seize illegal presses, and imprison offenders (*Common Journals*, ii. 402, 996–7).

---

[30] *The Humble Remonstrance of the Company of Stationers* (1643) sigs. A1^{r-v}, A4^r; Thomason's copy (British Library, E247 (23)) has the manuscript note, 'By Henry Parker esq.'. Blair Hoxby, 'The Trade of Truth Advanced: *Areopagitica*, Economic Discourse and Libertarian Reform', *Milton Studies*, 36 (1998), 177–202; and Smith, '*Areopagitica*: Voicing Contexts', describe how Milton seems at many points in *Areopagitica* to be answering this tract.

[31] *Commons Journals*, ii. 136, 208–9; Jason Peacey, *Politicians and Pamphleteers: Propaganda during the English Civil Wars and Interregnum* (Aldershot, 2004), 132–48.

[32] Mendle, 'De facto Freedom', 320–1, 329; *Commons Journals*, ii. 208–9, 739.

III

The June 1643 ordinance required that no books or pamphlets be printed unless they had been 'approved of and licensed' by men appointed by the Parliament, and entered in the register of the Stationers' Company 'according to ancient custom', with the printer's name attached.[33] On the same day that the Commons sought nominations for the licensors to be appointed under the ordinance, they sent for the royalist printer Richard Royston as a delinquent, and Walwyn claimed the ordinance was originally intended against royalist propaganda but 'by reason of the qualifications of the Licensers' it had 'stopt the mouthes of good men'. It would have been more honest to pass a measure against 'Anabaptisticall, Brownisticall, or Independent writings, then to have their mouthes stopt so subtlely and insensibly, and their liberty taken from them unawares'.[34] As Mendle has noted, *Areopagitica* was not an accurate picture of the impact of licensing in 1643–4, revealing fears for the future rather than the reality of the present.[35] However, both Walwyn and Milton might be seen as prophetic in their insistence that the main targets were those denounced as sectaries by orthodox Puritans.

Milton intermittently obeyed the provisions of the ordinance: *Of Education* and *The Judgement of Martin Bucer* had both been entered in the Stationers' Register before the publication of *Areopagitica*, and the *Poems* were entered in October 1645. As Secretary to the republic in the early 1650s, Milton himself acted as a licensor, to some later critical dismay.[36] But the regulation of the press was never complete. Even in the 1630s as many as 35 per cent of all works were never registered, and although the 1643 Ordinance effected a brief, temporary rise in registration, in 1644 only some 20 per cent of works were entered in the Stationers' Register, only 46 per cent carried a printer's name, and 32 per cent a bookseller's.[37] Thus the Presbyterian polemicist Thomas Edwards complained, 'never more dangerous unlicensed Books printed than since the Ordinance against unlicensed Printing'.[38] Why then did licensing matter, when it could so easily be circumvented? Edwards resented the respectability given to unorthodox books by a licence, blaming in particular John Bachelor, one of the few non-Presbyters among the licensers of divinity books. Bachelor had acted as a 'Man-midwife to bring forth more monsters begotten by the Divell and borne of the

---

[33] *Acts and Ordinances*, ed. Firth and Rait, 184.

[34] *Commons Journals*, iii. 131; Walwyn, *Compassionate Samaritane*, sig. A4[r–v].

[35] 'De facto Freedom', 331.

[36] French, *Records*, ii. 101, 105, 129; Sabrina Baron, 'Licensing Readers, Licensing Authorities in Seventeenth-Century England', in Jenny Andersen and Elizabeth Sauer (eds.), *Books and Readers in Early Modern England* (Philadelphia, 2002), 217–42; Abbe Blum, 'The Author's Authority: *Areopagitica* and the Labour of Licensing', in Margaret W. Ferguson and Mary Nyqyuist (eds.), *Remembering Milton* (New York and London, 1987), 74–96. Dobranski, *Milton, Authorship and the Book Trade*, 124, wisely asks why we expect consistency from Milton; see also Ann Hughes, 'Afterword' in Achinstein and Sauer (eds.), *Milton and Toleration*, 303.

[37] Mendle, 'De facto Freedom', 311; Dobranski, *Milton, Authorship and the Book Trade*, 111, drawing on the work of D. F. Mckenzie; Raymond, *Pamphlets and Pamphleteering*, 169–70.

[38] *Gangraena; Or, a Catalogue and Discovery of many of the Errours, Heresies, Blasphemies and pernicious Practices of the Sectaries of this time*, 3 pts. (1646), i, sig. a2[r].

Sectaries within these three last years' than the Bishops had managed in eighty. He had, for example, provided imprimaturs for works by John Goodwin and for Walwyn's attacks on Edwards.[39] Bachelor insisted, however: 'The Books which meet with harshest censure, such as the *Bloody Tenet*, the Treatise about *Divorce*, and others that have affinitie with these, I have been so farre from licensing, that I have not so much as seene or heard of them, till after they have been commonly sold abroad.'[40] For Milton, licensing also mattered because it deprived an author of his autonomy, depriving a man of his essential liberty. Whether books were actually suppressed was irrelevant; the requirement to go cap in hand to a licensor for permission, and the potential for suppression in itself turned virtuous, learned men into slaves, responsible adults into children. The bitter resentment in *Areopagitica* against a 'patriarchal licenser', and against dependency ('I hate a pupil teacher'), is testimony to the republican aspects of Milton's stance: 'He who is not trusted with his own actions, his drift not being known to be evil, and standing to the hazard of law and penalty, has no great argument to think himself reputed in the Commonwealth where he was born, for other then a fool or a foreigner' (*CPW*, ii. 533).[41]

These were issues of practice as well as theory. Even if licensing was only erratically enforced, there were risks for authors, printers, and publishers of unlicensed material, as Milton was aware. Soon after the publication of *Areopagitica*, the Stationers Company, in the course of an investigation into a 'scandalous pamphlet' illegally printed by an associate of Richard Overton, complained to the House of Lords about the 'frequent printing of scandalous Books by divers', specifically Hezekiah Woodward (who had written against the Presbyterians Prynne and Thomas Edwards) and John Milton. The two men were summoned for examination and Woodward was briefly imprisoned, but there is no evidence of any action against Milton, who professed to believe that his escape was a sign that Parliament wished 'to exalt the truth, and to depress the tyranny of error and ill custome' (*CPW*, ii. 579). Milton continued to feature in sensationalist Presbyterian polemic against error and heresy, attacked along with Baptists by Daniel Featley, and coupled again with Roger Williams in Ephraim Pagitt's Heresiography, which associated the 'bloody Tenet' with a 'tractate of divorce in which the bonds are let loose to inordinate lust'.[42]

[39] *Gangraena; Or, a Catalogue and Discovery of many of the Errours, Heresies, Blasphemies and pernicious Practices of the Sectaries of this time*, iii. 102; William Walwyn, *An Antidote against Master Edwards* (1646) includes an imprimatur from Bachelor dated 26 May 1646.

[40] Bachelor's imprimatur to John Goodwin, *Twelve Considerable Cautions*, published in Feb. 1646, quoted in French, *Records*, ii. 142–3. This passage has been taken to imply that Milton had sought a licence but been refused, but this seems to stretch the evidence (Baron, 'Licensing Readers, Licensing Authorities', 222).

[41] Martin Dzelzainis, 'Republicanism', in Corns (ed.), *Companion to Milton*, 294–308; Eric Nelson, ' "True Liberty": Isocrates and Milton's *Areopagitica*', *Milton Studies*, 40 (2001), 201–21; Norbrook, '*Areopagitica*, Censorship and the Early Modern Public Sphere'. See also Hoxby, '*Areopagitica* and Liberty', ch. 12 below.

[42] Ephraim Pagitt, *Heresiography* (1645 and later editions); Daniel Featley, *The Dippers Dipt* (1645). Milton also featured in Robert Baillie, *A Dissuasive from the Errours of the Time* (1645); see French, *Records*, ii. 122–3, 127–9, 132–3.

Bachelor's justification of his licensing activities, quoted above, indicates clearly that Milton's divorce tracts served as a marker of the unacceptable, even for an Independent sympathizer. They were denounced again in the longest, and most high-profile, Presbyterian heresiography, Thomas Edwards's *Gangraena*, published in three parts in 1646. Part I included garbled extracts from the *Doctrine and Discipline of Divorce*, mischievously associated with the argument that ''Tis lawfull for one man to have two wives at once'. In *The Second Part of Gangraena*, Milton was credited with inspiring a woman preacher of London, Mrs Attaway, who on the basis of 'Master Milton's Doctrine of Divorce' had abandoned her own 'unsanctified husband' and eloped with another married man.[43] By 1647 Milton's notoriety had reached the cheapest of print when 'A Divorcer' featured in an illustrated broadside catalogue of 'the severall sects and opinions in England'.[44]

The consequences for other books and other authors were more serious. In *Areopagitica* Milton declared:

Books are not absolutely dead things, but doe contain a potencie of life in them to be as active as that soule was whose progeny they are . . . as soon almost kill a Man as kill a good Book; who kills a Man kills a reasonable creature, Gods Image; but hee who destroyes a good Booke, kills reason it selfe, kills the Image of God, as it were in the Eye. (*CPW*, ii. 492)

In July 1645, Parliament ordered the destruction of a book, John Archer's *Comfort for Beleevers*, after the Assembly of Divines accused it of promulgating a 'scandalous, blasphemous Heresy' that God was the author of sin. Like Milton, although from a different perspective, the Assembly distinguished between book and man, noting that Archer, a minister, was dead and 'their Requests were nothing concerning his Person, but his Book'. This dangerous book was burnt in the chief places of sociability and debate in London, Westminster, St Paul's Churchyard, Smithfield, and the Exchange (*Commons Journals*, iv. 206).

By 1645–6, as the royalists were decisively defeated, printing was a formidable weapon for all sides in the increasingly bitter conflicts amongst parliamentarians, and control of printing a high-profile occasion of dispute. In the autumn of 1645 Presbyterians in London began a zealous campaign of publication and petitioning against Parliament's half-hearted religious settlement. Mobilization against this threatened Presbyterian dominance encompassed a broad range of independent and sectarian opinion and was spearheaded by men who were to become notorious as the leaders of the democratic 'Leveller' movement in 1647, John Lilburne, Richard Overton, and William Walwyn. Adherence to particular printed texts was crucial to the emergence of radical identities in London, and it was through print, above all, that Levellers sought to make their own individual sufferings emblematic of a broader parliamentary 'tyranny' and of Parliament's betrayal of their most loyal supporters. The sufferings of Lilburne and other Levellers arose directly from their

[43] Edwards, *Gangraena*, i. 34; ii. 11; Hughes, *Gangraena and the Struggle for the English Revolution*, 244–5.

[44] Hughes, *Gangraena and the Struggle for the English Revolution*, 272.

deployment of printed texts against the Presbyterians and then against a Parliament that sought to limit their freedom to publish. John Lilburne was imprisoned by Parliament from August until October 1645 for his anti-Presbyterian pamphlets, and his plight was the focus of a concerted campaign through Richard Overton's underground press and Thomas Paine's partly legitimate one. Parliamentary attempts to block radical publications were mostly unsuccessful; their main impact was to inspire radical critiques of the powers of the House of Lords, and demands for a political structure that truly represented the people.[45] The following year another radical printer, William Larner, was imprisoned on suspicion of involvement in publishing *The Last Warning to all the Inhabitants of London* (in fact a product of Overton's secret press). This attacked 'Presbyterian Prelates' and the willingness to 'receive the King in againe upon any conditions'; like Milton, the author of *The Last Warning* argued that limits on religious liberty led to 'vassallized judgement'.[46] Lilburne returned to prison in June 1646 and in July *The Remonstrance of Many Thousand Citizens*, a key radical manifesto probably written by Overton and Walwyn, incurred the wrath of Parliament's Committee for Examinations. Overton too was in prison by August. Like *Areopagitica*, *The Remonstrance* was directed to the Parliament, but specifically to the House of Commons, and with a much more aggressive tone: 'Wee are well assured, yet cannot forget, that the cause of our choosing you to be Parliament-men, was to deliver us from all kind of Bondage, and to preserve the Commonwealth in Peace and Happinesse.' The authors insisted that the Commons had 'only a Power of trust' which was 'ever revocable'.[47]

Regulation of printing was not the only weapon of Presbyterians and mainstream parliamentarians. In June 1645, for example, the Assembly went 'as a body' to Parliament to denounce the 'horrid blasphemies' of the anti-Trinitarian Paul Best. During an incarceration of more than two years, Best narrowly escaped a vote for his execution. A comprehensive ordinance against heresy and blasphemy was introduced in the House of Commons in September 1646 although it was not finally passed until May 1648.[48]

None of these measures could put a stop to parliamentarian fragmentation, and London, in particular, was an arena for lively speculation and rival mobilizations. Presbyterians were predictably alarmed. Prynne bemoaned the spread of error in 'this famous City' while Thomas Edwards condemned the 'abominable errours' preached in 'the heart of the City', and dispersed in printed books in 'all places', even Westminster Hall where the Parliament sat (*Gangraena*, i. 148–9). Milton, on the contrary, argued that it was better that diverse opinions were published openly than 'privily from house to house', and praised this same London as:

45 David R. Como, 'An Unattributed Pamphlet by William Walwyn: New Light on the Prehistory of the Leveller Movement', *Huntington Library Quarterly*, 69 (2006), 353–82.

46 *The Last Warning to all the Inhabitants of London* (n.p., dated by Thomason 20 Mar. 1645/6), 2, 3, 5; Como, 'An Unattributed Pamphlet', 371.

47 *A Remonstrance of Many Thousand Citizens* (n.p., 1646; Thomason adds London and 7 July); *Commons Journals*, iv. 482, 616.

48 Hughes, *Gangraena and the Struggle for the English Revolution*, 159–60, 364 n., 379–81.

this vast City; a City of refuge, the mansion house of liberty, encompast and surrounded with his protection; the shop of warre hath not there more anvils and hammers waking, to fashion out the plates and instruments of armed Justice in defence of beleaguer'd Truth, then there be pens and heads there, sitting by their studious lamps, musing, searching, revolving new notions and idea's wherewith to present, as with their homage and their fealty the approaching Reformation: others as fast reading, trying all things, assenting to the force of reason and convincement. (*CPW*, ii. 548, 533–4)

The Stationers' Company had complained in April 1643 that 'Printing hath of late been the fewell in some measure of this miserable Civill-Warre by deceiving the multitude', while William Walwyn claimed that Presbyterians sought to ensure 'that nothing may come to the Worlds view but what they please, unless men will runne the hazard of imprisonment'. Thomas Edwards indeed asked that 'the wicked books, printed of late years, (some whereof licensed, dispersed, cryed up) should be openly burnt by the hand of the hangman'. The list he conveniently provided included '*Mortality of Man, The Bloody Tenet, Compassionate Samaritan*', but none of Milton's works.[49] Presbyterians, and indeed most parliamentarians, wanted some control of the press, but in a context of polemical struggle, when many people were 'reading, trying all things', Presbyterians, like Independents or sectaries, had to engage in printed debate. Given that the wicked books existed, Presbyterians had to counter them and attempt to rally support to their cause through the press. Thus Thomas Edwards, like Walwyn and Milton, wanted active readers, inviting them to choose between his own arguments and those of John Goodwin or William Walwyn, confident that 'every judicious Reader, who hath but read M. Walwyns Pamphlets, out of them will acquit me, that I have said nothing of him but truth, he being out of his own mouth and writings condemned'.[50] If Presbyterian polemicists, against their natural inclinations, were forced to sanction open debate, much modern criticism has qualified the view of *Areopagitica* as a defence of freedom. As Thomas N. Corns has recently commented, *Areopagitica* has for some while 'seemed less like an iconic proclamation of core values of western liberalism and more like a series of problems to be explained away'.[51] Milton would not extend liberty to 'Popery and open superstition' and this last category might be wide indeed (*CPW*, ii. 565). He accepted that libellous and blasphemous books might be prosecuted after publication: the procedure which Parliament used for John Archer's book. The 'public sphere' that *Areopagitica* conjured up, where 'private persons', testing all things through conscience and reason, were thereby animated to give 'publick advice', had a complicated birth and a complex character. The fundamental divisions of the 1640s, and in particular the capacity for reflection, revision, and challenge within parliamentarianism (facilitated especially by print), do seem to have produced a novel public sphere where it was accepted as valid and necessary for an expanded political nation

---

[49] *The Humble Remonstrance*, sig. A4ʳ; Walwyn, *Compassionate Samaritane*, 39; Edwards, *Gangraena*, i. 171.

[50] *Gangraena*, ii. 26. See further Steven Dobranski, *Readers and Authorship in Early Modern England* (Cambridge, 2005), 207–9; Sharon Achinstein, *Milton and the Revolutionary Reader* (Princeton, 2004).

[51] Corns, 'John Milton, Roger Williams, and the Limits of Toleration', 72.

to engage in debate about the ends of government.[52] It was not simply that men like Milton and Walwyn were advocates of freedom opposed to authoritarian Presbyterians like Palmer or Edwards. The shift to a broader conception of the public sphere came from the powerful mixture of competing political and religious allegiances mobilized most consistently through new forms of print directed towards an expanding constituency of the literate. All participants had to contend with the rich and ultimately uncontrollable politicized press.

It would be misleading to conclude by blurring distinctions between Milton and Presbyterian polemicists. There were clear contrasts in their attitudes to division, and to truth. Milton, like Walwyn and John Goodwin, was immune to the terrors of 'sects and schisms' that populated the nightmares of Prynne, Calamy, and Edwards.[53] Milton ridiculed those 'who perpetually complain of schisms and sects', turning their own alarmist language against the Presbyterians: 'this obstructing violence meets for the most part with an event utterly opposite to the end which it drives at: instead of suppressing sects and schisms, it raises them, and invests them with a reputation' (*CPW*, ii. 550, 542). For Milton, division was inevitable, not a source of panic as it was to Edwards. In *Areopagitica*, Milton praised the radical parliamentarian peer Lord Brooke for his similarly relaxed attitude. Brooke had written in 1642 that 'it is clear in Reason, that Divisions, Sects, Schisms, and Heresies must come' and had rejected a forced 'Unity of Darknesse and Ignorance'.[54] Walwyn also agreed: 'All times have produced men of severall wayes and I beleeve no man thinks there will be an agreement of judgement as long as this world lasts.' If division was ever-present, debate and informed discussion were the only means of reaching the truth. For Walwyn, only 'the power and efficacie of Truth' could convince. It was tyranny 'to force men against their minde and judgment, to beleeve that other men conclude to be true' (*Compassionate Samaritane*, 41–2, 51). For Milton, too, truth was a 'streaming fountain', unlike the 'muddy pool of conformity and tradition'; 'A man may be a heretick in the truth; and if he beleeve things only because his Pastor sayes so, or the Assembly so determines, without knowing other reason, though his belief be true, yet the very truth he holds becomes his heresie' (*CPW*, ii. 543).

There remain tensions within Milton's position, here, as Norbrook has suggested, between 'Truth as absolute and Truth as process'. Most often truth 'emerges in dialogue' rather than being laid down by authority, as Prynne, Edwards, and Palmer insisted.[55] Throughout *Areopagitica*, the hostility to Presbyterian certainty is clear, and remarkably prescient, for the most aggressive assaults on sects and schism were more characteristic of 1645–7 than 1644:

---

[52] Peter Lake and Steve Pincus, 'Rethinking the Public Sphere in Early Modern England', *Journal of British Studies*, 45 (2006), 270–92 at 279–81.

[53] See Loewenstein, 'Toleration and the Specter of Heresy', for an eloquent exposition of this view.

[54] Robert Greville, Lord Brooke, *A Discourse Opening the Nature of that Episcopacie, which is Exercised in England* (1642), 88; *CPW*, ii. 560–1, 567.

[55] Norbrook, '*Areopagitica*, Censorship and the Early Modern Public Sphere', 23–4.

These are the men cry'd out against for schismaticks and sectaries; as if, while the Temple of the Lord was building, some cutting, some squaring the marble, others hewing the cedars, there should be a sort of irrational men who could not consider there must be many schisms and many dissections made in the quarry and in the timber, ere the house of God can be built. And when every stone is laid artfully together, it cannot be united into a continuity, it can but be contiguous in this world; neither can every peece of the building be of one form: nay rather the perfection consists in this, that out of many moderat varieties and brotherly dissimilitudes that are not vastly disproportional arises the goodly and the gracefull symmetry that commends the whole pile and structure. (*CPW*, ii. 555)

Here Milton rejects the scaremongering of Palmer and Prynne and accepts division, but there are nonetheless limits and hesitations, in confining difference to 'moderat varieties and brotherly dissimilitudes'. Here Milton has less in common with the open-minded sectary William Walwyn and more with mainstream independents like Oliver Cromwell, whose commitment to liberty of conscience was founded on the conviction that the godly could reach a common shared truth, though they might travel there by different roads.[56]

[56] Corns, 'John Milton, Roger Williams and the Limits of Toleration'; Smith, '*Areopagitica*: Voicing Contexts'; Blair Worden, 'Toleration and the Cromwellian Protectorate', in W. J. Sheils (ed.), *Persecution and Toleration* (Oxford, 1984), 199–233.

CHAPTER 12

....

AREOPAGITICA AND LIBERTY

....

BLAIR HOXBY

THE title page of *Areopagitica* (23 November 1644) presents the pamphlet as the sort of free political speech that was an integral part of Attic citizenship and liberty. Milton draws its epigram from a debate between Theseus and the Theban herald in Euripides' *The Suppliant Women*. When the Theban herald asks who the tyrant of the city is, Theseus retorts that there is none: Athens is a free republic. The herald is unimpressed. The common people cannot even speak properly, he says, much less guide a city. 'There is nothing more hostile to a city than a tyrant', responds Theseus.[1] He praises democracies in which laws are written down and citizens may express their enfranchisement and freedom in political speech. 'This is true Liberty', run his words on the title page of *Areopagitica*,

> when free born men
> Having to advise the public may speak free,
> Which he who can, and will, deserv's high praise,
> Who neither can nor will, may hold his peace;
> What can be juster in a State than this?[2]

The copy of Euripides that Milton used glossed this passage in terms of *parrhesia*, a form of free and bold speech in which the speaker typically offered sincere criticism

I would like to thank all the members of the Northeast Milton Seminar, and in particular John Leonard, Thomas Luxon, Jason Rosenblatt, Elizabeth Sauer, William Shullenberger, Nigel Smith, and Nicholas von Maltzhan, for their comments on an earlier version of this essay.

[1] Euripides, *The Suppliant Women*, l. 429, in *Euripides*, trans. David Kovacs, iii (Loeb Classical Library; Cambridge, Mass., and London, 1998).

[2] David Kovacs's translation reads: 'Freedom consists in this: "Who has a good proposal and wants to set it before the city?" He who wants to enjoys fame, while he who does not holds his peace. What is fairer for a city than this?'

of his audience at real risk to himself.[3] Although a philosopher who censured a tyrant could be said to use *parrhesia*, a speaker using it in democratic Athens would normally be a distinguished citizen addressing the *ecclesia*, or public assembly, and braving the disapproval of the majority. In *The Phoenician Women*, Euripides identifies the loss of this form of free and bold speech as the greatest sorrow of the exile. 'A slave's lot this,' says Jocasta, 'not saying what you think.' Polynices concurs, observing that a man exiled from his own polis must suppress his nature, endure the follies of his ruler, and play the slave.[4]

In his exordium, Milton presents himself as a *parrhesiastes* who, impelled by a love of liberty yet fearful of 'what will be the censure' (*CPW*, ii. 486), criticizes Parliament in public. The earnest of his own sincerity is the courage that he displays in addressing the assembly, and the evidence of his confidence in its members is his trust that they will play what Michel Foucault has described as the 'parrhesiastic game' by listening to the frank speech of a citizen convinced of the truth of what he says.[5] For those 'who wish and promote their Countries liberty', Milton's discourse may serve as a 'testimony' of what has already been achieved. For no man can expect to be free from grievances in a Commonwealth, but he can hope that 'complaints' will be 'freely heard, deeply consider'd, and speedily reform'd'. That is the 'utmost bound of civill liberty attain'd, that wise men looke for' (*CPW*, ii. 487).

One reason that Milton entitles his pamphlet *Areopagitica* is that he wants to recall one of the most famous examples of this sort of *parrhesia*. Holding up 'the old and elegant humanity of Greece' as a model for Parliament to follow in contrast to the 'barbarick pride of a *Hunnish* and *Norwegian* stateliness', Milton reminds the assembly that Isocrates once 'from his private house wrote that discours to the Parlament of *Athens*, that perswades them to change the forme of *Democraty* which was then establisht' (*CPW*, ii. 489). The sort of free, bold speech that Isocrates exercised in his written 'oration' and that Milton is exercising in the promulgation of his pamphlet should not be the exclusive privilege of Members of Parliament speaking in session. If it is in the interest of the 'Realme' and the 'Royall Estate' to permit every MP 'to discharge his conscience and boldly in every thing incident among us to declare his advice', as the Speaker of the Commons asserted at the opening of each session of Parliament when petitioning for free speech in the assembly, then surely, Milton suggests in his exordium, it would also be in their interest to hear from a countryman who can offer 'the industry of a life wholly dedicated to studious labours' (*CPW*, ii. 489–90).[6] Free speech should be extended to the realm of print and enjoyed as one of

---

[3] *Euripides tragoediae*, ed. Paulus Stephanus, 2 vols. (Geneva, 1602), ii, sig. Pii[v]. David Norbrook makes this point in *Writing the English Republic: Poetry, Rhetoric, and Politics, 1627–1660* (Cambridge, 1999), 127.

[4] See Euripides, *The Phoenician Women*, ll. 290–95, in *Euripides*, trans. David Kovacs, v (Loeb Classical Library; Cambridge, Mass., and London, 2002).

[5] See Michel Foucault, *Fearless Speech*, ed. Joseph Pearson (Los Angeles, 2001).

[6] The Speaker reiterated language first used by Thomas More when he was Speaker; see William Roper, *The Mirrour of Vertue in Wordly Greatnes. Or the Life of Syr Thomas More Knight, Sometime Lo. Chancellour of England* (Paris, 1626), 21–2.

the liberties of a people who are just as capable of directing their own affairs as the Athenians.

Milton's advice is that 'it would fare better with truth, with learning, and the Commonwealth' if Parliament's Licensing Order of 1643, which re-erected a system of pre-publication censorship that had effectively lapsed in 1640, 'were call'd in' (ii. 488). Under the Tudors and Stuarts, the Stationers' Company, the King's Printer, and the university presses had helped to suppress the dissemination of any books that had not received the approval of a licensor prior to publication because the maintenance of their lucrative exclusive privilege to print depended on their enforcement of these intellectual restrictions. Then in 1637 a Star Chamber decree had placed the Archbishop of Canterbury and the Bishop of London in charge of licensing the vast majority of books published in London, 'whether of Diuinity, Phisicke, Philosophie, Poetry, or whatsoever', and had placed the chancellors of Oxford and Cambridge in charge of licensing books printed at the universities. The punishment of offenders was to be determined by the Court of High Commission, the Court of Star Chamber, or the Privy Council.[7] This decree associated licensing firmly with William Laud in the popular imagination, for he was not only the Archbishop of Canterbury and Chancellor of Oxford but a powerful member of all the courts and councils that punished offenders. Once his role in the suppression of religious works became a contentious issue in his impeachment before Parliament in December of 1640, the Stationers' Company hesitated to use its powers of search and seizure, which had been authorized by the Crown and by Star Chamber, not by Parliament. Unlicensed publications grew apace.

But the majority of MPs never really intended to dispense with licensing, and by 1643 their alarm at the circulation of pamphlets written by both fervent royalists and radical reformers alike made them receptive to a petition from the Stationers' Company asking that licensing be reinstituted and their exclusive privileges upheld. Parliament duly passed an order 'for suppressing the great late abuses and frequent disorders in Printing many false forged, scandalous, seditious, libelous, and unlicensed Papers, Pamphlets, and Books to the great defamation of Religion and government' (*CPW*, ii. 797). Some of the assembly's warmest supporters considered this order a betrayal. In his *Liberty of Conscience* (24 March 1644), Henry Robinson argued that in religious controversies 'neither side must expect to have greater liberty of speech, writing, Printing, or whatsoever else, then the other', and in *The Compassionate Samaritane* (June–July? 1644), William Walwyn laid the blame on certain ministers of the Westminster Assembly, who wanted to squelch religious debate: the effect of the order would be to stop 'the mouthes of good men, who must either not write at all, or no more then is sutable to the judgements and interests of the Licensers'.[8]

---

[7] See *A Decree of Starre-Chamber, Concerning Printing* (1637); F. S. Siebert, *Freedom of the Press in England, 1476–1776* (Urbana, Ill., 1952), 127–46.

[8] Henry Robinson, *Liberty of Conscience* (1644), 17; William Walwyn, *Compassionate Samaritane* (1644), sig. A4ᵛ. On *Areopagitica*'s position amid other pleadings for free speech and liberty of conscience,

Milton entered the debate when the Stationers pursued him for the unlicensed publication of his divorce tracts. His response was to issue yet another unlicensed pamphlet—this time with his name printed boldly on the title page.[9] Like Walwyn and Robinson, Milton feared that the Licensing Order might be just the first of many efforts to restrict freedom of religion: soon the Westminster Assembly might become 'afraid of every conventicle', and shortly thereafter it might 'make a conventicle of every Christian meeting' (*CPW*, ii. 541). But *Areopagitica* is not a narrow defence of free religion. It is a broad vindication of liberty in which Milton seeks to fit together discrete 'liberties' that he finds in the Bible, the ancients, and the common law into a more capacious ideal that will remain incomplete unless it comprises 'the liberty to know, to utter, and to argue freely according to conscience'—the liberty that Milton asks for 'above all liberties' (ii. 560). It is Milton himself who offers us the best means to think about the way these discrete liberties and distinct intellectual traditions buttress his overarching claims: 'When every stone is laid artfully together, it cannot be united into a continuity, it can but be contiguous in this world; neither can every peece of the building be of one form; nay rather the perfection consists in this, that out of many moderat varieties and brotherly dissimilitudes that are not vastly disproportional arises the goodly and the graceful symmetry that commends the whole pile and structure' (ii. 555).

Christian Liberty and Roman Manhood

A central aim of *Areopagitica* is to persuade Parliament to 'foregoe this Prelaticall tradition of crowding free consciences and Christian liberties into canons and precepts of men' (*CPW*, ii. 554). It strives to expand the realm of 'things indifferent' and to argue that subjects should be left to make choices in these matters, not made to obey a particular protocol in the name of church discipline. Truth, Milton argues, may have more than one shape:

What else is all that rank of things indifferent, wherein Truth may be on this side, or on the other, without making her unlike her self. What but a vain shadow else is the abolition of *those*

---

see *Tracts on Liberty in the Puritan Revolution*, ed. William Haller, 3 vols. (New York, 1934); Ernest Sirluck, introduction and notes, in *CPW*, ii. 1–216, 480–570; Nigel Smith, '*Areopagitica*: Voicing Contexts, 1643–5', in David Lowenstein and James Grantham Turner (eds.), *Politics, Poetics, and Hermeneutics in Milton's Prose* (Cambridge, 1990), 103–22; and Thomas Fulton, '*Areopagitica* and the Roots of Liberal Epistemology', *English Literary Renaissance*, 34 (2004), 42–82.

[9] On the lost petition against Milton that the Stationers presented to the Commons, see Sirluck, introduction, in *CPW*, ii. 142. The petition was preceded by Herbert Palmer's sermon before Parliament (13 Aug. 1644), which attacked Milton. For Milton's complaints against intellectual restrictions in the divorce tracts, see the *Doctrine and Discipline of Divorce* (1 Aug. 1643) and *The Judgement of Martin Bucer* (15 July 1644), in *CPW*, ii. 223–6, 479.

ordinances, that hand writing nayl'd to the crosse, what great purchase is this Christian liberty which *Paul* so often boasts of. His doctrine is, that he who eats or eats not, regards a day, or regards it not, may doe either to the Lord. (*CPW*, ii. 563)

Paul developed this doctrine while intervening in the disputes of congregations in Rome, Corinth, and Galatia, where some Judaizing Christians were arguing that certain laws of the Jews such as circumcision ought to be observed by Jewish Christians or even by all Christians.[10] Paul countered that the time for the law had expired: it had been a 'schoolmaster *to bring us unto Christ*' (Gal. 3: 24), but it could not bind the liberty of Christians. Yet the fact that all things were lawful for Christians did not mean they were all expedient (1 Cor. 10: 23). 'All things indeed are pure', said Paul, but we should 'follow after the things which make for peace, and things wherewith one may edifie another.' Therefore '*it is* good neither to eat flesh, nor to drink wine, nor *any thing* whereby thy brother stumbleth, or is offended, or is made weak' (Rom. 14: 19–21). Thus Paul taught a doctrine not only of liberty but of forbearance and charity in which Christians could respect what Milton described as the 'neighboring differences, or rather indifferences' of their brethren (*CPW*, ii. 565). For Milton, the lesson was not that a Christian state must take extraordinary care to insulate its subjects from temptation or error—'For God sure esteems the growth and compleating of one vertuous person, more than the restraint of ten vitious' (ii. 528)—but that many 'things might be tolerated in peace, and left to conscience, had we but charity' (ii. 563; cf. 554).

Milton tells the story of an early bishop who ran afoul of a judgemental hypocrite who did not demonstrate such charity. 'A person of great name in the Church for piety and learning', Dionysius Alexandrinus had been used to 'avail himself much against hereticks by being conversant in their Books; untill a certain Presbyter laid it scrupulously to his conscience, how he durst venture himselfe among those defiling volumes' (*CPW*, ii. 511). Dionysius was perplexed until 'a vision sent from God ... confirm'd him in these words: Read any books what ever come to thy hands, for thou art sufficient both to judge aright, and to examine each matter' (ii. 511). The bishop 'assented' to this revelation because it agreed with a biblical injunction, 'Approve yourselves bankers of repute'. Perhaps because this text had since been relegated to the apocrypha, Milton has the bishop remember another passage often cited by apologists for liberty of the press, 1 Thessalonians 5: 21: 'Prove all things, hold fast that which is good.' And the bishop 'might have added another remarkable saying' of Paul, says Milton, referring to Titus 1: 15: 'To the pure all things are pure.' Milton maintains that Paul's apothegm applies not only to 'meats and drinks' but to 'all kinde of knowledge whether of good or evill' because 'the knowledge cannot defile,

---

[10] Paul's attitude towards the law remains contested. For some representative modern treatments, see E. P. Sanders, *Paul, the Law, and the Jewish People* (1985); Heikki Räisänen, *Paul and the Law*, 2nd edn. (Tübingen, 1987); Stephen Westerhom, *Israel's Law and the Church's Faith: Paul and his Recent Interpreters* (Grand Rapids, 1990); and Kari Kuula, *The Law, the Covenant, and God's Plan*, 2 vols. (Helsinki and Göttingen, 1999–2003).

nor consequently the books, if the will and conscience be not defil'd. For books are as meats and viands' (ii. 512).[11]

According to the dietary laws of the Jews, of course, not all meats and drinks were pure. God had imposed such restrictions on his chosen people, said Aristeas in one of the most famous ancient justifications of the Jewish law, in order to protect them from pollution: 'Therefore lest we should be corrupted by any abomination, or our lives be perverted by evil communications, [God] hedged us round on all sides by rules of purity, affecting alike what we eat, or drink, or touch, or hear, or see.'[12] Such strict observances would naturally have proved an obstacle to the first Christians who wished to evangelize among the Gentiles.

But as Milton reminds us, Simon Peter had a vision that dispensed with these dietary laws (*CPW*, ii. 512). According to Acts 10, Peter saw a vessel descend from heaven filled with

foure footed beasts of the earth, and wilde beasts, and creeping things, and foules of the ayre. And there came a voyce to him, Rise, Peter: kill, and eate. But Peter said, Not so, Lord; for I haue neuer eaten any thing that is common or vncleane. And the voice spake vnto him againe the second time, What God hath cleansed, that call not thou common.

Peter wondered at this vision until some messengers arrived requesting that he visit a virtuous Roman named Cornelius. At the house of Cornelius, Peter said, 'You know how that it is an vnlawfull thing for a man that is a Iewe, to keepe company or come vnto one of another nation: but God hath shewed me, that I should not call any man common or vncleane'. Just as Peter made the logical inference from meats to men, Milton extends that progression from meats to men to 'that season'd life of man preserv'd and stor'd up in Books' (ii. 493). Stressing the 'discretion' that God extended to each man in the matter of his diet, he concludes, 'when God did enlarge the universall diet of mans body, saving ever the rules of temperance, he then also, as before, left arbitrary the dyeting and repasting of our minds; as wherein every mature man might have to exercise his own leading capacity' (ii. 512–13).

The analogy between reading and eating makes profound sense if we consider the important role of diet and exercise in Galenic medicine.[13] Galenic physicians held

---

[11] This passage is crucial to Stanley Fish's reading of *Areopagitica*; he argues that 'the argument against licensing, which has always been read as an argument *for* books, is really an argument that renders books beside the point: books are no more going to save you than they are going to corrupt you; by denying their potency in one direction, Milton necessarily denies their potency in the other'. See *How Milton Works* (Cambridge, Mass., 2001), 187–214 at 195. Jason Rosenblatt observes usefully that 'Pauline verses authorized to abolish distinctions between forbidden and permitted foods and, more important, between Jew and gentile are used by Reformers to abolish distinctions between clergy and laity and to proclaim throughout the land the liberty to search scriptures'; he concludes that 'Milton uses a doctrinally unorthodox version of Christian liberty prevalent in Reformation texts on the Holy Scriptures to obliterate clerical privilege and to defend the universal right to read, a right that also exists under the Mosaic law. The essence of Christian liberty—rejection of the law of works and redemption in Christ—is alien to the ethos of this tract' (*Torah and the Law in 'Paradise Lost'* (Princeton, 1994), 113–22 at 114, 122).

[12] *The Letter of Aristeas*, trans. and ed. R. H. Charles (Oxford, 1913), 142–3.

[13] See Lawrence I. Conrad, Michael Neve, Vivian Nutton, Roy Porter, and Andrew Wear, *The Western Medical Tradition 800 BC to AD 1800* (Cambridge, 1995), chs. 1–3; Michael C. Schoenfeldt, *Bodies and*

that the physical health of the body was largely determined by the balance of the four humoral fluids that were produced by the body in the process of digesting food. The natural, vital, and animal spirits, which served as liaisons between the body and mind, were the results of further processes of refinement. Through these spirits, the body could dispose the mind, and the mind could affect the body. 'As the body works upon the mind by his bad humours, troubling the spirits, sending gross fumes into the brain, and so *per consequens* disturbing the soul, and all the faculties of it . . .', wrote Robert Burton, 'so, on the other side, the mind most effectually works upon the body producing by his passions and perturbations miraculous alterations, as melancholy, despair, cruel diseases, and sometimes death itself.'[14] Diet, exercise, and purgation assumed great importance because they appeared to be means to 'temper' one's 'complexion', or strike the right balance among one's humours, and therefore to maintain sound mental and physical health. Because such medical 'temperance' usually depended on eating and drinking in moderation, 'temperance' assumed the moral valence of a virtue among Stoics and Christians. But because everyone started out with a unique humoral disposition and was exposed to various airs, waters, and winds, each man had to minister to himself. 'Our owne experience is the best Physitian', wrote Burton. 'That diet which is most propitious to one, is often pernitious to another; such is the variety of palats, humors, and temperatures, let every man observe, and be a law unto himself.'[15] Just so, Milton wants to say, it is impossible for licensors to formulate a diet of the mind that will be salutary for everyone: let each man observe and be a law unto himself. The virtue that he must exercise is the same, whether he be consuming meats or books: temperance. This is a 'great' virtue, says Milton, 'yet God committs the managing so great trust, without particular Law or prescription, wholly to the demeanour of every grown man' (ii. 513).

A man can be temperate only if he knows his own body and mind, uses his reason, makes judicious choices, and maintains his self-control. Milton forgets or suppresses the fact that Spenser's model of 'true temperance' enters the Cave of Mammon without the Palmer, a figure of reason, because he wants to represent temperance not as a mere habit but as the result of reason exercised in choice: Guyon must 'see and know, and yet abstain' (*CPW*, ii. 516).[16] Yet without self-control, reason would be powerless to maintain a regimen of health. In 1 Corinthians 9: 25–7, Paul compares himself to an athlete training for a foot race or a boxing match: 'And every man that striveth for the mastery, is temperate in all things: Now they do it to obtain a corruptible crown, but we an incorruptible.' Milton likes both the regime of training and self-denial that Paul's image assumes and the *agon* that it anticipates. For Milton cannot praise a virtue that is 'unexercis'd & unbreath'd, that never sallies out and sees

Selves in Early Modern England: Physiology and Inwardness in Spenser, Shakespeare, Herbert, and Milton (Cambridge, 1999), 1–39 and (on *Areopagitica*) 132–5.

[14] Robert Burton, *The Anatomy of Melancholy* (1632), ed. Thomas C. Faulkner, Nicholas Kiessling, and Rhonda Blair, 2 vols. (Oxford, 1989), ii. 250.

[15] *Anatomy of Melancholy*, ii. 27.

[16] On Milton's error, see Ernest Sirluck, 'Milton Revises *The Faerie Queene*', *Modern Philology*, 48 (1950), 90–6.

her adversary, but slinks out of the race, where that immortall garland is to be run for, not without dust and heat' (ii. 515).

To deny men the freedom and responsibility of being temperate is to 'captivat' them 'under a perpetuall childhood of prescription' (*CPW*, ii. 514). Galatians 4: 1–5 attaches particular significance to such a childhood. There, Paul contrasts the servitude to the law that the Jews had to endure for a finite term with the state of adult liberty that Christians may now enjoy. For 'the heir', says Paul, 'as long as he is a child, differeth nothing from a servant, though he be lord of all; but is under tutors and governors until the time appointed of the father'. With the fulness of time, 'God sent forth his son . . . to redeem them that were under the law, that we might receive the adoption of sons' and cease to be 'servants'.

Like some biblical commentators, Milton appears to have interpreted this passage through the Roman law of persons.[17] In Milton's day, this law could not be studied in the *Institutes* of Gaius, which had yet to be rediscovered. But it could be found in the later *Institutes* of Justinian, which Milton read in the 1640s.[18] This codification and simplification of Roman law dating from the sixth century stated that all men were either free men or slaves. The former possessed a natural ability to do what they pleased unless prohibited by law, while the latter lacked freedom regardless of whether their movements were restricted or their actions coerced, for they remained 'in the power of their masters' (*in potestate dominorum*) and therefore subject to violence or death at any time. Yet even freeborn men and women could be placed under the care of a guardian (*in tutela*) until they reached puberty or, if they lacked the mental capacity to look after themselves, could be designated wards (*pupilli*) of a guardian who would make decisions for them. Thus Roman law suggested that those who were not free men were slaves and that those who were nominally free yet not under their own jurisdiction lacked the meaningful liberty of adult citizens. In his *Doctrine and Discipline of Divorce* Milton said that 'the time of the Law is compar'd to youth, and pupillage' because he read Galatians 4: 1–5 through the lens of the *Institutes*.

Unlike some Reformation theologians, Milton is not at pains to draw a distinction between Christian liberty and the ideal of civil liberty that he finds in the ancients. Commenting on Galatians 5: 1, 'Stand fast therefore in the liberty wherewith Christ hath made us free', Martin Luther insists that Christ has freed us 'not from an earthly bondage, or from the Babylonian captivity, or from the tyranny of the Turkes' but from God's wrath, so that Christian liberty rests 'in the conscience' only and goes 'no

---

[17] On the invocation of the Roman law of persons in Galatians 4, see W. S. Muntz, *Rome, St. Paul, and the Early Church: The Influence of Roman Law on St. Paul's Teaching* (1913), 71–2, 126 ff.

[18] On Milton's 'neo-Roman' conception of liberty, see Quentin Skinner, 'John Milton and the Politics of Slavery', in Graham Parry and Joad Raymond (eds.), *Milton and the Terms of Liberty* (Cambridge, 2002), 1–22. On Milton's use of Justinian's *Institutes* in *Areopagitica*, see Martin Dzelzainis, 'Republicanism', in Thomas N. Corns (ed.), *A Companion to Milton* (Oxford, 2001), 294–308 at 301–4; and id., 'Liberty and the Law', in Christophe Tournu and Neil Forsyth (eds.), *Milton, Rights, and Liberties* (Bern and New York, 2007), 57–68.

further': 'Christ hath made us free, not civilly, nor carnally, but divinely.'[19] Milton, in sharp contrast, would maintain in his later *Defence of the People of England* or *First Defence* (24 February 1651) that in 1 Corinthians 7: 21–3 Paul 'makes this assertion not of religious liberty alone, but also of political: "Are you called slave? Care not for that; but if you can become free, then use your freedom. You are bought for a price; be not the slaves of men"' (*CPW*, iv. 374).

In *Areopagitica* Milton argues that the Licensing Order is an affront to Englishmen because it deprives them of their Christian and their civil liberty in one fell blow. Seen as an instrument of tyranny, it imposes a form of 'bondage' and 'undeserved thralldom' that threatens to deepen the 'slavish print' that the 'yoke of outward conformity' has already left on their necks (*CPW*, ii. 568, 539, 564). It threatens, in other words, to turn them into a people with a servile disposition.[20] Even if interpreted charitably as a form of guardianship, it denies them the rights and responsibilities of men of riper years. 'What advantage is it to be a man over it is to be a boy at school', asks Milton, if even the author of 'serious and elaborat writings' is to be treated as if he were 'a Grammar lad under his Pedagogue' (ii. 531). An author who must be granted a 'pedantick license' is no true authority but a 'pupil teacher' who comes to the reader 'under the wardship of an overseeing fist' (ii. 533). Such a wardship treats authors and readers like fools or children.[21] To be sure, there may be some 'children and childish men, who have not the art to qualifie and prepare' the texts that Milton compares to 'working mineralls' but this is no reason to limit the access of more skilful adults to 'usefull drugs and materialls, wherewith to temper and compose effective and strong med'cins, which mans life cannot want' (ii. 521).

As if to prove that Englishmen do not deserve to be treated like children, Milton represents them as mirrors of manhood—an image that assumes both a spiritual and a civil significance. Inexperienced observers might misinterpret the division of the English people into 'parties and partitions' as a sign of weakness, he says, but the error would be theirs, for Englishmen are like the 'small divided maniples' of a Roman army—able to cut through 'a united and unwieldy brigade' at every angle (*CPW*, ii. 556). If a 'great and worthy stranger' were to behold them, 'he would cry out as *Pirrhus* did', admiring the 'docility and courage' of the soldiers of Rome, 'if such were my *Epirots*, I would not despair the greatest design that could be attempted to make a Church or Kingdom happy' (ii. 555). Indeed, the 'gallant bravery' that Londoners have shown as they dispute, reason, read, and invent despite rumours of impending battle makes Milton think that no small number possess the spirit of the Roman who bought the very piece of ground on which Hannibal had camped his hostile regiments—and at no diminution of the price, such was his confidence in the future of Rome (ii. 557). England is no land of children and punies but a 'noble and puissant Nation rousing herself like a strong man after sleep, and shaking her invincible locks' (ii. 558). In Samson—warrior, freedom fighter, and hero of faith—

---

[19] *A Commentarie of Master Doctor Martin Luther Vpon the Epistle of S. Paul to the Galathians*, 4th edn. (1644), fo. 231ᵛ.

[20] On the psychology of slavery, see Skinner, 'John Milton and the Politics of Slavery'.

[21] Dzelzainis, 'Republicanism', 303–4.

Milton finds the perfect image of an awakening, manly liberty that is both spiritual and civil, personal and national.

TYRANNY, MONOPOLY, AND THE LIBERTIES OF ENGLISH SUBJECTS

If *Areopagitica* depicts England as a chosen nation struggling for liberty, it denounces the Licensing Order as 'a servitude like that impos'd' on the Israelites 'by the Philistims, not to be allow'd the sharpning of our own axes and coulters, but we must repair from all quarters to twenty licensing forges' (*CPW*, ii. 536). By making all Englishmen repair to these 'forges', the authorities are not simply limiting their ability to make the intellectual weapons with which they might win their own spiritual and civil liberty, they are enforcing a monopoly.[22] But 'Truth and understanding are not such wares as to be monopoliz'd and traded in by tickets and statues, and standards', says Milton. 'We must not think to make a staple commodity of all the knowledge in the Land, to mark and licence it like our broad cloath, and our wooll packs' (ii. 535–6). That, however, is precisely the way the Licensing Order treats truth. It puts in place 'an *Oligarchy* of twenty ingrossers' (the licensors) and it empowers 'some old *patentees* and *monopolizers* in the trade of book-selling' (the Stationers). Whatever the Stationers may have said to the House of Commons, their real aim is 'to exercise a superiority over their neighbours' in the book trade, 'men who doe not therefore labour in an honest profession to which learning is indetted, that they should be made other mens vassalls' (ii. 558, 570).

A long history of legal argument and political complaint lies behind Milton's contention that monopolists deprive men of their liberties and turn freemen into bondmen. In *Darcy* v. *Allen* (1602), which Sir Edward Coke dubbed 'The Case of Monopolies', Nicholas Fuller successfully argued that when the queen granted exclusive manufacturing privileges to just one subject, she prevented others from working in their calling and fulfilling their godly obligation to earn their daily bread.[23]

---

[22] On *Areopagitica*'s attack on the Licensing Order as a monopoly, see Blair Hoxby, *Mammon's Music: Literature and Economics in the Age of Milton* (New Haven and London, 2002), ch. 1, and Joseph Loewenstein, *The Author's Due: Printing and the Prehistory of Copyright* (Chicago and London, 2002), 171–91. David Harris Sacks covers some of the same ground (without acknowledging Hoxby, *Mammon's Music*) in 'Adam's Curse and Adam's Freedom: Milton's Concept of Liberty', in Tournu and Forsyth (eds.), *Milton, Rights, and Liberties*, 69–98.

[23] The case may be followed in *English Reports*, 178 volumes (repr. Edinburgh, 1900–32); see 11 Co. Rep. 84b, 77 Eng. Rep. 1260 (1603); Moore 671, 72 Eng. Rep. 830 (1603); and Noy 173, 74 Eng. Rep. 1131 (1603). For an analysis of the case, see Jacob I. Corré, 'The Argument, Decision, and Report of *Darcy v. Allen*', *Emory Law Journal*, 45 (1996), 1261–1327; Hoxby, *Mammon's Music*, 27–31; and Loewenstein, *Author's Due*, 128–31.

A 'grant, ordinance, or law of any Christian king tending to prohibit some of his subjects' from labouring, Fuller said in Parliament when later summarizing the court's finding, was 'unlawful' and 'absurd' because it went 'directly against the law of God, which saith six days thou shall labor; so the grant and prohibition of any king tending to prohibit any of his subjects to labor in his lawful calling or trade . . . is contrary to the law of God and therefore . . . void'.[24] The monopolist was a *vir sanguinis*, or man of blood, because anyone who took away another man's means of living effectively took his life.[25]

In the process, he violated the liberties of the English subject that were guaranteed by Magna Carta. Fuller based this claim on *Davenant* v. *Hurdis* (1599), in which the queen's bench judged that an ordinance of the Company of Merchant Taylors requiring its members to put half their cloths out to other members to be dressed violated the twenty-ninth chapter of Magna Carta, which guaranteed, in part, that 'NO Freeman shall be taken or imprisoned, or be disseised of his Freehold, or Liberties, or free Customs, or be outlawed, or exiled, or any other wise destroyed'. Fuller argued that Darcy's monopoly similarly violated the Great Charter and took away what should have been the 'surest' form of subjects' property, the 'excellent skill in a trade' that they had acquired by their 'industry'.[26] He later used *Davenant* v. *Hurdis* and *Darcy* v. *Allen* to argue against other infringements of the liberties of Englishmen, including the impositions of James I and the power of the Church acting through High Commission to force men to testify truthfully without knowing what charge they faced. By arguing that the law of monopoly should be able to check the extension of prerogative powers, Fuller implied that there was an intimate connection between arbitrary will and monopoly power, and he cast both the king and the Church as monopolists who would coerce men, if not checked by the common law, into giving up their proprietary claims not only to their possessions but to their inmost thoughts.

The importance of these cases to the period's broader conception of liberty can scarcely be overstated. When glossing the word *libertates* in his commentary on the twenty-ninth chapter of Magna Carta—which had been suppressed by Charles I and only recently published by Parliamentary warrant in 1641—Coke cited only two cases to bolster his exposition, *Davenant* v. *Hurdis* and *Darcy* v. *Allen*, both of which concerned the freedom of Englishmen to contract their labour and use their property as they would.[27] Thus the common law made labour a proclamation of liberty when

---

[24] *Proceedings in Parliament, 1610*, ed. Elizabeth Reed Foster (New Haven, 1966), ii. 160.

[25] Noy 181, 74 Eng. Rep. 1138 (1603); 11 Co. Rep. 86b, 77 Eng. Rep. 1263 (1603). Sir Edward Coke explains the logic of this claim in *The Third Part of the Institutes of the Law* (1644): 'And the law of the Realm in this point is grounded upon the law of God, which saith *Non accipies loco pignoris inferiorem & superiorem molam, quia animam suam apposuit tibi* [Deut. 24: 6]. Thou shalt not take the nether or upper milstone to pledge, for he taketh a mans life to pledge. Whereby it appeareth that a mans trade is accounted his life, because it maintaineth his life' (p. 181).

[26] Magna Carta (1297) c. 9 25. Edw. 1. cc. 1. 9. 29; 11 Co. Rep. 86b, 77 Eng. Rep. 1263 (1603); Noy 180, 74 Eng. Rep. 1137 (1603).

[27] This is a point that John Lilburne drew to the attention of readers in *Innocency and Truth Justified* (1645), 61. On Coke's citation of these cases, see David Harris Sacks, 'Parliament, Liberty, and the

undertaken by freemen in a commonwealth and a confession of slavery when performed by subjects whose property in their persons, skills, and goods was not secure.

In the decades after *Darcy* v. *Allen*, when some of their opponents labelled companies like the Merchant Adventurers 'monopolies', advocates of freer trade began to lay stress on the deleterious effects that monopoly power had on the commonwealth. Whereas the companies maintained that their 'politic Government, Laws, and Orders' were the 'root and spring' of their 'incredible trade and traffic' and that trade that was thrown open to all Englishmen would be 'dispersed, straggling, and promiscuous', those in favour of opening up foreign trade claimed that 'if the number of traders were enlarged, trade itself would be enlarged'.[28] Whereas the companies attacked interloping merchants as 'disorderly and unskillful traders' who possessed 'neither skill nor patience', their opponents rejected the idea that skills were mysteries to be handed down within a secret society of merchants rather than acquired by 'active and industrious spirits' operating in the market place.[29] The best way to make goods more plentiful and of superior quality, the opponents of the guilds and companies insisted, was to encourage the emulation of craftsmen who were left free to rival one another.

Not only were monopolies listed among the principal grievances of the realm by the time the Long Parliament sat; the word 'monopoly' was a powerful term of opprobrium that implied tyranny, avarice, and the abuse of position and power.[30] Even prelates, courtiers, and aldermen who did not have patents could be labelled 'Prerogative-Monopolizing arbitrary-men'.[31] It is not surprising, therefore, that reformers opposed to the power of the prelates called, in Milton's words, for '*unmonopolizing* the rewards of *learning* and *industry*' (*CPW*, i. 613). 'Maintaine amongst us a free course of trading for eternall happinesse', appealed Thomas Hill in a sermon to the House of Commons in 1642,

set and keepe open those shops, such Pulpits, such mouthes, as any Prelaticall usurpations have, or would have, shut up. Secure to us not onely liberty of person and estate, but also liberty of Conscience from Church tyranny, that we be not pinched with ensnaring oathes, clogged with multiplyed subscriptions, or needlesse impositions.[32]

Such was the discursive atmosphere in which Henry Parker presented his petition on behalf of the Stationers' Company to the Long Parliament. While he had reason to

Commonwealth', in J. H. Hexter (ed.), *Parliament and Liberty from the Reign of Elizabeth to the Civil War* (Stanford, Calif., 1992), 85–121 at 95–6.

[28] John Wheeler, *A Treatise of Commerce* (1601), ed. with intro. George Burton Hotchkiss (New York, 1931), 338, 373; *Seventeenth-Century Economic Documents*, ed. Joan Thirsk and J. P. Cooper (Oxford, 1972), 20.

[29] *Seventeenth-Century Economic Documents*, ed. Thirsk and Cooper, 59; *A Discourse Consisting of Motives for the Enlargement and Freedome of Trade* (11 Apr. 1645), 27–8.

[30] David Harris Sacks, 'The Greed of Judas: Avarice, Monopoly, and the Moral Economy in England, c. 1350–c. 1600', *Journal of Medieval and Early Modern Studies*, 28 (1998), 263–307.

[31] John Lilburne, *Londons Liberty in Chains discovered* (1646), 40.

[32] Thomas Hill, *The Trade of Truth Advanced* (1642), 33; Hoxby, *Mammon's Music*, 31–5.

hope for a receptive hearing, he had to argue plausibly that a new licensing order would not erect a monopoly—either spiritual or economic. He contended that, because the Stationers' privileges were enjoyed by a considerable body of men, they did not qualify as an instance of a public good being driven into private hands. That the 'Mystery and Art of Printing' was of 'publike and great Importance' was not a reason for throwing it open but a reason for regulating it. A regulated press would be 'different in nature from the engrossing, or Monopolizing some other Commodities into the hands of a few, to the producing scarcity and dearth, amongst the generality'.[33] While Parker was acutely aware that some commodities like bread were thought to be too important to be monopolized, he also knew that the regulation of others like playing cards had been defended because they were 'not of any necessary use, but things of vanity'.[34] Parker consequently spoke of books as if they were playing cards: they were 'not of such generall use and necessity, as some staple Commodities are, which feed and cloath us . . . and many of them are rarities only and usefull only to a very few, and of no necessity to any'. Thus the Stationers' privileges could not harm the public as they might if they concerned 'Commodities of more publike use and necessity'.[35]

In *Areopagitica*, Milton insists, to the contrary, that this 'plot of licensing' causes the commonwealth 'incredible losse, and detriment', for 'more than if som enemy at sea should stop up all our hav'ns and ports, and creeks, it hinders and retards the importation of our richest Marchandize, Truth' and 'bring[s] a famine upon our minds' (*CPW*, ii. 548, 559). The suppression of books became commonplace only after the emperors of Rome became tyrants and the 'Popes of *Rome*' began 'engrossing what they pleas'd of Politicall rule into their own hands' (ii. 501–2). Licensing itself was invented by the Council of Trent and the Inquisition to suppress the Protestant Reformation. 'And this', says Milton, 'was the rare morsell so officiously snatcht up, and so illfavourdedly imitated by our inquisiturient Bishops' (ii. 507). Licensing, in other words, is the means by which the Catholic Church has tried to maintain its spiritual monopoly, and England's prelates and presbyters have adopted it with the same intention.

Milton's famous admonition, 'as good almost kill a Man as kill a good Book' (*CPW*, ii. 492), and his extended imagery of book suppression as homicide is meant to identify the Stationers and licensors alike as men of blood because they are monopolists:

We should be wary therefore what persecution we raise against the living labours of publick men, how we spill that season'd life of man perserv'd and stor'd up in Books; since we see a kinde of homicide may be thus committed, sometimes a martyrdome, and if it extend to the whole impression, a kinde of massacre, whereof the execution ends not in the slaying of an

---

[33] [Henry Parker], *Humble Remonstrance*, sigs. A1ᵛ, A1ʳ, A1ᵛ, A2ʳ, A3ʳ.
[34] 11 Co. Rep. 85b–86a, 77 Eng. Rep. 1261–2 (1603).
[35] [Parker], *Humble Remonstrance*, sig. A3ʳ⁻ᵛ.

elementall life, but strikes at that ethereall and fift essence, the breath of reason it selfe, slaies an immortality rather then a life. (ii. 493)

Milton identifies books as the 'living labours' of authors so that he may make his charge of monopoly clear: licensors and Stationers attack the livings of men and in doing so become *viri sanguinis*.[36] Yet to assert that the labour and the skill required to read and write need to be protected under the law as surely as any tradesman's livelihood is a remarkable claim that goes beyond anything that Coke could have anticipated in his report on 'The Case of Monopolies'. *Areopagitica* thus extends a project that Milton had already begun in *Of Reformation* (May 1641) when he asserted that 'Liberty consists in manly and honest labours' and cannot flourish when monopolists use their 'cruel authority' to oppress other men who are attempting to 'labour in the word' (i. 588, 856; see also Nigel Smith's essay, Ch. 8 above).

What it means to labour in the word *Areopagitica* vividly represents.[37] Writers display 'industry' and 'diligence' when they dedicate themselves to 'studious labours' like the 'labour of book-writing' (*CPW*, ii. 489–90, 532). To '*seek for wisdom as for hidd'n treasures*' means to perform 'the hardest labour in the deep mines of knowledge' (ii. 562). It entails both 'incessant labour to cull out, and sort asunder' good from evil (p. 514) and a willingness to contribute to the larger public project of building the Temple, 'some cutting, some squaring the marble, others hewing the cedar' (p. 555). It is precisely because books and pamphlets are 'publisht labours' and 'writt'n labours' that attacks on them may be seen as efforts to restrain men from undertaking their Godly duty to labour (pp. 493, 531). By insisting that reading and writing are labour, Milton asserts that to prevent any man from using his skill, invention, and industry to produce or consume texts is to deprive him of his fundamental liberties as a free Englishman.

Suspicious of any claim that the Crown, the Prelates, or even Parliament is skilful enough to govern for the good of the people, Milton is attracted to the idea that skill is dispersed widely and must be exercised in commerce with other men. By transvaluing the epithet *promiscuous*, which company merchants had often used to stigmatize unregulated trade, Milton suggests the extreme importance that he attaches to a state of intellectual free trade in which books may be 'promiscuously read' (*CPW*, ii. 517). His text creates the illusion that we are experiencing just such a free commerce in ideas by exposing us to such a bewildering variety of contradictory opinions. We do not sense that Milton's position is patently clear or indisputable, for truth and falsehood are as difficult to sort out as Psyche's seeds, but it seems to emerge from a multitude of alternatives as the best. We learn first hand that 'fast

---

[36] In her otherwise perceptive analysis of *Areopagitica*, Stevie Davies detects the extravagance of Milton's rhetoric in this passage without understanding its legal force: 'The passage goes on to argue, preposterously, that censorship is a kind of "homicide," "martyrdom," and indeed "massacre"'; *Milton* (New York, 1991), 30.

[37] On the imagery of labour, see Michael Wilding, 'Milton's *Areopagitica*: Liberty for the Sects', in Thomas N. Corns (ed.), *The Literature of Controversy* (1987), 7–38 at 16–18; Hoxby, *Mammon's Music*, 39–40.

reading, trying all things, assenting to the force of reason and convincement' is a form of exercise and discipline that may be found in a vibrant market place of ideas.

MILTON'S LIBERATING STYLE

That we are trucking and trading ideas even as we read is just one of the illusions that *Areopagitica* generates. That is why we still read Milton's tract—not because it was the first or the most reasonable defence of free speech and liberty of conscience to appear in England but because its style is liberating. Reading it makes us *feel* what it means to be free; and it especially makes us mindful of how central free speaking and reading are to an active and manly life. One way it does so is by attributing all the agency and personality normally reserved for men to books themselves:

I deny not, but that it is of greatest concernment in the Church and Commonwealth, to have a vigilant eye how Bookes demeane themselves, as well as men; and thereafter to confine, imprison, and do sharpest justice on them as malefactors: For Books are not absolutely dead things, but doe contain a potencie of life in them to be as active as that soule was whose progeny they are; nay they do preserve as in a violl the purest efficacie and extraction of that living intellect that bred them. I know they are as lively, and as vigorously productive, as those fabulous Dragons teeth; and being sown up and down, may chance to spring up armed men.[38] (*CPW*, ii. 492)

If books may comport themselves like men, all the perceptions, encounters, and experiences of our daily lives may likewise be compared to a book that we read as we lead our lives: 'what ever thing we hear or see, sitting, walking, travelling, or conversing may be fitly call'd our book, and is of the same effect that writings are' (ii. 528). By characterizing living as reading even while he describes reading and writing as the most vital forms of labouring and struggling, Milton implicitly denies the possibility that a meaningful agency could exist without the freedom of expression.

In certain passages, English words in all their Anglo-Saxon vigour assert themselves as representatives of the active, manly enjoyment of liberty that Milton wishes his readers to embrace as their birthright, while polysyllabic words of Latin extraction behave like nuncios of the slavish conformity that he associates with Catholicism, the Laudian church, and the practice of licensing:

Sometimes 5 *Imprimaturs* are seen together dialogue-wise in the Piatza of one Title page, complementing and ducking each to other with their shav'n reverences, whether the Author, who stands by in perplexity at the foot of his Epistle, shall to the Presse or to the spunge. These

---

[38] Stevie Davies observes: 'This act of blurring is a—perhaps, *the*—major premis[e] of *Areopagitica*, which brazenly insists that a book *is* a man, and that the same laws apply' (*Milton*, 30).

are the pretty responsories, these are the deare Antiphonies that so bewitcht of late our Prelats, and their Chaplaines with the goodly Eccho they made; and besotted us to the gay imitation of a lordly *Imprimatur*, one from Lambeth house, another from the West end of *Pauls*; so apishly Romanizing, that the word of command still was set downe in Latine; as if the learned Grammaticall pen that wrote it, would cast no ink without Latine: or perhaps, as they thought, because no vulgar tongue was worthy to expresse the pure conceit of an *Imprimatur*; but rather, as I hope, for that our English, the language of men ever famous, and formost in the atchievements of liberty, will not easily finde servile letters anow to spell such a dictatorie presumption English. (*CPW*, ii. 504–5)

This passage could serve as yet another example of Milton's elision of the distinction between books and life: it is hard to tell if we find ourselves on a title page or in a piazza, hedged in by the textual apparatus of licensing or surrounded by the servile churchmen who sit in judgement on books. But as Stevie Davies has observed, the passage also 'sets off charges of derisive Anglo-Saxon' by setting words like *ducking*, *shav'n*, and *English* 'against the imperialist invasive Latin' of *complementing*, *reverences*, and *dictatory presumption*, thus 'arraying what it presents as the sturdy, sterling down-to-earth plainness of English root words against the Latinate mannerisms of the prelates, their mouths rudely inflated with polysyllabic hot air'.[39] Milton's very choice of words seems to demonstrate the demystifying power of plain speech.

   In contrast to the prelates, who occupy themselves with custom and the preservation of ceremonies, Milton drives his plough over the bones of the dead. He generates metaphors only to discard them. The sheer abandon with which he erects and topples figures may best be demonstrated by comparing the use that he and William Walwyn make of the same image. 'Truth was not used to feare, or to seeke shifts or stratagems for its advancement!' writes Walwyn. 'I should rather thinke that they who are assured of her should desire that all mens mouthes should open, that so errour may discover its foulness and trueth become more glorious by a victorious conquest after a fight in open field; they shunne the battell that doubt their strength.'[40] For Walwyn, this is an isolated metaphor pressed into the service of a lucid and unadorned argument. For Milton, it is just one of the fleeting manifestations of Truth: 'And though all the windes of doctrin were let loose to play upon the earth, so Truth be in the field, we do injuriously by licensing and prohibiting to misdoubt her strength. Let her and Falshood grapple; who ever knew Truth put to the wors, in a free and open encounter.' Milton then imagines Truth as light shining through a casement window, as gold extracted from the deep mines of knowledge, as a cause for which authors fight like soldiers, calling their adversaries into the open plain, and then once again as a combatant who 'needs no policies, nor stratagems, nor licencings to make her victorious'. Not content to have returned full-circle, he reimagines her in new terms: 'give her but room, & do not bind her when she sleeps, for then she speaks not true, as the old *Proteus* did, who spake oracles only when he was caught & bound, but then rather she turns herself into all shapes, except her

---

[39] Ibid.
[40] Walwyn, *Compassionate Samaritane*, 58–9.

own, and perhaps tunes her voice according to the time, as *Micaiah* did before *Ahab'* (*CPW*, ii. 561–3).

The resistless surge of Milton's image-making has at least three effects. First, it demonstrates that Truth may have more shapes than one, and in doing so it implicitly argues for the expansion of 'that rank of things indifferent, wherein Truth may be on this side, or on the other, without being unlike herself' (*CPW*, ii. 563). Second, it presents Milton's prose as a performance of Christian liberty. The dead letter kills. But, as Lana Cable argues, 'Milton's kinetic images bear witness to something they themselves cannot contain'.[41] Finally, it suggests that we are living in conditions of continuing revelation: we cannot 'pitch our tent here', and anyone who believes we can 'is yet farre short of Truth' (ii. 549).

Some readers may doubt that Milton could really have intended his style to demonstrate the virtues that *Areopagitica* asks its readers to embrace. They should consider what the author says when he gets ahead of himself: 'See the ingenuity of Truth, who when she gets a free and willing hand, opens her self faster, then the pace of method and discourse can overtake her' (*CPW*, ii. 521). *Areopagitica* is a rhetorical performance of liberty, and Milton instructs us to read it as such.

LIBERTY, NOT LICENSE

Many critics have shared Ernest Sirluck's puzzlement that Milton should entitle his tract *Areopagitica* because his purpose seems to differ so strikingly from Isocrates'. The irony, as they see it, is that Milton 'nervously pleads with Parliament to lift controls' in an oration whose title invokes a famous attempt to increase the powers of the Court of Areopagus over 'the general censorship of manners' and thus to diminish liberty.[42] Yet to frame the puzzle in these terms is to ignore the fact that in Milton's day Isocrates' *Areopagiticus* was widely interpreted as an attempt to demonstrate how 'true liberty' might be preserved by avoiding the two plagues that always beset republics: tyranny, when magistrates preyed on the weak and gave leash to their own lust, avarice, and ambition; and anarchy, when the people, holding both the laws and the magistrates in contempt, assumed complete licence of action and speech.[43] Milton invokes Isocrates in *Areopagitica* not just because he wants to announce that he is publishing a written oration but because he wishes to promote a 'true liberty' that will not degenerate into licence. It is quite misguided to assert, as generations of Milton scholars have done, that the force of Milton's allusion to Isocrates is ironic.

---

[41] Lana Cable, *Carnal Rhetoric: Milton's Iconoclasm and the Poetics of Desire* (Durham, N.C., 1995), 118.

[42] *CPW*, ii. 486 n. 1; Joseph Wittreich,, 'Milton's *Areopagitica*: Its Isocratic and Ironic Contexts', *Milton Studies*, 4 (1972), 104, 103.

[43] See Eric Nelson, '"True Liberty": Isocrates and Milton's *Areopagitica*', *Milton Studies*, 40 (2001), 201–21.

Even in *Areopagitica*, Milton imagines that some form of censorship may be necessary to maintain true liberty. He notes that the Court of Areopagus probably censored libellous books and certainly banished Protagoras and burned his books because one of his discourses began 'with his confessing not to know *whether there were gods, or whether not*' (ii. 494). As we have seen, he freely concedes that 'it is of greatest concernment in the Church and Commonwealth, to have a vigilant eye how Bookes demeane themselves, as well as men; and thereafter to confine, imprison, and do sharpest justice on them as malefactors' (p. 492). He simply insists, as he later summarized the argument of *Areopagitica* in his *Second Defence of the English People* (30 May 1654), that 'the judgment of truth and falsehood, what should be printed and what suppressed, ought not to be in the hands of a few men (and these mostly ignorant and of vulgar discernment) charged with the inspection of books, at whose will or whim virtually everyone is prevented from publishing aught that surpasses the understanding of the mob' (*CPW*, iv. 626). All books should be published with the author's and publisher's name, and if any book that is published anonymously is found to be 'mischievous and libellous' once it has been made public, it may be committed to 'the fire and the executioner' (ii. 569). Given that the Court of Areopagus could tolerate the writings of the epicureans, libertines, and cynics despite their opinions tending to 'voluptuousnesse, and the denying of divine providence' (ii. 494–5), Milton supposes that such suppressions will not often be necessary, but he does not decry them on principle.

The Court of Areopagus as Isocrates describes it depended less on laws or punitive measures than on the habits of everyday life to maintain the virtue of the citizenry, and it believed that such habits could be formed most effectively by educating the youth of the republic and channelling their high-spirited desires into noble pursuits and congenial labour. Milton would likewise prefer to see 'those unwritt'n, or at least unconstraining laws of vertuous education, religious and civill nurture, which *Plato* there mentions, as the bonds and ligaments of the Commonwealth, the pillars and sustainers of every writt'n Statute', perform the work that the Licensing Order aims to accomplish (ii. 526–7). His argument is not just that 'preaching' and 'exhortation' should be sufficient to achieve what the Licensing Order would enforce by means of 'law and compulsion' (p. 514) but that true virtue can only be achieved by men who actively attempt to judge what is good and choose it, for the 'knowledge and survay of vice is . . . necessary to the constituting of human vertue, and the scanning of error to the confirmation of truth'. The advantage of books is that they permit young men to gain that experience by 'reading all manner of tractats, and hearing all manner of reason' rather than by 'scout[ing] into the regions of sin and falsity' in person (pp. 516–17). Milton is opposed to pre-publication censorship because it prevents future citizens from testing themselves in a wood of error and thus deprives the republic of virtuous adults who know what it means to exercise their reason, choice, and self-control. But he certainly shares Isocrates' view that the sagest and most virtuous members of the republic ought to oversee the 'education and morality of the young' (iv. 679).

If Milton's only interest in Isocrates' *Areopagiticus* had been its formal status as a published oration, he would not have returned to it on subsequent occasions when the republic threatened to degenerate into tyranny or anarchy. Yet he did. After Oliver Cromwell dismissed the Rump Parliament on 20 April 1653, for instance, Milton incorporated an address to his fellow countrymen in his *Second Defence*.[44] Although he denounced the theft, favouritism, and oppressive conduct of some of the Rump's members or officers in his address (*CPW*, iv. 680–1), he also justified the disenfranchisement of the sort of citizens whom Isocrates faulted in his orations *On the Peace* and *Areopagiticus*—those citizens who in deciding upon public affairs preferred as 'being better friends of the people, those who are drunk to those who are sober, those who are witless to those who are wise, and those who dole out the public money to those who perform public service at their own expense', those citizens, in short, who look 'upon insolence as democracy, lawlessness as liberty, impudence of speech as equality, and license to do what they please as happiness'.[45]

The tumultuous decade from 1644 to 1654 had not convinced Milton that the majority of Englishmen really knew what it meant to fight the wars of peace by governing themselves. 'Unless you expel avarice, ambition, and luxury from your minds', he warned, 'many tyrants, impossible to endure will from day to day hatch out from your very vitals' (*CPW*, iv. 680–1). Whereas Milton had bridled at the idea of being treated like a pupil or ward in 1644, he was now prepared to concede that Englishmen might have to endure a probationary period before they could earn the right of suffrage:

For why should anyone then claim for you freedom to vote or the power of sending to Parliament whomever you prefer? So that each of you could elect in the cities men of his own faction, or in the country towns choose that man, however unworthy, who has entertained you more lavishly at banquets and supplied farmers and peasants with more abundant drink? Under such circumstances, not wisdom or authority, but faction and gluttony would elect to Parliament in our name either inn-keepers and hucksters of the state from city taverns or from country districts ploughboys and veritable herdsmen. . . . Who could believe the masters and patrons of such thieves to be fit guardians of liberty, or think his own liberty enlarged one iota by such caretakers of the state (though the customary number of five hundred be thus elected from all the towns), since there would then be so few among the guardians and watchdogs of liberty who either knew how to enjoy, or deserved to possess, it? . . . Who would now be willing to fight, or even encounter the smallest danger, for the liberty of such men? It is not fitting, it is not meet, for such men to be free. However loudly they shout and boast about liberty, slaves they are at home and abroad, although they know it not. (iv. 682–3)

Rather than blame anyone else for their troubles, says Milton, the English should realize that 'to be free is precisely the same as to be pious, wise, just, and temperate, careful of one's property, aloof from another's, and, thus finally to be magnanimous and brave'; for 'to be the opposite of all these is to be the same as a slave' (iv. 684). If Englishmen could not learn to master themselves, 'then indeed, like a nation in wardship, you would rather be in need of some tutor, some brave and faithful

---

[44] For an attempt to date the composition of various sections of the *Second Defense*, see Blair Worden, *Literature and Politics in Cromwellian England: John Milton, Andrew Marvell, Marchamont Nedham* (Oxford, 2007), 262–88.

[45] *On the Peace*, 13, and *Areopagiticus*, 20, both in *Isocrates*, trans. George Norlin (Loeb Classical Library; Cambridge, Mass., 1929).

guardian of your affairs' (ibid.). That Milton was already capable of such a sentiment in 1644 may be suggested by his translation of Theseus' speech on the title page of *Areopagitica*, for whereas Euripides' Greek refers only to the *desire* to speak or remain silent, Milton's English implies that the speaker should not only desire to speak but be qualified to do so by his ability: 'Which he who can, and will, deserv's high praise, / Who neither can nor will, may hold his peace.' By 1654, Milton was prepared to contemplate the idea that his fellow citizens, who seemed to lack, as yet, the ability to speak for themselves and govern themselves, should endure a period of guardianship—provided that the state 'take more thought for the education and morality of the young than has yet been done' and 'permit those who wish to engage in free inquiry to publish their findings *at their own peril* without the private inspection of any petty magistrate' so that 'truth' might 'especially flourish' (iv. 679; my emphasis).

In *The Ready and Easie Way* (23–9 February 1660)—which he published when the restoration of Charles II seemed all but inevitable—Milton proposed another way to steer between the extremes of tyranny and anarchy in the republic. The popular clamour for elections could no longer be ignored, but Milton was still unwilling to surrender his belief that true liberty could be achieved only through temperance: like any Englishman who must be allowed to eat and read according to his conscience, to digest what he had consumed, and to purge himself, the body politic also had to be left free to engage in nutrition, refinement, and purification. Milton proposed a complex way to 'wel-qualifie and refine elections' so that the choice of senators need not be committed 'to the noise and shouting of a rude multitude' but might be selected in multiple stages 'till after a third or fourth sifting and refining of exactest choice, they only be left chosen who are the due number, and seem by most voices the worthiest' (*CPW*, vii. 442–3). Milton's electoral system was inspired in part by Isocrates' qualms about the selection of leaders by means of lot or popular acclamation, in part by the balloting processes of the Venetian republic, and in part by a medical analogy; for the body was thought to transform crude matter into natural, vital, and animal spirits (each more pure than the last) only by means of a series of refinements. Milton's goal was to return the body politic to the 'good plight and constitution' that he thought it was attaining when he described its fresh blood and 'pure and vigorous' spirits in *Areopagitica*, spirits that could support 'the acutest, and the pertest operations of wit and suttlety' (ii. 557).

From *Areopagitica* to *The Readie and Easie Way*, Milton never shrank from the idea that maintaining the health of the commonwealth might require careful management—and might even necessitate that a Protagoras be purged. Milton opposes pre-publication censorship because it denies men the opportunity to cultivate their own virtue and liberty and thus will have a deadening effect on the body politic, not because he thinks every citizen of a free republic can be preserved from peril, punishment, or even expulsion as dross. A system of free speech that is not *risk-free* speech may take a personal toll on some citizens, but it also extends an ethical benefit: it offers those virtuous men who have the courage of their own convictions the psychic reward of speaking boldly.

PART IV

REGICIDE, REPUBLICAN, AND RESTORATION PROSE, 1649–1673

CHAPTER 13

....

'THE STRANGEST PIECE OF REASON': MILTON'S *TENURE OF KINGS AND MAGISTRATES*

....

STEPHEN M. FALLON

THE *Tenure of Kings and Magistrates* appeared on 13 February 1649, a mere two weeks after the astonishing spectacle of the execution of Charles I. While simple and straightforward enough on its face in style and argument, the *Tenure* can be a challenging read. One key to its difficulty comes immediately in its subtitle: *Proving, That it is Lawfull, and hath been held so through all Ages, for any, who have the Power, to call to account a Tyrant, or wicked King, and after due conviction, to depose, and put him to death; if the ordinary Magistrate have neglected, or deny'd to doe it.* The subtitle points to an argument that, depending on one's perspective, is either inflammatory or inspiring, and both inflammation and inspiration disturb careful reading. One nineteenth-century editor of Milton's prose advised readers to stop at the title: 'Enunciation of this elaborate and wicked title is quite enough to deter any from

I am grateful to Thomas Fulton, John Rumrich, and John Sitter, as well as to the editors of the *Handbook*, for comments that have improved this chapter.

wasting time in the perusal of the treatise itself.'[1] Clement Walker, a victim of Pride's Purge, harshly dismissed the *Tenure* shortly after its appearance: 'There is lately come forth a Booke of *Iohn Meltons* (a Libertine that thinketh his Wife a Manacle, and his very Garters to be Shackles and Fetters to him: one that {after the Independent fashion} will be tied by no obligation to God or Man).'[2] If the wary editor and the purged MP are tempted, in the words of *Areopagitica*, to 'ding the book a quoit's distance', readers of the democratic and egalitarian sympathies predominant today might accept the work uncritically for its stirring tag lines: 'to say Kings are account-able to none but God, is the overturning of all Law and government' (*CPW*, iii. 204); 'he that bids a man reigne over him above Law, may bid as well a savage Beast' (p. 206). We are not surprised to hear that Jefferson admired Milton's political ideas, and that the *Tenure* influenced the wording of the Declaration of Independence.[3] When responses are coloured either by abhorrence at the text's defence of regicide or enthusiasm for its foreshadowings of modern democracy, it can be difficult to see what is really there.

And the reader's difficulty pales next to Milton's. The heroes of the New Model Army, having liberated the English from the thrall of tyranny, arbitrary government, and religious coercion, are prepared to lead the nation into the promised land of religious toleration and government by a godly people. The people, unfortunately, are proving recalcitrant. Facing furious resistance on one side from the Presbyterians, who would rather treat with Charles I than bring him to justice, and on the other side from the Levellers, who challenged the legitimacy of a body acting without the authority of the majority of the people, the Rump and the court it appointed to try Charles were acting for an English people who largely disowned their actions. Milton in the *Tenure* is simultaneously voicing cherished ideals and putting the best face on a bad business.[4] The strain marks the text throughout.

Addressing a salient manifestation of that strain, Martin Dzelzainis and Go Togashi have focused rightly on an arresting shift of argument in the pages added in the second edition of late 1649.[5] In whom is lodged the right to resist, and

[1] Revd James J. G. Graham, *Selections from the Prose Works of John Milton: With Critical Remarks and Elucidations* (1870), 230.

[2] Theodorus Verax (Clement Walker), *Anarchia Anglicana: or, The History of Independency. The Second Part* (1649), 99, quoted in W. R. Parker, *Milton's Contemporary Reputation* (1940; repr. New York, 1971), 82.

[3] John S. Tanner and Justin Collings, 'How Adams and Jefferson Read Milton and Milton Read Them', *Milton Quarterly*, 40 (2006), 207–19 at 214–15.

[4] Long ago Don M. Wolfe suggested that 'in writing the *Tenure* Milton was confronted, like the Independent party itself, with the dilemma of justifying at once military coercion and democratic ideology' (*Milton in the Puritan Revolution* (1941), 215).

[5] Martin Dzelzainis, 'Introduction', *John Milton: Political Writings*, ed. Dzelzainis (Cambridge, 1991), pp. xviii–xix; Go Togashi, 'Milton and the Presbyterian Opposition, 1649–1650: The Engagement Controversy and *The Tenure of Kings and Magistrates*, Second Edition (1649)', *Milton Quarterly*, 39 (2005), 59–81. For the date of the second edition of the *Tenure*, see John T. Shawcross, 'Milton's *Tenure of Kings and Magistrates*: Date of Composition, Editions, and Issues', *Papers of the Bibliographical Society of America*, 60 (1966), 1–8; id., 'A Survey of Milton's Prose Works', in Michael Lieb and John Shawcross (eds.), *Achievements of the Left Hand* (Amherst, Mass., 1974), 309–12; Campbell, *Chronology*, 102.

eventually execute justice upon, an errant ruler?[6] The Presbyterians, as Milton demonstrates at length in the tract, have resisted the king not merely with sermons but with parliamentary power and arms. Now they question the legitimacy of the Rump, from which their MPs have been purged, and of the tribunal. Near the beginning of the first edition of February 1649, Milton responds to attacks on the legitimacy of the recent proceedings against the king: 'when God out of his providence and high disposal hath deliver'd him [the king] into the hand of thir brethren, on a suddain and in a new garbe of Allegiance, which thir doings have long since cancell'd; they plead for him, pity him, extoll him, protest against those that talk of bringing him to the tryal of Justice, which is the Sword of God, superior to all mortal things, in whose hand soever by apparent signes his testified will is to put it' (*CPW*, iii. 193). If critics complain that the Rump and tribunal act as mere private persons, lacking the authority that belongs by right to inferior magistrates, Milton brushes aside the question of legitimacy by claiming that God himself, 'by apparent signs', has decided the question. One does not need a full Parliament, much less the king in Parliament. God places his sword 'in whose hand soever' he pleases, whether magistrate or private person. Near the end of the augmented edition of late 1649, however, after a survey of the opinion of Reformed authorities on resistance to monarchs, Milton significantly revises his position: 'indeed I find it generally the cleere and positive determination of them all, (not prelatical, or of this late faction subprelatical) who have writt'n on this argument; that to doe justice on a lawless King, is to a privat man unlawful, to an inferior Magistrate lawful' (iii. 257). Now it seems that private persons may not bring a monarch to justice; that role is reserved for the 'inferior magistrates', or Parliament. The new argument clashes not only with the argument of the beginning of the *Tenure*, but also with the work's subtitle.

One might attempt to save appearances by pointing out that Milton in the later passage characterizes the argument of the Protestant authorities he has quoted rather than his own views. But between the quoted passages and his description of their position on the lawfulness, Milton has himself endorsed the authorities upon whom he calls to endorse his position: 'These were the true Protestant Divines of *England*, our fathers in the faith we hold' (p. 252); 'we may follow them for faithful Guides, and without doubting may receive them, as Witnesses abundant of what wee heer affirme concerning Tyrants' (p. 257). Milton weaves together his own argument with that of the cited authorities so tightly that they become inextricable. The new argument conflicts with the first edition's argument for the lawfulness of actions against tyrants by private persons. And as Milton does not remove the earlier argument when he publishes the revised and expanded *Tenure*, the conflicting arguments uneasily share the same book, and even the same page.

Milton argues in the second edition that to make war upon a king, as the Presbyterians have done, but then to punish his subordinates while sparing the king himself, is the 'strangest peece of reason to be call'd human, that . . . ever yet

---

[6] On Milton's position on this issue, see further the essay by R. W. Serjeantson, Ch. 34 below.

was vented' (p. 254). His apparent about-face on whether private persons can bring tyrants to justice strains the logic of his own argument. The reason for the reversal, as Dzelzainis and Togashi point out, lies in the shifting political landscape. From the Presbyterian perspective, the purged Parliament of December 1648 and January 1649 was not a legitimate body of magistrates but an assemblage of private persons. Milton accordingly defended in early 1649 the right of private persons to bring a king to justice. But as the Rump exercised *de facto* and asserted *de jure* power as a body of magistrates, the danger now came precisely from private persons, primarily the Presbyterian ministers, agitating against that authority. One can find consistency in Milton despite the apparent contradiction. The bottom line is that the godly or 'uprighter sort' have the right to resist and punish a king, whether one thinks of them as private persons (as the Presbyterians viewed members of the purged Parliament) or as magistrates (as the Rump styled itself).

But it may be more difficult to rationalize another apparent contradiction in the *Tenure*. While the rapidly changing political landscape does help us to make sense of Milton's shifting position on the rights of private persons as opposed those of magistrates, as Dzelzainis and Togashi argue, it cannot account for the fact that the first edition of February 1649 is itself already contradictory and intractably divided. The gaps in the argument are highlighted by repeated claims of self-evidence, which I will examine in a moment. Stanley Fish has suggested that for Milton argument is irrelevant; if one has eyes to see, the truth will be plain, and if one does not, no amount of demonstration will make the truth visible.[7] This is the Milton of the *Reason of Church-Government*: 'I do not conclude that Prelaty is Antichristian, for what need I? the things themselves conclude it', and again 'Ile tell ye, or at least remember ye, for most of ye know it already' (*CPW*, i. 850–1).[8] But Fish tells only half the story, for Milton does make arguments in the *Reason of Church-Government* and elsewhere—certainly in the *Tenure*. In the *Tenure*, however, the strands of his argument unravel, leaving behind what is supposedly self-evident.

Lending force to Hobbes's claim that reading Greek and Roman political writers disposes men to rebellion,[9] Milton invokes Aristotle for one strand of his argument: 'Aristotle . . . [has] defin'd a King, [as] him who governs to the good and profit of his People, and not for his own ends' (*CPW*, iii. 202). Because he rules for the good and profit of his people, he is accountable not only to God, as royalists and now Presbyterians are claiming, but to the people. Milton quotes approvingly from Aristotle's Politics 10 in the expanded second edition: 'Monarchy unaccountable, is the worst sort of Tyranny; and least of all to be endur'd by free born men' (p. 204). To Aristotle's picture, Milton adds the biblical Fall. The need for governors arises

---

[7] This is the burden of Fish's *How Milton Works* (Cambridge, Mass., 2001).

[8] See Stanley Fish, 'Reason in *The Reason of Church Government*', in his *Self-Consuming Artifacts* (Berkeley, 1972), 265–302.

[9] Hobbes argues in ch. 21 of *Leviathan* ('Of the Liberty of Subjects') that men 'have gotten a habit (under a false shew of Liberty,) of favouring tumults, and of licentious controlling the actions of their Sovereigns' from reading anti-monarchical works by Aristotle, Cicero, and others; *Leviathan*, ed. C. B. Macpherson (Harmondsworth, 1968), 267.

because we must protect ourselves in a fallen world. The 'autoritie and power of self-defence' was originally vested in every person, but that authority and power were delegated to kings and magistrates, as Milton writes, 'for ease, for order, *and least* [i.e. *lest*] *each man should be his own partial Judge*', a phrase to which I will return (p. 199; my emphasis). Over time, as authority and power corrupted these public servants, the people, in whom the delegated authority essentially remained, framed laws to 'limit the autority of whom they chose to govern them: that so man, of whose failing they had proof, might no longer rule over them, but law and reason abstracted as much as might be from personal errors and frailties. While, as the Magistrate was set above the people, so the Law was set above the Magistrate' (p. 200). Like Aristotle, Milton stresses accountability. If the king rules for his own good rather than for the good of people, he should be deposed and punished. Romans 13: 1 may tell us that 'There is no power but of God' (p. 209) and thus that we should not resist earthly powers, but, in a move reminiscent of his divorce tracts, Milton argues that the powers ordained by God are only those powers that govern for the good of the people. One may not divorce a wife, but a wife is a wife only by virtue of fulfilling the purpose for which God instituted marriage; one may not resist a power ordained by God, but God ordains only those who rule for the good of their peoples.[10]

Again as in the divorce tracts, Milton straddles the divide between the postlapsarian and prelapsarian. Despite stipulating that we need governors because of the vicious tendencies arising at the Fall, Milton seems to yearn for the primitive freedom of Eden. He begins the paragraph in which he lays out the need for kings and magistrates with an articulation of that freedom: 'No man who knows ought, can be so stupid as to deny that all men naturally were borne free, being the image and resemblance of God himself, and were by privilege above all other creatures, born to command and not to obey' (*CPW*, iii. 198–9). Although he immediately goes on to add, 'and that they liv'd so. Till from the root of *Adams* transgression, falling among themselves to doe wrong and violence', he chafes throughout the tract at the idea that a free man would give up his right of self-determination to a monarch or magistrates. Any delegation of right and authority by a free man, Milton will argue, can be only provisional, and it must be immediately and easily revocable. In this he resembles the Leveller John Lilburne, who derives from the dignity and freedom of Adam and Eve, made in the image of God, the dignity and freedom of every man and woman, 'who are, and were, by nature all equal and alike in power, dignity, authority, and majesty, none of them having by nature any authority, dominion, or magisterial power one over and above another'.[11] Lilburne bypasses the Fall entirely here. Milton recalls the Fall, but he immediately seems to forget it. He derives from the Fall a contract theory of government, but he holds on to a vision of the dignity of the upright and godly that minimizes the very effects of the Fall that led in his own account to the need for

---

[10] To my knowledge, Arthur Barker was the first to draw the parallels between the arguments of the *Tenure* and of the divorce tracts, in *Milton and the Puritan Dilemma, 1641–1660* (Toronto, 1942), 123, 129.

[11] John Lilburne, *The Free-Man's Freedom Vindicated* (1646), excerpted in *Puritanism and Liberty: Being the Army Debates 1647–9 from the Clarke Manuscripts*, ed. A. S. P. Woodhouse (1938), 317.

submission to magistrates. According to William Poole, in the *Tenure* 'political identity is, like marital identity in the *Doctrine and Discipline of Divorce*, half in and half out of Eden'.[12] Because of their fallibility and tendency to sin, Milton seems to acknowledge, fallen human beings require the check of government, but that same check is an affront to primitive dignity and freedom, both of which Milton seems reluctant to surrender.

The tract veers between two arguments. On the one hand, Milton contends that subjects are within their rights to resist tyrants who act outside the law and who rule for themselves rather than for the people; on the other hand he maintains that subjects are free to change their governors at any time, for any reason. The two incompatible positions follow each other in close succession. Shortly after quoting Aristotle's condemnation of unaccountable monarchy as tyranny, on the threshold of his demonstration that one may resist unjust rulers, Milton unexpectedly suggests that one may resist a ruler even when there is no question of tyranny:

It follows lastly, that since the King or Magistrate holds his autoritie of the people, both originaly and naturally for their good in the first place, and not his own, then may the people as oft as they shall judge it for the best, either choose him or reject him, retaine him or depose him though no Tyrant, meerly by the liberty and right of free born Men, to be govern'd as seems to them best. (*CPW*, iii. 206)

In the same paragraph, responding to the injunction in 1 Peter 2: 13 to submit to civil power, Milton returns to the argument that opposition to constituted power is justified by that power's tyranny: 'But to any civil power unaccountable, unquestionable, and not to be resisted, no not in wickedness, and violent actions, how can we submitt as free men?' (p. 209). One may resist unjust, unaccountable power, and one may change rulers at any time and for no other reason beyond a free people's right of self-determination. The two arguments sit uneasily together not only in this paragraph but throughout the tract; if the former is more frequent, Milton never drops the latter. Towards the end of the first edition Milton asserts that without the right to 'remove, or to abolish' governors or governments, we enjoy only 'a ridiculous and painted freedom, fit to coz'n babies'.[13] Subjects lacking this right, he adds, 'though bearing high thir heads, they can in due esteem be thought no better than slaves and vassals born, in the tenure and occupation of another inheriting Lord. Whose government, *though not illegal, or intolerable*, hangs over them as a Lordly scourge, not as a free government' (pp. 236–7; my emphasis).[14] If a people can throw off kings or magistrates who rule legally and tolerably, it is not immediately clear why one

---

12 William Poole, *Milton and the Idea of the Fall* (Cambridge, 2005), 141.

13 Quentin Skinner demonstrates how Milton articulates the opposite of the free man through the imagery of slavery and childhood in 'John Milton and the Politics of Slavery', in Graham Parry and Joad Raymond (eds.), *Milton and the Terms of Liberty* (Cambridge, 2002), 1–22.

14 Thomas Fulton has astutely observed that Milton's 'use of "tenure" employs the rhetoric of ironic inversion . . . in which the discourse of his opponents is so wrong as to be completely upside down: it is the king and magistrates not the people, who are held in tenure' (*Historical Milton: Manuscript, Print, and Political Culture in Revolutionary England* (Amherst, Mass., forthcoming)).

needs to argue as strenuously as Milton does for the right to resist unjust, tyrannical rulers.

The linchpin for these two uneasily yoked arguments can be found, I think, in the tract's repeated claims of self-evidence. 'No man who knows ought, can be so stupid to deny that all men naturally were born free'; 'Against whom what the people lawfully may doe, as against a common pest, and destroyer of mankind, I suppose no man of cleare judgement need go furder to be guided then by the very principles of nature in him'; 'It must needs be clear to any man not avers from reason, that hostilitie and subjection are two direct and positive contraries'; 'No understanding man can bee ignorant that Covnants are ever made according to the present state of persons and of things' (iii. 198, 212, 230, 231–2). The truth is clear to those who can see. If others, who quail at the majesty of kings and who draw back from concluding what they have begun, need to be reminded of Charles's iniquity and of the right to depose and punish him, clear spirits need neither arguments to convince them nor even reasons to justify change of government. Freeborn and self-governing men— and only freeborn and self-governing men deserve and value good governors—do not need to be governed.

The gap between those who see immediately and those who must be persuaded threatens the coherence of the text as well as the stability of the nascent republic in 1649. Daniel Shore has recently argued that discontinuities in the text result from Milton's rhetorical accommodation of differing audiences:

> Much of the expository structure of *The Tenure of Kings and Magistrates* . . . is geared towards providing the kinds of argumentative proof demanded by disparate factions. . . . Even when the tract has progressed deep into the exposition of its argument the concern with audience largely determines its structure. . . . The argument, in short, develops as much through its relation to its plurality of audiences—successively addressing the concerns and standards of each constituency—as it does by any other internal logic.[15]

It is true that Milton is carefully attuned to audience, as Thomas Fulton demonstrates in his comparison of the language of the unpublished manuscript of the 'Digression' on the Long Parliament, probably written in 1648–9, with the rhetorically complex language of his public polemic.[16] But the discontinuity in the *Tenure* runs deeper than adjusting argumentative proof to convince differing factions. Milton does not merely use differing tactics to persuade differing groups of the wisdom of one political model, he offers two incompatible political models, one of which undoes the other. In one model, the legitimacy of deposing kings and overthrowing magistrates is grounded in a demonstration of their tyranny; in the other, no grounds for deposing are required, because the king or magistrates serve merely at the pleasure of the people. One model is applicable to the general run of fallen human-kind, the other to an imagined republic of godly individuals whose freedom of

---

[15] Daniel Shore, '*Eikonoklastes* and the Rhetoric of Audience', *Milton Studies*, 45 (2006), 129–48 at 143.

[16] Fulton, *Historical Milton*. See also Fulton, 'Edward Phillips and the Manuscript of the "Digression"', *Milton Studies*, 48 (2008), 95–112. On the date of the 'Digression', see the essay below by Martin Dzelzainis, Ch. 22.

self-determination must not be compromised.[17] The clash of two arguments is reminiscent of the dissonance in *Areopagitica* between the opening suggestion that offending books should be punished and the developing argument that virtuous readers can profit from reading bad books and that a 'naughty mind' can turn even a good book into an 'occasion for evil'; all books are good to a virtuous reader and no books are good to a vicious reader (*CPW*, ii. 512).

From the perspective of those not already sharing Milton's commitments, his argument that free men should be able to change their government 'though not illegal, or intolerable' must have seemed a prescription for anarchy. Milton claims for himself and for other right-minded men the 'authority and power of self-defence' that, though originally vested in every person, had been delegated to kings and magistrates, as Milton himself writes, 'for ease, for order, *and least* [*lest*] *each man should be his own partial judge*'. The danger of each man being his own partial judge is precisely what concerned Clement Walker, whose canny metaphor rebukes Milton for treating even necessary and indispensable ties as constricting chains: he takes 'his very Garters to be Shackles and Fetters', and he 'will be tied by no obligation to God or Man'. If obligation to governors is immediately dissoluble without cause, Walker has a point. When each man is his own partial judge, we have returned to the state of nature, or anarchy. Walker answers Milton as Oliver Cromwell answered Colonel Thomas Rainborough at Putney: 'No man says that you have a mind to anarchy, but the consequence of this rule tends to anarchy, must end in anarchy.'[18]

Milton's answer to the threat of anarchy is to invoke again the like-minded 'uprighter sort':

But who in particular is a Tyrant cannot be determin'd in a general discours, otherwise then by supposition; his particular charge, and the sufficient proof of it must determin that: which I leave to Magistrates, at least to the uprighter sort of them, and of the people, though in number less by many, in whom faction least hath prevaild above the Law of nature and right reason, to judge as they find cause. But this I dare owne as part of my faith, that if such a one there be, by whose Commission, whole massachers have been committed on his faithfull Subjects, his Provinces offerd to pawn or alienation, as the hire of those whom he had sollicited to come in and destroy whole Citties and Countries; be he King, or Tyrant, or Emperour, the Sword of Justice is above him; in whose hand soever is found sufficient power to avenge the effusion, and so great a deluge of innocent blood. (*CPW*, iii. 197)

Although Milton leaves judgement to the tribunal, his echoing in this passage of the terms of the indictment signals that his upright mind is thinking in concert with the uprighter sort among the people and magistrates. Again the test of a position is its acceptability by clear spirits, godly men, the well-affected, and one knows who clear spirits are by their acceptance of self-evident positions.

---

[17] For an exploration of the splintering of Milton's arguments resulting from his implicit self-understanding and self-representation in other works, notably in the divorce tracts, see Stephen Fallon, *Milton's Peculiar Grace: Self-representation and Authority* (Ithaca, N.Y., 2007), 110–45.

[18] *Puritanism and Liberty*, ed. Woodhouse, 59.

Milton's position is tenuous, nowhere more so than when he claims, in the wake of Army triumphs and the current trial of the king, that 'Justice and Victory' are the 'only warrants through all ages, next under immediat Revelation, to exercise supream power' (iii. 194). While one might recoil at Milton's version of 'might makes right', military victory at least has the advantage of being public, visible, and objective, or intersubjective. If justice, on the other hand, is to be a divine warrant to govern, the question of course will be 'whose justice?' This brings us right back to the problem that Milton is facing squarely in 1649, even if he addresses it only obliquely in his tract: the people of England do not recognize the justice of his cause.[19] An argument based on the right of the people to govern themselves can find no purchase among the people, so Milton must fall back on defining the people as the people at their best, as the 'uprighter sort'.[20]

Robert Filmer probes the weak spot in Milton's logic: 'Nay J. M. will not allow the major part of the Representors to be the people, but the *sounder and better part only* of them, & in right down terms he tells us *to determine who is a Tyrant, he leaves to Magistrates, at least to the uprighter sort of them and of the people, though in number less by many, to judge as they finde cause.* If the *sounder, the better, and the uprighter* part have the power of the people, how shall we know, or who shall judge who they be?'[21] Any successful appeal for deference to a minority of the 'uprighter sort' would depend on the majority's recognizing and acknowledging that they are not part of this honourable group. Milton is not being cynical or dishonest, but he is being entirely impractical. His rueful recognition that a majority of his countrymen are not ready to follow the path cleared by the New Model Army leaves its mark in the splintered argument of the tract. Filmer shrewdly observes, for example, that for all his condemnation of Charles's attempts to place himself above the law, Milton savages the Presbyterians for insisting on 'privileges, customs, forms, and . . . thir gibrish Lawes' (*CPW*, iii. 192–3; Filmer, 'Observations', 22).

For Milton, the truth is immediately available, by the kind of intuition that characterizes angelic discourse in *Paradise Lost*, to the uprighter sort, who have earned their spiritual and intellectual acuity by patient discipline and by their commitment, to use the words of 'Lycidas', 'To scorn delights and live laborious days' (l. 72). Others are disqualified by their failure to see. 'To these', Milton writes, 'I wish better instruction, . . . which . . . I shall indeavour, as my dutie is, to bestow on them' (*CPW*, iii. 194). He does not sound confident. To convince the naturally or

---

[19] Milton would address the lack of popular support more directly in 1660 in *The Readie and Easie Way*, where he argues explicitly for the right of the minority to exert its will on the majority by force, if necessary to preserve the minority's freedom.

[20] Blair Hoxby argues ingeniously that Milton has his eye on the prospective majority that will emerge to support his ideas once the free marketplace of ideas is allowed to do its work (*Mammon's Music: Literature and Economics in the Age of Milton* (New Haven and London, 2002), 55).

[21] 'Observations on Master Milton against Salmasius', in Robert Filmer, *Observations concerning the Originall of Government* (1652), 13, repr. in Parker, *Milton's Contemporary Reputation*, 279.

habitually servile, the opposite of the uprighter sort, is a difficult, perhaps a hercule-
an task. He fulfils a duty in the *Tenure*, to attempt to educate a recalcitrant public, but
his heart is elsewhere, with the virtuous and upright compatriots who see immediately. But Milton still labours to convince the rest. The problem is that the distance
between the attempts to convince and the statements of self-evidence open an
unbridgeable gap in the argument.

I close with the *Tenure*'s opening, where Milton, preparing for the task that is by
his own definition all but impossible, sets about clearing a small space out of the
chaos of public discourse where his truth can triumph immediately. 'If men within
themselves', Milton writes, 'would be govern'd by reason, and not generally give up
thir understanding to a double tyrannie, of Custom from without, and blind affections within, they would discerne better, what it is to favour and uphold the Tyrant of
a Nation. But being slaves within doors, no wonder that they strive so much to have
the public State conformably govern'd to the inward vitious rule, by which they
govern themselves' (*CPW*, iii. 190). Men are governed either by 'reason' or an 'inward
vitious rule'. As we have seen, those who are governed by reason do not need to be
constrained by kings and magistrates. Those who are governed by an 'inward vitious
rule' fall under and deserve tyrannical government. There is no place for inherited or
communal laws in the self-government of rational men. Good men do not need
them, and bad men cannot frame them and do not deserve them. For Milton, here as
elsewhere, only those who can govern themselves are fit to be citizens of a free society.
Unencumbered by passions and unwedded to outmoded and oppressive institutions,
they do not need the bridles and whips that their less virtuous contemporaries
require. When Milton adds that 'indeed none can love freedom heartilie, but good
men; the rest love not freedom, but license; which never hath more scope or more
indulgence then under Tyrants' (iii. 190), the argument is over before it begins. Those
'endu'd with fortitude and Heroick vertue' (p. 191), those in Milton's party, govern
themselves and thus already merit by (minority) acclamation the role of governors.
The rest are slavish by habit, inclined to favour the tyrants who will favour them.
While eventually they must be convinced, the legitimacy of the republican government with minority support does not depend on them. Milton in his opening words
has defined them out of the political equation.

Milton offers two political visions in the *Tenure*, one from the perspective of the
many who provide a government for themselves and the other from the perspective
of the individual governed. The first is a contract theory of government that is
predicated on the fall of man and that addresses the partiality, fallibility, and vice
inherited by fallen human beings. In this model the coercive authority of the king or
magistrate is essential to the functioning of government. For his second vision,
Milton falls back on his own perspective as a godly man subject to government.
The imagined citizens of this second model seem free from the vices that necessitated
the creation of kings and magistrates in the first place. They are free to change
governments at any time and for any reason, a freedom that could only undermine
the coercive power of kings and magistrates. This model tends to the utopian and the
anarchic: utopian because a change of governors would require the agreement of a

sufficient number of the godly (and as all would see themselves as godly and upright, this would really mean the support of a sufficient number of the people); and anarchic because fallen men even by Milton's own testimony need a coercive power to regulate civil society. The unravelling of the republican experiment in the years to come would measure the futility of Milton's political calculus.

CHAPTER 14

MILTON'S REGICIDE TRACTS AND THE USES OF SHAKESPEARE

NICHOLAS McDOWELL

SHAKESPEARE EXPELLED?

It would be richly ironic if Charles I, awaiting the judgement of Parliament on his life and sketching a book of meditations on his fate, found solace in the verse of the man who would soon be commissioned to defame his memory and discredit his book. Charles's copy of the second Shakespeare folio (1632) is today in the Royal Library at Windsor. The volume is of some interest in itself because Charles annotated the table of contents, renaming some of the plays after the characters that he apparently regarded as of leading interest: *As You Like It* becomes 'Rosalind', *A Midsummer Night's Dream* is retitled 'Pyramus and Thisbe', and, perhaps revealingly given his trouble with Puritans, *Twelfth Night* is remembered as 'Malvolio'. The poem that Milton published in the 1645 and 1673 *Poems* as 'On Shakespeare' appears, anonymously, in the 1632 folio as the second of the prefatory poems, entitled 'An Epitaph on the Admirable Dramatick Poet, W. Shakespeare'. According to Milton in *Eikonoklastes* (October 1649), Shakespeare was 'one whom we well know was the Closet Companion of these [the king's] solitudes' (*CPW*, iii. 361); and Milton goes on to contend that we can find a model for what he regards as the feigned piety of the

'King's Book', the *Eikon Basilike* (February 1649), in the character of Shakespeare's Richard III. A year earlier, with mortality on his mind and the notes for his book before him, Charles might have found consolation not only in Shakespeare but in Milton's conceit in his 'Epitaph' that a book can continue to elicit 'wonder and astonishment', more so than the splendour of any actual tomb, even a king's, long after the author's demise:

> What neede my *Shakespeare* for his honour'd bones,
> The labour of an Age, in piled stones
> Or that his hallow'd Reliques should be hid
> Vnder a starre-ypointing Pyramid?
> Deare Sonne of Memory, great Heire of *Fame*,
> What needst thou such dull witnesse of thy Name?
> Thou in our wonder and astonishment
> Hast built thy selfe a lasting Monument:
> For whil'st to th' shame of slow-endevouring Art
> Thy easie numbers flow, and that each part,
> Hath from the leaves of thy unvalued Booke,
> Those Delphicke Lines with deepe Impression tooke
> Then thou our fancy of her selfe bereaving,
> Dost make us Marble with too much conceiving,
> And so Sepulcher'd in such pompe dost lie
> That Kings for such a Tombe would wish to die.

The 'deepe Impression' which the folio makes on the hearts of Shakespeare's readers transforms 'us' into his tombstone, or rather a multitude of tombstones: each reader becomes a memorial to the affective power of Shakespeare's words. Royalists looked to just such images of the internalized monument when they sought to describe the effect of Charles's death on the English people:

Madam, I am confident that I may, without adulation say, that your Royall Fathers death, gave a life to Vertue. And as we have a sufficient cause to deplore the absence of his Person, so we have an undeniable reason to rejoice for the presence of his perfections, which will build everlasting Pyramids in the hearts of those, which were his loyall Subjects.[1]

In the New Testament *eikon* is used to describe 'Christ, who is the image of God' (2 Cor. 4: 4), as Paul explains how the converted who find God within their hearts are transformed into the living image of Christ. With its repeated identification of the regicide with the passion of Christ, the explicit aim of the *Eikon Basilike* was to place the living image of the dead king in the hearts of all his 'loyall Subjects' and convert them to the Stuart cause, soon to be resurrected in the form of the king's son.

After his execution Charles's copy of the second folio fell into the possession of Sir Thomas Herbert, who after the Scots handed the king over to the Parliamentary Army in 1647 was appointed groom to Charles in his captivity. T. A. Birrell suggests that Herbert essentially stole the Shakespeare, along with several other books, and

---

[1] John Quarles, dedication to Princess Elizabeth, in *Regale Lectum Miseriae* (1649), sig. a2ᵛ.

that Herbert was 'the source for the story that Charles I was reading Shakespeare and Ben Jonson in his last days: the story that was made so much of by Milton and the other Puritan pamphleteers'. But Birrell also observes that the second folio 'is, like every book belonging to Charles I, not just a book, it is a relic of a martyr'.[2] The *Eikon Basilike* first appeared only days after the regicide and presented itself precisely as 'a relic of a martyr'; it was this representation that Milton sought to expose as false and idolatrous in *Eikonoklastes*. For Milton, the image of the Stuart king as Christ-like martyr was not the Pauline *eikon*, the internalized Christian image, but *eidolon*, the empty, idolatrous form: the 'image of the Beast' worshipped by those who will 'drink of the wine of the wrath of God' (Rev. 14: 9–10).[3] The charge that Shakespeare had been Charles's 'closet Companion' while he sketched his meditations is one aspect of Milton's strategy of attacking the *Eikon Basilike* as a piece of theatre, briefly transfixing but insubstantial and dangerously manipulative of its audience's passions:

And how much their intent, who publish'd these overlate Apologies and Meditations of the dead king, drives to the same end of stirring up the people to bring him that honour, that affection, and by consequence, that revenge to his dead Corps, which hee himself living could never gain to his person, it appears both by the conceited portraiture before his Book, drawn out to the full measure of a Masking Scene, and set there to catch fools and silly gazers . . . for though the Picture sett in Front would Martyr him and Saint him to befool the people, yet the Latin motto in the end, which they understand not, leaves him, as it were a politic contriver to bring about that interest by faire and plausible words, which the force of Armes deny'd him. But quaint Emblems and devices begg'd from old Pageantry of some Twelf-nights entertainment at *Whitehall*, will doe but ill to make a Saint or Martyr: and if the People resolve to take him Sainted at the rate of such a Canonizing, I shall suspect thir Calender more than the *Gregorian*. (*CPW*, iii. 342–3)

Milton calls upon the language of Puritan anti-theatricalism to identify the King's Book, and in particular the famous frontispiece showing Charles in a pose of Davidic, penitential meditation, exchanging his earthly for a heavenly crown, as a form of popish idol. The *Eikon Basilike* is presented as a decorous textual statue of the king which, like a model of a saint or the Virgin Mary in Catholic practice, turns devotion into passive, 'silly' gazing on a meaningless visual sign, when it should instead take the form of active intellectual engagement with the Word of God in the Scriptures. Milton's emphasis on the Latin motto continues the association with Catholicism but the reference to popular ignorance ('which they understand not') also introduces the disdain that resurfaces throughout *Eikonoklastes* for 'an inconstant, irrational, and Image-doting rabble' (*CPW*, iii. 601), whose appetite for the King's Book—it went through thirty-five editions within a year—shows their reason to be enslaved to their passions, skillfully 'stirr[ed] up' within them by the Machiavellian clerics behind its

---

² *English Monarchs and their Books: from Henry VIII to Charles II* (1987), 44–7.

³ A point made by Florence Sandler, 'Icon and Iconoclast', in Michael Lieb and John T. Shawcross (eds.), *Achievements of the Left Hand: Essays on the Prose of John Milton* (Amherst, Mass., 1974), 160–84 at 161.

publication.[4] While Milton presumably has the Stuart court masques of Jonson, Davenant, and Shirley in mind in the passage above rather than Shakespeare's *Twelfth Night* (1601)—although that play was indeed performed at court on Candlemas, 1623, under the title of 'Malvolio' preferred by Charles—Milton more likely recalls earlier in the same passage how Shakespeare's Mark Anthony whips up the passions of the Roman crowds after he has read Caesar's will, turning the corpse into a site of religious devotion as he implores them to 'go kiss dead Caesar's wounds / And dip their napkins in his sacred blood, / Yea, beg a hair of him for memory' (III. II. 129–31): 'And among other examples we finde that the last will of Caesar being read to the people, and what bounteous Legacies he had bequeath'd them, wrought more in that Vulgar audience to the avenging of his death, then all the art he could ever use, to win thir favour in his life-time' (iii. 342).[5] The reference to Mark Anthony's calculated working on the passions of the 'vulgar' through exploitation both of Caesar's corpse and of a text Caesar has supposedly left behind prepares the way for the doubt Milton casts throughout on Charles's authorship of 'these Soliloquies' (p. 346). We now know that Milton was right to the extent that the Presbyterian cleric John Gauden apparently edited notes made by Charles; but the question mark over authorship matters to Milton only insofar as it allows him to present the dead king as both an actor and a prop in a drama directed by 'secret *Coadjutors*', plotting to bring down the new Commonwealth regime (pp. 338, 346).[6]

It has been forcefully argued by Steven N. Zwicker that the 'association of the king's person with learning and aristocratic refinement, with poetry, drama, and visual culture, forced Milton to trivialize the artistic forms and genres most closely identified with Charles I'. Zwicker sees Milton as 'forced' into a rhetorical position, with which, as a poet, he was profoundly uneasy: this uneasiness is one of the reasons why *Eikonoklastes* fails as effective polemic.[7] In fact Milton was returning to the polemical strategies of Parliamentarian propaganda of the first civil war. One of the distinctive aspects of the work of Marchamont Nedham, who in 1650 would join Milton as the leading propagandist for the new Commonwealth, had been his claim that the royalists' self-deluding fantasies about their successes in the war were an anachronistic and incongruous continuation of the distracting illusions peddled by

---

[4] For an excellent discussion of the treatment of pathos in *Eikonoklastes*, see John Staines, 'Compassion in the Public Sphere of Milton and Charles', in Gail Kern Paster, Katherine Rowe, and Mary Floyd-Wilson (eds.), *Reading the Early Modern Passions: Essays in the Cultural History of Emotion* (Philadelphia, 2004), 89–110.

[5] All references to Shakespeare are to *The Arden Shakespeare Complete Works*, ed. Richard Proudfoot, Ann Thompson, and David Scott Kastan, rev. edn. (2001).

[6] There is a helpful discussion of the authorship question in the most recent edition of the *Eikon Basilike*, ed. Jim Daems and Holly Faith Nelson (Petersborough, Ont., 2006), 16–21.

[7] *Lines of Authority: Politics and Literary Culture, 1649–89* (New York, 1993), 39. Kevin Sharpe also argues that Milton was 'forced', and failed, to 'critique the *Eikon Basilike* as text: as a work of literature and authorial performance' ('The King's Writ: Royal Authors and Royal Authority in Early Modern England', in Sharpe and Peter Lake (eds.), *Culture and Politics in Early Stuart England* (Basingstoke, 1994), 117–38).

early Stuart theatrical culture. In the newsbook *Mercurius Britanicus* Nedham mocked his royalist rival *Mercurius Aulicus* as

a woefull spectacle and object of dullness and tribulation, not to be recovered by the Protestant or *Catholique* liquor, either Ale or strong beer, or Sack, or Claret, or Hippocras, or Muscadine, or Rosasolis, which hath been reputed formerly by his Grand Father *Ben Johnson*, and his Uncle *Shakespeare*, and his Couzen Germains *Fletcher* and *Beaumont*, and nose-lesse *Davenant*, and Frier *Sherley* the Poets, the onely blossoms for the brain, the restoratives for the wit, the bathing of the wine muses, but none of these are now able either to warme him into a quibble, or to inflame him into a sparkle of invention[.][8]

If the royalists are the 'sons of Ben', or rather the grandsons, Shakespeare is also cited as a direct literary ancestor of the royalist polemicists, presumably because he was also the recipient of Stuart patronage. Less surprisingly, perhaps, royalists appropriated Shakespeare in their efforts to portray England's new rulers as stereo-typically Puritan philistines, as Malvolio's and Zeal-of-the-Land Busy's. In its prefa-tory verses the anonymous play-pamphlet *The Famous Tragedie of King Charles I* (1649) reminds its readers that

> Though *Johnson*, *Shakespeare*, *Goffe*, and *Davenant*,
> Brave *Sucklin*, Beaumont, Fletcher, *Shurley* want
> The life of action, and their learned lines
> Are loathed, by the Monsters of the times;
> Yet your refined Soules can penetrate
> Their depth of merit[.] (sig. A3[r])

   Consequently more convincing than Zwicker's argument that Milton was forced to 'trivialize' the literary culture associated with the Stuarts, including Shakespeare, is Nigel Smith's claim that, partly as a consequence of 'his contempt of Charles I's own love of Shakespeare', Milton's 'regicide tracts mark the beginning of his expulsion of Shakespeare from his dramatic inventiveness, and his attempt to create a new theatre for the republic'.[9] In other words, Milton seeks in the regicide tracts the reform of literary culture at the moment of both political and religious reformation, and he looks beyond an English theatrical culture tainted by Stuart patronage to the political and moral lessons of classical, anti-tyrannical closet drama. Smith quotes the invo-cation of Seneca's version of Euripides' *Heracles furens* in *The Tenure of Kings and Magistrates*:

Greeks and Romans, as their prime Authors witness, held it not onely lawfull, but a glorious and Heroic deed, rewarded publicly with Statues and Garlands, to kill an infamous Tyrant at any tyme without tryal: and but reason, that he who trod down all Law, should not be voutsaf'd the benefit of Law. Insomuch that Seneca the Tragedian brings in Hercules the grand suppressor of Tyrants, thus speaking:

---

8 *Mercurius Britanicus*, 20 (4–11 Jan. 1644), 152.
9 *Literature and Revolution in England, 1640–1660* (New Haven and London, 1994), 16–17.

> — Victima haud ulla amplior
> Potest, magisque optima mactari Jovi
> Quam Rex iniquus —
> — There can be slaine
> — No sacrifice to God more acceptable
> Then an unjust and wicked King — (CPW, iii. 213)

The example is repeated in the *First Defence* (1651), where Samson is cited along with Hercules as an example of a heroic tyrant killer, and the Euripidean and Senecan Hercules would become one of the models for Milton's own closet drama *Samson Agonistes*—a rebuke, among other things, to a debased Restoration theatre, with its restagings and rewritings of Shakespeare by the likes of Dryden and William Davenant.[10]

The idea of a Miltonic 'expulsion' of Shakespeare after the regicide would not be accepted by those who have argued for a strong and positive Shakespearean presence in *Paradise Lost*.[11] But the idea of 'expulsion' also assumes a renunciation of an earlier allegiance, and several critics have argued that 'On Shakespeare' itself displays a deep, if not yet politicized nor probably fully conscious, suspicion of the Shakespearean example. For John Guillory, lines 13–14 ('Then thou our fancy of her selfe bereaving, / Dost make us Marble with too much conceiving') subvert the performance of epitaphic praise and disclose Milton's resistance to Shakespearean 'fancy', or a notion of 'natural' poetic creativity divorced from divine authorization. In reading Shakespeare's book, his words are written on our heart and our imagination is overpowered by his, turning us into memorial statues to his art; but such a 'condition of arrest or paralysis is everywhere morally suspect in Milton's poetry'.[12] And, we might add, though Guillory does not, in Milton's prose: *Eikonoklastes* is also in effect an apostrophe to a deceased entity whose posthumous book has overwhelmed its readers' conceptual capacities with its affective rhetoric, turning them into 'blockish' idolaters who lose the liberty of thought and action that defines their humanity:

But now, with a besotted and degenerate baseness of spirit, except some few, who yet retain in them the old English fortitude and love of Freedom, and have testifi'd it by thir matchless deeds, the rest, imbastardized from the ancient nobleness of thir Ancestors, are ready to fall flat and give adoration to the Image and Memory of this Man, who hath offer'd at more cunning fetches to undermine our Liberties, and putt Tyranny into an Art, then any British King before him. (*CPW*, iii. 344)

Guillory suggests that the capacity of Milton's Shakespeare to manipulate men's imaginations prefigures 'the tempter's magical power' in *A Maske Performed at Ludlow Castle*, and refers to the 'numerous Shakespearean echoes' associated with

---

[10] See e.g. Stella P. Revard, 'The Politics of Milton's Hercules', *Milton Studies*, 32 (1995), 217–45. On the politics of Davenant's *Macbeth* (1663), see Lois Potter, *Secret Rites and Secret Writing: Royalist Literature, 1641–1660* (Cambridge, 1989), 203–7.

[11] I am thinking pre-eminently of Paul Stevens, *Imagination and the Presence of Shakespeare in Paradise Lost* (Madison, Wis., 1985).

[12] *Poetic Authority: Spenser, Milton, and Literary History* (New York, 1983), 19.

Comus and his magic (p. 19). Comus is the offspring of Bacchus and Circe, 'Whose charmed cup / Whoever tasted, lost his upright shape, / And downward fell into a grovelling swine'; Comus 'Excels his mother at her mighty art' (*A Maske*, ll. 51–3, 63). As soon as men drink from Comus's potion 'their human countenance, / The express resemblance of the gods, is changed / Into some brutish form' (ll. 68–70): enslaved to the *eidolon* or empty, material form, the true, embodied image or *eikon* of God—'So God created man in his own image' (Gen. 1: 27)—is disfigured and God-given liberty is lost. The Circe story is for Milton, even in 1634, a mythical lesson in the workings of idolatry, showing how it originates in men's susceptibility to sensual comfort, and has an essential link with slavery.[13] The connection with slavery is made explicit in *Eikonoklastes* in Milton's lament that 'so many sober Englishmen . . . like men enchanted with the *Circean* cup of servitude, will not be held back from running their own heads into the Yoke of Bondage' (*CPW*, iii. 488). In the devastating final lines of the second, 1650 edition of *Eikonoklastes* (which shows, presumably because of the continued popularity of the *Eikon Basilike*, an even greater scorn for the rational capacities of the common people than the first), Milton attacks those taken in by the King's Book as

a credulous and hapless herd, begott'n to servility, and inchanted with these popular institutes of Tyranny, [who] subscrib'd with a new device of the King's Picture at his praiers, hold out both thir eares with such delight and ravishment to be stigmatiz'd and board through in witness of their own voluntary and beloved baseness. (iii. 601)

Milton seems to recall here the public mutilations performed under the Laudian church on the Puritan activists John Bastwick, Henry Burton, and William Prynne in 1637; Prynne had previously had his ears cropped for his attack in *Histromastix* (1634) on the theatrical culture of the court. The people who become 'inchanted' by the King's Book are reduced to an inhuman state (a 'herd'), as Odysseus' men were turned to pigs by Circe, and voluntarily return themselves to the conditions of tyrannical rule from which they had sought to free themselves in the 1640s. But the facial mutilation that Milton recalls from life under Stuart monarchy in the 1630s is also a literal manifestation of the defacement of the *eikon* of God that gives humanity its shape.[14]

Do the prose tracts then make conscious and explicit a suspicion of Shakespearean 'fancy' that is unconscious and implicit in the early poetry? Does the identification of Shakespeare with royalism and above all with Charles enable Milton to formulate a long-standing doubt about the moral value of Shakespearean art? Paul Stevens responds to Guillory by objecting, first, that the Shakespearean echoes in the *Maske*, composed four years after 'On Shakespeare', are 'not associated predominantly or even exclusively with Comus's magic'. While there have been claims for echoes

---

[13] For an overview of the connection between idolatry and slavery throughout the poetry and prose, see Barbara K. Lewalski, 'Milton and Idolatry', *Studies in English Literature, 1500–1900*, 43 (2003), 213–32. See also the essay below by Regina Schwartz, Ch. 35.

[14] John Leonard argues for the impact of the 1637 punishment of Bastwick, Burton, and Prynne on 'Lycidas' in '"Trembling ears": The Historical Moment of *Lycidas*', *Journal of Medieval and Renaissance Studies*, 21 (1991), 59–81.

in the *Maske* of numerous Shakespeare plays, the influence of *The Tempest*, in particular, has long been recognized, and Stevens points to the association between Ariel and the Attendant Spirit.[15] He also points out that 'the figure of "Divinest Melancholy"' in 'Il Penseroso', 'whose soul is enraptured in a "holy passion", is urged to intensify her contemplative activity and "Forget thy self to marble"' (ll. 12, 41–2). 'Stasis here', argues Stevens, 'does not indicate moral paralysis but *ex stasis*, the ecstasy that Donne's lovers parody [in "The Ecstasy"] when their self-absorption is so intense they appear to outsiders like "sepulchral statues".'[16] Stevens also offers a convincing source for Milton's 'bereaving/conceiving' rhyme in Spenser's 'Hymne of Heavenly Beautie', published in *Fowre Hymnes* (1596), and specifically its description of those deemed worthy to contemplate the face of Sapience, enthroned in heaven:

> None thereof worthy be, but those whom she
> Vouchsafeth to her presence to receive,
> And letteth them her lovely face to see,
> Whereof such wondrous pleasures they conceive,
> And sweet contentment, that it doth bereave
> Their soul of sense, through infinite delight,
> And them transport from flesh into the spright. (ll. 253–9)

Guillory's Miltonic opposition of a secular Shakespearean 'fancy' and a divinely authorized Spenserian inspiration seems to fade in this light. The memory of Spenser in 'On Shakespeare' suggests that in reading Shakespeare's book rightly, we can glimpse on earth the wondrous face of heavenly wisdom—the true Christian *eikon*—and this can be a transformational spiritual experience. If we now return to the prose, can we find a Shakespeare who offers us divine guidance in the struggle against the temptation to idolatry? A Shakespeare who may be the favourite reading of tyrants but who can teach *us* about tyranny if we devoutly contemplate lines possessed of the power to transport 'from flesh into the spright'?

MILTON'S *MACBETH*

Thomas N. Corns has found that the 1649 prose 'exhibits a new stylistic austerity, as unusual collocations become much rarer than formerly, [Milton's] incidence of imagery falls quite sharply, and the imagery he does use sheds the luxuriance that

---

[15] 'Subversion and Wonder in Milton's Epitaph "On Shakespeare"', *English Literary Renaissance*, 19 (1989), 375–88 at 382–3. On the *Maske* and *The Tempest*, see e.g. John M. Major, '*Comus* and *The Tempest*', *Shakespeare Quarterly*, 10 (1959), 177–83; David Norbrook, '"What Cares These Roarers for the Name of King": Language and Utopia in *The Tempest*', in Gordon McMullan and Jonathan Hope (eds.), *The Politics of Tragicomedy: Shakespeare and After* (London and New York, 1992), 21–54.

[16] 'Subversion and Wonder', 383.

had characterized it before'. Corns links this newly austere prose style with Milton's engagement as a (salaried, from 15 March 1649) propagandist for the Commonwealth, who is charged with converting political innovation into 'a new orthodoxy, commanding wide assent'.[17] Certainly the 1649 prose lacks the poetic flights of self-representation in several of the anti-prelatical tracts, or the linguistically creative vituperation of the divorce tracts. But, as Zwicker's argument about Milton's 'trivializing' of the aesthetic suggests, *Eikonoklastes* is the prose work in which Milton most engages with English literary history, through explicit references to Sidney and Spenser as well as Shakespeare. Moreover the Shakespearean allusions in *The Tenure of Kings and Magistrates* hint at a wilder, more radical attitude towards monarchy contained by the 'austere' analysis of what Milton himself later called 'an abstract consideration of the question, what might be done against tyrants . . . written rather to reconcile the minds of the people to the event, than to discuss the legitimacy of that particular sentence'. In this same passage in the *Second Defence* Milton tells us that he was driven to write the *Tenure* by the backsliding of the Presbyterian clergy, who had supported the first civil war only to 'become jealous of the growth of the Independents and of their ascendency in Parliament, [and] most tumultuously clamoured against the sentence [on the king], and did all in their power to prevent the execution'.[18] Milton's detestation of the Presbyterians with whom he had earlier sided in the anti-prelatical tracts is the most consistent theme of his writing of the 1640s after the *Doctrine and Discipline of Divorce* was publicly condemned as libertine and heretical by the 'high' Presbyterian clergy such as Thomas Edwards.[19] From the prose of late 1644–5 to the unpublished satirical sonnets of 1646–7 to the regicide tracts, Milton aims his most virulent abuse at the Presbyterians, whom he charges with ignorance, intolerance, and constancy only in the promotion of their self-interest. In Milton's history of priestcraft in *Areopagitica* the 'apishly Romanizing' bishops have themselves been imitated by the Presbyterian clergy, who have 'mastered the Episcopal arts' to 'execute the most *Dominican* part of the Inquisition over us' (*CPW*, ii. 504). Or as the dismissive final line of 'On the New Forcers of Conscience Under the Long Parliament' (1646?) has it: 'New *Presbyter* is but old *Priest* writ large.'[20] The Presbyterians, in other words, threaten to impose on the English people the same slavery to empty religious forms as the Laudians and Catholics before them, and they will similarly deface Christian liberty by the maintaining of their tyrannous power through censorship and physical persecution.

---

[17] 'Milton's *Observations Upon the Articles of Peace*: Ireland under English Eyes', in David Loewenstein and James Grantham Turner (eds.), *Politics, Poetics, and Hermeneutics in Milton's Prose* (Cambridge, 1990), 123–34 at 129, summarizing the arguments in Corns, *The Development of Milton's Prose Style* (Oxford, 1982), 67–79, 83–101.

[18] I prefer here the translation in Milton, *Complete Poems and Major Prose*, ed. Merritt Y. Hughes (1957; Indianapolis, Ind., 2003), 831.

[19] See the essays above by Sharon Achinstein (Ch. 9) and Ann Hughes (Ch. 11).

[20] On Milton's anti-Presbyterianism and its relation to his ideas of a poetic career, see Nicholas McDowell, *Poetry and Allegiance in the English Civil Wars: Marvell and the Cause of Wit* (Oxford, 2008), 69–89.

In the opening paragraph of the *Tenure* Milton immediately identifies his primary polemical target as not the diehard royalists but 'these men' who

after they juggl'd and palter'd with the world, bandied and born armes against thir King, devested him, disannointed him, nay curs'd him all over in thir Pulpits and thir Pamphlets, to the ingaging of sincere and real men, beyond what is possible or honest to retreat from, not only turne revolters from those principles, which could only at first move them, but lay the staine of disloyaltie, and worse, on those proceedings, which are the necessary consequence of thir own former actions[.] (*CPW*, iii. 191)

The Presbyterian clerics are here implicitly compared to the witches in *Macbeth* (1606) as they are described by Macbeth when he finally accepts the witches' prophecies were always designed to trick him, and moments before he is killed by Macduff:

> And be these juggling fiends no more believed,
> That palter with us in a double sense,
> That keep the word of promise to our ear
> And break it to our hope.[21] (V. ix. 19–22)

The Presbyterians are like Shakespeare's Scottish witches in their demonic equivocation over the regicide, and in this they are also like Jesuit priests, notorious in England for their doctrine of duplicity, exemplified by the discovery in the aftermath of the Gunpowder plot of the Jesuit manual 'A Treatise of Equivocation'. The connection between the witches and Jesuits seems to have been one that Shakespeare expected his audience to make—in II. iii the drunken porter, welcoming imaginary visitors at the gate of hell, alias Inverness Castle, invokes the memory of Henry Garnet, the author of the 'Treatise' who was tried and executed in 1606, when he exclaims 'Faith, here's an equivocator that could swear in both the scales against either scale, who committed treason enough for God's sake, yet could not equivocate to heaven' (pp. 7–11).[22] As we have seen, Milton had come to see Presbyterians and Jesuits as different forms of the same spirit of clerical tyranny: the allusion to *Macbeth* not only associates the Presbyterians with sorcery but suggests how for Milton the Presbyterians are as responsible, for all their feigned outrage, for the execution of Charles Stuart as the Jesuits were for the attempted assassination of his father. There seems to be an echo in the repeated *d*s of the passage from the *Tenure* quoted above ('divested him, disannointed him') of the famous charge made by Edward Coke against Garnet at his trial that he was 'a Doctor of Dissimulation, Deposing of Princes, Disposing of Kingdoms, Daunting and deterring of subjects, and Destruction'.[23]

---

[21] The allusion was first noted by Martin Dzelzainis, 'Milton, *Macbeth*, and Buchanan', *Seventeenth Century*, 4 (1989), 55–66.

[22] See Gary Wills, *Witches and Jesuits: Shakespeare's* Macbeth (New York, 1995), 22–3, 93–9.

[23] *A True and Perfect Relation of the Whole Proceedings Against the Late Most Barbarous Traitors, Garnet a Jesuit and His Confederates* (1606), 162.

It has been found puzzling that *Macbeth* 'never seems to be quoted in the literature of 1640–60', despite its ostensible appeal to royalists as a play about regicide and its monstrous consequences. In fact Milton may again have picked up on the polemical strategies of Marchamont Nedham's newsbooks—except this time when Nedham was writing for the royalist cause, after switching allegiance in 1647. In *Mercurius Pragmaticus* in 1648 we find Nedham advising Cromwell that it is not in his or Parliament's interest to ally with the Presbyterians: 'Yet let them *Juggle* and do what they can, I warrant you *Oliver* is more wise, than to admit of a *Scottish* Presbyterie in England, since wheresoever it settles, it layes an intolerable *Burthen* upon all, from the *King* to the *Beggar*, without exception.'[24] The logic of Nedham's allusion aligns Cromwell with Macbeth, the future regicide, but, where Nedham is warning Cromwell not to follow Macbeth's route, Milton of course makes a very different point. Given he is himself explicitly defending the execution of a Stuart monarch, Milton can hardly identify the Presbyterians with the Jesuit gunpowder plotters merely on the grounds that they both wanted to kill a king; rather he is concerned to emphasize the Presbyterians' Jesuitical dissimulation and will to clerical tyranny, and on this Milton and Nedham were united: their shared anti-Presbyterianism is one of the reasons that they could work together in the Commonwealth's press office, for all Nedham's earlier royalist activities.[25] The allusion to the 'Scottish play' also encapsulates one of the recurring preoccupations of the anti-Presbyterian rhetoric of both Nedham's controversial writing in all its guises and Milton's regicide tracts. Milton had for five years been damning Presbyterianism as a specifically Scottish, and thus as an alien, threat to true English values of liberty of conscience and expression. He was perhaps even more outspoken in private verse than in published prose, as is illustrated by the sonnets 'On the New Forcers of Conscience' and 'A book was writ of late call'd *Tetrachordon*', both unpublished until 1673. In these sonnets, as Howard Erskine-Hill has put it, 'mental despotism assumes a pronounced Scottish accent and Presbyterian form':[26]

> Dare ye for this adjure the civil sword
>   To force our consciences that Christ set free,
>   And ride us with a classic hierarchy
>   Taught ye by mere A. S. and Rutherford?
> Men, whose life, learning, faith and pure intent
>   Would have been held in high esteem with Paul
>   Must now be named and printed heretics
> By shallow Edwards and Scotch What-d'ye-call[.]
>   ('On the New Forcers of Conscience', ll. 5–12)

---

[24] Potter, *Secret Rites and Secret Writing*, 203; *Mercurius Pragmaticus* (10 Oct. 1648), in *Making the News: An Anthology of the Newsbooks of Revolutionary England*, ed. Joad Raymond (Moreton-in-Marsh, 1993), 357.

[25] On Nedham's anti-Presbyterianism as the consistent theme in a career marked by apparent switches of political allegiance, see Jeffrey R. Collins, *The Allegiance of Thomas Hobbes* (Oxford, 2005), 198–9; Blair Worden, *Literature and Politics in Cromwellian England: John Milton, Andrew Marvell, Marchamont Nedham* (Oxford, 2007), 14–53.

[26] *Poetry and the Realm of Politics: Shakespeare to Dryden* (Oxford, 1996), 159.

The philistine and persecutory ethos of the clergy has been transmitted from priest to prelate to Presbyter, and this ethos is shown to be not only anti-Christian but un-English through association with both Continental Catholicism and the Scottish Presbyterian divines Adam Stewart, Samuel Rutherford, and (probably) Robert Bailie, 'Scotch What-d'ye-call'. In 'A book was writ of late' Milton apostrophizes the great Greek scholar Sir John Cheke to lament an age in which booksellers and readers complain about Milton's use of difficult Greek words while they are happy to pronounce equally foreign Scottish names: 'Why is it harder sirs than Gordon, / Colkitto, or Macdonnel, or Galasp?' (ll. 8–9) While the first three names refer to officers in the royalist army of Montrose, the last is to George Gillespie, a prominent Presbyterian member of the Westminster Assembly. The sonnets equate the Scottish influence on English affairs with intellectual and cultural decline as well as religious repression.

It has been noted in recent years that the first commissioned piece of propaganda that Milton completed for the Commonwealth, his *Observations* upon the *Articles of Peace Made and Concluded with the Irish Rebels, and Papists, by James Earle of Ormond, For and in behalfe of the late King* (16 May 1649), is a work only 'opportunistically' about the alliance between Catholics and royalists in Ireland 'and more deliberatively about Presbyterianism and the Scots'.[27] Milton devoted less than five of the twenty-one pages of his work to responding to the thirty-three pages of Ormond's treaty of peace with the Irish Catholics, but spends thirteen pages on the four-page *Representation . . . by the Presbytery at Belfast*. He did not complete the first commission given him by the Council, on 26 March, to respond to a Leveller tract. We might, if we wanted to see ideological consistency in Milton, suppose that he felt uncomfortable attacking the Levellers, who agreed with his arguments about liberty of conscience and shared his anti-Presbyterianism, while he recognized in the Irish commission the chance to maintain his assault on Presbyterian intolerance. The brief from the Council on 28 March was to write 'some observations upon the Complicacion of interest w[hi]ch is now amongst the severall designers against the peace of this Commonwealth' (French, *Records*, iv. 234–50). In collapsing together Irish Catholics, Scottish Presbyterians, English Presbyterians, and English royalists as a rebellious threat to the English state, Milton was faithfully following this brief. As in the satirical sonnets, the threatening forces are represented as both literally foreign (Irish and Scottish) but they also embody persecutory religions—Catholicism, Presbyterianism—that are foreign to the native English tendency to religious toleration. In their enslaving of the English people to idolatrous forms, the Shakespearean Scottish witches of the *Tenure* are no different, then, from the Homeric royalist Circe's of *Eikonoklastes*: 'the Prelats and thir fellow teachers, though of another Name and Sect' have in 'thir Pulpit stuff, both first and last, bin the Doctrin and perpetual infusion of servility and wretchedness to all hearers' (CPW, iii. 344).

In the *Observations*—published anonymously but with the imprint 'by Authority'—Milton reverses the charge of rebellion aimed at the regicides by grouping the

---

[27] Joad Raymond, 'Complications of Interest: Milton, Scotland, Ireland, and National Identity in 1649', *Review of English Studies*, 55 (2004), 315–45; see also Corns, 'Milton's *Observations*'.

English royalists and the Presbyterians with the Irish Catholics, traditional enemies of Protestant England, as 'rebels' to the legitimate Protestant state of the Common-wealth. Later in the *Tenure* Milton again looks to *Macbeth* for images of guilt and dissimulation that he can apply to the Presbyterians to undermine their polemical rhetoric of rebellion:

> But this I doubt not to affirme, that the Presbyterians, who now so much condemn deposing, were the men themselves that deposd the King, and cannot with all thir shifting and relapsing, wash off the guiltiness from thir owne hands. For they themselves, by these thir late doings have made it guiltiness, and turnd thir owne warrantable actions into Rebellion. (*CPW*, iii. 227)

Milton projects onto the Presbyterians the guilt that haunts Shakespeare's Scottish king-killers by recalling Lady Macbeth's mental disintegration under the guilt of her involvement in the murder: 'What will these hands ne'er be clean? . . . Here's the smell of blood still' (V. I. 44, 51). Milton of course suffers from no such guilt because he is convinced that he has done the right thing—the implication is that it is not the killing of the king, either in Shakespeare's play or Milton's England, that is in itself a matter for guiltiness, but rather guilt is the consequence of hypocritical regret and effeminate retreat from principle, of 'shifting and relapsing'. The Presbyterians are like Lady Macbeth when she pathetically and hopelessly seeks to wash the bloodstains from her hands; but they should be like Lady Macbeth when she urges her husband on to do the deed like a true man:

> Art thou afeard
> To be the same in thine own act and valour
> As thou art in desire?
> . . .
> When thou durst do it, then you were a man. (I. VII. 39–41, 49)

This rather unsettlingly puts Milton in the role of the Lady Macbeth who taunts her husband for his failed masculinity; and indeed just before the allusion to *Macbeth*'s witches, Milton combines sexual with anti-clerical politics: 'neither let milde and tender dispositions be foolishly softn'd from thir duty and perse-verance with the unmasculine Rhetorick of any puling Priest or Chaplain' (*CPW*, iii. 195).

Fifty years ago Patrick Cruttwell asked us to imagine

> a *Macbeth* written after the execution of King Charles. It would have been quite impossible to preserve, as Shakespeare does, both the mystical reverence for legitimate kingship, the sense that its destruction involves a violation of the divine and the natural orders, and the sympathetic dramatic presentation of the murderous usurper.[28]

Some recent scholars have been sceptical that Shakespeare preserves such a sense of political balance, arguing that the tragedy, with its image in the witches' mirror of the line of kings descending directly from Banquo to James I, explicitly legitimates Stuart

---

[28] Cruttwell, *The Shakespearean Moment* (1954), 202.

divine-right monarchy and may even have been designed to counter the arguments against hereditary kingship produced out of Scottish history in George Buchanan's *Rerum Scoticarum historia* (1582).[29] Is Milton—who uses Buchanan on the legitimacy of resistance to tyrants in the *Tenure*, and on several occasions quotes his *History*, as part of his strategy of reminding the Presbyterian Scots of the radical heritage that they are betraying—consequently reading *Macbeth* against the grain of Shakespeare's own intentions, as some modern political critics have done (*CPW*, iii. 225–6)?[30] Does the subtext of the *Tenure* validate in its allusions to Shakespeare's tragedy even the regicidal act of Macbeth and his wife against the saintly Duncan—an act that Shakespeare represents as elementally unnatural—simply because Duncan is a *king*, and therefore jeopardizes the people's liberty 'not merely by actual but by possible constraint'?[31] Milton is nonetheless concerned on the surface of the text to deny the charge of rebellion alleged against Parliament and to redefine the regicide as justified resistance to a tyrant:

Therefore when the people or any part of them shall rise against the King and his autority executing the Law in any thing establishd civil or Ecclesiastical, I doe not say it is rebellion, if the thing commanded though establishd be unlawfull, and that they sought first all due means of redress. (p. 228)

Given the implicit if unmistakable nature of the allusions to *Macbeth* in the *Tenure*, it is not clear how conscious this against-the-grain reading might be; the issue is complicated by the fact that Milton outlined plans for his own play about Macbeth, probably sometime in the early 1640s (under the revealing heading 'Scotch Stories or rather brittish of the north parts'), which might suggest either dissatisfaction with Shakespeare's play, or that he was inspired to develop aspects of the tragedy, or both.[32] He thought to open his *Macbeth* with the meeting of Macduff and Malcolm in England, suggesting his version would have focused on the proper action to take against Macbeth's tyranny, and also that it would have been written either to reflect the need for an English–Scottish alliance to overthrow tyranny in the three kingdoms, or predominantly from an English perspective on an endlessly dysfunctional, endemically barbaric Scotland. The former is more likely if we accept the conventional date of 1639–42 for Milton's outline of potential topics for plays, before the hostile Presbyterian reaction to the divorce tracts.

---

[29] Alan Sinfield, '*Macbeth*: History, Ideology, and Intellectuals', *Critical Quarterly*, 28 (1986), 63–77; David Norbrook, '*Macbeth* and the Politics of Historiography', in Kevin Sharpe and Steven N. Zwicker (eds.), *Politics of Discourse: the Literature and History of Seventeenth-Century England* (Berkeley, 1987), 78–116.

[30] Sinfield argues that the traces of Buchanan in *Macbeth* allow the anti-monarchical viewer/reader to reconstruct from the play a Buchananesque argument against hereditary monarchy ('*Macbeth*: History, Ideology, and Intellectuals'). On Milton and Buchanan in the *Tenure*, see also Dzelzainis, 'Milton, *Macbeth*, and Buchanan'.

[31] The phrase is from Quentin Skinner's influential argument for a 'neo-Roman' idea of liberty in the regicide tracts in 'John Milton and the Politics of Slavery', in Graham Parry and Joad Raymond (eds.), *Milton and the Terms of Liberty* (Cambridge, 2002), 1–22 at 18.

[32] Milton, *Poems: Reproduced in Facsimile from the Manuscript in Trinity College, Cambridge* (Menston, 1970), 39.

The latter view of the Macbeth story was promoted, however, by another of the Commonwealth's leading propagandists, John Hall, hired two months after Milton. While acting as an official reporter on Cromwell's Scottish campaign in 1650, Hall compiled and then published in Edinburgh and then London *The Grounds and Reasons of Monarchy Considered. In a Review of the Scotch Story, gathered out of their best Authours and Records.* Hall turns the history of Scottish kings into a polemical Gothic narrative of rape, murder, madness, and witchcraft, designed to demonstrate to the Scots that they can only be prevented from 'enslaving and ruining themselves' under a 'Tyrannizing Nobilitie and Clergie' by incorporation into a British republic. His discussion of Macbeth shows him to have been reading Shakespeare's play as well as Buchanan's *History*:

> *Donald* . . . a good natur'd and unactive Prince, who with a stratagem of sleepy drink, destroyed a *Danish* Army that had invaded and distressed him, but at last being insnared by his Kinsman *Mackbeth* (who was pricked forward by Ambition, and a former vision of three women of a Sour-humane shape, whereof one saluted him, *Thane* of *Angus*, another of *Murray* the third King) he was beheaded. The severity and cruelty of *Mackbeth* was so known, that both the sons of the murthered King were forced to retire, and yield to the times, whilest he courted the Nobility with largesses: The first ten years he spent virtuously, but the remainder was so savage and Tyrannicall, that *Macduff Thone* of *Fife* fled into *England* to *Milcolm*, son of *Donald*, who by his perswasions, and the assistance of the King of *England*, enterd *Scotland*, where he found such great accessions to his party, that *Mackbeth* was forced to fly, his death is hid in a such a mist of *Fables*, that it is not certainly known.[33]

Hall recalls the conclusion of Macbeth's first soliloquy ('I have no spur / To prick the sides of my intent, but only / Vaulting ambition which o'erleaps itself / And falls on th'other' (I. VII. 25–8)). If Milton can identify, in his scorn for the 'unmasculine' backsliding of the Presbyterians, with the Lady Macbeth who urges her husband on to the murder of Duncan as an act of masculine valour, his ideas for a new version of the play centred on the problem of Macbeth's tyranny, coupled with the use of *Macbeth* by his fellow Commonwealth propagandist Hall, suggest that English republicans came to see in *Macbeth* a linguistically powerful *exemplum* of the cycle of overleaping ambition, violence, and tyranny fostered by kingship.

SHAKESPEAREAN LESSONS

The submerged presence of *Macbeth* in the *Tenure* does not offer us a sound basis on which to argue for or against the beginnings of a Miltonic expulsion of Shakespeare,

---

[33] *The Grounds and Reasons of Monarchy*, 2nd edn. (1651), 86–7.

although the bias of my argument has been towards Milton's reading against the grain of *Macbeth*'s pro-Stuart and divine-right sympathies. What is clear, however, is that Milton found Shakespeare *useful* in offering him an affective language for his argument and animus against the Presbyterians and the Scots. If we return to *Eikonoklastes*, we can now see more clearly that while Charles and the royalists may find specious models of duplicitous behaviour in Shakespeare, reading his lines in the idolatrous way they read what Milton dismisses as 'the easy literature of custom', Shakespeare can yet, like Milton's own book, offer 'entertainment' or education in the ways of tyranny and idolatry to those readers, 'few perhaps' but of 'value and substantial worth, as truth and wisdom, not respecting numbers and bigg names, have bin ever wont in all ages to be contented with' (*CPW*, iii. 339–40; this sentence was added to the 2nd edn.).[34] We saw earlier how in the preface to *Eikonoklastes* the 'besotted and degenerate baseness of spirit' of the mass of the English people is exemplified by their devotion to the false pieties of the King's Book, 'except some few, who yet retain in them the old English fortitude and love of Freedom, and have testifi'd it by thir matchless deeds, the rest, imbastardized from the ancient nobleness of thir Ancestors, are ready to fall flat and give adoration to the Image and Memory of this Man'. 'Fall flatt' points us to *The Tempest* (1611) and Caliban's encounter with Trinculo and Stephano, whom he initially presumes to be minions of Prospero: 'Here comes a spirit of his, and to torment me / For bringing wood in slowly. I'll fall flat; / Perchance he will not mind me' (II. II. 15–17).[35] While Caliban's posture here is one of self-protection it soon turns into one of self-debasement after Stephano pours wine into his mouth: 'I do adore thee . . . And I will kiss thy foot. I prithree, be my god . . . I'll swear myself thy subject' (ll. 138, 147, 150). The blasphemy of Caliban's adoration of these ridiculous false gods is encapsulated in Stephano's repeated injunctions that Caliban must 'kiss the book' (ll. 129, 140, 155). The drinking of the wine becomes a parodic, idolatrous version of swearing an oath on the Bible, with a parodic echo also of sacramental ceremony that Milton the religious anti-formalist might have particularly appreciated, if not necessarily for the reasons Shakespeare intended.

In *Eikonoklastes* the 'besotted' English fall flat like savage Calibans before the image of the king in the *Eikon Basilike*, idolatrously kissing his book, which blasphemously masquerades as a form of Scripture in its numerous analogies with the Psalms and the Passion narratives. Milton recognizes in this scene in *The Tempest* a retelling of

---

[34] My argument here about right reading has some overlap with David Ainsworth's discussion of 'Spiritual Reading in Milton's *Eikonoklastes*', *Studies in English Literature, 1500–1900*, 45 (2005), 157–89. As Ainsworth points out, those who argue for the failure of *Eikonoklastes* as propaganda need to reckon with Milton's insistence that his book will anyway only be read properly by the virtuous 'few'; although Ainsworth himself does not sufficiently recognize the extent to which this invocation of an elite 'spiritual' readership is added to the 1650 second edition, after the first edition had apparently made little impact on the popularity of the *Eikon Basilike*.

[35] The possible allusion to *The Tempest* was brought to my attention by Karen Edwards's stimulating paper, 'Falling Flat: Tyranny and Tragicomedy', at the Eighth International Milton Symposium in Grenoble, July 2005. Her subsequent argument—that Milton sees the tragedy of *The Tempest* in the return of the tyrant Prospero to power—proceeds quite differently from my own.

the Circe myth, except Caliban is already only half a man ('What have we here, a man or a fish?' (ll. 24–5)) and Stephano and Trinculo are pathetic parodies of the seductive Circe. As in *Eikonoklastes*, it is hard to tell whether the idolater's monstrosity ('A most poor credulous monster!' (l. 144)) leads to his idolatry or vice versa. Milton is careful to characterize the idolatry of the King's Book as papist and therefore foreign to 'the old English fortitude and love of Freedom', retained only by 'some few'. In the *Observations*, as we have seen, he runs together Scottish Presbyterians and English royalists with Irish Catholics as a foreign threat, in their idolatry and intolerance, to English Protestant values. Ormond leads 'a mixt Rabble, part Papists, part Fugitives, and part Savages' (*CPW*, iii. 315). In the attack on the Irish in the *Observations* which has most in common with stereotypical early modern English representations of a savage island, Milton finds in Irish farming practices evidence of 'a disposition not onely sottish but inducible and averse from all Civility and amendment ... [they] preferred their own absurd and savage Customes before the most convincing evidence of reason and demonstration' (*CPW*, iii. 304). Milton here sounds rather like Prospero and Miranda damning Caliban as 'Abhorred slave, / which any print of goodness wilt not take' (I. II. 352–3). Several critics have indeed argued that 'Ireland provides the richest historical analogue for [*The Tempest's*] colonial theme'.[36] Milton seems to identify Caliban's brutish susceptibility to idolatry with an un-English 'baseness of spirit' among Presbyterians and royalists that only a few months earlier he had linked with the savage 'inducible' nature of the Irish. Indeed Sir John Davies, in *A Discoverie of the True Causes why Ireland was never entirely Subdued* (1612), had called on the Circe myth to convey his disgust at how the 'old' English settlers who had come to Ireland in the 1530s seeking to 'make a perfect conquest of the Irish, were by them perfectly and absolutely conquered': having left behind

the Ciuill and Honorable Lawes and Customes of *England*...they became degenerate and metamorphosed like *Nabuchadnezzar:* who although he had the face of a man, had the heart of a Beast; or like those who had drunke of *Circes* Cuppe, and were turned into very Beasts; and yet tooke such pleasure in their beastly manner of life, as they would not returne to their shape of men againe. (pp. 164, 182)

In *Eikonoklastes* one of Milton's most serious charges against Charles is that he fomented the Irish rebellion of 1641: his wider point is that in the idolatry of their worship of the king the royalists are no more civil than, and just as un-English as, the Catholic Irish.

In the *Observations* Milton maintains that the Irish 'by their endlesse treasons and revolts have deserv'd to hold no Parlament at all, but to be govern'd by Edicts and Garrisons, as absolute and supreme in that Assembly as the People of *England* in their own Land' (*CPW*, iii. 303). This echoes the suggestion in Spenser's dialogue *A View of the Present State of Ireland* (*c*.1596; first publ. 1633) that Ireland might best be

---

[36] Dympna Callaghan, 'Irish Memories in the *The Tempest'*, in her *Shakespeare without Women: Representing Gender and Race on the Renaissance Stage* (2000), 100. See also Paul Brown, '"This thing of darkness I acknowledge mine": *The Tempest* and the Discourse of Colonialism', in Jonathan Dollimore and Alan Sinfield (eds.), *Political Shakespeare: Essays in Cultural Materialism*, 2nd edn. (1994), 48–71.

controlled by a form of martial law imposed by four garrisons placed at strategic points across the island. Milton cites Spenser's *View* in his Commonplace Book in the early 1640s but does not refer to it in the *Observations*, perhaps because his tract 'chiefly uses the Irish to censure the parties with whom they share a professed interest' in overthrowing the Commonwealth—the royalists and the Presbyterians (*CPW*, i. 495–6).[37] Indeed a later allusion to Spenser's *View* at the end of the *Observations* helps to condemn the Scottish Presbyterians as tainted by the same Celtic degeneracy as the Irish Catholics, exemplified by their common support for the Irish rebel leader Owen Roe O'Neill. 'By thir actions we might rather judge them [the Belfast Presbyterians] to be a generation of High-land theevs and Red-shanks' recalls Spenser on how the 'O-Neales are neerlye allyed . . . to the Earl of Argile, from whom they use to have all theyr succours of those Scots and Reddshankes' (*CPW*, iii. 333 n. 96). In *Eikonoklastes* Milton does refer directly to Spenser but to *The Faerie Queene*, in a moment revealing of both his frustration with the legal process of the trial of the king, with the opportunity it gave Charles to adopt the pose of martyr, and of his identification of the popular idolatry of the King's Book with the sort of religious and moral degeneracy stereotypically ascribed to the Irish:

If there were a man of iron, such as *Talus*, by our Poet *Spencer*, is fain'd to be page of Justice, who with his iron flaile could doe all this, and expeditiously, without those deceitfull formes and circumstances of Law, worse than those ceremonies of Religion; I say God send it don, whether by one *Talus*, or by a thousand. (iii. 390)

In Book V of *The Faerie Queene* Artegall, 'Champion of true justice', is helped by the ferociously iconoclastic 'yron man' Talus—'Immoveable, resistlesse, without end. / Who in his hand an yron flale did hould, / With which he thresht out falsehood, and did truth unfould'—to save the virgin Irena, a figure of Elizabeth's rule in Ireland, from the tyrant Grantorto. At one point Artegall has to restrain Talus from 'slaughter' of their defeated enemies but nonetheless in his determination to 'reforme that ragged commonweale' he sends Talus to search out those 'who did rebell gainst lawfull government; / On whome he did inflict most grievous punishment'.[38] Milton goes on to remind his readers how it was 'this iron flaile the People' that 'threw down' all 'those Papistical innovations' in the Church as well as tyrannous organs of government such as the Star Chamber (iii. 391). But the 'iron flaile' that had so recently purged Parliament and paved the way for the execution of the King was not 'the People' but the New Model Army. As Milton implicitly identifies with the bloodthirsty regicide Lady Macbeth in the *Tenure*, the approving reference to Talus evokes violent Miltonic fantasies of the annihilation of the idolatrous enemies of liberty, without regard to the traps and snares of the law—in *Eikonoklastes* those enemies often include the people themselves, who have lost their humanity

---

[37] Raymond, 'Complications of Interest', 324–5. See also Willy Maley, 'How Milton and Some Contemporaries Read Spenser's *View*', in Brendan Bradshaw, Andrew Hadfield, and Willy Maley (eds.), *Representing Ireland: Literature and the Origins of Conflict, 1534–1660* (Cambridge, 1993), 191–208; John Kerrigan, *Archipelagic English: Literature, History, and Politics, 1603–1707* (Oxford, 2008), 231–2.

[38] *The Faerie Queene*, ed. Thomas P. Roche, Jr. (Harmondsworth, 1987), V. i. 12, xii. 26.

in their adoration of the King's Book and so become like the degenerate, 'inducible', slavish Irish.

The allusions to *Macbeth* in the *Tenure* and to *The Tempest* in *Eikonoklastes* show us that, if Milton now associated Shakespeare with Stuart court culture, he nonetheless still found 'Delphicke lines' in the plays. The plays offer him useful fictive analogues and vivid poetic language as he engages with issues of tyranny, regicide, popular allegiance, and national identity—and in particular the British dimension of the civil wars, which has attracted increased attention in recent years and is certainly crucial to understanding Milton's polemical concerns in the regicide tracts.[39] We can return now to the only explicit reference to Shakespeare in the tracts, the charge that Charles learned how 'the deepest policy of a Tyrant [is] to counterfeit Religious' from Shakespeare's *Richard III* (1597):

> From Stories of this nature both Ancient and Modern which abound, the Poets also, and som English, have bin in this point so mindfull of *Decorum*, as to put never more pious words in the mouth of any person, then of a Tyrant. I shall not instance an abstruse Author, wherein the King might be less conversant, but one whom we well know was the Closet Companion of these his solitudes, *William Shakespeare*; who introduces the Person of *Richard* the third, speaking in as high a strain of pietie, and mortification, as is utterd in any passage of this Book; and sometimes to the same sense and purpose with some words in this place, *I intended*, he saith, *not onely to oblige my Friends but mine enemies*. The like saith *Richard, Act 2. Scene 1*,
>
> > *I doe not know that Englishman alive*
> > *With whom my soule is any jott at odds,*
> > *More then the Infant that is borne to night;*
> > *I thank my God for my humilitie.*
>
> Other stuff of this sort may be read throughout the whole Tragedie, wherein the Poet us'd not much licence in departing from the truth of History, which delivers him a deep dissembler, not of his affections onely, but of Religion. (*CPW*, iii. 361–2)

The passage is worth quoting at length because it becomes clear that, regardless of the idolatrous readings of Shakespeare by the King and his cronies—and Milton immediately goes on to make his famous charge that Charles's book substitutes heathen idolatry for Christian inspiration by its unacknowledged appropriation of a prayer from Sidney's *Arcadia* (first publ. 1590)—the plays offer the right or 'spiritual' reader lessons in the workings of tyranny. Just as Mark Anthony's speech in *Julius Caesar* offers us a dramatic, affective example of how self-interested politicians have exploited the body and writing of a dead tyrant to turn him into a martyr, so *Richard III* offers a powerful case study in how the most murderous tyrants exert power by simulating piety. By remembering Shakespeare's dramatization of their history, the English can learn from their mistakes and avoid repeating them by falling for the mock devotions of the *Eikon Basilike*. In terms of the 'other stuff of this sort' in *Richard III*, Milton likely has in mind III. VII, in which Richard appears before the Lord Mayor and citizens of London, presenting himself, on the advice

---

[39] See most recently Kerrigan, *Archipelagic English*.

of his spin-doctor Buckingham, as an image of the Christian prince: 'And look you get a prayer-book in your hand, / And stand between two churchmen, good my lord: / For on that ground I'll build a holy descant' (III. VII. 46–8). The image of Richard created by Buckingham and the bishops which appears before the citizens, like the image of Charles created by his prelatical advisors, is *eidolon* not *eikon*—the frontispiece of *Eikon Alethine* (August 1649) or the 'true image', the first concerted attack on the King's Book, has a curtain being drawn to reveal the 'Presumptuous Priest' who would make the 'King his Bastard issue own'.[40] It is worth dwelling for a moment on Buckingham's declaration that he will 'build a holy descant'. In the first line of *Eikonoklastes* Milton insists that 'To descant on the misfortunes of a person fall'n from so high a dignity, who hath also payd his final debt both to Nature and and his Faults, is neither of it self a thing commendable, nor the intention of this discours' (*CPW*, iii. 337). Zwicker finds the use of 'descant' odd, suggesting the notion it introduces of singing 'variations on a theme' may be ironic, as 'there is surely nothing lyric about *Eikonoklastes*'. But he goes on to note that 'the phrase "misfortunes of a person fall'n from so high a dignity" announces literary matter, tragic forms and themes'.[41] Although Zwicker does not make the link, 'descant' appears in one of the most memorable phrases of the 'Now is the winter of our discontent' soliloquy which opens *Richard III*:

> Why I, in this weak piping time of peace,
> Have no delight to pass away the time,
> Unless to spy my shadow in the sun,
> And descant on mine own deformity. (I. I. 24–7)

Milton announces in his preface that he will not spare to attack Charles directly so that those readers who 'are so much affatuated, not with his person onely, but with his palpable faults, and dote upon his deformities, may have none to blame but thir own folly' (*CPW*, iii. 341–2). The heavenly wisdom given dramatic form in Shakespeare's book can help us see the demonic deformity of the tyrant behind the beautiful but false image of the martyr king.

---

[40] There are extracts from *Eikon Alethine* in *Eikon Basilike*, ed. Daems and Nelson, 285–91.
[41] *Lines of Authority*, 46.

CHAPTER 15

···

JOHN MILTON, EUROPEAN: THE RHETORIC OF MILTON'S DEFENCES

···

JOAD RAYMOND

Indeed, I have learnt, I have observed, I have read—the writings of the wisest and most illustrious men in this republic and in other states have recorded for our use, that the same men are not always bound to defend the same opinions, but such as may be required by the state of the nation, the bent of the times, and by a regard to union. (Cicero, *Pro Planci*, quoted in Milton, *Defensio secunda*)[1]

The three Latin prose tracts about the regicide and the republic that Milton wrote in his capacity as Secretary for Foreign Tongues—*Pro populo Anglicano defensio* (1651), *Defensio secunda* (1654), and *Pro se defensio* (1655)—are collectively known as the defences (or 'Defences'), and are usually seen as a series of arguments legitimizing the republic that increasingly focus on Milton himself. According to some accounts they trace in *sotto voce* his growing doubts concerning the state and Oliver Cromwell. They have a great deal in common: they are written in an imposing neo-Roman Latin to counter

---

[1] *CW*, viii. 166–9; cf. *CPW*, iv. 643. Translations of *Defensio secunda* and *Pro se defensio* are from *CW*, which I have modified in places.

Latin polemics against the republic written and printed elsewhere in Europe; they speak to both a British and an overseas audience; they are satirical and rebarbative; they champion the ideal of political liberty, and present the author as a reluctant but selflessly dedicated enemy of the commonwealth's detractors. There are, however, profound differences between the three works, and between their language, style, and rhetoric (as a consecutive reading clearly demonstrates). Milton wrote very different kinds of responses to different circumstances, and this is reflected in the literary modes he adopted. The tendency has been to collapse the three defences into a single prose enterprise, one which, importantly for narratives of Milton's life, drew him away from his profound vocation, his long-term ambition to write an English epic. The purpose of this essay is to examine the language, style, and rhetoric of the three tracts, to consider their decorums and indecorousness, and to suggest what these qualities reveal about the intentions behind these diversely flavoured works.

'THE EXCELLENT DEEDS OF MY FELLOW COUNTRYMEN': *DEFENSIO*

Milton accepted a government post in March 1649, a post he was offered in part because of his recent *Tenure of Kings and Magistrates*. During his first year he produced, following commissions, *Articles of Peace, Made and Concluded with the Irish Rebels, and Papists, by James Earle of Ormond, For and in behalfe of the late King, and by vertue of his Autoritie. Also a Letter sent by Ormond to Col. Jones, Governour of Dublin, with his Answer thereunto. And a Representation of the Scotch Presbytery at Belfast in Ireland. Upon all which are added Observations*, usually known simply as *Observations* (May 1649); and *Eikonoklastes* (October 1649, with a revised edition in 1650), a rebuttal of the *Eikon Basilike* attributed to Charles I. *Observations* had little impact, and was hack work in which he took little pride; but *Eikonoklastes* was a fervid and rhetorically and intellectually compelling dissection of the king's posthumous propaganda masterpiece. Milton was unable to convert the king's supporters, however, and confronted unfavourable sentiments and allegiances. While his arguments are unquestionably powerful, his work achieved none of the commercial success and long-term popularity that the king's book did. In addition to these polemical labours Milton drafted and translated official documents, undertaking routine duties for the Council of State.

In January 1650 the Council of State ordered Milton to write a response to *Defensio Regia* by the French humanist scholar Claudius Salmasius. The outcome, published in February 1651, was *Pro Populo Anglicano Defensio* (hereafter *Defensio*, though sometimes known as *Defensio prima* or *First Defence*). Milton was now known within Britain as a polemicist, and not only as a scandalous defender of divorce. The story in mainland Europe was quite different, however: despite his reputation as a poet and a companion in the Florentine *accademia* in 1638–9, he was comparatively unknown outside his mother tongue. This is one of the many layers of significance in the presentation of his name on the title page of *Defensio*: 'Joannis MiltonI Angli'.[2]

Defensio changed these circumstances, and that was one of Milton's intentions in writing it. His first duty, certainly, was to refute Salmasius' arguments and to champion the cause of liberty as reflected in England's new constitutional arrangements in 1649–51. The brilliance of Milton's prose, and his status as a humanist scholar, were ethical proofs that gave force to that cause.[3] *Defensio* consists of animadversions against Salmasius' *Defensio Regia*. These animadversions are *ad locum* and selective: Milton does not quote his opponent's text in entirety, but he does deal with most of its arguments, using quotation where the phrasing is relevant and where words fall to his advantage. He does, however, follow the sequence of *Defensio Regia*, and therefore his rhetorical structure in large part depends on his adversary's. He writes in his peroration: 'And I have not knowingly passed over without reply any argument or testimony brought by my opponent which seemed indeed to have any solidity at all to it or any power of proof. Perhaps I have gone closer to the opposite kind of fault . . .' ('neque ullum sine responso vel argumentum, vel exemplum, vel testimonium ab adversario allatum sciens prætermisi, quod quidem firmitatis in se quicquam, aut probationis vim ullam habere videretur; in alteram fortasse partem culpæ proprior . . .').[4]

We are not well disposed to animadversion in the twenty-first century. It seems a cumbersome and mechanical way of proceeding, and one likely to give too much credence to the intellectual rationale and point of view of one's opponent. But it was an essential foundation of early-modern printed debate. Milton does it brilliantly, and his remorselessness and repetitions are integral to his skill. Thus much might be said of the rhetoric of *Eikonoklastes*. What *Defensio* has in addition is the learning, the mastery of exempla, and the inventive wordplay of *Tenure*. It is a work of humanist scholarship, though at times the voice seems to be that of a vernacular pamphleteer. The tone is dazzlingly varied: the scholarly voice is sufficiently confident to move between Ciceronian oratory, satire, burlesque, and *paranomasia*.

One of the shaping characteristics of the defences is the multiplicity of the audiences they address. Through much of the text *Defensio* addresses Salmasius in the second person. The adversary is the primary audience. While the direct address to the opponent is often for display, Salmasius—and Alexander More and Peter Du

---

[2] On Milton's role as Secretary for Foreign Tongues, see Robert T. Fallon, *Milton in Government* (University Park, Pa., 1993); Leo Miller, *John Milton and the Oldenburg Safeguard* (New York, 1985); Leo Miller, *John Milton's Writings in the Anglo-Dutch Negotiations, 1651–1654* (Pittsburgh, Pa., 1992); on *Observations*, see Joad Raymond, 'Complications of Interest: Milton, Scotland, Ireland, and National Identity in 1649', *Review of English Studies*, 55 (2004), 315–45.

[3] For considerations of the artfulness of Milton's Latin see Estelle Haan's essay in the present volume, Ch. 3; *John Milton, Latin Writings: A Selection*, ed. and trans. John K. Hale (Assen, 1998); and the works in n. 9.

[4] Milton, *Political Writings*, ed. Martin Dzelzainis, trans. Claire Gruzelier (Cambridge, 1991), 251; for *Defensio* I use this translation. *CW*, vii. 550.

Moulin, authors Milton would refute in the subsequent defences—were real readers of the text, and while Milton did not need to persuade them, he certainly needed to anticipate them. Milton describes himself waiting for More's *Supplementum* to *Fides Publica*, the two tracts that Milton animadverted against in the third of his defences, *Pro se defensio* (*CW*, ix. 228; *CPW*, iv. 796–7). He mocks Salmasius' reading habits (*Political Writings*, 119; *CW*, vii. 186). This address to individual readers belongs to the conventions of the virtual republic of letters that humanists created through their printed epistolary exchanges (a device De Moulin played to considerable effect through the various epistles prefaced to his *Clamor*). Nevertheless, this is both an imaginary audience and a real one. Milton's arguments had to be Salmasius-proof.

A second audience is implicit here: the Europe-wide audience before whom Milton must confute his opponent. This strategy is common in much English pamphleteering from 1641 onwards. The author-speaker and the direct addressee are understood to be in view of a reading public, whose duty it is to judge between the contestants.[5] At times Milton switches his focus from his adversaries and speaks to his European readers, seeking their agreement on some point he has made, and Salmasius is referred to in third person:

What then will you do, wretch? With this keenness of yours you have clearly ruined the young king; for upon your own opinion, I will torture you to confess that this power in England which now is has been ordained by God, and then that all Englishmen within the boundaries of the same commonwealth ought to be subject to the same power. So wait, critics, and keep your hands off, this is a new emendation by Salmasius on the epistle to the Romans; he has discovered that it should not be rendered the powers which are, 'but which now exist'; so he might show that all ought to have been subject to the tyrant Nero who was then emperor indeed.

Quid autem facies miser? acumine hoc tuo regem adolescentem planè perdisti; ab ipsa enim tua sententia extorquebo ut fatearis, hanc potestatem in Anglia, quæ nunc est, à Deo ordinatam esse; atque omnes proinde Anglos intra ejusdem reipublicæ fines eidem potestati subjectos esse debere. Attendite igitur Critici, et manus abstinete, Salmasii nova hæc emendatio est, in epistola ad Romanos; non quæ sunt potestates, sed quæ nunc existunt, reddi debere adinvenit; ut Neroni tyranno tunc scilicet imperanti subjectos esse omnes oportuisse demonstraret.[6] (*Political Writings*, 115; *CW*, vii. 172)

The rhetoric brings to mind a council chamber, public forum, or parliament, as Milton had evoked in *Areopagitica* (1644), a pamphlet written and printed in the form of a mock parliamentary speech; alternatively it might suggest a courtroom, in which Milton and his adversary are advocates. Though the terminology of legal procedure has a stronger presence in *Pro se defensio*, much of the argument of

---

[5] Sharon Achinstein, *Milton and the Revolutionary Reader* (Princeton, 1994), 27–70; Joad Raymond, *The Invention of the Newspaper: English Newsbooks, 1641–1649* (Oxford, 1996), 80–126; id., *Pamphlets and Pamphleteering in Early Modern Britain* (Cambridge, 2003), 202–85. Many pamphlets had multiple prefaces to address multiple audiences, or to guide readers into choosing to ally themselves with a particular category (ibid. 282, 284–6); see also Heidi Brayman Hackel, *Reading Material in Early Modern England: Print, Gender, and Literacy* (Cambridge, 2005), 116–24.

[6] Another fine example is where Milton interrupts his second-person harangue of Salmasius with an unexpected direct address to his readers (*Political Writings*, 125; *CW*, vii. 200–2).

Defensio concerns precedent, natural law, and legal right. The overwhelming rhetorical mode of *Defensio*—I shall come to some exceptions—is forensic, the mode of the court room according to Cicero.[7]

There are more audiences. The third is the English people, Latin-reading and otherwise, who are repeatedly separated from the European readership. Milton demarcates them from time to time with appeals to nationhood and its corollaries, especially in the exordium and the peroration to the tract, where he is less restricted by the conventions of animadversion. Milton states that Salmasius' accusations would be self-evidently false to Englishmen familiar with recent history and local politics, and therefore need no refutation: 'if he had produced these things which he has now written in Latin, such as it is, amongst the English and in our own language, I believe there would scarcely be anyone who judged the effort was needed to reply . . .' ('Et sanè hæc quæ jam Latinè utcunque scripsit, si inter Anglos, et nostro sermone protulisset, vix esset, credo, qui de responso laborandum esse judicaret . . .') (*Political Writings*, 53; *CW*, vii. 8). The readership is distinctively Latin-formed, then. However, this sits side by side with repeated contempt for Salmasius not only as a Frenchman but as a foreigner (foreign born, *alienigena*), and, paradoxically, for foreigners in general: 'you know how to rattle off certain worthless lectures and trash at such a great price among foreigners' (though perhaps he means strangers: 'quod frivolas quasdam prælectiones et nugamenta scis tanta mercede apud exteros effutire' (*Political Writings*, 62; *CW*, vii. 34)).

There is perhaps a fourth readership: those who gave Milton his commission. The first commission he received from the Council of State, on 28 March 1649, was to write 'some observations upon the Complicacion of interest wch is now amongst the severall designers against the peace of this Commonwealth'. They wanted a treatise that would repudiate arguments against a major military expedition to Ireland. Milton produced *Observations*, a tract which probably failed to meet the Council's expectation, not least because it seems more engaged with English and Scottish politics, and the Presbyterian betrayal of the republic, than the threat the Irish and Scots collectively represented in Ireland. The Council of State may have indicated their dissatisfaction when they ordered Milton, in January 1650, to assist Thomas Waring in publishing his *A Brief Narration of the Plotting, Beginning & Carrying on of that Execrable Rebellion and Butcherie in Ireland* (1650), a work that denounced Irish barbarity with much greater relish.[8] Milton may have understood from this that his writings on behalf of the government, if not subject to censorship, should at least meet the expectations of his paymasters. Moreover, in seeking to guide through praise, thereby fulfilling the traditional humanist role of counsellor, he evidently seeks to be read and appraised. In *Defensio* he seeks not so much the Council's

---

[7] See Martin Dzelzainis, 'Milton and the Limits of Ciceronian Rhetoric', in Neil Rhodes (ed.), *English Renaissance Prose: History Language and Politics* (Medieval and Renaissance Texts and Studies, 164; Tempe, Ariz., 1997), 203–26, and 'Milton and Forensic Oratory', paper delivered at Milton and the Law symposium, Queen Mary University of London, 29 June 2007; I am grateful to Martin Dzelzainis for supplying me with a copy of this.

[8] French, *Records*, iv. 234–50; Raymond, 'Complications', 316–28.

sanction as its approval of the case he makes for English parliamentary liberty. This fourth readership, Milton's paymasters the commonwealth's Council of State, would later play a more central role in *Defensio secunda*.

The depth of Milton's concern with a domestic readership is particularly evident in the peroration, where his prose achieves its most sonorous effects:

So far I seem now to have completed with God's good aid the task which I had set out in the beginning—to defend the excellent deeds of my fellow countrymen against the mad and most spiteful rage of this raving sophist both at *home and abroad*, and to assert the common right of the people against the unjust domination of kings, not indeed out of hatred of kings, but of tyrants . . .

Hactenus, quod initio institueram ut meorum civium facta egregia contra insanam et lividissimam furentis sophistæ rabiem et domi et foris defenderem, júsque populi commune ab injusto regum dominatu assererem, non id quidem regum odio, sed tyrannorum, Deo bene juvante, videor jam mihi absolvisse . . . (*Political Writings*, 251; *CW*, vii. 550)

The emphasis is mine: Milton's readers at home and abroad equally need to be disabused. This seems to be a clear declaration of Milton's intention. But then he cranks up the eloquence another register, and adopts an epideictic voice (he does so at several points in the tract, but here most clearly in tone and intention). *Defensio* both repudiates the accusations of Salmasius and celebrates the achievements of the English people in overthrowing tyranny and choosing liberty. In this respect, it offers a combination of forensic and epideictic rhetoric:

One thing remains, perhaps the most important—which is that you too, my countrymen, yourselves refute this opponent of yours; and I see no other way of doing this than by striving forever to surpass the evil words of all men by your own best deeds . . . After so shining a deed, you will have to think and do nothing mean and narrow, nothing that is not great and lofty. To attain this glory there is one path to walk upon . . .

Unum restat, et fortasse maximum, ut vos quoque, ô Cives, adversarium hunc vestrum ipsi refutetis; quod nulla alia ratione video posse fieri, nisi omnium maledicta vestris optime factis exuperare perpetuò contentandis . . . Post hoc facinus tam illustre, nihil humile aut angustum, nihil non magnum atque excelsum et cogitare et facere debebitis. Quam laudem ut assequamini, hac sola incedendum est via . . . (*Political Writings*, 251–2; *CW*, vii. 550–2)

It is glorious though full of warnings. A few words later this praise becomes the exhortation of a Jeremiah: 'But if—which, good God, may you not allow—you have otherwise in mind' ('Sin autem, quod, bone Deus, ne unquam siveris, aliter in animum induxeritis') (*Political Writings*, 252; *CW*, vii. 554). And he tells the English that should they fail, their enemies will have spoken truly, God will show himself angry, and even spokesperson Milton will be unable to defend them.

Milton had spoken in the voice of a Jeremiah before, in *The Reason of Church-Government* (1642), where it is similarly partnered with a privileged poetic voice, a voice that celebrates the English people (*CW*, iii. 230–1). He would do so again: most audibly in *The Readie & Easie Way*, but also, I argue below, in *Defensio secunda*.[9]

---

[9] Laura Lunger Knoppers, 'Milton's *The Readie and Easie Way* and the English Jeremiad', in David Loewenstein and James Grantham Turner (eds.), *Politics, Poetics, and Hermeneutics in Milton's Prose*

Praise was often accompanied by, or inflected with, criticism in early-modern writing, but Milton's exploitation of this convention was strident to the point of discordance. Sometimes he seems to expect failure. It will be your fault, and yours only, he seems to say, watch me fail to persuade you again.

This rhetorical turn to jeremiad was emphasized in an addition to the peroration in the 1658 revised edition of *Defensio* (often, and oddly, chosen as the copy-text for modern editions). Milton's final words declare the power of his own rhetoric: just as events he celebrated could not have been performed without God's support, so too his praises of them were inspired. His success was accordingly recognized not only by fellow-citizens but by foreigners ('non meorum modò civium, sed exterorum etiam hominum' (*CW*, vii. 556)). Yet there is a melancholy edge to this triumph. Milton was singing old praises in a new context. This edition of *Defensio* appeared in October 1658. Cromwell had died the preceding month, having nominated his son as successor. The republic that Milton defended in 1651 had been replaced, following Cromwell's forced dissolution of Parliament, by an interim settlement with a nominated parliament, then, in December 1653, by the Protectorate, with Cromwell himself as Lord Protector.[10] The original constitution of this government—which Milton celebrated in *Defensio secunda*—had been modified by successive expedient measures that compromised its republican integrity. The most recent of these had been the Humble Petition and Advice of 1657, which reintroduced an upper, non-elected House, gave power of nominating a successor to the Protector, increased Cromwell's prerogative, and instigated a more ceremonial mode of rule. The republic was looking more like a monarchy. Hence when Milton republished his defence of regicide and panegyric to liberty in 1658, the praise remained as vital as ever, though the object of praise was spectral.

'A MONUMENT, WHICH WILL NOT SPEEDILY PERISH': *DEFENSIO SECUNDA*

Milton wrote *Defensio secunda* in response to one of the tracts that attacked his *Defensio*, *Regii Sanguinis Clamor ad Coelum* (1652). This anonymous tract was written by Peter du Moulin, though Milton understood it (at least initially) to have been written by Alexander More, and the polemic of *Defensio secunda* relies heavily on this mistaken attribution. It follows its predecessor in form: it consists of

(Cambridge, 1990), 213–25; Raymond, 'Complications', 328; id., 'The Cracking of the Republican Spokes', *Prose Studies*, 19 (1996), 255–74.

[10] Austin Woolrych, *Commonwealth to Protectorate* (Oxford, 1982), esp. 352–86; Samuel Rawson Gardiner, *History of the Commonwealth and Protectorate*, 4 vols. (1903; Adlestrop, 1988–9), ii. 316–30.

animadversions, and combines forensic with epideictic rhetoric, excoriating a critic and singing the praises of the republic. Otherwise the rhetorical texture is entirely different. Milton pays limited attention to the detail of his opponents' (plural because other authors supplied additional texts printed in the book) arguments, and instead focuses on his own merits. The detailed political argument is supplanted by charged articulations of epic ambitions, and a powerful evocation of a free republic. David Loewenstein suggests that it is 'centrally concerned with the role of literary discourse in the new social order'.[11] It is a tract in which grand literary aspirations replace mundane polemic.

Two circumstances had changed since 1651 that profoundly shaped Milton's rhetoric. First, he had established a reputation in Europe as a brilliant Latinist and polemicist (French, *Records*, ii. 340–63, iii. 14–126). He was no longer the underdog, if not unknown at least not blooded, who wrote *Defensio*. Two things follow: first, on this occasion his learning was recognized, and could therefore be deployed within the encounter as a known reality rather than something that needed to be proved; secondly, the potential role of ethical proof was enhanced. Perhaps this is the reason that *Defensio secunda* contains a great deal about Milton himself. Though there is evidence that Milton's employers were part of his implied readership, there is no official record that Milton was ordered to write this rebuttal, though he states in *Pro se defensio* that *Defensio secunda* was commissioned (*CW*, ix. 164, *CPW*, iv. 767).

The second change in circumstance was that the republic he had praised in 1651 had been transformed into a Protectorate, with a written constitution, drafted according to classical republican theory but without parliamentary legitimacy, having been introduced by the Nominated Assembly and the force of the army. Even if Milton believed this to be a just government, many other republicans had distanced themselves from it, articulating suspicion of Cromwell's ambitions; and it was not the government of the people that Milton had idealized. It needed a different kind of rhetorical legitimation.

Defensio secunda appears at first, much like *Defensio*, to have a formal rhetorical structure. The exordium—marked by the phrase 'in ipso limine orationis' (*CW*, viii. 2), 'on the entrance to this oration'—begins with thanks to God for his own successes, and moves to praise of the English people: 'And what can be more for the honour or glory of any country, than liberty, restored alike to civil life, and divine worship?' ('quid patriæ cujusquam esse magis decori aut gloriæ potest, quàm libertas, non civili tantùm vitæ, sed divino etiam cultui restituta?' (*CW*, viii. 6–7)). Milton presents himself as a spokesperson quite different in persona from three years earlier. The ambitious expansion in his role merits quoting at length:

I confess it is with difficulty I restrain myself from soaring to a more daring height than is suitable to the purpose of an exordium . . . for, to whatever degree I am surpassed (of which there can be little doubt) by the ancient, illustrious orators, not only as an orator, but also as a

---

[11] David Loewenstein, 'Milton and the Poetics of Defense', in Loewenstein and Turner (eds.), *Politics, Poetics, and Hermeneutics*, 171–92 at 177.

linguist (and particularly in a foreign tongue . . .) I shall surpass no less the orators of all ages in the nobleness and instructiveness of my subject. This it is, which has imparted such expectation, such celebrity to this theme, that I now feel myself not in the forum or on the rostrum, surrounded by a single people only, whether Roman or Athenian, but, as it were, by listening Europe, attending, and passing judgement. I feel that I addressed myself in my former defence, and that I shall again address myself in this, to all sittings and assemblies, wherever are to be found men of the highest authority; wherever there are cities and nations. I imagine myself to have set out upon my travels . . . Here is presented to my eyes the manly strength of the Germans, disdainful of slavery; there the lively and generous impetuosity of the Franks, worthily so called; on this side, the considerate virtue of the Spaniards; on that, the sedate and composed magnanimity of the Italians . . . Encompassed by such countless multitudes, it seems to me, that, from the columns of Hercules to the farthest borders of India, that throughout this vast expanse, I am bringing back, bringing home to every nation, liberty, so long driven out, so long an exile . . . that I am spreading abroad among the cities, the kingdoms, and nations, the restored culture of citizenship and freedom of life.

quoties animum refero, fateor me mihi vix temperare, quin altiùs atque audentiùs quam pro exordii ratione insurgam . . . quandoquidem oratores illos antiquos & insignes, quantum ego ab illis non dicendi solum, sed & loquendi facultate, (in extranea præsertim . . . linguâ . . .) haud dubiè vincor, tantùm omnes omnium ætatum, materiæ nobilitate & argumento vincam. Quod & rei tantam expectationem ac celebritatem adjecit, ut jam ipse me sentiam non in foro aut rostris, uno duntaxat populo, vel Romano, vel Atheniensi circumfusum; sed attentâ, & considente quasi totâ penè Europâ, & judicium ferente, ad universos quacunque gravissi-morum hominum, urbium, gentium, consessus atque conventus, & priore defensione, dixisse, & hac rursus dicturum. Jam videor mihi, ingresses iter . . . Hinc Germanorum virile & infestum servituti robur, indè Francorum vividi digníque nomine liberales impetus, hinc Hispanorum consulta virtus, Italorum inde sedata suíque compos magnanimitas ob oculus versatur . . . Videor jam mihi, tantis circumseptus copiis, ab Herculeis usque columnis, ad extremos Liberi Patris terminos, libertatem diu pulsam atque exulem, longo intervallo domum ubique gentium reducere . . . restitutum nempe civilem liberúmque vitæ cultum, per urbes, per regna, pérque nationes disseminare. (*CW*, viii. 12–15)

His audience has expanded beyond any forums or parliaments, and now he speaks to all peoples, threatening kings and the enemies of liberty everywhere. His vision has extended beyond confuting individual, mortal opponents. This is a humanist's reflection on the power of print to create a virtual audience beyond the reach of any voice. But it also articulates an ideal of shared values contained within the different national characters of Europe. These are ancient values, long in exile, now being restored (*restitutum*), a sentiment that anticipates the 'Note on the Verse' of *Paradise Lost*. He expresses modesty about his eloquence, but accepts the reflected merit of his topic. He is nonetheless a spokesperson for—not only speaking to but on behalf of— 'the universal race of man, against the enemies of man's freedom' ('pro universo potiùs hominum genere, contra humanæ libertatis hostes') (*CW*, viii. 18–19).

Consequently Milton feels no compunction to observe the decorum of animadversion. With the conclusion of this breathtaking exordium he turns to Du Moulin's book (though here, of course, attributed to More), first dealing with his enemy's anonymity, then the crucial distinction (maintained in *Tenure* and in *Defensio*) between a king and a tyrant, and then offering a character sketch of More, the erroneously revealed author. He begins to tackle the prefatory materials to *Clamor*, and thus briefly employs animadversion. But this entails responding to *ad hominem* insults, and so Milton returns again to himself, one of his favourite topics.[12] He discusses his physical appearance, his blindness and its significance, before returning to the text. He is almost halfway through his own book, and he has only dealt with the prefatory materials to *Clamor*. Within a handful of pages he is reflecting upon the risks he took in responding to Salmasius, and then spends five pages praising Queen Christina of Sweden in what he acknowledges to be a 'digressum' (*CPW*, iv. 602–6; *CW*, viii. 102–9 at 108). Shortly thereafter he offers the longest and most systematic autobiography of many in his writings, tracing his education and his public service up to his appointment by the Council of State and the commission to refute Salmasius (*CW*, viii. 118–39; *CPW*, iv. 612–29). This narrative appears too late in the work for a conventional *captatio benevolentiae*, and if the strategy is to establish his ethical authority, he belatedly does so at the mid-point of the text. There follows the most sustained series of responses to Du Moulin's arguments, which are broken up by the famous series of panegyrics that bring the tract towards its conclusion: of John Bradshaw, Cromwell, Sir Thomas Fairfax. These portraits counterbalance the negative 'characters' of Milton's detractors that appear earlier in the text. The effect is not unlike John Dryden's satirical poem *Absalom and Achitophel* (1681), with its juxtaposition of heroic and villainous sketches. *Defensio secunda* then concludes with five pieces of advice to Cromwell, one of which involves praise of other citizens in the republic, and then an address to his fellow countrymen (the European audience have disappeared by this point) warning of the dangers of returning to tyranny. Like *Defensio* it concludes as a jeremiad, with Milton as the poet who bears testimony to what might have been: the republic that is endangered by the shortcomings of his countrymen.

Defensio secunda, then, observes neither the imitative, *ad locum* structure of animadversion, nor the formal structure of a classical oration, carefully followed in the *Tenure*. Milton refutes his opponent less by analysis or logical proof than by narration. The denigration of England's republican worthies, including Milton, by Du Moulin certainly provides the occasion for the extended passages of praise and autobiography, but these are by no means restricted to the immediate purpose. Instead *Defensio secunda* is a work that shirks the rigours of argument and instead offers an artful series of digressions.

This is made possible in part by Milton's own change in status. He no longer has to prove his grasp of historical and biblical precedent or classical philology. And in order to achieve his purpose mere wangling with Du Moulin's insults and antithetical political allegiances would not suffice. Instead he sings in praise of liberty—forensic oratory providing the occasion for epideictic—and doing so effectively requires a poet. Having established his literary credentials throughout, in the peroration he

---

[12] Stephen M. Fallon, *Milton's Peculiar Grace: Self-Representation and Authority* (Ithaca, N.Y., 2007).

declares that he has written an epic. As he worries that his countrymen will fail to live up to their initial promise, so he articulates his own fulfilment of it:

I have celebrated, as a testimony to them, I had almost said, a monument, which will not speedily perish, actions which were glorious, lofty, which were almost above all praise; and if I have done nothing else, I have assuredly discharged my trust. But as the poet, who is styled [a weak word for 'vocatur'] epic, if he adhere strictly to established rules, undertakes to embellish not the whole life of the hero whom he proposes to celebrate in song, but, usually, one particular action of his life, as for example, that of Achilles at Troy, or the return of Ulysses, or the arrival of Æneas in Italy, and leaves alone the rest; so likewise will it suffice for my duty and excuse, that I have at least embellished one of the heroic actions of my countrymen. The rest I pass by: for who could do justice to all the great actions of an entire people?

ego quæ eximia, quæ excelsa, quæ omni laude propè majora fuere, iis testimonium, prope dixerim monumentum, perhibui, haud citò interiturum; & si aliud nihil, certè fidem meam liveravi. Quemadmodum autem poeta is qui Epicus vocatur, si quis paulò accuratior, minimèque abnormis est, quem Heroem versibus canendum sibi proponit, ejus non vitam omnem, sed unam ferè vitæ actionem, Achillis putà ad Troiam, vel Ulissis reditum, vel Æneæ in Italiam adventum ornandum sibi sumit, reliquas prætermittit; ita mihi quoque vel ad officium, vel ad excusationem satis fuerit, unam saltem popularium meorum heroicè rem gestam exornasse; reliqua prætereo; omni universi populi præstare quis possit? (*CW*, viii. 252–3)

Throughout his writings, in print and manuscript, Milton articulated his ambition to write a great literary work. He wished to write an epic, something that aftertimes would not let die. It is for this reason that the period during which he more or less committed himself to prose, 1641–60, has been described by critics, following Milton's rhetorical cue, as a diversion from or suspension of his poetic ambitions, a distraction from greatness while pursuing 'achievements of the left hand', as he put it in *Reason of Church-Government*.[13] The conclusion of *Defensio secunda* suggests that he has in some part achieved these ambitions, having found a topic worthy of celebrating, a hero, and a style appropriate to the matter. The form is also that of an epic poem, which focuses on a single event in the life of a hero, and places this in context through patterns of digression. The ambition of *Defensio secunda* is too great to be realized by focusing too narrowly on silencing *Clamor*. In the summer of 1654, on receiving a copy of *Defensio secunda*, Marvell wrote to its author praising 'the Height of the Roman eloquence' he found therein, and characterizing its Roman sublime: 'When I consider how equally it turnes and rises with so many figures, it seems to me a Trajans columne in whose winding ascent we see imboss'd the severall

---

[13] 'I should not choose this manner of writing [prose] wherein knowing myself inferior to myself, led by the genial power of nature to another task, I have the use, as I may account it, but of my left hand . . . a poet soaring in the high region of his fancies with his garland and singing robes about him might without apology speak more of himself than I mean to do . . . sitting here below in the cool element of prose' (*CPW*, i. 808). For interpretations that complicate this critical narrative by suggesting continuities between the poetry and the Latin prose, see Loewenstein, 'Milton and the Poetics of Defense'; David Norbrook, *Writing the English Republic: Poetry, Rhetoric and Politics, 1627–1660* (Cambridge, 1999), 209–11, 331–7; and John K. Hale, *Milton's Languages: The Impact of Multilingualism on Style* (Cambridge, 1997), 82–98.

Monuments of your learned victoryes.'[14] Marvell recognized the poetry of *Defensio secunda*, though he seems to have thought Milton, rather than the English people, was its hero.

Milton's epic ambitions are sung in a curiously elegiac context. He might have called it a monument ('prope dixerim monumentum'), as it will be a great subject of grief if the English people fail. At least 'there was not wanting one, who could give good counsel' ('non defuisse qui monere recta . . . potuerit') (*CW*, viii. 252–5). Milton seems to anticipate collective failures with some enthusiasm, but the discordance here is even greater than at the end of *Defensio*. The tone reflects the new and uncertain circumstances of 1654. The introduction of the written constitution named 'The Instrument of Government', and the inauguration of Cromwell as Lord Protector, divided republican opinion. Edmund Ludlow later wrote that the Protectorate was ushered in as 'a work of darkness'.[15] There is consensus that at some point between 1653 and 1659, when he appears to describe the Protectorate as 'a short but scandalous night of interruption' in the history of the commonwealth, Milton became disillusioned with Cromwell, and found himself withdrawing from official duties, and even reflecting subversively on the Protectorate in print in 1658 (*CPW*, vii. 274, 85–7).[16] While Robert Fallon painstakingly argues that Milton was a supporter of Cromwell and the republic, and demonstrated this support in his meticulous work for the government, others suggest that the portraits of republican worthies that appear towards the end of *Defensio secunda*, some of whom were out of favour with or had distanced themselves from the new regime, intimate Milton's dissatisfaction with the Protectorate.[17] Much hangs on the interlinear critique of these passages and the identification of irony in the praise of Cromwell, including the narrative of Milton's allegiances throughout the 1650s, and political interpretations of *Paradise Lost* as the work of an unswerving or disillusioned republican.

Praise and blame are conjoined in Renaissance rhetoric. Praise of a person, a virtue, an action or an event, was well understood to communicate advice, guidance, and even criticism.[18] Thus epideictic literature frequently undertook the humanist

---

[14] *Poems and Letters of Andrew Marvell*, ed. H. M. Margoliouth, 2 vols. (Oxford, 1952), ii. 293.

[15] *The Memoirs of Edmund Ludlow*, ed. C. H. Firth, 2 vols. (Oxford, 1894), i. 371.

[16] Austin Woolrych, 'Milton and Cromwell: "A Short but Scandalous Night of Interruption?"', in Michael Lieb and John T. Shawcross (eds.), *Achievements of the Left Hand: Essays on Milton's Prose* (Amherst, Mass., 1974), 200–9; though contrast Norbrook, *Writing the English Republic*, 395; Don M. Wolfe, *Milton in the Puritan Revolution* (1941; 1963), 287–9; Christopher Hill, *Milton and the English Revolution* (1977), 189–97; Nigel Smith, *Literature and Revolution in England, 1640–1660* (New Haven and London, 1994), 189–96; Martin Dzelzainis, 'Milton and the Protectorate in 1658'; and David Armitage, 'John Milton: Poet against Empire', in David Armitage, Armand Himy, and Quentin Skinner (eds.), *Milton and Republicanism* (Cambridge, 1995), 181–205 and 206–25.

[17] Fallon, *Milton in Government*, 6, 181–4, 188–9, 202–3, and *passim*; Andrew Milner, *John Milton and the English Revolution: A Study in the Sociology of Literature* (1981); perhaps Christopher Kendrick, *Milton: A Study in Ideology and Form* (New York and London, 1986), a study of the 'revolutionary' Milton which only mentions Cromwell twice; likewise Charles R. Geisst, *The Political Thought of John Milton* (London, 1984), 45, 59, according to which Cromwell was Milton's hero; Parker, i. 415–50.

[18] Kevin Sharpe, *Criticism and Compliment: The Politics of Literature in the England of Charles I* (Cambridge, 1987).

role of offering counsel to princes. Milton's praise of Cromwell is genuine: his victories are impressive, his godliness sincere. Cromwell is fit to rule, but not as a king. Milton's praise invites us to see an implicit admonition:

if, after becoming so great, you should be captivated with a name, which, as a private man, you were able to subjugate, to reduce to a cipher, it would be all one, as if, after subduing, by the help of the true God, an idolatrous nation, you were to worship as gods those whom you had brought under subjection.

quod enim nomen, privatus sub jugum mittere, & ad nihilum planè redegere potuisti, eo si tantus vir factus caperere, idem penè faceres, atque si gentem aliquam Idololatram Dei veri ope cùm subegisses, victos abs te coleres deos.

Milton is anxious about the very survival of the commonwealth, adding, with some temerity: 'respect yourself, and suffer not that liberty, which you have gained with so many hardships, so many dangers, to be violated by yourself, or in any wise impaired by others' ('teipsum . . . reverere, ut pro quâ adipiscendâ libertate, tot ærumnas pertulisti, tot pericula adiisti, eam adeptus, violatam per te, aut ullâ in parte imminutam aliis, ne sinas esse') (*CW*, viii. 224–5, 226–7; cf. *CPW*, iv. 672, 673). This fits within the scope of Renaissance praise, if at the more abrasive and strident end of the spectrum.

Milton proceeds to praise others who had recently opposed Cromwell or expressed reservations about the new constitution. They include John Bradshaw:

no one could even desire an advocate, or a friend, more able, more intrepid, more eloquent: for he has found one, whom no threats can turn aside from rectitude, whom neither intimidation nor bribes can bend from his duty and virtuous purpose, can move from an unshaken steadiness of mind and of countenance

non patronum, non amicum, vel idoneum magis & intrepidum, vel disertiorem alium quisquam sibi optet; habet, quem non minæ dimovere recto, non metus aut munera proposito bono atque officio, vultùsque ac menti firmissimo statu dejicere valeant (CW, viii. 158–61; cf. *CPW*, iv. 637–9)

These are strong words to describe someone who had fallen out with Cromwell. He also praises Sir Thomas Fairfax (who had retired from public life) at length, more briefly Robert Overton (who would shortly be arrested for planning an insurrection), and others who rejected the trial of the king altogether. Cromwell, Milton advises, needs to listen to these good counsellors. He does not go so far as praising Thomas Harrison, a personal enemy of Cromwell (*CW*, viii. 216–9, 232–3; cf. *CPW*, iv. 669, 675–8).

In reading this passage we need to make a distinction between Cromwell and the republic itself, a distinction explicit in the Instrument of Government, and implicit in Milton's rhetoric. Milton pointedly praises Cromwell for rejecting 'haughty titles', but also allowing himself to 'be forced as it were into the ranks' ('& velut in ordinem cogi, publico commodo, & sensisti & sustinuisti') (CW, viii. 224–5; *CPW*, iv. 672). The phrase is echoed in Marvell's *First Anniversary* (1655), a poem on the political circumstances of 1654:

> For to be Cromwell was a greater thing,
> Then ought below, or yet above a King:

> Therefore thou rather didst thy Self depress,
> Yielding to Rule, because it made thee Less.[19]

The echo suggests a similar understanding of the relationship between republic and Protector. The constitution places limits on Cromwell's prerogative. In 1654 some were concerned that these limits would be ineffectual, and however republican the forty-two carefully drafted articles of the Instrument of Government seemed on paper, the danger was that Cromwell was greater than any force in place to secure them.[20] Milton praises Cromwell as a servant of the republic. He also commends the Instrument of Government, and his praise of Cromwell, who was subordinate to the Council of State and Parliament in both legislative and executive authority, is shaped by his view of the constitution.[21] Milton nonetheless firmly admonishes Cromwell of the danger of further ambition:

if the patron himself of liberty, and as it were, her tutelary genius—if he, than whom none is esteemed a more just, a holier, a better man, should at last offer violence to her whom he has defended, this must, of necessity, be destructive and deadly not to himself alone, but, in a manner, to the very cause of all virtue and piety.

At verò, si patronus ipse libertatis, & quasi tutelaris dues, si is, quo nemo justior, nemo sanctior est habitus, nemo vir melior, quam vindicavit ipse, eam postmodùm invaserit, id non ipsi tantùm, sed universæ virtutis ac pietatis rationi perniciosum ac lethale propemodum sit necesse est. (*CW*, viii. 226–7; *CPW*, iv. 673).

We should not call this unbounded praise. Nor is it implicit criticism—though it clearly speaks Milton's anxieties—so much as an expression of qualified support. Milton proceeds to offer Cromwell five pieces of advice on which his support is suspended: admit good counsellors; keep church separate from secular authority and property; educate the young; allow freedom of expression; listen to those who support freedom. Then he concludes with his jeremiad.

One brief passage in *Defensio secunda* merits some attention, not least because it does seem to utter a quiet statement of the author's political position. Discussing the treacheries of the Scots, a favourite topic that he had already covered in *Tenure*, *Observations*, and *Eikonoklastes*, and the agreements made between the English and Scottish parliaments concerning the treatment of the king, he asserts that 'a parliament or a senate is at liberty, according to expediency, to change its counsels'

---

[19] Marvell, *Poems*, ed. Nigel Smith (2003), 293, ll. 225–8.

[20] See Norbrook, *Writing the English Republic*, 331–7; Joad Raymond, 'Framing Liberty: Marvell's *First Anniversary* and the Instrument of Government', *Huntington Library Quarterly*, 62 (2001), 313–50.

[21] Contemporary commentaries approved the dissolution of the Rump and of the Nominated Assembly; Milton likewise emphasizes the slowness of their work, attendant upon gradual corruption into self-interest (CW, viii. 220–3; CPW, iv. 671). Perhaps his main concern is religious toleration, which was guaranteed by the Instrument. He also commends the limitation of new laws as a means of enabling the cultivation of virtue and liberty. Marchamont Nedham, in a text with many parallels with *Defensio Secunda*, had argued that perpetual parliaments, unlike triennial parliaments, led to the proliferation of laws and destruction of liberty: Milton's sentiment appears to recognize one of the virtues of the Instrument as identified by Nedham (CW, viii. 234–7; CPW, iv. 678–9; Nedham, *True State of the Commonwealth, Stated* (1654), 23–5).

('Licere autem Parlamento ver Senatui, prout expedit, consilia mutare'). He refers Salmasius, and the general reader, to Cicero's *Pro Plancio*, where the Roman advises that someone standing on the wheel of political life or in a circle of the common-wealth must adapt himself to its rotation. He then offers the sententia quoted as the epigraph to this chapter (*CW*, viii. 166–7; *CPW*, iv. 643).[22] The argument is itself something of an expedient: the rotations in government between April and December 1653, to which Milton is obliged to respond in his answer to Du Moulin, demanded a degree of flexibility among republican supporters of the government. Nonetheless Milton was among those who thought that continued support of the Protectorate was better than opposition, though the political realities might have fallen short of the reformist ideals they held between 1649 and 1653.

This advocacy of pragmatism, or at least a practical-mindedness with respect to constitutional arrangements, was not intended to persuade More, Milton's direct addressee, so much as a British audience. The advice to Cromwell is addressed both to the man himself and to the citizenship. The peroration is addressed to the people of England, or in reality the Latin-literate ones. The overall movement of the tract is away from a European audience towards a more purely local one. This cannot be justified on rhetorical grounds, nor on tactical ones. This narrowing of focus probably discloses Milton's anxieties: though his aesthetic ambitions seek recognition of his eloquence across Europe, he is more concerned to persuade his fellow-country-men than foreigners, as it is they who represent the greater threat to the survival of the republic.

'NO FISH STRUGGLES UNLESS HE IS CAUGHT': *PRO SE DEFENSIO*

Milton had heard from his friend Samuel Hartlib that Alexander More was probably not the author of *Clamor* before he had published *Defensio secunda*, but he stuck to the false attribution. In doing so Milton exposed himself to further attack.[23] More's polemic of self-exoneration, *Fides publica contra calumnies Joannis Miltoni* (1654), together with his

---

[22] We can find a similar pragmatism in the peroration to *Pro se defensio*, where Milton notes that private enmities can sometimes lead to the correction of public vices, so the self-interested motive of the critic is independent of the virtue of the public action (*CW*, ix. 226–7).

[23] *CPW*, iv. 274–83; Paul R. Sellin, 'Alexander Morus before the Hof van Holland: Some Insight into Seventeenth-Century Polemics with John Milton', in Martinus A. Bakker and Beverly H. Morrison (eds.), *Studies in Netherlandic Culture and Literature* (Lanham, Md., 1994), 1–11, 'Alexander Morus and John Milton (II): Milton, Morus, and Infanticide', in William Z. Shetter and Inge Van der Cruysse (eds.), *Contemporary Explorations in the Culture of the Low Countries* (Lanham, Md., 1996), 277–86, and 'Alexander Morus before the Synod of Utrecht', *Huntington Library Quarterly*, 58 (1996), 239–48. For a chronology, see Campbell, *Chronology*, 142–58.

subsequent *Supplementum* (1655), provided another occasion for Milton to write about himself. He seems at first glance to be on a trajectory towards increasingly introspective polemical work; *Pro se defensio*, however, is less reliant on autobiography and self-presentation than its predecessor. Instead it is a set of animadversions against *Fides publica* that make their case not through quotation and refutation so much as through further calumniation and the elaboration of defamatory narratives. Milton imagines and dramatizes the key scenes in the story that he and More are disputing, such as More's last meeting with the serving girl Pontia, with whom More allegedly had a sexual liaison. It is animadversion cross-bred with romance.

The effect is frequently funny, though Milton loses the expanse of vision of the earlier defences. His audience narrows: despite his complaints about More and Salmasius involving themselves in the matters of foreign localities, sometimes it seems that he writes only for More and the councillors of Geneva, whom he wanted publicly to censure More for alleged sexual misconduct. Never does it seem that he speaks to Europe, or even, convincingly in defence of liberty. The rhetoric is almost exclusively forensic, without epideictic. Milton introduces a new strain, however, of legal terminology, which suggests that he had been concerned with the law, especially Roman law, over preceding months. He reminds his readers that in many legal systems only men of proven virtue were permitted to harangue the people. He quotes Justinian's Institutes on authorship, publication, and defamation. Imperial law on defamation provides the context for understanding the legitimacy of Milton's censure of More, and the weakness of More's response; which stands at some distance from the rhetoric of *Areopagitica*. Elsewhere he notes the relevance of the law requiring two witnesses as a standard of proof for an imputation (*CW*, ix. 146–9, 30–1, 138–9, 36–41, 60–1). He invites the reader to consider his rencounter with More as taking place within a courtroom, with the reader as jury. This rhetorical stratum is reinforced when Milton switches from denouncing More in second person to directly addressing the reader for concurrence. The letters and documents both cite are witnesses (e.g. *CW*, ix. 182–3, 28–9, 194–7).

It is not Milton's most impressive performance. The bravura is lifted in the peroration (the closing section of the main body of the text, which is extended, without an eye to the overall architecture, by a response to More's *Supplementum*) with a discussion of the role of rhetoric and education in the public servant:

We, who as boys are accustomed under so many masters to sweat in the shade at eloquence, and who are convinced that its persuasive power consists in censure no less than in applause, may, it is true, safely and valiantly batter the names of ancient tyrants.

Nos qui adolescentes tot sub magistris exudare in umbra eloquentiam solemus, vímque ejus demonstrativam in vituperatione haud minùs, quàm in laude arbitramur esse positam, tyrannorum antiqua nomina fortiter sanè ad pluteum concidimus.

Killing tyrants in figures of speech is fitting for children:

But yet, it was expected that those who thus spent a good part of their prime in mere pastime in the shade, should, at some after period, when the country, when the republic stood in need of their services, throw aside their foils, and dare the sun, and the dust, and the field; that they should at last have the courage to use in their contests hands and arms of flesh and blood, to brandish real weapons, to encounter a real enemy.

Atqui oportuit aut non in ludicro primam ferè ætatem umbratiles consumpisse, aut aliquando cùm patriæ, cùm Reipublicæ est opus, relictus rudibus, in solem ac pulverum atque aciem audere; aliquando veros lacertos contendere, vera arma vibrare, verum hostem petere. (*CW*, ix. 222–5)

The language is reminiscent of *Areopagitica* ('I cannot praise a fugitive and cloistered virtue . . .'), articulating the humanist ideal that the *otium* of education prepares a man for the *negotium* of public life. The emphasis is not on counsel or the arts of peace; the potency of language lies in its capacity to celebrate virtue, to denounce tyrants, to confute opponents. Here also, somewhat belatedly Milton justifies the use of jest in earnest political argument, which is not, according to Cicero, contrary to the decorum of a grave oration (*CW*, ix. 174–7). It is a sign of the influence of English pamphlet controversy over the preceding fifteen years—years in which a vital and vituperative pamphlet culture had thrived and shaped national events—that Milton conceives of his weighty and learned Latin defences as generically mixed, spoken interventions to an invisible public.[24]

Why did Milton respond to More? In *Pro se defensio* he explains, in answer to More's prompting, that he responded to the anonymous *Clamor* rather than the many other works attacking *Defensio*, because he was ordered to by his employers (*CW*, ix. 164–5; the order is not extant; we rely on Milton's own testimony). No such order existed for *Pro se defensio*, and, given its shortfall of magnanimous public-spirited rhetoric, one wonders why Milton troubled himself, and why *Fides publica* merited such attention. Milton's *amor propre* may have influenced his decision, and he certainly enjoyed writing about himself. The result here is not compelling, and the critical neglect of this work can probably be justified. However, *Pro de defensio* gave Milton the opportunity to work through a problem that also troubled *Defensio secunda*. The anxiety breaks out again and again in the tract: what is the relationship between being a public-spirited champion of liberty and writing for hire? It is this concern that engaged Milton on this project.

In *Defensio secunda* Milton declares that while his opponents wrote for hire, bribes, and in pursuit of promotion (*CW*, viii. 28–9, 140–1, 144–5; *CPW*, iv. 563, 629, 632), his own decision to write, and the substance of his writing, were not 'moved by ambition, by lucre, or by glory; but solely by a sense of duty, of grace [or honour], and of devotion to my country' ('nullâ ambitione, lucro, aut gloriâ ductus; sed officii, sed honesti, sed pietatis in patriam ratione solâ') (*CW*, viii. 66–7; *CPW*, iv. 587).[25] While maintaining this essential polarity between public duty and private appetite, Milton increases the temperature in the later work. 'Is there any reason why

---

[24] For general discussion, see Smith, *Literature and Revolution*; Raymond, *Pamphlets and Pamphleteering*; Jason Peacey, *Politicians and Pamphleteers: Propaganda during the English Civil Wars and Interregnum* (Aldershot, 2004).

[25] Cf. the suggestion in *Defensio* that in the *Eikon Basilike* (1649) Charles 'tried to sell himself to the people' (*Political Writings*, 53).

you, a preacher for hire, should be able to advise better than I, who deliver gratuitous, and as I trust, sounder admonitions?' ('non est, quam ob rem te mercede concionantem, quàm me gratis monentem rectiora putem posse suadere') (*CW*, ix. 176–9). More felt the sting of the earlier accusation that he was a mercenary, and his protestations provide occasion for Milton to flesh out the image of greed. More claims to preach 'gratis'; Milton responds that 'on the offer of more abundant hire, you quitted the office of pastor, and became professor of sacred history' ('ex quo videlicet ampliore mercede propositâ, relicto Pastoris munere, sacrarum Historiarum Professor factus es') (*CW*, ix. 282–3). There is a bilingual pun here: 'professor' becomes a term of abuse in *Pro se defensio*, because it suggests a sinecure procured through patronage rather than intellectual merit or virtue; in English in the 1650s it additionally connoted one who makes an open declaration of religious commitment, but whose inner faith is suspect.[26] As in his poetry, so in his Latin prose Milton exploited etymology, semantic equivalence, and homophones to comic and satirical effect. For example: he compares his own humour to salt to rub over More's corruption, and continues, 'that professor's ignorance of yours, which is not seasoned with one particle of salt . . .' ('tuámque putredinem perfricanti sales concessos non negaverint, tum quidem tua professoris insulsi ignorantia') (*CW*, ix. 174–5). *Sal* acts here not only as a preserving and flavouring agent, but as the origin of *salarium* (literally 'salt money') or salary, reminding us of More's motivation: he is anything but an unsalted professor.

In contrast Milton portrays himself as reluctant to enter debate, as stooping ('descendi') into unrewarding contention out of necessity, driven 'by a public order and by private injury' ('& publicè jussus & privatim læsus') (*CW*, ix. 220–3). There is an evident tension here. While Milton writes his own views, and does so because of public-spiritedness, he cannot obscure the order that lay behind *Defensio* (and perhaps it serves to deflect suspicions of egotism); and while there is no evidence of a similar order for *Defensio secunda* or *Pro se defensio*, he was nonetheless a salaried employee of the republic, whose brief included writing polemic as well as drafting state papers and translations. The themes of moral honesty, public virtue, self-interest, and the corruption of the hireling resonate throughout these polemics, and Milton reflects on them, and shapes his abuse according to the values they represent, but he never confronts the distinction between them, nor quite shakes off the discomfort that being a hired pen involves. Perhaps this is because he was too well aware of his own political doubts, and the contradiction embedded in his claims to write only out of a commitment to the public good.[27]

---

[26] On the effects of Milton's multilingualism, see Hale, *Milton's Languages*, 99–102 and *passim*.

[27] This thread of the later two defences anticipates Milton's later tract *Considerations Touching the Likeliest Means to Remove Hirelings from the Church* (1659): it is possible that his opposition to tithes inflects his arguments about secular virtue here.

CONCLUSION

Though Milton's political and religious ideals remained consistent through this period, his articulation of them was thoroughly sensitive to his immediate context. The rhetoric of the defences was responsive, adapting to the texts to which Milton answered, through animadversion that was increasingly indirect in nature. However, the subtext of this rhetoric also speaks of Milton's own relationship with the republican governments in the first half of the 1650s. His ability to speak on behalf of the English people, to the citizens of Europe, had diminished by 1655. Just as it is important to recognize the literary merits of the defences, and not to regard them as a prosaic distraction from the deep-seated ambition to write a great epic, so it is necessary to acknowledge that his published writings in this period were complemented by a more mundane engagement with the duties of a civil servant, drafting documents, translating to and from several languages, and liaising with representatives of the book trade, all of which seemed to him a significant contribution to the public good. However, it was as a champion of liberty in a Europe-wide context that Milton wanted himself to be seen, as an orator and an Englishman among wider non-national networks. In 1655 he also wrote a sonnet to Cyriack Skinner in which the loss of his sight is ameliorated by the reflection that he lost it 'In liberty's defence, my noble task / Of which all Europe talks from side to side' ('To Mr Cyriack Skinner Upon his Blindness', ll. 11–12). That liberty's defence was not only poetic and heroic but also sometimes evasive, vituperative, and open to accusations of self-serving did not make it any less noble.

CHAPTER 16

....

DEFENSIO PRIMA AND THE LATIN POETS

....

ESTELLE HAAN

WHILE Milton's Latin poetry has inspired a rich tradition of critical investigation, his Latin prose defences have, with only one or two notable exceptions, failed to attract similar attention.[1] *Defensio Prima* in particular has never really recovered from Parker's uncharacteristic misreading as 'one of the dullest, most pedestrian of all his writings', one in which Milton fails to lift the argument above a 'plodding, authority-quoting, precedent-hunting' methodology (*Milton*, i. 383). This viewpoint is perhaps all too symptomatic of a tendency on the part of critics to bisect the Miltonic corpus into the poetry/the prose; the English/the Latin; the inspired bard/ the skilful polemicist. But surely among the most insightful readings is one which can demonstrate cross-fertilization between the poetry and prose and vice versa? Thus David Loewenstein has usefully highlighted the aesthetic and potentially poetic dimension of *Defensio Secunda*.[2] Such a dimension is also discernible, even if in a

---

[1] On the Latin poetry, see, among others, the essays on 'Urbane Milton' in *Milton Studies*, 19 (1984); Stella P. Revard, *Milton and the Tangles of Neaera's Hair* (Columbia, Mo., 1997); Estelle Haan, *From Academia to Amicitia: Milton's Latin Writings and the Italian Academies* (Philadelphia, 1998). On the Latin prose, see David Loewenstein, 'Milton and the Poetics of Defense', in David Loewenstein and James Grantham Turner (eds.), *Politics, Poetics, and Hermeneutics in Milton's Prose* (Cambridge, 1990), 171–92; M. V. Ronnick, 'Milton's Vituperative Technique: Claude Saumaise and Martial's Olus in the *Defensio Prima*', *Notes and Queries*, NS 40 (Sept. 1993), 314–15; ead., 'Salmacis and Salmasius: *Pro Populo Anglicano Defensio Secunda* 1. 38.8–11', *Notes and Queries*, NS 42 (Mar. 1995), 32–4.

[2] See Loewenstein, 'Milton and the Poetics of Defense'.

rather different way, in *Defensio Prima*, a work which, it will be argued, rises above Parker's criticism through its integration of and interaction with Latin poetry, embracing *inter alios* Plautus, Terence, Horace, Ovid, Martial, and Milton's own Latin verses.

The present chapter will selectively examine ways in which Milton's recourse to Latin poetry in *Defensio Prima* serves a much deeper purpose than that of merely illustrating or lending authority to his argument. Rather, it will be suggested, the *Defensio* engages with a variety of Latin intertexts, which in turn give birth to a range of dramatis personae, with whom Salmasius is ironically and somewhat kaleidoscopically equated. This methodology lends particular force to Milton's rhetoric of invective while hopefully laying to rest the fallacy that his Latin prose writings were writing during a period of 'poetic inactivity'.[3] For this is a prose work that is poetically as well as politically aware.

The citation of poetic 'authority' in a prose defence need come as no surprise. Cicero and Quintilian emphasize on more than one occasion the potential affinity between the two disciplines of oratory and poetry. Thus in *De Oratore* the poet is very closely affiliated to the orator (*est enim finitimus oratori poeta*) and while matching his powers of ornamentation, possesses greater verbal licence.[4] Quintilian juxtaposes the two, citing Theophrastus' recommendation that the orator should read poetry.[5] What is beyond doubt is that the 'oratorical' Milton readily cites Dante, Petrarch, Ariosto, and Chaucer to lend authority to his statements in his prose writings.[6] And once again there is classical precedent for this methodology. Cicero after all had cited Latin poetry in his political speeches (indeed *Defensio Prima* even alludes to this), turning for the most part to works that would have been familiar to his audience.[7] This is perhaps best exemplified by his inclusion in *Pro Caelio* of an extract from Terence's *Adelphoe* as a way of contrasting two different fathers in Roman comedy: the lenient father versus the stern authoritarian. But here, as R. G. Austin has remarked, Cicero cites Terentian authority with 'apparent impartiality'.[8] The poetic quotation serves to illustrate a point rather than functioning on an intertextual level. The obverse of this is true in Milton's case. While Milton's 'self-fashioning' in *Defensio Prima* is frequently that of a second Cicero, as opposed to the failed Cicero that is Salmasius, he moves beyond his classical

---

[3] See e.g. Richard Helgerson, *Self-Crowned Laureates: Spenser, Jonson, Milton, and the Literary System* (Berkeley, 1983), 242–3, 269, 273–80.

[4] Cicero, *De Oratore*, 1. 16. 70. Text is that of Cicero, *De Oratore*, ed. E. W. Sutton (Cambridge, MA, 1948). Cf. Loewenstein, 'Milton and the Poetics of Defense', 177.

[5] Quintilian, *Institutiones Oratoriae*, 10. 1. 27.

[6] See e.g. *Of Reformation* in *CPW*, i. 558–60, 579–80, 595.

[7] 'aliaque huiusmodi ex poetis ibidem recitat'—an allusion to the fact that in the *Pro Rabirio Postumo* Cicero cites such poets as Ennius (*Ioannis Miltoni Angli Pro Populo Anglicano Defensio Contra Claudii Anonymi, Alias Salmasii, Defensionem Regiam* (1652), 35; all quotations from *Defensio Prima* are from this edition).

[8] Cicero, *Pro Caelio*, ed. R. G. Austin (Oxford, 1933), 37, 80. See L. P. Wilkinson, 'Cicero and the Relationship of Oratory to Literature', in E. J. Kenney and W. V. Clausen (eds.), *Cambridge History of Classical Literature*, ii, Pt. 2: *The Late Republic* (Cambridge, 1982), 230–67 at 232.

predecessor in a number of respects.[9] Now the poetic intertexts (frequently a fusion of more than one classical author) resonate and function as a means of enhancing the sardonic tone of his argument. And more than that: Milton's criticism of Salmasius' misinterpretation of classical Latin poetry, a misinterpretation that is itself couched in flawed Latin prose, is ironically set against a backdrop in which his opponent is depicted as assuming a variety of pseudo-classical roles. In effect, Salmasius becomes the dramatis personae of a Miltonic drama enacted upon a stage of defence. It is a stage that is frequently poetic.

This is not to deny that Latin verse can serve on the purely functional level of argument. But even this occurs with something of a twist. Milton turns Salmasius' citations of Latin poetry against him, thereby exposing the pedant's failed scholarship, his abstraction of quotation from literary context, and ultimately his misunderstanding and misappropriation of classical Latin verse. And he goes further by reworking these citations into an ironic criticism or wry comment at his opponent's expense. A few examples will give some flavour of this technique: (1) Where Salmasius had cited Virgil's description of Aeneas' hair standing on end and his voice sticking in his throat, and had done so to compare foreign reaction to a regicide which is now equated with a thunderbolt, Milton pours ridicule upon this misapplication of the verse (which in its original context described Aeneas' reaction to a divine rebuke rather than to a thunderbolt).[10] Proclaiming that scientists would be very surprised to hear that thunderbolts can make one's hair stand on end, he transforms the whole into a wish that Salmasius' own voice would stick in his throat since all that he utters are curses![11] (2) Where Salmasius cites the bees of Virgil's *Georgics* supposedly as proof that Eastern kings ruled with supreme power, Milton refutes this by means of a further Virgilian quotation,[12] and turns the whole upon its head, for now it is Salmasius who is contrasted with bees, equated instead with the drone seeking to live off the produce of others.[13] (3) Where Salmasius quotes Tibullus' description of iron-hearted men (*feros ac ferreos*) Milton applies this by way of a macaronic pun on *tinnulus* and 'tin' to Salmasius himself: a *tinnulus orator* (*Defensio Prima*, 10).[14] By contrast the Miltonic orator is rendered eloquent, appropriately didactic, and even heroic.

[9] On Milton's recourse to Cicero in support of his argument, see e.g. *Defensio Prima*, 13, 21, 60, 62, 66, 133. On Salmasius as a failed Cicero, see *Defensio Prima*, 15–17.

[10] 'arrectaeque horrore comae et vox faucibus haesit' (Virgil, *Aeneid*, 4. 280) cited at *Defensio Regia*, 3 and *Defensio Prima*, 9. All quotations from Virgil are from *P. Vergilii Maronis Opera*, ed. R. A. B. Mynors (Oxford, 1969). All quotations from *Defensio Regia* are from *Defensio Regia Pro Carolo I Ad Serenissimum Magnae Britanniae Regem Carolum II* (Leiden, 1652).

[11] *Defensio Prima*, 9: 'vox tamen, ut tu modo aiebas, "faucibus haesit"; atque haesisset utinam in hunc usque diem'.

[12] Virgil, *Georgics*, 4. 210–12; *Defensio Regia*, 40; 'magnis agitant sub legibus aevum' (*Georgics*, 4. 154), cited at *Defensio Prima*, 33.

[13] 'Tridentinae enim licet sint, fucum te esse indicant' (*Defensio Prima*, 33). On the drone in Virgil, see *Georgics*, 4. 168; *Aeneid*, 1. 435.

[14] Tibullus, 1. 10. 12: 'quis fuit, horrendos primus qui protulit enses? / quam ferus et vere ferreus ille fuit' (Tibullus, *Carmina*, ed. Georg Luck (Stuttgart, 1988)). Cf. *Defensio Regia*, 3.

That the *Defensio* opens in a quasi-heroic and even poetic 'grand style' is beyond question. Indeed its resemblance to an epic invocation has been noted by Loewen-stein.[15] And the argument can be taken further. The *Praefatio* is characterized by a confident, assertive, and pseudo-poetic didacticism. The speaker assumes a pioneer-ing voice which is quasi-Lucretian in essence, promising to free human minds from the evil of superstition. Thus the Miltonic aim 'ad levandos magna superstitione hominum animos' articulates a purpose not very far removed from the Lucretian endeavour: 'et artis/religionum animum nodis exsolvere pergo' (i. 931–2), a recurring leitmotif of the *De Rerum Natura*.[16] Central to that endeavour was the exposition of the philosophy of Epicurus, invoked as a god who was the first to raise light out of darkness, the guide whose footsteps the Lucretian speaker professedly follows.[17] Whereas the misguided Salmasius is frequently enshrouded in imagery of metaphor-ical darkness,[18] the Miltonic speaker and his fellow countrymen possess an illumi-nating guide in God himself, whose footsteps they have venerated and who has revealed to them a path of light.[19] And Milton takes this one stage further, praising such illumination and freedom from superstition as qualities inherent in and ema-nating from the English people, who have shone (*eluxit . . . effulgebat*) with a majesty surpassing that of any monarch. In making the king accountable to his own laws, they have in fact fulfilled the Lucretian aim of shaking off an inveterate and enduring superstition ('excussa illa veteri superstitione quae diu invaluerat') (*Defensio Prima*, 4). In short, the British people mirror on a microcosmic level that freedom from superstition effected by the power of God and hymned in the work's soaring conclusion.[20]

But if Milton turns to the elevated language of classical epic and didactic poetry, so too is his vituperative rhetoric of invective voiced in the vulgar colloquialisms of Roman comedy. At times he reverts to such expressions as 'I do not care a straw for' (*non flocci facimus*)[21] or else he ridicules his opponent via such Plautine and Terentian terms of abuse as gallows-bird (*furcifer*),[22] thrice gallows-bird

---

[15] 'Milton and the Poetics of Defense', 177.

[16] *Defensio Prima*, 3. Cf. 168: 'quorum animos . . . superstitio occupavit'. The lines are repeated verbatim at *De Rerum Natura*, 4. 6–7. See e.g. 'humana ante oculos foede cum vita iaceret / in terris oppressa gravi sub religione' (*De Rerum Natura*, 1. 62–3). All quotations from Lucretius are from *De Rerum Natura*, ed. Cyril Bailey (Oxford, 1947).

[17] 'e tenebris tantis tam clarum extollere lumen / qui primus potuisti inlustrans commoda vitae' (*De Rerum Natura*, 3. 1–2); 'inque tuis nunc / ficta pedum pono pressis vestigia signis' (*De Rerum Natura*, 3. 3–4).

[18] See e.g. *Defensio Prima*, 18, 99: 'at hercle etiam in tenebris es'; 'quae te mentis caligo in hanc impulit fraudem?'

[19] 'Illius nos manifesto numine ad salutem et libertatem prope amissam subito erecti; illum ducem secuti, et impressa passim divina vestigia venerantes, viam haud obscuram, sed illustrem, illius auspiciis commonstratam et patefactam ingressi sumus' (*Defensio Prima*, 4).

[20] 'Quae duo in vita hominum mala sane maxima sunt, et virtuti damnosissima, Tyrannis et superstitio, iis vos gentium primos gloriose liberavit' (*Defensio Prima*, 192).

[21] *Defensio Prima*, 9. Cf. Plautus, *Mostellaria*, 76; *Rudens*, 795; *Trinummus*, 918; Terence, *Eunuchus*, 303.

[22] *Defensio Prima*, 8. Cf. Plautus, *Amphitruo*, 539; *Rudens*, 717.

(*trifurcifer*),[23] man of three letters (i.e. *fur*) (*trium literarum hominem*),[24] and little weevil (*curculiunculus*).[25] Salmasius, moreover, is frequently identified with a range of low-life stock characters from Roman drama: the pimp (*leno*),[26] the parasite (*parasitus*)[27] the prostitute (*meretrix*),[28] the branded slave,[29] while his ability to transform himself into different shapes is conveyed by the same adjective (*versipellis*)[30] used by Plautus to describe Jupiter's assumption of the guise of Amphitruo[31] in order to seduce Alcmena, Amphitruo's wife. Indeed it is in his interconnected roles as seducer and potential rapist that Salmasius assumes a more specific role upon a Miltonic stage.

At an interesting moment in the *Defensio* Milton, in drawing attention to Salmasius' erratic and inconsequential citation of poetry, makes a rather telling point: we should have regard not so much for what a poet says, as for the character in the poem who says it.[32] This acknowledgement of the importance of contextualizing a poet's words, of situating those words in relation to character and circumstance, is quite significant, and may enhance an understanding of the variety of ways in which Salmasius is equated with a range of *personae* from Latin poetry, embracing Roman comedy, myth, and satire.

Salmasius, Danae, and the *Eunuchus*: A Terentian Intertext

One aspect of Milton's invective lies in his criticism of Salmasius' materialism and in particular his willing acceptance of coins of payment (Jacobuses: *illos aureos*)[33] for the *Defensio Regia*—coins which, Milton states, were brought in a money-bag

---

[23] *Defensio Prima*, 120. Cf. Plautus *Aulularia*, 326; *Rudens*, 734.

[24] *Defensio Prima*, 178. Cf. Plautus, *Aulularia*, 325–6.

[25] *Defensio Prima*, 26. Cf. Plautus, *Rudens*, 1325; *Curculio, passim*.

[26] 'servitutis tam foedum procuratorem ac lenonem publicum' (*Defensio Prima*, 129). On the *leno* in Roman comedy, cf. Plautus, *Asinaria*, 70; *Rudens, passim*; Terence, *Phormio*, 83. See, among others, G. E. Duckworth, *The Nature of Roman Comedy* (Princeton, 1971), 262–4.

[27] 'euge parasite, lenones iam omnes et propudia aulica hac voce demeruisti; O quam lepide simul et parasitaris, et eadem opera lenocinaris!' (*Defensio Prima*, 136). Cf. Plautus, *Bacchides*, 573; *Curculio*, 67.

[28] Salmasius is described in the *Praefatio* as an orator who is for sale: 'O te venalem oratorem et sumptuosum!' (6). Cf. 'sumptibus regiis conductum' (7); 'mercedula conductum' (126); 'pretio . . . qui te conduxit' (140). Cf. Plautus, *Mostellaria*, 286; Terence, *Adelphoe*, 747.

[29] *Defensio Prima*, 23. The identification recurs at 81 and 129.

[30] 'O vafrum et versipellem' (*Defensio Prima*, 11).

[31] Plautus, *Amphitruo*, 123: 'ita versipellem se facit quando lubet'.

[32] *Defensio Prima*, 110: 'Scito, inquam, non quid Poeta, sed quis apud Poetam, quidque dicat, spectandum esse: variae enim personae inducuntur, nunc bonae, nunc malae, nunc sapientes, nunc simplices, non semper quid Poetae videatur, sed quid cuique maxime conveniat loquentes.'

[33] On Milton's persistent criticism of this supposed monetary reward received by Salmasius from (the future) Charles II, see *Defensio Prima*, 137, 165, 168. The theme is ironically expounded in Milton's Latin verses on the subject inserted in *Defensio Prima* (and modelled after Perseus' Prologue to his choriambi). See *Defensio Prima*, 150.

(*crumena*) to his very house (*Defensio Prima*, 7). While not naming the messenger, Milton describes him as the King's chaplain (*Sacellanus*). This sacred term, denoting a custodian of a shrine, contrasts sharply, as Hale has noted, with the vulgarity of *crumena* (a word pertaining to the world of Roman comedy).[34] But it also contains a pun on *sacellus* (purse) as if to highlight the intrinsic, if incongruous, affinity between chaplain and coin, between the godly and the material. And as the payment is received, the language is eroticized, with Salmasius stretching forth his greedy hands and pretending to 'embrace' (*ut . . . amplecterere*) the chaplain when in effect embracing the gift itself.[35] Moreover, upon receipt of this single payment he drains the entire treasury dry![36] Salmasius as recipient is also, as it were, a willing participant in this seduction scene. Then in what would seem at first glance to be something of a non sequitur Milton heralds the entrance of a classical actor ('sed eccum ipsum, crepant fores, prodit histrio in proscenium') onto a seventeenth-century stage that is also and essentially Terentian: 'Date operam et cum silentio animadvertite, / Ut pernoscatis quid sibi Eunuchus velit.'[37] The quotation, from the Prologue to Terence's *Eunuchus*, functions perhaps as the key to a fuller understanding of the intertextuality of Milton's own 'Prologue'. And upon closer inspection its applicability to the Miltonic argument becomes apparent. Included in the plot of Terence's play is the rape of a young girl (Pamphila) within her mistress's household. This crime, moreover, is associated with and even instigated by its perpetrator's beholding a work of art, the contents of which seem to be mirrored in Milton's description of the reception of gold by Salmasius from a chaplain, supposedly a man of God.

Part of the deception in Terence's play lies in the fact that the lascivious Chaerea will ultimately disguise himself as the eponymous eunuch with the purpose of gaining admission to the household of the beautiful Pamphila, of whom he is enamoured. When at last he sees her she is gazing upon a painting of the rape of Danae by Jupiter in the guise of a shower of gold (*imbrem aureum*).[38] Chaerea likewise begins to stare at the painting and, as he later boasts, he thinks that what is good enough for the supreme god Jupiter is good enough for him (*Eunuchus*, 590–1). The god had, after all, secretly entered the dwelling of another and had used a disguise to commit his act of rape. Chaerea's lust is intensified by the focus of the male gaze, and his crime is partially instigated by this iconographical representation of the king of the gods disguised as a shower of gold and thereby raping a human

---

[34] John K. Hale, *Milton's Languages: The Impact of Multilingualism on Style* (Cambridge, 1997), 96; Plautus, *Asinaria* 653; *Epidicus* 360; *Truculentus* 956.

[35] 'novimus qui te avaras manus porrigentem vidit, in speciem quidem ut Sacellanum Regis missum cum munere, re vera ut ipsum munus amplecterere' (*Defensio Prima*, 7).

[36] 'et una tantum mercede accepta totum pene aerarium exinanires' (*Defensio Prima*, 7).

[37] *Defensio Prima*, 7, citing Terence, *Eunuchus*, Prologue, 44–5. Most modern editions read *animum attendite* for *animadvertite*.

[38] 'Virgo in conclavi sedet / suspectans tabulam quandam pictam: ibi inerat pictura haec, Iovem / quo pacto Danaae misisse aiunt quondam in gremium imbrem aureum' (*Eunuchus*, 583–5). All quotations from the *Eunuchus* are from *Terence*, trans. John Sargeaunt (Cambridge, Mass., 1964).

victim (his boastful citation of this precedent would later infuriate St Augustine).[39] And aspects of the drama's rape scene (of Pamphila by Chaerea) and of its essentially domestic setting are not without relevance to the Salmasius/chaplain episode. In Terence, the eunuch is explicitly proffered as a gift (*donum*) to a household (*domus*) (see *Eunuchus* 352, 354–5, 362). Thus Parmeno's announcement of his intention to conduct the eunuch to Thais' home (*Eunuchus*, 363–4) is met with the following *makarismos* from Chaerea: 'O fortunatum istum eunuchum qui quidem in hanc detur domum!' (l. 365). Likewise Chaerea, upon usurping the eunuch's place, boasts of the welcome reception he met with at the hands of Thais, who leads him into her home (*Eunuchus*, 575–6). In Milton, the chaplain's gold both here and elsewhere is depicted as a gift ('cum munere . . . ipsum munus') which has been delivered to Salmasius' home ('novimus qui illos aureos domum attulit tuam') except that now the Jovian shower of gold has, as it were, materialized into actual golden coins proffered by a minister of God. And as the Miltonic doors creak and the Terentian eunuch enters, his invasion of the *Defensio*'s domestic space, so to speak, seems to mirror the invasion of the female body in Terence. But with an important difference. For if the King's chaplain is to some degree a second Jupiter offering gold to his potential victim, that 'victim' (now transformed by gender inversion into the male Salmasius) is in this instance a willing participant in the sexual act, 'embracing' that gold. Rapacity on the part of victim and rape on the part of agent seem to proceed hand in hand. Indeed with his subsequent 'draining' of the treasury, his despoiling of his guest, the role reversal seems complete as victim becomes agent.

By the mid-seventeenth century the Danae myth had been reconceived somewhat ambivalently in terms of both iconographical and literary representation. As Julie Sanders has observed, 'Danae was simultaneously read as a female victim and as agent in her narrative trajectory'.[40] For example, she is depicted as sexually open by Titian in his 1545 painting, while her rape is perhaps most eloquently euphemized in Jonson's *The Alchemist*.[41] It is interesting to note, moreover, that in the late sixteenth and early seventeenth centuries the divine shower of gold had become money in its most tangible of forms.[42] Jupiter's shower of gold is equated in Jonson's *Volpone* with a 'purely fiscal action', and contextualized in *The Alchemist* to suggest the process of sublimation itself.[43] As Katherine Maus remarks, the myth was increasingly employed in the Renaissance to 'suggest both prostitution and the descent of divine grace'.[44]

---

[39] Augustine, *Confessions*, 1. 16: 'et vide, quemadmodum se concitat ad libidinem quasi caelesti magisterio' (Augustine, *Confessions*, trans. William Watts (Cambridge, Mass., 1950)).

[40] ' "Powdered with Golden Rain": The Myth of Danae in Early Modern Drama', *Early Modern Literary Studies*, 9/2 (Sept. 2002), 1. 1–23 at 4.

[41] *The Alchemist*, IV. I. 24–30. For Danae as a willing 'victim' of the golden shower of materialism, see Ben Jonson's *Catiline*, II. I. 176–85.

[42] Sanders, 'The Myth of Danae', compares Gustav Klimt's painting of Danae in which 'the coins flowing into the female protagonist's vagina . . . are far from ambiguous signifiers' (p. 1).

[43] Ibid. 6. See Jonson, *Volpone*, V. II. 98–104. As Sanders notes, the sublimation process takes place in a Danae-like tower.

[44] Katherine E. Maus, *Ben Jonson and the Roman Frame of Mind* (Princeton, 1984), 89.

To some degree there may be precedent for this in Horace's demythologizing of the Danae episode in *Odes*, 3. 16, where it functions as a critique of political corruption. Indeed that incongruity between the Terentian god and gold or between the Miltonic chaplain and coin is brilliantly encapsulated in the Horatian phrase *converso in pretium deo* (*Odes*, 3. 16, l. 8). But Milton's gendered role reversal has homoerotic undertones as the heterosexual union of god and woman is transformed into a same-sex encounter between a chaplain and Salmasius.

Salmasius, moreover, is envisaged in terms that seem to suggest the actions of a Terentian rapist. Milton turns once again to Terence's *Eunuchus* to lend weight to his criticism of his opponent's barbaric Latin, his haughty pride, and his cowardice. Thus Salmasius shields himself by the rude barbaric structure of a book and, like Terence's soldier, lurks behind the ranks.[45] The Terentian precedent is afforded by Thraso, the *miles gloriosus* of the *Eunuchus*. Attempting to snatch a girl from her dwelling, Thraso threatens to storm the house, and then summons his protectors Dorax and Simalio. They are to advance and draw up the men in battle array while he will hide behind the second rank.[46] Thraso's choice of a location for himself *post principia* betrays his cowardice, for he has in effect selected the safest place in his army. The sturdy human protectors in Terence are replaced in Milton's reinvention by books, the massive literary barrier (*moles*) behind which the cowardly Salmasius lurks and hides. Gnatho had remarked on the shrewd cunning of Thraso's stance ('illuc est sapere: ut hosce instruxit, ipse sibi cavit loco' (l. 782)). Milton, making a Gnatho-like observation, likewise describes Salmasius' plan as a cunning one (*callido sane consilio*) (*Defensio Prima*, 10).

And the equation can be taken further. For is not Salmasius a seventeenth-century *miles gloriosus* of sorts? Thraso abounds in self-praise, proclaiming that everything he enacts is a cause for gratitude (*Eunuchus*, 396). Salmasius is frequently depicted as 'swelling' whether upon the huge page (*grandi pagina turgescat*) or as an excessively arrogant man ('superbia et fastidio...supra modum turget') or as a strutting scholar (*circumferre se tumidum*) (*Defensio Prima*, 5, 10, 106). And the ironic appropriateness underlying the parallel becomes more obvious when it is remembered that Thraso, like Salmasius, is a royalist of sorts, boasting in the special privileges he has enjoyed from a *rex* who used to regard him as a confidant, granting him unique privileges, entrusting to him his very army and stratagems, and even dining with him (*Eunuchus*, 397–8, 402–3, 407). In the play's concluding lines, however, he is exposed as a fool, duped and ridiculed behind his back by Gnatho, who describes him as silly, boring, sluggish, and as one who snores by day and night ('fatuus est, insulsus, tardus: stertit noctesque et dies' (l. 1079)). It is hardly coincidental that Salmasius, the royalist, is likewise described as *fatuus* (*tune, fatue*), as a snorer (*stertentem te tam prope finem*), whose behaviour

---

[45] 'ni mole tantum libri inconcinna atque incondita se protegeret, et veluti miles ille Terentianus post principia lateret' (*Defensio Prima*, 10).

[46] 'tu hosce instrue; ego ero hic post principia: inde omnibus signum dabo' (*Eunuchus*, 781).

and failed scholarship are characterized by *infantia, deliramenta,* and *ineptiae.*[47] As a second Thraso Salmasius is potential rapist, royalist, coward, and ultimately dupe.

FROM MIDAS TO EUCLIO: SALMASIUS' GOLD AND THE PLAUTINE MISER

Salmasius' rapacity and materialism are emphasized by reference to two further characters from Latin literature: Ovid's Midas and Plautus' Euclio. In Salmasius' case, moreover, it is a materialism that is multifaceted, operating on a grammatical, pedagogical, literary, as well as a pecuniary level. Milton frequently emphasizes the co-existence or interdependence of monetary and verbal excess as this miser accumulates hoards of grammatical errors, piles of worthless verbiage, and heaps of useless books.[48]

In Ovid's *Metamorphoses* Midas had prayed (to Bacchus) that whatever he touched would turn into gold. His prayer, however, is presented as doomed from the outset. This is achieved via the authorial comment: *ille male usurus donis* preceding the prayer itself: 'effice, quicquid / corpore contigero, fulvum vertatur in aurum'.[49] Midas' wish was famously granted: everything he touched became gold, but the gift granted to him would ultimately prove his undoing (*nocituraque munera* (l. 104)) with the result that he could not even properly wash his hands. Instead when he tried to do so, the water turned into gold, which, Ovid states, could have eluded even Danae (ll. 116–17). Eventually Midas grows to detest his wealth. Salmasius, the very perversion of Danae, is also and initially, it would seem, a Midas-like character, longing for and embracing those golden coins, but this rapacity is also replicated on a pedagogical and grammatical level. Milton explicitly invokes the Midas myth, stating that it is as though Salmasius has uttered a prayer to some god or other, a prayer more foolish than that of Midas himself ('nihil nisi grammaticus es: immo ac si deo cuilibet votum ipso Mida stultius nuncupasses') (*Defensio Prima,* 26). But the nature

---

[47] *Defensio Prima,* 22, 184. 'quantas ineptias atque infantias toto opere congesserit, qui tam densas, ubi minime decuit, in ipsa fronte collocavit' (*Defensio Prima,* 10). Cf. *stuporis et insaniae* (p. 72).

[48] This co-existence underlies Milton's criticism of Salmasius' predilection for stylistic quantity over quality (*Defensio Prima,* 15). Here he compares him to Crispinus (*veluti Crispinus alter*), a long-winded poet of Stoic persuasion, cited by Horace as an example of prolixity ('iam satis est: ne me Crispini scrinia lippi / compilasse putes, verbum non amplius addam') (*Satires,* ed. Frances Mueck (Warminster, 1993), 1. 1, ll. 120–1). It is no coincidence that *Satire* 1. 1 constitutes a diatribe against the evils of accumulating material possessions. *Compilasse* mirrors the satire's pervasive imagery of hoarding (e.g. *immensum... argenti pondus et auri* (41), *acervo* (34), *quid habet pulchri constructus acervus?* (44), *at suave est ex magno tollere acervo* (51)).

[49] Ovid, *Metamorphoses,* trans. F. J. Miller (Cambridge, Mass., 1916), 11. 102–3.

and consequences of that prayer are very different from the wish uttered by his classical prototype: whatever he touches becomes 'pedagogical' except when it is 'grammatical': 'quicquid attrectas, nisi cum soloecismos facis, Grammatica est'. The image is of a rapacious pedagogue infiltrating with grammatical errors everything he touches, resembling Midas in that he uses his 'gifts' badly, gifts that possess a harm of their own, except that in this instance pedagogical corruption has taken the place of gold itself. Even as a Midas character Salmasius seems doomed to failure.[50]

Milton's emphasis upon the co-existence of material and verbal accumulation recurs in his contextualization of Salmasius within a Plautine drama: the *Aulularia*. And once again in a *contaminatio* of sorts he fuses this with other classical intertexts. In Plautus' play the paranoid miser Euclio, eager to preserve his gold from all possible danger, complains that his dunghill cock (*gallus gallinacius*) almost proved the ruination of him in that it began to scratch with its claws at the potential site of the gold's burial. Euclio becomes so exasperated that he takes a stick and knocks off the cock's head, believing that his cooks have offered the cock a reward if he should discover the gold.[51] The heap of dung in which Plautus' cock rummages is developed by Milton (*stercorarium . . . sterquilinia . . . stercoreo*) and reworked on a metaphorical level whereby it is applied to the multitude of worthless books accumulated by Salmasius. And it is a heap over which he 'crows'.[52] Punning on *Gallus* (Frenchman) and *gallus* (cock),[53] Milton depicts his opponent as a raucous bird, deafening everyone with his cock-crow of dung.[54] In Plautus, Euclio had feared that his gold was hidden in the heap in which the cock was scratching about with its claws ('ubi erat haec defossa, occepit ibi scalpurrire ungulis' (l. 467)). Salmasius differs from his Plautine equivalent in that he has actually unearthed the gold—one hundred gold sovereigns. What is more, he has escaped the fate of decapitation, although, says Milton, he deserved death by Euclio's stick far more so than the poor little bird in Plautus ('cum Euclionis fuste potius, quo misellus ille

---

[50] Milton does not let escape an opportunity to ridicule another potentially Midas-like attribute of his opponent: Apollo did not permit Midas' *aures stolidas* (Ovid, *Metamorphoses*, 11. 174–5) to retain their human form, transforming them instead into those of a donkey. Responding to Salmasius' complaint in *Defensio Regia* that news of the regicide wounded his ears but even more so his mind (p. 3), Milton by way of a pun turns this against him: those ears (*aures auritissimae*) must have been long in that they could be wounded from such a distance (*Defensio Prima*, 7). See also *auritus . . . asellus* (Ovid, *Amores*, 2. 7, l. 15; *Ars Amatoria*, 1. 547).

[51] 'ita mihi pectus peracuit: / capio fustem, obtrunco gallum, furem manufestarium' (Plautus, *Aulularia*, ed. E. J. Thomas (Oxford, 1913), 468–9).

[52] *Defensio Prima*, 101. On the recurring metaphor of Salmasius' accumulation of heaps or piles, see in particular p. 190, in which Milton states that he has accumulated such a heap that he supposes he wishes to predict the downfall of his work. See also pp. 12, 68, 120, 167.

[53] 'sed stercorarium quendam esse Gallum oportet. Pro libris certe nemo te maiora edit sterquilinia, et gallicinio tuo stercoreo omnes obtundis; hoc unicum galli gallinacei habes' (*Defensio Prima*, 101). Cf. the equation of Salmasius with a chicken at pp. 22–3.

[54] 'cum tu ipse Gallus, et, ut ferunt, vel nimium gallinaceus' (*Defensio Prima*, 101). On the cock (*gallus*) in Milton, see Karen Edwards, 'Milton's Reformed Animals; An Early Modern Bestiary', *Milton Quarterly*, 39 (2005), 183–292 at 253–7. On the multiple meanings of *gallus*, see Quintilian, *Institutiones Oratoriae*, 7. 9. 2. The pun permeates William Gager's *Allusio in Stemma Gentilitium Serenissimae et Illustrissimae Reginae Elizabethae et Domini Guilelmi Cordeli Archivorum Principis*. See *William Gager: The Complete Works*, ed. and trans. Dana F. Sutton, 4 vols. (New York and London, 1994), iii. 118–19.

Plautinus, obtruncari dignior sis') (*Defensio Prima*, 101). Salmasius, the Euclio-like miser, has become the Plautine cock meriting decapitation (teasingly appropriate given the fate of Charles I), while the theme of kingship implicit in Salmasius' statement that the cock rules all males and females is picked up and inverted in Milton's description both here and elsewhere of his opponent as a hen-pecked husband, and thereby emasculated.[55] It is the hen who lords it over him (*non tuae gallinae, sed illa tibi imperitet*) and *in te regnum exerceat*. But even if the cock is *plurium feminarum rex*, Salmasius is, as it were, a failed *rex* deserving of decapitation but not actually receiving it![56]

But Milton moves beyond Plautus in his promise to give Salmasius a multitude of chickenfeed (*multa hordei grana*) on the off-chance that Salmasius can produce even a single 'gem' for him (*vel unam mihi gemmam*) as he rummages in the dunghill.[57] The *gemma* here, while hinting at the hidden gold in Plautus, operates on a metaphorical level. The passage interacts with a pseudo-Aesopian fable about a cock and a jewel, aptly alluded to by Milton at this point (*ut Aesopicus ille, simplex et frugi gallus*) (*Defensio Prima*, 101). In the fable, a cock while strutting up and down a farmyard spies something gleaming beneath the straw. After rooting it out, the cock observes that it is a pearl, and remarks that while this is a treasure to men, he would rather have a single barleycorn. The invocation at this juncture of this particular fable as a means of attacking the pedantic verbiage of Salmasius, the would-be pedagogue, is noteworthy. For a Latin version of this fable had been cited by the Renaissance educator John Brinsley not only as a useful text illustrating 'the foolish contempt of learning and virtue', but also as a methodological *exemplum* (via Latin translation) of the ideal interpretation of Aesop in the Renaissance classroom.[58] Likewise Renaissance commentators and educational theorists interpreted the whole as an allegory: the cock symbolizing a foolish man or one given over to pleasure; the precious stone (*gemma*) symbolizing art or the wise man bestowing grace or else epitomizing the kingdom of heaven.[59] Such allegorical readings were frequently set within a

---

[55] '"Gallus gallinaceus" inquis "tam maribus quam feminis imperitat"' (*Defensio Prima*, 101; *Defensio Regia*, 137). Gallus was also an emasculated priest of Cybele, the Magna Mater (Martial, *Epigrams*, 3. 81). On the emasculation of Salmasius, see *Defensio Prima*, 23, in which he is depicted as a *grammaticus* in labour and calling upon Lucina, goddess of childbirth; at 141 he is described as a *semivir* possessing a wife as his husband (*semivirum Gallum cum uxore viro*). See also his connection with Salmacis and Hermaphroditus (*Defensio Prima*, 9), highlighted by Ronnick, 'Salmacis and Salmasius'.

[56] Throughout the work Milton depicts Salmasius in terms ironically associated with kingship and regicide: in his self-contradictions his *acumen* has destroyed his *regem adolescentem* (*Defensio Prima*, 63). He is also a self-assassin (*tuus tibi ipse sicarius es* (p. 72)), and his wife has royal rights over him.

[57] 'Iam ego multa hordei grana daturum me tibi promitto, si totum hoc vertendo sterquilinium tuum, vel unam mihi gemmam ostenderis' (*Defensio Prima*, 101). For *sterquilinium* as a term of abuse, see Plautus, *Persa*, 407.

[58] See *Aesopi Phrygis Fabulae* (Cambridge, 1633); John Brinsley, *Ludus Literarius Or The Grammar Schoole* (1612), ed. E. T. Campagnac (Liverpool, 1917), 145.

[59] See *Aesopi Phrygis Fabulae*: 'Moral: Per gemmam, artem sapientiamque intellige. Per gallum, hominem stolidum et voluptuarium' (p. 1); *Fabulae Aesopi cum Commento* (1514): 'Allegoria: per gallum aliquem stultum intellige; per margaritam sapientem donans gratiam dei vel regnum caelorum' (sig. 1ᵛ).

pedagogical context. For example, in 1617 a translation of Aesop 'for Grammar-Schools' regarded the fable as symbolizing 'the foolishnesse of men, especially of children preferring play before learning, a little pleasure and folly, before the most excellent wisdome', and its moral was 'to teach them to followe after and to embrace learning and wisdome, even from their tender yeares, and to be ashamed of mis-spending their precious time in play and idle vanities'.[60] Milton is thus turning pedagogy against the seeming pedagogue. And the irony is not lost, for throughout the *Defensio* Salmasius is consistently portrayed as a failed *grammaticus* (*Defensio Prima*, 5, 26, 165), a degraded grammarian, whose barbaric Latin offends the ears of true *grammatici*[61] and whose solecisms engulf the English nation as a whole.[62] Punning on the twofold meaning of the Latin term *grammaticus* as both grammarian and pedagogue, Milton locates Salmasius in a seventeenth-century classroom of sorts, pronouncing his uncouth Latin from the teacher's chair,[63] but as blabbering pedagogue becomes incompetent pupil,[64] he is depicted as deserving a caning from his pupils (who are envisaged as breaking their sticks on his back) since one single volume contains so many barbarisms.[65]

SALMASIUS, ST BERNARD, AND DAMASIPPUS

As a failed pedagogue Salmasius assumes the role of two further *dramatis personae*, and once again this is achieved through the fusion of a number of Latin intertexts. Citing his opponent's comment that the sun has never seen a more wicked deed than this regicide, Milton ironically addresses him as 'good teacher' (*bone magister*), stating that the sun 'has seen many things which Bernardus did not see' ('multa Sol aspexit, bone magister, quae Bernardus non vidit'), and remarking that Salmasius is in need of some warmth since the *Defensio Regia* will meet with a chilly reception (*Defensio Prima*, 18). Indeed, says Milton, one might otherwise think of him as an *umbraticus doctor*—a teacher who lives in the shade. Paul Blackford has suggested that *Bernardus* may be a Latinized form of 'barnard' or 'bernard', the cony-catching

---

[60] *Aesops Fables Translated Grammatically . . . for Grammar-Schools* (London, 1617), Epistle Dedicatory, sigs. A2ᵛ–A3ʳ.

[61] 'quique omnium Grammaticorum et Criticorum aures, modo teretes habent et doctas, atrociori vulnere si non perculerit' (p. 7); see also 123: 'succurrite grammatici grammatico laboranti'.

[62] See *Defensio Prima*, 126: 'O scelerate! hoccine erat, quod deminutus capite Grammaticus in nostram rempub. te ingerere cupiebas, ut soloecismis nos tuis et barbarismis oppleres?'

[63] *Defensio Prima*, 14: 'te vero in illa tua exedra infantissime rhetoricantem quae fiducia provexit . . . ullum vel inter pueros regem commovere te posse'.

[64] At *Defensio Prima*, 10, Milton states that even a little schoolboy could have proclaimed the subject in better Latin: 'at quis interim e ludo fere puer . . . casum hunc regis non multo disertius, imo Latinius hoc oratore regio declamitasset?'

[65] *Defensio Prima*, 151: 'profecto omnes puerorum ferulas in te frangi oportet'.

pamphleteers' term for a 'lurking cozener' (*CPW*, iv/i, 326). In fact it alludes to St Bernard of Clairvaux (b. 1091) and an associated Latin proverb (*Bernardus non vidit omnia*) replicated in hagiographical writings and also in Chaucer's *Legend of Good Women*.[66] According to the *Vita Prima*, the saint's contemporary biography,[67] Bernard used to remark jokingly to his friends that he had oak and beech trees as his sole teachers.[68] Hoffman suggests that this was the source of the proverb.[69] But the *Vita Prima* cites several instances when Bernard *non vidit omnia*: thus his devotion to spiritual matters was so intense that he distanced himself from the senses with the result that although seeing, he did not see; although hearing, he did not hear (*videns non videbat, audiens non audiebat*). His spiritual absorption was so intense that although spending a whole year in the cell of the novices, he could not say whether or not there was a vaulted ceiling; although spending many hours in the church, he thought that there was only one window to the sanctuary when in reality there were three. If he did happen to behold something, he did not notice it because of his mental preoccupation.[70]

Milton ironically asks if Salmasius' style is *simpliciter narrare*. As *praeceptor bonus* and *magister* he seems initially to parallel the oak and beech trees which St Bernard used to say functioned as his teachers. But is he not also an ironic version of the saint himself? Like Bernard, he is engrossed in a world of his own except that the saint's spiritual abstraction has now become a pedant's preoccupation and obsession with literary and pedagogical niceties. Like the saint, he lives in the shade of trees, albeit metaphorically, and is in need of the sun, but does not receive it. He is, says Milton, an *umbraticus doctor*.[71] The phrase occurs in Petronius to describe the prolix philosopher who destroys men's intellects, as opposed to Sophocles and Euripides, who could easily find the words they wanted in order to express ideas. Petronius laments the decline in literary and stylistic standards: overblown verbosity has invaded Athens from Asia, and, like a malignant star, is blasting the minds of young men.[72] The passage, moreover, had already articulated the ideal style: one which is not turgid or overloaded with ornament, but elevated

---

[66] 'Bernard the monk ne saugh nat al, pardee!' (Chaucer, *Legend of Good Women*, 16). See W. W. Skeat '"Bernardus non vidit omnia": "Bling Bayard"', *Notes and Queries*, 2 (June 1900), 441.

[67] *Sancti Bernardi Abbatis Clarae-Vallensis Vita et Res Gestae*, in J. P. Migne, *Patrologia Latina*, 185 (Paris, 1879), 225–416. See in general G. Hüffer, *Der Heilige Bernhard von Clairvaux* (Münster, 1886), and Elphège Vacandard, *Vie de Saint Bernard Abbé de Clairvaux* (Paris, 1895).

[68] 'nullos aliquando se magistros habuisse, nisi quercus et fagos, ioco illo suo gratioso inter amicos dicere solet' (Migne, *Pat. Lat.* 185, 240). Cf. Petrarch, *De Vita Solitaria*, 2. 14; Baptista Mantuanus, *Carmen Encomiasticum in Vitam et Obitum B. Bernardi Clarae-Vallensis Coenobii Primi Abbatis*, ll. 23–6: 'secum / assiduo meditans, sine praeceptoribus ullis / scivit, ei idcirco silvas habuisse magistros / se dicebat'.

[69] J. J. Holfmann, *Lexicon Universale* (Basel, 1677), s.v. Bernardus: 'Nullos habuit praeceptores praeter quercus et fagos. Hinc proverb: Neque enim Bernardus vidit omnia.'

[70] Migne, *Pat. Lat.*, 185, 238.

[71] See the *Oxford Latin Dictionary*, ed. P. G. W. Glare (Oxford, 1982), sv. *umbraticus*: 'that lives in the shade (as being devoted to sheltered or unpractical pursuits); also of activities'.

[72] 'nondum umbraticus doctor ingenia deleverat, cum Pindarus novemque lyrici Homericis versibus canere timuerunt' (*Petronii Arbitri Satyricon Reliquiae*, ed. Konrad Müller (Stuttgart and Leipzig, 1995), 2).

in virtue of its own natural beauty.[73] In fact it is everything that Salmasius' style is not. Indeed as an *umbraticus doctor,* the prolix Salmasius both echoes and epitomizes the very target of Petronius's criticism.

And the passage neatly dovetails into Milton's criticism of his opponent's deranged ramblings. Where Petronius attacks the insanity that afflicts declaimers,[74] Milton echoes a Horatian satire on the theme of madness. Alluding to Salmasius' remark that 'kings are coeval with the sun's creation' Milton responds: 'Dii te, Damasippe, deaeque solstitio donent, quo te calfacias' (*Defensio Prima,* 18)—a reinvention of Horace, *Satires,* 2. 3, l. 16, in which an initial curse is transformed into a wish.[75] Here Salmasius is equated with Damasippus, a failed speculator, contemporary of Cicero, and chief exponent in the poem of the Stoic paradox that all fools are mad. Thus avarice, ambition, extravagance, love, and superstition are all forms of insanity. But once again roles are reversed. For in Milton, it is Salmasius whose brain is deranged, his empty head encircled and set whirling by all his foolish trifles.[76] The upshot of this is that he does not know what should be said first or later or in conclusion. And in place of Damasippus' beard (the physical mark of the philosopher) Milton substitutes the heat of the sun.[77] The Stoic philosopher who outlines and inveighs against different forms of insanity has now become a long-winded, babbling, and verbose speaker. Here, as elsewhere, Salmasius' persistent misreading of the Latin poets is mirrored by his ironic equation with the *variae...personae* contained therein. For no matter what part he plays, this is an actor who ultimately falters upon a stage that is classical, Miltonic, and frequently poetic.

---

[73] 'grandis et ut ita dicam pudica oratio non est maculosa nec turgida, sed naturali pulchritudine exsurgit' (Petronius, *Satyricon,* 2).

[74] 'num alio genere furiarum declamatores inquietantur?' (Petronius, *Satyricon,* 1).

[75] 'di te, Damasippe, deaeque / verum ob consilium donent tonsore' (Horace, *Satires,* 2. 3, ll. 16–17).

[76] *Defensio Prima,* 18. On the recurring theme of Salmasius' insanity, see the description of him as in a bacchic frenzy (*debaccharis* (p. 45)), beset by Furies (p. 128), and possessing *rabies* (p. 191). For fuller development of the theme, see p. 121: where madness turned Hecuba into a dog, it has turned Salmasius into a cuckoo. Horace, *Satires,* 2. 3 is cited later at *Defensio Prima,* 184–5 in relation to the respective insanity of sinners and tyrants.

[77] See e.g. Horace, *Satires,* 1. 3, l. 133; Juvenal, *Satires,* 14, l. 12.

CHAPTER 17

'NOTHING NOBLER THEN A FREE COMMONWEALTH': MILTON'S LATER VERNACULAR REPUBLICAN TRACTS

N. H. KEEBLE

OF CIVIL POWER: MILTON AND THE PROTECTORATE, SEPTEMBER 1658–MARCH 1659

'Cromwell, our chief of men':[1] in the early 1650s Milton shared with a large body of radical and republican opinion in England an admiration for Oliver Cromwell as the agent of religious and political transformation. 'Brave' Cromwell, the conqueror of

---

[1] 'To the Lord General Cromwell' (1652), l. 1. The quotation in the title is in *CPW*, vii. 482. All references to Milton's prose are to *CPW*.

Ireland, had figured in the *Defence of the English People* of 1651 (iv/i. 458), and in the *Second Defence* of 1654, in which Milton takes the insult that he is '"worse than Cromwell"' as 'the highest praise you could bestow on me' (iv/i. 595), the Lord Protector is famously eulogized as the one man upon whom the state depends (pp. 666–72).[2] Thereafter, however, Milton kept his counsel. His silence on the occasion of Cromwell's death on 3 September 1658, and, apparently, for the four preceding years, has exercised commentators concerned to determine whether Milton's earlier laudatory view of Cromwell survived the experience of the Protector's later rule, with its Privy Council, second chamber indistinguishable from a House of Lords, courtly etiquette, and increasingly monarchical characteristics. Though some have held that it did,[3] the prevailing view has been that Milton's silence betokens disillusion.[4]

In fact, Milton was not silent during 1658. He took two opportunities obliquely to signal a changed view of Cromwell's achievement and to demonstrate that, since 1654, he had been 'very cautiously distancing himself from the Protectorate'.[5] In 1658 he put a brief preface to *The Cabinet-Council*, a collection of pieces of political advice published as by Sir Walter Raleigh though the extracts were taken from a number of European scholars and commentators (none of them Raleigh, or, indeed, English). Noting the incongruity of Milton's name prefacing a courtly advice book, and the allusion to the demise of the Roman republic in the work's epigraph from Horace (almost certainly of Milton's choosing), Martin Dzelzainis has persuasively argued that we have here 'a tract for the times' that highlights the degeneration of the Protectorate from the republican ideal by ironically addressing to it the kind of advice that imperial and monarchical regimes had traditionally received. Similarly, the revised 1658 edition of the *Defence of the English People*, the pre-eminent apologia for the Commonwealth, implicitly underscored how far short the Protectorate now fell from the ideals that text had first celebrated in 1651.[6] Among the additions to the

---

[2] For the view that in these texts Milton's praise of Cromwell is nevertheless cautious and qualified, see e.g. Blair Worden, 'Milton and Marchamont Nedham', in David Armitage, Armand Himy, and Quentin Skinner (eds.), *Milton and Republicanism* (Cambridge, 1995), 175–8; David Norbrook, *Writing the English Republic: Poetry, Rhetoric and Politics, 1627–1660* (Cambridge, 1999), 331–7.

[3] See e.g. David Masson, *The Life of John Milton*, 7 vols. (1859–94), v. 577–80; William B. Hunter, 'Milton and Richard Cromwell', *English Language Notes*, 3 (1966), 252–9; Robert Thomas Fallon, 'Milton in the Anarchy, 1659–60: A Question of Consistency', *Studies in English Literature*, 21 (1981), 123–46; Laura Lunger Knoppers, 'Late Political Prose', in Thomas N. Corns (ed.), *A Companion to Milton* (Oxford, 2001), 309–25.

[4] See e.g. Arthur Barker, *Milton and the Puritan Dilemma* (Toronto, 1942), 196; Don M. Wolfe, *Milton in the Puritan Revolution* (New York, 1941), 289–90; Barbara Lewalski, 'Milton: Political Beliefs and Polemical Methods', *Publications of the Modern Language Society of America*, 74 (1959), 192–3; Michael Fixler, *Milton and the Kingdoms of God* (1964), 198–9; Austin Woolrych, 'Milton and Cromwell: "A Short but Scandalous Night of Interruption"?', in Michael Lieb and John T. Shawcross (eds.), *Achievements of the Left Hand: Essays on the Prose of John Milton* (Amherst, Mass., 1974), 185–218, and 'Historical Introduction' to *CPW*, vii. 85–7; Blair Worden, 'John Milton and Oliver Cromwell', in Ian Gentles et al. (eds.), *Soldiers, Writers, and Statesmen of the English Revolution* (Cambridge, 1998), 243–64.

[5] Norbrook, *Writing the English Republic*, 395.

[6] Martin Dzelzainis, 'Milton and the Protectorate in 1658', in Armitage, Himy, and Skinner (ed.), *Milton and Republicanism*, 181–205, from which this paragraph derives. See further the contrary view of Paul Stevens, 'Milton's "Renunciation" of Cromwell: The Problem of Raleigh's Cabinet-Council', *Modern*

new edition was the pointed assertion that 'there will hardly be found anyone' who has defended 'civil freedom' 'in a greater or more glorious case' than Milton in this 'memorial', the 'highest' of his labours that 'will not easily die'.[7] Whatever the Protectorate may have achieved in the cause of freedom is clearly secondary to the achievements of the exemplary Commonwealth. Fit readers might thus discern in both publications renewed affirmations of republican allegiance.

This makes it easier to understand the sudden revival of Milton's vernacular prose career and why, throughout the bewildering succession of three military coups and six changes of regime that succeeded Cromwell's death, he sought repeatedly to identify an opportunity to secure the commonwealth on non-monarchical founda-tions.[8] Following Cromwell's death, 'All the commonwealth party', recorded Gilbert Burnet, 'cried out upon [Richard Cromwell's] assuming the protectorship, as a high usurpation' and a continuance of the perversion of the Good Old Cause into the tyranny of rule by a single person.[9] This was the context for Milton's return to pamphleteering in February 1659 with his first vernacular tract for ten years, *A Treatise of Civil Powers in Ecclesiastical Causes*.[10] Particularly after the election of the Parliament that met in January 1659, a reinvigorated republican opposition stimulated political debate, not only in the House but in London's coffee houses and clubs. These Milton may well have frequented, including perhaps, later in the year, James Harrington's Rota Club meeting in Miles's coffee house.[11] A resurgence of republican petitioning and pamphleteering, of the writing and publication of politi-cal tracts, constitutional models, republican newsbooks, and translations of classical

---

Philology, 98 (2001), 363–92, and Blair Worden, *Literature and Politics in Cromwellian England* (Oxford, 2007), which holds that 'Dzelzainis's hypothesis can be neither proved nor disproved' (p. 325). *The Cabinet Council* was registered on 4 May 1658, and the second edition of the *Defence* was published in October (Campbell, *Chronology*, 179, 181).

[7] John Milton, *Political Writings*, ed. Martin Dzelzainis (Cambridge, 1991), 253. The Latin text (without translation) is in *CPW*, iv/ii. 1138–9.

[8] These were: the Protectorate of Richard Cromwell (4 Sept. 1658–22 Apr. 1659); the restored Rump (7 May–13 Oct. 1659); the Committee of Safety (27 Oct.–25 Dec. 1659); the Rump restored for the second time (26 Dec. 1659–20 Feb. 1660); the restored Long Parliament (21 Feb.–16 Mar. 1660); the Convention parliament (met on 25 Apr., 1660), which on 1 May voted to restore monarchy and recall Charles II (who landed at Dover on 25 May and entered London on his thirtieth birthday, 29 May). For full accounts see Godfrey Davies, *The Restoration of Charles II, 1658–1660* (1955; repr. Oxford, 1969); Ronald Hutton, *The Restoration: A Political and Religious History of England and Wales, 1658–1667* (Oxford, 1985); Ruth E. Mayers, *1659: The Crisis of the Commonwealth* (Woodbridge, Suffolk, 2004); Austin Woolrych, 'Introduction' to *CPW*, vii. 1–228; and, for a briefer account, N. H. Keeble, *The Restoration: England in the 1660s* (Oxford, 2002), 5–31.

[9] Gilbert Burnet, *Burnet's History of My Own Time, Part I: The Reign of Charles the Second*, ed. Osmund Airy, 2 vols. (Oxford, 1897–1900), i. 147.

[10] This was advertised on 14 Feb. and registered for publication two days later (*CPW*, vii. 236; Campbell, *Chronology*, 182).

[11] See Stephen B. Dobranksi, '"Where Men of Diffring Judgements Croud": Milton and the Culture of the Coffee House', *Seventeenth Century*, 9 (1994), 34–56, which plausibly suggests (p. 44) that Milton may be quoting discussion at the Rota Club when in *The Readie and Easie Way*, with reference to the ideas of Harrington and his circle, he uses a phrase not found in Harrington's writing: 'this they call *partial rotation*' (*CPW*, vii. 434–5).

republican texts called for the restoration to Parliament of supreme power within the constitution and for freedom of conscience.[12]

These were dear Miltonic themes, the former announced in the first line of his tract's prefatory address to Parliament, which is hailed as '*supream Councel*' (vii. 239), and the second in the tract's subtitle, *Shewing That it is not lawfull for any power on earth to compell in matters of Religion* (p. 238). This combination of parliamentary supremacy and religious freedom defines the parameters of Milton's thinking, but so, too, does the subordination of the political to the religious: for Milton, as Barbara Lewalski has observed, 'the absolute value was religious liberty'.[13] This was a direct consequence of his dynamic conception of Christian commitment. 'Truth', he had written in *Areopagitica*, referring to Psalm 85: 11, 'is compar'd in Scripture to a streaming fountain; if her waters flow not in a perpetuall progression, they sick'n into a muddy pool of conformity and tradition' (ii. 543). What animates *Areopagitica* is not the revelation of truth but the excitement of its pursuit through interrogation and debate. Christian faith imposes the responsibility of independent intellectual endeavour: 'to be still searching what we know not, by what we know, still closing up truth to truth as we find it . . . is the golden rule in *Theology*' (ii. 551). The antithesis of this vibrant Christianity is conservatism, complacency, and subservience to prescriptive authority. Hence, paradoxically but understandably, for Milton a person 'may be a heretick in the truth . . . if he beleeves things only because his Pastor sayes so . . . though his belief be true, yet the very truth he holds becomes his heresie' (ii. 543). It is the business of government to prevent this heresy by facilitating believers' exercise of their intellectual independence: parliamentary supremacy is but a means to this end of religious toleration, but with one exception. By tyrannically insisting upon obedience to its ecclesiastical authority, Roman Catholicism subordinated individual witness to communal uniformity of opinion and practice and so, on Milton's view, made it impossible to be a sincere Roman Catholic. Popery is excluded as 'the only or greatest Heresie' (viii. 420–1) from the toleration he advocated for Protestants of any persuasion in *Of True Religion* (1673).

Just these positions are adopted in *Of Civil Power*:

he who holds in religion that beleef or those opinions which to his conscience and utmost understanding appeer with most evidence or probabilitie in the scripture, though to others he seem erroneous, can no more be justly censur'd for a heretic then his censurers . . . To protestants therfore whose common rule and touchstone is the scripture, nothing can with more conscience, more equitie, nothing more protestantly can be permitted then a free and lawful debate at all times by writing, conference or disputation of what opinion soever,

---

[12] For surveys of this material, see Norbrook, *Writing the English Republic*, 396–407; Elizabeth Skerpan, *The Rhetoric of Politics in the English Revolution, 1642–1660* (Columbia, Mo., 1992), 207–36; Jonathan Scott, *Commonwealth Principles: Republican Writing of the English Revolution* (Cambridge, 2004), 294–309; Joad Raymond, *Pamphlets and Pamphleteering in Early Modern Britain* (Cambridge, 2003), 251–5; Austin Woolrych, 'The Good Old Cause and the Fall of the Protectorate', *Cambridge Historical Journal*, 13 (1957), 133–61, and 'Introduction' to *CPW*, vii. 19–26, 66–8, 101–7.

[13] Barbara Lewalski, 'Foreword to The Political and Religious Tracts of 1659–60', in J. Max Patrick (ed.), *The Prose of John Milton* (New York 1968), 440.

disputable by scripture: concluding, that no man in religion is properly a heretic at this day, but he who maintains traditions or opinions not probably by scripture; who, for aught I know, is the papist only; he only heretic, who counts all heretics but himself. (vii. 251)

It follows that 'for beleef or practise in religion according to ... conscientious perswasion no man ought [to] be punished or molested by any outward force on earth whatsoever' (p. 242). To secure this fundamental and unlimited 'Christian and evangelic liberty' (p. 271) Milton was prepared severely to limit civil liberty: while the former encompasses all (biblically derived) opinions, in the public sphere only a very restricted range of political views is admitted. Milton's supreme council would not be freely elected: only those who can properly distinguish between civil and religious power, and who do not use the former to impose upon the latter, '*shall be admitted to govern*' (p. 240). To prevent the prescription of religious opinion Milton prescribes the limits of political opinion.

The elitism and exclusivity that are consequent marks of Miltonic republicanism were biblically founded.[14] Milton shared with many radical Puritans a fondness for the Old Testament notion of the 'godly remnant', reserved by the Lord to fulfil his purposes despite the ungodly and hostile majority.[15] Just so, in *The Tenure of Kings and Magistrates* he had justified the exercise of unrepresentative power in bringing Charles I to trial and execution: 'If God and a good cause give them Victory' then these 'Worthies' are justified in pressing ahead regardless of 'the throng and noises of Vulgar and irrational men' (iii. 192). By empowering Milton to dismiss the views of the 'rable' who objected to rule by a small and unrepresentative junto (vii. 365–6), this conviction that 'God hath yet his remnant' (p. 363) fatally undermined the polemical force and political persuasiveness of the 1659/60 tracts: it was precisely the right of the 'revolutionary elite' to exercise power that royalists and Presbyterians did not accept and was the point to be argued.[16]

THE LIKELIEST MEANS: MILTON AND THE RESTORED RUMP, APRIL–AUGUST 1659

Richard Cromwell succeeded his father in name only. Released from the dominating power of Oliver Cromwell, what the Presbyterian pamphleteer William Prynne styled

---

[14] Cf. Norbrook, *Writing the English Republic*, 397, quoting George Bishop, *Mene Tekel* (1659), 4: 'For many religious radicals, however, "the *Good Old Cause*, was (chiefly) *Liberty of Conscience*", and political forms were subordinate ... if secular institutions proved resistant to tolerating the godly, the elect might have to take power into their own hands and rule as a spiritual elite.'

[15] See e.g. Isa. 10: 20–6; Jer. 23: 3; Micah 5: 7–8; Zeph. 3: 13; Zech. 8: 12.

[16] The phrase is from Thomas N. Corns, *Uncloistered Virtue: English Political Literature, 1640–1660* (Oxford, 1992), 197, which quotes this passage.

'the confederated *Triumvirate* of *Republicans, Sectaries,* and *Souldiers*' recovered the confidence to challenge the adequacy of the Protectorate's constitution to embody the republican ideal.[17] Pressure for the restoration of supreme authority to a uni-cameral parliament led finally to Richard's being forced by the Army high command to dissolve his parliament on 22 April. His resignation as Lord Protector followed on 25 May, but well before that, on 6 May, at the insistence of their junior officers and troops, the Army's General Council had invited members of the Rump Parliament to resume their seats to carry on the 'Great Work' of the Good Old Cause. Curiously little mention was made of the fact that it had been their failure to discharge this very commission that had led Oliver Cromwell and the Army forcibly to turn out these same members six years before, on 20 April 1653.

There being, in John Aubrey's words, 'as to human foresight . . . no possibility of the king's returne' following the overthrow of Richard Cromwell's authority,[18] the fall of the Protectorate provided 'a fruitful intellectual context' for what, Jonathan Scott has claimed, became 'the "*annus mirabilis*" of republican writing'. David Norbrook has similarly argued that, with the collapse of 'one form of monarchism' (that is, the Protectorate), the 'anarchy' of 1659 so deplored by conservatives of Presbyterian and royalist stamp could from another point of view be seen 'as a return to first principles; this chaos might be creative'.[19] The suggestion that the year's constitutional turmoil did indeed represent just such a creative return to the unlimited potentialities of the revolutionary 1640s is articulated with growing confidence by Milton as he recovers the rhetoric and optimism of *Areopagitica* in *Considerations Touching the Likeliest Means to Remove Hirelings Out of the Church*, the second of his two tracts published in 1659.[20]

This is evident in Milton's self-presentation. His friend Moses Wall, who had begun to wonder whether Milton's public service for the Cromwellian Protectorate had weakened his republicanism, had been reassured by the publication of *Of Civil Power*: 'I was uncerten whether yor Relation to the Court, (though I think a Commonwealth was more friendly to you than a Court) had not clouded yor former Light, but yor last Book resolved that Doubt' (vii. 510–11). Wall must have taken heart from the fact that, though Milton might appear to have acquiesced in the continuation of the Protectorate by addressing *Of Civil Power* to Richard Cromwell's parliament, he did so with a republican formulation ('To the Parlament of the Commonwealth of England with the Dominions Thereof' (vii. 239)) that ignored both the Protector and the Protectorate.[21] Perhaps, too, Wall was encouraged by the return to print of that familiar republican author 'J. M.' (p. 238), not identified on a

---

[17] William Prynne, *The Re-publicans and Others Spurious Good Cause . . . Anatomised* (1659), 1, quoted by Woolrych in *CPW,* vii. 19.

[18] John Aubrey, *Brief Lives and Other Selected Writings,* ed. Anthony Powell (1949), 265.

[19] Scott, *Commonwealth Principles,* 296; Norbrook, *Writing the English Republic,* 379.

[20] Cf. the comment in Norbrook, *Writing the English Republic,* 404, that in *The Likeliest Means* Milton 'often reverts to the language of *Areopagitica*'.

[21] Masson, v. 587 reads *Of Civil Power* 'as an effort on Milton's part, Protectorist and Court-official though he was, to renew his relations with the old Republican party in the Parliament'.

title page since Milton's last vernacular prose tract, the regicide apologetic *Eikonoklastes* in 1649.[22] If so, he would have been further encouraged by J.M.'s explicit affirmation of unchanged republican allegiance in its companion piece,[23] *The Likeliest Means*, which appeared in the late summer of 1659.[24] In *Of Civil Power* Milton had returned to vernacular pamphleteering with the reminder to his readers that '*Of civil libertie I have written heretofore by the appointment, and not without the approbation of civil power*' (vii. 240), but in this next tract, published under the restored Commonwealth, he is altogether more assertive about his role as the man who formerly 'defended the publick cause of this commonwealth to foreiners' and who 'som years past' convinced 'the uningag'd of other nations in the justice of your doings' in bringing Charles I to the scaffold (vii. 275).

With this confidence goes a new optimism about the prospects now appearing. These Milton associates with the heady early days of revolution. Appealing to 'this libertie of writing' which, 'through your protection, supream Senat', he has 'us'd these 18 years on all occasions to assert the just rights and freedoms both of church and state', he salutes the Rumpers as the men 'whose magnanimous councels first opend and unbound the age from a double bondage under prelatical and regal tyrannie'. 'By a new dawning of Gods miraculous providence', these 'authors and best patrons of religious and civil libertie, that ever these Ilands brought forth' are now, 'after a short but scandalous night of interruption', once again to assume responsibility for England's 'peace and safety' (vii. 274).[25] The implication is clear: what they achieved once in the late 1640s and early 1650s they can achieve again; and as Milton was there then to advise them in his anti-prelatical and regicide tracts, so he is there now to advise them how best to take advantage of this providential opportunity to rekindle the republican flame.

To conjure this revolutionary prospect Milton writes as though, with his support, a single regime had driven forward the republican agenda since the early 1640s. This was very far from the case.[26] It was not the regime restored in May 1659 that had set England

[22] The three intervening Latin apologias were published as by John Milton (*Johannis Miltoni*). In the preface to *Of Civil Power* Milton explicitly called attention to his return to the vernacular (vii. 239).

[23] In *Of Civil Power* Milton gave notice of a second tract to complete his treatment of Christian liberty, and later in *The Likeliest Means* he refers back to the first tract (*CPW*, vii. 241, 277).

[24] The tract was advertised in the first week of September, but Thomason dated his copy 'August' and Woolrych, in *CPW*, vii. 84–5, points out that the text appears to refer to the Rump's debates about tithes in June, and to be answered by James Harrington's undated *Aphorisms Political*, which Thomason obtained on 31 Aug. 1659; cf. Campbell, *Chronology*, 185.

[25] The duration of the 'short night' has been much debated, whether from Cromwell's forcible dissolution of the Rump in 1653 to the Army's restoration of it in the late spring of 1659 (so including the full term of the government Milton had himself served) or whether the two weeks between the Army's ejection of Richard Cromwell's parliament and the restoration of the Rump, or the period of the Second Protectorate. For the first, see Woolrych, 'Milton and Cromwell', 200–9, and in *CPW*, vii. 85–7, 274; Norbrook, *Writing the English Republic*, 403; Lewalski, *Life*, 367–8. For contrary views, see Masson, *Life*, v. 606–7; Hunter, 'Milton and Richard Cromwell', 252–9; Fallon, 'Milton in the Anarchy', 131–2; Corns, *Uncloistered Virtue*, 274; Wolfe, *Milton in the Revolution*, 289.

[26] Citing Milton's use in *The Likeliest Means* of the same style of prefatory address 'To the Parlament of the Commonwealth' as in *Of Civil Power*, Robert Fallon argues that for Milton the sitting of the Parliament, however constituted, and the continuity of a core of republican members throughout the 1650s, did indeed define the Interregnum as a single republican regime ('Milton in the Anarchy', 132–3).

on its revolutionary course eighteen years before, as Milton suggests, but the Presbyterian Long Parliament. Far from protecting Milton, that body and its supporters had been appalled by the proliferation of such heterodox pamphlets as his own divorce tracts, as at the time he had himself bitterly recognized in the exclamation that 'New *Presbyter* is but old *Priest* writ large' ('On the New Forcers of Conscience under the Long Parliament', l. 20). Milton had defended the 'freedoms both of church and state' on behalf of the Rump, and as much against the Presbyterian members of the Long Parliament as against royalists. And finally, the parliament restored in May 1659 was but a rump of a rump: forty or so members took their seats on 7 May, out of a total of perhaps seventy members of the Rump still alive, outnumbered four to one by surviving members of the Long Parliament. Milton's version of history would persuade none who did not already share his partiality, but he makes no attempt to justify his elisions and ellipses. His historiographical business is less to persuade the public than to spur Parliament and convinced republicans to take the opportunity now provided to recover the momentum of the Good Old Cause.

A LETTER TO A FRIEND: MILTON AND THE ARMY, SEPTEMBER–OCTOBER 1659

In the summer of 1659 Milton (and not only Milton) may have entertained hopes that 1649 was come again, but the argument of *The Likeliest Means* against a publicly funded ministry had no more effect on the religious policy of the restored Rump than had *Of Civil Power* on its predecessor. In the preface to *Of Civil Power* he could remark on his having been witness to debates in the Council of State of the Commonwealth (vii. 240), but those days were long gone. He now lived a secluded life with very little first-hand contact with leading political figures or Army commanders: in a letter of 18 December 1657 he wrote that 'my influential friends are very few (since I stay nearly always at home . . .)' (vii. 507).[27] Later in 1659 he described himself as one who, 'without doors' (vii. 327), no longer had access to the corridors of power and had resigned himself 'to the wisdome & care of those who had the government . . . not finding that either God or the publick required more of me then my prayers for them that govern' (p. 324). This is a little disingenuous—the 1659 tracts did not rely on prayers to guide the government— but it was true that he no longer knew the 'bottome' of public affairs (p. 327). In *The Likeliest Means* he badly misread the political situation: what he took to be the beginnings of a new phase of revolutionary development was no such thing.

---

[27] Milton's last state letters were dated 15 May 1659, and he drew his final salary as Secretary of Foreign Tongues in October that year (Campbell, *Chronology*, 184, 186 (but see also 185, under 30 June)).

The Rumpers might have been expected judiciously to cultivate those to whom they owed their power: they were perilously dependent for their survival upon the Army that had first created the Rump in December 1648 and had now returned it to power. They could sit as the sole legislative body only as long as the military guard at the door of the House admitted them and denied access to the secluded members of the Long Parliament, and they knew full well that the Army was as capable of ejecting them as it was of restoring them; it had done both once already. With fatal misjudgement, however, the Rump sought to reduce its vulnerability not by meeting the Army's demands for arrears of pay, a republican constitution, and a newly elected legislature, but by weakening the Army, cashiering its officers, and controlling its deployment. Frustration at the lack of progress finally resulted in a *coup d'état* when, on 13 October, Major-General John Lambert locked out the Rump.

Under the shock of this intervention, on 20 October Milton wrote an unpublished *Letter to a Friend, Concerning the Ruptures of the Commonwealth*, advising how best to respond to the consequent crisis. The friend has not been identified;[28] indeed, there may have been no 'friend' since *letters to a friend* constituted a recognized pamphleteering genre of comment on current affairs.[29] Although the text begins in apparently autobiographical incidental detail ('Sir upon the sad & serious discourse which we fell into last night... (vii. 324)), it was a common rhetorical strategy thus to situate published counsel within the context of a private conversation. On the other hand, though apparently finished (it is signed and dated), the text is very brief and stylistically unpolished, and it concludes by telling its addressee that 'With this you may doe what you please: put out, put in, communicate or suppresse' (p. 332),[30] all of which suggests that the text is indeed what it purports to be, a quickly written summary of Milton's views in response to a personal request to 'set downe my opinion' following a conversation the night before (p. 324).

So great is Milton's dismay that nearly half the *Letter*'s 1,500 or so words are passed in exclamation and lament before it turns to 'what remedies may be likelyest to save us from approaching ruine' (vii. 329). The Milton who in May had been 'overjoyed' at the Army's 'restoring the old famous parlament, which they had without just autority dissolved',[31] is now 'amaze[d]' that that same

---

[28] Suggested identifications include Sir Henry Vane (Barker, *Milton and the Puritan Dilemma*, 260) and John Bradshaw (*CPW*, vii. 121).

[29] See Raymond, *Pamphlets and Pamphleteering*, 214–18.

[30] In the event, it remained unpublished until it appeared in John Toland's 1698 three-volume edition of Milton's *Historical, Political and Miscellaneous Works* (ii. 779–81). *CPW* prints a text from the 17th-c. collection of copies of some of Milton's state papers, letters, and other texts known as the 'Columbia Manuscript' from its provenance in the Columbia University Library (MS X823M64/S52). Though this manuscript copy carries the same date as Toland's text (20 Oct. 1659), it differs from it in some particulars (some variations in wording and accidentals, and some slight omissions).

[31] As Woolrych in *CPW*, vii. 121, and others have noted, this is a reversal of Milton's applause in the *Second Defence* (*CPW*, iv/i. 671, 682–5) for Cromwell's forcible dissolution of the Rump in 1653 and is an explicit dissociation of himself from the Protectorate.

Army, 'lately so renowned for the civilest & best ordered in the world', is 'backsliding' as it had in 1653 by dissolving 'that parlament which they themselves reestablished & acknowledged for the supreme power', the more especially since there is plain evidence that 'God was pleased with their restitution, signing it as he did, with such a signall victory' (pp. 324–7).[32] The political nation at large was increasingly contemplating the restoration of monarchy as the way to resolve these successive constitutional crises, or, as Milton put it, 'were desperately conspir'd to call back again their Egyptian bondage' (p. 325). He, however, proposed, the state 'Being now in Anarchy without a counselling & governing power', that 'a senate or generall Councell of State' must be convened 'with all speed' either by recalling the Rump or by constituting a new council (p. 329). In either case, the Army, 'since they only now have the power' (ibid.) must be the agent, and in either case, the two key points enunciated in *Of Civil Power* must obtain in determining the membership of this ruling assembly: 'The termes to be stood on are Liberty of conscience to all professing Scripture the rule of their faith & worship, And the Abjuracion of a single person' (p. 330).

This is familiar enough, but, after his outrage and disappointment at the Army's action, Milton's solution to the problem of instability and his response to the exercise of military power are unexpected. The Rump or Council and Army must enter into 'a mutuall league & oath private or publick not to desert one another till death: that is to say, that the Army be kept up & all these officers in their places during life, & so likewise the parlament men or counsellors of State; which wilbe no wayes unjust considering their knowne merits on either side in councell or in field' (vii. 330–1). To turn from stigmatizing the Army's rejection of civilian authority as 'most illegall & scandalous, I fear me barbarous' (p. 327) to the proposal that, on the grounds of its 'knowne merits', that Army's military power should serve as the guarantor of a future republican government appears an all but desperate expedient. Milton, however, had formerly been prepared to recognize in the New Model Army a force for republican good and to prefer military might over popular opinion when he defended Pride's Purge on the grounds that the men of the Army were not merely soldiers but 'citizens, forming a great part of the people' who 'acted with the consent and by the will of most of the rest' (iv/i. 457). This was no more the case in late 1659 than it had been in late 1648 but the claim demonstrates Milton's willingness to invest the Army's political interventions with legitimacy: 'If a majority in Parliament prefer enslavement and putting the commonwealth up for sale, is it not right for a minority to prevent it if they can'?, he had asked, responding to Salmasius' straightforward statement that 'The officers did it with their troops' with the assertion: 'We should then thank the officers for standing by the state, and for driving off the raging mob of London hirelings and hucksters' (iv/i. 457–8).

---

[32] i.e. the victory achieved by John Lambert on 19 Aug. 1659, at Winnington Bridge, Cheshire, on behalf of the restored Rump over the royalist rising of Sir George Booth.

Distrust of the general populace, confidence in a perpetual council of right-minded men, and reliance upon army support are the defining features of Milton's political thinking in the last months of the Interregnum. In the *Letter* he does prevaricate over lifelong tenure for senators when, in an oddly uninterested dismissal of a fundamental constitutional question, he observes that 'whether the civill government be an annuall democracy or a perpetuall Aristocracy, is too nice a consideration for the extremities wherein wee are' (vii. 331). To prevent his scheme resulting in 'an Oligarchy or the faction of a few', he proposes that the governing senate should be of some scale, and that 'the well ordered committies of their faithfullest adherents in every county may give this government the resemblance & effects of a perfect democracie' (p. 331). It is not much of a resemblance: with membership of the senate limited to those who accepted Milton's two key principles and the county committees restricted to their followers, government by the right-minded few on the basis of minority support remains Milton's preferred model.

PROPOSALLS OF CERTAIN EXPEDIENTS: MILTON AND THE COMMITTEE OF SAFETY, NOVEMBER 1659

Lambert's was to prove the briefest of the several hegemonies of 1659. His action was so sudden that it caught everyone unprepared, including his fellow Army officers. Whether the Rump was suspended or dissolved no one knew. During the two weeks following the coup, the Council of State gradually withered and ceased to meet, while power passed to the Army's Council of Officers. To fill the constitutional vacuum the Army Council finally established a twenty-three-member Committee of Safety on 27 October. During the final months of the year, as the Committee of Safety failed to agree on a constitutional settlement, General George Monck, the supreme army commander in Scotland and a declared supporter of the Rump (but not, at this stage, of the full Long Parliament, still less of monarchy), moved his troops to the Scottish border. On 3 November Lambert marched north to confront him.

Milton was in a dilemma. On the one hand, the Rump represented that 'old famous parlament' and the best hope of republicanism; yet it had failed to implement full religious toleration or to abolish tithes, the two policies Milton had promoted as essential in *Of Civil Power* and *The Likeliest Means*, and its apparent champion, Monck, was a conservative Presbyterian who had 'purged' his regiments of radical elements. On the other hand, the officers and men of the Army did indeed support liberty of conscience, and in the *Letter to a Friend* Milton had himself argued that the Army was essential to future stability; yet its actions represented brute force and constitutional chaos, and there was more than a suspicion abroad that Lambert was aiming to perpetuate military rule with himself as Lord Protector.[33]

This conundrum perhaps explains the more restrained tone of Milton's *Proposalls of Certaine Expedients for the Preventing of a Civill War now Feard, & the Settling of a Firme Government*. Like the *Letter to Friend*, this was unpublished in his lifetime.[34] Briefer and scrappier even than the *Letter*, it too may have been a private note of advice to a political friend, or perhaps a first draft or sketch of what Milton might have intended to be a printed tract, a plan subsequently overtaken by events (as *The Readie & Easie Way* was to be). Written when the Committee of Safety was in office (vii. 336), and probably in November,[35] it avoids the *Letter*'s expressions of dismay. In addressing the present 'distracted anarchy' (p. 336), however, its political position has hardened a good deal. It proposes that the Rump should be reconvened, though, since *parliament* is 'a Norman or French word, a monument of our Ancient Servitude', perhaps better called by the title 'Grand or Supreme Counsell' (p. 337), with membership conditional upon subscription to the two key Miltonic principles: 'the main condicions of their agreement be full liberty of conscience to all who professe their faith & worship by the scriptures only, & against single government by any one person in cheif & house of Lords' (p. 336). Army officers are again to be confirmed in their commissions for life (p. 337). However, whereas Milton had havered in the *Letter*, he is now firm on the need for lifelong terms of office for councillors: citing Rome and Venice as precedents, his Supreme Council is to be perpetual, sitting 'indissolubly', and present and future members are to 'retaine their places during life' (p. 336). Whereas the possibility of annual elections and county representation had remained in the *Letter*, Milton will not now risk entrusting republican government to such democratic forces: vacancies in the Supreme Council should be filled by persons either 'nominated by the grand Councell, & elected by the well affected people, or nominated by those of the people & elected by the grand Councell' (pp. 337–8). Finally, the Council is to choose from those 'of eminent ability' among its own members an executive Council of State (p. 338). The question 'whether the civill government be an annuall democracy or a perpetuall Aristocracy' that had been put to one side in the *Letter* as 'too nice' for the times is now no question at all. There is no longer any doubt that Milton's republic is indeed a 'perpetuall Aristocracy'.

---

[33] Cf. Norbrook, *Writing the English Republic*, 407: 'The . . . split between Parliamentary and military forces left Milton . . . virtually paralysed by the difficulty of taking sides.'

[34] But, unlike the *Letter*, it remained unpublished until it was included in *CW*, xviii. 3–7, the text taken from the Columbia manuscript.

[35] The Committee of Safety lasted from 27 Oct. until 26 Dec. 1659. Civil war became a distinct possibility only after Lambert left London on 3 Nov. See further *CPW*, vii. 140, 334; Campbell, *Chronology*, 186.

THE READIE AND EASIE WAY: MILTON AND THE RESTORED LONG PARLIAMENT, DECEMBER 1659–FEBRUARY 1660

While Monck bided his time in the North, chaos in London as law courts closed, trade ceased, and public demonstrations and protests grew increasingly violent fuelled the clamour for a restoration of representative parliamentary rule. Its advocates, who were in touch with Monck, sought not merely the restoration of the Rump but of 'a full and free Parliament', that is, either the Long Parliament, with its Presbyterian majority willing to treat with Charles II, or a newly elected House, with an almost certain royalist majority. With the Committee of Safety and the Army's Council of Officers both failing to devise a constitutional settlement, with Lambert's troops deserting and his attempt at a military engagement with Monck in the North abandoned, on 26 December the Army, at a loss how else now to govern the country, once more restored the Rump. Monck and his army finally crossed the Tweed into England on 1 January and in the course of his progress south—for it was this, rather than a march, still less an invasion—he was deluged with letters, petitions, and pamphlets exhorting him to effect the constitutional settlement that the re-restored Rump still seemed to put second to securing its own hold on power. Monck, however, played his cards very close to his chest. His contemporary biographer declared that when he 'came out of *Scotland* . . . no man knew what he would do, or declare'. On 18 January Pepys noted in his diary that 'All the world is now at a loss to think what Monck will do'.[36] Monck, now indisputably the most powerful man in Britain, reached London on 3 February. A week later, on 11 February, he required the Rump by the next Friday (the 17th) to issue writs to fill its vacancies, to dissolve itself by 6 May, and to arrange for the election of a new parliament. Bell-ringing, bonfires, and roasting of rumps of beef in the streets of London greeted this turn of events, but Monck was not yet done. On 17 February the Rump did agree to issue writs for elections, but on 18 February it so restricted the eligibility to stand in those elections as to exclude royalist and Presbyterian candidates and to ensure its own continuance under another guise. This proved a fatal miscalculation: in a reversal of Pride's Purge, on Tuesday 21 February Monck withdrew the guard from the House and had his soldiers escort the secluded members into the chamber. He maintained to this now fully restored Long Parliament that a commonwealth was the only way to secure the nation, but he could hardly have been unaware that Londoners' popular applause for his actions strongly suggested rather different expectations.

Its first paragraph provides the *terminus ad quem* for the composition of *The Readie and Easie Way to Establish a Free Commonwealth*:

---

[36] Thomas Gumble, *The Life of General Monck* (1671), 166; *The Diary of Samuel Pepys*, ed. Robert Latham and William Matthews, 11 vols. (1970–83), i. 22.

Although since the writing of this treatise, the face of things hath had some change, writs for new elections have bin recall'd, and the members at first chosen, readmitted from exclusion, to sit again in Parlament, yet not a little rejoicing to hear declar'd, the resolutions of all those who are now in power, jointly tending to the establishment of a free Commonwealth, and to remove if it be possible this unsound humour of returning to old bondage . . . I thought best not to suppress what I had written, hoping it may perhaps (the Parlament now sitting more full and frequent) be now much more useful then before: yet submitting what hath reference to the state of things as they then stood, to present constitutions; and so the same end be persu'd, not insisting on this or that means to obtain it. The treatise was thus written as follows. (vii. 352–4)

This establishes that the body of the text was written before this first paragraph, and before the secluded members were 'readmitted from exclusion' to the House on 21 February. Milton's central argument—that the way to secure the Commonwealth is to perpetuate the Rump, the embodiment of the 'Good Old Cause'—hence derives from the period in January and early February when it appeared that Monck might indeed secure the continuance of the Rump.[37] By the time the text went to print, it was evident that he had no such intention. Though, in Milton's understated formulation, 'the face of things hath had some change', the opening paragraph that was then added clings to the possibility that the tract still has relevance, but it can do so only by conceding that, with the Presbyterian majority of the Long Parliament now restored to power, there is not the least chance of the proposed ready and easy way being adopted: means appropriate to 'present constitutions' will have to be adopted. When, however, to propose the Rump as the only suitable means was precisely the point of the tract, it is very hard to see what else in it Milton thought might still be applicable. Even the opening paragraph was overtaken by events: its supposition that the parliament would now 'sit more full and frequent' could hardly have been entertained once, on 22 February, the Long Parliament voted that a new parliament should be summoned to meet on 25 April.[38]

It was already apparent that this new parliament would (if freely elected) vote for the restoration of monarchy. Milton recognized that 'the inconsiderate multitude' were now 'madd upon' monarchy and wished 'to creep back . . . to thir once abjur'd and detested thraldom of kingship' (vii. 356–7, 375) but, writing before 21 February, when 'our old Patriots, the first Assertours of our religious and civil rights' were 'wonderfully now the third time brought together' in the Rump (p. 356) and when its avowed supporter Monck was marching south with an army, he ignored popular opinion to address a moment of high republican hope: 'now is the opportunitie, now the very season wherein we may obtain a free Commonwealth, and establish it forever in the land, without difficulty or much delay' (p. 367). To this end, *The Readie and*

---

[37] As Robert W. Ayers in *CPW*, vii. 343, points out, reference within the body of the text to elections conducted according to the 'just and necessarie qualifications decreed in Parlament' that would have restricted eligibility for standing to fill vacant places in the Rump to its own supporters (p. 368) shows that it was completed after 18 Feb., and perhaps even written between the 18th and the 21st, since it was after the 18th that the perpetuation of the Rump (or its equivalent) appeared most likely: 'but what Milton seized upon as a last chance, Monck looked on as a last straw' (p. 344).

[38] The first paragraph can hence be dated precisely to 21 Feb.

Easie Way proposes, like its two predecessors, a national 'Grand or General Councel' (p. 373)—that is, the Rump, which had (then) 'voted to fill up their number' (vii. 367)—whose membership is perpetual and which elects from its members an executive Council of State. Precedents are the Jewish Sanhedrin, the Athenian Areopagus, the thirty Ancients of Sparta, the Roman Senate, and the Venetian Senate. Milton rejects 'successive Parlaments' as likely 'to breed commotions, changes, novelties and uncertainties' (p. 369), but he does develop, if loosely, the idea floated in the *Letter* of county-based local government: in the 'little commonwealth' of each county the 'nobilitie and chief gentry', from 'houses and palaces, befitting their qualitie', should 'bear part in the government, make their own judicial laws, and execute them' without reference to national government, with, in their cities, 'schools and academies at thir own choice' offering educational programmes that extend far beyond 'grammar only' (pp. 383–4). In this decentralized legislative, administrative, and judicial system, based upon hereditary county gentry, lies the promise for the future membership of the Grand Council. As far as that Council is concerned, Milton will, if needs must, concede a rotation every two or three years whereby 'a hundred or some such number may go out by lot or suffrage of the rest', their places to be supplied by elections, 'but in my opinion better nothing mov'd, unless by death or just accusation' (pp. 369–70). It was perhaps wariness of Monck's Presbyterian credentials and of his authority that led Milton to compromise on the line taken in earlier tracts by omitting any reference to religious toleration as essential in Council members (p. 368) and by dropping the proposal that army officers should serve for life. Certainly, the suspicion that Monck might himself be aiming at something like Cromwellian power seems to lie behind the warning against 'the fond conceit of somthing like a duke of *Venice*, put lately into many mens heads, by som one or other suttly driving on under that prettie notion his own ambitious ends to a crown' (pp. 374–5).

These notions echo the previous tracts, but what is new in *The Readie and Easie Way* is its literary texture. There is every sign of haste, in its style and its printing (to which Milton himself refers in the second edition (vii. 409)), but there is no mistaking its figurative patterning and affective ambition: as the scope for political invention narrows, that for literary invention broadens.[39] With its central political proposal rendered irrelevant by events (as its first paragraph all but acknowledges), the tract yet has a claim on readers' attention: it comes to assume the character of prophetic testimony, a bearing of witness against a backsliding nation.[40] Milton had ended *The*

---

[39] For discussion of the literary qualities of *The Readie and Easie Way* in relation to the stylistic plainness of Milton's other late tracts—'in matters of religion he is learnedest who is planest' he says in *Of Civil Power* (*CPW*, vii. 272)—see Thomas N. Corns, *The Development of Milton's Prose Style* (Oxford, 1982), *passim*; James Egan, 'Milton's Aesthetics of Plainness, 1659–1673', *Seventeenth Century*, 12 (197), 57–83; Stanley Stewart, 'Milton Revises *The Readie and Easie Way*', *Milton Studies*, 20 (1984), 205–20.

[40] For this view, see Robert W. Ayers in *CPW*, vii. 402–3; James Holstun, *A Rational Millennium: Puritan Utopias of Seventeenth-Century England and America* (Oxford, 1987), 246–65; Skerpan, *Rhetoric of Politics*, 200–1, 233; Laura Lunger Knoppers, 'Milton's *Readie and Easie Way* and the English Jeremiad', in David Loewenstein and James Grantham Turner (eds.), *Politics, Poetics and Hermeneutics in Milton's Prose* (Cambridge, 1990), 213–25. Corns is less impressed by prophetic aspects or the utility of the generic category of the jeremiad (*Uncloistered Virtue*, 283–4).

Likeliest Means with just such an affirmation: 'If I be not heard nor beleevd, the event will bear me witnes to have spoken truth: and I in the mean while have borne my witnes not out of season to the church and to my country' (vii. 321). Now again:

What I have spoken, is the language of the good old cause: if it seem strange to any, it will not seem more strange, I hope, then convincing to back-sliders. Thus much I should perhaps have said though I were sure I should have spoken only to trees and stones, and had none to cry to, but with the Prophet, *O earth, earth, earth*: to tell the verie soil it self, what God hath determined of *Coniah* and his seed for ever. (vii. 387–9)[41]

This witness is structured by a binary rhetoric that opposes, on the one hand, 'the noblest, the manliest, the equallest, the justest government, the most agreeable to all due libertie and proportiond equalitie, both humane, civil and Christian' (p. 359), conducted by men who 'are not elevated above thir brethren, live soberly in thir families, walk the streets as other men, may be spoken to freely, familiarly, friendly, without adoration' (p. 360), against, on the other, the government of a king who

must be ador'd like a Demigod, with a dissolute and haughtie court about him, of vast expence and luxurie . . . to set a pompous face upon the superficial actings of State, to pageant himself up and down in progress among the perpetual bowings and cringings of an abject people, on either side deifying and adoring him. (pp. 360–1)

This opposition between republican freedom and monarchical servitude is re-worked and reinforced insistently, less in political terms than through metaphor, metonymy, and association. Within the register of the former lie: manliness, strength, resilience, nobility, freedom, glory, friendship, confidence, service, mag-nanimity, integrity, order, naturalness, plainness; and within the latter: womanli-ness, weakness, softness, debasement, enslavement, ignominy, sycophancy, fear, tyranny, indulgence, hypocrisy, chaos, monstrosity, affectation.[42] This conviction that courts typify the antithesis of the moral life is a constant in Milton. Twenty-five years before it had been in Comus's 'stately palace' that the Lady, who prefers the 'honest-offered courtesy' of 'lowly sheds' to the 'courts of princes', found herself trapped and threatened with rape (*A Maske*, ll. 319–24, stage direction at l. 657); and Satan was perhaps already 'exalted' 'High on his throne of royal state, which far / Outshone the wealth of Ormus or of Ind, / Or where the gorgeous East with richest hand / Showers on her kings barbaric pearl and gold' (*Paradise Lost*, ii. 12. 1–5).[43]

---

[41] Jer. 22: 24–9. Milton implicitly identifies Charles II with the despised King Coniah, whose death in exile is prophesied, and Charles I with his father the evil Jehoiakim, lamentation for whom is forbidden.

[42] Cf. the comment in Norbrook, *Writing the English Republic*, 412: 'Milton both practises and preaches a commitment to the power and the value of republican language.'

[43] See *FPL*, 5 for evidence that Milton was composing the poem at this time.

THE PRESENT MEANS: MILTON AND MONCK, FEBRUARY–MARCH 1660

The restored Long Parliament promptly set about undoing the work of the Rump. On 21 February, the day of the secluded members' readmission, it voted to erase from the record all decisions surrounding Pride's Purge (including the refusal to treat with Charles I) and to annul the Rump's vote to restrict eligibility to stand in the forthcoming elections. On 1 March it voted to dissolve on 15 March (in the event, 16 March). On 5 March it reinstated the Presbyterian Solemn League and Covenant and agreed that the Presbyterian Westminster confession should be the confession of faith for the Church of England. On 13 March it voted to annul the Engagement, the 1650 oath of loyalty to the Commonwealth 'as it is now established, without a King or House of Lords', imposed upon all adult men. On the 14th it agreed to broaden considerably the eligibility criteria for parliamentary candidates and on 17 March writs for elections to a new parliament to meet on 25 April were issued. At the beginning of March Pepys recorded that 'Great is the talk of a single person', though at this stage Richard Cromwell, Monck, and Charles II were all possibilities; when the Long Parliament dissolved on 16 March, however, people began 'to talk loud of the King'; by 19 March, 'All the discourse nowadays is that the King will come again; and for all I see, it is the wishes of all and do believe that it will be so'.[44]

Seeking to prevent what Pepys and many others now believed would come to be, Milton once again sought to enlist the support of military power: after Cromwell and Lambert, now Monck. In *The Present Means, and Brief Delineation of a Free Commonwealth, Easy to be Put in Practice, and Without Delay. In a Letter to General Monk*, a rough draft of less than 1,000 words of either a pamphlet or an actual letter to Monck,[45] written after 22 February,[46] Milton sought to have Monck ensure a republican outcome to the elections. Eligibility to stand for election should be confined to those 'already firm, or inclinable to . . . a free Commonwealth . . . without single person or House of Lords' for otherwise, 'who foresees not, that our

---

[44] Pepys, *Diary*, i. 74, 89, 92.

[45] Like the *Letter* but unlike the *Proposalls*, *The Present Means* was first published in 1698 in Toland, *Works*, ii. 799–800, but, unlike both the *Letter* and the *Proposalls*, no manuscript copy survives. It and the *Letter* were, says Toland, 'communicated to me by a worthy friend who, a little after the author's death, had them from his nephew, and I imparted them to the publishers of the new edition of his Works in folio'. His comment that the text was 'addressed, I suppose, to Monk' indicates that the words *In a Letter to General Monk* were not in the title in the manuscript and were presumably added by Toland himself. The identification is accepted by Woolrych (*CPW*, vii. 189). There is no evidence that the text was ever finished, sent, or printed in Milton's lifetime.

[46] The *terminus a quo* of 22 Feb. is established by references to the 'ensuing Elections' and to the argument for a perpetual council in 'that Book', namely *The Readie and Easie Way* (*CPW*, vii. 392, 394); the *terminus ad quem* seems to be mid-Mar. since the text's trust in Monck's public statements of support for a commonwealth could hardly have survived the Presbyterian votes of 5 Mar., the annulling of the Engagement on 13 Mar., and the opening up of parliamentary candidature to Presbyterians and royalists on 14 Mar.

Liberties will be utterly lost in this next Parlament' (vii. 392–3). The 'Danger and Confusion of readmitting Kingship' (p. 393) and the probability of revenge by a restored Stuart regime should be impressed upon the county gentry to ensure public support, but if, nevertheless, they 'refuse these fair and noble Offers of immediate Liberty' there will, Milton adds ominously, doubtless 'be enough in every County who will thankfully accept them', this being Monck's 'Mind, and [you] having a faithful Veteran Army, so ready, and glad to assist you in the prosecution thereof' (p. 395).[47] Something very like a military dictatorship now appears to be the condition of freedom.

The Second Edition of *The Readie and Easie Way*: Milton and Elections to the Convention, March 1660

The second edition of *The Readie and Easie Way* was explicitly directed to the voting public 'in the midst of our Elections to a free Parlament' (*CPW*, vii. 408). To anticipate publication during the elections of late March and early April, Milton would have had to have worked on the text during March; a reference to the issuing of writs (p. 430) suggests that some at least of the work of revision post-dated 17 March, and Milton's hope that it would be 'freely published' (p. 408) perhaps suggests it was completed before 28 March, when, for 'seditious and treasonable publishing', a warrant was issued for the arrest of Livewell Chapman, the publisher of the tract's first edition (and of *The Likeliest Means*).[48]

There was not the least doubt that the elections would result in an overwhelmingly royalist parliament. The only live political question was whether Charles II would return unconditionally or (as Presbyterians continued to hope) pledged to a reformed national church and a constitutional monarchy. This question Milton refuses to admit, still less answer, but he does sufficiently recognize political reality to work to accommodate Presbyterian opinion in his attempt, even now, to forestall the restoration of monarchy. All references to the Rump are excised, with attendant passages. A long inserted passage surveying the history of the previous twenty years evokes a Puritan heritage shared by Presbyterians and Independents alike. Milton speaks appreciatively of the Presbyterians' attempts to resolve differences with

---

[47] Cf. the reading of the 'admittedly ambiguous jottings' of *The Present Means* as 'advice on a military coup should the elections go against the republicans' (Corns, *Uncloistered Virtue*, 285–6).

[48] In the event, the second edition was surreptitiously printed with the uninformative (and so illegal) imprint 'Printed for the Author, 1660', presumably at Milton's own expense, appearing probably in the first week of April, as argued by Robert W. Ayers in *CPW*, vii. 398–400.

Charles I and of the intentions of the Solemn League and Covenant (pp. 411–22), sentiments the author of *The Tenure of Kings and Magistrates* could never have entertained. There is, too, a shared vulnerability to the threat of Stuart revenge by 'our newly animated common enemies' (p. 452) and 'a standing armie... of the fiercest Cavaliers' (p. 454).[49] There are other shared enemies: the spectres of France and of Popery now haunt the tract (e.g. p. 426).

Nevertheless, Milton's republicanism is not only unqualified but yet more vehemently expressed than in the first edition. Expatiations on the corruptions of what is now explicitly an 'hereditarie' monarchy (vii. 427) add to the extortions of the king those of a royal family: 'There will be a queen also of no less charge; in most likelihood outlandish and a Papist; besides a queen mother... with both thir courts and numerous train: then a royal issue, and ere long severally thir sumptuous courts...' (p. 425). These, with passages arguing for a perpetual senate, nearly double the length of the work. Something of the vituperative and coruscating irony of the 1640s returns: advocates of monarchy are 'tigers of Bacchus... fanatics of not the preaching but the sweating-tub, inspir'd with nothing holier then the Venereal pox' (pp. 452–3). The aristocratic bias of Milton's republicanism remains unchanged. Though he cites historical precedents for his Grand Council, he rejects the democratic corollary of those precedents: while the 'perpetual Senats' of Athens, Sparta, and Rome 'had also popular remedies against thir growing too imperious' in the Athenian citizens' council, the ephors and the tribunes, 'the event tels us, that these remedies either little availd the people, or brought them to such a licentious and unbridl'd democratie, as in fine ruind themselves with thir own excessive power' (p. 438). Rather than allowing 'the noise and shouting of a rude multitude' to determine the outcome of elections 'only those of them who are rightly qualifi'd' should choose (pp. 442–3). And if the resulting Council is unrepresentative, no matter: 'most voices ought not always to prevail where main matters are in question'; what counts is weight of argument, not weight of numbers, 'there being in number little vertue' (p. 415).

And yet, even as the tract works to unite Puritan and oppositional opinion and to reiterate the outlines of a Miltonic constitution, it anticipates its own futility. The tone is now much darker. If the people's 'absolute determination be to enthrall us, before so long a Lent of Servitude, they may permitt us a little Shroving-time, wherin to speak freely, and to take our leaves of Libertie' (vii. 408–9). That valedictory note, here sounded at the end of the first paragraph, recurs throughout the tract, most poignantly in what are almost its final words: Milton should have written as he has 'though what I have spoke, should happn... to be the last words of our expiring libertie' (p. 463). In this last paragraph he now adopts not merely 'the language of the good old cause' (p. 387) but of 'that which is not call'd amiss *the good Old Cause*' (p. 462). To add that pointed affirmation was to bear the resolute and solitary witness of the 'constant' Abdiel and of the 'unchanged' epic poet of *Paradise Lost* (v. 896–903, vi. 29–37, vii. 24)

---

[49] As noted by Corns, *Uncloistered Virtue*, 288–9, which is drawn on here.

BRIEF NOTES: MILTON AND RULE
BY A SINGLE PERSON, APRIL 1660

There was a sad coda to this magnificent peroration. *Brief Notes Upon a Late Sermon*, Milton's final pre-Restoration piece, was written in reply to an intemperately royalist sermon preached on 25 March by an episcopalian cleric, Matthew Griffith, formerly a chaplain to Charles I. Fiercely hostile to the parliamentary cause in the Civil War and to the Interregnum regimes, the sermon looked to a restored Charles II to avenge these evils. When the sermon was published it bore a prefatory dedication to Monck calling on him to complete the work of restoring monarchy upon which he had begun. At this delicate stage, Monck could not yet risk alienating the Army in particular and the body of Presbyterian and republican opinion in general by appearing to accept association with the unconditional return of Charles II. His public commitment was still to a commonwealth. Griffith was committed to Newgate on 5 April. Though immoderate, however, the sermon spoke for an increasingly vocal body of opinion (and, as it turned out, for Monck's own private opinion).

In his response, written in early April,[50] Milton again addresses the Presbyterians, who are 'well forewarnd' by Griffith of the true character of a royalist regime (vii. 485). While he 'trusts' that Monck's actions will be of a piece with his public declarations of support for a commonwealth (p. 471) it seems unlikely that Milton seriously entertained the possibility that these offered good hopes for the future for, in what was surely a despairing moment, he is reduced to proposing that, though there is 'nothing nobler then a free Commonwealth', if the English must prefer the 'thraldom' of government by a single person, then, rather than Charles Stuart, far better a person of their own choosing, 'out of our own number one who hath best aided the people, and best merited against tyrannie', that is, implicitly Monck. By this expedient, 'the space of a raign or two we may chance to live happily anough, or tolerably' (p. 482). Such low expectations are small recommendation: Milton's disappointment is palpable. Even so, what in the first edition of *The Readie and Easie Way* had been dismissed as 'The fond conceit of something like a duke of Venice' to answer 'ambitious ends to a crown' (vii. 375) is now all that can be hoped for. At the last, Milton is reduced to proposing something very like a return to Oliver Cromwell's Protectorate.

---

[50] Reference within *Brief Notes* to Griffith's imprisonment (*CPW*, vii. 486) indicates that it was composed after 5 Apr. and by 20 Apr., the date on the title page of Roger L'Estrange's response, *No Blind Guides*, by which time it must have been in print sufficiently long for L'Estrange to have written his tract.

CHAPTER 18

....

DISESTABLISHMENT, TOLERATION, THE NEW TESTAMENT NATION: MILTON'S LATE RELIGIOUS TRACTS

....

ELIZABETH SAUER

THE critical reception of John Milton's *A Treatise of Civil Power in Ecclesiastical Causes* (1659) and *Considerations Touching the Likeliest Means to Remove Hirelings Out of the Church* (1659) consists of a handful of studies that situate the works in relation to their historico-political and religious contexts and questions of liberty, conscience, and the polemics and poetics of election. This chapter examines more specifically the conjunctions between toleration and nationhood in these late religious tracts and in related literature by Milton's contemporaries.[1] In *The Likeliest Means*, Milton refers,

---

[1] Victoria Silver develops the links between epistemology, legal theory, theology, and equity in 'Milton's Equitable Grounds of Toleration', in Sharon Achinstein and Elizabeth Sauer (eds.), *Milton and Toleration* (Oxford, 2007), 144–70; Susanne Woods studies the form and stylistic features of the tracts as they influence author–text–reader interactions, the destabilization of cultural identity, and definitions of liberty ('Elective Poetics and Milton's Prose: *A Treatise of Civil Power* and *Considerations Touching the Likeliest Means to Remove Hirelings Out of the Church*', in David Loewenstein and James Grantham

as do other advocates of disestablishment, to the 'just petition of many thousands' who offer the Restored Rump in 1659 'new modells of a commonwealth' (*CPW*, vii. 275).[2] Both the 1659 religious tracts interrogate church and state relations in a period when the terms of toleration were central to the formation of nationhood, as evidenced by contemporary writings on the topical issues of church politics, establishment, religious settlement, and the status and rights of subjects.[3] Milton's distinctive contributions to debates on civil and ecclesiastical power and corresponding arguments on toleration are primarily couched in political theology rather than political philosophy.[4] His efforts are ultimately directed at exposing obstructions to the 'freedom' of the church, whose 'better constituting' (vi. 275) is for Milton the foundation for an 'undisturbd' Christian commonwealth (p. 276).

Milton's theory of toleration is discussed here in terms of the relationships between spiritual and temporal authority and the biblical precedents he puts forth for imagining the nation. Applying a largely negative concept of toleration—a resistance to constraints—Milton's religious tracts challenge the forced legal, religious, and dogmatic *settlement* of a nation: a settlement founded on what he judged as a remnant of Deuteronomic law, upheld by English constitutional law. The tracts in turn advance concepts of nationhood that John Lucas characterizes as 'necessarily oppositional' in subsequent decades when the championing of 'private conscience . . . and the spirit of the Commonwealth' threatened the dream of a cohesive nation.[5] Milton uses his polemics on toleration to develop an alternative foundation, typological narrative, and conscience for a New Testament nation.[6]

Turner (eds.), *Politics, Poetics, and Hermeneutics in Milton's Prose* (Cambridge, 1990), 193–211). Compare Harry Smallenburg's stylistic analysis in 'Government of the Spirit', in Michael Lieb and John T. Shawcross (eds.), *Achievements of the Left Hand: Essays on the Prose of John Milton* (Amherst, Mass., 1974), 219–37. See also Barbara K. Lewalski, 'Milton: Political Beliefs and Polemical Methods, 1659–60', *Publications of the Modern Language Association*, 74 (1959), 191–202.

    [2] *Englands settlement, upon the two solid foundations of the peoples civil and religion liberties* (1659) mentions the petition of 12 May 1659, and that of many '*Thousand Gentlemen, Freeholders, &c. Of the County of Kent and City of Canterbury*' (p. 24).

    [3] The crises over toleration were directly related to the uncertain future of the republic and the safeguarding of liberty. See Martin Dzelzainis, 'Milton and the Protectorate in 1658', in David Armitage, Armand Himy, and Quentin Skinner (eds.), *Milton and Republicanism* (Cambridge, 1995), 181–205 at 182.

    [4] See Sharon Achinstein, *Literature and Dissent in Milton's England* (Cambridge, 2003), 129–30; Michael P. Zuckert, *Natural Rights and New Republicanism* (Princeton, 1994), 79; and Robert Thomas Fallon, who maintains that liberty of conscience was for Milton the condition for political freedom (*Milton in Government* (University Park, Pa., 1993), 179, 188, 212).

    [5] John Lucas, *England and Englishness: Ideas of Nationhood in English Poetry, 1688–1900* (Iowa City, Ia., 1990), 12.

    [6] See Adrian Hastings, *The Construction of Nationhood: Ethnicity, Religion and Nationalism* (Cambridge, 1997), 3, and Claire McEachern, *The Poetics of English Nationhood, 1590–1612* (Cambridge, 1996), 12.

I

The competing interests of the early modern nation included civil, religious, and political liberties, as well as 'state and church-government' relations that ranged from disestablishment to comprehension—an ecclesiastical settlement potentially accommodating divergent opinions on non-essential issues in a single institution.[7] The history of the relationship between the temporal and religious powers originated in the Old Testament, as Milton and his contemporaries maintained, and as the political and ecclesiastical documents of the early modern period underscored.[8] Reassessing Old Testament models of law, nationhood, and spiritual and secular authority, Milton's late religious tracts exploit the associations between Judaic–papist practices and monarchical tyranny that reformers and radicals first associated with Henry VIII's supremacy over the English Church. Despite the efforts by the mid-seventeenth-century Interregnum government to grant liberty of conscience by condoning practices and doctrines not in violation of fundamental truths deemed essential to salvation, the founding of a national church through the promulgation of Erastian ecclesiology and the settlement of civic and ecclesiastical power became an integral part of Oliver Cromwell's religious and political policy.[9] Consolidation not mutual respect for difference delineated national boundaries.[10] Furthermore, while intolerance was often reproved, toleration was rarely accorded a positive value.

Milton's identification of the nation with the fight for freedom of conscience and with resistance to a settled religion and nation-state not only prompted the production of *A Treatise of Civil Power* and *The Likeliest Means* but also laid the groundwork for *De Doctrina Christiana*. His major theological treatise continues the work of distinguishing between ecclesiastical and civil power (*CPW*, vi. 611–13) or the policy of the state towards religious dissent and the authority of the civil magistrate. At the same time, the writing of the nation entailed for Milton engagement with documents that discouraged toleration and the exercise of Christian liberty—the foundation for a free commonwealth. Among such documents were the *Humble Petition and Advice* (1657), which demanded a public declaration of faith as confirmation of one's fitness for 'any Civill Trust, Imployment or Promotion in these Nations'; the 1658 *Savoy Declaration of Faith and Order*—a settlement between moderate Independents and Presbyterians, which promoted liberty of conscience, while granting authority in

---

[7] Alexandra Walsham, *Charitable Hatred: Tolerance and Intolerance in England, 1500–1700* (Manchester, 2006), 234. See also John Coffey, *Persecution and Toleration in Protestant England, 1558–1689* (Harlow, 2000).

[8] *Of Civil Power*, in *CPW*, vii, rev. edn., 251; *The humble Advice of the Assembly of Divines . . . sitting at Westminster, Concerning a Confession of Faith* (1647), chs. 20 (pp. 35–6) and 23 (pp. 41–2).

[9] Blair Worden, 'Toleration and the Cromwellian Protectorate', in W. J. Sheils (ed.), *Persecution and Toleration* (Oxford, 1984), 199–233 at 209. On the rise of the Erastian state and the ideal of a national Church, see Walsham, *Charitable Hatred*, 49–92.

[10] Cromwell wanted liberty of conscience only for the 'peculiar interest' of the people of God (*The Writings and Speeches of Oliver Cromwell*, ed. W. C. Abbott, 4 vols. (New York, 1970), iv. 260, 271).

religious matters to civil magistrates—and the Westminster Assembly's *Confession of Faith* on which the *Savoy Declaration* drew, and which in April 1659 was again 'held forth as the public profession of the nation'.[11] In *The Likeliest Means* Milton adds the influential writings of William Prynne, who grounds his argument for tithing in Old Testament traditions, and Henry Spelman, who uses the weight of constitutional history to support his case. Primacy of conscience led Milton in the religious tracts to refute both lines of argument and to situate the controversy over tithing in terms of theories of nationhood and disestablishment.

This commitment to a disestablishment position, on which Milton's theories of toleration and nationhood are based, evolves gradually during his career and shifts in accordance with the historico-political contexts and the inventions demanded by topical issues. Initially Milton had associated the civil magistrate with 'the full and perfet reformation of [God's] Church' (*CPW*, i. 928), though as early as 'Lycidas' he already vilified ministers who serve 'for their bellies' sake' (l. 114). *The Reason of Church-Government* (1642) contains a passage arguing for separation (i. 831–2), while championing popular participation in ecclesiastical government that would grant the regenerate their allotted place 'upon the tabernacle as the rightfull Clergy of Christ, a chosen generation, a royal Priesthood' (p. 838). At the end of the decade, Milton inserts a paragraph in his *Observations* upon the *Articles of Peace* reminiscent of that in *Church-Government* (*CPW*, iii. 310–11). 'On the New Forcers of Conscience' (1646) anticipates *A Treatise of Civil Power* in demanding that the Westminster Assembly 'abjure the civil sword / To force our consciences that Christ set free' (ll. 5–6). Along the same lines, 'To the Lord General Cromwell', responding to the Committee for the Propagation of the Gospel, urges Cromwell to 'save free conscience from the paw / Of hireling wolves' (ll. 13–14). The *Defensio Secunda* (1654; *CPW*, iv. 678) and the 1652 sonnet to Henry Vane also take up this theme, with the latter commending the statesman's awareness of 'Both spiritual power and civil, what each means / What severs each' (ll. 10–11). Earlier in his *Doctrine and Discipline of Divorce*, Milton accorded magistrates—still identified as 'Christian Magistrate[s]' (*CPW*, ii. 239)—a role in upholding Mosaic Law on matters of divorce. By the end of the next decade, Milton renounced Old Testament precedents, particularly as they were used to justify tithing and the magistrate's jurisdiction in ecclesiastical affairs. While Milton's anti-establishment views can be traced in the pre-1659 works, they were not paramount, as Balachandra Rajan reminds us, until Milton confronted the growing scope and complexity of the crisis over toleration.[12] In the year leading up to the Restoration, Milton also fused for a final time his political ambition to defend the Good Old Cause of republicanism, as N. H. Keeble has cogently argued, with the cause of reformation and toleration, which he channelled into the anti-Erastian

---

[11] *The Humble Petition and Advice* (1657), 14; Austin Woolrych, 'Milton and Cromwell, "A Short But Scandalous Night of Interruption"?', in Lieb and Shawcross (eds.), *Achievements of the Left Hand*, 185–218 at 200.

[12] *Milton and the Climates of Reading: Essays by Balachandra Rajan*, ed. Elizabeth Sauer (Toronto, 2006), 143.

sentiment of the 1659 tracts and thereafter into an aggressive assault on popery in *Of True Religion* (1673).[13]

Occupying different positions on the scale of toleration, the writers of the nation in Milton's day turned specifically to questions of church–state relations and the magistrate's authority. While preaching before the House of Commons in May 1647, Thomas Case decried liberty of conscience on the basis that '*freed from the power of Parliaments*, and . . . *Kings* . . . *Liberty of Conscience* (falsly so called) may in good time, improve it self into *liberty* of *estates*, and . . . *houses*, and . . . *wives*'.[14] In stark contrast, Roger Williams, who divorces church and state in a manner unprecedented in the mid-seventeenth century, advocates wide toleration, and presses for disestablishment of the ministry. In *Hireling Ministry None of Christs*, Williams protests against any incursion of the state into spiritual affairs by differentiating between nation-states and the elect nation: 'The body of a civill State or Nation, and the elect or chosen of God out of each Nation, must be rightly distinguished.'[15] The Baptist minister and soon-to-be Quaker Samuel Fisher recommends in *Christianismus redivivus* (1655) that magistrates 'give protection to men . . . without respect to their Religions, whether true or false . . . And . . . to allow Tolleration to all men to practise according to their principles, the practise of whose principles is not directly destructive to the true Religion . . . peace and safety of the Common-wealth.'[16] Among the anti-Baptists whose arguments Fisher refutes is Stephen Marshall—a moderate Presbyterian known to Milton as a Smectymnuuan (see Nigel Smith's essay above, Ch. 8). *The Power of the Civil Magistrate*, a posthumous sermon by Marshall, ascribes the moral well-being of the nation to the rule of magistrates on the basis of Isaiah 60: 12: 'For the Nation and Kingdome that will not serve thee, shall perish; yea those Nations shall be utterly wasted.' Quoting the Congregationalist Divine John Norton, Giles Firmin, the former New Englander and publisher of *The Power of the Civil Magistrate*, concedes: 'It is true what Learned Mr. *Norton* saith, *to Tolerate all things, and tolerate nothing, are both intolerable.*' In conceptualizing toleration negatively, Firmin applies the early modern definition of toleration as limited permission granted by a temporal or ecclesiastical authority: 'When States will make Acts for Toleration in matters of Religion, they had need . . . to declare *what they will NOT Tolerate*: they had need make good fences about the Vitals of Religion, or else we shall have errors arise.'[17]

Central to the debate on toleration was the anatomy of the nation-state and body politic, the conventional view of which the English churchman Robert South endorsed: 'There is a great Analogy between the Body Natural and Politick; in which the

---

[13] See the essay above by N. H. Keeble, Ch. 17.

[14] Thomas Case, *Spirituall Whoredom Discovered in a sermon preach'd before the Honourable House of Commons* (1647), 34.

[15] Roger Williams, *Hireling Ministry None of Christs, or A Discourse touching the Propagating the Gospel* (1652), 18.

[16] Samuel Fisher, *Christianismus Redivivus, Christndom Both un-christ'ned and new-christ'ned* (1655), 537.

[17] Stephen Marshall, *The Power of the Civil Magistrate In matters of Religion, Vindicated* (1657), 3, 21, 21.

Ecclesiastical or Spiritual part, justly supplyes the part of the soul; and the violent separation of this from the other . . . leaves the Body of the Commonwealth a carcass, noysom, and exposed to be devoured by Birds of Prey.'[18] Thomas Collier in *The Decision & Clearing of the great Point now in Controversie* (1659) insists, by contrast, that liberty involves 'untwist[ing] this knot, i.e. unity of Church and State'.[19] Milton more than agrees; transferring his argument from *Tetrachordon* (*CPW*, ii. 651) that it is 'detestable to joyne that . . . which God hath put asunder' to the question of the magistrate's jurisdiction, Milton states in *A Treatise*: 'If church and state shall be made one flesh again as under the law, let it be withall considerd, that God who then joind them hath now severd them' (*CPW*, vii. 260). Indeed the remarriage of church and state which God 'hath now severd' is an act of fornication. In *The Likeliest Means* Milton portrays a state-dominated church as a monstrous 'political head on an ecclesiastical bodie; which at length by such heterogeneal, such incestuous conjunction, transformes her oft-times into a beast of many heads' (vii. 308).

Implied in the argument for disestablishment is a new concept of the Christian church. The early church reformers whose example Milton invokes had imagined the counter-cultural, anti-establishment New Testament community as 'an *ecclesia* called out from among the nations, not a community coterminous with national populations'.[20] In this respect as well the proponents of the New Testament church resisted the idea of a nation-state—involving 'an identity of character between state and people'.[21] In his early polemics on the traditions of the Church of England, Milton maintained that the Christian church was distinct from the Jewish Temple. He continued in this vein in the late religious tracts, insisting in *The Likeliest Means* that the prescriptive Law of Moses was abrogated with the destruction of the temple (vii. 289) and that the true church, unlike that of the Jews with its 'many incomplete synagogues' (p. 292), is independent of a national identity: 'the Christian church is universal; not ti'd to nation, dioces or parish, but consisting of many particular churches complete in themselves' (ibid.). The multifarious corporate identity Milton imagines here thus contrasts with the settled nation-state in consisting of 'many particular congregations, subject to many changes' (p. 308).

The early forms of nationhood were derived from a religious nationalism, 'experienced by the English people as a revival of Old Testament nationalism' and 'inspired by their self-identification with the Hebrews'.[22] But in championing disestablishment, radical tolerationists of Milton's day proposed models based on principles of nature and natural law and resistant to any incursion of civil authorities into

[18] Robert South, *Ecclesiasticall Policy the Best Policy, in Interest Deposed, and Truth Restored . . . in Two Sermons* (Oxford, 1660), 11.

[19] Thomas Collier, *The Decision & Clearing of the great Point now in Controversie about . . . the Civill Magistrate* (1659), 16.

[20] John Coffey, 'Puritanism and Liberty Revisited: The Case for Toleration in the English Revolution', *Historical Journal*, 41 (1998), 961–85 at 973.

[21] Hastings, *The Construction of Nationhood*, 3.

[22] Ernest Barker, *Oliver Cromwell and the English People* (Cambridge, 1937), 167–8.

ecclesiastical affairs, especially as justified by Mosaic Law.[23] Challenging the applicability of the Israel parallel to the primitive church and present-day church in a larger argument that anatomizes William Prynne's proposal for an episcopal government and a national Presbyterian Church, the author of *Certaine briefe Observations and Antiquaeries* (1644) determines that 'The Nationall Church of the Jewes cannot be a patterne for us now, because the covenant of the Gospell is not made with any one particular Nation, as with the Jewes, but to all persons that embrace the Gospell'. Henry Robinson (and Henry Burton) likewise observes that 'in all the New Testament you finde no Nationall Churches, but severall Independent ones'.[24] Rehearsing the argument he presented in an earlier treatise, Roger Williams determines in *Hirelings Ministry* that 'The *Civill* state of the *Nations* . . . cannot (Christianly) be called *Christian States*, after the patterne of that holy and typical Land of *Canaan*, which I have proved at large in the *Bloudy Tenent*, to be a *Non-such*' (p. 3), or, as Milton judges in *The Likeliest Means*, God 'hath now alienated that holy land' (*CPW*, vii. 288).

II

The concepts of Protestant nationhood and citizenship that distinguish Milton's 1659 religious tracts are thus derived from a reformulation of the Old–New Israel parallel. In *A Treatise of Civil Power* Milton repudiates the use of civil power in ecclesiastical causes and transfers authority to the individual conscience. That Milton regards his mission as a writer and polemicist as a national one is underscored by reference to his service to his country, and notably the censure of Salmasius in the *Pro Populo Anglicano Defensio*, which is now converted into a tirade against '*Erastus* and state-tyranie over the church' (*CPW*, vii. 252). In *A Treatise* he pleads for Christian liberty—the freedom won from the bondage of the law and the birthright enjoyed by Christians (vii. 262, 265)—as distinct both from '*civil libertie [of which] I have written heretofore*' (p. 240) in the *Defensio*, and from a birthright enjoyed by citizens of the commonwealth. Indeed the tract foregrounds religious over civil discourses. Conscience serves 'the advancement of religion' in being answerable only to 'the will of God & his Holy Spirit within us, which we ought to follow much rather then any law of man' (vii. 242). Without the separation of civil from religious power,

---

[23] Coffey, 'Puritanism and Liberty Revisited', 976.

[24] *Certaine briefe Observations and Antiquaeries* (1644), 7–8; Henry Robinson [and Henry Burton], *An Answer to Mr. William Prynn's Twelve Questions concerning Church Government* (1644), 7. John Coffey rules out John Goodwin as the author of *Certaine briefe Observations*, suggesting instead Robinson or John Price (*John Goodwin and the Puritan Revolution: Religion and Intellectual Change in Seventeenth-Century England* (Woodbridge, Suffolk, 2006), 301).

'true religion' will succumb to '*inward decay* and will ultimately be overthrown by a *common enemy*' (p. 240).

Given the threats to toleration, Milton's appeals are often rooted as much in a negative toleration as in an embrace of heterodoxy, and involve an assault on error. Thus he admonishes false prophets through 'instant and powerfull demonstration to the contrarie; by opposing truth to error, no unequal match' (*CPW*, vii. 261) and situates 'the right of Christian and evangelic liberty' in contradistinction to 'all those pretended consequences of license and confusion' (p. 270). His earlier polemics against custom and conformity are here directed at the settlement of religion by civil power as justified by Old Testament practices. Whereas Old Israel 'had a commonwealth by [Moses] deliverd them, incorporated with a national church . . . so as that the church might be calld a commonwealth and the whole commonwealth a church', the same, Milton contends, cannot be said of the Christian church 'deliverd without the help of magistrates, yea in the midst of thir opposition' (p. 251). Yet the Protestant reformers who adopted the Old Testament model of governance 'assumed that Protestant churches should also be national, state churches'.[25] Coffey explains that radical tolerationists considered the magisterial reformers' adherence to Old Testament laws an act of 'Judaizing'.[26] In *The Likeliest Means* Milton likewise remarks that the primitive church (until the time of Constantine) did not practise tithing, though 'error' thereafter 'miserably Judaiz'd the church' through the reinstatement of 'priests, altars and oblations' (vii. 290).

Advancing his argument in *A Treatise of Civil Power*, Milton outlines his objections to the office of the magistrates and their acts of compulsion (*CPW*, vii. 256) on the basis that 'our whole practical dutie in religion is contained in charitie, or the love of God and our neighbour, no way to be forc'd, yet the fufilling of the whole law'. He thus denounces Deuteronomic laws, while nevertheless equating freedom from the Law with its fulfilment (ibid.).[27] Settlement and restraint of conscience violate an active faith, the principle of toleration, and the oft-rehearsed Pauline dictate in Romans 13 that '*every soul be subject to the higher powers*' (p. 250). Those who judge the gospel unsafe

unless it be enacted and settled, as they call it, by the state, a statute or a state-religion . . . understand not that the church it self cannot . . . settle or impose one tittle of religion upon our obedience . . . unless they mean to . . . give to the state in thir settling petition that command of our implicit beleef, which they deny in thir setled confession both to the state and to the church. (*CPW*, vii. 257–8)

Milton's derisive references to 'settling' call to mind the *Humble Petition and Advice*, a work that prompted his rebuke of the petitioners' plea that God use Cromwell and the army 'in the Setling and Securing [of] our Liberties' (*Humble Petition*, 2). Upon chastising 'those magistrates who think it their work to settle religion', Milton

---

[25] Coffey, 'Puritanism and Liberty Revisited', 972.

[26] Ibid.

[27] Joan S. Bennett, *Reviving Liberty: Radical Christian Humanism in Milton's Great Poems* (Cambridge, Mass., 1989), 129.

reclaims settlement for 'each particular church by perswasive and spiritual means within it self' (*CPW*, vii. 271). Membership in the true church is dependent upon the exercise of Christian liberty, defined as a birthright (vii. 262, 265), and possible only under the condition of toleration.[28] In turn Milton presents scriptural proofs that underscore the right to religious freedom by relegating authority to God: Romans 14: 6, Galatians 4: 10; Colossians 2: 16, Acts 10: 15; Galatians 5: 13, among others (vii. 263). Recourse to biblical authority, the differentiation between Christian birthright and state citizenship, and the critical engagement with state-issued declarations and legislation underwrite Milton's Christian nation.

Hotly contested in the press and pulpit of the day, the rights of subjects, the authority of magistrates, and the theories and policies on establishment fuelled controversies over the bounds of toleration in the pre-Restoration nation. Marshall's *Power of the Civil Magistrate* (1657) ascribes the health of the nation to the magistrates' role: 'They are to look to the preservation and restauration of Religion: as the Physitian either aimes at the preservation, or restauration of health' (p. 6). Correspondingly, magistrates are morally and legally entitled to 'publique rovisions by Glebes, Tythes, and such publike *stipendia* already setled by law' (p. 7). Giles Firmin, who takes the liberty of adding notes to John Marshall's sermon, cites '*Deut.* 17: 18. a text commonly brought to prove that the Magistrate is *keeper of both Tables*' (p. 10) and insists that 'The Duties of the second table [are] the sinews of Commonwealths' (p. 19)—the second table constituting commandments 6–10 and prohibiting social and civic transgressions. Milton by contrast reminds Parliament of the differences between the state of religion under the gospel and under the law (*CPW*, vii. 259). In the fourth section of *A Treatise*, which argues against the use of compulsion (p. 265), he refutes the teaching 'that the Christian Magistrate is *custos utriusque tabulæ*, keeper of both tables' (p. 271). The magistrates' jurisdiction does not extend to what Milton refers to as the 'inward man', to conscience or religion, on which he bases his arguments for tolerance. Milton, though, is less radical than Roger Williams in still conceding a function for magistrates as civil authorities, specifically in the exorcising of a politicized popery and idolatry (p. 254).

The fight for toleration and disestablishment and the corresponding resistance to the settlement of the national church and ministry take the form of an anti-tithe argument in the sequel to *A Treatise of Civil Power. Considerations Touching the Likeliest Means to Remove Hirelings* appeared in August 1659, following Richard Cromwell's abdication and the reconstitution of the Long Parliament, the Rump, when the ethical and legal question of tithing again came to the fore in the disputes over church–state relations. Petitions from 'many thousands best affected both to religion and to this your returne' are cited by Milton (*CPW*, vii. 275), who addresses the reconvened Parliament. That *The Likeliest Means* is a response to the crises over toleration in an increasingly

---

[28] By instituting Sabbatarianism in particular, the English state 'turnd quite against all other Protestants' (*CPW*, vii. 263). 'An Act of the better observation of the Lord's Day' was passed on 26 June 1657 (*Acts and Ordinances of the Interregnum 1642–1660*, ed. C. H. Firth and R. S. Rait, 3 vols. (1911), ii. 1162–70 at 1167).

oppressed and oppressive nation is evident in a reminder to Milton by Moses Wall about Milton's complaints on 'the Non-progressency of the nation, and of its retrograde Motion of late, in Liberty and Spiritual Truths'. Wall urges Milton to fulfil his promise in *A Treatise of Civil Power* to write a companion treatise on the injustices of hire in the church, on the assumption that economic reforms were most needed to ensure national progress. Fearing that England's leaders may 'lead us back to Egypt', he recommends the 'improving of o^r native Comodities, as our manufacturers... [which] wold give the body of the nation a comfortable Subsistence... [and] breaking that cursed yoak of Tythes wold much help y^{r}to'.[29] While commercial interests and justifications were, along with the biblical, legal, and historically based arguments, central to the anti-tithe movement, Milton steers clear of economic concerns. Rather he broaches the question of toleration in terms of the difference between Old and New Testament models of nationhood and the degree of liberty enjoyed by the subjects thereof. As the Old Israelites had subjected themselves to Egypt, so are the New Israelites enslaved by tithing, Milton judges. John K. Hale recognizes that Milton in 1659 'could expect his fellow religionists to resent the return to an "Egypt" of monarchy, bishops, and tithing'. Accordingly, 'to limit the new Israel to England was impossible to the sincere tolerationist'.[30] The Israel–England parallel remains most relevant for Milton, but from here on it is used to illustrate how far from the peculiar status and from the ideal commonwealth the intolerant, backsliding English had deviated.[31]

The two arms of Antichrist are compulsion and hire, but given the state policy on hirelings, Milton resigns himself to proposing ways of limiting the number of hirelings and curtailing the abuses of hire in the church. His argument is further founded on negative toleration, as underscored by its three parts, in which he contests the recompense due to church ministers, then considers the question of who is responsible for the maintenance of ministers, and finally reviews the administration of the recompense. His strategy throughout involves driving a wedge between the Old and New Testament practices on the basis that 'our ministers at this day, being neither priests nor Levites... can have no just title or pretence to tithes' (p. 284)—an invalidation of *jure divino,* the Mosiac law that awarded the tenth to Levites. Only a New Testament nation—here defined in opposition to a national church modelled on an Old Testament type—can secure liberty of conscience for the people. Reproaching those who support 'their old Papistical tithes' and the 'Judaical or ceremonial law' that justifies tithing, Milton cites 'an express ordinance of the gospel, founded not on any type, or that municipal law of *Moses* [particular to

---

[29] 'Moses Wall to Milton', *CPW*, vii. 510–13 at 511.

[30] John K. Hale, 'England as Israel in Milton's Writings', *Early Modern Literary Studies*, 2/2 (1996), 3. 1–54 at 46.

[31] As Milton's sense of the English nation's peculiar status had been compromised, Christopher Hill's contention that Milton always 'assumed that God had a special interest in the English people' requires qualification (*Milton and the English Revolution* (1977), 282).

Israel] but on moral, and general equitie, given us instead: 1 Cor. 9. 13, 14' (p. 289). Gospel equity is distinguished from the legal equity, as Milton insists that 'a rule of common equitie' does not grant the labourer 'a legal right' to tithes (p. 290).

Anti-tithe advocates like Milton drew on John Selden's *History of Tithes* (1618) to bolster the case for the self-sufficiency of Scripture, expose the injustices of forced tithing throughout history, and to urge the abrogation of Mosaic Law by the New Testament. At the same time, Milton channels his energies into discrediting historically rooted arguments for tithing that determined the direction of and advanced state policy on the subject in his day, notably the Anglican Henry Spelman's 1639 *Concilia, Decreta, Leges, Constitutiones, in re Ecclesiarum Orbis Britannici*, which grounds tithing practices in legal history, beginning with pre-Conquest Britain. Further, Milton refutes the Presbyterian William Prynne's 1653 *A Gospel Plea . . . for the Ancient Settled Maintenance and Tithes* and his 1659 *Ten Considerable Quaeries about Tithes*, which appeared in the month he began composing *The Likeliest Means*. Milton proceeds by challenging justifications for tithing founded on the laws of Saxons and kings whose ancient constitutions were derived from Athelstan (*CPW*, vii. 294), and he exposes the contradictions of 'our new reformed English presbyterian divines' who ransack the authorities they reference and betray the reformation and liberty of conscience by preserving Mosaic laws.

Prynne, who in 1653 uses Spelman as an authority to argue that the maintenance of the ministers was instituted by 'religious Christian Kings and Ancestors' and by divine and civil right, accuses anti-tithe supporters of betraying the public faith and the nation-state. The motives of the opposition, he determines, 'proceed not from any reall grounds of Piety or Conscience' but from a 'designe to subvert and ruine our Ministers, Church and Religion' and thereby 'our Nation'.[32] He complains further that these 'Anabaptists', along with their popish supporters, revile tithing as 'Jewish and Antichristian'. To illustrate his point, Prynne cites a 'new Voice from the Alehouses' by John Canne, 'the old Anabaptist', Canne's *A Voice from the Temple to the Higher Powers* having appeared in June 1653 and his *Second Voyce from the Temple* in August.[33] *A Second Voyce* locates the origins of tithing in popery and decries the present-day 'vest[ing] & settl[ing] [of tithing] in persons Ecclesiastical' by English common law' (p. 12). 'To retein tythes, is to keepe up and give honour to the Jewish shadowes, which by Christs death were taken away' (p. 15), Canne maintains, in line with those who condemned tithing in supporting New Testament nationhood. In his characteristically bombastic retort that features Canne as one of many targets, Prynne brands the opposition as traitors to the nation. The Pope too, Prynne warns, hopes 'to see England perfectly reduced to her former obedience to the See of Rome'; he and his home-grown supporters, the 'professed Enemies of our Church, Religion, Nation', must be prevented from sowing their 'seeds of ruine and desolation amongst us' (sig. b3). That Prynne's indictment of Canne might be extended to

---

[32] William Prynne, *A Gospel Plea . . . for . . . the Ancient Settled Maintenance and Tithes of the Ministers of the Gospel* (Sept. 1653), 4.

[33] Prynne, 'To the Reader', *Gospel Plea*, sig. b1^r.

Milton is suggested by Prynne's attack, several months before the publication of *The Likeliest Means*, on 'Melton', whose subversive writings helped 'justif[y], maintain[], the very highest, worst treasonablest . . . tenents', including the 'subverting of Kingdoms', 'the altering of all setled Laws', and the breaching of the commandments of the second table.[34]

Milton in contrast attributes national upheaval to the betrayal of national election. Peculiar status becomes for him not a confirmation of England's Old Testament nationalism but a condition for the health of the true church comprised of voluntary members in a New Testament 'covnant of union' (*CPW*, vii. 245). In *The Likeliest Means*, the argument for the establishment of the new covenant is overshadowed by an emphasis on the abrogation of the Mosaic Law. National election is thus negatively defined as a rejection of tithes and Old Testament types: '1 *Pet*. 2. 5 signifying the Christian true and *holy priesthood, to offer up spiritual sacrifice*; it follows hence, that we are now justly exempt from paying tithes, to any who claim from *Aaron*, since that priesthood is in us now real, which in him was but a shaddow' (p. 283). Peter razes the social and ecclesiastical hierarchy: 'we are now under Christ a royal priesthood, 1 *Pet*. 2. 9, as we are coheirs, kings and priests with him' (p. 286), a reference which underscores the principle of New Testament equity. However, that chosen status has been misappropriated ever since the days of the early Church by ministers who 'affected to be calld a clergie', and become 'a peculiar tribe of levites, a partie, a distinct order in the commonwealth' (p. 319). This defiled commonwealth has been settled by law and the compulsion of 'notorious hirelings' who assert 'that if ye settle not our maintenance by law, farwell the gospel' (p. 318). By failing to exercise their birthright or their Christian liberty, the nation has become 'as lay-papists are to their priests': a condition which will exacerbate the 'infinit disturbances in the state' (p. 320), Milton prophesies in witnessing to a church and state whose 'settlement' was now again imminent.

III

Debates about the limits of toleration and the terms of national stability continued through the eve of the Restoration. Parliament declared a fast day to appease a God outraged by the heresies that were plaguing the kingdom and by the civil magistrates' failure to enforce the law.[35] In contrast, tracts like *Englands settlement, upon the two solid foundations* associated divine judgements and visitations upon the nation with intolerance and compulsion: '*foul Tyranny* or Coercive power over Mens

---

[34] William Prynne, *A true and perfect Narrative of What was done* (1659), 50, quoted in French, *Records*, iv. 266.

[35] Woolrych, 'Milton and Cromwell', 200.

Consciences, is the principall sin that has drawn down these judgements from Heaven'.[36] According to *Englands settlement*, the settling of 'this state and Government' demands the securing of 'just Civil Liberty' (p. 5), which has, however, been violated by the installation of 'a new Supream Magistrate', the miscarriage of justice which has led to many unwarranted imprisonments, and by excessive taxation (p. 6). The other pillar upon which the nation rests is 'spirituall liberty' (p. 8), secured by 'an innocent Toleration' (p. 9) or an 'in-offensive Toleration in matters of Religion' (p. 11). A nation-state that denies spiritual liberty is in danger of 'ruine and subversion' (p. 10). The author acknowledges Henry Vane, 'H. S.' (Henry Stubbe), and the aforementioned work by Thomas Collier, *The Decision & Clearing*, which opposes the ecclesiastical authority of the magistrate on the basis that the New Testament unlike the Old offers no such precedent (p. 7). *Englands settlement* further refers to the 'Good old cause' as that of toleration (pp. 16, 25), as does Henry Stubbe, who defends 'a just and innocent *Toleration*'.[37] Religious persecution is 'a Bad new Cause'. Even Turks practise conscionable toleration.[38] Milton likewise frames the question of toleration in national and international terms, claiming that persecutory English Protestants betray their moral responsibility on the international stage, and by their example invite other nations to compel them against their conscience (vii. 318).

The competition over the conditions and limits of toleration generated an immediate and blunt retort to *Englands settlement*, titled *Englands settlement mistaken*, which accuses the author of the former of instigating sedition. The confuter insists that magistrates be charged with 'restrain[ing] . . . all Religions, but the true[,] . . . knowing that if variety of Religions be suffered to get footing in a Nation, they will unsettle the peace of the nation'.[39] Since there is only one true religion, dissent is intolerable. Implied disputations between Erastians and proponents of disestablishment are integrated into both of Milton's 1659 religious tracts, with the exchange in *A Treatise* focused primarily on countering the arsenal of biblical support for Erastian arguments, and that in *The Likeliest Means* on the practice by magistrates of exacting fees for weddings and funerals (*CPW*, vii. 298–9). As for generating actual dialogues, there is little evidence that *The Likeliest Means*, like its predecessor, had any impact in its day, though James Harrington refutes some of its key tenets in his insistence that a commonwealth, in conjunction with its Old Testament type, must have a national religion, tithes, and an endowed clergy in order to guarantee liberty of conscience.[40]

---

[36] *Englands settlement, upon the two solid foundations of the peoples civil and religion liberties* (1659), 2, 3.

[37] H.[enry] S.[tube], *The Common-wealth of Israel, or A brief account of Mr. Prynne's anatomy of the good old cause* (1659), 2. Several days beforehand, on 13 May 1659, Prynne published *The re-publicans and others spurious good old cause, briefly and truly anatomized*.

[38] *Englands settlement*, 25, 16, 17.

[39] *Englands settlement mistaken, or, A short survey of a pamphlet called England's settlement* (1660), 9.

[40] See Woolrych, 'Introduction', *CPW*, vii. 55, 94. Harrington's 1659 *Aphorisms Political* probably offers a corrective to *Considerations* (see *Aphorisms*, 35, 37, 38; *CPW*, vii. 521) and *The Censure of the Rota* (1660) reviled Milton as a Church robber (pp. 8–9). In terms of *Of True Religion*, Raymond Tumbleson maintains that Milton's recourse to religious liberty when the political nation was moving on explains the tract's poor reception ('Of True Religion and False Politics: Milton and the Uses of Anti-Catholicism', *Prose Studies*, 15 (1992), 253–70 at 266).

Indeed the Restoration saw the re-establishment of the Church of England, the reinstatement of the Book of Common Prayer, and reinforcement of the civil magistrate's role in securing obedience to the law and ecclesiastical hierarchy. In 1662, the Commons legislated, outside of monarchic jurisdiction, adherence to the Act of Uniformity that identified 'the settling of peace in this nation' with 'the honour of our religion and propagation thereof'.[41] The discourses of uniformity in fact served as sutures for a Restoration nationhood resistant to toleration. Roger L'Estrange, Surveyor of the Press, maintained in his 1663 *Toleration discuss'd* that religious union was 'the Ciment of both Christian, and Civil Societies: Take That away, and the Parts drop from the Body' (p. 86). 'Uniformity if it were carefully maintained, and diligently looked after', as Thomas Tomkins would declare several year later, would 'recall our Ancient Unity'.[42] In 1669 Samuel Parker underscored the necessity of 'severe government over men's consciences and Religious perswasions' on the basis that it was 'absolutely necessary to the Peace and Happiness of... Kingdom'.[43] In the Restoration, moderate Independents like John Owen, Philip Nye, and John Humfrey distinguished between the public sphere and that of the individual, while balancing the subject's liberties with the civil and ecclesiastical jurisdiction of magistrates.[44] Milton persists in advocating a divorce between temporal and spiritual power, though *Of True Religion* accommodates conciliatory gestures, including a declaration of allegiance to the universally held Protestant 'Principles of true Religion' (*CPW*, viii. 420).[45] His primary strategy involves consolidating and galvanizing the Protestant community through an anti-popery campaign designed to extend the bounds of toleration to the nonconformist-minded.

More forcibly than in the 1659 tracts, Milton establishes the case for toleration negatively in arguing against Popish tyranny. *Of True Religion* was produced in reaction to the use of civil power in ecclesiastical causes and in particular to the 1673 Test Act that was implemented to protect the state, quiet the minds of the king's 'good subjects', and enforce uniformity by requiring office holders to demonstrate publicly their allegiance to the established Church, thus targeting Catholics and inadvertently Nonconformists.[46] Milton further decries Anglican policies towards Nonconformists, fines for religion being against 'the Clemency of the Gospel, more then what appertains to the security of the State' (*CPW*, viii. 431). Again his appeal for toleration is founded on claims of conscience, scriptural authority (p. 423), as well as

---

[41] *English Historical Documents 1660–1714*, ed. Andrew Browning (1953), 377–82 at 378.

[42] Roger L'Estrange, *Toleration discuss'd. By Roger L'Estrange* (1663), 86; Thomas Tomkins, *The Inconveniences of Toleration* (1667), 6.

[43] Gordon Schochet, 'Samuel Parker, Religious Diversity, and the Ideology of Persecution', in Roger D. Lund (ed.), *The Margins of Orthodoxy: Heterodox Writing and the Cultural Response, 1660–1750* (Cambridge, 1995), 119–48 at 132–4.

[44] Gary S. De Krey, 'Rethinking the Restoration: Dissenting Cases for Conscience, 1667–72', *Historical Journal*, 38 (1995), 53–83 at 57–60.

[45] See Elizabeth Sauer, 'Milton's *Of True Religion*, Protestant Nationhood, and the Negotiation of Liberty', *Milton Quarterly*, 40 (2006), 1–19 at 9–12.

[46] 'An Act for preventing dangers which may happen from Popish recusants' (1673), in *The Stuart Constitution: Documents and Commentary*, ed. J. P. Kenyon, 2nd edn. (Cambridge, 1986), 385.

in anti-Catholic sentiment. Citing a politicized popery as the worst example of the enmeshing of secular and religious authority, Milton can in good conscience concede to the magistrates a role in resisting this 'Roman principalitie' as a civil offence and national threat: 'supported mainly by a civil, and, except in *Rome*, by a forein power', Catholicism is 'justly therfore to be suspected, not tolerated by the magistrate of another countrey', Milton stated in *A Treatise* (*CPW*, vii. 254). In *Of True Religion*, magistrates are urged to root out popery even more aggressively on the basis that the Pope has sought 'to destroy both King and Parliament'. 'Whether therefore it be fit or reasonable, to tolerate men this principl'd in Religion towards the State', Milton continues, 'I submit it to the consideration of all Magistrates . . . As for tolerating the exercise of their Religion . . . I answer, that Toleration is either public or private; and the exercise of their Religion, as far as it is Idolatrous, can be tolerated neither way' (viii. 430). The intensified hostility towards Catholicism in the Restoration treatise is evident in the differences between this statement and his earlier remarks on the policing of Catholicism: 'a magistrate can hardly err in prohibiting and quite removing at least the publick and scandalous use' of idolatry (vii. 254–5). In *Of True Religion*, papists have relinquished their right not only to public but also private worship; in both spheres, they have indentured themselves to external, foreign authorities. Milton simultaneously seizes the opportunity to attack Charles II's 1672 indulgence of Catholics 'in the common Exemption from the execution of the Penal Laws, and the Exercise of their Worship in their private Houses'.[47] Translating what he calls 'state-tyranie' in *A Treatise* (vii. 252) into an attack on popery in *Of True Religion*, one for which he anticipated wide support, Milton reins in toleration in order to argue from a position of strength and accommodation in a Protestant nation.

A contrast between the New Testament church and the Jewish state church is the basis for the distinction between a catholic Protestantism and the parochial 'Roman principalitie': 'Catholic in Greek signifies universal: and the Christian Church was so call'd, as consisting of all Nations to whom the Gospel was to be preach't, in contradistinction to the Jewish Church, which consisted for the most part of Jews only' (*CPW*, viii. 422). John Hale validly observes that 'advocating liberty of worship predisposes the poet against the Israelite analogy, which in practice if not in principle also resisted universalization'.[48] In the case of *Of True Religion*, the universality of the Christian Church is specifically established through its opposition to 'the common adversary' (p. 420), and its differences from Judaism.

Among the expressions of comprehension and solidarity in *Of True Religion* are appeals to a shared Protestant faith and concessions to a theological reductionism that identifies commonalities among the co-religious and national documents that institutionalize the faith. Milton's uncharacteristic defence of the Church of England's Articles of Religion (*CPW*, viii. 419)—which contrasts with his rebutting of scriptural proofs in the Articles' previous dogmatic and confessional

---

[47] *His Majesties Declaration to all his Loving Subjects, March 15th 1671/2* (1672), 7.
[48] 'England as Israel', 6.

incarnations—can be explained by his efforts to align Nonconformist religious principles with the national religion largely by opposing them with Catholic dogma. Recourse to Scripture and scriptural authorities provides the platform from which he lashes out at popery and pleads for toleration of sects: 'Another means to abate Popery arises from the constant reading of Scripture, wherein Beleivers who agree in the main, are every where exhorted to mutual forbearance and charity one towards the other, though dissenting in some opinions' (viii. 435). Milton reminds his readers in *Of True Religion* that 'Our Church . . . hath proposd [the Bible] to all men, and to this end translated it into English' (p. 434), an extension of his claim in *The Likeliest Means* that Protestantism 'make[s] more easie the attainment of Christian religion by the meanest: the entire scripture translated into English with plenty of notes' (vii. 304). His diatribes in *The Likeliest Means* (pp. 302, 320) against Protestants who fail to practise an active faith are likewise recalled in *Of True Religion*, in which their remissness has national implications and consequences: scriptural ignorance which 'cheifly upholds Popery' threatens to ruin the Reformation nation, both as a religious and political entity (viii. 435).

What are the outer limits of toleration for Protestants? 'If it be askt how far they should be tolerated? I answer doubtless equally, as being all Protestants . . . For if the *French* and *Polonian* Protestants injoy all this liberty among Papists [of public speaking, writing, and printing], much more may a Protestant justly expect it among Protestants' (*CPW*, viii. 426–7). Toleration is commanded by the gospel, Milton avers, and yet as he concedes at the heart of his pamphlet, 'some times here among us, the one persecutes the other upon every slight Pretence' (p. 427). A moral and international awareness about English policies on toleration gives way to an injunction to purge popish practices among the natives, with the weight of judgement falling on English Protestant intolerance and a compromised national election: 'it is a general complaint that this Nation of late years, is grown more numerously and excessively vitious . . . no wonder if Popery also grow a pace' (viii. 438–9). 'The heaviest of all Gods Judgements, Popery' (p. 440), Milton prophesies, will be visited upon the nation for the collusion between church and state and for its moral degeneracy.

The Old Israel–New Israel parallel that characterizes the literature on English nationhood is not ultimately invalidated by the complication and reassessment of peculiar status; the parallel serves rather as a tragic reminder of New Israel's violation of its rights and obligations as a tolerant nation. The marriage of Crown and Church had once been imaginable when the Church constituted the nation in Hebrew society (*CPW*, vii. 292) and when the civil magistrate could ensure the 'reformation of his Church' (*CPW*, i. 928). But disestablishment emerged as the only conscionable solution in a time of corruption and climate of intolerance. Justification for this separation had less to do with complaints about the Judaizing practices of officials— which reformers nevertheless cited since the days of John Foxe—than with the betrayal of the modern nation's elect status. In *A Treatise of Civil Power*, Milton chides the Erastians for propping up their case for establishment with examples of Old Testament rulers who exercised both ecclesiastical and state authority. Times have now changed, retorts Milton: 'To little purpose will they here instance *Moses*, who did all by immediate divine direction, no nor yet *Asa*, *Jehosaphat*, or *Josia*, who both might when they pleasd receive answer from God, and had a commonwealth by him deliverd them, incorporated with a national church' (*CPW*, vii. 251). Though Milton equates idolatrous Judaic and papist rituals throughout his writings, including in the late religious tracts, his argument for disestablishment is founded on his reproof of the magistrates' inability or failure to imitate their godly Old Testament counterparts. In an era when toleration was vital to the health of a liberty-loving English nation, the state had overstepped its authority by policing matters of conscience.

This chapter has sought to assess the competing and correspondent relationships of toleration and nationhood in the pre- and early Restoration years, as negotiated in Milton's late religious tracts. At a time when the majority supported establishment and the reinstatement of a national religion, Milton upheld a minority, oppositional position, that severed Christianity and national election from Jewish antecedents. The sinews for the regenerate commonwealth Milton imagines are reasoned biblically based arguments that expound New Testament values, gospel equity, and freedom of conscience, and that are conveyed in the vernacular and in a consciously unadorned style. In turn Milton identifies the subject and architect of the nation as one who is answerable to spiritual authority independent of temporal power. Furthermore, in the midst of the crises over toleration, he envisages a disembodied nation in contradistinction to the body politic and settled nation-state.[49] During the Restoration, a turbulent era of national self-fashioning, the polemicist modulates that antithetical relationship into an argument for the comprehension of all Protestants, including Nonconformists. At the same time *Of True Religion* is the product of a particular moment of fierce anti-Catholic agitation. In championing a common national cause, Milton offers a programme of reform based on a dialectical model of toleration and politicized anti-popery, captured in his judgement that Protestants, by adhering to the 'Word of God only' and renouncing an implicit popish faith, would 'cut off many Debates and Contentions, Schisms and Persecutions,... and more firmly unite against the common adversary' (*CPW*, viii. 420); indeed 'no true Protestant can persecute, or not tolerate his fellow Protestant, though dissenting from him in som opinions, but he must flatly deny and Renounce these two his own main Principles, whereon true Religion is founded' (pp. 420–1).

---

[49] Christopher Hill, 'The Protestant Nation', in *The Collected Essays of Christopher Hill*, ii: *Religion and Politics in Seventeenth-Century England* (Brighton, 1986), 21–36 at 28.

CHAPTER 19

....

MILTON AND NATIONAL IDENTITY

....

PAUL STEVENS

AT a critical moment in *The Tenure of Kings and Magistrates* (1649) Milton insists that principle transcends national identity—that affiliation to one's country is simply not enough:

Who knows not that there is a mutual bond of amity and brother-hood between man and man over all the World. . . . Nor is it distance of place that makes enmitie, but enmity that makes distance. He therfore that keeps peace with me, neer or remote, of whatsoever Nation, is to mee as farr as all civil and human offices an Englishman and a neighbour: but if an Englishman forgetting all Laws, human, civil and religious, offend against life and liberty, to him offended and to the Law in his behalf, though born in the same womb, he is no better then a Turk, a Sarasin, a Heathen. (*CPW*, iii. 214–15)

This often quoted passage, together with one from the poet's response to Peter Heimbach in August 1666, has come to constitute the *locus classicus* for Milton's abjuration of what we might call English 'nationalism'.[1] No one doubts his early

---

[1] For more discussion of these passages, see e.g. the separate essays by David Loewenstein, Joad Raymond, and Paul Stevens in David Loewenstein and Paul Stevens (eds.), *Early Modern Nationalism and Milton's England* (Toronto, 2008). On Milton and nationalism in general, see Lawrence Lipking, 'The Genius of the Shore: "Lycidas", Adamastor, and the Poetics of Nationalism', *Publications of the Modern Language Association*, 111 (1996), 205–21; Paul Stevens, ' "Leviticus Thinking" and the Rhetoric of Early Modern Colonialism', *Criticism*, 35 (1993), 441–61; 'Milton's Janus-Faced Nationalism', *Journal of English and Germanic Philology*, 100 (2001), 247–68; 'Milton's "Renunciation" of Cromwell: The Problem of Raleigh's *Cabinet-Council*', *Modern Philology*, 98 (2001), 363–92; 'Milton's Nationalism and the Rights of

investment in the English nation, but from the evidence of passages such as these it seems clear that by 1649 he was increasingly capable of reflecting on the limitations of national identity and by 1666 quite indifferent to the particular nation that had betrayed his best hopes. None of the three great Restoration poems on which his historic reputation rests seems centrally or directly concerned with England. In the Latin letter to Heimbach, written just after the worst of the Great Plague was over, he sounds philosophical. He takes the virtues the unctuous German councillor attributes to him and focuses on 'the one you call *Policy*' but which 'I would prefer you call *Patriotism*' (*CPW*, viii. 4). While the other virtues have sustained him, he says, the siren sounds of Patriotism have led him adrift: 'having allured me by her lovely name, [Patriotism] has almost *expatriated* me, as it were'. Devotion to his country has ironically led to the loss of that country. As he was church-outed by the prelates so many years before, he now feels excluded by his own nation. This, as it turns out, so the letter infers, is not such a bad thing. The singing of the other virtues—such universals as Charity, Piety, Prudence, Learning, and 'fairest' Humanity—all sound so 'well together', he concludes, that one's *Patria* may not be a geographical place at all, but 'wherever it is well with him', that is, wherever those virtues are (viii. 2, 4). As he dictates his letter to a boy who knows no Latin, he imagines himself a member of a community of the virtuous, an ideal *Patria* beyond nation or state. Neither of these moments of transcendence is, however, quite what it appears to be. For at no point in his career, so I want to suggest, does Milton forsake his simultaneous commitment to both the absolute and universal, on the one hand, and the contingent and particular, on the other. For all his musing, he never quite leaves England behind, and once these passages are contextualized they begin to look surprisingly different.

Milton's impassioned insistence on principle over national identity in the *Tenure* is, of course, highly problematic, since the universal brotherhood he appeals to does not extend to Turks, Saracens, or other non-Christians. This solecism is important for a number of reasons. First, it suggests the haste, the speed and energy, with which he writes. The *Tenure* was written in three or four weeks during January–February 1649 (*CPW*, iii. 184–8). As with so many of his pamphlets, Milton writes 'vehemently', that is, like Luther he writes out of the ardency of his spirit (i. 901).[2] This means that

---

Memory', in Elizabeth J. Bellamy, Patrick Cheney, and Michael Schoenfeldt (eds.), *Imagining Death in Spenser and Milton* (2003), 171–84; 'Intolerance and the Virtues of Sacred Vehemence', in Sharon Achinstein and Elizabeth Sauer (eds.), *Milton and Toleration* (Oxford, 2007), 243–67; 'Milton's Polish Pamphlet and the Duke of Monmouth: Longing for a Hero', *Milton Studies*, 48 (2008), 72–94; Nicholas von Maltzahn, 'The War in Heaven and the Miltonic Sublime', in Alan Houston and Steve Pincus (eds.), *A Nation Transformed: England after the Restoration* (Cambridge, 2001), ch. 6; Johann P. Sommerville, 'Literature and National Identity', and Derek Hirst, 'Literature and National Identity', in David Loewenstein and Janel Mueller (eds.), *The Cambridge History of Early Modern English Literature* (Cambridge, 2002), chs. 15 and. 21; Andrew Escobedo, *Nationalism and Historical Loss in Renaissance England: Foxe, Dee, Spenser, Milton* (Ithaca, N.Y., 2004), chs. 4–5; Elizabeth Sauer, 'Milton's *Of True Religion*, Protestant Nationhood, and the Negotiation of Liberty', *Milton Quarterly*, 40 (2006), 1–19; Rachel J. Trubowitz, 'Body Politics in *Paradise Lost*', *Publications of the Modern Language Association*, 121 (2006), 388–404.

² See Stevens, 'Intolerance and the Virtues of Sacred Vehemence', 251–6.

there is a high degree to which his work is what we would call journalistic, occasional, not quite under the kind of control he routinely claims for it. He often betrays sentiments he might well disown on careful reflection. Not long after dismissing national identity as a guiding principle in the *Tenure*, for instance, he is happy to revert to his native English strain, forget the universal brotherhood of man, and in his 1651 *Pro Populo Anglicano Defensio* revile his French adversary Salmasius (Claude de Saumaise) explicitly for his foreignness: 'I tell you, you foreigner who are a complete stranger to our affairs, I, an eye-witness and a native, tell you that we "removed from our midst" a king who was neither "good" nor "just", but a tyrant.'[3] Distance of place now seems to matter a great deal, and distance clearly makes for enmity, as is evident in the Frenchman's antipathy, like that of Shakespeare's French aristocrats before Agincourt, to the English as bloody and remorseless hounds. Far from transcending the national slur, Milton returns it in kind: 'It offends you now, being a Frenchman and a vagabond, that the English are "more ferocious than their own hounds", as your doglike eloquence has it' (*Political Writings*, 74–5).[4] Increasingly, in a highly charged text like the *Defensio* the discussion of principle, even in the presence of an international audience, gets caught up in a weakness for national stereotyping.[5]

Equally important, Milton's exclusion of Turks and Saracens from universal brotherhood in the *Tenure* reveals a deep-rooted orientalism. This contempt for the East and its various nations is not merely a function of his Christian aversion to heathens but much more pointedly of his classical disdain for Asiatics. As he explains in the *Defensio*, both Aristotle and Cicero bear witness that while all 'the peoples of Asia easily endure servitude' some like the Jews and Syrians 'have been born to it' (*Political Writings*, 80).[6] But if Asian nations are the weakest, the most prone to slavery, then they are merely part of a continuum: the truth is that most nations, whether from East or West, are doomed never to remember the civility, the 'Laws, human, civil and religious' considered so fundamental in the *Tenure*—few 'want their freedom', that is, the true liberty made possible by law, 'or are able to make use of it' (p. 80), he argues, but among those few are the English. Their revolution and the removal of the tyrant Charles I, he insists, was truly exceptional: 'with such greatness of mind as has scarcely been heard of in any record, [the English] struggled out of and overcame not only armed enemies, but the inwardly hostile—that is,

---

[3] *John Milton: Political Writings*, ed. Martin Dzelzainis (Cambridge, 1991), 3.

[4] Milton is responding most immediately to Salmasius' identification of the English with the Molossian hounds of Lucretius' *De Rerum Natura*, 5. 1063, but given Milton's familiarity with *Henry V* it is difficult not to imagine he is also thinking of Orleans's gibe in III. VIII. 128.

[5] In the *Philippics*, Milton's model for the *Defensio*, it is true that Cicero indulges a taste for nationalist contempt. In *Philippic* 5, for instance, he reviles his antagonist, M. Antonius, for appointing Greeks to serve as jurymen in Roman courts: 'My heart yearns to plead for a defendant in that court', he says ('Avet animus apud consilium illud pro reo dicere'; 5. 5. 14). The point is, however, that Cicero is addressing a Roman not an international audience. Cicero is quoted from *Philippics*, trans. Walter C. A. Ker (1926; repr. Cambridge, Mass., 1957).

[6] On Milton's responses to the East, see e.g Robert Markley, *The Far East and the English Imagination, 1600–1730* (Cambridge, 2006), esp. ch. 2, and Gerald Maclean, 'Milton, Islam, and the Ottomans', in *Milton and Toleration*, 284–98.

superstitious—opinions of the mob, and created for themselves in general the title of Deliverers thereafter amongst all peoples' (p. 75). For Milton, in the early republic, Englishness is repeatedly associated with the heroic refusal to 'offend against life and liberty', and the passage from the *Tenure* might be read not so much as a rejection of national identity as a call to live up to its promise. The period of the early republic may be the high point of Milton's nationalism but, despite many arguments to the contrary, it never completely disappears.[7]

Most dramatically, in *Of True Religion* (March 1673), seven years after his letter to Heimbach and only eighteen months before his death, Milton feels anything but expatriated. He rejoices in what he considers England's national recovery: 'God hath giv'n a heart to the people' (*CPW*, viii. 417). In forcing Charles II to cancel his 1672 Declaration of Indulgence—a piece of prerogative legislation that in granting limited toleration to dissenters had also offered relief to Catholics—English Protestants, both conforming Anglicans and dissenters themselves, had come together to oppose the growth of popery. For Milton, the English had remembered who they were—a people defined by their desire for freedom, by their historic deliverance from 'Popish thralldom' and their ability to value the enabling gift of the gospel, 'so freely and so peaceably injoy'd among them' (viii. 417). Milton happily offers to rejoin the national community in its efforts to defend itself against Rome: 'I thought it no less then a common duty to lend my hand', he says, 'how unable soever, to so good a Purpose' (viii. 417–18). Though considerably more subdued and narrowly focused on religious toleration than in the heady days of the early republic, Milton seems confident that the English are undergoing some kind of regeneration. The key phrase with which the pamphlet opens, 'God hath giv'n a heart to the people', is an allusion to the reversal of Israel's fate and its rebirth in Ezekiel's valley of dry bones: 'A new heart also will I give you, and a new spirit will I put within you: and I will take away the stony heart out of your flesh, and I will give you an heart of flesh' (36: 26). It is the same passage that God the Father invokes in *Paradise Lost* to articulate the workings of prevenient grace: 'I will clear their senses dark, / What may suffice, and soften stony hearts' (iii. 188–9). The Father speaks these words in response to the Son's intercession on behalf of humankind: the Son's critical speech comes at the point in the poem where Milton, imitating Venus' intercession on behalf of the Trojans in the *Aeneid* (i. 223–96), offers a God's-eye perspective and reverses humankind's fate to show that Satan's apparently triumphant story is merely a part of God's own providential narrative.[8] Here in *Of True Religion* the same kind of reversal seems to be under way. What seems most remarkable, then, is that despite England's innumerable failures and Milton's other-worldly concerns, the 'nation' remains a central category through which he continues to think and feel right up to the end of his life.

---

[7] See e.g. Thomas N. Corns, 'Milton and the Limits of Englishness', in *Early Modern Nationalism and Milton's England*.

[8] For more on the relation of Milton's divine council to those of the *Iliad*, *Odyssey*, and *Aeneid*, see Paul Stevens, *Imagination and the Presence of Shakespeare in 'Paradise Lost'* (Madison, Wis., 1985), 145–77. See also Martin Dzelzainis's essay on *Paradise Lost* below, Ch. 31.

What I want to do in this essay is come to a better understanding of why exactly this is the case.

Milton clearly inherited a rich and powerful sense of national identity, that is, a very specific sense of what it meant to be an Englishman, but what makes him so interesting is his agonistic relation to the nation from which he derived that identity—agonistic both in terms of his idealistic determination to develop and reshape the identity he had inherited and his complex response to the various pressures that would try and disrupt his community-inspired self-fashioning project, especially during the tumultuous period of the Commonwealth. My analysis thus seeks to answer three questions: first, what was the national identity he inherited? Second, how did he try to reimagine it? And third, how did he react to the collapse of popular support for the Commonwealth over its course between 1649 and 1660? Let me begin with the national story into which he was born.

INHERITANCE: ENGLAND'S STORY

During his second year at Cambridge, probably in the autumn of 1626, the 17-year-old Milton wrote a miniature epic poem in Latin celebrating the anniversary of the thwarted Gunpowder Plot, 'In Quintum Novembris'. The fifth of November had by this time become one of the focal points of England's new national narrative, a narrative that was rapidly writing over, assimilating, and soon to replace the old British narrative inherited from Geoffrey of Monmouth and embellished by early Tudor propaganda. While the old story, the story of Britain from its foundation by Brutus through a long line of kings to its *Götterdammerung* under King Arthur in the days of the encroaching Saxons, could be adapted for the purposes of the Reformed religion, the new story was exclusively Protestant. The old story, recast in its most sophisticated form by Spenser, persists in Milton certainly through the 1640s, especially when he wants to think of England in its most expansive form as the senior polity among the British archipelago's three kingdoms.[9] When he does so, England becomes, somewhat confusingly, 'Britain', 'these British Islands', or even '*this Britannick Empire*' built up to such a 'glorious and enviable height, with all her Daughter-Ilands about her' (*Of Reformation, CPW*, i. 614). But here, in 'In Quintum Novembris', the focus is almost entirely on the new narrative, and the poem assumes its audience's complete familiarity with this emphatically Protestant story.[10]

---

[9] And, of course, the principality of Wales, 'An old, and haughty nation proud in arms' (*A Maske*, l. 33).

[10] On the power and resilience of the old story, see e.g. Graham Parry, *The Trophies of Time: English Antiquarians in the Seventeenth Century* (1995; repr. 2007); Escobedo, *Nationalism and Historical Loss*; and Philip Schwyzer, *Literature, Nationalism and Memory in Early Modern England and Wales* (Cambridge, 2004). On the establishment of the new narrative, see e.g. David Cressy, *Bonfires and Bells: National Memory and the Protestant Calendar in Elizabethan and Stuart England* (1989).

As Ernest Renan suggests in his remarkable account of nation-formation, national cultures draw enormous strength and definition from the memory of some original disaster: 'suffering in common unifies more than joy does', he argues, and where 'national memories are concerned, griefs are of more value than triumphs, for they impose duties, and require a common effort'.[11] In the new English narrative, the original disaster or holocaust was the Marian persecution of 1553–8. In representations such as Foxe's *Acts and Monuments*, the fires of Smithfield are apocalyptic precisely because they reveal the demonic reality of Catholicism—its superstition, cruelty, and irredeemable tyranny, the degree to which it is in fact only a parody of true religion. The Gunpowder Plot was as important as it was in the national imaginary because its horrors as detailed in what we would call the media—in sermons and broadsides, in such popular works as Francis Herring's *Pietas Pontificia* (1605) and its various translations, and uncritically reproduced in works like Milton's poem—promised to renew that original disaster at an unprecedented level.[12] As the adolescent Milton's Satan explains to his agent, the Pope, 'If you explode gunpowder under the foundations of the building in which they [King and Parliament] are assembled you will be able to tear them limb from limb and limb, scatter them in the air and burn them to cinders.'[13] At one blow, you will thus destroy the nation's governing elite. Then, after either French or Spanish troops have overwhelmed the 'still panic-stricken' people, 'the Marian regime [*Saecula Mariana*] will at last be re-established in that land'.[14]

England's story is not without its triumphs but these appear as acts of God's saving grace, moments of providential deliverance from the impending threat of Catholicism. The threat is always there and requires constant vigilance. The most important of these triumphs, second only to the thwarting of the November plot, was the defeat of the Spanish Armada in 1588. Hence Milton's Pope is urged to remember the past: 'Avenge the scattered Spanish fleet! Avenge the Iberian standards overwhelmed in the deep and the bodies of so many saints nailed to the shameful cross during the Amazonian virgin's recent reign.'[15] What defines the English is then not their ethnicity, nor even, per se, their language, manners, or laws, but their story. It is a story that announces the English as a nation foremost in God's favor, possessing a character uniquely inclined to the pursuit of religious liberty, jealous of its political sovereignty, and confident in its civility. England is no longer the distant home of

---

[11] Ernest Renan, 'What is a Nation?' (1882), in *Nation and Narration*, ed. Homi K. Bhabha (1990), 19. Benedict Anderson's influential concept of nations as 'imagined communities' clearly owes much to Renan's seminal essay, *Imagined Communities: Reflections on the Origin and Spread of Nationalism* (1983; rev. edn., 1991), esp. 187–206, and also Antony Easthope, *Englishness and National Culture* (1999), esp. 33–5.

[12] See e.g. Cressy, *Bonfires and Bells*, 141–55, and Richard F. Hardin, 'The Early Poetry of the Gunpowder Plot: Myth in the Making', *English Literary Renaissance*, 22 (1992), 62–79.

[13] 'Hos tu membratim poteris conspergere in auras, / Atque dare in cineres, nitrati pulveris igne / Aedibus iniecto, qua convenere, sub imis' (ll. 119–21).

[14] 'Perculsosque metu subito, casumque stupentes / Invadat vel Gallus atrox, vel saevus Iberus. / Saecula sic illic tandem Mariana redibunt, / Tuque in belligeros iterum dominaberis Anglos' (ll. 125–8).

[15] 'Et memor Hesperiae disiectam ulciscere classem, / Mersaque Iberorum lato vexilla profundo, / Sanctorumque cruci tot corpora fixa probrosae, / Thermodoontea nuper regnante puella' (ll. 102–5).

Virgil's barbarous British tribes, 'wholly sundered from all the world', but in its Reformation history, in its opposition to Satan and the servility of Rome, the locus of an exceptional nation.[16] Milton invokes the testimony of Satan to confirm this point: 'I have wandered over the whole world', the Devil says, 'and this is the only thing that brings tears to my eyes; this is the only nation that rebels against me, spurns my government and is mightier than my crafts.'[17]

In his magisterial *Forms of Nationhood* Richard Helgerson suggests the degree to which the identity produced by this story at its most apocalyptic or impatient of constituted worldly authority was not unconflicted.[18] Against the narrative as articulated most powerfully in Foxe's *Acts* (1563), he opposes the apologetic historicism of Hooker's *Laws of Ecclesiastical Polity* (1593), a text that rejects the typological confidence of Foxe's history and insists on looking at events in all their contingency and 'circumstantial particularity'.[19] At the end of Book 4, for instance, when Hooker considers 'God's special Providence over England', he is struck by its unpredictability. The Marian persecution baffles him. After the signal achievements of 'Edward the Saint', all is suddenly lost. 'But what ensued?' he asks in some confusion. All the great work of reformation 'was in short space so overthrown, as if almost it had never been'.[20] The persecution continues unabated until equally unpredictably God reverses things: God

whose property is to shew his mercies then greatest when they are nearest to be utterly despaired of, caused in the depth of discomfort and darkness a most glorious star [Queen Elizabeth] to arise, and on her head settled the crown, whom himself had kept as a lamb from the slaughter of those bloody times; that the experience of his goodness in her own deliverance might cause her merciful disposition to take so much delight in saving others, whom the like necessity should press. (i. 487)

This focus on God's unknowability, on the way he keeps the Elizabethan settlement 'so strangely' (p. 488), allows Hooker space for the free play of his historicist inclinations, and somewhat paradoxically, he deploys this method, so Helgerson argues, to empty time, demystify change, and establish a vision of England that is more synchronic than diachronic, a vision in which the emphasis falls on the precariousness of the order to be preserved rather than the promise of its millenarian end. It is in the tension between Hooker and Foxe, in these two distinct but related Protestant views of England that Helgerson sees the genesis of the Civil War, the division between those who felt reform had gone far enough and those who felt it had only begun. Unlike his vision, Hooker's historicist way of reasoning, his insistence that events signify themselves and nothing else, will play an increasingly important

---

[16] 'et penitus toto divisos orbe Britanno' (*Eclogues*, 1. 66). Virgil is quoted from *Eclogues, Georgics, Aeneid*, trans. H. Rushton Fairclough, 2 vols. (Cambridge, Mass., 1999–2000).

[17] 'Atque pererrato solum hoc lacrymabile mundo / Inveni, dixit, gens haec mihi sola rebellis, / Contemtrixque iugi, nostraque, potentior arte' (ll. 40–2).

[18] Richard Helgerson, *Forms of Nationhood: The Elizabethan Writing of England* (Chicago, 1992), 249–94.

[19] Helgerson is quoting Debora Shuger, *Habits of Thought in the English Renaissance: Religion, Politics, and the Dominant Culture* (Berkeley, 1990), 32–3.

[20] *The Works of Mr. Richard Hooker*, ed. John Keble, 3 vols., 5th edn. (Oxford, 1865), i. 487.

role in Milton's thinking, but in 1626, in 'In Quintum Novembris', just as Hooker refuses to challenge the overall shape of the Elizabethan settlement's heroic narrative, so Milton is happy to reproduce the same narrative as though it had already achieved its purpose. Milton's poem ends in triumph, bonfires blaze, and young people dance in crowds: 'in all the year', he concludes, 'there is no day more celebrated than the fifth of November' ('quintoque Novembris / Nulla dies toto occurrit celebrator anno') (ll. 225–6).

At this point, then, the narrative is normative: it embraces the most divisive range of Protestant constituencies and is not confined to an educated elite. As David Cressy has shown, the narrative is naturalized and extended to all in the transformation of the nation's annual calendar. The annual progress of holidays is changed to make the memory of national events coincide with the cycle of the seasons: for most English people time past comes to be experienced as a drama 'written by God, a succession of warning disasters and providential escapes', says Linda Colley, which the English act out every year as a way of reminding themselves who they are.[21] Most importantly, it functions as a common framework through which all kinds of Protestant confessional identities can be expressed. And in Milton's case, it provides the public framework through which 'John Milton, Englishman' or 'Joannes Miltonius, Anglus', as he began styling himself in 1638, comes to understand his personal development and most treasured identity.[22]

One of the most striking features of 'In Quintum Novembris' is the degree to which it anticipates Milton's greatest and in many ways most personal poem, *Paradise Lost*. The national story of the English as it is told in 1626 adumbrates and in certain specific ways makes possible the universal story of humankind as it is told in 1667/1674—the earlier poem provides a template for the plot of the later one. If Milton's paradise in the later poem, his 'happy rural seat of various view' (iv. 247), is, as John Broadbent pointed out many years ago, 'almost laughably the England of Penshurst, Cooper's Hill and Appleton House', then Milton's Jacobean England in the Latin poem is quite clearly a version of paradise.[23] As Satan roams the world, he discovers Albion: suddenly 'white cliffs and rocks with roaring breakers come into view' and '[a]s soon as he catches sight of the island, blessed with wealth and joyful peace, with its fields cram-full of Ceres's gifts and—what pained him even more—its people worshipping the sacred powers of the true God, he breaks into sighs that stink of hellish flames and yellow sulpher'.[24] It is England's paradisal happiness, just as it will be Adam and Eve's 'happier Eden' (iv. 507), that excites Satan's anger and envy, and precipitates his epic plan to subdue the inhabitants and, in this case, re-establish his rule through the '*Saecula Mariana*'. But just as it is in *Paradise Lost*, so here Satan's

[21] Linda Colley, *Britons: Forging the Nation, 1707–1837* (1992; repr. 1996), 20, summarizing Cressy's argument.

[22] French, *Records*, i. 419, and Stevens, 'Milton's Janus-Faced Nationalism', 255.

[23] John B. Broadbent, *Some Graver Subject: An Essay on 'Paradise Lost'* (1960), 184.

[24] 'Iamque fluentisonis albentia rupibus arva / Apparent . . . At simul hanc opibusque et festa pace beatam / Aspicit, et pingues donis Cerealibus agros, / Quodque magis doluit, venerantem numina veri / Sancta Dei populum, tandem suspiria rupit / Tartareos ignes et luridum olentia sulphur' (ll. 25–6, 31–5).

disorder turns out to be merely a part of God's order. At a pivotal point in the poem, a point which looks back to the divine council in Book 1 of the *Aeneid* and rehearses the great reversal of perspective in Book 3 of *Paradise Lost*, God is discovered watching Satan's plan as it unfolds: he 'looks down and laughs at the vain attempts of the evil mob', for he already has it in mind 'to defend His people's cause Himself'.[25] And so he does, not through the agency of the Son, and the heroic struggle of our first parents to hear and respond to God's Word, but here somewhat anti-climactically through the confused words of rumour. If it is true that only in *Paradise Lost* does Milton fully realize what he considers his God-given vocation, his true identity, then that identity is quite literally inscribed in his country's story—critically, it is inscribed in the reversals guaranteed by God's special providence over England. All this is made explicit in the famous introduction to the second book of *The Reason of Church-Government* (1642), where it becomes clear that the national identity that Milton inherited is not so much a state of being as one of becoming.

REIMAGINATION

England's Discipline and Milton's Calling

While 'In Quintum Novembris' ends in triumph, sixteen years later *The Reason of Church-Government* opens in a state of enormous tension. Things look different now. On the eve of the Civil War, England and its identity seem anything but secure. As Milton has matured in understanding, and as Charles I's personal rule has consigned the English—not the king, as Milton pretends—to grind like blind Samson 'in the prison house of their [the Bishops'] sinister ends and practices' (*CPW*, i. 859), so Foxe's diachronic view of England and its revolutionary potential, his emphasis on the continuing struggle for reform, has broken the consensus and reasserted itself.[26] For Milton change is imperative. England may be a great and warlike nation, but its defining story is in danger—so much so that it may in fact be illusory. The year before in his first ever political pamphlet, *Of Reformation*, Milton had expressed his doubts very clearly. The contemplation of England's past glory now produces dismay; it leads him into 'a serious question and debatement with my selfe' (i. 525):

how should it come to passe that *England* (having had the *grace* and *honour* from God to bee the first that should set up a Standard for the recovery of *lost Truth*, and blow the first

---

[25] 'Interea longo flectens curvamine coelos / Despicit aetherea dominus qui fulgurat arce, / Vanaque perversae ridet conamina turbae, / atque sui causam populi volet ipse tueri' (ll. 166–9).

[26] The role of Samson is formally assigned to Charles but Milton is, fairly obviously, using the king as a synecdoche for the people. On Foxe, see e.g. Paul Christianson, *Reformers and Babylon: English Apocalyptic Visions from the Reformation to the Eve of the Civil War* (Toronto, 1978).

Evangelick Trumpet to the *Nations*, holding up as from a Hill, the new Lampe of *saving light* to all Christendome) should now be last, and mostly unsettled in the ways of *Peace*, whereof she taught the way to others. (ibid.)

Like Hooker, he is baffled by the way things have turned out: 'the *Precedencie* which God gave this *Iland*, to be the first *Restorer* of *buried Truth*, should have been followed with more happy successe, and sooner attain'd Perfection' (p. 526). But unlike Hooker, his response is more openly active. The problem now becomes pressing: how are the English to facilitate the kind of reversal, the revolutionary response to saving grace, imagined in the national story and given such prominence in both 'In Quintum Novembris' and *Paradise Lost*? Milton's solution is evident in the answer to a more immediate question.

It is difficult to read *The Reason of Church-Government* without wondering why in the midst of a public tract written against a particular form of ecclesiastical government Milton should suddenly choose to disclose his most private, poetic vocation. What's poetry got to do with it? The problem is exacerbated by the way the celebrated autobiographical passage is routinely abstracted from its polemical context and anthologized. Milton offers many tactical reasons why he should 'venture and divulge unusual things of my selfe' (*CPW*, i. 808), largely to do with establishing his integrity or 'the ethos of the rhetor', but the strategic answer to this apparent discontinuity between the tract's argument and the poet's disclosure lies in the concept of 'discipline'. By discipline Milton means the ordering of those practices by which doctrine, which is the substance of true religion, may be taught and put into effect; that is, the practical means by which the grace which will return England's story to its proper course may be heard and acted on. Unlike discipline as command and control, the kind of juridical, Presbyterian discipline Hooker both admires and suspects in Calvin, discipline in Milton is from the beginning a matter of preaching that is emphatically pedagogical.[27]

Discipline as a form of teaching itself needs to be immediate, practical, hands-on, and in order to underline this, Milton regularly characterizes instruction as though it were the work of a medical doctor. In *Of Reformation*, for instance, discipline is 'the execution and applying of doctrine home', not the salve itself but the means of laying 'the salve to the very *Orifice* of the *wound*' (i. 526). In *The Reason of Church-Government*, it is the 'practick' work of instruction 'directed and apply'd as is most requisite to particular duty', that is, a matter of feeling pulses and making out prescriptions (i. 755–6). Milton is most immediately concerned with the confessional community of the church, but at the beginning of the tract he very deliberately extends the concept to explain the workings of all communities: 'He that hath read with judgment, of Nations and Common-wealths, of Cities and Camps of peace and

---

[27] What Hooker suspects is the universal claims Calvin makes for his particular form of church government: 'That which Calvin did for establishment of his discipline, seemeth more commendable than that which he taught for the countenancing of it established' (i. 138). For Arthur Barker, *Milton and the Puritan Dilemma* (Toronto, 1942), Milton is already distinguishing himself from his Presbyterian allies by substituting a 'democratical' for an 'aristocratical' form of discipline (p. 32).

warre, sea and land, will readily agree that the flourishing and decaying of all civill societies, all the moments and turnings of humane occasions are mov'd to and fro as upon the axle of discipline' (i. 751). It soon becomes clear that the government of the church cannot be divorced from the discipline of the nation: 'I shall . . . not cease to hope', he says, 'that England shortly is to belong, neither to See Patriarchall, nor to See Prelaticall, but to the faithfull feeding and disciplining of that Ministeriall order' first constituted by the apostles (p. 749). Only the faithful feeding and disciplining of the English can save the nation, both church and state. After agonizing for years over what he was to do with his life—'as yet obscure, & unserviceable to mankind', he says to a friend in 1633 (*CPW*, i. 319)—he becomes even more confident that poetry might be seen as a practical form of preaching and that his own poetry is the peculiar means by which he might contribute to the discipline of the nation. His personal identity as a poet is thus validated by the needs of his country's identity. This, the degree to which the nation liberates the subject's desire, is at the heart of Milton's nationalism: thoughts of writing a poem that posterity would 'not willingly let die' (i. 810) have possessed him 'ever since I could conceiv my self any thing worth to my Countrie' (p. 820)—that is, conceiving or being himself is to a critically important extent a matter of being of worth to his country, and writing himself becomes a matter of writing the nation. As Louis Althusser might have put it, Milton is 'interpellated' or called into being by the nation.[28]

According to Colin Kidd in his influential book, *British Identities before Nationalism*, 'nationalist thinking is alien to the early modern period'.[29] But the case of Milton, as of so many others, suggests otherwise. It suggests, as I have argued elsewhere, that the imagined community of the nation is not contingent on any narrow sense of English ethnicity—that it does not stand in opposition to the 'claims of church, confession, kingdom, and constitution' (p. 1), as Kidd contends, but rather, in the nation's extraordinarily powerful and already deep-rooted narrative, it comes to serve as their matrix or crucible.[30] Milton's confession in *The Reason of Church-Government* makes this perfectly clear. His inchoate desire to 'conceiv' or realize himself and fulfil his vocation is given form and coherence by the urgency of the crisis in which his country now finds itself. The poetry that reveals who he is may be deeply expressive and ambitiously aesthetic, but it is immediately legitimized by being pragmatic—that is, by having a practical purpose in the world, and that purpose is national. '[C]ontent with these British Ilands as my world', he now knows that he must write a poem 'doctrinal and exemplary to a Nation' (i. 812, 815). He has to contribute to the faithful feeding and disciplining of the English by producing poetry as though it were some form of medical practice: he must work 'to imbreed and cherish in a great people the seeds of vertu, and publick civility, to allay

---

[28] See Louis Althusser, *Lenin and Philosophy and Other Essays* (1971; repr. New York, 2001).

[29] Colin Kidd, *British Identities before Nationalism: Ethnicity and Nationhood in the Atlantic World, 1600–1800* (Cambridge, 1999), 5.

[30] See Paul Stevens, 'How Milton's Nationalism Works', in Loewenstein and Stevens (eds.), *Early Modern Nationalism and Milton's England*.

the perturbations of the mind, and set the affections in right tune' (pp. 816–17). What's poetry got to do with it? If 'discipline is the practick work of preaching' (p. 755), then poetry, to the extent that it is of 'power beside the office of a pulpit' (p. 816), is disciplinary. It can, in fact, help turn the axle of the nation's discipline towards the reception of God's redemptive grace.

England's Academy, or the Nation Reimagined

In the event, disciplining the nation turns out to be a process of reimagining it, for if the nation's story and its needs give form to individual aspiration, then equally so that desire gives form to the nation. Milton's vision of England developed dramatically over the course of the 1640s—if not in poetry itself, then in prose often so poetic that, as David Norbrook has suggested, Milton's emphasis on the distinction 'should not be taken fully at face value'.[31] In that poetic prose, discipline and doctrine come increasingly to mirror each other—there is a degree to which the medium becomes the message. As Milton dedicates himself to disciplining the nation, it comes to be recreated in the image and likeness of the kind of community he knows best; that is, the kind of pedagogical community that had most enabled him. It may be a republic but it is a republic of letters. It is a humanist academy where teaching is revealed as an intensely dialogic activity and liberty is the power to imitate God's own creativity in the 'industry of free reasoning' (*Doctrine and Discipline of Divorce*, CPW, ii. 224).

At the height of the Civil War, in November 1644, Milton published *Areopagitica*. For Norbrook, this is Milton at his most sublime. Milton's England, he argues, is recreated in the image of Athenian democracy with all the cultural and political capital that the identification of parliamentary England with the elegant humanity of Greece might generate.[32] So it is, but it is a very bookish Athens, and there are moments when it seems more accurate to say it is recreated in the image of an idealized St Paul's School, Christ's College, or Hartlib circle. As England responds to God's prevenient grace, as it turns on the axle of discipline and succeeds 'beyond a *Roman* recovery' in reversing 'the very steepe disadvantage of tyranny and superstition' (ii. 487), Milton urges Parliament to reflect on who exactly the English are: 'Lords and Commons of England, consider what Nation it is wherof ye are, and wherof ye are the governours' (ii. 551). Not surprisingly, it appears as a remarkably educable nation, one whose academic inclinations and intellectual acuity are a lot like Milton's own: just as he sees his own life 'wholly dedicated to studious labours' (ii. 489–90), so England appears similarly committed. At this point, England seems like an unusually gifted student, 'a Nation not slow and dull, but of a quick,

---

[31] David Norbrook, *Writing the English Republic: Poetry, Rhetoric and Politics, 1627–1660* (Cambridge, 1999), 136.

[32] Ibid. 118–39.

ingenious, and piercing spirit, acute to invent, suttle and sinewy to discours, not beneath the reach of any point the highest that human capacity can soar to' (ii. 551). Indeed, if the war is to be won, the intellectual authority of the people and all this energy has to be acknowledged and unleashed. To a degree that would have as-tounded war leaders, both contemporary and more recent, the arsenal of democracy or 'shop of warre' is felt to be of less importance than the bustling conference of scholars who seem to populate the public sphere of Milton's polis—the 'pens and heads', sitting 'by their studious lamps, musing, searching, revolving new notions and idea's wherewith to present, as with their homage and their fealty the approaching Reformation' (ii. 554). Most importantly here, this intellectual energy is made the enabling condition, if not the direct cause, of the grace that will return England to its proper course. England's intellectual vitality and history of 'learning in her deepest Sciences' clearly has something to do with the special favour and love God has for us: Why else was England chosen to initiate the original Reformation? Milton asks. 'Why else was this Nation chos'n before any other' (ii. 551–2)? The critical point is the relation between education and grace, the relation at the heart of civility and made explicit by Milton just before the publication of *Areopagitica* in his tract *Of Education* (June 1644):

The end then of learning is to repair the ruins of our first parents by regaining to know God aright, and out of that knowledge to love him, to imitate him, to be like him, as we may the neerest by possessing our souls of true vertue, which being united with the heavenly grace of faith makes up the highest perfection. (ii. 367)

Education is imagined as both being facilitated by and facilitating grace. It is this relation which, according to Milton, ultimately explains the triumph of the Revolu-tion and the heroic success of the English of 1649 in remembering 'all Laws, human, civil and religious', and refusing to 'offend against life and liberty' (*CPW*, iii. 214–15). This is what he means by their 'greatness of mind' (*Political Writings*, 75) and what leads him to invest so heavily in the sovereignty of their will (iii. 202–3).

There is clearly a degree to which Milton's vision of England is solipsistic but that solipsism is as important as it is because it is the key to the nation's extraordinarily *affective* power. It is worth remembering, says Benedict Anderson, 'that nations inspire love, and often profoundly self-sacrificing love'.[33] The English nation is the object of such emotional intensity in Milton, not because it is a particular kind of polity, an abstract republic or free commonwealth, but because it can be reimagined as one: that is, his own native community, the one he grew up in with all its innumerable and indefinable sensible associations, historically 'ever famous, and formost in the atchievements of liberty' (*CPW*, ii. 505), has the potential, once reimagined, to give private citizens like himself what they most lack. The nation, increasingly refigured as a republic or free commonwealth, answers directly to Milton's impassioned desire for liberty of conscience and the unfettered pursuit of learning: 'Give me the liberty to know, to utter, and to argue freely according to

---

[33] *Imagined Communities*, 141.

conscience above all liberties' (*CPW*, ii. 560). This individualistic vision is not, however, entirely solipsistic. Among those pens and studious heads he idealizes are real people, admired friends and sympathizers as diverse as Lady Margaret Ley and the great scholar John Selden, the late Lord Brooke, the bookseller George Thomason and his wife Catherine, students like Cyriack Skinner and Edward Phillips. According to Ernest Renan, a nation is defined by two principal elements: first, 'a rich legacy of memories' held in common, or what I have been calling England's story; and second, 'present-day consent, the desire to live together, the will to perpetuate the value of the heritage that one has received in an undivided form'.[34] For Milton, the defining value of the nation's memories or heritage is, in a way it was not for many poorer English Protestants, the enabling relation between education and grace, and what I have been calling England's discipline is the means by which this value may achieve common consent among the nation's people.[35] Milton's republicanism begins as a function of his nationalism in the specific sense that a free commonwealth emerges as the proper form to perpetuate what he imagines to be the nation's historic values. Norbrook acknowledges that 'English republicanism emerged in part as a vehicle for English nationalism',[36] but he does so only to emphasize the English republic's tendency to aggressive expansion. My point is quite different. I make the relation between republicanism and nationalism to emphasize the republic's potential to *enable* all those various forms of individual liberty, religious, political, and social, which Milton at his most optimistic felt to be rooted in the English nation's providential story. This vision, moving as it is, leads Milton to a radical overestimation of both the learning of the people and the related conviction that the temple of the reimagined nation might be constructed out of 'many moderat varieties and brotherly dissimilitudes' (ii. 555). The period 1649–60 is the bruising story of the consequences of this act of overestimation.

REACTION

England's 'People' and its Discontents

For many years, Milton considered his greatest achievement to be the *Defensio*, his 1651 defence of the English people. He gloried in the book's success and republished a fuller version of it in October 1658 a few weeks after Cromwell's death. At the end of his *Defensio Secunda* of 1654, he represented the work of both books as an epic

---

[34] 'What is a Nation?', 19.
[35] See Paul Stevens, 'John Bunyan, the Great War, and the Political Ways of Grace', *Review of English Studies*, 59 (2008), 701–21.
[36] *Writing the English Republic*, 20.

achievement, implying that he had perhaps effectively redeemed his promise in *The Reason of Church-Government* to write a poem 'doctrinal and exemplary' to the nation: 'I have borne witness', he says, likening himself to an epic poet, 'I might say I have erected a monument that will not soon pass away, to those deeds [of my fellow countrymen] that were illustrious, that were glorious, that were almost beyond any praise, and if I have done nothing else, I have surely redeemed my pledge' (*CPW*, iv/i. 685). The subject of the epic story is the Revolution, the casting off of tyranny in the state and superstition in the church, and the hero of the story is the English people, a hero every bit as worthy, so he says, as Achilles, Ulysses, or Aeneas. The implication is that the English have so turned the axle of discipline that God's grace has brought about a deliverance even greater than that of 1588 or 1605.[37] Milton's determination to write contemporary history in an epic strain, to explain England's success in terms of her people's 'greatness of mind', forces him to emphasize their learning or educability. As a result, when Salmasius insists otherwise, when he repeatedly points to the ignorance and vulgarity of the English, he brings Milton's *agon* to the surface.

Milton's immediate response to his French adversary is, as we saw above, one of scorn and defiance, slight regard and contempt: 'Now see how I, one of those Englishmen whom you often dare to call "frenzied, unlearned, unknown and wicked," scorn and mock you' (*Political Writings*, 77). But Milton's grand gesture of solidarity with the humblest of his countrymen belies the weakness of his argument: 'Whoever from those "dregs of the common people"', he admonishes Salmasius, has persuaded himself 'that he was born not for the benefit of kings, but for God and his country, should be judged much more learned indeed than you, much wiser, much more honest and useful for every life. For he is learned without letters, [just as] you are lettered without learning' (ibid.). The assertion that it is adequate for the people to be 'learned without letters' cuts right at the heart of Milton's great argument, for it is precisely the industry of free reasoning, the trial of intellectual effort within the bounds of faith, that makes the English who they are. Without the effort of learning, the people's understanding, their very agency, is not their own, but merely 'implicit' or 'imputed'. They are anything but true warfaring Christians. As the Royalist commentator, Sir Robert Filmer, pointed out shortly after the publication of the *Defensio*, the argumentation gets even weaker when Milton has to respond to Salmasius' charge that the Revolution was not so much the will of a sovereign people as a coup, the violent act of a military faction.[38] In Milton's less than impressive

---

[37] Milton makes the point this way at the beginning of *Defensio Secunda*: 'First [I am grateful] that I was born at a time in the history of my country when her citizens, with pre-eminent virtue and a nobility and steadfastness surpassing all the glory of their ancestors, invoked the Lord, followed his manifest guidance, and after accomplishing the most heroic and exemplary achievements since the foundation of the world, freed the state from grievous tyranny and the church from unworthy servitude' (*CPW*, v/i. 548–9).

[38] *The Originall of Government* (Feb. 1652), in Sir Robert Filmer, *Patriarcha and Other Writings*, ed. Johann P. Sommerville (Cambridge, 1991). References cited in the text. On Filmer's response to Milton, see *Political Writings*, pp. xxiii–xxv, and Victoria Kahn, 'Milton's Disappointed Nationalism', in Loewenstein and Stevens (eds.), *Early Modern Nationalism and Milton's England*. See also *CPW*, iv/i. 112–23.

response, the people gradually disappear: the soldiers who took part in Pride's Purge of December 1648 first represent the majority of the people, then a minority, even though the 'better' or 'healthier' part, and finally, merely their own officers who were determined to protect the now cleansed house of Parliament from 'the unruly workmen and shopkeepers of London' bent on besieging it (*Political Writings*, 181–2). The people are only the people, a sceptic might say, when they agree with the policies Milton, now a paid spokesman for the government, endorses. Martin Dzelzainis may be right to point out just how conventional it was for advocates of popular sovereignty to speak of the people in qualitative terms, that is, in terms of 'the weightier part' legitimately representing the whole (*Political Writings*, p. xxiv), but no matter how conventional, the argument does not answer Filmer's telling objection. If a state is to invest sovereignty in the will of the people, it is crucial to know who exactly the people are, and in this case, says Filmer, even the most learned cannot agree on the term's meaning (p. 197). If it is not the whole, if it is only 'the "sounder, the better, and uprighter" part [who] have the power of the people, [then] how shall we know, or who shall judge who they be?' (pp. 198–9). Milton's solipsism, the English people as a projection of his own learned self, has come home to roost, and Filmer can hardly contain his laughter.

What Milton will not admit in the *Defensio*, what ultimately makes it, in Ernest Sirluck's words, such 'a radically inconsistent book', is that like his fellow humanist, his adversary and secret sharer, Salmasius, he now has little or no confidence in the English people as a whole.[39] This has been a long time coming. In his darkest moments over the course of the 1640s, even while extolling the natural pliancy and proneness of the English 'to seek after knowledge' (*Areopagitica*, *CPW*, ii. 554), he frequently doubts their ability to learn. Most famously, possibly as early as 1648, before the Army's purge, as his own Hooker-like historical research into England's origins and the machinations of the Presbyterian-led Long Parliament coincide, he wonders about the natural aptitude of his countrymen. In the digression originally placed at the head of Book 3 of *The History of Britain* but never published in his lifetime, he puts it this way:

For Britain (to speake a truth not oft spok'n) as it is a land fruitful enough of men stout and courageous in warr, so is it naturallie not over fertil of men able to govern justly & prudently in peace . . . Valiant indeed and prosperous to winn a field, but to know the end and reason of winning, unjudicious and unwise, in good or bad success alike unteachable. (*CPW*, v/i. 451)[40]

Milton's anguish is palpable. The only solution he seems to be able to imagine at this point is the importation of learning from abroad, but even as he searches for an answer he begins to reformulate his understanding of the English people. According to Sirluck, over the period 1649–54, under pressure from the people's repeated

[39] Ernest Sirluck, 'Milton's Political Thought: The First Cycle', *Modern Philology*, 61 (1964), 209–24 at 214.

[40] See Nicholas von Maltzahn, *Milton's* History of Britain: *Republican Historiography in the English Revolution* (Oxford, 1991), ch. 2.

failures and despite what he represents as their epic success, Milton makes two critical moves: first, the definition of popular sovereignty quietly shifts from the 'sovereignty of the people's will' to that of their 'welfare';[41] and second, the custodianship of that welfare shifts from the elected representatives of the people in Parliament to the 'regenerate', those so transformed by grace whether inside or outside Parliament that it could not be doubted.[42] In the digression, the first move, the shift to the sovereignty of the people's welfare, is evident in the way he asserts that change will be effected, not by the people themselves, but only by an educated elite—only if our affairs are conducted by 'men more then vulgar, bred up . . . in the knowledge of Antient and illustrious deeds, invincible against money, and vaine titles, impartial to friends and relations' (CPW, v/i. 451). Popular sovereignty redefined as the sovereignty of the people's welfare renders Filmer's objection irrelevant. The people can now be the whole people again because their very divisions and confusion only testify to the need for a strong hand not to deny their educability but to direct it. The 'moderat varieties and brotherly similitudes' are not to be suppressed but orchestrated by a leadership that is clearly identifiable as regenerate, and in the *Defensio Secunda* such leadership, Milton feels, is mercifully provided by Cromwell.

England's Hero and the Nation's Defining Value

What is remarkable about Milton's retreat from 'the sovereignty of the people's will' is, then, that his reimagination of England's historical identity, with its emphasis on the relation between education and grace, is not so much abandoned as refocused or displaced. As David Loewenstein puts it, Milton 'carried his ideal of England with him' through a bewildering range of political vicissitudes.[43] After whatever real support there was for the Revolution began to wither, after the dissolution of the Rump Parliament in April 1653 and the inauguration of the Protectorate the following December, Milton placed that ideal, the potential of the English people to be educated into true liberty and so realize their destined end, in the custody of the Lord Protector. In the final pages of the *Defensio Secunda*, Milton acknowledges the failure of the Rump and emphasizes the regenerate nature of Cromwell's leadership. In its refusal to dissolve itself and honour the people's trust, so he says, the Rump had revealed just how much it had become the creature of 'private interest' (CPW, v/i. 671). At the same time, Cromwell's sanctification appears self-evident. Whoever now doubted the safety of the nation, he assures Cromwell, 'does not have sufficient faith even in God himself', especially when 'he sees God everywhere so favorable to you, so unmistakably on your side' (p. 670). In a move that returns us to the core of Milton's

---

[41] 'Milton's Political Thought', 233.

[42] Ibid. 234.

[43] David Loewenstein, 'Milton's Nationalism and the English Revolution: Strains and Contradictions', in Loewenstein and Stevens (eds.), *Early Modern Nationalism and Milton's England*, 43.

thought, Cromwell's sanctification or providential *virtù* is understood as having been facilitated by his virtue, itself a function of his moral education. Grace cannot be earned but learning virtuously pursued can make one more able to hear and respond to God's guidance, and so Cromwell's astounding military success in reuniting all three of Britain's kingdoms is paradoxically unremarkable (v/i. 667–8). The conquest of England and Wales (1648), Ireland (1649–50), and Scotland (1650–1) is prefigured in his complete conquest of himself: 'Commander first over himself . . . he had learned to achieve over himself the most effective triumph, and so, on the very first day that he took service against an external foe, he entered camp a veteran and past-master in all that concerned the soldier's life' (v/i. 668). In Milton's fertile imagination, Cromwell is not a necessary evil, but a new manifestation of the nation; that is, in the way this unique individual is identified with the national community, the Lord Protector's *virtù* is made to embody and reassert England's exceptionalism. Nowhere is this more evident than in Milton's appropriation of the republican notion of reduction.

In David Norbrook's *Writing the English Republic* 'reduction' is a recurrent concern. As he points out, the concept comes from Machiavelli's *Discourses*.[44] In terms of the state it refers to the frequent need to reduce the polity to first grounds or first principles (*ridurre ai principii*) in order to maintain or restore it. In terms of the individual it means self-abnegation, and reduction to first principles in governance is often brought about by individual acts of self-abnegation. Machiavelli's great example from antiquity, Norbrook notes, is Lucius Junius Brutus' 'calling for the death sentence on his own sons to be executed when they resisted the republican government'.[45] Most strikingly, Norbrook deploys this concept of reduction to bring to light the republican tenor of God's sacrifice of his Son in *Paradise Lost*. The Son reduces himself by becoming mortal in order to restore humankind to its original condition—the divine hero's act of reduction enabling the human community's elevation and so precipitating the great reversal in humankind's fortunes.[46] Abdiel understands the very begetting of the Son in Book 5 as a prefiguration of this climactic act of elevating reduction. The purpose of the begetting was not to 'make us less', he patiently explains to Satan, but 'rather to exalt / Our happy state under one head more near united': 'he the head / One of our number thus reduced becomes, / His Laws our laws, all honour to him done / Returns our own' (v. 828–31, 842–5). This is a wonderfully suggestive argument, but for whatever reason Norbrook chooses not to emphasize the degree to which Milton's Cromwell in the *Defensio Secunda* anticipates the Son's reduction. He certainly discusses the key passage, but his interest seems to lie elsewhere.[47]

---

[44] Norbrook (*Writing the English Republic*, 97) acknowledges his debt to Victoria Kahn, 'Reduction and the Praise of Disunion in Machiavelli's *Discourses*', *Journal of Medieval and Renaissance Studies*, 18 (1988), 1–19, for bringing the concept to his attention.

[45] *Writing the English Republic*, 97.

[46] Ibid. 472–9.

[47] Ibid. 335–7.

Before God the Son offers to reduce himself, to become 'mortal to redeem / Man's mortal crime' (iii. 214–15), he makes an extraordinary act of faith in God the Father's grace (iii. 144–66). What is extraordinary about it is the way in which the speech-act's *illocutionary* force seems at odds with its *perlocutionary* force. That is, the Son expresses himself as someone whose very being is defined by his faith in the Father's actions even as he pointedly warns the Father against not performing those actions. The speech-act splits between affirmation and admonition. To a degree that seems remarkably revealing about the intensity of Milton's commitment to the English nation, the Son's speech rehearses Milton's own act of faith in Cromwell's providential *virtù*, a speech-act that similarly splits between affirmation and admonition. The Son expresses complete confidence in the Father's determination to save humankind even as he threateningly warns him that 'should man finally be lost ... So should thy goodness and thy greatness both / Be questioned and blasphemed without defence' (iii. 150, 165–6). At the same time, just as he challenges the Father, he reasserts his faith by representing himself as the antitype or fulfilment of Abraham before Sodom and Gomorrah in Genesis 18: 25: to abandon humankind, says the Son paraphrasing Abraham, 'That be from thee far, / That far be from thee, Father, who art judge / Of all things made, and judgest only right' (iii. 153–5). In the *Defensio Secunda*, a similar pattern occurs. Milton expresses complete faith in Cromwell's determination to save the nation even as he pointedly warns him against failing to do so. Cromwell is explicitly identified with the republican hero L. J. Brutus (*CPW*, iv/i. 682) and Milton's faith is focused on Cromwell's Brutus-like act of reduction. Since his deeds 'surpass all degrees, not only of admiration, but surely of titles too', in accepting the title and the practical, disciplinary role of Lord Protector, he appears not only Brutus-like but Christ-like: 'You have suffered and allowed yourself, not indeed to be borne aloft, but to come down so many degrees from the heights and be forced into a definite rank, so to speak, for the public good' (iv/i. 672). Had he not done so, however, had he not spurned the 'name of king', Milton admonishes him, had he been 'captivated by the title which as a private citizen you were able to send under the yoke and reduce to nothing', he would have proved himself little more than an idolator and been rightly reviled without defence. At the same time, just as he warns Cromwell, he reasserts his faith in England's national hero: 'You, the liberator of your country, the author of liberty, and likewise its guardian and savior, can undertake no more distinguished role and none more august [than serving as Lord Protector]' (p. 672). Most importantly, Cromwell has become not only the custodian of the people's welfare but the saviour of the nation's defining value: that which our dear mother, 'our native land, ... once sought from the most distinguished men of the entire nation', Milton says, 'she now seeks from you alone and through you alone hopes to achieve' (p. 673). The nation's defining value is, of course, liberty, but the full significance of what exactly that means is most succinctly caught in the Son's syntactically conflicted speech-act.

As I suggested above, the passage from Ezekiel that announces the reversal of England's fortunes in 1673—'God hath giv'n a heart to the people' (*CPW*, viii. 417)—also animates God the Father's response to the Son's speech-act: it explains the workings of 'offered grace' (*PL*, iii. 187) and precipitates the great narrative reversal in *Paradise Lost*. Ezekiel's Yahweh represents himself as a surgeon: 'I will take away the stony heart out of your flesh, and I will give you an heart of flesh' (36: 26). When Milton's God the Father reproduces these words, he represents himself as much like a teacher as a medical doctor:

> I will clear their senses dark,
> What may suffice, and soften stony hearts
> To pray, repent, and bring obedience due.
> To prayer, repentance and obedience due,
> Though but endeavoured with sincere intent,
> Mine ear shall not be slow, mine eye not shut. (iii. 188–93)

The key to the Father's teaching practice lies in the repetition and transformation of 'To pray, repent, and bring obedience due' into 'To prayer, repentance and obedience due'. The switch in perspective is most immediately meant to suggest how grace both facilitates and is facilitated by these actions, but since repetition and transformation, imitation and originality, are at the heart of humanist educational practice, it is also meant to suggest a reciprocity that is pedagogical, dynamically dialogic. Humankind is not expected to parrot God's words, but to imitate the creativity of their production. This is made clear in the Son's speech-act which does not simply repeat the grace-note at the end of the Father's 'sovereign sentence' (iii. 145), but re-sounds and amplifies it in such a way that it becomes a challenge and so establishes the Son's independence, his originality and autonomous individuality. The Father's immediate response to the Son's industry of free reasoning is that of a good, if somewhat overbearing, pedagogue: 'All hast thou spoken as my thoughts are' (iii. 171). If the critical relation is, as I am suggesting, that between education and grace, then it should come as no surprise that the reforms Cromwell's reduction are meant to implement focus on facilitating the dialogism of free reasoning: the church should be left to the church, more thought should be given to 'the education and morality of the young', those who wish to engage in 'free inquiry' should be allowed to publish without the 'private inspection of any petty magistrate', and the Lord Protector should refuse to listen to those who 'do not believe themselves free unless they deny freedom in others' (*CPW*, iv/i. 678–9).

Cromwell is not God the Father nor Milton God the Son. But Milton's response to the Lord Protector's power, his simultaneous affirmation and admonition, acts out the creative dialogism, the educational practice, at the heart of his concept of liberty, and most memorably articulated in the Son's response to the Father in *Paradise Lost*. Most importantly for the present argument, it suggests how much of Milton's deepest thought as it appears in a text like *Paradise Lost*, a poem that apparently transcends any form of nationalism, has been conceived in the service of perpetuating the nation's defining value. In the same way that the great reversal of humankind's fortunes in Book 3 of *Paradise Lost* is prefigured in that of England's in 'In Quintum Novembris', so here God the Son's elevating reduction is prefigured in that of a national hero like Cromwell. England is imagined as a quotidian type or vehicle of these transcendent truths, a place where if the nation is true to its promise then the industry of free reasoning may be pursued in full confidence that God's truth will not be subverted but shine 'Substantially expressed' by it (*PL*, iii. 140). Milton's epic poem, written over the period of the collapse of the Commonwealth between 1658 and 1663, cannot escape the traces of its genesis in the struggle to rewrite the nation.[48] Milton signals this in defiantly refusing to write his epic poem in Latin or Italian, but in his native tongue. In what he may have conceived as a climactic contribution to England's discipline, risking censorship, he wrote *Paradise Lost* as a poem 'doctrinal and exemplary' to the nation, addressed to 'mine own Citizens' in their 'mother dialect' (*CPW*, i. 815, 812).

National Identity and Principle

The political cycle that Ernest Sirluck identifies in 1649–54 repeats itself in the last days of the Commonwealth over the period 1659–60. Milton continues to focus on the sovereignty of the people's welfare, but after the death of Cromwell and the final collapse of the Protectorate in April 1659, he reinvests his hopes in the reconstituted Rump Parliament as the new locus of the regenerate: 'I persuade me that God was pleased with their restitution' (*CPW*, vii. 325). When that fails, despite his new-found determination to abjure the rule of a 'single person' and his vain attempts at hatching a new constitution in *The Readie & Easie Way* (February and April 1660), his hopes come to rest once again in the *virtù* of a national hero. This time it is George Monck, a former Royalist officer turned Cromwellian general whom Milton in desperation urges to make himself king (*CPW*, vii. 482). The pattern is evident again in 1673–4 when after the false dawn of the cancellation of the Declaration of Indulgence in March 1673, Milton advertises the advantages of elective monarchy in his English translation of the extravagant praise of Poland's new king, General John Sobieski, in *A Declaration, or Letters Patents* in July 1674 (*CPW*, viii. 445–53)—a leader powerful enough, so Milton may have thought, to guarantee religious toleration (pp. 426–7).[49] As Milton makes clear in his letter to an unknown friend in October 1659, the precise constitution of the Commonwealth matters little to him as long as it protects the nation's defining value: 'whether the civill government be an annuall democracy or a perpetual Aristocracy is too nice a consideracion for the extremities wherein wee are' (*CPW*, vii. 331). That defining value is not majority rule or even representative rule— it is not in this sense truly republican at all. England's defining value is liberty of conscience or what I have been calling the industry of free reasoning practised within the analogy of faith. It is exactly what we see the Son do in Book 3 of *Paradise Lost* and Adam and Eve as they undergo a painful process of regeneration in Book 10.

---

[48] On the date of composition, see Lewalski, *Life*, 351, 432.
[49] See Stevens, 'Milton's Polish Pamphlet'.

It is a principle inspired by the protocols of humanist education, but understood by Milton from an early and formative age as the peculiar moral of England's great Reformation story.

What I have been trying to do in this essay is show how Milton's writings, often in despite of themselves, routinely deconstruct the binary opposition with which we began, the antithesis between national identity and principle. For only by doing so can one understand why the category of the nation is central to his thinking. England is only truly England to the extent that it articulates its great principle—but it is critical to emphasize that what makes Milton a nationalist is the very desire to define national identity in terms of a transcendent principle. It is in this more than anything else that Milton anticipates the nationalism that comes to shape modernity.

At the high point of modern European nationalism, J. G. Fichte in his *Addresses to the German Nation* (1807–8) emphasizes the relation between national identity and principle.[50] The German nation is awakening, he argues, coming to consciousness of itself: a mirror is 'being held up to this nation, in which it may recognize and form a clear conception of that which it has hitherto become by nature without being distinctly conscious of it, and to which it is called by nature'. The German nation expresses a universal principle. That principle is the one it enacts—that nations are organic bodies; they grow naturally and consciousness of this process can bring it to fruition—hence 'a proposal is being made to this nation to make it wholly and completely what it ought to be, to do this according to that clear conception and with free and deliberate art'.[51] Milton offers only a very limited sense of nations growing organically, but he does offer a coherent vision of the nation constantly renewing itself and reversing its fortunes through its defining principle, the relation between education and the agency of God's grace. Against Fichte's 'naturally supernatural' nationalism, Milton offers a kind of regenerate nationalism, a divinely inspired narrative in which the stony can always be taken out of the nation's heart should the nation prove responsive to God's grace. Milton's ideal England stands not as anybody growing into consciousness, but as a specifically righteous individual transformed by grace: as he puts it in *Areopagitica*, the nation stands like the regenerate Samson: 'Methinks I see in my mind a noble and puissant Nation rousing herself like a strong man after sleep, and shaking her invincible locks' (*CPW*, ii. 557–8). In *Samson Agonistes* itself, as the hero feels certain rousing motions within him, and even as English dissenters in London rise to contest the 1670 Conventicle Act, Samson expresses a sense of identity that Milton seemed to have longed for. 'Our God, our Law, my nation, or myself' (l. 1425) are at one.

---

[50] Fichte is quoted in Easthope, *Englishness and National Culture*, 21.
[51] Ibid.

PART V

WRITINGS ON
EDUCATION,
HISTORY,
THEOLOGY

CHAPTER 20

THE GENRES OF MILTON'S COMMONPLACE BOOK

WILLIAM POOLE

PROVENANCE

Milton's Commonplace Book (CPB) is for serious Miltonists an indispensable if slightly forbidding document.[1] It is a manuscript, compiled over three decades (1630s–1660s), and scribed by several different hands in five different languages: Latin, Greek, English, French, and Italian. One of the scribes is Milton himself, his italic hand modulating with his age; the other hands are mainly those of amanuenses, some of whom we can identify, some of whom we cannot. The presence of these amanuenses is largely explained by Milton's complete blindness after 1652. Following a classic 1921 article by J. H. Hanford, we can establish a fairly precise chronology for most of the entries in the manuscript, in which they are ordered into various strata

---

[1] The first edition, without translation, was prepared by Alfred J. Horwood (1876; corrected edn., 1877). He also produced an extremely useful facsimile (1876). *CW* (1938) next provided a basic text and translation. *CPW* (1953) printed only a translation, but with indispensable commentary. Its editor, Ruth Mohl, subsequently published a monograph arising from her edition, *John Milton and his Commonplace Book* (New York, 1969). Important corrections to Mohl's scholarship were offered by Leo Miller, *John Milton among the Polygamophiles* (New York, 1974). I usually follow Mohl's translation in this article.

based on hand and position.[2] But for a manuscript commonplace book in use over three decades, the CPB is a surprisingly sparse affair, comprising perhaps around 14,000 words of Miltonic origin; two-thirds of the available pages in the manuscript are blank. Some headings are followed by only one or two entries; conversely a few, such as those on for instance 'Divorce', 'Marriage', 'King', 'Laws', and 'Tyrant', receive thicker annotation. More will be said about the organization of this manuscript in due course.

The CPB was the last major Miltonic document to be recovered into the public or semi-public domain, after the chiefly poetical Trinity College Manuscript (recognized in the early eighteenth century, before 1726) and Milton's essay in theological systematics, the *De Doctrina Christiana* (discovered among the State Papers in 1823). We know too that Milton compiled a Latin lexicon in manuscript, lost, and it is likely for reasons that we will come to that Milton also maintained further commonplace books, also lost (Darbishire, 4). The CPB itself refers to an 'Index Theologicus' on several occasions, into which Milton, it seems, abstracted from his theological reading material. It is obvious that these materials addressed points of controversy between the Reformed and Roman Catholic churches, and Gordon Campbell has therefore suggested that the 'Index Theologicus' was compiled for the purpose of writing a polemical work against Cardinal Bellarmine.[3] It may be, however, that structuring an 'Index Theologicus' under polemical headings against Bellarmine was a standard way of organizing such manuscripts, and indeed I have located a few such theological commonplace books that bear instructive comparison with Milton's lost manuscript.[4] The CPB itself was rediscovered in 1874 by Alfred J. Horwood among the papers of Sir Frederick Graham, 3rd Baronet of Netherby, Cumberland, in the course of one of his many investigations for the Historical Manuscripts Commission. Although the manuscript was unsigned by Milton, folded into it were two other Miltonic documents that assisted attribution: a manuscript of an early prolusion with an attribution to Milton, and a letter to Milton from Henry Lawes enclosing

---

[2] J. H. Hanford, 'The Chronology of Milton's Private Studies', *Publications of the Modern Language Association*, 36 (1921), 251–314. Dated commonplace book entries referred to in the main text follow Hanford unless otherwise indicated. Edward Jones, ' "Filling in a Blank in the Canvas": Milton, Horton, and the Kedermister Library', *Review of English Studies*, 53 (2002), 31–60, speculates that Milton may have started off the reading that went into the CPB (BL Add. MS 36354) by using the Kedermister Library near Horton in his immediate post-Cambridge years. Jackson Campbell Boswell's *Milton's Library: A Catalogue of the Remains of John Milton's Library and an Annotated Reconstruction of Milton's Library and Ancillary Reading* (New York, 1975) is a useful if mistitled reference work.

[3] CPB, 197 ('Vide Indicem Theologiam'), 221 ('in indice altero'), and cross-references to headings not witnessed in CPB on 12, 112, 183, 244, 246; Gordon Campbell, 'Milton's *Index Theologicus* and Bellarmine's *Disputationes De Controversiis Christianae Fidei Adversus Huius Temporis Haereticos*', *Milton Quarterly*, 11 (1977), 12–16. Campbell observes of the phrase 'in indice altero' that *alter* must mean the other of *two*, not of many indexes; but for my conjecture that Milton may nevertheless have maintained other commonplace books in unconnected disciplines, see below. On Milton's manuscripts see Peter Beal, 'Milton, John', in his *Index of English Literary Manuscripts*, ii: *1625–1700, part 2. Lee–Wycherly* (1993).

[4] Bodleian Library, MS Rawlinson D 1323, structured as a series of *quæstiones*; MS Rawlinson D 1425, an unsigned 'Disputationum Roberti Bell: de controversijs Christianæ fidei Analysis'; and further MS Rawlinson D 1266, a theological commonplace book containing various headings with Bellarmine *contra* and Calvin *pro*. All three are roughly contemporaneous with Milton's lost MS.

Milton's passport for foreign travel, signed by the Lord Warden of the Cinque Ports. The manuscript was eventually acquired in 1900 by the British Museum from Sir Richard James Graham, 4th Baronet of Netherby, along with the rest of the Netherby Library; it is now Additional MS 36354.[5]

The Netherby library was dominated by the papers of Sir Frederick Graham's direct lineal ancestor, the statesman, diplomat, and Jacobite conspirator Richard Graham, 1st Viscount Preston (1648–95), and Milton's manuscript contains several clearly distinguishable entries in Preston's own hand, following Milton's common-placing format, and largely of juristic interest. The manuscript must have passed from Milton to Preston at some point in the two decades separating the two men's deaths. The likely intermediary is Daniel Skinner, 'a scholar and a Bold Young Man whoe...cull'd out w^t he thought fitt' from Milton's papers after the latter's death.[6] He certainly took the *De Doctrina* and a manuscript of the Latin Letters of State; he quite probably removed the CPB and the documents with it; and indeed, as Maurice Kelley has suggested, he may also have taken the Trinity College Manuscript.[7] But why would Skinner send Milton's CPB to a Jacobite politician? Skinner and Preston had been old schoolmates at Westminster, and two formal letters (in shaky French) from Skinner to his powerful old acquaintance survive from 1682.[8] These letters are attempts to win Preston's patronage or favour—though the evidence of the seal on one of the letters led Kelley to suspect that Skinner was spying for Preston[9]—and Skinner possibly sold or gave the CPB manuscript to Preston as part of the same programme of ingratiation.[10] But Skinner failed to win Preston's favour, and precisely what role this manuscript served in their interactions remains obscure.

So much for the provenance of this manuscript, which is important chiefly for showing us that Milton's manuscript was used after his death for a similar purpose by a politically hostile contemporary who nonetheless failed to show any interest in the Miltonic seam of his acquisition beyond aping its format. For Preston, this was not a hallowed object but a scrapbook that he recycled and then laid aside, to be forgotten

---

[5] *Catalogue of Additions to the Manuscripts in the British Museum in the Years MDCCCC–MDCCCCV* (1907).

[6] Longleat House, Coventry Papers, fo. 60 (undated latter, written between Nov. 1676 and Jan. 1677). Extracts quoted by J. E. Jackson in *Notes and Queries*, ser. iv, 3 (1869), 144; and Gordon Campbell, Thomas N. Corns, John K. Hale, David Holmes, and Fiona Tweedie, 'The Provenance of *De Doctrina Christiana*', *Milton Quarterly*, 31 (1997), 67–117. They comment: 'The letter was written by an anonymous informant and sent either to [Henry] Coventry or to his secretary, H. F. Thynne.'

[7] Maurice Kelley, 'Daniel Skinner and Milton's Trinity College Manuscript', *Notes and Queries*, 222 (1977), 206–7. Examination of Milton's Euripides (Bodleian Library, Don. d. 27, 28) convinces me that we should retire the idea that Skinner lifted this (valuably annotated) edition too: we may conclude that Skinner was a 'liberator' of manuscripts, not printed works.

[8] Add. MS 63766, fos. 10^r–11^v, 95^r–96^v (the second letter appears to be scribal, further increasing doubts as to Skinner's linguistic proficiency).

[9] Maurice Kelley, 'Addendum: The Later Career of Daniel Skinner', *Publications of the Modern Language Association*, 55 (1940), 116–18.

[10] Maurice Kelley, 'Daniel Skinner, Lord Preston, and Milton's Commonplace Book', *Modern Language Notes*, 64 (1949), 522–5.

for nearly two centuries. We turn now to some standard ideas in the period concerning the practice of commonplacing.

COMMONPLACING

All scholarly minded early moderns took notes when they read.[11] Sometimes they inserted these into the margins, flyleaves, or endpapers of their books (there are some Miltonic examples); sometimes they wrote them on disconnected pieces of paper; sometimes they entered them into separate, rough notebooks; and sometimes they organized these notes in a commonplace book. Most, indeed, employed all four systems. What distinguished a commonplace book from the prior methods of note-taking was the idea of an order governing the practice of excerpting which did not itself rely on the organization of the book in hand. The preferred form of repository was the bound and blank book organized into sections or headings reflecting an intellectual arrangement appropriate to some particular genre or genres of reading. These books, as incrementally generated objects, were usually entirely handwritten, but there was also a tradition of the printed commonplace book, in which the headings were supplied in type, the owner subsequently adding appropriate entries by hand.

It was probably while Milton was at Cambridge that a St John's College don, Richard Holdsworth, composed one of the few student advice manuals surviving from Cambridge from this period.[12] Holdsworth devoted a chapter of his 'Directions for a Student in the Universitie' to the art of taking notes, and to the 'commendable endeavour to make Common place books, in w:^ch they might recorde the best of theyr studies to certain heads of future use and memorie'. Holdsworth was emphatic that all students ought to take notes, but he drew a distinction between the miscellaneous notes a student might make in his rough notebooks, and the material fit for the commonplace book proper. He thought that the latter should only be commenced when the student had elected to specialize in theology, law, or medicine, the three

---

[11] The literature on commonplacing is substantial, but for two important contemporary sites on commonplacing, see Desiderius Erasmus, *De Copia*, book 2, in *Collected Works of Erasmus*, xxiv (Literary and Educational Writings, vol. 2), ed. Craig R. Thompson (Toronto, 1978), 635–48 (and compare *De Ratione Studii*, ibid. 672); Bartholomäus Keckermann, 'De locis communibus...', in *Gymnasium Logicum... Libri Tres* (1606), 199–211 (where the ethical/economical/political subdivisions can be seen). Useful modern discussions include Joan Marie Lechner, *Renaissance Concepts of the Commonplaces* (New York, 1962); Peter Beal, 'Notions in Garrison: The Seventeenth-Century Commonplace Book', in W. Speed Hill (ed.), *New Ways of Looking at Old Texts* (Binghamton, N.Y., 1993), 131–47; Ann Moss, *Printed Commonplace Books and the Structuring of Renaissance Thought* (Oxford, 1996).

[12] For the general background, see William T. Costello, *The Scholastic Curriculum at Early Seventeenth-Century Cambridge* (Cambridge, Mass., 1958); for Milton's place in it, see H. F. Fletcher, *The Intellectual Development of John Milton*, 2 vols. (Urbana, Ill., 1956–61). Although restricted to Oxford, Mordechai Feingold's chapter on 'The Humanities' in Nicholas Tyacke (ed.), *The History of the University of Oxford: Seventeenth-Century Oxford* (Oxford, 1997), is invaluable.

higher faculties. Until this decision had been made, the rougher form of the note-book would suffice; a sophomore uncertain of his vocation, Holdsworth maintained, should not have to reach for 'a great Folio book, & toss it and turn it for evry little passage y^t is to be writt downe'.[13]

Holdsworth's fussiness was typically ignored. Yet his discussion underscores for us what an important tool the early-modern commonplace book was—for 'future use and memorie', and emphatically not a mere scrapbook. Milton's CPB conforms to this ideal, both in its tightly controlled range, and in the heavy use Milton made of it when composing (especially) his prose works. And as the internal order of many early-modern commonplace books reflects the external rationale of the academic curriculum of the time, this parallelism can be exploited to allow us to identify what kind of commonplace book Milton maintained.

What Kind of Commonplace Book did Milton Keep?

Since its rediscovery, this untitled manuscript has been correctly termed Milton's 'Commonplace Book', but it can be given a yet more exact designation, based on its internal subdivisions. Milton splits his manuscript up into three parts headed respectively 'Index Ethicus', 'Index Oeconomicus', and 'Index Politicus', and supplies an index that likewise observes this tripartite distinction. Within these subdivisions, he devotes most space to politics.[14] Now any educated contemporary of Milton's would immediately recognize these three headings as the standard subdivisions of the academic discipline termed either 'moral philosophy', 'practical philosophy', or simply 'ethics'.[15] This stems from the Aristotelian distinction of all philosophy into

---

[13] John A. Trentman, 'The Authorship of *Directions for a Student in the Universitie*', *Transactions of the Cambridge Bibliographical Society*, 7 (1978), 170–83. Text from Emmanuel College MS 48, reproduced in Fletcher, *Intellectual Development*, ii, App. II, p. 651. (Holdsworth's own commonplace book may well be Cambridge University Library MS Dd.IV.5; it certainly bears his name (fo. 95^v), among others.)

[14] Reducing all duplications to a single heading, as Milton's own index does, we obtain Ethical (24 headings), Economic (12), and Political (27) sections in an exact ratio of 8: 4: 9. (The one exception is Milton's repetition of the 'Subditus' page (183) under the 'Libertas' (183, 190) heading in his index; as these were in origin two separate headings they are counted as such.) But the large number of duplications (four pages on 'King', two on 'Laws', two on 'Tyrant') in the political section shows that it was in the event used much more heavily than the ethical index, and the political section on its own accounts for well over half the words of the whole MS. Finally, although the political section takes the lion's share, it must be recalled that the two pages on 'Marriage' in the economic section, cross-referenced by Milton as they are to the 'Divorce' heading, stand behind the publications that would make him notorious in the mid-1640s, as the contents of the political index would serve in the next decade.

[15] Jill Kraye, 'Moral Philosophy', in Charles B. Schmitt (gen. ed.), *The Cambridge History of Renaissance Philosophy* (Cambridge, 1988), 303–86, esp. 305.

'speculative' versus 'practical' philosophy. Speculative philosophy is divided into metaphysics, physics, and mathematics, whereas practical philosophy is divided into a 'common' part, *ethics*, and a 'special' part, which contains *politics* and *economics*. (Occasionally we also encounter 'monastic' and 'ecclesiastic' divisions in moral philosophy too, but Protestant writers of Milton's day subsume such issues under 'politics', as Milton does.[16]) Practical philosophy resides in the practical understanding (*intellectus*), the function of which is to know things inasmuch as they are good or bad, to distinguish them, and to propose to our will what we must seek after, and what we must shun. Practical philosophy is therefore not an art but a matter of prudence. It concerns what the Greeks call *ēthicē*, in Latin *moralis*, and that is why practical philosophy, moral philosophy, and ethics are interchangeable terms. In sum, moral philosophy may be defined as prudence directing human passions (*affectiones*), insofar as is possible in this life, so that we may live well, and blessedly.

The rationale behind the tripartite division of moral philosophy is this: ethics deals not with statements about particular people but the general principles of ethical behaviour; it is therefore 'common' in the sense of 'shared'. Its 'special' part descends to particulars, either as they pertain to the household (*œconomia*) or to the state (*politica*). Milton may also have appreciated the distinction that Aristotle himself had made between economics and politics in the opening paragraphs of both the *Politics* and the (pseudo-Aristotelian) *Economics*: whereas the former sphere was ruled over by one person alone, the latter required a group of men for good government. We may note too that as well as raiding historical texts, active philosophy might also 'borrow' an ancillary discipline from the mathematical arts—geography. History is the eye of the politician; and, as the saying went, geography and chronology are the eyes of the historian. This explains why Milton excerpts so readily from John Speed, for instance, whose 'history' is also a work of 'chorography', that part of geography dealing with individual places and their (human as well as physical) traditions.[17] Finally, alongside history, poetry is also to be considered relevant to moral philosophy insofar as both poetry and history provide moral *exempla*.[18] Thus both Milton's ethics/economics/politics division and the genres excerpted under these headings conform to the educational dictates of Milton's time.[19] Milton's CPB is thus a highly coherent object in contemporary terms.

---

[16] To take three examples from textbooks studied in Milton's Cambridge: Eustachius of St Paul used the terms 'ethical' and 'monastic' interchangeably (*Ethica* (1666), 5–6); John Case treated 'monastic' as a further subdivision (*Ancilla Philosophiæ* (Oxford, 1599), 6); but Robert Sanderson insisted that 'monastic' and 'ecclesiastic' were properly placed under 'politics' (*Artis Logicæ Compendium* (Oxford, 1615), 'Appendix Prima', 106).

[17] Lesley B. Cormack, 'Good Fences Make Good Neighbors: Geography as Self-Definition in Early Modern England', *Isis*, 82 (1991), 639–61.

[18] Sanderson, *Artis Logicæ Compendium*, 'Appendix Prima', 106.

[19] I have taken the definitions in this and the previous paragraph from textbooks popular in the Christ's College of Milton's time: Franciscus Burgersdijk, *Idea Philosophiæ tum Naturalis tum Moralis* (Oxford, 1631), 1–5; Burgersdijk, *Idea Philosophiæ Moralis* (Oxford, 1631), 1–7; Bartholomäus Keckermann, *Systema Ethicæ* (1607), 1; Keckermann, *Systema Compendiosum Totius Mathematices* (Hanover, 1617), 412. On Keckermann at Christ's, see Fletcher, *Intellectual Development*, ii. 147–8; Quentin

Indeed this piece of curricular Aristotelianism survives intact in Milton's *Of Education* (1644), where we find the study of ethics, economics, and politics sequentially organized as in the CPB manuscript:

By this time, yeers and good generall precepts will have furnisht them more distinctly with that act of reason which in *Ethics* is call'd *Proairesis*: that they may with some judgement contemplat upon morall good and evill. Then will be requir'd a speciall reinforcement of constant and sound endoctrinating to set them right and firm, instructing them more amply in the knowledge of vertue and the hatred of vice: while their young and pliant affections are led through all the morall works of *Plato, Xenophon, Cicero, Plutarch, Laertius,* and those *Locrian* remnants ... Being perfit in the knowledge of personall duty, they may then begin the study of Economics. ... The next remove must be to the study of *Politics*; to know the beginning, end, and reasons of politicall societies; that they may not in a dangerous fit of the commonwealth be such poor, shaken, uncertain reeds, of such a tottering conscience, as many of our great counsellers have lately shewn themselves, but stedfast pillars of the State.[20] (*CPW,* ii. 396–8)

Interestingly, Milton's rigorously classical reading list was not the one he followed in his own commonplacing habits, where he preferred to excerpt from the church historians and more recent writers, probably because of the polemical nature of the work he was himself about to undertake or actually undertaking. At any rate, *Of Education* once again proves more conservative in tone than either Milton's own literary behaviour or that of the Hartlibian educational reformers with whom he briefly intersected in the 1640s. By contrast, the CPB starts to look like a more specialized—even 'weaponized'—operation than *Of Education*'s Erasmian ideal of a *cursus* of classical authors, all (to adopt Anthony Grafton's recent terminology) processed and stored for future consumption.[21]

So Milton's CPB may more exactly be styled his 'commonplace book *in moral philosophy*'; this is the subject represented by Milton's three named indexes in this manuscript, and it is an association reproduced in the ideal curriculum of *Of Education*. Miltonists who neglect this basic correlation with the curricular practice of the time will fall into a good deal of unnecessary speculation about why we have no scientific, musical, or biblical, and few classical, excerpts in this manuscript. These, we now see, are irrelevant to its precise genre. Again, Milton's expansive account of his private study in *An Apology against a Pamphlet* (1642) exceeds the portion represented by the CPB, which cannot therefore be taken to contain all his serious

Skinner, 'The Generation of John Milton', in David Reynolds (ed.), *Christ's: A Cambridge College over Five Centuries* (2005), 41–72.

[20] This instruction would take place at the end of the third or fourth year of the eight envisaged by Milton between the ages of 12 and 20. Although Milton then treats Law as following on after Ethics, Economics, and Politics, in CPB he cites a good deal of material from the Roman legists. In CPB Milton therefore appears to have included legal material within the moral philosophical ambit, circumstantial evidence that the so-called 'Legal Index' occasionally attributed to Milton has nothing to do with him, as Kelley (overcautiously) argued (*CPW,* i, app. A).

[21] Anthony Grafton, *What Was History? The Art of History in Early Modern Europe* (Cambridge, 2007), 208–16.

reading (i. 888–91).[22] And the variety and accuracy of Milton's astronomical and mythological knowledge as displayed in *Paradise Lost* and elsewhere suggest that he kept commonplace books suitable to those areas, and that they have been lost. (Manuscript hunters, for instance, would do very well to keep their eyes peeled for an unattributed commonplace book containing a breakdown of the astronomical controversy between John Wilkins and Alexander Ross, for instance, or another full of references to John Selden's *De Dis Syris* (1617).)[23]

A final point to conclude this section is that the declared purpose of both the serious commonplace book and of moral philosophy itself is *action*. The action of the commonplace book may appear largely linguistic (for better arming one's arguments in speech or writing), as opposed to the direct action of moral philosophy—how to live the good life both in domestic and political spaces. But for Milton, well-chosen words were political actions, a Ciceronian stance on the status of rhetoric that would drive him to present even his plea for the restriction of pre-publication censorship, the *Areopagitica* (1644), as a hypothetical oration delivered before an attentive Parliament.[24] (*Areopagitica* is probably a feminine singular adjective, so what suppressed noun does it qualify? Perhaps *oratio*, 'speech'?) Now and then this sense of immediacy breaks through into Milton's excerpting. After citations from John Stow and John Speed on the folly of imitating foreign fashions—here explicitly French customs, in Edward the Confessor's time—Milton adds his own prayer: 'god turn the omen from these days'. Again, citing Stow on King Alfred's translation of the laws into the vernacular, Milton complained of the Law French still in use in his day: 'I would he liv'd now to rid us of this norman gibbrish.'[25] (We see here a favourite national prejudice, especially virulent in the days of Henrietta Maria.) Milton's CPB is therefore a manuscript *for doing things with*, and that must be remembered by modern readers used to the debased notion of the commonplace book as a mere miscellany of colourful snippets.

MILTON'S BEHAVIOUR

Now we have established what kind of commonplace book Milton's manuscript is, we will next want to know some more precise information about how he manoeuvred within this classification. We have already seen that his own practice differed

---

[22] Milton commented in the *Second Defence* merely that he 'devoted [him]self entirely to the study of Greek and Latin writers' (*CPW*, iv/i. 614).

[23] Grant McColley, 'The Ross–Wilkins Controversy', *Annals of Science*, 3 (1938), 153–89; Milton's demonology surely derives from Selden.

[24] On early-modern uses of Ciceronian rhetoric, see Quentin Skinner, *Reason and Rhetoric in the Philosophy of Hobbes* (Cambridge, 1996).

[25] CPB, 179, 180. On such interventions Lewalski, *Life*, 65–6, 126–7, 160–1.

from his precepts in *Of Education*. So we might next ask whether Milton's headings differ from or conform to other examples of contemporary practice. The answer appears to be that Milton's behaviour is pretty standard. To take a prominent example of a printed commonplace book, John Foxe's *Pandectæ* of 1572, almost every single one of Milton's headings appears as a printed heading in Foxe's (significantly broader) compilation.[26] The very few that do not can mostly be pieced together by splicing two of Foxe's designedly basic headings. Turning to later manuscript commonplace books where the headings are more likely to be more personally tailored, we still see a similar overlap, for instance in a seventeenth-century ethical commonplace book now in the Rawlinson Manuscripts and used at different points by at least three people.[27]

If, then, we can conclude that both Milton's organization and his coverage are conventional, we will still want to know how he filled up his commonplace book, as it is here and not elsewhere that we see what is 'Miltonic' about this manuscript. So when did Milton do his reading? How many authors did he cite? What kinds of genres did he subdue to his general ethical priorities?

Milton probably started the reading that would be excerpted in the CPB in the mid-1630s round about the time in 1636 when he moved with his father from Hammersmith to Horton. Just perhaps he used the nearby library at Eton or the Kedermister Library at Langley; it is likely he set about purchasing his own copies too. In a late 1637 letter to Charles Diodati, Milton commented on how 'by continued reading' he had worked his way through Greek and Italian history, and this signals that he had been reading hard for some time by that point.[28] It was most probably in this year that he started the CPB itself.[29] By his 1638 Italian trip he had crawled through the church historians and various patristic authors, as well as the more pleasant territory of Dante and Ariosto.[30] But it was in the early years of the 1640s

---

[26] For a heavily used exemplar of Foxe's *Pandectæ*, see British Library, Add. MS 6038, the commonplace book of Sir Julius Caesar (1558–1636). Foxe's title alludes to Conrad Gesner's alphabetical index of *loci* at the end of his classified list of subject headings, the *Pandectarum sive partitionum universalium libri XXI* (Zurich, 1548).

[27] Bodleian Library, MS Rawlinson D 1407 (commonplace book of John Howson, James Hamilton, and Lyonell Gwillims). Headings witnessed also in Milton include: 'Adulatio', 'Avaritia', 'Castitas', 'Consultatio', 'Curiositas', 'Ebrietas', 'Fides', 'Fortitudo', 'Furtum', 'Gula', 'Iustitia', 'Libido', 'Maladicentia', 'Mendacium', 'Mors', 'Poeta', 'Rhetores', 'Reprehensio', 'Virtus', 'Voluntas'.

[28] Letter of 23 Sept. [probably Nov.] 1637, in *CPW*, i. 327. The previous letter to Diodati (*CPW*, i. 322–5) also shows that Milton's commonplace-oriented reading was well under way by this point, even if he had not started abstracting notes into the CPB itself.

[29] Masahiko Agari, 'A Note on Milton's Trinity MS', *English Language Notes*, 22 (1984), 23–6 at 26; *pace* Parker, *Milton: A Biography*, ii. 801, proposing a start in 1635 (as had Hanford) or even 1634. See also John Shawcross, *John Milton: The Self and the World* (Lexington, Ky., 1993), esp. 76–82, and Appendix A, for the later date.

[30] Hanford, 'Chronology', provides sequential lists of Milton's authors, and I follow these; Campbell contextualizes this data with some additional detail in *Chronology*, 56–7, 66, 67–8, 70–1, 79, 104. See also Parker, *Milton*, 145–50, 248–50, 295–6, and accompanying commentary. The pre-/post-Italian entries were distinguished using the classic observation that Milton deliberately recast his Greek 'e' to an Italic 'e' after his Italian trip; but it is now thought that this shift in hand should be dated to autumn 1637. It is not known if Milton carried the CPB with him on his foreign travels, but I am inclined to doubt it.

that Milton seriously set about gathering ethical material geared to his polemic interests, and he now turned chiefly to England, working his way systematically through the gruelling folios of Bede, William of Malmesbury, Stow, Holinshead, Speed, and Camden. This he complemented with Continental history, both on the British Isles themselves (Du Chesne), as well as on the various European national histories (Sleidan, Jovius, Sarpi, Girard, Thuanus, and others). Reading in these genres continued into Campion and Spenser on Ireland. Milton also embarked on Samuel Purchas's famous 1625 collection of travel narratives, *Purchas his Pilgrimes*, and Walter Ralegh's *History of the World* (1614). And although all that survives of this reading are Milton's own use of these authors in his other writings and the CPB entries themselves, he does appear to have had some grand publication projects in mind too. Theodore Haak—who was later to translate a good deal of *Paradise Lost* into German[31]—told Samuel Hartlib in 1648 that 'Milton is not only writing a Vniv*ersal* History of Engl*and* but also an Epitome of all Purcha's volumes.'[32] Nothing appears to have come of this latter project, but the CPB bears out the plausibility of Haak's claim. These years also saw more poetic reading in English, notably in the older writers Chaucer and Gower, whose vocabulary must have been getting pretty tough for the seventeenth-century reader, and whose metrics were universally misunderstood. Legal research into Justinian was another important site of reading in this period, and among the many other authors and texts read by Milton in the 1640s we should mention John Selden's *Uxor Ebraica* (printed 1646, but completed by 1640), probably not known to Milton in time for *The Doctrine and Discipline of Divorce*, but possibly read in manuscript for *Tetrachordon*.[33] In the 1650s, Milton's use of the CPB slumped, and of course he was using scribes by this point, but one author in particular now received closer attention—Machiavelli, a fact of considerable importance for thinking about Milton's political ideas in the wake of the regicide.[34] Thereafter Milton had notes entered up until at least the mid-1660s, but only very intermittently. The heyday of this manuscript therefore lies in the years of Milton's first, furious entry into the world of polemical prose. All in all, Milton's CPB shows him turning over the pages—seemingly all the pages—of some ninety-five authors. And this, we have seen, can only represent one (albeit important) corner of his reading. Yet reading the CPB without access to the texts behind it can be difficult. Milton's notes frequently lasso together passages separated in their original texts, and he is often content to remind himself to go back to a given work rather than copy out the passage in full. Indeed, on occasion there is no way of telling *what* Milton thought

---

[31] Pamela Barnett, *Theodore Haak, F.R.S. (1605–1690): The First German Translator of 'Paradise Lost'* (The Hague, 1962). In passing, Haak's own, fairly densely emended copy of the first complete German translation of the epic, *Das Verlustigte Paradeis*, trans. Ernst Gottlieb von Berge (Zerbst, 1682), is now Bodleian Library, 8° G 100 Linc.

[32] *The Hartlib Papers*, ed. Judith Crawford et al., 2nd edn., 2 CD-ROMs (Ann Arbor, 1995), 32/21/21A.

[33] Eivion Owen, 'Milton and Selden on Divorce', *Studies in Philology*, 43 (1946), 233–57.

[34] Cedric Brown, 'Great Senates and Godly Education: Politics and Cultural Renewal in Some Pre- and Post-revolutionary Texts of Milton', in David Armitage, Armand Himy, and Quentin Skinner (eds.), *Milton and Republicanism* (Cambridge, 1995), 43–60.

was noteworthy without checking his reference, as he himself would presumably have had to do. Finally, it is crucial to note that the consistent and almost continuous contact between Milton's entries to the CPB, and allusion to or quotation of these entries in his own writings, shows that the CPB was to a high degree a document not for private meditation but for public use. In this respect it is not really a typical, personal 'Commonplace Book' at all, for scholarly and mnemonic development, but a digest eventually to be stomached by others. Milton's integration of so many of his commonplace entries into his later works thus removes his own example of the genre to the outer extremes of its kind.

MILTON'S USE OF HIS READING—THE EXAMPLE OF LACTANTIUS

Now that we have a sense both of what kind of commonplace book Milton maintained, and of his own habits as a note-taker, we will want to see how some of his reading connects up to his own writing, and for this purpose I carry out a tiny case study of Milton's ongoing engagement with Lactantius, an engagement that takes its origin in some early entries to the CPB.

Lactantius, the third- to fourth-century African Church Father, was a theologian and moralist with whom Milton has a great deal in common.[35] Milton read his Lactantius properly, probably just after his Tertullian (another, slightly earlier Latin African Father), in the years around 1640—in other words, probably just after his return from Italy, and while he was preparing his first string of prose polemics. Lactantius was one of the most celebrated stylists among the Fathers, and as such Milton was in theory supposed to have read him as a young boy at St Paul's.[36] Whether or not he did so, his encounter with Lactantius in his early 30s was chiefly ethical.[37] He cited with approval Lactantius' comments on the evils of pederasty, for instance, and that courage flowed from reason rather than mere physical strength. In a fascinating passage in the Political Index he also took issue with Lactantius' denunciation of drama in terms that may be juxtaposed with Milton's public denunciation of the academic drama, acted by budding ecclesiastics 'writhing and unboning their Clergie limmes', and with his (post-Restoration, with the ethical

---

[35] Kathleen Hartwell, *Lactantius and Milton* (Cambridge, Mass., 1929).

[36] Donald L. Clark, *Milton at St. Paul's School: A Study of Ancient Rhetoric in English Renaissance Education* (New York, 1948), 100–1, 125–6. (Given that Lactantius is named in the company of Juvencus and Sedulius, however, it may be the poetic *Phoenix* that is meant, and not the prose.)

[37] CPB, 4 (two integrated citations on the problem of evil), 5 (the good man exercises patience), 14 (pederasty), 18 (courage depends on reason), 178 (patriotism should not prompt plunder), 241 (plays and acting).

horrors of its own revived theatre) insistence that *Samson Agonistes* was a drama of the page, not the stage (*An Apology*, *CPW*, i. 887). But in the CPB Milton insists, in terms that in context must apply to performance, that an outright ban of drama would be absurd:

although the corruptions of the theatre deservedly should be removed, it is by no means necessary for that reason that all practice [*usus*] of the dramatic arts should be completely done away with; on the contrary it would rather be absurd beyond measure. For what in all philosophy is more important or more sacred or more exalted than a tragedy rightly produced [*constituta*], what more useful for seeing [*spectandos*] at a single view the events and changes of human life? (CPB, 241; Latin supplied from the MS)

This text makes it rather more difficult to believe Milton when he writes in *An Apology* (1642) only a few years later that as a student at Cambridge he had watched his fellow-students act solely because he 'thought them fools'; that he 'laught' at them; that he 'mislik't' them, and 'hist'.[38] Milton may want us to believe that only rough comedy was performed in Cambridge, but this is untrue. On its own, this passage is preening and supercilious; but when combined with Milton's generous, passionate defence of tragedy in the CPB, it simply rings false.[39] Such discrepancies remind us not to read Milton's polemical voices as uncomplicatedly autobiographical.

But Milton's most important engagement with Lactantius concerns the problem of evil. One of the earliest entries in the CPB states in terse form Milton's governing ethical principle:

Why does God permit evil? So that reasoning and virtue may be correlated [*ut ratio virtuti constare possit*]. For the good is made known, is made clear, and is exercised by evil. As Lactantius says, Book 5. c[hapter] 7, that reason and intelligence may have the opportunity to exercise themselves by choosing the things that are good, by fleeing from the things that are evil. Lactan de ira dei. c[hapter] 13.[40]

Now the notion that good can only be revealed through a process of moral struggle is perhaps Milton's most important principle. 'For if there were no opposition where were the triall of an unfained goodnesse and magnanimity?' (*CPW*, i. 795), Milton wrote in *The Reason of Church-Government* (1642), and the principle had already supplied the moral structure of *A Maske* (1634). As God ringingly declares in *Paradise Lost* (1667) not just of Adam and Eve but of 'all th'Ethereal Powers / And Spirits':

> Freely they stood who stood, and fell who fell.
> Not free, what proof could they have givn sincere
> Of true allegiance, constant Faith or Love,
> Where onely what they needs must do, appeard,
> Not what they would? (iii. 100–6; 1674 text)

---

[38] But in *The Reason of Church-Government* (*CPW*, i. 240) he had included 'theatres' in his list of institutions to be reformed—not abolished—for recreation and moral exhortation.

[39] Compare Milton on Philip Sidney's *Arcadia* in CPB ('exquisite reasoning', 16), and in *Eikonoklastes* (1649) ('vaine amatorious Poem', in *CPW*, iii. 362).

[40] CPB, 363, Latin from manuscript and translation adjusted from Mohl.

Examples can be multiplied from all genres and periods of Milton's writing. Perhaps the most forceful, after God's words above, is the celebrated passage in *Areopagitica* (1644): 'I cannot praise a fugitive and cloister'd vertue, unexercis'd & unbreath'd, that never sallies out and sees her adversary, but slinks out of the race, where that immortall garland is to be run for, not without dust and heat' (*CPW*, ii. 516). But for all this Milton was troubled about how such freedom could be squared with God's absolute foreknowledge, a worry that must take its origin from the opposing theology of the growing Calvinist convictions of his early adulthood.[41] He followed his extract from Lactantius in the CPB with the revealing qualification: 'however much these things fail to satisfy [*quamvis et haec non satisfaciunt*]'.[42] This moment of doubt in the CPB can be referred back to the central dramatic problem of *A Maske*: namely, that despite all her fine ethical language, the Lady remains stuck to her chair, and cannot rise out of it by her own power. From his earliest work, Milton was troubled not just by the necessity of moral freedom but the difficulty of demonstrating that such freedom was invariably available. Indeed, by Milton's death this emphasis on moral choice as requiring freedom had become a central tenet of Anglican rational theology too, and had Milton not rendered his Arminianism explicit in *Paradise Lost*—he was content to veil or at least dissemble his more outlandish heresies—his epic would not have won the audience it did throughout the eighteenth and nineteenth centuries.[43] The germ of this lies in his brief entry early on in the CPB—but, equally importantly, so too does his unease at Lactantius' brusque solution.

FATIGUE

The CPB also witnesses to the fatigue of reading. When Milton wrote of his exhaustion with patristics, he was thinking precisely of the reading he had undertaken in order to compile the CPB: 'Whatsoever time or the heedless hand of blind chance hath drawn from of old to this present in her huge Dragnet, whether Fish or Sea-weed, Shells or Shrubbs, unpicked, unchosen, those are the Fathers' (*Of Prelatical Episcopacy* (1641), in *CPW*, i. 626). Milton had toiled over their 'immeasurable, innumerable, and therefore unnecessary and unmerciful volumes', and all he had found were: 'crabbed . . . abstruse . . . knotty Africanisms, the pamper'd metafors; the intricat, and involv'd sentences . . . the fantastick, and declamatory flashes; the

---

[41] Gordon Campbell, 'The Theology of the Manuscript', in Thomas N. Corns, John K. Hale, and Fiona Tweedie, *Milton and the Manuscript of 'De Doctrina Christiana'* (Oxford, 2007), 90–1.

[42] The interpretation of these words has been controversial: see William Poole, *Milton and the Idea of the Fall* (Cambridge, 2005), 139.

[43] Henry G. Van Leeuwen, *The Problem of Certainty in English Thought 1630–1690* (The Hague, 1963), 68 (on John Wilkins).

crosse-jingling periods which cannot but disturb, and come thwart a setl'd devotion worse then the din of bells, and rattles' (*Of Reformation* (1641), in *CPW*, i. 568).[44]

Now indeed Milton had polemic cause to attack the authority of the Fathers, as arguments for Presbyterian church organization had since Thomas Cartwright's 1570s Cambridge lectures rested on a reaffirmation of the terminology of Scripture, particularly from the book of Acts, over later patristic texts. But for all that we can still hear clearly the plaintive tone of scholarly exhaustion. Milton had spent his childhood reading, seven years at Cambridge reading, and then five more reading at Hammersmith and Horton, more or less in self-imposed isolation.[45] And he did indeed use huge volumes. Suitably bound, his 1612 collection of the early church historians, the 1612 Geneva *Historiae Ecclesiasticae Scriptores Graeci*, or his 1634 Paris Tertullian *Opera*, for instance, could flatten a child.[46]

CONCLUSION

Most Miltonists visit the CPB on the hunt for parallels to Milton's other, more formally public works—parallels to his poetry, to an extent, but most of all to his prose polemics. This reasonable course of action is encouraged by the fact that Milton used his CPB most heavily throughout the first half of the 1640s, his most intense period of prose publication. But in this brief introduction I have attempted first and foremost to respect the CPB as an object in its own right, structured not just by Milton's own polemic concerns, but by his educational background and the priorities it continued to exert. I have indeed also supplied some examples of cross-readings of Milton using the CPB, and these may be multiplied by careful use of the *CPW* commentary and subsequent work. Diligent rereading of all Milton's commonplaced authors is sure to throw up new material that can be paralleled in his other writings, even when no entry was made in the CPB. Such findings will have to be judged on a case-by-case basis.[47] To conclude, however, I will offer one further parallel, this time between the structure of the CPB and Milton's later account of his studies.

---

[44] These passages also reflect an unacknowledged debt to Jean Daillé's celebrated *Traicté de l'Employ des Saincts Pères* (1632).

[45] Gordon Campbell, in his article on Milton for the *ODNB*, elegantly suggests that Milton's five-year private course of reading was to fulfil his MA oath that he would study for a further five years in preparation for holy orders. 'Church-outed by the Prelats' (*CPW*, i. 823), Milton would nevertheless keep true to the spirit if not the letter of his oath.

[46] Bodleian Library, H 1.4 Th. Seld (*Scriptores Graeci*), M 1.5 Th. Seld (Tertullian), the copies of John Selden, a scholar much admired and excerpted by Milton (CPB, 109, 110).

[47] See e.g. J. H. Hanford, 'Milton and the Art of War', *Studies in Philology*, 18 (1921), 232–66, versus Robert Fallon, *Captain or Colonel: The Soldier in Milton's Life and Art* (Columbia, Mo., 1984), 57–9, concerning Milton's use of Robert Ward, *Animadversions of Warre* (1639), cited in CPB, 18.

In a famous passage of his *Second Defence* (1654), Milton retrospectively sought to bestow some order on his prose publications of 1640–4. As he wrote:

Since, then, I observed that there are, in all, three varieties of liberty without which civilized life is scarcely possible, namely ecclesiastical liberty, domestic or personal liberty, and civil liberty, and since I had already written about the first, while I saw that the magistrates were vigorously attending to the third, I took as my province the remaining one, the second or domestic kind. (*CPW*, iv/i. 624)

Milton here gives the impression of a systematic, almost impersonal approach to the pursuit of liberty. Over a decade later, he recalls that he had perceived three spaces of liberty, and selflessly turned his pen towards those areas unaddressed by his own previous work or the labours of others.

Now this passage may strike readers as suspiciously pompous. Milton projects a version of himself that seems a little too in control of his intellectual trajectory. But in certain ways the CPB bears out this self-projection—Milton, the CPB demonstrates, was already collecting texts on marriage *before* his first, initially disastrous marriage, and his decision to defend conjugal liberty, therefore, indeed involved reflecting on previous reading as well as simply lamenting an over-hasty marriage and collecting material on divorce. But there is a more important way in which the self-projection of the *Second Defence* is anchored into the world of the CPB. As we have seen, the vocabulary of 'liberty' and 'civilized life' is the language of moral philosophy. And Milton's 'ecclesiastical', 'domestic', and 'civil' categories in the *Second Defence* answer to the twin economic ('domestic') and political ('ecclesiastical' and 'civil') subdivisions of the 'special' part of moral philosophy covered by the CPB. (For Milton, of course, religious and civil questions in the early 1640s were not in practice distinguishable.) One level deeper, Milton's subsequent subdivision of the economic space into matters of 'the nature of marriage', 'the education of the children', and 'the freedom to express oneself' (iv/i. 624) answers in its first two components to precise headings within the Economic Index: 'marriage', 'divorce', and 'the education of children'. But Milton's defence of 'the freedom to express oneself', we may note, was more contextually driven than his recollection insinuates—in *Areopagitica* he was worried about specific and sudden legislation (*CPW*, ii. 158–64), and it is notable that there is no corresponding entry for this subject in the CPB. So we can conclude that if Milton was retrospectively tidying up the contingencies of his literary past in the *Second Defence*, then there are still some loose ends. But, finally, the *Second Defence's* autobiography was an exercise in retrospective self-structuring that had nevertheless largely originated in, and had been sustained by, the Commonplace Book in Moral Philosophy. The CPB, therefore, witnesses not only to the evolution of Milton's interests, but to the large-scale, static presuppositions about intellectual organization that he had inherited from his education.

CHAPTER 21

MILTON, THE HARTLIB CIRCLE, AND THE EDUCATION OF THE ARISTOCRACY

TIMOTHY RAYLOR

THE modern reader approaching Milton's tract *Of Education* for the first time is likely to be puzzled by two things. The first is the vast range and stupefying ambition of Milton's curriculum, with readings in classical authors ranging from Aratus to Zaleucus. The second is its oddity: just what kind of an institution might include the study of biblical Aramaic alongside instruction in music, fortification, and wrestling? These difficulties raise the question of the character of the proposal. Was it, as some have thought, a mere paper project, from which one should not expect much by way of plausibility? Or did Milton imagine that there was a real chance his plan might be put into practice? In this chapter, I suggest that we take seriously the institutional aspect of Milton's sketch. Although in some respects eccentric and certainly overambitious, it nevertheless represented a genuine proposal to establish

For their support of my research I am grateful to the Dean and President of Carleton College and indebted in many ways to my unstintingly generous colleagues in the Department of English. For comments on this essay, I thank Richard DuRocher.

in England a version of the French noble academy which was then enjoying great popularity among the English upper classes. Milton's was in fact just one in a series of efforts to bring such academies to England: an effort distinctive for its attempt to reform the noble academy in order to produce a new breed of reformed aristocrat. To see Milton's proposal in this light encourages us to recognize its continuities with his reformist aristocratic entertainments of the 1630s,[1] and to discern more precisely than hitherto both the nature of his proposed institution and the character of its connection with the schemes of the educational reformer Samuel Hartlib, at whose request Milton wrote the tract. For in efforts to establish such academies in England, Hartlib and his associates played a significant role; in doing so, moreover, they were profoundly influenced by Milton's work.

I

There is a strong temptation, when faced with the range of texts and languages Milton's boys were to master, to dismiss his curriculum as a pipe dream. Such, famously, was the reaction of Dr Johnson.[2] But Johnson—himself a failed pedagogue—lived through what was almost certainly the nadir of English education; what seemed impractical to the mid-eighteenth century did not necessarily appear so to the mid-seventeenth. It has often been noted that Milton's pedagogical practice in the instruction of his nephews and a small group of young boys during the early to mid-1640s traced large areas of the curriculum he sketched in his tract.[3] Such evidence suggests that we should take his sketch seriously.

But how exactly should we take it? What kind of institution did it imply? Students of Milton have long wrestled with the nature and character of his projected academy. That it embodies, in a general way, the Renaissance aim of offering an education in virtue: modelling young men of standing into perfect scholar-soldiers, prepared to take a

---

[1] The reformist impulse in these entertainments is demonstrated by Cedric C. Brown, *John Milton's Aristocratic Entertainments* (Cambridge, 1985); for the broader context, see Barbara K. Lewalski, 'How Radical was the Young Milton?', in Steven B. Dobranski and John P. Rumrich (eds.), *Milton and Heresy* (Cambridge, 1998), 49–72.

[2] James Boswell, *Life of Johnson*, ed. R. W. Chapman, rev. J. D. Fleeman (Oxford, 1980), 999; Samuel Johnson, *Lives of the English Poets*, ed. George Birkbeck Hill, 3 vols. (Oxford, 1905), i. 18–19.

[3] See e.g. David Masson, *The Life of John Milton: Narrated in Connexion with the Political, Ecclesiastical, and Literary History of his Time*, 6 vols. (1859–80), iii. 253–4; Oliver Morley Ainsworth, *Milton on Education* (Cornell Studies in English, 12; New Haven, 1928), 15–16; Donald Lemen Clark, *John Milton at St. Paul's School* (New York, 1948), 251; *Of Education*, ed. Thomas R. Hartmann, in *The Prose of John Milton*, ed. J. Max Patrick (New York, 1967), 220–2. For the full text of Phillips's biographical account, see Darbishire, 60–1; Gordon Campbell helpfully presents an annotated version of this part of it, which may be readily compared with Milton's essay, in Milton, *Complete English Poems, 'Of Education', 'Areopagitica'*, ed. Gordon Campbell (1990), 570–1.

leading role in public affairs, has been recognized.[4] Milton's comment on the goal and scope of his proposal comprises a classic statement of the aims of this kind of education. Milton claims to be showing how to provide 'a compleate and generous Education', which he defines, conventionally, as 'that which fits a man to perform justly, skillfully and magnanimously all the offices both private and publike of peace and war'.[5] He also reveals his commitment by dividing the curriculum into two parts, with 'studies' on the one hand and 'exercises' on the other (*CPW*, ii. 381), thereby representing two of the three aspects of the archetypical Renaissance gentlemanly education (the third aspect— 'manners', a vital part of the Italian, courtly version of the tradition—he completely ignores, for reasons we shall discuss in due course).[6] In addition to recognizing that it falls squarely within the tradition of the Renaissance education of the aristocrat for public service, there is also a strong consensus that, in its emphasis on the primacy of literary training, *Of Education* is also indebted to the humanist education Milton had himself received at St Paul's School—even, perhaps, extending a humanist grammar-school approach through university.[7] Having started his boys five years later than normal (at 12 as opposed to 7), the tract takes them through the grammar-school curriculum and beyond: through to the age of majority (21), covering large areas of the undergraduate arts course: the mathematical and natural sciences, ethics and politics, logic and rhetoric, but all by way of classical literature.

The institution adumbrated in *Of Education* cannot, however, be understood as a kind of extended grammar school, from which it differs in three fundamental respects. The first is its emphasis on the practical application of the disciplines—as in the applied mathematics of 'Fortification, *Architecture*, Enginry, or navigation' (*CPW*, ii. 392); this emphasis on utility is quite out of step with the speculative bias of both grammar-school and university approaches to learning. The second is its inclusion of physical exercises: at least an hour and a half a day devoted to swordsmanship and wrestling, followed by practice in music; two hours before supper on infantry or cavalry manoeuvres—the latter implying mastery of and therefore

---

[4] See e.g. William Harrison Woodward, *Studies in Education during the Age of the Renaissance, 1400–1600* (Cambridge, 1906), 296; Elbert N. S. Thompson, 'Milton's *Of Education*', *Studies in Philology*, 15 (1918), 159–75; Harris Francis Fletcher, *The Intellectual Development of John Milton*, 2 vols. (Urbana, Ill., 1956–61), i. 73–88. See also *CPW*, iv. 625.

[5] *CPW*, ii. 378–9. Compare 'this institution of breeding . . . shall be equally good both for Peace and warre' (*CPW*, ii. 408). Similarly phrased statements appear in *The Institucion of a Gentleman* (1555), sig. c5ʳ, quoted in Ruth Kelso, *The Doctrine of the English Gentleman in the Sixteenth Century* (University of Illinois Studies in Language and Literature, 14; Urbana, Ill., 1929), 39; in Roger Ascham, *The Schoolmaster (1570)*, ed. Lawrence V. Ryan (Charlottesville, Va., 1967), 49, and in the writings of Antoine de Pluvinel (see below, n. 26). The general context is well sketched by Kelso, *Doctrine*, 111–62.

[6] Kenneth Charlton, *Education in Renaissance England* (1965), 82, 221. The terms 'study' and 'exercise' come from the Latin 'studium' and 'exercitus' and are standard in the tradition: see Pier Paulo Vergerio, 'The Character and Studies Befitting a Free-Born Youth', in *Humanist Educational Treatises*, ed. Craig W. Kallendorf (Cambridge, Mass., 2002), 36–7, 66–7, 76–82; Richard Mulcaster, *Positions Concerning the Training Up of Children*, ed. William Barker (Toronto, Buffalo, and London, 1994), 60–3; and compare Sir Thomas Elyot, *The Governor*, ed. S. E. Lehmberg (1962), 59.

[7] Clark, *Milton at St. Paul's*, 250–1; Sirluck, *CPW*, ii. 213–14; Fletcher, *Intellectual Development*, i. 152.

training in horsemanship.[8] None of this features in any known grammar-school curriculum.[9] Finally, and most fundamentally, unlike either grammar school or university, Milton's institution is designed for the instruction of the upper classes: 'These are the studies wherein our noble and our gentle youth ought to bestow their time' (ii. 406).

The last aspect of Milton's proposal has often been noticed, but is generally regarded with embarrassment and treated with equivocation by modern scholars, keen to read the inclusiveness and meritocracy of contemporary liberal education back onto Milton's 'compleate and generous Education'.[10] In the Yale edition of the tract, for instance, Donald C. Dorian quite properly glosses 'generous' as 'appropriate to one of noble birth or spirit'; but he goes on, in an accompanying exposition, to loosen its focus, implying that Milton is *not* drawing a strict class distinction here: 'Milton's deliberate intention is to provide a plan of education for those boys suited by birth *or character* to become leaders' (ii. 378 n. 56; my emphasis). The additional evidence Dorian musters does not, however, support his suggestion that character alone might fit one for such an education. He cites, for example, Milton's revived proposal, in *The Readie & Easie Way*, for the establishment of 'schools and academies' which would teach both 'liberal arts and exercises' to the sons of 'the nobilitie and chief gentry'. It is hard to see how such phrasing might be construed as referring to character rather than class.[11] Contemporary evidence about Milton's proposal supports a narrow reading. John Phillips—the poet's nephew—was absolutely clear on the matter, describing the educational programme of the tract as 'an easy and delightful method for training up Gentry'; he does not write: 'those of gentle spirit' (Darbishire, 24). This does not, of course, mean that Milton intended to institute some kind of genealogical entry requirement; the point is that he conceives of his curriculum as appropriate for aristocrats and leading gentlemen and makes no effort to urge its utility for those of lower rank. Some sense of the social standing, and also the range, of the anticipated clientele may be gauged from Milton's known pupils during the early 1640s, among whom were an Anglo-Irish aristocrat, an Essex

[8] In his notes to the Yale edition, Dorian points out the distinctiveness of both Milton's proposal for the teaching of mathematics and his emphasis on military training, drawing parallels in both cases with Gilbert's 'Queene Elizabethes Achademy' (on which, see below) (386–7 n. 82, 411 n. 26).

[9] J. Howard Brown, *Elizabethan Schooldays* (Oxford, 1933), 135–6; but compare Joan Simon, *Education and Society in Tudor England* (Cambridge, 1966), 365–6. Mulcaster was one of the few educational theorists who recommended instruction in physical exercises at the grammar school—he emphasized wrestling; his recent editor, however, shows that he wrote with little or no first-hand understanding of the implications of his recommendations, which were lifted wholesale from an earlier source (*Positions*, pp. xxii–xxviiii).

[10] Charles Webster quietly condemns the academy by the adjective 'élitist' (*Samuel Hartlib and the Advancement of Learning* (Cambridge, 1970), 42); and William Riley Parker ignores its class restrictions, noting merely that it is designed to produce public leaders (*Milton*, i. 255); but compare, for a more clear-sighted view, '*Areopagitica*' and '*Of Education*', ed. K. M. Lea (Oxford, 1973), pp. xiv–xv, and Perez Zagorin, *Milton: Aristocrat and Rebel* (Rochester, N.Y., and Woodbridge, 1992), 61.

[11] Milton, *CPW*, vii. 383–4, 458–9, 460. I do not see that this represents, as has been suggested by Arthur E. Barker, a 'return to the humanistic confidence of *Of Education*' (*Milton and the Puritan Dilemma 1641–1660* (1942), 281); this is to mistake a class distinction for a change of mind.

gentleman, and two of the poet's own nephews (Parker, *Milton*, i. 296–7, ii. 922–5). Milton is nothing if not sceptical about the virtue of hereditary nobility; but he is clear-sighted about the fact that there is a governing class, and proposes means of reforming it.[12]

While the concern with applied science, the practice of exercises with a military aspect, and its noble student body distinguish Milton's projected institution from the English grammar school or university, these are all features of a largely forgotten contemporary institution: the French aristocratic academy. Historians of education have in fact long since recognized that the institution Milton sketched in *Of Education* was a version of such an academy.[13] But perhaps because of the lack of any comprehensive overview of the academies—and also, perhaps, because of a long tradition of whiggishness in Milton studies—students of the poet have been reluctant to pursue this line of enquiry.[14]

II

The origins of the noble academy lie in the tension that emerged in the Renaissance between the clerical education offered at the universities and the demand by growing numbers of the nobility and gentry (who had traditionally tended to ignore institutions of higher education in favour of private tutors and pageships) for access to the universities and, once there, for an education for leadership in public life—in the camp or the provinces, in public assemblies or at court: an education in practical philosophy, in ethics and politics; in the government of the mind and of the body— the kind of education first sketched by Sir Thomas Elyot in *The Governour* and imitated in successors like James Cleland's *Institution of a Young Nobleman* and Henry Peacham's *Complete Gentleman*. Such an education the universities—still primarily clerical seminaries, dominated in England by faculties of law and (after the Reformation) theology—were neither designed nor well equipped to provide.[15]

---

[12] For Milton's scepticism about hereditary nobility, see, for example, his remarks in the Commonplace Book (*CPW*, i. 471–3) and *An Apology against a Pamphlet* (*CPW*, i. 922–3).

[13] John William Adamson, *Pioneers of Modern Education in the Seventeenth Century* (Cambridge, 1921), 182–5; Patricia-Ann Lee, 'Some English Academies: An Experiment in the Education of Renaissance Gentlemen', *History of Education Quarterly*, 10 (1970), 273–86 at 281–2.

[14] In his introduction to the Yale edition of the tract, Sirluck gestured briefly towards the existence of such institutions and marked them out as 'a promising field' for future research (ii. 214); I am not aware that any student of Milton has ever followed up on his suggestion. Thompson had earlier discussed the French academies in relation to Milton, but rejected any possible influence on the grounds of Milton's well-known dislike of French culture ('Milton's *Of Education*', 170–1).

[15] The classic statements of this view are J. H. Hexter, *Reappraisals in History* (1961), 45–70; Laurence Stone, 'The Educational Revolution in England, 1560–1640', *Past and Present*, 28 (1964), 41–80; Charlton, *Education in Renaissance England*, 16–19, 132–57, 213–15; Simon, *Education and Society*, 340–53; Hugh Kearney, *Scholars and Gentlemen: Universities and Society* (1970), 25–33.

In the early sixteenth century, proposals for alternative systems of aristocratic education were mooted. As the century wore on, however, and increasing numbers of gentry and aristocracy repaired to the university, the colleges, at least, made efforts to provide such an education, reconfiguring themselves from societies of graduates to institutions of undergraduate instruction.[16] And student demand for instruction in fencing and dancing encouraged independent professors of those arts to set up shop in university towns—not always with the blessing of the university authorities.[17]

A classic statement of the aristocratic point of view can be found in the autobiography of Edward, Lord Herbert of Cherbury, who received his early education just prior to the first great flourishing of the French academies (he matriculated from University College, Oxford in 1596). In reflecting on his upbringing, Lord Herbert entered into a lengthy digression on education, from which it is apparent that he regarded his own as being split into two discrete parts. On the one hand were his studies, first with private tutors and then at university; on the other—and quite outside the official institutions of learning—came his independent mastery of modern languages and music, and his practice, under 'masters' in both England and France, of the exercises of fencing and horsemanship. Herbert dismissed the undergraduate arts course as unsuitable for a gentleman. Its emphasis on elaborate logical disputations and pre-professional training turned students into 'excellent wranglers, which Art though it may bee tollerable in a mercenary Lawyer I can by noe meanes commend it in a sober and well gouerned Gentleman'.[18] The kind of education required by a gentleman was altogether different. It featured Greek literature at school for the universal knowledge contained therein. Afterwards, enough logic to test the strength of his own and others' reasoning (six months at the most); a nodding acquaintance with Plato and Aristotle; geography, to understand the nations of the world—their situations, manners, religions, and governments, both ancient and modern; enough arithmetic to keep accounts and enough geometry to understand the science of fortifications; sufficient medicine to undertake diagnoses and enough botany to compose cures; moral philosophy and theology to guide conduct; and rhetoric for eloquence (though not in the over-schematized and artificial manner of the schools). In addition to his intellectual development, the student should pursue, under the tutelage of appropriate masters (preferably French),

---

[16] For the seminal statement of the view (much contested) that the universities successfully responded to the new demands, see M. H. Curtis, *Oxford and Cambridge in Transition 1558–1642* (Oxford, 1959), 17–148, but see Charlton, *Education in Renaissance England*, 144–50; Simon, *Education and Society*, 357–61; Rosemary O'Day, *Education and Society 1500–1800* (London and New York, 1982), 81–97, 106–18; and James McConica (ed.), *The History of the University of Oxford: The Collegiate University* (Oxford, 1986), 179–80, 693–721. Extensive research on 17th-c. Oxford by Mordechai Feingold tends to support Curtis's thesis, for the later period, at least ('The Humanities', and 'The Mathematical Sciences and New Philosophies', in Nicholas Tyacke (ed.), *The History of the University of Oxford: Seventeenth-Century Oxford* (Oxford, 1997), 211–357, 359–448.

[17] McConica (ed.), *The Collegiate University*, 652; Tyacke (ed.), *Seventeenth-Century Oxford*, 70; John Earle, *Microcosmography*, ed. Harold Osborne (n.d.), 61, 155.

[18] *The Life of Edward, First Lord Herbert of Cherbury Written by Himself*, ed. J. M. Shuttleworth (1976), 19, 16–17, 31–5.

physical 'exercises' in the following order: dancing (to render the body graceful), fencing (not before the age of 11), and the manège (the riding of the great horse: a valuable courtly discipline in its own right, which also provided training for duelling and warfare).[19]

Lord Herbert did not himself enrol in an academy on reaching Paris in 1608, but he was impressed by them, and continued to practise his music, fencing, and horsemanship there.[20] The educational plan he sketched in his autobiography was an idealized version of the kind of education the academies were, by then, ostensibly providing—a practical education for an active nobility.

III

The French academies emerged in the wake of the wars of religion, after figures like François de la Noue generated proposals to reverse the decline of the aristocracy by way of improved education.[21] The first academy was established, with royal approval (though not, apparently, under direct royal authority), at Paris by Antoine de Pluvinel, 'écuyer du roi', in 1594. This was primarily a riding school fashioned after the Italian model (Pluvinel had studied in Naples under Pignatelli); it taught the manège according to Pluvinel's new 'method of the pillars'.[22] But Pluvinel had larger ambitions. In the version of his fictionalized dialogue with Louis XIII published posthumously in 1625, he advocated the establishment of four academies under royal authority: one at Paris, and others in leading provincial cities.[23] Such academies were

---

[19] Ibid. 18–35; see also Kelso, *Doctrine of the English Gentleman.* One might compare Lord Herbert's sketch with James Cleland, *Institution of a Young Noble-Man*, ed. Max Molyneux (New York, 1948), 74–97, and Henry Percy, 9th earl of Northumberland, *Advice to his Son*, ed. G. B. Harrison (1930), 67–72.

[20] He tells us that he was privately instructed in the manège by Disancour and Menou, respectively the personal écuyer and the page of Henri, duc de Montmorency. The first of these was a horseman, Herbert insists, 'not inferior to Pluvenel or La-brove'; the second, Herbert takes pains to point out, 'keepes now an Academy at Paris'; on Pluvinel, see below; Salomon La Broue was a leading horseman, author of the influential *Cavalerice François* (Herbert of Cherbury, *Life*, 49, 45).

[21] There is no adequate general survey of these institutions, which are not to be confused with the literary and learned societies of the 16th and later 17th cc. Useful overviews (with valuable bibliographical references) are Roger Chartier, Dominique Julia, and Marie-Madeleine Compère, *L'Éducation en France du XVIe au XVIIIe siècle* (Paris, 1976), 168–71, 181–5; Ellery Schalk, *From Valor to Pedigree: Ideas of Nobility in France in the Sixteenth and Seventeenth Centuries* (Princeton, 1986), 174–201; Mark Motley, *Becoming a French Aristocrat: The Education of the Court Nobility 1580–1715* (Princeton, 1990), 123–68. From the point of view of the English traveller, the most useful sources are John Stoye, *English Travellers Abroad, 1604–1667*, rev. edn. (New Haven and London, 1989), 31–9, 311, 313, 333, and John Lough, *France Observed in the Seventeenth Century by British Travellers* (Stocksfield, 1985), 284–5.

[22] Schalk, *From Valor to Pedigree*, 181–8.

[23] Pluvinel, *L'Instruction du roy en l'exercice de monter à cheval* (Amsterdam, 1666), 152.

to be more than mere riding-schools; each was to be a complete 'escole de vertu'.[24] Housing its students in 'a lodging large and spacious enough to accommodate gentlemen', each academy would develop body and mind for service and command.[25] Through physical training in fencing, horsemanship, and dancing students would master the arts of the camp and the court; through mental training in ethics and politics, they would come to understand the full range of their duties, both civil and martial, and learn how to enact them: 'either to command or to obey, as also how to serve their master, either in an embassy, or in some other affair; in brief, to try in this way to render them capable of serving their prince well, either in peace or in war'.[26]

Pluvinel's idea of state control was not taken up, but his academy itself was an instant success, spawning imitations at Paris and in the provinces: at Toulouse (1598), Angers (by 1601), Aix (1611), and elsewhere.[27] At their apogee, around 1680, there were apparently seven or eight academies in Paris and as many as twenty in the provinces.[28]

Entrance to the academies was limited to members of the nobility, though we do not know how rigorously a student's credentials were examined.[29] No doubt to increase enrolments in a limited home market, the academies soon began to attract and admit foreign students. The first Englishman to enrol in Pluvinel's academy seems to have been Henry, Lord Clifford, in 1610; others soon followed suit.[30] We cannot be sure of the numbers involved—most of the registers are lost; but some sense of the scale of the English presence may be gauged from the lists of foreign students at the academy of Angers, analysed by Willem Frijhoff. Frijhoff found that

---

[24] *L'Instruction du Roy en l'exercice de monter à cheval* (Paris, 1625); all quotations are from the Amsterdam edition of 1666. This posthumous work underwent substantial editorial attention by Pluvinel's literary executor, Menou de Charnizay, on which see the comments of Hilda Nelson in Pluvinel, *The Maneige Royal*, trans. Hilda Nelson (1989), pp. v–vi, xi n. 8, and those of Schalk, *From Valor to Pedigree*, 186. It is impossible to know exactly when the dialogue was written, and how much Menou was responsible for its final form. Its emphasis on the financial independence and moral qualities necessary for the head of an academy, and its dismissive remarks about those who currently ran such institutions (*L'Instruction*, 153), suggests that Pluvinel was pushing for regulatory authority over the burgeoning academies; the crown did eventually, in the late 17th c., secure such authority: Motley, *Becoming a French Aristocrat*, 127–33.

[25] 'un logis grand & spacieux pour loger les Gentils-hommes' (*L'Instruction*, 154).

[26] 'soit pour commander, soit pour obeyr: comme quoy servir son Maistre, soit en Ambassade, soit en quelqu'autre affaire particuliere: bref, tascher par ce moyen de les rendre capables de bien servir leur Prince, soit en paix, soit en guerre' (ibid. 155).

[27] For Toulouse and Aix, see Schalk, *From Valor to Pedigree*, 182 n. 18, 188; for Angers, see Willem Frijhoff, 'Étudiants étrangers à l'académie d'équitation d'Angers au XVIIᵉ siècle', *LIAS*, 4 (1977), 1–84 at 1–2.

[28] Chartier et al., *L'Éducation*, 181; Motley, *Becoming a French Aristocrat*, 126–7. The number might even have been higher. Writing to Samuel Hartlib in 1648, Sir Balthazar Gerbier claimed that there were twelve academies in Paris alone; Sheffield University Library, Hartlib Papers, 36/1/18A; quoted from the CD-ROM edition, *The Hartlib Papers*, 2nd edn. (Sheffield, 2002); further references to the Hartlib Papers are by bundle and leaf number. Gerbier repeated the claim in his dedication to *A Publique Lecture on all the Languages, Arts, Sciences, and Noble Exercises* (London, 1650), sig. A2ᵛ; but since his purpose was clearly promotional his estimate cannot be regarded as disinterested.

[29] Schalk, *From Valor to Pedigree*, 194–5; Schalk notes the possible exception of Aix (188).

[30] Stoye, *English Travellers Abroad*, 31–9.

eighty-four English or Scottish students enrolled in the academy between 1601 and 1635, making up 12 per cent of its student body (well behind the Germanic visitors and those from the Low Countries, but ahead of the Scandinavians); most (forty-seven) registered between 1606 and 1613.[31] Frijhoff's figures may be slightly high, since they lump visiting aristocrats together with their travelling tutors: the incongruous figure of John Dury—Hartlib's future associate as educational reformer and roving advocate of Protestant union—appears as a student in 1623 (no. 457); he was in fact travelling as tutor to the son of a Dutch gentleman, Barthelemy Panhuysen (= P[eter?]; no. 122).[32] Even allowing for some inflation, however, the numbers involved, though small, are substantial. And since Angers was only one of up to twenty provincial academies, with perhaps eight more in Paris itself, the number of English aristocrats enrolled in the French academies during this period may have reached the low thousands. In all likelihood it did not climb so high; few even among the aristocracy or gentry could afford the expense—over £100 per year in 1642, according to one estimate.[33]

The course of tuition offered in the academies appears to have been basically that outlined in Pluvinel's dialogue: horsemanship, supplemented by some combination of fencing, vaulting (= the art of leaping onto horses), dancing, applied mathematics (for fortifications), moral and political philosophy, drawing and painting, writing and music.[34] Thomas Lorkin, travelling tutor to Sir Thomas Puckering, furnishes details of a typical day at Pluvinel's academy in November 1610: two hours each morning on horsemanship, one on weapon-handling, one on French, and one on Latin; a two-hour dinner break (from twelve until two o'clock), featuring some arms-related recreation; an hour of dancing followed by two more on Latin. After supper, a review of the day's studies.[35]

Lorkin's account surprises slightly by its reference to Latin; a frequent criticism of the academies was that they failed to provide an adequate training in traditional academic 'studies'. Alternative ways of doing so were soon proposed.

---

[31] The list features some very grand names: Cecil, Devereux, and Godolphin (Sidney: student no. 460; registered in 1630); Percy, Vaux, and Villiers (George, first duke of Buckingham: student no. 510, registered in 1611, along with his brother, John: no. 511) (Frijhoff, 'Étudiants étrangers', 19, 43–5).

[32] J. Minton Batten, *John Dury: Advocate of Christian Reunion* (Chicago, 1944), 15. A similar explanation accounts for the presence of Nathaniel Brent (no. 439), fellow and future warden of Merton College, Oxford, who enrolled in 1613, while travelling as tutor to Lord Cromwell (no. 452); Cromwell's registration date is, however, given as 1611 rather than 1613. The same is probably true also of the future biblical scholar Herbert Thorndike (no. 504; enrolled 1630) (A. J. Hegarty, 'Brent, Sir Nathaniel', *ODNB*).

[33] In 1610 Clifford's tutor estimated the cost of enrolment in Pluvinel's academy alone at £70 per year, his full expenses totalling £500 (tuition and private lodgings outside the academy came to £150; the lodging cost £80) (Stoye, *English Travellers Abroad*, 31; Charlton, *Education in Renaissance England*, 221–2). In 1642, James Howell estimated that £110 would cover tuition, diet, and lodging in a Parisian academy for a student and his servant (Howell, *Instructions for Forreine Travell*, ed. Edward Arber (1869), 27).

[34] Schalk, *From Valor to Pedigree*, 190–1; Frances A. Yates, *The French Academies of the Sixteenth Century* (1947, 1988), 278 (painting); compare the accounts of James Howell, John Evelyn, and Sir John Reresby, referenced below.

[35] Charlton, *Education in Renaissance England*, 220–1.

In 1636, Cardinal Richelieu established twenty scholarships for poor nobles to enrol at Benjamin's academy (Benjamin was Pluvinel's successor) while also undertaking the kind of studies associated with the university arts course: logic, physics, and metaphysics; ethics and history—all with an emphasis on the vernacular. Richelieu was not entirely satisfied with this solution, and went on to propose his own academies, which would blend academy with college; in 1640 he established one in the town of Richelieu. This offered a six-year course, in the vernacular, on a range of trivial, quadrivial, and modern studies, ranging from grammar, poetry, and rhetoric in the first year, through (*inter alia*) mechanics, optics, astronomy, and gnomonics, to moral philosophy, economics, politics, and metaphysics in the final year. In Richelieu's academy, 'studies' effectively dethroned 'exercises', which were to be undertaken twice a day, in the afternoons, as they might be fitted in ('aux heures les plus commodes'). There was even provision for instruction in Greek and Latin grammar in the evenings. This shift in emphasis did not adversely affect enrolments; the academy took 200 students in its first year and 400 in its second. But its success had more to do with the prestige of its founder than the attractiveness of its new curriculum; on the cardinal's death, it quickly dwindled.[36]

Nor did Richelieu's initiatives have any discernible impact on the other academies. James Howell's 1642 account of the Parisian academies mentioned only the traditional bodily exercises, along with mathematics.[37] And when, in early April 1644, the learned virtuoso John Evelyn visited the academies of Du Plessis and de Veau to watch students riding the great horse, he noted their emphasis on such exercises, along with the development of 'some skill in Fortification & the Mathematics', and approved it: 'truely the designe is admirable & very worthy'.[38] Indeed, Evelyn regarded the academies as an important source of French military prowess.[39] Some visitors did, however, register concern about the neglect of learning in the academies. After visiting France in the mid-1650s Sir John Reresby—no great intellectual—wrote that 'The gentry are well bred, but no scholars, being usually taken from their studies at about fourteen, then put in the academy to learn their exercises, as fencing, dancing, music, riding the great horse, and the like.'[40] To Reresby, the academies offered an alternative to rather than a means of study. Similar criticisms would be levelled by many of the educational projectors who sought to create English rivals to the French academies.

[36] Chartier, et al., *L'Éducation*, 183–5; Schalk, *From Valor to Pedigree*, 192–5.
[37] Howell, *Instructions*, 27.
[38] John Evelyn, *The Diary of John Evelyn*, ed. E. S. De Beer, 6 vols. (Oxford, 1955), ii. 134. Lord Willoughby was enrolled in de Vaux's academy in 1647 (Lough, *France Observed*, 284); for others enrolled there in 1650 see Evelyn, *Diary*, iii. 8.
[39] Lough, *France Observed*, 181, 285: quoting Evelyn, *Diary*, i. 88, and his *State of France* (1652), 87–8.
[40] Sir John Reresby, *Memoirs and Travels of Sir John Reresby*, ed. Albert Ivatt (1904), 37.

IV

....

From their earliest days the French academies, with their provision of instruction in martial exercises and courtly accomplishments, greatly appealed to the English nobility and gentry, who enrolled in considerable numbers, usually in the course of a broader programme of travel and instruction: an embryonic grand tour, which served as the final phase of a young man's education, adding experience and polish to precepts learned in study under a tutor or at university.[41] This was not the most efficient or economical method of education. If the universities were to offer instruction in noble exercises and courtly accomplishments, the recourse to foreign academies would be unnecessary. But the universities had not the slightest interest in offering such instruction; indeed, they fought hard to suppress it. The story of the attempt to establish the academies in England is, in consequence, that of a series of private initiatives to seek royal patronage or state support for the creation of alternative educational institutions: institutions that would furnish practical instruction for the minds and bodies of an active nobility; an education civic, martial, and (often) courtly, rather than scholastic.[42] These projectors tended to focus their arguments around two points: the inadequacy of the university curriculum and those of the French academies; and the dangers (moral and physical), expense, and incommodities of foreign travel.[43]

The first formal proposal for an English noble academy appears to pre-date the French institutions. It is Sir Humphrey Gilbert's proposal for 'Queene Elizabethes Achademy', a manuscript of uncertain date, apparently submitted to the Queen or at least to her advisers, perhaps around 1572.[44] Gilbert's proposal is a blueprint for the education of the Queen's wards, along with 'others the youth of nobility and gentlemen', from the age of 12 until their majority, in a curriculum designed for civil and military action rather than scholarship: 'wheareas in the vniuersities men study only *schole learninges*, in this *Achademy* they shall study matters of accion meet for present practize, both of peace and warre'.[45] The academy was to feature instruction in

---

[41] Charlton, *Education in Renaissance England*, 215–17. One work of advice recommended 25 as the most suitable age at which to travel; but this was in response to the fact that many went abroad younger; Charlton, *Education in Renaissance England*, 217–18, 220. Students at Angers ranged from age 16 to 30, with almost 66 per cent being aged between 20 and 24 (Frijhoff, 'Étudiants étrangers', 23).

[42] On the attempts to establish English academies there is no full and satisfactory modern study. In addition to the particular references cited below, the most helpful overviews are T. W. J., 'Dr. Wallis' Letter against Mr. Maidwell. 1700', *Collectanea*, 1st ser., ed. C. R. L. Fletcher (Oxford Historical Society, Publications, 5; 1885), 271–305; Foster Watson, *The Beginnings of the Teaching of Modern Subjects in England* (1909), pp. xxxii–xxxiv, *et passim*; Adamson, *Pioneers*, 175–90, and Lee, 'Some English Academies'. In addition, W. A. L. Vincent, *The Grammar Schools: Their Continuing Tradition 1660–1714* (1969), 199–201, contains some useful information about the later period.

[43] Lee, 'Some English Academies', 283.

[44] Ibid. 278.

[45] Sir Humphrey Gilbert, 'Queene Elizabethes Achademy', ed. F. J. Furnivall, in *Early English Texts*, Extra Series, 8 (1869), 1–12 at 1, 10; I have silently expanded conventional abbreviations. Further references are given in text.

traditional grammar-school subjects like Greek, Latin, and Hebrew, along with modern languages and studies in the university arts courses; the boys were also to be given exposure to the higher disciplines: law, divinity, and medicine (pp. 2–7). Instruction in these subjects was to have a practical slant, with a view to civil and military applications. Thus, orations were to be in English, and on political and military matters (p. 2); the moral philosopher was to read only 'the *politique parte* thereof', alternating between civil and martial policy (pp. 3–4); the mathematicians were to teach geometry for '*Imbattelinges, fortificacions, and matters of warre, with the practiz of Artillery*' (p. 4); and the physician was to teach physic, surgery, and the preparation of medicines (pp. 5–6). The 'achademy' also gave due weight to military exercises and courtly accomplishments, offering instruction in horsemanship, arms, 'dancing and vawting', and music (pp. 4–5, 7). Perhaps inevitably, given the hefty price tag Gilbert attached to it (£2,966. 13s. 6d. per annum; p. 9), the proposal came to nothing.[46]

Though Gilbert's proposal vanished, the need for an effective means of educating the aristocracy continued to be felt, along with the sense that an academy in the French sense was its appropriate institutional form. The idea flourished briefly at the short-lived court of Prince Henry, itself eulogized by James Cleland in 1607 as an '*Academie*... where young Nobles may learne the first elements to be a *Privie Counseller*, a *Generall* of an Armie, to rule in peace, & to commande in warre'.[47] But Prince Henry's household incorporated no formal academic structure; it would be some years before another proposal for the formal establishment of such an institution would surface. It did so under the patronage of Buckingham (an alumnus of the Angers academy), who, in the House of Lords on 5 March 1621, solicited voluntary contributions towards the establishment of 'an Academy, for the breeding and bringing up of the Nobility and Gentry of this Kingdom'.[48] A committee was established to investigate the proposal, but the idea did not long survive its sponsor.[49]

The middle decades of the century saw a number of private initiatives, a few of which achieved temporary realization. The first of these was Sir Francis Kynaston's 'Musaeum Minervae', a pilot version of which was established with royal approval and some financial support in 1635.[50] Based in Covent Garden, Kynaston's academy was designed to demonstrate that England could host an institution to rival the academies of the Continent, thus obviating the need for young Englishmen to endure the danger and expense of foreign travel (Kynaston, *Constitutions*, sig. ¶2ʳ–¶3ʳ). It

---

[46] Lee, 'Some English Academies', 278.

[47] *The Institution of a Young Noble Man*, 35; pp. xx–xxvi, 35–7 (conventional abbreviations silently expanded); see also Roy Strong, *Henry, Prince of Wales and England's Lost Renaissance* (1986), 8, 215.

[48] *Journal of the House of Lords*, iii. 36.

[49] The scheme was not always clearly distinguished from a related proposal, associated with the name of Edmund Bolton, for a national academy, which was to be a research rather than a teaching institute; see Ethel M. Portal, 'The Academ Roial of King James I', *Proceedings of the British Academy* (1915–16), 189–208 at 192.

[50] Sir Francis Kynaston, *The Consitutions of the Musaeum Minervae* (1636); G. H. Turnbull, 'Samuel Hartlib's Connection with Sir Francis Kynaston's "Musaeum Minervae"', *Notes and Queries*, 197 (1952), 33–7; Charles Webster, *The Great Instauration: Science, Medicine and Reform 1626–1660* (1975), 218–19.

was a courtly academy on the French model, aiming to provide the sons of the
nobility and gentry with an education in active virtue, marrying, as its choice of
patron suggests, arms and arts, and polishing the combination with a pleasing
courtly gloss.[51] It did so by way of a seven-year course taught by a regent and six
professors—all of them English (8)—which offered the usual balance of intellectual
and corporal pursuits (4). Studies exhibited the typical emphasis on gentlemanly
utility: modern languages as well as ancient; applied mathematics (emphasizing
fortification and architecture); astronomy, optics, navigation, and cosmography;
heraldry, common law, and husbandry (4–5); the similarities with Richelieu's academy are striking. Martial exercises were in the care of a 'Professor of Defence', who
would teach wrestling and the use of weapons. Instruction in courtly 'manners' was
called for—though without any indication that there were means to provide it:
'*Riding* shall be taught; *Dancing* and behaviour, *Painting, Sculpture, Writing*' (5).
The Musaeum quickly ran into financial difficulties and folded after Kynaston's death
in 1642.[52]

Among those who took a particular interest in Kynaston's design was Samuel
Hartlib. It may initially be something of a surprise to find this earnest Puritan
millenarian and tireless promoter of universal education concerning himself with
so elite a scheme as Kynaston's. But Hartlib's educational interests should not be
construed in narrowly Baconian or Comenian terms, as if he were exclusively
concerned with vocational training and the promotion of technical colleges.[53] His
aims and interests were broad, and he clearly saw the education of the nobility and
gentry as a discrete problem in need of reform.[54] Hartlib's earliest pedagogical
undertaking had been the establishment, with the mathematician John Pell, of a
reformed, Puritan version of a noble academy at Chichester, emphasizing piety and
morality rather than martial exercises or courtly accomplishments; he later described
it in his petition to Charles II as 'a little Academie for the Education of the Gentrie of
this Nation, to advance Pietie, Learning, Moralitie, & other Exercises of Industrie not
vsuall then in Common Schooles'.[55] Hartlib's academy was short lived (it lasted little
more than a year); but the idea of a Puritan academy for the nobility and gentry
would resurface in the educational proposals of his maturity.

Although Hartlib hoped, in the auspicious early days of the Long Parliament, to
see the immediate realization of Comenius's 'pansophia', after the collapse of civil
order dashed his utopian dreams, he and the adaptable John Dury retrenched,

---

[51] For the aspirations of the academy, see Kynaston's masque of 27 Feb. 1635[/6], *Corona Minervae*
('1635'[1636]).

[52] On the academy's financial difficulties, see the undated documents of [1637?], National Archives, SP
16/376/8.

[53] As, for instance, in Sirluck's memorable description of him as 'that indefatigable bureau of
Comenian propaganda' (*CPW*, ii. 205).

[54] See also Webster, *Samuel Hartlib*, 42.

[55] Sheffield University Library, Hartlib Papers, 7/19A; G. H. Turnbull, *Hartlib, Dury, and Comenius:
Gleanings from Hartlib's Papers* (1947), 16–20; Noel Malcolm and Jacqueline Stedall, *John Pell (1611–1685)
and his Correspondence with Sir Charles Cavendish* (Oxford, 2005), 30–3.

retailoring their goals and their proposals to suit less propitious circumstances. Universalist aspirations were abandoned in favour of localized plans for the establishment of particular educational institutions—reformed colleges of various kinds.[56] Underlying this shift in emphasis was Hartlib's awareness of the growing bank of confiscated royalist estates and Parliament's promise (dating back to 1641) to employ dean and chapter lands for 'the Advancement of Learning and Piety'.[57] Nothing came of such promises, but Hartlib and his associates regularly recurred to the notion that vulnerable institutions might be appropriated: the Charterhouse, the Savoy Hospital, and, above all, the well-situated but institutionally weak and under-endowed Chelsea College.[58] In reform proposals of the later 1640s, Hartlib and Dury drew up blueprints for networks of reformed educational institutions, often earmarking existing foundations like Chelsea for conversion (in the most elaborate of these—c.1647–9—several institutions were joined to form a collegiate University of London), and invariably including 'academies' for the education of the nobility and gentry—academies associated, in more than one version, with the name of Kynaston.[59]

For some within the circle, such proposals were driven by explicitly political motives. In a semi-legible note on 'means' at the end of a draft plan for various colleges containing material dating from February 1646[/7], Hartlib jotted a proposal to use parliamentary influence to identify a leading royalist (a 'Grand Vn-discoverd delinquent') whose estate might be used for the purpose; this he justifies, in a further note, apparently ascribed to Benjamin Worsley (the name is hard to decipher): 'bec [ause] the Nobilite et Gentry haue so much assisted the k[ing] and beene the org. therefor for there better breeding for the Common Service of their Country to take out of their Delinquencies' (Hartlib Papers, 47/9/35A). By means of a reformed academy, paid for by their sequestered estates, the nobility and gentry were to be reeducated for service in the public interest.

During the later 1640s, Hartlib assisted several projectors in plans to establish reformed noble academies in England.[60] Probably during the period 1645 to 1648 two Huguenot exiles, Hugh l'Amy and Peter le Pruvost, proposed 'vne Academie a la francoise' to be founded at London—or perhaps in an appropriated college at one of the universities.[61] L'Amy and Le Pruvost deployed familiar arguments to justify their academy (e.g. the dangers of foreign travel), but gave it a reformed spin, affording pride of place not to the master of the horse (equitation looks like an afterthought—'Et est aussy possible d'auoir . . . esquiers pour dresser a monter a cheual etc.'), but to a doctor

---

[56] Webster aptly describes the years 1643–6 'as a period of readjustment and consolidation' (*Samuel Hartlib*, 41).

[57] *Journals of the House of Commons*, ii. 159: Webster, *Samuel Hartlib*, 28–9.

[58] On Chelsea College, see Robert Fitzgibbon Young, *Comenius in England* (1932), 43 n. 4, 54; Turnbull, *Hartlib, Dury, and Comenius*, 48–9, 101, 314, 361; Webster, *Samuel Hartlib*, 36, 59; Webster, *Great Instauration*, 49, 71, 221, 223.

[59] Hartlib Papers, 47/9/16B, 21A, 32A–B; Webster, *Samuel Hartlib*, 60; Webster, *Great Instauration*, 223.

[60] For an overview of his activities in this field, see, in addition to the particular sources cited below, Turnbull, *Hartlib, Dury, and Comenius*, 57–64; Webster, *Great Instauration*, 218–19.

[61] Hartlib Papers, 12/101A. Parliament had announced plans to reform the universities as early as 1641 (Webster, *Samuel Hartlib*, 36); Cambridge underwent parliamentary visitation in 1644, Oxford in 1648.

of divinity. There was, however, to be the usual instruction (in French) in physic and logic, ethics, economics, and fortifications, together with exercises in the use of arms.[62]

Hartlib is often mentioned as a leading supporter of the academy established at Bethnal Green in 1650 by Sir Balthazar Gerbier, that courtly entrepreneur and shameless self-publicist.[63] Encouraged by news that the Duke of York was about to enter a French academy, Gerbier proposed, in the summer of 1648, to establish an academy in England; this would avert the usual problems: foreign travel, expense, the superficial French curriculum.[64] But Gerbier went further: soon, foreigners would be travelling to England to study with him.[65] There is, however, no evidence from the various proposals, prospectuses, and specimen lectures he printed up that his curriculum differed in any significant respect from the norm. It included the usual courtly exercises—dancing, painting, riding the great horse; and it was absurdly ambitious: cosmography, geography, and languages were all to be covered on Tuesday mornings.[66] Its distinctive feature was the fact that Gerbier planned to teach most of its courses himself—a decision reflecting limited resources more than breadth of learning. The academy opened in the summer of 1649 and ran for a short time, first at Bethnal Green and subsequently in Whitefriars, before folding in February 1650.[67]

True, Gerbier had sought Hartlib's help in establishing the academy, bombarding him with drafts, proposals, and demands: for the distribution of publicity material, for assistance in gaining a pass to re-enter the country; for help in dealing with creditors, in finding a site for the academy, in printing publicity materials.[68] But there is little evidence that Hartlib did much to help him. Hartlibian influence might be detected in Gerbier's inclusion of 'experimental natural Philosophy', and in his eventual dropping of Latin from the curriculum, to avert the ire of the universities.[69]

---

[62] Hartlib Papers, 12/101A–102B; Turnbull, *Hartlib, Dury, and Comenius*, 63; Webster, *Great Instauration*, 219. The proposal is not dated, but probably belongs to the period 1645–8, during which Hartlib was assisting l'Amy and le Pruvost with their schemes for improved fishing, husbandry, and plantations; Turnbull, *Hartlib, Dury, and Comenius*, 68, 257; Webster, *Great Instauration*, 78, 371–2.

[63] Turnbull, *Hartlib, Dury, and Comenius*, 57–63; Webster, *Great Instauration*, 219; M. J. Power, 'Sir Balthazar Gerbier's Academy at Bethnal Green', *East London Papers*, 10 (1967), 19–34. On Gerbier in general, see Donald G. Wing, 'Sir Balthazar Gerbier', in *To Doctor R.: Essays Here Collected and Published in Honor of the Seventieth Birthday of Dr. A. W. S. Rosenbach* (Philadelphia, 1946), 241–9; Hugh Ross Williamson, 'Sir Balthazar Gerbier', in *Four Stuart Portraits* (1949), 26–60, 143–50; Edward Chaney, 'Notes towards a Biography of Balthazar Gerbier', in *The Evolution of the Grand Tour: Anglo-Italian Cultural Relations Since the Renaissance* (2000), 215–25. Jeremy Wood's *Oxford Dictionary of National Biography* entry on Gerbier is unreliable on this aspect of his work (Wood's suggestion that the academy's emphasis on horsemanship, foreign languages, and military technology made it 'a school for spies' is fanciful).

[64] Hartlib Papers, 10/2/4A (Gerbier to Hartlib, 27 Aug. 1648); Gerbier, *To All Fathers of Noble Families, and lovers of Vertue* ([London], [1648]; Wing G573); Turnbull, *Hartlib, Dury, and Comenius*, 58, 61–2.

[65] Gerbier, *To All Fathers of Noble Families, and lovers of Vertue* ([London], [1649]; Wing G574), 5–6.

[66] Ibid. 2–3; 7.

[67] Power, 'Gerbier's Academy', 31, 29, 32.

[68] Hartlib Papers, 10/2/1–47; Power, 'Gerbier's Academy'.

[69] See Gerbier's instructions to Hartlib of 31 Oct. 1648: Hartlib Papers, 10/2/20A; and examples of the prospectus with Latin—e.g. Hartlib Papers, 10/2/36A; *To All Fathers* (Wing G574), 2; *To All Fathers of Noble Families and Lovers of Vertue* (London, [1649]; Wing G575), and without it—e.g. *To All Fathers* (Wing G573).

In general, however, Hartlib's response appears to have been discouraging: the universities would move against him as they had done against Kynaston; a parliamentary monopoly would be impossible to secure (Gerbier claimed not to want one); another academy was soon to open, in St James's.[70] The location of this latter academy, mentioned by Hartlib in a lost letter of 11 January 1649, suggests a link to John Dury, then living at St James's palace, where he was (until May) in charge of educating the king's younger children.[71] If Dury were at this time planning to launch his own academy this would explain Hartlib's rather lukewarm response to Gerbier.[72]

A cluster of documents shows that, during the same period, Hartlib offered substantial editorial assistance to the musician Colonel John Humphrey (uncle of the composer Pelham Humphrey) in framing a petition to Parliament for 'some fitt place & accomodation' in which to set up his academy, which was designed to prevent the need for nobles and gentlemen to travel abroad in order to receive a fit education.[73] The documents are undated, but Hartlib's intrusion of a reference to the teaching of 'double-writing' points to a date in or soon after 1647, when William Petty patented his 'instrument' for this purpose.[74] Humphrey's was in most respects a typical curriculum, divided into studies and exercises, but with a strong intellectual emphasis. Its inclusion of experimental philosophy suggests the influence of Hartlib, who subjected Humphrey's curriculum to revision, adding Hebrew and double-writing—presumably using Petty's new device.[75] Humphrey's academy seems to have been up and running in London in a limited fashion by the summer of 1650, when William Spenser referred to it as an 'Academy of Musick' (Hartlib Papers, 46/7/5A; Spenser to Hartlib, 16 June 1650). Nothing more is heard of it, however, and we may presume that it too failed to take root.

Although efforts to establish English academies for the nobility and gentry yielded no lasting results, we should not leap too quickly to the conclusion that they were follies and inevitably doomed. The sense that there was a need for a discrete kind of education aimed at preparing the nobility and gentry for action in peace and war—a kind of education not provided by the universities—remained strong through the end of the century. The debate focused on how best to provide it. The French academies were its most notable sources; but there were concerns over the solidity

---

[70] Hartlib Papers, 36/1/18A–19A (Gerbier to Hartlib, 9 Sept. 1648); 10/2/10A–11B (Gerbier to Hartlib, 16/26 Sept. 1648); 10/2/28A (Gerbier to Hartlib, 24 Mar. 1649); Turnbull, *Hartlib, Dury, and Comenius*, 59 and n. 1, 61.

[71] 10/2/28A (Gerbier to Hartlib, 24 Mar. 1649); Turnbull, *Hartlib, Dury, and Comenius*, 61, 258–9, 266.

[72] The removal of the royal children from his care in May might also explain why nothing further came of the idea.

[73] Hartlib Papers, 47/8/5A8B; Turnbull, *Hartlib, Dury, and Comenius*, 57; Webster, *Great Instauration*, 218–19.

[74] Petty announced his invention in his *Advice of W. P. to Mr. Samuel Hartlib* of 1648 (Webster, *Great Instauration*, 164).

[75] Hartlib Papers, 47/8/5A, 7A, 9A. Hartlib seems to have toyed with including several more of his pet notions: 'A Vniversal Method of Ordering the Thoughts to finde out by our owne industry any truth as yet vnknown, and to Resolue any Question which may be proposed in Nature, as the Object of a Rational Meditation' appears in one version of the proposal (47/8/9A–9B).

and depth of their curricula;[76] continued arguments over the value as against the expense, incommodities, and dangers of foreign travel; and repeated efforts to bring the best of the academies to England. The arguments on each side are given a careful hearing—but no clear resolution—in Clarendon's late 'Dialogue . . . concerning Education', a discussion which incorporates yet another sketch for a Crown-sponsored domestic academy for gentlemen.[77] Attempts to design or establish such academies continued to occupy educationalists and projectors. John Aubrey began to sketch out an ideal for one in the late 1660s; he was heavily influenced by Milton's tract.[78] A metropolitan academy run by Henry de Foubert flourished in the 1680s.[79] Another was proposed by Lewis Maidwell, who sought public funding for it in 1700, only to meet with energetic opposition from John Wallis, defending the interests of the University of Oxford.[80]

The failure of the academies to take root in England was probably due not to any inherent absurdity in their design but to several interrelated external factors. One was their sponsors' failure to secure adequate official backing to give credibility, guarantee protection, and offset their substantial set-up and operating costs. Another was the vigorous opposition of the universities, which lobbied at every turn to put down the academies as threats to their monopoly on post-grammar-school education.[81] Closely connected with the unversities' offensive action was the apparent success of their defence: their adaptation, at the college level, to the new curricular demands placed upon them by the influx of gentle and noble students.[82] But such a makeshift accommodation could have succeeded only if the gentry and nobility were not seriously troubled by the inefficiencies of a two-stage system, separating studies from exercises. That they were not seems clear. The explanation for this probably lies in the growing fashion for and gradual institutionalization of the grand tour. Against the growing social cachet of the tour, arguments about the dangers of foreign

---

[76] See e.g. John Aubrey, *Aubrey on Education*, ed. J. E Stephens (1972), 19–20, and T. W. J., 'Dr. Wallis' Letter against Mr. Maidwell', 295.

[77] 'A Dialogue . . . concerning Education', in Edward Hyde, earl of Clarendon, *Miscellaneous Works* (1751), 313–48; repr. in *Two Dialogues*, intro. Martine Watson Brownley (Augustan Reprint Society, 227–8; Los Angeles, 1984), pp. vi–vii, 292–321.

[78] See Aubrey, *Aubrey on Education*, 94, 123, 156, 159 n. 5.

[79] Vincent, *The Grammar Schools*, 199–200.

[80] T. W. J., 'Dr. Wallis' Letter against Mr. Maidwell', 269–337. Wallis argued that the university was already providing the kind of individualized attention Maidwell promised; that students could take extra-curricular lessons in riding or fencing if they wished; and that the public financing Maidwell sought would render his academy a burden on the nation. His comments about the ease of taking private lessons in the university towns were disingenuous. While university towns usually housed fencing and dancing masters (see above) riding schools seem to have been rare. The efforts of a Mr Crofts to set one up in Oxford in 1637 were successfully resisted by the university Chancellor, Archbishop Laud (Curtis, *Oxford and Cambridge in Transition*, 144); in his response to Maidwell's petition, Wallis claimed that there had been 'not many years since' a teacher of the manège in Oxford, but could not remember his name (T. W. J., 'Dr. Wallis' Letter against Mr. Maidwell', 319).

[81] In addition to the efforts by Laud and Wallis already noticed, we should give weight to Hartlib's continued concern to alert his projectors to the jealousies of the universities; Turnbull, *Hartlib, Dury, and Comenius*, 59 and n. 1, 60, 63, and Hartlib Papers, 36/1/18A–19A (Gerbier to Hartlib, 9 Sept. 1648).

[82] Lee, 'Some English Academies', 283–4; Feingold, 'Humanities'.

travel carried little weight—though this did not prevent them from being urged.[83] In the end, however, the most significant reason for the ultimate failure for the academies to take root was almost certainly the eventual fall from fashion of the manège, the riding of the great horse, itself.[84]

V

The institution Milton proposed to establish in *Of Education* was a version of a noble academy—a distinctly English, reformed, and Miltonic version, to be sure; but a version nonetheless. This is clear from its conception, its presentation, and its curriculum. In the introduction of his design, Milton refers to his projected establishment as an academy, and—as Pluvinel had earlier done—notes the need for a house of sufficient amplitude and with adequate grounds (evidently for the performance of exercises): 'a spacious house and ground about it fit for an *Academy*' (*CPW*, ii. 379).[85] Contemporaries clearly regarded it as such: Edward Phillips, for instance, refers to it as an 'Academical Institution' (Darbishire, 68). As I have argued above, Milton, like other projectors of academies, regarded his institution as a means of training the sons of the upper classes ('our noble and our gentle youth'; ii. 406) for action: 'to perform justly, skillfully and magnanimously all the offices both private and publike of peace and war' (p. 379). The proximity of Milton's phrasing to that of Pluvinel ('to render them capable of serving their prince well, either in peace or in war'), Gilbert ('they shall study matters of accion meet for present practize, both of peace and warre'), and Cleland ('to rule in peace, & to commande in warre') is striking; but such language is typical of accounts of noble education;[86] it derives from Aristotle's *Politics* (7. 14; 1333^{b}1–5).[87] Like the French academicians, Milton envisages his institution as an aristocrat's alternative to the university.[88] Like other English projectors, Milton criticizes the university arts course for its excessive abstraction, its emphasis on scholastic metaphysics failing to produce virtuous discipline in its students (ii. 374–6). Like the other English projectors also, Milton presents his academy as a means of obviating the need for English students to venture to Paris

---

[83] In addition to Clarendon, see, for instance, Gilbert Burnet's objections against foreign travel, appended to his posthumously published *Thoughts on Education*; John Clarke, *Bishop Gilbert Burnet as Educationist* (Aberdeen, 1914), 77–81.

[84] See Kelso, *Doctrine*, 156.

[85] Compare Pluvinel's demand for 'un logis grand & spacieux pour loger les Gentils-hommes' (*L'Instruction*, 154).

[86] See also the anonymous *Institucion of a Gentleman* (1555), sig. c5^r, cit. Kelso, *Doctrine*, 39.

[87] As noted by Dorian 379 n. 58 (citing vii. 8) and Hartmann, in *Prose of John Milton*, 241 n. 11.

[88] It is not, Parker suggests (*Milton*, i. 255), designed as a general replacement for the university. Milton had little use for the universities, but such academies are clearly distinct from the schools Milton later envisaged (in *The Likeliest Means*) as providing for clerical education (*CPW*, vii. 90–1, 183–4, 305).

to seek a superficial instruction, whence they return corrupted: 'Nor shall we then need the *Mounsieurs* of *Paris* to take in our hopefull youth into thir slight and prodigall custodies and send them over back again transform'd into mimics, apes & Kicshoes' (p. 414).[89] This passage is usually glossed as a general critique of French culture; I think it makes more sense to read it as a specific gibe at the expensive and insubstantial education offered by the Parisian masters. Like Gerbier, Milton goes further: domestic academies on his model might attract foreigners to come and study in England—or even to imitate his version of the academy: 'And perhaps then other Nations will be glad to visit us for their breeding, or else to imitate us in their own Country' (p. 414). Finally, Milton's hope that academies on his model would be instituted 'in every City throughout this land' (p. 381) echoes the petitions of figures like Pluvinel and Gilbert for Crown- or State-sponsored academies throughout the provinces.[90]

It is in terms of the noble academy that Milton's curriculum can best be understood. Milton's was of course not absolutely typical—it differs in some crucial ways from the French norm; but its most important and distinctive features can best be accounted for by reference to that standard. This is clear first of all from the tract's division of the curriculum into studies and exercises. Although there is no doubt some validity in the tradition of explaining Milton's decision to include military exercises by reference to the poor showing of the parliamentary army at this stage in the Civil War, such an ad hoc explanation misses the larger congruence between Milton's curriculum and the Renaissance ideal of aristocratic education embodied in the academies.[91] It also ignores the fact that even before the outbreak of hostilities Milton had, in *The Reason of Church-Government* (1642), been urging mandatory public participation in 'martial exercises' to enhance 'warlike skil and performance' (*CPW*, i. 819).

The exercises Milton envisages for his students are largely those of the academies: fencing and music; 'military motions' (*CPW*, ii. 411). There are, however, some significant alterations. One is the expectation that the entire student body will turn out and engage in drills and manoeuvres; I am not aware that anything quite this ambitious was attempted in the French academies—not, at least, before they metamorphosed into military academies; but we have already noted that Evelyn's suggestion that the academies explained French military prowess. Milton's idea for military drills is ambitious; but one is not quite sure how seriously to take it. By comparison with his painstaking lists of graduated readings, Milton's account of his students' exercises is thin, and its sequencing not entirely unclear: as, for example, on the

---

[89] Cf. Adamson, *Pioneers*, 184. Gerbier, Humphrey, and l'Amy and le Pruvost refer to the moral dangers of travel to Paris (Hartlib Papers 36/1/18A; 47/8/7A; 12/101A); Howell mentions the danger that young travellers will return from the Continent 'mere *Mimiques*' (*Instructions*), 63.

[90] Like Pluvinel, Milton had evidently not thought through the precise institutional structure that might underpin such an initiative (ii. 381 n. 62).

[91] Compare R. T. Fallon, *Captain or Colonel: The Soldier in Milton's Life and Art* (Columbia, Mo., 1984), 64–7, with J. H. Hanford, 'Milton and the Art of War', in *John Milton: Poet and Humanist* (Cleveland, Ohio, 1966), 185–223 at 186–7, and Dorian, *CPW*, ii. 408 n. 11; 411 n. 26.

question of when the boys would learn the riding skills they would need in order to perform their cavalry manoeuvres. That this aspect of the proposal is not well thought through no doubt reflects the constraints of Milton's circumstances: the city garden of his rented house in Aldersgate Street being too small to allow him to engage his current students in the practice of exercises—hence the demand in *Of Education* for 'a spatious house and ground about it'.[92] Even though they are not drawn up with great precision, Milton's exercises were to absorb a significant part— about three and a half hours—of the school day. This time is squeezed in between periods of study; but it would represent little less than a full morning's work at a Parisian academy.

Milton's most substantial alteration to the French model is his prioritizing of studies over exercises. Whereas Pluvinel's students were to spend the bulk of their time on their exercises, Milton's would focus on their studies. In this shift of emphasis Milton aligns his academy with the reforms of Richelieu, creating an institution that would blend academy and college. Indeed, like Richelieu, Milton extends his curriculum to cover those areas of the university arts course he wished to preserve: logic and rhetoric (the latter habitually taken to include poetics); natural, moral, and civil philosophy. But Milton's curriculum is both more substantial and more classically humanist than Richelieu's. Its extra breadth can be explained in part by the length and rigour of his anticipated school day and in part by the fact that his is to be a nine-year course—three years longer than Richelieu's (*CPW*, ii. 381–2 n. 65). But even this will not fully account for its greater scope, which aims to improve also upon what Milton sees as the restricted and ponderous curriculum of the English grammar school (pp. 370–1). Nor will it explain his emphasis on ancient literature in subjects where one might expect to find modern vernacular textbooks. Where the French and English academies taught quadrivial and modern subjects for practice— arithmetic, geometry, astronomy, and geography; at a higher level, fortification and navigation—and did so primarily in the vernacular—Milton, who shared this practical emphasis and followed the same sequence, taught them by way of classical authorities: Geminus, Solinus, Mela, Frontinus, and so on. Milton's curriculum— this portion of it, at least—is that of a noble academy; but his courses are to be taught by a humanist.

Other changes of focus establish Milton's as a reformed, Puritan academy. A godly emphasis informs the first of the two definitions of learning he offers in the tract: 'The end then of learning is to repair the ruins of our first parents by regaining to know God aright' (*CPW*, ii. 366–7); it informs the nightly scriptural readings that serve to frame and orient the day's work (p. 397); and it explains the banishment of scholastic metaphysics, the introduction of Hebrew (as in the more ambitious grammar schools and academies), and also, in another instance of Miltonic ambition, that of the Old Testament languages of Aramaic and Syriac (p. 400). Milton's academy also diverges from its French prototypes by virtue of a strong strain of anti-

---

[92] Parker, *Milton*, i. 192; there is no mention of any such exercises in the biographical accounts of John or Edward Phillips.

courtliness. Milton completely banishes courtly 'manners': those graceful accomplishments of dancing, painting, and 'behaviour' that had been so important a part of the tradition deriving from Castiglione. By the same token, he gives prominence to an exercise absent from the French academies and disdained even by most English theorists of noble education as too vulgar for courtly use: the traditional English sport of wrestling (p. 409 n. 15).[93] The anti-court note is struck early, in the attack on the university arts course for its production of effete courtiers, lacking in civic virtue: 'others betake them to State affairs, with souls so unprincipl'd in vertue, and true generous breeding, that flattery, and court shifts and tyrannous aphorismes appear to them the highest points of wisdom' (pp. 375–6). By its emphasis on Bible study and wrestling as opposed to deportment and dancing Milton's reformed, Puritan academy firmly divorces the robust, godly governor from the effete courtier.

There are, of course, some idiosyncratic aspects to Milton's proposal: most striking is its apparent sequencing of the curriculum to place poetics at or near its climax, alongside rhetoric: 'To which Poetry would be made subsequent, or indeed rather precedent' (ii. 403). His ambiguous phrasing both here and in the surrounding text has been much debated.[94] It yields fertile ground to those who would dismiss the entire curriculum as an impractical formula for mini-Miltons. But this objection can be at least partly rebutted by recalling that poetics was generally considered and taught as a part of rhetoric, and that it is—in true humanist fashion—oratory (rather than poetry) that forms the climax of Milton's discussion (pp. 405–6); the paean to poetry can reasonably be seen as a heart-felt digression which is not structurally integral to the curriculum.[95]

Despite its idiosyncrasies, Milton's plan should, I think, be regarded as a practical proposal to institute in England a reformed version of a recognizable kind of educational institution. Milton had a motive for thinking practically about such matters. When he presented his letter to Hartlib in May or early June of 1644, he was living off a modest private income and searching for a public role (Parker, *Milton*, i. 229). The public success of figures like Pluvinel modelled the notion that such a role might lie in the field of aristocratic education—especially if such academies were, as Milton recommended (ii. 380–1), to be planted throughout the land. Circumstantial evidence favours the view that *Of Education* was intended practically. We have noticed Hartlib's general interest in appropriating houses or colleges for educational purposes, and his particular support of Humphrey's petition to Parliament for a building to house his academy. By the spring of 1643 Parliament had begun to turn its attention to reforming the University of Cambridge; this was the time Milton first made Hartlib's acquaintance and began to discuss with him his 'projects and

---

[93] Its introduction was not entirely unprecedented: La Noue had recommended it (Chartier et al., *L'Éducation*, 170); and Kynaston had included it in the Musaeum Minervae (*Constitutions*), 5.

[94] See esp. Balachandra Rajan, 'Simple, Sensuous, and Passionate', *Review of English Studies*, 21 (1945), 289–301; repr. in Arthur E. Barker (ed.), *Milton: Modern Essays in Criticism* (1965), 3–20; '*Areopagitica*' and '*Of Education*', ed. Lea, 78–9; and William G. Riggs, 'Poetry and Method in Milton's *Of Education*', *Studies in Philology*, 89 (1992), 445–69.

[95] As is brilliantly argued by Riggs, 'Poetry and Method'.

inventions'; it must have seemed that with Parliament finally taking action on its promise to advance learning, the moment might soon be opportune to press for the appropriation of institutions like Chelsea College.[96] With its six acres of land on the banks of the Thames, Chelsea would nicely have answered Milton's call for space for up to 150 people.[97] That Milton may have had something like this in mind is suggested by his reference to the high repute in which Hartlib stands with 'some of highest authority among us', which must surely be an allusion to Hartlib's standing with powerful parliamentary leaders (ii. 363). Further evidence for the view that Milton was thinking seriously about expanding his academy along the lines sketched in *Of Education* is furnished by the fact that he subsequently did do so, on a more modest scale. In the spring of 1645 he rented a 'great house' in the Barbican, apparently in order to increase the number of his pupils; Parker plausibly detects the hand of Hartlib behind this move (Darbishire, 24, 66–8; Parker, *Milton*, i. 286–7, ii. 896 n. 115).

That Hartlib's encouragement underlay Milton's expansion of his academy for the aristocracy and gentry is likely; in its blueprint for such an academy, *Of Education* was much more closely aligned with the Hartlib Circle's schemes of the later 1640s than we have hitherto recognized. Ever since Masson established the framework for modern understanding of the relationship between Milton and Hartlib, scholarly debate has focused on the degree to which Milton did or did not subscribe to the educational initiatives of Hartlib's mentor, the educational reformer Jan Amos Comenius.[98] Subsequent scholarship by Sirluck and more recently Lewalski has dismantled most of Masson's claims, showing that Milton was fundamentally opposed to the central Comenian proposals, including the use of epitomes and the banishment of classical literature, and demonstrating that apparent similarities are more often than not insignificant.[99] Nor is Milton's tract quite so progressively utilitarian as is sometimes thought; even its apparently experimental, Baconian touches often turn out to have a humanist pedigree. For instance, Milton's inclusion of the study of agriculture is not necessarily connected with the Hartlibian promotion of agricultural reform, which was not yet in full swing; it more probably reflects the traditional view that an aristocrat ought to have some converse with the requirements of running a country estate.[100] And although his recommendation that such students should seek the practical expertise of 'Hunters, fowlers, Fishermen, Shepherds, Gardeners, *Apothecaries*', and so forth (ii. 394) may sound Baconian, it probably derives from the

---

[96] Masson, *Life*, iii. 32; Turnbull, *Hartlib, Dury, and Comenius*, 39–40. On Chelsea College, see above n. 58.

[97] Barbara K. Lewalski suggests that in proposing a national network of such institutions, Milton has in mind Parliament's promise to employ church estates to advance learning: 'Milton and the Hartlib Circle: Educational Projects and Epic *Paideia*', in Diana Treviño Benet and Michael Lieb (eds.), *Literary Milton: Text, Pretext, Context* (Pittsburgh, Pa., 1994), 202–19 at 209.

[98] Masson, *Life*, iii. 231–52.

[99] Sirluck, in *CP W*, ii. 184–216; Lewalski, 'Milton and the Hartlib Circle', 202–11; see also William Poole, 'Milton and Science: A Caveat', *Milton Quarterly*, 38 (2004), 18–34 at 19.

[100] Clarke, *Burnet as Educationist*, 73; Kelso, *Doctrine*, 60; Charlton, *Education in Renaissance England*, 288–92.

humanist pedagogy of Vives, who suggested in *De tradendis disciplinis* that students of nature have recourse 'to gardeners, husbandmen, shepherds and hunters'.[101]

From his demonstration of Milton's opposition to Comenianism, Sirluck drew the conclusion that Hartlib could not have approved his tract and must have refused to publish it, forcing the poet to have it printed himself. Charles Webster responded by suggesting that Milton's tract should be seen in terms of Hartlib's sponsorship of 'specialist works dealing with the education of all social classes'; and I have argued elsewhere that Sirluck's arguments are not well founded: there is little evidence within the Hartlib Circle for fundamental objections to the tract, little evidence that Hartlib did not publish it, and some that he did.[102] I hope now to have shown that Milton's proposal should be taken seriously as an attempt to sketch a reformed, English, Puritan version of the French noble academy; I hope also to have demonstrated that in his tractate Milton was, without being sympathetic to Comenianism, nevertheless working within the mainstream of Hartlibian educational reform as it was conceived during the 1640s. The reform of gentle and aristocratic education was a discrete area of concern to the Hartlibians; it has not been sufficiently recognized by modern scholarship. I wish to conclude this discussion by suggesting that Milton's tract played a significant part in shaping the Hartlibians' understanding of the institutional and curricular structure of a reformed institution of aristocratic education.

Evidence for Milton's importance to the Hartlib Circle in its understanding of the reformed aristocratic academy lies in the demonstrable influence of *Of Education* on the Hartlibian schemes promoted in its wake. Responses to Milton's tract by Hartlib's associates expressed not disagreement—as one might expect were Milton's anti-Comenianism an issue for them—but either approval or the criticism that it was too brief and insufficiently detailed, or both. To John Hall of Durham it was simply 'excellent'; to John Dury it was 'brief & generall'; to Sir Cheney Culpeper it had 'some good sprincklings' but not 'descendinge enowght into particulars'.[103] In his criticism, Dury remarked on the need to tailor ambitions to circumstances: the tract had, he wrote, 'many requisits which I doubt will hardly bee obtained in a tyme of Peace[;] it is wisdome to doe what may be done in an easie waye'.[104] In the summer of 1644, with war still raging, the time was, in Dury's view, unripe; but by the end of the following year, after a series of stunning parliamentary victories, peace was inevitable. In the new year, Hartlib and his associates returned in earnest to the reform of education. But they no longer envisaged the universal institution of pansophy; instead they tailored their aims, as Dury had suggested, to the possible: proposing the

---

[101] Juan Luis Vives, *On Education*, ed. and trans. Foster Watson (Cambridge, 1913), 170, 209. Watson long ago proposed *De tradendis* as a source for *Of Education* (pp. cxxviii n. 2, cli).

[102] Webster, *Samuel Hartlib*, 42; Timothy Raylor, 'New Light on Milton and Hartlib', *Milton Quarterly*, 27 (1993), 19–31 at 22–3.

[103] Hartlib Papers, 60/14/6A (Hall to Hartlib, 21 Dec. [1646]); 13/122A (Culpeper to Hartlib, 13 Nov. 1645); 3/2/43B (Dury to Hartlib, 11/21 July 1644); Turnbull, *Hartlib, Dury, and Comenius*, 39.

[104] Hartlib Papers, 3/2/43B (Dury to Hartlib, 11/21 July 1644); the manuscript is slightly cropped at the right edge; I have inferred the loss of a punctuation mark and supplied one.

establishment of reformed institutions in appropriated houses, colleges, and estates. By spring, hopes were running high; Dury began to ruminate upon 'education in the Academie', drafting some notes on the education of the nobility and gentry.[105] Milton's continued importance to the Hartlibians at this time is suggested by the appearance of his name at the head of a list of educational desiderata probably dating from 1647; this is headed: 'Mr. Miltons Academie'—though for reasons that have never been satisfactorily explained Milton's name is crossed out and underneath is inserted an alternative: 'Mr Lawrence Academie'.[106]

Although Dury's essay on the subject of aristocratic education was pushed aside by more pressing commitments, he returned to the issue after losing his post as royal tutor, integrating his thoughts into a comprehensive, two-tiered educational system in *The Reformed School* (1650): a system based on the opposition between what he would later term 'noble' (or, as we would say, 'liberal') and 'mechanical' education.[107] In erecting this division, Dury introduced a degree of meritocracy, opening up schools designed primarily for the gentry and nobility to talented members of the middle classes.[108] There should, he wrote in 1649, be 'a school for the Gentry and Nobility whereunto also the most Gentle spirits of the vulgar ought to be received'.[109] Although this marks a significant departure from the exclusivity (at the conceptual level at least) of Milton's academy, the conception, the rhetorical presentation, and the post-elementary curriculum of Dury's reformed school are, as H. M. Knox has painstakingly illustrated, heavily indebted to Milton.[110] Dury's academic curriculum moves, like Milton's (and for the same reasons) from sensory to abstract; its subjects are largely the same and are ranged in largely the same order as Milton's; and its readings are frequently those recommended in *Of Education*.[111] Absent, however, is the prominence of aristocratic training

---

[105] Webster, *Samuel Hartlib*, 42; Hartlib Papers, 3/3/13B (Dury to Hartlib, 24 Apr. 1646); HDC 256; Thomas H. H. Rae, *John Dury and the Royal Road to Piety* (Frankfurt-am-Main, 1998), 125–6. Dury's draft survives as British Library, MS Sloane 649, fos. 82–3.

[106] Hartlib Papers, 47/9/34A; Turnbull, *Hartlib, Dury, and Comenius*, 40.

[107] On the opposition between 'noble' (liberal) and mechanical education, see 'Some Proposalls towards the Advancement of Learning' (1653), Hartlib Papers, 47/2; printed in part in Webster, *Samuel Hartlib*, 165–92 at 179–80; Webster, *Great Instauration*, 213–17.

[108] See Rae, *John Dury*, 118–20; though Rae errs in arguing that no social distinction is implied by Dury's use of the term 'noble' (p. 119).

[109] *A Seasonable Discourse* (1649), 8. Compare his 'Supplement' to *The Reformed School*, in which he explains that his reformed school is 'proper to such of the nobility, gentry and better sort of citizens which are fit to be made capable to bear offices in the Commonwealth' (*The Reformed School*, ed. H. M. Knox (Liverpool, 1958), 69–70); and his 1653 'Proposalls' (Hartlib Papers, 47/2/8A–8B; Webster, *Samuel Hartlib*, 165–92; for Webster's 'incapable of the best breeding' (p. 182) read 'capable ~'). In 1653, however, Dury also envisaged the possible provision of at least some academies expressly for the nobility and gentry in addition to his 'noble' schools ('Proposalls', Hartlib Papers, 47/2/12A; Webster, *Samuel Hartlib*, 190–1; Rae, *John Dury*, 119–20).

[110] *The Reformed School*, 8, 77–82.

[111] Ibid. 46–9. Compare Milton, 'the Authors of *Agriculture*, Cato, Varro, and *Columella*' (*CPW*, ii. 387–8); with Dury's 'The Latin authors of agriculture, Cato, Varro, Columella' (*The Reformed School*, 48). See also Richard J. DuRocher, *Milton among the Romans: The Pedagogy and Influence of Milton's Latin Curriculum* (Pittsburgh, Pa., 2001), 10–12; I disagree with DuRocher's suggestion that Milton's readings differ by being contemplative as opposed to practical.

in the use of arms.[112] Barbara Lewalski has proposed that Dury's borrowings represented 'a gesture of accommodation' with Milton.[113] But a gesture would have required
only some respectful acknowledgement, of which there is in fact none. What we find
rather is (as Lewalski notes) appropriation, at the level of curricular structure, and in
sequencing, content, and set-texts. Dury's debt to Milton here is fundamental and
profound. Within the elaborate ground plan of Dury's reformed school—the most
important, coherent, and detailed account of educational reform of the entire revolutionary period—we can discern the outline of Milton's reformed academy.

[112] Dury mentions 'military employments' as only one among several possible kinds of bodily
exercise; the others (husbandry and manufactures) are more mechanical in emphasis (*The Reformed
School*, 32).
[113] 'Milton and the Hartlib Circle', 210.

CHAPTER 22

....

CONQUEST AND SLAVERY IN MILTON'S *HISTORY OF BRITAIN*

....

MARTIN DZELZAINIS

At Dover on 29 May 1670, Charles II simultaneously celebrated his birthday, the tenth anniversary of his restoration, and—though this was known only to very few members of his inner circle—the initialling a week before of a treaty with Louis XIV of France. The so-called secret treaty of Dover brought into being a defensive and offensive alliance between the two countries. It required Charles to declare his conversion to Catholicism and join France in a war against the Dutch republic. In return, Louis promised Charles annual subsidies to pay for the English fleet and to deal with any adverse domestic reaction to his reconciliation with Rome. The fact of an alliance (though not the terms of the treaty itself) became public knowledge at the start of the third Anglo–Dutch war in 1672. For Charles, however, Dover arguably proved to be 'the most serious error of his reign'.[1] He had given a hostage to fortune such that 'for the rest of his life [he] would be a French client and prey to constant anxiety that Louis would leak the details of their agreement'.[2] It was at this critical juncture for the

---

[1] Ronald Hutton, 'The Making of the Secret Treaty of Dover 1668–1670', *Historical Journal*, 29 (1986), 318.

[2] John Spurr, *England in the 1670s: 'This Masquerading Age'* (Oxford, 2000), 13.

restored monarchy, as it embarked upon what would prove to be fifteen years of clientage, that John Milton put the finishing touches to his longest English prose work, *The History of Britain, That part especially now called England. From the first Traditional Beginning, Continued to the Norman Conquest*, which was in print by 1 November. By this stage, Milton had been working on the *History* for over twenty years—beginning and then laying it aside at some point in the late 1640s, picking it up again in the later 1650s as his official duties as secretary for foreign tongues decreased, and finally revisiting the manuscript in the late 1660s to make it ready for the press.[3] Few things he published were quite so long in the making and it is hardly surprising that as a result commentators have sought to find in the *History* a reflection of his changing 'judgement on contemporary events'. In Hugh Trevor-Roper's phrase, it can be read as a 'barometer of his political mood' during these decades.[4]

This being the case, it is hard to overlook the fact that, in the concluding book of the *History*, Milton introduces his narrative of events leading up to the Norman Conquest with an account of the self-subjugation of the English to the French. He lays particular blame on Edward the Confessor, whose

imprudence laid the foundation of a far worse mischeif to the English; while studying gratitude to those Normans, who to him in exile had bin helpfull, he call'd them over to public Offices heer, whom better he might have repaid out of his privat purse; by this means exasperating either Nation one against the other, and making way by degrees to the Norman Conquest. *Robert* a Monk of that Country, who had bin serviceable to him there in time of need, he made Bishop, first of *London*, then of *Canterbury*; *William* his Chaplain Bishop of *Dorchester*. Then began the English to lay aside thir own antient Customes, and in many things to imitate French manners, the great Peers to speak French in thir Houses, in French to write thir Bills and Letters, as a great peece of Gentility, asham'd of thir own: a presage of thir subjection shortly to that people, whose fashions and language they affected so slavishly. (*CPW*, v. 377)

In other words, a slavish embrace of all things French preceded enslavement by the French. However, it seems to be a clear if unstated implication of what Milton is saying that one state of affairs did not just prefigure the other but was somehow its causal antecedent. And the nature of that causal relationship—of how and why one thing leads to another in the *History*—is the central subject of this essay.

---

[3] For recent discussions of the composition of the *History*, see French Fogle, 'Introduction', *CPW*, v, pp. xxxvii–xliii; Nicholas von Maltzahn, *Milton's 'History of Britain': Republican Historiography in the English Revolution* (Oxford, 1991), 22–47, 168–76; and Blair Worden, *Literature and Politics in Cromwellian England: John Milton, Andrew Marvell, Marchamont Nedham* (Oxford, 2007), 410–26.

[4] Michael Fixler, *Milton and the Kingdoms of God* ([Evanston. Ill.], 1964), 196; Hugh Trevor-Roper, *Catholics, Anglicans and Puritans: Seventeenth-Century Essays* (1989), 272.

I

Milton in fact signs off the *History* with another vehement denunciation of how the English 'were constrein'd to take the Yoke of an out-landish Conquerer'. As before, however, these constraints appear to have been in some measure self-imposed. For what Milton seeks to underline in his account of the Saxons on the eve of the Conquest is 'With what minds and by what course of life they had *fitted themselves* for this servitude' (my emphasis). The clergy, he observes, 'had lost all good literature and Religion', while the 'great men' were

giv'n to gluttony and dissolute life, made a prey of the common people, abuseing thir Daughters whom they had in service, then turning them off to the Stews, the meaner sort tipling together night and day, spent all they had in Drunk'ness, attended with other Vices which effeminate mens minds. Whence it came to pass, that carried on with fury and rashness more then any true fortitude or skill of War, they gave to *William* thir Conqueror so easie a Conquest. Not but that some few of all sorts were much better among them; but such was the generality. *And as the long suffering of God permits bad men to enjoy prosperous daies with the good, so his severity oft times exempts not good men from thir share in evil times with the bad.*

If these were the Causes of such misery and thraldom to those our Ancestors, with what better close can be concluded, then here in fit season to remember this Age in the midst of her security, to fear from like Vices without amendment the Revolution of like Calamities. (CPW, v. 402–3)[5]

It has sometimes been suggested that Milton added the final paragraph as the work went to press, in which case he was issuing a last-minute warning to his contemporaries that their irreligious and vicious way of life was exposing them to the possibility of a new 'thraldom' along the lines of the Norman Conquest.[6] But how likely is it that Milton was deploying the *History* in this highly topical way? Rather than voicing alarm at the prospect of a *rapprochement* with France, was he not just busy clearing his desk, as the appearance in print of works like *Accedence Commenc't Grammar* (1669), *Artis Logicae Plenior Institutio* (1672), and *Epistolarum Familiarium Liber Unus: Quibus Accesserunt . . . Prolusiones Quaedam Oratoriae* (1674) towards the end of his life would suggest?

This was, moreover, not the first time Milton had voiced anti-French sentiments. One of the advantages he claimed for the programme of instruction set out in *Of Education* (1644) was precisely that it would obviate the 'need' for those he scornfully calls 'the *Mounsieurs* of *Paris* to take our hopefull youth into thir slight and prodigall custodies and send them over back again transform'd into mimics, apes & Kicshoes'; on the contrary, 'other Nations will be glad to visit us for their breeding, or else imitate us in their own Country' (*CPW,* ii. 414).[7] Furthermore, while Francophobia

---

[5] The final paragraph is not italicized in the Yale edition even though it is in both states of the first edition of the *History* (Wing M2119 and M2120).

[6] But see Maltzahn, *Milton's 'History of Britain'*, 171–4, for scepticism about the supposed topicality of the *History.*

[7] Though it should be noted that *Of Education* was appended to a new edition of the *Poems* in 1673, making it the only one of his Civil War prose works that he had reprinted after the Restoration.

increased in the course of the third Anglo–Dutch war it was not until peace was imminent in 1674 that the political nation finally became more preoccupied by the threat from the French than that from the Dutch.[8] It follows that if cultural and political anxieties about France were fuelling Milton's concluding remarks in the *History* then they should be seen as retrospective rather than proleptic; that is to say, as related to an earlier phase of hostility to the French in the 1660s that had been provoked by the sale of Dunkirk to Louis XIV in 1662, aggravated in 1666 by the entry of France into the second Anglo–Dutch war of 1665–7 on the side of the Dutch, and further magnified by the ominous ease with which the French overran the Spanish Netherlands in 1667–8.[9] This earlier round in the 'culture war' between England and France was fought out largely in theatrical terms. James Howard's *The English Mounsieur*, for example, staged in July 1663, satirized the mania for French fashions in the character of Mr Frenchlove.[10] John Dryden set his dialogic *Of Dramatick Poesie, An Essay* (1668) against the backdrop of the outbreak of the second Anglo–Dutch war in June 1665; from their barge on the Thames the interlocutors can hear the noise of the cannon at the battle of Lowestoft. Yet for all the alleged importance of this English naval victory over the Dutch ('a day wherein the two most mighty and best appointed Fleets which any age had ever seen, disputed the command of the greater half of the Globe, the commerce of Nations, and the riches of the Universe'), Dryden turns out to be far more concerned 'to vindicate the honour of our English Writers, from the censure of those who unjustly prefer the French before them'. One of the four participants, Eugenius (Lord Buckhurst) militantly declares that he is 'at all times ready to defend the honour of my Countrey against the French, and to maintain, we are as well able to vanquish them with our Pens as our Ancestors have been with their swords', though he actually delegates the task of arguing the case to Neander (Dryden himself).[11] But in this event it might well be asked what if anything differentiates Milton's Francophobic attitudes from those seemingly endemic in English culture at the time.

In fact, royalists and republicans differed sharply on the nature of the threat posed by France. A case in point is the critique of absolutism produced in the mid-1660s by Milton's former colleague Algernon Sidney, who cast his *Court Maxims, Discussed and Refelled* in the form of a dialogue between a courtier, Philalethes, and a republican diehard, Eunomius. In the tenth dialogue, they discuss what is alleged to be a favourite maxim of Charles II and his advisers to the effect that 'Union with France and war with Holland is necessary to uphold Monarchy in England[;] or thus, a strict friendship is to be held with the French that their customs may be introduced and the people by their example brought to beggary and slavery quietly.'[12] With remarkable

---

[8] See Steven Pincus, 'From Butterboxes to Wooden Shoes: The Shift in English Popular Sentiment from Anti-Dutch to Anti-French in the 1670s', *Historical Journal*, 38 (1995), 333–61.

[9] See Jeremy Black, *A System of Ambition? British Foreign Policy 1660–1793* (Stroud, 2000), 22, 143–9.

[10] See P. Vander Motten, 'Howard, James (c.1640–1669)', *ODNB*.

[11] John Dryden, *Of Dramatick Poesie, An Essay* (1668), sig. A4ᵛ, 1, 26.

[12] Algernon Sidney, *Court Maxims*, ed. Hans W. Blom, Eco Haitsma Mulier, and Ronald Janse (Cambridge, 1996), 152. *Court Maxims* remained in manuscript until published in this edition.

candour, Philalethes confirms that these precepts govern the foreign and domestic policy of Charles II, whose aim it is 'to bring in the vices of the French, to corrupt our young nobility, gentry, and people', adding that 'those are most favoured at court that conform to the French manners and fashions in all things' (p. 153). Eunomius replies that this policy runs counter to the 'true interest' of 'the people' who are, moreover, mindful that the 'English nation ever contended with France for superiority, often with good success, and will horribly detest any that renders it dependent on and subservient to [France's] interest'. He fears nevertheless that the strategy may prove effective, and despairingly warns Philalethes that 'if your design succeed of bringing the people to such poverty, misery, slavery and baseness, the king of France will look on, perhaps, and when no virtue, vigour, or power is left in the nation, will make an easy conquest of it. *So you may live and die his slaves*' (p. 154; emphasis in original). Sidney thus agrees with Milton that a slavish disposition towards the French is a precondition of enslavement by them. Indeed, the main difference between their accounts of the actual and anticipated conquests of William I and Louis XIV respectively is that, whereas Milton sees the corruption of the English by the French as having happened unintentionally, for Sidney it is the centrepiece of a deliberate policy of enfeebling the nation so as to make it more compliant with the royal will.

This makes it all the more striking that Milton and Sidney were sometimes concerned instead to minimize the political consequences of what happened in 1066. The need for them to do so arose from the fact that in the early modern period one of the most powerful ideological weapons in the hands of those seeking to restrain their rulers was the doctrine of the ancient constitution, which in England took the form of the claim that the common law and Parliament were 'immemorial and therefore beyond the king's power to alter or annul'.[13] Yet this doctrine flew in the face of the fact that the Norman Conquest represented a complete rupture in the alleged continuity of these institutions. The response from those seeking to uphold the doctrine, and from common lawyers in particular, was simply to deny that that had ever been a Conquest at all; William, they argued, had a valid claim to the throne; had not introduced an alien legal system since the feudal usages thought to typify it actually antedated the Conquest; and had in any case sworn to uphold the laws of Edward the Confessor. During the Civil War, however, the doctrine came under renewed assault from several sides; there were royalists who pointed to the Conquest as proof that the powers of the monarchy had never been constrained in the manner alleged by the parliamentarians; there were radicals like the Levellers who wished to sweep away the legal, social, and political injustices which they traced to the imposition of the Norman Yoke; and, after the overthrow of the monarchy in 1649, there were apologists for the new republican regime who sought to ground its claim to *de facto* sovereignty in conquest theory.[14] Faced with these various incompatible

[13] J. G. A. Pocock, *The Ancient Constitution and the Feudal Law: A Study of English Historical Thought in the Seventeenth Century. A Reissue with a Retrospect* (Cambridge, 1987), 16.

[14] See Quentin Skinner, 'History and Ideology in the English Revolution', in *Visions of Politics*, 3 vols. (Cambridge, 2002), iii. 238 (this is a revised version of the essay in *Historical Journal*, 8 (1965), 151–78);

theories, Milton and Sidney fell back on the arguments used earlier by defenders of the ancient constitution. Thus in *The Tenure of Kings and Magistrates* (1649), Milton brusquely pointed out that '*William* the Norman though a Conqueror, and not unsworn at his Coronation, was compell'd the second time to take oath at S. *Albanes*, ere the people would be brought to yeild obedience', and in *Pro Populo Anglicano Defensio* (1651) he even argued that the English might have carried on fighting after their defeat at Hastings but 'preferred to accept a king rather than endure a conquering tyrant'; whatever rights of conquest William may have had were thereby extinguished (*CPW*, iii. 201; iv. 480). Sidney, who was familiar with Milton's work, follows exactly the same line of argument. When Philalethes asks Eunomius 'what think you of the right of conquest by which many kings hold their crowns, and particularly ours from William the Conqueror?', he is scornfully assured that this surname was conferred on him by his 'flattering servitors' whereas the truth was that 'A good part of the nobles and commons of England did from the first make him their head and leader.'[15] Unembarrassed by the historical implausibility of their arguments, Milton and Sidney actually sought to turn the Conquest into a demonstration of the principles of popular sovereignty in action.

This demarche in Milton's political thought certainly complicates the question of what to make of the conclusion of the *History*, where the narrative shows little or no trace of these principles. It is true that Milton says that before William was crowned he gave 'his Oath at the Altar in presence of all the people, to defend the Church, well govern the people, maintain right Law; prohibit rapine and unjust judgment'. Yet this does not obviate the brute fact that the English—as Milton concedes in his very next sentence—had been 'constrein'd to take the Yoke of an out-landish Conquerer' (*CPW*, v. 402). Milton thus affirms in the *History* what he denies elsewhere: that the English were completely subjugated by the Normans. This discrepancy might conceivably be attributed to official interference with the text were it not for the fact that Edward Phillips (our principal source for the information that the *History* was censored before publication) says only that the licenser took exception to 'some Passages' that he 'thought too sharp against the Clergy'; anticlericalism, not politics, is what got the work into trouble (Darbishire, 75). There is, moreover, good reason for thinking that—at least in this case—what we are reading is what Milton wrote. For, when he surveyed these historical materials with the eyes of a moralist rather than a political apologist, Milton came to the conclusion that the English had deserved to be conquered for their failings, and this in turn meant that the

---

Christopher Hill, *Puritanism and Revolution* (1958), 75–82; Johann Sommerville, 'History and Theory: The Norman Conquest in Early Stuart Political Thought', *Political Studies*, 34 (1986), 249–61. The most important (and neglected) royalist exponent of conquest theory was Dudley Digges, or Diggs (1613–43); see Digges, *The Vnlawfulnesse of Subjects taking up Armes against their Soveraigne in what case soever* (n.p., 1643), 81–3, 116–19. The treatise was reprinted in 1644, 1647, 1662, 1664, and 1679; see Martin Dzelzainis, 'The Ideological Context of John Milton's *History of Britain*' (Ph.D thesis, University of Cambridge, 1984), 127–55 (ch. 4: 'Royalist Theories of Conquest').

[15] Sidney, *Court Maxims*, 14–15; cf. Sidney, *Discourses Concerning Government*, ed. Thomas G. West (Indianapolis, Ind., 1996), 107, 377, 414–15.

constitutionalist fiction of a non-Conquest that he and Sidney were prepared to canvass on other occasions had to be discarded.

II

If Milton was not an exponent of conquest theory this is not to say that he lacked a theory of conquest. Its outlines can be seen in his theological treatise *De Doctrina Christiana*. Discussing the legitimacy of warfare in the concluding chapter of Book 2, he declares that

Obedience to God's commandments makes commonwealths prosperous in every respect; see Lev. xxvi. It makes them fortunate, wealthy and victorious, Deut. xv. 4–6, and lords over other nations; see Deut. xv. 6 and xxvi. 17–19, and particularly xxviii. 1, etc. Politicians should read over and over again Deut. xxix. and iv; Judges ii and iii; Psal. xxxiii. 12: *blessed is the nation whose God is Jehovah*; Prov. xi. 11: *a city is made to prosper by the blessing of the righteous*, and xiv. 34: *righteousness exalts a nation* . . . , and xxviii. 2: *when a land is in difficulties because of transgression* . . . ; Isa. iii. and xxiv. And xlviii. 18: *if only you had listened* . . . ; Jer. v; Ezek. vii. (*CPW*, vi. 804; slightly adapted; ellipses in the original)[16]

Since there is no passage corresponding to this in Johannes Wolleb's *Compendium Theologiae Christianae* (1625), the work which supplied Milton with the template for Book 2 of the treatise, we are on relatively safe ground in treating these remarks as a guide to his own thinking. His main contention is that success for commonwealths or states ('respublicas') is something that depends entirely on remaining obedient to God. And the principal way in which they can manifest this obedience is by avoiding idolatry—a point made several times over by the various scriptural proof-texts Milton cites. What is particularly striking, however, is that the rewards of such spiritual righteousness are figured in wholly material terms: states that do not seek after false gods will prosper by becoming not only wealthy and powerful ('opulentas') but also the conquerors and lords of other nations ('victrices . . . et dominas gentium'). From one point of view, this is merely a Miltonic extrapolation from God's promise to those who remain obedient that 'thou shalt reign over many nations, but they shall not reign over

---

[16] 'Florentissimas undequaque reddit respublicas mandatorum Dei observatio: Lev. xxvi. per totum caput: fortunatas et opulentas et victrices gentium, Deut. xv. 4, 5, 6. et dominas gentium, v. 6. et cap. xxvi. 17, 18, 19. et insigne, cap. xxviii. 1, &c. Politicis etiam atque etiam legendum, cap. xxix. et iv. Iudic. ii. et iii. Psal. xxxiii. 12. *beata gens illa, cuius Iehova Deus est*. Prov. xi. 11. *benedictione rectorum effertur urbs*. et xiv. 34. *iustitia exaltat gentem–*. et xxviii. 2. *ubi defectione laborat regio–*. Isa. iii. et xxiv. et xlviii. 18. *o si attendisses–*. Ier. v. Ezech. vii' (*CW*, xvii. 412). Overriding punctuation and capitalization, the Yale and Columbia translators incorrectly suggest that what 'should be read over and over again' by politicians is the immediately preceding material from Deuteronomy 28 rather than the succeeding material from Deuteronomy (29 and 4), Judges, Psalms, Proverbs, Isaiah, Jeremiah, and Ezekiel. My thanks to John Hale for confirming the textual details of the *Doctrina* manuscript.

thee' (Deut. 15: 6).[17] From another angle, however, it looks more like laying the scriptural foundations of an ideology of godly conquest and imperialism.

Milton then turns to making the same point in negative terms. He does this by citing passages from Isaiah (3: 8; 42: 13, 14, 17), Hosea (5: 13; 7: 11, 12; 12: 2), and Habbakuk (2: 12) that are said to be directly opposed ('Opposita sunt') to the ones he has just adduced (*CPW*, vi. 804; *CW*, xiv. 412–13). What these new texts do is demonstrate the terrible consequences for Israel of apostasy: spiritual defection inevitably leads to national ruin. The citations of the prophet Hosea are especially interesting in this respect since his book as a whole is noted for its stark equation of religious and sexual transgression: one kind of infidelity is systematically figured in terms of the other. But, according to Hosea, these transgressions also have a political analogue in the form of the mistaken alliances that Israel makes with heathen nations. One of the more obscure verses cited by Milton, Hosea 7: 11 ('Ephraim [Israel] is like a silly dove without heart: they call to Egypt, they go to Assyria'), for example, embodies a warning against the pusillanimity that will lead Israel into dependency upon its faithless and godless neighbours.[18] For Milton, the moral of the story was that no nation that is foolish (*fatuus*) and mindless (*demens*) can hope to avoid subjugation by its more hawkish rivals.

However, these pronouncements raise questions not only about how the threats and promises made by God come to pass in the world but also about the justice of the threats and promises themselves. Milton's silence at this point is explained by the fact that he had already considered these issues thoroughly when discussing divine decrees in chapter 3 of the first book of *De Doctrina Christiana*. Much of what is said there is applied directly to the plight of Adam, and the chapter is accordingly often read as a gloss on the theodicy articulated by Milton—more or less contemporaneously—in Book 3 of *Paradise Lost*; in the treatise, as in the poem, he is anxious to reconcile the claim that God created men and angels with free will with the fact that He also foreknew with absolute certainty that they would fall.

In effecting this reconciliation, Milton starts from the premiss that 'God made no absolute decrees about anything which he left in the power of men, for men have freedom of action' (*CPW*, vi. 155).[19] The conditional nature of these decrees is evident from the history of God's dealings with Israel—rescinding benefits which had been promised when it turned out that 'that nation did not keep the condition upon which the decree depended' or, conversely, remitting punishments which had been threatened when the people showed themselves capable of reform (vi. 155). However, this conditionality exposes Milton's project to two contrasting objections. The first is

---

[17] Authorized Version; 'poteris dominari in gentes multas, neque in te dominaturæ sunt' (*Testamenti Veteris Biblia Sacra, sive, Libri canonici priscae Iudaeorum Ecclesiae à Deo traditi, Latini recèns ex Hebraeo facti, brevibúsque scholiis illustrati ab Immanuele Tremellio & Francisco Junio* [London, 1593], 162b). The Junius–Tremellius Bible, available in many editions, was the version favoured by Milton.

[18] Authorized Version; 'Sed est Ephrajim similis columbæ fatuæ, demens: Ægyptium vocant, Assyrium adeunt' (*Testamenti Veteris Biblia Sacra*, 106b).

[19] 'Nihil itaque Deus decrevisse absolute censendus est, quod in potestate libere agentium reliquit' (*CW*, xiv. 64).

that to introduce an element of contingency into the equation is to imply that 'God does not know everything' that is going to happen, meaning He cannot be omniscient (vi. 165). This cavil is dismissed out of hand by Milton. Instead of offering a rebuttal, he merely reiterates the view that, as he phrased it in an earlier chapter, 'God has complete foreknowledge, so he knows what men, who are free in their actions, will think and do, even before they are born and even though these thoughts and deeds will not take place until many centuries have passed' (vi. 150).[20] But to adopt this uncompromising stance is to invite the opposite objection that 'all future events must happen by necessity because God has foreknown them', meaning that men are not free after all. Milton clearly regards this as much the more serious objection of the two, and deploys an array of counter-arguments. While it may be foreknown with absolute certainty that something will happen, it does not happen, he insists, *because* it was foreknown: 'A thing which is going to happen quite freely in the course of events is not then produced as a result of God's foreknowledge, but arises from the free action of its own causes, and God knows in what direction these will, of their own accord tend.' To illustrate the point that certainty is not the same thing as necessity, Milton briefly dwells on the familiar example of Adam, who God knew for a fact 'would, of his own accord, fall'. That is to say, God's unerring knowledge of how the relevant causes would play out in Adam's case meant that 'it was certain he would fall, but it was not necessary' that he did so in consequence of its being foreknown. Milton then considers at greater length the implications of God's foreknowing 'that the Israelites would lapse from their true religion to alien Gods', as reported in Deuteronomy 31: 16. He admits that 'If their lapse was a necessity, caused by God's foreknowledge, then it was exceedingly unjust of him to threaten to afflict them with numerous evils' (vi. 165). But this was not what had happened: 'the Israelites did not revolt because God knew that they would: rather, God knew that they would because he knew the causes of their revolt. It was certain, as a result of these, that they would revolt, although they were free agents' (vi. 165–6).[21] The Israelites could not be held accountable for their actions unless they were able to act otherwise than they did, and this had been the case even though there was an omniscient observer who knew (and had known from all time) that they were going to act as they did and not otherwise.

Notwithstanding Milton's reputation as an original thinker, it would be true to say that there was little that was new in his view of human freedom. His position is in many respects indistinguishable from that of John Bramhall, Bishop of Derry, whose famous debate on the topic with his fellow-royalist Thomas Hobbes began privately during their exile in Paris in 1645 before exploding into a full-scale controversy in print a decade later.[22] Like Bramhall, Milton was an incompatibilist; that is to say, he

[20] 'prænovit etiam Deus, quæ eius absoluta præscientia est, et cogitationes et facta hominum libere agentium, etiam nondum natorum, etiam multis post sæculis futura' (*CW*, xiv. 56).

[21] 'non ergo desciverunt Israelitæ quia Deus hoc prænovit, sed inde Deus prænovit quod ex causis sibi notis, quamvis libere agentes, certo tamen erant defecturi' (*CW*, xiv. 86).

[22] For a cogent survey of the controversy, see *Hobbes and Bramhall on Liberty and Necessity*, ed. Vere Chappell (Cambridge, 1999), pp. ix–xxiii. Hobbes's last word on the matter was *The Questions Concerning Liberty, Necessity and Chance* (1656), to which Bramhall responded with his *Castigations of Mr. Hobbes*

regarded freedom as logically inconsistent with necessitation, and in particular believed that the workings of the will were not necessitated by something outside itself (unlike the compatibilist Hobbes, who believed both that human mental processes and the actions to which they gave rise were physically caused and that as long as such actions were not externally impeded then they were free). Nor is there anything odd about the fact that Milton should have shared his incompatibilist metaphysics with an Anglican bishop since both of them were also Arminians, for whom a commitment to the idea of free will went hand in hand with a rejection of Calvinist doctrines of predestination and grace.

As I hope to show in the next section, these are the theological and metaphysical foundations upon which the *History of Britain* ultimately rests. Indeed it would be no exaggeration to say that most of the narrative dealing with the course of events following the arrival of Christianity in Britain—which means everything from two-thirds of the way through Book 2 onwards—is shaped by Milton's sense of what happens to nations which do or do not deviate from the path of true religion. This was because he saw the sequence of invasions that dominate British history from Roman times until 1066 largely through the lens of the theory of conquest articulated in *De Doctrina Christiana*. However, we should bear in mind that Milton was probably working on the theological treatise in tandem with *Paradise Lost* between 1658 and 1665 and that this was *after* he would have finished drafting almost the whole of the *History*.[23] The likelihood is therefore that when Milton came to assemble the final chapter of the *De Doctrina Christiana* his thinking was conditioned by his recent reflections on the history of God's dealings with the English as well as the Israelites; *De Doctrina Christiana* is at least as much informed by the *History* at this point as the *History* is by *De Doctrina Christiana*.

III

The extent to which the structure of the *History* is determined by the topic of conquest should be apparent from a brief summary of the contents of its six books. After disposing of the phase of legendary pre-history in the opening (and shortest) book, Milton turns in Book 2 to the Roman conquest and colonization of Britain. Book 3 deals with the plight of the Britons after the Roman withdrawal and

---

(1657). It is possible that Hobbes's reply is being alluded to in *Paradise Lost* when God describes his own 'goodness, which is free / To act or not, necessity and chance / Approach not me, and what I will is fate' (vii. 171–3).

[23] See Lewalski, *Life*, 416. However, if Blair Worden's conjectural reconstruction of the layers of composition in the *History* is right, then it may be the case that some of the passages from the *History* discussed below were composed after the relevant portions of the *Doctrina* had been drafted (*Literature and Politics in Cromwellian England*, 420–5).

their fatal decision to try to stave off the incursions of the Scots and the Picts by inviting in the pagan Saxons. The story of how the Saxons were eventually Christianized despite their frequent lapses into their old religion takes up most of Book 4. Book 5—which may at one point have been intended to be the final book, taking the story through to the events of 1066—opens with an account of the unified monarchy of Ecbert, before charting the long process of decline which eventually rendered the Saxons vulnerable to conquest first by the Danes and then by the Normans, the 'double Conquest' that forms the subject matter of Book 6 (*CPW*, v. 328).

Milton underlines the importance of conquest to his work in two ways. The first is via the set-piece passages found mostly at the start or the end of the various books, where he turns aside from the immediate demands of the narrative to reflect on the quality of his historical materials and, more importantly (though not unconnectedly), the moral significance of the story they have to tell. These passages of reflection are also markedly 'Hosean', registering divine displeasure with nations which stray from the path of virtue and true religion.[24] As we have seen, the *History* ends with just such a commentary on how the irreligion and vice of the native English effectively brought about their conquest by the Normans. Another example is when Milton signs off Book 3 with the following summary:

Thus omitting Fables, we have the veiw of what with reason can be rely'd on for truth, don in *Britain*, since the *Romans* forsook it. Wherin we have heard the many miseries and desolations, brought by divine hand on a perverse Nation; driv'n, when nothing else would reform them, out of a fair Country, into a Mountanous and Barren Corner, by Strangers and Pagans. So much more tolerable in the Eye of Heav'n is Infidelity profess't, then Christian Faith and Religion dishonoured by unchristian works. (*CPW*, v. 183)

According to Milton, once the fabular has been excluded, what we are left facing is the truth—in this case, the melancholy truth that the various calamities suffered by the ancient Britons were actually punishments meted out by a 'divine hand'. Thus God began to visit them with these 'miseries and desolations' after they entered into an alliance with the unbelieving Saxons just as the Israelites had with the Egyptians and the Assyrians. Yet this Hosean scenario is less straightforward than it at first appears. For what Book 3 shows us is that the Saxons, to whom the Britons had turned for help, quickly became their nemesis; the punishment for involvement with pagans proved to be an even deeper involvement with them. This being so, what characterizes divine retribution, on Milton's account of it, is the economy of means with which it operates; the punishment fits the crime so closely because the crime is its own punishment. At the same time, we might ask, if it was appropriate for the Britons to be chastised in this way for their 'unchristian' behaviour, how is it possible to account for the success of the Saxons, who did not believe in Christianity at all?

---

[24] Although I have labelled such moralizing 'Hosean', a more immediate source was probably the 5th- or 6th-c. historian Gildas, from whose *De excidio et conquestu Britanniae* ('On the ruin and conquest of Britain') Milton quotes liberally (see Maltzahn, *Milton's 'History of Britain'*, 116–40). However, Milton frequently adopts this tone in the *History* and elsewhere and it may be that he was drawn to Gildas's work precisely because it chimed with views he had already formed.

Resolving this conundrum leads Milton to make a remarkable statement: 'Infidelity profess't', he announces, is surely 'more tolerable' in the sight of God 'then Christian Faith and Religion dishonoured by unchristian works.' That is to say, an honest admission that one lacks faith is preferable to professions of religious commitment that are belied by one's actions. In short, religious hypocrisy is far worse than blatant infidelity.[25]

The most imposing and complex of these set-pieces is the one that opens Book 5, where Milton pauses to reflect on the topic of conquest at some length. He begins by sounding an optimistic note about the prospects for a newly unified Saxon monarchy:

> The summe of things in this Iland, or the best part therof, reduc't now under the power of one man; and him one of the worthiest, which, as far as can be found in good Authors, was by none attain'd at any time heer before unless in Fables; men might with some reason have expected from such Union, peace and plenty, greatness, and the flourishing of all Estates and Degrees: but far the contrary fell out soon after, Invasion, Spoil, Desolation, slaughter of many, slavery of the rest, by the forcible landing of a fierce Nation; *Danes* commonly call'd, and somtimes *Dacians*, by others, the same with *Normans*; as barbarous as the *Saxons* themselves were at first reputed, and much more; for the *Saxons* first invited came hither to dwell; these unsent for, unprovok'd, came only to destroy. But if the *Saxons*, as is above related, came most of them from *Jutland* and *Anglen*, a part of *Denmarke*, as *Danish* Writers affirm, and that *Danes* and *Normans* are the same; then in this invasion, *Danes* drove out *Danes*, thir own posterity. And *Normans* afterwards, none but antienter *Normans*. Which invasion perhaps, had the Heptarchie stood divided as it was, had either not bin attempted, or not uneasily resisted; while each Prince and people, excited by thir neerest concernments, had more industriously defended thir own bounds, then depending on the neglect of a deputed Governour, sent oft-times from the remote residence of a secure Monarch. (*CPW*, v. 257–8)

The disquisition quickly becomes an exercise in irony. While a unified monarchy might be expected to enhance national security and prosperity, this proves not to be the case. Indeed, by the end of the passage Milton has turned the argument on its head: a heptarchy might have deterred or resisted invaders more effectively than a centralized monarchy did. The invaders too are subjected to ironic scrutiny. Since the Saxons and the Danes both originally came from Denmark, and since the Danes and Normans were also closely related, it follows that the successive conquests of one by the other were literally self-defeating. On this view, the Norman Conquest was a case neither of the Normans suppressing Saxon liberties nor of the Saxons reaffirming their liberties notwithstanding their defeat by Duke William, but of Normans unwittingly displacing 'antienter *Normans*'. Although Milton adopts a rather facetious tone when making these remarks, their ideological significance is clear; for to rewrite 1066 in these terms is to render it incompatible with any of the standard versions of conquest theory.

---

[25] Milton may partly owe this unexpectedly relativistic point of view to Sir Henry Vane the Younger, whose *Zeal Examined* (1652) he much admired; see my essay on 'The Politics of *Paradise Lost*' below, Ch. 31.

Milton then goes on to give the reader the real—which is to say, Hosean—story of why the Saxons succumbed to the Danes:

when God hath decreed servitude on a sinful Nation, fitted by thir own vices for no condition but servile, all Estates of Government are alike unable to avoid it. God had purpos'd to punish our instrumental punishers, though now Christians, by other Heathen, according to his Divine retaliation; invasion for invasion, spoil for spoil, destruction for destruction. The *Saxons* were now full as wicked as the *Britans* were at their arrival, brok'n with luxury and sloth, either secular or superstitious; for laying aside the exercise of Arms, and the study of all vertuous knowledge, some betook them to over-worldly or vitious practice, others to religious Idleness and Solitude, which brought forth nothing but vain and delusive visions; easily perceav'd such, by thir commanding of things, either not belonging to the Gospel, or utterly forbidden, Ceremonies, Reliques, Monasteries, Masses, Idols, add to these ostentation of Alms, got ofttimes by rapine and oppression, or intermixt with violent and lustfull deeds, sometimes prodigally bestow'd as the expiation of cruelty and bloodshed. What longer suffering could there be, when Religion it self grew so void of sincerity, and the greatest shews of purity were impur'd? (v. 259)

This account represents a further intensification of the irony. Indeed, irony might well be thought of as the narrative leitmotiv of the *History*. Or, to put it another way, the *History* shows God to be somewhat of an ironist. For the scheme of 'divine retaliation' is such that since the Saxons are now as corrupt in their religious beliefs and practices as the Britons once were they must be punished in exactly the same way, 'invasion for invasion'. And being heathens—just as the Saxons once were—is precisely what makes the Danes the appropriate means 'to punish our instrumental punishers'.

Disparaging the Saxon church in this comprehensive fashion was one of the aspects of the *History* that contributed to the official view that the work was 'too sharp against the clergy'. For Milton himself, however, the historical moment with the greatest contemporary resonance was probably neither the Danish nor the Norman Conquest but the withdrawal of the Romans from Britain, an episode that, as he puts it at the start of Book 3, 'may deserve attention more than common' from those 'who can judiciously read'. What he had in mind was the parallel that could be drawn between post-imperial Britain in the fifth century and post-civil war Britain in the late 1640s, given that

the late civil broils had cast us into a condition not much unlike to what the *Britans* then were in, when the imperial jurisdiction departing hence left them to the sway of thir own Councils; which times by comparing seriously with these later, and that confused Anarchy with this intereign, we may be able from two such remarkable turns of State, producing like events among us, to raise a knowledg of our selves both great and weighty . . . (v. 129–30)

This looks like a promise to begin a comparative exercise at once, but Milton seems to have delayed doing so until he reached the point in Book 3 when the Britons finally implore the Saxons to assist them. However, the resulting 2,000-word 'Digression' did not see the light of day until 1681 when it was printed as *Mr John Miltons Character of the Long Parliament and Assembly of Divines in MDCXLI* from papers which had come into the possession of Roger L'Estrange, the Surveyor of the Press, presumably around the time the *History* was being cleared for publication. It is nevertheless more likely that its omission in 1670 was the result of self-censorship on Milton's part rather than L'Estrange's intervention as licenser since the note prefixed to the *Character* says that the text was going to be printed '*But out of tenderness to a Party . . . was struck out for some harshness, being only such a Digression, as the History it self would not be discomposed by its omission: which I suppose will be easily discerned, by reading over the beginning of the Third Book of the said History, very near which place this Character is to come in*' (*CPW*, iv. 440). The implication is that Milton himself thought better of allowing this highly critical account of the Long Parliament and the Westminster Assembly to appear in print, although the precise point at which it should have featured in the first edition of the *History* is recorded at the head of a seventeenth-century manuscript of the Digression.[26]

But when was the Digression itself composed? To ask this question is actually to raise two distinct issues. On the one hand, if it is assumed it was written at the same time as Book 3, then the question becomes one of when Book 3 was composed, with scholars differing as to whether this was before or after the execution of Charles I in January 1649. On the other hand, if the composition of the Digression can be detached from that of Book 3, then there is in principle no reason why it cannot have been written in 1660 or even as late as 1670.[27] The choice is between seeing the Digression as a commentary on a revolution in progress or a work of retrospection situated at a lesser or greater distance from the events it considers. But while there is no conclusive evidence either way, it is worth noting that although the manuscript Digression begins by asserting that 'the gaining or loosing of libertie is the greatest change to better or to worse that may befall a nation', its focus thereafter is exclusively on the former of these transformations of political fortune. What it seeks to explain above all is the Britons' failure to seize the 'occasion' provided by their 'manumission' from slavery (*CPW*, v. 441). This being so, the relevant issue is when Milton was more likely to have been preoccupied by thoughts of what happens when a nation is liberated from the rule of a conqueror than what happens when it is subjected to it. And the answer is surely that the matter of 'gaining . . . libertie' was uppermost in his mind during the early years of the English republic, for in both *The Tenure of Kings and Magistrates* (1649) and *Defensio Pro Populo Anglicano* (1651) he invokes the crucial moment when the Romans 'quitted and relinquishd what right they had by

---

[26] For the best account of the *Character*, see Maltzahn, *Milton's 'History of Britain'*, 1–21. On Harvard MS Eng 901, see now Thomas Fulton, 'Edward Phillips and the Manuscript of the "Digression"', *Milton Studies*, 48 (2008), 95–112.

[27] For these various possibilities, see Austin Woolrych, 'The Date of the Digression in Milton's *History of Britain*', in *For Veronica Wedgwood These: Studies in Seventeenth-Century History*, ed. Richard Ollard and Pamela Tudor-Craig (1986), 217–46; Maltzahn, *Milton's 'History of Britain'*, 22–48, and 'Dating the Digression in Milton's *History of Britain*', *Historical Journal*, 36 (1993), 945–56; Austin Woolrych, 'Dating Milton's *History of Britain*', ibid. 929–43; Worden, *Literature and Politics in Cromwellian England*, 414–20; Martin Dzelzainis, 'Dating and Meaning: *Samson Agonistes* and the "Digression" to Milton's *History of Britain*', *Milton Studies*, 48 (2008), 160–77.

Conquest to this Iland, and resign'd it all into the peoples hands' (*CPW*, iii. 221; cf. iv. 479).

Milton's preoccupation with the theme of conquest is far from being exhausted in these grandly orchestrated passages. Indeed, it would be true to say that, in answering the question of *why* the Britons and their successors incurred divine displeasure and hence became liable to being conquered, Milton for the most part confines himself to examining the way in which the relevant secondary causes played themselves out. His aim in doing so is to supply less-elevated explanations of why our forebears behaved as they did and not as they might otherwise have done. The form these explanations accordingly take is that of moral psychology. For it is one of Milton's central beliefs as a historian that to identify the moral strengths and weaknesses of one's ancestors is to equip oneself with the master key to understanding their actions. As we have already seen, the fact that the Saxons were 'brok'n with luxury and sloth' and, instead of practising 'Arms' or pursuing 'vertuous knowledge', gave themselves over to 'vitious practice' or 'religious Idleness' explains why the Danes were able to overcome them. Similarly, for the English to surrender themselves to the full range of 'Vices which effeminate mens minds' was what 'gave to *William* thir Conqueror so easie a Conquest' (*CPW*, v. 259, 402–3).

Such moralizing is not confined to the set-pieces, but dispersed throughout the text. In fact, one of the most striking features of the *History* is the changes that Milton continually rings on just a few key terms. The most important of these is 'courage', which is used on no fewer than fourteen occasions, together with cognates like 'encourag'd', 'encouragement', 'reincourag'd', 'discourag'd', and 'discouragement'.[28] There are even more variants upon the closely related term 'heart': 'hart'n', 'heart'ns', 'hartning', 'faint-hearted', and 'heartless'.[29] Adverse winds, we are told, 'disheartn'd' the Roman invasion fleet under Claudius, though the appearance of a meteor meant they 'tooke heart againe', and when the Danish invader Edric managed to 'dishart'n' the Saxons by tricking them into believing that their leader, Edmund, was dead, Edmund's reappearance among them meant 'they recoverd heart' at once. Conversely, when Harold, having fought 'with unspeakable courage', is shot with an arrow, the effect is to leave 'his Souldiers without heart' (*CPW*, v. 65, 354–5, 401). Also part of this nexus are 'spirit' (used six times), and 'animated' and 'animating'.[30] Time and again in the *History*, military and political success is shown to depend on possessing courage, heart, and spirit while the absence of these qualities leads to disaster. What is required therefore is the cardinal virtue of fortitude, the key elements of which are courage and magnanimity—that is to say, the opposite of the fearfulness and pusillanimity displayed by the Israelites in their dealings with Assyria and Egypt.[31]

---

[28] See *CPW*, v. 53, 58, 66, 70, 75, 77, 79, 88, 89, 131, 153, 187, 261, 273, 299, 311, 315, 337, 344, 355, 357, 398, 400, 401.

[29] See *CPW*, v. 45, 133, 139, 80, 293, 343.

[30] See *CPW*, v. 124, 133, 158, 317, 326, 330, 351, 372.

[31] On Milton and fortitude, see Martin Dzelzainis, 'Milton's Classical Republicanism', in David Armitage, Armand Himy, and Quentin Skinner (eds.), *Milton and Republicanism* (Cambridge, 1995),

Since Milton's preoccupation with fortitude has its origins in his engagement with Roman historians and moralists, it is no surprise that his reliance on this lexicon in the *History* first becomes noticeable at the point in Book 2 where he begins to draw heavily on works by Tacitus—the *Annals*, the *Histories*, and especially *Agricola*, the biography of his father-in-law, Julius Agricola, the governor who completed the Roman conquest of Britain. Throughout these writings, Tacitus himself relies on a key pair of terms to explain the course of events: *virtus* (courage, strength, manliness) and *animus* (heart, spirit, courage). Not only does Milton follow suit, he does not hesitate to bring out in full the gendered implications of this terminology: to display courage (*virtus*), he says, is equivalent to showing 'down right manhood' or being 'like men resolv'd', and when Suetonius Paulinus 'heart'ns his men' in the face of Boadicea's army this is so that they will 'strike manfully this headless rabble' (v. 66, 69, 80). Milton is also attentive to the tactics used by Agricola, chief among which was the sustained use of terror to make the Britons lose heart. Thus after his decisive victory at Mons Graupius, Agricola deliberately returns to winter quarters 'with slow marches, that his delay in passing might serve to awe those new conquer'd Nations' (v. 91; cf. Tacitus, *Agricola*, 38). Arguably, however, what impressed Milton most was the subtle way in which Agricola deployed what might today be called 'soft power' so as to undermine the independent spirit of the Britons. His version of Tacitus' account of Agricola's policy of 'Romanization' is notably full:

The Winter he spent all in worthie actions; teaching and promoting like a public Father the institutes and customes of civil life. The Inhabitants rude and scatter'd, and by that the proner to Warr, he so perswaded as to build Houses, Temples, and Seats of Justice; and by praysing the forward, quick'ning the slow, assisting all, turn'd the name of necessitie into an emulation. He caus'd moreover the Noblemens Sons to be bred up in liberal Arts; and by preferring the Witts of *Britain*, before the Studies of *Gallia*, brought them to affect the Latine Eloquence, who before hated the Language. Then were the *Roman* fashions imitated, and the Gown; after a while the incitements also and materials of Vice, and voluptuous life, proud Buildings, Baths, and the elegance of Banqueting; which the foolisher sort call'd civilitie, but was indeed a secret Art to prepare them for bondage. (v. 85)[32]

Whereas Tacitus states only that Agricola's promotion of *humanitas* was a further aspect of the Britons' slavery ('pars servitutis esset'), Milton dilates upon the phrase so as to attribute a sinister agency to him; that he was in fact exercising 'a secret Art to prepare them for bondage'. However, this was to do no more than make explicit what Tacitus—with his habitual reserve—had left unspoken. The two historians are in fact

---

12–13, and 'Milton's Politics', in Dennis Danielson (ed.), *The Cambridge Companion to Milton*, 2nd edn. (Cambridge, 1999), 73–5.

[32] 'sequens hiems saluberrimis consiliis absumpta. namque ut homines dispersi ac rudes eoque in bella faciles quieti et otio per voluptates adsuescerent, hortari privatim, adiuvare publice, ut templa fora domos extruerent, laudando promptos, castigando segnis: ita honoris aemulatio pro necessitate erat. iam vero principum filios liberalibus artibus erudire, et ingenia Britannorum studiis Gallorum anteferre, ut qui modo linguam Romanam abnuebant, eloquentiam concupiscerent. inde etiam habitus nostri honor et frequens toga; paulatimque discessum ad delenimenta vitiorum, porticus et balinea et conviviorum elegantiam. idque apud imperitos humanitas vocabatur, cum pars servitutis esset' (Tacitus, *Agricola*, 21).

equally ambivalent about the benefits of 'civilitie' and, more particularly, have in common a specifically republican fear about the loss of virtue (and hence effeminacy) to which luxury leads. As we saw earlier, Algernon Sidney, who was no less heavily influenced by Tacitus, said very similar things about the insidious court culture of Louis XIV. And it is indeed very striking that, embedded in the passage from *Agricola*, we already find a juxtaposition between the 'Witts of *Britain*' and the 'Studies of *Gallia*' ('ingenia Britannorum studiis Gallorum'). The anti-French dimension of republicanism had a long pedigree.

By the time we reach the end of the *History*, the relation between slavery and slavishness has been shown to work both ways. On the one hand, it is certainly the case that Milton sometimes adopts the view of the Roman historians and moralists to the effect that, as Quentin Skinner puts it, the 'imposition of slavery invariably breeds servility and slavishness'.[33] This is the idea clearly being invoked at the start of Book 3 when Milton attributes the Britons' failure 'to use and maintain true libertie' after the departure of the Romans to their having become, 'through long subjection, servile in mind'. But the point Milton emphasizes rather more often is that it is slavishness that leads to slavery; it is only because the Saxons are already 'fitted by thir own vices for no condition but servile' that God 'decreed servitude' on them (*CPW*, v. 130, 259). Indeed, the perception that servility of mind results in slavery is what the *History* ultimately has in common with works like *Defensio Secunda*, *De Doctrina Christiana*, and *Paradise Lost*.

[33] Quentin Skinner, 'John Milton and the Politics of Slavery', in *Visions of Politics*, 3 vols. (Cambridge), ii. 304.

CHAPTER 23

....

DE DOCTRINA CHRISTIANA: AN ENGLAND THAT MIGHT HAVE BEEN

....

GORDON CAMPBELL

THOMAS N. CORNS

I

....

The work we now know as *De Doctrina Christiana* opens with an epistle to the reader in which Milton describes the origin of the treatise. Reflecting on his earliest engagement with controversial theology, he explains that, after long study of the biblical languages, he immersed himself in a series of short systematic accounts of theology. Having mastered the genre, he began to construct a theological commonplace book (now lost), which assembled biblical texts under doctrinal heads. On his account, his confidence and autonomy grew alongside his dissatisfaction with his work so far and he turned to the study of more substantial ordonnances, and eventually embarked on gathering his own readings and interpretations into a consolidated account. He stresses that his purpose, initially, was simply the clarification of his own thinking to strengthen the intellectual foundation of his own faith. In a formula echoed throughout the Protestant tradition, Milton asserts the primacy of the biblical texts; the work, he insists, draws on 'the Bible alone' (*solo dei verbo*) (CW, xiv. 6).

The date at which this process began is a matter of surmise; sometime in the late 1640s would be compatible with what we know of his other commitments. The process of formal Bible study and research would thus fit between the flurry of pamphleteering in which he had been engaged from 1641 to 1645 and inception early in 1649 of his career as a public servant. It is likeliest that the decision, which he describes in the epistle, to vouchsafe the treatise which resulted from his sustained study to a wider public was reached towards the end of the English republic. William R. Parker goes so far as to suggest that the extreme tolerationism of *Of Civil Power* (1659) perhaps marked Milton's attempt to prepare the way for publication of so apparently heterodox a treatise (Parker, *Milton*, 518–22).

Scribal evidence also points to a dating shortly before the Restoration. The principal *in vita* scribe of the manuscript, Jeremie Picard, is clearly associated with Milton in life records which date from the late 1650s and into 1660; thereafter, he is not to be found. Picard was evidently engaged by Milton on the project over an extended period, and the manuscript he produced gives clear answers to the old and obvious question: how could the blind Milton have produced a tract which incorporates approximately 8,000 biblical references? The answer, in a word, is 'fascicules'.

The manuscript at the National Archives and catalogued as State Papers 9/61 is currently bound into three soft-covered volumes. The authors of this chapter were allowed access to the text cut from its bindings while the document was in preparation for digitization. This unique opportunity readily disclosed what had been obscured by an earlier generation of conservators, who had cut the folios on which the text had been for most part transcribed and pasted individual leaves, in a staggered way, on thick stubs. We noticed first, that each chapter had evidently been worked on as a separate fascicule, or manuscript booklet of folio sheets stitched together. This was evident both from the quiring (how the manuscript pages were folded and fitted together), which we could work out from the watermarks, and from the state of the outside pages, which were both faded and stained, no doubt from the hands of the scribes who worked on it. Every chapter begins on a recto page. Moreover, the original pagination was continuous only within the fascicules, and they in turn corresponded to chapters.

Our discovery of Picard's way of working enables us to understand how Milton mitigated the problems of blindness. The key to his practice was concentration on individual chapters, most of which are quite short, which could be accessed by any of his evidently considerable network of helpers, who could select an individual chapter which Milton could then hear, reflect on, and augment. While most additional material, added frequently interlineally or in the wide margins of the manuscript, is in the hand of Picard, numerous other hands of occasional assistants have been identified. Early biographers tell us of Milton's fine memory and methodical way of working.

Our unique access to the manuscript disclosed another insight: even within chapters leaves may differ significantly in size. Also, line density varies considerably, again even within a single chapter. These facts point towards another aspect of Milton's working practice. From time to time, when a leaf was replete with additional material, some of it inserted vertically, Milton had it recopied by Picard, the original leaf was cut out of the fascicule, and the new leaf inserted. Sometimes, it would seem, whole fascicules have been recopied, as if to ready them for publication, though even these contain further additions in their margins.

It appears from what we have identified as the earliest drafts that at one time manuscript circulation may have been envisaged. We see Picard demonstrating his full decorative range as a skilled scribe, and showing, too, three principal varieties of his hand, a large hand, for emphasis and headings and the like, his normal hand, and, for the quotations, an italic hand. In sections which are plainly later copies incorporating additional material, the scribal range is more or less restricted to his normal hand and, for quoted material, italic, thus anticipating the principal fonts used in printed books, and rejecting the graphic potential present in manuscripts intended for circulation.[1] What Milton had begun as a private exercise, perhaps had been reconceived as one appropriate for manuscript circulation to a fit audience though few, before work began on preparing the text for print publication.

The scribal evidence points us to another important conclusion: the work of preparing this manuscript for the press was not completed in Milton's lifetime. The strongest evidence is that Picard and Milton were still adding material to fascicules which had been already fair copied. Moreover, some sections are in no condition to be handed to a printing house. Indeed, the early section has been recopied by Daniel Skinner, of whom more shortly, almost certainly because those pages required attention before a printer could begin to set them. It is instructive to consider the two pages for which we have both Skinner's version and the state in which Picard had left it (pp. 308 and 308A).[2] There are strong arguments for assuming that the pages at the beginning of the treatise, which Skinner thought it appropriate to copy, were as dishevelled as page 308A. There is a sharp contrast between the fouler papers of SP 9/61 and the near-perfect fair copy of *Paradise Lost*, Book 1, which is preserved in the Pierpont Morgan Library, New York, and from which its first edition was set.

All the evidence points towards Milton abandoning, not completing, the project round about the time of the Restoration. Why should he have given over what he famously described as his 'best and dearest'? The reasons are not hard to find. Milton, as an apologist for regicide, could have expected the malign attention of a restored monarchy. Indeed, he was added only very late to those excused prosecution by the Act of Oblivion, and, contrary to the spirit of that law, he was for a while incarcerated. Republican supporters had every reason to suppose their papers would be examined and perhaps confiscated. Such was the practice of successive regimes through the mid-century. William Prynne had examined the papers of William Laud. At the Restoration, John Thurloe, Milton's line manager in the civil service of the 1650s, carefully concealed his own papers in the ceiling of his Lincoln's Inn

---

[1] See Peter Beal, *In Praise of Scribes: Manuscripts and their Makers in Seventeenth-Century England* (Oxford, 1998).

[2] Gordon Campbell, Thomas N. Corns, John K. Hale, and Fiona Tweedie, *Milton and the Manuscript of* De Doctrina Christiana (Oxford, 2007), 42–3.

chambers in anticipation of their seizure. In 1661 James Harrington's arrest included the confiscation of his own manuscripts. The practice continued well into the latter part of the century. The manuscript of Algernon Sidney's *Discourses*, found when he was taken into custody, was used in the trial against him. Milton at the Restoration spent some time in hiding, faced expropriation of property, and the possibilities of a far worse fate. His manuscript could, at best, have been lost; at worst, its heterodoxy could have been used against him in any subsequent prosecution and trial.

At his death, Milton's family at least had been reunited with the manuscript. The likeliest route for its transmission was through Edward Phillips, his nephew, who according to John Aubrey had possession of his unpublished manuscripts. At this point, Daniel Skinner enters the history of the work. Skinner, a junior fellow of Trinity College, Cambridge, conceived the notion of taking the manuscript, together with his own transcription of Miltonic state papers, to the United Provinces for publication. To that end, he made a fair copy of the first fascicules of the treatise. On whose authority he did this is unclear. Perhaps he was acting for Phillips or for Milton's widow; just possibly he acted to discharge a promise made to the ailing Milton, though no lifetime record connects him to the poet.

His decision soon proved imprudent, since it provoked the obloquy of Sir Joseph Williamson, the implacable secretary of state for the Northern Department, whose responsibilities included diplomatic relations with northern Europe and national security. He was, thus, well placed to track Skinner down and to bring to bear sufficient pressure to ensure his cooperation in surrendering the two Miltonic manuscripts into his hands. Williamson, no doubt with satisfaction at suppressing the *Nachlass* of the man he termed 'that villain, Milton', placed the documents in a 'press' or cupboard in the Old State Paper Office in the Middle Treasury Gallery in Whitehall.[3]

There they remained till November 1823. Milton by then was perceived and represented as the iconic poet of English Protestantism. Joseph Addison's assiduous work at cleaning up the reputation of the old republican apologist still had its effect. The newly discovered treatise posed an obvious problem: Milton's heterodoxy could no longer, with facility, be glossed over. One immediate response was to dispute its authorship. Thomas Burgess, bishop of Salisbury, insisted this apparently Unitarian work could not be the work of Milton as he was contemporaneously perceived. Since the 1990s that doubt has been rehearsed again, most influentially in the writings of William B. Hunter. Recent research, including stylometric analysis, has demonstrated beyond reasonable doubt the Miltonic provenance of the treatise, though its derivative nature, a feature of the genre, means it has close verbal affinities with the work of other systematic theologians of the Reformation period, pre-eminently William Ames and Johannes Wolleb.[4]

---

[3] For Williamson's views on Milton and his attempts to secure and suppress the manuscript of *De Doctrina Christiana*, see Campbell et al., *Milton and the Manuscript of* De Doctrina Christiana, 10–29.

[4] See William B. Hunter, *Visitation Unimplor'd: Milton and the Authorship of* De Doctrina Christiana (Pittsburgh, Pa., 1998). On Milton's relations to the tradition of Protestant systematic theology in general and to the work of Ames and Wolleb in particular, see Campbell et al., *Milton and the Manuscript of* De Doctrina Christiana, esp. ch. 5.

Why did Milton choose to write in Latin? In the case of his three defences, *Defensio Pro Populo Anglicana* (1651), *Defensio Secunda* (1654), and *Pro Se Defensio* (1655), the decision was in part determined by the medium chosen by those critics of the English regicide that he was obliged to refute. They served the political objective of defending the English republic before continental Europe, and their content in part reflected the diplomatic priorities of Milton's political masters. The first defence seems to show concern with influencing a Dutch readership, a little ahead of the republic's first major embassy abroad, which was to the United Provinces. The second reflects the currently congenial relations with Sweden; his panegyric to Queen Christiana, surprisingly cordial for a republican spokesman, reflects governmental enthusiasm for strengthening those ties. The point is that these are genuinely targeted at a foreign audience, and are couched in the *lingua franca* of international communication.

The decision to write *De Doctrina Christiana* in Latin probably reflected some of the same priorities, but may have been shaped also by the early history of the project. As he explained in his epistle, when Milton drew material from the great systematic theologians of early modern Protestantism, he was consolidating writing that was itself in Latin. As he assembled his proof-texts, drawing on the word of God alone, he did so using the Junius–Tremellius Latin translation of the Scriptures favoured by Protestant scholars. If the early work was indeed an aid to private study, reflection, and devotion, the overwhelming probability is that it was in Latin. Latin, moreover, meant that, when he was ready to address a readership, he targeted the larger world of continental European theologians, as well as the learned among his countrymen. Certainly Milton in 1659 in *Of Civil Power* defends the rights of relatively uneducated laymen to preach and to lead Christian worship; but in *De Doctrina Christiana* the scholar speaks to fellow scholars, across frontiers, and in their common language. That is, moreover, the common language of all the major systematic theologies. Milton, of course, had used English for his first, highly controversial theological treatise, the *Doctrine and Discipline of Divorce* (1643; 1644). But that tract was aimed at swaying English decision-making institutions, pre-eminently the Westminster Assembly of Divines and the Long Parliament itself, towards the replacement of canon law provision with new legislation. The issues were English issues, albeit that he invokes the supporting judgements of Continental divines in the second edition and in *The Judgement of Martin Bucer* (1644). His own Latin treatise, though, aims to contribute to the higher discourse where Ames and Wolleb, and before them Calvin, Beza, and Melanchthon, operated, and the opinions he seeks to sway are those of elite, professional theologians.

The style of *De Doctrina Christiana* has been subjected to recent scrutiny. Milton's Latin exhibits considerable variation.[5] Much of the work is more or less transcribed from the Junius–Tremellius Bible; Milton indeed often allows the word of God to be interpreted in relatively unmediated form. He has, too, a plain style for routine matters of exposition, for definitions, divisions into parts, and exegesis. But he

---

[5] Campbell et al., *Milton and the Manuscript of* De Doctrina Christiana, ch. 4.

commands, also, a grander idiom manifest in the high rhetoric of the epistle and in the second preface composed for the long and contentious chapter *De Filio*. Throughout, as one would expect from the writer of the defences, the lexis and syntax are admirable in their impeccable Latinity, while the highest style aspires to a Ciceronian copiousness and keeps to a noticeably Ciceronian word-order.

II

We turn now to the theological arguments of the treatise. Heterodoxy is dissent from orthodoxy, and there are several orthodoxies against which the theology of *De Doctrina* can be set. As we have noted, when Bishop Burgess considered the work in the 1820s, it seemed to him a treatise that supported the unitarianism of which he was a committed foe; indeed, the theology of the treatise was so inimical to his own brand of Anglicanism that he declared it to be non-Miltonic. In the late twentieth century the theology was seen by some Christian evangelicals as broadly consistent with their own thinking and by some secular leftists as indicative of a Miltonic radicalism of which they thoroughly approved. When in the 1990s the authorship of the treatise was questioned, the authors of this chapter were sometimes said to be conspiring to reclaim Milton for Anglicanism.

In the seventeenth century there were other orthodoxies. The treatise has been read by students of English literature in the context of radical theological thinking in mid-seventeenth-century England. There are certainly points of analogy, but in our view it is inappropriate to judge the orthodoxy of a Latin treatise against the vernacular writings of English radicals. The appropriate context is rather that of systematic theology, which is almost exclusively a Continental Latin genre. Many theologians from Luther and Calvin onwards wrote both in Latin and their chosen vernacular, and the differences between these two types of writings are striking. Vernacular theology takes various forms, of which the most popular was biblical theology, the patient and detailed exposition of biblical texts, often undertaken by theologians with some command of the biblical languages. Such writing embodies theological perspectives, but it is consensual in tone, and rarely heterodox. Systematic theology, on the other hand, is a genre in which argument is cast in a learned language that will not be accessible to ordinary believers, whose faith might be destabilized by debate. It is this genre in which theologians remove the kid gloves with which they treat vernacular readers, instead indulging in some bare-knuckle encounters with fellow professionals. It is therefore a genre characterized by views that range from the eccentric to the heretical. In this context, the theology of *De Doctrina Christiana* is for the most part unexceptionable, but on a few doctrines, some central (e.g. Christology) and some clearly adiaphorous (e.g. mortalism), Milton adopts minority positions.

One of the reasons that Latin ordonnances of the period seem quite similar is that they share a common methodology based on the logic of Petrus Ramus, which means that they classify propositions in order of generality, proceeding from the most general to the most specific. A second reason is that systematic theologians read each other in much the same way that secular modern scholars do. Milton acknowledged that he read the treatises of Ames and Wolleb, and from time to time mentions other theologians, such as Thomas Cartwright and Dudley Fenner; we have considered treatises by these theologians, and by others such as William Perkins, Johann Gerhard, Johann-Heinrich Alsted, Théodore de Bèze, Johannes Piscator, and Ramus.

For modern readers, the most contentious aspect of the theology of *De Doctrina* is its anti-trinitarianism. Indeed, twenty-first-century Christians tend to see it as heretical, because trinitarianism is now enshrined in all confessions of faith with the exception of Unitarianism. In the seventeenth century there was no such consensus: Milton was far from alone in observing that the biblical evidence for the trinity was virtually non-existent. Indeed, the only unequivocal biblical text, as Milton and many others pointed out, is a medieval forgery. The verse known to scholars as the Johannine Comma and to Bible readers as 1 John 5: 7 ringingly proclaims that 'there are three that bear witness in heaven, the Father, the Word and the Holy Ghost; and these three are one'. The difficulty is that the verse first appears in the twelfth century, when it was inserted to buttress a doctrine that lacked any significant biblical foundation.

Once freed from the constraining hegemony of trinitarian thought, radicals moved in various directions. Milton's dissent from traditional forms of trinitarianism was relatively cautious (he did not, for example, deny the divinity of Jesus), but it affected both his Christology and his pneumatology. In the case of the former, which was an extremely sensitive issue, Milton wrote a special preface to the chapter (I. 5) in which he sets out his position. At the core of his Christology is the technical view that God the Son is consubstantial with God the Father, but not co-essential: he shares the divine substance but has his own essence. The distinction is a complicated one, in part because there is not a stable relationship between Greek, Latin, and English terminology. In Patristic Greek theology a distinction is drawn between the substratum of the godhead (*ousia*) and its modes of existence (*hypostaseis*). At first *ousia* was correctly translated into Latin *essentia* and *hypostasis* (plural *hypostaseis*) as *substantia*, but soon the Latin terms became muddled and were sometimes reversed or conflated. Augustine therefore proposed to translate *hypostasis* as *persona*, thus enabling theologians to declare that the Trinity consisted of one *essentia* (or one *substantia*) and three *personae*. In English, the problem was exacerbated by the practice (common but not usual) of translating *essentia* as 'substance' and *substantia* as 'essence'. Milton's contribution to the confusion was to translate *ousia* as *substantia* but, unusually, to translate *hypostasis* as *essentia*; his source seems to have been Tremellius, who in his Latin translation of the Syriac New Testament, in which *hypostasis* is translated as Syriac *qnoma*, decided to translate *qnoma* into Latin as *essentia*.

All of this may seem incomprehensible to a modern secular reader, but in the early modern period it was highly controversial (people were burned for anti-trinitarianism), and the formulation Milton adopts was deemed to be demeaning to the Son.

Certainly aspects of his Christology seem to be reductive: he argues, for example, that because the Son was begotten in time, he should be described as perpetual rather than eternal; similarly, he denies the ubiquity of the human nature of the exalted Son, insisting that his human nature now exists in one place. Milton's position should not be confused with Arianism, because, although he agrees with Arius that the Son is not eternal, he does not believe that the Son was created out of nothing, but was rather begotten out of the substance of God the Father.[6] Similarly, he does not deny the pre-existence of the Son, nor is he troubled by the anti-adorationist position taken by Transylvanian Unitarians. This position is sufficiently orthodox to have been embodied in the second verse of 'O come all ye faithful', in which the Son is said to be 'very God, begotten not created' and the audience is invited to adore him.

In the late twentieth century, literary critics who wanted to distance Milton from Arius in order to make his Christology more palatable to contemporary Christian tastes declared Milton to be a subordinationist, which was a position commended as a halfway point between heretical Arianism and orthodox trinitarianism. The subordinationist snake has been adeptly scotched by John Rumrich, who observed that subordination is a nineteenth-century concept designed to denote a tendency in some Patristic theologians to deny the co-equality of the persons of the trinity.[7] In short, it is a tendency rather than a doctrine, and it is futile to associate Milton with it.

The status of the Holy Spirit was also the subject of technical distinctions: whereas the world was said to have been created and the Son to have proceeded from God the Father by generation, the Spirit, in the language of pneumatology, was deemed to have proceeded by spiration. The font of this spiration became a matter of dispute that was eventually to divide the church. At the Third Council of Toledo in 589, the Greek delegates insisted that the Spirit proceeded from God the Father, but Western delegates insisted on adding the word *filioque* ('and the Son') to the Creed, so that the Spirit was deemed to have proceeded conjointly from Father and Son. Western insistence on the double procession of the Holy Spirit led to a rift with the Orthodox Church, and the two have remained estranged throughout succeeding centuries. In *De Doctrina* Milton argues that the Spirit shares the substance but not the essence of God the Father, but on the mode of procession he is distinctly undogmatic, because biblical evidence is wanting: he dismisses procession by spiration, and declares himself unable to decide between the other two options (generation and creation) because neither has scriptural warrant.

Four other doctrines have achieved prominence in discussions of the theology of *De Doctrina*: creation, soteriology, mortalism, and polygamy.

That the world was created was not at issue. The difficulties arose from four secondary questions: of what was it created? who created it? what relation does the creation bear to the advent of time? were souls still being created? Many Christian

---

[6] On Milton and Arianism, compare the essays on *Paradise Lost* by Nigel Smith and John Rogers below, Chs. 28 and 33.

[7] John P. Rumrich, 'Milton's Arianism: Why It Matters', in Stephen B. Dobranski and John P. Rumrich (eds.), *Milton and Heresy* (Cambridge, 1998), 81–2.

theologians argued that the world was first created from nothing (*creatio ex nihilo*) and then shaped by the hand of God; advocates of this two-stage creation included Trelcatius and Wolleb. Milton's position was subtly different, in that he rejects *creatio ex nihilo* in favour of what he variously calls *creatio ex Deo* or *creatio a Deo*. The preposition matters, because, as Augustine explains in *De natura boni*, 'from him' (*ex ipso*) does not mean the same as 'of him' (*de ipso*); the latter preposition is reserved for the Son. On the question of who effected the creation, the formulation of the Nicene Creed that it was the Son through whom all things were made (*per quem omnia facta sunt*) was widely accepted, but Milton dissented; his anti-Trinitarian logic led him to the conclusion that the Son had only a secondary role in the creation. On the relation to the advent of time, the consensus was that time began as the world was created. Milton disagreed, arguing that the creation certainly took place after the generation of the Son and probably after the fall of the angels, and so was an event embedded in time rather than one that marked the inception of time. On the creation of the soul, there were two principal positions: those called creationists (a usage wholly distinct from the modern meaning) argued that God created a fresh soul every time a new human was born; those called traducianists, of whom Milton was one, thought that the soul extended to all parts of the body, including bodily fluids, and that the soul of Adam was transmitted to successive generations through the semen of fathers. This doctrine had an important consequence for Milton's hamartiology, in that traducianism meant that sin was inherited; creationists, on the other hand, took the view that humans were born in a state of innocence and then fell inevitably into sin.

Soteriology was the founding doctrine of the Reformation. Luther insisted that salvation must be secured by faith alone (*sola fide*), and most Protestant groups united in support of this view. The fissiparous nature of Protestantism did not affect this central doctrine, but certainly occasioned divisions in the two principal components of soteriology: the atonement, which is the means by which God effects salvation, and grace, which is the means by which humans secure salvation. The four rival theories of the atonement are known as the recapitulation, ransom, satisfaction, and forensic theories. The first, which is associated with Irenaeus, depicts Jesus as recapitulating the entire human race in his person; the race fell through Adam, and was redeemed by Jesus, the second Adam. The second depicts Jesus as a ransom paid to Satan to pay for the sins of humankind; elaborations of this theory depicted Jesus as a mousetrap (so Augustine) or fishhook (so Gregory the Great) whose ransom led to the defeat of Satan. The third, which was memorably formulated by Anselm, depicts Jesus as the penalty paid to God the Father as reparation for the dishonour caused by the fall; the wrath of God was deemed to be satisfied by the death of his son. The fourth, which emerged at the Reformation (and is also known as the penal-substitutionary theory), represents the soterial act as a trial in which God the Father is judge and Jesus is the barrister who represents fallen mankind and then volunteers to bear the penalty on behalf of his client, so mollifying the just anger of the judge. Milton's thinking on many theological issues changed during the course of his life, but he was always a supporter of the forensic theory of the atonement. Advocates of that theory were divided into those who thought that Jesus died for all (universal atonement, often supported by Arminians) or only for the elect (limited atonement, often supported by Calvinists); Milton's position in *De Doctrina* (I. 16) is broadly supportive of the Arminians, though his mortalism (of which more below) is a radical element in an otherwise mainstream position.

The doctrine of grace had divided the church since late antiquity, and in Milton's time was still a deeply contentious issue. Everyone agreed on the necessity of grace, which by common consent was the transformation of the sinner on the initiative of God. There were, however, deep disagreements about the freedom of the human will (i.e. whether or not grace was irresistible) and about predestination (were the saved chosen before they were born?) and reprobation (were the damned chosen before they were born?). Grace was subdivided (prevenient, subsequent, sufficient, efficacious, habitual, actual, and congruent were the main categories), as was the Calvinist position (supralapsarians, antelapsarians, infralapsarians, postlapsarians). Arminius revived the compromise (between the Augustinian and Pelagian positions) proposed by John Cassian, who in the position known as semi-Pelagianism accepted Augustine's doctrine of original sin but rejected total depravity and the irresistibility of grace in order to assert the freedom of the human will to choose. This Arminian–Cassian doctrine became the theology of Laudian Arminianism, and so the ceremonial and sacramental theology of the young Milton.[8] By the time he wrote *De Doctrina* Milton had abandoned sacramental Arminianism in favour of a remarkably independent Arminian position. In his advocacy of general rather than particular election he was at one with a host of prominent Arminians (notably Episcopius, Curcellaeus, and Limborchus, the last of whom had been asked in the later 1670s to advise on whether *De Doctrina* should be published), but he parted company with other learned Arminians on the subject of reprobation.[9] Milton's position, which is that reprobation is not simply the exercise of the divine will but is also the obstinacy of the human will, is one that he shared with radical Arminians such as John Goodwin, and even Servetus.

Mortalism was a doctrine that arose to fill the awkward gap created by the abolition of Purgatory by Protestants. Where did one go between the death of the body and the Last Judgement? The heretical answer to this question was mortalism, which came in three variants: thnetopsychism (the soul dies with the body but is resurrected at the Last Judgement), psychopannychism (the soul sleeps from the moment of death and is awakened at the Last Judgement), and annihilationism (the soul dies with the body and permanently ceases to exist). As late as the 1640s, Milton took the conventional view that the dead were in heaven, so he assumes in the preface to *The Judgement of Martin Bucer* (1644) that Bucer is listening to the debate. From the 1650s, however, Milton championed thnetopsychism, and that is the view set out in *De Doctrina*.

---

[8] See Gordon Campbell and Thomas N. Corns, *John Milton: Life, Work, and Thought* (Oxford, 2008), chs. 3–6.

[9] Campbell et al., *Milton and the Manuscript of* De Doctrina Christiana, 7.

Polygamy interested Milton throughout his adult life. His insistence in *De Doctrina* that polygamy is licit is unique among systematic theologians of the seventeenth century, but has sixteenth-century antecedents both among the early Reformers (Luther had condoned the bigamy of Philip of Hesse) and radical Anabaptists such as John of Leiden. Advocacy of polygamy is more than a male fantasy, because it has important theological consequences. Milton was not an advocate of Galenic embryology, but rather stressed the centrality of the male seed in procreation; for Protestants, this had the advantage of reducing the role of the Virgin Mary, who became only the nourisher of the divine seed. In Milton's case the advocacy of polygamy coloured his hamartiology as well as his Christology, because the soul and the sin of Adam were passed through the male line.

III

De Doctrina Christiana has provoked much debate in recent years, though the crucial questions have now been answered (at least to our general satisfaction). The history of the manuscript firmly ties it to a Miltonic provenance. Its transmission can be traced from the unpublished works of the late poet, through the hands of Daniel Skinner and the Dutch publisher with whom he tried to place it, into the keeping of Sir Joseph Williamson. Stylometric analysis shows clear affinities with Milton's undisputedly canonical works and offers no evidence to dispute its provenance, though it also discloses an important characteristic of the genre, namely the habitual appropriation of earlier writing. The physical condition of the manuscript gives plenty of insight into how a blind man could work on so challenging a project. By working in fascicules, each one containing a chapter, Milton broke the effort down into easily located components, which, with the help of a sound support network, he could amend, revise, and supplement in methodical fashion. That way of working was so important to him that even as sections were recopied to incorporate addenda his principal scribe laboured to retain those physical divisions. But there is also ample evidence that the manuscript, in the state in which Milton left it at his death, was some way from readiness for submission to the press. Moreover, the life records of Milton and of his principal scribe show no evidence of his working on the manuscript later than 1660, and it resonates with the optimistic and expansive tolerationism of *Of Civil Power*, written in the Indian summer of English republicanism. Both its unfinished status and its relatively early date could well explain discrepancies in its argument and the theology of *Paradise Lost*, and further caution against too straightforward a reliance on the treatise as an interpretative aid to understanding the epic. Certainly in several key areas the treatise expounds significantly heterodox positions. But many systematic theologians, respected in the own age and subsequently for their Protestant orthodoxy, also accommodate within their own treatises ideas which reflect their own new thinking or else the challenging views of a minority. After all, if a theologian had nothing new to add, no original perspectives and interpretations, then there was scant motivation to add another tome to the pile. As we concluded the study we co-authored with Fiona Tweedie and John Hale, 'Seen as a text of the late 1650s, [*De Doctrina Christiana*] points, perhaps, to a different lost paradise, that of a republican England that could have been characterized by a genuinely broad toleration, where no orthodoxy would go untested, where all would worship according to their own inner conviction, and none need fear the tithing priest and his ally, the persecuting magistrate.'[10] *De Doctrina Christiana* memorializes an England that might have been.

---

[10] Ibid. 161.

PART VI

PARADISE LOST

CHAPTER 24

WRITING EPIC: *PARADISE LOST*

CHARLES MARTINDALE

Without stopping to qualify the averment, the Old World has had the poems of myths, fictions, feudalism, conquest, caste, dynastic wars, and splendid exceptional characters and affairs, which have been great; but the New World needs the poems of realities and science and of the democratic average and basic equality, which shall be greater. In the centre of all, and object of all, stands the Human Being, towards whose heroic and spiritual evolution poems and everything directly or indirectly tend, Old World or New.

Walt Whitman, prefatory letter to *Leaves of Grass* (1889)

In the proem to *Paradise Lost* 9, at the turning point of the epic, Milton gives three potential hindrances to the completion of his heroic task (ll. 41–6). The first—for he is one of God's Englishmen—is the weather. Like many before and since, the Italophile Milton believed that the climate of the Mediterranean was more propitious for art and culture than that of the cold North among what Dr Johnson satirically terms a 'lagging race of frosty grovellers';[1] in *The History of Britain* Milton argues that 'civility' has to be introduced from countries where 'the sun, which we want, ripens wits as well as fruits' (*CPW*, v/i. 451).[2] The other two hindrances are both aspects of

I would like to thank Colin Burrow, John Hale, David Hopkins, and Liz Prettejohn for help, advice, and encouragement.

[1] Samuel Johnson, *The Lives of the Most Eminent English Poets; with Critical Observations on their Works*, ed. Roger Lonsdale, 4 vols. (Oxford, 2005), i. 267 (cited in text as *Lives of the Poets*). Throughout this chapter I have modernized spelling and punctuation in all citations.

[2] See Nicholas von Maltzahn, *Milton's History of Britain: Republican Historiography in the English Revolution* (Oxford, 1991), 189–90.

belatedness: Milton's own advancing years, and 'an age too late' (some believed that the world had been decaying since the Fall, a view of which Milton made imaginative use in *Paradise Lost*, though he had previously argued against it).[3] Even as a young man, in Sonnet VII ('How soon hath time the subtle thief of youth'), Milton was worrying that the 'hasting days' might make impossible the achievement of his as yet unfocused aspirations. Now, in his fifties, to complete his epic he depended on the nightly visits of the Heavenly Muse, his 'celestial patroness', and, according to his nephew Edward Phillips, this inspiration was confined to the period from the autumn to the spring equinox.[4] Jonathan Richardson tells us that Milton often lay awake whole nights unable to compose a single line, whereas at other times the verses flowed easy 'with a certain *impetus*'.[5] Clearly there were cogent reasons for anxiety.

From a later perspective, and on a Hegelian notion of literary history, by the late seventeenth century writing an epic on the classical model might seem not so much belated as already out of date, even if few realized it at the time. Dryden begins the *Dedication* to his version of the *Aeneid* (1697) with the resounding sentence 'A heroic poem, truly such, is undoubtedly the greatest work which the soul of man is capable to perform', and eighty years later Dr Johnson was still to concur: 'By the general consent of critics, the first praise of genius is due to the writer of an epic poem, as it requires an assemblage of all the powers which are singly sufficient for other compositions.'[6] But Dryden had to be content with translating another man's epic; likewise Pope, after the enormous success of his *Iliad* (1717), moralized his song, projecting but never realizing a heroic poem of his own on a British theme, his energies concentrated rather on satire and epistle. By the nineteenth century it had become clear that much of the old epic impulse had migrated to the junior and more amorphous genre of the novel.

How then did Milton succeed in composing the last wholly convincing European vernacular epic 'truly such' where so many others had failed or (like Sir Richard Blackmore with his *Prince Arthur* (1695)) were to fail? My answer would be that it was the sheer extent and intensity of Milton's long-pondered engagement with the classical epic tradition, probably beyond that of any other modern poet, which made this possible. Later Friedrich Schiller was to argue that the modern artist should turn away from the conformities of the present and find inspiration in antiquity for a *revolutionary* art: 'Then, when he has become a man, let him return, a stranger, to his own century; not, however, to gladden it by his appearance, but

---

[3] William Poole, *Milton and the Idea of the Fall* (Cambridge, 2005), 1–6.

[4] Darbishire, 73. In view of Milton's insistence on the importance of sunshine, some have argued that Phillips must be mistaken, and that the period should rather be from spring to autumn.

[5] J. Richardson, Father and Son, *Explanatory Notes and Remarks on Milton's Paradise Lost* (1734; facsimile repr. New York, 1973), 114.

[6] *Selected Essays of John Dryden*, ed. W. P. Ker, 2 vols. (Oxford, 1926), i. 154 (Dryden is here closely echoing the French critic René Rapin; see *Rapin's Reflexions on Aristotle's Treatise of Poesie, Containing the Necessary, Rational, and Universal Rules for Epic, Dramatic, and other Sorts of Poetry*, trans. Thomas Rymer (1674), 72); Johnson, *Lives of the Poets*, 282. Another crucial text for the period's view of epic is René Le Bossu's *Traité du poème épique* (1675).

rather, terrible like Agamemnon's son, to cleanse and to purify it.'[7] In just such a manner Milton in *Paradise Lost* produced something radically new by a peculiarly profound engagement with 'that epic form whereof the two poems of Homer, and those other two of Virgil and Tasso are a diffuse...model' (*Reason of Church-Government*; *CPW*, i. 813), rethinking epic from the bottom up in an act of sustained imitation (Spenser's relationship with the ancients is much more relaxed, genial, and opportunistic by comparison).[8] The results, while in one sense owing so much to the tradition, are at the same time so disconcertingly new that Dryden was moved to deny that the poem, with its fusion of epic and tragic structures ('I now must change / Those notes to tragic...sad task, yet argument / Not less but more heroic...' (*PL* ix. 5–6, 13–14)), was an epic at all: Milton, he writes, would have 'a better plea' for being considered the successor of Virgil 'if the Devil had not been his hero, instead of Adam; if the giant had not foiled the knight, and driven him out of his stronghold, to wander through the world with his lady errant; and if there had not been more machining persons than human in his poem'.[9] *Paradise Lost* is on such an account the most modern of epics precisely because it is the most fully engaged with antiquity (the revolutionary canvases of the French painter David would be an analogy in a different medium). Thus it is not the paradox it might seem that this in one sense most backward-looking of poets is also the poet who most insistently looks forward to future literary developments. *Paradise Lost* is stamped everywhere with Milton's opinions and with his personality, in the manner of a Romantic or post-Romantic poet (for example, the Wordsworth who egotistically charts the growth of the poet's mind), but the poem is also much larger than Milton, in part because he underwent the discipline of a traditional form. Authority is thus variously inscribed, not only in the prophetic voice of the *vates* inspired by God— it is also located *from the first* in the Western epic tradition descending from Homer. There may be transumption— Christianity is of course superior to paganism within this discourse—but paganism has its own measure of validity.

   Paradise Lost is often seen today as the inevitable climax of Milton's poetic career. Indeed Milton himself may have come to think so ('this subject for heroic

---

[7] *Friedrich Schiller: On the Aesthetic Education of Man in a Series of Letters*, ed. Elizabeth M. Wilkinson and L. A. Willoughby (Oxford, 1967), 57.

[8] For Milton and the classics see Davis P. Harding, *The Club of Hercules: Studies in the Classical Background of Paradise Lost* (Urbana, Ill., 1962); Charles Martindale, *John Milton and the Transformation of Ancient Epic* (London and Sydney, 1986; 2nd edn., Bristol, 2002); Colin Burrow, *Epic Romance: Homer to Milton* (Oxford, 1993); André Verbart, *Fellowship in Paradise Lost: Vergil, Milton, Wordsworth* (Amsterdam and Atlanta, Ga., 1995), with a useful appendix of Virgilian parallels.

[9] *Essays of John Dryden*, ed. Ker, ii. 165 (from *Dedication of the Aeneis*); cf. ii. 29 from *A Discourse concerning the Original and Progress of Satire*: 'As for Mr. Milton, whom we all admire with so much justice, his subject is not that of an Heroic Poem, properly so called. His design is the losing of our happiness; his event is not prosperous, like that of all other epic works; his heavenly machines are many, and his human persons are but two.' It is true that the opportunistic statements in Dryden's prose are not always at one with his deeper beliefs reflected in his own poetic practice. According to Richardson (*Notes and Remarks*, 119–20), sent *Paradise Lost* by the Earl of Dorset, Dryden averred 'This man cuts us all out, and the ancients too'; the story has been doubted, but it is still interesting that this view should have been attributed to Dryden.

song / Pleased me long choosing, and beginning late' (ix. 25–6)). The two major disasters of his life—his blindness, and the ultimate failure of the political cause to which he had given so much energy—could readily be reconfigured as enabling conditions for his epic: Milton had in truth become the English Homer, the blind poet-prophet who could sing to his countrymen, who had yet again gone astray, of things invisible to mortal sight. The Virgilian triad, Virgil's seemingly relentless upward march from lesser to higher genre (itself a *post-factum* construction), had from the first served as a potential model. Milton always wished to be famous and to achieve something of prime literary note, for which he prepared himself by years of careful reading—'the wearisome labours and studious watchings, wherein I have spent and tired out almost a whole youth' (*An Apology*; *CPW*, i. 869). At the end of 'Lycidas' (1637), he gestures towards the 'pastures new' of a possible epic future, in a passage of *ottava rima* (the metre of Tasso's *Gerusalemme liberata*); this could be part of a Virgilian progression or a gesture of deferral that was already a generic topos. A couple of years later, in *Mansus* (ll. 80–4), addressed to a patron of Tasso, and *Epitaphium Damonis* (ll. 162–8), he is more specific, sketching themes from early British history (though we cannot be sure he is not thinking of an epic in Latin). In *The Reason of Church-Government* (1642), very probably as part of a conscious strategy of presenting himself as a learned humanist, not a vulgar pamphleteer, he ranges over possible literary projects in the vernacular whereby he might undertake 'what the greatest and choicest wits of Athens, Rome, or modern Italy, and those Hebrews of old did for their country', first in epic, then tragedy, then lyric, to produce 'something so written to aftertimes, as they should not willingly let it die', but without indication of where his ultimate preference will alight (*CPW*, i. 812, 810). Perhaps at one stage he seriously envisaged an *Arthuriad* or the like (with a 'king or knight' providing 'the pattern of a Christian hero'), but if so it would doubtless have been highly Spenserian in style and conception (i. 813–14). By the time he wrote the *History of Britain* Milton had lost all confidence in the truth-value of early British history, a history 'either wholly unknown, or obscured and blemished with fables' (*CPW*, v/i. 1; by contrast in *PL* viii. 6–7 Raphael is termed 'divine historian', since he can tell what actually happened, if in a form accommodated to Adam's and our understanding). The Trinity Manuscript contains lists of potential plots (compiled ? 1639–42), sixty-seven of them biblical, including *Paradise Lost* and *Adam Unparadised* among several based on Genesis, and thirty-eight from British and Scottish history, but these are for tragedies, not epics (*CPW*, viii. 554–85).[10]

All this occasions Richard Helgerson's quip: 'Like the middle class, Milton is always rising and never getting anywhere.'[11] As with Virgil, the culminating epic only became inevitable once it had been completed, and only retrospectively does the

---

[10] At British tragedies plot 24 (p. 571) Milton writes: 'A heroical poem may be founded somewhere in Alfred's reign, especially at his issuing out of Edelingsey on the Danes; whose actions are well like those of Ulysses.'

[11] Richard Helgerson, *Self-Crowned Laureates: Spenser, Jonson, Milton and the Literary System* (Berkeley, 1983), 270.

poet's career cohere, for himself and for his readers. And whatever Milton's early inchoate plans, everything had changed with the execution of Charles I (1649). For a decade Milton wrote virtually no poetry, and may well have completely revised his sense of his own career trajectory. There is no mention of poetry in the autobiographical sections of the *Second Defence* (or of Homer in his list of the virtuous blind[12]), and more than a little hostility to it and to 'the polluted orts and refuse of *Arcadias* and Romances' in *Eikonoklastes*; admittedly, as is always the case with Milton, considerations of genre are at work—one of his objections to the King's book is that it becomes, indecorously for a work of politics, 'a piece of poetry' where 'there wanted only rhyme' (*CPW*, iii. 364, 406). There are good reasons for thinking that Milton may have conceived his *Second Defence* as a prose substitute for epic; thus he praises Cromwell for surpassing 'not only the achievement of our kings, but even the legends [*fabulas*] of our heroes', and compares himself to an epic poet who observes the rules about unity of plot by praising 'one heroic achievement of my countrymen' (*CPW*, iv/i. 672, 685).[13] Contingent events again changed the course of Milton's life, and brought him at last to an epic of a very different stamp from anything he had imagined earlier (there is some evidence that Milton began *Paradise Lost* in 1658, the year of Cromwell's death, but it must mainly have been written during the Restoration).[14] It is not easy, in secular history present or past, to determine whose side God is on, and no longer will Britain be 'the praise and the heroic song of all posterity' (*Of Reformation*; *CPW*, i. 597). Defeat may have helped to give Milton the imaginative freedom he needed as an epic poet.[15]

Paradise Lost was not largely ignored on its appearance, as is sometimes believed. On the contrary the early editions sold well, and the poem had keen admirers from the first. Dryden echoes it with increasing frequency in his verse, as well as adapting it for the stage in *A State of Innocence* (publ. 1677).[16] Nonetheless it is true that it was the publishers, editors, critics, and biographers of the eighteenth century who firmly established its reputation as an English classic, a heroic poem truly such and of European importance. The first commentary, indeed the first extended commentary on any English poem, appeared (to accompany a text put out by Jacob Tonson, who obtained the copyright) as early as 1695: *Annotations on Milton's Paradise Lost* by Patrick Hume, 'wherein the texts of Sacred Writ, relating to the poem, are quoted; the

---

[12] 'Bards' in *CPW*, iv/i. 584 for *vates* should surely rather be 'prophets', since the examples given are Teiresias and Phineus, and Homer is conspicuous by his absence.

[13] See further David Loewenstein, 'Milton and the Poetics of Defense', and James Grantham Turner, 'The Poetics of Engagement', in David Loewenstein and James Grantham Turner (eds.), *Politics, Poetics, and Hermeneutics in Milton's Prose* (Cambridge, 1990), 171–92, 257–75.

[14] The argument of this paragraph owes much to a lecture given by Blair Worden at the University of Bristol in 2007.

[15] Helgerson, *Self-Crowned Laureates*, 250–1; Blair Worden, 'Milton's Republicanism and the Tyranny of Heaven', in Gisela Bock, Quentin Skinner, and Maurizio Viroli (eds.), *Machiavelli and Republicanism* (Cambridge, 1990), 225–45; for an opposing view see David Norbrook, *Writing the English Republic: Poetry, Rhetoric, and Politics 1627–1660* (Cambridge, 1999).

[16] The evidence is set out in full in J. R. Mason, 'To Milton through Dryden and Pope' (Ph.D. diss., University of Cambridge, 1987).

parallel places and imitations of the most excellent Homer and Virgil cited and compared; all the obscure parts rendered in phrases more familiar; the old and obsolete words, with their originals, explained and made easy to the English reader'. Marcus Walsh, in his study of eighteenth-century editing, argues that Hume took English biblical commentary as his model; it is much more plausible to say that Hume simply provided for Milton the kind of scholarly apparatus long available for Homer, Virgil, and other classical poets.[17] A series of commentaries followed culminating in Thomas Newton's important variorum edition of 1749, designed, as the Preface puts it, to present the poem 'as the work of a classic author cum notis variorum' and published by the younger Tonson. With extensive notes under the text *Paradise Lost* now *looked* exactly like a classical epic. The standing of the poem gained even from the wayward attentions of Richard Bentley, the greatest classical scholar of the age; his implied criticisms[18] only served to stimulate skilful defences, and he was quickly figured as, precisely, a Satanic reader, since, in the words of the author of *Milton Restored, and Bentley Deposed* (1732), 'this way of restoring, i.e. interpolating by guess, is so sacrilegious an intrusion that, as it had its rise, so it is hoped it will have its fall with you'.[19]

In this reception of *Paradise Lost* as the great English epic, perhaps the key work is the series of eighteen essays published by Joseph Addison in the *Spectator* in 1712, comprising six papers on general issues, and one on each of the twelve books. Published together in 1719 and often reprinted, they constituted something startlingly novel: in effect a short monograph on a modern English writer.[20] Voltaire scarcely exaggerated when he wrote that Addison 'pointed out the most hidden beauties of the *Paradise Lost*, and settled for ever its reputation'.[21] It was a commonplace to make a complimentary comparison of an English writer, however minor, with one of the ancients. Dryden had produced an epigram for Tonson's 1688 edition, ingeniously turned after a Latin original by Selvaggi (now identified with an expatriate Englishman, David Codner):

> Three poets, in three distant ages born,
> Greece, Italy, and England, did adorn.
> The first in loftiness of thought surpassed;
> The next in majesty; in both the last.
> The force of nature could no further go:
> To make a third, she joined the former two.

---

[17] Marcus Walsh, *Shakespeare, Milton, and Eighteenth-Century Literary Editing: The Beginnings of Interpretative Scholarship* (Cambridge, 1997), 57–8.

[18] Lewis Theobald, the editor of Shakespeare, was probably right to suggest that Bentley is covertly criticizing Milton, not really correcting him; see *Milton 1732–1801: The Critical Heritage*, ed. John T. Shawcross (London and Boston, 1972), 66.

[19] Cited in Walsh, *Shakespeare, Milton, and Eighteenth-Century Literary Editing*, 77.

[20] The only real precedent is Dennis's hostile account of Blackmore's *Prince Arthur: Remarks on a book, entitled Prince Arthur, an Heroic Poem, with some several general critical observations, and several new remarks upon Virgil* (1696), in *The Critical Works of John Dennis*, ed. Edward Niles Hooker (Baltimore, 1939), i. 46–144.

[21] *Milton: The Critical Heritage*, ed. John T. Shawcross (1970), 251. This volume contains the full text of Addison's papers (pp. 147–220). Hereafter cited as Shawcross.

But a man is not on oath in a conventional laudatory poem, and there is plenty of evidence that Dryden did not think Milton the equal of Homer or Virgil. Addison is making a different kind of claim, that in sober truth Milton's epic is a work comparable in scope and stature only with those of Homer and Virgil, and indeed in certain respects superior to them, and he sets out to show *in detail* how such a claim can be made good. At the beginning of the first paper he quotes the words with which Propertius (2. 34. 65) had greeted, in advance of its publication, Virgil's *Aeneid*: *cedite Romani scriptores, cedite Grai* ('yield you Roman writers, yield you Greek')— the following line hangs for the cognoscenti in the air: *nescio quid maius nascitur Iliade* ('something or other greater than the *Iliad* is being born'). Given the extraordinary standing of Homer and Virgil at the time, Addison's claim is far indeed from being the commonplace which, through the quality of his demonstration and his authority as a critic, it soon became.

Addison writes in a very different critical idiom from ours; he has a respect for the 'rules' we find it difficult to share, and, while he points to individual 'beauties', he does not include passages of close reading of the kind with which we have become familiar (for these one must go to the commentators, particularly the Richardsons, in what are still the most sensitive notes on the poem). But Addison will be a particularly useful guide for considering *Paradise Lost* as epic writing for four main reasons.[22] First, as someone soaked from early days in classical literature he has an instinctive feeling for where Milton is imitating the ancients that perhaps no modern reader (even a scholar) can fully share (he also of course knows the Bible intimately, and admires its literary qualities). Secondly, although not a contemporary, and belonging to a very different political milieu (one in which Milton's political radicalism and unorthodox religious beliefs are censured or downplayed), Addison is far closer than we are to much that Milton and his contemporaries took for granted in relation to classical literature and the critical debates involved in its reception. It is sometimes said that the 'neo-classical' Addison could not understand the 'baroque' sensibilities of Milton; this is misleading—the whole period from 1580 to 1780 can properly be seen as the neo-classical phase of our literature. Even where Addison censures some 'fault' in *Paradise Lost* (for example, the puns or the allegorical episodes involving Sin and Death), Milton would have had no difficulty in understanding the basis of the criticism (he was well versed in Italian and other debates about the application of Aristotle's doctrines and the nature of epic). Thirdly, Addison always treats *Paradise Lost* first and foremost as a work of imaginative literature. Modern critics often fall into the trap of explaining the poem wholly by way of the prose works; but in the poem we find a more open, more generous, and multifaceted writer than in much of the prose (with its tendency to overstatement). Thus the Milton who so relishes attacking his enemies, at length and with no holds

---

[22] It will be clear that I reject any idea of Addison as 'perversely influential' (Mindele Anne Treip, *Allegorical Poetics and the Epic: The Renaissance Tradition to Paradise Lost* (Lexington, Ky., 1994), 110) or an exemplar of 'the malign legacy of eighteenth-century scholarship' in general (Thomas N. Corns, 'Milton's English', in Thomas N. Corns (ed.), *A Companion to Milton* (Oxford, 2001), 90–106 at 90).

barred, is largely (though not wholly) absent. Likewise that Milton believed he was inspired does not entail that he thought *Paradise Lost* had the status of Scripture; it is an epic poem on a Christian subject, not a definitive work of systematic Christian theology (hence in part its greater orthodoxy than *De Doctrina Christiana*, usually put down to fear of censorship). In *De Doctrina Christiana* we can read what Milton (if he it is) thinks was involved, theologically, in the Fall of Man (*CPW*, vi. 382–92); the poem shows us this in action, sympathetically, psychologically, with human generosity and delicacy, not so far from the manner of a novel.

Finally, Addison exhibits more catholicity of taste than most of his successors. To an extent the history of Milton criticism will prove to be the history of a narrowing of response. Where F. R. Leavis perversely found in *Paradise Lost* only a monotonous uniformity of grandeur that 'functions by rote', Addison rightly insisted on various-ness: 'I have endeavoured to show how some passages are beautiful by being sublime, others by being soft, others by being natural; which of them are recommended by the passion, which by the moral, which by the sentiment, and which by the expression.'[23] Many readers today think that Milton's devil has all the best tunes, and that these tunes generally come courtesy of the Greek and Latin classics. But Milton clearly valued the Bible for literary as well as for theological reasons, though perhaps it is the case that he was more often inspired by the Old Testament than by the New. C. S. Lewis thought that you needed to have a 'romantic' taste to be attracted to the Bible as literature, and Milton certainly responded to its combination of boldness, simplicity, and the sublime.[24] The evocative lines about Jacob's ladder, some of the finest in the poem, are a good illustration:

> The stairs were such as whereon Jacob saw
> Angels ascending and descending, bands
> Of guardians bright, when he from Esau fled
> To Padan-Aram in the field of Luz,
> Dreaming by night under the open sky,
> And waking cried, *This is the gate of heaven*. (iii. 510–15)

'This is the gate of heaven' is a direct quotation from Genesis (28: 17), and Milton retains the simple vocabulary of the English Bible and employs a straightforward, unconfusing syntax, while relishing the resonant biblical names, and enhancing the sense of wonder and wistfulness. This is sublime, but it is a biblical as much as a classicizing sublime, conveying the aspect of Genesis to which alone in classical antiquity the author we call Longinus rather surprisingly responded.[25] True, these lines come from a passage about Satan, on whose exclusion from heaven they may thus bestow some pathos, but their flavour is far indeed from the maimed Satanic

---

[23] F. R. Leavis, *Revaluation: Tradition and Development in English Poetry* (1969), 43–4; Shawcross, 220.

[24] 'The Literary Impact of the Authorized Version', in *C. S. Lewis: Selected Literary Essays*, ed. Walter Hooper (Cambridge, 1969), 126–45.

[25] *Peri Hypsous* (*On the Sublime*), 9. 9; since the 18th c. the passage has been regarded by some, with insufficient justification, as a later addition. For Longinus and Milton (though unduly privileging the political aspect) see Annabel M. Patterson, *Reading between the Lines* (Madison, 1993), 256–72.

sublime as it unfolds in the opening scenes in Hell. The greatness of *Paradise Lost* derives from the intensity of Milton's love of both the Bible and classical epic, and his various strategies for mediating between them.

It is significant in this regard that, whereas the biblical Book 7 is comparatively neglected by modern critics, Addison by contrast rightly saw it as one of the wonders of the poem. In it we find 'an instance of that sublime which is not mixed and worked up with passion' (in contrast to the preceding War in Heaven, which Addison also greatly admired, some excesses aside, finding it, too, sublime, in contrast to many moderns who see the writing as pitched just this side of absurdity, closer to mock than genuine heroic). Scripture is again the main source, but, Addison suggests, Milton also imagines how Homer might have treated the subject of Creation, testing the connections between two different traditions of sublime writing (the compasses, for example, are 'conceived altogether in Homer's spirit'). The vividness of the writing (an example of what the theorists of antiquity called *enargeia*) exhibits 'the whole energy of our tongue', and means that 'the reader seems present at this wonderful work' (Shawcross, 195–9). The book is a genial and joyous expansion of the opening of Genesis, which indeed displays much of Milton's long-breathed mastery:

> Forthwith the sounds and seas, each creek and bay
> With fry innumerable swarm, and shoals
> Of fish that with their fins and shining scales
> Glide under the green wave, in schools that oft
> Bank the mid-sea; part single or with mate
> Graze the seaweed their pasture, and through groves
> Of coral stray, or sporting with quick glance
> Show to the sun their waved coats dropped with gold,
> Or in their pearly shells at ease attend
> Moist nutriment, or under rocks their food
> In jointed armour watch . . . (vii. 399–409)

Writing like this (which also owes something to Ovid) inspired some of the best descriptive poetry of the eighteenth century, as well as one of the greatest musical works of all time, Haydn's *Creation*. There is an enormous sense of the plenitude of the world —'air, water, earth, / By fowl, fish, beast, was flown, was swam, was walked / Frequent' (ll. 502–4)—and of Milton's gratitude for it, a gratitude that fostered such linguistic daring and that we, like Addison, might want to share. But gratitude, as Christopher Ricks has reminded us, though one of the things 'literature lives to realize', is not a Satanic characteristic:

Even the fallen natural world may be alive to this paradisal possibility. A hope, at least, is to be scented. There are wafted 'Sabean Odours from the spicie shoare / Of Arabie the blest', whereupon 'many a league / Cheard with the grateful smell old Ocean smiles'. With how fine an air 'the grateful *smell*' turns to and into '*smiles*'. We should be grateful to Milton, and so we are. Meanwhile Satan, the great ingrate, in this his unsmiling passage into the Garden of Eden, was seeking to darken this very passage of Milton.[26]

---

[26] Inaugural Lecture as Oxford Professor of Poetry, *Times Literary Supplement*, 25 Feb. 2005, p. 13.

This is finely said, and in addition a fine piece of literary criticism. But gratitude, as Ricks goes on to say, is no easy thing, rather it is all too fatally easy for us to share in Satan's darkening. Clearly Milton himself felt the full force of the attraction (there is much of Milton in his Satan—as in his Eve, and indeed his God), but, unlike many of his modern critics, he did not surrender entirely to it.

Addison's initial papers deal with *Paradise Lost* under four aspects: the fable, the characters, the sentiments, and the language. These are traditional categories,[27] and Addison touches on many topics about which others had written at greater length, including Tasso in his *Discorsi del poema eroico* (1594), which Milton is likely to have studied with care, as he did the *Liberata* itself.[28] In both its ten- and its twelve-book versions *Paradise Lost* was subtitled simply 'a poem'.[29] Addison starts his discussion by saying that those who would deny that it is properly heroic may call it a 'divine poem' if they please: 'for those who allege it is not an heroic poem, they advance no more to the diminution of it than if they should say Adam is not Aeneas, nor Eve Helen'. But just as Milton starts *Paradise Lost* by ostentatious and emulous imitation of the openings of the *Iliad* and *Aeneid* (including a sustained play on the word 'first' that implies that his belated poem is in another sense primary), so Addison examines it 'by the rules of epic poetry' (Shawcross, 147). For the early modern critics of epic, the 'fable', encompassing what we would call both plot and structure, came first. Ben Jonson (*Discoveries*, 3317) gives elegant expression to the orthodoxy: 'The fable is called the imitation of one entire and perfect action, whose parts are so joined and knit together as nothing in the structure can be changed, or taken away, without impairing or troubling the whole, of which there is a proportionable magnitude in the members.' That fable should also be verisimilar, probable; *Paradise Lost*, even if it contains figurations of various kinds, is not (*pace* many modern critics) an allegorical narrative, at least not in the manner of Spenser or even Dante. Addison stresses the enormous skill with which Milton constructs such an epic fable out of the opening chapters of Genesis and other parts of the Bible, despite having 'to proceed with the greatest caution in everything that he added out of his own invention', given the choice of a scriptural subject; 'indeed', he continues, 'notwithstanding all the restraints he was under, he has filled his story with so many surprising incidents, which bear so close analogy with what is delivered in Holy Writ, that it is capable of pleasing the most delicate reader, without giving offence to the most scrupulous' (Shawcross, 150–1). Johnson thought that 'considered with respect to design' *Paradise Lost* 'may

---

[27] So e.g. Tasso; see *Torquato Tasso: Discourses on the Heroic Poem*, ed. Mariella Cavalchini and Irene Samuel (Oxford, 1973), 17.

[28] See Judith A. Kates, *Tasso and Milton: The Problem of Christian Epic* (London and Toronto, 1983); Treip, *Allegorical Poetics and the Epic*, especially chs. 5–7, 12. Addison knows that Milton frequently echoes Tasso, but does not give instances, partly because he regards Tasso as inferior to Milton and thus not 'a sufficient voucher', and partly because Tasso is of less interest to his readers than the classical poets (Shawcross, 220).

[29] The twelve-book format is Virgilian; the suggestion (made by the present author among others) that the earlier version was designed to bring to mind the Republican Lucan is problematical, since the *Pharsalia* is in ten books only because it was unfinished—structural symmetry may have been the issue.

claim the first place...among the productions of the human mind' (that is, even above Homer's *Iliad*): 'He has involved in his account of the fall of Man the events which preceded and those that were to follow it; he has interwoven the whole system of theology with such propriety that every part appears to be necessary' (*Lives of the Poets*, i. 282–3). Many early modern critics, following Aristotle, argued that the unified epic plot needed to be such that it could be taken in at an overall view, producing what Addison calls 'an agreeable story sufficient to employ the memory without overcharging it' (one could contrast the meandering, easily forgotten, multiple story lines of Ariosto or Spenser[30]). Coleridge is thus being a good neo-Aristotelian when he comments: 'The *story* of Milton might be told in two pages—it is this which distinguishes an *Epic Poem* from a *Romance in metre*.'[31] Indeed, from the fourth issue of the first edition brief prose arguments were provided (originally printed together, but from 1674 dispersed among the books), which show clearly the articulation of the fable.

Milton, in accordance with Horatian prescript and in imitation of Homer and Virgil, starts the action, with powerful immediacy, in the middle, with the fallen angels cast out of Heaven; preceding events are subsequently described in flashback. But this is no mere imitation for imitation's sake (however skilful); rather the structure is connected to the crucial role of time in *Paradise Lost*. It allows Milton to make man's first disobedience, as the poem's subject, the climax of the action, while also showing its prehistory (which renders it intelligible) and its consequences (which involve us all); Raphael's retrospective narrative is elegantly balanced by Michael's prospective one. It also allows us to approach the unfallen Adam and Eve gradually and in the first instance through the eyes of the fallen Satan, which we must learn to see beyond. There are at least two distinct strokes of genius in all this. First, the fall of the angels is skilfully linked with the fall of man (in a way that is parallel, as Addison observes, to the link between the rise of Carthage and the rise of Rome in the *Aeneid*). Addison comments: 'its running parallel with the great action of the poem hinders it from breaking the unity so much as another episode would have done that had not so great an affinity with the principal subject' (Shawcross, 149). Secondly the 'machining persons' become integral to the action rather than mere decorative additions, too obviously copied after Homer and Virgil (Milton's devils and angels, as Addison observes, are moreover characterized variously and with great skill).[32] The use of a scriptural plot was controversial (Tasso had advised against it), as was

---

[30] Shawcross, 150. Aristotle is talking about tragedy, but he uses the Homeric poems to illustrate unity of plot.

[31] Joseph Anthony Wittreich, Jr., *The Romantics on Milton: Formal Essays and Critical Asides* (Cleveland, Ohio and London, 1970), 159.

[32] For the early modern debate about the machines in modern (Christian) poetry see Dryden's 'A Discourse concerning the Original and Progress of Satire' (*Essays*, ii. 30–7), with the notes in *The Poems of John Dryden*, ed. Paul Hammond and David Hopkins, 5 vols. (Harlow, 1995–2005), iii. 339–48; Tom Mason, 'A Noble Poem of the Epique Kind? *Palamon and Arcite*: Neoclassic Theory and Poetical Experience', in Michael Kenneally, Holger Klein, and Wolfgang Zach (eds.), *Dryden and the World of Neoclassicism* (Tübingen, 2001), 181–91.

the proper role of the gods (if any) in a modern epic (Tasso argued that, for reasons of verisimilitude, Christian machines are needed to provide the epic marvellous, since we no longer believe in the pagan gods). There was much debate about the best subject matter; for Tasso stories about Arthur or Charlemagne or the Crusades were particularly suitable, as events in Christian history neither too remote nor too recent. Milton's bold solution to this whole set of problems seems easy and inevitable once arrived at, but nothing better illustrates his radical reshaping of the genre. The opening of the *Liberata* is merely dutifully imitative in comparison; after the invocation God despatches Gabriel (decked out like Virgil's Mercury) to urge Goffredo into action, and this is followed by council of war and catalogue. Tasso has not thought hard enough about how to combine the pagan and the Christian, and as a result is here controlled by, rather than controlling, his ancient models.

Addison turns next to the actors. Here he awards the palm to Homer, who 'has excelled all the heroic poets that ever wrote in the multitude and variety of his characters'; Virgil, by contrast, 'falls infinitely short . . . both as to their variety and novelty'. As for Milton, 'he has introduced all the variety his fable was capable of receiving'. The contrast between the fallen and unfallen Adam and Eve means that there are as it were four characters in the poem, and moreover it is 'impossible for any of its readers, whatever nation, country, or people he may belong to, not to be related' to 'the principal actors' as being 'not only our progenitors, but our representatives' (in Aristotelian terms 'like us'): 'no less than our utmost happiness is concerned, and lies at stake in all their behaviour'.[33] Johnson famously claimed that 'the want of human interest is always felt' (*Lives of the Poets*, 290). Addison by contrast shows how the poem is chock-full throughout of human interest. Famously Satan (who in Addison's view outclasses Homer's Odysseus in subtlety and variety of stratagem), though grander than most human beings, is human enough (all too human) and humanly attractive enough to explain the Satanist interpretation. And the poem is also full of things human beings are interested in—including ideas. The extended epic similes, with their varied subject matter, some of it taken from the modern world (what other epic makes room for Galileo's telescope?), are one prime means by which the poem's scope is extended in marvellously varied ways (we shall return to them). We might recall that *Paradise Lost* was one of the few books from which Frankenstein's monster received an education instructing him about humanity and human culture.

Addison also touches on another much debated matter: the identity of the hero of *Paradise Lost*. Over the years many candidates have been proposed, for reasons that often reflect the varying ideologies of the proposer: Adam, Adam and Eve, Eve, Satan, the Son (Addison's eventual, somewhat pious choice[34]), the reader, Milton. If

---

[33] Shawcross, 151–4. Cf. the Richardsons at viii. 653 on the narrative of the Fall: 'Now the heart is called upon, every line is important to us, and cries aloud "Thou art the man".'

[34] Shawcross, 166; for a defence of this view see Hideyuki Shitaka, *Milton's Idea of the Son in the Shaping of 'Paradise Lost' as a Christian Epic* (Tokyo, 1996). Contrast the Richardsons, *Notes and Remarks*, p. clxvi (misprint for cxlvi): ''tis Adam, Adam, the first, the representative of Human Race'.

we must have a hero (or rather heroes), it surely has to be 'our grand parents' as protagonists of the principal action. But it is not clear that the question is well formulated. Aristotle called not for a single hero but for a single action, praising Homer over the poets of *Heracleids* and *Theseids* that covered the whole lives of their protagonists (*Poetics* 1451). The *Iliad* has at least two protagonists, likewise the *Liberata*; Lucan's *Pharsalia* (as the epic of Republicanism, a key if still comparatively neglected intertext for *Paradise Lost*) has three.[35] One might rather say that Milton's fable sets out and tests and revaluates different models of the heroic (the great epics had always done this); the proem to Book 9 assails previous epics for their defective vision, recommending 'the better fortitude / Of patience and heroic martyrdom / Unsung' (ll. 31–3). Satan is, more closely than other characters, associated with the classical warrior hero. Hazlitt observes that 'Milton has got rid of the horns and tail, the vulgar and physical *insignia* of the devil, and clothed him with other greater and intellectual terrors, reconciling beauty and sublimity, and converting the grotesque and deformed into the *ideal* and classical', while for Coleridge Satan exhibits 'a singularity of daring, a grandeur of sufferance and a ruined splendour'.[36] In ii. 445–56 for persuasive effect Satan recycles, or rather taints in advance, Sarpedon's famous enunciation of the heroic code of *noblesse oblige* (*Iliad*, 12. 310–28); Milton in general showed little concern with honour—'liberty' is always the word of power for him—and the narrative makes clear that Satan's motives are far from disinterested. Satan's heroism is clearly flawed, like that of the Englishmen in *A Brief History of Moscovia* who discovered Russia by the Northern Ocean in what 'might have seemed an enterprise almost heroic if any higher end than the excessive love of gain and traffic had animated the design' (*CPW*, viii. 524). Nonetheless David Reid is right to say that Satan's heroism is in its way genuine (if tragically misapplied) because he is an individual, not an allegorical type, just as the poem charts 'a human action, not just a rhetorical scheme disguised as fiction' (we can link all this with Milton's belief in free will).[37]

Abdiel, by contrast, like Cato in the *Pharsalia* (opponent of the ever-moving Caesar), represents, in a poem of action, virtuous immobility: 'Among the faithless, faithful only he; / Among innumerable false, unmoved' (v. 897–8). Like Jesus in *Paradise Regained* he is heroic not for acting but for 'standing', for resisting the pressure to act (if Eve had rebuffed Satan, that would have been heroism of this type).

---

[35] See Martindale, *John Milton and the Transformation of Ancient Epic*, ch. 5; Norbrook, *Writing the English Republic*, esp. 438–67. The comparatively lower status of the *Pharsalia* in the period means that Milton does not signal his indebtedness in obvious programmatic ways, as with Homer and Virgil.

[36] Wittreich, *Romantics on Milton*, 389, 244. An emphasis on Satan long pre-dates the Romantics. For example, for John Dennis 'the most delightful and most admirable part of the sublimest of all our poets is that which relates the rebellion and fall of these evil angels', and 'the Devil is properly his hero, because he bests the better' (Shawcross, 112, 129). For Hugh Blair (1759–60) Satan is 'the best drawn character in the poem', while for Daniel Webb (1762) its 'principal beauties' are 'thrown on the person of Satan' (Shawcross, *Milton 1732–1801*, 246, 256).

[37] David Reid, *The Humanism of Milton's Paradise Lost* (Edinburgh, 1993), 127, 80. Johnson ascribes to Milton himself the Satanic qualities of 'an envious hatred of greatness' and 'pride disdainful of superiority' (*Lives of the Poets*, 276).

One may feel a particularly strong identification on Milton's part here, but he was attracted also to more dynamic models. The Son not only makes his heroic offer of self-sacrifice (previously parodied, when Satan volunteers to make the hazardous journey to earth), but is presented as a conquering hero in the War in Heaven (though in biblical not classical terms). 'Domestic' Adam (ix. 318) and Eve, who represent a non-militaristic model of heroism (that anticipates features of the novel), have shown an ability to grow and develop and engage in varied activity (love-making, gardening, education through conversing, creating new forms of prayer and love poetry) even in their short time in Paradise; after the Fall they again display their continued capacity for change through repentance (a process pioneered by Eve).[38] Tasso had sanctioned love as well as wrath as subject matter wholly proper for epic,[39] and from its wrathful opening *Paradise Lost* gradually mutates into the great epic of love; Milton, excoriated by Johnson for 'something like a Turkish contempt of females' (*Lives of the Poets*, 276), becomes in the process the author of some of the world's greatest love poetry. In the words of David Quint, 'it is the free choice of Adam and Eve to accept grace and to love one another again that has impressed many readers to be the most signal . . . act of heroism in *Paradise Lost*'.[40] Again revised epic form and new content work together: 'only the unique subject of the Fall allows the poet of *Paradise Lost* to invent a poetry of the mind that still reads like epic because it can subsume traditional epic structures and styles into its revelation of the soul's history'.[41]

Addison's third and fourth categories are the sentiments (where in 'the sublimity of his thoughts' Milton 'triumphs over all the poets both modern and ancient, Homer only excepted') and the language.[42] Addison acknowledges that, in respect of the style of *Paradise Lost*, 'the learned world is very much divided' (Shawcross, 158). Modern readers (because of the prestige of Shakespeare and later developments in English poetry influenced by Milton) often do not realize how radical and controversial was Milton's choice of blank verse as the metre for a modern epic (Johnson devotes considerable space to the issue, only eventually conceding that 'I cannot prevail on myself to wish that Milton had been a rhymer'; *Lives of the Poets*, 294). There were few precedents, and these insufficiently weighty or positively discouraging: Surrey's version of two books of the *Aeneid*, Marlowe's of *Lucan's First Book* (a work that merits more attention from Miltonists), Trissino's *L'Italia liberata dai goti*, an over-conscientious imitation of Homer which, in Tasso's words, 'few mention and still fewer read' (in contrast to the success of Ariosto's rule-breaking epic romance).[43] Tasso himself, on numerological grounds, strongly recommended the virtues of *ottava rima* (though in a different genre he employed blank

---

[38] On Eve's heroism see Barbara K. Lewalski, 'Milton On Women—Yet Again', in Sally Minoghue (ed.), *Problems for Feminist Criticism* (London and New York, 1990), 46–69.

[39] *Tasso: Discourses*, 48–9; Burrow, *Epic Romance*, 84–5.

[40] David Quint, 'Recent Studies in the English Renaissance', *Studies in English Literature*, 38 (1998), 173–205 at 186.

[41] Kates, *Tasso and Milton*, 156.

[42] Shawcross, 156; for the section on style, 158–62.

[43] *Tasso: Discourses*, 66.

verse for his hexameral *Sette giornate del mondo creato*),[44] and by 1660 there was an almost universal assumption that non-dramatic verse required rhyme among English poets and critics. For the second edition Milton supplied an eloquent defence of his unorthodox decision:

The measure is English heroic verse without rhyme, as that of Homer in Greek, and of Virgil in Latin; rhyme being no necessary adjunct or true ornament of poem or good verse, in longer works especially, but the invention of a barbarous age, to set off wretched matter and lame metre. . . . Not without cause therefore some both Italian and Spanish poets of prime note have rejected rhyme . . . as a thing of itself, to all judicious ears, trivial and of no true musical delight; which consists only in apt numbers, fit quantity of syllables, and the sense variously drawn out from one verse into another . . . This neglect then of rhyme so little is to be taken for a defect . . . that it rather is to be esteemed an example set, the first in English, of ancient liberty recovered to heroic poem from the troublesome and modern bondage of rhyming.

One can imagine the poet relishing the frisson in his evocation of 'ancient liberty', and some modern scholars have concluded that the overriding reason for his choice of metre was political. But unrhyming verse on the model of the ancients had long been a humanist aspiration (Roger Ascham in *The Schoolmaster* urged his country-man to 'understand rightfully our rude beggarly rhyming, brought first into Italy by Goths and Huns, when all good verses, and all good learning too were destroyed by them');[45] and Milton may have been influenced too by the freedom of Hebrew verse. Politics and poetics cannot so easily be elided: in 1667 the royalist Dryden used the image of the 'slavery' of rhyme.[46] Rather, blank verse, with frequent use of enjamb-ment and variation in the position of the caesura, enabled Milton, uniquely, to write an epic that was truly comparable in style to the *Iliad* or *Aeneid*, that successfully Englished Virgil's majestic paragraphs and variety of verse movement, and the ongoing forward motion of Homer (by contrast the Spenserian stanza in its very shape suits the complex windings of romantic epic).[47] From his 'careful' education Milton had, from 'the best and elegantest authors of the learned tongues', obtained 'an ear that could measure a just cadence, and scan without articulating' (*An Apology*; *CPW*, i. 914). T. S. Eliot, who called Milton 'the greatest master in our language of freedom within form', describes the results well:

It is the period, the sentence and still more the paragraph, that is the unit of Milton's verse; and emphasis on the line structure is the minimum necessary to provide a counter-pattern to the period structure. . . . The peculiar feeling, almost a physical sensation of a breathless leap,

---

[44] Ibid. 201.

[45] 'On Imitation', in *English Renaissance Literary Criticism*, ed. Brian Vickers (Oxford, 1999), 157. For Daniel's reply, and the possible political entailments of the dispute, see Richard Helgerson, *Forms of Nationhood: The Elizabethan Writing of England* (Chicago and London, 1992), ch. 1.

[46] *Preface to Annus Mirabilis*, in *Essays*, i. 12; for this 'heroic' poem Dryden uses quatrains with alternate rhymes, after the example of Davenant's *Gondibert*. On the Republican side Lucy Hutchinson employs rhyming couplets for her biblical poem (or epic?) on the book of Genesis, *Order and Disorder*, subtitled 'Meditations upon the Creation and the Fall' and composed at about the same time as *Paradise Lost*.

[47] Leigh Hunt gives an excellent example (Wittreich, *Romantics on Milton*, 446).

communicated by Milton's long periods, and by his alone, is impossible to procure from rhymed verse.[48]

For a classicist no other modern epic feels much if at all like Homer or Virgil.

Many early readers found Milton's verse insufficiently smooth (indeed he sought to carry into English the calculated roughness and difficulty, the *asprezza* sought by the Italians Tasso and Giovanni Della Casa for heroic poetry[49]), or felt that blank verse was designed for the eye not the ear and was too close to prose (hence its appropriateness for drama)—throwing it 'off from prose', as Addison puts it, accordingly requires 'pomp of sound, and energy of expression' (Shawcross, 161). Addison, like other early critics, was guided by Longinus' treatise *On the Sublime* to a sense of Milton's achievement (the work is on Milton's ideal school syllabus in *Of Education*, but its influence hugely increased as a result of Boileau's translation of 1674). Addison argued that the style of epic needed to be 'both perspicuous and sublime'; sublimity required that it 'deviate from the common forms and ordinary phrases of speech' (Shawcross, 158, 159), without falling into the opposite vice of grandiloquent bombast (the fault of Statius—and Shakespeare). Addison details after Aristotle some of the ways that this deformation can be achieved, including metaphor, the use of old words and coinages, extension or contraction of particular words (as with 'eremite' for 'hermit'); in chapter 5 of Tasso's *Discorsi* Milton could find detailed advice on how to achieve the grand manner, illustrated in particular from Virgil and Petrarch. Most controversial, then as now, was Milton's resort to foreign idioms, which Addison explains with succinct precision:

Another way of raising the language, and giving it a poetical turn, is to make use of the idioms of other tongues. . . . Milton in conformity with the practice of the ancient poets and with Aristotle's rule, has infused a great many Latinisms as well as Graecisms, and sometimes Hebraisms, into the language of his poem. . . . Under this head may be reckoned the placing the adjective after the substantive, the transposition of words, the turning the adjective into a substantive, with several other foreign modes of speech, which this poet has naturalized to give his verse the greater sound and throw it out of prose. (Shawcross, 160)

For example, in 'Yet oft his heart, divine of something ill, / Misgave him' (ix. 845–6) the rare use of 'divine' to mean 'foreseeing', followed by a genitive (like *divinus* in Latin, as in Horace's Ode 3. 27. 10), constitutes a small defamiliarizing touch to heighten a passage which might otherwise be overly prosaic[50] (moderns may argue that such a notion of decorum is outdated, but even today you could translate the opening words of the *Aeneid* 'arms and the bloke I sing' only in parody). Eighteenth-century critics and editors all agreed that Milton made extensive use in particular of Latinate diction and syntax. Modern scholars, including Alastair Fowler and Thomas Corns, reacting to the attacks on Milton's style by Leavis and Eliot, have sought to

---

[48] 'Milton II', in *Selected Prose of T. S. Eliot*, ed. Frank Kermode (1975), 273, 271.
[49] See F. T. Prince, *The Italian Element in Milton's Verse* (Oxford, 1954).
[50] See John K. Hale, *Milton's Languages: The Impact of Multilingualism on Style* (Cambridge, 1997), 109–10.

minimize the number and importance of Milton's supposed Latinisms.[51] Because ordinary English and the English poetic tradition in general owes so much to Latin, the matter is difficult to determine with any exactitude, but the instincts of Addison and the rest (much better read than we are in classical literature) are not lightly to be ignored. Fowler goes so far as to call *Paradise Lost* 'the most colloquial secondary epic ever written'.[52] This cannot be quite right (one thinks of the poem's sixteen-line opening sentence, even grander than its equivalent in the *Aeneid*, or the glamorous magniloquence associated with Satan), though it is true that Milton often employs very plain diction (much of it of Anglo-Saxon origin) and can write with astonishing simplicity (after the manner of his favourite Homer).[53] Where ordinary prose would run 'Thus saying, she softly withdrew her hand from her husband's hand', Milton creates supreme poetry by the slightest alteration of 'normal' syntax, with the verb held back to the end and the adverbial use of the adjective (both, as it happens, features of Latin—the rhythm tells against Ricks's view that 'soft' might also be an adjective[54]), the two hands close together before the final parting, though with a caesura between them: 'Thus saying, from her husband's hand her hand / Soft she withdrew' (ix. 385–6); but this moving directness (in the Richardsons' words, 'a master-touch of tenderness in few words') is further enhanced by the contrast with the richer and more complex movement of what follows. The language of *Paradise Lost* is strikingly varied, matching the variety of content, in accordance with the underlying principle of decorum, 'the grand masterpiece to observe' (*Of Education*, *CPW*, ii. 405); epic style, Tasso observes, allows considerable flexibility, encompassing both 'the solemnity of the tragic' and 'a lyrical floweriness'.[55]

Arguments about whether a particular Miltonic usage is strictly speaking a 'Latinism' or not (with varying definitions of the term) can become rather sterile. John Hale, in one of the finest books on *Paradise Lost* of the last decade, suggests that a more profitable approach would be to acknowledge the all-pervading importance of Milton's multilingualism on his style. Milton knew at least ten languages, translating from five, and composing poetry in four, and this 'polyglot versatility' left its mark on all his work.[56] The very title of *Paradise Lost* (brilliantly chosen, though easily taken for granted) is an interlingual gesture: paraphrasable as 'the losing of Paradise',

---

[51] *FPL*, 13–23; Thomas N. Corns, *Milton's Language* (Oxford, 1990); Corns, *Regaining 'Paradise Lost'* (Harlow, 1994). On the style C. S. Lewis, *A Preface to Paradise Lost* (1942), 40–61 and Christopher Ricks, *Milton's Grand Style* (1963) remain fundamental. For Latinisms see Verbart, *Fellowship in Paradise Lost*, 5–28; Hale, *Milton's Languages*; Kenneth Haynes, *English Literature and Ancient Languages* (Oxford, 2003).

[52] John Carey and Alastair Fowler, *The Poems of Milton* (Harlow, 1968), 433; in *FPL* Fowler modifies this sentence to 'the most direct of secondary epics' (p. 17).

[53] In his note on *Iliad* 2. 552 Pope observes that Milton imitates the lowness (offensive to 'a modern critic') of some of Homer's similes: 'Milton, who was a close imitator of our author, has often copied him in these humble comparisons.'

[54] Ricks, *Milton's Grand Style*, 90.

[55] *Tasso: Discourses*, 137; Tasso also observes (pp. 84, 191) that Homer combines all three styles (high, middle, low).

[56] *Milton's Languages*, p. xi.

it successfully naturalizes the Latin *ab urbe condita* construction ('from the founding of the city'), while hinting at a key generic analogue whose title had the identical grammatical form, *Gerusalemme liberata* ('the liberating of Jerusalem'); but at the same time the monosyllabic finality of the past participle conveys our irrevocable exclusion from Eden. Milton had an intense love for words, their etymologies, their ambiguities and interconnections, their exfoliating significations. In his metaphrastic translation of Horace's Pyrrha Ode he tested the relationship between English and Latin almost to destruction; 'precisely because he could think in Latin or English, or both or neither, he cared about their differences and limits'.[57] In *Paradise Lost* he used his knowledge of other languages not to write English 'on a perverse and pedantic principle' as Dr Johnson maintained (*Lives of the Poets*, 293), but to energize it, to maximize and extend its expressive potential (from time to time the bold experimentation may fall flat, but, as Longinus insisted in a much invoked passage, genius that incurs danger is always preferable to successful mediocrity). So 'liquid' becomes a word of much greater linguistic resource because Milton is intimate with the various ways *liquidus* was used in Latin;[58] something similar can be said about much of the poem's vocabulary, for example 'ruin' (always in *Paradise Lost* with some sense of falling, from the Latin *ruo*), or 'rapture' (which in vii. 36, in connection with Orpheus and the maenads, means 'transport of delight' but glances at both prophetic inspiration and dismemberment).[59] On occasion the simultaneous evocation of different meanings congeals into the kind of wordplay of which many eighteenth-century critics inclined to disapprove, for example 'casual fruition' (iv. 767), where 'casual', from the Latin *casus*, punningly alludes to the Fall. Sparks are struck off words as they combine; in 'for nature here / Wantoned as in her prime, and played at will / Her virgin fancies, pouring forth more sweet, / Wild above rule or art; enormous bliss' (v. 294–7), 'wantoned' clashes with 'virgin', the pent-up energies reaching an immense resolution in 'enormous', which unites the meaning 'huge' with the etymological 'outside the ordinary' (Latin *norma*)—precisely 'above rule' (the Richardsons comment: 'what shall I call it? A monstrous bliss! It was before said Nature here wantoned as a girl; now she is stark wild, so profuse is she of her beauties. Words cannot carry an idea beyond this'). The result is 'an incessant, sometimes obtrusive, activity of mind' which prevents the magnificent style from becoming bland or pompous.[60]

Even if his brief discussion involves simplification, Addison also has a better sense than many moderns of how Milton's epic similes work, quite unlike 'the quaint

---

[57]   *Milton's Languages*, 14.

[58]   See Verbart, *Fellowship in Paradise Lost*, 16–19.

[59]   On 'ruin' in 1. 46 the Richardsons comment: 'Milton . . . chooses to use words in the most ancient and learned sense; and thus "ruin" includes the idea of rushing with violence, noise, tumult, and velocity.' On 'rapture' see Rachel Falconer, *Orpheus Dis(re)membered: Milton and the Myth of the Poet-Hero* (Sheffield, 1996), 131–2; John Leonard, *Naming in Paradise: Milton and the Language of Adam and Eve* (Oxford, 1990), 236–9.

[60]   Prince, *The Italian Element in Milton's Verse*, 123.

similes and little turns of wit, which are so much in vogue among modern poets':
Milton, by contrast,

never quits his simile till it rises to some very great idea, which is often foreign to the occasion
that gave birth to it. . . . The resemblance does not, perhaps, last above a line or two, but the
poet runs on with the hint, till he has raised out of it some glorious image or sentiment,
proper to inflame the mind of the reader, and to give it that sublime kind of entertainment,
which is suitable to the nature of an heroic poem.

Addison continues by quoting with approval Boileau's defence of Homer's 'long-
tailed' similes as properly designed 'to relieve and diversify his subjects' (Shawcross,
172–3). Modern critics are generally unhappy with this notion of 'relief', perhaps
wrongly confusing it with inattention (in the often-quoted words of Jonathan
Richardson, the reader of Milton 'must be always upon duty',[61] in the similes as
much as elsewhere); they are more concerned to find precise correspondences
between simile and narrative, and often turn similes into miniature theological
allegories.[62] Addison and the eighteenth-century critics by contrast grant greater
imaginative freedom to both poet and reader. In his note on *Iliad* 5. 116 Pope observes
that Homer in his similes 'affects . . . rather to present the mind with a great image
than to fix it down to an exact one' (a mark of sublimity). Johnson writes in similar
vein of Milton:

he does not confine himself within the limits of rigorous comparison: his great excellence is
amplitude, and he expands the adventitious image beyond the dimensions which the occasion
required. Thus, comparing the shield of Satan to the orb of the moon, he crowds the
imagination with the discovery of the telescope, and all the wonders which the telescope
discovers. (*Lives of the Poets*, 287)

In ix. 1099 ff. Adam and Eve use leaves of the fig tree to cover their nakedness:

> not that kind for fruit renowned,
> But such as at this day to Indians known
> In Malabar or Decan spreads her arms
> Branching so broad and long, that in the ground
> The bended twigs take root, and daughters grow
> Above the mother tree, a pillared shade
> High overarched, and echoing walks between;
> There oft the Indian herdsman shunning heat
> Shelters in cool, and tends his pasturing herds
> At loop-holes cut through thickest shade . . .

This passage (which Coleridge chose to illustrate how 'imagination' differs from
'fancy', praising in particular the 'echoing walks between'[63]) is structured like a

---

[61] Richardsons, *Notes and Remarks*, p. cxliv (Coleridge was so struck by these words that he made
them, literally, his own (Wittreich, *Romantics on Milton*, 159)).

[62] A good introduction to current approaches is Linda Gregerson, *The Reformation of the Subject: Spenser,
Milton, and the English Protestant Epic* (Cambridge, 1995), 245–59 (with bibliography at 245 n. 19).

[63] Wittreich, *Romantics on Milton*, 225.

long-tailed simile whether or not it should be strictly so categorized (the leaves may be those of the banyan tree, or they may be like them). As such, along with a number of similes, it brings into the poem the romance of exotic geography and ethnography. A few lines further on Adam and Eve are likened to the Native Americans discovered by Columbus (1115–18); these comparisons produce a striking shift of perspective in our sense of our 'grand parents', not previously presented as in any way distanced or 'primitive' or foreign. Fowler's note proposes various strategies for increasing the passage's relevance to the context or the poem's themes, including the suggestions that 'the proliferating tree may figure ramifying original sin' or is 'a tree of life, with loopholes letting in general grace', or that the herdsman is 'an antitype, in his pastoral care, to the corrupt clergy'. This is to turn the passage into a theological cryptogram. It seems better to invoke the Kantian free-play of the mental faculties in the aesthetic that does not result in strict determination, a free-play encouraged by the dialectic of similarity and difference necessarily involved in a simile (which in practice readers will construe differently). Certainly the passage may resonate suggestively with others in the poem, for example the nuptial bower ('the roof / Of thickest covert was inwoven shade', iv. 692–3) or the Vallombrosa simile ('where the Etrurian shades / High overarched embower', i. 303–4), but without reductive closure. Crowding the imagination will do very well to describe the experience.[64]

The similes of *Paradise Lost* are one of the poem's 'beauties', and vastly extend its reach and scope; in this too they are like the similes of the *Iliad*—indeed their subject matter is more various. At the end of Book 1 the devils are compared to elves (777–90):

> Behold a wonder! They but now who seemed
> In bigness to surpass Earth's giant sons
> Now less than smallest dwarfs, in narrow room
> Throng numberless, like that pygmean race
> Beyond the Indian mount, or fairie elves,
> Whose midnight revels, by a forest side,
> Or fountain some belated peasant sees,
> Or dreams he sees, while overhead the moon
> Sits arbitress, and nearer to the earth
> Wheels her pale course, they on their mirth and dance
> Intent, with jocund music charm his ear:
> At once with joy and fear his heart rebounds.
> Thus incorporeal spirits to smallest forms
> Reduced their shapes immense, and were at large . . .

The simile can be read (as it was by Voltaire) as straightforwardly satirizing the devils by comparing them with something small and insignificant (but is not an easy equation of the two itself Satanic?); certainly the pun on 'at large' puts the devils in their place, while the dizzyingly swift shifts in scale disorient the reader (Kant later

---

[64] Cf. Immanuel Kant, *The Critique of Judgement*, trans. James Creed Meredith (Oxford, 1952), 178 (§49): 'the imagination . . . stirs up a crowd of sensations and secondary representations for which no expression can be found'.

called this 'the mathematical sublime'[65]). But the Richardsons are also right to say in their note that 'the picture is exceeding pretty and delightful', providing a contrast to the desolations of Hell. The metamorphosis of the devils is presented as something marvellous; we may recall that, according to Tasso, the epic ought to arouse delight through wonder.[66] The strength of Milton's engagement is shown by the potent double allusion to two loved authors: to the ill-meeting by moonlight of Oberon and Titania in *A Midsummer Night's Dream*, II. I. 60 ff. ('midnight revels' echoes 'moonlight revels', while the moon, the forest, the fountain, the dance, the music, and perhaps the Indian, call to mind Shakespeare's play) and to the solemn scene in *Aeneid* 6. 440 ff. when Aeneas recognizes Dido again in the darkness of the Underworld like one 'who sees or thinks he sees' (*videt aut vidisse putat*) the moon rising among the clouds at the month's beginning. Allusion is never a figure of stability, since the relationship between the texts can always be reconfigured. We can say, if we like, that, by evoking them in this context, Milton is in part associating Virgil and Shakespeare with the dangerous glamour of Satan, but the beauty of their writings is fully savoured and reproduced (the peasant, 'belated' in a secondary sense perhaps as belonging to the literary past, feels joy as well as fear).[67] The similes, rather than establishing fixed correspondences (Satan is like Dido or whatever), colour our sense of the action in just such complex ways.

Paradise Lost could not have been written without Milton's profound knowledge of ancient epic; but it is a modern poem, in no sense a pastiche of the classical. This is partly because it reflects so many contemporary concerns and incorporates (perhaps unexpectedly) so much material from the modern world, partly because the biblical subject matter brings with it a matching range of biblical styles to complement the classical and at times to conflict with it (one could contrast Vida's neo-Latin *Christiad* (1527), wholly Virgilian in diction, where there is no stylistic pressure from the Bible). Much of the prestige of the epic has subsequently migrated to the novel. When the two forms are contrasted, epic (bad) is usually characterized as ancient, authoritarian, teleological, backward-looking, objective, religious, univocal, and aristocratic, novel (good) as modern, democratic, anti-teleological, subjective, secular, dialogic, bourgeois. *Paradise Lost* clearly cuts across a number of these categories. For Hegel, whose *Aesthetics* plots the supposedly progressive unfolding of *Geist* in different literary forms (first epic, then tragedy, then lyric), epic and modernity are at odds; epic 'presents what is itself objective in its objectivity' (inevitably its 'original and unsurpassed perfection' is found in Greece), and Milton errs in incorporating didactic and lyric features that conflict with this objectivity;[68] the 'un-epic' interiority is also evident in Satan's solipsistic involutions. According to

---

[65] *Critique of Judgement*, 94–101 (§§25–6).
[66] *Tasso: Discourses*, 15–17.
[67] See John Guillory, *Poetic Authority: Spenser, Milton, and Literary History* (New York, 1983), 140–3.
[68] *Hegel's Aesthetics: Lectures on Fine Art*, ed. T. M. Knox, ii (Oxford, 1975), 1037, 1094, 1075–9, 1109.

Bakhtin, 'absolute conclusiveness and closedness is the outstanding feature of the temporally valorized epic past'.[69] In one sense *Paradise Lost* might seem the perfect illustration: nothing could be further in the past or more finished and separate from us than Eden. But the drive to origination and closedness is matched by a counter-movement that seeks to address an open-ended present and brings back into the poem the multiple contingencies of history, contingencies that press upon the poet and his wayfaring readers for whom nothing is yet finished (Bahktin's epic, by contrast, lacks 'any gradual, purely temporal progressions that might connect it with the present').[70] In Linda Gregerson's words, 'inspiration in *Paradise Lost* is patently plural, mediated, incomplete'; part of the poem's essential truthfulness is that it acknowledges its own fallen status, while pointing, with great sensuousness, towards a felicity that is strictly beyond our ken'.[71] An epic that adopts a teleological structure more all-encompassing even than the Virgilian trajectory from Troy to a Roman *imperium sine fine* also ends with the 'wandering steps and slow' of Adam and Eve as they enter our world of time and change and choice (where 'wandering' is the key word for the anti-teleological tendencies of romance).[72] The intertextual fecundities of a poem which is a sort of compendium of European genres mean that a vast number of voices (though organized into a coherent whole) speak from within its polyphony; fragments of other texts are everywhere, bringing with them their own complications (the metamorphic Ovid, for example, alongside the end-directed Virgil).[73] All this connects with Milton's intense commitment to free will and readerly freedom, which produces a corresponding dialogism in his epic. In viii. 595–614 Adam, rebuked by Raphael for excessive uxoriousness, responds with a moving expression of his experience in loving Eve. In ix. 205–385 Eve uses arguments not unlike those advanced in *Areopagitica* to answer Adam's objections to her going out alone (there can be no sin in her doing so, since she has not yet fallen). In both instances critics divide between those for whom the issue of authority is clear cut—Raphael in the first case, Adam in the second—and those who think that Milton, of the devil's party but without knowing it, unconsciously undermines that authority. But in both cases it is better to see designed and genuine dialogue, with the arguments finely balanced; it is not the poet's business to tell fit readers what to think but to encourage them in the responsibility to think for themselves, through an educative process which has the capacity 'to repair the ruins of our first parents'

[69] M. M. Bakhtin, *The Dialogic Imagination: Four Essays*, trans. Caryl Emerson and Michael Holquist (Austin, Tex., 1981), 16. It is doubtful how far Bakhtin's unsupported assertions apply even to classical epic; see R. Bracht Branham (ed.), *Bakhtin and the Classics* (Evanston, Ill., 2002), pt. 2: 'Bakhtin on Homer'.

[70] Ibid. 15.

[71] *Reformation of the Subject*, 225.

[72] For the complex entanglements of epic and romance see Burrow, *Epic Romance*, and David Quint, *Epic and Empire: Politics and Generic Form from Virgil to Milton* (Princeton, 1993), esp. ch. 7.

[73] See e.g. Barbara Kiefer Lewalski, 'The Genres of *Paradise Lost*', in Dennis Danielson (ed.), *The Cambridge Companion to Milton*, 2nd edn. (Cambridge, 1999), 113–29.

(*Of Education*; *CPW*, i. 366–7).[74] Learning through dialogue is central to Milton's epic, 'a poem directed at the spiritual discipline of his countrymen'.[75]

Milton's achievement in making an epic out of one of the West's major myths was of European scope and vision. The emphasis of our new historicists on the particular and the local risks making the early modern period seem more parochial than it is. The parochialism is rather ours; the dislodgement of Milton hailed by Dr Leavis (unlikely ever to be a friend of epic) was conducted in the name of an Englishness (not altogether convincingly associated with Shakespeare) that is rather easily re-figured as a form of little Englandism. Milton's multilingual dexterity, with its 'intensely imaged multicultural fusings of perception',[76] makes him in some ways a more exemplary figure for our current needs even than Shakespeare (his only equal in the poetic handling of the English language). Felipe Fernández-Armesto asks 'what might winkle most Britons out of their bleak, dim, monoglot little worlds';[77] could restoring *Paradise Lost* to a central position in the curriculum be the start of an answer?

[74] For the reader in Milton see Sharon Achinstein, *Milton and the Revolutionary Reader* (Princeton, 1994); Tilottama Rajan, 'The Other Reading: Transactional Epic in Milton, Blake, and Wordsworth', in Lisa Low and Anthony John Harding (eds.), *Milton, the Metaphysicals, and Romanticism* (Cambridge, 1994), 20–46.

[75] Cedric C. Brown, 'Great Senates and Godly Education: Politics and Cultural Renewal in Some Pre- and Post-Revolutionary Texts of Milton', in David Armitage, Armand Himy, and Quentin Skinner (eds.), *Milton and Republicanism* (Cambridge, 1995), 43–60 at 58.

[76] Hale, *Milton's Languages*, 40.

[77] *Times Higher Education Supplement*, 13 Oct. 2006, p. 13.

CHAPTER 25

....

'A MIND OF MOST EXCEPTIONAL ENERGY': VERSE RHYTHM IN *PARADISE LOST*

....

JOHN CREASER

T. S. ELIOT, a conservative in politics and religion, never overcame his acknowledged antipathy to Milton the man, but responded finely to what he calls 'the peculiar feeling, almost a physical sensation of a breathless leap, communicated by Milton's long periods, and by his alone. . . . To be able to control so many words at once is the token of a mind of most exceptional energy.'[1] Celebration of the energies pulsing through *Paradise Lost* originates in the commendatory poems by Barrow and Marvell in the 1674 edition. Similar praise runs through writings as diverse as Jonathan Richardson in *Explanatory Notes and Remarks on Paradise Lost* (1734)[2] and Blake's audacious *The Marriage of Heaven and Hell*, where the Devil is the embodiment of creative energy and Milton is 'a true poet, and of the Devil's party without knowing it'.[3]

---

[1] 'Milton (1947)', in *Milton Criticism: Selections from Four Centuries*, ed. James Thorpe (1965), 312, 324.
[2] For Richardson, poetry 'supposes energy as well as beauty' (p. clv) and his notes have many comments such as ''tis all nerve and energy' (p. 371) and 'an abounding fullness of expression . . . adding force and energy' (p. 462).
[3] *Blake: The Complete Poems*, ed. W. H. Stevenson, 2nd edn. (Harlow, 1989), 107.

The dynamism of the poem is found in the cosmic scope of the fable and the sublime intensity of local images, with the matching force of the characters suggested by Shelley's claim: 'Nothing can exceed the energy and magnificence of the character of Satan as expressed in *Paradise Lost*.'[4] Mental energy is everywhere apparent in force of argument, while the poem is charged with political and theological shock-waves from the cultural conflicts of its day. But all this would be inert without the all-pervading energy and rhythm of the language. From the energy concentrated within individual lines to the steady onward pressure of the verse and the 'breathless leaps' of the great passages, the rhythm of the verse is the lifeblood of the poem.

This could hardly be claimed for the few earlier English narrative poems in blank verse, notably the epic translations of Surrey and Marlowe and the first original poem, *The Steel Glass* (1576) by George Gascoigne, a determined but cautious pioneer, where a typical passage reads:

> That age is dead, and vanished long ago,
> Which thought that steel, both trusty was and true,
> And needed not, a foil of contraries,
> But showed all things, even as they were indeed.
> Instead whereof, our curious years can find
> The crystal glass, which glimpseth brave and bright,
> And shows the thing, much better than it is,
> Beguiled with foils, of sundry subtle sights,
> So that they seem, and covet not to be.[5]

Everything has its predictable place in these iambic pentameters: stress, beat, phrase, and line all coincide. The prevailingly monosyllabic lines, each with five full and even stresses, are alike in cadence. Every pair of syllables is in rising rhythm, moving from lighter to heavier emphasis; every line falls into a pattern of four syllables followed by six; elision is infrequent and straightforward ('*ev'n*', 'cur-*ious*'); every line but one is end-stopped; there are no hypermetrical syllables or feminine endings. The verse is a series of discrete lines, each shaped so that Gascoigne's readers, familiar only with rhymed verse, know where they are.

These simple norms continue to underlie later verse, and the vigour of more adventurous writing comes in deviating from them. Their very simplicity permits wide variation, and the supreme masters, Shakespeare and Milton, react in almost antithetical ways. In a nutshell, one line in five by the mature Shakespeare dislocates these prosodic norms, and in *Paradise Lost* one line in 265. Broadly speaking, metre governs rhythm in sixteenth-century blank verse (including the young Shakespeare) and the rhythms of the language are adapted to the metrical pattern, but with mature Shakespeare comes a new expressive freedom: colloquial rhythm governs metre, and the phrase, the sentence, and the speech become predominant.

---

[4] 'A Defence of Poetry', in *Milton Criticism*, ed. Thorpe, 358.
[5] *Complete Works of George Gascoigne*, ed. John W. Cunliffe, 2 vols. (Cambridge, 1907–10), ii. 147–8 (punctuation original, spelling modernized).

Consequently, as George T. Wright records in detail, Shakespeare's later plays jeopardize our sense of the iambic pentameter, and are free to the point of licentiousness.[6] For example, Prospero's greatest and most disturbed speech begins with a nine-syllable line incompatible with iambic verse: 'You do look, my son, in a mov'd sort' (*The Tempest*, IV. I. 146), and soon there is a line which, while metrically regular, is rhythmically shapeless in isolation: '(As I foretold you) were all spirits, and' (l. 149). In general, there are many short lines—even some scenes, as many speeches, end mid-line—and there are various other licences, such as headless lines (initial off-beat omitted), broken-backed lines (off-beat omitted at the caesura), and triple rhythms where duple would be orthodox. Long as well as short lines occur: as many as one line in twenty-one in the verse of *Measure for Measure* is a hexameter, while from *Twelfth Night* onwards, one line in twenty-one also contains an 'epic caesura', an extra, unstressed syllable at the pause within the line (as in 'Wake Duncan with thy knock-*ing*! I would thou couldst!', *Macbeth*, II. II. 71[7]). Inevitably, feminine endings are common, rising from about one line in ten in the early work to about one in three in the late plays.[8] The integrity of the line frequently yields to the immediacy of passion, with the ending apparently thrown away on a weak word, such as an unstressed 'and' or 'that'. After the early plays, Shakespeare is no longer content to write sequences of regular pentameters: something irregular is always liable to happen, although the sense of the norm is never quite lost, because four out of five lines remain regular in essentials.

What does it mean to say that a line of blank verse is licentious or is 'regular in essentials'? An answer is best approached through the theories of Derek Attridge, based as they are on two major tendencies of the spoken language: towards isochrony or the equal timing of stress, and towards duple rhythm, the alternation of syllables lighter and heavier in stress.[9] Carefully uttering a phrase of strongly stressed syllables such as 'quick brown fox', for example, we tend to give each syllable equal time, but maintain a duple movement by giving the outer words slightly more weight—equal weight for 'brown' would make the word stand out, as if drawing a distinction with, say, a red fox. Similarly, a careful speaker of the phrase 'tennis on the lawn' would tend to give 'on', as the second of three unstressed syllables, slightly more time or weight than in the phrase 'tea on the lawn'. In the accentual-syllabic prosody of most literary verse, where every syllable counts, the prevailing lines are the iambic pentameter and tetrameter, and, as is clear in every line by Gascoigne quoted above, these combine isochrony with the duple tendency. Attridge shows that the incalculable variety of movement in regular iambic verse since the sixteenth century is released by only three deviations from duple alternation. First, the 'quick brown fox' pattern,

---

6 *Shakespeare's Metrical Art* (Berkeley, 1988), 105–6.

7 Ibid. 292–3, 165.

8 Ibid. 160–1.

9 See especially Derek Attridge, *The Rhythms of English Poetry* (Harlow, 1982), and *Poetic Rhythm: An Introduction* (Cambridge, 1995). A fuller account of his theories, and of much of the prosodic detail in this chapter, is given in my article '"Service is Perfect Freedom": Paradox and Prosodic Style in *Paradise Lost*', *Review of English Studies*, 58 (2007), 268–315, cited hereafter as 'Service'.

with equal time for all three stressed syllables but less weight for the second, becomes in verse the *demotion* of the second of three consecutive stresses, as in: 'Say first, for HEAVEN *HIDES* NOTH-ing from thy view' (i. 27).[10] (Roman capitals indicate full stresses and italic capitals demotions.) A demoted syllable is a stressed off-beat, an addition to the line's five beats required by the metre (which here are 'first', 'Heav'n', 'noth-', 'view', and either 'from' or 'thy'); through isochrony, it makes for a slower and more weighty line.

The obverse of demotion is the *promotion* of the second of three non-stresses by a lengthening or pause, as with 'from' in 'NOTH-ing FROM thy VIEW'. A promoted syllable (indicated by small capitals) is usually a pronoun or preposition colloquially given only subsidiary emphasis but which, by its placing, is allotted (or felt as being allotted) the time and a little of the weight of a metrical beat. The third deviation is *pairing*, where there are only two adjacent stresses, both of them beats. The phrase just cited might also be read as a pairing: 'NOTH-ing from THY VIEW'. Two stresses do not permit demotion, and as they disrupt the duple flow of iambic verse and push a line off balance, the imbalance is kept as brief as possible by immediately preceding or following the pair with two non-stresses. Pairings may be *stress-final*, as in 'Favoured of heaven so high-ly to FALL OFF' (i. 30), or *stress-initial*, as in 'For one re-STRAINT, LORDS of the world besides' (i. 32). (The four syllables of a pairing are identified by underlining.)

A significant nuance is that, under precise conditions, the pause of the line-turn may act as a syllable, stressed or unstressed, and make deviation possible, so that two rather than three syllables may permit promotion or demotion, and a single stress may permit pairing. In iambics, promotion occurs at the end of the line: 'That to the height of this great ARG-u-MENT [x]' (i. 24). Conversely, demotion may occur at the start of the line: '[/] *BROUGHT* DEATH into the world, and all our woe' (i. 3). Pairing occurs as the common reversal of stress at the beginning of a line: '[/] ROSE out of chaos: Or if Sion hill' (i. 10). These deviations are made possible by the pause at the turn, not by the end or beginning of an adjacent line. The demotion opening ii. 256, '*HARD* LIB-erty before the easy yoke', is not begun by the preceding beat, since line 255 has a feminine ending, 'preferring'. Indeed, the pause of the turn creates an absolute metrical barrier between adjoining lines, however fluid the syntax. While rhythm depends at least as much on perception as on measurable sounds, the audible reality of the line-turn, as of demotion and promotion, is borne out by experiment.[11]

Attridge's methods are a marked advance on the familiar division of lines into so-called disyllabic 'feet', a mode of analysis not taken seriously by metrical theorists for decades. As his prosody responds to the realities of English speech, it records meaningful rather than arbitrary sequences of syllables; it establishes the line-turn as a real presence in English verse; it adds the distinction between the structural functions of beat and off-beat to the distinction between spoken stress and non-stress; and, coming back

---

[10] Quotations are from the Scolar Press facsimile of *Paradise Lost 1667* (Menston, 1968), with spelling modernized but with the original punctuation. Line-numbers are adjusted to the division into twelve books.

[11] Ada L. F. Snell, 'An Objective Study of Syllabic Quantity in English Verse', *PMLA* 33 (1918), 396–408.

to the question from which this technical discussion began, it can draw fine distinctions between degrees of irregularity, between lines that are deviant and those that are aberrant. A 'deviant' line may exploit promotion, demotion, and pairing—even very freely—but is felt as an acceptable variation on the prosodic base, while an 'aberrant' line goes beyond deviations into dislocations and is felt as exceptional. Indeed, an aberrant line seems clumsy unless it has some expressive purpose.

For example, why—to contrast lines evoking divine power in the cosmos—does the rhythm of how eternal wrath 'Burnt after them to the bottomless pit' (vi. 866) seem aberrant, while it seems merely deviant that the light of heaven 'Shoots far into the bosom of dim night' (ii. 1036)? The second line scans '*SHOOTS* <u>FAR IN</u>-to the BOS-<u>om</u> of <u>DIM NIGHT</u>': it begins with a line-turn demotion, continues with a stress-initial pairing (it is more propulsive here to stress 'into' on the first syllable), and concludes with a stress-final pairing. Though rhythmically striking, it is free rather than aberrant: it packs energy into the start and finish to emphasize the power of divine light shooting towards our universe, and it touchingly isolates the intimacy of 'bosom' in mid-line. But vi. 866 cannot be assimilated to the deviation rules. Its ten syllables have five potential stresses ('burnt', 'af-', 'them', 'bot-', 'pit'), but only four can be realized as metrical beats in one orthodox reading: if 'af-' is stressed then 'burnt' is demoted; if 'burnt' is given the full stress and also the beat that it seems to require, there is a reversed opening, with no beat on 'after'. Either way, there is no sequence of three non-stresses to make a promotion and so a fifth beat possible. It would have been easy for Milton to have produced an orthodox line such as 'BURNT after THEM to <u>HELL'S BOT</u>-tomless PIT', but the only ways to give the actual line five beats in a pattern compatible with the norms would be through an absurd emphasis, such as: 'BURNT after THEM to <u>THE BOT</u>-tomless PIT'. Consequently, the line is likely to be read by insisting on five beats in abnormal sequence, 'BURNT AF-ter THEM to the BOT-tomless PIT', or read as an alien line of four-beat accentual verse (where the structural principle is solely the number of beats in a line): 'BURNT after THEM to the BOT-tomless PIT'. Both of these work expressively: the grating against metrical norms in the first is apt for the unimaginable horror of the fall from heaven. The second, missing a beat, makes a vertiginous climax to a passage evoking a fall through chaos. As accentual verse, moreover, the line reads as accelerating throughout, with only two stresses in the last six syllables, before coming to an abrupt and early halt—as if echoing the unnatural pace of the rebels' descent before its terrible ending. Orthodox prosodists have failed to normalize this line; a new approach makes it possible to appreciate Milton's audacity and power.[12]

This sketch of prosodic theory will help to clarify how the blank verse of *Paradise Lost* is virtually a new beginning and transmits a quite un-Shakespearean energy. Its prosodic style is as self-conscious a creation as Gascoigne's, and beside Shakespeare's may seem strict to the point of austerity. A hypothetical blank-verse poem matching the 10,565 lines of *Paradise Lost* in the manner of the late Shakespeare would have over 2,000 aberrant lines; in *Paradise Lost*, only some forty lines are at all aberrant.

---

[12] 'Service', 273, 283.

A mere handful of these deviate markedly from the norm of five metrical beats in ten metrical syllables (discounting elisions and feminine endings). There are, for example, no tetrameters or hexameters.[13] Even the so-called 'epic caesura', which was common in *Comus*, is here eschewed. Not a single line falls below the syllable-count of ten (although two lines, through their reversed endings, seem to be one *metrical* syllable short).[14] Scarcely any line exceeds the norm, though a near exception is the twelve-syllable line 'Because thou hast he heark'nd to the voice of thy wife' (x. 198), which becomes metrically ten only if one reads '*thou'st*' and '*to'th*'', forms of elision rejected elsewhere in the poem. A straightforward reading of the line gives the divine judge a grotesque gallop of accentual verse: 'Be-CAUSE thou hast HEARK'nd to the VOICE of thy WIFE', but read as blank verse the line remains clumsy, scanning: 'Be-CAUSE thou'st HEARK-'nd TOTH' VOICE of thy WIFE', with 'to the' not only forced into elision but given an unnatural emphasis. Such a line, where the rhythm is tricky for no expressive end, is almost unique.[15]

A line of verse is determined by its ending. The handling of the turn colours the whole movement, and metrically the strongest points of a line of iambic verse are the words given the first and final beats. A firm final stress maintains a sense of the prosodic integrity of the individual line, especially if it coincides with a unit of sense. A weaker ending, such as a closing promotion—or the extra and uncompleted movement of a feminine ending—lessens that sense of integrity and isolation, and encourages a sense of the passage rather than the line. Whereas Shakespeare is prepared to sacrifice the line to the speech, *Paradise Lost* maintains the integrity of the line, with a driving clarity of movement, line by line—even when characters are said to be faltering in their speech.[16] Consequently, no line-ending is thrown away on a mere function word, and very few lines end even with a polysyllable and hence the relative weakness of a promotion; most end on a stressed monosyllable, and almost all the others on a disyllable with second-syllable stress. In keeping with such discipline, every single paragraph ends at the end of a line. Similarly, most speeches open and close at line-boundaries, and the exceptions are absorbed into the prevailing regularity by a narrative introduction or conclusion, not exposed in dramatic cut and thrust. In such ways, the poem keeps us conscious of its simple prosodic base. For this reason, feminine endings, with the dissolution of the line-boundary that they tend to create, are rare, occurring on average barely more than once in a hundred lines, and absent from long stretches of the poem.[17]

[13] At x. 989–90, as printed in editions up to 1695, a tetrameter is followed by a hexameter. This has been seen as expressive, but is probably a printing error for two pentameters ('Service', 292).

[14] The lines 'Which of us who beholds the bright surface' (vi. 472) and 'Beyond all past example and future' (x. 840) are aberrant, nine-syllable lines plus feminine ending unless 'surface' and 'future' are artificially stressed on the second syllable ('Service', 300–1).

[15] Some stressings which read awkwardly to modern ears, such as 'inDISsolUbly' (vi. 69) and 'inEXpliCAble' (x. 754) are readily paralleled in contemporary verse.

[16] For example, 'the anarch old' at ii. 988–1009.

[17] See J. C. Smith, 'Feminine Endings in Milton's Blank Verse', *Times Literary Supplement*, 5 Dec. 1936, p. 1016; S. Ernest Sprott, *Milton's Art of Prosody* (Oxford, 1953), ch. 6; and André Verbart, 'Measure and Hypermetricality in *Paradise Lost*', *English Studies*, 80 (1999), 428–48.

Such disciplined continuity is apt for epic, an art of presentation. Permeating our response to characters and situations, however passionate, is a constant awareness not so much of the narrator as of the narration. These are not the characters of drama living in apparent autonomy; they, even God, are the poem's creatures and speak in its manner. For all the sophistication of this 'tertiary epic', the radical remains the vocal continuity of the singer of tales, not the theatre's versatility of voice and perspective.

How, having developed prosody of such austerity, order, and closure, does Milton manage to convey such a sense of energy? Is his appeal to liberty in the note on 'The Verse' justified, or has he swapped 'the troublesome and modern bondage of rhyming' for another straitjacket?

Prosodic analysis shows that Milton ranges freely within his chosen limits: there is no iambic jog-trot, and the rhythms are endlessly varied. Approximate though such figures inevitably are, it is worth recording that a passage of 200 lines will contain on average 166 deviations—promotions, demotions, pairings, and their line-turn varia-tions—decidedly more than in earlier writers of narrative blank verse. In effect, five lines out of six are liable to be in some way deviant.[18] Regular lines working within the standard deviations vary, for example, between three words and ten and between three full spoken stresses and eight ('Im-MUT-a-BLE, im-MORT-al, IN-fin-ITE', iii. 373; '*ROCKS*, CAVES, *LAKES*, FENS, *BOGS*, DENS, and SHADES of DEATH', ii. 621).

Moreover, all this unpredictable variety of movement is not variety for variety's sake. Unlike the lulling sameness of Gascoigne, it enforces attention, and is inex-haustibly there for expressive purpose. In the lines just cited, for example, the presence of only three words and three full stresses in the address to God leads one to compensate by giving extra weight to each word and dwelling on the ineffable mysteries implied, while, through isochrony, the eight stresses of the line on the hell discovered by the fallen angels mean that the line stretches on and on, as horror succeeds horror. Readers open to the presence of pairing in the verse—a deviation often overlooked because incompatible with traditional prosody—not only escape monotony but also discover innumerable apt nuances of emphasis. These two lines from Satan's Niphates soliloquy, for example,

> I 'sdained subjec-tion, and THOUGHT ONE step higher (iv. 50)
> None left but by submiss-ion; and THAT WORD (iv. 81)

might be read with an iambic tread. But to stress 'thought' rather than 'and' brings out the pain of Satan's new self-knowledge, and to stress 'that' rather than the second 'and' brings out his disdain for the merest hint of submission. The lines

> The FIRST SORT by their own suggestion fell (iii. 129)
> For WHAT GOD after better worse would build? (ix. 102)

are striking if read as indicated, with the normally pivotal second beat on the fourth syllable anticipated off-balance in the third. The first line brings out God's contempt

---

[18] 'Service', 295 ff.

for the fallen angels, and the second invites dwelling on the complex of emotions evoked when Satan mentions deity.

Such nuances enliven thousands of individual lines with the energy of intensive meaning. For example, an untypical lack of rhythmic clarity becomes expressive in the account of the indeterminate and warring causes within chaos, 'mixt / Confused-ly, and which thus must ever fight' (ii. 914): the rhythm meanders ambiguously and is unstable until the eighth syllable. A completely different rhythmic effect cuts strange-ly into Adam's soliloquy of despair in Book 10: 'O fleeting joys / Of paradise, dear bought with lasting woes' (741–2)—the apostrophe, with a phrase of four beats followed by a phrase of three, brings a poignant echo of the common metre of hymns and psalms into the tragic bitterness.

There are also prosodic effects larger in scale. For example, there is a rare cluster of demotions in the course of Adam and Eve's morning psalm to '*HIM* FIRST, *HIM* LAST, *HIM* MIDST, and without end' (v. 165) as they 'Vary to OUR *GREAT* MAK-er STILL *NEW* PRAISE' (184). In the score of lines from v. 164 there are eighteen demotions, almost as many as on average occur in some 200 lines. Milton here adopts a slow and weighty movement, because this is a rare passage lacking narrative drive; it evokes a creation of changeless bliss, uttering universal and unending praise of him who is 'without end'.

Moreover, Milton is no slave to his prosodic norms. He is quite prepared for small licences, such as a pairing across an elision, as in: 'Hypocrisy, the ON-*LY'EV*-il that walks (iii. 683). A more occasional licence, showing Milton's Shakespearean confi-dence in handling his rhythms, is a paradoxical three-beat pairing, a sequence of three beats (beats and not stresses, so there can be no demotion), where the first two complete a stress-final pairing and, pivoting on the second, the final two open a stress-initial pairing: 'When the FIERCE FOE HUNG on our broken rear' (ii. 78). The cluster of beats enforces the relentlessness of the enemy angels.

Sometimes he is prepared to show an off-handed mastery and take his rhythms to the limits of the tolerable. Lurking beneath the iambic pentameter is always the risk of collapse into the four-beat accentual verse of much popular writing. A few lines in *Paradise Lost* avoid this only if a syllable normally given little stress does duty as a beat in a pairing. For example, viii. 292 is notionally kept regular by having the preposi-tion 'at' as a beat ('When sudd-enly STOOD AT my head a dream'), but read straightforwardly the line emphasizes the suddenness by accelerating into accentual verse ('When SUDD-enly STOOD at my HEAD a DREAM'). Reading aloud, one rhythm or the other must be chosen, but those with the text before their eyes can sense the coexistence of both. Practised readers can feel various valid possibilities even as they read aloud or as if aloud, with the mind's ear alert. Almost unique is a line of ten syllables impossible to shape into an iambic pentameter: 'Be-FORE thy FELL-ows, am-BIT-ious to WIN' (vi. 160). Here, in the flyting before the war in heaven, it seems plausible to claim that, as Satan accuses Abdiel of thrusting himself prematurely on his old leader, the alleged presumption is evoked in the disrupted rhythm: the line, lacking a beat, hurries to an abrupt conclusion.

Most aberrations are, however, milder than this, being versions of unbalanced pairings, where the off-beats are detached from their matching beats. In the whole poem, out of well over a thousand pairings, there are barely more than half a dozen straightforward instances of this, for example: 'On the other SIDE, AD-am, soon as he heard' (ix. 888). The effect here is to put extra stress on 'soon', emphasizing just how quick the shocked Adam is to respond to the falling Eve. Somewhat less rare is what may be termed the 1–3–6 sequence, a dual reversed opening, with beats on the first and third syllables and the line out of balance until the sixth. I have observed no more than twenty-three possible examples in the whole epic, as opposed to about 1,750 standard reversed openings, and an orthodox alternative stressing is possible for several of these twenty-three. Almost all must be calculated abnormalities. For example, the raw alienation of the newly fallen Adam and Eve when they emerge reluctantly into the divine presence at x. 111 is marked by the extra stress on 'not' brought by the aberrant rhythm: 'LOVE was NOT in their LOOKS, either to God'. Similarly, when Eve opens the gardening debate with the line 'AD-am, WELL may we LAB-our still to dress . . .' (ix. 205), the presumption within her apparently reasonable proposal of gardening apart is revealed not only by her speaking first for the first time and addressing Adam bluntly, without any of the loving periphrases of the unfallen world, but also by the abnormal stress giving a quizzical tone to 'well'.

This versatile handling of rhythm within and occasionally beyond the prosodic norms is only one major mode of freedom in Milton's versification. The places established for the caesura by poets and critics such as Gascoigne were after the fourth and sixth syllables, but Milton makes his verse at once weighty and flexible through caesuras both frequent and unorthodox. They are present in three out of four lines, and less than half fall in the conventional positions. Otherwise, there is an even spread across the second to eighth places, with fully a third of the total being 'lyric caesuras', falling after odd syllables. This variety gives the verse energy as well as weight and flexibility, since verse that is straightforward in rhythm and moves forward regularly lacks the propulsiveness of tension. The telling exception is Samson's nadir of despair at 590–8 ('All otherwise to me my thoughts portend . . .'), where the emotional flatness is expressed in a sequence of nine end-stopped lines varied by merely two caesuras, one each at the fourth and sixth syllable.[19]

Another sign of flexibility is Milton's readiness to deviate from the firm convention of ending a sentence at a line-end. Whereas virtually all sentences in earlier writers of narrative blank verse end there, just over a quarter of Milton's end mid-line (even though he always ends a paragraph at a line-end), an innovation responding to Shakespeare. This, together with his frequent placing of other heavy pauses within the line, puts Milton at the opposite extreme from Gascoigne's predictable cadences.

Another source of the continuous variety within an apparently strict system is the pervasive elision. This adds new permutations of rhythm, since invariably the elided syllable is glided into its neighbour rather than cut out. On a full count, for example,

---

[19] 'Service', 305–6.

'Embryos and idiots, eremites and friars' (iii. 474) has thirteen syllables. Although the
metre entails elisions at *bry-os*, *i-ots*, and *i-ars*, no syllable is quite lost; the i-glides
remain audible presences and so add rhythmic nuance. Milton varies his decasylla-
bles with fleeting hypermetrical presences. There is all the more variety because some
of his elisions can be no more than notional, with syllables to be elided separated by
punctuation, for example x. 762, 'Wherefore didst thou beget *me? I* sought it not', or
xi. 336, 'Not this rock on-*ly; his* omnipresence fills'. Such hypothetical elisions are in
effect epic caesuras, in an epic that rejects this familiar licence. At vii. 411, 'Wall-*owing*
unwield-*y, e*-normous in their gait', Milton exploits such elision to evoke the ga-
lumphing sea-creatures. These virtual elisions can even be found away from the
caesura, as at xi. 772: 'Him or his children, ev-*il he* may be sure'. Such examples
epitomize how Milton squares the circle of combining austerity with licence.

The feminine ending is another instance. Its rarity must be deliberate, since it is
much more common in *Comus* and *Samson Agonistes*—there are sixty-one in the 270
lines of vehement exchange between Samson and Dalila. Nevertheless, such as there
are in *Paradise Lost* make their mark, because from the outset they are just frequent
enough to be noticed as unusual. Early in the first book, one finds three of them:

> Of rebel angels, by whose aid aspiring (l. 38)
>
> And high disdain, from sense of injured merit (l. 98)
>
> That durst dislike his reign, and me preferring (l. 102)

In this way, the feminine ending is associated with over-reaching and with opposition to the law of God. There is not a single instance in the first scene in heaven, until
the significant line: 'But yet all is not done; man disobeying' (iii. 203), while they
cluster at the crisis of the fall. There are, as Weismiller points out, more feminine
endings in Books 9 and 10 than in the rest of the poem put together.[20] That Milton
gives so much significance to occasional nuances shows both his minute concern for
prosodic effect and his liberated use of a strict system.

So much for Milton's freedoms within the line. If we now consider how the verse
moves on from line to line, then its expressive freedoms become still more striking.
The verse of *Paradise Lost* is distinguished by the sustained length of its sentences,
which are on average about ten lines long, despite the frequent use of short sentences
for rhetorical effect. And the verse is even more distinguished by what Milton's note
draws to our attention among the sources of 'true musical delight' as 'the sense
variously drawn out from one verse into another'. On average, as many as three lines
in five run on,[21] and overall there are far more mid-line pauses than end-stops.
Milton has brought the unprecedented freedoms of mature Shakespeare into the
relative formality of epic. Because the verse is no longer moving line by line, syntax is
released from metrical regularity; word-order and syntactical form can be endlessly
varied. Moreover, enjambement is indeed 'variously' used. In particular, he ranges

[20] Edward R. Weismiller, 'Blank Verse', in *A Milton Encyclopedia*, gen. ed. W. B. Hunter, Jr., 9 vols.
(Lewisburg, Pa., 1978–), i. 186.
[21] Weismiller, 'Versification', in *A Milton Encyclopedia*, viii. 133.

continually from a break between phrases ('for heaven hides nothing from thy view / Nor the deep tract of hell'), to what, unusually, is the commonest break in the poem, that between segments of a phrase ('the fruit / Of that forbidden tree, whose mortal taste / Brought death', plus over half the lines of the opening invocation), to, much less common, a break within a segment of a phrase ('The originals of nature in their crude / Conception', vi. 511–12). Such variety at the line-turn blends with ceaseless changes of movement within the line to create the continuous modulations of cadence. Milton's insistence on a firm prosodic ending to the line, usually through a stressed monosyllable, makes readers aware of all these modulations by the guidance of a clear norm.

Moreover, the firm ending leads us to dwell on words that reward deliberation and emphasis. For example, if Satan on Mount Niphates had reached the conclusion:

> But say I could repent and therefore could
> Obtain by grace my former state; how soon
> Would height recall high thoughts, and I how soon
> Unsay what feigned submission swore:

the repetitions of 'could' and 'how soon' would have seemed mechanical. In Milton's version, the line-turns are alive to the urgency of Satan's thinking at his most sincere, as he moves from the possibility of hope to the apparent inevitability of despair:

> But say I could repent and could *obtain*
> By act of grace my former state; how *soon*
> Would height recall high thoughts, how soon *unsay*
> What feigned submission swore: (iv. 92–5)

Such prosodic variety brings with it a matching variety of effect. The marked emjambement at i. 508–9, 'The Ionian gods, of Javan's issue held / Gods', creates a sardonic pause. The first two paragraphs of Book 11 are a signal instance of Milton's quiet audacity: all but nine of these forty-four lines run on. Apart from the paragraph endings, only one line ends with a full stop; otherwise lines end in four commas, a semicolon, and a bracket closing a parenthesis. The verse flows on with ease, especially the first paragraph, which comprises a single sentence of twenty-one lines, end-stopped before the close by a mere two commas. This fluency is sustained within the individual lines, since there are numerous promotions but only two pairings, while, until the last few lines of the second paragraph, more of the forty-two caesuras indicated by punctuation are lyric rather than ordinary or 'masculine'. These two paragraphs mark the transition from human penitence to divine compassion. Adam and Eve are suspended in prayer, while the Son makes the remarkable proposal to God that there is after all something fortunate about their fall, for their prayers are 'Fruits of more pleasing savour from thy seed / Sown with contrition in his heart, than those / Which his own hand manuring all the trees / Of Paradise could have produced, ere fall'n / From innocence' (ll. 26–30). As the poem hovers for the first time 'Betwixt the world destroyed and world restored' (xii. 3), the ease of movement empties this tremendous turning from the first to the second dispensation of human history of any dramatic tension. The fluidity of the verse prepares us for the spontaneous outpouring of divine grace, and the compassion within unavoidable judgement that will be shown the erring pair in God's answering words and the rest of the poem.[22]

The other expressive freedom as the verse swings from line to line is less innovative but also, after Milton's note on the verse, more surprising. Having presented his blank verse as 'ancient liberty' recovered from rhyme, Milton adds to the aural density of his already packed verse with occasional rhymes. To take another moment of transition, Book 8 opens with the pause that follows on Raphael's account of the creation: 'The angel ended, and in Adam's ear / So charming left his voice, that he awhile / Thought him still speaking, still stood fixed to hear' (ll. 1–3). Adam's suspension in absorbed ecstasy is enacted in one of the least tense and progressive rhymes in the language, a rhyme with only the slightest semantic and aural distinction—for what does the ear do but hear?

In sum, the blank verse of *Paradise Lost* is a deliberate and distinctive creation, influenced by but antithetical to late Shakespeare through working within a strict discipline. This metrical austerity is essential to the poem's dynamism and expressive freedom, in the way a skier is energized by a strict slalom course. It was 'by the known *rules* of ancient liberty' (my italics) that Milton, in one of his crucial distinctions, sought to bring home to the unruly mob that 'licence they mean when they cry liberty' (Sonnet XII, l. 11). Modern writers of free verse have to work hard for rhythmic energy and expressive variety within and between lines, because each line is formally a new beginning, rhythmically unique, and the poet has to find ways of doing something with it or the verse will be lethargic. But a poet working with a given form creates a point of energy and tension with any deviation from the norm, and the clearer the form, the more energy even a minor deviation can release. Milton's verse is energized by the constant, expressively apt variations within his sequences of ten syllables.

Moreover, this disciplined freedom expands into the 'breathless leaps' of the long periods. The exceptional length of the sentences and the pervasiveness of enjambement drive the intensive energy of the individual line into the extensive energy of the period and paragraph. A comparison with as exhilarating a passage as any in sixteenth-century blank verse should illuminate this. In the first part of Marlowe's *Tamburlaine*, performed 1587, only a decade after *The Steel Glass* was published, blank verse is suddenly alive, here in a sentence of twelve lines and over eighty words where the conqueror justifies his opportunism:

> Nature that framed us of four elements,
> Warring within our breasts for regiment,
> Doth teach us all to have aspiring minds:
> Our souls, whose faculties can comprehend
> The wondrous architecture of the world:

---

[22] For a fuller account of expressive enjambement, see Archie Burnett, ' "Sense Variously Drawn Out": The Line in *Paradise Lost*', *Literary Imagination*, 5 (2003), 69–92, plus studies cited there.

> And measure every wandering planet's course:
> Still climbing after knowledge infinite,
> And always moving as the restless spheres,
> Wills us to wear ourselves and never rest,
> Until we reach the ripest fruit of all,
> That perfect bliss and sole felicity,
> The sweet fruition of an earthly crown. (II. vii. 18–29)[23]

Line by line, this is very simple verse, appropriate for Tamburlaine's monolithic image of himself. The original punctuation reproduced above, where every line except one is end-stopped, emphasizes the integrity of the individual lines, while only the fourth has a marked caesura (there might have been another after 'Nature' in line 1). Consequently, the lines are very regular and alike in movement, especially as there is a verb in every line but one of the first nine and a string of noun-phrases in the last three. The rhythm is straightforward; there is only one demotion ('*STILL CLIMB-*'), and only one pairing ('<u>us of FOUR EL</u>-'), although there are the implied pairings of three reversed openings ('Nature, Warring, Wills'). The slight traces of elision are commonplace ('ev'ry', 'wand'ring'). On the other hand, there is a promotion in almost every line, with as many as five at the line-turn ('elements, regiment, comprehend, infinite, felicity'), making for a movement that is light and fleet, although at risk of monotony.

What makes this nevertheless one of the most thrilling periods in English verse is the forceful but shapely syntactic energy, through patterns of progressive expansion. Much of it consists of two segments in parallel, with the subjects ('Nature', 'Our souls') opening one line and separated by relative clauses from predicates each filling a complete line ('Doth teach us all to have aspiring minds'; 'Wills us to wear ourselves and never rest'). The first segment is expanded to three lines by a relative and a participial clause; the second is doubled to six lines by two pairs of relative and participial clauses. The suspension of almost five lines between the second subject and its verb 'Wills' creates immense tension in reader or listener, as if we ourselves were climbing and moving, waiting and waiting for the subject to be resolved. But even when it is, we cannot relax, but must enter a second three-line segment, a fourfold ascent through synonyms, with the simple parallels of 'bliss' and 'felicity' enclosed between parallel phrases: 'the ripest fruit of all' and the ultimate climax, given a line to itself, the 'sweet fruition of an earthly crown'. The speech endorses Donald Davie's claim that 'a movement of syntax can render, immediately present, the curve of destiny through a life or the path of an energy through the mind'.[24]

The passage is a triumph of extensive rather than intensive energies, working not through local intensities of phrase and rhythm, but through fusing twelve lines into a simple and elegant shape, expressing a mind at once dynamic and apparently under complete control. It invites a response not of appraisal but of amazement. Only with

---

[23] Spelling modernized from *Complete Works of Christopher Marlowe*, v, ed. David Fuller (Oxford, 1998); original punctuation retained.
[24] Donald Davie, *Articulate Energy: An Enquiry into the Syntax of English Poetry* (1955), 157.

hindsight can one begin to perceive that the rhetorical climax, the deliberate blasphemy of 'an earthly crown', is an anti-climax after language of such aspiration, and an early crack in the monolith presented by Tamburlaine.

At the opening paragraph of *Paradise Lost*, the language of aspiration is of comparable syntactic grandeur, and there is again a large simplicity in the overall structure, with the passage divided harmoniously into sentences of sixteen and ten lines. As Lee Johnson points out,[25] this pattern of 10:16:16:26 is as close as possible to what was seen as the most harmonious relation of all, the 'divine proportion' or Golden Section.

> Of man's first disobedience, and the fruit
> Of that forbidden tree, whose mortal taste
> Brought death into the world, and all our woe,
> With loss of Eden, till one greater man
> Restore us, and regain the blissful seat,   5
> Sing heavenly Muse, that on the secret top
> Of Oreb, or of Sinai, didst inspire
> That shepherd, who first taught the chosen seed,
> In the beginning how the heavens and earth
> Rose out of chaos: or if Sion hill   10
> Delight thee more, and Siloa's brook that flowed
> Fast by the oracle of God; I thence
> Invoke thy aid to my advent'rous song,
> That with no middle flight intends to soar
> Above the Aonian mount, while it pursues   15
> Things unattempted yet in prose or rhyme.
> And chiefly thou O Spirit, that dost prefer
> Before all temples the upright heart and pure,
> Instruct me, for thou know'st; thou from the first
> Wast present, and with mighty wings outspread   20
> Dove-like sat'st brooding on the vast abyss
> And mad'st it pregnant: what in me is dark
> Illumine, what is low raise and support;
> That to the height of this great argument
> I may assert eternal providence,   25
> And justify the ways of God to men.

Being very different in mentality and hence in movement, however, this verse is altogether more complex than Marlowe's in rhythmic as in thematic organization. The sentences flow together in the parallel addresses to the Muse and the Spirit,

---

[25] Lee M. Johnson, 'Milton's Epic Style: The Invocations in *Paradise Lost*', in Dennis Danielson (ed.), *The Cambridge Companion to Milton* (Cambridge, 1989), 65–78 at 71. The 'divine proportion' or Golden Section, much celebrated in the Renaissance, is the proportion in which a line or rectangle is divided so that the ratio of the smaller segment to the larger equals that of the larger to the whole. It is inexpressible as finite numbers, but approximates to 8:13. The proportion was believed to correspond with divine law for the structure of the universe, and to be the secret of visual harmony.

celestial beings who may well be one and the same,[26] and the division into two is obscured by the resumptive 'And chiefly thou' of line 17. Within them, Milton blends diverse syntactic structures. The opening is periodic and left-branching, with the subject and main verb, 'Sing heavenly Muse', attained only after five lines and thirty-eight words. Whereas Tamburlaine's five-line suspension is clearly structured, Milton's opening soon deviates into a complex of subordinate clauses ('whose mortal taste . . . With loss of Eden . . .') and leads us into a vast process, an epitome of fall and redemption, before the syntax begins to take shape. The sense of rhythmic energy is created by the energies demanded of the reader, who must keep the whole complex in play. The longer the passage continues without the resolution of subject and verb, the greater the tension created and the more energy engendered as, reading aloud or as if aloud, we manage or imagine ourselves managing our breath, while keeping ourselves open to the growing possibilities of meaning. As an action and as a poem, everything in *Paradise Lost* is to be intricately interwoven, and the opening lines epitomize how we must be open to the slow growth into unity.

With subject and verb established, Milton proceeds into a loose and right-branching sentence, a typical series of subordinate clauses ('that . . . didst inspire / That shepherd') and sub-clauses ('That shepherd, who first taught . . .'). As Tom Corns has shown, Milton's periods are distinctive in length and sustained vigour through their growth into clause after clause and especially sub-clause after sub-clause.[27] The sentence proceeds, also characteristically, through loops of association: the essence of the first subordinate clause is the inspiring of Moses the shepherd, and logically the place of that inspiration—'the secret top / Or Oreb or of Sinai'—is secondary. But the next clause builds on place—'or if Sion hill / Delight thee more'—and this develops into the ambition of soaring above yet another summit, 'the Aonian mount', the art of ancient paganism. Finally, after line 18 proclaims the preference of the Spirit for a pure heart rather than any outer place of worship, the peaks of inspiration become a state of mind: 'What in me . . . / . . . is low raise and support: / That to the *height* of this great argument . . .'.

Faced with an uncomprehending response to his visual art as obscure, William Blake replied: 'What is Grand is necessarily obscure to Weak men. . . . The wisest of the Ancients consider'd what is not too Explicit as the fittest for Instruction, because it rouzes the faculties to act.'[28] Milton similarly 'rouzes' the faculties and energizes the mind, not through an idiosyncratic symbolism such as Blake's but through the sustained intricacy of his syntax and, in this passage, the density of allusion. We have to maintain an alert, open-minded equilibrium through passages syntactically prolonged and dense with information until the temporary release of a full stop.

---

[26] As John Leonard notes: 'If *chiefly* refers to *thou*, Spirit and Muse are distinct; if to *Instruct* (19), they are identical' (Milton, *Complete Poems* (Harmondsworth, 1998), 713). The latter possibility seems stronger.

[27] Thomas N. Corns, *Milton's Language* (Oxford, 1990), 22–3.

[28] *The Letters of William Blake*, ed. Geoffrey Keynes (1956), 34.

But the sustained prosodic inventiveness is as energizing as the syntax, and where Milton's invocation is most distinct from the even rhythms of Tamburlaine. Although there are more straightforward iambic pentameters (such as lines 2 or 7) than in many of Milton's paragraphs, the reader is never lulled into a comfortable rhythm. Standard deviations bring the verse alive, as in the drawn-out intensities of line 3 and its misery: '*BROUGHT* DEATH in-TO the WORLD, and ALL *OUR* WOE'. Milton also goes to the very limits of deviation and even beyond. At the reversed opening of line 21, 'DOVE-like *SAT'ST* BROOD-ing', there is a marked sense of weight and stasis through the unusual, and apt, presence of an extra, subordinate stress on 'sat'st'—enhanced by the density of the consonants and the careful articulation required. At line 19, 'In-STRUCT me, for THOU KNOW'ST; THOU from the FIRST', there is one of the rare 'three-beat pairings' mentioned above, pivoting on 'know'st' and drawing out the powers of the Spirit through the dual emphasis on 'thou'.

Unpredictability of rhythm challenges the reader from the start: 'Of man's first disobedience, and the fruit . . .'. The second to fourth syllables are all stressed, and this would conventionally lead to the demotion of 'first'. But precisely because this is the first and all-changing sin, the word demands a full stress. While there might in consequence be a stress-initial pairing on 'MANS FIRST diso-', the negative prefix 'dis-' must also be prominent, and we are left with a six-beat line with an abnormal sequence of stresses: 'Of MAN'S FIRST DIS-o-BED-ience AND the FRUIT', a rhythm found nowhere else in the poem. The first moral and spiritual dereliction by man is reflected in a slight but disquieting prosodic dislocation. The paragraph reaches a climactic expansiveness in the three final lines' distinctive and uncharacteristic though not aberrant rhythm. Not only are these lines flowing and simple in syntax and unbroken by any caesura, but there are also successive lines ending in lengthy trisyllables and hence promotions ('AR-gu-MENT' and 'PRO-vid-ENCE'). Promotions ending successive lines are extremely rare in the poem, and their use is almost always expressive. There is no other clear example until iii. 372–3: 'Thee Father first they sung omnipotent, / Immutable, immortal, infinite'. Both passages transform the weak ending normally avoided by Milton into sublime and unpredictable emphases through the echoing rhythm of the key words.[29] In the opening paragraph, the trisyllables also re-echo in the 'justify' of the otherwise monosyllabic final line, a word standing out further because it deprives the line of a full stress on the pivotal fourth syllable. In consequence the reader is invited to make up the stress by pausing or dwelling on 'justify', a theologically rich term at the heart of the poem's theodicy. David Daiches has argued that the previous expression of hope in the paragraph, 'With loss of Eden, till one greater man / Restore us, and regain the blissful seat' (ll. 4–5), is 'deliberately routine'—an impression that must come primarily from the lines' iambic regularity, especially after the agonized density of line 3.[30] In the disposition of the invocation as a whole, the reason for this blandness is now

[29] I pass over occasional instances of exotic words with a subsidiary but firm emphasis on the final syllable, e.g. i. 583–4 ('Montalban/Trebisond'), ii. 516 ('cherubim').

[30] 'The Opening of *Paradise Lost*', in Frank Kermode (ed.), *The Living Milton* (1960), 55–69 at 59.

apparent: an early outburst of confidence would dilute the climactic aspirations of the final lines.

It is the interweaving of the rhythmic life of individual lines such as these with the prolonged spans of syntax that gives such energy to Milton's verse. Their convergence is most telling at the line-turn, marked so often by a weighty final beat. In theory, this brings some risk of monotony and static containment, and this must be the basis of F. R. Leavis's distaste for what he hears, strangely, as 'the routine gesture . . . of the verse', 'the foreseen thud', and the 'automatic ritual'.[31] In practice, any such risk is easily surpassed, even discounting the incessant modulation of cadence within the line: first, continual enjambement keeps the verse moving, with the line-turns marking the norms for variation. Secondly, many line-turns are exploited by inviting a conspicuous emphasis: 'I *thence* / Invoke', 'What in me is *dark* / Illumine'. Thirdly, Milton concentrates syntactic energy at the line-turn by placing so many of his verbs there. Since two of the five beats in a pentameter adjoin the line-turn, there is no lack of precedent for this in blank verse, and there are examples even in the conscientiously inert lines from Gascoigne cited earlier. But the degree of Milton's concentration of syntactic energy around the line-turn is unprecedented: as many as nineteen of the twenty-five verbs in the opening paragraph (as opposed to six of Marlowe's eleven) occur at the end or the beginning of the line, and where a verb does occur mid-line there is almost always another at the turn. Moreover, many of these verbs are charged with vigour: 'how the heavens and earth / *Rose* out of chaos'; 'That with no middle flight intends to *soar* / Above the Aonian mount, while it *pursues* / Things unattempted . . .'. In this way, Milton's verbs push the verse over the turn or along the line. The apt exception proving the rule is the heavily static mid-line phrase: 'sat'st brooding'.

Prosody and syntax are almost inseparable in effect in *Paradise Lost* because they have the same functions while they work within and against orthodox expectations. Both make for continuity: their structures move us alike on towards the end of line, sentence, and paragraph. For example, in the strong momentum of the opening invocation the reader is encouraged onward by the frequent enjambement between the segments of a phrase, and also by the presence of twelve lyric caesuras, plus one after an eighth syllable, as opposed to only six in the conventional positions after the fourth and sixth syllables. Similarly, Milton's gathering of his periods into lengthy compound sentences makes for onward momentum. The invocation, for example, might have been divided at lines 10, 16, 19, and 22 into five rather than two sentences. At iii. 555–87, a modernizing editor like A. W. Verity snips Satan's flight through our universe to land on the sun neatly into five sentences,[32] whereas Milton has it swirl onward in one enormous period. Such a span 'rouzes the faculties to act', summoning mental energy as well as narrative continuity. Moreover, as amply demonstrated above, prosody and syntax make alike for both emphasis and mimesis. That Milton is

---

[31] *Revaluation: Tradition and Development in English Poetry* (Harmondsworth, 1964), 43–4.
[32] *Paradise Lost*, ed. A. W. Verity (Cambridge, 1910). See Mindele Treip, *Milton's Punctuation and Changing English Usage 1582–1676* (1970), 115–17.

very conscious of what he is doing is manifest from the opening lines' holding back of 'Sing heavenly Muse'. Similarly, at ii. 552–5, when fallen angels seek to allay hell in music

> Their song was partial, but the harmony
> (What could it less when spirits immortal sing?)
> Suspended hell, and took with ravishment
> The thronging audience . . .

the suspension of syntax wittily and poignantly echoes the brief suspension of their agonies.[33]

This leads, in conclusion, to a qualification of Eliot's evocative image with which I began. Eliot goes on to speak of Milton's control, but his striking phrase 'almost a physical sensation of a breathless leap' implies a wilful and risky act, whereas the disciplined energies of Milton's verse resemble more the mastery of the virtuoso skier, diver, or gymnast. Blake plays on the ambiguity of 'bound' in asserting in *The Marriage of Heaven and Hell* that 'reason is the bound or outward circumference of energy'.[34] It is Milton's rational control of prosody and syntax that puts the spring of energy into his bounding lines.

[33] A point first made in Thomas Newton's 1749 edition.
[34] *Complete Poems*, 106.

....

CHAPTER 26

EDITING MILTON: THE CASE AGAINST MODERNIZATION

....

STEPHEN B. DOBRANSKI

You know my method. It is founded upon the observance of trifles.
Sherlock Holmes, 'The Boscombe Valley Mystery'

When Eve in *Paradise Lost* returns to Adam after eating the forbidden fruit, she tells her first lie: 'Thee I have misst' (ix. 857).[1] In truth, Eve has been too busy thinking about herself to yearn for Adam's company. Having 'Greedily . . . ingorg'd without restraint', she begins to worship the tree—'Sovran, vertuous, precious'—before her thoughts turn to Adam (ix. 791, 795). Then she does not long to be with him but instead worries about revealing her new-found knowledge: 'Shall I to him make known / As yet my change?' (ix. 817–18).

Eve's sibilant response in this passage, 'Thee I have misst', momentarily echoes the serpent's seductive hiss and helps to dramatize her fall: just as she begins to act like the serpent, she also begins to sound like him. Readers of both the first and second editions of *Paradise Lost* might have also noticed that the archaic spelling 'misst' enhances this subtle resemblance; it punningly associates Eve with the rank, 'rising Mist' that Satan uses to re-enter Paradise (ix. 75). While the specific form 'misst' could merely reflect the vagaries of seventeenth-century orthography, the past tense

---

[1] This and all subsequent references to the text, unless otherwise indicated, are taken from Milton, *Paradise Lost*, 2nd edn. (1674).

of 'miss' is spelled 'miss'd' (vi. 499) and 'missd' (xi. 15) in all other places in both the first and second editions of the epic, and all the other uses of 'mist' in Book 9 specifically describe Satan: he later appears 'wrapt in mist' (l. 158) and resembles a 'black mist low creeping' (l. 180).[2]

Modern editors coming across Eve's lie while preparing a new edition of *Paradise Lost* must decide whether to modernize the spelling 'misst' and, if so, whether, like Eve, to 'make known' any change they render. In this passage, an editor has four basic choices:

1. to retain the original spelling, 'misst', without comment;
2. to retain the original spelling and describe the pun in a note;
3. to modernize the spelling of 'misst' without comment; or,
4. to modernize the spelling and explain in a note what the original spelling implied.

Presumably the solution the editor prefers—and the possibilities are not limited to these four—will depend on the edition's intended audience and the broader theoretical method the editor has adopted for that audience. Whereas a seasoned literary critic, say, might wish to explore the nuances of Milton's seventeenth-century text with minimal editorial assistance (or, in the critic's mind, with minimal editorial interference), other, less experienced readers would likely appreciate the familiarity of a modernized text and might rely on an editor who highlights such possible wordplay. Both categories of readers might also reasonably question whether Milton supervised the spelling of his printed texts and, regardless of who was responsible for 'misst', whether seventeenth-century readers would have been attuned to such orthographical subtleties.

The decision of how to edit even such a minor passage as 'Thee I have misst' thus raises various overlapping issues: the weight that can hang on a single editorial choice, the loss that can occur by smoothing away variant spellings, and the value of establishing an audience-based methodology. Given the evocative implications of this one word, we may be surprised how often recent editors of Milton have summarily dis-missed the significance of retaining such details. In an edition of Milton's works for the Oxford Author Series, Stephen Orgel and Jonathan Goldberg claim that modernizing 'Milton's spelling' merely means 'a loss of quaintness', while in the Longman edition of *Paradise Lost* Alastair Fowler reasons: 'the original spelling cannot be shown to represent Milton's preferences, and so has not been retained . . . even where a distinct pronunciation may conceivably be indicated'.[3]

---

[2] We could also note that elsewhere in the epic Milton consistently associates the noun 'mist' with disease or deception. The narrator calls upon 'Celestial light', for example, to 'Shine inward' and 'all mist from thence / Purge and disperse' (iii. 51–4). See also v. 434–6 and x. 693–5. Only the description of God's creation in *Paradise Lost* sounds innocent, when 'a dewie Mist / Went up and waterd all the ground' (vii. 333–4), but a threat even lurks behind the cherubim's descent with Michael: they take their positions, 'Gliding meteorous, as Ev'ning Mist / Ris'n from a River o're the marish glides, / And gathers ground fast at the Labourers heel / Homeward returning' (xii. 629–32).

[3] *John Milton*, ed. Stephen Orgel and Jonathan Goldberg (Oxford, 1991), p. xxxi; *FPL*, 8. Still other editors announce without explanation, 'Spelling has been modernized'.

In this essay, I examine modern editing practices of Milton's poetry and argue for the need to respect the evidence of his original publications—both the accidentals and the bibliographical context.[4] Surveying the approaches taken by recent editors, I wish to show, most simply, that form matters: the edition in which readers experience Milton's poetry can influence their interpretations. While a market persists for an accessible, modernized version of Milton's works, I am proposing a widely available specialist text, one that does not treat bibliographical evidence as if it existed in a realm distinct from poetic meaning. Admittedly, to duplicate Milton's original publications in all their features would be impractical. But, as the use of 'misst' in *Paradise Lost* suggests, editions that remain sensitive to the appearance of Milton's publications can help readers discover new interpretations. If editing, like politics, requires compromise, then I am calling for a practical middle ground: an edited text but one that acknowledges the material history of Milton's writings.

While the eminent textual critic W. W. Greg once brushed aside the bibliography of *Paradise Lost* as 'child's play' compared to the textual complexities in some of Shakespeare's works, editors of Milton nevertheless face a series of daunting challenges.[5] In most cases, the difficulty arises not because, as with Shakespeare's plays, so many of Milton's poems and pamphlets were printed in radically different versions during the Renaissance. With the possible exception of *A Maske Presented at Ludlow Castle*, we can compare the contemporary editions of Milton's works and confidently ascertain the author's intentions. Certainly it was Milton who revised and expanded the second editions of the *Doctrine and Discipline of Divorce* (1643, 1644), *The Tenure of Kings and Magistrates* (1649, 1650), *Eikonoklastes* (1649, 1650), *Pro Populo Anglicano Defensio* (1651, 1658), and *The Readie and Easie Way to Establish a Free Commonwealth* (February and April 1660). Refusing to accept publication as the final step in the creation of a work, Milton also continued to improve *Paradise Lost* after it was printed. In a reissue of the first edition, he added a short defence of his verse and the arguments that summarize each book; then for the second edition (1674) he restructured his epic according to Virgil's twelve-book model, adding eight lines (viii. 1–3; xii. 1–5), revising one line (viii. 4), and dividing the original Book 8 into Books 7 and 8 and the original Book 10 into Books 11 and 12.[6]

But if the wholesale revisions in these works clearly indicate Milton's changing intentions, the difficulty for an editor rests instead with the multitude of minute

---

[4] W. W. Greg introduced the influential term 'accidentals' to define readings in a text 'affecting mainly its formal presentation'. In contrast, Greg defined 'substantive' readings as 'those . . . that affect the author's meaning or the essence of his expression'. See Greg, 'The Rationale of Copy-Text', *Studies in Bibliography*, 3 (1950–1), 19–36; repr. with some revisions in Greg, *Collected Papers*, ed. J. C. Maxwell (Oxford, 1966), 374–91 at 376.

[5] W. W. Greg, review of Harris Francis Fletcher, *John Milton's Complete Poetical Works Reproduced in Photographic Facsimile*, in *Modern Language Review*, 42 (1947), 133–7 at 134.

[6] Milton also appears to have made at least four other substantive revisions (i. 504–5, v. 636–41, xi. 485, 551), while another approximately thirty-seven, comparatively minor changes made between the first and second edition—'founded' versus 'found out' (i. 703), for example, or 'where' versus 'were' (ii. 282)—may or may not have been authorial. For a discussion of the individual differences between the two editions, see R. G. Moyles, *The Text of* Paradise Lost: *A Study in Editorial Procedure* (Toronto, 1985), 21–8.

variations in Milton's surviving texts and the long-standing belief that he oversaw his texts' minor details. Perhaps because Milton wrote so often about himself, or because in *Areopagitica* he specifically addresses the printing trade, critics and editors have traditionally assumed that Milton supervised the publication of his works and strove to control all aspects, from the subtlest poetic effects to the layout of his title pages. Even the theoretically sophisticated editors Orgel and Goldberg overlook the social process of material production and assert that the author's 1645 *Poems* represents 'Milton as he presented himself'.[7] That many of Milton's shorter poems survive in both print and manuscript has also encouraged this misapprehension: whereas Shakespeare's plays grew out of the protean world of the theatre, Milton's works are associated with the quiet and solitude of the poet's study. We consequently excuse the inconsistencies in Shakespeare's plays because their author was less invested in print publication, but we try to puzzle out what Milton may have intended with each variant.[8] Any poet capable of writing such exquisite and diverse works as the Nativity Ode, 'Lycidas', *Paradise Lost, Paradise Regain'd*, and *Samson Agonistes*—surely, we suppose, he could do anything. Milton must have chosen 'misst'; just as he must have had a good reason in 'Lycidas' for writing 'Comes the blind *Fury*' (l. 75) when the passage would seem to require 'Comes the blind *Fate*'; just as it must have been Milton who insisted on spelling 'ye' as 'yee', and 'we' as 'wee' in some places in *Paradise Lost*.[9]

The notion of Milton's exacting control over his works' printing is a fiction, however. In the case of *Paradise Lost* and Eve's lie, 'Thee I have misst', the way to edit and/or annotate such passages would typically be decided by attempting to discern the author's final intentions: how did Milton wish the line to appear? But while textual critics such as Helen Darbishire and B. A. Wright have tried to portray Milton as preternaturally vigilant—going so far as to devise a complex system of punctuation and orthography that Milton purportedly used to enhance pronunciation and metre—the fact is that we still cannot distinguish Milton's spelling, italics, punctuation, and capitalization from his compositors' preferences.[10] Milton did use some forms more than others, and, as Mindele Treip has shown, much of the punctuation in the surviving manuscript of *Paradise Lost*, Book 1, also seems distinctively authorial.[11] But we have insufficient evidence, as has been repeatedly shown, to support the notion that Milton tried to control the minor variants in his printed works or that he wished to oversee his books' design or layout.[12]

---

[7] *John Milton*, ed. Orgel and Goldberg, p. xxxi.

[8] The long-standing belief that Shakespeare wrote only for the stage and thus ignored the readership of his printed works has been challenged by Lukas Erne, *Shakespeare as Literary Dramatist* (Cambridge, 2003).

[9] All quotations of Milton's shorter poetry, unless otherwise indicated, are taken from *Poems of Mr. John Milton, both English and Latin, Compos'd at Several Times* (1645).

[10] *The Poetical Works of John Milton*, ed. Helen Darbishire, 2 vols. (Oxford, 1952–5), i, pp. ix–xxxxv; *Milton: Poems*, ed. B. A. Wright (London, 1956).

[11] Mindele Treip, *Milton's Punctuation and Changing English Usage 1582–1676* (1970), 54–64.

[12] See e.g. Robert Adams, *Ikon: John Milton and the Modern Critics* (Ithaca, N.Y., 1955), 60–111; Moyles, *The Text of* Paradise Lost, 18–29; and John Creaser, 'Editorial Problems in Milton', *Review of English*

In general, decisions about such details were the province of the printing house during the seventeenth century. Compositors would attempt to follow an author's manuscript copy, but their work could be influenced by personal preferences, honest mistakes, and house styles. A compositor might also alter a writer's words based on the availability of type or the need to fill out or 'justify' a line, perhaps adding a final 'e' to some words (so as to lengthen the line), or creating abbreviations or contractions (so as to shorten the line). In *Mechanick Exercises of the Whole Art of Printing* (1683–4), Joseph Moxon describes how a seventeenth-century compositor '*is strictly to follow his* Copy' but also may incorporate changes according to '*a Custom, which among them is look'd upon as a task and duty incumbent on the* Compositer, *viz. to discern and amend the bad* Spelling *and* Pointing *of his* Copy, *if it be English*'.[13] What constituted '*bad* Spelling *and* Pointing' at a time when no widely accepted standards yet existed was evidently left to the compositor's discretion. Moxon goes on to explain that each compositor should

> be a good English Schollar at least; and that he know the present traditional Spelling of all English Words, and that he have so much Sence and Reason, as to Point his Sentences properly: when to begin a Word with a Capital Letter, when (to render the Sence of the Author more intelligent to the Reader) to Set some Words or Sentences in Italick or English Letters, &c. (Moxon, *Mechanick Exercises*, 193)

Nothing in Milton's writings suggests that he and his books' creators deviated from such a collaborative arrangement.[14] Comparing the surviving manuscript of *Paradise Lost*, Book 1, with the same text in the first printed edition of 1667 reveals more than 1,000 changes in spelling and roughly 133 changes in punctuation—all apparently attempts by members of the printing house to normalize, albeit inconsistently, Milton's manuscript.[15] None of these changes indicates authorial supervision. Given, too, that Milton had gone blind by 1652 and would have had to rely on amanuenses to compose his works and, if he wished, on agents to supervise the publication, the notion that Milton insisted on every comma, case change, or variant spelling becomes even less plausible.

Which does not mean that contemporary printers ignored the minor variants in Milton's manuscripts. If we return to the spelling of 'misst' in *Paradise Lost*, Milton's amanuenses and compositors could have followed his specific preference in this and other instances, even while they accepted responsibility for many of the publication's minor details. As John Shawcross has shown, for example, the compositors of

Studies, 34 (1983), 279–303 and 35 (1984), 45–60. In this paragraph and the preceding one, I am drawing on arguments from Stephen B. Dobranski, *Milton, Authorship, and the Book Trade* (Cambridge, 1999).

[13] Joseph Moxon, *Mechanick Exercises of the Whole Art of Printing (1683–4)*, ed. Herbert Davies and Harry Carter, 2nd edn. (1962), 192.

[14] For Milton's collaborative practices of authorship, see Dobranski, *Milton, Authorship, and the Book Trade*.

[15] See *The Manuscript of Milton's* Paradise Lost, *Book I*, ed. Helen Darbishire (Oxford, 1931), pp. xxiii–xxxvii; and Moyles, *The Text of* Paradise Lost, 80–116. I arrived at the latter number from Treip, *Milton's Punctuation*, 150–2.

Paradise Lost in both 1667 and 1674 mostly respected Milton's idiosyncratic spelling of 'their' as 'thir', and the creators of Milton's 1645 *Poems* regularly followed the poet's preference of dropping the final 'e' in 'som', 'com', and 'welcom'.[16] Moreover, that the list of errata added to the first edition of *Paradise Lost* asks readers to repair, for example, 'we' to 'wee' suggests that the press's corrector tried to respect Milton's manuscript in even some of its smallest details.[17] While Helen Darbishire may have erred in using this specific emendation to make a larger case that Milton intended 'ee' to signify the emphatic, stressed form of some pronouns, the presence of this apparently inconsequential change reveals that at least someone in Samuel Simmons's printing house thought such features valuable (*Poetical Works of John Milton*, i. xxxiii).

We should also not assume that Milton entirely ignored his works' spelling and punctuation. According to Milton's nephew, Edward Phillips, the blind author cared about at least some of his manuscripts' accidentals. Phillips reports that during the composition of *Paradise Lost*: 'I had the perusal of it from the very beginning; for some years, as I went from time to time, to Visit him, in a Parcel of Ten, Twenty, or Thirty Verses at a Time, which being Written by whatever hand came next, might possibly want Correction as to the Orthography and Pointing' (Darbishire, 73). While Phillips's use of 'Correction' could refer to the poet's efforts to remove only the most egregious blunders from a rough copy, this account still suggests that before Milton handed over his manuscript to the printer he understood spelling and punctuation as having a correct form—and he took pains to repair these details. Milton himself in one of his letters, dated 15 August 1666, also suggests that he cared about his works' appearance: he tells Peter Heimbach, 'if you find anything incorrectly written or without punctuation here, . . . impute that to the boy who has taken it down from my dictation, and who is utterly ignorant of Latin, so that I was forced, while dictating, not without misery, to spell out the letters of the words one by one' (*CW*, xii. 115). If Milton troubled himself with such small matters in a personal letter, we might expect him to have overseen comparable details before he went blind in, for example, the first collected edition of his poetry.

But exactly how many of Milton's preferred forms seeped into his published texts we do not know—a fact that recent editors have used to justify their decision to modernize his writings. Since his publications' spelling, italics, punctuation, and capitalization cannot be established as definitively authorial, they are not retained. Why should modern editors and their readers bother with such minutiae when

---

[16] John T. Shawcross, 'One Aspect of Milton's Spelling: Idle Final "E"', *Publications of the Modern Language Association*, 78 (1963), 501–10, and Shawcross, 'Orthography and the Text of *Paradise Lost*', in *Language and Style in Milton*, ed. Ronald David Emma and John T. Shawcross (New York, 1967), 120–53.

[17] The brief errata list comprises a total of thirteen corrections, mostly misspellings (for example, 'lost' is corrected to 'last') and transpositions (for example, 'and Band' is corrected to 'Band and'). The list concludes with the general admonition: 'Other literal faults the Reader of himself may Correct.' We should also note that this revised spelling of 'wee' was not, for whatever reason, preserved in the 1674 text.

Milton himself, as R. G. Moyles concludes, took only a 'casual' interest in supervising the accidentals in his greatest work, *Paradise Lost*.[18] And the operative word is 'bother': modernizing editors claim that the texts' original features are not only meaningless but also distracting. To preserve a text's original appearance would 'dim' Milton's works, as John Creaser puts it, in 'a haze of quaintness'.[19]

I would suggest, however, that the uncertainty surrounding Milton's contemporary texts may itself be significant. If the traditional motive for reproducing the original spelling, italics, punctuation, and capitalization is that these elements more closely express an author's intentions, the uncertain authority of Milton's accidentals could support the argument for less, not more, editorial intervention. Given that Milton seems to have cared about the spelling and punctuation in his surviving manuscripts; given that we can also establish some of the spellings in Milton's printed texts as his preferred forms; and given that compositors would have had little reason to change a manuscript's pointing—all these facts should encourage readers to hesitate before accepting a generalized rule for modernizing the physical appearance of Milton's publications. Even within the same work, Milton may have insisted on some of the accidentals and not worried about others; perhaps apparently minor details such as 'misst' also reveal his influence. We know that Milton sometimes incorporated slight adjustments in his poems, revising, for example, two out of 244 lines in 'On the Morning of Christ's Nativity' between 1645 and 1673, and during the same period fine-tuning four out of more than 1,020 lines in *A Maske Presented at Ludlow Castle*. He also cared enough about the appearance of his publications to compose a Greek epigraph in 1645 when William Marshall's frontispiece portrait did not meet his approval, and, according to the errata list in Milton's 1673 *Poems*, the author took an interest in the book's organization: readers are asked to imagine that 'At a Vacation Exercise' appears earlier in the collection, between 'On the Death of a Fair Infant' and 'The Passion'—instead of where it actually is printed, after 'Ad Pyrrham Ode V' and before 'On the New Forcers of Conscience under the Long Parliament'.[20]

Perhaps, then, other details in Milton's original publications that modernizing editors obscure or omit also deserve attention. Milton, for example, may have rearranged the line in Sonnet VIII from 'If *ever* deed of honour did thee please' in 1645 (l. 3) to 'If deed of honour did thee *ever* please' in 1673 (my emphasis). Or, perhaps, for the second edition of his *Poems* Milton repaired 'At a Solemn Musick' by replacing 'That undisturbed Song of pure *content*' (l. 6) with the reading from the three copies in the Trinity Manuscript, 'That undisturbed Song of pure *concent*' (my emphasis). Milton also may have purposefully written in *Paradise Lost*, 'Let th'Earth bring forth Fowle living in her kinde, / Cattel and Creeping things, and Beast of the Earth, / Each in their kinde' (vii. 451–3). While modern editors in this latter passage consistently

---

[18] Moyles, *The Text of* Paradise Lost, 28.

[19] Creaser, 'Editorial Problems in Milton', 303.

[20] Milton, *Poems, &c. upon Several Occasions. By Mr. John Milton: Both English and Latin, &c. Composed at Several Times* (1673), sig. ᵖA4ᵛ.

follow Richard Bentley's emendation and replace 'Fowle' with 'soul', Milton could have used 'Fowle', an obsolete form of 'foal' to signify a young quadruped.[21]

Modern readers of Milton should at least have the opportunity to make these types of decisions and peruse the evidence that modernizing editors often silently consult. Specialist readers in particular, rather than ceding their authority to an editor, can make new discoveries by determining for themselves whether a specific spelling, case change, or punctuation appears meaningful. Roy Flannagan has argued for an old-spelling edition in terms of preserving the 'texture' of Milton's original publications. Flannagan acknowledges that such an edition may initially look unfamiliar, but, he asserts, 'Milton's texts should be distanced from his modern readers, because they are distanced by time and by the evolution and the fluidity of the English language.'[22] I would emphasize that modernizing also obscures puns, blunts rhymes, and gives undue authority to the editor in determining whether an ambiguous passage needs correcting.[23] It divorces us, more generally, from an early modern reader's experience by falsely suggesting that a text's physical appearance has no effect on its poetic meaning.

In an attempt to address these concerns and bring modern readers closer to an author's original writings, new theories and practices of editing have arisen in recent years that accommodate textual multiplicity. The dominant method of scholarly editing has traditionally been to remove outside influences from a literary work and produce a clean, stable text. These editions are called 'eclectic' or 'intentionalist' because editors piece together features from all of a work's surviving versions (also called 'witnesses') so as to fulfil what, the editor believes, the author would have ideally wanted, without the contaminating contributions of acquaintances and amanuenses, or printers and publishers. As G. Thomas Tanselle explains, the result-ing edition 'may not correspond with any text that ever existed in tangible form, because the goal is what once existed in the author's mind'.[24]

Other, more recent editorial practices, fuelled by the play of meaning associated with post-structuralism and the pliable forms offered by new literacy technologies, begin with the premiss that all literary works are necessarily material and all authors engage in a collaborative process of production.[25] Whereas the intentionalist editor tries to distil and clarify a series of texts so as to arrive at the author's original ideas, the revisionist critic emphasizes textual variance and acknowledges that readers often do judge a book by its cover—as well as by its physical design, layout, and typogra-phy. Removing these original elements, collectively called a work's 'bibliographical context', would deny modern readers of essential information that may or may not have been dictated by the writer but that was produced out of a material process in

---

[21] The text reads 'Fowle' in 1667 and 'Foul' in 1674; I am quoting these lines from Milton, *Paradise Lost* (1667), sig. Aa4ʳ. See also *Milton's* Paradise Lost: *A New Edition*, ed. Richard Bentley (1732; New York, 1974), 234. Adams first made this point in *Ikon: John Milton and the Modern Critics*, 95.

[22] *The Riverside Milton*, ed. Roy Flannagan (Boston, 1998), pp. vii, viii.

[23] I am echoing here both Philip Gaskell and John T. Shawcross. See Gaskell, *From Writer to Reader* (Oxford, 1978), 8; and Shawcross, preface, *Riverside Milton*, p. xxvii.

[24] G. Thomas Tanselle, *A Rationale of Textual Criticism* (Philadelphia, 1989), 90.

[25] See e.g. Jerome J. McGann, *A Critique of Modern Textual Criticism* (Chicago, 1983).

which the writer participated. Given that all of a text's material features impart meaning, the editor accepts that a writer's acquaintances do not contaminate but instead help to create the final product.

Both of these approaches have merit for today's readers of Milton. Because Milton did not exclusively control the appearance of his printed texts, editors have licence to assemble forthright modernized editions. Moreover, because some of the poet's accepted preferences—spelling 'thir' for 'their', say, or 'som', 'com', and 'welcom' without the final 'e'—do not affect his works' metre or meaning, an editor could argue that retaining these features adds little for a modern audience. John Creaser, for example, concludes from his study of modern editing practices that reproducing Milton's preferred forms—Creaser calls them 'hallowed Miltonisms'—diminishes the poet's 'immediacy' and 'distracts attention from meaning to variant spellings (and sometimes variant pronunciations) . . . which only the passage of time has made at all remarkable'.[26] According to this way of thinking, modernizing Milton's texts more closely approximates the experience of contemporary readers, who would not have been concerned about the works' minor variants. In the case of Eve's lie, 'Thee I have misst' (ix. 857), both the first and second editions of *Paradise Lost* actually include the '∫' in 'mi∫st', one of various typographical conventions from the seventeenth century that would almost certainly distance modern readers without advancing their understanding. All modern editors accordingly update ∫ to s, modernize u to v, and ignore all ligatures.

But in advocating this more thorough editorial approach to Milton's works, editors have ignored or downplayed the implications of his texts' other material details. If we linger on Creaser's argument for a moment, he asserts that 'for the sake of rhythm' modernizing editors can occasionally retain an original feature or draw attention to it in a note: 'The apparent clumsiness is in fact an advantage, because it enables the modernizing editor to pick out the puns, rhymes, and ambiguities which seem definitely worth attention.'[27] Creaser is, of course, right that a modernizing editor can make such decisions—but, I would suggest, specialist readers may not wish to give over this authority to an editor. Readers of *Paradise Lost* can choose whether to consult an editor's commentary to understand, for example, the historical significance of '*Siloa*'s Brook' (i. 11) or the '*Punic* Coast' (v. 340). But the kind of editing that Creaser advocates seems un-Miltonic in its denial of our interpretative free will. Readers can no longer determine for themselves which lines contain puns and ambiguities; the editor, not the reader, has already decided what is 'definitely worth attention'.

Modernizing editors have also not been scrupulously consistent. While basing their decision to modernize Milton's texts on an intentionalist argument—that is, Milton did not supervise his works' printing, so his works may be modernized—editors nevertheless include in their editions of *Paradise Lost* both the defence of the verse and the arguments that summarize each book. Milton, however, did not

---

[26] 'Editorial Problems in Milton', 303.
[27] Ibid. 300–1.

'intend' either of these features. As the printer/publisher Samuel Simmons explains in a reissue of the first edition: '*Courteous Reader*, There was no Argument at first intended to the Book, but for the satisfaction of many that have desired it, I have procur'd it, and withall a reason of that which stumbled many others, why the Poem Rimes not. *S. Simmons*'.[28] According to this announcement, Simmons and the readers who 'stumbled' through the first issue of *Paradise Lost* helped to create a text different than the one Milton 'first intended'. Should an intentionalist editor then reproduce these features in a modern edition?

For G. Thomas Tanselle, the answer is no. As the current and most eloquent spokesperson for intentionalist editing, Tanselle argues that editors should pursue 'the minds in which works originate', and for Tanselle the minds that matter belong to individual writers, not readers or members of the book trade.[29] Editors thus ought not accept any revisions that an author incorporates at another person's prompting—even when the author willingly undertakes such changes and regardless of whether the changes prove beneficial. Tanselle classifies this type of revision as authorial 'acquiescence', which he distinguishes from the editor's ultimate goal: mining texts for an author's Platonic 'intentions'.[30]

My point is not that I agree with Tanselle's distinction, nor that we should fault editors who include Milton's revisions in modern editions of *Paradise Lost*. On the contrary, editors should respect the fact that Milton followed Simmons's advice. These addenda suggest that Milton willingly modified his works according to readers' responses and that he intended to share responsibility for the creation of his works. The value of Tanselle's theory is that it points up the larger problem confronting Milton's editors: Milton's literary works cannot always be seamlessly extracted from his material texts, and his individual will cannot always be isolated from his works' collaborative genesis.

We do not know, for example, who composed the explanatory tags that accompany some of Milton's poems in his 1645 collection. The epigraph at the conclusion of 'The Passion' explains: '*This subject the Author finding to be above the yeers he had, when he wrote it, and nothing satisfi'd with what was begun, left it unfinisht*'; in like manner, the headnote added to 'Lycidas' in 1645 provides valuable contextual information: it identifies 'Lycidas' as a monody, highlights the critique of the clergy, and describes the poem's original occasion.[31] While Milton must have supplied all of

---

[28] *Paradise Lost* (1667), sig. ᵖA2ʳ. The arguments were first printed in a group at the beginning of *Paradise Lost*, like an annotated table of contents, and for the second edition were moved to their current position at the start of each of the epic's respective books.

[29] Tanselle, *A Rationale of Textual Criticism*, 75.

[30] Ibid. 84. Tanselle develops this argument in 'The Editorial Problem of Final Authorial Intention', *Studies in Bibliography*, 29 (1976), 167–211, esp. 193–4.

[31] *Poems of Mr. John Milton*, sigs. B2ʳ, D5ʳ. While the copy of 'Lycidas' in the Trinity Manuscript includes part of the 1645 headnote, it has been hastily added and could have been inserted after the *Poems* went to press. The manuscript note reads 'Novemb: 1637. In this Monodie the author bewails a lerned freind unfortunatly drownd in his passage from Chester on the Irish seas 1637'. See *John Milton's Poetical Works Reproduced in Photographic Facsimile*, ed. Harris Francis Fletcher, 4 vols. (Urbana, Ill., 1943), i. 436–7.

these details to the book's publisher, Humphrey Moseley, the collection's tags refer to the author in the third person, which raises the possibility that Moseley or another member of the printing house requested and/or composed these statements. By comparison, some of the explanatory tags printed in Milton's 1673 *Poems* appear more personal and are written in the first person.[32] But whereas modern editions typically include only the longer notes associated with 'The Passion' and 'Lycidas' from 1645, I would propose that all of the explanatory tags from his 1645 and 1673 collections represent crucial parts of Milton's texts. Regardless of their uncertain provenance, these tags belong in modern editions because they reflect the collaborative origins of Milton's works and potentially bear on how we understand what his poems mean.

Or, to take another example: that Milton's *Paradise Regain'd* and *Samson Agonistes* were published together and in that order in 1671 seems to have originated with Milton.[33] The author also presumably chose the quotation from Aristotle's *Poetics* on *Samson*'s title page, and he may have deliberately requested that the ten extra lines from *Samson* be printed at the end of the book with detailed directions for readers to insert them.[34] Yet no modern edition that I have examined retains all these features from the 1671 text. The Columbia edition of Milton's works goes so far as to split the two poems into separate volumes: *Samson* is incorporated with Milton's shorter poems, and *Paradise Regain'd* is joined with *Paradise Lost*.[35] Again, I would suggest that a modern text should respect the original bibliographical context of Milton's works so that readers can experience how these material details bear on the poems' individual meanings and intertextual relationship. If modern editions of *Paradise Lost* include the arguments and the defence of verse—elements that depended on a printer's prompting—then surely these other bibliographical details deserve our scrutiny.

---

[32] The translations of Psalms 80–8, for example, begin with a headnote that is signed by the author, 'April. 1648. J. M.' (sig. I8ʳ), and the notes accompanying 'Ad Joannem Rousium' represent the first time in the two editions that Milton speaks directly to readers about his poetic intentions. To explain the poem's form and context, he uses the first person plural, describing how 'we have divided' the strophes and antistrophes ('secuimus', sig. R2ᵛ) and referring to 'others of our books in the public library' ('cum aliis nostris in Bibliotheca publica', sig. Q8ᵛ).

[33] On the poems' interrelationship, see e.g. Balachandra Rajan, ' "To Which Is Added *Samson Agonistes*—" ', in *The Prison and the Pinnacle*, ed. Balachandra Rajan (Toronto, 1973), 82–110; Mary Ann Radzinowicz, *Toward* Samson Agonistes: *The Growth of Milton's Mind* (Princeton, 1978), 227–60; John T. Shawcross, Paradise Regain'd: *Worthy T'Have Not Remain'd So Long Unsung* (Pittsburgh, Pa., 1988), 102–15, and Joseph Wittreich, *Interpreting* Samson Agonistes (Princeton, 1986), 329–85.

[34] For the evidence of Milton's role in the book's creation and the interpretive implications of the volume's material design, see Stephen B. Dobranski, *Readers and Authorship in Early Modern England* (Cambridge, 2005), 183–209.

[35] In *CW*, *Samson Agonistes* is printed in pt. II of vol. i, and *Paradise Regain'd* is printed in pt. II of vol. ii. While the separate publication of *Samson Agonistes* was a phenomenon of the late 18th c., a Dublin edition of 1724 first paired *Paradise Lost . . . Together with Paradise Regain'd* in two volumes that could be sold separately. See K. A. Coleridge, *A Descriptive Catalogue of the Milton Collection in the Alexander Turnbull Library, Wellington, New Zealand* (Oxford, 1980), 224–5.

No doubt we can attribute some of these inconsistencies in modernized editions to the market pressures of academic publishing. Today's editors resemble Milton in that they, too, do not have complete control over their works, and they must create their editions within their own collaborative circumstances. Still, one wishes that some recent editions of Milton's poems were conceived with a more precise sense of audience. The superb scholarly annotations and introductory essays included in modern editions speak most forcefully to specialized readers, but the modernized versions of Milton's poetry that these books contain often seem more suitable for students.

To illustrate more fully the consequences of modernization, I have copied below two versions of the proem from *Paradise Lost*, Book 1, one of the epic's best-known passages. On the left appears a transcription from the second edition of 1674; on the right, a recent modernized version of these same lines as edited by David Scott Kastan:[36]

Of Mans First Disobedience, and the Fruit	Of man's first disobedience and the fruit
Of that Forbidden Tree, whose mortal tast	Of that forbidden tree, whose mortal taste
Brought Death into the World, and all our woe,	Brought death into the world and all our woe,
With loss of *Eden*, till one greater Man	With loss of Eden, till one greater man
Restore us, and regain the blissful Seat,	Restore us and regain the blissful seat, 5
Sing Heav'nly Muse, that on the secret top	Sing heavenly muse, that on the secret top
Of *Oreb*, or of *Sinai*, didst inspire	Of Oreb, or of Sinai, didst inspire
That Shepherd, who first taught the chosen Seed,	That shepherd who first taught the chosen seed,
In the Beginning how the Heav'ns and Earth	In the beginning how the heavens and earth
Rose out of *Chaos*: Or if *Sion* Hill	Rose out of chaos; or if Sion hill 10
Delight thee more, and *Siloa's* Brook that flow'd	Delight thee more, and Siloa's brook that flowed
Fast by the Oracle of God; I thence	Fast by the oracle of God, I thence
Invoke thy aid to my adventrous Song,	Invoke thy aid to my adventurous song,
That with no middle flight intends to soar	That with no middle flight intends to soar
Above th' *Aonian* Mount, while it pursues	Above the Aonian mount while it pursues 15
Things unattempted yet in Prose or Rhime.	Things unattempted yet in prose or rhyme.
And chiefly Thou, O Spirit, that dost prefer	And chiefly thou, O spirit, that dost prefer
Before all Temples th' upright heart and pure,	Before all temples the upright heart and pure,
Instruct me, for Thou know'st; Thou from the first	Instruct me, for thou know'st; thou from the first
Wast present, and with mighty wings outspread	Wast present, and, with mighty wings outspread, 20
Dove-like satst brooding on the vast Abyss	Dove-like sat'st brooding on the vast abyss
And mad'st it pregnant: What in me is dark	And mad'st it pregnant. What in me is dark
Illumin, what is low raise and support;	Illumine, what is low raise and support,
That to the highth of this great Argument	That to the height of this great argument
I may assert Eternal Providence,	I may assert eternal providence 25
And justifie the wayes of God to men.	And justify the ways of God to men.

---

[36] *Paradise Lost*, ed. David Scott Kastan (Indianapolis, Ind., 2005), 6–8. All subsequent quotations from this text are cited parenthetically by page number.

At first glance, comparing these two versions may suggest that a modern edition changes the letters but not the spirit of Milton's poetry. Most obviously, Kastan has modernized the original spelling, so that in the final line, for example, 'justifie' becomes 'justify', and 'wayes' becomes 'ways'. He has also regularized the use of italics and upper-case letters according to modern standards; in the seventeenth century, by comparison, all substantives were usually capitalized, and proper nouns were commonly printed with italic type. Moreover, in treating Milton's use of elision, Kastan has regularized forms that are inconsistently abbreviated, such as 'Heav'ns' / 'heavens' (l. 9), and he has spelled out other expressions, so that 'th' upright heart' becomes 'the upright heart' (l. 18).

Kastan to his credit announces at the start of his edition that he has based his text of Milton's epic on what he calls Merritt Hughes's 'classic edition' (p. iii), and he also notes that he has undertaken a 'more thoroughgoing' modernization than Hughes attempted (p. lxvii). Whereas most modernizing editors, for example, approach the punctuation in Milton's original texts more cautiously than his other accidentals, Kastan has also tried to improve *Paradise Lost*'s pointing. He believes that the original punctuation would 'inevitably make the meaning of the poem less rather than more clear' (p. lxxiv), and he suggests that previous editors have 'rationalized' their conservative approach to Milton's pointing because they lacked initiative: 'My (no longer) secret sense has been that its retention is more pragmatic than principled: modernization of the punctuation of Milton's meandering sentences and verse paragraphs is extremely difficult' (p. lxxiii).

The problem with Kastan's more rigorous editorial policy lies in its disruption of the epic's tone and rhythm. In the proem to Book 1, for example, the addition of an extra syllable in 'adventurous' (l. 13) spoils the line's regular, iambic metre, and the removal of four rhetorical commas so close together (ll. 3, 5, 8) needlessly mars the passage's more deliberate, almost ruminative pacing. Even the omission of upper-case letters—regardless of whether Milton himself chose these forms—diminishes the effect of the proem's final lines: the cumulative force of the successive capitalized terms, 'Argument', 'Eternal Providence', and 'God', is softened in the text's modernized version.

More important, such efforts to modernize Milton's works inevitably affect the meaning. Kastan, for example, removes two commas, after 'shepherd' and 'seed'. Once again, the 1674 text appears on the left, and Kastan's version appears on the right:

Sing Heav'nly Muse, that on the secret top	Sing heavenly muse, that on the secret top 6
Of *Oreb*, or of *Sinai*, didst inspire	Of Oreb, or of Sinai, didst inspire
That Shepherd, who first taught the chosen Seed,	That shepherd who first taught the chosen seed
In the Beginning how the Heav'ns and Earth	In the beginning how the heavens and earth
Rose out of *Chaos*	Rose out of chaos 10

While such a slight change may initially seem inconsequential, the modernized text turns a restrictive into a non-restrictive clause: 'who first taught the chosen seed' now modifies only 'shepherd', but in the 1674 text it could simultaneously modify the 'Heav'nly Muse'. Removing the commas also closes off the fleeting possibility that 'In the beginning' modifies when the muse 'didst inspire / That shepherd', whereas in the modernized text it only describes what 'That shepherd' told 'the chosen seed'. Perhaps Milton intended the momentary temporal conflation to reinforce the muse's comprehensiveness.

Kastan has also added a comma after 'outspread' (l. 20), another apparently minor adjustment:

And chiefly Thou, O Spirit, that dost prefer	And chiefly thou, O spirit, that dost prefer
Before all Temples th' upright heart and pure,	Before all temples the upright heart and pure,
Instruct me, for Thou know'st; Thou from the first	Instruct me, for thou know'st; thou from the first
Wast present, and with mighty wings outspread	Wast present, and, with mighty wings outspread, 20
Dove-like satst brooding on the vast Abyss	Dove-like sat'st brooding on the vast abyss
And mad'st it pregnant: What in me is dark	And mad'st it pregnant. What in me is dark
Illumin, what is low raise and support;	Illumine, what is low raise and support,
That to the highth of this great Argument	That to the height of this great argument
I may assert Eternal Providence,	I may assert eternal providence, 25
And justifie the wayes of God to men.	And justify the ways of God to men.

But the insertion of this comma again changes the poem's meaning; it insists that 'Dove-like' modifies how the spirit 'satst', whereas in the original text the absence of a comma implied both that the spirit 'Dove-like sat'st' and that the spirit's wings were 'out-spread / Dove-like'. Nor does Kastan mention that some copies of the second edition of *Paradise Lost* read, as above, 'And chiefly Thou, O Spirit', but other copies agree with the manuscript and first edition in omitting the comma between 'Thou' and 'O'. The presence of this slight pause, isolating the first part of the line, may encourage readers to see 'chiefly' as an adjective modifying 'Thou', but its absence makes more likely that 'chiefly' is an adverb modifying 'Instruct' (l. 19). While Kastan acknowledges in a footnote the uncertainty of what this word modifies, the evidence of the original texts more clearly allows for both possibilities and enables readers to make their own interpretative choices.

My point in all these instances is not that I disagree with Kastan's readings: an excellent scholar, he has much to offer readers of Milton's epic. Instead, I wish to illustrate how modernizing can impose such readings onto a work before readers can formulate their own ideas. I would add that the efforts of modernizing editors may not be strictly necessary: I have yet to teach a student who has been confused by the spelling, italics, punctuation, or capitalization in Milton's original texts. Students struggle with Milton's syntax and allusions, and they need time to adjust to early modern typographic conventions such as using 'ſ' to signify 's'. But I am not convinced that a modern editor should sacrifice fidelity to Milton's original publications for the sake of consistency or in an effort to aid even beginning readers of Milton. Especially in a semester-long course on Milton, or when reading *Paradise Lost* in its entirety, students need relatively little help before they become acclimated to the appearance of Milton's writings. Today's students need even less assistance in 'reading' the other material aspects of Milton's works, such as the title pages and frontispiece portraits. Already steeped in visual culture, students not only can gain new insights from perusing the material parts of Milton's texts but also can become more enthusiastic about early modern poetry by examining these more familiar features.

Whereas Stanley Fish has recently argued that 'there is no . . . relationship' between 'the details of composition and publication . . . and what the published product means',[37] I am instead proposing that they are dynamically interdependent. Certainly Fish is right to establish a sharp distinction between a work's material form and its literary content—so long as we accept his narrow definition of what 'composition and publication' entail: 'How long did it take to write? To whom were various drafts shown? What were Milton's negotiations with his printer?'[38] But Fish here asks all the wrong questions. Readers should instead begin by examining what exactly constitutes *Paradise Lost*—the ten-book epic that Milton published in 1667, or the twelve-book epic from 1674? Or, are there two *Paradise Lost*s? Does the work also comprise the title page that identifies it as a 'poem' instead of an 'epic'? And should modern readers read the features that were added to the second edition: the frontispiece portrait and the introductory encomiastic poems by the court physician Samuel Barrow and Milton's protégé, Andrew Marvell? The editors of the *Norton Anthology of English Literature*, for example, claim to present 'John Milton's *Paradise Lost* . . . in its entirety', but their edition then omits all these introductory materials, including Milton's prose arguments summarizing each book.[39] Evidently, in these editors' minds, the author's own summaries do not qualify as part of the work. By comparison, Kastan in his edition includes Milton's arguments, the defence of the verse, the original title page, and the introductory encomiastic poems by Barrow and Marvell. He omits, however, the second edition's frontispiece portrait—and then inserts, without explanation, Simmons's note about the addition of the arguments, which was only included in some copies of a reissue of the first edition.

These inconsistencies in modern editorial practices demonstrate once again the need for a specialist text that accepts the collaborative genesis of Milton's works and respects his works' material history. Although we may be tempted, like Fish, to draw a firm, reassuring line between the material form and poetic meaning of Milton's works, an examination of his original publications reveals a productively more complex relationship. Readers can thus decide for themselves, for example, whether 'misst' is a pun in *Paradise Lost*, or whether the textual differences matter between

---

[37] Stanley Fish, 'Why Milton Matters', *Milton Studies*, 44 (2005), 1–12 at 7.

[38] Ibid.

[39] *The Norton Anthology of English Literature*, 8th edn., vol. B, ed. Stephen Greenblatt (New York, 2005), p. xxviii. The editors include the argument for Book 1, apparently as an example of what they have otherwise omitted (pp. 1831–2).

Milton's *A Maske* as copied in the Trinity and Bridgewater manuscripts and as printed in 1637, 1645, or 1673. Fish himself in *How Milton Works* might have bolstered his argument for the alleged pun of 'raised'/'razed' in *Paradise Lost* had he attended to the material form of Milton's epic and noticed that a nearby passage invites precisely this wordplay: the surviving manuscript reads 'raz'd' but was changed to 'ras'd' when the poem was published (i. 362).[40]

The challenge facing today's editors is to discover new ways of effectively presenting such nuances of meaning along with the bibliographical context of Milton's publications. If good editing, like a musical accompaniment, ought to enhance without overpowering, to render intelligible without calling attention to itself, then modern editors must not emend or annotate a text so intrusively that it becomes distorted or cluttered. In addition to exploring new forms of online publication that would grant readers easy access to all of a text's variants, Milton's editors might follow the model of some Shakespeare editions that include a separate, running commentary at the bottom of the page to record not only alternative contemporary readings but also the salient choices made by past editors.

Milton's revision of the episode of Mammon's Cave from *The Faerie Queene* provides an apt metaphor for an editor's proper function. Whereas Spenser depicts Guyon entering alone into Mammon's Cave, Milton in *Areopagitica* rewrites Spenser's text by having the Palmer accompany Guyon 'that he might see and know, and yet abstain' (*CPW*, ii. 516). Modern readers similarly need to have Milton's texts gently edited and annotated so that they, like Guyon, can benefit from the practical wisdom that the Palmer embodies. Instead of venturing forth alone into the intricacies of Milton's syntax and allusions, readers can rely on an editor so that they, too, can see, know, and avoid careless errors.

But if editing this passage from *Areopagitica* would deserve mention only in a footnote, other textual details in Milton's works do not offer such obvious solutions. When complexities arise—even apparently minor ones—readers should expect editors to gloss, but not to gloss over, the work's variants. And when the editor attempts to correct what he judges to be an error in Milton's texts, readers should be given enough information to question the editor's judgement. If we borrow yet another passage from *Areopagitica*, Milton warns that a true Christian must not resolve 'to give over toyling, and to find himself out som factor, to whose care and credit he may commit the whole managing of his religious affairs' (p. 544). Similarly, readers of Milton must not resolve to give over their toiling and to find some editorial agent to manage his works' ambiguities. Like Milton's admonishment against the 'heretick in the truth' who 'beleeve[s] things only because his Pastor sayes so, or the Assembly so determins' (*CPW*, ii. 543), today's students and specialists should not unthinkingly depend on editors' modernizations. Only by looking anew at the old forms of Milton's publications can we fully understand the meaning of his poems and make, perhaps for the first time, our own interpretative discoveries.

---

[40] Fish, *How Milton Works* (Cambridge, Mass., 2001), 479–80. John Leonard offers a cogent challenge to Fish's reading of this passage in his review article, 'Did Milton Go to the Devil's Party?', *New York Review of Books*, 49 (18 July 2002), 28–31.

CHAPTER 27

THE 'WORLD' OF
PARADISE LOST

KAREN L. EDWARDS

AT the centre of the vast cosmography of *Paradise Lost* is the bower of Adam and Eve, as if John Milton has translated into a structural principle for epic the declaration of the lover in John Donne's 'The Sun Rising': 'the world's contracted thus'.[1] The imaginative rendering of the bower in Book 4 emphasizes its discreteness, interiority, and privacy. '[T]he roof / Of thickest covert was inwoven shade'; '[a]canthus, and . . . bushy shrub / Fenced up the verdant wall'; '[h]ere in close recess' Eve strews the nuptial bed with flowers; here, no 'other creature . . . durst enter' (iv. 692–3, 696–7, 708, 704). When after their day's work, Adam and Eve walk hand in hand to their enclosed bower for the night, we expect to read that in their lovemaking they constitute a world unto themselves, that (in Donne's words) 'Nothing else is' (l. 22). There *is*, however, much else. I am not referring simply to the great symbolic places of the poem, Heaven, Hell, Chaos, and Earth, crucial though they are. To think of the world of the poem only in these terms is to limit oneself to a single plane, that of the story, or fiction. Other planes cut through the plane of the fiction; we may call them other worlds. Reflecting on their relationship to the story is part of a mature reading of *Paradise Lost*. These other worlds are the 'much else' a reader encounters even in the representation of Adam and Eve's intimate and secluded bower. Thus, before they arrive at it, the narrator compares the bower to those of the Romans' woodland gods:

---

[1] John Donne, 'The Sun Rising', in *John Donne*, ed. John Carey (Oxford, 1990), 92–3, l. 26. All further quotations from Donne's poem are from this edition.

> In shadier bower
> More sacred and sequestered, though but feigned,
> Pan or Silvanus never slept, nor nymph,
> Nor Faunus haunted. (*PL*, iv. 705–8)

That the pagan world of ancient Rome intrudes here, that 'salvage and beastly Deities, and acknowledg'd *feign'd*, are brought here in Comparison; and their wild Grottos forsooth are [called] *Sacred*, is shocking to Milton's eighteenth-century editor, Richard Bentley.[2] In 1935 William Empson, agreeing with Bentley's insight (though not with his indignation), commented that the lines above are 'the most firmly "pagan"' (as well as 'the most beautiful') of all the poem's comparisons.[3] This world is left behind at the resumption of the narrative at line 720 ('Thus at their shady lodge arrived, both stood'). Then, at the very moment that Adam and Eve turn to each other with pure desire (ll. 741–3), the world of the poem's composition suddenly and forcefully intrudes as the narrator denounces those who pervert the role of God-given sexuality (ll. 744–75). The condemnation of both promiscuity ('Casual fruition') and a prudish refusal of sexual intercourse ('hypocrites . . . Defaming as impure what God declares / Pure') responds directly and polemically to Milton's seventeenth-century context (*PL* iv. 767, 744–7). At its conclusion, the narration proper resumes (l. 776): Adam and Eve lie sleeping, and guardian angels take up their nightly posts.

The nuptial bower is thus depicted as separate, unique, and inviolable *and* as intimately connected to other represented worlds. This representational paradox is characteristic of the poem. The 'world' of *Paradise Lost*, a creation responsible for readers' sense of being immersed in a wholly imagined reality when they read the poem, is in fact composed of the interaction of multiple imagined worlds. A comparison with the mode of 'The Sun Rising' is instructive. There, the lovers in their bed are said to constitute a world unto themselves. Yet those elements declared external to that world—'Late schoolboys, and sour prentices . . . court-huntsmen . . . country ants' (ll. 6–8)—are in fact continuous with it, with each other, and with the reader. There is but one world in Donne's poem, and the lovers are part of it, despite the speaker's declarations to the contrary. The wit of the poem lies partly in that contradiction. In contrast, the fictive world of *Paradise Lost*, the imagined world in which the story takes place and which operates according to certain laws, is intruded upon by other worlds experienced by readers as distinct and separate. Two are primary, as the passage from Book 4 suggests: the metaphoric world imported into the poem through similes and comparisons, and the world of seventeenth-century England in which the poem was written.[4] The interaction of these worlds, the subject

---

[2] *Milton's 'Paradise Lost': A New Edition*, ed. Richard Bentley (1732), *PL* iv. 705 n.

[3] William Empson, *Some Versions of Pastoral* (1935), 190.

[4] In its conception and execution, *Paradise Lost* is necessarily a product of the 17th c.; hence it would be fair to say that the poem as a whole and in all of its details responds to the cultural conditions of Milton's day. But in this essay I am interested in those passages, like the passage on wedded love in Book 4, which explicitly and polemically engage with issues of concern to Milton and his contemporaries.

of my essay, creates what I am calling the 'world' of *Paradise Lost*. It can best (and perhaps only) be apprehended through close attention to the details of an extended passage, to a consideration of how the segments of the passage are related to each other. I will concentrate on two passages: Satan at the threshold of the universe, *PL* iii. 418–97, and his approach to the garden of Eden, iv. 153–66. These are rich passages, their usefulness for my purpose deriving from the extraordinary efflorescence of imagined worlds that occurs whenever the fallen Satan prepares a new assault on an unfallen Creation. We might call them 'articulated' passages: they are composed of distinct worlds that work together to elaborate the full meaning of Satan's incursions. They trace their manifestations in mythic history, project them into a future, and reflect on their shaping of Milton's own era.

Bringing the poem's multiple worlds into play allows one to see what various critical approaches have to offer and how it is possible to learn from each without accepting wholly the lines of argument it proposes. The passage above on the bowers of nymphs and fauns, for instance, may be overlooked by those scholars who are primarily interested in how *Paradise Lost* responds to political and religious developments in the Civil War period and the Restoration. On the other hand, scholars with this historical approach, associated most closely with the work of Christopher Hill, have illuminated the contemporary context of Milton's condemnation of those who do not properly value God-given sexuality.[5] Empson, who is always looking for ways in which Milton may contradict himself, teaches readers to be attentive to those passages apparently incidental to such explicit ideological interventions, or indeed to the plot. His adjective 'pagan' opens up the possibility that Milton responded deeply (and against his Christianity) to the residue of primitive, chthonic beliefs effortlessly available to classical poets. Empson's attentiveness, that is, may lead us to enquire more deeply into the relationship between 'feign'd' and 'sacred' in the context of the highly artificial bower and paganism's apparently 'natural' worship of the earth. Christopher Ricks, concerned like Empson with the verbal texture of the poem, turns Bentley's indignant criticisms on their head to demonstrate Milton's coherence and artistic control.[6] This position allows him to engage with the language of the poem without getting tangled in general theories. His attentiveness to individual words, admired and adopted by Hill, constantly brings rich insights to the surface; Hill presses those insights for their political implications. Empson, Ricks, and Hill, along with Stanley Fish, may be thought of as founders of the critical discourses that currently shape the study of Milton's poetry.[7] To study the articulation of worlds in

---

[5] See William Haller, 'Hail Wedded Love', *English Literary History*, 13 (1946), 79–97; David Aers and Bob Hodge, ' "Rational burning": Milton on Sex and Marriage', *Milton Studies*, 13 (1979), 3–33; James Grantham Turner, *One Flesh: Paradisal Marriage and Sexual Relations in the Age of Milton* (Oxford, 1987). Christopher Hill's analysis of *Paradise Lost* is most fully set out in *Milton and the English Revolution* (New York, 1977), 354–412.

[6] See Christopher Ricks, *Milton's Grand Style* (Oxford, 1963).

[7] Fish's impact on Milton studies has been largely through his *Surprised by Sin: The Reader in 'Paradise Lost'* (1967; Berkeley, 1971). His argument—that the experience of reading *Paradise Lost* convicts us of our fallenness by making us conscious of our limitations and defective understanding—defines a reader as

the 'world' of *Paradise Lost*, a reader must draw upon the insights yielded by all these scholarly approaches.

I

In Book 3, after Chaos directs his perilous odyssey through Night, Satan arrives at the outside of the universe and alights on its convex shell (ll. 418–29). God has already declared that the fiend's attempt to destroy humankind will be in vain, that it 'shall redound / Upon his own rebellious head' (iii. 85–6). Vanity conditions the account of Satan's meditated entry into the universe. The universe itself is imagined as a giant globe, though but a pinprick in size compared to Heaven, from which it hangs by a golden chain. The outer surface of 'this pendant world' is inhospitable. It

> seems a boundless continent
> Dark, waste, and wild, under the frown of Night
> Starless exposed, and ever-threatening storms
> Of Chaos blustering round, inclement sky;
> Save on that side which from the wall of heaven
> Though distant far some small reflection gains
> Of glimmering air less vexed with tempest loud:
> Here walked the fiend at large in spacious field. (iii. 423–30)

This convex shell is a liminal space between Creation (formed matter) and Chaos (formless matter). Barren, vacuous, and insatiable, the wind that ceaselessly blows here perfectly embodies the vanity that motivates Satan. From Latin *vanus*, 'empty', 'without substance' (related to *vaccuus*, 'vacant', and *vastus*, 'waste'), the word 'vain' characterizes Satan from the beginning of *Paradise Lost*: he, 'with ambitious aim / Against the throne and monarchy of God / Raised impious war in heaven and battle proud / With vain attempt' (i. 41–4). The place, a 'windy sea of land', and the being, who 'has freedom without self-discipline, dynamic energy and driving individualism with no recognition of limits', are one.[8] Vanity is a satanic version of *spiritus*, divine inspiration, the vital, creative, form-endowing breath of God. In contrast to God's performative utterance ('Let there be light: and there was light', Gen. 1: 3), Satan's words, like his actions, are unproductive; he is titled, appropriately, both 'the Prince of the Air' and 'the Father of Lies'.

---

religious rather than historical. Whereas Empson, Ricks, and Hill find ambiguity that opens up meaning, Fish finds verbal traps that put meaning out of reach, a perspective equivalent, finally, to the repression of the poetry. Fish's mode of reading *Paradise Lost*—his detachment of the world of the reader from the poem's other worlds—has contributed to this essay by stimulating me to argue against his assumptions.

[8] Hill, *Milton and the English Revolution*, 367.

The elaborate simile that interrupts the narrative at *Paradise Lost* iii. 431 has windy tales, or lies, at its base, both ancient lies (those stemming from traditional lore) and new ones (the incredible stories produced by the age of exploration):

> As when a vulture on Imaus bred,
> Whose snowy ridge the roving Tartar bounds,
> Dislodging from a region scarce of prey
> To gorge the flesh of lambs or yeanling kids
> On hills where flocks are fed, flies toward the springs
> Of Ganges or Hydaspes, Indian streams;
> But in his way lights on the barren plains
> Of Sericana, where Chineses drive
> With sails and wind their cany wagons light: (iii. 431–9)

The world of the simile is nightmarishly limited to a sterile, gusty plain resembling the shell of the universe. Buffeted by the winds of chance that offer occasions for predation, it is a world guided by opportunism and the breaching of unacknowledged boundaries. Truth has no place here. The murderous vulture that alights 'on the barren plains' was anciently thought to be conceived by the wind.[9] By Milton's day the theory of its windy conception (or anaemophily) was understood to be just that—a windy conception.[10] In contrast to ancient lore about the vulture, Chinese land ships were known to early modern England through the account of Juan González de Mendoza, whose name (evocative of L. *mendax, mendacis*, 'given to lying'), nationality (Spanish), and profession (Jesuit priest) would have signified for Milton the untrustworthiness of the account.[11] The propellant for the tale of these 'wind-wagons', we might say, is hot air. The simile depicts a world in which vanity and chaos, sterility and rapaciousness, reign; even the innocuous term 'wagons' is compromised by implying, untruthfully, that the vehicles are practically designed to carry loads. The simile, in short, projects the archfiend's mind onto a landscape that resembles barren parts of the earth. It shows what the windy outside of the world would look like if it were folded into itself and became 'our' world.

The narrative of Satan's solitary walk resumes at line 440: 'So on this windy sea of land, the fiend / Walked up and down alone bent on his prey, / Alone, for other

---

[9] See Aelian, *On the Characteristics of Animals*, trans. A. F. Schofield, 3 vols. (Loeb Classical Library; 1958–9), iii. 145. Cf. Aristotle, *History of Animals*, 3 vols, trans. A. L. Peck (vol. i: Books 1–3, and vol. ii: Books 4–6) and D. M. Balme (vol. xi: Books 7–9) (Loeb Classical Library; 1965–91), ii. 542, on the partridge. The Loeb editors observe: 'The belief that animals can be impregnated by the wind is very ancient and very widespread' (ii. 110–12 n.). On the history of the concept, see Conway Zirkle, 'Animals Impregnated by the Wind', *Isis*, 25 (1936), 95–130. Zirkle discusses four creatures (mares, hens, vultures, and women) especially liable to anaemophily; vultures are discussed at 104–11.

[10] See Thomas Browne, *Pseudodoxia Epidemica*, ed. Robin Robbins, 2 vols. (Oxford, 1981), i. 420; and John Ray, *The Ornithology of Francis Willughby* (1678), 66.

[11] Mendoza's book (originally published in Spanish in 1585) was translated by Robert Parke as *The Historie of the Great and Mighty Kingdome of China* (1588). Evidently uneasy about seeming to endorse a Roman Catholic's opinions, the printer warns readers that 'Spaniards . . . doo usually in all their writings extoll their owne actions, even to the setting forth of many untruthes and incredible things' (sig. A3ʳ). The account of the 'landship' is on p. 32. See Frank L. Huntley, 'Milton, Mendoza, and the Chinese Land-Ship', *Modern Language Notes*, 69 (1954), 404–7.

creature in this place / Living or lifeless to be found was none' (iii. 440–3). Then, as with an afterthought—'None *yet*' (l. 444, emphasis added)—the narrative is again interrupted, this time by a burlesque satire on vanity so lengthy and apparently unrelated to what precedes it that it is often called a digression (ll. 444–97). The Paradise of Fools or Limbo of Vanity depicted by the satire *would* exist in the poem (in the way that Hell, Chaos, and Heaven exist) if the story continued all the way to the author's own day. The satire conjures up an image of 'all things transitory and vain' blowing around the outside of the universe (l. 446), among them:

> Embryos and idiots, eremites and friars
> White, black and gray, with all their trumpery.
> Here pilgrims roam, that strayed so far to seek
> In Golgotha him dead, who lives in heaven;
> And they who to be sure of paradise
> Dying put on the weeds of Dominic,
> Or in Franciscan think to pass disguised;
> . . .
> A violent cross wind from either coast
> Blows them transverse ten thousand leagues awry
> Into the devious air; then might ye see
> Cowls, hoods and habits with their wearers tossed
> And fluttered into rags, then relics, beads,
> Indulgences, dispenses, pardons, bulls,
> The sport of winds: all these upwhirled aloft
> Fly o'er the backside of the world . . . (iii. 474–80, 487–94)

All these are tokens of superstition, by definition empty and (literally) insignificant. What John King calls 'symbolic flatulence' functions here, as elsewhere in the poem, 'to represent the corrupt offensiveness' of false belief.[12]

For Milton, the centre of such corruption is papal Rome. King observes that Milton's jeering at 'eremites and friars / White, black and gray' belongs to 'a tradition of anti-fraternal satire that stretches back into the Middle Ages'.[13] The addition of 'all their trumpery' (iii. 475), argues King, brings the satire up to the 1630s and early 1640s, the period of Laudian controversy in England. The term 'trumpery', he notes, 'invokes the vernacular rhetoric of revolutionary broadsides that celebrated the downfall of Archbishop Laud, whose introduction of liturgical changes evoked the specter of Catholic "peril" in the minds of militant Protestants'.[14] It is likely, however, that by 1667 Milton had another, more immediately relevant, target in mind. After the Restoration, Milton's old enemies, the Anglican prelates, began to appropriate

---

[12] John N. King, 'Milton's Paradise of Fools: Ecclesiastical Satire in *Paradise Lost*', in Arthur F. Marotti (ed.), *Catholicism and Anti-Catholicism in Early Modern English Texts* (Basingstoke, 1999), 198–217 at 206. For other studies relating the Limbo of Vanity to Milton's cultural context, see especially Catherine Gimelli Martin, ' "What If the Sun Be Centre to the World?": Milton's Epistemology, Cosmology, and Paradise of Fools Reconsidered', *Modern Philology*, 99 (2001), 231–65, and John Wooten, 'From Purgatory to the Paradise of Fools: Dante, Ariosto, and Milton', *English Literary History*, 49 (1982), 741–50.

[13] 'Milton's Paradise of Fools', 201.

[14] Ibid. 203.

the Reformation (including Reformation wit and satire) for the Church of England. The process led eventually, for instance, to Bishop Burnet's publication in 1679 of *The History of the Reformation of the Church of England*, and Sir Roger L'Estrange's translation and publication of *Twenty Select Colloquies* of Erasmus in 1680. These are among many signs that after the Restoration the Anglican Church worked to position itself as the perfect Reformed Church, the true inheritor of the Reformation. By including Anglican trumpery in the Limbo of Vanity—itself modelled upon savage, witty, outraged Reformed satire—Milton in effect reclaims the Reformation for non-sacramental, non-sacerdotal Christianity.

The satirical picture of friars and bishops in chaotic orbit around the shell of the universe is severe in its condemnation of spiritual vanity. But calling the satire a 'digression'—or, less obviously, to consider it as a separable, uniquely political passage—is to miss how much its severity owes to the two worlds with which it is juxtaposed. In the world of the poem's story, Satan's vanity corresponds to the wind-swept emptiness of the universe's outside; its lifelessness is a portrait of his spiritual state. The world of the simile, claustrophobic despite its evocation of great distances, is utterly dominated by vanity's avatars, the wind and the sterile plain. The deadliness and futility of both worlds underlies the Limbo of Vanity, 'placed', in any case, on the shell of the universe that belongs to the poem's plot. The interweaving of worlds shows that it is inadvisable to dismiss as irrelevant Milton's satire on his contemporaries, the 'eremites and friars', imagined spinning around the backside of the universe. They are, as the overlapping worlds of story, simile, and satire suggest, not only the rightful occupants but the creators of a world dominated by death. Like Satan, they are destroyers of 'true life' (iv. 196).

II

Foul, wasteful, and destructive, wind is the product and signifier of vanity in the three worlds we have looked at in Book 3. Divine inspiration, in contrast, manifests itself in pure, sweet air and the creative utterance. In Book 4 of the poem Satan smells the air of the garden of Eden as he approaches the boundary wall.

> and of pure now purer air
> Meets his approach, and to the heart inspires
> Vernal delight and joy, able to drive
> All sadness but despair: now gentle gales
> Fanning their odoriferous wings dispense
> Native perfúmes, and whisper whence they stole
> Those balmy spoils. (iv. 153–9)

Bearing fragrance, the air 'meets' him as he moves towards paradise. The account of the meeting of air and angel, interrupted by the simile that begins halfway through line 159, concludes at line 166: 'So entertained those odorous sweets the fiend / Who came their bane'. 'Entertained' was more strongly associated in the past than it is today with receiving guests and providing for all their needs.[15] Indeed, the language in which fallen archangel and paradisal air encounter each other evokes the ancient Near Eastern treatment of guests as recorded in the Bible. Genesis 18: 2 tells of the approach of three strangers as Abraham sits at the door of his tent, whereupon he 'ran to meet them' and offer them food. The three, it turns out, are angels. In Hebrews 13: 2, Paul draws the lesson: 'Be not forgetful to entertain strangers: for thereby some have entertained angels unawares.' The angels whom Abraham entertains promise a son to him; their arrival can be said to inaugurate a change in history. Does Satan's entertainment of 'those odorous sweets' signal the possibility of a change even more momentous, his repentance and return to obedience of God?

That this possibility needs at least to be considered arises from the poem's monism, the fact that Milton conceives Creation—the substance of the created world and its creatures, from rocks to angels—to be *ex Deo* ('from God') rather than *ex nihilo* ('from nothing'), as orthodox Christianity holds.[16] The crucial poetic consequence of this unorthodox view of Creation is that all matter is shown to be alive with spirit, or, to put it another way, the figurative and the literal, the spiritual and the material, are not discontinuous. Milton explains in *De Doctrina Christiana* that the breath of life that God breathes into Adam's nostrils at Genesis 2: 7 is *not* a metaphor for 'a part of the divine essence' or for 'the soul'; rather, 'the breath of life' is 'a kind of air or breath of divine virtue, fit for the maintenance of life and reason and infused into the organic body' (*CPW*, vi. 318). In Book 5 of *Paradise Lost*, the archangel Raphael, entertained in the garden by Adam and Eve, offers a fuller explanation of monistic ontology (or 'animist materialism') to his host.[17]

> O Adam, one almighty is, from whom
> All things proceed, and up to him return,
> If not depraved from good, created all
> Such to perfection, one first matter all,
> Indued with various forms, various degrees
> Of substance, and in things that live, of life;
> But more refined, more spirituous, and pure,
> As nearer to him placed or nearer tending
> Each in their several active spheres assigned,
> Till body up to spirit work, in bounds
> Proportioned to each kind. So from the root

---

[15] See *OED*, s.v. entertain, v., senses 12 and 13; s.v. entertainment, senses 11.a., b., and c.

[16] Milton discusses creation *ex Deo* in Book 1, ch. 7 of *De Doctrina Christiana*. See *CPW*, vi. 305–11.

[17] For the political, religious, and scientific background and implications of Milton's animist materialism, see especially John Rogers, *The Matter of Revolution: Science, Poetry, and Politics in the Age of Milton* (Ithaca, N.Y., 1998), 103–76, and Stephen M. Fallon, *Milton among the Philosophers: Poetry and Materialism in Seventeenth-Century England* (Ithaca, N.Y., 1991).

> Springs lighter the green stalk, from thence the leaves
> More airy, last the bright consummate flower
> Spirits odorous breathes: ... (v. 469–82)

Raphael's simile suggests that the pure air flowing out to meet Satan as he approaches paradise in Book 4—air that partakes of the divine breath of life— *might* have inspired him (as he inspires, or breathes, it) to return to his Creator. *Might* have. In a monistic universe, Creation is good, reminding us that grace is freely available to all. Raphael's 'So from the root / Springs lighter the green stalk' is more than a simile: the flowering plant he describes *enacts* matter's return to spirit. The created world is full of such models, reminding us that choosing obedience is always possible. Monism thus supports Arminianism, the doctrine that salvation is open to all who choose to receive it and return 'up' to God (in contrast to predestinarianism, which holds that God has determined from eternity whether an individual is to be saved or damned). Christopher Hill remarks: 'This is Arminian doctrine. Milton endowed Satan with conscience ... and appears to envisage the possibility of his repenting.'[18] The appearance of the word 'odorous' at line 166 ('So entertained those odorous sweets the fiend') is perhaps a reminder of Raphael's simile. The line may in fact be read in two ways, as it is perfectly ambiguous. Hill, acknowledging his debt to Empson and Ricks, observes that 'Milton is the great equivocator ... equivocation is at the heart of his greatest poetry'.[19] We might say that equivocation, ambiguity, syntactical fluidity, what Ricks calls 'liquid texture'—all the qualities of Milton's poetry, in short, which prevent a reader from settling on a single, paraphrasable meaning—are the stylistic equivalent of Arminianism: choice always remains.[20] Line 166 allows a reader simultaneously to see Creation reaching out to the fallen creature and the fallen creature ignoring the invitation. When 'odorous sweets' is the subject of the sentence, the line shows the sweet air of paradise to be capable of receiving and inspiring Satan, vanquishing his despair and renewing his love of the Creator. When 'the fiend' is the subject, the line shows us that Satan enjoys paradisal air merely as a brief but pleasant distraction from his sadness. Offered 'purer air' he takes 'despair', the rhyme insisting, even at this last moment, that hopelessness is a choice.

The fact that 'despair' occurs in the middle of line 156—or, rather, that line 156 extends beyond 'despair'—further undermines the finality that is superstitiously associated with the term.[21] Lines 156b to 159a, moreover, continue the description

---

[18] Hill, *Milton and the English Revolution*, 367.

[19] Ibid. 472. Fish's Milton, in contrast, presents readers with an *apparent* interpretive choice, but when, inevitably, they make the wrong choice, the poem corrects them, bringing them to contrition and recognition of their sinfulness. This construction of Milton, which loses sight of his Arminianism, is particularly inadequate for dealing with those instances in which a fallen character encounters an unfallen Creation. There, a sustained double perspective is the point.

[20] Ricks, *Milton's Grand Style*, 81–7.

[21] Despair was regarded by the Catholic Church as a mortal sin. Reformed Protestantism posited two kinds of despair: one, a profound sorrow at one's sinfulness, which leads to repentance and salvation; the other, a spiritual paralysis or worldly sorrow that has pride at its base. For an excellent, concise account of early modern Protestant attitudes towards despair, see *The Spenser Encyclopedia*, ed. A. C. Hamilton et al. (Toronto, 1990), q.v. despair (pp. 213–14).

of paradisal air ('now gentle gales / Fanning their odoriferous wings...'), as if to imply that the offering of grace does not cease. These strange and complex lines, like the description of sylvan bowers in Book 4, are too easily disregarded. Let us ask to what world the gales belong. 'Now', introducing them, implies that they belong to Satan's growing experiential knowledge of the garden and hence to the fictive world of the poem. First, pure air 'runs to meet' him; then, gentle gales fan him with perfumed 'wings' and whisper secrets to him. The erotic quality of the lines hints at Satan's ability to derive illicit pleasure from an innocent source;[22] and 'stole' and 'spoils'—unexpected in the context of the prelapsarian garden—point to the rapaciousness that vainly seeks to fill spiritual emptiness. Like the pure air that bespeaks and partakes of divine inspiration, the garden's fragrant gales also declare the Creator. Fragrance in the form of incense is associated with the worship of Jehovah in the Old Testament; in the New Testament, at 2 Corinthians 2: 15, Paul speaks figuratively of 'a sweet savour of Christ, in them that are saved, and in them that perish'.[23] In the monistic fictional world of *Paradise Lost*, the 'sweet savour' of the garden's air is both literal and figurative, a union reinforced by the sibilance of the lines. But the fact that 'stole' and 'spoils' participate in the sibilance suggests the profound nature of the corruption that Satan represents, or the swiftness with which that corruption works. Christopher Ricks's concept of infected language, which would lead to the argument that the 'fallen' sense of 'stole' and 'spoils' is elicited only to be excluded by fit readers, needs to be turned around here.[24] 'Stole' and 'spoils' do not have an unfallen sense in the way, for instance, that 'err' and 'wanton' do.[25] In Thomas Newton's 1750 edition of *Paradise Lost*, lines 158–9 are compared to canto 34, stanza 51, of Ariosto's *Orlando furioso* with the comment: 'this expression of the air's stealing and dispersing the sweets of flowers is very common in the best Italian poets'.[26] If so, Milton makes the commonplace uncommon. The narrator's 'stole' and 'spoils' (used, after all, of the air, which is inexhaustible, incorruptible, and freely available) seem to be linguistic realizations of the plundering that is uppermost in Satan's mind as he moves towards paradise.

The lines describing the 'gentle gales' of paradise thus function as Wittgenstein's 'duck-rabbit': they allow readers to move back and forth between fallen and unfallen perspectives within the fictive world of the poem.[27] They also prepare for the metaphoric world of the simile with its emphasis on wind-driven ships of prey:

---

[22] The hint is developed at *PL* ix. 444–70, when Satan is shown to be voyeuristically susceptible to Eve's beauty.

[23] The New Revised Standard Version renders the verse as follows: 'For we are the aroma of Christ to God among those who are being saved and among those who are perishing' (*The New Oxford Annotated Bible*, ed. Bruce M. Metzger and Roland E. Murphy (New York, 1991)). The editors suggest that Paul has in mind not only the incense of sacrifice but also of Roman triumphal processions (2 Cor. 2: 14 n.).

[24] Thus, as Ricks puts it, we are made conscious again of 'what has happened to the word, and the world, since' (*Milton's Grand Style*, 111).

[25] Ibid. 110–12.

[26] *Paradise Lost: A Poem in Twelve Books by John Milton*, ed. Thomas Newton, 2nd edn. (1750), iv. 158–9 n.

[27] Ludwig Wittgenstein, *Philosophical Investigations*, trans. G. E. M. Anscombe (Oxford, 1968), 194e.

>   As when to them who sail
>   Beyond the Cape of Hope, and now are past
>   Mozámbic, off at sea north-east winds blow
>   Sabean odours from the spicy shore
>   Of Arabie the blest, with such delay
>   Well pleased they slack their course, and many a league
>   Cheered with the grateful smell old Ocean smiles. (iv. 159–65)

David Quint has argued that 'the principal subtext' for the simile is 'the journey of Vasco da Gama around the Cape of Good Hope to India' as recounted in Luis de Camões's epic, *Os Lusíadas*.[28] An English translation by Richard Fanshawe was published in London in 1655 as *The Lusiad, or Portugals Historicall Poem*. Milton's achievement, Quint argues, is to disclose what actual voyages and the romance adventures depicted in Renaissance epic have in common—that both are inherently mercantile (p. 266). Milton's rejection of a Spenserian or romance form for his epic, in this view, registers resistance to early capitalism and the emergence of a merchant class (p. 265). Quint reads the simile, in short, as crystallizing a double rejection: 'Milton's fiction, by recasting the events of the *Lusíadas* into Satan's journey, suggests that the voyages are the work of the devil' (p. 255).

Quint's argument usefully identifies the relevance of da Gama's voyage and Camões's epic to the simile. But the simile itself puts those voyages in a much wider perspective, which undermines his argument. 'Sabean odours' (l. 162) alludes to the mysterious biblical land of Saba, or Sheba, kingdom of the queen who comes to Solomon 'with a very great train, with camels that bare spices, and very much gold, and precious stones' (1 Kings 10: 2). The name Saba, according to Pliny, 'in the Greek tongue signifieth a mystery'.[29] 'Arabie the blest' evokes the description of *Arabia Felix* by the ancient historian Diodorus Siculus, who tells of the country's perfumed winds blowing across the sea. Diodorus acknowledges that much of his material is legendary.[30] Milton cites Diodorus as justification for his own use of 'relations heertofore accounted fabulous' in *The History of Britain*. Such fabulous tales, he asserts, 'have bin after found to contain in them many footsteps and reliques of somthing true' (*CPW*, v. 3). That which is not actual, in other words, may nonetheless be true, a conclusion that holds for the world depicted in the simile. It points to an alternating pattern in human voyaging, in which, at least occasionally, graspingness is waylaid by inspiration, and the spirit that informs matter can no longer be denied. In the English version of Diodorus' history, Sheba is full of 'Palme-trees, Canes, Cinamon, and other such like odoriferous things . . . so that the odours, which come to our sences from those Trees, seeme to be somewhat that is truly Divine'.[31]

To argue that the simile offers an alternative to the despair embraced by Satan is not to suggest that the world it paints is rosy. Indeed, Quint's concentration on the

---

[28] David Quint, *Epic and Empire: Politics and Generic Form from Virgil to Milton* (Princeton, 1993), 253.
[29] Pliny [Plinius Secundus], *The Historie of the World*, trans. Philemon Holland (1601), i. 366.
[30] Diodorus Siculus, *The History of Diodorus Siculus*, trans. H[enry] C[ogan] (1653), 142.
[31] Ibid. 141.

sailors' mercantile aims causes him to underestimate the profound darkness of that world. Let us remember that the main function of lines 159–65 is to reveal Satan's state of mind when he first breathes the sweet air of paradise. There is very little of the merchant about his intentions. Indeed, what connects the fictive world of the archfiend and the metaphoric world of the Iberian sailors is both fragrant air and a determination to despoil—a monistic reminder that rapacious materialism deforms spirituality. The subtitle of Fanshaw's translation, *Portugals Historicall Poem*, warns seventeenth-century readers that this is the national epic of a *Catholic* country. By evoking *The Lusiad*, the simile points to the Roman Catholic Church as the spiritually corrupt power behind voyages to the East (and West) Indies. Milton is explicit on this point in 1641. *Of Reformation* represents Philip II of Spain, 'that sad Intelligencing Tyrant', as the very type of those whose greed for gold and silver is employed to halt the ongoing work of Reformation. He 'mischiefes the World with his Mines of *Ophir*', says Milton: Spanish galleons carry New World gold back to Europe for gilding cathedrals and funding the war against Protestantism (*CPW*, i. 615). When in the same tract Milton satirically compares Anglican bishops to ships, he implies that the prelates are going about the same work. They would prefer 'that we would burst our *midriffes*', jeers Milton, 'rather then laugh to see them under Sayl in all their Lawn, and Sarcenet, their shrouds, and tackle' (p. 612). Bishops and Spanish galleons are driven by the wind of vanity in their search for material gain: bishops' 'mouths cannot open without the strong breath, and loud stench of avarice, Simony, and Sacrilege, embezling the treasury of the Church on painted, and guilded walles of Temples wherein God hath testified to have no delight' (pp. 610–11). As their allegiance is to Mammon rather than God, to 'lucre and preferment' and 'belly-cheere' rather than to piety, they are 'hinderers of *Reformation*' who teach their congregations not true spiritual worship but 'sensuall Idolatry' (pp. 719, 541, 520).

In 1641 Milton saw the Reformation in England as incomplete. By 1667 he saw it as betrayed, with Catholicism tolerated at court and Anglicanism (with its leanings towards popery) resurgent. In this fraught context, a single word may carry great political weight. Christopher Hill calls attention to Milton's pun on the adjective 'pontifical' at *PL* x. 313 'to describe the causeway constructed by Sin and Death between hell and earth: "bridge-building" and "episcopal"';[32] and Alastair Fowler observes that one of the Pope's titles is 'Pontifex' (*PL* x. 313 n.). 'There is nothing in the Bible, but much in post-Restoration England, to justify the pun', remarks Hill.[33] The word 'odoriferous' in the description of 'gentle gales' in Book 4 contains another such lexical signal that superstition has prevailed over spirituality. If the entire passage is Janus-faced, the word 'odoriferous' is the hinge. The term does not otherwise occur in *Paradise Lost* or elsewhere in Milton's poetry, although it appears once in his prose. The very fact that 'odorous' occurs three times in Book 4 (at lines 166, 248, and 696) draws attention to the unusual form 'odoriferous'. Fowler remarks that it 'was a familiar word' in Milton's day (*PL* iv. 156–8 n.). It was familiar, however,

---

[32] Hill, *Milton and the English Revolution*, 391.
[33] Ibid.

in only two contexts: as a modifier for aromatic plants and gardens (usually with a connection to the East), and for the bodies of saints and martyrs.[34] We have seen the word in Diodorus' description of Saba; it appears also in his description of Araby: winds 'waft the air from off that land, perfumed with sweet odours of myrrh and other odoriferous plants, to the adjacent part of the sea'.[35] The word appears in adverbial form in Milton's *History of Moscovia*, in a description of the markets of 'Yara', which 'smell odoriferously with Spices' (*CPW*, viii. 509).[36] The fact that the gentle gales of paradise have odoriferous wings thus helps shift our viewpoint from the garden of Eden (in which fragrance signifies holiness) to the world of spice trading evoked in the simile at iv. 159 (in which fragrance can be bought and sold).

'Odoriferous' also evokes Catholic sanctification, however. Instead of the stench and putrefaction associated with a normal corpse, the body of a saint was believed to exude a sweet scent, the reversal of the ordinary human situation testifying to the saint's extreme godliness.[37] Thus in *The Life and Death of Sir Thomas Moore*, written in 1631 by his great-grandson and republished in 1642, those family members who come to kiss the body of the saint 'wittnessed that they smelt a most odoriferous smell to come from him'.[38] The sentence ends with a reference to Genesis 27: 27, in which the blind Isaac, thinking that his elder son Esau is before him, blesses his younger son Jacob instead. Isaac says, in the Authorized Version, 'See, the smell of my son *is* as the smell of a field which the Lord hath blessed'. For Milton, the literalism that lies behind a belief in odoriferous corpses epitomizes the superstition perpetrated by Roman Catholicism. The distance between 'odorous' and 'odoriferous', that is, measures the distance between understanding that matter is infused with spirit and valuing matter to the exclusion of spirit. The latter is idolatry. Idolatry, not the rising merchant class, is the danger lurking in Satan's erasure of the Creator from his reading of Creation. Idolatry conditions the world of the simile (a world constructed in the image of Satan's mind), and that world is connected to Milton's own through the historical fact that early modern Iberian explorations were directed towards upholding the material position of the Roman Catholic Church, now re-establishing itself in England. Reformation hindered is now Reformation postponed and indefinitely delayed.

As Christopher Hill puts it, 'the lessons of history are discouraging'.[39] Yet the seeds of renewal have time to germinate in what seems to be the waste of delay. The slackened speed enforced by the 'adverse' winds gives the opportunity for 'them who sail' to change their minds and their direction. Satan's entertainment of the pure air of the garden might have dissuaded him from 'the ascent of that steep savage hill' and the corruption of humankind (*PL* iv. 172). England's abolition of an episcopal state

---

[34] See *OED*, s.v. odoriferous, for historical examples of the term's use.

[35] *The History of Diodorus Siculus*, 142.

[36] 'Yara is thought to be Süan-hwa-fu' (*CPW*, viii. 508 n. 18).

[37] See Piero Camporesi, *The Incorruptible Flesh: Bodily Mutilation and Mortification in Religion and Folklore*, trans. Tania Croft-Murray (Cambridge, 1988), 25–35.

[38] Cresacre More, *The Life and Death of Sir Thomas Moore* ([Antwerp,] 1631; repr. Antwerp, 1642), 343.

[39] *Milton and the English Revolution*, 385.

church might have led its population to true spiritual freedom. In none of the three imagined worlds is the pause in 'business as usual' seized upon for a new course: just as Satan holds to despair, so the merchant-explorers sail '*Beyond* the Cape of *Hope*, and now are *past*' (emphasis added), and Anglicanism with its 'sensuall Idolatry' is welcomed back with the monarch. But there is no inevitability here. Different choices might have been made—and perhaps, with the help of *Paradise Lost*, *will* be made in future.[40] There is after all one more world that helps make up the 'world' of the poem, and that is the world of the reader. To quote Christopher Hill in a different context than he intended it, Milton was indeed 'fascinated by contemporary discussions on the possibility of a plurality of worlds'.[41] As Satan travels from the edge of the universe to the earth, wending 'his oblique way' among the 'innumerable stars', they seem to him to be other worlds (iii. 564–5). '[B]ut who dwelt happy there / He stayed not to inquire' (iii. 570–1). The statement echoes the famous opening of Francis Bacon's essay, 'Of Truth': '"What is truth?" said jesting Pilate; and would not stay for an answer.'[42] What Satan and Pilate (and vultures, bishops, and Iberian sailors) fail to do—staying to inquire—is the essential mode for apprehending the multiple worlds of *Paradise Lost* in their complex interaction. Each world serves as a commentary on the other, the poem thus providing glosses on itself. It teaches us how to read it; it encourages us to pause and think about how its worlds cohere, and in their coherence, to see that matter is alive with spirit. Raphael reminds Adam that 'knowledge is as food' (vii. 126). Without proper digestion, which necessarily takes time, wisdom turns to folly, nourishment to wind. Staying to inquire is both the subject of the poem and the proper way to consume it.

[40] See Hill on Milton's use of 'perhaps' as a way of making readers ponder (*Milton and the English Revolution*, 408–9).

[41] *Milton and the English Revolution*, 399.

[42] Francis Bacon, 'Of Truth', in *The Essayes or Counsels, Ciuill and Morall* (1625), 1.

CHAPTER 28

PARADISE LOST AND HERESY

NIGEL SMITH

MILTON held unorthodox religious views relating to a wide variety of matters: the law of marriage and the relationship between men and women, the nature of God, Jesus Christ, and the Holy Spirit, the relationship between the soul and the body, the nature of the created universe, the role of human free will in the matter of salvation. These views were set out in his published prose tracts of the 1640s and 1650s, and in his compendious theological statement *De Doctrina Christiana*, which was not known until the nineteenth century. These works are discussed in several of the contributions in this handbook. Milton did not abandon these views by the time he came to write *Paradise Lost*. Rather he located these views in the narrative and structure of his epic, although often apparently in a more pessimistic way than had been the case in the prose tracts.

In *Of Education* and *Areopagitica* Milton had already made a forceful plea for a return to the original meaning of 'heresy' in Greek philosophy: choice, from Greek *proairesis*. Rather than the Augustinian understanding of heresy as that which is forbidden and to be expunged from believers, making them if need be the object of persecution, heresy becomes a fundamental part of a Christian's life of faith: to choose good from evil and to make a trial of virtue in an active life as opposed to a withdrawn, contemplative one. While Milton's poem articulates heresy in the Augustinian sense of theological doctrine, the drama of the dilemmas facing each of the characters in *Paradise Lost* is also a demonstration of the operation of true heresy: choosing good from evil, or, as it happened, not.

CREATION

Adam asks Raphael to narrate the creation of the universe at the start of Book 7:

> relate
> What may no less perhaps avail us known,
> How first began this heaven which we behold
> Distant so high, with moving fires adorned
> Innumerable, and this which yields or fills
> All space, the ambient air. (vii. 84–9)

The creation of nearly everything in the universe comes from God himself, *ex deo*, because God is nearly everything that is in space out there:

> Boundless the deep, because I am who fill
> Infinitude, nor vacuous the space.
> Though I uncircumscribed my self retire,
> And put not forth my goodness, which is free
> To act or not, necessity and chance
> Approach not me, and what I will is fate. (vii. 168–73)

In orthodox theology, God created out of nothing, *ex nihilo*, which also means that whatever the 'nothing' was it has nothing to do with Him. But to create out of himself means logically that everything that exists was originally part of God: the matter of God, so to speak. The creation of the earth, and everything therein, including the humans, is in order to repopulate heaven. God says that the race of men will eventually return to heaven by merit (the Fall and its consequences are interestingly absent in this passage) and make up the deficit left by the fallen angels, surrounding Him with his own substance, sufficiently refined (vii. 150–60).

What actually happens when the world is created? God says to the Son: 'My overshadowing Spirit and might with thee / I send along, ride forth, and bid the deep / Within appointed bounds be heaven and earth' (vii. 165–7). These lines have been used as evidence that Milton was an orthodox Trinitarian, and so it seems, for the Son and Spirit are there doing the acts of creation united with God and apparently in the Godhead, who is present at the creation of the earth in the sense that He is omnipotent. But Milton calls it the 'filial Godhead', which means that there is within it an inferiority relationship at the very least: there is a father and a son. And when the Son passes through the gates of heaven to do the creating, he does not look much like the Son as we have seen him so far: 'to let forth / The king of glory in his powerful Word / And Spirit coming to create new worlds' (vii. 207–9). So is the Son the 'king of glory', or is he God himself? The Son is at this point the Word. The matter to realize is that Milton will have us see that the Son is not part of the substance of the Father; although divine, when on earth he is not God incarnate. This refusal of the doctrine of the Holy Trinity (where the Father, Son, and Spirit are part of one substantial, eternal godhead, and which had been dominant in church teaching since the Council of Nicaea), was seen by the orthodox in Milton's time be they Anglican or Puritan as capable of dissolving the glue that held society together. How could Jesus be obeyed if he was merely a man?

When the business of creation is done, the Son returns to heaven. It is as if he has become indeed God: 'The great creator from his work returned / Magnificent, his six days' work, a world' (vii. 567–78). To say this is to commit one of the greatest acts of heresy (in the Augustinian sense): to give human form to that which is beyond such animation, an apparently idolatrous act. This is a direct consequence of Milton's development of his mythic account of creation. The narrative suggests Trinitarian dimensions, but especially since we know these ideas are also challenged elsewhere in the poem, we note also that godliness in the sense of the power of creation falls on a figure who is not God, and who has been given human dimensions during the course of creation. The tension of identities within the poem is evident in a sentence that has notoriously confused editors:

> The filial power arrived, and sat him down
> With his great Father (for he also went
> Invisible, yet stayed, such privilege
> Hath omnipresence) and the work ordained,
> Author and end of all things. (vii. 587–91)

Early editors made 'Father' the subject of 'ordained' and hence the 'author and end' but Hebrews 12: 2 refers to Christ as 'author and finisher', thereby suggesting an elevation of the Son to the status of creator within Milton's sentence.

The fact that it is God and not the Son who does the naming allows Milton to follow a far more conventional description of the creation of the elements, nature, and the animals. The Bible is a strong source here as well as popular vernacular creation poems, especially Josuah Sylvester's translation of the French Protestant du Bartas's *Les Semaines* (1578–1603; trans. 1592–1608). The Son's role is more evident at the point where man is created (vii. 519–34) but Raphael's narration does not at this stage go into details. Nonetheless, God speaks 'audibly' to the Son, addressing the joint project: 'Let us make now man in our image' (vii. 519). And man is created, we are told three times in this short passage, in the image of God, as a 'similitude'. Does this mean that God is a man, visible in a human form (and/or that man is a version of the Father), lessening the sense we have in Book 3 that Milton's angry God is a metaphorical portrayal of what is incomprehensible to fallen humans? The charge against some of the English Socinians, the anti-Trinitarians whom Milton broadly supported, is that they had anthropomorphically depicted God, as opposed to accepting scriptural metaphor as a necessary way of explaining sacred matters to frail, sublunary human intelligence.[1]

The problem continues with the role of the Son, and in particular his intercession. Milton has to reinvent the atonement, especially since he downplays the crucifixion.

---

[1] Despite Milton's anti-Trinitarian beliefs and sympathies (he licensed a Latin edition of the Socinian Racovian Catechism), John Rogers identifies a precise attack by Milton on the Socinians (see his essay below) and regards Milton as generally Arian (after the followers of the patristic period anti-Trinitarian Arius) in his views on the Trinity. Compare also the essay by Campbell and Corns, Ch. 23 above.

In Books 3 and 10–11, the atonement occurs as a conversation between God and the Son, in which the Son offers to undergo death in order to pay the ransom for mankind's sins. And in Book 10, it is not God, or accurately speaking, 'the voice of the Lord God' (Genesis 3: 8) that confronts Adam and Eve after their temptation but the Son. Adam and Eve hear the voice of God, but it is the Son who makes contact possible by being physically present (x. 85–102). As the Son facilitates the voice of God in Eden, promising that the seed of the woman will bruise the serpent's head (Genesis 3: 15), so he is able to see the future when Jesus will defeat Satan (x. 182–92).

A more extensive episode of intercession occurs early in Book 11 when the Son is moved by the penitent prayers of Adam and Eve. Milton bases his text, it has been argued, on Hebrews 9: 24, where Christ is said 'to appear in the presence of God for us'. This refers to Christ's ascension after his resurrection, and some of the Socinians imagined this to mean that Christ interceded on behalf of mankind after his crucifixion, as opposed to the crucifixion being the sacrifice that buys man grace. Since they also believed that the Son was created for the first time when he was born of a woman, the episode as Milton describes it, coming shortly after the Fall but a long time before most of the events recounted in the Old Testament, cannot in their view have taken place. It has been conjectured that the Son's intercession in this way is in fact an adaptation by Milton of the Socinian position, and that it is a crucial part of Milton's downgrading of the crucifixion in his explanation of the atonement.[2] After all, the Son hears the prayers of Adam and Eve, which are 'engrafted' onto his own payment, and then offered up to God, who receives them and grants immortal life to those who follow his ways. Adam and Eve, we are told, have been moved to prayer by the 'prevenient grace' that has wafted down from heaven and that presumably has been in existence since the Son first offered himself as a redemptive sacrifice for mankind in Book 3. The Passion of Christ is squashed into four lines, and seemingly replaced in significance with an immediately postlapsarian intercession. One can see in Milton's text the kinds of objections made to the Socinian position: that with grace bought at this point, why did the Son need to die?; in making Adam and Eve so active in already unwinding the consequences of the Fall, isn't Milton denying the special place of Christian witness, and even more, showing little difference between Jews and Christians?

In *Paradise Lost* so much poetic energy has been directed at showing the proximity of unfallen man to God, and of giving human shape to the Son if not also to God, that we begin to feel an anthropomorphizing energy throughout the poem.[3] Thus, at the sentencing of man in Book 11 of *Paradise Lost*, man's crime is to have become like God and the angels: 'like one of us man is become' (xi. 84). To eat the fruit of the Tree of Life would be to live for ever, or, so Milton adds to Genesis, to 'dream at least to live / For ever' (xi. 95–6), which seems to repeat how things had been before the Fall

---

[2] John Rogers, 'Milton and the Heretical Priesthood of Christ', in David Loewenstein and John Marshall (eds.), *Heresy, Literature, and Politics in Early Modern English Culture* (Cambridge, 2006), 203–20.

[3] See Abraham Stoll, 'Discontinuous Wound: Milton and Theism', *Milton Studies*, 44 (2005), 179–202. See also Gordon Teskey, *Delirious Milton: The Fate of the Poet in Modernity* (Cambridge, Mass., 2006), 87.

anyway, but the point here is the proximity in standing of the 'sons' of God (xi. 84):
the angels and mankind, and with a more distant prospect, the fallen angels, yet more
'sons', once blessed. How far are we from the story of the Sons of God in the
pseudepigraphic Book of Enoch (known to Milton through a Latin translation of
the Dutch humanist Guilielmus Henricus Vorstius), who came down from a mountain, made love to the women, and bred a race of giants, or to the early commentaries
on Genesis 6 that assumed fallen angels had mated with women (Milton alludes to
the Scripture at xi. 621–2)? Adam and Eve first appear as 'Godlike erect', meaning, one
initially supposes, that they are as beautiful as the pagan gods (iv. 289–90), perhaps
also alluding to traditions of iconography in painting. But can that be right? Are they
not made in the image of God, and has Milton not slipped to saying that they look
like Him? When Adam says that in his dream he could see that Eve was less a
resemblance of God than he was (viii. 543–4), is he not talking in the most literal
of senses?

To create is to seize material from Chaos, and in this respect the epic yokes the
imperial themes of exploration with the cosmological reapportioning necessary for
creation that Chaos himself resists. Not for the first time do we find ourselves in
sympathy with Satan as he battles through the contesting elements of chaos in search
of the Earth: after all, it nearly defeats him ('on all sides round / Environed wins his
way; harder beset / And more endangered' (ii. 1015–17)). It is for Milton a poetic
triumph involving the imitation of not merely Ovid's representation of chaos, but
also the energetic, atomistic poetry of Lucretius. Both are surpassed by the mytho-
poeia of Satan's final triumphant journey (only the second to last time he will have a
triumph) through the adversity of the elements:

> He ceased; and Satan stayed not to reply,
> But glad that now his sea should find a shore,
> With fresh alacrity and force renewed
> Springs upward like a pyramid of fire
> Into the wild expanse, and through the shock
> Of fighting elements, on all sides round
> Environed wins his way; harder beset
> And more endangered, than when Argo passed
> Through Bosporus betwixt the jostling rocks:
> Or when Ulysses on the larboard shunned
> Charybdis, and by the other whirlpool steered.
> So he with difficulty and labour hard
> Moved on, with difficulty and labour he;
> But he once past, soon after when man fell,
> Strange alteration! (ii. 1010–24)

At the end of his journey through Chaos, Satan 'lands' on the outer sphere ('the
firm opacous globe' (iii. 418)) that surrounds the earth (and contains the stars and
the planets) in the universe as Milton conceives of it. What had seemed a globe in
distance is now experienced by Satan as a waste wilderness. While we are impressed
with the epic similes of Satan as vulture waiting to prey on the young of sheep and

goats and as a Chinese land ship, we also confront the fact that Milton is describing space travel. As Satan 'walks' on this 'surface' (for it is a surface appropriate for his substance), Milton uses Satan's experience of God's creation as the lens through which we gain this knowledge. Satan is therefore a figure for education at this point in the poem. It is through Satan that we view Milton's Protestant limbo, created by the 'vain things' that fly up from the earth into the higher atmosphere, empty vessels all but waiting for recipients in the future history of mankind. Even with nothing present for Satan to confront, we are shown a colourful collection of monstrosities, the begetters of outrageously proud projects like Babel, and mistaken philosophers, to say nothing of the hosts of Roman Catholic religious orders, or, more alarmingly, those whose faith is so misguided they make an earthly pilgrimage, rather than seek immediate access to God.

The first section of Book 8 contains Raphael's overview of astronomical theory, with Adam willingly following his hint to leave these speculations for higher beings. That may be well enough for Adam, but is it enough for us the reader? The questions—whether the earth rises on the sun or vice versa; how the planets move; Copernicus's three motions of the earth; whether there is an invisible *primum mobile*—are certainly there for our contemplation. Soon we are going to see innocent, dutiful Adam failed by his faithfulness. Is not Milton implicitly introducing double-think into his poem: that knowledge of the heavens might well help to save us in future? Milton was proposed in 1667 as a possible author for a poem on the Royal Society and its achievements.[4] Contrary to the limit Raphael imposes on Adam, the first parent is clearly an exponent of the *prisca theologia*, the idea that God had placed in Adam the uncorrupted name and knowledge of every object in creation; by looking at each one Adam could name them.

Since Milton believes that the entire universe is one substance, and is not divided into the material and the immaterial, any more than bodies are divisible from souls, Paradise is an entirely fulfilled entity: exactly the place that God designed for unfallen man. So long as Adam and Eve remain innocent they can look forward to an unending perfect life, during which time the earth would become populated with their perfect children and they would, according to Raphael, ascend to the status of angels. The Fall brings death as punishment, which gives Milton a chance to spell out his mortalist position: that the soul dies with the body until the general resurrection.[5] When Cain is killed by Abel, he 'groaned out his soul' (xi. 447), which might be taken as a description of the separation of soul from body at death, or simply as an expression of pain at death, but there is no doubt that, echoing Genesis 3: 19, Adam will 'return unto the ground . . . For dust thou art, and shalt to dust return' (x. 206–8). Furthermore, the Fall is a great wounding of the earth severing the wholeness of its former self, pitching it from perpetual spring/summer into seasonal cycles and hence a certain amount of decay. Adam and Eve also lose their sense of

---

[4] British Library, Evelyn Collection MS Letters, John Beale to John Evelyn, Nov. 1667–Feb. 1671.

[5] See William W. Kerrigan, 'The Heretical Milton: From Assumption to Mortalism', *English Literary Renaissance*, 5 (1975), 125–66.

place, and it is this double loss—their home and the wounding of the paradisal earth—that has seemed to some to add an ecological dimension to Milton's view of Eden.[6] The legacy of the fallen angels is the treatment of creation for purely acquisitive ends, having forgotten that they are creatures with a responsibility to creation. Milton is the first to represent Adam and Eve as literal gardeners, stewards of God's earth in their labours. The Fall is an ecological disaster.

LOVE IN PARADISE

Adam argues for the partner who will help him enjoy paradise; it is easy to concur with him that this is a matter of the exercise of free will, less easy to believe that God was merely testing Adam's powers of judgement in denying him one for as long as he does. Yet all this while Adam has been talking directly with God. Raphael instructs Adam to resist the deposition of reason that Eve's attractive presence exerts over him, but it is this unbounded pull that stays with the reader: 'here passion first I felt / Commotion strange, in all enjoyments else / Superior and unmoved, here only weak.... All higher knowledge in her presence falls / Degraded' (viii. 530–2, 551–2). Is this not the consequence of both free will and desire? Does free will only have to be a regulatory power? Raphael's denial of 'carnal pleasure' does not reveal an adequate understanding of Adam's feelings, which might already as 'passions' be partaking of the higher love that the angel praises. After all, the angels love by having angelic intercourse (viii. 620–9).

The culmination of the passion is the consummation of the paradisal marriage, and an uneasiness where sexual passion is acknowledged ('Commotion strange') but which Raphael warns is deceptive and bestial, and might spoil the proper exercise of free will: far better to find more refined 'true love', that 'refines / The thoughts, and heart enlarges' (viii. 589–90). Is this not what we have just witnessed between God, angel, and man, requiring a supreme act of loving from God, who after all is solitary? Now we see with surprise that passion has just been redefined. No longer is passion the act of suffering in the crucifixion, but the desire of the first man for the first woman. No small event in the history of semantics (Milton is particularly on the ball here: *OED* gives the first dating for 'passion' meaning sexual desire as 1641), and in Milton's view it is the end of the act of God's creation, rather than the response to Satan's sometime victory.

---

[6] See Ken Hiltner, *Milton and Ecology* (Cambridge, 2003), pt. 1; Diane Kelsey McColley, *Poetry and Ecology in the Age of Milton and Marvell* (Aldershot and Burlington, Vt., 2007), ch. 7; Nigel Smith, *Literature and Revolution in England 1640–1660* (New Haven and London, 1994), ch. 8; Timothy Morton, *Ecology without Nature: Rethinking Environmental Aesthetics* (Cambridge, Mass., 2007), 16, 18.

Even as an elderly man, Milton presents the Fall of Man in *Paradise Lost* strung between two moments of sexual utopianism. First, Milton's unconventional but not unprecedented view, expounded openly and literally when we first meet Adam and Eve, that there was coition in Paradise:

> nor turned I ween
> Adam from his fair spouse, nor Eve the rites
> Mysterious of connubial love refused:
> Whatever hypocrites austerely talk
> Of purity and place and innocence,
> Defaming as impure what God declares
> Pure, and commands to some, leaves free to all.
> Our maker bids increase, who bids abstain
> But our destroyer, foe to God and man?
> Hail wedded love, mysterious law, true source
> Of human offspring, sole propriety,
> In Paradise of all things common else.
> By thee adulterous lust was driven from men
> Among the bestial herds to range, by thee
> Founded in reason, loyal, just, and pure,
> Relations dear, and all the charities
> Of father, son, and brother first were known. (iv. 741–57)[7]

Then there is the joyous vision of angelic sex imparted by Raphael at viii. 618–29: frictionless sex involving the occupation of one angelic being by another. While Milton eschews conventional forms of sexual ardour, as he would have known it from courtly literature, and probably also an Italianate literature that praised the courtesan, a very high premium is put upon the special delights of sex in marriage. The examples in *Paradise Lost* suggest that this is over and against the view that sex was tainted with original sin, and therefore a necessity only for the purposes of reproduction. The conventional view of marriage, widely taught throughout Christendom, and repeated in the passage from *Paradise Lost*, Book 4, quoted above, was that marriage was for procreation. Milton instead argues that marriage is for 'fit conversation', by which he meant that the woman was there to fill a lack in man, so avoiding the 'evil of solitary life' (*CPW*, ii. 235). If such a conversation was impossible, that is, if the partners were, as we would put it, incompatible, then divorce was a remedy.

These views are tested in *Paradise Lost*. Book 4 presents Adam and Eve as exemplars of the mutuality that Milton idealizes in the divorce tracts. It is reported that Adam chased Eve when he first saw her, but unlike the rapes that ended such chases in classical literature, Adam chases Eve to have a conversation. The intention is to suggest that we too can become like Adam and Eve in their innocent sexuality, insofar as we can surmount the consequences of the Fall. Milton achieves this by

---

[7] See esp. James Grantham Turner, *One Flesh: Paradisal Marriage and Sexual Relations in the Age of Milton* (Oxford, 1987).

having the first people symbolically replicate the appearance and piety of his contemporary Puritans:

> in their looks divine
> The image of their glorious maker shone,
> Truth, wisdom, sanctitude severe and pure,
> Severe, but in true filial freedom placed;
> Whence true authority in men; though both
> Not equal, as their sex not equal seemed;
> For contemplation he and valour formed,
> For softness she and sweet attractive grace,
> He for God only, she for God in him:
> His fair large front and eye sublime declared
> Absolute rule; and hyacinthine locks
> Round from his parted forelock manly hung
> Clustering, but not beneath his shoulders broad:
> She as a veil down to the slender waste
> Her unadornèd golden tresses wore
> Dishevelled, but in wanton ringlets waved
> As the vine curls her tendrils, which implied
> Subjection, but required with gentle sway,
> And by her yielded, by him best received,
> Yielded with coy submission, modest pride,
> And sweet reluctant amorous delay. (iv. 291–311)

Hair to the shoulder but not below for the man, while Eve's cloth-like tresses figure the veil worn by primitive Christian and later godly women in church services. All hint of lewdness is supposed to be absent because we are in a prelapsarian world. Nonetheless, we cannot help thinking about those later fallen associations: this is a crucial part of the poem's duality (see further Susan Wiseman's essay below). Yet still, they live naked, work as gardeners, and eat as vegetarians, the latter feature replicating the idealism of some of Milton's co-religionists.[8]

The relationship between Adam and Eve turns on the meaning of 'one flesh'. As Milton gives us his adumbrated version of Genesis, they literally are a somatic continuum, since Eve was formed out of one of Adam's ribs. The text continually makes us feel that sympathy and companionship between the two is a reflex of their material co-extension. In Adam's view they are always one continuous being, 'one flesh'; he does not admit of divorce, and Adam and Eve's oneness anticipates the apocalyptic reversal of divorce that will come with the last days, when all within the boundaries of salvation will be as one and reconciled with each other. The crunch comes with the Fall. Where much of the growing difference of opinion between Adam and Eve focuses upon the understanding of free will, Adam's astonishing speech at the point of his Fall (Eve has already been successfully tempted) involves the fusing of emotions, passions, and flesh that is now familiar, and familiarly vexed:

---

[8] See Smith, *Literature and Revolution*, 327–36; and, more generally, Tristram Stuart, *The Bloodless Revolution: A Cultural History of Vegetarianism from 1600 to Modern Times* (New York, 2007).

How can I live without thee, how forgo
Thy sweet converse and love so dearly joined,
To live again in these wild woods forlorn?
Should God create another Eve, and I
Another rib afford, yet loss of thee
Would never from my heart; no no, I feel
The link of nature draw me: flesh of flesh,
Bone of my bone thou art, and from thy state
Mine never shall be parted, bliss or woe. (ix. 908–16)

It may be Latinate syntax, but in English, Adam's sense of loss feels like a grammatical absence: at l. 913, 'would never' *what* from his heart? The abrupt caesura that follows, and the emotionally disturbed 'no, no' underlines the point. Some forty lines later, Adam rationalizes his decision:

I with thee have fixed my lot,
Certain to undergo like doom, if death
Consort with thee, death is to me as life;
So forcible within my heart I feel
The bond of nature draw me to my own,
My own in thee, for what thou art is mine;
Our state cannot be severed, we are one,
One flesh; to lose thee were to lose my self. (ix. 952–9)

Of course, in choosing to stay with Eve, Adam is divorcing himself from God, and it has been argued that this affirmation of faith in the 'bond of nature' (it has been 'bond' rather than 'link' in these lines), whether it be a psycho-physical continuum, or merely a bond of affection, is self-deceptive. Adam should really obey the advice of *Tetrachordon* (1645), which was not to lose oneself, and not to lose oneself meant to divorce. This opposition is highly pointed and very deliberate. Moreover Eve is a separate intelligence from Adam, and in that sense beyond 'one flesh'. And what of that?

In *Paradise Lost*, the creation of the world in Book 7 is also rendered as a gendered process where Mother Earth has within her womb all the objects of creation, but where nothing will appear until God gives permission. The oceans ferment the hard crust of the earth to produce life, but God has not yet spoken. Then he does:

The Earth was formed, but in the womb as yet
Of waters, embryon immature involved,
Appeared not: over all the face of earth
Main ocean flowed, not idle, but with warm
Prolific humour softening all her globe,
Fermented the great mother to conceive,
Satiate with genial moisture, when God said
Be gathered now ye waters under heaven
Into one place, and let dry land appear. (vii. 276–84)

This is highly charged sexual language, if not exactly erotic. What we are seeing is God's 'divorcing' command as divorce or separation is written into the making of objects in the natural world. Since, in Milton's heretical universe, all matter was originally part of the body of God, and God is present in it unless he chooses not to be in it, we are witnessing a description of, so to speak, divine sexuality. The sexual sensuality of the description of creation augurs no less whether mountains or animals are the subjects. Fecundity in nature is not to be had without this charged element of description, even if some of the vocabulary has its roots in alchemy or philosophy. This is, as it were, axiomatic sexuality, as opposed to the personal sexuality of Adam and Eve, and men and women thereafter. It recalls the sexual imagery of creation at the beginning of Book 1, which describes creation as the Holy Spirit's impregnation of Chaos: 'thou from the first / Wast present, and with mighty wings outspread / Dove-like satst brooding on the vast abyss / And mad'st it pregnant' (ll. 19–22). Since Milton held that God created the universe out of himself we have to assume that this is a description of a sexual act of one entity with itself. Later in Book 8, Milton has Raphael suggest that there might be other worlds, so divided between 'the two great sexes' (viii. 151), not merely in terms of original (male) and reflected (female) light, but of a universe utterly divided by gender.

We leave Adam and Eve at the end of *Paradise Lost* very much in a state of fallen mutuality: 'hand in hand with wandering steps and slow, / Through *Eden* took their solitary way' (xii. 648–9). We have not witnessed the divorce of Adam and Eve, but, with all the sense of a tragic catharsis behind us, we have witnessed the end of 'one flesh', with Satan playing the role of putative adulterer.

Scepticism and Free Will

By fusing classical form with biblical subject matter, *Paradise Lost* also contains a very large number of points where an informed reader can discern a deep irony behind a biblical or otherwise Judaeo-Christian sacred material. It may be mocking of the fallen angels for the narrator to laugh ('Behold a wonder!', l. 777) at their rapid downsizing at the end of Book I, and this has certainly been seen as Protestant disapproval of Roman Catholic infernal angelology. But this treatment also suggests laughter at sacredness *tout court*; the poem begins to partake of sceptical unbelief, of the kind generated by the use of pagan perceptions and art forms, and by the findings of the humanist scholars. In the world of mid-seventeenth-century intellectual life, such perceptions were very common. Although they are a long way away from Protestant heresy as most would have known it, there is a relationship which comes together most evidently in Milton's epic. Neither should we discount the presence of humour, which is not a quality usually associated with Milton.

It is very much Milton's version of events, his own particular Scripture that we are given in the poem. This is especially so when there is no biblical source for the events described, such as the creation of Pandemonium towards the end of Book 1. Here one of the fallen angels is the Greek God Mulciber (or Hephaistos, or Vulcan), whose name in Heaven we never learn. What Milton does tell us is that the myth of his casting down by Jove, as told by Homer (*Iliad*, 1. 591–5), is an error; in fact Mulciber 'Fell long before' (i. 748), with Satan and the other fallen angels. But later on the ancient myths of punished giants function as a way of explaining the fall of the rebel angels (ii. 174–84). Bible and ancient epic elements become interdependent in Milton's narrative: they certainly make *Paradise Lost* what it is, they reinforce each other, but they also undermine each other.

That Satan is wrong in the bigger scheme of things, however much we feel sympathy in places for him, makes the liberty he speaks for seem like both a heresy (in the Augustinian sense) and a blasphemy; just so when Mammon sees the fallen angels' predicament as a struggle between fate and chance (ii. 232–3), or when Satan plots his revenge by proposing the seduction of mankind (ii. 345–75). This is a matter for discussion in respect of the politics of the poem. Similarly, the licence in *Paradise Lost* for Raphael to liken 'spiritual things to corporal' means that Satan's rebellion is figured as a republican revolt against imposed monarchy. Nowhere is this more startlingly expressed than in King Moloch's rousing call to overwhelm God's throne:

> No, let us rather choose
> Armed with hell flames and fury all at once
> O'er heaven's high towers to force resistless way,
> Turning our tortures into horrid arms
> Against the torturer; when to meet the noise
> Of his almighty engine he shall hear
> Infernal thunder, and for lightning see
> Black fire and horror shot with equal rage
> Among his angels; and his throne itself
> Mixed with Tartarean sulphur, and strange fire,
> His own invented torments. (ii. 60–70)

Let there be no mistake of the sheer daring of these lines: Milton has one of his characters imagine the destruction of God. No less startling is Belial's imagining of annihilation (as opposed to punishment) as the ultimate end of God's justice, and it sounds like the denial of consciousness so valued in *Areopagitica*: 'this intellectual being, / Those thoughts that wander through eternity' (ii. 147–8). Just as Cartesian thought is associated with Satan elsewhere in the poem, scepticism leads on to nihilism. On the one hand, these positions come to us through the mouths of infernal agents; on the other hand, there they are as discernible thoughts.

At the heart of *Paradise Lost* is Milton's free will theology, the belief that man can choose between good and evil; Satan rebelled of his own free will, Adam chose fatally the wrong way, and although postlapsarian man is much reduced on that account, we still have the obligation through our faith to choose good from evil. We are certainly not predestined either to damnation or salvation (although Milton did not discountenance the possibility of the latter). Much has been written of free will in Milton's epic, and the large extent to which it drives the poem. Whether or not it counts as a heresy is another matter. In Milton's view, it was a vital part of what made heresy heresy.

Thus, Milton explicitly exempts God's foreknowledge (he does not mention predestination) from having any impact on the Fall, howsoever He foreknew it:

> they themselves decreed
> Their own revolt, not I: if I foreknew,
> Foreknowledge had no influence on their fault,
> Which had no less proved certain unforeknown.
> So without least impulse or shadow of fate,
> Or aught by me immutably foreseen,
> They trespass, authors to themselves in all
> Both what they judge and what they choose; for so
> I formed them free, and free they must remain,
> Till they enthrall themselves. (iii. 116–25)

Satan's language in Book 2 of *Paradise Lost* is distinctly that of free will, right, and merit. Yet Satan does not know, or has lost the ability to understand, the theological universe in which he exists. Thus, it is God who prescribes him in stark terms at the beginning of Book 3. Satan believes his defeat is a consequence of fate, and God knows he rules the universe. In terms of dramatic, classical, and theological tradition, Satan is a tragic hero in a voluntarist universe. 'Just right' is his first explanation for his wicked eminence as leader of the angelic rebellion, but the second cause is 'free choice', which in a sense is true—Satan has chosen to fall (ii. 18–24). The fallen angels 'complain that fate / Free virtue should enthral to force or chance' (ii. 550–1), but this is ancient *virtus*, manliness, not choice. Nonetheless, other fallen angels discuss 'providence, foreknowledge, will and fate, / Fixt fate, free will, foreknowledge absolute' (ii. 559–60) but cannot conclude, cheer themselves up with false surmises, and in general are lost, sliding first in the absence of scriptural authority to mere scholastic debate (as chastised in *Areopagitica*) and then to Stoic philosophy 'Vain wisdom all, and false' (ii. 565), which the Son will deride in *Paradise Regained* (iv. 274–330). In *Paradise Lost*, Book 5, Raphael explains to Adam and Eve how it is for angels and men:

> Our voluntary service he requires,
> Not our necessitated, such with him
> Finds no acceptance, nor can find, for how
> Can hearts, not free, be tried whether they serve
> Willing or no, who will but what they must
> By destiny, and can no other choose? (v. 529–34)

Free will makes full sense when it is conjunct with obedience: 'freely we serve / Because we freely love, as in our will / To love or not; in this we stand or fall' (v. 538–40). It is when Eve explains her faith in God's support, that he would surely not have subjected them to temptation without some kind of guard, that our attention should be triggered: 'And what is faith, love, virtue unassayed / Alone, without exterior help sustained?' (ix. 335–6). It seems a good argument, but Adam is more cautious:

> But God left free the will, for what obeys
> Reason, is free, and reason he made right,

> But bid her well beware, and still erect,
> Lest by some fair appearing good surprised
> She dictate false, and misinform the will
> To do what God expressly hath forbid,
> Not then mistrust, but tender love enjoins,
> That I should mind thee oft, and mind thou me.
> Firm we subsist, yet possible to swerve
> Since reason not impossibly may meet
> Some specious object by the foe suborned,
> And fall into deception unaware,
> Not keeping strictest watch. (ix. 351–63)

Adam introduces the concept of 'right reason' here: the power to choose but also one that always puts obedience to God first and foremost. Satan is the first to alienate right reason. But Adam is caught since he cannot compel Eve to stay: that would be a compromise of her innocence. So he must let her go to face the trial of her innocence:

> But if thou think, trial unsought may find
> Us both securer then thus warned thou seemst,
> Go; for thy stay, not free, absents thee more;
> Go in thy native innocence, rely
> On what thou hast of virtue, summon all,
> For God towards thee hath done his part, do thine. (ix. 370–5)

The whole poem, and Milton's view of the history of mankind, turns on these lines, and they have been much discussed in respect of whether Eve was presumptuous or Adam insufficiently responsible in not restraining her. Leaving the choice so balanced deliberately conveys the dilemma in the theological issue, and the only crucial difference between God and Adam at this point and on this issue is that Adam does not have foreknowledge. Later on, Eve's suggestion that she and Adam commit suicide is a final beggary of free will (x. 1001–6).

Most orthodoxy in the Church of England since Queen Elizabeth's reign had in fact accepted predestination theology: it was enshrined in the seventeenth of the Thirty-Nine Articles of the Church of England. It is a matter of some debate whether this article was drafted under the influence of Calvin or reflects a looser and far less serious interest in the matter.[9] The commitment to Calvinism remained strong among the senior Anglican churchmen until the 1620s when the influence of Jacobus Arminius was felt, particularly among those followers of William Laud, Bishop of London and then Archbishop of Canterbury, who sought a return in some measure to focus upon ceremonies and the veneration of the 'beauty of holiness'. Laud's abhorrence of predestination is quite clear. But free will theology was also the preference of some Puritan divines and some of the radical Puritan and separatist groups. William Ames stands out as a distinguished theologian who had an influence upon Milton as well as many others, while the General Baptists, who had their origins in the early seventeenth century were also free willers, perhaps through early contact

---

[9] Thanks to John N. Wall, Charles Carlton, and Peter Lake for information on this matter.

with Dutch Anabaptists. Resistance to orthodox, Calvinistically focused Puritanism might result in general allegiance to free will principles, and the Quakers stand as the most influential group of this kind, with whom the older Milton had some close connections. Some of the most influential Puritan preachers during the 1640s and 1650s accepted free will as a foundation from which to mount toleration arguments. The most significant here was the prolific Congregationalist John Goodwin, whose church in Coleman Street, London, was close to Milton's residences in the 1640s. Free will cannot be seen as a heresy in the Augustinian sense in Milton's lifetime, despite the noise made by orthodox Calvinists, especially Presbyterians, about it. No one was persecuted under the blasphemy act for being an Arminian in the 1650s. So many different groups manifested an interest in it, at all levels of the church, and from some of its most orthodox and traditional parts. Nonetheless, it was a force of considerable theological change and Milton's poem alongside much more of his writing registers that most centrally.

Conclusion

Paradise Lost, then, is a heresy machine: it produces heresies as we readers make sense of the epic. This follows from Milton's very position on heresy—in itself unusual in his time—as the act of choosing by the believer when confronted by the evidence in the first and second scriptures: the Bible and the Book of Nature. Many of Milton's heretical views were shared with his more unorthodox contemporaries, be they curious intellectuals or fervent sectaries, Thomas Hobbes or Gerrard Winstanley and the Diggers. The very innovative form of *Paradise Lost*, a kind of literary heresy (in Miltonic terms) itself, becomes a site for these heterodox views and necessarily their embodiment. And the extremely human terms of the poem bring those heterodox views right home to us, the reader, poignantly in the characters of Adam and Eve, and painfully in the character of Satan. Finally, they live in us for better or for worse as we internalize the teaching of free will theology and free will epic.

CHAPTER 29

···

GOD

···

STUART CURRAN

MICHAEL Lieb argues persuasively that Milton reimagined the nature and function of God every time he wrote about him.[1] This proposition, however, simple as it seems, carries major implications, immediately subverting any concerted attempt or even felt need to find a consistent theological position that would determine Milton's understanding of the deity across his career. A further implication to the argument is that there is no necessary progression implicit in Milton's renderings of God—that, for all we can discern, God's character in any work is determined by narrative or generic pressures more than dogmatic certainty. Nor need we, in this view, chart a theological trajectory by which Milton might be supposed to develop an ever more refined conception of God over his career (which is particularly useful where so little certainty can be brought to the exact dating of his major writings in verse). It is assuredly true, if we accept the common though still much debated consensus that Milton was the actual author of *De Doctrina Christiana*, that in that work he sought to deduce from an exact interrogation of Scripture the nature of God and to see all the rest of creation, including the Son, in a subordinate position (*CPW*, vi. 274–80). That might seem to agree with the relation of Father and Son in *Paradise Regained* where Jesus is resolutely humanized, but it is of little purport to what follows in the same volume, *Samson Agonistes*, a work where God's absence and with it a lack of assured redemption is the central and tragic driving force. And it simply cannot be considered the ideological premiss of *Paradise Lost*, where the Son constitutes an aspect, extension, and embodiment of God: his 'Word, [his] wisdom, and effectual might' (iii. 170) and thus a second self.

[1] *Theological Milton: Deity, Discourse and Heresy in the Miltonic Canon* (Pittsburgh, Pa., 2006), 10.

The God of *Paradise Lost* exists, first and foremost, as a character, a highly problematic one for many readers. It has been asserted, by Harold Bloom, that 'God's failure as a literary character is the only blemish' in the work.[2] But that is hard to square with the return of critic after critic to how God is expressed and expresses himself in the poem. There are definitely elements to this being that are difficult to fathom and even to reconcile; and in the end, however firm the faith of a figure like Milton, beneath his justification of God yawns a deep incertitude. In this respect God is a much more complex figure than the sublime emblem of self-deception and reactionary despair we encounter in Satan. He might therefore be construed as actually the greater 'character', at once clear and enigmatic, declaratively candid yet always hidden, an authoritative voice but one at once undercut and counter-balanced by the Son who is also God. C. S Lewis, though overly dismissive in tone of those who had forgotten their Anglican catechism, is surely right in his famous declaration that those who don't like Milton's God simply don't like God, not because Milton's God is a traditional Anglican deity (far from it), but because he is the intentional embodiment of all the paradoxes, which is to say seeming contradictions, of many centuries of Judaeo-Christian thought.[3] Indeed, it appears to be the contention of twenty-first-century critical revisionism[4] that Milton deliberately accentuates these paradoxes as a means of freeing Christianity from externally imposed sectarian dogma or critics striving for authority through authoritarian tactics.[5]

Rather than either an off-the-cuff dismissal of God as a character or an abject determination of his rectitude, then, it would seem more respectful of Milton as the greatest of literary artists in English to record and rightly understand the elements essential to his characterization. First, on the supposition that God is all-knowing, omnipotent, and eternal, Milton cannot construe him within any of the categories by which Kant would assert we conceptualize reality on a human plane. We are introduced to God in Book 3 doing what no other figure in the epic (except, it would appear, the Son) could replicate, looking down from Heaven on an overlaid montage of perspectives, 'His own works and their works at once to view' (iii. 59), as simultaneously he surveys Eden, Hell, and the edge of Chaos where Satan is at this point entering into the newly created universe. The verse paragraph ends by returning us to the centre of God's prospect, 'Wherein past, present, and future he beholds' (iii. 78); and, as God then utters his first words to his Son, Milton shifts from a spatial to a likewise multiple temporal perspective, with God describing Satan's expedition to corrupt Eden. For twelve lines his discourse flows in an anticipated present tense, recapitulating what we had learned in Book 2 of Satan's plan 'By force . . . or . . . / By some false guile [to] pervert' (iii. 91–2) Adam and Eve; then, suddenly, 'and shall pervert' (iii. 92), God declares, striking out for five lines into a future tense that

---

[2] *The Book of J.* (New York, 1990), 316–17.
[3] *A Preface to 'Paradise Lost'* (1942), 130.
[4] See Lieb, *Theological Milton*; Michael Bryson, *The Tyranny of Heaven: Milton's Rejection of God as King* (Newark, Del., 2004); Peter C. Herman, *Destabilizing Milton: 'Paradise Lost' and the Poetics of Incertitude* (New York and Basingstoke, 2005).
[5] See Lewis, *A Preface*; Stanley Fish, *Surprised by Sin: The Reader in 'Paradise Lost'* (1967).

encapsulates the entire epic, from which abruptly he shifts to a past perfect (which assimilates Adam and Eve into the singular creation of Genesis 1: 27)—'he had of me / All he could have' (iii. 97–8)—then an imperfect: 'I made him just and right' (iii. 98). The remainder of God's opening speech mixes present and past tenses, as if there were no distinctions between them—as, of course, there are not from an eternal perspective. If everywhere in *Paradise Lost* we are confronted with an over-determined postlapsarian language from which it is impossible for readers truly to conceptualize the nature of prelapsarian Eden or even Heaven, Milton's initial representation of God places us likewise outside the normative ken of the reality we inhabit, which is where God exists, inscrutably.

If we do not conceptualize in the manner of God, it goes without saying that we will not talk like him either, and it is not simply because his discourse is that of a 'school divine', as Pope wittily remarked.[6] Although it may be true that Milton's God is capable of hate, as Lieb argues,[7] it is not the kind of hatred (of God, of Adam and Eve, of superiors in a hierarchy, of contradiction in general) that animates Satan. God's is an intellectual not a passionate hatred: within the text of *Paradise Lost* he is unsusceptible to passion, whose Greek root links it to suffering. And accordingly he does not resort to passion to explain himself. Satan is the master rhetorician in both *Paradise Lost* and *Paradise Regained*. We are not likely to be seduced by his words in the brief epic because Jesus does such a notable job of puncturing his arguments. But every reader is swayed by the power of Satan's rhetoric in *Paradise Lost*. The exception is God, who 'reads' Satan thoroughly and remains untouched, because God is a logician, not a rhetorician. The operative principle of his universe in conception and operation is pure reason, and Satan, from his wandering first speech lacking a syntactic centre on to his unanticipated reduction to a reptile in Book 10, for all his interrogating rhetoric, is profoundly irrational. God, on the other hand, however he mixes his tenses, never speaks in conditional clauses ('If thou beest he', i. 84), never asks questions that cannot be answered ('knowledge forbidden? / Suspicious, reasonless. Why should their Lord / Envy them that? Can it be sin to know? / Can it be death? . . . ' (iv. 515–18)). We respond so powerfully to Satan because, unlike God, he talks like us; it is Milton's quiet achievement to make us uncomfortable with a deity who trades only in right reason.

And then, too, however often Satan shifts his shape, from 'stripling cherub' in Book 3 (l. 636), to towering giant in Book 4 (ll. 986–90), to serpent in Books 9 (ll. 494 ff.) and 10 (ll. 511–14), he always is physically definable. Indeed, his very physicality, we eventually come to see, is an index of his fallen nature. God, in contrast, exists within a dazzling fountain of light, which no being in the universe can penetrate except the Son, who 'Account[s himself] man' (iii. 238), according to the angels who celebrate his bold heroism, to 'end the strife / Of mercy and justice in [God's] face discerned' (iii. 406–7). This, of course, is consonant with the Son's theological role as

---

6 'Imitation of Horace, First Epistle of the Second Book', in *Poetical Works*, ed. Herbert Davis (Oxford, 1978), 364, l. 102.
7 Lieb, *Theological Milton*, 163–83.

mediator between the pure essence who is God and the material creation he has substantiated. But if only the Son, in this vast universe, can visualize God, how can any of us—or them—actually know God? To give an example of how radically ignorant is every other being, even the archangels, one need only look to Raphael's explanation late in his four-book account of the war in heaven and the creation of the universe. In Book 8 he admits to having missed Adam's creation (also, of course, Eve's, which may account for his unswervingly male-centred understanding of the nature of things). He was, he says, sent on an excursion to see that Hell's gates remained barred 'while God was in his work' (viii. 234) of creation: 'Lest he incensed at such eruption bold, / Destruction with Creation might have mixed' (viii. 235–6). This is at once very sloppy theology, given the account of creation he has just given in Book 7, and a misreading of the nature of Eden, which not only has the potentiality for destruction mixed with its creation but embodies it in a second, fatal tree next to the Tree of Life. In Books 11 and 12 Michael envisages and recounts postlapsarian human history to Adam: not that he knows any of it. God slips in the clause, 'As I shall thee enlighten' (xi. 115), to send him on his way to earth. God here likewise in advance firmly discredits the *felix culpa* (xi. 86–9) that Michael blithely endorses (xii. 575–87).

But Adam and Eve, it would appear, in their innocent stage, do know God. Yet this is not exactly true. They know the Son: it is he, who coming to judge Adam and Eve after the fall introduces himself thus—'Where art thou, Adam, wont with joy to meet / My coming seen far off?' (x. 103–4). And presumably it is likewise the Son who interrupts Eve's contemplation of her own beauty in iv. 467–76, and leads her to Adam. Yet it is a 'voice' (iv. 467) she hears, and she is 'invisibly thus led' (iv. 476) to her consort. When Adam recounts the scene, he likewise emphasizes the lack of substantiality: 'on she came, / Led by her Heav'nly Maker, though unseen / And guided by his voice' (viii. 484–6). And in his account of his own first recollection, he perceives his Maker initially in a 'dream' (viii. 292), then when he awakens as a 'Presence divine' (l. 314), then as a 'vision bright' (l. 367), and finally as a 'gracious voice divine' (l. 436). However firmly, then, the Son recounts his physicality when he comes to judge Adam and Eve, in terms of their creation he is decidedly, like his Father, insubstantial.

A pattern such as this always in Milton has a purpose, and the purpose here, it would seem, is insistently to remind us that the Son is a 'Divine Similitude' (iii. 384), like the Father, an extension of the Father, 'Image of [God] in all things' (vi. 736), not a wholly separate being. And though he appears in Book 3 in the guise of a debating opponent, the crucial rendering of the inverse trinity of Book 2—Satan, Sin, and Death—ought to have prepared us to read this debate allegorically, as God, beyond space and time, the 'I am who fill[s] / Infinitude' (vii. 168–9), ponders the dynamics of his new creation: on the one hand—on the other hand. But the contrary voices in their turn point to an insistent dialectical kinesis that constitutes Milton's attempt to explain, and to justify, God's nature. The dialectical, it should be emphasized, is the very essence of paradox, of all those centuries of paradox written into Judaeo-Christian theology.

But the question remains, since the idea of a Son of God occurs fairly late in the Old Testament, among the prophets, why Milton should so insistently present his God in a dialectical posture. And its corollary is why God should have decided to recreate himself, as it were, as a dialectical union of essence and substance necessitating an entire universe in which to play out its tensions. One key to this is represented by the exchange between the newly created Adam and his Maker in Book 8. There Milton goes out of his way to represent God—though it must be the voice of the Son we hear—as occupying a unique state of unconnectedness in his universe. But the attentive reader cannot miss the slippage, and, as with the many like instances where Milton depends on us to navigate his textual echoes, we may surmise that he has a purpose in alerting us to what neither Adam nor Raphael quite fathoms.

Adam, arguing that his solitary condition goes against the norms of God's creation, questions 'Among unequals what society / Can sort, what harmony or true delight?' (iii. 383–4). He has no being with whom to 'converse' (viii. 396), Adam stipulates (born as he is with a refined sense of Latin roots), and his creator replies in kind:

> What think'st thou then of me, and this my state,
> Seem I to thee sufficiently possessed
> Of happiness, or not? who am alone
> From all eternity, for none I know
> Second to me or like, equal much less.
> How have I then with whom to hold converse
> Save with the creatures which I made . . . ? (viii. 403–9)

Adam counters by remarking his own lack of a comparable creative ability: 'I by conversing cannot these erect / From prone, nor in their ways complacence find' (viii. 432–3).

So, is God too, in his supreme aloneness, without 'complacence'? If not, where would he look, sole as he is, to satisfy it? Where but in the Son, whom God apostrophizes in Book 3 as 'thou, / My sole complacence' (iii. 275–6), which leaves Adam's echo resounding with unmistakable precision. And where has God found one 'Second to me, or like, equal [no] less', indeed, but in the Son, whom God explicitly represents as 'throned in highest bliss / Equal to God, and equally enjoying / God-like fruition' (iii. 305–7)? Though it is the Son who speaks here as God's Word, it is therefore God who likewise speaks, for he solely converses, is conversant, in every sense, with the Son. With the other angels he decrees, commands, and commends but never holds an open interchange. Milton has it on Paul's authority that God cannot lie (Titus 1: 2, Hebrews 6: 18), but he makes it appear that he does so in order that the startled reader will perceive a pattern not just linking the first and second Adams, but linking them in parallel ways, in their creation and in their innate identity. A secondary value to the seeming prevarication is that it shines a penetrating light on just how and where God may be understood to participate in the dynamics of his own universe.

The most striking aspect of *Paradise Lost*, one that Milton not only does not gloss over but rather accentuates, is that the events it recounts, whatever the sanction of the Bible, did not have to happen. God could have been content with enacting C. S. Lewis's notion of his placid orthodoxy right from the start. That would have saved him from a prelacy of Lewis-like defenders and occasional upstart anticlericals, epitomized by William Empson's now infamous comparison of God with Stalin.[8] In short, God would not have had to lose a third of the heavenly angels if he had not decided that his original heaven was not all it could be. To rectify its if not inherent inadequacies, at least its limitations as to range and variety, 'on a day' (v. 579), as Raphael off-handedly relates it, he decides to create a second self; a radically reconstructed and enlarged universe, containing all manner of diverse life forms; and a new race of sentient, intelligent, pro-creative, and, above all, independent beings; also a realm of un-creation, which is Hell, and a set of reactionary, un-creating beings to inhabit it in a shadowy mirroring of the life of heaven. And he so foresees the results of this profusion of his creativity that he makes it essential that his own Son, his 'Word . . . wisdom, and . . . effectual might' should converse with—that is, convert himself into—this new order of creation: 'Account me man' (iii. 28), says the 'omnific Word' (vii. 217).

There are doubtless church fathers and later theologians in whom one might attempt to justify the audacity of Milton's conception of God's simultaneous and parallel acts of creation—Augustine's *Confessions* immediately leaps to mind with its daring parallelism between the saint's coming to his self-understanding and the seven days of God's creation—but the originary impulse to Milton's thinking may derive not from any particular intellectual forebear but from his recognition of the sheer mythological oddity of the second account of the creation of human beings offered in Genesis 2: 21–2. Instead of 'Male and Female created he them' (1: 27), we have Eve's secondary creation, which in Milton's conception may perhaps be seen less as concerning gender equality—whether justifying both Adam and Raphael's facile assumptions about male superiority or Adam's tendency to idolatry, with Eve as the 'last and best / Of all God's works' (ix. 896–7)—and more as identifying an element essential to the very notion of God's creativity, one with a powerful typological import, being, indeed, the first point in the Bible registering the forward thrust of Christian typology. What most fundamentally matters is that Adam must sacrifice of himself to enable Eve's creation: 'Account me woman', so to speak.

Moreover and most importantly, God himself sets the example that Adam retraces in having Eve configured from a part of his own identity. In order for God to create this new race of beings, to begin with, he must knowingly be prepared to sacrifice a third of the heavenly angels of his original creation, those who cannot deeply read, and reading thereupon commit themselves to the logic underlying, the new order of things. And, more essential yet, he must, as that logic construes its extremities, be prepared to sacrifice himself. It is easy, as the critical literature reminds us, to be so alienated by God's hectoring tone in Book 3 as to overlook the structural schema by which the book develops, which increasingly centres on the necessity and nature of

---

[8] William Empson, *Milton's God* (1965), 146.

the atonement for the contemplated originary human sin. And though the Father defines atonement in terms of the demands of eternal, immutable justice, the Son places the emphasis in radically different terms:

> Account me man; I for his sake will leave
> Thy bosom, and this glory next to thee
> Freely put off, and for him lastly die
>
> . . .
>
> Then with the multitude of my redeemed
> Shall enter Heaven long absent, and return,
> Father, to see thy face. (iii. 238–40; 260–2)

'[L]ong absent', the 'Divine Similitude' (iii. 384), having been 'Freely put off', will reappear; but still, it will have been 'long absent', with God during that period being first divided, then in part reviled and executed before becoming reassimilated into a unified supreme being. God himself figures this loss in almost homely, domestic terms: for the sake of man, he says, 'I spare / Thee from my bosom and right hand, to save, / By losing thee awhile, the whole race lost' (iii. 278–80). At the end of the conversation of Father and Son in Book 3 the gathered angels hymn this self-sacrifice as 'unexampled love, / Love nowhere to be found less than divine!' (iii. 410–11). Later, after the Fall, the Son, in preparing to honour the Father's justice, returns to the nature of his mission: 'I go to judge / On earth these thy transgressors, but thou know'st, / Whoever judged, the worst on me must light, / When time shall be' (x. 71–4). What does it mean that 'the worst on [him] must light'? Adam and Eve are judged to die of natural causes, after a long and vigorous existence; the Son of God submits himself to a short, ignominious life span whose culmination is his own sacrifice: 'the worst on me must light'. One can only speculate, in this account, on what must have been God's condition during his thirty-three years of self-division. It is, perhaps, telling that Milton, with all these dynamics still in mind, should in *Paradise Regained* have presented his deity as virtually tongue-tied, speaking but nine words in Satan's memory (i. 85), ten in that of Jesus (i. 285–6). God in *Paradise Regained* is literally without his Word.

If God's willing self-sacrifice is the heart of the logic of creation, and Dennis Danielson begins from this premiss in his examination of the God of *Paradise Lost* (though without tracing its ramifications beyond the traditional understanding of the crucifixion), those ramifications in the work itself are everywhere to be discerned.[9] Adam's sacrifice of a part of himself to bring Eve into being is the first human action in Eden, necessary not just for his having a helpmeet with whom to converse but also to their mutual procreation of the human race. But God's renewed universe is so ordered that all acts of privation, even all satanic negations, issue in a greater profusion of the forces of life, just as all pruning in the garden of Eden results in a greater abundance of fruition. It may be that the conspicuous, non-biblical presence of Chaos in the poem, as Joan Webber long ago argued (seconded since by

---

[9] Dennis Danielson, *Milton's Good God: A Study in Literary Theodicy* (Cambridge, 1982).

numerous others),[10] is there to ensure that we readers understand God's creation as always foregrounding potentiality over mere achievement, with no end in sight for eternity, in the same way that there are always more words possible in the vocabulary of the divine Logos than have yet been uttered. But the kinetic energy driving this ceaseless creativity is self-sacrifice.

The alternative metaphor that Milton employs to configure this logic is that of debt. The Son's 'Account me man' is wonderfully, if unknowingly, expounded upon in the ensuing book by Satan on Mount Niphates. He has reneged, he understands, on 'The debt immense of endless gratitude, / ... still paying, still to owe' (iv. 52–3), even as he acknowledges 'that a grateful mind / By owing owes not, but still pays, at once / Indebted and discharged' (iv. 55–7). This is the economy of God's new universe, the energy that keeps all elements in a commerce of debt, a commerce God does not just regulate but of which he is always the source and in which he too participates. The great chain of being is, indeed, not linear but circular in its dimensions, as each being is indebted to the next in an unceasing interchange of obedience to an external good. The autonomy that Satan pictures to himself and propounds as a politics of individuality to his followers is against the principle of mutual dependencies and conversations instilled by God in his recreation of his universe. Any beings claiming autonomy, like the Satanic legions, by that claim determinedly cast themselves (vi. 864) out of heaven. The essential purpose, God says, as he prepares the Son to begin the process of creation, is always a reaching outward, forward, and upward, with an 'upright heart' (i.18). The new world will contain a race of beings who may, so Raphael opines, 'by degrees of merit raised / ... open to themselves at length the way / Up' (vii. 157–9) to heaven. As Raphael represents God's creation in a way understandable to innocent human apprehension, the emphasis is less on staying 'lowly wise' (viii. 173) tending the garden than on perpetual self-betterment and taking responsibility for one's own initiative. The consequences, of course, of what Raphael instils as independent initiative and a continual reaching upward, are a disastrous hubris; but even after the Fall a second Archangel, Michael in Book 12, still represents this as the aim of God's creation, an aim that, whatever the obstacles to its success—and the history recounted in Books 11 and 12 suggests that they are truly formidable—has by no means been abandoned.

So much, then, one might say, for 'justify[ing] the ways of God to men' (i. 26). And yet, as all but the most orthodox of readers of *Paradise Lost* have asked for centuries, why does God's replacing the bland cosmic comedy of passive obedience with insistent, painful choice necessitate such tragic repercussions? Does a dynamic of being required at every juncture to ask 'where to choose' (xii. 646) by its nature determine that we all—angels no less than humans—transact a 'solitary way' (xii. 649) in doing so? In other words, how does this creation by self-sacrifice operate beyond the perimeters of the poem, or, at the very least, of the traditional Judaic myth of creation. Milton offers a clear signal of this extension in how the question of

---

[10] Joan M. Webber, *Milton and his Epic Tradition* (Seattle, 1979).

atonement in Book 3 of *Paradise Lost* is introduced. In the proem Milton does not just abandon the pose of irradiated power with which he introduced his project in Book 1; he represents himself in a state of abject privation from it:

> ...cloud, instead and ever-during dark
> Surrounds me, from the cheerful ways of men
> Cut off, and for the Book of Knowledge fair
> Presented with a universal blank
> Of Nature's works to me expunged and razed
> And wisdom at one entrance quite shut out. (iii. 45–50)

'Cut off; shut out', an exemplar of unconnectedness, perhaps in the likeness that God will portray to Adam in Book 8. But no—'So much the rather thou celestial Light / Shine inward, and the mind through all her powers / Irradiate' (iii. 51–3). The avatar of potentiality, who assembled the components of Old and New Testament, as well as classical, authority in the proem to the first book, is still capable, though he can no longer read, of being flooded with light. Milton claims his connection to God on the same principle on which God posits his creation, by his own accepted martyrdom, which from this point establishes the pattern of his self-representation in the subsequent proems in Books 7 and 9. And if we can thus move outside the mythology of the poem into its surrounding actual and, by projection, its political context, we observe how Milton portrays himself in this same guise of heroic martyr as he digresses into the autobiographical representation of the *Second Defence*. There, confronted with the choice of abandoning his duty or his eyesight, Milton deliberately chooses blindness in the exchange by which he serves his people, the 'populus Anglicanus', which in this quasi-mythic account the writer, who stands as keeper of the Logos and himself bearer of the Divine image, is helping to create.

CHAPTER 30

....

EVE, *PARADISE LOST*, AND FEMALE INTERPRETATION

....

SUSAN WISEMAN

> Not equal, as their sex not equal seem'd;
> For contemplation hee and valour form'd,
> For softness shee and sweet attractive Grace,
> Hee for God only, shee for God in him. (*PL*, iv. 296–9)

This is only one of several representations of Adam and Eve found in *Paradise Lost*. Milton's response to the story of Eve is so rich and complex that 'Milton's Eve' is often discussed solely in relation to the epic she uneasily inhabits and with particular focus on Books 4, 8, and 9. For contemporaries, however, *Paradise Lost* took its place alongside other kinds of writing which use Eve to debate social, theological, and political issues. Eve was an example—a figure used by writers and readers to test and assert views on social and political organization. Reading about Eve now readers are inevitably reminded of the modern debate about the equality between men and women. But as Constance Jordan reminds us, in seventeenth-century England 'the idea of an *equality* of authority and power between different kinds of persons, and notably between men and women, had for the most part no endorsement'.[1] The modern debate is both distinct from seventeenth-century debates and yet also grew from post-Reformation commentary on the Bible. Eve grew in importance at the

I am grateful to the editors for their very extensive work on this essay.

[1] Constance Jordan, *Renaissance Feminism: Literary Texts and Political Models* (Ithaca, N.Y., 1990), 5.

Reformation when women were invited to see their sufferings in childbirth not so much in terms of the power of the Virgin to redeem—a belief associated with Catholic birthing practices, construed as magical—but in terms of Eve's transgression.[2] Eve's disobedience to God made her an exemplary figure for the drama of obedience and disobedience in a society in which, in theory at least, obedience was an ideal. Milton's view of Eve seems momentarily clear when he takes trouble here to remind his reader that Eve was, specifically, 'not equal'. Yet, not only is this representation of Eve qualified by other parts of *Paradise Lost*, but also by the other representations of Eve the poem's contemporary readers might have encountered. Rather than surveying the pervasive presence of Eve in theological commentary, this essay situates the Eve of *Paradise Lost* in the specific context of writing on obedience by seventeenth-century women, exploring different ways in which Eve was an object of public interpretation for women as well as men in the period. I consider how Milton deals with the question of Eve, obedience, and the Fall in relation to the interpretations of the poet Aemillia Lanyer, the polemicist Rachel Speght, the prophet Anna Trapnel, and the Quaker Margaret Fell.

One reason for Eve's importance as an exemplary figure is the complex and potentially contradictory way in which her creation is described in the Bible. The description of how 'the rib, which the Lord God had taken from man' was made into 'woman' was normally taken to show that Eve's coming into existence consolidated the priority of Adam. Yet it was also argued, without scriptural sanction, that the rib taken from Adam was crooked, and so Eve too was like the bough that did not grow straight—she had a 'crooked disposition'.[3] In *Paradise Lost*, after the Fall, Adam realizes that the rib taken from his left or 'sinister' side to create Eve was in fact crooked: 'but a rib / Crooked by nature, bent, as now appears, / More to the part sinister from me drawn' (x. 884–6). The phrase 'Crooked by nature' echoes the claims of Joseph Swetnam, who in his 1615 pamphlet *The arraignment of lewd, idle, froward, and unconstant women* declared that 'a ribbe is a crooked thing good for nothing else, and women are crooked by nature' (p. 1). In a 1617 response to Swetnam, published under the name 'Esther Sowernam' (a pseudonym, with Esther invoking the biblical queen and 'Sowernam' a play on 'Swetnam'), the author retorted: 'So if women received her crookedness from the rib, and consequently from the Man, how much doth man excel in crookedness, who hath more of those crooked ribs!'[4] However, Eve's emergence could also be seen as making Adam perfect; as the Geneva Bible (1560) commented in its margins on Genesis 2: 22: 'Signifying that mankind was perfect when the woman was created, which before was like an imperfect building.' From this point of view, Eve's creation brought a moment of perfection and with it a promise of

---

[2] Mary E. Fissell, *Vernacular Bodies: The Politics of Reproduction in Early Modern England* (Oxford, 2004), 43. This tendency is evident in Milton's reference in his Sonnet XIX, 'Methought I saw my late espoused saint', to the 'spot of childbed taint' (l. 5).

[3] See e.g. Philip C. Almond, *Adam and Eve in Seventeenth-Century Thought* (Cambridge, 1999), 146–9.

[4] 'Esther Sowernam', *Esther hath hang'd Haman* (1617), 3. See further *Half-Humankind: Contexts and Texts of the Controversy about Women in England, 1560–1640*, ed. Katherine U. Henderson and Barbara F. McManus (Urbana, Ill., 1985).

salvation for the reader, for it was prophesied that her seed—Christ—should tread on the head of the serpent (Genesis 3: 15).

This message of hope and redemption embodied in Eve was in tension with her transgression: arguments about which aspect of Eve took precedence occurred in both poetry and vernacular polemic during the seventeenth century, as well as in theological disputes, and women as well as men contributed to the controversy. In *Salve Deus Rex Judaeorum* (1611), Aemillia Lanyer explores the dual potential of Eve:

> Till now your indiscretion sets us free,
> And makes our former fault much less appeare,
> Our Mother *Eve*, who tasted of the Tree,
> Giving to *Adam* what shee held most deare.
> Was simply good, and had no power to see,
> The after-coming harme did not appeare:
> The subtile Serpent that our Sex betraide,
> Before our fall so sure a plot had laide.[5]

For Lanyer, the story of Christ's Passion becomes a tale of the *obedience* of women as compared with the disobedience of men, and her examples run from Eve to Pilate's wife, from whose imagined speech pleading for Jesus' life the lines above are taken. Lanyer nonetheless accepts that the Genesis story implies Eve's subordination and makes her giving of the apple to Adam into a testimony to her obedience: 'Giving to *Adam* what shee held most deare.' The story of Adam and Eve did not in itself offer answers to the problem of obedience but rather offered a narrative understood as speaking of those concerns. That Lanyer can inflect the story to fit her chosen emphasis is bound up with the narrative's perceived need for, and openness to, interpretation.

During the second decade of the seventeenth century a pamphlet debate sparked by Swetnam over the nature and proper role of women developed and, inevitably, the implications of Genesis for women's status as social and political subjects featured in the controversy. In *A Mouzell for Melastomus* (1617) Rachel Speght asserts that Eve, 'excepting man, is the most excellent creature vnder the Canopie of heuen'.[6] Speght's argument, structured as answers to a whole series of objections, demonstrates Eve's position as the key example of obedience and its opposite—and therefore a figure rich in argumentative potential. The first objection she imagines takes us to the heart of how Eve was debated: 'that woman, though created good, yet by giuing eare to Sathan's temptations, brought death & misery vpon all her posterity' (p. 3). In response to this objection Speght answers that:

Sathan first assailed the woman, because where the hedge is lowest, most easie it is to get ouer, and she being the weaker vessel was with more facility to be seduced: Like as a Cristall glasse sooner receiues a cracke then a strong stone pot. Yet we shall finde the offence of *Adam* and *Eve* almost to parallel: For as an ambitious desire of being made like unto God, was the motiue which caused her to eate, so likewise was it his[.] (p. 4)

---

[5] Aemillia Lanyer, *Salve Deus Rex Judaeorum* in *The Poems of Aemilia Lanyer*, ed. Suzanne Woods (Oxford, 1993), ll. 761–8.

[6] Rachel Speght, *A Mouzell for Melastomus* (1617), 3.

Both have the ambitious desire but, for Speght, in going along with Eve, Adam is like a man who burns his hands in a fire. Satan has kindled the fire, and Eve has 'blowne' it, but it is Adam's decision to put his hand in (p. 5). Importantly, Speght argues, against the authority of St Augustine, for the positive implications of the Fall:

The offence therefore of *Adam* and *Eve* is by Saint *Augustine* thus distinguished, *the woman sinned against God, her selfe, and her husband*: yet in her giuing of the fruit to eate had she no malicious intent towards him, but did therein show a desire to make her husband partaker of that happinesse, which she thought by their eating they should both have enjoyed. This her giuing to *Adam* of that sawce, wherewith Sathan had serued her, whose sowrenesse afore he had eaten, she did not perceiue, was that, which made her sinne to exceed his: wherefore, that she might not of him, who ought to honour her, be abhorred, the first promise was made in Paradise, God makes to woman, that by her Seede should the Serpents head be broken: whereupon *Adam* calles her *Heuah, life*, that as the woman had beene an occasion of his sinne, so should woman bring foorth the Sauiour from sinne. (p. 6)

Eve had no intention to harm Adam but, as importantly, any harm was temporary because of God's decision that (lest Adam come to abhor Eve), her offspring, their offspring, should become the promise of Satan's defeat. Thus, some fifty years before the publication of *Paradise Lost* we find Eve playing a crucial part in a popular pamphlet debate on the status of women. Of course Milton's epic does not respond very directly to the Jacobean 'woman controversy'.[7] However, the texts from these years indicate the significance of Eve as an example in published vernacular debate in seventeenth-century England.

It seems more likely that in imagining Eve Milton responded to the controversy over women's preaching and participation in the separatist and sectarian congregations which proliferated during the English Civil Wars. Once the established, national, church began to disintegrate in the early 1640s women's role—in the congregation, in biblical interpretation and 'prophecy', even in ministry—was increasingly under discussion. London in the 1640s saw women like Katherine Chidley, Sara Wight, and Anna Trapnel working with ministers in the gathered churches and putting forward interpretations of the Bible in speech and writing. Such interpretations were not, necessarily, focused on the question of gender but inevitably that issue was important for the interpreters of the women's actions. During the revolutionary period women were active as prophets: while 'prophecy' might include the predictive it was more likely to imply inspired biblical exegesis.[8] The 'prophesies' of a number of women

---

[7] Although it is argued Milton does respond directly to the controversy in Shannon Miller, 'Serpentine Eve: Milton and the Seventeenth-Century Woman Debate', *Milton Quarterly*, 42 (2008), 44–68.

[8] See e.g. Teresa Feroli, *Political Speaking Justified: Women Prophets and the English Revolution* (Newark, Del., 2006); Diane Watt, *Secretaries of God: Women Prophets in Late Medieval and Early Modern England* (Cambridge, 1997); Hilary Hinds, *God's Englishwomen: Seventeenth-Century Radical Sectarian Writing and Feminist Criticism* (Manchester, 1996); Nigel Smith, *Perfection Proclaimed: Language and Literature in English Radical Religion, 1640–1660* (Oxford, 1989); Elaine Hobby, *Virtue of Necessity* (1988); Phyllis Mack, *Visionary Women: Ecstatic Prophecy in Seventeenth-Century England* (Berkeley and Los Angeles, 1994).

from the gathered churches were delivered at moments of political pressure during the 1640s and 1650s: there appear to have been as many as 300 female prophets active during the period.[9] A significant figure among the many prophets is Trapnel, who in the winter of 1653 attended the examination of the Fifth Monarchist preacher Vavasour Powell by the Council of State at Whitehall. In response to events in his trial, Trapnel fell into a trance and was carried to a house nearby where, eating nothing and drinking little, she prayed and prophesied for several days. Trapnel's audience was both supportive and sceptical.[10] Trapnel's prophesies were written down by a 'relator' who was, he says, listening 'in the chamber where she lay', and published in 1654 as *The Cry of a Stone or a relation of Something Spoken in Whitehall* (p. 16). Eden is invoked in Trapnel's attack on merchants, where she addresses 'you that are proud, and with stout necks / And mincingly do go':

> But oh the spiritual do see,
> They do hate it and spew.
> They cannot endure your company,
> Oh cover then your skins,
> Remember when that Adam fell,
> He covered was leaves in.
> His nakedness with leavy skins
> At length must be his clothes;
> Oh therefore all you naked ones,
> Oh do not scripture oppose.

The merchants' showy, rich clothes, 'black spots and powdered locks' remind Trapnel of the Fall from innocent nakedness (p. 31). Her criticism may play or pun on the (fruitless) attempts of deceived or deceitful men to cover their nakedness with untrue language or scriptures. It is male commercial society that here embodies the Fall and false knowledge. Trapnel's version of the Fall absents Eve from a highly masculine scene of sin and discovery as she focuses the reader's attention on the way the merchants' adornment replays the Fall, in which Adam's clothes paradoxically come to signal the very sin they attempt to hide. Trapnel's effacing of Eve's sin while recalling Adam's (as re-enacted by merchant manners) makes Eve conspicuous by her absence. Certainly, the reader can hardly avoid the implication, frequently made explicit in Trapnel's prophecies, that her own prophetic speaking is justified precisely by her plainness and lowliness as a simple and unadorned (either by learning or wealth) woman. It was in such biblical phrases as 'God hath chosen the weak things of the world to confound the things that are mighty' (1 Corinthians 1: 27) that female prophets found authorization for their conviction that 'the weaker vessel', woman (1 Peter 3: 7), might be thought particularly likely to carry God's word.[11]

---

[9] Mack, *Visionary Women*, 24.

[10] Anna Trapnel, *The Cry of a Stone* (1654), ed. Hilary Hinds (Tempe, Ariz., 2000), p. xvii.

[11] Elaine Hoby, 'Prophecy, Enthusiasm, and Female Pamphleteers', in N. H. Keeble (ed.), *The Cambridge Companion to Writing of the English Revolution* (Cambridge, 2001), 162–78 at 162.

Finally, in 1666, just a year before Milton's epic, an account of Eve appeared in the Quaker Margaret Fell's *Women's Speaking Justified*. Fell wrote to support the position that women had as strong an inner revelation of Christ as men and should be heard in Quaker congregations. Fell's justification rests on the argument that a proper interpretation of Scripture supports women's access to a public or political or congregational voice. It is those who are 'ignorant of the scriptures' who are 'against Women's speaking', but as the Church is Christ's wife, so 'in it do Daughters prophesie'.[12] Fell's argument underpinning this position begins with a reading of Eve. She intervenes at the key points in the Genesis narrative: creation, temptation, and Fall, enmity between women's seed and the serpent. When Fell writes 'in the Image of God created he them, male and female', slightly rewriting the first account of creation in Genesis 1: 27 ('So God created man in his *own* image, in the image of God he created him; male and female he created them'), she implies an answer to Eve's supposed secondariness: both Adam and Eve are to be considered as made in God's image and Eve is not at more of a distance from that image. Divine and human apprehensions of gender differ because, simply, God makes 'no such distinctions and differences as men do'; for him there are 'no such difference between the Male and Female as men would make' (sig. A2^r). Having dealt summarily with a subject of huge debate, Fell's discussion of temptation and the Fall is equally adroit. 'It is true', she announces, that the serpent came to the woman in his 'subtilty discerning her to be more inclinable to hearken to him, when he said, *If ye eat your eyes shall be opened*'. In mitigation Fell proposes only that when asked about her sin by God Eve confessed: 'Here the woman spoke the truth unto the Lord: See what the Lord saith, vers. 15. after he had pronounced sentence on the serpent; *I will put enmity between thee and the Woman, and between thy Seed and her Seed; it shall bruise thy head, and thou shalt bruise his heel*, Gen. 3' (sig. A2^v). Fell's emphasis on God's promise allows her to naturalize women's speaking:

Let this Word of the Lord, which was from the beginning, stop the mouth of all that oppose Womens Speaking in the Power of the Lord; for he hath put an enmity between the Woman and the Serpent; and if the Seed of the Woman speak not, the Seed of the Serpent speaks; for God hath put enmity between the two Seeds, and it is manifest, that those that speak against the woman and her Seed Speaking, speak out of the enmity of the old Serpent's Seed; and God hath fulfilled his Word and his Promise. (p. 4)

Although Speght and Fell are using Eve differently, both focus on her potential after the events in paradise; both insist on her prophesied redemptive role as the factor which should influence interpretation of Eve in the present. Fell strongly emphasizes the happy outcome of the Fall for mankind and the high spiritual status of women. The promise that future generations shall bruise the serpent's head reinforces the case that, although Eve has sinned, the outcome of such sin is to be measured against the promise of redemption.

---

[12] Margaret Fell, *Womens Speaking Justified* (1667), ed. David Latt (Los Angeles, 1979), 17.

If Fell's Quaker theology, with its emphasis on the certainty of earthly redemption through revelation of the inner light, allows her to emphasize the restorative properties of the Fall story, it is still the case that, like Speght and Trapnel, she feels the need to shape the implications of that story for her readers. Eve was a topic which allowed, even demanded, interpretation both because of the dual emphasis on transgression and promise to be found in the biblical accounts and because of the wealth of both scholarly and popular commentary for and against her. Whether Milton read these vernacular materials or not is not the point; rather, what is crucial is that these and many other interpretations of Eve were circulating in the world inhabited by *Paradise Lost*'s first readers. When Milton comes to Eve he is making interpretations that, like those of Speght, Trapnel, and Fell, have implications for women's relationship to religious, social, and political hierarchy.

Margaret Fell wrote *Women's Speaking Justified* in the years immediately after the restoration of monarchy but also in the aftermath of the unprecedented public activity of Quaker and other women like during the Civil Wars. Some critics have seen the Civil Wars and the regicide as 'intervening' in Milton's poetic processes, but, equally, we can see the cataclysmic events of these years as giving his writing vital impetus that cannot be directly tracked.[13] When Milton turns to Eve in *Paradise Lost*, his poem does seem to be marked by the vocal presence of women in religious and political life during the 1640s and 1650s. The versions in *Paradise Lost* of the two key scenes discussed above, creation and transgression, allow us to consider what Milton's interpretations do and do not share with those of his female contemporaries. Let us return to the description of Adam and Eve in Book 4:

> Godlike erect, with native Honour clad
> In nak'd Majesty seem'd Lords of all,
> And worthy seem'd, for in their looks Divine
> The image of their glorious maker shone,
> Truth, wisdom, sanctitude severe and pure,
> Severe but true filial freedom placed;
> Whence true authority in men; though both
> Not equal, as their sex not equal seem'd;
> For contemplation hee and valour form'd,
> For softness shee and sweet attractive Grace,
> Hee for God only, shee for God in him:
> His fair large Front and Eye sublime declar'd
> Absolute rule; and Hyacinthine Locks
> Round from his parted forelock manly hung
> Clust'ring, but not beneath his shoulders broad:
> Shee as a veil down to the slender waist
> Her unadorned golden tresses wore
> Dishevell'd but in wanton ringlets wav'd
> As the Vine curls her tendrils, which impli'd
> Subjection, but required with gentle sway,

---

[13] Christopher Ricks, 'Introduction', *Paradise Lost* (Harmondsworth, 1968), p. xi.

> And by her yielded, by him best receiv'd,
> Yielded with coy submission, modest pride,
> And sweet reluctant amorous delay. (ll. 289–311)

While many critics have noted that Eve is introduced with words like 'coy' and 'wanton', and that these words invite the reader to consider the 'movement from innocence to experience and sin', the question of both Adam and Eve's 'seeming' is less often discussed.[14] They are 'clad' in honour, 'seem' lords of all, and 'seem' worthy (not unlike the London merchants in Trapnel's prophecy). Their inequality is a matter of both appearance and 'seeming'. Words like 'seems' are all the more noticeably ambiguous in relation to Eve's 'unadorn'd' hair, the ringlets of which 'imply' hierarchical 'subjection' but 'gentle' subjection of an unfallen, pre-contractual, nature. If the question of seeming reminds us of the ever-present problem of the Fall, it also prompts us to remember the problem of seeming as introduced in the person of Satan in Book 4: the 'first / Who practis'd falsehood under saintly show' (l. 123) and whose 'borrow'd visage' (l. 116) is found out by Uriel. Given that much of the reader's attention in the opening of Book 4 is directed to recalling Satan's shape-shifting from Book 1, the description of Adam and Eve in Book 4 alerts us to the possibility that all is not, indeed, as it 'seems'.

As with other language clustering around Eve, 'seems' poses for the reader the problem of how to respond to implied qualifications of the Edenic state. What the reader does with the word, whether we read it as a hint of a Fall to come, depends on what we see as most important about the question of time. Does 'seeming' imply that the Fall is inevitably coming, or that (because it is inevitably coming), it has to all intents and purposes already happened—as indeed, in the time-of-reading it has (though so also has the new dispensation of salvation)? The extended description in Book 4 shows that Adam is subject to some of the same ambiguous, question-prompting language as Eve but that she is much more intensely and densely framed by such 'fallen' words. Indeed, when it comes to the question of the pair's nakedness the poem tells us explicitly to acknowledge both their spotless innocence and remember that 'guilty shame, dishonest shame / Of nature's works, honour dishonourable, / Sin-bred' (ll. 313–15) is on its way. Milton's poem subtly but continually reminds readers that Eve was the agent of the Fall, and so raises questions about how blameworthy she was before the Fall actually happened. Should we see the description of Eve (as well as her own speech) as significantly typological, always reminding the reader that she is going to fall?[15] Milton needs to 'characterize a perfect Adam and Eve who yield plausibly to the temptation to eat the forbidden fruit' and this presents him with the problem of making their disobedience and sin plausible in psychological and literary terms, but also theologically.[16] The couple must be perfect before the Fall, yet how can the author represent the nature of a perfection which

---

[14] Stanley Fish, *Surprised by Sin: The Reader in 'Paradise Lost'*, 2nd edn. (Cambridge, Mass., 1997), 93.

[15] On fallen and unfallen language in Milton's representation of Eden, see especially John Leonard, *Naming in Paradise: Milton and the Language of Adam and Eve* (Oxford, 1990).

[16] George Musacchio, *Milton's Adam and Eve* (New York, 1991), 1–8.

nonetheless allows for (perhaps inevitably leads to) a use of free will that is sinful? Some maintain that Adam and Eve are still innocent even as the language of the Fall—our own, fallen language—describes them.[17] If we follow God's account in Book 3, as presumably Milton intends us to, we must understand the text's events as taking place within a paradoxical double time where the fall is both pre-ordained (in some sense) and, crucially, the product of free will. And, furthermore, we may also need to remain aware that the poem itself is the product of language after the Fall. Rather than see Adam and Eve as fallen or unfallen we can read them as both and neither. But Milton's narrative strategy, unlike the defences of Eve which put the Fall in the past and focus instead on the prophecies of her redemptive role, inevitably places the emphasis on the reader's knowledge that the Fall is to come and that Eve will be the first transgressor.

These questions about the Fall are a crucial constituent of readers' encounters with the densely layered descriptions of Eve, nowhere denser than in the pool scene in Book 4 where we encounter the falling, fallen, unfallen, redeemed, unredeemed time and language inhabited by Eve. Her memory of her first moments involves a memory of her own reflection. Eve is in charge of the narration, describing to her 'Guide / And Head' how she came to him (ll. 442–3). 'I first awak't', she tells him, and 'much wond'ring where / And what I was' (ll. 450–2), she hears a 'murmuring sound' of waters flowing into 'a liquid Plain' and into which she gazes:

> As I bent down to look, just opposite,
> A shape within the wat'ry gleam appear'd
> Bending to look on me, I started back,
> It started back, but pleas'd I soon return'd,
> Pleas'd it return'd as soon with answering looks
> Of sympathy and love, there I had fix't
> Mine eyes till now, and pin'd with vain desire,
> Had not a voice thus warn'd me, What thou seest,
> What there thou seest fair Creature is thyself,
> With thee it came and goes: but follow me,
> And I will bring thee where no shadow stays
> Thy coming, and thy soft embraces, hee
> Whose image thou art, him thou shalt enjoy
> Inseparably thine, to him shalt bear
> Multitudes like thyself, and thence be called
> Mother of human race[.] (ll. 460–75)

However, even with the voice of her creator prompting her to her destiny Eve finds Adam, though 'fair indeed and tall', a disappointment—'Less winning soft, less amiably mild' (l. 479)—and she turns back until she yields to his words and hand. Eve only turns to Adam after considerable verbal prompting by her maker and by Adam; 'I yielded' (l. 489), she tells him and successfully embraces 'conjugal attraction' (l. 493).

---

[17] These questions are discussed by Diane Kelsey McColley, *Milton's Eve* (Urbana, Ill., 1983).

The tension between obedience and disobedience is present even in Eve's very beginning. In reminding readers of the fate, as told in Ovid's *Metamorphoses*, of the beautiful boy Narcissus who dies by falling in love with his own reflection, Milton calls our attention to more than the obvious problems of the eye. If Eve, self-desiring and desired by others, refigures Narcissus and focuses our attention on the role of looking, then in Ovid's story the female figure of the nymph Echo, who, rejected by Narcissus, pines away until 'nought is left but voice and bones', is as important and directs our attention to the female voice and to the problems of communication.[18] Milton's best-known interrogation of communication between man and wife is in the divorce tracts, where fit 'conversation' between man and wife is essential to the man's ability to assemble and shape a self of manly vigour ready to serve the commonwealth. Failure or success of conversation is at the heart of marriage, making or breaking the link between household and government.[19] Eve's first coming to consciousness invokes the story of Echo's fruitless, failed speech and hints at an association between women's narcissistic imagination or fancy, female transgression and disobedience, and the dangers, but also the importance, of conversation between man and wife.

The weakness of female 'fancy' is further emphasized in Book 4 in the context of the dreams inspired by Satan, who is discovered by the angels Ithuriel and Zephon:

> Squat like a toad, close at the ear of Eve;
> Assaying by his devilish art to reach
> The organs of her fancy, and with them forge
> Illusions as he list, phantasms and dreams,
> Or if, inspiring venom, he might taint
> The animal spirits that from pure blood arise
> Like gentle breaths from rivers pure, thence raise
> At least distempered, discontented thoughts,
> Vain hopes, vain aims, inordinate desires
> Blown up with high conceits engendering pride. (ll. 800–9)

As I have suggested elsewhere, Milton here gives Eve a morally depraved dream of 'flight' and 'high exhaltation' (v. 89–90).[20] When she tells the story of the dream it is as if she is partially in its grip. Adam is alarmed by 'This uncouth dream, of evil sprung, I fear' (l. 98), and diagnoses the presence of evil in Eve's soul '[c]reated pure' as caused by 'fancy', which takes over when reason retires: 'mimic fancy wakes / To imitate her; but misjoining shapes, / Wild work produces oft' (ll. 110–12). The prophetic speech and visions of figures such as Trapnel and Fell were dismissed by their clerical critics in these terms; what was claimed as a vision from God was ascribed to disordered fancy or melancholy—an effect of bodily instability rather than a spiritual state. In hostile sermons and pamphlets vulnerability to false

---

[18] *Ovid's Metamorphoses*, trans. Arthur Golding (1567), ed. Madeleine Forey (Harmondsworth, 2002), 3. l. 496.

[19] Joan M. Weber, 'The Politics of Poetry: Feminism and *Paradise Lost*', *Milton Studies*, 14 (1980), 3–24.

[20] Susan Wiseman, *Conspiracy and Virtue: Women, Writing, and Politics in Seventeenth-Century England* (Oxford, 2006), 165.

prophecy either as a prophet or a listener was associated particularly with those who were regarded as lacking the rationality instilled by education to control their fanciful passions—artisans and women.[21]

Milton's Eve is a female reasoner and so subject to the tyranny of fancy, manifested in demonic 'uncouth' dreams rather than true prophetic visions; her faulty reasoning leads her to transform Satanic fancy into sinful reality through the crucial act of disobedience, described in Book 9:

> So saying, her rash hand in evil hour
> Forth reaching to the Fruit, she pluck'd, she ate:
> Earth felt the wound, and Nature from her seat
> Sighing through all her Works gave signs of woe,
> That all was lost. (ll. 780–4)

This moment arguably partially resolves some of the productive tensions we find in the unfallen Eve. Her 'sapience' (l. 797)—a word fusing knowledge and taste—reframes her and orients the reader towards the coming fall of Adam and, to some extent, the ensuing drama of redemption. Any comparison between Milton's Eve and those of his contemporaries reminds us that Milton's representation of both Adam and particularly Eve is complicating and multilayered, where the women we have cited seek to simplify, and to defend. As an epic, Milton's poem deals with the time of Eve's fall in a quite different way from the other texts examined here. Adam and Eve's story is both retrospective and unfolding in a poetic present. Within this framework, Eve's fall exists in more than one time and, as we have seen, the poem constantly plays on that doubleness. As William Poole points out, *Paradise Lost* 'consistently inverts the order of the history it tells, giving us the fallen before the unfallen', with the implication, inevitably, that the Fall (rather than the promise of redemption to mankind, and of the woman's seed treading on the head of the serpent) is the climax of the story.[22] Even the title of Milton's text reminds us, anticipatorily, of the loss rather than the redemption.

If we return to the section of Lanyer's *Salve Deus Rex Judaeorum* designated 'Eve's Apology', Lanyer sets Eve's sin against that of those men who condemned Jesus: 'Let not us Women glory in Mens fall, / Who had power given to over-rule us all.' (ll. 759–60) Lanyer's framing of the Genesis story within that of the greater sin of the rejection of Christ by men, and her claim that that rejection should be seen as compromising the authority of men's rule, add up to a precise and polemical re-evaluation of the Fall. Though Eve is sinful, there are mitigating factors and her sin is massively eclipsed by that which it foreshadows—the betrayal of Christ. Milton's account offers a very different emphasis. If *Paradise Lost* is extremely sophisticated in its prolonged invitation to emotional engagement with the story of Adam and Eve, our attention is

---

[21] Smith, *Perfection Proclaimed*, 28–30; see 83–4 for comparison between Eve's dream in Book 5 and the prophetic dream of 'Mrs T. P.' as recorded by the leading 'Ranter' Abiezer Coppe in *Some Sweet Sips, of Some Spiritual Wine* (1649). See further William Poole, *Milton and the Idea of the Fall* (Cambridge, 2005), 173.

[22] *Milton and the Idea of the Fall*, 158. I am very grateful to Dr Ed Paleit for discussion of this matter.

focused sustainedly on the way Eve is persuaded to eat and then on what happens to her as a consequence of eating. Immediately she tastes the fruit Eve becomes a compulsive, greedy eater. Next she reasons, deviously, about whether to keep the joy of knowledge for herself:

> so to add what wants
> In Female Sex, the more to draw his Love,
> And render me more equal, and perhaps,
> A thing not undesirable, sometime
> Superior; for inferior who is free? (ix. 821–5)

Eve's new reasoning is now fully subject to her passion, producing a huge intensification of appetite, irresponsible desire for power, and an understanding of her own position as unequal political subject. As Milton introduces the reader to the Fall long before the inhabitants of Eden enter the unfallen world—indeed in the first four words of the poem, 'Of man's first disobedience'—there is an additional force to the act of transgression in Book 9. It is what we have known was coming, not simply because we know the story, but because of the way Milton's poem structures our expectations, making Eve's transgression the event for which we have always been waiting. If the language of the Fall presses in upon Eve before the event, then her having fallen, as it were, proves the pattern of expectation set up by the poem.

When, finally, with Adam, 'hand in hand with wand'ring steps and slow' Eve makes her 'solitary way', she is in a newly distant, more fully human, relationship to Adam and to God (xii. 648–9). Eve has both survived and been destroyed by the Fall. Critics tend to balance Eve's sin against the vision of renewal in this final book. Two points can be made on the basis of the female readings of the Fall against which we have set *Paradise Lost*. First, seventeenth-century readers of *Paradise Lost* might have been rather differently engaged than us by Eve's drama; they would have been aware of other writing on Eve, including in vernacular and popular print, and might well have measured Milton's version against others available. Second, at least some of those other interpretations and representations by women, although many are more literal in their approaches to Eve, also give her a role with very different religious and social implications. From this point of view, Milton's Eve must make a specific intervention in a debate about obedience and disobedience. *Paradise Lost* makes Eve's transgression the focal point of the epic, in part through the reader's encounter with fallen language even in paradise, but also makes it absolutely central to the poem's emotional dynamic. Milton locates the problem of Eve in Eve herself rather than in the question of where she should be placed, as an example, in a narrative which encompasses creation, transgression, and redemption. In this very personification of the problem of Eve in 'Eve' as a developed narrative subject, *Paradise Lost* can remind us that, for some readers at least, the issues of Eve's sin and disobedience, and of the spiritual equality of man and woman, were—as Margaret Fell's insistence that a righteous woman could be spiritually superior to an unrighteous man illustrates—increasingly problematic in the world into which Milton's text emerged.

Comparing *Paradise Lost* with some women's writings on Eve has not delivered to us a unified feminist view, shared by women, to set against Milton's poem. There are certainly similarities in the way post-Reformation writers see Eve as a problem of interpretation. If we think of Speght's Adam choosing to put his hand in the fire, we can see how important godly reasoning was for all of our interpreters. And this emphasis on interpretation illuminates something specific to Milton's poem, something which may be a consequence of the new prominence of women in the revolutionary period in which Milton began to write his epic. For, if Eve's encounter with her watery reflection shows her to be a misty reasoner, she is, nevertheless, given a second chance to dream. In Book 12, Eve dreams again, explaining that though she is now distant from God, yet 'God is also in sleep, and Dreams advise, / Which he hath sent propitious, some great good / Presaging, since with sorrow and heart's distress / Wearied I fell asleep' (ll. 611–14). But Eve has learned that she cannot be an interpreter of her own dreams or prophecies:

> But now lead on;
> In me there is no delay; with thee to go,
> Is to stay here; without thee to stay,
> Is to go hence unwilling; thou to me
> Are all things under heaven, all places thou,
> Who for my wilful crime art banished hence.
> This further consolation yet secure
> I carry hence; though by me all is lost,
> Such favour I unworthy am vouchsafed,
> By me the promised seed shall be restored. (ll. 614–23)

The Fall has rescued Eve from her 'fancy'—she has learned to give over the matter of interpretation to Adam. So, if Eve poses a question of interpretation for Milton's contemporaries, it seems that one aspect of her development in *Paradise Lost* is to relinquish the act of interpretation, or 'prophecy', to the superior reasoner—Adam: 'So spake our mother Eve, and Adam heard / Well pleased, but answered not' (ll. 624–5). If Eve's story demands its readers become interpreters of the key biblical texts, one of the things 'learned' by Milton's Eve is the limit of female interpretation.

CHAPTER 31

....

THE POLITICS OF *PARADISE LOST*

....

MARTIN DZELZAINIS

In the 'Life of John Milton' prefixed to the 1698 *Complete Collection* of Milton's prose works, the republican freethinker John Toland proclaimed that the 'chief design of his *Paradise Lost*' was 'to display the different Effects of Liberty and Tyranny' (Darbishire, 182). However, Toland's eagerness to co-opt the cultural prestige of Milton's epic for the radical Whig cause highlights the surprising lack of any explanation by him of *how* it displays 'the different Effects of Liberty and Tyranny'. There is no suggestion that Satan might embody the tyrannical principles of a Charles I or a Cromwell, and no discussion of how the obedience enjoined upon Adam and Eve is consistent with their freedom. Instead, what Toland appends by way of commentary is the rhapsodical conclusion to Milton's *Of Reformation* (1641) in which he prophesied that the bishops

shall be thrown down eternally into the darkest and deepest Gulf of Hell, where under the despitful controul, the trample, and spurn of all the other Damn'd, that in the anguish of their torture shall have no other ease than to exercise a raving and bestial Tyranny over them as their Slaves and Negros, they shall remain in that plight for ever, the basest, the lowermost, the most dejected, most underfoot, and downtrodden Vassals of Perdition. (Darbishire, 183; cf. *CPW*, i. 617)

The switch from poetry to prose, from a post-Restoration to a pre-Civil War work, and from politics to religion appears wilful, even whimsical. But that is only how it seems to us. To a freethinker like Toland, the bishops personified the most insidious tyranny of all: 'priestcraft', or the power and influence of organized religion. Nor is it likely Milton would have disagreed with Toland's implied reading of *Paradise Lost*: after all, much of Book 12 is given over to the Archangel Michael's prophetic account of the decline of the primitive church until finally appropriated by clerical 'wolves' who seek to 'force the spirit of grace itself, and bind / His consort Liberty' (xii. 508,

525–6). Toland's considered juxtaposition of texts should remind us that the politics of *Paradise Lost* are those of the seventeenth century and not those of today.

Most recent accounts of the politics of the poem have accordingly focused on the question of what political statement Milton was or was not making when he first published it in 1667. According to Hugh Wilson, for example, it was an 'act of resistance' by a 'dissident' who chose a moment when the restored monarchy was weakened by the humiliating outcome of the second Anglo–Dutch War of 1665–7.[1] Similarly, David Loewenstein finds that Abdiel 'captures the spirit of seventeenth-century resistance writing' in his exchanges with Satan, while for David Norbrook Adam, in his conversation with Michael about Nimrod (see *PL*, xii. 24–104), shows himself, like the unfallen angels, to be a 'natural republican'—further evidence that 'far from retiring into political resignation, Milton made every effort to intervene in the now-diminished public sphere' of the Restoration.[2] And Barbara Lewalski is if anything even more categorical when she asserts that Milton 'stages the Nimrod episode as an overt statement of republican principles'.[3]

Admittedly, these views do not command universal assent. William Walker has recently challenged the consensus that Milton was a republican in any of the senses in which the term is usually deployed (he was actually, it seems, an antiformalist and a meritocrat), while Paul Rahe has questioned whether republicanism itself was quite what it has been taken to be.[4] There is, it must be said, a tendency for discussions of Milton's republicanism to turn into exercises in taxonomy, and perhaps this is part of the reason why some commentators have lately begun to question whether *Paradise Lost* is political at all. For Stanley Fish, this is largely a matter of rejecting a misconceived historicism that seeks to illuminate its politics by appealing to the historical archive. This does not mean that Fish wants to depoliticize the poem altogether; rather he wants to draw our attention to what he calls its 'politics of being', which is centred on maintaining 'an interior disposition' to the world rather than attempting to intervene in the flux of events.[5] For Annabel Patterson, however, depoliticization is precisely what Milton was aiming at, since he 'made a sustained effort, during his entire life, to prevent his poetry from being contaminated by—that is to say, read in the light of—his polemical prose'. It is no accident that attempts to read the prose into the poems generally prove frustrating—indeed, Patterson warns that what Michael says about Nimrod actually *reverses* the political theory of Milton's *The Tenure of Kings and Magistrates* (1649). Toland, it follows, was simply among the

---

[1] Hugh Wilson, 'The Publication of *Paradise Lost*, the Occasion of the First Edition: Censorship and Resistance', *Milton Studies*, 37 (1999), 18–41 at 18, 21.

[2] David Loewenstein, *Representing Revolution in Milton and his Contemporaries: Religion, Politics and Polemics in Radical Puritanism* (Cambridge, 2001), 226; David Norbrook, *Writing the English Republic* (Cambridge, 1999), 434, 487.

[3] Lewalski, *Life*, 470. For evidence that this was how the passage was seen by some early readers, see Nicholas von Maltzahn, 'The First Reception of *Paradise Lost*', *Review of English Studies*, 47 (1996), 479–99.

[4] See William Walker, '*Paradise Lost* and the Forms of Government', *History of Political Thought*, 22 (2001), 270–99; Paul Rahe, 'The Classical Republicanism of John Milton', ibid., 25 (2004), 243–75.

[5] Stanley Fish, *Surprised by Sin: The Reader in 'Paradise Lost'*, 2nd edn. (Basingstoke, 1998), p. lv.

first of many mistakenly seeking to align *Paradise Lost* 'with the political positions [Milton] took during the revolutionary era'.[6]

What these ways of politicizing and depoliticizing *Paradise Lost* fail to shed much light on is the politics of—by which I mean politics as depicted in—the poem. The main exception is the parallel often drawn between earthly and infernal parliaments. In the opening two books, we are assured, Milton procedurally and rhetorically reproduces the parliamentary process from summons to debate to final vote, and shows it being manipulated at every stage by Satan and Beelzebub.[7] Yet Milton consistently refers to Satan's 'great consult' with the fallen angels as a council rather than a parliament (i. 798; see i. Argument, 755; ii. Argument, 506). And while there is no evidence that Milton ever heard (as distinct from reading) a parliamentary speech, he did witness debates in the Council of State, the executive arm of the new republic that he served as secretary of foreign tongues from March 1649 onwards.[8] My aim in this essay is accordingly to illuminate aspects of the executive political culture to which Milton belonged, and in which he was still immersed when he began sustained work on *Paradise Lost* towards the end of the 1650s, and to suggest some ways in which it informed the poem. In doing so, it may be that a less familiar—and less congenial—image of Milton comes into view.

The best place to begin is with two of Milton's sonnets from these years. The one addressed to Cyriack Skinner in 1654 or 1655 invites his former pupil and now friend and amanuensis to put serious matters aside and relax:

> Today deep thoughts resolve with me to drench
> In mirth, that after no repenting draws;
> Let Euclid rest and Archimedes pause,
> And what the Swede intend, and what the French. (ll. 5–8)

At first sight, mathematics and diplomacy appear to have little connection—so little that editors see no need even to try to establish one. That they were related is evident from Milton's *Of Education* (1644), where students in his ideal academy 'having thus past the principles of *Arithmetic, Geometry, Astronomy,* and *Geography* with a generall compact of Physics . . . may descend in *Mathematicks* to the instrumentall science of *Trigonometry,* and from thence to Fortification, *Architecture,* Enginry, or navigation' (*CPW,* ii. 391–2). In the seventeenth century, geometry and mathematics indeed found some of their most important applications in warfare.[9] They were

---

[6] Annabel Patterson, 'Why is there no Rights Talk in Milton's Poetry?', in Christophe Tournu and Neil Forsyth (eds.), *Milton, Rights and Liberties* (Bern, 2007), 197–212 at 202.

[7] See Michael Wilding, *Dragon's Teeth: Literature in the English Revolution* (Oxford, 1987), and Sharon Achinstein, *Milton and the Revolutionary Reader* (Princeton, 1994), esp. 177–223.

[8] See Martin Dzelzainis, 'History and Ideology: Milton, the Levellers, and the Council of State in 1649', in Paulina Kewes (ed.), *The Uses of History in Early Modern England* (San Marino, Calif., 2006), 265–83. However, from Feb. 1651 the Council routinely excluded officials other than its secretary and his assistant from meetings; see Leo Miller, *John Milton's Writings in the Anglo-Dutch Negotiations, 1651–1654* (Pittsburgh, Pa., 1992), 5.

[9] See e.g. the material on fortification and gunnery appended to Richard Elton, *The Compleat Body of the Art Military* (1668), 239, 245.

indispensable both for understanding ballistics—the science which then as now underpinned foreign policy—and for designing fortifications that could withstand siege artillery. Diplomacy and the new military technologies went hand in hand. Notwithstanding its dissuasive intent, what the sonnet captures is something of the way those at the heart of the republican regime thought and talked about geopolitics.

The other sonnet was sent to Sir Henry Vane the Younger (1613–62) on 3 July 1652. While its sestet praises Vane for distinguishing between 'spiritual power and civil' as 'few have done' (ll. 10–11), the opening octave celebrates him as politician and administrator:

> Vane, young in years, but in sage counsel old,
>> Than whom a better senator ne'er held
>> The helm of Rome, when gowns not arms repelled
>> The fierce Epirot and the African bold.
> Whether to settle peace or to unfold
>> The drift of hollow states, hard to be spelled,
>> Then to advise how war may best, upheld,
>> Move by her two main nerves, iron and gold...
>>>> thou hast learned. (ll. 1–8, 11)

Under discussion is the Commonwealth's diplomatic and naval strategy, in framing which Vane played a central part by virtue of his long experience in both fields (he was sent to Vienna on his first diplomatic mission at the age of 18 and oversaw English naval finances from 1639). On 19 May 1652, an English fleet commanded by Blake clashed with a much larger Dutch force under Tromp even though the two northern maritime republics had been negotiating a treaty in London since December. Following representations from the Dutch, the Council of State (of which Vane was then President) set up a committee on 4 June to prepare a response and the next day Vane reported to Parliament with a draft answer which was then translated into Latin by Milton.[10] It accused the United Provinces of having an 'Intention...by force to Usurp the known Rights of *England* in the Seas, to destroy the Fleets that are, under God, their Walls and Bulwarks, and thereby expose this Commonwealth to invasion at their Pleasure, as by this late Action they have attempted to do.'[11] In short, the Dutch had mounted a pre-emptive strike under cover of the treaty.

Milton gives Vane full credit for catching the 'drift' of Dutch intentions ('hollow states' puns on 'Holland' and 'States-General', the governing body of the confederation). However, when George Sikes first published the sonnet in 1662 in *The Life and Death of Sir Henry Vane* his commentary took a different turn: 'In the former part of these verses, notice is taken of a kind of angelical intuitiveness and sagacity he was furnished with, for spying out and unridling the subdolous intentions of hollow-hearted States, however disguised with colourable pretexts of Friendship.'[12] The rare

---

[10] See Miller, *John Milton's Writings in the Anglo-Dutch Negotiations*, 61–2.

[11] A *Declaration of the Parliament of the Commonwealth of England* (1652), 16 (Miller, *John Milton's Writings*, 204); for Milton's Latin, see *Scriptum Parlamenti Reipublicae Angliae* (1652), 16 (ibid. 232).

[12] George Sikes, *The Life and Death of Sir Henry Vane* (n.p., 1662), 94.

term 'subdolous', derived directly from the Latin *subdolus*, means cunning, sly, subtle, and deceptive; Vane's specialism was thus the unmasking of deceit.[13] But to Sikes this acuity betokened spiritual as much as political gifts, and he accordingly attributed an 'angelical intuitiveness and sagacity' to Vane, rather as if he were one of the 'pure / Intelligential substances' (v. 407–8) who inhabit *Paradise Lost*.[14] The piety informing Sikes's account is, however, absent from Milton's austerely secular portrait that casts Vane not as an angel but as a Roman senator. His points of reference are not the Scriptures, but Cicero and Machiavelli. Moreover, Milton's allusion to Machiavelli's *Discorsi* is actually by way of *contradicting* Machiavelli's claim that war is waged with iron rather than gold, suggesting that he was becoming more attuned to early modern theorists of the fiscal-military state like Justus Lipsius (1547–1606) than to a previous generation of political thinkers still preoccupied with the Italian city-republics.

Vane and Milton were less on the side of the angels than might be imagined. Something about Vane's personal style—perhaps what Sikes calls his tendency to 'keep silence even from good'—led others to assume he was agreeing with them when he was not (Sikes, *Life*, 9). While Governor of Massachusetts (1636–7), he acquired a sinister reputation in some quarters because of what John Winthrop called 'his secret underminings' of the colony.[15] Similarly, Clarendon remarked on the 'rare dissimulation' with which Vane concealed his objectives during negotiations with the Scots over the Solemn League and Covenant in 1643: 'There needs no more be said of his ability than that he was chosen to cozen and deceive a whole nation which excelled in craft and dissembling.'[16] Trusted by the Scots as their 'most intime friend', Vane slipped the phrase 'according to the Word of God' into the opening clause of the Covenant that dealt with church reform: it turned out to be the 'politick engyn' that hindered the introduction of the presbyterian system which the Scots had intended the clause to promote.[17] Milton not only came to share Vane's dislike of Presbyterianism but was also unusually permissive about lying to those who are not one's friends. In *De Doctrina Christiana*, the theological treatise he was working on in the 1650s in tandem with *Paradise Lost*, he discarded the standard definition of a lie as an untruth told with an intention to deceive, and substituted a more complex one of his own: 'FALSEHOOD must arise from EVIL INTENT ['DOLO MALO'] and entails EITHER THE DELIBERATE MISREPRESENTATION OF THE TRUTH OR THE TELLING OF AN ACTUAL LIE TO SOMEONE, TO WHOM IT IS THE SPEAKER'S

---

[13] In 'In Quintum Novembris' (l. 90) Milton calls Satan 'subdolus'; i.e. 'Full of deceit and wiles, deceitful, crafty, sly, cunning', according to [Adam Littleton], *Linguae Romanae Dictionarium Luculentum Novum* (Cambridge, 1693), s.v. *subdolus*. According to the prefatory note (sig. A2ᵛ), the dictionary was prepared with the assistance of Milton's MS Latin thesaurus.

[14] Vane refers to 'Angels and intellectual Substances' in a letter to his wife in Mar. 1662 (*Two Treatises* (n.p., 1662), 95).

[15] Quoted in Michael P. Winship, *Making Heretics: Militant Protestantism and Free Grace in Massachusetts, 1636–1641* (Princeton and Oxford, 2002), 146.

[16] Edward Hyde, Earl of Clarendon, *History of the Rebellion*, ed. W. D. Macray, 6 vols. (Oxford, 1888), iii. 267.

[17] See Ruth E. Mayers, 'Vane, Sir Henry, the younger (1613–1662)', *ODNB*.

DUTY TO BE TRUTHFUL' (*CPW*, vi. 760; *CW*, xvii. 300). This shifts the emphasis from the intention *to* deceive to intention *in* deceiving. For there to be falsehood now requires not just intent but an 'evil intent'. That is to say, where the intention in deceiving is good (as when a doctor humanely withholds information from a patient), then there is no falsehood. And falsehood itself now takes two forms; one negative, the other positive. The former involves misrepresentation or concealment of the truth. Such dissimulation does not necessarily require any action on our part (as when not saying something allows another to form or persist in a false belief) whereas an outright lie requires us positively to state an untruth—to simulate rather than dissimulate. Finally, Milton stipulates that all this applies only when we owe a duty of truthfulness to our interlocutors. Where no such duty exists, then the issue of falsehood simply does not arise. And such a duty, he was clear, exists only in the case of our neighbours: 'If, then, we are commanded to speak the truth only to our neighbor, it is clear that we are not forbidden to tell lies, as often as need be, to those who have not earned the name of neighbor' (*CPW*, vi. 762) On this view, the commandment not to bear false witness against your neighbour left you pretty much free to lie to all and sundry.

As Milton's view of lying might lead us to expect, his attitude to the practice of analysing politics in terms of *ragion di stato* (reason of state) was ambivalent.[18] What theorists of reason of state maintained was that in situations where rulers had to choose between what was honest and what was profitable, they might legitimately choose the latter if it served their best interests or those of the state. Writers in this tradition understood politics in terms of the pursuit of interest (another favourite term), and characteristically delivered their insights in a dense, aphoristic style that owed much to Tacitus, who in his histories had unlocked the mysteries of state— *arcana imperii*—at the heart of imperial Rome. It is true that Milton often fulminated against this style of politics (or political style), condemning, for example, Virgilio Malvezzi's *Discorsi sopra Cornelio Tacitus* (1622) for cutting '*Tacitus* into slivers and steaks' before dismissing 'all the Tribe of *Aphorismers*' (*CPW*, i. 573, 598). However, a distinction was often made—especially by Jesuits—between acceptable and unacceptable forms of reason of state, and Milton did the same, denying toleration to Catholics on these grounds in *A Treatise of Civil Power* (1659): 'if they ought not to be tolerated, it is for just reason of state more then of religion' (*CPW*, vii. 254).[19] What he valued in Vane was precisely an ability to penetrate arcana and calculate interests. And it is significant that Milton says that for 'many years' he kept on file a manuscript that he took to be by Sir Walter Raleigh that encapsulated virtually the entire literature of reason of state, and which he published in 1658 as *The Cabinet-Council: Containing the Cheif Arts of Empire and Mysteries of State; Discabineted in Political and Polemical Aphorisms*. Without Milton already having displayed some interest in

---

[18] For the best recent summary of this tradition, see Noel Malcolm, *Reason of State, Propaganda, and the Thirty Years' War* (Oxford, 2007), 92–123.

[19] For this distinction, see ibid. 98–100.

statecraft, it is hard to see why he should have been given the manuscript by 'a Learned Man at his Death'.[20]

Sometimes Milton assumed political and ethical positions going beyond those of the reason of state theorists. Here chapters 13–24 of *The Cabinet-Council*, which derive from Lipsius's hugely influential contribution to the genre, *Politicorum sive Civilis Doctrinae Libri Sex* (1589), can serve as a benchmark. Unlike the Jesuits, Lipsius saw no prospect of a sanitized form of reason of state, accepting that there would always be an element of vice in what he called 'mixed prudence'. His experiences in the war-torn Netherlands made him mindful of the supreme value of peace and the need to preserve political authority, even if this meant that princes might have to disregard laws and conventional morality. Ultimately, the survival of the state depended on the ruler's ability to secure supplies of arms and money and to deploy these in the most efficient way; accordingly, in Lipsius's view, 'The Art Military [*Militarem aut Prudentiam*] is of all other qualities most necessary for Princes' (*CC*, 127).[21] But while stressing the need for military prudence, Lipsius insisted that 'No Warr . . . is to be made but such as is just'. What he had in mind was self-defence, which is 'natural and necessary', and the 'repossession by force' of lands or goods that have been wrongfully seized if peaceful methods have failed. For Lipsius, this ruled out all wars of aggression (with one major exception, as we shall see), and he was especially adamant that 'no desire of Honor [*Gloria*] or Empire [*Imperium*], are any lawful causes of War' (*CC*, 57; Lipsius, 148). Milton's discussion of these topics in the concluding chapter of *De Doctrina Christiana* is strikingly different. War, he begins by saying, 'is to be undertaken only after extremely careful consideration' ('ut prudentissimis consiliis suscipitur'), and then goes on to specify that it is 'to be waged knowledgeably and skilfully', 'with moderation', and 'in godly fashion'— stipulations that are followed by a fifth to the effect that 'a cruel enemy should not be spared'. But, astonishingly, at no point does Milton stipulate that the war itself must be just. Although its justness might be inferred from the further injunction that when fighting 'we should not trust in the strength of our forces, but in God alone', all he says we need to be sure of *before* hostilities commence is that the matter has been considered with the utmost prudence (*CPW*, vi. 802; *CW*, xvii. 406). In other words, Milton's concern is not so much with the right to wage war (what was called the *ius ad bellum*) as with ensuring that it is waged in the right way (the *ius in bello*).

The question of what the rules of war permitted was widely discussed at the time, and Lipsius devotes a separate chapter to defending the use of stratagems. For while he regards it as beyond question that 'out of the War covertly to kill a particular

---

[20] *The Cabinet-Council: Containing the Cheif Arts of Empire and Mysteries of State; Discabineted in Political and Polemical Aphorisms*, ed. John Milton (London, 1658), sig A2^{r-v}. hereafter cited as *CC*. For a full discussion, see Martin Dzelzainis, 'Milton and the Protectorate in 1658', in David Armitage, Armand Himy, and Quentin Skinner (eds.), *Milton and Republicanism* (Cambridge, 1995), 181–205. For an alternative view, see Paul Stevens, 'Milton's "Renunciation" of Cromwell: The Problem of Raleigh's *Cabinet-Council*', *Modern Philology*, 98 (2001), 363–92.

[21] The Latin is quoted from Lipsius, *Politicorum sive Civilis Doctrinae Libri Sex* (1590), 142. Hereafter cited as 'Lipsius'.

enemy by secret Assault or Practice, is not warrantable, either by Faith or Honor; yet to use all craft, cunning, and subtility in open War, is both allowable and praisable; and so is thought by Christian Writers'. And he buttresses this with a quotation from Augustine to the effect that once you have entered upon a just war it makes no difference to its justness whether you win in open combat or by guile (*CC*, 75).[22] It is clear from *Of Education* that Milton was well versed in these aspects of warfare: students were to acquire 'all the skill of embattailing, marching, encamping, fortifying, besieging, and battering, with all the helps of ancient and modern stratagems, *Tactiks*, and warlike maxims' (*CPW*, ii. 411–12).[23] He also thought it was legitimate to deploy such skills in combat since, as he notes in *De Doctrina Christiana*, it is universally agreed that 'the stratagems and tactics [*dolos*] of warfare, provided that they do not involve treachery or perjury, do not constitute falsehood' (*CPW*, vi. 761; *CW*, xvii. 302). But Milton goes further than Lipsius by insisting that we have no duty of truthfulness whatsoever towards an enemy: 'stratagems', he says,

> are allowable, even when they entail falsehood, because if it is not our duty to tell someone the truth, it does not matter if we lie to him whenever it is convenient. Moreover I do not see why this should apply to peace any less than to war, especially when we may, by a salutary and commendable falsehood, save ourselves or our neighbor from harm or danger. (*CPW*, vi. 761–2)

Milton was thus willing for deceptions which most theorists would contemplate (if at all) only in wartime to be permitted during peace.

Broadly there were two ways of thinking about international relations in the seventeenth century: the scholastic and the humanist.[24] The former tradition was the one in which the doctrine of the just war developed, basic to which was the distinction between defensive and offensive action. While anyone was allowed to defend themselves from attack, taking the offensive was permitted only to punish a crime or to secure reparation; belligerence for the sake of acquiring glory or empire was wholly disavowed. As we saw, these were the tenets invoked by Lipsius (somewhat atypically for a humanist). Generally, the humanists, with whom Milton aligned himself, were much less inhibited about the use of force. Violence was not only legitimate when responding to something that had already happened; pre-emptive strikes motivated by fear of what might happen were also permitted. In maintaining this, the humanists were reviving a view that had been widespread in the ancient world. One of the best summaries of this school of thought was supplied by Francis Bacon (1561–1626) in his *Considerations Touching a Warre with Spaine*, written in 1624, where he defended the proposition 'that a *iust Feare*, (without an Actuall Inuasion or Offence,) is a sufficient Ground of a *War*, and in the Nature of a true *Defensiue*'. Drawing on examples from Thucydides, Plato, and Livy, he argued that

---

[22] 'Cum iustum bellum suscipitur, ut aperte pugnet quis aut ex insidiis, nihil ad iustitiam interest' (Lipsius, 197; Augustine, *Quaestiones in Heptateuchum*, VI. x).

[23] Milton's nephew, Edward Phillips, read '*Frontinus* his Stratagems . . . *Ælian's Tacticks*; and *Polyænus* his Warlike Stratagems' under Milton's direction (Darbishire, 60).

[24] See the excellent account by Richard Tuck, to which I am greatly indebted, in *The Rights of War and Peace: Political Thought and the International Order from Grotius to Kant* (Oxford, 1999), 16–77.

the threat posed by 'ambitious States'—of which the Turks and Spain were the salient modern examples—was always such that 'other *States* (assuredly) cannot be iustly accused, for not staying the first Blow', whereas by clinging to the principle that 'euery *Offensiue Warre* . . . presupposeth a precedent Assault', the scholastics showed that they were 'fitter to guide Penkniues, than Swords'.[25] Milton, who greatly admired Bacon, deployed this humanist doctrine in *The Tenure*, the work that secured his appointment to the Council of State. When the Presbyterians attempted to evade responsibility for the regicide by claiming that they had only engaged in a defensive, and not an offensive, war against the king, Milton dismissed this as a distinction without a difference: 'Have they not levied all these Warrs against him whether offensive or defensive (for defence in Warr equally offends, and most prudently before hand)' (*CPW*, iii. 230). As the parenthetical remark reveals, Milton agreed with Bacon that in a situation where there was nothing to choose between defence and attack, the most prudent course of action would be to launch a pre-emptive strike.

However, the humanists countenanced wars of aggression against other people even when neither provoked by nor living in fear of them. Religious or cultural differences might be enough to justify violent intervention in their lives. As Lipsius put it, 'invasion is lawfull against Barbarians, whose Religion and Impiety ought to be abhorred, chiefly if they be potent and apt to offend; for the cause of such Warr is compulsion and suppression of evil' (*CC*, 58).[26] The view that barbarians could be conquered and enslaved with a view to civilizing and converting them was in stark contrast to the beliefs of the scholastics, and especially the theologians and jurists who belonged to the so-called 'School of Salamanca'. Its founder, Francisco de Vitoria (*c*.1485–1546), systematically dismantled the justifications usually offered for Spain's colonization of the New World, denying that Christians could attack non-Christians simply on the grounds of their infidelity, and rejecting the claim made by John Mair in 1510 that the Indians were in effect the 'slaves by nature' discussed by Aristotle in his *Politics*. According to Aristotle, the state ultimately grew out of the family or household (*oikos*) headed by a freeman ruling over his wife, children, and slaves. These arrangements had arisen naturally from the duality between ruling and subject elements found in all living things. In the case of the soul and the body, the first 'is by nature the ruler and the other the subject'. And the same was true of the sexes, where the 'male is by nature superior, and the female inferior; and the one rules, and the other is ruled', and masters and slaves, where 'some men are by nature free and others slaves, and . . . for these latter slavery is both expedient and right'. What made the difference in each case was the level of rationality of which men, women, and slaves were respectively thought capable. A master ruled by virtue of his superior rationality whereas what made a slave a slave was his limited capacity for reason: enough to

---

[25] Francis Bacon, *Certaine Miscellany Works of the Right Honourable Francis Lo. Verulam, Viscount S. Alban*, ed. William Rawley (1629), 12, 15, 20, 21. Tuck (*Rights*, 127) suggests that Thomas Hobbes may have drafted the *Considerations* for Bacon.

[26] The translation in *CC* simplifies Lipsius: 'Iam & Inuasio legitima videtur, etiam sine iniuria. vt in Barbaros, & moribus aut religione prorsum a nobis abhorrentes: maxime si potentes ij, & aliena ipsi inuaserunt aut inuadunt. Caussa [*sic*] enim hic est, Coerctio, & in malo repressio' (p. 148).

apprehend it in others without possessing it himself—enough, that is, to carry out commands but not to formulate them. Aristotle spelled out the brutal implications of this when he came to consider the related arts of war and acquisition. The latter included 'hunting, an art which we ought to practise against wild beasts, and against men who, though intended by nature to be governed, will not submit; for war of such a kind is naturally just'.[27] Hence to characterize the Indians as slaves by nature because incapable of ruling themselves was tantamount to asserting that they were open to conquest and enslavement. Vitoria's reply was that this misrepresented the Indians' actually rather complex way of life, and that since they manifestly 'have some order in their affairs' and 'have judgment like other men' it followed that they 'possessed as true dominion, both public and private, as any Christians'.[28]

While the argument from natural slavery was rejected at the Valladolid conference summoned by Charles V in 1550 to determine the legitimacy of Spanish conquests, it remained a central feature of French, Dutch, and English apologies for colonization and religious war. Bacon again provides a conspectus of humanist thinking in his unfinished dialogue of 1622, *An Advertisement Touching an Holy Warre*, in which he explores the rationale for a war against the Turks, though the discussion itself relates mostly to the Americas. The principal speaker, Zebedaeus (a Catholic), begins by remarking that Aristotle is 'no ill Interpreter' of the law of nature and then rehearses the principle that 'if there can be found, such an Inequality betweene Man and Man, as there is betweene Man and Beast, or betweene Soule and Body, it inuesteth a Right of Gouernment'. He admits, however, that while it is true that the 'more Intelligent' should rule, intelligence is only one of the qualities required, and this means that establishing 'Fitnesse to gouerne, is a Perplexed Businesse'. Zebedaeus accordingly suggests that the principle should be used negatively, as a criterion of *unfitness* to govern, something that would in turn serve to identify that '*Nation*, or *Society* of *Men*, against whom it is lawfull to make a *Warre*, without a *Precedent Iuiury* or *Prouocation*'. A hypothetical example would be a society of Amazons—'a Preposterous *Gouernment*', which, since it is 'against the first Order of Nature, for *Women* to rule ouer *Men*', would be 'in it selfe void, and to be suppressed'.[29] But before it can be established whether the Turks fall into this category the dialogue comes to a premature end.

Unlike Lipsius and Bacon, Milton was utterly averse to the idea of using violence to enforce religious belief. However, his admiration for Aristotle as 'one of the best interpreters of nature and morality' and among 'the best of Political writers' made it easy for him to subscribe to the rest of the humanist agenda (*CPW*, iii. 202, 204). He believed those who were naturally superior should rule, and initially supported Cromwell's elevation to Lord Protector on just those grounds: 'there is nothing in human society more pleasing to God, or more agreeable to reason, nothing in the state more just, nothing more expedient, than the rule of the man most fit to

[27] Aristotle, *The Politics*, ed. Stephen Everson (Cambridge, 1988), 6–7, 11.
[28] Francisco de Vitoria, *Political Writings*, ed. Anthony Pagden and Jeremy Lawrance (Cambridge, 1991), 250; but cf. 290–1.
[29] Bacon, *Certaine Miscellany Works*, 118, 119, 120, 121, 129.

rule'—and in 1653 Cromwell was that man (*CPW*, iv. 671–2). Correspondingly, not only did Milton condone the institution of slavery, as the discussion in *De Doctrina Christiana* strongly implies, but even endorsed the idea that it was natural.[30] In *Eikonoklastes* (1649), he observed that if the people were to seek to restore kings they 'would shew themselves to be by nature slaves and arrant beasts; not fitt for that liberty which they cri'd out and bellow'd for' (*CPW*, iii. 581). The account of the Irish in the *Observations* upon the *Articles of Peace* (1649) is couched in terms which suggest that Milton regarded them much as other humanists (and he himself) saw Indians or Turks; their preference for 'their own absurd and savage Customes' is said to be 'a testimony of their true Barbarisme' (*CPW*, iii. 304).[31] And in *Defensio Secunda* (1654) he contemplates with horror the possibility of the common people sinking 'to a barbarism fouler than that which stains the Indians, themselves the most stupid of mortals . . . who worship as gods malevolent demons whom they cannot exorcise' (*CPW*, iv. 551). Citing Aristotle and Cicero, he remarks in *The Tenure* that 'generally the people of Asia, and with them the Jews also . . . are noted by wise authors much inclinable to slavery', and repeats the point in *Pro Populo Anglicano Defensio* (1651), adding, however, that as a matter of fact most people were inclined that way (*CPW*, iii. 202–3; iv. 343).

These tenets underpinned all of Milton's social and political views. In the divorce tracts, the place assigned to women in the household is ultimately determined by the Aristotelian principle of differential rationality. This emerges with particular clarity in *Tetrachordon* (1645) where Milton endorses the Pauline view that 'the head of the woman is the man' (1 Corinthians 11: 3). While this does not mean that the man can 'hold her as a servant', and indeed should admit 'her into a part of that empire' given him by God, Milton nonetheless insists that she is 'made subject to him'. This arrangement can be departed from if and only 'if she exceed her husband in prudence and dexterity, and he contentedly yeeld, for then a superior and more naturall law comes in, that the wiser should govern the lesse wise, whether male or female' (*CPW*,

---

[30] This point is unfortunately obscured in the existing Yale and Columbia translations of the relevant passage in Book 2, ch. 15 of *De Doctrina*, where Milton discusses the respective duties of masters and slaves in completely neutral tones: 'HERI officia . . . De possessione et iure in servos'. John Carey (Yale) translates this as 'The Duties of a MASTER . . . On the subject of the possession and lawful treatment of slaves', while Charles Sumner (Columbia) renders it 'The duties of MASTERS . . . Respecting the possession of slaves, and the extent of the master's authority' (*CW*, xvii. 366–9; *CPW*, vi. 787–8). An *erus* or *herus* was a master of a house or family, or simply its owner, though interestingly Milton does not use the obvious term for that: *dominus*. As for 'De possessione et iure in servos', both Carey and Sumner seem to me to overstep the mark in expanding upon the original, respectively extracting 'lawful treatment of slaves' and 'the extent of the master's authority' from the single word 'iure'. The term itself derives from the Roman law of persons according to which everyone either possesses power or is in the power of another: thus a slave is someone who is not *sui iuris*, not within his own power, but *alieni iuris*, in another's power. By 'iure' Milton therefore simply means the power that an *erus* has over slaves. What Milton does not do at any point in *De Doctrina Christiana* is condemn the institution of slavery as such. See also the very illuminating essay by Steven Jablonski, 'Ham's Vicious Race: Slavery and John Milton', *Studies in English Literature*, 37 (1997), 173–90.

[31] See Nicholas Canny, 'The Ideology of English Colonization: From Ireland to America', *William and Mary Quarterly*, 30 (1973), 575–98.

ii. 589). But since this is the exception that proves the rule, and since Aristotle himself had said as much anyway (see Aristotle, *Politics*, 17), the effect of the concession is to underline how closely Milton otherwise adhered to this view of gender politics.

Milton did, however, have at his disposal a richer vocabulary than Aristotle's for the purpose of differentiating between the various kinds of rational incapacity that render individuals unable to manage their own lives and hence liable to be ruled by others. He acquired this terminology from the Roman law of persons, which dealt exhaustively with a range of topics from the relationship between masters and slaves to the appointment of tutors or curators to look after the interests of the underage, the lunatic, or the spend-thrift. In one sense, this was a counter-intuitive move for Milton to have made since the *Institutes* (the text with which he was most familiar) categorically deny that slavery is natural, even if permitted by the law of nations (*ius gentium*): 'Servitude . . . is an institution of the law of nations whereby one man is, contrary to nature, subject to the dominion of another.'[32] So how did Milton reconcile these conflicting positions? How could he simultaneously subscribe to an Aristotelian theory of natural slavery *and* to a neo-Roman theory of natural liberty? One answer lies in the Renaissance habit of syncretism: after all, Aristotle was often translated into Latin—notably by Juan Ginés Sepúlveda, the notorious defender of natural slavery at Valladolid—and thereby assimilated to different cultural norms. But more important for Milton's purposes was the standard distinction between fallen and unfallen nature.[33] He first drew this in *Tetrachordon*, arguing that while 'prime Nature made us all equall, made us all equall coheirs by common right and dominion over all creatures', the result of the Fall was that God permitted a number of practices which fell under the *ius gentium*, in particular suffering 'his owne people to wast and spoyle and slay by warre, to lead captives, to be som maisters, som servants, som to be princes, others to be subjects' (*CPW*, ii. 661). In other words, slavery was unnatural only in that it would never have existed but for the Fall, though in that respect it was no different from other institutions like war, political subjection, private property, or usury.

Having effected this accommodation between Aristotle and the Roman law, Milton was able to provide a much more detailed account of how people fell into, or freed themselves from, various states of dependence on others up to and including the condition of slavery. We can see this clearly in a passage in *Defensio Secunda* where an Aristotelian argument about self-government, and how those incapable of self-rule become the slaves of others, is recast in juridical terms:

a nation which cannot rule and govern itself, but has delivered itself into slavery to its own lusts, is enslaved also to other masters whom it does not choose, and serves not only voluntarily but also against its will. Such is the decree of law and nature itself, that he who cannot control himself, who through poverty of intellect or madness [*per inopiam mentis aut furorem*] cannot properly administer his own affairs, should not be his own master [*in sua*

---

[32] *The Institutes of Justinian: Text, Translation and Commentary*, ed. and trans. J. A. C. Thomas (Amsterdam and Oxford, 1975), 13.

[33] See Jablonski, 'Ham's Vicious Race', 182–5.

potestate ne sit], but like a ward [*pupillus*] be given over into the power of another. (*CPW*, iv. 684; *CW*, viii. 170)

Conversely, the first step for those who do not wish to be slaves or wish to remain free is to 'learn to obey right reason, to master yourselves' ('rectae rationi obtemperare discite, vestrum esse compotes'). Milton does not underestimate the difficulty of doing so, but the stark alternative, he warns his English audience, is to remain 'a nation in wardship' ('pupilla gens') (*CPW*, iv. 684; *CW*, viii. 170–1). Taken together, these contentions about freedom and slavery represent the heart and nerve and sinew of his political thought.

Milton was thus surprisingly at ease with a humanist ethos that tolerated violence, slavery, fraud, and falsehood. He was evidently a willing servant of the fiscal–military state. Yet he saw dangers in an executive political culture that valued only 'the ability to devise the cleverest means of putting vast sums of money into the treasury, the power readily to equip land and sea forces, to deal shrewdly with ambassadors from abroad, and to contract judicious alliances and treaties' (*CPW*, iv. 681). *Defensio Secunda* in fact closes with a list of desiderata that risked being overlooked in the drive for bureaucratic efficiency: the separation of church and state, religious liberty, legal reform, and freedom from censorship. In most other respects, however, the politics of the executive were perfectly compatible with Milton's commitment to the republic.[34] Thus the non-democratic aspect of republicanism necessarily followed from the principle of differential rationality; as Milton expressed the point in *Defensio Secunda*, majorities are defined qualitatively not numerically so that those who possess wisdom and virtue will, 'however small their number, be a majority' (*CPW*, iv. 636). The same went for the masculine bias of republican ideology. Nor was republicanism inconsistent with imperialism. Although it is open to debate whether Milton approved or disapproved of the 'Western Design'—the abortive attack on Spanish colonial possessions in the West Indies in 1655—it is unlikely that he would have found much to quarrel with in the declaration that justified the Cromwellian project.[35] As the peroration reveals, its aims were quintessentially humanist: to mount a pre-emptive strike before Spain could 'recover again a power . . . to become as intolerable and dangerous as heretofore', and to do so for the greater glory of God.[36] What we must consider next is how these themes played out in *Paradise Lost*.

Toland's admiration of Milton's stance on liberty and tyranny was not shared by all. The Tory philosopher Mary Astell quickly pounced on what she saw as an obvious

---

[34] For the claim that during the 'Civil War reason of state became a normative and persuasive description of what politics involved, not a clandestine art', see Geoff Baldwin, 'Reason of State and English Parliaments, 1610–42', *History of Political Thought*, 35 (2004), 620–41.

[35] For contrasting views, see Robert Fallon, *Milton in Government* (University Park, Pa., 1993), 88–100, and 'Cromwell, Milton, and the Western Design', in Balachandra Rajan and Elizabeth Sauer (eds.), *Milton and the Imperial Vision* (Pittsburgh, Pa., 1999), 33–54, and David Armitage, 'John Milton: Poet against Empire', in Armitage et al., *Milton and Republicanism*, 206–25.

[36] *A Declaration of His Highness by the Advice of His Council; Setting forth on the Behalf of this Commonwealth, the Justice of Their Cause against Spain* (1655), 141; cf. *Scriptum Dom. Protectoris Reipublicae Angliae, Scotiae, Hiberniae* (1655), 40.

inconsistency; for 'how much soever Arbitrary Power may be dislik'd on a Throne, Not *Milton* himself wou'd cry up Liberty to poor *Female Slaves*, or plead for the Lawfulness of Resisting a Private Tyranny'. She thereby opened up what seemed to be a gap between the private and the public aspect of Milton's politics that has never been closed. Concerned as Astell was with the plight of the married women who typically 'puts herself entirely into her Husband's Power', she probably had the divorce tracts in mind, but it is far from certain that reading *Paradise Lost* would have changed her view significantly.[37] This is because at the centre of the poem is a straightforwardly Aristotelian narrative of gender inversion.

Although Adam and Eve are portrayed as man and wife, marriage is not the only institution they exemplify. Their rights in each other are a form of private property—indeed, as Milton insists, they are the 'sole propriety, / In Paradise of all things common else' (iv. 751–2). Furthermore, notwithstanding the absence of slaves and offspring, the couple also constitute a household in which Adam occupies a paternal position by virtue of the fact that Eve is the 'Daughter of God and man' (iv. 660).[38] He thus incurs the responsibilities not only of a husband but also those of household management (*oikonomia*) consequent upon being what Milton elsewhere in his divorce tracts and political writings calls a 'Maister of Family' (see *CPW*, ii. 353; iii. 237). While this complicates his relationship with Eve, it also reinforces his dominance. Their unequal positions are summed up in the Pauline formula, 'He for God only, she for God in him', but are also manifested physically; Adam's 'fair large front and eye sublime declared / Absolute rule' while Eve's 'golden tresses . . . implied / Subjection' (iv. 299, 300–1, 307–8). (Adam's capacity for rule, we note, is actively 'declared', while Eve's disposition to be ruled is passively 'implied'.) The rationale for this difference in status is moreover fully transparent to the humans themselves. Eve expressly confirms to Adam the twofold respect in which she is subordinate to him:

> My author and disposer, what thou bidst
> Unargued I obey; so God ordains,
> God is thy law, thou mine: to know no more
> Is woman's happiest knowledge and her praise. (iv. 635–8)

Likewise Adam, in conversation with Raphael, rehearses the grounds of his superiority to her:

> For well I understand in the prime end
> Of nature her the inferior, in the mind
> And inward faculties, which most excel,
> In outward also her resembling less
> His image who made both, and less expressing

---

[37] Mary Astell, *Some Reflections upon Marriage* (1700), 28–9.

[38] As for the absence of slaves, J. Martin Evans, *Milton's Imperial Epic: 'Paradise Lost' and the Discourse of Colonialism* (Ithaca, N.Y. and London, 1996), 57, suggests that Adam's relationship with the animals is 'essentially colonial' in that he has been given dominion over them while they in return 'pay . . . fealty / With low subjection' (*PL* viii. 344–5).

> The character of that dominion given
> O'er other creatures. (viii. 540–6)

Inwardly and outwardly, Adam is naturally superior to Eve, and Eve recognizes this. The trouble is that in the event neither of them can sustain this understanding. For whenever Adam approaches Eve, he goes on to tell Raphael,

> All higher knowledge in her presence falls
> Degraded, wisdom in discourse with her
> Looses discountenanced, and like folly shows;
> Authority and reason on her wait,
> As one intended first, not after made
> Occasionally. (viii. 551–6)

Each element in the rationale rehearsed in the first part of his speech is systematically inverted in the rest. Adam's self-analysis at this point renders the Fall to come intelligible as a lapse in proper management of himself and hence of Eve. The Fall is among other things a failure in—because of an exchange of—gender roles. Or, in the words of the Son when delivering judgement, Adam resigned his 'manhood' and placed himself in 'subjection' (x. 148, 153) to Eve, whose particular

> gifts
> Were such as under government well seemed,
> Unseemly to bear rule, which was thy part
> And person, hadst thou known thy self aright. (x. 153–6)

The Son's impeccably Aristotelian summary of the relationship between Adam and Eve underlines the fact that it could not but be politicized from the beginning in consequence of their differential qualities: any account of politics in the poem has to accommodate its sexual politics.

After eating the apple Eve wonders how best to deploy her changed capabilities; that is, whether to share her new knowledge with Adam or to 'keep the odds' stacked in her favour so as to 'render me more equal, and perhaps, / A thing not undesirable, sometime / Superior; for inferior who is free?' (ix. 820, 823–5). Eve rejects inferiority just as Adam surrenders superiority. Once they have fallen, however, there is no way back to the marriage they previously enjoyed: the status quo ante cannot be restored. Thus the Son tells Eve that 'to thy husband's will / Thine shall submit, he over thee shall rule' (x. 195–6). What makes this punitive is that she is henceforth subject to Adam's will rather than his reason and wisdom. Rule that was merely absolute now becomes arbitrary or even despotic (cf. *Samson Agonistes*, l. 1054). This is what Milton means when he says in *De Doctrina Christiana* that the 'husband's authority became still greater after the fall' (*CPW*, vi. 355).

Although this Aristotelian drama unfolds in an ostensibly pastoral setting, the garden itself is a militarized zone. After Adam and Eve retire to their bower, prompting the narrator's celebration of 'wedded love' (iv. 750), the angelic guards based at the eastern gate of paradise carry out a counterinsurgency sweep to apprehend Satan. For their part, the couple know that 'Millions of spiritual creatures walk the earth' and are aware (if only subliminally) of their protective function—of how the angelic 'bands' sing or play instruments as they 'keep watch' or 'rounding walk' and 'divide the night' between them (iv. 677, 684–5, 688). The musical–martial puns embedded in this passage are completely in keeping with the lexis of the poem as a whole.[39] Indeed, very little escapes being rendered in these terms. Not only landscapes but moral and psychological phenomena are militarized. Thus in what proves to be a tragically self-deluding figure of speech Adam assures Raphael that Eve's qualities of magnanimity and nobleness 'create an awe / About her, as a guard angelic placed' (viii. 558–9). Or take the term 'torment', which in the poem is invariably associated with fallenness and with Satan in particular (see 1. 56; ii. 70, 196, 274; iv. 88, 505, 510; vi. 244; viii. 244; x. 781, 998; xi. 769). Milton derived the noun from the Latin *tormentum* meaning 'torture; pain, grief' *and* 'an engin of war to cast stones or darts . . . also any piece of Ordnance, a Cannon or great Gun' ([Littleton], *Dictionarium*, s.v. *tormentum*). When expressing the anguish caused by the delights of the garden, Satan draws on both main senses: 'the more I see / Pleasures about me, so much more I feel / Torment within me, as from the hateful siege / Of contraries' (ix. 119–22). External pleasures are implicitly figured as darts being hurled into his psyche by a siege engine—a torment-causing *tormentum*.

Such usages also infiltrate Milton's accounts of heaven. It is already apparent prior to Satan's rebellion that the polity is organized along military lines. The angels' response to being summoned to the Son's exaltation is a cross between an army parade and an ecclesiastical procession; they appear 'in orders' with 'ensigns high advanced' and 'Standards and gonfalons twixt van and rear'. And afterwards we are told how 'the angelic throng / Dispersed in bands and files their camp extend' (v. 587–9, 650–1) There is too the twice-mentioned 'armoury of god' from which Michael is equipped with a sword and the Son with animated chariots (vi. 321; vii. 200). Even after the rebellion has been defeated, God is determined to maintain military discipline for the sake of it, sending the angels on otherwise pointless expeditions, as Raphael puts it, merely 'to inure / Our prompt obedience' (viii. 239–40). As all this suggests, while Milton may have had nothing but contempt for naked militarism (exemplified in the poem by Moloch as it was in the Europe of the 1650s by Charles X of Sweden), he was very far from endorsing pacifism.[40] That, however, still left ample scope for the legitimate use of force.

When God orders Michael to drive the rebel angels from Heaven, there can be no doubt that this is a just war in the scholastic sense.[41] However, it should be noted that Milton himself insists in humanist manner that the objective on *both* sides is to achieve

---

[39] See especially the notes in John Milton, *Paradise Lost and Paradise Regained*, ed. Christopher Ricks (New York, 1968), and James A. Freeman, *Milton and the Martial Muse: 'Paradise Lost' and European Traditions of War* (Princeton, 1980), *passim*.

[40] See Martin Dzelzainis, 'Juvenal, Charles X Gustavus and Milton's letter to Richard Jones', *Seventeenth Century*, 9 (1994), 25–34.

[41] See John Coffey, 'Pacifist Quietist, or Patient Militant? John Milton and the Restoration', *Milton Studies*, 42 (2003), 149–74 at 155–8.

glory, however differently it may be defined by them.[42] As the Argument to Book 6 puts it, the 'tumult' not having ended after two days, 'God on the third day sends Messiah the Son, for whom he had reserved the glory of that victory.' In other words, the military stalemate has been engineered precisely so that when 'War wearied hath performed what war can do', the Son will have the 'glory . . . Of ending this great war' and thereby manifesting himself 'worthiest . . . to be heir and to be king' (vi. 695, 701–2, 707–8). Indeed, the completely counter-productive nature of the uprising is apparent before its inception, when the Son pronounces that it is 'Matter to me of glory, whom their hate / Illustrates' (v. 738–9). But Satan too systematically seeks glory. His reply to Michael's condemnation of the 'hateful strife' for which he holds him responsible is that 'The strife which thou call'st evil . . . we style / The strife of glory' (vi. 264, 289–90). He reiterates the claim when rallying his troops after defeat, even if now obliged to employ litotes: the 'strife / Was not inglorious, though the event was dire' (i. 623–4). And subsequently the aim of achieving glory is transferred to the project of destroying or subverting the new world. To a large extent this is a matter of personal ambition, as Satan discloses in his soliloquy at the start of Book 9: 'To me shall be the glory sole among / The infernal powers, in one day to have marred / What he almighty styled, six nights and days / Continued making' (ix. 135–9). However, he also invokes a public dimension when spurring himself on in Book 4: 'yet public reason just, / Honour and empire with revenge enlarged, / By conquering this new world, compels me now / To do what else though damned I should abhor' (iv. 389–92). A revealing gloss on this passage is provided by the *Cabinet-Council*, where, as we saw, it was insisted 'That no revenge, no desire of Honor or Empire, are any lawful causes of War' (*CC*, 59). If we turn to the sequence of rhetorical questions posed in the Lipsian original, the similarities with Satan's phrasing become more striking still: 'Quid si enim Vltio tibi proposita? quid si Gloria, aut Imperium? peccas' ('What if thou set before thee reuenge? What if thy intent be glorie, or a kingdome? Thou doest erre').[43] However, the conclusion Satan reaches— that reason of state and the pursuit of *gloria* and *imperium* by way of revenge override any personal scruples he may have—is exactly the opposite of what Lipsius maintained.

   Once the war in heaven has begun, the question of *ius in bello* immediately arises: what do the rules of war permit? After the rebel angels have been repulsed on the first day, they spend the night manufacturing gunpowder and constructing what the Argument to Book 6 calls 'the machines of Satan'. But it turns out that the kind of 'machine' to which Milton is alluding here is the Latin *machina*; that is to say, both 'engine of war' and a 'device, trick, shift, invention to bring about some end' ([Littleton], *Dictionarium*, s.v. *machina*). Accordingly, the next morning the rebel army advances 'in hollow cube / Training his devilish enginery, impaled / On every side with shadowing squadrons deep, / To hide the fraud' (vi. 552–5). Whereas the loyal angels the previous day had 'In cubic phalanx firm advanced entire' (vi. 399), the rebels' formation is deceptively 'hollow'. And the 'fraud' to which they resort in concealing their artillery is in fact a

   [42] For a full discussion, see John Rumrich, *Matter of Glory: A New Preface to 'Paradise Lost'* (Pittsburgh, Pa., 1987).
   [43] Lipsius, 148; Lipsius, *Six Bookes of Politickes or Civil Doctrine*, trans. William Jones (1594), 133.

spectacular instance of what Lipsius and humanist jurists like Alberico Gentili and Hugo Grotius had in mind when they considered—and, like Milton, for the most part enthusiastically endorsed—the use of *dolus* in warfare.[44] It is also to some extent a reprise of Milton's youthful miniature epic on the Gunpowder Plot, 'In Quintum Novembris', where the 'subdolus' (l. 90) Satan, disguised as a Franciscan friar, urges the Pope to foment 'plots' ('dolos'; l. 213) and 'secret treachery' ('caecis / Insidiis' (ll. 215–16).[45] But it is more clearly still an embedded memory of the events of May 1652 that led to the outbreak of the first Anglo–Dutch war. As we saw, the allegation against the Dutch at the time was that they had mounted a pre-emptive strike under cover of negotiating a treaty. It is therefore telling that Satan, rather than firing his cannon at once, indulges in a bout of 'scoffing in ambiguous words', playing repeatedly on the language of diplomacy ('peace and composure', 'overture', and 'propound') (vi. 560, 562, 567, 568). The outcome is that the loyal angels are left completely baffled at the sight of the open mouths of the cannon

> Portending hollow truce; at each behind
> A seraph stood, and in his hand a reed
> Stood waving tipped with fire; while we suspense,
> Collected stood within our thoughts amused. (vi. 578–81)

'Hollow' means insincere, but inevitably echoes the related pun in the sonnet to Vane, just as 'truce' recalls the negotiations with the Dutch. 'Amused', as several editors have noted, is a military term, meaning to divert the attention of the enemy from one's real designs, and this was precisely the sense in which the verb also featured in the parliamentary *Declaration* of 1652 when protesting against Dutch attempts 'to Amuse the Parliament'. However, since there was no exact Latin equivalent for 'amuse', Milton translated the relevant phrase as 'ut Parlamentum suspenso animo tenerent', and this wording surely lies behind Raphael's account of how the good angels 'suspense, / Collected stood within our thoughts amused' before being levelled by the first volley from the rebels (*Declaration*, 8; *Scriptum Parlamenti*, 8; Miller, *John Milton's Writings*, 200, 236).[46] This being the case, the second day of the civil war in heaven is perhaps best visualized as a kind of mid-air version of the naval engagement between the sister-republics that took place off the Downs in the spring of 1652.

The implicit figuration of Satan as the Dutch commander Tromp comes as no surprise since on two occasions the archfiend is also associated with the East Indies trade route that was at the centre of Anglo–Dutch commercial rivalry throughout the

---

[44] See Alberico Gentili, *De Iure Belli Libri Tres*, ed. C. Phillipson and trans. J. C. Rolfe, 2 vols. (Oxford, 1933), i. 228–32 ('De dolo, & stragematis' ['Of Craft and Strategy']); 232–9 ('De dolo verborum' ['Of Deception by Words']); 239–49 ('De mendaciis' ['Of Falsehoods']); ii. 142–54; Hugo Grotius, *The Rights of War and Peace*, ed. Richard Tuck, 3 vols. (Indianapolis, 2005), iii. 1185–1230 (III. 1. 1–22). For possible historical analogues, see Harold H. Scudder, 'Satan's Artillery', *Notes and Queries*, 195 (1950), 334–7, and Michael Murrin, *History and Warfare in Renaissance Epic* (Chicago and London, 1994), 131–2.

[45] See Macon Cheek, 'Milton's *In Quintum Novembris*: An Epic Foreshadowing', *Studies in Philology*, 54 (1957), 172–84, and Stella Revard, *The War in Heaven: 'Paradise Lost' and the Tradition of Satan's Rebellion* (Ithaca, N.Y. and London, 1980), 86–107.

[46] The French translation by Lewis Rosin (see Miller, *John Milton's Writings*, 58–9) reads 'pour amuzer le Parlement' (*La Declaration du Parlement de la Republique D'Angleterre* (1652), 8).

century (see *PL* i. 634–42; iv. 159–65). Furthermore, to identify him with one of the most notorious instances of state treachery in living memory was in keeping with his designated role in the poem as the 'artificer of fraud' who 'was the first / That practised falsehood under saintly show, / Deep malice to conceal' (iv. 121–4). This view of Satan as the prototypical fraudster was of course hardly novel—Milton himself had long ago labelled him a 'past-master of trickery' ('fraudumque magister') in 'In Quintum Novembris' (l. 17). But it is still absolutely fundamental to the way politics is conceived of in *Paradise Lost*—which is to say, as a matter not so much of the abstract exposition of ideologies (though there is a good deal of that) as of a pragmatic commitment to the realm of deceit and illusion. Paradise, God tells the Son, will be lost not through violence but, what is 'worse, / By some false guile' (iii. 91–2; cf. v. 242–3), and the terms 'guile' and 'fraud' accordingly resonate throughout the text. Indeed, the 'great consult' in Pandaemonium that takes up the first half of Book 2 is expressly devoted to this very topic; for, as Satan says, 'Whether of open war or covert guile, / We now debate: who can advise, may speak' (ii. 41–2). In tabling the motion, Satan echoes the advice dispensed to the pope by his earlier incarnation to the effect that he should launch a pre-emptive strike against King James I's growing strength, though rather than challenging him 'to war or open combat' ('bellis et aperto Marte') it would be better to 'use trickery' ('utere fraude') ('In Quintum Novembris', ll. 113–14). It is also true, however, that he is selectively quoting St Augustine's dictum that if a war is just to begin with it does not matter whether you subsequently win it in open combat or by guile. For what the fallen angels do not ever get to debate is the question of the justice of their war against heaven. They focus exclusively on the means rather than the end, forgetting (or choosing to ignore) that it is only the end which validates the means.

What of the first fraudster's first victims? It is often remarked that, as soon as Adam and Eve experience guilt and shame, Milton feels impelled to resort to images of contemporary Asian and American natives to depict their fallen state; thus he describes them hiding beneath a 'fig-tree' of the kind 'at this day to Indians known / In Malabar or Decan' and clothing themselves with its leaves, and adds that 'of late / Columbus found the American so girt' (ix. 1101, 1102–3, 115–16). The significance of this is taken to be that they have suddenly become natural slaves of the kind described by Mair, Sepúlveda, and others.[47] There is, however, nothing intrinsic to the images themselves that demands such a conclusion. After all, when preparing the frontispiece to *De Cive* (1642), Thomas Hobbes adapted Theodore de Bry's famous engraving of an Algonquian chief to illustrate what he meant by a state of natural *liberty*.[48] But while Milton was far from agreeing with the Hobbesian account of the state of nature, and certainly endorsed Aristotle's views on natural slavery, his position was rather less straightforward than might appear. It is sometimes assumed (partly on the strength of the passage from *Tetrachordon* quoted earlier) that Milton

[47] See Evans, *Milton's Imperial Epic*, 100–1, and Paul Stevens, '*Paradise Lost* and the Colonial Imperative', *Milton Studies*, 34 (1996), 3–21 at 14–15.

[48] See Quentin Skinner, *Hobbes and Republican Liberty* (Cambridge, 2008), 98–103.

represents Adam and Eve before the Fall as living in a wholly pre-political condition. In fact, politics for Milton is not an exclusively fallen phenomenon; just as he goes out of his way to legitimate sex and work by showing them to be part of the unfallen world, so there is a true prelapsarian political order of things. The Fall represents not so much the introduction of politics into the world as the subversion of a politics that already existed, whether in heaven, or inside the Edenic household, or within the individual beings of Adam and Eve. The psychological consequences of sin are represented as—because they actually are—political events:

> high winds worse within
> Began to rise, high passions, anger, hate,
> Mistrust, suspicion, discord, and shook sore
> Their inward state of mind, calm region once
> And full of peace, now tossed and turbulent:
> For understanding ruled not, and the will
> Heard not her lore, both in subjection now
> To sensual appetite, who from beneath
> Usurping over sovereign reason claimed
> Superior sway. (ix. 1122–31)

In short, the Fall is an internal *coup d'état*.

Its wider political consequences soon become apparent. Book 12 opens with Michael foretelling that the post-Noachian order of 'families and tribes / Under paternal rule' will be terminally disrupted when

> one shall rise
> Of proud ambitious heart, who not content
> With fair equality, fraternal state,
> Will arrogate dominion undeserved
> Over his brethren, and quite dispossess
> Concord and law of nature from the earth,
> Hunting (and men not beasts shall be his game)
> With war and hostile snare such as refuse
> Subjection to his empire tyrannous:
> A mighty hunter thence he shall be styled
> Before the Lord, as in despite of heaven,
> Or from heaven claiming second sovereignty (xii. 23–35)

Nimrod is the key agent in the transition from the natural world of patriarchy to the political realm of dominion, empire, and sovereignty. However, embedded in this passage is an obvious allusion to Aristotle's notorious endorsement of the practice of slave-hunting. The difference is that whereas the acquisition of slaves in antiquity and the present alike was thought to be just insofar as it concerned itself with those who are slaves by nature—that is to say, differentiated by their evident propensity to be subjected to others—Nimrod made slaves of those who were living in an undifferentiated 'fair equality' and who were therefore fully entitled to 'refuse / Subjection'.

Adam at once issues a 'fatherly' reproof of his 'execrable son' for 'assuming / Authority usurped' (xii. 63, 64, 65–6). God, he correctly points out, gave man

'Dominion absolute' only over the animal world, 'but man over men / He made not Lord; such title to himself / Reserving, human left from human free' (xii. 68, 69–71). However, this protest elicits a lesson in politics from Michael. While Adam is quite right to abhor Nimrod, what he says applies only to the prelapsarian state of affairs; he needs to adapt his thinking to what is newly true of the world:

> Since thy original lapse, true liberty
> Is lost, which always with right reason dwells
> Twinned, and from her hath no dividual being:
> Reason in man obscured, or not obeyed,
> Immediately inordinate desires
> And upstart passions catch the government
> From reason, and to servitude reduce
> Man till then free. Therefore since he permits
> Within himself unworthy powers to reign
> Over free reason, God in judgment just
> Subjects him from without to violent lords;
> Who oft as undeservedly enthral
> His outward freedom: tyranny must be,
> Though to the tyrant thereby no excuse.
> Yet sometimes nations will decline so low
> From virtue, which is reason, that no wrong,
> But justice, and some fatal curse annexed
> Deprives them of their outward liberty,
> Their inward lost: witness the irreverent son
> Of him who built the ark, who for the shame
> Done to his father, heard this heavy curse,
> *Servant of servants*, on his vicious race. (xii. 83–104)

What Adam has to learn is that outward political realities are simply the corollary of internal ones. The only exception to the rule whereby a failure in self-government ultimately leads, via God's judgement, to servitude to others is the case of those nations deemed incorrigibly lacking in reason and virtue; because inherently incapable of governing themselves they are permanently—and justly—deprived of their liberty. The scriptural warrant for this is provided by the curse upon Canaan, son of Ham and grandson of Noah (see Genesis 9: 25). As for the modern-day sons of Ham, it appears that Milton identified them with black Africans, as indeed the casual conjoining of 'Slaves and Negros' in the passage from *Of Reformation* quoted by Toland would suggest.[49]

Virtually nothing in this harsh archangelical lecture should surprise an attentive reader of what Milton had written in the 1650s. The political theory it articulates is that of *Defensio Secunda* and Milton's other writings on behalf of the Commonwealth and Protectorate. The language and the events of the poem resonate with the politics of that decade. On the one hand, there is certainly an element of continuity, of keeping faith with what was called the Good Old Cause of religious and political

---

[49] See Jablonski, 'Ham's Vicious Race', 179–81.

liberty. And yet, on the other hand, it would be hard to deny that the politics of the executive are actively at work in the poem: much of what Satan says and does is simply unintelligible without an understanding of what went on at the heart of the regime to which Milton devoted a decade of his life. This is not at all to suggest, as Blake did, that Milton was of the devil's party without knowing it. But it is to call to mind the truism that it takes one to know one.

PART VII

1671 POEMS:
PARADISE REGAINED
AND
SAMSON AGONISTES

CHAPTER 32

'ENGLANDS CASE': CONTEXTS OF THE 1671 POEMS

LAURA LUNGER KNOPPERS

On 2 July 1670, Milton's final two poems, *Paradise Regain'd* and *Samson Agonistes*, were licensed for publication.[1] Entered into the Stationers Register on 10 September, the jointly published poems (though dated 1671) had most likely appeared by late autumn 1670.[2] The slim octavo volume might well have generated interest due to its notorious author alone. While Milton's writings defending the regicide had been published two decades earlier, he had been briefly imprisoned by the restored regime in autumn 1660 and his prose writings were variously denounced, banned, and burned in the early Restoration.[3] The subject of the two poems—the temptation of

---

[1] The 1662 Licensing Act (14 Car. II, c. 33) required that every book be read and approved prior to publication by the appropriate mandated authority and then entered (for a fee) into the Register of the Stationers' Company; *The Statutes of the Realm*, ed. A. Luders, T. E. Tomlins, et al., 11 vols. (1810–28), v. 428–33. Following the further stipulation of the Act that the licence should be printed at the beginning of each book, we find on the first leaf of Milton's text the words 'Licensed, *July* 2. 1670'. On Restoration print control and censorship, see J. Walker, 'The Censorship of the Press during the Reign of Charles II', *History*, NS 35 (1950), 219–38; Harold Weber, *Paper Bullets: Print and Kingship under Charles II* (Lexington, Ky., 1996), 131–71; and N. H. Keeble, *The Restoration: England in the 1660s* (Oxford, 2002), 148–54.

[2] *A Transcript of the Registers of the Worshipful Company of Stationers from 1640–1708*, ed. G. E. Briscoe Eyre, 3 vols. (1913–14), ii. 415. While the imprint on the title page of Milton's volume reads MDCLXXI, it was not uncommon for printers to post-date title pages for books published late in a given year, hence keeping the titles fresh.

[3] On Milton's reputation in the 1660s, see the narrative in Lewalski, *Life*, 398–415. Also valuable is David Masson's classic treatment of Milton in the early Restoration, *The Life of John Milton: Narrated in*

Jesus in the wilderness and the final days of the Hebraic hero Samson—might seem innocuous enough. But the volume's plain appearance (no dedication or frontispiece) and the genres of brief epic and classical tragedy were unusual in 1670–1, amid printed drama and poetry, sermons and psalters, ballads and broadsides, devotional guides and cookery books. What would contemporary readers have made of Milton's texts? What contexts are most relevant for understanding and interpreting the two poems?

READING MILTON'S REPUBLICANISM

As a lens into how Milton's contemporaries were reading the 1671 poems, two unique indexes in a contemporary or near-contemporary hand are particularly instructive.[4] The indexes (Pl. 1 and 2) are written in a neat hand, perhaps imitating print in its separated letters and lack of a cursive quality. Using a straightforward, commonplacing style, the indexes show an early modern reader's interest in the broadly ethical and moral concerns of the poems, listed by topic and page number: for *Paradise Regain'd*, for example, 'Flaws 103', 'Riches 52', 'Beauty 39', and 'women 36', and for *Samson Agonistes*, 'women 48 62', and 'Hypocrisie 55'.[5] Other concerns are theological or religious: for *Paradise Regain'd*, 'Son of God, 105', and for *Samson Agonistes*, 'Atheist 24'. Yet among the index entries marking ethical issues, social concerns, and religious matters, one entry seems strikingly anomalous: 'Englands Case 23'. Hence, a marginal line appears alongside Samson's castigation of Israel for rejecting its divinely appointed deliverer and acquiescing in its own servitude to the Philistines:

> But what more oft in Nations grown corrupt,
> And by thir vices brought to servitude,
> Then to love Bondage more then Liberty,
> Bondage with ease then strenuous liberty. (ll. 268–71)

Connexion with the Political, Ecclesiastical, and Literary History of his Time, 7 vols. (New York, 1822–90), vi. 162–217.

[4] The indexes appear in *Paradise Regain'd* and *Samson Agonistes* (1671), the Rare Book and Manuscript Library of the University of Illinois at Urbana-Champaign, call no. 821 M64 M3 1671, copy 23, bound with *Paradise Lost* (1674), call no. 821 M64 M1 1674, copy 11. The index labelled 'Paradice regaind' is on sig. H8^v/p. 112 (verso of the final page of *Paradise Regain'd*), while the index 'Sampson Agonistes' is on the recto of the flyleaf following the Errata Page. Materials on this index and on other early readers' markings are further explored in *The Complete Works of John Milton*, ii: *The 1671 Poems: Paradise Regain'd and Samson Agonistes*, ed. Laura Lunger Knoppers (Oxford, 2008), pp. lviii–lxxv.

[5] For those wishing to correlate the index entries with Milton's text, the original pagination of the 1671 poems can be found in copies on Early English Books Online or in Harris Francis Fletcher, *John Milton's Complete Poetical Works, Reproduced in Photographic Facsimile*, 4 vols. (Urbana, Ill., 1948), iv. My quotations from Milton's poetry are taken from Fletcher and are cited parenthetically in the text by act and line number (*Paradise Regain'd*) or by line number (*Samson Agonistes*).

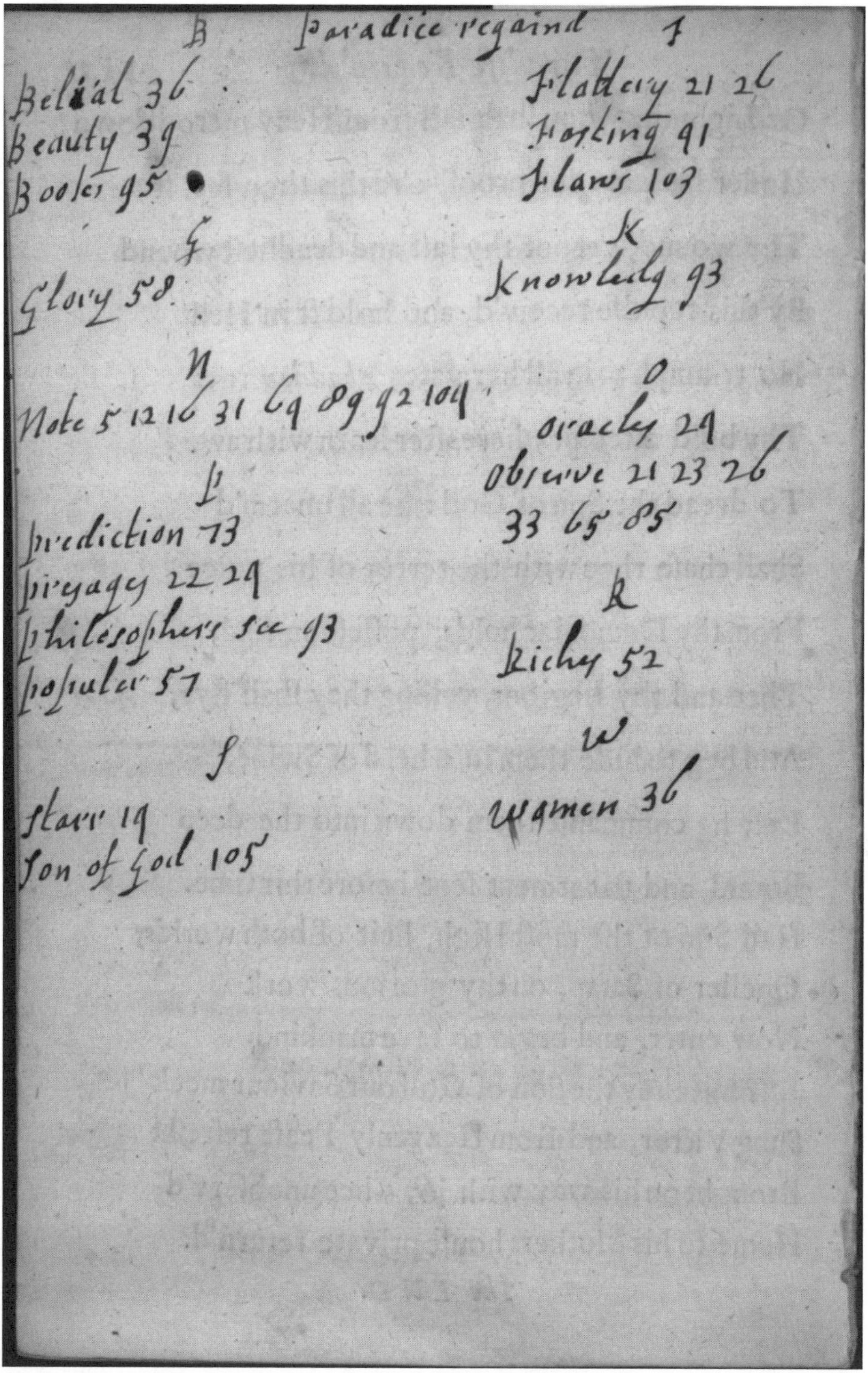

Paradice regaind

B

Belial 36
Beauty 39
Booke 95

F

Flattery 21 26
Forking 91
flaws 103

G

Glory 58

K

Knowledg 93

N

Note 5 12 16 31 69 89 92 104

O

oracle 29
observe 21 23 26
33 65 85

P

prediction 73
presages 22 24
philosophers see 93
popular 57

R

Riches 52

S

starr 19
Son of God 105

W

women 36

PL. 1. Early reader's index for *Paradise Regain'd* (1671)

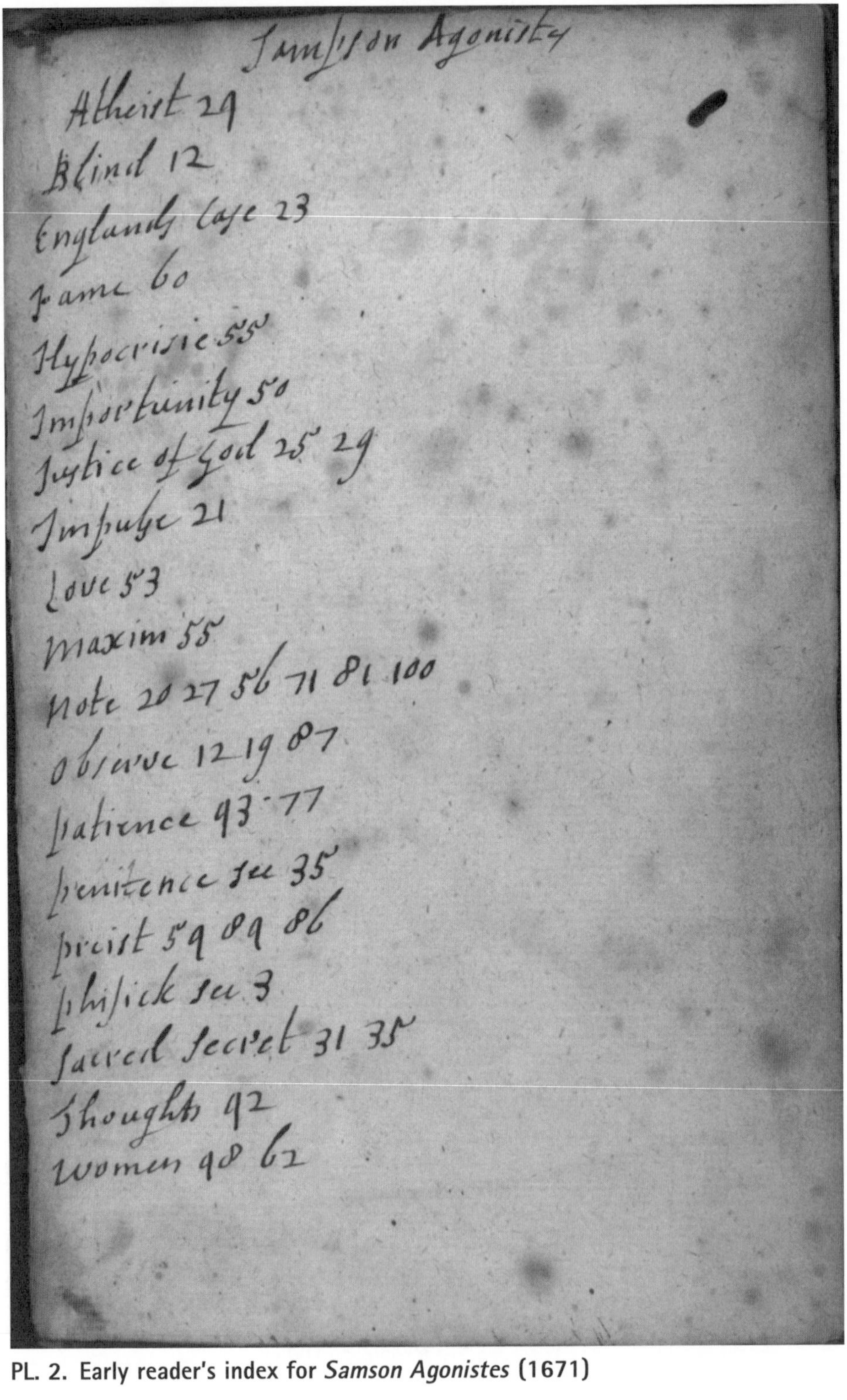

Samson Agonistes

Atheist 29
Blind 12
Englands Case 23
Fame 60
Hypocrisie 55
Importunity 50
Justice of God 25 29
Impulse 21
Love 53
Maxim 55
Note 20 27 56 71 81 100
Observe 12 19 87
Patience 93 77
Penitence see 35
Preist 59 89 86
Phisick see 3
Sacred secret 31 35
Thoughts 92
Women 48 62

PL. 2. Early reader's index for *Samson Agonistes* (1671)

This strikingly republican passage parallels the Son's denunciation, in *Paradise Regain'd*, of the captive tribes of Israel: 'let them serve / Thir enemies, who serve Idols with God' (iii. 431–2), and of the Romans, luxurious and effeminate in triumph: 'What wise and valiant man would seek to free / These thus degenerate, by themselves enslav'd, / Or could of inward slaves make outward free?' (iv. 143–45).[6] And, for this indexing reader, corruption and self-enslavement characterize not only Samson's Israel but the England of his own time.

As the reader perhaps intuits, the republican sentiment that loss of virtue brings loss of liberty also marks Milton's own bitter disappointment in his fellow countrymen who, after deliverance from the bondage of kingship into the liberty of a republic, had backslid into monarchy. Throughout his prose works, Milton linked virtue with liberty, drawing on both biblical and classical republicanism, especially Cicero, Sallust, Tacitus, and Livy.[7] Yet as early as the regicidal tracts, he began to fear that the English might be unworthy of liberty. In *Eikonoklastes* (1649), his official response to the overwhelmingly popular *Eikon Basilike* that had transformed Charles I into a martyr, Milton denounces the image-seeking rabble, who 'like a credulous and hapless herd, begott'n to servility, and inchanted with these popular institutes of Tyranny . . . hold out both thir eares with such delight and ravishment to be stigmatiz'd and board through in witness of thir own voluntary and beloved baseness' (*CPW*, iii. 601). Late in the *Second Defence*, his oration to a European audience on behalf of the fledgling Commonwealth, Milton takes up the issue of character and liberty, directly warning his fellow countrymen that 'Unless you expel avarice, ambition, and luxury from your minds, yes, and extravagance from your families as well, you will find at home and within that tyrant who, you believed, was to be sought abroad and in the field—now even more stubborn' (*CPW*, iv/i. 680). Learning from the negative exemplum of the Romans, who after being freed from absolute monarchy were corrupted in the late Republic and returned to the rule of the Caesars, the English people must cultivate virtue to preserve their freedom. If they should backslide, 'no one, not even Cromwell himself, nor a whole tribe of liberating

---

[6] Quentin Skinner links the Samson passage with Milton's use of Roman 'republican' historiography, particularly Sallust's view (cited in Milton's earlier prose) of virtue as vitiated under absolute monarchy, bringing about such servility and torpor in the people that they may indeed prefer a state of bondage ('John Milton and the Politics of Slavery', in Graham Parry and Joad Raymond (eds.), *Milton and the Terms of Liberty* (Cambridge, 2002), 1–22). Similarly, on *Paradise Regain'd*, Stella P. Revard comments that Milton has given us a 'Jesus with republican principles'; like Skinner on *Samson Agonistes*, she points to classical sources, in this case Tacitus' account of the corruption of the Roman republic, underlying the denunciation of the corrupt Romans in *Paradise Regain'd* ('Milton and Classical Rome: The Political Context of *Paradise Regained* ', in P. A. Ramsey (ed.), *Rome in the Renaissance: The City and the Myth* (Binghamton, N.Y., 1982), 414–16).

[7] For important work that establishes the classical sources, particular configuration, and fundamental continuities of Milton's republicanism, see Skinner, 'John Milton and the Politics of Slavery'; Martin Dzelzainis, 'Milton's Classical Republicanism', in David Armitage, Armand Himy, and Quentin Skinner (eds.), *Milton and Republicanism* (Cambridge, 1995), 3–24; and id., 'Republicanism', in Thomas N. Corns (ed.), *A Companion to Milton* (Oxford, 2001), 294–308. Walter S. H. Lim, *John Milton, Radical Politics, and Biblical Republicanism* (Newark, N.J., 2006), stresses that Milton's republicanism is drawn not only from classical but from biblical texts.

Brutuses, if Brutus were to come to life again, either could if they would, or would if they could, free you a second time, once you had been so easily corrupted' (p. 682).

And by 1659, after the collapse of the Protectorate, months of chaos, General Monck's march to London with his Scottish army, and (with Monck's backing) writs for a new parliamentary election that virtually ensured the return of Charles II, Milton saw a nation unworthy to be free.[8] Nonetheless, in *The Readie and Easie Way*, Milton makes a last, desperate attempt 'to remove, if it be possible, this noxious humor of returning to bondage'.[9] But the emphasis falls on the backsliding and self-enslaved people. For the English, 'so valorous and courageous to winn thir liberty in the field', now 'basely and besottedly to run their necks again into the yoke which they have broken, and prostrate all the fruits of thir victorie for naught at the feet of the vanquishd' will be 'an ignomine if it befall us, that never yet befell any nation possessd of thir libertie; worthie indeed themselves, whatsoever they be, to be for ever slaves' (*CPW*, vii. 428).

After the return of the king, however, Milton could no longer speak so freely and openly. In *Samson Agonistes*, Samson's denunciation of the nation that by losing its virtue has lost its liberty provides a biblical analogue to Milton's own time: 'Englands Case'. But what precisely was the case of England in the early 1670s? What did the monarchy look like in 1670? What liberties were threatened or lost? In what ways did 'Bondage with ease' characterize the majority of the English nation? Who, if anyone, still fought for 'strenuous liberty'?

'THE HIGHEST PITCH OF WANT AND LUXURY': KING AND COURT, 1670–1671

As 1670 opened, three bills stood before the House of Commons: a much-debated subsidy bill, a bill to regulate conventicles (the private meetings of Nonconformists), and the seemingly innocuous 'Lord Roos' divorce bill.[10] Each of these bills gives a window into the tensions that had developed a decade after the Stuart monarch had returned to England, seemingly to universal joy and celebration. Between that virtually unconditional return, hailed as divinely providential, and the present time

---

[8] On these events, see Knoppers, 'Late Political Prose', in Corns (ed.), *A Companion to Milton*, 309–25.

[9] *The Readie and Easie Way to Establish a Free Commonwealth*, *CPW*, vii. 407. The second, revised edition was boldly published in late Apr. 1660, less than a month before the return of King Charles II.

[10] Important primary sources for parliamentary politics in this period include *Debates of the House of Commons, from the Year 1667 to the Year 1694*, ed. Anchitell Grey, 10 vols. (1763); *The Poems and Letters of Andrew Marvell*, ed. H. M. Margoliouth, 3rd edn., rev. P. Legouis and E. E. Duncan-Jones, 2 vols. (Oxford, 1971); and Edward Dering, *The Parliamentary Diary of Sir Edward Dering, 1670–1673*, ed. Basil Duke Henning (New Haven, 1940). For a helpful and detailed narrative of 1670–2, see John Spurr, *England in the 1670s: 'This Masquerading Age'* (Oxford, 2000), 9–32.

stood a decade of anxiety and unsettlement, including continued tensions over the religious and political issues that had earlier sparked civil war as well as new conflicts over sovereignty, finance, and foreign and domestic policies.[11] In 1660, the most severe reprisals were limited to the actual regicides (signers of the death warrant for King Charles I), ten of whom were hanged, drawn, and quartered in gruesome displays of restored state power in mid-October.[12] Yet more pervasive and long-lasting were a series of measures that ejected Nonconformists from the Church of England and outlawed worship outside it.[13] At the same time, the new licensing act and a newly established Surveyor of the Press, Roger L'Estrange, sought to control sedition and religious dissent (repeatedly linked together) through control of print.[14] A devastating plague of 1665, the Great Fire of London in 1666, and humiliation in the Second Dutch War when, in June 1667, the Dutch advanced up the Medway and captured the English fleet, seemed ominous signs of divine wrath against England: although royalists and dissenters disagreed sharply on whose sins were being punished.[15] With the fall of the Lord Chancellor, Edward Hyde, Earl of Clarendon in 1667, the seemingly more tolerant rule of the loosely configured 'Cabal' cabinet, and the government in general on the defensive, new hopes—and fears—of toleration were raised.[16] A temporary loosening of press controls opened up debate in print, in the pulpit, and in the streets.

[11] While the 1660s were long viewed as a period of peace between the 'revolutions' of 1649 and 1688–9, recent historians have focused more on the instabilities of the period. Gary De Krey, *London and the Restoration, 1659–1683* (Cambridge, 2005), 69–115, treats the disruption of civic affairs with the contest against coercion; Tim Harris, *Restoration: Charles II and his Kingdoms, 1660–1685* (2005), 43–84, examines the weaknesses of the Restoration monarchy, including the Civil War legacy of political and religious division, practical restraints on Charles II that frustrated efforts to rebuild royal authority, and the loss of royal prestige; and N. H. Keeble, *The Restoration*, shows how anxiety and insecurity dominated contemporary experience of the period, as documented in diaries, journals, memoirs, polemical tracts, and newsbooks. Richard L. Greaves looks at continued militant activities and defiance of the law in *Deliver Us from Evil: The Radical Underground in Britain, 1660–1663* (New York and Oxford, 1986) and in *Enemies under his Feet: Radicals and Nonconformists in Britain, 1664–1677* (Stanford, Calif., 1990).

[12] On the execution of the regicides and corresponding themes of treason and justice in Milton's *Samson Agonistes*, see Knoppers, *Historicizing Milton: Spectacle, Power, and Poetry in Restoration England* (Athens, Ga., 1994), ch. 2.

[13] The historical circumstances of Nonconformity (or dissent) up through the early 1670s have received detailed treatment in Douglas Lacey, *Dissent and Parliamentary Politics in England, 1661–1689* (New Brunswick, N.J., 1969), 15–70; John Spurr, *The Restoration Church of England, 1646–1689* (New Haven, 1991), 29–61; N. H. Keeble, *The Literary Culture of Nonconformity in the Later Seventeenth Century* (Athens, Ga., 1987), 25–67; Keeble, *The Restoration*, 132–58; and De Krey, *London and the Restoration*, 69–115.

[14] See the accounts of L'Estrange in the *ODNB*; Lois G. Schwoerer, *The Ingenious Mr. Henry Care, Restoration Publicist* (Baltimore and London, 2001), 1–18; and Peter Hinds, '"A Vast Ill Nature": Roger L'Estrange, Reputation, and the Credibility of Political Discourse in the Late Seventeenth Century', *Seventeenth Century*, 21 (2006), 335–63.

[15] On jeremiads over the plague, fire, and war correlated with the paradigm of sin, punishment, and repentance in *Samson Agonistes*, see Knoppers, *Historicizing Milton*, ch. 6.

[16] The loosely configured 'Cabal' government (1668–73) was so called after the initial letters of the names of the leading ministers after Clarendon's fall: Clifford, Arlington, Buckingham, Ashley Cooper, and Lauderdale. On the toleration debates of 1667–72, see Greaves, *Enemies under his Feet*, 142–51.

We return, then, to Parliament and three major bills on the legislative agenda in early 1670: the year in which Milton's last two poems proceeded through publication. First, how was it that a seemingly private bill, sponsored by Lord Roos, who sought a parliamentary divorce and sanction to remarry, had national implications? For that indeed was the case. By 1670, it had become plain that the King would not produce legitimate heirs by his queen, Catherine of Braganza. Almost from the beginning of his reign but more notoriously after the fall of the censorious Clarendon, the King flaunted a series of royal mistresses, mostly Catholic and mostly grasping for financial emoluments and political influence. Indeed, Charles managed to sire some fourteen illegitimate children. The royal marriage and the expected heir to the throne, however, were another story. As the long-suffering Catherine failed to produce an heir, the suspected Catholicism of the king's brother and thus heir apparent, James, Duke of York, caused not only increasing anxiety but considerable speculation over whether or not the king would attempt to divorce his queen, or, possibly, declare his first-born illegitimate son, the popular James, Duke of Monmouth, legitimate.

Lord Roos's bill, to divorce an unfaithful wife and remarry (at a time when only separation from bed and board was allowed), could hence be seen as a kind of trial run for the King's own divorce.[17] Gilbert Burnet, Bishop of Salisbury, chaplain to Charles II, and later historian, writes that 'The duke [of York] and all his party apprehended the consequences of a parliamentary divorce: so they opposed this with great heat . . . And the king was as earnest in the setting it on, as the duke was in opposing it.' Although Burnet adds that, after the bill had passed, 'some moved the king that he would order a bill to be brought in, to divorce him from the queen', Charles did not, in the event, pursue a royal divorce.[18] Rather, the king pursued even more energetically a series of mistresses, English and French, from court beauties to French ladies-in-waiting to English actresses.

This last group is relevant to an ominous incident which ended the year 1670 and showed both the licentiousness of the court and the consequences of even the mildest reproof. As the poet and prose writer Andrew Marvell, Member of Parliament for Hull, explained it to his nephew, William Popple, in the course of the Commons's debate on the perennial question of how to raise funding for the king, 'Sir John Coventry having moved for an Imposition on the Playhouses, Sir John Berkenhead, to excuse them, sayed they had been of great Service to the King'. In reply, Coventry 'desired that Gentleman to explain, whether he meant the Men or Women Players', an obvious slur on the king's profligacy. It was a comment that he would soon regret. Shortly thereafter, members of the duke of Monmouth's troop in the guards laid in

---

[17] On Lord Roos's bill, see *Debates*, ed. Grey, i. 251–3; Marvell, *Poems and Letters*, ii. 136, 315; and Lawrence Stone, *Road to Divorce: England, 1530–1987* (Oxford, 1990), 309–11. Milton's early anonymous biographer claims in his *Life of Milton* that 'when the Subject of Divorce was under consideration with the Lords, upon the account of the Lord Ross, [Milton] was consulted by an eminent Member of that house' (Darbishire, 33).

[18] Burnet, *Bishop Burnet's History of his Own Time: From the Restoration of King Charles the Second to the Treaty of Peace at Utrecht* (1850), 177.

wait for Coventry and, in Marvell's words, 'as he returned from the *Cock*, where he supped, to his own House, they threw him down, and with a Knife cut off almost all the End of his Nos'.[19] The Commons was outraged, and Marvell concludes that 'The Court is at the highest Pitch of Want and Luxury, and the People full of Discontent'.[20]

'A SUM OF MONEY': ANGLO–FRENCH ALLIANCE IN THE SECRET TREATY OF DOVER

The second parliamentary bill, for supplies, gives a window into one of the key causes of conflict after 1660: the disputed boundaries of sovereignty between Parliament and the monarch, and the monarch's related frustration with a perpetual lack of funds, given inadequate parliamentary subsidies and the court's often extravagant expenditures. Charles II ultimately got his subsidies once again: through a combination of charm, coercion, and concessions (the most notable being his agreement to the second Conventicle Act). But the king chafed under the need to make concessions to gain parliamentary supply, and financial independence was probably one of the admittedly murky motives that led Charles, in late spring 1670, to meet with his sister, Henriette Anne, at Dover and negotiate a treaty with the powerful and ambitious French Catholic monarch, Louis XIV (to whose brother, the Duke of Orléans, Henriette was married).

Although Henriette's visit was passed off as a lavish family reunion, suspicions were rife. Marvell speculated on a new potential marriage: '*Madame*, our King's Sister . . . is to come as far as *Canterbury*. There will doubtless be Family Counsels then. Some talk of a *French* Queen to be then invented for our King. Some talk of a Sister of *Denmark*; others of a good virtuous Protestant here at Home.'[21] Others suspected more dire consequences. A full year earlier, on 25 April 1669, Samuel Pepys heard court rumors 'that for a sum of money we shall enter into a league with the King of France'. The likely consequences—that the king would then 'not need the Parliament' and that the English would be forced to break with their new alliance with the Dutch (and Swedes)—would, Pepys feared, 'undo us': 'this is a thing that will make the Parliament and Kingdom mad, and will turn to our ruine—for with this money the King shall wanton away his time in pleasures, and think nothing of the main till it be too late'.[22]

---

[19] Marvell, *Poems and Letters*, ii. 321.

[20] Ibid. 322.

[21] Ibid. 317.

[22] Pepys, *The Diary of Samuel Pepys*, ed. Robert Latham and William Matthews, 11 vols. (Berkeley and Los Angeles, 1970–83), ix. 536.

Indeed, such fears were closer to the truth. In a treaty concealed from other European states and from his own subjects, Charles pledged to align his British kingdoms with France against the Dutch in return for an annual French subsidy.[23] In even more secret provisions, known only to the king and two top ministers Arlington and Clifford, Charles promised to convert publicly to Catholicism and to reconcile his three kingdoms to Rome: in return, Louis XIV would provide further subsidies and, if necessary, French troops to subdue a restive nation. Charles's commitment to the secret Treaty of Dover would influence his actions for the remainder of his reign, including the third Anglo–Dutch War of 1672–4 and the king's 1672 Declaration of Indulgence permitting dissenters to take out licences for public worship and Catholics to worship in private. When Parliament not only forced Charles to withdraw the Declaration but passed a Test Act that required all office-holders to deny transubstantiation and take Anglican communion at least once a year, the resultant exposure of the Catholicism of James, Duke of York, added to increasing fears of popery and arbitrary government. And while popish-leaning Court and prelates triumphed, the godly had been forced out into the wilderness.

'Worse than Nebuchadnezzar': Coercion, Conflict, and the Second Conventicle Act

As member for Hull, Marvell had also watched with dismay as the new bill on conventicles, 'the Quintessence of arbitrary Malice', made its way through the Houses of Parliament in spring 1670.[24] The Conventicle Act replaced an earlier act that had expired in March 1669. This initial act was part of the 'Clarendon Code' put into effect by the Cavalier Parliament that sought both to ensure uniformity within the Church of England and to suppress religious observance outside of it. Despite Charles's promise of liberty for tender consciences in the Declaration of Breda that preceded his return to England, the king was hampered in his natural inclinations towards toleration (of both Nonconformists and Catholics) by a partisan Parliament and by churchmen such as Gilbert Sheldon and Matthew Wren with long memories and many grievances. The 1670 Conventicle Act instituted stiffer fines for dissenting preachers and for landowners who allowed dissenters to meet on their property. Implicitly recognizing the lack of enthusiasm for enforcing the laws against dissenters, the act gave financial incentives to informers and imposed fines on justices of the peace who neglected enforcement. An equally harsh addition was that offenders

---

[23] See Ronald Hutton, 'The Making of the Secret Treaty of Dover, 1668–1670', *Historical Journal*, 29 (1986), 297–318.

[24] *Poems and Letters*, ii. 314.

could be tried before a single justice of the peace, rather than the traditional trial by jury. Passed in April 1670, the Act was to go into effect on 15 May.[25]

There was much resistance to the new Conventicle Act in London and elsewhere in England in spring and summer 1670, as Milton's final poems were being printed, licensed, and registered. On 23 May 1670, Charles Whittington explained in a letter to Sir Joseph Williamson, Secretary of State, that 'the Act for suppressing conventicles had so exasperated' the inhabitants of Derbyshire, that

nothing short of a sudden insurrection is threatened. They complain of the great misery and loss the nation has received by the Stuarts, ever since Elizabeth, and say that if some course is not taken, the nation will be ruined, as the great sins of the Court cannot go unpunished; they endeavour to render the King as odious as they can, being a most factious and discontented people.[26]

Widespread opposition to the Act and the reluctance of many local constables and justices of the peace to enforce it were not the only headaches facing Williamson, who oversaw a large intelligence network. July 1670 produced a kind of showdown in London, with many preachers and their flocks coming into town. Reports varied. On 24 July, Francis Rainsford, deputy-lieutenant of the Tower, sent Williamson an optimistic account:

All the meeting-places in London have been secured by the military and peace officers, so that there was no teaching or disturbance. The preacher and hearers at a Quakers' meeting in Spitalfields were all convicted; the justices and military dispersed another, and an Anabaptists' meeting in Southwark, and sent the preachers, and half a score more, to gaol, for refusing to take the oath of allegiance. There was a great meeting in Little Moorfields, but it was dispersed by the Life Guards, and some Foot. (*CSPD*, x. 343)

Yet the very next day, Joseph Binckes wrote to Williamson that the 'people still persist in meeting in the open streets, and with more ardent resolutions than heretofore. I do not understand the doings of the justices, but know that all they suppress to-day are at liberty to-morrow' (p. 344).

Reports coming into Williamson showed at least rhetorical violence. On 12 May, one Nicholas Cox, an Anabaptist, of Cross Lane, St Giles, was reported as saying 'that he would not submit to the new Act made against conventicles; that he would be hanged at his own door before he would change his religion, and that he usually went to meetings and conventicles' and further 'that the King had acted worse than Nebuchadnezzar, as he acted in ignorance, but the King had acted wilfully, to pull down violence upon his own head' (*CSPD*, x. 220). Informers met with contempt, if not threatened violence. On 10 July, 'one John Tanton and his wife, of Westbury, asked [the informers] why they disturbed meetings which were according to God's law, while the informers' proceedings were those of the Devil, for which they would burn in hell fire' (p. 370). On 14

---

[25] 22 Car. II, c. 1, *Statutes of the Realm*, v. 648–51.

[26] *Calendar of State Papers, Domestic Series, of the Reign of Charles II*, 12 vols. (1860–95), x. 233 (cited hereafter as *CSPD*).

August, when authorities attempted to break up a meeting at the house of John Selcock, he 'called them informing rogues, and threatened to knock out their brains if they approached nearer'. On that same date, John Love of Stoford, and Tobias Hacker, an Anabaptist, called the informers 'vile and scurrilous names' (p. 370). Others responded with mockery. On 2 September 1670, writing to the Bishop of Salisbury of the 'great disorders committed in these parts', John Eyre noted that the distrainment (confiscation) of property had been an abject failure, for 'Many distresses have been made against those convicted, and the things were offered for sale in the markets and fairs, yet not one penny has been bid, but by way of a sneer; as 6*d*. or 13½*d*. for a cow, and such like, save what I bought myself, without occasion, but chiefly to encourage others' (*CSPD*, x. 417).

Aware of such problems, Parliament, upon reconvening in October 1670, appointed a committee to examine the new Conventicle Act. In November, Marvell wrote to his nephew of the increased powers of the London authorities to act against conventicles, as well as of the resistance they had been facing: 'To say Truth, they met in numerous open Assemblys, without any Dread of Government. But the Train Bands in the City, and Soldiery in *Southwark* and Suburbs, harassed and abused them continually; they wounded many, and killed some Quakers, especially while they took all patiently.'[27] Marvell goes on to mention two widely publicized cases: the arrests of civic dissenting leaders James Hayes and John Jekyll and of Quaker leaders William Penn and William Mead. After being arrested in June 1670, Hayes and Jekyll refused to post sureties for good behaviour; in turn, they sued the London magistrates for false imprisonment, hence challenging the enforcement of the Conventicle Act and raising broader questions of liberty and the rights of subjects.[28]

Penn and Mead, arrested when their preaching at the Grace-church meeting allegedly caused a tumult, brought an even more severe and widely publicized challenge to the Conventicle Act in their court trial.[29] Because the jury would not find the defendants guilty, they were, in Marvell's words, 'kept without Meat or Drink some three Days, till almost starved, but would not alter their Verdict; so fined and imprisoned'.[30] Penn and Mead publicized the trial, including the court's bullying of the jury, in *The Peoples Ancient and Just Liberties Asserted* (1670). The tract's inflammatory content included an exchange in which the Recorder, frustrated by the intransigence of the two defendants, (allegedly) blurted out that 'Till now I never understood the Reason of the Policy and Prudence of the Spaniards, in suffering the Inquisition among them; And

[27] *Poems and Letters*, ii. 317–18.

[28] The case reached the Commons, to whom Hayes and Jekyll appealed. *Debates*, ed. Grey, i. 294–300, 303–10; Dering, *Diary*, 4–7, 9–12; and Marvell, *Poems and Letters*, ii. 117–18; 317–18. De Krey, *London and the Restoration*, 112, gives a good account of the incident.

[29] *A Complete Collection of State Trials*, ed. Thomas B. Howell, 28 vols. (1809–20), vi, columns 951–1000; De Krey, *London and the Restoration*, 112–14.

[30] *Poems and Letters*, ii. 318.

certainly it will never be well with us, till something like unto the Spanish Inquisition be in England' (p. 3). For the godly, this outburst showed the true character of the persecutory state and church authorities. Aligned with that archetype of popery, the Spanish Inquisition, the Recorder's remark was a glimpse of the cloven hoof.

'Strenuous Liberty': *Paradise Regain'd* and *Samson Agonistes* in their Political and Religious Contexts

A king and court widely viewed as luxurious and dissolute. Conflicts over sovereignty, ongoing financial excess, and a court that seemed to tolerate popery. A volatile domestic situation in which repression only seemed to strengthen the resolve of Nonconformists. Widely publicized court cases that showed parliamentary Acts against dissent to be a threat to English liberty, property, and rights. In this context of unrest, resistance, and debate—rather than simply defeat—Milton published his brief epic and his classical tragedy.[31]

Under a regime, as well, of censorship and surveillance, Milton's literary texts take on multiple meanings, working through allusion and indirection, metaphor and paradigm.[32] Milton's own publisher, John Starkey, was involved in the underground press and would later be forced to flee into exile for attempting to publish what was judged a seditious, anti-monarchical work.[33] Although Milton's poems—*Paradise Lost*

---

[31] On Milton in defeat, see the influential work of Christopher Hill, esp. *The Experience of Defeat: Milton and Some Contemporaries* (New York, 1984) and '*Samson Agonistes* Again', *Literature and History*, 1 (1990), 24–39.

[32] On the 'functional ambiguity' of literary language, see Annabel Patterson, *Censorship and Interpretation: The Conditions of Writing and Reading in Early Modern England* (Madison, Wis., 1984); and Christopher Hill, 'Censorship and English Literature', in *The Collected Essays of Christopher Hill* (Brighton, 1985), i. 32–71.

[33] Starkey's publications included such republican texts as James Harrington's *The Rota* (1660) and Machiavelli's *Works* (1675). In 1682, Starkey fled the country after attempting to republish two anti-monarchical works by Nathaniel Bacon, *An Historicall Discourse of the Uniformity of the Government of England* (originally published in 1647) and *The Continuation of An Historicall Discourse* (originally published in 1651). See the entry for Starkey in the *ODNB*. In ground-breaking studies, Mark Knights, 'John Starkey and Ideological Networks in Late Seventeenth-Century England', *Media History*, 11 (2005), 127–45, places Starkey in overlapping political discourses of classical republicanism and Lockean contractual theory; and Annabel Patterson, 'Milton's Radical Publisher(s)', paper presented at the Canada Milton Seminar, Apr. 2006, compares Starkey's scofflaw activities with his seemingly innocuous booklists, showing how Milton's books take on radical resonance by keeping company with the works of Machiavelli, James Harrington, Henry Neville, and other republican theorists. On Starkey's scribal newsletters and his radical print activities, see also *The 1671 Poems*, ed. Knoppers, pp. xix–l.

as well as *Paradise Regain'd* and *Samson Agonistes*—passed the licensing scrutiny of Thomas Tomkins, they could nonetheless carry political meaning, working allusively and indirectly.[34]

The indexes are a further distinctive, indeed unique, corroboration of the ways in which Milton's late poems were shaped by and responsive to political and religious contexts: and indeed, *were recognized* as doing so by a seventeenth-century reader.[35] In correcting the Errata, marking the *Omissa*, making sensitive stylistic emendations, and adding indexes, early readers engaged actively with Milton's 1671 poems.[36] For all their straightforward, even simple, common-placing content—and with only nineteen entries (albeit some with multiple page numbers) for each of the poems—the indexes still manage to point to a broad range of issues: theological, moral, social, ethical, and political. Indeed, a return to our indexes—and the 1671 poems—shows that in fact it is not just the entry for 'Englands Case' that provides important commentary on Milton's own time. Rather, the reader looks to *Paradise Regain'd* and *Samson Agonistes* for models of faith and patience under persecution, for exposure of ungodly prelates and priests, and for possible violent revenge closely linked with the concerns of dissent and republicanism.[37] As such, Milton's final two

---

[34] Nicholas von Maltzahn's discussion of Tomkin's licensing of *Paradise Lost* is helpful for the 1671 volume as well; 'The First Reception of *Paradise Lost* (1667)', *Review of English Studies*, NS 47 (1996), 481–7.

[35] For all of the interest in Milton's hypothetical, idealized, or assumed readers, little attention has been given to actual readers of his texts. Important exceptions, however, have pointed to active readers whose literary responses are inseparable from political and religious judgements. Hence, Nicholas von Maltzahn's ground-breaking study showed how the clergyman and Royal Society member John Beale was preoccupied with Milton's republicanism and Calvinism even while recognizing and wanting to harness his considerable literary abilities ('Laureate, Republican, Calvinist: An Early Response to Milton and *Paradise Lost* (1667)', *Milton Studies*, 29 (1992), 181–98). Subsequently, William Poole has shown how the scientific virtuosi read Milton with suspicion, regarding him as a profound but dangerous talent ('Two Early Readers of Milton: John Beale and Abraham Hill', *Milton Quarterly*, 38 (2004), 76–99). In an important study of early modern readers that includes Milton, Steven N. Zwicker finds that marginalia on two copies of *Paradise Lost* shows memory- and devotionally oriented notations that also assumed political topicality (' "What every literate man once knew": Tracing Readers in Early Modern England', in Robin Myers, Michael Harris, and Giles Mandelbrote (eds.), *Owners, Annotators and the Signs of Reading* (Newcastle, 2005), 75–90).

[36] For an excellent account of early modern readers broadly considered, see Heidi Brayman Hackel, *Reading Material in Early Modern England: Print, Gender, and Literacy* (Cambridge, 2005); also helpful is William H. Sherman's elucidation of readers' marginalia and other textual markings, 'What Did Renaissance Readers Write in their Books?' in Jennifer Andersen and Elizabeth Sauer (eds.), *Books and Readers in Early Modern England: Material Studies* (Philadelphia, 2002), 119–37. On early readers of *Paradise Regain'd* and *Samson Agonistes*, see *The 1671 Poems*, ed. Knoppers, pp. lviii–lxxv.

[37] Significantly, this 17th-c. index correlates with a number of the points that scholars have made in linking Milton's final poems with dissent, albeit without treating actual readers. Most relevant, N. H. Keeble, *The Literary Culture of Nonconformity*, 187–214, discusses Nonconformist internalization, introspection, and individualism; and Keeble posits the wilderness of *Paradise Regain'd* as both a refuge from and challenge to the restored regime, in 'Wilderness Exercises: Adversity, Temptation, and Trial in *Paradise Regained*', *Milton Studies*, 42 (2002), 86–105. Sharon Achinstein looks at *Paradise Regain'd* as a model of faith and patience, as well as an oblique attack on false prelacy, and at the concern with cases of conscience and divinely inspired motions in *Samson Agonistes* (*Literature and Dissent in Milton's England* (Cambridge, 2003), 130–53). David Loewenstein stresses violent apocalypticism, imagined in *Paradise Regain'd* and enacted in *Samson Agonistes* (*Representing Revolution in Milton and his Contemporaries: Religion, Politics, and Polemics in Radical Puritanism* (Cambridge, 2001) chs. 8 and 9).

poems complement as much as contrast with one another, depicting both present and future action.

In *Paradise Regain'd*, the Son's obedient perseverance in the wilderness is a model of true martyrdom, of faith under persecution, of a kind of militant patience. The early reader underscores in his index the poem's unknown, solitary protagonist, who does not seek fame on earth. An index entry for 'popular 57' marks a passage critiquing the ignorance of the masses—'They praise and they admire they know not what' (iii. 52)—while 'Glory 58' points to Job as a model of true glory in heaven: 'Famous he was in Heaven, on Earth less known; / Where glory is false glory, attributed / To things not glorious, men not worthy of fame' (iii. 68–70). The Son, like many a dissenting minister forced out into fields and barns, eschews book learning for true, divinely given knowledge.[38] Hence, the reader notes 'Knowledg 93', pointing to the Son's perhaps otherwise puzzling rejection of Greek literature and philosophy:

> Think not but that I know these things, or think
> I know them not; not therefore am I short
> Of knowing what I aught: he who receives
> Light from above, from the fountain of light,
> No other doctrine needs, though granted true. (iv. 286–90)

At the same time that *Paradise Regain'd* holds up patience, faith, and an inner light, it also exposes Satan as a false minister, misleading and deceiving the people: 'presages 22 24' points to Satan as he claims to 'lend them oft my aid, / Oft my advice by presages and signs, / And answers, oracles, portents and dreams' (i. 393–5), as well as to the Son's rebuke of false priestcraft: 'But what have been thy answers, what but dark / Ambiguous and with double sense deluding' (i. 434–5). Suspicion of prelacy and priestcraft also seem to be behind the indexing of 'oracles 24': 'all Oracles / By thee are giv'n, and what confest more true / Among the Nations? that hath been thy craft, / By mixing somewhat true to vent more lyes' (i. 430–3). 'Flattery 21 26' marks Satan's boast to be of service to God himself, giving the wicked Israelite king Ahab false portents of success in battle: 'I undertook that office, and the tongues / Of all his flattering Prophets glibb'd with lyes / To his destruction, as I had in charge. / For what he bids I do' (i. 374–7). The second reference to flattery highlights Satan's claim that misery has made him a liar: forced to 'Say and unsay, feign, flatter, or abjure' (i. 474). Both instances evoke false priestcraft: whether Episcopal prelate or Roman pontiff.[39]

---

[38] I owe this formulation of the Son as a dissenting minister to Marshall Grossman. Significantly, when the first Conventicle Act (16 Car. II, c. 4) banned meetings of 'five persons or more assembled together over and above those of the same *household*' (*Statutes of the Realm*, v. 516, my emphasis), dissenters met in fields and open spaces to avoid the letter of the law. The Second Conventicle Bill (22 Car. II, c. 1) was emended to close the loophole. Following the words 'over and above those of the same household' was added 'if it be in a House where there is a Family inhabiting, or if it be in a House, Feild, or place where there is noe Family inhabiting' (*Statutes of the Realm*, v. 648).

[39] Achinstein notes that Restoration dissenting texts linked the flattering prophets of Ahab with the tyrannous and idolatrous state church (*Literature and Dissent*, 133–4).

As with *Paradise Regain'd*, the index to *Samson Agonistes* picks up the theme of patience and perseverance. 'Patience 43 77' draws attention to the Chorus's commendation of 'Patience as the truest fortitude' (l. 654), as well as its recognition (despite hopes for action) that

> patience is more oft the exercise
> Of Saints, the trial of thir fortitude,
> Making them each his own Deliverer,
> And Victor over all
> That tyrannie or fortune can inflict. (ll. 1287–91)

Barring some kind of divine intervention, the blinded Samson might be one of those 'Whom Patience finally must crown' (l. 1296).

Again, as with *Paradise Regain'd*, the index to *Samson Agonistes* notes not only the models of patience and faith but also the abuses of the ungodly. Hence, three page references under the index entry 'preist 54 84 86' underscore how Milton's drama—unlike anything in the Book of Judges—blames priests for suborning Dalila to betray her husband, for refusing to release the blinded and seemingly harmless Samson, and for egging on the idolatrous triumph over the defeated godly. The references begin with Dalila's excuse for betraying her husband, a parody of true religious piety:

> and the Priest
> Was not behind, but ever at my ear,
> Preaching how meritorious with the gods
> It would be to ensnare an irreligious
> Dishonourer of *Dagon* (ll. 857–61)

Similarly negative is Samson's concern that the sight of him at the festival of Dagon may exasperate his foes: 'Lords are Lordliest in thir wine; / And the well-feasted Priest then soonest fir'd / With zeal, if aught Religion seem concern'd' (ll. 1418–20). And, finally, as he attempts to ransom his son, Manoa finds that the Philistines who are most averse—'Contemptuous, proud, set on revenge and spite' (l. 1462)—are those most uphold their country's false religion: 'That part most reverenc'd *Dagon* and his Priests' (l. 1463).

Yet, as we saw earlier with the index entry on 'Englands Case', Milton's two final poems do not simply put forward a model of godly patience and ungodly persecution. Rather, they offer a republican critique of both the individual and nation as responsible for their own servitude. External bondage—whether Israel's bondage under the Philistines, the Romans under Tiberius, or the Jews under Roman rule in Christ's time—correlates with inner servility, the loss of virtue. Index entries on such topics as divine justice underscore that the erring nation—and the erring Samson—have brought upon themselves their own punishment. Divine justice, if questioned by Samson in moments of despair, is ultimately affirmed by both Samson and the Chorus in *Samson Agonistes*. Hence, 'Justice of God, 25, 29', marks both the Chorus's denigration of the disbelievers 'who doubt his ways not just' (l. 300) and Samson's acknowledgement that 'Nothing of all these evils hath befall'n me / But justly' (ll. 374–5).

And as such the poems indicate a possible way beyond crime and punishment. Hence, the index marks 'penitence see 35', Manoa's advice to Samson to 'Be penitent and for thy fault contrite, / But act not in thy own affliction, Son' (502–3). Equally significant, 'Impulse 21' points to Samson's comment on his first marriage to the Woman of Timna: 'I knew / From intimate impulse, and therefore urg'd / The Marriage on; that by occasion hence / I might begin *Israel's* Deliverance' (ll. 222–5). Waiting upon the Spirit of God, receiving divine impulse, and knowing when the time to act is right are crucial in both of Milton's poems: and of major concern in Restoration dissent.[40]

In *Samson Agonistes*, when the time is right, a Samson who has moved, however unevenly and incompletely, from bitterness and despair through confession and repentance to new faith is ready to act. The Chorus's hopes for a time when 'God into the hands of thir deliverer / Puts invincible might / To quell the mighty of the Earth, th' oppressour' (ll. 1270–2) seem fulfilled in the bloody offstage finale, reported by the Messenger, as Samson pulls down the Temple of Dagon upon the idolatrous Philistines—and on himself. But, the Chorus—upon hearing the offstage noise—initially envisages an even more dramatic victory, questioning whether Samson, his eyesight 'by miracle restor'd' (l. 1528), might be 'dealing dole among his foes, / And over heaps of slaughter'd walk his way?' (ll. 1529–30). This apocalyptic vision was originally placed not in the main text, but on a final *Omissa* page, perhaps added strategically late to evade the licenser.[41] Again, the same copy of the 1671 poems that we have been examining gives evidence that the *Omissa* was taken seriously, as the pertinent page of the text (p. 89/sig. O5) has been marked with three asterisks and with the notation: 'V[ide] the Omissa at yᵉ End'.[42]

Precisely how this imagined apocalyptic victory in the *Omissa* and the actual catastrophe of Samson's pulling down the Temple upon himself and the exultant Philistine lords and ladies relate to the political and religious contexts of Milton's 1671 poems is ambiguous, no doubt deliberately so. The vast majority of religious dissenters, after all, resisted passively, did not resort to armed violence, and indeed professed loyalty to the King. Yet more militant action always remained a possibility, and, as the censorship laws and L'Estrange's attempts to suppress illicit publications inadvertently showed, print was a powerful weapon for shaping public opinion in the Restoration period. Milton's poems can be seen as part of oppositional discourse, fostering hope and fortifying resistance in dissenters and political radicals. The Son's patience and perseverance and Samson's hard-earned recovery are models for the

---

[40] David Norbrook shows how *Paradise Regain'd* and *Samson Agonistes* are concerned with ascertaining the right occasion for action, in 'Republican Occasions in *Paradise Regained* and *Samson Agonistes*', *Milton Studies*, 42 (2002), 122–48.

[41] This is the important contribution made by Stephen B. Dobranski, who persuasively argues that the ten omitted lines could not be the result of a compositor's or printer's error and thus represent an authorial intervention, possibly a late addition after the work had already been licensed (*Milton, Authorship, and the Book Trade* (Cambridge, 1999), 41–61).

[42] The marking of the *Omissa* as well as of the Errata and other stylistic changes on this copy appears to be in a different hand than that of the indexer.

godly few who—faced with a corrupted nation that prefers 'Bondage with ease'—are ready, even eager for the exertions of 'strenuous liberty'.

In his Restoration poetry, then, Milton continues to engage political and religious issues, indirectly and allusively, as part of the meaning of his biblical narratives, classical forms, and resonant poetic language. Investigation of the political, religious, social, literary, and economic contexts of *Paradise Regain'd* and *Samson Agonistes* has proved and no doubt will continue to prove fruitful for understanding Milton's rich and complex late poems. In this endeavour, we have the models not only of academic scholarship, but of readers of Milton's own time, whose textual traces likewise merit our continued interest and attention.

CHAPTER 33

PARADISE REGAINED AND THE MEMORY OF *PARADISE LOST*

JOHN ROGERS

IT is generally acknowledged that sequels are rarely greater than the original works whose stories they continue. Perhaps a certain diminished appeal could even be asserted as a necessary and inevitable fact of the sequel. But whatever our ultimate judgement of the relative merits of Milton's *Paradise Lost* (1667) and the poem that appeared four years later, *Paradise Regained* (1671), we can assume that the disappointment that typically accompanies the reading of a sequel must have been a phenomenon of which Milton was unusually aware. Thomas Ellwood, a young Quaker who served as one of the blind Milton's amanuenses, claimed, years after the poet's death, that *he* had been responsible for Milton's composition of the great epic's sequel. Ellwood recorded having told Milton, after having been shown an early manuscript copy of *Paradise Lost*: 'Thou hast said much here of *Paradise lost*; but what hast thou to say of *Paradise found*.' Milton, Ellwood continued, in his account of this alleged conversation, 'made me no answer but sate some time in a Muse'.[1] The majority of Milton scholars have understandably looked with some suspicion on Ellwood's assertion that it was he, and not Milton himself, who generated the idea of a sequel to *Paradise Lost*: the prospect of the sequel, of *regaining* the paradise lost, is,

---

[1] *History of the Life of Thomas Ellwood* (1714), 233–4.

after all, in sight within the first lines of *Paradise Lost*, which opens by instructing the Heavenly Muse to sing of the act of disobedience that brought 'Death into the World' and 'loss of Eden, till one greater Man / Restore us, and regain the blissful Seat' (i. 3–5). But it is likely that Ellwood's comment on his role in the genesis of the later poem is so widely cited in the critical literature—even when it is ultimately dismissed—for good reason. Milton's readers seem often to be searching for some *excuse* for Milton's composition of the briefer, less lively, 'epic' *Paradise Regained*, which presents itself as a continuation of the much grander poem's account of Judaeo-Christian history. While Milton's readers have never, in the main, shown a preference for the sequel, the poet himself, it would seem, was of a different mind. Milton's nephew Edward Phillips described the way in which readers even in Milton's lifetime judged the sequel to be the weaker of the two works: *Paradise Regained* 'is generally censur'd to be much inferiour to the other, though he [Milton] could not hear with patience any such thing when related to him' (Darbishire, 75–6). This idea of the old Milton, impatient with any comment that might belittle the accomplishment of his sequel, is a moving one. And if the biographical information offered by Milton's nephew is trustworthy, then it is worth pursuing the reason for which Milton himself might have considered the sequel, far from 'inferiour to the other', the greater of the two works. This essay, which sets out to understand the import of Milton's *Paradise Regained* by shining a new light on that poem's famously opaque climactic action, will attempt to explain a way in which the poet crafted his sequel to serve not just as the culmination, but, in a remarkable way, the actual *revelation*, of the story of Christian history he began in *Paradise Lost*.

I

Surely the first thing we notice in reading the sequel to *Paradise Lost* is the radical difference of its style. The rhetorical texture of *Paradise Regained* constitutes perhaps its greatest departure from *Paradise Lost*. And although most readers of *Paradise Regained* find it less stylistically pleasing than *Paradise Lost*, Milton has inarguably imposed on his poetic style, and on his general literary inclinations towards a visionary mode of mythopoesis, a deliberate set of constraints. This poet has clipped his long, wandering sentences into shorter, less equivocal declarations, replacing the lush polyvalence of the epic similes that so marked the ornamental quality of *Paradise Lost* with the puritan austerity of simple argument and statement of fact.[2]

---

[2] Barbara Kiefer Lewalski, *Milton's Brief Epic: The Genre, Meaning, and Art of Paradise Regained* (Providence, R.I., 1966), summarizes (without approving) this conventional sentiment: 'The language of *Paradise Regained* is usually said to be flat, colorless, and austere in comparison with that of *Paradise Lost*' (p. 332).

How odd, then, that this poem, seemingly written in a stylistic mode as plain and unambiguous as Milton appears to have been capable of producing, conjures for us a world in which so few matters of consequence can be simply or clearly understood. Each of the two central characters of *Paradise Regained*, Satan and the Son of God— each having undergone a radical alteration in substance and demeanor from his earlier appearance in *Paradise Lost*—betrays a striking degree of ignorance concerning the Son's true identity. Each of them appears as well, at one point or another, to fail to comprehend the full significance of a divine declaration (the Father's baptismal proclamation, 'This is my beloved Son') that appears at least to have been uttered with perfect perspicacity. If a certain degree of ignorance marks the central characters of Milton's *Paradise Regained*, we, too, as readers, have historically found ourselves at a loss to understand precisely what is accomplished or learned at the poem's climax: Satan's final temptation of the Son situated near the poem's end. Milton begins *Paradise Regained* with an implicit promise that Jesus will emerge by the end of the poem 'By proof th' undoubted Son of God' (i. 11); the promise to prove Jesus' sonship is seen shortly afterward to have echoed the words the Father issued to Gabriel, after the baptism, when he promised that 'doubting' angel (i. 137) that 'this day by *proof* thou shalt behold . . . how I begin / To verifie that solemn message' (my italics) that Gabriel had delivered to Mary, 'that she should bear a son / Great in Renown, and call'd the Son of God' (i. 130–6). But readers of Milton's poem have never found any interpretation, let alone any 'proof', of the hero's emergence as the 'Son of God' that has gone 'undoubted'. There has been nothing like consensus about what it is in the poem by way of establishing Jesus' status as the Son of God that actually qualifies as proof; nor has there even been a consensus concerning the more general question of why Jesus' identity as the Son of God, a fact that nearly all readers, regardless of religious sensibility, have assumed the poem has taken as a matter of faith, needs to be proven at all.

Of Satan's three temptations of the Son of God in *Paradise Regained*, which Milton bases on the version of the story from the Gospel of Luke, and which comprise what is essentially the entire plot of the sequel, the third and final temptation (iv. 500–59), which 'has generated more disagreement than any other in the poem', is the one that precipitates the poem's conclusion (*CSP*, 418). In Milton's hands, Satan structures this final temptation as a paternity test, a means by which he can determine, once and for all, who—and whose—this so-called Son of God is. It is here that Satan takes the Son to the top of the temple, to the pinnacle of 'the Father's house' to prove not simply that this 'Son' before him is the 'Son of God' (Satan notes, rightly, that 'All men are Sons of God' (iv. 520)); he stages the temptation to ascertain, rather, what specific relevance this common title, 'Son of God', might have with respect to this particular Son, Jesus: 'I thought thee worth my nearer view / And narrower Scrutiny, that I might learn / In what degree or meaning thou art call'd / The Son of God, which bears no single sence' (iv. 514–17). When Satan then asks the Son to cast himself down, Milton tells us, with astonishing simplicity: 'To whom thus Jesus: also it is written, / Tempt not the Lord thy God, he said and stood. / But Satan smitten with amazement fell' (iv. 560–3). The Son of God performs no action here other than quoting a verse from Deuteronomy (6: 16) and then standing. And it is this spare, almost negligible, quotation of Scripture, followed by the seemingly passive action of standing—or the action, perhaps, of merely *remaining* standing—that, quite remarkably, precipitates the Son's conquest of Satan and effects the redemption of fallen man, or what Milton refers to in this sequel to *Paradise Lost* as the regaining of Paradise.

What, exactly, is accomplished at the moment the Son successfully resists this final temptation of Satan's on the top of the temple? Is, as has often been argued, the last of Satan's temptations a final attempt to confirm a terrible suspicion of Jesus' divine nature? Does Satan's violent positioning of the Son on the pinnacle work ultimately to prove that the Son of God is the second person of the Trinity, coequal and coeternal with the Father? Or is it, as A. H. Gilbert brilliantly argued many years ago, the fact that the Son's manhood is indeed perfect, and that perfect manhood is itself divine, that Satan realizes when he is smitten with amazement at the Son's ability to stand?[3] These speculations concerning the Son's nature and origin, which historically fall under the long-standing theological heading of 'the person of Christ', have surely been approached from every conceivable angle. In a provocative recent essay by Regina Schwartz, this perennial question for scholars of Milton's brief epic poem has been dismissed—and it has to be said that almost any amount of time spent with the critical literature on this poem written over the course of the last forty years will convince one that Schwartz has a point—as a series of 'tired controversies over the person of Christ'.[4]

As will become clear later in this essay, I agree with Schwartz that, on some level, the scholarly determination to solve the confounding Christology of Milton's poem has served as a critical bogey, blinding us to questions and problems no less pressing or urgent. But, ultimately, my argument must counter Schwartz's suggestion, since it is virtually impossible to deny that a central thrust of Satan's temptation is some attempt to determine, or at the very least to *pretend* to determine, the precise nature of the 'person of Christ'. 'His first-begot we know, and sore have felt', Satan tells his counsel of fallen angels, remembering his painful defeat at the hands of the Son in the War in Heaven, 'when his fierce thunder drove us to the deep'; 'Who *this* is', Satan continues, referring to this messianic figure, Jesus, immediately after the scene of his baptism which opens *Paradise Regained*, 'we must learn' (i. 89–91; emphasis mine). *Why* Satan, and for that matter, why we as readers, 'must learn' the identity of this Jesus is a long-standing, if rarely articulated, critical question, and one that has never been adequately answered. But to arrive at our own understanding of the poem's investment in the problem of learning the Son's identity, we must understand as precisely as possible what it is that Satan needs to know.

His problem is not, surely, a simple one of memory, however reluctant Satan may be to recall his ancient interaction with the Son of God in heaven. Satan had begun his address to the 'mighty Peers' of his 'gloomy Consistory' (i. 40–2) with a reflection

---

[3] Allan H. Gilbert, 'The Temptation in *Paradise Regained*', *Journal of English and Germanic Philology*, 15 (1916), 603–5.

[4] Regina Schwartz, 'Redemption and *Paradise Regained*', *Milton Studies*, 42 (2003), 26–49.

on the pain of any memory of their defeat: 'For much more willingly I mention Air, / This our old Conquest, then remember Hell / Our hated habitation' (i. 45–7). For all the anguish aroused by his recollection, Satan's memory of hell, and of the defeat that led him there, is firmly intact. And that memory will, in fact, continue to surface at precisely those moments in which Satan is most committed to determining the Son's identity: in a later address to the council of peers, he will announce that 'such an Enemy / Is ris'n to invade us, who no less / Threat'ns then our expulsion down to Hell' (ii. 126–8). The cognitive challenge Milton establishes for Satan in *Paradise Regained* is not, then, simply one of remembering; it is rather the establishment of the *relation* of those remembered events to the current circumstances inaugurated by the Father's declaration at the baptism. Satan's challenge is to conceive of the Son as one who occupies the identity both of this present Messiah and of the Son of painful memory, to understand the temporal continuity of person that links the exalted Son of the earlier poem, whom he clearly remembers, and this newly risen enemy, this messianic Son of God, with whom he is confronted at the present moment. Milton's inventive narrativization of a cognitive lapse so severe that the full identity of the hero escapes the evident grasp of both the hero and the villain is without question one of his greatest literary achievements. And it is my hope to propose a way of thinking about the later poem's unusual problematization of the Son's identity that moves past the traditional theological question of the 'person of Christ'—the Christological problem of *who this is* or even, more specifically, *who this has been*—and addresses instead the larger epistemological question of how and when and why Milton permits us, or fails to permit us, to *know* what is at stake in the relation between who this is and who this has been.

Satan's confusion as to the identity of the Son has been matched, if not bested, by the confusion on this matter evinced by the readers of *Paradise Regained*. Not only are readers uncertain as to the question of the Son's divinity or humanity, there is no critical agreement concerning the process by which the Son arrives at, or develops, whatever knowledge (if any) he may have of the full truth of his nature. If, as I and many other critics believe, following Barbara Lewalski's ground-breaking argument in *Milton's Brief Epic*, a sense of his own identity as *the* Son of God is something that the Son comes to only by the end of the poem (and it is possible, as I will suggest later, that he may not come to it at all), it is still not clear exactly when, or how, the Son arrives at the knowledge that the vast majority of Milton's readers have assumed he has possessed all along.

As Lewalski's reading makes clear, what the Son *begins* the poem knowing of his identity cannot be in dispute. The initial stage of his coming into Christological knowledge the Son himself narrates clearly in his opening soliloquy, where we learn that, since the age of 11, upon visiting the Temple 'to hear / The teachers of our Law' (i. 211–12), he had begun experiencing 'growing thoughts' of his desire and potential for messianic conquest. The Son proceeds to recall how these adolescent thoughts would be matched, and refined, by the certain (though partial) knowledge his mother shared with him of his divine pedigree. 'For know, thou art no Son of mortal man', Mary revealed to Jesus, upon 'perceiving' the son's messianic desires made strangely manifest 'by words at times cast forth' (i. 234, 227–8); 'Thy Father', she continued, 'is the Eternal King, who rules / All Heaven and Earth' (i. 236–7). The Son describes, too, the scholarly bent that moved him, upon hearing what the angel Gabriel had told his mother at his conception, to verify her words; he returned immediately to his study of 'The Law and Prophets, searching what was writ / Concerning the Messiah' (i. 260–1), a return to the scriptural text that enabled the young Jesus, after a careful collation of his mother's revelation with the revelation of Scripture, to find 'of whom they spake / I am' (i. 262–3). The Son's knowledge of who he is and who he will be (the Messiah, sired by none other than God himself, destined to be the future king of Israel and deliverer of mankind) is indisputably established for him by the time his 'age / Had measur'd twice six years' (i. 209–10), and is never seriously questioned by any character in *Paradise Regained*.

But it is not the knowledge of who the Son is, but who the Son *was*, that is the unacknowledged object of the unacknowledged quest that structures Milton's poem. Up to the moment of the event of the baptism, the acquisition of the knowledge of his past is something whose importance has clearly never impressed itself on the poem's hero. The conveyor of revealed truth most important to *Paradise Regained* is unquestionably Hebrew Scripture, a set of texts the Son knows well and to which he will repeatedly resort in his temptation by Satan. But these texts say nothing of the Son's pre-existence; and absent any revelation either oral or written of an existence in heaven before his earthly nativity, this man, with his perfect knowledge of his messianic future, is afforded no evident means by which he can understand his past, by which he can identify himself as one whose existence pre-dated his modest Bethlehem birth and who had heroically brought to its conclusion a war among the angels in heaven.[5] The drama of *Paradise Regained*, as Lewalski's study makes clear, lies in Milton's original representation of an event at which the Son arrives at his non-scriptural knowledge of his past identity as the first begotten of the Father's creatures.

It should be pointed out that Milton himself betrays no uncertainty about the identity of the pre-existent Son with the human Messiah in his theological treatise *De Doctrina Christiana*, a work he is likely to have written either contemporaneously with, or shortly before, *Paradise Lost*. He devotes considerable attention to proving his theology of the person of Christ, which boldly confronts the orthodox account of the Son's equality and co-eternity with the Father, insisting heretically in the treatise that the Son, who must be thought inferior to the Father, had not existed from eternity, but 'that he was the first of created things' (*CPW*, vi. 207). Armed with the written revelation of the New Testament, a body of evidence available to neither Satan nor the Son in *Paradise Regained*, Milton appears in the *De Doctrina* to be amply satisfied with the Christian scriptural evidence for the continuity of identity

---

[5] To the extent that any important interpretative question concerning *Paradise Regained* has been resolved, it is now generally agreed that Milton's Son betrays no memory of his heavenly life before his incarnation. As John Carey notes, the one moment in the text that had for some critics suggested otherwise (ll. 410–20) does not in fact indicate the Son's experiential memory of a life in heaven (*CSP*, 440 n.). Carey cites as support Lewalski's argument that the Son's speech in that passage is 'an imaginative recreation of the scene based upon traditional (Christian) exegesis of the Job story' (*Brief Epic*, 212).

between the pre-existent Logos and the human Jesus. He is able thereby to dismiss the assumptions held by those ancient theologians, most notably the adoptionists (or those often referred to as Samosatenians), who had posited the idea that Jesus was but a man, fathered by the carpenter Joseph, who was only at his baptism adopted by the Father as the Son of God and invested with the Logos. And Milton is able to dismiss as well the more recent, contemporary adherents of anti-trinitarianism, the Socinians (to whom he refers in the treatise as 'modern thinkers' (*moderni*)), who had, like the adoptionists, dated Christ's origin to the nativity, but who had insisted that this created Messiah was nonetheless the Son of God, having been born of Mary but conceived by the Father. Having ruled incorrect these low theological assessments of the person of Christ, Milton, finally, is able to assert his own 'higher' Christology, a version of Arianism, an ancient Christian theology which had propounded the Son's creation by the Father but which dated that creation to a moment in time well before the nativity of Jesus.[6] Milton can prove his higher (though still heretical) Christology of the created Son's pre-existence in heaven by means of a comprehensive review in the *De Doctrina* of those passages in the New Testament that reveal to his satisfaction that it was through the created Son that 'all other things, both in heaven and earth, were afterwards made' (*CPW*, vi. 206).

It is clearly the Christian, and not the Hebrew, scriptural record to which Milton turned in the *De Doctrina Christiana* for undoubted evidence of the unity of person between the Messiah Christ and the pre-existent Son of God. But when he takes up the same question in his sequel to *Paradise Lost*, he sets himself the extraordinary challenge of establishing the unity of person between the pre-existent Son and Jesus of Nazareth without any evidentiary recourse to the revelations of the New Testament. Imposing upon his brief epic the same epistemological constraints under which the historical Jesus would likely have laboured, Milton crafts a narrative which is at once charged to prove the fact of the Messiah's pre-existence and denied any access to the Christian scriptural sources upon which Milton himself relied to make the same point in his theological treatise. The brief epic will, furthermore, deny itself the most obvious way of establishing Jesus' identity with the pre-existent Son. Just as the recall of Hebrew Scripture can do nothing to assist the unspoken labour of establishing the facts of the Son's pre-existence, so too does personal memory prove a failure as a form of reliable evidence. The Satan of *Paradise Regained* clearly remembers the first-begotten Son of God and his chariot-driven triumph that ended the War in Heaven (i. 89–90), although he cannot, as we have seen, understand the relevance of that memory to his current situation. But the Son himself betrays no

---

[6] Despite the resistance among many Milton scholars to bestow upon Milton's admittedly idiosyncratic heterodox Christology the historical name that comes closest to describing it, I use the term 'Arian', compelled by the strong case for the use of that term by John P. Rumrich, in *Milton Unbound: Controversy and Reinterpretation* (Cambridge, 1996), 24–9. See, too, Rumrich's 'Milton's Arianism: Why It Matters', in Stephen B. Dobranski and John P. Rumrich (eds.), *Milton and Heresy* (Cambridge, 1998), 75–92. Michael Bauman provides a comprehensive review of Miltonic heresy in Michael Bauman, *Milton's Arianism* (Frankfurt am Main, 1987). For an alternative view, see the essay above by Gordon Campbell and Thomas N. Corns, Ch. 23.

direct experiential knowledge of a heavenly pre-existence before his birth as Jesus, his memory, we can only assume, having been emptied out along with his divinity at the kenosis of his incarnation as a man: the Son of *Paradise Regained*, quite simply, knows no time when he was not as now.[7] And as a consequence of the cognitive and memorial lapses suffered by the two central characters of the poem, what strikes nearly every reader as the painfully obvious facts—of the identity of *this* latter-day Jesus Son of God with *that* pre-existent Son of God, and of the intimate relation of this brief epic with its longer predecessor—present themselves in *Paradise Regained* as culminating revelations towards which the poem's entire plot, such as it is, moves.

II

The critics of *Paradise Regained* who have followed in Lewalski's steps disagree among themselves as to when the Son of God comes into his knowledge of the connection of his present, past, and future existence. Is it that miraculous moment on the pinnacle at which he *stands*? Is it the moment, or perhaps the moment just after, he utters the word 'God' in his Deuteronomic citation, 'Tempt not the Lord thy God'? Or is it the moment after *that*, when the angelic choir reveals what no one, including the narrator himself, has yet revealed, which is for all readers of Milton the excruciatingly obvious fact that this son of God, Jesus, is that same 'Son of God' that *we* remember as the conquering hero from the War in Heaven represented in Book 6 of *Paradise Lost*? Addressing the Son, the angels sing that 'long of old thou didst debel' Satan, saving for the end of the poem the first acknowledgement by anyone but Satan and the narrator that there is a connection between the events represented in *this* poem, *Paradise Regained*, and those represented in the poem *Paradise Lost* of which it so self-consciously serves as the sequel. And, finally, it must be said, given the fact that the Son, while the putative addressee of these 'Angelic Quires' and their revelatory 'Heavenly Anthems' (iv. 593–4), is never shown to be startled or even enlightened by the information imparted in the celestial hymn (perhaps because he is feeding at the time at the 'table of Celestial Food' (iv. 588)), the Lewalski thesis could also support a more radical reading of the poem's contribution to the theology of the 'person of Christ': it is possible that the Son of God, at least by the point in his earthly career reached by the end of the poem, never learns, or if he learns is not actually concerned with, either the general fact of his existence before his earthly nativity or the specific fact of his pre-existent victory in an ancient war among the angels in heaven.

---

[7] See Lewalski, *Brief Epic*, 135: The Son 'has no consciousness of himself as the "first-begot" or of any pre-existent state in heaven'.

Before we can understand why Milton has made the culminating action of *Paradise Regained* so difficult to identify or understand, we need to recognize that this is not the first time that Milton has staged the process, with some degree of obscurity, whereby the true, Arian understanding of the 'person of Christ' comes gradually to be revealed. When Milton is writing formal theology, in the *De Doctrina Christiana*, he is able to assert categorically his Arian Christology of the created Son's preexistence, which he confidently distinguishes from those low Christologies, such as adoptionism or Socinianism, which he views, quite simply, as wrong. But one of the most striking, though critically unexamined, ways in which *Paradise Regained* makes itself felt as a sequel to *Paradise Lost* (the last books in particular) is in the degree to which it presents the revelation of its official Christology not as a singular event, but as an elaborate cognitive process. Christological truth emerges as the product of successive revelations whereby both the fictional characters and the reader are guided through a sequence of heretical Christologies, none of which receive dismissal (as in the *De Doctrina*) as wrong, but which are shown at the poems' ending merely to be incomplete, to be provisional Christologies waiting simply for the gentle correction supplied by the presumably final revelation of the true, higher theology, Miltonic Arianism. As if committed to the revelation of the true understanding of the person of Christ as an inescapably successive movement from shadowy types to truth, both poems stage a march through a series of provisional theological positions, each one developmentally appropriate given the stage at which Adam, in *Paradise Lost*, or the Son, in *Paradise Regained*, finds himself at any given point in the story: Adam and the Son move from a low form of Jewish messianism, to an earnest presentation of an adoptionist reality, with its assumption of the Son's manhood, to an even more amplified presentation of a Socinian world view, which accepts the adoptionist theory that the Son has only been in existence since his nativity as Jesus, but augments it with the revelation that the Son was actually fathered by God. And Adam and the Son both find themselves by the end of their poems in possession, presumably, of the final truth of Miltonic Arianism, which builds on the Socinian thesis of the Son's divine paternity by adding the crucial additional revelation that this Son had in fact been created by the Father in Heaven at a point in time before his birth—now seen as his incarnation—as Jesus.

In *Paradise Lost*, each heretical step of the slow instruction into the true nature of the person of Christ is delivered with utter authenticity by the archangel Michael, since he himself receives only gradual Christological 'enlightenment' from the Father (xi. 115). Milton's narrator, too (and this will be the case as well in *Paradise Regained*), seems no less dependent than Michael on a gradual enlightenment on the topic of the person of Christ, as he never exposes any higher knowledge of the Son's identity than that which Michael and Adam possess at any given point in the story of Adam's Christological instruction. But the epic's first introduction to the question of the unity of person between the pre-existent Son and the earthly Christ emerges in Book 10, before Michael begins his slow series of revelations for the benefit of Adam. It is, ironically, the Son himself who in *Paradise Lost* first brings to our attention the matter of his identity. Assuming the role of 'God', and known by Adam and Eve as well as by the narrator as the 'Lord God', the Son has descended to the Garden to issue the judgements of the Father, and delivers Satan, in the hearing of Adam and Eve, the prophecy, derived by Milton from Genesis 3: 14 and known as the 'proto-evangelium', of Satan's ultimate destruction by the woman's 'Seed' (x. 180; see further Susan Wiseman's essay above, Ch. 30). Carefully preparing us for the lesson we will have to learn, or relearn, when we read the sequel, Milton's first reference to the figure we of course recognize as the Christian redeemer reveals not even the slightest sense that the Son, who is speaking, or the narrator, who is relaying the Son's speech, understands its Christological implications. The Son, assuming his provisionally authorized role as the 'Lord God', but betraying no sense that he has anything like the Father's full awareness of the implications of his speech, declares to Satan that the woman's 'Seed shall bruise thy head, thou bruise his heel' (x. 181). Evincing the same degree of Christological naivety as the Son, Milton's narrator follows the judgement with these words carefully crafted, surely, to set the stage for the epistemological problems that will be expanded upon in much greater detail in *Paradise Regained*:

> So spake this Oracle, then verifi'd
> When *Jesus* son of *Mary* second *Eve*,
> Saw Satan fall like Lightning down from Heav'n,
> Prince of the Air. (x. 182–5)

The Son, posing as God as he judges Satan, Adam, and Eve, may qualify as an 'Oracle' in issuing the protoevangelium, but he manifests no more oracular a sense of the Christological implications of his prophecy of the Seed than does the narrator at this point. Ignorant of any future incarnation as man, knowing only that he has volunteered to make himself 'mortal', to redeem man's mortal crime, the Son of God has no more knowledge at the time he issues his judgement than (apparently) has the narrator that he, the Son, will in fact prove identical to the person with whom he is compared in Milton's brief narrative of typological verification: '*Jesus* son of *Mary* second *Eve*'. Nor can the Son (or apparently the narrator) know at this point that the future sight that this son of Mary and Eve will have of Satan's fall will itself be but a repetition of the event, unrecorded but for the sequel that has not yet been written, of his sight of Satan's amazed fall from the pinnacle of the temple in *Paradise Regained*.

In the final books of *Paradise Lost*, Adam's instinctive sense that the Messiah—or, as he is initially taught to call him, the 'woman's Seed'—is merely one of many possible divinely begotten Sons of God and Man, is promiscuously encouraged by the archangel Michael. Adam is never given any reason to assume the identity of the earthly Messiah with that divine being, called the 'Son', he had learned about from Raphael. In fact, Michael's first introduction to Adam of the Messiah suggests, if anything, that deliverer's exclusive manhood (xii. 148–50). Some 150 lines later in Book 12, Michael will reveal that the Messiah's name will be Jesus, and that this man, Jesus, will be none other than the prophesied Seed who will bruise the serpent's head (ll. 310–13). At this early point in Michael's lesson in Christian history, the Christology to which Adam is introduced is the lowest form possible: it is adoptionism, the belief in Jesus' exclusive manhood until his adoption by the Father, which Adam has no choice at this point but to embrace, and which would come to characterize later in the eighteenth century the credo of many Unitarians.

But, of course, we know that Milton's Jesus, just like the mid-seventeenth-century Socinian Jesus, is not exclusively human.[8] It is the raising of the bar from the extremely low Christology of adoptionism to the slightly higher Christology of Socinianism to which Michael turns next. When, at the end of Michael's narration of the Messiah story in Book 12 we are given the information that the Messiah has been fathered by God himself, Michael and Adam still betray no certain knowledge that this anointed one is identical to the pre-incarnate Son of Raphael's long narration. In fact this new Christological information is not even delivered by Michael himself, but emerges rather (much as the key Christological information emerges in *Paradise Regained*) by means of the vehicle of an angelic choir, whose prophesied song to the simple shepherds hasting to the manger at the nativity Michael quotes:

> They gladly thither haste, and by a Quire
> Of squadrond Angels hear his Carol sung.
> A virgin is his Mother, but his Sire
> The Power of the most High; he shall ascend
> The Throne hereditary, and bound his Reign
> With earths wide bounds, his glory with the Heav'ns. (xii. 366–71)

To be sure, this strange point and news of the Son's heavenly paternity ('his Sire / The Power of the most High') hits Adam with a Christological revelation so forceful that he is led to experience it as a final truth, unquestionably higher than his earlier, incomplete assumptions of the earthly ancestry of the Messiah and the Seed. But this choral revelation of the identity of the Son's most high father still falls short of the true Arian Christology of Milton's Son: this new information, that the Messiah has been begotten by the Heavenly Father upon a mortal virgin, confers upon the Son no higher Christological identity than that he is assumed to have by Satan in *Paradise Regained* or by any Socinian contemporary of Milton's. That Jesus is a man of special

---

[8] Milton, we know, appears in the *De Doctrina Christiana* to take a swipe at the Socinians, when he complains of the modern thinkers who consider Jesus a 'mere man'. But he would have been more than aware of the fact that the majority of his Socinian contemporaries believed no such thing. In fact, the Racovian catechism argues for Jesus' divine paternity and against his 'meer manhood'. Milton writes in the *De Doctrina* that 'It follows that he [Christ] must have existed before his incarnation, whatever subtleties may have been invented to provide an escape from this conclusion, by those [the Socinians, or possibly the more ancient antitrinitarians, the adoptionists] who argue that Christ was a mere man' (*CPW*, vi. 419). But the Socinian catechism, with which Milton was surely familiar, answered precisely that question, 'Is the Lord Jesus then a meer man', with this assertion of Jesus's divine paternity: 'By no means. For he was conceived of the Holy Spirit, and born of the Virgin Mary, and therefore is from his very conception and birth the Son of God, as we read, Luke 1. 35. where the Angell thus speaketh to the Virgin Mary, The Holy Spirit shall come upon thee, and the power of the highest shall overshadow thee, wherefore also that Holy Thing Generated shall be called the Son of God' (*Racovian Catechisme* (Amsterdam, 1652), 27–8). As Milton rightly notes in the late work *Of True Religion* (1673), Arians and Socinians, for all their denial of his co-eternity with the Father, 'acknowledge [Christ] both God and their Saviour' (*CPW*, viii. 425).

birth and power, born of a virgin, and fathered by God, is a claim—easy to miss—perfectly construable as truth by any character, including Satan, at any point in *Paradise Regained*: Satan, we recall, begins *Paradise Regained* by concluding, after the baptism, that 'His Mother then is mortal, but his Sire, / He who obtains the Monarchy of Heav'n' (i. 85–7). That we are told in *Paradise Lost* that 'he shall ascend / The Throne hereditary, and bound his Reign / With earths wide bounds' (xii. 369–71) bears no relevance on the fact of his pre-existence, as the claim of his future kingship is simply information established in the Davidic prophecies, and information in fact that Michael had already made plain to Adam (xii. 325–30).

But this new information concerning the Messiah's heavenly paternity, although 'merely' Socinian, is nonetheless offered to us as a Christological advance of unquestionable interest to Adam. Given that Adam, up to this point in the last book of *Paradise Lost*, has had no reason to assume that the Messiah was anything other than a son of David, Michael's carefully released news of the Messiah's heavenly paternity, a fact that Adam would have been incapable of determining on the basis of reason alone, elicits from the first parent what may be the most exuberant burst of excitement in the entire book:

> O Prophet of glad tidings, finisher
> Of utmost hope! Now clear I understand
> What oft my steddiest thoughts have searcht in vain,
> Why our great expectation should be call'd
> The seed of Woman: Virgin Mother, Hail,
> High in the love of Heav'n, yet from my Loyns
> Thou shalt proceed, and from thy Womb the Son
> Of God most High; so God with man unites. (xii. 375–82)

It is at this point in *Paradise Lost*, and not before this point, that the 'Seed' of the protoevangelium whom Adam has only been recently taught to identify as the 'Messiah' (xii. 244), can be confidently referred to by humanity as the 'Son'. This new designation of the Seed as the 'Son' is evidence—of that there can be no doubt—of Christological progress. But, to cite the Father's words to the Son in Book 3, 'all is not done' (iii. 203). Despite the fact that scholars of the poem have reproduced Adam's enthusiastic sense that his Christological instruction at the hands of Michael (the 'finisher / Of utmost hope') is now complete, there is still no firm indication, yet, of Adam's full comprehension of Milton's Arian Christology.[9] Adam knows now that the Seed is the Messiah, and that the Messiah has been sired by the Father; and he is about to learn from Michael that this Son of God will fulfil his 'Obedience to the Law of God', will suffer the penalty of death, and will be raised from the dead by the Father, as an example to those who believe and prepare their minds for the martyr's death, 'like that which the redeemed dy'd' (xii. 445). It is this cluster of facts about the

---

[9] See Hugh MacCallum, *Milton and the Sons of God: The Divine Image in Milton's Poetry* (Toronto, 1986). Although claiming that Adam's instruction into the truth of Milton's theology of the Son is complete at this point, MacCallum's is still the best account of the Christological import of Michael's tutelage.

prophesied Seed that elicits from Adam the enthusiastic response we have just seen. But we cannot deny the fact that what it is that so excites Adam is essentially a Christological conviction in the earthly Messiah's heavenly paternity with which nearly all of Milton's contemporary Socinians would feel comfortable. Milton's theological treatise, as I have noted, may have seemed confident in its dismissal of the Socinian view of the Son's origin at his earthly conception, but *Paradise Lost*, perhaps not unlike a consideration of heresy in Milton's late treatise *Of True Religion* (*CPW*, viii. 437), reveals a marked, perhaps surprising, sympathy for contemporary anti-trinitarianism, despite the failure of that 'modern' theology to acknowledge the ancient, Arian truth of the Son's pre-existence.[10]

Committed ultimately to the Arian thesis of the created son's pre-existence in heaven, Milton naturally does not leave Adam, or us, in this uncertain state of an uncorrected Socinianism, in a state of knowing that the Messiah is a Son of God but still ignorant of the additional truth that he is but the earthly incarnation of *the* Son of God whose story lies at the centre of *Paradise Lost*. It is not until the full story of this Messiah/Son is told, including the event of his final victory over Satan at the end of time, that Milton permits Michael to prove or verify the ultimate truth of the Son's identity. It is only at the end of the story, at which the Son's triumphant heroism is fully articulated, that the Arian pedigree of the Messiah Son is delivered, this time unmistakably, to Adam:

> Then to the Heav'n of Heav'ns he shall ascend
> With victory, triumphing through the air
> Over his foes and thine, there shall surprise
> The Serpent, Prince of air, and drag in Chains
> Through all his Realm, and there confounded leave;
> Then enter into glory, and *resume*
> *His Seat at Gods right hand*, exalted high
> Above all names in Heav'n. (xii. 451–8; my italics)

How does Adam, and how do we, *know*, that the Seed *cum* Messiah *cum* Son is none other than the Son of God whose story filled the pages of Raphael's portion of *Paradise Lost*? Revealing in these final lines the fact that this victorious messianic Son will '*resume* / His Seat at Gods right hand, exalted high / Above all names in Heav'n' (emphasis mine), Michael subtly, but with absolute perspicuity, establishes the identity of *this* Son with the Son whose elevation to his session at the Father's right hand is the inaugural point in the poem's story, and the only aspect of Michael's story of the Son that intersects with any aspect of the narrative of that pre-existent being that Raphael had delivered to Adam.

To be sure, this event of Adam's recognition of the Son's true identity is situated in a narrative structure that directs us to anticipate Adam's educational development as a process culminating in a satisfying acquisition of knowledge. And given the

---

[10] See Martin Dzelzainis, 'Milton and Antitrinitarianism', in Sharon Achinstein and Elizabeth Sauer (eds.), *Milton and Toleration* (Oxford, 2007), 171–85, for a comprehensive account of Milton's sympathetic encounters with anti-trinitarianism in general, and of the tolerant view of Socinianism he expresses in *Of True Religion* in particular (pp. 174–5).

attention the poem has devoted to the discovery of the Son's identity, it is hard to imagine an event in the last two books that should be more culminating than that moment in which fallen Adam comes to know that the redeemer of fallen man is none other than the pre-existent Son of God, the very hero of Milton's *Paradise Lost.* That said, we have no choice but to acknowledge the fact that what should be, by virtue of our generic expectations, an explosive moment of anagnorisis is shockingly easy to miss. One could imagine a reasonable argument (however inadequate) that this scene may not be one of distinct recognition at all, since there is no earlier point in the last books of which we can say with certainty that Adam did *not* know that the Seed/Messiah/Son whose earthly presence was prophesied by Michael was none other than the 'only' Son of God whose exaltation to his headship over the angels was narrated in Book 5. And it would be senseless to damn as irredeemable the vast majority of critics who appear silently to have assumed that Adam understands the poem's official Christology at some point in the final books *before* line 456 of Book 12. But it is nonetheless indisputable that there is no prior moment (before xii. 456) in Michael's lesson in Christian history that authoritatively establishes the identity of the Messiah whose story he is presently relating with that of the Son whose compelling narrative had constituted the bulk of Books 5 to 7 of *Paradise Lost.* The moment (if any) of Adam's recognition of the poem's final Christological truth has not only been delayed to an almost embarrassing degree, but, more important, its actual appearance in the narrative has been radically obscured, its thematic and theological import radically minimized. 'O goodness infinite, goodness immense!', Adam replies, upon receiving Michael's final confirmation of the poem's Arian Christology. But as Adam amplifies his sense of immense goodness ('That all this good of evil shall produce, / And evil turn to good; more wonderful / Then that which by creation first brought forth' (xii. 469–72)), Milton in no way permits us to feel confident that Adam's exclamatory praise has anything whatsoever to do with this final acquisition of knowledge—so extraordinarily long in the making, and from any theological perspective so enormously important—about the person of Christ.

We are, in short, never in *Paradise Lost* afforded anything like the moment that Michael's carefully calibrated release of information concerning the Son leads us to expect, a moment in which the finally Christologically enlightened Adam might say to Michael, 'Goodness Immense! So *this* Son of God of whom you speak is that *same* Son of God that Raphael told me about!' And, similarly, and no less frustrating, from the perspective at least of our conventional generic expectations—though Milton's Michael is never in Books 11 and 12 reluctant to chide Adam for his faulty or incomplete theological understanding—we are never offered the converse moment in which Michael makes explicit any aspect of Adam's obviously disjunctive misunderstanding of the Son's identity: there is no parallel in the last book of *Paradise Lost* of the manifest cognitive occlusion with which the Satan of *Paradise Regained* will embarrass himself: 'his first-begot we know . . . who *this* is we must learn' (i. 89–91). And while Adam was undoubtedly, and explicitly, thrilled to acquire the Socinian truth of the Son's heavenly paternity, Milton will not convey anything like a strong sense that Adam, if he indeed learns the higher truth of the Son's Arian pre-existence, really *cares* that the redeemer of his fallen progeny will prove to have been the same being as that figure exalted high above the other angels and placed at the Father's right hand. The final Christological revelation does not explode with a bang, but dribbles out of Michael's narrative with an anticlimactic whimper. Adam's coming into the poem's official, Arian Christological knowledge probably *happens*, we have to assume; but exactly when, and how, and why that knowledge is acquired remains clouded in obscurity.

Quite remarkably, for a theologian who devoted far more pages of his theological treatise on the topic of the person of Christ than he did on any other subject, Milton has managed to fashion in *Paradise Lost* an Adam, a Michael, and even a reader, who remain to the end fundamentally indifferent to the final form taken by the theological truth of Milton's Arianism. While Milton, Michael, and Adam are all manifestly attentive to the importance of the minimal faith of Socinianism—the fundamental doctrine that the human Son has been fathered by the Father himself, the doctrine whose revelation lifts Adam's lesson in future Christian history to its highest emotional pitch—any question concerning the person of Christ that reaches for the higher Christology of Miltonic Arianism, seems, at least so far as the indifferent Adam is concerned, to fall in the catch-all theological category of *adiaphora*, of 'things indifferent'. In his late treatise *Of True Religion* Milton had rightly noted that Arians and Socinians alike 'acknowledge [Christ] both God and their Saviour'. And it is no more than this minimal Christological acknowledgement, acceptable to any Socinian, that the Arian Milton will require at the conclusion of *Paradise Lost* as the 'sum / Of wisdom' (xii. 575–6), as the Christological knowledge sufficient for Adam's virtuous and pious life outside the gates of paradise: Michael asks Adam simply to wait for the return of 'The Womans seed, obscurely then foretold, / Now amplier known thy Saviour and thy Lord' (xii. 543–4), and Adam responds, in his last lines of the poem, with an unmistakably Socinian claim for the exemplary status of the Son, 'whom I now / Acknowledge my Redeemer ever blest' (xii. 569–73). The higher fact of the Son's pre-existence, available of course to Milton and now to Milton's reader, does not emerge at the poem's conclusion as core doctrine, but as an object of knowledge, however true in itself, potentially superfluous to the conduct of the faithful and obedient life: 'Greatly instructed I shall hence depart', Adam exclaims, 'and have my fill / Of knowledge, what this Vessel can containe; / Beyond which was my folly to aspire' (xii. 557–60).

III

If *Paradise Lost* takes pains, as we have seen, to avoid presenting the thesis of the Son's pre-existence as a necessary component of the Christian faith, such cannot be said of that poem's sequel. Among the many other things *Paradise Regained* accomplishes, the sequel makes the revelation of the Son's pre-existence coincident with nothing less than the redemption of man. How, then, to explain the boldness with which *Paradise Regained* asserts not just the fact, but the importance, of the recognition of the unity of person tying the pre-existent Son to the earthly Jesus? Why is the sequel able to overcome the seeming reluctance of *Paradise Lost* to assert the identity of the ancient with the current Son of God? One way to understand the difference with which the two poems approach this central question is to consider the difference in the authorities on which the two poems are able to rely for proof or verification. Because the climactic revelation of the Son's past in *Paradise Regained* is tied specifically to the role he played as the military hero in *Paradise Lost*, the Hebrew Scriptures are of no avail in illuminating the truth of the present Messiah's identity with a pre-existent Logos. The Son tells us in *Paradise Regained* that upon learning from his mother that he was the Messiah, he

> strait . . . again revolv'd
> The Law and Prophets, searching what was writ
> Concerning the Messiah, to our Scribes
> Known partly, and soon found of whom they spake
> I am. (i. 259–63)

Reviewing the Scriptures, the Son has no problem confirming the connection between the messianic prophecies and his mother's story of the 'glorious Quire / Of Angels' who at his nativity told the local shepherds that 'the Messiah now was born' (i. 242–5); by collating Scripture with the testimony of his mother, he is able quickly and unceremoniously to confirm his identity as the prophesied Messiah. But, as the Son indicates here, the full understanding of the Messiah was only 'Known partly' by the Hebrew Scribes, and even the most thorough review of the law and the prophets would fail to inform the Son of his pre-incarnational existence or of the specific truth of his pre-incarnational victory over Satan in the War in Heaven. Even if the Son had had access to the Book of Revelation (which of course could only have been written after he died), he could never on his own have determined his role in the War in Heaven, since, according to Revelation, it was the archangel Michael, and not the Son of God, who destroyed Satan in that celestial conflict. The only text whose revolving by the Son could have afforded him the information adequate to the truth of his status as the heroic 'debeller' of Satan is *Paradise Lost*, since it is that text alone in which the Son's role in the War in Heaven can be read. (As we have seen, not even Milton's own *De Doctrina Christiana*, had it been available to the Son, could have enlightened him on that point.) The recovered memory of the earlier epic offered by the angelic choir at the end of the later one is focused almost entirely on the Son's role in the War in Heaven. It is the singular Christology of *Paradise Lost*, and in particular Milton's wildly original contribution, in Book 6, to the story of the Son, that provides the key to the mystery of the identity of its sequel's hero.

   Nowhere in *Paradise Regained* is the pressure applied by the events recounted in *Paradise Lost* so powerfully felt (and so negligibly understood) as at the sequel's opening event. Milton returns us to that originary scene of the Son's exaltation to his Headship over the angels, at which the Father in *Paradise Lost* had declared to all the angels: 'This day I have begot whom I declare / My onely Son' (*PL*, v. 603–4). The Father at the opening of *Paradise Regained* rehearses that earlier declaration, at the baptism of Jesus, and 'From Heav'n pronounc'd him his beloved Son' (i. 31–2). Satan rushes to the congregation of angels assembled at the River Jordan to hear the 'high attest' that God was bestowing upon this man from Nazareth, this man who was 'the son of *Joseph* deem'd' (i. 23). Satan, who unlike the Son brings with him at least a partial memory of the events of *Paradise Lost*, reacts to this belated repetition of the Father's exaltative pronouncement with utter astonishment:

> That heard the adversary, who roving still
> About the world, at that assembly fam'd
> Would not be last, and with the voice divine
> Nigh Thunder-struck, th'exalted man, to whom
> Such high attest was giv'n, a while survey'd
> With wonder. (*PR*, i. 33–8)

That Milton tells us that Satan is astonished, or 'Thunder-struck', must be attended to, if only because the poet gives us so little by way of poetic metaphor in the generally restrained verse of *Paradise Regained*.[11] The word 'Thunder-struck' can in fact be seen as all the more striking, given that Milton has used it in only one other instance in his poetry. A perfect memory of *Paradise Lost* (which of course none of the characters of *Paradise Regained* can boast) would identify that earlier occurrence in Raphael's account of the climactic moment in the War in Heaven in Book 6, the moment at which the Son of God assumes the chariot of paternal deity and proceeds to put a decisive end to the battle with the rebel angels:

> The overthrown he rais'd, and as a Heard
> Of Goats or timerous flock together throng'd
> Drove them before him Thunder-struck, pursu'd
> With terrors and with furies to the bounds
> And Chrystal wall of Heav'n. (*PL*, vi. 856–60)

It is at this terrible moment of being *thunderstruck* by the awesome power of the Son that the rebel angels throw themselves 'headlong . . . / Down from the verge of Heav'n' (vi. 864–5).

By repeating in *Paradise Regained* this very specific word he used to such effect in *Paradise Lost*, Milton signals a connection between the horrifying moment of the Son's victory over Satan in the earlier poem, and the Son's new victory over Satan that begins at this moment, centuries later, of the Son's baptism. But while we as readers might be struck by the importance of the sequel's careful echo of the original, an echo by means of which that climactic moment in *Paradise Lost* is brought to mind, it is a literary echo that the sequel itself, *Paradise Regained*, is not yet able to do

---

[11] Of the adjective 'Thunderstruck' Barbara Lewalski writes that the narrator 'calls upon the vivid metaphorical meaning, struck by thunder, and suggests also the Titans or the falling Vulcan struck by Jove's thunder: this latter implication is reinforced a little later as Satan recalls how "his fierce thunder drove us to the deep"' (*Brief Epic*, 341).

anything with. Satan may be thunderstruck at the baptism, just as he was thunderstruck at the War in Heaven, but he is incapable of understanding how these two moments of astonishment, or how these two astonishing opponents, might in any way be related. As if struck with amnesia at this initial action in the sequel, Satan would appear at this very moment to have been robbed of any memory of his first having been thunderstruck.

It is not simply the case that the two main characters of *Paradise Regained* have forgotten the epic celestial events recounted in *Paradise Lost* (forgotten, that is, in the kenotically amnesiac Son's case, and repressed, perhaps, in Satan's). The poet, too, or at least the poem's narrator, appears to have forgotten the sublime *epic* content of that earlier poem. In beginning the brief epic by identifying himself as 'I who erewhile the happy garden sung', Milton places himself in the Virgilian, and Spenserian, position of opening an epic poem by reminding his readers of his earlier, more youthful, commitment to pastoral:

> I who erewhile the happy Garden sung
> By one mans disobedience lost, now sing
> Recovered Paradise to all mankind,
> By one mans firm obedience fully tried. (i. 1–4)

Milton is obviously drawing our attention to his earlier achievement, the glorious epic that had begun with that prepositional phrase, 'Of man's first disobedience'. As scholars have long noted, Milton marks the magnificent achievement of his composition of *Paradise Lost* by alluding to the opening of Virgil's *Aeneid* and its imitation by Spenser in the opening of *The Faerie Queene*. Virgil and Spenser had begun their vast and ambitious epic projects by identifying themselves to their readers as poets who had sung of happy gardens, who had been content writing diminutive pastoral poems, but who are now embarking on the more consequential genre of epic, the form given to the putatively more mature subject matter of wars and heroism. But given the fact that Milton had already written an *epic* poem, what sense does it make for him to begin *Paradise Regained* with the conventional, Virgilian gesture of self-consciously modest literary self-identification? Not only had Milton already written his epic, but he had written his pastoral verses, his own songs of the 'happy Garden', long before *that*, some thirty years earlier in his 'L'Allegro', *Arcades*, *Maske*, and 'Lycidas'. To identify *Paradise Lost* as a simple pastoral lyric is obviously, and profoundly, to misrecognize the generic essence of that work. If the Satan of the sequel had somehow managed to suppress the fact that his present opponent, the Son of God, had been the very Son of God who had brought him to the brink of destruction in the War in Heaven, then the poet of the sequel joins him in this activity of suppression: Milton appears to have forgotten that *Paradise Lost* was an epic, a poem featuring the epic subject of war.

That is, Milton appears to have forgotten the epic content of *Paradise Lost* up to the moment of the sequel's extraordinary culminating action, at which Satan urges the Son to leap off the pinnacle, tempting thereby the Father to save him. Here, at the poem's climax, the Son responds to Satan's final temptation with his citation from

Deuteronomy: 'Tempt not the Lord thy God.' This utterly straightforward, and characteristic, response to Satan's temptation—delivered by the Son with what degree of irony or self-knowledge we will never know—appears to have the extraordinary effect of pushing Satan to repeat the consequences of his own temptation of the Father's wrath over the course of his rebellion against the Father's throne as recounted in *Paradise Lost*. Reminded perhaps of the Son's terrifying arrival in the War in Heaven, 'in his right hand / Grasping ten thousand Thunders, which he sent / Before him' (vi. 835–7), at which point Satan and his followers 'astonisht all resistance lost' (l. 838), Satan, at the present moment in the sequel, is once again astonished, thunder-struck. In this surprising repetition of that initial state of astonishment, the identity of *this* Son of God with *that* Son of God—the Father's heroic vicegerent who had from the Father's chariot thunderously manoeuvered Satan and his followers to throw 'headlong themselves . . . Down from the verge of Heaven' (vi. 863–4)—is established. Thunder-struck, 'all resistance' once again 'lost', Satan finds himself, a second time, falling headlong to his destruction. Can Satan at this second defeat be said at least to enjoy, finally, the certain knowledge of the Arian identity of the Son, the confident identification of the Son of the sequel with the Son of the earlier epic? Probably not: Milton's mysterious adjectival phrase, 'smitten with amazement', used to describe Satan's reaction to the Son's response to the third temptation in *Paradise Regained*, is likelier to name a deeper state of confusion than a fresh state of cognitive mastery in its attempt to describe Satan's response to the apparent connection between the two Sons whom he has battled, and the two traumatic defeats he has suffered. But if Satan is not granted a vision of Christological enlightenment at this moment in *Paradise Regained*, the poem itself, surely, is. At this climactic event of the sequel's reproduction of one of the most crucial actions of *Paradise Lost*, the poem, the poet, the narrator can all be seen to have been meaningfully struck with the memory of the earlier poem's most daringly unscriptural contribution to the mythology of the Son of God, its fashioning of the Son as the epic hero, who, in an event recorded nowhere in the law nor in the prophets, assumed the mantle of warrior and debelled Satan and the rebel angels in the first, and therefore the most glorious, war ever recorded.

This revelation of the Son's identity, which is the first articulation in *Paradise Regained* of the poem's official doctrine of Arianism, may be no less astonishing for this 'Quire / Of squadrond Angels', newly regathered since their earlier performance at the Son's nativity, than it is for Satan himself. At the nativity, we remember from *Paradise Lost*, it was this angelic choir that established the doctrinally crucial Socinian fact that while 'A Virgin is his Mother', his 'Sire [is] / The Power of the most High' (xii. 368–9). But here at this cataclysmic repetition of Satan's initial fall, the angels find themselves singing for the first time—whether directly to the Son, or to themselves, we are not told—of the higher truth of the Son's Arian credentials, of his heroic life before the incarnation:

> him long of old
> Thou didst debel, and down from Heav'n cast

> With all his Army; now thou hast aveng'd
> Suplanted *Adam*, and by vanquishing
> Temptation, hast regain'd lost Paradise. (iv. 605–8)

Not only does this hymn constitute the first and only instance in *Paradise Regained* at which the poem acknowledges the Son's agency in the War in Heaven, it is the first and only instance in which the poem acknowledges the Miltonic theological truth that the Son had a pre-existence in Heaven at all. For this information, the angelic choir in *Paradise Regained* is reliant on no knowledge revealed in the law or the prophets. The only source Milton can tap here for the angelic revelation of the facts of the Son's pre-incarnational victory over Satan is nothing other than this sequel's original, his own poem, *Paradise Lost*, which is exalted at the singing of this heavenly anthem to the status of Scripture. No longer merely the poem of the happy garden that John Milton, Londoner, has written 'erewhile', *Paradise Lost*, by the time we reach the hymn of the angelic choir in *Paradise Regained*, has managed to assert itself as a newly verified source of previously unrecorded Christological truth.

Here, finally, the connection between *Paradise Lost* and *Paradise Regained* is indisputably established: the condensed phrase 'regain'd lost Paradise' of line 608 packs into three words the titles of both works, sealing the conjunction between the two poems. One of the greatest revelation scenes in all of Western literature, this moment in *Paradise Regained* reveals not merely the true identity of a particular character, the Son of God, but the identity of an entire text, *Paradise Lost*, which can now be acknowledged as having recorded what in the universe of these two poems circulates as Christological truth. *Paradise Lost*, that poem about which Milton has prophesied decades before that 'aftertimes should not willingly let it die' (*CPW*, i. 810), a poem recognizable now as one not just about a happy garden but about the Son of God's heroic comportment in the War in Heaven, is here at the sequel's conclusion shown 'Worthy t' have not remain'd so long unsung'. If, as his nephew tells us, Milton could not hear with patience any comment concerning the inferiority of *Paradise Regained* to *Paradise Lost*, his impatience may be owing to a higher understanding of the interdependence of the two works: if the sequel depends for its culminating truth on that original poem's bold introduction of the pre-existent Son's glorious participation in the War in Heaven, then the original epic comes to depend on the sequel for the verification of the quasi-scriptural status of its own most daring mythology.

IV

Perhaps it makes sense to consider now why these Christological articulations, so important to both *Paradise Lost* and *Paradise Regained*, have not managed successfully, for a few centuries now, to register with Milton's readers. It has been convincingly demonstrated that some early readers of *Paradise Lost*, those perhaps most attuned to the dissenting and heretical energies of their culture, were struck by the poem's unavowed Arianism.[12] But most readers, early and late, it can be assumed, would probably accept the judgement of C. S. Lewis, who claimed even in the face of his knowledge of Milton's heretical leanings that *Paradise Lost* 'gives the great central tradition'.[13] It is certainly the case that Milton's careful staging, in the last books of *Paradise Lost*, and in the entirety of *Paradise Regained*, of our gradual development of Christological knowledge from adoptionism, through Socinianism, and finally to Arianism, has never fully risen, in the modern scholarly study of Milton, to the plane of legibility. And this disjunction between what it is the poems attempt to teach us, and what it is we are in a position readily to learn, has taken an indisputable toll on the full critical appreciation of *Paradise Regained*. One way of considering this disjunction, I propose, is to consider the difference between Milton's actual readers, readers who have either anticipated or acceded to Lewis's claim that Milton's poetry 'gives the great central tradition', and the quite different assembly of readers that Milton posits, as if in fantasy, as the 'fit audience' for whom he is putatively writing the poem. With few exceptions, most readers now, just like most of Milton's contemporary readers, approach a work such as *Paradise Regained* with an unquestioned, perhaps even unshakeable, presumption of the Son's identity *as* God, or at the very least of the earthly Messiah's identity with the pre-existent Son of God.[14] Given the relative ignorance of the outcast heretical movements that had for centuries questioned the long-standing orthodoxy of the shared essence and the co-eternity of the Father and the Son, an unthinking internalization of the orthodox Christology of the Nicene Creed has shaped Milton's modern, more likely than not secular, audience almost as powerfully as it had the original, presumably pious, readers of both the great and the brief epic.

The interpretative problems troubling the appreciation of Milton's carefully staged development from one heterodox Christology to another in the last books of *Paradise Lost* and *Paradise Regained* begin the minute that his actual readers, whom we can safely assume to bring to those poems a conventional assumption that the Christian Messiah is the pre-existent Son of God, fail fully to recognize that the fictional world

---

[12] The best account of the early identification of the heretical theologies of *Paradise Lost* is in Bauman, *Milton's Arianism*, 276–89. Bauman cites John Toland's 1698 suggestion of a widespread readerly assumption of the poem's 'heresy and impiety' (p. 277); Charles Leslie's 1698 criticism that Milton's 'scheme of the Angels revolt cannot answer . . . to the eternal Generation of the Son' (p. 279); John Dennis's 1704 suggestion that *Paradise Lost*, iii. 383, shows Milton to have been 'a little tainted with Socinianism' (p. 280); the Earl of Shaftesbury's complaint that Milton had presumed to represent in *Paradise Lost* 'the birth, procedure, generation and personal distinction of the divinity' (pp. 281–2); and Daniel Defoe's insistence that the poem's representation of the Exaltation of the Son in Book 5 'lays an avowed foundation for the corrupt doctrine of Arius' (p. 285).

[13] C. S. Lewis, *A Preface to Paradise Lost* (Oxford, 1961), 92.

[14] See Lewalski, *Brief Epic*: 'The proper view of Christ's nature is indeed implicit in the poem itself, but the fact that many readers for nearly two centuries found strictest orthodoxy in *Paradise Lost* indicates how easily theological concepts and terms not explicitly defined in a work of art may be accorded the value most familiar and most agreeable to the reader' (p. 138).

they are inhabiting is founded on a set of rules quite foreign to, and in fact anterior to, any of the theological 'truths' established by the ancient Nicene or other councils on the godhead. Readers absorbed by the hegemonic cultural discourse—if not the actual theological confession—of the equality and co-eternity of the Father and Son, have found themselves incapable of finding their way in the much lower, quite different, theological world by which the natural, rational, pre-revelatory under-standing of the Christian Messiah is initially adoptionist, in its lowest form, and Arian, in its highest. (Fallen Adam, we remember, starts out an adoptionist, con-vinced of the exclusive manhood of the Seed, while Satan and the Son begin *Paradise Regained* as Socinians, aware of the Messiah's heavenly paternity, but ignorant of his pre-existence.) The relatively low Christological baseline of Milton's final poems has proven surprisingly invisible in the face of the unexamined, culturally entrenched Christological expectations of the readers constitutive of Milton's actual, as opposed to his projected, 'fit' audience.

It did not have to be this way. It would have been much easier for Milton to have configured differently, and more straightforwardly, his role as teacher and our role as pupils. In fact, when Milton takes on the cultural behemoth that is Trinitarian orthodoxy in the fifth chapter of the first book of the *De Doctrina Christiana*, he appears rhetorically to have assumed an audience, steeped in wrong-headed Chris-tological lore, badly in need of his heretical instruction. With skillful heuristic care he dismantles the institution of the Trinity by a methodical argument against all those mistaken readings of scripture that have worked for over a millennium to bolster the case for the wrongheaded faith in the equality and co-eternity of the Father and the Son. But what seems so remarkable, and so puzzling, about the very different type of theological work performed by *Paradise Lost* and *Paradise Regained*, is the fact that neither of those epics appears to betray, as does the theological treatise, the author's presumption that the majority of his readers are steeped in the wrong-headed logic of trinitarianism. Quite unlike the explicitly anti-Trinitarian argumen-tative strategy of the *De Doctrina*, the narratively encoded theological arguments of the two epics cannot technically be called *anti*-Trinitarian at all, since they unfold without any sign that Milton is arguing a case for the benefit of the actual readers he surely must know he *has*: Trinitarians, men and women who perhaps unquestion-ingly take as a matter of faith the Son's co-eternity with the Father, and who would obviously be, from Milton's perspective, in need of theological correction.

Instead of performing the much more straightforward gesture, as he did in the *De Doctrina*, of assuming a more or less orthodox audience whose understanding of the Son needs to be lowered to a belief in the Son's status as a created being, Milton, I suggest, takes a quite different tack. He willfully misrecognizes the fit audience of *Paradise Lost* and *Paradise Regained* as Christologically lower believers, as Socinians, perhaps, or more likely, subscribers to the even lower creed of adoptionism. He writes the end of *Paradise Lost* and the entirety of *Paradise Regained* for an imagined readership whose Christology is so low that it requires the successive revelations the poet will offer of a *higher*, rather than a lower, truth, the Socinian doctrine, first, of the Messiah's heavenly paternity, and then, finally, the Arian doctrine of the fact of the Son's pre-existence. It is by means of this staggeringly counter-intuitive strategy that Milton levels, in the register of poetic fiction, a powerful, dialectically structured attack on the orthodox Christology with which we know he so vigorously took issue, in the very different register of theological argument, in the *De Doctrina Christiana*. It is almost as if, in *Paradise Regained* and the ending of *Paradise Lost*, Milton attempts to disprove an inimical Christological orthodoxy by ignoring it entirely, dismissing it *in absentia*, and thereby rendering it irrelevant. And the key to this ingenious theological strategy is a fiction of *forgetting*: Milton the poet of *Paradise Lost* and *Paradise Regained* writes as if he had *forgotten* that the age too late in which he had no choice but to live and write was an almost inescapably Trinitarian one.

But can it be said, in the end, that Milton's two epics succeed in their subtle dialectical attempt to wipe orthodox Christology off the map? The answer would have to be no. The very fact that the culminating revelation of *Paradise Regained* had proven invisible to readers for nearly three hundred years, waiting for Barbara Lewalski to identify its essential plot as one worthy to have not remained so long unsung, might, in the end, suggest a considerable miscalculation on Milton's part. Underestimating, it would seem, the hegemony orthodox Christology held (and would continue to hold) over the Christian imagination, Milton seems also to have overestimated his ability to reshape his readers' surprisingly tenacious preconceptions concerning the person of Christ. The 'fit audience . . . though few' that Milton imagined he could conjure for the *Paradise* poems turn out to be, alas, *too* few. If the history of the criticism of those poems is any indication, Milton managed to hail all too few members of his audience into the appropriate state of fitness. Too few readers for too long would be able to appreciate the progressive tutorials Milton orchestrated to reveal the true relation of the earthly Messiah with the pre-existent Son of God, as well as the corollary relation, whose revelation was to be no less redemptive, of the sequel, *Paradise Regained*, to the original, *Paradise Lost*.

So there exists the possibility that the failure of the critical tradition to detect the delicate modulations of heresy rung in the *Paradise* poems resulted from the poet's inability ultimately to fashion his audience into a state of theological awareness sufficiently astute that its members could meaningfully be called 'fit'. But with what confidence can one make any claim concerning what a reader knows or does not know about *Paradise Lost* or *Paradise Regained*, two poems whose equivocations on the problem of knowledge are of an almost infinite complexity? While the long history of the misinterpretation of the heretical energies of these poems may be laid at the door of the poet who misjudged his readers, it can at the same time yield to a very different sort of analysis. Is it not just as likely that the centuries-old failure to discern the heresy of Milton's poem is a failure that Milton had himself anticipated, and perhaps even cultivated, in his composition of *Paradise Regained*? Milton, as I suggested earlier, may well have concluded the brief epic having deliberately with-held any explicit representation of the plot's long-awaited Christological enlightenment of either the hero or the antagonist. On the central question of whether either character in *Paradise Regained* possesses in the end full knowledge of the Son's past relation to Satan, the poem is as maddeningly agnostic as it is on many another important matter. If we were to ask what it is Satan and the Son actually come to *know* of the Son's identity, the poem would sagely reply as the Son replies to Satan during the temptation of Athens: think not but that they know these things, or think they know them not. Given the poem's outsized commitment to epistemological equivocation, we can certainly venture the argument that Milton had deliberately laid the foundation for the failure of interpretation to which *Paradise Regained* would be subject over the next few centuries. As we have seen, the Christological secrets of *Paradise Lost* surface in *Paradise Regained,* like the previously unrecorded events in the life of Jesus, as 'Worthy t' have not remain'd so long unsung'. Surely it is possible that Milton, having troubled to craft a narrative of heretical theological development that would barely rise to a level of perceptibility, could imagine that his fragile story of the recognition of the Son's Arian nature might itself remain long unread, and long unsung.

CHAPTER 34

··

SAMSON AGONISTES AND 'SINGLE REBELLION'

··

R. W. SERJEANTSON

How should we interpret the acts of violence perpetrated in Milton's *Samson Agonistes*? In answer to this large question two broad interpretative traditions have emerged. The first sees Samson's slaughter of the Philistines in, so to speak, positive terms: a typological indication of Samson's regeneration,[1] or an emblem of hope for godly Nonconformists experiencing persecution by a Philistine prelatical party,[2] and

I am grateful to Nicholas McDowell, Deirdre Serjeantson, Martin Dzelzainis, and Anthony Grafton for their helpful comments on previous drafts of this chapter, and to Ceri Sullivan in particular for encouraging me to write it. Translations are my own unless otherwise acknowledged.

[1] John M. Steadman, '"Faithful Champion": The Theological Basis of Milton's Hero of Faith', *Anglia*, 77 (1959), 12–28; Anthony Low, *The Blaze of Noon: A Reading of 'Samson Agonistes'* (New York, 1974), esp. 102; Sharon Achinstein, '*Samson Agonistes* and the Politics of Memory', in Joseph Wittreich and Mark Kelley (eds.), *Altering Eyes: New Perspectives on 'Samson Agonistes'* (2002), 168–91 at 179–83; Mary Ann Radzinowicz, *Toward 'Samson Agonistes': The Growth of Milton's Mind* (Princeton, 1978), attempts to leave behind this tradition (see 277 n. 15); Feisal G. Mohamed, 'Confronting Religious Violence: Milton's *Samson Agonistes*', *Publications of the Modern Language Association*, 120 (2005), 327–40 may be regarded as in part an extension of it.

[2] Christopher Hill, *The Experience of Defeat: Milton and Some Contemporaries* (1984); Sharon Achinstein, '*Samson Agonistes* and the Drama of Dissent', *Milton Studies*, 33 (1997), 133–58; David Loewenstein, 'The Revenge of the Saint: Radical Religion and Politics in *Samson Agonistes*', *Milton Studies*, 33 (1997), 159–203; Janel Mueller, 'The Figure and the Ground: Samson as a Hero of London

for quiescent but attentive republicans.[3] The other broad interpretative tradition, by contrast, sees Samson's killing of the Philistines in negative terms: as destructive, fallen, and perhaps also ultimately suggestive of the failure of the Good Old Cause.[4] Behind the debate lies the important question of whether or not to accord a divine origin to the 'rouzing motions' that Samson professes to feel before he tugs down the Philistine theatre. The first tradition has tended to garner more support; but several important voices have been prominent in arguing for the second. More recently, too, a number of interpretations have stressed the inherent ambivalence of *Samson Agonistes*'s dramatization of the Samson story. These accounts have drawn attention, and with good reason, to the 'evident ambiguity of Milton's representation of Samson's final action'.[5]

The present chapter contributes to this far-reaching debate by asking a political question about Samson's actions. Is his slaughter of the Philistines—and also of himself—legitimate?[6] This is the kind of question, after all, that Milton undertook to answer in respect of a different act of violence—the regicide—in *The Tenure of Kings and Magistrates* (1649) and in his two *Defensiones* of the English people (1651, 1654). But it is also a question that is canvassed extensively in the course of *Samson Agonistes* itself—in Samson's debate with Harapha, and in the final discussion of his death between Manoa, the Messenger, and the Danite Chorus.

What the drama itself does not give us, however, is sure ground from which to assess these arguments. It is possible, of course, to judge Samson's actions simply on the moral intuitions of the present, and of this kind of approach to Milton's writings we do not want. But it is also possible to approach the matter from a more scholarly perspective. We can ask by what moral and political standpoints available to Milton Samson's actions might be judged. The answer to this question will lead us into later sixteenth- and seventeenth-century literatures of political resistance. Above all,

Nonconformity, 1662–1667', in Graham Parry and Joad Raymond (eds.), *Milton and the Terms of Liberty* (Cambridge, 2002), 137–62; John Coffey, 'Pacifist, Quietist or Patient Militant? John Milton and the Restoration', *Milton Studies*, 42 (2003), 149–74; Sharon Achinstein, *Literature and Dissent in Milton's England* (Cambridge, 2003).

[3] Blair Worden, 'Milton, *Samson Agonistes*, and the Restoration', in Gerald MacLean (ed.), *Culture and Society in the Stuart Restoration* (Cambridge, 1995), 111–36; David Norbrook, *Writing the English Republic: Poetry, Rhetoric and Politics, 1627–1660* (Cambridge, 1999), 435, 491; id., 'Republican Occasions in *Paradise Regained* and *Samson Agonistes*', *Milton Studies*, 42 (2003), 122–48.

[4] John Carey, *Milton* (1969), 138–46; Irene Samuel, '*Samson Agonistes* as Tragedy', in Joseph Wittreich (ed.), *Calm of Mind: Tercentenary Essays on 'Paradise Regained' and 'Samson Agonistes' in Honor of John S. Diekhoff* (Cleveland, Ohio, 1971), 235–57; Joseph Wittreich, *Interpreting 'Samson Agonistes'* (Princeton, 1986); Jane Melbourne, 'Biblical Intertextuality in *Samson Agonistes*', *Studies in English Literature, 1500–1900*, 26 (1996), 111–27.

[5] John Rogers, 'The Secret of *Samson Agonistes*', *Milton Studies*, 33 (1997), 111–32 at 111. See also George McLoone, '"True Religion" and Tragedy: Milton's Insights in *Samson Agonistes*', *Mosaic*, 28 (1995), 1–29; Joseph Wittreich, *Shifting Contexts: Reinterpreting 'Samson Agonistes'* (Pittsburgh, Pa., 2002). John T. Shawcross, *The Uncertain World of 'Samson Agonistes'* (Cambridge, 2001); Derek Wood, *'Exiled from Light': Divine Law, Morality and Violence in Milton's 'Samson Agonistes'* (Toronto, 2001), esp. pp. xxii, 88, 139.

[6] A similar question is raised, from a different perspective, by Robert Thomas Fallon, *Divided Empire: Milton's Political Imagery* (University Park, Pa., 1995), 169–79.

however, it will take us into the genre of commentaries upon the source of Milton's drama: the book of Judges in the Old Testament.[7]

The question of the legitimacy of Samson's actions was one that also preoccupied a large number of sixteenth- and seventeenth-century commentators on the episode. This was a hero widely compared to Hercules, and whom St Paul had numbered among the faithful. But—as Jean Calvin put it—he had also been overcome by the 'blandishments of a concubine' (*concubinae blanditiae*) and 'recklessly betrayed his own and an entire peoples' safety' (*suam & totius populi salutem inconsiderate prodit*).[8] Was this in fact praiseworthy? Or, as Philipp Heinrich Friedlieb (d. 1663) put it in his *Theologia exegetica* of 1649: 'Is this person, who dishonours the commands of the Lord, truly a saint?' (*Illene sanctus, qui violat praecepta Domini?*).[9] Our own debates, that is to say, on the quality of Samson's actions are of long standing. The ambiguities of Milton's *Samson*, which deserve the emphasis they have received, are also those of an established early modern interpretative tradition, particularly in the hands of its more Reformed exponents. Indeed, we may go further: Milton exploited the debates of the Reformed interpretative tradition over the legitimacy of Samson's actions to help create the dramatic masterpiece of *Samson Agonistes*.

'A MURTHERER, A REVOLTER, AND A ROBBER'

The question of the legitimacy of Samson's violent actions is raised quite deliberately at the centre of the tragedy in the course of his great debate with the non-biblical figure of the Philistine giant Harapha.[10] The point at issue is not the final slaughter of the Philistines in their spacious theatre, which has yet to occur. Instead, the crime

---

[7] It seems that no extended study of *Samson Agonistes* in the light of commentaries on Judges has been undertaken since the work of Michael F. Krouse, *Milton's Samson and the Christian Tradition* (Princeton, 1949). The present study differs from Krouse's in stressing the importance of the Reformed tradition of commentary for Milton's understanding of the politics of the Samson episode, rather than its Christian typology. George N. Conklin, *Biblical Criticism and Heresy in Milton* (New York, 1949) offered a rather clearer sense than Krouse of what commentaries Milton might actually have known, but is not primarily concerned with *Samson Agonistes*. Peter Martyr's commentary on Judges (in its English translation) is discussed in the context of *Samson Agonistes* by Barbara Kiefer Lewalski in '*Samson Agonistes* and the "Tragedy" of the Apocalypse', *Publications of the Modern Language Association*, 85 (1970), 1050–62 at 1055–6; and for an argument deriving Milton's 'self-begott'n bird' (l. 1699) from Joannes de Pineda's *Commentariorum in Iob libri tredecim* (1598), see Sanford Budick, 'Milton's Joban Phoenix in *Samson Agonistes*', *Early Modern Literary Studies*, 11 (2005), 5.1–15 <http://purl.oclc.org/emls/11-2/budiphoe.htm>.

[8] Jean Calvin, *Commentarii in omnes Epistolas S. Pauli Apostoli, atque etiam in Epistolam ad Hebraeos: nec non in Epistolas Canonicas* (Amsterdam, 1667), 579 (on Hebr. 11: 32).

[9] Philipp Heinrich Friedlieb, *Theologia exegetica, seu observationes Biblicae* (Stralsund, 1649), 315 (on Judg. 16: 1).

[10] For the argument that the encounter between Samson and Harapha is a counterpart of Milton's quarrel with Claude de Saumaise, see Michael Lieb, *Milton and the Culture of Violence* (Ithaca, N.Y., 1994), 244.

with which Harapha taxes Samson is his slaughter of the thirty spies after the nuptial feast in Timna. For Harapha, this deed makes Samson straightforwardly 'A Murtherer, a Revolter, and a Robber' (l. 1180).

Samson's answer to Harapha's 'shifts' (l. 1220) does not deny the fact of his actions. Instead he refutes their status *de jure*. Far from being the civil crimes Harapha charges him with, Samson's actions were legitimate. Those he killed were his 'enemies' and he 'took thir spoil / To pay my underminers in thir coin' (ll. 1202–4). Hence he is neither a robber nor a murderer. But it is the charge of rebellion that Samson is most concerned to refute. In answer to Harapha's objection (as re-posed by Samson) that 'My Nation was subjected to your Lords', Samson asserts that the Philistines' conquest of Israel legitimized his own violent response: 'It was the force of Conquest; force with force / Is well ejected when the Conquer'd can' (ll. 1205–7). Here again, however, Samson poses another of Harapha's objections to his vindication of himself. What if his actions were not those of the liberator of a conquered people, but rather of a private individual acting contrary to the orders of his nation? 'But I a private person, whom my Countrey / As a league-breaker gave up bound, presum'd / Single Rebellion and did Hostile Acts' (ll. 1208–10). Samson answers this objection with what is perhaps his most problematic claim: he was acting neither as a private person, nor on the orders of his country, but upon divine command:

> I was no private but a person rais'd
> With strength sufficient and command from Heav'n
> To free my Countrey;
>
> . . .
>
> I was to do my part from Heav'n assign'd (ll. 1211–17)

The slaughter of the thirty was therefore neither theft, nor rebellion, nor 'Notorious murder' (l. 1186): it was the work of a national saviour who possessed the sanction of God.[11]

The question, however, remains of how we are to take Samson's claims. It is evident that Harapha's charges, levelled at his actions against the thirty spies, will also take on a direct relevance for Samson's final act of destruction: the 'Self-violence' which also engulfs the 'choice nobility and flower' of the Philistines (ll. 1585, 1654). Yet there is also an extra-dramatic reason why Milton should have made the slaughter of the thirty men of Ashkelon the central point at issue between Harapha and Samson. Sixteenth- and seventeenth-century commentators on the book of Judges had found the legitimacy of Samson's violence at this point (Judges 14: 19) a particular occasion for doubt. One tradition, invoked by the Calvinist Hebraeist Johannes Drusius (Jan van den Driesche, 1550–1615), had noted Samson's status as a Nazarite dedicated to God, and wondered how he could lawfully touch the slaughtered bodies when he 'took thir spoil' (l. 1203).[12]

---

[11] Cf. Stuart Sim and David Walker, *The Discourse of Sovereignty, Hobbes to Fielding: The State of Nature and the Nature of the State* (Aldershot: Ashgate, 2003), 54; Robert L. Entzminger, '*Samson Agonistes* and the Recovery of Metaphor', *Studies in English Literature, 1500–1900*, 22 (1982), 137–56 at 148.

[12] Johannes Drusius, *Ad loca difficiliora Iosuae, Iudicum, & Samuelem commentarius liber* (Franeker, 1618), 306 (on Judg. 14: 19). It is possible, at least, that Milton derived his knowledge of the rabinnical

A more far-reaching tradition of biblical commentary, however, had asked simply if this slaughter was a lawful thing to do (*an recte fecit?*).[13] As we shall see, the answer to this question was not straightforward.

'MY NATION WAS SUBJECTED'

Harapha's first charge is that Samson's nation was 'subject to our Lords' (l. 1182), and hence that Samson was a 'Revolter'. This charge was, in fact, a well-established one: it had been influentially made by Nicholas of Lyra (*c.*1270–1349), whose postils on the entire text of the Bible remained prominent in both Catholic and Protestant commentaries of the early modern period.[14] Nicholas had argued that there were certain agreements or treaties (*pacta*) that had been made between the Hebrews and the Philistines 'which were not rashly to be violated' (*quae temere non erant violanda*). One author who noted this view on the matter was Peter Martyr Vermigli (1499–1562), in his elaborate commentary on Judges, first published in 1561.[15] Vermigli has a certain importance for our subject, because his is the only Judges's commentary that we can say with certainty Milton knew: drawing in the *Tenure of Kings and Magistrates* (1649) upon a Commonplace Book entry he had made six years or so earlier, Milton had approvingly recorded the views on kingship of '*Peter Martyr* a Divine of formost rank, on the third of *Judges*'.[16] This well-known suggestion of a treaty between the Israelites and the Philistines may help shed some light on Harapha's accusation that Samson was a 'League-breaker' (l. 1184).

Another author who argued against Nicholas of Lyra's view that there was some kind of pact between the Israelites and the Philistines was the Reformed theologian David Pareus (1548–1622), whose commentaries, as it happens, had obtained a degree of notoriety in earlier seventeenth-century England. In his account of chapter 13 of the Epistle to the Romans, Pareus had defended resistance by inferior magistrates to the superior magistrate on grounds of tyranny. This doctrine had been picked up by certain rash disputants in the divinity schools of the English universities, leading to

gloss of Kimchi (David Kimhi) on Judg. 19: 2 from Drusius; see further Conklin, *Biblical Criticism and Heresy*, 64–5.

[13] *Synopsis criticorum aliorumque S. Scripturae interpretum*, ed. Matthew Poole, i: *Complectens Libros omnes a Genesi ad Jobum* (1669), col. 1167 (on Judg. 14: 19) and further references cited below.

[14] On Nicholas of Lyra's allegorizing treatment of the Samson story see Krouse, *Milton's Samson*, 68.

[15] Peter Martyr Vermigli, *In librum Judicium . . . commentarii doctissimi* (Zurich, 1561), fo. 153ᵛ (on Judg. 14: 6) (trans. from Vermigli, *Most fruitfull & learned Commentaries* (London, 1564), fo. 213ᵛ).

[16] Milton, *Tenure of Kings and Magistrates*, in *CPW*, iii. 221; Commonplace Book, *CPW*, i. 455–6. Vermigli is also cited approvingly in *Judgement of Martin Bucer*, *CPW*, ii. 478. See further Jackson Campbell Boswell, *Milton's Library: A Catalogue of the Remains of John Milton's Library and an Annotated Reconstruction of Milton's Library and Ancilliary Readings* (New York, 1975), §1446. (NB, however, that this work is a rather a reconstruction of Milton's reading than of his physical library.)

its swift condemnation in Cambridge in 1619 and again in the 'Directions Concerning Preachers' (1622).[17] For reasons not unconnected with this, however, Pareus's biblical commentaries possessed a particular importance for John Milton. He cites them repeatedly on the matter of marriage in *The Doctrine and Discipline of Divorce* (1643) and in *Tetrachordon* (1645), and he duly quotes the offensive comment upon Romans in *The Tenure of Kings and Magistrates*.[18] But the most obvious indication of the significance of Pareus's biblical commentary for *Samson Agonistes* is that Milton cites Pareus on Revelation in his account 'Of that sort of Dramatic Poem which is call'd Tragedy' which prefaces his drama.[19] We cannot be certain that Milton had also read Pareus's annotations on the book of Judges, but there must be a strong presumption that he did so. Certainly the riposte his Samson returns to Harapha shares with Pareus's account the desire to deny the thought that the Israelites owed subjection to the Philistines. Indeed, Samson's defiant claim to have been raised 'to free my Countrey' might be taken to echo Pareus's assertion that Samson 'knew that he was appointed from the womb to be the freer of his people' (*liberator populi*).[20]

Pareus also suggests that a sufficient 'occasion' had been provided for Samson against the Philistines by their being simply 'enemies of the people of God' and thereby 'destined for ruin' for their possession of land that was promised to the Israelites.[21] This last view was shared by the author (whose identity is unfortunately unknown) of the commentary on Judges that was published in the fuller second edition of the Westminster Assembly's *Annotations upon all the Books of the Old and New Testament* (1651). For this commentator, it was indeed 'lawfull' for Samson to slay the thirty men of Ashkelon, 'because they were of those cursed nations which God long before had sentenced to death and destruction'.[22]

Milton's Samson, however, emphasizes the political as well as the providential legitimacy of his actions, and he does so (somewhat anachronistically) by quoting Roman law. Samson's contention that 'force with force / Is well ejected' (ll. 1206–7) derives ultimately from the *Digest* of Justinian, in which it appears several times, most significantly in the jurist Ulpian's endorsement of the view that 'to repel force with force' (*vim vi repellere*) was a law of nature (D 43. 16. 1. 27). From this essentially private law

---

[17] W. B. Patterson, *King James VI and I and the Reunion of Christendom* (Cambridge, 1997), 192; Leo F. Solt, *Church and State in Early Modern England, 1509–1640* (New York, 1990), 166.

[18] References in Boswell, *Milton's Library*, §§1074–8; Milton, *Tenure*, in *CPW*, iii. 247–8.

[19] Milton, 'Prose Preliminary to *Samson Agonistes*', in *CPW*, viii. 134. On this point see also Lewalski, '*Samson Agonistes* and the "Tragedy" of the Apocalypse'; Lynn Veach Sadler, 'Typological Imagery in *Samson Agonistes*: Noon and the Dragon', *English Literary History*, 37 (1970), 195–210 at 196.

[20] David Pareus, *Primarii operum theologicorum partes quatuor: in quibus commentarii et adversaria Biblica*, 4 vols. (Frankfurt am Main, 1647), i. 491 (on Judg. 14: 19).

[21] Ibid. (on Judg. 14: 4).

[22] *Annotations upon all the Books of the Old and New Testament*, 2nd edn. (1651), sig. Iii4ʳ (on Judg. 14: 19) (henceforth 'Westminster *Annotations*'). Although the authors of the commentaries on most of the other books can be identified, the identity of the author of those on Judges remains unknown. See Richard A. Muller and Rowland S. Ward, *Scripture and Worship: Biblical Interpretation and the Directory for Public Worship* (Phillipsburg, N.J., 2007), 21; also D. G. Lampros, 'A New Set of Spectacles: The Assembly's *Annotations*, 1645–1657', *Renaissance and Reformation*, 19 (1995), 33–46. (I am grateful to Chad van Dixhoorn for his help on this point.)

source the doctrine that it was allowable to return force with force came in the later sixteenth century to take on particular political importance for Calvinists concerned to defend themselves, and their religion, against what they regarded as tyrannical oppression. The Roman law maxim plays a prominent part in the argument of the anonymous *Vindiciae, contra tyrannos* (1579).[23] From works such as this it was picked up by the Presbyterian Samuel Rutherford as a ground of government and as a defence against tyranny in his anonymously published *Lex Rex* of 1644.[24] Most pertinently, however, Milton himself had employed the maxim in his Commonplace Book to describe another such work, François Hotman's *Francogallia* (1573): 'in which it is shown that subjects have the right to repel with force any force exerted against them illegally, even by magistrates'.[25] Milton, that is to say, has Samson assert the Israelites' right to resist the Philistines with arguments to which he is elsewhere sympathetic.[26]

There was a further argument for the legitimacy of Samson's actions available to early modern readers of the Old Testament which did not fail to be canvassed in the commentary tradition. We are twice told (Judges 15: 20 and 16: 31) that Samson ruled Israel for twenty years as a Judge. As such, his actions could be interpreted as being those of a public magistrate lawfully resisting Philistine oppression. This was a defence that was widely endorsed by commentators on the book of Judges, among them Martin Bucer (1491–1551), whose writings had in 1644 furnished Milton with arguments for the legitimacy of divorce. According to Bucer, speaking in Ciceronian terms, Samson 'bore a public person' (*publica personam gerebat*), and hence the commonwealth (*respublica*) was necessarily involved in any injury to him; the wrong done to him was 'an injustice and an ignominy to the entire people' (*totius populi injuria et ignominia*).[27] The Catholic commentator Estius (Willem Hessels van Est, 1542–1613) similarly argued that Samson's status as a Judge made any injury to him a public injury.[28] Peter Martyr Vermigli, too, asserted Samson to be 'declared a Magistrate by God' (*Magistratus a deo…declaratus*),[29] while the Jesuit Jacobus Bonfrerius (Jacques Bonfrère, 1573–1642) found the slaughter of the thirty men of Ashkelon allowable for the same reason: 'Samson was then made a Judge of the

---

[23] *Pace* the misconceived account of Anne McLaren, 'Rethinking Republicanism: *Vindiciae, contra tyrannos* in Context', *Historical Journal*, 49 (2006), 23–52. See *Vindiciae, contra tyrannos*, ed. and trans. George Garnett (Cambridge, 1994), 45, 92, 105, 149, and further Garnett, 'Law in the *Vindiciae contra tyrannos*: A Vindication', *Historical Journal*, 49 (2006), 877–91.

[24] [Samuel Rutherford], *Lex, Rex: The Law and the Prince* (London, 1644), 4, 260.

[25] Milton, Commonplace Book, *CPW*, i. 501 (trans. from *CW*, xviii. 213). On the nature of Milton's surviving Commonplace Book see the essay in this volume by William Poole, Ch. 20.

[26] On this general point see also the valuable account of Joan S. Bennett, '"A Person Rais'd": Public and Private Cause in *Samson Agonistes*', *Studies in English Literature, 1500–1900*, 18 (1978), 155–68 at 168.

[27] Martin Bucer, *Psalmorum libri quinque ad Hebraicam veritatem traducti, et…enarrati…. Commentarii in librum Iudicium, & in Sophoniam Prophetam* (Olewig, 1554), 514 (on Judg. 16: 30). On the Ciceronian notion of 'bearing a person', and its uptake in early modern English theories of political representation, see Quentin Skinner, 'Hobbes on Representation', *European Journal of Philosophy*, 13 (2005), 155–84 at 161–2.

[28] Guilelmus Estius, *Annotationes a Ureae in praecipua ac difficiliora Sacrae Scripturae loca* (Cologne, 1622), 169 (on Judg. 16: 19).

[29] Vermigli, *Commentarii*, fo. 163ʳ.

people by God' (*Samson tunc populi Judex a Deo factus est*).[30] And the author of the Westminster *Annotations* on Judges also agreed that it was lawful for Samson to do this deed, 'because he was called now of God to be a Judge, to deliver his people, and to avenge them on their enemies'.[31]

In this light it is striking that the defence that he is a Judge of Israel is nonetheless not one that Milton's Samson avails himself of. As a number of scholars have correctly observed (although others again have missed it), Milton writes Samson's judicial function out of *Samson Agonistes*.[32] A good reason for why he might have done this is offered by the attractive reading that sees the tragedy in part as a dramatization of the experience of the defeated Nonconformists after the Restoration, and perhaps specifically (on Janel Muller's interpretation in 'The Figure and the Ground') after the plague (1665) and the Great Fire (1666). If this identification is to work, then it would clearly be inappropriate, in the light of the Uniformity (1662), Conventicle (1664), and Five Mile Acts (1665) disabling Dissenters, to endow Samson with magisterial authority.

Yet there is an intriguing analogue among one of the commentators on Judges with the political defence that Milton's Samson offers of the legitimacy of his actions. In his *Annotations*, the Westminster commentator on Judges offers a suspiciously timely justification for Samson's acts of violence: what made it a 'publique quarrel between both the whole nations' was the fact that the Philistines had—apparently, although there is no obvious biblical warrant for this—raised 'a great Army' against the Israelites when they came to search for Samson.[33] It is hard to avoid the thought that this gloss owes less to the text of Judges than it does to the manner in which Parliament had justified its actions as self-defence against Charles I's own raising of an army in 1642.[34] If this is right, then Samson's example was already being invoked by the godly against the royalist cause under the English Commonwealth.

'A PRIVATE PERSON'

So much for Samson's political defence of his actions. Yet from the perspective of the commentary tradition there remained a major objection to Samson's defence that he

---

[30] Bonfrère's gloss is reported in *Synopsis criticorum*, ed. Poole, col. 1167 (on Judg. 14: 19).

[31] Westminster *Annotations*, sig. Iii4ʳ (on Judg. 14: 19); see also sig. Iii4ʳ⁻ᵛ (on Judg. 15: 7).

[32] Camille Wells Slights, 'A Hero of Conscience: *Samson Agonistes* and Casuistry', *Publications of the Modern Language Association*, 90 (1975), 395–413 at 404. This point is missed by Lewalski, '*Samson Agonistes* and the "Tragedy" of the Apocalypse', 1058, and John Spencer Hill, *John Milton: Poet, Priest and Prophet: A Study of Divine Vocation in Milton's Poetry and Prose* (1979), 153.

[33] Westminster *Annotations*, sig. Iii4ᵛ (on Judg. 15: 9). This gloss is not present in the first edition of the *Annotations* (1645).

[34] See esp. 'A Declaration of the Lords and Commons now assembled in Parliament' (4 Aug. 1642), in *An Exact Collection of all Remonstrances, Declarations . . . and other remarkable passages betweene the Kings most excellent Majesty, and his high court of Parliament* (1642), 491–8.

was acting as a national liberator, and Milton again did not fail to raise it. As we have seen, Harapha charged Samson with acting as 'a private person', whose rebellion was not that of his people but of a single individual (l. 1208). The distinction invoked here was a very standard one in early modern European jurisprudence and political philosophy, used to distinguish between, on the one hand, subjects or citizens in their private capacity and, on the other, public magistrates who acted with the authority of the state or of those they represented—such as the 'Public Officer' of the Philistines in *Samson Agonistes* (l. 1306).[35]

The question of the lawfulness of private violence in the service of political and religious ends had again been raised most insistently in the controversial literature generated in the 1570s by the French wars of religion. Huguenot authors such as Theodore Beza (Théodore de Bèze, 1519–1605) and François Hotman (1524–90) had an obvious interest in legitimating the violent resistance of French Calvinists, particularly after the St Bartholomew Day massacre of 1572. But they also had to take into account St Paul's injunction to obey 'the powers that be' in Romans 13: 1. The answer they arrived at, developing a hint offered by Calvin in the last book of his *Institutio Christianae religionis* (1536), was that resistance was only legitimate when authorized by a 'popular' magistrate, although that magistrate could be inferior to the monarch.[36] Calvin had given the example of the Spartan ephors.[37] In the French context, this ephoral magistrate was commonly interpreted in terms of the Estates General. In 1640s England, the doctrine of inferior magistracy would be understood as giving Parliament licence to resist the Crown.

An indication of the significance of the charge that Samson acted as a 'private person' is again offered by the most notorious (although not the most radical) development of Calvin's ephoral suggestion: in the *Vindiciae, contra tyrannos*, written either by Philippe du Plessis-Mornay or by Hubert Languet, or perhaps by both of them, and first published in 1579.[38] As well as being the most notorious, this was also one of the longest-lived of these works of resistance theory. As John Salmon showed fifty years ago, the *Vindiciae* was extensively deployed in English political writings in the period up to the regicide.[39] An English translation of the book was rushed into print in March 1648.[40] The *Vindiciae* smouldered alongside Milton's own works in the University of Oxford's loyal bonfire of seditious books in

---

[35] It follows that Ashraf H. Rushdy, *The Empty Garden: The Subject of Late Milton* (Pittsburgh, Pa., 1992), 332, has misunderstood Milton's use of 'private' here.

[36] See Quentin Skinner, *The Foundations of Modern Political Thought*, 2 vols., ii: *The Age of Reformation* (Cambridge, 1978).

[37] Jean Calvin, *Institutes of the Christian Religion* (Book 4, ch. 20), in *Luther and Calvin on Secular Authority*, ed. and trans. Harro Höpfl (Cambridge, 1991), 45–86 at 82.

[38] 'Stephanus Junius Brutus, Celtus', *Vindiciae, contra tyrannos* ('Edinburgh' [*recte* Basle?], 1579). On the question of authorship see George Garnett, 'Editor's Introduction', to *Vindiciae, contra tyrannos* (1994), pp. lv–lxxvi. See further Quentin Skinner, 'Humanism, Scholasticism and Popular Sovereignty', in *Visions of Politics*, 3 vols., ii: *Renaissance Virtues* (Cambridge, 2002), 245–63 (esp. 247).

[39] J. H. M. Salmon, *The French Religious Wars in English Political Thought* (Oxford, 1959).

[40] *Vindiciae contra Tyrannos: A Defence of Liberty against Tyrants* (1648). Thomason's copy is dated 1 Mar. 1647 (i.e. 1648). The prevalence of misprints suggests the haste with which the book was produced.

1683.[41] And the book was republished again in 1689 as a vindication of that year's Revolution.[42] Milton, who mentions the work in the *Defensio secunda* (1654), was certainly familiar with it.[43]

The *Vindiciae*'s answer to the question 'Whether it be lawfull to take Armes for Religion' (*an arma ista pro Religione capiantur?*) provided a *locus classicus* on the question for subsequent generations. It argued that it was lawful to defend true religion with violence, both under the law and under the Gospel. Moreover, it went on, it was in fact a sin for those in authority not to resist a king who 'seekes to corrupt the Law of God' (*legem dei corrumpens*). But the *Vindiciae* is generally very careful to emphasize that resistance may only be offered by princes or magistrates, albeit that these may be only 'a small handful of people' (*pars aliquantula populi*). Private persons (*privati*), by contrast, have no right to take up arms without the authority of the magistrate.[44] Indeed, it was for this that Hubert Languet himself had admonished Philip Sidney when Sidney went, as a 'private person', to fight for the cause of international Calvinism under Casimir in the Spanish Netherlands. According to Languet, only Sidney's prince and magistrate, Elizabeth I, could lawfully authorize such an action.[45]

The language of the *Vindiciae*, then, is the language of Samson's reply to Harapha. And it is also the language of the Reformed commentary tradition on Judges. Perhaps also following Peter Martyr Vermigli's insistence on the matter, a number of Calvinist commentators had all prominently raised the question of whether Samson acted as a private man or not. David Pareus insisted that Samson's actions were lawful, 'because he is not to be considered as a private person' (*persona privata*).[46] David Chytraeus (1530–1600) noted that although the biblical Samson's claim to have done unto the Philistines as they did unto him (Judg. 15: 11) might constitute forbidden private vengeance (*vindicta privata*), in the case of 'this hero' who sought to avenge the injuries of God's people it was a 'noble and praiseworthy' (*generosa et laudabilis*) revenge.[47] But perhaps the most striking treatment of the question is provided by Johannes Piscator (Fischer, 1546–1625), who in response to the question of whether Samson's slaughters were 'justified' (*justa*) answered that 'insofar as he was revenging a private injury, he seems to have sinned' (*quatenus privatam injuriam ulciscebatur, videtur peccasse*).[48] This Reformed preoccupation with Samson's status was in due

---

[41] *The Judgment and Decree of the University of Oxford . . . against certain pernicious books* ([Oxford], 1683), 3.

[42] *Vindiciae contra Tyrannos: A Defence of Liberty against Tyrants. Or, Of the lawful power of the Prince over the People, and of the People over the Prince* (1689).

[43] *Defensio secunda*, in *CW*, viii. 198; Milton here ascribes the authorship of the *Vindiciae* to Theodore Beza.

[44] *Vindiciae, contra tyrannos* (1579), 69, 74, 51 (trans. in *A Defence of Liberty against Tyrants* (1648), 42, 45, 31).

[45] Blair Worden, *The Sound of Virtue: Philip Sidney's 'Arcadia' and Elizabethan Politics* (New Haven, 1996), 283.

[46] Pareus, *Opera*, i. 491 (on Judg. 15: 4–5).

[47] Chytraeus's views are reported by Friedlieb, *Theologia exegetica*, 315 (on Judg. 15: 11).

[48] Johannes Piscator, *Commentarii in omnes libros Veteris Testamenti*, 3 vols. (Herborn, 1646), ii. 86 (on Judg. 15: 11).

course given particular consideration in the Westminster *Annotations*, whose author was highly exercised by the question of whether Samson set out to do 'publique and hostile actions' or whether his deeds were merely a 'private and personall way of taking revenge'.[49] Milton had invoked just this distinction in *The Tenure of Kings and Magistrates* and the first *Defensio* to explain David's refusal to kill Saul.[50]

It is worth emphasizing the centrality of the concern over Samson's status as a 'private person' in the Reformed commentary tradition, since its presence here offers a rather more plausible explanation for Milton's own emphasis on it than has been offered elsewhere. There is no reason, that is to say, to suppose that Milton is invoking a specifically 'classical' distinction.[51] Nor do I find any evidence to suggest that Milton's Samson is here invoking a natural-law defence of his actions that derives from the ideas of Hugo Grotius (1583–1645).[52] It is true that, in his commentary on Judges, Grotius does explain Samson's actions in terms of his taking revenge for a wrong done to himself, something which 'neither natural law (*ius naturae*) nor the law of nations (*ius gentium*) prohibits'—although Grotius does go on to say that, because such revenge tends to get out of hand, it is forbidden by civil laws.[53] And indeed Grotius even invokes the example of Samson in the passage in his *De jure belli ac pacis* (1625) in which he discusses private vengeance.[54] But although Milton evidently admired Grotius's annotations on the New Testament, upon which he draws more than once in the divorce tracts,[55] there is little evidence that Grotian natural law provides a key to *Samson Agonistes*.[56] (The case for Milton's sympathy with Grotius's *Christus Patiens* (1608) is stronger.[57]) In fact, I believe we may go so far as to say that, in having Samson defend himself against the charge of private revenge, Milton again directly reflects the preoccupations of the Reformed commentary tradition on Judges.

There is, however, a potential objection to this argument which needs to be addressed. The view from *Samson Agonistes* would seem to indicate that Milton

[49] Westminster *Annotations*, sig. Iii3ʳ (on Judg. 14: 4).

[50] Milton, *Tenure*, in *CPW*, iii. 216; *A Defence*, in *CPW*, iv. 402–3.

[51] *Pace* John Guillory, 'Dalila's House: *Samson Agonistes* and the Sexual Division of Labour', in Margaret W. Ferguson, Maureen Quilligan, and Nancy Vickers (eds.), *Rewriting the Renaissance: The Discourses of Sexual Difference in Early Modern Europe* (Chicago, 1986), 106–22 at 109.

[52] *Pace* Elizabeth Oldman, 'Milton, Grotius, and the Law of War: A Reading of *Paradise Regained* and *Samson Agonistes*', *Studies in Philology*, 104 (2007), 340–75 at 364–6; also Victoria Kahn, *Wayward Contracts: The Crisis of Political Obligation in England, 1640–1674* (Princeton, 2004), 252; Leonard Tennenhouse, 'The Case of the Resistant Captive', *South Atlantic Quarterly*, 95 (1996), 916–46.

[53] Hugo Grotius, *Annotata ad Vetus Testamentum*, 3 vols. (Paris, 1644), i. 203 (on Judg. 15: 3).

[54] Hugo Grotius, *De iure belli ac pacis libri tres*, 3rd edn. (Amsterdam, 1646), 320 (2. 20. 8). This passage is overlooked by Oldman, 'Milton, Grotius, and the Law of War'.

[55] See esp. Milton, *Doctrine and Discipline of Divorce*, in *CPW*, ii. 329; *Judgement of Martin Bucer*, in *CPW*, ii. 433–4; *Tetrachordon*, in *CPW*, ii. 715. *Doctrine and Discipline*, in *CPW*, ii. 335, cites Grotius's opinion on Judg. 19: 2, but from his commentary on Matthew.

[56] *Pace* Wittreich, *Shifting Contexts*, 94, Samson's 'Against the law of nature, law of nations' (l. 890) might equally well be taken to allude to John Selden's *De jure naturali et gentium, juxta disciplinam Ebraeorum* (1640) as to Grotius's *De jure belli ac pacis*—or to neither.

[57] Russell Hillier, 'Grotius's *Christus Patiens* and Milton's *Samson Agonistes*', *The Explicator*, 65 (2006), 9–13.

took the Calvinist tradition's prohibition of private resistance but legitimation of divinely sanctioned violence seriously. But in a subtle and penetrating account Martin Dzelzainis has argued that in the first (although not the second) edition of *The Tenure of Kings and Magistrates* (February 1649) Milton had in fact devoted himself to 'challenging and reversing' the 'key assumption' of Protestant resistance theories: that it was always unlawful for private persons to act independently of the inferior magistrate. On this account, Milton 'begins to leave the Calvinist agenda behind altogether' in order to 'affirm the lawfulness of individual private action and so furnish a defence of the Army's conduct'.[58]

This striking and important case is characteristically carefully argued. But it may possibly be pressed a little too far. How far is it in fact the case that Milton in the *Tenure* wished to allow political violence by private persons? The best evidence for this comes from the title page itself of the first edition: 'proving, That it is Lawfull . . . for any, who have the Power, to call to account a Tyrant . . . if the ordinary magistrate hath neglected, or deny'd to do it'.[59] But we have already seen that in the first edition Milton invokes the prohibition on 'privat enmity' to explain David's refusal to lift his hand against Saul. And Dzelzainis himself has pointed out the explicit reappearance in the second edition (October 1649) of the tenet that 'to doe justice on a lawless King, is to a privat man unlawfull, to an inferior Magistrate lawfull'.[60] Moreover, Milton never goes so far in the *Tenure* as to state explicitly that the actions of the Army are those of 'private persons'. Indeed, in the first edition he couples 'the Parlament and Military Councel' as the bodies responsible for the regicide, and in the second edition he also suggests that the 'protestant State' did the deed (*CPW*, iii. 237).

The case for private rebellion in the *Tenure*, then, seems oblique in the first edition, and was denied in the second. But however we interpret that book, it seems right to regard *Samson Agonistes* as reaffirming the standard tenets of the Calvinist prohibition on private rebellion.[61] Milton apparently wished Samson to present the classic version of the argument, even if on Dzelzainis's account of the first *Tenure* he did not need to. Or, to put it another way, however attractive the parallels are that Blair Worden has pointed out between Samson's 'single' status and the 'single . . . witness' of the regicide Sir Henry Vane, Samson himself in fact denies that he 'presum'd / Single Rebellion' (ll. 1209–10).[62]

---

[58] Martin Dzelzainis, 'Introduction', in John Milton, *Political Writings* (Cambridge, 1991), pp. ix–xxv at xii–xv; id., 'Milton's Politics', in Dennis Danielson (ed.), *The Cambridge Companion to Milton* (Cambridge, 1999), 71–83 at 79–81.

[59] Milton, *Tenure*, in *CPW*, iii. 189. Dzelzainis, 'Introduction', p. xv.

[60] Milton, *Tenure*, in *CPW*, iii. 215, 216, 257. Togashi Go, 'Milton and the Presbyterian Opposition, 1649–1650: The Engagement Controversy and *The Tenure of Kings and Magistrates*, Second Edition (1649)', *Milton Quarterly*, 39 (2005), 59–81, offers an effective case for the renewed prominence of this argument in the second edition.

[61] *Pace* Slights, 'A Hero of Conscience', 404.

[62] Blair Worden, *Literature and Politics in Cromwellian England: John Milton, Andrew Marvell, Marchamont Nedham* (Oxford, 2007), 363–4.

'A PERSON RAIS'D'

But if Samson is not a private 'Revolter', this still leaves us with a further vital question: what is the significance of his claim to be 'raised' by God? Like Milton in the *Tenure of Kings and Magistrates*, and like the Calvinist exponents of resistance by popular or inferior magistrates, no Reformed commentator on Judges known to me allowed that private revenge could in itself be lawful. But both the author of the *Vindiciae* and these commentators on the Samson episode did permit one important exception to this interdiction. Private violence was permitted only in the case of persons who had an 'extraordinary vocation' from God.[63] In the *Vindiciae* it was just such an extraordinary vocation that justified the rebellions of such exemplars as Moses, Jehu (2 Kings 9), Ehud (Judges 3), and Deborah (Judges 4). It was this divine calling that protected these figures from the charge that they had acted *ultra vires*.[64]

Samson, however, is not mentioned in the *Vindiciae*, and his example is also not commonly encountered in the later literature of resistance by Reformed authors—unlike Jehu or Ehud, both of whom Milton invokes in the *Tenure*.[65] One reason for this general silence about Samson may simply be that he did not visit his violence upon a king, and it was a justification for resistance to monarchical tyranny that most of these authors sought. Samson's enemies (both in Judges and in *Samson Agonistes*) are the Philistine 'lords', not a tyrannical monarch arisen from the Israelites themselves.[66] Another reason, however, may have been that Samson provided a rather ambiguous exemplar of a figure who possessed divine authorization for his acts of violence.

This ambiguity is certainly reflected in the commentary tradition on Judges. Commentators of all stripes were conscious that Samson was by no means a wholly admirable figure: it is this that lies behind the often-expressed doubts as to whether his actions are lawful (*recte*) or not. The revenge Samson took on the Philistines by burning their crops was 'rather harsh' (*satis crudelis*) and 'expressly against the Law' (*expresse contra Legem*), thought Martin Bucer in his extensive commentary.[67] Johannes Piscator confessed that it 'seems difficult to determine' (*difficile videtur pronuntiare*) on the question of whether Samson's earlier revenges were justified.[68] And David Pareus's judgement on Samson is particularly fierce: his 'heinous sins'

---

[63] *Vindiciae, contra tyrannos*, 74 (trans. in *A Defence of Liberty against Tyrants* (1648), 45).

[64] *Vindiciae, contra tyrannos*, 68 (cf. *A Defence of Liberty against Tyrants* (1648), 41).

[65] Milton, *Tenure*, in *CPW*, iii. 215. But see Dzelzainis, 'Introduction', pp. xii–xv, on how Milton's account of Ehud differs from that of his predecessors.

[66] For a fascinating and scholarly account of the origins of Milton's view that republics were the only legitimate regimes, see further Eric Nelson, '"Talmudical Commonwealthsmen" and the Rise of Republican Exclusivism', *Historical Journal*, 50 (2007), 809–36.

[67] Bucer, *Commentarii*, 508 (on Judg. 15: 3). Bucer goes on to remind his readers that in this cruelty Samson's actions are like divine vengeance, which we all deserve.

[68] Piscator, *Commentarii*, ii. 86 (on Judg. 15: 11). Piscator's doubts on the matter were noticed by Friedlieb, *Theologia exegetica*, 317. Piscator is less equivocal in his less ambitious *Expositio brevis dictorum selectorum ex libris Veteris Testamenti* (Herborn, 1598), 66 (on Judg. 16: 30).

(*peccata atrocia*) of adultery, scortation, and the betrayal of his Nazarite vows brought his destruction upon him.[69]

Yet if Samson was an ambiguous examplar of pious resistance for some, he was not so for Milton in the *Pro populo Anglicano defensio* (1651). Here Milton not only again gave the example of Ehud; he also invoked the figure of Samson, who had slain 'not one but a host of his country's tyrants', and who 'therefore thought it not impious but pious to kill those masters who were tyrants over his country'.[70] The author of the Westminster *Annotations* on the book of Judges—again, perhaps with the example of recent English history in mind—had asserted that the Philistines had 'tyrannized' over the Israelites; so too here does Milton. For both of them, in the context of tyranny, Samson's slaughters are acts of pious justice, not the terrible crimes that Harapha charges him with.[71]

The fact that Milton's Samson speaks in just the terms that were applied to the godly revengers of the Reformed tradition would seem to support this interpretation. Samson vaunts of 'those great acts which God had done / Singly by me' (ll. 243–4). He goes on to speak of himself as one 'Whom God hath of his special favour rais'd' as a deliverer of the Israelites (l. 273). Above all, Samson asserts to Harapha that he was 'a person rais'd' with 'command from Heav'n / To free my Countrey' (ll. 1211–13). Moreover, it is in just these terms that Samson had also been defended by the Reformed commentators on Judges, above all by the most remorselessly providentialist of all of them, David Pareus—the tutelary commentator of *Samson Agonistes*. Pareus is clear that God, 'either by an express command, or by a secret inspiration' (*sive expresso oraculo, sive arcano instinctu*), 'guided and persuaded' (*regebat et flectebat*) Samson's mind.[72] Samson's deeds were just, because he was from birth a divinely inspired 'defender' (*vindex*) and 'freer' (*liberator*) of his people.[73] For Friedlieb too (following David Chytraeus) Samson was a 'hero raised by heaven' (*heros divinitus excitatus*).[74] For Piscator, Samson was an 'extraordinary defender' (*extraordinarius vindex*) of God's people.[75] For the Rostock Lutheran Johann Quistorp (d. 1669), God had similarly 'raised' (*excitare*) Samson as a 'defender' (*vindex*) of the Israelites and a chastiser of the Philistines.[76] The Westminster annotator also spoke of Samson acting by an 'extraordinary motion and instinct of Gods Spirit'.[77] This consensus was also shared by the Swiss Calvinist Giovanni Diodati (1576–1649),

---

[69] Pareus, *Opera*, i. 492 (on Judg. 16). Vermigli, *Commentarii*, fos. 163ʳ ff. (trans. in Vermigli, *Fruitfull & learned Commentaries*, fos. 229ʳ ff.), takes occasion here to furnish an elaborate reflection on the impropriety of scortation ('whoredom').

[70] Milton, *Pro populo Anglicano defensio*, in *CPW*, iv. 401–2. On this point, see also Bennett, 'Public and Private Cause', 165.

[71] Westminster *Annotations*, sig. 3K1ʳ (on Judg. 15: 20).

[72] Pareus, *Opera*, i. 491 (on Judg. 14: 4).

[73] Ibid. (on Judg. 15: 4–5 and 14: 19).

[74] Friedlieb, *Theologia exegetica*, 315 (on Judg. 15: 11).

[75] Piscator, *Expositio brevis*, 66 (on Judg. 16: 30).

[76] Johannes Quistorpius, *Annotationes in omnes libros Biblicos* (Frankfurst and Rostock, 1648), 254 (on Judg. 15: 11).

[77] Westminster *Annotations*, sig. 3K2ʳ (on Judg. 16: 30).

whom Milton had met in Geneva in 1639, and whose biblical commentary was sufficiently admired in 1640s England to receive a vernacular translation which went through several editions (Parker, *Milton*, i. 181). Milton cites Diodati's commentary at several points in *Tetrachordon* and the *Pro se defensio*, and Paul Sellin has specifically argued that Milton made use of Diodati's interpretation of Judges 16: 25.[78] Diodati, too, was clear that 'the Spirit of God having a hand', Samson 'had power to execute his vengeance upon the accursed and tyrannicall nation'.[79]

When Samson asserts, therefore, that he acted not as a private person, but as one who felt 'rouzing motions' that disposed him to 'something extraordinary' (ll. 1382–3), he is very precisely making the point that, by all the accepted canons of good Protestant political theory, his actions are just.[80] It follows that, if you acknowledge the truth of Samson's claims to be raised by God, then you must regard his deeds as legitimate.

'AMONG THY SLAIN SELF-KILL'D'

One last question about the legitimacy of Samson's actions remains. It is not raised in the course of the debate with Harapha, because it could not be. But it is canvassed at length by the protagonists at the end of Milton's drama. In what ways should Samson's death by 'Self-violence' be distinguished from suicide? Like Manoa, that is to say, the commentators on Judges also want to know 'How dy'd he?' (l. 1579). Here again the question was prompted by the commentary of Nicholas of Lyra.[81] But the analysis of Samson's death in the tragedy again echoes most strongly the distinctions made in the Reformed commentary tradition. All the commentators, indeed, agree with Manoa that Samson took his revenge (*ultio*) upon the Philistines, indeed, that he was 'on his Enemies / Fully reveng'd' (ll. 1711–12). David Pareus was even concerned to refute the thought that Samson might appear 'greedy for revenge' (*cupidus vindictae*).[82]

The protagonists of Milton's drama also stress that Samson's self-destruction was 'inevitably' involved with that of the Philistines (l. 1657), and that his death came 'Not willingly, but tangl'd in the fold, / Of dire necessity' (ll. 1665–6). There is a Horatian echo here, but there are also echoes of the biblical commentators' efforts to explain

---

[78] Milton, *Tetrachordon*, in *CPW*, ii. 615; *Pro se defensio*, in *CPW*, iv. 748, 787, 799, 817. Paul R. Sellin, 'Milton's Epithet *Agonistes*', *Studies in English Literature, 1500–1900*, 4 (1964), 137–62 at 161.

[79] Giovanni Diodati, *Pious and Learned Annotations upon the Holy Bible* (London, 1651), sig. 2B3ᵛ (on Judg. 14: 18).

[80] The attempt of Abraham Stoll to relate Samson's 'motions' to the writings of Edward Herbert is accordingly implausible ('Milton Stages Cherbury: Revelation and Polytheism in *Samson Agonistes*', in Wittreich and Kelley (eds.), *Altering Eyes: New Perspectives on Samson Agonistes*, 281–306). On the documented reception of Herbert's *De veritate* see R. W. Serjeantson, 'Herbert of Cherbury before Deism: The Early Reception of the *De veritate*', *Seventeenth Century*, 16 (2001), 217–38.

[81] See Drusius, *Ad loca difficiliora*, 321 (on Judg. 16: 30), quoting Nicholas of Lyra.

[82] Pareus, *Opera*, i. 492 (on Judg. 16).

why Samson's death was not that of a suicide.[83] 'What Sampson here did,' explained the Westminster *Annotator* on Judges,

was done by an extraordinary motion and instinct of Gods Spirit; neither was it the primarie and principall end at which he aymed, to kill himself, but the death and destruction of Gods and his Churches enemies, unto which he was called and consecrated as a publique person, and a Judge.

Samson's death, continued this author, in a logical analysis beloved of the Reformed hermeneutic tradition to which Milton's *Artis logicae plenior institutio* (1672) is a late contribution, 'did follow as a necessary consequent'.[84]

Among the commentators Martin Bucer offers an especially elaborate meditation on the meanings of Samson's death. In particular, he ascribes its volition, not to Samson ('Not willingly'), but to God, who 'did not want him to live any longer' (*nolebat eum diutius vivere*).[85] The English divine Matthew Poole's compendium of biblical commentaries, the *Synopsis criticorum* (1669), reproduces the assessment of more scholastic and Catholic commentators, including Cornelius à Lapide (Cornelis Cornelissen van den Steen, 1567–1637), in whose opinion 'Samson did not kill himself specifically and physically (*physice*); but engulfed himself indirectly and permissively in a disaster (*clades*) which he could not avoid'.[86] Poole also offers the scholastic suggestion (he quotes Lessius on the matter) that although it is not lawful to procure one's own death 'directly' (*directe*), it is permissible to do so 'indirectly' (*indirecte*) if a 'good and honest' goal cannot be obtained without bringing about one's own death—something of which martyrs and brave soldiers daily offer examples.[87] A similar thought had been offered by Peter Martyr Vermigli: Samson 'dyd not rashly incurre death, but followeth hys vocation', like soldiers who may justly say 'we seeke not death but victorye'.[88] This thought in its turn was echoed by the author of the anonymous commentary on the Old Testament published by Anthony Scattergood in 1653 from a manuscript he had found in the library of the (ejected) Archbishop of York, John Williams. For this commentator, Samson did not 'straightforwardly' (*simpliciter*) long for death, but rather carried on fearlessly in his calling (*vocatio*) like a soldier among a horde of enemies.[89]

[83] Horace, *Odes*, 3. 24. 6: *dira necessitas*. See *CSP*, commentary on ll. 1665–6. George F. Butler, 'Donne's *Biathanatos* and *Samson Agonistes*: Ambivalence and Ambiguity', *Milton Studies*, 34 (1997), 199–219 at 210–11, observes that the major dramatic analogues of Milton's tragedy, by contrast, do not stress the inevitability of his death.

[84] Westminster *Annotations*, sig. 3K2^r (on Judg. 16: 30). Cf. the account of efficient causation in Milton, *Art of Logic*, in *CPW*, viii. 226–7.

[85] Bucer, *Commentarii*, 514 (on Judg. 16: 30).

[86] *Synopsis criticorum*, ed. Poole, col. 1185 (reporting Cornelius à Lapide on Judg. 16: 30).

[87] Ibid. (on Judg. 16: 30).

[88] Vermigli, *Commentarii*, fo. 169^v (on Judg. 16: 30) (trans. in Vermigli, *Fruitfull & learned Commentaries*, fo. 236^r).

[89] *Annotationes in Vetus Testamentum . . . Incerto autore*, ed. Anthony Scattergood (London, 1653), 194. See further Hugh de Quehen, 'Scattergood, Anthony (*bap.* 1611, *d.* 1687)', *ODNB*.

This is not to say that Samson's act of heroism could not also be seen as a punishment. Certain of the commentators emphasize that Samson's death, while in itself lawful, was nonetheless also a punishment for his former sins. Cornelius à Lapide suggests that, as Samson's final slaughter was a great act of bravery, so it was also 'a great punishment for past sins' (*magna pro praeteritis culpis poena fuit*).[90] And from the opposite end of the confessional spectrum, David Pareus speaks (as we have seen) of the 'heinous sins' by which Samson 'brought destruction upon himself' (*sibi exitium attraxit*).[91] Other commentators, however, are more positive about the nature of Samson's death. Several emphasize, as Manoa also does, its heroic quality: '*Samson* hath quit himself / Like *Samson*, and heroicly hath finish'd / A life Heroic' (ll. 1709–11). Bucer in particular was adamant that Samson's was 'an heroic death' (*heroica mors erat*).[92] Johann Piscator also found in it 'a further example of an heroic deed' (*heroicum facinus*).[93] The heroic parallel between Samson and Hercules was well explored in the commentary tradition—above all in the *Synopsis criticorum*—and has been well established by scholars of *Samson Agonistes*.[94] But it may also be appropriate to invoke here not only Samson's heroism but also his nobility. In the Commonplace Book, under the heading of *Nobilitas*, Milton had extended the humanist argument that virtue constituted true nobility into one that asserted that nobility should derive 'from the spirit of God' (*a dei spiritu*), not from ancestors or human laws.[95] For Manoa, as well as being heroic, Samson's is 'a death so noble' (l. 1724), and it may therefore be that here too we should find evidence for the providentialist interpretation of the drama.[96]

The strongest assertion in the drama that Samson's death was accompanied by his rapprochement with the god of the Hebrews is again made by Manoa: 'And which is best and happiest yet, all this / With God not parted from him, as was feard' (ll. 1718–19). Manoa's optimism on this score echoes that of the commentators, all of whom also ultimately emphasize Samson's return to divine favour in his final act of vengeance. Martin Bucer draws attention to Samson's plea to be avenged for the loss of his sight (Judges 16: 28) and allows Samson to have prepared himself with 'pious and faithful prayer' (*precatio pia et fidelis*) which sought not 'private revenge' (*ultio privata*) but legitimate divine vengeance. For Bucer Samson's actions would not have been successful if they had not been approved (*probatus*) by God.[97] Indeed, there is a strong consensus among the commentators that God did indeed hearken to

---

[90] *Synopsis criticorum*, ed. Poole, col. 1185 (reporting Cornelius à Lapide on Judg. 16: 30).

[91] Pareus, *Opera*, i. 492 (on Judg. 16).

[92] Bucer, *Commentarii*, 514 (on Judg. 16: 30).

[93] Piscator, *Commentarii*, ii. 88 (on Judg. 16: 30).

[94] See *Synopsis criticorum*, ed. Poole, col. 1186 (on Judg. 16: 30). See also Krouse, *Milton's Samson*, 44–5, 78–9.

[95] Milton, Commonplace Book, *CPW*, i. 471. On the humanist argument see Quentin Skinner, 'Thomas More's *Utopia* and the Virtue of True Nobility', in *Renaissance Virtues*, 213–44.

[96] Further evidence is offered by Michael Lieb, *Theological Milton: Deity, Discourse and Heresy in the Miltonic Canon* (Pittsburgh, Pa., 2006), 201–3.

[97] Bucer, *Commentarii*, 514 (on Judg. 16: 30).

(*exaudire*) Samson's prayer.[98] What doubts they might possess are widely laid to rest by Samson's appearance among the catalogue of the faithful in the Epistle to the Hebrews (11: 32).[99] Few are as eloquent as Martin Bucer, but all concur in the end in the sentiment that Samson was a figure who threw himself into danger for the sake of the commonwealth and for the glory of God, 'to redeem and protect his people, to vindicate God's cause, and to avenge his enemies' (*populum redimere, et servare, Dei causam vindicare, et hostes ulcisci*).[100] This too is the Samson presented by Milton in *Samson Agonistes*.

Epilogue

Defenders of the negative interpretation of *Samson Agonistes* have sometimes pointed out that Samson's slaughter does not immediately result in 'Honour . . . and freedom' for Israel (l. 1715).[101] Yet this was not a stumbling block for early-modern interpreters of Judges. They acknowledged that (as Carlo Sigonio put it in his commentary on Sulpicius Severus's *Historia sacra*) Samson 'did not entirely liberate Israel from the servitude of the Philistines'.[102] But they knew that he had begun a task that was, as Giovanni Diodati put it, 'reserved for *David* to do'.[103] For these authors the Israelites did ultimately 'Find courage to lay hold on this occasion' (l. 1717).

Several of the episodes in Samson's angry and heroic life may have been questionable. But as we have seen, the circumstances of his death, above all for Reformed commentators on Judges, were unambiguously legitimate. And it is to these authors, I have suggested, that we should look to help us grasp the political valence of Samson's actions. It is nonetheless true that one can find other contemporaries of Milton who took a different view of the legitimacy of Samson's example. Wittreich has duly drawn attention to Herbert Thorndike's (1597?–1672) scathing assessment of Samson in 1659. But Thorndike also published in the same year an elegy for the 'present calamity' of the established Church whose expressions of sympathy for

[98] Ibid.; Vermigli, *Commentarii*, fo. 169ᵛ; Piscator, *Expositio brevis*, 66; Piscator *Comentarii*, ii. 88; Pareus, *Opera*, i. 492 (all on Judg. 16: 30).

[99] Vermigli, *Commentarii*, fo. 153ʳ (on Judg. 14: 3); Pareus, *Opera*, i. 491 (on Judg. 14: 4); Piscator, *Commentarii*, ii. 88; Friedlieb, *Theologia exegetica*, 318; Quistorpius, *Annotationes*, 256 (all on Judg. 16: 30).

[100] Bucer, *Commentarii*, 514 (on Judg. 16: 30).

[101] See e.g. Fallon, *Divided Empire*. On this point see also Norbrook, 'Republican Occasions in *Paradise Regained* and *Samson Agonistes*', 144.

[102] Carlo Sigonio, *De antiquo iure civium Romanorum . . . libri XI. . . . Quibus adiecti . . . De republica Hebraeorum, libri septem: et in B. Sulpicii Severi historicos libros duos, commentarii duo* (Frankfurt, 1593), 787. Milton read Sulpicius Severus's history but not in this edition (*CPW*, i. 416).

[103] Diodati, *Annotations*, sig. 2B3ᵛ (on Judg. 15: 20). See also Quistorpius, *Annotationes*, 253 (on Judg. 13: 5).

Catholicism startled even members of his own episcopal party.[104] The thought of the prelatical Thorndike helping us to understand the resolutely Independent and republican Milton is quite implausible.

The fundamental legitimacy of Samson's actions in the commentary tradition out of which Milton in part forged his tragedy emerges particularly clearly in the comparisons these authors occasionally allow themselves to draw between Samson's situation and political struggles with which they were themselves familiar. Peter Martyr Vermigli, for instance, found the Philistines' gloating over the blind Samson reminiscent of 'the conquerying of *Constantinople*, wherein the Turkes when they had gotten the city, caried about in derision the image of Christ'.[105] And in his commentary on Samson's death Johannes Quistorp quoted the opinion of Johann Conrad Dannhauer: 'Samson died bravely. It is just as if a courageous man should throw himself into the midst of a Turkish army, in vindication of divine glory (*ut si vir fortis se in confertissimam Turcarum aciem inferret, in vindictam gloriae divinae*).'[106] Samson, that is to say, was a hero of legitimate violence for religious ends. For all their questions, this was ultimately the meaning of his story for the Reformed commentary tradition, and the evidence I have presented here suggests that this was also its meaning for John Milton.

---

[104] Wittreich, *Shifting Contexts*, 171 (where he is called 'Henry'), 174–5. But Wittreich does not cite Thorndike's *Epilogue to the Tragedy of the Church of England* (1659). See further W. B. Patterson, 'Thorndike, Herbert (*bap.* 1597?, *d.* 1672)', *ODNB*.

[105] Vermigli, *Fruitfull & learned Commentaries*, fo. 235ʳ (on Judg. 16: 30).

[106] Quistorpius, *Annotationes*, 256 (on Judg. 16: 30), citing Johann Conrad Dannhauer, *Collegium Decalogicum* (Strasbourg, 1638).

CHAPTER 35

SAMSON AGONISTES: THE FORCE OF JUSTICE AND THE VIOLENCE OF IDOLATRY

REGINA M. SCHWARTZ

Why was the First Temple destroyed? Because of three sins: idolatry, immorality, and bloodshed. But why was the Second Temple destroyed, seeing that during the time it stood people occupied themselves with Torah, with observance of *mitzvot* [commandments], and with the practice of *tzedakah* [charity]? Because during the time the Second Temple stood, *sinat hinam* [baseless hatred] prevailed. This teaches us that baseless hatred is deemed as grave as the sins of idolatry, immorality, and bloodshed combined.

Talmud, Yoma 9b

THE FORCE OF JUSTICE

How we understand Samson's violence depends upon how we understand justice. If the wellspring of Samson's act of destruction is vengeance, we have ample evidence that Milton himself often disdains that motive; in *Paradise Lost*, he casts revenge as the very root of evil, the 'cause' of Satan's commitment to destroy mankind and the earth:

> say first what cause
> Moved our Grand Parents in that happy State,
> Favoured of Heaven so highly, to fall off
> From thir Creator, and transgress his Will
> For one restraint, Lords of the World besides?
> Who first seduced them to that foul revolt?
> The infernal Serpent; he it was, whose guile
> Stird up with Envy and Revenge, deceived
> The Mother of Mankind . . . (i. 28–36)

Of course violence can be framed in radically different ways: revenge against an enemy is not the same as liberation from an oppressor. If Samson were *only* seeking vengeance, presumably, his violence would be Satanic.[1] But if his motive is liberation, his violence is not only justified, but obliged. While Milton wrote in *The Reason of Church-Government* (1642) that 'Surely to every good and peaceable man it must in nature needs be a hateful thing to be the displeaser and the molester of thousands', he added:

But when God commands to take the trumpet, and blow a dolorous or jarring blast, it lies not in man's will what he shall say, or what he shall conceal . . . If the prelates have leave to say the worst that can be said, or do the worst that can be done . . . no man can be justly offended with him that shall endeavour to impart and bestow, without any gain to himself, those sharp and saving words which would be a terror and a torment in him to keep back. (*CPW*, i. 598)

Milton will defend more than sharp words: when 'the earth itself hath too long groan'd under the burd'n of their injustice, disorder, and irreligion', it is time '*To bind thir Kings in Chaines and thir Nobels in links of Iron* [Gen. 10: 10]'. This must be understood as an 'honour belonging to his Saints . . . not to build *Babel* (which was Nimrods work the first King, *and the beginning of his Kingdom was Babel*) but to destroy it' (*Eikonoklastes*, *CPW*, iii. 598). In the Geneva Bible, marginalia for Judges tend to turn the story of Samson into one of divinely inspired resistance to alien tyranny. The faithful must be actively defended against the infidel: 'they by God's just judgments are made slaves to infidels which neglect their vocation in defending the faithful' (Judges 16: 25); it was Samson's vocation 'to execute God's judgments upon the wicked' (16: 29). Furthermore, the notes insist that Samson's violent actions against the Philistines were committed 'in faith, and so with a true zeal to glorify God

---

[1] Many critics have noted that Milton omits the motive of revenge for losing his eyes offered in the biblical narrative of Samson: 'O Sovereign LORD, remember me. O God, please strengthen me just once more, and let me with one blow get revenge on the Philistines for my two eyes' (Judg. 16: 28). Milton not only omits this motive, he alludes to the prayer nervously, even ambiguously, with a third-person report that Samson looked 'as one who prayed' (l. 1637). This has spawned much debate about whether Samson or God was the source of the 'rousing motion' that leads to the Temple's destruction, but it is plausible that it is the content of the prayer that Milton is avoiding, rather than doubting the source of Samson's inspiration and strength.

and deliver his country' (14: 18). Presumably, this is why Paul numbers Samson among the 'heroes of faith' (Hebrews 11: 32).

Reflecting these differences, the critical response to the work is deeply divided, with some scholars arguing that the slaughter and slaughterer are being held up for critique by Milton, or even despite Milton, and others arguing that the drama fully justifies Samson's actions. Michael Lieb is one of the critics who do not shy away from the violence in the drama. He describes the God of the drama as a God of vengeance and shows how the very name of God, 'the Dread' or *pachad* of God, descends on the people to obliterate them in holy wrath.[2] John Carey has dared to compare the biblical Samson with the airline hijackers of 11 September: 'Like them he destroys many innocent victims, whose lives, hopes, and loves are all quite unknown to him personally. He is, in effect, a suicide bomber, and like the suicide bombers, he believes that his massacre is an expression of God's will.'[3] Both positions, Samson as holy warrior in the cause of right and Samson as violent slaughterer of innocents, have clearly generated strong readings, each with their respective legitimacies: one man's terrorist is another man's freedom fighter. As Joseph Wittreich summarizes: 'the issue for criticism now is whether Milton, through *Samson Agonistes*, condones or criticizes, underwrites or undermines, his own culture of violence'.[4]

Many of the other questions that haunt the drama flow from whether we understand this violence as revenge or redemption. Does Samson undergo a process of regeneration in the course of the play and emerge spiritually victorious, a recipient of divine grace? Or is he, having violated divine commands, abandoned by God and hence killed in a desperate act of suicide? Is Samson caught tragically between two imperatives, to fulfil the law not to kill, and yet to defend God, his Law, and his people against their enemies? Or is he fulfilling the Law of God at the highest level by heeding a direct prompting from God, as Abraham did when he was willing to

[2] Michael Lieb, *Theological Milton: Deity, Discourse, and Heresy in the Miltonic Canon* (Pittsburgh, Pa., 2006), 187–209.

[3] John Carey, 'A Work in Praise of Terrorism? September 11 and *Samson Agonistes*', *Times Literary Supplement*, 6 Sept. 2002. Miltonists are deeply engaged in the *agon* of how to read Samson Agonistes. Joseph Wittreich is considerably less inflammatory, but clearly sides with those who believe the violence of Samson is disturbing, even disturbing enough to undermine his heroism; see *Interpreting Samson Agonistes* (Princeton, 1986). In stark contrast, Mary Anne Radzinowicz sees Samson engaging in an exemplary process of enlightenment, showing the reader the way as he gains understanding of how God makes his presence known in the heart (*Toward Samson Agonistes: The Growth of Milton's Mind* (Princeton, 1978)). David Loewenstein argues against the regeneration of Samson, insisting that *Samson Agonistes* centres on an impulse to devastate one's enemies by means of a spectacular act; rather than muting the devastation depicted in the Book of Judges, Milton's account heightens it (*Representing Revolution in Milton and his Contemporaries: Religion, Politics, and Polemics in Radical Puritanism* (Cambridge, 2001), 269–95, and 'Samson Agonistes and the Culture of Religious Terror', in Michael Lieb and Albert C. Labriola (eds.), *Milton and the Age of Fish: Essays on Authorship, Text and Terrorism* (Pittsburgh, Pa., 2006)). Loewenstein understands the iconoclastic ending as a violent clash between God and Dagon—a 'theomachic confrontation', as Michael Lieb describes it. Lieb argues that *Samson Agonistes* is not only 'a work of harsh and uncompromising violence', but, indeed, 'a work that exults in violence while it gives expression to profound and deeply disturbing elements of vehemence and rage' (*Theological Milton*, 186).

[4] Joseph Wittreich, *Shifting Contexts: Reinterpreting Samson Agonistes* (Pittsburgh, Pa., 2002), p. xxii.

sacrifice his son? Is this drama centred on human responses to evil—to fight tyranny requires violence—instead of messianic ones, and is Samson's story of fighting tyranny with violence paired with the story of Jesus's non-violent response, *Paradise Regained*, to offer the alternatives? Is Samson, rather, an apocalyptic figure, and as such, a precursor, even a type for the anti-type of the sword-bearing Redeemer of Revelation? These questions deepen into strong disagreement among critics on the way Milton regards the slaughter of the Philistines: is this an exemplary act of piety, the execution of a divine will that is communicated directly to Samson through 'rousing motions' (l. 1382), and so is Samson like those revolutionaries who took their political course from divine promptings? Or does Samson act with independent or 'private' agency, so committing murder and suicide?

The political, theological, and generic implications of the violence in *Samson Agonistes* have been extensively explored in a rich variety of contexts: among them, the revolutionary zeal of his period, dissent during the Restoration, the thought of Hugo Grotius, Christian theology, Rabbinic commentary, the work of Josephus, the problem of theological wrath, the suffering of Christ, Aristotelian cartharsis, and Euripidean and Senecan tragedy.[5] Here, I will approach Milton's Samson in the context of biblical violence, for the question that violence raises is also the pressing question of Samson's violence: when is violence just? The answer to that question in turn will suggest whether we are to understand Samson as a saviour or destroyer, a success or failure. Furthermore, the problem of the justice of his violence has wider implications beyond the figure of Samson: it asks us to understand the depiction of community in the drama, for his regeneration is certainly not private, like Job's; rather, he acts against a people, the Philistines, on behalf of another people, the Israelites. In the story of Samson what is at stake, then, is also the wider question of the violence between peoples and of under what conditions such violence may be not only acceptable, but propitious.

Understanding massacre as divinely willed would not surprise many of Milton's contemporaries: the *Annotations Upon all of the Books of the Old and New Testament* of 1645, written by a notable committee of Puritan clergy, asserts that Samson was 'the instrument under God of executing vengeance upon God's and the church's enemies'. According to the 'Annotations', God 'brought blind Samson to a sight of his sin, that he might unfeignedly repent', and an 'extraordinary motion of God' gave him supernatural strength—Milton's 'rousing motions'—'to glorify God and give deliverance to his people' (Judges 14). Even those who criticized Samson's sexual behaviour applauded his violence: Joseph Hall, Milton's early polemical opponent, wrote that Samson was 'a slave to lewd desires' but 'I never read that Samson slew any but by the motion and assistance of the spirit of God'. And as for the massacre of Philistines in the Temple, Hall specifically distinguishes violence in the service of faith from violence in the service of hate: 'it is zeal that moves him, not malice'.[6] To John

---

[5] Wittreich's *Shifting Contexts* is especially helpful at highlighting the wealth and variety of these readings.

[6] Joseph Hall, *Contemplations on the Old Testament* (1612–28), in *Works . . . of Jospeh Hall*, ed. Josiah Pratt, 10 vols. (1808), i. 224, 228.

Sadler, a member of Samuel Hartlib's network of reformers, taking away Samson's strength was like robbing the people of their power.[7] The regicide Thomas Scott compared Samson to the honest Puritans who, once united, will pull the house down on idolaters.[8]

To engage the problem of how to understand Milton's *Samson Agonistes*, then, is to approach the problem of divinely sanctioned violence. Those who are troubled by the depiction of Samson's act in Milton's drama would doubtless worry too about other cultural and political depictions of God as destroying his enemies and rejoicing at their defeat: the God who was invoked at the Crusades to kill Muslims, during the Spanish Inquisition to expel Jews, during the conquest of the New World to destroy natives, during 'ethnic cleansing' (a horrific phrase) in Bosnia. This rhetoric of violence may invoke the holy, but the violence is anything but holy: it often seems nakedly political, the result of nervously forging collective identity negatively, against some other, when 'us' understood as distinguished from 'them' turns easily into 'us vs. them', or, in religious parlance, believers vs. idolaters or faithful vs. infidels, Christians vs. pagans, the civilized vs. barbarians, and even the human vs. the subhuman.[9]

Let us surmise that for the Bible, as well as for Milton, the Philistines are not part of a pluralistic society that includes many equally legitimate cultures, that the Philistines are not innocent like the victims of terrorists, and that instead they are richly deserving of destruction to avoid greater destruction at their hands. In *Samson Agonistes*, the Chorus addresses the problem head-on. According to them, there is just cause for Samson to set his people free from such an enemy. Hence, the violence committed against that enemy is more the eradication of an evil blight, the clearing away of an oppressor, than revenge. The stones that crush the Philistines bring liberty, as surely as the Egyptian oppressors were drowned in the Red Sea. There is, in fact, every reason to understand the Philistine as another instalment in Israel's long narrative of oppression. What Samson offers in that story, he says explicitly, is deliverance, and what frustrates him about Israel's governors is that although they see the great acts which God had done through him, they fail to recognize them as offers of deliverance from bondage. To these efforts 'Had Judah that day joined, or one whole tribe, / They had by this possessed the towers of Gath, / And lorded over them whom now they serve' (ll. 265–7). This complaint of an opportunity missed for deliverance is surely directed at Milton's compatriots who failed him when he offered a 'ready and easy way' to establish a free commonwealth as the restoration of the tyranny of monarchy was immanent.

Modelled on both the Book of Job and Greek tragedy, *Samson Agonistes* takes up the question of justice explicitly: '*Just* are the ways of God / And *justifiable* to men'

---

[7] John Sadler, *A Word in Season* (1646), 5.

[8] T. W. Hayes, entry for Thomas Scott in *Biographical Dictionary of British Radicals in the Seventeenth Century*, ed. R. L. Greaves and R. Zaller, 3 vols. (Brighton, 1982–4), iii. 147.

[9] For further discussion of the relation between religious identity and violence, see Regina Schwartz, *The Curse of Cain: The Violent Legacy of Monotheism* (Chicago, 1997).

(ll. 293–4; my emphasis), asserts the Chorus when Samson complains that even if his nation abandoned him, they were wrong to neglect deliverance of the nation itself:

> Yet more there be who doubt his ways not just,
> As to his own edicts, found contradicting,
> Then give the reigns to wandering thought,
> Regardless of his glory's diminution;
> Till by their own perplexities involved
> They ravel more, still less resolved,
> But never find self-satisfying solution. (ll. 300–6)

Those who doubt the justice of God are like the philosophers of Hell in *Paradise Lost*, condemned to eternal confusion, in 'wandering mazes lost' (ii. 561).

But what does 'the justice of God' signify in the world of *Samson Agonistes*? Is it, in the end, virtually synonymous with 'the terror of God', with vengeance on the enemies of God? Lieb has astutely honed in on the appellation 'our living Dread' for God, the description used by the semi-chorus upon the news of the destruction of the temple of Dagon, tracing its debt to the 'fear of God' or *pachad* in 1 Samuel 11: 7; Job 13: 11, and Job 4: 13–14, and the patriarchal understanding of divine dread in Genesis 31: 42, 53. 'The God of the patriarchs is thereby redefined most fearsomely as very dread, indeed, dread deified'; the name is meant to 'sow terror among his enemies'.[10] In Genesis, we discover a wrongly accused Jacob, indeed, one who has been wrongly treated, defending himself by invoking his divine protector: 'Except the God of my father, the God of Abraham, and the fear of Isaac (*pachad vitschaq*), had been with me, surely thou hadst sent me away now empty' (Genesis 31: 42). The dread of God is joined to the justice of God; when he sees injustice, he asserts justice with force, if need be. And this restorative justice is not the same as revenge. Retributive justice has the aim of paying back, returning aggression with aggression. Restorative justice aims less to punish than to repair, to correct a deficit. Liberation from slavery is not framed as retributive—as motivated by the desire to punish, to repay—but as restorative, regaining the dignity that has been denied by enslavement.

In this light, we might helpfully disentangle vengeance from violence, and try to understand Samson's violence, not as retributive, but as redemptive. This requires a further distinction between 'force' and 'violence'. Force has an integral relation to justice; it is the way that we en-force justice, that is, make sure it comes into being. Whether this force is legal (sanctioned by state), or revolutionary, it can be marshalled to the service of pursuing justice. The force of justice is not violence for its own sake. In 'Force of Law' Derrida writes that

there is no law that does not imply *in itself, a priori, in the analytic structure of its concept*, the possibility of being 'enforced', applied by force. . . . There are, to be sure, laws (*lois*) that are not enforced, but there is no law (*loi*) without enforceability and no applicability or enforceability of the law (*loi*) without force, whether this force be direct or indirect, physical or symbolic,

---

[10] *Theological Milton*, 189.

exterior or interior, brutal or subtly discursive—even hermeneutic—coercive or regulative, and so forth.[11]

Milton's understanding of the force of justice is inflected by Exodus where God turns forcefully and swiftly against Israel when she is idolatrous, less to punish than to engage in a full-scale effort to deliver her from her own worst impulses. When Moses comes down from the mountain to offer his community the law of justice, he discovers them violating it—that is, they are in the midst of violating the very first command they are given, against idol worship. With the law broken even as it is given, it is as if the Israelites are not ready to receive this law. Having forged a molten idol they can bribe, they are still enslaved to a system of thought that is alien to the new justice. They would also choose a captain back to Egypt, to the house of slavery.

With stunning simplicity, the Decalogue establishes the logic between deliverance from slavery and idolatry: 'I am the Lord your God who brought you out of the land of Egypt, out of the House of bondage. Thou shalt have no other gods before me' (Exodus 20: 2–3). Milton's contemporaries understood the bondage of the nation, the bondage of the will, and the bondage of the heart to be all idolatrous.[12] For Milton, the only way out of the house of slavery, in all these senses, is the radical rejection of idolatry, a subject that preoccupies him from the Nativity Ode to *Samson Agonistes*, as well as throughout his polemical prose and his doctrinal theology.

According to Samson, from his first marriage on, his mission is to begin Israel's deliverance. Deliverance, here, as throughout Milton's prose, suggests a rescue from bondage—of a people from a tyrant, of the will from the tyranny of custom, of reason from the tyranny of passion, and of all from the spiritual bondage of idolatry. Deliverance is Samson's mission in a drama obsessed with slavery: Samson is Delilah's bond-slave, and his enslavement to her issues in his enslavement to the Philistines. Importantly and innovatively, Milton makes us meet Samson in bondage—not in his announced heroic birth, and not in any of his heroic, if excessive, adventures. Samson himself chooses to frame his experience as bondage: his *servile* mind was rewarded with *servile* punishment. And yet, once imprisoned, he does not succumb to the tyranny of the Philistines, to the manipulations of Delilah, to the tauntings of Harapha, or even to the customs of his own people. Imprisoned though he may be, Samson is no longer enslaved to passion. His final act is no private rage or vengeance, but an act moved by the spirit of God on behalf of delivering his people.

---

[11] Jacques Derrida, 'Force of Law: The "Mystical Foundation of Authority"', in Gil Anidjar (ed.), *Acts of Religion* (New York and London, 2002), 228–98 at 233.

[12] Studies of idolatry with special emphasis on the visual include Ernest Gilman, *Iconoclasm and Poetry in the English Reformation: Down Went Dagon* (Chicago, 1986); Michael O'Connell, *The Idolatrous Eye* (New York, 2000); David Hawkes, *Idols of the Marketplace: Idolatry and Commodity Fetishism in English Literature 1580–1680* (New York and Basingstoke, 2001).

THE VIOLENCE OF IDOLATRY

Idolatry brought the Heathen to hainous trangressions . . . and hainous trangressions ofttimes bring the slight professors of true religion to gross Idolatry.[13]

Samson does not just spectacularly destroy *anything*; he destroys a *temple* to Dagon and all his worshippers: as such, Samson is an iconoclast, eradicating idolatry.[14] And Samson's destruction of the temple is his encore to his performance at the festivities to honor Dagon:[15] 'While their hearts were jocund and sublime, / *Drunk with idolatry*, drunk with wine / And fat regorged of bulls and goats, / *Chanting their idol*' (ll. 1669–72; my emphasis). To imagine this as genuine worship, when they are drunk with wine, gorged with fat, chanting their idol—in contrast to singing songs of praise to divinity—is delusional. The contrast is drawn explicitly: 'preferring [Dagon in his temple] / Before our living dread who dwells / In Silo his bright sanctuary' (ll. 1672–4).

Idolatry encompasses many concepts, some almost at odds with each other. And the tension in the concept is as old as the ancient Hebrew, where *avodah zara* suggests both strange gods and strange ways of worshipping God. With reference to worshipping the one god of ancient Israel, idolatry suggests belief in and reverence towards foreign gods, with all the threats that foreignness entails. That loyalty should be to the God of Israel and to none other. Worshipping another god, the god of another people, is worshipping an idol, and idolatry is understood as betrayal of the exclusive relationship with the God of Israel. The other is figured as a seducer who leads one away from his exclusive loyalty, and idolatry is figured as adultery. Throughout biblical prophecy, the idolater is the unfaithful wife who must be 'put away', cast out—even in the hope of her regeneration—or destroyed violently. The marriage between Israel and God is betrayed by the idolatrous Israel, and the metaphor at the opening of the book of Hosea—'Go, take unto thee a wife of whoredoms and children of whoredoms: for the land hath committed great whoredoms, *departing* from the Lord' (1: 2)—is so shocking that Maimonides and Ibn Ezra consider the entire story of chapters 1–3 as a visionary dream. Jeremiah offers another vivid example of this rhetoric: 'And I saw, when for all the causes whereby backsliding Israel committed adultery, I had put her away, and given her a bill of divorce; yet her treacherous sister Judah feared not, but went and played the harlot also' (3: 8). But

---

[13] *Of True Religion* (1673), in *CPW*, viii. 439–40.

[14] Barbara Lewalski has written a perceptive survey of the subject ('Milton and Idolatry', *Studies in English Literature, 1500–1900*, 43 (2003), 213–32). She demonstrates how preoccupied Reformist Protestants were with the category, and how frequently they accused Catholicism of idolatry: 'The Puritan response to contemporary idolatry found extreme expression during the English Civil War, especially in the winter of 1643–44, when William Dowsing and Francis Jessups led regiments of the army on a campaign of wanton destruction of religious statuary and stained glass in English cathedrals and churches, in accordance with a decree of Parliament (26 August, 1643) that "all Crucifixes, Crosses, and all Images ad Pictures of Saints . . . shal be taken away and defaced"' (p. 214).

[15] As Joseph G. Mayer observes: 'In an extraordinary exercise of invention as well as strength, he combines the antithetical identities of God's champion and glorifier of Dagon' (*Between Two Pillars: The Hero's Plight in 'Samson Agonistes' and 'Paradise Regained'* (Lanham, Md., 2004), 27).

Ezekiel 16, the extended allegory of Israel as a harlot, is the most graphic: she is born vulnerable, nurtured by God and when she reaches maturity, protected by God: 'thy breasts are fashioned, and thine hair is grown... I spread my skirt over thee, and covered thy nakedness: yea, I sware unto thee, and entered into a covenant with thee' (7–8). But Israel is unfaithful, committing idolatry with all of Israel's enemies:

And it came to pass after all thy wickedness, (woe, woe unto thee! saith the Lord GOD;) That thou hast also built unto thee an eminent place, and hast made thee an high place in every street. Thou hast built thy high place at every head of the way, and hast made thy beauty to be abhorred, and hast opened thy feet to every one that passed by, and multiplied thy whore-doms. Thou hast also committed fornication with the Egyptians thy neighbours, great of flesh; and hast increased thy whoredoms, to provoke me to anger. Behold, therefore I have stretched out my hand over thee, and have diminished thine ordinary food, and delivered thee unto the will of them that hate thee, the daughters of the Philistines, which are ashamed of thy lewd way. Thou hast played the whore also with the Assyrians, because thou wast unsatiable; yea, thou hast played the harlot with them, and yet couldest not be satisfied. Thou hast moreover multiplied thy fornication in the land of Canaan unto Chaldea; and yet thou wast not satisfied herewith. (23–9)

In this allegory, the ensuing response by the husband/God is unsparingly violent:

Thus saith the Lord GOD; Because thy filthiness was poured out, and thy nakedness discov-ered through thy whoredoms with thy lovers, and with all the idols of thy abominations, and by the blood of thy children, which thou didst give unto them; Behold, therefore I will gather all thy lovers, with whom thou hast taken pleasure, and all them that thou hast loved, with all them that thou hast hated; I will even gather them round about against thee, and will discover thy nakedness unto them, that they may see all thy nakedness. And I will judge thee, as women that break wedlock and shed blood are judged; and I will give thee blood in fury and jealousy. And I will also give thee into their hand, and they shall throw down thine eminent place, and shall break down thy high places: they shall strip thee also of thy clothes, and shall take thy fair jewels, and leave thee naked and bare. They shall also bring up a company against thee, and they shall stone thee with stones, and thrust thee through with their swords. (36–40)

This lurid rhetoric betrays an obsession, not just with the threat of foreign gods, but with national identity: Israel must renounce the foreign gods, the Baals and Astartes, to establish and preserve her identity. Indeed, the emphasis is more on identity than religious belief, for this figuration of idolatry as adultery, as pollution by foreigners, has a strong ideological and political character—even more than a metaphysical one, say, about the nature of being, or a theological one, about the nature of the divine. 'Political idolatry', as I will call it, is especially concerned with relations between peoples, often fraught relations. The political aspect comes into view when the terms infidel, pagan, barbarian, and idolater are used, often interchangeably, to denigrate the foreigner. After all, one man's idol is another's God. 'The world is split into two camps, the camp of believers and the camp of infidels': this sounds less like a genuine theological observation than a politically incendiary one—in fact, it was recently made by Osama bin Laden.

In Milton's age, the charge of idolatry was ubiquitous: anything associated with the Roman religion was idolatrous, the Irish were idolaters, the Mass was idolatrous, the vestments, the images, statues, and paintings—all occasions for idolatry. And the foreign idol was not only without, in Rome and Ireland, but within. Anything in the Church of England that was deemed to have Catholic association was similarly labelled idolatrous by Puritans—making comparison with ancient Israel, where idols were worshipped in the very sanctuary of the Lord, especially apt. And this comparison gave way to the desecration of images, especially during the Civil War. But, as Barbara Lewalski notes, 'unlike Oliver Cromwell's soldiers, Milton Icono-clastes did not lop off the heads of saints in cathedrals, he sought rather to topple idols with his pen, by unmasking and denouncing their evil'.[16]

A different but related sense of idolatry verges on contradicting this political, ideological emphasis on foreign gods, on adultery, and on the dangers of the foreigner, especially the foreign woman, who lures the Israelite into her idolatrous practices and beliefs. This other sense is also biblical, but has had a long theological and philosophical career: idolatry as nothingness, as void, as vanity. In Jeremiah, God complains: 'For my people have committed two evils; they have forsaken me the fountain of living waters, and hewed them out cisterns, broken cisterns, that can hold no water' (2: 13): the idol as broken cistern instead of the adulterer. Isaiah also associates idols with nothing: 'They that make a graven image are all of them vanity; and their delectable things shall not profit; and they are their own witnesses; they see not, nor know; that they may be ashamed' (44: 9). By Paul, the association of nothingness with idols had grown strong:

As concerning therefore the eating of those things that are offered in sacrifice unto idols, we know that an idol is nothing in the world, and that there is none other God but one. For though there be that are called gods, whether in heaven or in earth, (as there be gods many, and lords many,) But to us there is but one God, the Father, of whom are all things, and we in him; and one Lord Jesus Christ, by whom are all things, and we by him. (1 Corinthians 8: 4–6)

And a few chapters later:

What say I then? that the idol is any thing, or that which is offered in sacrifice to idols is any thing? But I say, that the things which the Gentiles sacrifice, they sacrifice to devils, and not to God: and I would not that ye should have fellowship with devils. Ye cannot drink the cup of the Lord, and the cup of devils: ye cannot be partakers of the Lord's table, and of the table of devils. (1 Corinthians 10: 19–21)

To worship nothingness is to be attached to illusion, to falsehood. In this under-standing of idolatry, the question is not the lure of the foreigner, nor even religious pluralism, so much as misguided thinking—although they often overlap. This sense of falsehood deepens into error, and much of the suspicion of representation that attends the discourse on idolatry concerns error: the image is conceived of as an error, as not successfully representing the referent who is unrepresentable; the venerator is conceived as falling into the error of mistaking the object, the icon, for the true God.

---

[16] 'Milton and Idolatry', 214.

For many thinkers, including many reformers, idolatry is the 'invisible made visible', and that process involves the fundamental error of trying to render visible what cannot be seen. According to Milton in *Of Reformation*, whether the forces are old or new, the molten calf or the idol of the Mass, both 'draw downe all the Divine intercourse, betwixt God, and the soule, yea, the very shape of God himselfe, into an exterior, and bodily forme' (*CPW*, i. 520). This is because, as Luther explained, the internal idolatry of spiritual fornication with sin produces external manifestations, the idolatry of images and idols that pollute the world. In Henry More's description, idolatry is a 'grievous Disease of the Soul' vilely debasing her and sinking her into Sensuality and Materiality, keeping her at a distance from 'the true sense and bright knowledge of God'.[17] This visibility of the idol is not only understood as a material representation, but also as a conceptual representation of God—the idol of the brain. Calvin saw the mind of man as 'a perpetuall manufactory of idols': he wrote of how the 'mind of man, being full of pride and temerity, dares to conceive of God according to its own standard, and being...immersed in profound ignorance, imagines a vain and ridiculous phantom instead of God'.[18] What visibility confers is an access to the divine, including manipulation over it, enabling idolaters to instrumentalize God. They invent a concept or image of God to justify their ends, to reflect their passions, and—not least—to endorse their error. Instead of moving beyond their interests to a higher concept of the good, they depict their interests *as* the divine good. As such, the rationality of idolaters is enslaved to falsehood, as the spirituality of idolaters is enslaved to illusion.

In the course of Christian thought, this sense of error deepens into the gravest error, sin. Idolatry is a symptom of the power and success of the Antichrist. In his short but important treatise 'On Idolatry', Tertullian describes the sin of idolatry as so comprehensive that it includes virtually all other sins: the idolater is a murderer, fornicator, adulterer, committer of fraud and contumely, and altogether unrighteous: 'For what more unrighteous than it, which knows not the Father of righteousness?' In idolatry resides the 'concupiscence of the world': idolatry is characterized by vanity, 'since its whole substance is false'.[19] Augustine expands concupiscence to signal all desire that eclipses the rational tendencies of the soul: 'Men bind themselves to images by the chains of their own lusts.' 'In worshipping idols, men are in reality worshipping demons' who seduce them, lure them into an infection of the will.[20] Understanding idols as demons who infect the will persists into Milton's time: Joseph Mede, Milton's tutor at Christ's College, writes that 'idolatry or Spiritual Whoredom' is the 'storm of the Devil'; 'the very Soul of the Apostasie under the Man of sin' and

---

[17] 'An Antidote Against Idolatry', pt. 2 of *An Exposition of the Seven Epistles to the Seven Churches* (1669), 4–5, 14.

[18] *Institutes of the Christian Religion*, trans. John Allen, 2 vols. (Philadelphia, 1813), i. 104–5.

[19] *Ante-Nicene Christian Library: Translation of the Writings of the Fathers down to A.D. 325*, ed. Alexander Roberts and James Donaldson (Edinburgh, 1869), xi. 141–2.

[20] *A Select Library of the Nicene and Post-Nicene Fathers*, ed. Philip Schaff and Henry Wace (Grand Rapids, Mich., 1956), ii. 162.

'the main Character of the Churches Apostasie'.[21] But the bottom line is that, in Tertullian's phrase, 'idolatry savours of opposition to God'. Instead of obeying a divine law, idolaters 'obey' themselves. This understanding was well articulated by Thomas Bilson in *The True Difference Betweeene Christian Subjection and Unchristian Rebellion* (1585): Saint Paul 'called the couetous man a worshipperer of idols: of others hee saith, which God is their bellie, teaching us, that whatsoeuer we loue, serue, or obey against the commandement of God, we make it our God by preferring it before the will and precepts of the true God' (551–2).

Idolatry is not just any error but injustice, and specifically the injustice of slavery. Even as Milton inveighs against Roman liturgy and ceremony, and against the English prelates who have adopted these rituals, in his anti-prelatical tracts, he emphasizes that these idolatrous acts breed slavishness and servility, not the freedom intended for a Christian. This complaint is behind his description of the prelate's Mass in *Of Reformation* (1641):

that feast of free grace and adoption to which Christ invited his Disciples to sit as Brethren, and co-heires of the happy Covenant...even that Feast of love and heavenly admitted fellowship, the Sealle of filiall grace, became the subject of horror, and glouting adoration, pageanted about like a dreadful Idol. (*CPW*, i. 522–3)

The risk of enslavement is so great that in *Of Civil Power* (1659), where he seeks to separate the prerogatives of the civil from the religious leader, he makes an exception of idolatry: 'a magistrate can hardly err in prohibiting and quite removing at least the public and scandalous use thereof'. He continues:

Their religion [Catholicism], the more considered, the less can be acknowledged a religion, but a Roman principality rather, endeavoring to keep up her old universal dominion under a new name and mere shadow of a catholic religion: being indeed more rightly named a catholic heresy against the scripture, supported mainly by a civil and, except in Rome, by a foreign power: justly therefore to be suspected, not tolerated, by the magistrate of another country. (*CPW*, vii. 255)

Even in this overtly political context, Milton is not imagining only vengeance against an enemy, but also the assertion of truth—the Roman problem is not only their foreignness, but also their 'heresy against the scripture'.

While the political question of the nation of England and the moral question of sin are never separable—England must be a country devoted to true religion, a nation of free and virtuous citizens who fulfil the national aspiration of republicanism because only that is the true political expression of their religious freedom—it is also the case that when Milton's writing is most concerned with the national political project, he becomes most preoccupied with the threat of the foreign idolater: Rome, of course, and Ireland, as well as what he deemed papist tendencies within England, and these threats are represented through the rhetoric of the foreign seductress. When he is anxious about England's self-definition, its future as a holy polity, he writes of

---

[21] *The Apostasy of these Latter Times* (1641), 643.

idolatry as the threat of foreign gods, and even specifically as the threat of a foreign wife luring one into idolatry. The anxiety surfaces in his prose in, among other places, *Eikonoklastes*, *Of Civil Power*, and *Of True Religion*. In his explicitly political tracts, idolatry is the sin of the State; he counts himself among the Iconoclastes, which is 'the famous Surname of the Greek Emperors, who in thir zeal to the command of God, after long tradition of Idolatry in the Church, took courage, and broke all superstitious Images to peeces'. The King's Image, the *Eikon Basilike*, was no 'better Oracle than a Babylonish gold'n image' (*CPW*, iii. 343). *Eikonoklastes* seeks to free readers' minds from the bondage of servility towards the Crown, in part by portraying Charles himself as enslaved to an 'idolatrous consort', his French and Catholic queen Henrietta Maria:[22]

He [Charles] ascribes...all vertue to his Wife, in straines that come almost to Sonnetting: How fitt to govern men, undervaluing and aspersing the great Counsel of his Kingdom, in comparison of one Woman. Examples are not farr to seek, how great mischeif and dishonour hath befall'n to Nations under the Government of effeminate and Uxorious Magistrates. Who being themselves govern'd and overswaid at home under a Female usurpation, cannot but be far short of spirit and autority without dores, to govern a whole Nation. (*CPW*, iii. 420–2)

In Chapter 21 of *Eikonoklastes*, after enumerating Catholic plots from abroad and royalist plans for a foreign invasion, Milton writes: 'to sum up all, they shew'd him govern'd by a Woman...All which though suspected vehemently before, and from good grounds beleev'd, yet by him and his adherents peremptorily deny'd, were, by the op'ning of that Cabinet, visible to all men under his own hand' (iii. 538–9).[23] As Milton put it in the *First Defense*: 'Solomon was lured to idolatry by many wives; Charles by one' ('Solomon a plurimis uxoribus ad Idolorum cultum pellectus est; hic ab una') (*CPW*, iv/i. 372).

In general, when Milton has more difficulty imagining England throwing off the yoke of oppression, he speaks of Idolatry as Error—no longer in the sense of enslavement to foreign idolaters, but the inward idolatry that infects the will, that enslaves reason to illusion, virtue to sin, and humankind to Satan himself. So, while *Paradise Lost* will include a catalogue of pagan, foreign deities, the point he drives home about them is that they are all devils, and they are engaged collectively in the deadly project of destroying humankind. After the fall, these devils will be 'adored for deities'. With this shift in focus from idolatry as foreignness to idolatry as error, the emphasis falls on self-enslavement, on one's own responsibility, on the failure to ward off the temptations of the devil. Instead of the outsider, Englishmen must look within and accept their own responsibility for the idolatrous return to monarchy. In *Paradise Lost* when Eve falls, she is depicted as an idolater. All this was Satan's intention: he had planted false religion into the mind of Eve in Book 5, praising the forbidden tree: 'on that fair tree he also gazed; / And O fair plant, said he, with

---

[22] Cedric Brown, 'Milton and the Idolatrous Consort', *Criticism*, 35 (1993), 441–62.

[23] Milton is alluding to the provocative decision of Parliament to publish intercepted letters between the King and Queen in *The King's Cabinet Opened* (1645).

fruit surcharged' (ll. 57–8). In Book 9, Satan builds idolatrous rhetoric into his temptation of Eve:

> O sacred, wise, and wisdom-giving plant,
> Mother of science, now I feel thy power
> Within me clear, not only to discern
> Things in their causes, but to trace the ways
> Of highest agents, deemed however wise. (ll. 679–83)

Eve takes the cue, first in her speech:

> O sovereign, virtuous, precious of all trees
> In Paradise, of operation blest
> To sapience, hitherto obscured, infamed,
> And thy fair fruit let hang, as to no end
> Created. (ll. 795–9)

and then by idolatrous act: 'So saying, from the tree she turned, / But first low reverence done, as to the power / That dwelt therin' (ll. 834–6). It is also true that Adam is an idolater in putting Eve before God, and in this way effectively enslaving himself to her will. 'Was she thy god', he is rebuked, 'that her thou didst obey / Before his [God's] voice' (x. 145–6). This is why he speaks, after she has fallen, as if he has no freedom of choice. 'I feel / The link of nature draw me' (ix. 913–14): he has been lured by an idolatrous consort, one whom he should have divorced according to his own doctrine.

In *Paradise Regained*, the temptation of the foreign idol appears but plays a relatively minor role compared to the great temptations of the idols of wealth, power, and knowledge, all of which can be purchased by worshipping Satan: 'Women, when nothing else, beguiled the heart / Of wisest Solomon, and made him build, / And made him bow to the gods of his wives' (ii. 169–71). But the relation of political idolatry to the idolatry of falsehood is especially compelling in *Samson Agonistes*, for they come together most powerfully, and troublingly, in this drama, where Milton's project is to bring together the concepts of idols as the foreign gods and idolatry as injustice. He chooses a plot that can do this most effectively: the biblical narrative of a national figure who is chosen to redeem his people from idolaters, from the foreign pollution of the enslaving Philistines, but who must wrestle first with his own enemy within, must withstand the temptations of idolatry offered by his Job-ian friends to renew his strength to fight the idolatry of the other. The implication in *Paradise Lost* and *Paradise Regained* is that restoration is only achievable by each person's embrace of virtue—their refusal of the temptations of the idol. In *Samson*, the act of heroism can still save others, but only after he has refused the idols, internal and external, that plague him. He must release himself from the snare of the idolatrous consort, Dalila, to begin his journey towards freedom and to become an example to the enslaved Israelites.

The book of Amos is among the many biblical sites where the equation of idolatry and injustice is apparent:

Though ye offer me burnt offerings and your meat offerings, I will not accept them: neither will I regard the peace offerings of your fat beasts. Take thou away from me the noise of thy songs; for I will not hear the melody of thy viols. But let judgment run down as waters, and righteousness as a mighty stream. Have ye offered unto me sacrifices and offerings in the wilderness forty years, O house of Israel? But ye have borne the tabernacle of your Moloch and Chiun your images, the star of your god, which ye made to yourselves. (Amos 5: 22–6)

In this light, Samson disobeys in the darkest sense: he not only disobeys the Law, violates the command of his Nazarite vow, he also betrays the divine mystery of his power when he tells Dalila his secret. He gives the mystery of God to idolaters, and that issues in their enhanced capacity to worship a false god. *A worse thing yet remains*, says Manoa, worse than all the terrible degradation his son has suffered, and what is worse is enabling the Philistine festival of idolatry:

> This day the Philistines a popular feast
> Here celebrate in Gaza, and proclaim
> Great pomp, and sacrifice, and praises loud
> To Dagon, as their god
> . . .
>
> So Dagon shall be magnified, and God,
> Besides whom is no god, compared with idols,
> Disglorified, blasphemed, and had in scorn
> By the *idolatrous rout* amidst their wine. (ll. 434–7, 440–3; my emphasis)

The wine is no incidental detail: when Eve worships the tree, she is drunk, 'heightened as with wine, jocund and boon' (ix. 793). To be drunk with idolatry is to have lost right reason. Tertullian understood idolatry to include 'lasciviousness and drunkenness; since it is, for the most part, for the sake of food and stomach and appetites that these solemnities are frequented'.[24]

Samson understands his facilitating of idolatry as the worst of his sins:

> Father, I do acknowledge and confess
> That I this honour, I this pomp have brought
> To Dagon, and advanced his praises high
> Among the heathen round; to God have brought
> Dishonour, obloquy, and oped the mouths
> Of idolists, and atheists; have brought scandal
> To Israel, diffidence of God, and doubt
> In feeble hearts, propense enough before
> To waver, or fall off *and join with idols;*
> *Which is my chief affliction, shame and sorrow* . . . (ll. 448–57; my emphasis)

Clearly idolatry is not only about the worship of false gods. It encompasses wider meanings than the idolatry of 'replacement' wherein worship of the wrong object is substituted for worship of the right one. It also includes the radical understanding voiced succinctly by Wittgenstein: 'All that philosophy can do is to destroy idols. And

---

[24] *Ante-Nicene Christian Library*, xi. 142.

that means not making any new ones, say, out of the absence of idols.'[25] Under the general subject of 'Worship or Love of God' in *De Doctrina Christiana*, Milton states that 'idolatry consists in the making, worshipping, or trusting in idols *whether considered as representations of the true god or a false one*' (*CPW*, vi. 180; my emphasis). Throughout the treatise, 'worship' is both internal and external. Milton would distinguish between the object and the manner of worship—a drunken lust for God, a seizing and appropriating of God to authorize one's own purposes, identity, and violence. In this sense, we can seem to have come full circle: the distinction is subtle, so subtle that it may not be discernible: it is idols that authorize violence against *our* enemies while God authorizes force against the enemies of God.

When Samson responds to 'rousing motions'—killing, against the custom of his people and against his own inclination—he is no longer grasping a god-idol for his own purposes. As Loewenstein has put it, Milton's *Samson* offers one of the most daring depictions of providence in Puritan literature.[26] The contest between idol and God is explicit, and the aim of the drama is to assert the victory of God, even when we least anticipate it. Our reason is faulty, but the motions of the inner spirit are to be trusted. Many revolutionaries cited Samson as the illustrious example of one who destroyed the idolaters in his time by 'pulling away the pillars whereby the building was supported, whereupon the whole frame toppled to the ground: So the Lord intending the ruine of that mighty power, whose top seems to reach to heaven, will do it pulling away the pillars and supporters of it, after which it cannot stand one moment'.[27] Manoa understands that his son's death is victorious: God had not abandoned him in the end: there is the world of difference between a hidden God and an idol. The grasping of God, the possession of him, can be helpfully contrasted to the willing obedience that does not grasp God, the kind Abraham shows when he cannot comprehend the divine purpose but nonetheless obeys in binding Isaac.

To choose between Dagon and God is not to choose between two gods, or two idols; it is to choose between the idol and the divine. For Milton, diversity of opinion is fine, for in dialogue, in a field of contest, men will strive towards truth. But Milton is not living in a multicultural, pluralistic space where all religions are equally valid. In his writing, we encounter, again and again, and with much discomfort, the limits of toleration. And those limits are always idolatry. Milton unleashes, both in his prose and in *Samson Agonistes*, fury against the bondage of idolatry—and this helps to explain the remarkable appeal of his writing down the ages to those enslaved to the tyrants of nations or to the tyranny of instrumental worship:

If men within themselves would be governed by reason, and not generally give up their understanding to a double tyrannie, of Custom from without, and blind affections within, they would discerne better what it is to favour and uphold the Tyrant of a Nation. But being

---

[25] Wittgenstein, *Culture and Value* (Oxford, 1988), 31.

[26] *Representing Revolution in Milton and his Contemporaries*, 276–81.

[27] John Owen, *The Shaking and Translating of Heaven and Earth* (1649), 27. This was a sermon preached before the Commonwealth Parliament.

slaves within doors, no wonder that they strive so much to have the public State conformably govern'd to the inward vitious rule, by which they govern themselves. (*CPW*, iii. 190)

A frightening thought cannot be ignored by today's reader: what if the Philistines, the Royalists, the Catholics—believed to be so riddled with error and devoted to sin, unquestionable and unredeemable idolaters of falsehood—were not evil at all, but only, after all, 'political idolaters', i.e. enemies? Surely that conclusion is compelling from our current cultural and historical perspective. But if one man's idol is another's god, how would we know idolaters when we see them? It is unlikely that they are coterminus with any whole group of people; indeed, to think so would be tantamount to the religious bigotry that so embarrasses us about Milton's age. Instead, they may be those persons, or those moments in a person's life, who use God, and by extension other people and the world itself, instrumentally, for self-interest, instead of living under a horizon of justice. The distinction is not easy. It is, in fact, the labour of the moral life: to cull and sort asunder, like the confused seeds of Psyche, the true from the false, the good from the evil.

CHAPTER 36

....

SAMSON AGONISTES AND MILTON'S SENSIBLE ETHICS

....

ELIZABETH D. HARVEY

MARY Ann Radzinowicz remarked thirty years ago that *Samson Agonistes* is a work notable for its 'outward stillness' and 'inward movement'. Samson is, she asserts, 'enchained, encased in sightless silence, confined to a single bank, enclosed in a dark dungeon of a body, assaulted by numberless inward griefs'.[1] Where such critics as David Quint and David Norbrook have perceptively claimed that Samson's terrible vengeance against his enemies is cognate with Milton's imaginative resistance to the restored monarchy of Charles II in 1660 and to the religious uniformity it imposed,[2] Radzinowicz's psychosocial characterization channels the action of the tragedy inward, not only to the 'prison-house' of the body, but also to 'th'inmost mind' (ll. 922, 611). The nature of Samson's interior state has continued to preoccupy critics, as in, for example, Stanley Fish's contention that Milton's poem is about the inscrutability of Samson's interior, a mind that, like the poem itself, grapples with

I am grateful for the work of two superb research assistants, Timothy Harrison and Adele Wilson, and to Fran Dolan and Theresa Krier for their generous suggestions and perceptive criticism.

[1] Mary Ann Radzinowicz, *Toward* Samson Agonistes: *The Growth of Milton's Mind* (Princeton, 1987), 15.

[2] David Quint, *Epic and Empire* (Princeton, 1993), 278–80; David Norbrook, *Writing the English Republic: Poetry, Rhetoric and Politics, 1627–1660* (Cambridge, 1999), 435, 491.

irresolvable interpretative ambiguity.[3] Sharon Achinstein, too, recognizes the 'unan-swerable questions' that shape the poem, but she historicizes Samson's inner struggle for meaning through her engagement with Restoration debates around religious dissent.[4] Victoria Kahn has argued recently in a brilliant consideration of Milton's tragic poem that *Samson* participates in seventeenth-century debates about political obligations in ways that engage not only cognition but also affect; her account renders the passions central to the poem's political motivations.[5]

Samson's interior state is, as the interpretative history of the poem shows, deeply entwined with the poem's political engagements.[6] The interiorizing movement that Radzinowicz and others describe maps the interstitial space between individual subjectivity and the ethical and political obligations of the nation, and between the physicality of Samson's 'incorporate' flesh and the operations of the mind's inward-ness. I will explore here the poem's anatomization of this liminal territory, for I argue that the interface between body and mind (or soul), what some early moderns termed the subtle body, and between the individual and the communal context, is one of the poem's animating ideas.[7] This interface is, I claim, manifested in the poem's quite remarkable attention to the array of sensory experience: it describes in vivid perceptual detail Samson's imaging of the dark prison of his blindness, Dalila's seductive fragrance, and the vulnerability and acuity of the acoustic organs, as Samson attempts to 'fence' his ears against Dalila's sorceries (l. 937). Early in the poem, for instance, Samson's lament for his lost sight poignantly contrasts the dissipation of touch throughout the surface of the body with the contraction of vision, suspended in the vulnerable optical organs:

> why was the sight
> To such a tender ball as the eye confined?
> So obvious and so easy to be quenched,
> And not as feeling through all parts diffused
> That she might look at will through every pore? (ll. 93–7)

The distribution of the haptic sense throughout the organ of the skin captures the ubiquitous corporeal scattering associated with early modern representations of touch: tactility is said to be everywhere and nowhere, for unlike the other senses, it is not

---

[3] Stanley Fish, 'Spectacle and Evidence in *Samson Agonistes*', *Critical Inquiry*, 15 (1989), 556–86.

[4] Sharon Achinstein, '*Samson Agonistes* and the Drama of Dissent', *Milton Studies*, 32 (1997), 133–57.

[5] Victoria Kahn, *Wayward Contracts: The Crisis of Obligation in England, 1640–1674* (Princeton, 2004).

[6] Recent interpretations of *Samson Agonistes* enlarge the political dimensions of the play's violence through analogies with the present. In a now vigorously debated essay, John Carey likened Samson's demolition of the temple and the ensuing massacre of the Philistines to the hijackers' destruction of the World Trade Center ('A Work in Praise of Terrorism? September 11 and *Samson Agonistes*', *Times Literary Supplement*, 6 September 2002, pp. 15–16). For a useful analysis of political partisanship and the poem's interpretative tradition, see Feisal G. Mohamed, 'Confronting Religious Violence: Milton's *Samson Agonistes*', *Publications of the Modern Language Association*, 120 (2005), 327–40.

[7] The subtle body has a complex history that derives from Platonic, Neoplatonic, gnostic, alchemical, and medical traditions. G. R. S. Mead, an influential member of the Theosophical Society, explains the genesis of this idea in philosophical thought in *The Doctrine of the Subtle Body in Western Tradition: An Outline of what the Philosophers Thought and Christians Taught on the Subject* (1919). See also D. P. Walker, 'The Astral Body in Renaissance Medicine', *Journal of the Warburg and Courtauld Institutes*, 12 (1958), 119–33.

confined to a discrete organ.[8] The 'quenched' eye is in this optative moment diverted into a synaesthetic register, as if touch could install an eye in every pore, as if the sheath of skin that bounds the body could become an Argus-eyed instrument of seeing.

Samson's phenomenological experience of his physicality is revealed through the play's fascination with the senses, its use of sensory language, and its depiction of the passions, figurations that simultaneously chart the boundary between human subjects and the world they inhabit. The border between the self and the social community is the domain of ethics and politics, influentially explored by Aristotle in the *Nicomachean Ethics*.[9] Aristotle's writings on the senses in *De anima* and *De sensu et sensibilibus* was central to early modern understanding of sensory experience, and in Book 3 of the *Nicomachean Ethics*, Aristotle links emotion and the senses in his discussion of temperance and voluntary action, a connection that is, as we shall see, crucial to *Samson Agonistes*. Milton's understanding of sensory and passional experience situates *Samson* within seventeenth-century debates about the physiology of sensation and emotion, controversies that reveal the nature of the poem's preoccupation with agency, suffering, and the ethical implications of suicide.

The English anatomist Helkiah Crooke called the senses 'intelligencers between the body and the soule'.[10] Cesare Ripa's emblem of a spy in his *Iconologia* joins the political aspect of espionage with the sensory faculties; the cloak that envelops his figure of the intelligencer is inscribed with eyes, ears, and tongues, and the wings on the spy's heel link him to Hermes, messenger, go-between, and interpreter.[11] Sensation marks the interface between the body and the world, the moment when the organs of sensibility receive and interpret environmental signals. Early modern philosophers and physicians were fascinated by the relationship between the senses and affect, a conjunction that was central to their understanding of human subjectivity. The linkage was theorized by René Descartes in his 1649 treatise *The Passions of the Soul* in ways that offer fresh understanding not only of Milton's own figuring of sensory and passional experience in *Samson Agonistes*, but also of the relationships among epistemology, faith, and ethical action on the one hand, and riddling and prophetic language on the other. If phenomenology relies on the recognition that all human knowing is embodied and that the apprehension of corporeal knowing entails a radical dissolution of the distinction between the perceiving subject and the

---

[8] Phineas Fletcher sums up this paradox: '*Tactus*... [h]ath his abode in none, yet every place' (*The Purple Island*, in *Giles and Phineas Fletcher: Poetical Works*, ed. Fredrick S. Boas (Cambridge, 1909), v. 55).

[9] For a discussion of the passions and the *Nicomachean Ethics* in *Samson Agonistes*, see Richard DuRocher, 'Samson's "Rousing Motions": What They Are, How They Work, and Why They Matter', *Literature Compass*, 3 (2006), 453–69.

[10] Helkiah Crooke, *Mikrokosmographia. A Description of the Body of Man. Together with the Controversies thereto Belonging. Collected and Translated out of all the Best Authors of Anatomy, Especially out of Gasper Bauhinus and Andreas Laurentius* (1615), 6. I have silently modernized i, j, u, v, and long s, and expanded contractions.

[11] Cæsar Ripa, *Iconologia: Or, Moral Emblems* (1709), fig. 290. Isaac Oliver immortalized the iconography of political and sensory espionage in his representation of Elizabeth I in the so-called 'Rainbow Portrait', depicting the queen's cloak strewn with disembodied eyes and ears, emblems of her visual and acoustic vigilance.

perceived object, recent work in historical phenomenology recognizes that the nature of that epistemological incarnation is intimately anchored in history.[12] *Samson Agonistes*, a poem suffused with descriptions of sensory experience, yields especially well to this approach, particularly in its linkage of the epistemological and sensory-psychic registers with ethical considerations and their contextualization in social and historical registers. The poem evokes a series of speculations: how are the data of the senses distilled into understanding? How are the senses, like the play's political spies, capable of perverting and distorting truth? How do prophecy and riddles, God's inscrutable language, manifest themselves in 'incorporate' form and make themselves accessible to human apprehension and understanding? In what ways are the senses and passions faculties of agency? And finally, how does the tragedy itself draw on a language of the senses and the passions in order to engage the reader in its imaginative work?

I

Samson Agonistes is a drama that was never meant to be performed. Although Milton invokes Aristotle on tragedy and filiates his 'dramatic poem' with the classical precedents of Euripides, Sophocles, and Aeschylus, he never intended it for the stage. Instead, the dramatic action is compressed, distilled through Samson's psychological and physiological experience, a corporeal trajectory that is theorized in two ways in Milton's brief introduction to the poem. First, when he cites Aristotle's definition of tragedy, Milton alters a crucial word: if tragedy's power operates 'by raising pity and fear, or terror, to purge the mind of those and such like passions', Milton says, it does so by 'tempering' and 'reducing' 'them to just measure with a kind of delight, stirr'd up by reading or seeing those well imitated'. Whereas in the *Poetics*, Aristotle says 'actions well imitated', Milton substitutes 'passions', a word that is, as we shall see, central to the 'action' of the drama (*CSP*, 341). Indeed, as I will argue, passion *is* the action.[13] Milton reveals this transmutation of emotion in his description of passional homeopathy, where we can see the process of interiorization

---

[12] For the philosophical background, see Maurice Merleau-Ponty, *The Primacy of Perception*, ed. James M. Edie (Evanston, Ill., 1964) and *Phenomenology of Perception*, trans. Colin Smith (1945; repr. 2002). Historical phenomenology in the early modern period is exemplified by such works as Bruce R. Smith's 'Mouthpieces: Native American Voices in Thomas Harriot's *True and Brief Report of . . . Virginia*, Gaspar Pérez de Villagrá's *Historia de la Nueva México*, and John Smith's *General History of Virginia*', *New Literary History*, 32 (2001), 501–17, and Gail Kern Paster's *Humoring the Body: Emotions and the Shakespearean Stage* (Chicago, 2004).

[13] This claim is closely aligned with Victoria Kahn's persuasive analysis of contract theory and *Samson Agonistes*. She suggests that Milton's poem is 'about the power of mimesis or representation to turn passion into action' (*Wayward Contracts*, 272), but whereas her emphasis is on the passions and political dimension of the aesthetic, my own focus is on sensible ethics and the phenomenology of the passions.

at work. He likens tragedy to medicine: 'for so in Physic things of melancholic hue and quality are us'd against melancholy, sowr against sowr, salt to remove salt humours'. By extension, the representation of the passions can effect an Aristotelian catharsis, purging the listeners or readers of the very emotions that are depicted. Milton may well have known Antonio Minturno's *Arte poetica*, for the Italian critic also joins homeopathic principles with Aristotle's theory of tragedy. Victoria Kahn suggests that Milton differs from Minturno, however, for whereas Minturno argues that pity and fear can purge and moderate the passions in general, Milton insists on the specifically mimetic and aesthetic nature of catharsis.[14] Milton develops this kernel of theory in great detail in *Samson Agonistes*. The extraordinary concentration in the tragedy on sensory experience is central to this purgation of the passions because the senses are central to aesthetic experience. The poem repeatedly foregrounds the reception of sensation as a process that is as actively interpretative as it is evocative of the passions.

Passion is a word with powerful etymological resonances. Derived from the Latin *patior*, to suffer, which is in turn a translation of the Greek *pathos*, it evokes emotional experience, a condition of intense affective receptivity. The singular form would have elicited for Milton's readers the passion of Christ, a natural association both because Samson was a typological precursor of Christ, and because the poem was bound together with *Paradise Regained* in the 1671 edition.[15] Passion's cognate, pathology, propels the idea of suffering into a medical context, apparent in such descriptions of Samson's grief as the 'tumors of a troubl'd mind' (l. 185), as a 'lingring disease', and as 'wounds immedicable' that 'Ranckle, and fester, and gangrene, / To black mortifica-tion' (ll. 618–22). These designations of pain shuttle between the body and the mind: 'mortification' suggests the gangrenous necrosis of flesh, as well as eliciting the active subjection of the senses and the passions cultivated by ascetic religious practice. 'Black' inevitably calls up the constellation of physiological and psychologi-cal symptoms associated with melancholy and a surfeit of black bile.[16] In addition to signifying extreme emotion in the seventeenth century, passion also denoted gram-matical passivity, the syntactical position of being acted upon (*OED*, III. 11a). Suffering or passion thus encodes an economy of subject and object, a reciprocal ligature of agency and reception, a subordination of the object to the force exerted upon it. The convergence of the medical and the grammatical meanings of passivity is expressed in Milton's iterative use of the word 'patient', a term employed both to describe Samson's tribulations and a designation for the virtue of patience, the ability

---

[14] *Wayward Contracts*, 271–2.

[15] For an account of typological controversies and *Samson Agonistes*, see Lynn Veach Sadler, 'Regeneration and Typology: *Samson Agonistes* and its Relation to *De Doctrina Christiana, Paradise Lost,* and *Paradise Regained*', *Studies in English Literature, 1500–1900*, 12 (1972), 141–56.

[16] Important recent studies of early modern melancholy include Giorgio Agamben, *Stanzas: Word and Phantasm in Western Culture*, trans. Ronald L. Martinez (Minneapolis, 1993); Douglas Trevor, *The Poetics of Melancholy in Early Modern England* (Cambridge, 2004), and Juliana Schiesari, *The Gendering of Melancholia: Feminism, Psychoanalysis, and the Symbolics of Loss in Renaissance Literature* (Ithaca, N.Y., 1992).

to sustain pain and hardship: the Chorus extols 'patience as the truest fortitude' (l. 654), reminding us that 'patience is more oft the exercise / Of Saints, the trial of their fortitude' (ll. 1287–8). Samson berates Dalila for trying to ascertain 'how far urged his patience bears' (l. 755), and the messenger tells at the end of the poem how the Philistine guards led Samson 'patient but undaunted' to the temple (l. 1623). Patience is the art of endurance, the capacity to submit, to bear passively, as Milton also reminds us in his sonnet on his blindness ('They also serve who only stand and wait'). The Chorus's formulation couples ostensibly oxymoronic terms (glossing patience as 'fortitude', a word whose derivation designates physical strength), revealing the poem's paradoxical purpose to convert one into the other, passive suffering into moral strength.[17]

This conception of heroism is, according to Mary Beth Rose, a specifically seven-teenth-century phenomenon that is aligned with the division of private and public spheres. Where ideals of heroism were conventionally associated with war, politics, and public life, she follows Max Weber and Norbert Elias in tracing the social and economic changes that render the figure of the heroic warrior in the Renaissance both residual and elegiac. She identifies an important counter-discourse, exemplified by Milton's Samson, that valorizes a private, inner heroism based on endurance rather than military exploit or conquest, a kind of fortitude that is feminized and linked to the social subordination of slavery.[18] Samson initially laments his loss of physical strength, a power that '[m]ight have subdued the earth' (l. 174), and he equates his vulnerability with Dalila's feminine frailty: 'Let weakness then with weakness come to parle' (l. 785), he tells her bitterly. The words Milton chooses to depict Samson's dispossession—'blind, disheartened, shamed, dishonoured, quelled' (l. 563)—are negative descriptors that systematically erase sight and extinguish hope and honour. The transformation of weakness into potency, of passion into action, expresses itself through a linguistic formulation: the messenger's response to Manoa's dawning comprehension of Samson's suicide as 'at variance with himself' invokes both passive and active voices: 'Inevitable cause / At once both to destroy and be destroyed' (l. 1587). The issues of agency that lie at the heart of the poem are expressed in Milton's representation of the senses, for they are cognate with the early modern debates on the activity and passivity of perception. The echo of 'destroy' first as a verb whose object is the Philistines and then as a passive form in which the consequence of his feat rebounds upon Samson superimposes the gram-matical forms, epitomizing Samson's strength of agency even as he simultaneously becomes the object of his own predicate.

The questions of agency and receptivity that are epitomized by Samson's suicide feature centrally in the philosophical and physiological discussion of sensory

---

[17] John Arthos makes a similar point in 'Milton and the Passions: A Study of *Samson Agonistes*', *Modern Philology*, 69 (1972), 209–21 at 213.

[18] Mary Beth Rose, *Gender and Heroism in Early Modern Literature* (Chicago, 2002). See also Mary Nyquist's important essay on gender in *Samson Agonistes*, 'Textual Overlapping and Dalilah's Harlot-Lap', in Patricia Parker and David Quint (eds.), *Literary Theory/Renaissance Texts* (Baltimore, 1986), 341–72.

perception which begins with Plato and Aristotle.[19] The sixteenth-century Paduan anatomist Julius Casserius Placentinus summarized this debate in his treatise on the senses, which was translated by Helkiah Crooke in his massive vernacular anatomy of 1615, *Mikrocosmographia*. Does sensation occur because the organ of sense acts upon an object, or is the object itself the agent, making the sense organ merely a passive receptor? Aristotle maintained in *De anima* and *De sensu*, Placentinus tells us, that the act of sensation is produced both by the sensory faculty and by the sensible object, which '*excite and provoke the senses into action*' (Crooke, *Mikrokosmographia*, 657). According to Aristotle, a sensation such as sound originates in the external world, through such actions as the striking of hard objects together, and the ear then receives this auditory perception through the medium of air.[20] The organ of sense in this formulation is not simply the recipient of the action, but must be instead a complex mixture of action and reception, a dialectical interplay between the subject and the ambient world. When Samson hears his friends, the play's Chorus, approach, he provides us with a kind of auditory anatomy: 'I hear the sound of words, thir sense the air / Dissolves unjointed e're it reach my ear' (ll. 176–7). Milton understands the air as a medium that transports auditory noise, and the disruption of this process, the acoustic 'unjointing' of sound, is marked by the disarticulation of its passage and reception as raw auditory data.[21] It is as if the moment of sensible reception had been slowed down or suspended, caught in its passage and as yet unfiltered by the *sensus communis*, the central organ that processes all sensation. The sound Samson hears is literally inarticulate, for it is audible as noise but not comprehensible as the discrete, jointed parts that make up interpretable speech. Samson's intensified sense of sound may paradoxically derive from his loss of sight, a sensory rechannelling, just as Milton's blindness could have heightened his remaining four senses and his acute understanding of sensory perception. Milton's dissection of the acoustic in *Comus* is pertinent here: the lady reflexively analyses the noises she hears (ll. 170–6), and Comus seems to hear through his feet rather than his ears, feeling the Lady's approach rather than hearing it (ll. 145–6). The wood and its noises in the masque reproduce the ear's mazes, a progressive entry through what Placentinus calls the 'winding burroughs', the 'Labyrinth', the 'Snaile-shell' to the 'Auditory nerve', which conveys sound 'unto the common Sense as unto his Censor and Judge' (Crooke, *Mikrokosmographia*, 696).

---

[19] George F. Butler provides an analysis of early modern positions on suicide and a comparison of the similarities between Milton's *Samson Agonistes* and John Donne's treatment of Samson in *Biathanatos* in 'Donne's *Biathanatos* and *Samson Agonistes*: Ambivalence and Ambiguity', *Milton Studies*, 34 (1997), 199–219.

[20] Aristotle, *De anima*, in *Aristotle: On the Soul, Parva Naturalia, On Breath*, trans. W. S. Hett (Cambridge, Mass., 1936; repr. 1995), 419^b–420^b.

[21] For a powerful analysis of the 'acoustic mystery' at the end of the play and its relationship to the faculty of personal and political memory, see Sharon Achinstein, '*Samson Agonistes* and the Politics of Memory', in Mark R. Kelly and Joseph Wittreich (eds.), *Altering Eyes: New Perspectives on* Samson Agonistes (Newark, N.J., 2002), 168–91. Bruce R. Smith's magisterial study, *The Acoustic World of Early Modern England: Attending to the O-Factor* (Chicago, 1999), offers a rich survey of acoustic life, particularly his chapter 'Re: Membering' for his analysis of the links between language, bodies, and sound.

Samson's description of hearing is subtended by early modern theories of acoustic sensation that oppose and complicate the materialist and mechanist model that Hobbes proposes in *Leviathan*, where external objects pressing on the sensory organs convey this pressure by the mediation of 'nerves and strings' in order to produce 'sense'.[22] Placentinus's discussion of sensation offers a physiology of feeling that links the senses to the passions: the action of the senses is, he says, '*a motien through a body which suffers in the Sensation*' (Crooke, *Mikrokosmographia*, 656). Suffering turns out to be reciprocal, not unlike Merleau-Ponty's discussion of mutual touching, where to touch is also to be touched.[23] For Crooke and Placentinus, sensation happens when the sense is converted into the nature of the sensible thing, that is, through an alteration.[24] The sensible object changes the faculty of sensation, transforming it to its own nature, and it is this conversion of essence that causes suffering. In *Samson Agonistes*, the sensory register of feeling is for Samson a literal suffering in which physical pain is translated into contiguous or analogous melancholy passion:

> O that torment should not be confin'd
> To the bodies wounds and sores
> With maladies innumerable
> In heart, head, brest, and reins;
> But must secret passage find
> To th' inmost mind,
> There exercise all his fierce accidents,
> And on her purest spirits prey,
> As on entrails, joints, and limbs,
> With answerable pains, but more intense,
> Though void of corporal sense. (ll. 606–16)

The passage traces the metaphorical movement from outward to inward and back, from physiological agony to psychic suffering to bodily affliction. The trajectory is 'answerable', that is, body and mind are knit together through the action of the senses; although 'void of corporal sense', Samson borrows the language of fleshly sensation to portray a suffering that exceeds sensory experience, a comparison that appropriates and surpasses the somatic register even as it seems to discard it. While Samson ostensibly rails against a mental pain more debilitating than the physical ailments he so graphically describes, the analogies couple inner and outer as answerable versions of each other, mutually implicated in origin and effect.

The sensitive faculties occupied the space that Milton maps through these metaphorical exchanges between body and spirit, a domain that early modern physicians designated as the subtle body. Helkiah Crooke, following Hippocrates, Galen, and the Stoics, defined this body as a spirit or 'intermediate Nature' by which 'through a

---

[22] Thomas Hobbes, *Leviathan*, ed. G. A. J. Rogers and Karl Scuhmann (Bristol, 2003), 13–14.

[23] *Phenomenology of Perception*, 106.

[24] For a discussion of passion and alteration, see Timothy Hampton, 'Strange Alteration: Physiology and Psychology from Galen to Rabelais', in Gail Kern Paster, Katherine Rowe, and Mary Floyd-Wilson (eds.), *Reading the Early Modern Passions: Essays in the Cultural History of Emotion* (Philadelphia, 2004), 272–93.

stronge though not indissoluble bonde the Divine soule might be tyed to the bodie of Earth' (Crooke, *Mikrokosmographia*, 173–4). Whereas some have designated this medium as an 'Aetheriall' or even astral body, Crooke insisted that these spirits are rather a '*subtle or thinne body always moveable, engendred of blood and vapour, and the vehicle or carriage of the Faculties of the soule*' (p. 174).[25] Although Crooke makes it clear that this threshold body is corporeal, it is, he asserts, composed of the 'subtillest substance', vapours that move through secret channels in the body. Milton associated these spirits with the breath that God inspires into human beings, a life principle that is manifested in the 'vital or sensitive or rational faculty, or some action or affection belonging to them' (*CPW*, vi. 317). He claims that, far from being separable, body and soul are contiguous, composed as they are of the same substance. Milton's monism, what Stephen Fallon terms his animist materialism, is thus deeply sensible.[26] Its foundation is Aristotle's conception of the tripartite soul, for the 'breath of life mentioned in Genesis' is not, Milton says in *Christian Doctrine*, 'a part of the divine essence'. Rather, he cites 1 Corinthians 15: 45 as his authority, glossing the 'soul' as 'animal', since it has all the attributes assigned in common to the body, such as touch. If one speaks of the body as a 'merely physical trunk', Milton asserts, 'then the "soul" may mean either the spirit or its secondary faculties, such as the vital or sensitive faculty' (vi. 318). As Raphael explains to Adam in his discourse on angelic digestion in *Paradise Lost*, intelligential and rational substance contains all the lower faculties of sense 'whereby they hear, see, smell, touch, taste / Tasting concoct, digest, assimilate, / And corporeal to incorporeal turn' (v. 410–13). The senses operate at the interface of the corporeal and the incorporeal for Milton, with taste, a form of touch, here providing the assimilative linkage that joins body and spirit.

As Aristotle recognized in *De anima* and *Nicomachean Ethics*, sensation is closely tied to the passions. Sensation produces pleasure and pain, and the repetition of these experiences engender 'feelings', such as desire or fear.[27] Thomas Wright in his 1601 treatise *Passions of the Mind* calls the passions and the senses 'two naughty servants', for the passions are 'drowned in corporall organs and instruments, as well as sense'.[28] The passions, aided by their 'cousin german', the senses, are the body's rebels, mutinous forces that must be controlled by the will and reason. It is this description of the passions, familiar from scholastic and Stoic doctrine, that

---

[25] D. P. Walker usefully distinguishes the tradition of medical spirits from the Neoplatonic astral body in 'The Astral Body in Renaissance Medicine'.

[26] Stephen M. Fallon, *Milton among the Philosophers: Poetry and Materialism in Seventeenth-Century England* (Ithaca, N.Y., 1991).

[27] Aristotle, *Nicomachean Ethics*, Book 2; *De anima*, 3. 6–12.

[28] Thomas Wright, *The Passions of the Mind* (1601), 15–16. Indeed, Wright suggests that since the time of our infancy and childhood, the senses have been 'joint-friends' with the passions: 'whatsoever delighted sense, pleased the passions; and whosoever was hurtfull to the one, was an enemy to the other; and so, by long agreement and familaritie, the passions had so engaged themselves to sense, and with such bondes and seales of sensuall habites confirmed their friendship, that as soone as reason came to possession of her kingdome, they beganne presently to make rebellions for right reason oftentimes deprived sense of those pleasures he had of long time enjoyed'.

Descartes's book, *The Passions of the Soul,* published a few weeks before his death in 1649, begins to challenge. Descartes is known as the proponent of a dualist metaphysics, who with his *cogito ergo sum* cleft the body and mind, dividing substance into *res cogitans,* 'thinking substance', and *res extensa,* 'extended substance', but scholars have more recently begun to reassess the definitiveness of that rupture.[29] *The Passions of the Soul* is instrumental to that revision because it provides a fundamentally different conception of the passions. Whereas earlier understandings of Descartes centred on *The Discourse of Method* and the *Meditations,* his later work reintroduces the body, no longer alienated and mechanized, as the basis of an ethics that is grounded in a passional and sensible corporeality.[30] When Milton invokes Cartesian dualism in *Paradise Lost,* it is associated with Satan's infernal world. Satan becomes a kind of parody of *res cogitans,* imprisoned within an unalterable mind that cannot change even when his physical circumstances do.[31] In *The Passions of the Soul* and in his posthumous work, *L'Homme,* Descartes theorizes what he understood to be the hinge between body and mind, the pineal gland, which contains the *sensus communis,*[32] the faculty that unifies and interprets sensation.[33] For Descartes, however, both sensation and affect are produced by the *sensus communis*; both emerge from corporeality, and the function of the communal faculty is to regulate the physiological and ethical aspects of passional and sensational experience. It is this later Cartesian theorization of the senses that animates Milton's anatomization of sensory experience in *Samson Agonistes.*

If sensation marks the boundary between the human subject and the world, ethics demarcates the border between the individual and the social or communal world. Ethics must work in concert with a 'medico-physiological' understanding of the body and the passions, and in *The Passions of the Soul* Descartes aims to provide just this knowledge. If shaping the passions is foundational for a Cartesian ethics, it is nevertheless a fundamentally different process from the controlling effort advocated by

[29] See Susan James, *Passion and Action: The Emotions in Seventeenth-Century Philosophy* (Oxford, 1997) and Erec R. Koch, 'Cartesian Corporeality and (Aesth)Ethics', *Publications of the Modern Language Association,* 121 (2006), 405–20. Luce Irigaray makes Descartes's theorization of wonder the foundation of her feminist ethics, a radically different response from her scathing critique of him in *Speculum of the Other Woman* (see Elizabeth D. Harvey, ' "Mutuall Elements": Irigaray's Donne', in Theresa Krier and Elizabeth D. Harvey (eds.), *Luce Irigaray and Premodern Culture: Thresholds of History* (2004), 66–87).

[30] *The Passions of the Soul* is the book that emerged from Descartes's 1643–9 correspondence with Elisabeth of Bohemia. The epistolary exchange began as a conversation about the metaphysics of mind and body, but it ultimately focused on the crucial point of contact between soma and mental faculty, the passions. The purpose of the correspondence was both philosophical and therapeutic, for Descartes sought to find a cure that would alleviate Elisabeth's melancholic suffering. The letters and *The Passions of the Soul* thus have a practical purpose that not only anatomizes but also seeks to regulate passional pathology.

[31] Fallon, *Milton Among the Philosophers,* 203–4.

[32] According to Aristotle, this common sensibility harmonizes sensation, distilling such attributes as colour, size, and distance, and although the sensitive faculty subsequently attributes pleasure or pain to these sensory data, he does not locate the passions in this unifying faculty (Koch, 'Cartesian Corporeality', 407).

[33] René Descartes, *The Passions of the Soul,* trans. Stephen Voss (Indianapolis, Ind., 1989), art. 31–5.

Stoicism.[34] Whereas the Stoics advocated the cultivation of *apatheia* or apathy, the banishing of passionate feeling, Descartes is closer in *The Passions of the Soul* to an Augustinian position that redirects the passions towards decorous ends.[35] What is especially pertinent for my purposes in this Cartesian account of the passions is the intricate relationship between the senses and the passions, and therefore the role that the senses might play in altering or regulating the passions. The senses distinguish objects that are pleasurable or painful, but the passions saturate those sensory judgements with emotional value, prolonging the effect of sensory judgement.[36] The passions thus extend sensation into imagination and memory, faculties that store and recycle sensory experience. One of the examples that Descartes gives for intervention in the passions by means of the senses is theatre: 'one naturally takes pleasure in feeling moved to all sorts of Passions, even Sadness and Hatred, when those passions are caused only by the unusual adventures one sees represented on a stage . . . which, not being able to harm us in any way, seem to titillate our soul in affecting it' (*The Passions of the Soul*, art. 94). *Samson Agonistes* offers an analogous use of the passions, one that works through the explicit mediation of the senses, a cultivation of their imaginative or aesthetic effects for the purpose of producing ethical behaviour through art.

II

I want now to return to *Samson Agonistes* in order to gauge how the reader is implicated in the sensory and passional experience of the tragedy. Let us begin with the sensory experience of the poem, a movement in which the poem draws its reader into the 'vacant interlunar' cave of Samson's blindness. It does so by refusing to provide what it seems to offer. That is, it proclaims itself to be a tragic drama, but it is a tragedy that insists on the cultivation of the reader's imaginative evocation of the senses, for the sensory satisfaction that performance promises is never given. The poem substitutes instead a plethora of sensory effects that call on the reader's imagination. The play opens with touch, the faculty that Aristotle and Placentinus proclaimed was fundamental to life itself. As Samson makes his way from the common prison, he says to his invisible companion: 'lend thy guiding hand / To

---

[34] Descartes begins with an intellectual inventory of the passions, which he provides in *The Passions of the Soul*; he subsequently advocates a channelling, an imaginative and intellectual redirection that produces desirable kinds of social and ethical behaviour: 'even those who have the weakest souls could acquire a quite absolute dominion over all their passions if one employed enough skill in training and guiding them' (*The Passions of the Soul*, art. 50).

[35] See Michael Schoenfeldt, '"Commotion Strange": Passion in *Paradise Lost*', in Paster et al. (eds.), *Reading the Early Modern Passions*, 43–67 at 53.

[36] David Summers has an excellent discussion of this point in '*Cogito* Embodied: Force and Counterforce in René Descartes's *Les passions de l'âme*', in Richard Meyer (ed.), *Representing the Passions: Histories, Bodies, Visions* (Los Angeles, 2003), 13–36 at 16–18.

these dark steps, a little further on'. The escort's hand is a synecdoche for touch, which here substitutes for Samson's extinguished eyes:

> For yonder bank hath choice of sun or shade,
> There I am wont to sit, when any chance
> Relieves me from my task of servile toil,
> Daily in the common Prison else enjoined me,
> Where I a prisoner chained, scarce freely draw
> The air imprisoned also, close and damp,
> Unwholesome draught: but here I feel amends,
> The breath of heaven fresh blowing, pure and sweet,
> With day-spring born; here leave me to respire. (ll. 1–11)

The air in the prison was 'close and damp', an 'unwholesome draught', whereas 'yonder bank' allows Samson both choice of sun or shade and the 'breath of heaven fresh blowing, pure and sweet' (l. 10). In the first eleven lines of the poem, the reader comes to inhabit an imaginative world of sensory deprivation that is Samson's blindness. The poem immediately compensates, for just as the other senses intensify in a blind person, augmenting their powers to recompense the loss of sight, so does the poem's language insist on alternative sensory experience.[37] We are made to *feel* rather than see the difference between sun and shade—a distinction that becomes a function of temperature rather than light—just as we are also made to smell and sense the difference between the fetid air of the prison and the fragrant breeze of the bank.

When at the beginning of the poem, Samson bids his unseen guide leave him, he stages a retirement from the 'popular noise', a progressive retreat to solitude, to this 'unfrequented place', and then to the innerness of his mind. Unlike the annihilating pastoral consciousness of Marvell's 'The Garden', Samson's mind turns out to be Spenser's buzzing chamber of imagination. No sooner is he alone than his restless thoughts 'like a deadly swarm / Of hornets armed' 'rush upon [him] thronging' (ll. 19–21). Like the Son in *Paradise Regained* whose 'multitude of thoughts' (i. 196–7) swarm him, Samson's anguish afflicts him with a kind of restless sensory babble. The image of the mind as teeming with thought cannot but recall Spenser's ventricle of imagination in *The Faerie Queene*. Phantastes, the personification of imagination, presides over the chamber; he secures the connection between the profusion of past and present sense impressions and the mind's imaginative creation. His room, painted with 'sundry colours' on which 'were writ / Infinite shapes of things' fashioned by fantasy, is filled with buzzing flies that 'encombred all mens eares and eyes', like swarms of bees about 'their hives with honny'.[38] The stanzas describing Phantastes's chamber are dense with sensory images: the room is drenched in colour, crowded with images and idle thoughts, and thronged with buzzing flies that accost the senses. Imagination is, as Hobbes memorably said, 'nothing but decaying sense',

---

[37] See Susannah B. Mintz, 'Dalila's Touch: Disability and Recognition in *Samson Agonistes*', *Milton Studies*, 40 (2002), 150–80, for an analysis of Samson's blindness as sensory deprivation.

[38] Edmund Spenser, *The Faerie Queene*, ed. Thomas P. Roche, Jr. (New Haven, 1981), II. ix. 50–1.

a formulation that draws on a long tradition of understanding imagination as a collection of sense impressions, imprints of sensible experience that form a residue in the mind and provide the material that feeds the imagination (*Leviathan*, 16). The vividness of these figurations exemplifies both the way the senses are besieged by unedited sensory information and the way the poetic imagination can create the illusion of sensory data through the vestigial but phantasmatic residue of these impressions. Samson's mind, too, is assaulted by old sense impressions: memories of the prophecies at his birth and his consecration as a Nazarite, when, endowed with 'heav'n-gifted strength', he was destined by God for 'great exploits' (ll. 33, 36). He 'suffers' sensation in ways that augment and literalize Placentinus's description of sensory reception. The senses and the passions are at the beginning of the poem both contiguous and disordered, and it is only at the end that suffering as sensation is conjoined with passion and action and, as Descartes advocates, trained and guided (*The Passions of the Soul*, art. 50).

As his lament for his lost sight makes clear, Samson is afflicted with the passion of sadness, what Descartes classifies as one of the six primitive passions (*The Passions of the Soul*, art. 69):

> O dark, dark, dark, amid the blaze of noon,
> Irrecoverably dark, total eclipse
> Without all hope of day!
> O first created beam, and thou great word,
> Let there be light, and light was over all;
> Why am I thus bereaved thy prime decree?
> The Sun to me is dark
> And silent as the moon,
> When she deserts the night
> Hid in her vacant interlunar cave. (ll. 80–9)

Samson's language invokes a rhetoric of erasure, a negative creation. If God's generation of light was his 'prime decree', the withdrawal of that light undoes creation, extinguishing both heavenly orbs, and banishing them to the dark interval between moons. The movement is not only a darkening and a silencing, but it is also a diminution of the universe to human size, a shrinkage of the 'vacant interlunar' cave to Samson's empty eye sockets. 'Exiled from light' (l. 97), Samson's body becomes his grave and prison, a metonymic conversion of his incarceration at Gaza, a body without its primary sensory conduit to the world:

> Which shall I first bewail,
> Thy bondage or lost sight,
> Prison within prison
> Inseparably dark?
> Thou art become (O worst imprisonment!)
> The dungeon of they self; thy soul
> (Which men enjoying sight oft without cause complain)
> Imprisoned now indeed,
> In real darkness of the body dwells,

> Shut up from outward light
> To incorporate with gloomy night;
> For inward light alas
> Puts forth no visual beam. (ll. 151–64)

This last phrase, 'puts forth no visual beam', refers to theories of extramission (in which rays of light emanate from the eye and actively engage the objects of vision), which were advocated by Plato, rejected by Aristotle, and then influentially championed by Galen and others. In this passage, the occlusion of the 'visual beam' has the effect of withdrawing Samson's sensory engagement with the world, a consequence that intensifies the multiple meanings of incorporate: to become unembodied, to be without substance; to copulate with night and thus to usher darkness into the body's interior; to seal up the soul within the dense materiality of the body. Samson's visual deprivation paradoxically intensifies the sensory aspects of the poem by heightening the importance of the other senses and engaging the reader through the very sensory faculty that has been extinguished in Samson; this strategy intensifies pathos and accentuates the vulnerability of the reader/viewer's eyes. Milton's representation of Samson's blindness as a 'prison within prison' filiates the body with a philosophical tradition, influentially inaugurated by Plato, of representing the fleshly body as a dungeon. Here, however, Milton alludes ironically, I would argue, to the *Phaedo*, the dialogue in which Phaedo visits Socrates in prison and witnesses Socrates' death, his liberation from the immurement of his body. Whereas in the *Phaedo* the senses collude in the body's somatic incarceration, fanning the passions through their delusive gathering of deceptive information, it is, by contrast, the loss of a sensory faculty, Samson's sight, that creates his dark confinement.[39] The senses and the passions have the potential to imprison, but they can also be the instruments of liberation, as they ultimately are for Samson and potentially for the readers of Milton's poem.

Milton uses the acoustic register in the poem not only to map theatrical onstage/ offstage space, but also to demarcate the body's boundaries. The ear is, after the already eradicated 'tender ball of th' eye' (l. 94), the most vulnerable sensory organ in the poem. Samson tells Dalila that he has learnt to 'fence his ear' against her 'sorceries', but his fortifications against her counterfeit 'Hyaena' voice replicate the imagery of the attack of the senses from Spenser's Castle of Alma. Dalila's own rhetoric is a parodic version of Samson's: she hints at the force that constrained her betrayal, offering to detail the 'assaults', the 'snares', the 'sieges' that 'girt [her] round' (ll. 845–6). Just as Maleger's rabblement stormed Alma's castle, so was Dalila encircled and overwhelmed by the 'magistrates / And princes', who came to her in person and 'Solicited, commanded, threatened, urged', 'Adjured', and 'pressed' her. The pile-up of verbs and enjambed lines enacts the urgency of their petitions for

---

[39] Plato, *Phaedo* in *The Collected Dialogues of Plato*, ed. Edith Hamilton and Huntington Cairns (Princeton, 1961), 66. Stephen Fallon suggests that we can trace a trajectory in Milton's work from the dualism of *Comus* to the monism of *Paradise Lost*, a trajectory that would support Milton's critique of the Platonic dualism in this passage (*Milton among the Philosophers*, 81).

betrayal. The Priest was not just 'behind', Dalila says, 'but ever at my ear' (l. 858). How was she to resist such 'powerful arguments', she asks piteously, to 'fence' her own ears (to borrow Samson's words) against their supplications? Dalila's account of how she was made into a tool of political infiltration replicates her own seductive besieging of Samson, an insinuation that conjoins the erotic and the political. She is sent to gather intelligence about the secret of Samson's strength, and her embodiment of sensory temptation aligns her with the early modern figuration of the senses as the body's spies. Sensation, particularly erotic sensation, accentuates the body's vulnerability, its inability to defend itself against sensory stimuli. It is fitting, therefore, that the two uses of the word 'spies' in the poem occur in the context of Samson's first marriage (ll. 386, 1197). At his wedding to the woman of Timna, Samson tells us that she was corrupted by the 'Spies' and 'Rivals' who sought the meaning of Samson's riddle: 'Out of the eater came forth meat, and out of the strong came forth sweetness.' A riddle contains hidden meaning that is wrapped in enigmatic language, and the signification of the conundrum eluded Samson's enemies until his wife bombarded him 'With blandished parleys, feminine assaults, / Tongue-batteries, she surceased not day nor night / To storm me over-watched, and wearied out' (ll. 403–5). The discourse of sensory attack here couples politics and sex; Samson's sensual indulgence, his inability to barricade himself against the assault of 'flattering prayers and sighs', causes him to betray his secret. Just as a riddle wraps meaning in obscure words, hiding its truth in opaque language, so is the secret of Samson's vigour hidden from Dalila. Dalila and Samson's first wife, the woman of Timna, extort the hidden heart of the riddle or secret through sexual and sensory sieges ('The secret wrested from me in her height / of nuptial love professed' (ll. 384–5)) and translate it into language. The mechanism of extraction in both cases is sensory infiltration.

Dalila is the character who most closely embodies the senses, not only because of the extraordinary array of sensory imagery associated with her, but also because she operates as a political intelligencer, a spy who moves between Samson and the Philistines and between Samson's outer, physical and private, psychic selves. Dalila's seductions are insidiously sensual. The Chorus describes her approach first as visual ('bedecked, ornate, and gay' (l. 712)), then olfactory ('An Amber sent of odorous perfume' (l. 720)), then auditory, with her cunning and seductive speech, and finally tactile, when she offers to approach and touch Samson's hand (l. 951). Samson's vehement response captures the alluring dangers of that contact: 'Not for thy life, lest fierce remembrance wake / My sudden rage to tear thee joint by joint' (ll. 952–3). But Dalila's most potent temptations are acoustic, for the arguments she makes, particularly her final pitch, stage powerful appeals to the senses:

> ... only what remains past cure
> Bear not too sensibly, nor still insist
> To afflict thy self in vain: though sight be lost,
> Life yet hath many solaces, enjoyed
> Where other senses want not their delights
> At home in leisure and domestic ease,
> Exempt from many a care and chance to which

Eyesight exposes daily men abroad.
I to the Lords will intercede, not doubting
Their favourable ear, that I may fetch thee
From forth this loathsom prison-house ... (ll. 912–22)

Her remedy for Samson's afflictions is a kind of domestic imprisonment, a cultivation of the remaining senses as compensatory solace, an exemption from the 'care and chance' of visual exposure by means of her strategic acoustic intervention ('favourable ear'). Her admonition to Samson to '[b]ear not too sensibly' his travails invokes the discourse of sensation as suffering and passion, but the leisured prison-house into which she promises to conduct him offers none of the release through sensation and passion that ultimately effects his apparent redemption at the end of the poem. The paradise that Dalila proposes is a shuttered world of sensory indulgence, an enslavement with 'dotage', as the Chorus puts it, a depravity of 'sense' (ll. 1041–2).

The Chorus images Samson's wives, and women in general, as similar to riddles: they initially seem 'all heavenly', 'under virgin veil', 'Soft, modest, meek, demure' (ll. 1035–6). Once 'joined', however, they become a 'cleaving mischief, and a 'thorn / Intestine' (ll. 1037–9). The word 'cleave', meaning at once 'to join' and also 'to separate', epitomizes the way Dalila insinuates herself into Samson's confidence and affection and then divides him from himself, his secret from his inner nature, making him, as he says, 'traitor to myself' (l. 401). Dalila's self-description, as 'importune / Of secrets' (l. 775), offers a potent connection with the sensory tradition that I have been tracing. The word and its variants are repeated seven times in the poem. The verb 'importune' means to solicit or annoy; as an adjective, it captures the insatiable curiosity and inquisitiveness attributed to the feminine sex. It is etymologically cognate with port and portal, suggesting the body's boundedness by gates or portals.[40] The iconography of the senses is rich in imagery of the five sensory portals, ranging from Spenser's five bulwarks in the Castle of Alma to 'five imaginary forts' of Marvell's 'Upon Appleton House' to the five gates of the senses that bound the city in Bartolomeo del Bene's philosophical dream poem *Civitas Veri sive Morum Mori* (1609), a text that refashions Aristotle's *Nicomachean Ethics*.[41] In Del Bene's poem, the soul is represented as a city, which can be entered by five portals or gateways. The incorporated soul animates the body or kingdom, a familiar image that sutures theories of government, the body politic, to philosophical and medical understandings of the somatic–psychic nexus, the body natural. In order to gather intelligence from the outer reaches of the kingdom, the prince dispatches sensory spies, and the ability to process this information determines his success in governing. Dalila, who depicts herself as enduring a sensory assault when the 'princes' and 'magistrates'

---

[40] The root of 'importune' links it to Portunus, the protector god of harbours. In addition to the imagery of the five sensory portals of the body that the word elicits, it may also evoke England's Cinque Ports, the five strategic harbours that provide access to the nation's body. Andrew Marvell makes exactly this connection in 'Upon Appleton House': 'But he preferred to the Cinque Ports / These five imaginary forts' (ll. 349–50).

[41] For discussions of this poem, see Frances A. Yates, *The French Academies of the Sixteenth Century* (1947), 111, and Bruce R. Smith, *The Acoustic World of Early Modern England*, 101–2.

solicit her aid, succumbs finally to arguments that privilege the public, civic, and religious good over private need (ll. 867–8). Her work as an intelligencer joins the sensory and political functions of espionage, an occupation that relies on the gathering of knowledge by means of a secret insinuation through the portals of the senses into the interior of a nation, a body, a mind.

Nowhere is the work of the senses more apparent than at the end of the poem. When Manoa hears a terrible noise, he asks, 'What hideous noise was that? / Horribly loud, unlike the former shout' (ll. 1509–10). The Chorus attempts to describe the sound, to give an interpretation of the sensory data: 'Noise call you it or universal groan / As if the whole inhabitation perish'd, / Blood, death, and deathful deeds are in that noise' (ll. 1510–13). As Manoa speaks with the Chorus, attempting to gloss the noise, they see a messenger running towards them. The Messenger's language is instructive, for it displays the marks of sensory and passional incoherence: 'The sight of this so horrid spectacle / Which erst my eyes beheld and yet behold; / For dire imagination still persues me' (ll. 1543–5). The force of the report that the messenger is about to give is emotionally intensified by its remove from the actual destruction of the temple, for it is filtered not only though the fragmented second-hand accounts that emerge in pieces, but through language saturated with sensory description that replicates and multiplies the horror of the event:

> Ah Manoa I refrain, too suddenly
> To utter what will come at last too soon;
> Lest evil tidings with too rude irruption
> Hitting thy aged ear should pierce too deep. (ll. 1565–8)

Milton's strategy of dispersal and fragmentation mimics the sensory confusion of the tragedy, piercing the ears of his readers and auditors in an act of sensible violence. This moment augments the illusion of theatricality, since it is spoken, not written, language that strikes or pierces the ear. Milton's attention to the potential violence of sensory reception evokes both the dramatic nature of the poem and the action the play imitates through his attention to the auditory, a conjuring of spectacle through the vividness of the acoustic register.

When the Philistines summon Samson, the Semichorus tells us, they are 'Drunk with Idolatry, drunk with Wine, / And fat regorged of bulls and goats' (ll. 1670–1). Like the ancients whom Placentinus chastises for becoming so 'ensnared with the allurement of their Senses' that they deserved to be branded 'with the ignominious Title of Epicurean Hogges' (Crooke, *Mikrokosmographia*, 646), the sensory indulgence of the Philistines brings about their own demise. Motivated by a 'spirit of frenzy', they 'call in haste for their destroyer', and thus 'unweetingly importuned / Their own destruction' (ll. 1675–81). The self-reflexivity of their command and the complicity in their own destruction echoes the depiction of Samson's final moment, 'At once both to destroy and be destroyed' (l. 1587). Significantly, the verb Milton uses to describe the Philistines' command is 'importune', a word associated with Dalila's solicitations. More importantly, the adverb 'unweetingly' suggests not only a lack of conscious knowledge, but it also carries within it the root of 'wit', a reference to the five wits or senses in general, or to 'wit' as one of the five internal senses, a term that often designated common wit or the *sensus communis*. Without this filter and guide, the Philistines are the target of their own sensory gratification, and it is thus not surprising to see that the ruin they invite upon themselves leaves them 'insensate', 'or to sense reprobate'. These terms figure the obliteration of their own sensibility, an inanimation, and a withdrawal or rejection by sensory experience. Struck with internal blindness, the Philistines exchange through a sensory chiasmus their faculty of vision, for although Samson's physical blindness remains, he is 'illuminated' with 'inward eyes' (l. 1689).

We often doubt what God's work seems to be, the Chorus pronounces, and although he frequently 'seems to hides his face', yet he 'unexpectedly returns' (ll. 1749–50). As Samson told Harapha earlier in the poem, the divine organs of sense are always accessible: 'Whose ear is ever open; and his eye / Gracious to readmit the suppliant' (1173–4). Although divine sensibility is unoccluded, the sensory faculties of human beings require training and guidance before they can be reliable sources of information. Like riddles, the senses, often in concert with the passions, are both dangerous and inscrutable. The spectators to the tragedy in Gaza have with 'new aquist' of 'true experience' spent their 'passion' (ll. 1755–8), a cathartic process that Descartes envisaged in *The Passions of the Soul*: just as hunting dogs can be trained to redirect their sensory responses, so might it be possible 'even for those who have the weakest souls . . . [to] acquire a quite absolute dominion over all their passions if one employed enough skill in training and guiding them' (*Passions of the Soul*, art. 50). *Samson Agonistes* cultivates the sensory perception of its readers in just this way, engaging the senses and the passions through the dramatic form, not to purge the emotions that are raised, but to 'temper' and 'reduce' them. Milton here activates the Latinate meaning of 'reduce' as an educative process, a leading or channelling of sensory and emotional turbulence towards the 'calm of mind' (l. 1758) that describes the spectators at Gaza, and by extension, Milton's readers. The poem is less an incitement to violence, then, than it is a homeopathic remedy, a poetic and dramatic method for guiding powerful feeling through the theatre of the mind into ethically responsible ways of being.

PART VIII

....

ASPECTS
OF INFLUENCE

....

CHAPTER 37

....

MILTON EPIC AND BUCOLIC: EMPIRE AND READINGS OF *PARADISE LOST*, 1667–1837

....

ANNE-JULIA ZWIERLEIN

INTRODUCTION: MILTON EPIC AND BUCOLIC

....

'Of Man's first disobedience . . . / Let nobler poets sing': The proem to James Hurdis's *The Village Curate* (1788), a long poem highly reliant in style and structure on *Paradise Lost*, ostentatiously opposes the humble subject matter of English country life to Milton's universal theme.[1] Hurdis, the vicar for the West Sussex village of Burpham (and in 1793 appointed Professor of Poetry at Oxford University), here offers a partly autobiographical description of the self-contented daily routines of a village curate. 'Attend[ing] the garden studious', the clergyman and his 'fair' are modelled on Milton's Adam and Eve in paradise. However, the poem is coloured by a postlapsarian awareness of the wider world: the pastoral idyll of the English countryside inhabited by this new version of the biblical pair is contrasted with 'all the wealth of Ind', but at the

---

[1] James Hurdis, *The Village Curate, a Poem* (1788), 1.

same time Adam and Eve enjoy whiling away long winter evenings reading travel writings and battle accounts—proudly tracing the voyage of Britain's 'thund'ring fleets' to, precisely, 'farthest Ind' (*The Village Curate*, 74, 1, 121–2). The sense of snug safety in an English rural enclave is heightened by exciting reading matter provided by expanding British imperial horizons. Even the curate's handling of his library has militaristic overtones: he is shown proudly surveying his numerous volumes, like their 'commander, like the vanquish'd fiend, / Out-cast of heav'n, [who] oft thro' their armed files / Darts an experience'd eye, and feels his heart / Distend with pride to be their only chief' (*The Village Curate*, 7). This is taken nearly verbatim from Milton's description of Satan, the 'mighty chief', surveying his armed forces in hell. A private space, a country clergyman's library, thus becomes political, and Miltonic language turns Hurdis's curate into a military commander, even a Satanic one, in slippers—an apt if somewhat ambiguous image of British bourgeois support of the empire.[2]

Throughout Hurdis's poem, there is a nearly schizophrenic deployment of Milton, symptomatic of the eighteenth-century reception of Milton as a whole: on the one hand, Milton is styled as a pastoral poet, whose descriptions of nature's beauties give pleasure to the curate's household as they recognize in them their own English countryside, complete with 'roses', 'flocks', and 'herds'. On the other hand, Milton's war in heaven and details such as the 'everlasting show'r of burning hail' are employed to describe the victories of the British fleet (*The Village Curate*, 131, 121–2). At the root of this two-sided Milton interpretation is a particular construction of poetic genealogy: at least since John Dryden's introductory verses to the 1695 *Poetical Works of Mr John Milton*, Milton was seen as a British successor to Homer and especially Virgil. The Roman poet's two-sided personality, as a bucolic poet in his *Eclogues* and *Georgics* and as a national and imperial poet in his *Aeneid*, provided an apt parallel for the contrasting ways in which the eighteenth-century British audience read Milton's *Paradise Lost*, alternatively highlighting Milton's idyllic descriptions of paradise and his accounts of warfare and the growth of nations.

This divided image of the seventeenth-century poet was also linked to the peculiar eighteenth-century British conception of empire, the 'blue-water policy' of naval protection which ostentatiously preferred maritime commerce over conquest and contributed to preserving a vision of homely British insularity, even while the acquisition of colonies in America, the Caribbean, and later India was in full swing.[3] From an ideological stance comparable to Hurdis's, yet another village curate, Richard Jago, in his four-book topographical poem *Edge-Hill, or the Rural Prospect Delineated and Moralized* (1767), depicts Britain's fleet in Miltonic terms as 'Eden's nightly guards' which make the blissful pastoral idyll at home possible through their military presence.[4] Britain, the new worldly paradise, is guarded by her navy in the same way that in

---

[2] Compare *PL*, i. 566–72. On the 18th-c. bourgeois support of empire see Paul Langford, *A Polite and Commercial People: England 1727–1783* (Oxford, 1989), 68–71.

[3] See Daniel A. Baugh, 'Great Britain's "Blue-Water" Policy, 1689–1815', *International History Review*, 10 (1988), 33–58.

[4] Richard Jago, *Edge-Hill, or the Rural Prospect Delineated and Moralized* (1767), in *The Works of the English Poets from Chaucer to Cowper*, ed. Alexander Chalmers (1810), repr. *Anglistica & Americana*, 51, 21

Paradise Lost the entrance to paradise is guarded by God's angels. Milton is thus implicitly seen as combining Virgil's bucolic and epic sides.

In what follows I will first trace the political subtexts of the British reception of Milton—especially the reception of *Paradise Lost*—during the 'Long Eighteenth Century', the period from the first publication of the epic in 1667 to the accession of Queen Victoria in 1837, attending to the ways in which *Paradise Lost* was both 'classicized' and 'anglicized' at the same time. I will demonstrate that as a result of this process of reception Milton was constructed to appear simultaneously imperial *and* domestic. I will then show how *Paradise Lost* was adapted in eighteenth-century English georgics and pastorals, and concentrate especially on Milton's role in eighteenth-century critical discourses on taste and landscape gardening. The eighteenth-century enclosure movement and its repercussions in Miltonizing poetry will serve as a case study of the 'empire at home': Even in the pastoral or georgic mode, eighteenth-century Miltonizing poetry was always also 'imperial'.

MILTON RECEPTION: A NATIONAL AND IMPERIAL POET

One of the central authors of the evolving literary canon, the eighteenth-century Milton had metamorphosed from a republican regicide into a symbol of Britishness under the restored monarchy of a new 'Great Britain', successively 'unified' in 1707 and 1801. Whether we see Milton as a 'poet against empire', as David Quint and David Armitage have done, or whether we endorse Paul Stevens's proposition that '*Paradise Lost* authorizes colonial activity even while it satirizes the abuses of early modern colonialism', it was certainly in the course of a long and complicated process of reception that Milton became 'a national and then imperial poet' for eighteenth- and nineteenth-century British readers.[5] In his 1839 essay 'Milton', Thomas De Quincey maintained that what the seventeenth-century poet signified at the beginning of the nineteenth century had been determined by 'all who have quoted him, copied him, echoed him, lectured about him, disputed about him, quarrelled about him'—in other words, Milton's key position in the canon was the result of critical engagements

---

vols. (Hildesheim, 1971), xvii. 287–307 at 287. Jago's footnote refers the reader to 'Milton. Paradise Lost, book iv'.

   [5] See David Quint, *Epic and Empire: Politics and Generic Form from Virgil to Milton* (Princeton, 1993), and David Armitage, 'John Milton: Poet against Empire', in David Armitage, Armand Himy, and Quentin Skinner (eds.), *Milton and Republicanism* (Cambridge, 1995), 206–25. Paul Stevens, '*Paradise Lost* and the Colonial Imperative', *Milton Studies*, 34 (1996), 3–21 at 3. Nicholas von Maltzahn, 'Acts of Kind Service: Milton and the Patriot Literature of Empire', in Balachandra Rajan and Elizabeth Sauer (eds.), *Milton and the Imperial Vision* (Pittsburgh, Pa., 1999), 233–54 at 234.

with and poetic appropriations of his works.[6] *Paradise Lost* was slowly redefined as a '*Classic* in the *English* tongue', equal to the epics of Roman and Greek antiquity.[7] Milton himself, by deciding to write in his native English rather than Latin, had initiated this literary competition with the classics, dissociating his work from the subordinate mode of a former Roman colony. When during the Long Eighteenth Century Britain became a colonizer and an exporter of 'culture' in her own right, Milton's epic therefore offered itself as 'a poetry fit for empire'.[8]

While the first recorded reactions to *Paradise Lost* demonstrated 'a peculiar sensitivity to how Milton's poetry might revive the sedition of his prose', and while early readers such as John Hobart welcomed the epic explicitly as a Christian counterweight to the irreligious culture of the Restoration court, the 'translation of Godly politics into Whig ideology' slowly began to change the ways in which Milton's epic was read—and that was 'increasingly as an Augustan contribution favouring empire'.[9] Nicholas von Maltzahn has shown in detail how Milton's writings were turned into cultural capital which then served in the struggle with France for imperial—and cultural—predominance.[10] Next to the 'newly exhumed and cosmeticized Saxons', as Gerald Newman points out, Shakespeare and Milton were rediscovered as 'heroic "role models"', omnipresent in eighteenth-century British literary discourse.[11] Although poetic apotheoses, for instance by Nahum Tate and William Hayley, often had Milton regret his participation in the regicide from heavenly hindsight and make his peace with the new king, the fact that there was so much obviously problematic biographical information perhaps helped to concentrate the attention more strongly on Milton's poetical works.[12] From the influential *Spectator* essays by Joseph Addison in 1711–12 there emerged a 'polished and sublime' Milton; in fact, Addison 'popularized Milton's epic at the cost of domesticating the poet's radical ideas'. His introductory statement to the *Spectator* essays announced that the reader would find in them not 'a single Word of News, a Reflection in Politicks, nor a Stroke of Party'.[13] He transformed *Paradise Lost* into a classic by cleansing it from all suspicions of political and religious bias, organizing his essays around notions of

---

[6] Thomas De Quincey, 'Milton' (1839), in *De Quincey as Critic*, ed. John E. Jordan (1973), 250–65 at 253–4.

[7] William Massey, *Remarks upon Milton's Paradise Lost* (1761), 'Advertisement to the Reader', pp. iii–vii at iii.

[8] Nicholas von Maltzahn, 'Milton's Readers', in Dennis Danielson (ed.), *The Cambridge Companion to Milton*, 2nd edn. (Cambridge, 1999), 236–52 at 248.

[9] Nicholas von Maltzahn, 'The First Reception of *Paradise Lost* (1667)', *Review of English Studies*, 47 (1996), 479–99 at 494, 490; id., 'Acts of Kind Service', 235. See also George F. Sensabaugh, *That Grand Whig Milton* (Stanford, Calif., 1952).

[10] See von Maltzahn, 'Acts of Kind Service'; 'Milton's Readers'.

[11] Gerald Newman, *The Rise of English Nationalism: A Cultural History, 1740–1830* (1987), 151–2.

[12] See Nahum Tate, *A Poem, Occasioned by His Majesty's Voyage to Holland* (1691), 5, and William Hayley, *The Life of Milton, in Three Parts. To which are added, Conjectures on the Origin of Paradise Lost* (1796), repr. in *English Literary Criticism of the Eighteenth Century*, 51 (New York, 1971), 185, 215.

[13] Trevor Ross, 'Addison Reads Milton', in *The Making of the English Literary Canon: From the Middle Ages to the Late Eighteenth Century* (Montreal, 1998), 213–20 at 213; Joseph Addison, *Criticism on Milton's Paradise Lost; from The Spectator, 31 December 1711–3 May 1712*, English Reprints, 8 vols., ed. Edward Arber (1869; repr. New York, 1966), ii. 9–152 at 9 (31 Dec. 1711).

'politeness' and 'refined taste', the new values of the burgeoning British middle class. Of course, in the context of Whig nationalism, the aestheticization of Milton was everything but apolitical. De Quincey saw this clearly when in 1839 he claimed that 'Addison ... did a service to Milton incomparably greater than all other critics collectively', gaining him 'popular acceptation' and giving 'the initial bias to the national mind' ('Milton', 260).

During the eighteenth century 'the great commercial interest in Milton centered in *Paradise Lost*, as perhaps the "best seller" of the market'.[14] The commercial success of the fourth edition of *Paradise Lost* in 1688, the entrepreneurial endeavours of the new owner of the copyright for Milton's poetry, Jacob Tonson, and the resulting accessibility of Milton's epic through large print runs 'made *Paradise Lost* the modern classic', often mentioned in the same breath as Virgil.[15] After the Tonsons' copyright expired in the 1750s, selections from Milton proliferated, along with a variety of annotated and illustrated editions, some of them intended for a specific readership such as women, children, or the poor. *Paradise Lost* was now 'published annually or more often, in Britain and abroad. ... Milton's English epic was distinguished by its wide availability as well as by its great sublimity'.[16] As the numerous contemporary abbreviated versions and paraphrases demonstrate, no extensive knowledge of the text was necessary to acquire the cultural capital that was 'Milton'. Scraps and quotations from Milton's texts circulated freely in contemporary discourse in the same way as references to Shakespeare. In fact, the 'gradual extension of the reading class affected the development of the literature addressed to them'; *Paradise Lost* was now frequently repackaged for easier access.[17] James Paterson in 1744 explicitly justified his paraphrase of *Paradise Lost* by pointing to the needs of a larger readership; John Marchant's professed aim in compiling his 1751 variorum edition was to present the epic to people 'who may not have Leisure, or Capacity, or Learning sufficient to understand [Milton] in all Points'; and the Methodist educator John Wesley addressed his 1763 annotated edition, *An Extract from Milton's Paradise Lost with Notes*, to 'persons of a common Education'. These had now become part of what Johnson in 1781, still somewhat hyperbolically, called 'a nation of readers'.[18]

---

[14] John Walter Good, *Studies in the Milton Tradition* (1913; repr. New York, 1971), 249.

[15] Von Maltzahn, 'Milton's Readers', 246. Milton's epic was now increasingly parsed in the schoolroom, like a piece of classical literature. See Bernard Sharratt, 'The Appropriation of Milton', *Essays and Studies*, 35 (1982), 30–44 at 34. Milton was also occasionally translated into Latin; Dustin Griffin, *Regaining Paradise: Milton and the Eighteenth Century* (Cambridge, 1986), 63–4, cites more than twelve Latin translations for the Long Eighteenth Century.

[16] Von Maltzahn, 'Milton's Readers', 247.

[17] Leslie Stephen, *English Literature and Society in the Eighteenth Century* (1910), 26. See also Langford, 'Books and the Bourgeoisie', in *A Polite and Commercial People*, 90–9.

[18] *A Complete Commentary ... on Milton's Paradise Lost*, ed. James Paterson (1744): 'without such a Work the *Poem* is useless to most Readers of it' (title page); *Paradise Lost*, ed. Marchant, 'Preface'; *An Extract from Milton's Paradise Lost with Notes*, ed. John Wesley (1763), 'Preface'. See also Oscar Sherwin, 'Milton for the Masses: John Wesley's Edition of *Paradise Lost*', *Modern Language Quarterly*, 12 (1951), 267–85 at 269, and Marcus Walsh, *Shakespeare, Milton, and Eighteenth-Century Literary Editing: The Beginnings of Interpretative Scholarship* (Cambridge, 1997), 56. Samuel Johnson, *Life of Swift* (1781), in *Lives of the English Poets*, ed. George Birkbeck Hill, 3 vols. (Oxford, 1905), iii. 1–74 at 19.

Milton was now increasingly seen as a 'national treasure' that had to be defended against encroachments from outside. In 1691, Anthony à Wood, in his short biography of Milton, had still deplored that '[Milton] was more admired abroad, and by Foreigners, than at home', and Richard Blackmore had similarly regretted, in his 1716 'Essay on the Nature and Constitution of Epick Poetry', that 'Paradise Lost, *an admirable Work of* [Epick Poetry], *publish'd by Mr.* Milton, *the great Ornament of his Age and Country, lay many Years unspoken of, and entirely disregarded*'.[19] But by the mid-eighteenth century, so well established was Milton's position as the national English poet that William Lauder's fabricated attack against the 'authenticity' of *Paradise Lost* was rebuked nearly unanimously as an attack against the nation. Richard Richardson, for instance, reproached Lauder with a '*Mean officious zeal to strip the deserved laurel from his* own countryman, *to grace the brows of a few* obscure foreigners!' Similarly, an anonymous correspondent to the *Gentleman's Magazine* in 1747 stated that 'the question, whether *Milton* borrow'd from *Masenius*, concerns, in my opinion, the whole nation', praising Milton explicitly as 'a poet, who does us more honour by his writings, than our arms have done some years past'. Even Samuel Johnson, who had originally helped Lauder launch his attack, recognized that to 'lessen the reputation of Milton' would 'diminish in some degree the honour of our country'.[20] As late as 1847, De Quincey, defending Milton against Walter Savage Landor's critical attacks, styled himself as a 'British gentleman', defending a 'noble vessel, from the Thames or the Clyde' against foreign pirates.[21] As Milton's poetry became one of Britain's most valuable cultural assets, he had to be protected against external—and internal—foes.

The overwhelming majority of eighteenth-century British adaptations of Milton rewrote *Paradise Lost* as an imperial epic, redeploying in new contexts Miltonic motifs such as Satan's council in hell, Satan's 'colonialist' raid of paradise, the fall of Adam and Eve, or Adam's mountain vision. Robert Thyer, in his 1749 commentary notes on *Paradise Lost*, deplored the lack of a Virgilian vision of the glories of empire in Milton's epic, and Hayley, in his *Essay on Epic Poetry* (1782), claimed '*a national Epic Poem* [to be] *the great desideratum in English literature*'.[22] Their appeals did not go unheard: according to Stuart Curran, the 'truly amazing phenomenon' of the Romantic period was 'the proliferation of epics in England, which is unique in the

---

[19] Darbishire, 48; Richard Blackmore, 'An Essay on the Nature and Constitution of Epick Poetry', in *Essays upon Several Subjects* (1716), pp. iii–viii at iv.

[20] Richard Richardson, *Zoilomastix: or, a Vindication of Milton* (1747), 24. Anon., [no title], *Gentleman's Magazine*, 17 (1747), 567. Samuel Johnson, *Life of Milton* (1779), in *Milton Criticism: Selections from Four Centuries*, ed. James Thorpe (1951), 65–88 at 72. For Johnson's support of Lauder, see Samuel Johnson, 'Preface to Lauder's *Essay on Milton's Use and Imitation of the Moderns*' (1750), in *Selections from Samuel Johnson, 1709–1784*, ed. R. W. Chapman (1962), 143–4.

[21] Thomas De Quincey, 'Milton versus Southey and Landor' (1847), in *De Quincey as Critic*, ed. Jordan, 465–82 at 465.

[22] Thyer's notes, first incorporated in Thomas Newton's 1749 edition, were frequently reused; I quote from *Paradise Lost*, ed. Marchant, 712–13. William Hayley, *An Essay on Epic Poetry* (1782), 96, 'Argument to the fifth epistle'.

history of Western literature'.[23] Not only poets laureate but also 'minor poets' such as schoolmasters, college deans, and curates like Hurdis were eager to show their patriotism in mixtures of Miltonic and Virgilian language. Miltonizing nationalist epics such as John Ogilvie's twenty-book epic *Britannia* (1801) or Henry Hart Milman's twelve-book epic *Samor, Lord of the Bright City* (1818) attempted, by painting a heroic picture of the ancient Britons, to supply what Milton, even in his *History of Britain* (1671), had largely 'left unsung'.[24]

However, Milton interpretations remained variegated: for instance, the resonant image of Satan's fallen glory from Book 1 of *Paradise Lost* was repeatedly used in (not necessarily anti-imperial) Miltonizing epics to warn British readers against an impending ruin of the empire; the British Society for the Abolition of Slavery relied in their pamphlets on passages such as the claim that God 'human left from human free' (*PL*, xii. 71); William Wordsworth in his early Jacobin phase persisted in reading Milton as a radical revolutionary, and William Blake, especially in *Milton* (1804), simultaneously attempted to create an anti-imperial epic and to retrieve Milton's identity as a prophet and visionary.[25]

At the same time, Milton also became part of New England literature: He 'was the most widely read author in eighteenth-century America. . . . If a home in the American colonies possessed any books besides the Bible, they were likely to be *The Pilgrim's Progress* and *Paradise Lost*.'[26] During the fight for independence Milton's epic was adapted, for instance by Thomas Paine and Thomas Jefferson, to support the cause of the revolutionaries, and later, Miltonizing American epics conjured up visions of territorial expansion across the American continent in the same way that British national epics had deployed Milton as a 'Virgilian' national epic poet.[27] The Virgilian concept of *translatio imperii et studii*—the idea that the imperial nation disseminates 'culture' to the remotest regions—was transferred to the influence of Milton's epic, the essence of British culture, on foreign literatures. Even after the loss of the American

---

[23] Stuart Curran, *Poetic Form and British Romanticism* (Oxford, 1986), 158.

[24] I borrow the phrase from William Wordsworth's declaration in the 1805 *Prelude* that his is a topic 'by Milton left unsung' (1. 180). On Milton's aborted attempts at describing 'Britain's legendary beginnings' see David Loewenstein, *Milton and the Drama of History: Historical Vision, Iconoclasm, and the Literary Imagination* (Cambridge, 1990), 97.

[25] On Miltonizing poems in the 'Ruins of Rome' genre see Anne-Julia Zwierlein, *Majestick Milton: British Imperial Expansion and Transformations of Paradise Lost, 1667–1837* (Muenster, 2001), 73–9; on the abolitionists' use of Milton see 353–98. On Wordsworth see Matthew Biberman, ' "The Earth Is All Before Me": Wordsworth, Milton, and the Christian Hebraic Roots of English Republicanism', in Ghislaine McDayter, Guinn Batten, and Barry Milligan (eds.), *Romantic Generations: Essays in Honor of Robert F. Gleckner* (Cranbury, N.J., 2001), 102–28. On Blake, see e.g. Joseph Anthony Wittreich, Jr., *Angel of Apocalypse: Blake's Idea of Milton* (Madison, 1975), and Jackie DiSalvo, *War of Titans: Blake's Critique of Milton and the Politics of Religion* (Pittsburgh, Pa., 1983).

[26] Nancy Armstrong and Leonard Tennenhouse, *The Imaginary Puritan: Literature, Intellectual Labor, and the Origins of Personal Life* (Berkeley, 1992), 11.

[27] See Tony Davies, 'Borrowed Language: Milton, Jefferson, Mirabeau', in Armitage et al., *Milton and Republicanism*, 254–71; Jay Fliegelman, *Prodigals and Pilgrims: The American Revolution against Patriarchal Authority, 1750–1800* (Cambridge, 1982), 157; Keith W. F. Stavely, *Puritan Legacies: Paradise Lost and the New England Tradition, 1630–1890* (Ithaca, N.Y., 1987); and Lydia Dittler Shulman, *Paradise Lost and the Rise of the American Republic* (Boston, 1992).

colonies, British cultural ascendancy over America was still emphasized as a given by British poets, exemplified by Anna Letitia Barbauld's vision in her epic *Eighteen Hundred and Eleven* (1812) that 'Milton's tones [shall] the raptured ear enthrall, / Mixt with the roaring of Niagara's fall'. In his *Life of Milton* (1796), written twenty years after the Declaration of Independence, William Hayley had similarly maintained: 'the triumph of [Milton's] genius . . . though it aspired only to the praise of these British islands, is already grown an object of universal admiration, and may find hereafter, in the western world, the amplest theatre of his glory'. Samuel Taylor Coleridge in 1833 endorsed the same vision of British cultural hegemony, embodied in Milton, reaching 'into the remotest seclusion of the civilized world. . . . Even the lone Icelander, placed "Far amid the melancholy main", has listened in his own tongue to the Story of Paradise. As a poet, [Milton's] genius was universal.'[28] Milton's 'universality', implicitly coterminous with the 'universality' of the Christian religion and Western civilization, thus became an asset in the battle for international predominance. While the 'civilized world' was envisaged by Coleridge as an audience for Milton's song, this was a proleptic image: the world became civilized, Coleridge was in fact saying, by listening to Milton.

A CRITICAL DILEMMA: MILTON DOMESTIC AND EXOTIC

However, the British imperial Milton also had an intensely domestic side: In this section I will look more closely at the ways in which Milton critics deployed the languages of both the imperial and the domestic sphere, sometimes alternating imperceptibly between the two. Throughout, critics and editors proudly compared Milton to the ancient classics but simultaneously aimed to reclaim him for a nativist tradition. Similarly Milton commentators who attempted to 'anglicize' *Paradise Lost* were at the same time also clearly fascinated by Milton's surveys of exotic regions and customs. I will start by taking a look at eighteenth-century comments on Milton's language and subject matter, proposing that debates about aestheticism, about Milton's diction and versification, his sublimity, or his deviance from the newly invented norms of neoclassical aesthetics also had political significance.[29]

---

[28] Anna Letitia Barbauld, *Eighteen Hundred and Eleven* (1812), repr. in *The Poems of Anna Letitia Barbauld*, ed. William McCarthy and Elizabeth Kraft (Athens, Ga., 1994), 153–61, ll. 95–6. On the rise of a 'new American Milton' see the pieces listed in Good, *Studies in the Milton Tradition*, nos. 129, 160, 174, 176, 190. Hayley, *Life of Milton*, 40. Samuel Taylor Coleridge, *Conversations*, June 1833, quoted in Joseph Anthony Wittreich, Jr. (ed.), *The Romantics on Milton: Formal Essays and Critical Asides* (Cleveland, Ohio, 1970), 274–5.

[29] For a survey of such comments, see also John T. Shawcross, 'The Deleterious and the Exalted: Milton's Poetry in the Eighteenth Century', in Mark R. Kelley, Michael Lieb, and John T. Shawcross (eds.), *Milton and the Grounds of Contention* (Pittsburgh, Pa., 2003), 11–36.

In Milton criticism there were persistent attempts at expunging from Milton's language its numerous 'un-English' elements, or the exotic subject matter from his narrative. Through his archaisms, etymological figures, and Latinizing style Milton was arguably commemorating a time before the linguistic confusion at Babel; his epic has to be read in the wider context of 'renaissance multilingualism'.[30] But in the eyes of some eighteenth-century critics and editors this meant that *Paradise Lost* was not English enough. In 1692 John Dennis complained that Milton's language was not '*as pure as the Images are vast and daring*'. Alexander Pope likewise objected to Milton's 'exotic style', claiming that through his Latinisms and other linguistic 'imports' Milton had created 'a second *Babel*', and Johnson, although he was otherwise highly interested in the 'derivation of languages' as 'the most indubitable proof of the traduction of nations, and the genealogy of mankind', called Milton's language, in nearly the same words, 'a *Babylonish Dialect*'.[31]

But on the other hand, very frequently throughout the Long Eighteenth Century critics and commentators saw Milton's epic as an example of successful linguistic appropriation. An early case is Dryden, who in 1690 had still accused Milton of using 'old words . . . with too free a hand, even sometimes to the obscuring of his sense'. However, in 1693 he was talking about Milton's 'admirable *Grecisms*';[32] in 1695, as we have seen, he contributed verses to Tonson's *Poetical Works of Mr John Milton*, in which he cast Milton as the modern embodiment of Homer and Virgil, and again in the 1697 dedicatory introduction to his own translation of the *Aeneid*, he himself had to answer the accusation that he 'latinized too much'. By emphasizing that 'when I want at home, I must seek abroad', he repeated Milton's advice from the Digression to the *History of Britain*, published as *The Character of the Long Parliament*, that due to the relative backwardness of England, 'ripe Understanding, and many civil Vertues' have to be imported from 'Forreign Writings' (*CPW*, v. 450). Importation, according to Dryden, is a gain, even a conquest: 'I carry not out the Treasure of the Nation, which is never to return: but what I bring from *Italy*, I spend in *England*: Here it remains, and here it circulates.'[33] These metaphors betray the influence of the early mercantilist idea that 'the quantity of wealth in the world is a constant' and that therefore 'a country could gain only at the expense of other countries'.[34] However,

[30] John K. Hale, *Milton's Languages: The Impact of Multilingualism on Style* (Cambridge, 1997), 1.

[31] John Dennis, *The Passion of Byblis, from Ovid, Made English* (1692), 'Preface', quoted in Nicholas von Maltzahn, 'The Whig Milton, 1667–1700', in Armitage et al. (eds.), *Milton and Republicanism*, 229–53 at 243. Alexander Pope, *Anecdotes, Observations, and Characters, of Books and Men, collected from the Conversation of Mr. Pope*, coll. Joseph Spence, ed. Samuel Weller Singer (1820), Section IV, 134–81 at 174. Samuel Johnson, Letter of 13 Aug. 1766 to William Drummond, in *Selected Letters of Samuel Johnson* (Oxford, 1925), 64–6 at 64; Johnson, *Life of Milton*, 86.

[32] John Dryden, 'The Preface to *Don Sebastian*' (1690), in *The Works of John Dryden*, gen. ed. Alan Roper, 20 vols. (Berkeley, 1956–96), xv. 65–72 at 67; Dryden, 'Discourse Concerning the Original and Progress of Satire' (1693), in *Works*, iv. 3–90 at 85.

[33] John Dryden, 'To the Most Honourable John, Lord Marquess of *Normandy*, Earl of Mulgrave, etc. and Knight of the *Most Noble Order of the Garter* [Dedication of the *Aeneis*]', in *Works*, v. 335–6.

[34] Jacob Viner, 'Power Versus Plenty as Objectives of Foreign Policy in the Seventeenth and Eighteenth Centuries' (1949), repr. in David Armitage (ed.), *Theories of Empire, 1450–1800* (Aldershot, 1998), 277–305 at 285.

Dryden ends on a note of warning: the 'License' for linguistic innovation through importation must be used 'very sparingly; for if too many Foreign Words are pour'd in upon us, it looks as if they were design'd not to assist the Natives, but to Conquer them' (p. 336). Here, traces of Britain's former status as a Roman colony resurface in the anxiety that importing goods—or words—from abroad might be the same thing as inviting the colonizers into the country.

Tonson's 1695 edition with commentary notes by Patrick Hume treated *Paradise Lost* as equal to the epics of classical antiquity, but at the same time Hume distanced himself, like Milton, from imperial visions, denouncing Virgil's 'vainglorious Boastings' about '*Roman* Conquerors' and emphasizing that Milton's epic points beyond present political and social issues to a 'better [World]'. Hume also acknowledged, like Dryden, the linguistic diversity of *Paradise Lost* as a 'Commerce' in words, thus taking up the political context of Britain's 'blue-water policy': 'why may we not presume that our Island Ancestors, by situation inclined to Commerce, might bring home and adopt into their Language many Greek Words, as probably as their Sailing-Successors daily transport Foreign Commodities and Fashions'.[35] Richardson, in the 'Life of the Author' appended to his Milton commentary, likewise saw Milton's language as 'Enrich'd and Strengthen'd with *Attick* and *Roman* Spoils, in Words, Phrases, and Idiom'; he even claimed Milton's capacity for assimilating foreign idioms to be superior to Virgil's, ending with a nationalist flourish by insisting that 'there is yet a further Pleasure in Thinking [*Paradise Lost*] is the Work of Our Friend, Our Country-Man'.[36] James Paterson, vice versa, stated that the richness of Milton's English might now in its own turn become useful to travellers, traders, and learners of English as a foreign language: '*And therefore I humbly recommend [Paradise Lost] to all* Parents, Schoolmasters, Tutors, Travellers, Merchants, Foreigners, . . . *both at* Home *and* Abroad'.[37]

However, where Milton's subject matter, and not his language, was concerned, the purists remained vociferous. Most eighteenth-century critics and commentators, it appears, did not have the scruples voiced by Coleridge in 1817 that 'it would be scarcely more difficult to push a stone out from the pyramids with the bare hand, than to alter a word, or the position of a word, in Milton or Shakspeare, (in their most important works at least) without making the author say something else, or something worse, than he does say'.[38] For instance, Richard Bentley's notorious 1732

---

[35] Patrick Hume, *Annotations on Milton's Paradise Lost, in The Poetical Works of Mr. John Milton. Containing, Paradise Lost, Paradise Regain'd, Sampson Agonistes, and his Poems on several Occasions. Together with Explanatory Notes on each Book of the Paradise Lost, and a Table never before Printed* (1695), 300 (between xi. 433–6) and 53 at ii. 289.

[36] Jonathan Richardson, Father and Son, *Explanatory Notes and Remarks on Milton's Paradise Lost, With the Life of the Author, and a Discourse on the Poem by Jonathan Richardson Senior* (1734), in Darbishire, 210, 326. For the comparison with Virgil see p. 320. On Warton's similar judgement see also Mark Thackeray, 'Christopher Pitt, Joseph Warton, and Virgil', *Review of English Studies*, 43 (1992), 329–46 at 340.

[37] *Complete Commentary*, p. viii.

[38] Samuel Taylor Coleridge, *Biographia Literaria, or, Biographical Sketches of My Literary Life and Opinions* (1817), in *The Collected Works of Samuel Taylor Coleridge*, gen. ed. Kathleen Coburn, 16 vols. (Princeton, 1983), vii/i. 23.

critical edition of *Paradise Lost* was both a repackaging of the epic as a classical text, subjected to the same kind of textual criticism that Bentley had applied to his Horace (1711) and Terence (1726), and an attempt at 'modernizing' Milton and salvaging him for a nativist tradition. Thus Milton's famous simile of Satan as a merchant traveller 'Close sailing from . . . the isles / Of Ternate and Tidore' (*PL*, ii. 638–9) met with Bentley's utter disapproval: 'why those exotic Names, *Bengala, Ternate* and *Tidore*? A vain Ostentation of the most vulgar Knowledge; when a Ship at home in our own Channel would serve the turn better. . . . why must the *Aethiopic* Sea be it? when the *Europaean* Seas carry ten times the Trade.'[39] George Smith Green in *A New Version of the Paradise Lost: or, Milton Paraphrased* (Oxford, 1756), in a similar vein, took exception to Milton's famous lines on Vallombrosa (*PL*, i. 302–4), declaring that an English epic could do without such foreign allusions: 'As few English Readers know the Brooks in *Vallambrosa* . . . and we have Woods of our own that in Autumn shed Leaves enough to raise an Idea of Multitude, that *foreign* Parade is omitted, and the Image brought within the understanding of a common Reader' (p. 47). This debate about 'Englishness' and 'one's own' English landscapes also left its marks on Wordsworth's annotations to *Paradise Lost*, made between 1798 and 1800. At *PL*, iii. 543–50, the passage on Satan's first view of the earth after his voyage through chaos, a 'scout' discovers from the 'brow of some high-climbing hill . . . The goodly prospect of some foreign land / First seen, or some renowned metropolis / With glistering spires and pinnacles adorned'. According to Wordsworth, Milton here deplorably prefers 'some foreign land' to English scenes: 'This part of the picture might have been improved by . . . <a simple introduction> of some of the most interesting rural images of an extensive prospect viewed at daybreak <such as> Hamlets cottages & woods with reaches of a river, all . . . <lifting themselves> here & there thro the morning vapour.' Wordsworth, who in his famous 1802 sonnet on 'Milton' uttered his pride in Milton's 'faith and morals' as an undying legacy to his countrymen, here domesticated his epic by wishing for a specifically English countryside, epitomized in the stock ingredients of 'Hamlets cottages & woods'.[40]

The domestic and the exotic, however, became increasingly intertwined as eighteenth-century Milton critics paradoxically tried to 'anglicize' Milton's epic and to 'explore' its arcane and foreign allusions at the same time. Milton fuelled many enthusiasms: during the eighteenth century, *Paradise Lost* became a standard text for painters and engravers; British tourists travelled through Europe 'in Milton's footsteps', for instance—Smith Green would not have liked this—to Vallombrosa (although it is quite certain that the poet had never been there); John Keats enthused

---

[39] *Milton's Paradise Lost: A New Edition*, ed. Richard Bentley (1732), at ii. 636. Coming to Milton from his classical editions, Bentley claimed that he set out to restore the '*Poet's own Words . . . not from a Manuscript, (for none exists) but by Sagacity, and happy Conjecture*' (Preface, sig. a2ᵛ), although in fact he extensively used the manuscript of the first book, then in Tonson's possession (R. G. Moyles, *The Text of Paradise Lost: A Study in Editorial Procedure* (Toronto, 1985), 18–20).

[40] William Wordsworth, Annotations to *Paradise Lost* (1798–1800), in Wittreich (ed.), *The Romantics on Milton*, 104; William Wordsworth, 'Milton' (1802), in *Wordsworth: Complete Poetical Works* (1904), ed. Thomas Hutchinson, 2nd edn. (Oxford, 1936), 244.

over 'a lock of Milton's hair'; Blake and his wife, naked in their garden, read Adam and Eve's dialogues to each other, and Richard Steele in *The Tatler* translated the marital strife between Milton's first pair (*PL*, ix. 1134–89) 'out of heroics . . . into domestic style', poking dubious fun at 'refined' eighteenth-century wives.[41] The ('un-English') plurality and richness of Milton's epic cosmos inspired eighteenth-century Milton commentators to give attention to (more or less authentic) travellers' accounts. Paterson expressed the hope that the still insufficient explanation of Milton's exotic terminology might animate '*ingenious* Travellers' to research foreign languages, and his appeal met with an eager response throughout the Long Eighteenth Century.[42] Virtually every Milton commentary from Hume onwards drew on the experience of travellers to explain passages in *Paradise Lost*, in increasing consonance with the spirit of scientific inquiry characteristic of the age. On the 'asphaltick Pool' in hell, in 1750 Callender of Craigforth offered 'Dr. Pocock's travel account', which 'confirms the truth of that extraordinary property of these waters, that no living bodies will sink in them, having tried the experiment himself by swimming'. Marchant in his 1751 commentary presented an anecdote first recounted in Thomas Newton's 1749 edition about 'a Man lately at *Bath*' who attempted to recreate the Chinese mode of transportation mentioned by Milton: 'the barren plains / Of Sericana, where Chineses drive / With sails and wind their cany wagons light' (*PL*, iii. 437–9). This English citizen, it was reported, 'could really drive his Machine without Horses, by the Help of Wind and Sails, upon *Marlborough* Downs, but it would not serve upon the Road; it did well enough upon the Plain, but he could not make it go up-hill'.[43]

Milton commentaries also started to reflect the British colonial experience. In fact, Milton's exotic locations had already come much closer to the British homeland in Hume's 1695 annotations, where, for instance, Milton's '*Ternate* and *Tydore*' were described as those islands 'whence our Merchants bring the *East-India* Spices'. Paterson emphasized that some parts of *Paradise Lost* were more familiar to eighteenth-century readers than they had been to Milton's contemporaries: any of the countries presented to Adam by Michael 'were not then in Being, and others not discovered nor known to the *Europeans* and other *Nations*, till of late'. In Miss Christian Cann's *Scriptural and Allegorical Glossary to Milton's Paradise Lost* (1828), which contained many pieces of advice about living conditions in British colonies, 'Asia' was annotated as 'the richest and most fruitful part of the world, [which] supplies us with the richest spices, drugs, diamonds and other precious stones; with

[41] See Edward Chaney, 'The Visit to Vallombrosa: A Literary Tradition', in Mario A. Di Cesare (ed.), *Milton in Italy: Contexts, Images, Contradictions* (Binghamton, 1991), 113–46 at 115. See also Robin Jarvis, 'Wordsworth at Vallombrosa', *Studies in Romanticism*, 25 (1986), 483–504. John Keats, 'On Seeing a Lock of Milton's Hair', in *Keats: Poetical Works*, ed. H. W. Garrod (Oxford, 1970), 377–8. Reminiscence by Blake's friend and patron Thomas Butts, recorded in *Blake Records*, ed. G. E. Bentley, Jr. (Oxford, 1969), 53–4. Richard Steele, 'Scolds—with an Illustration from the Garden of Eden' (1710), in *The Tatler*, ed. Lewis Gibbs (1953), 218–22.

[42] *Complete Commentary*, p. vi.

[43] *Milton's Paradise Lost, Book I*, ed. Callender of Craigforth (Glasgow, 1750), 69. *Paradise Lost*, ed. Marchant, 239–40.

silks, muslins, coffee, tea, &c'. These exotic luxuries had here become fully integrated into the framework of domestic commodities and necessities. Milton's 'Ganges', she claimed, was now a British dominion, in its 'whole navigable course...from its entrance into the plains of Hindoostan to the sea...possessed by the British, their allies and tributaries'.[44]

The pervasive orientalism of the late eighteenth and early nineteenth centuries also produced numerous epics describing in Miltonic style voyages into exotic regions. Robert Southey's epics *Madoc* (1805) and *The Curse of Kehama* (1810), as well as their predecessor, Walter Landor's *Gebir* (1798), were examples of this new wave of epic writing. The increasingly aggressive nineteenth-century ideology of British cultural and religious interventionism resulted in fascinated accounts of allegedly barbarous pagan rituals, in epic writing as well as in commentary notes on Milton's exotic passages.[45] What Milton himself had culled from travellers' accounts such as Richard Hakluyt's *Principal Navigations, Voyages and Discoveries of the English Nation* (1589) or Samuel Purchas's *Purchas His Pilgrimage* (1613) now fed back into eighteenth-century exoticist discourse, and eighteenth- and nineteenth-century Milton editions emphasized the here and now of the evolving empire.

THE EMPIRE AT HOME

In this final section I will return to the dichotomous image of Milton as a successor to both the bucolic and the imperial versions of Virgil, looking specifically at writing on 'taste', landscape gardening, and enclosure in eighteenth-century Miltonizing pastoral and georgic. Here, the imperial vision continually encroached upon the seemingly secluded English countryside idylls: the eighteenth-century genre of 'imperial georgic' was marked by a 'growing awareness of the British Empire', and its depiction of the 'agricultural landscape was imbued with a sense of spatial and economic continuity with the wider imperial world'.[46] The pervasive presence of the empire throughout the British isles during the eighteenth century is also evidenced by the wide range of exotic products that were on offer in local shops, or by the records of circulating libraries in provincial towns, which demonstrate a shift in the interests of

---

[44] Hume, *Annotations on Milton's Paradise Lost*, 78 at ii. 637; Paterson (ed.), *Complete Commentary*, 443 at xi. 367; Miss Christian Cann, *A Scriptural and Allegorical Glossary to Milton's Paradise Lost* (1828), at ii. 2, ix. 81.

[45] See e.g. Josiah Conder, *The Star in the East; with Other Poems* (1824), ll. 119–25, or the commentary by James Prendeville in *John Milton, Paradise Lost*, ed. Prendeville (Paris, 1841), 19.

[46] Karen O'Brien, 'Imperial Georgic, 1660–1789', in Gerald MacLean, Donna Landry, and Joseph P. Ward (eds.), *The Country and the City Revisited: England and the Politics of Culture, 1550–1850* (Cambridge, 1999) 160–79 at 162.

the rural population away from religious literature to travel reports—as witnessed by Hurdis's *The Village Curate*.[47]

To take only a few examples, the bucolic and the epic genre, Virgil's *Georgics* and Milton's *Paradise Lost*, were merged in a central passage of T. C. Rickman's poem *The Fallen Cottage* (1793), his celebration of peasant life: 'Happy, thrice happy clowns! Who thus in peace / Enjoy the earth's best gifts, with them content!' This has ominous overtones, as both God's angels and Satan had used nearly identical words to describe Adam and Eve's as yet unfallen but precarious state of innocence.[48] Behind these Miltonic passages is the self-contented happiness of Virgil's rustic swains in the *Georgics*: 'O fortunatos nimium, sua si bona norint, / agricolas! Quibus ipsa, procul discordibus armis, / fundit humo facilem victum iustissima tellus' (*Georgics*, 2. 458–60). The seclusion from outward strife and from the world of luxury goods (*Georgics*, 2. 463–6) are the most important points in Virgil's celebration of rustic happiness. In a similar vein, the fall in Rickman's poem is the consequence of foreign travel and commerce; here, luxury goods 'furnish riot, and debase / Our nature', exactly as Virgil and Milton claimed they did.[49] But the poem is a belated epitaph to 'old England'; the new, commercial, empire was already an all-pervasive force. Similarly, the earlier poem *Cider*, by John Philips (1708), which sings 'thy gift, Pomona, in Miltonian verse', on the one hand celebrates the secluded idyll of the English countryside as opposed to exotic overseas locations, an 'Albion . . . sever'd from the world / By Nature's wise indulgence, indigent / Of nothing from without'. On the other hand and very incongruously, Philips translates Satan's voyage from *Paradise Lost* into a part of Britain's imperialist mission: the British navy 'through the ocean vast / Shall wave her double cross, t'extremest climes / Terrific, and return with odorous spoils / Of Araby well fraught, or Indus' wealth, / Pearl, and barbaric Gold'.[50] This exotic vision combines Milton's description of Satan 'High on a throne of royal state' with its 'barbaric pearl and gold' (*PL*, ii. 1–4), and the 'odoriferous wings' of the winds, the 'native perfumes' and 'balmy spoils' perceived by Satan as he approaches the earth (*PL*, iv. 157–9).[51] Britain's domestic idyll is revealed to be dependent on resources from the exotic world abroad. However, visions of imperial ruin through excessive luxury were countered by discussions of conspicuous consumption in eighteenth-century magazines: the press 'increasingly developed a nice

---

[47] See John E. Wills, Jr., 'European Consumption and Asian Production in the Seventeenth and Eighteenth Centuries', in John Brewer and Roy Porter (eds.), *Consumption and the World of Goods* (1993), 133–47, and Gerald MacLean, Donna Landry, and Joseph P. Ward, 'Introduction', in MacLean et al. (eds.), *The Country and the City Revisited*, 1–23 at 11.

[48] T. C. Rickman, *The Fallen Cottage* (Philadelphia, 1793), 13. See *PL*, vii. 631–2: 'thrice happy if they know / Their happiness, and persevere upright', and *PL*, iv. 370–1: 'Happy, but for so happy ill secured / Long to continue'.

[49] Rickman, *The Fallen Cottage*, 14. See Milton on the trade in goods that foster 'luxury and riot' (*PL*, xi. 715).

[50] John Philips, *Cider* (1708), in *The Works of the English Poets from Chaucer to Cowper*, ed. Alexander Chalmers (1810), repr. *Anglistica & Americana*, 51, viii. 385–96 at 393, 395.

[51] On this passage see also Karen L. Edwards's essay, Ch. 27 above.

(and often desperate) distinction between the good luxury of the tasteful and the bad luxury of the vulgar'.[52]

Thus the evolving eighteenth-century discourse on 'taste', seemingly confined to the realm of aesthetics, also had strong colonialist and imperialist overtones. Again, the bucolic and epic genres were combined by eighteenth-century critics, who reinvented Milton's landscapes to express contemporary notions of the 'tasteful', and, with perhaps even more emphasis, the 'useful'. His paradisiacal 'happy rural seat of various view' (*PL*, iv. 247) was reproduced in eighteenth-century landed estates, designed to express the new rationality of the age in a well-ordered and productive countryside.[53] Horace Walpole, claiming that Milton 'seems with the prophetic eye of taste ... to have conceived, to have foreseen modern gardening', thereby recruited Milton for eighteenth-century cultural politics. Joseph Warton similarly claimed that Milton, 'superior to the prejudices of his times ... exhibited in his EDEN, the first hints and outlines of what a beautiful garden should be', thus showing himself 'free from the unnatural and *narrow* taste of [his] countrymen'.[54] So omnipresent was the eighteenth-century rage for Miltonic landscape gardening that in 1798 John Aikin found it necessary to produce an essay 'On Milton's Garden of Eden, as a Supposed Prototype of Modern English Gardening' in which he demonstrated that 'the plan of Milton's Paradise ... by no means was intended to serve as a model for gardens made by human hands'.[55] Natural description in Milton criticism always also conveyed an ideological point of view; 'landscape and country representations', as Sharon Achinstein reminds us, are also 'stories about other significant economic and social relations, for instance, the colonial slave trade, consumerism, urbanism, enclosure, and the effects of capitalism upon the rural poor'.[56]

The debate on Miltonic gardening was perceptibly coloured by Britain's status as an imperial power. Anna Seward, in a 1794 letter, pointed to Milton's 'description of the primeval garden' as a literary manifestation of 'the rational spirit of improvement'. Capability Brown, she claimed, had realized this Miltonic rationality to

[52] John Brewer and Roy Porter, 'Introduction', in Brewer and Porter (eds.), *Consumption and the World of Goods*, 1–17 at 8.

[53] See John Prest, *The Garden of Eden: The Botanic Garden and the Recreation of Paradise* (New Haven, 1981), Max F. Schulz, *Paradise Preserved: Recreations of Eden in Eighteenth- and Nineteenth-Century England* (Cambridge, 1985), and Douglas Chambers, 'The Garden of the World Erewhile: Husbandry, Pastoral, and Georgic', in *The Reinvention of the World: English Writing, 1650–1750* (1996), 78–107.

[54] Horace Walpole, 'On Modern Gardening', in *The Works of Horace Walpole, Earl of Orford*, 5 vols. (1798), repr. *Anglistica & Americana*, 157, pp. 517–45 at 527–8; Joseph Warton, *An Essay on the Genius and Writings of Pope*, 2 vols. (1782; repr. New York, 1974), ii. 183.

[55] John Aikin, 'On Milton's Garden of Eden, as a Supposed Prototype of Modern English Gardening', in *Letters from a Father to His Son, on Various Topics, relative to Literature and the Conduct of Life*, 2 vols. (1796, 1800), repr. in *English Literary Criticism of the Eighteenth Century*, iii–iv (New York, 1971), Letter VI, ii. 99–113 at 102.

[56] Sharon Achinstein, ' "Pleasure by Description": Elizabeth Singer Rowe's Enlightened Milton', in Mark R. Kelley, Michael Lieb, and John T. Shawcross (eds.), *Milton and the Grounds of Contention* (Pittsburgh, Pa., 2003), 64–87 at 79–80. See also James Turner, *Politics of Landscape: Rural Scenery and Society in English Poetry, 1630–1660* (Oxford, 1979), and Tim Fulford, *Landscape, Liberty and Authority: Poetry, Criticism and Politics from Thomson to Wordsworth* (Cambridge, 1996).

perfection, maintaining in his landscaped gardens the balance between art and nature and rendering 'Britain the Eden of Europe'. Seward's political convictions and Whig concepts of 'liberty' were intertwined with her aesthetic positions: 'the gardens of England are as much more natural, free, and beautiful, than those of any other country, as its constitution diffuses more genuine liberty'.[57] William Mason's Miltonic poem *The English Garden* (1781) was another telling instance of how Milton was utilized as an epitome of Englishness; here, a poetical essay on gardening styles became a general lesson in 'native' authenticity. 'Great Nature scorns control', Mason counselled his readers; 'she will not bear / One beauty foreign to the spot or soil'. The poem was partly influenced by the 'Gothic revival', which celebrated an alleged nativist tradition, and 'British antiquity', in explicit opposition to the Greek and Roman legacy. Thus Mason was strongly opposed to the fake Roman ruins so fashionable in eighteenth-century gardening, preferring more truthful 'Saxon piles': 'form they a rude, 'tis yet an English whole'.[58] Arguing for a whole-scale redesign of British parks and gardens after the Miltonic model, the Scottish critic Lord Kames, in his *Elements of Criticism* (1762), likewise rejected such 'Roman' accessories in gardening, claiming that they would look like remnants from the time of Rome's conquest of Britain. To the new insistence on indigenous 'purity', Kames added the anxiety of a former colony.[59]

Responding to the new situation of a commercial empire, critics like Addison, Steele, and the Earl of Shaftesbury developed a language of 'politeness' and a 'Whiggish politics of manners'.[60] Revealing to their readership the hidden beauties of both literary works and landscapes, these literary critics simultaneously restricted the potential for any 'deeper' appreciation of art or nature to a select segment of the population. Most famously, Addison in his *Spectator* essays insisted that *Paradise Lost* contained 'Multitudes of Beauties', most of which 'are not so obvious to ordinary Readers'. Addison established a connection between the learned appreciation of literary works and the refined gaze upon landscapes:

A Man of a Polite Imagination . . . meets with a secret Refreshment in a Description, and often feels a greater Satisfaction in the Prospect of Fields and Meadows, than another does in the Possession. It gives him, indeed, a kind of Property in every thing he sees, and makes the most rude uncultivated Parts of Nature administer to his Pleasures.[61]

---

[57] Anna Seward, Letter to J. Johnson, 20 Sept. 1794, in *Letters of Anna Seward, Written between the Years 1784 and 1807*, 6 vols. (Edinburgh, 1811), iv. 3–12 at 10.

[58] William Mason, *The English Garden: A Poem in Four Books* (1781), in Chalmers (ed.), *Works of the English Poets*, xviii. 379–97 at 379, 395. See Kenneth Clark, *The Gothic Revival: An Essay in the History of Taste* (1928), p. vii, and Newman, *The Rise of English Nationalism*, 110–12.

[59] [Lord Kames] Henry Home (pseud.), 'Gardening and Architecture', in *Elements of Criticism*, 3 vols., 2nd edn. (Edinburgh, 1763), iii. 326–400 at 347.

[60] Lawrence E. Klein, 'Property and Politeness in the Early Eighteenth-Century Whig Moralists: The Case of the *Spectator*', in John Brewer and Susan Staves (eds.), *Early Modern Conceptions of Property* (1995), 221–33 at 221.

[61] Addison, *Criticism on Milton's Paradise Lost*, 75 (8 Mar. 1712); 182 (21 June 1712). On this elitist discourse about 'concealed beauties' see also Ross, 'Addison Reads Milton', 213.

This was, in fact, a sophisticated transposition of the language of imperialist appropriation: aesthetic pleasure became conducive to an exclusive kind of spiritual, if not actual, 'Property', turning even 'rude uncultivated' nature into a prelapsarian paradise. Mary Louise Pratt recounts how in the eighteenth century a European 'planetary consciousness' manifested itself in a landscape discourse that shunned overt attitudes of conquest but, in the very acts of seeing and appreciating, took possession of foreign regions—or, for that matter, of one's own countryside.[62] These metaphors of hidden beauties in nature and literature were further developed by later critics, who kept referring to Addison's essays as the originating moment of refined literary criticism; thus Jonathan Richardson in his *Explanatory Notes and Remarks on Milton's Paradise Lost* (1734) claimed that Milton 'Expresses himself So Concisely, Employs Words So Sparingly, that whoever will Possess His Ideas must Dig for them, and Oftentimes pretty far below the Surface'. Milton's literary landscape, he insisted, was 'Well Separated and Regularly Order'd' but had to be explored and exploited by dutiful and careful readers. In his *Discourse on the Dignity, Certainty, Pleasure and Advantage of the Science of a Connoisseur* (1719), he maintained that by learning to appreciate literary works of art, for instance Milton's description of paradise, readers would also be taught the right way to respond to nature; in an expanded reference to Milton, he compared the 'connoisseur' to Adam 'after the angel had removed the film from [his] eyes, and purged with euphrane and rue the visual nerve'.[63]

There was a concrete political context for these debates on aesthetics: the contemporary agitation for enclosure, the privatization of so-called 'waste commons'. W. J. T. Mitchell has argued that the 'Enclosure movement . . . [was] an internal colonization of the home country, its transformation from what Blake called "a green & pleasant land" into a landscape.'[64] Writing on the conceptual relationship between the English country house and the colonial estate, Bruce McLeod argues that 'the need to control space in external possessions leads to similar regulation at home'.[65] While Milton's description of paradise, and florilegia such as Adam and Eve's morning hymn, were frequently used by eighteenth-century readers to describe their own sense of the divine in nature,[66] at the same time topographical poetry by Country Whig poets turned paradise, anachronistically, into a result of the enclosure movement. An anonymous 1769 broadside poem, for instance, called, simply,

---

[62] Mary Louise Pratt, *Imperial Eyes: Travel Writing and Transculturation* (1992), 5.

[63] Richardson, *Explanatory Notes and Remarks on Milton's Paradise Lost*, 315–16; Jonathan Richardson, *A Discourse on the Dignity, Certainty, Pleasure and Advantage of the Science of a Connoisseur* (1719), in *The Works of Mr. Jonathan Richardson, consisting of I. The Theory of Painting, II. Essay on the Art of Criticism, so far as it relates to Painting, III. The Science of a Connoisseur*, ed. Jonathan Richardson, Jr., (1773), repr. *Anglistica & Americana*, 37, pp. 241–346 at 323–4.

[64] 'Imperial Landscape', in W. J. T. Mitchell (ed.), *Landscape and Power* (Chicago, 1994), 13–27 at 17. See also Raymond Williams, *The Country and the City* (1973), 101, and Pamela Horn, *Life and Labour in Rural England, 1760–1850* (1987), 47.

[65] Rephrased by Andrew Hadfield, 'Colonial Roots in English Gardens', review of Bruce McLeod, *The Geography of Empire in English Literature 1580–1745* (Cambridge, 1999), *Times Literary Supplement*, 17 Dec. 1999, p. 24.

[66] Achinstein, ' "Pleasure by Description" ', 74.

Paradise, and '*undertaken at the desire of the Gentleman who raised the elegant Villa, whose various scenery it is intended to describe*', directly linked the fruitful landscape of a 'Paradise restored' to the fact of enclosure: 'where yon lengthening waste / (An age o'erlook'd;) no rich inclosure graced; ... an Eden bloom'd a-new' (p. 26). John Gilbert Cooper's *Letters Concerning Taste* (1755) likewise rewrote an English landscape as a utilitarian paradise. The speaker transforms, before his reader's mental eyes, an idyllic garden landscape into an agricultural landscape, a 'merely' beautiful scene into a useful one. It soon transpires that the hidden material qualities of the landscape, 'Minerals in the Mountains; future Navies in the Woods', all along had been the cause behind the—initially superficial—impression of beauty:

Now to heighten this beautiful Landscape, let us throw in Corn Fields, here and there a Country Seat, and, at proper Distances, small Hamlets, together with Spires and Towers, as MILTON describes them, 'bosom'd high in tufted Trees'. Does not an additional Rapture flow in from this Adjunct, of which Reason will afterwards discover the latent Cause... Truth, Beauty, and Utility are inseparable.[67]

In Miltonic manner, the signs of human civilization, 'Spires and Towers', are here harmoniously embedded into the natural environment, 'bosom'd high in tufted Trees' ('L'Allegro', ll. 77–8), producing the scene that Wordsworth had demanded from Milton, English 'Hamlets cottages & woods'. Moreover, Cooper's 'intellectual Powers' here assign everything to its 'proper' use. It is 'Reason' that discovers these 'latent Cause[s]' of nature's beauty, connecting aesthetic value and utility. Milton's works have been updated to suit the reality of a commercial empire. In *Paradise Lost*, it should be kept in mind, there is no clear-cut distinction between secluded garden idylls and a world of exotic riches; even before the fall, Milton's paradise contains oriental goods of proleptically sinister connotations.[68] In the eighteenth century, then, a pervasive consciousness of being part of a wider empire rendered all poetic attempts at depicting a self-sufficient English countryside hopelessly anachronistic. Thus as we survey Milton's 'afterlife' during the Long Eighteenth Century, it becomes apparent that when Milton critics talked about language and aesthetics, or writers talked about enclosures and gardening in the Miltonic style, they were also talking about the wider political context of their own imperial nation. In eighteenth-century Miltonizing texts and Milton criticism, both versions of Milton's classical precursor, bucolic and imperial Virgil, were indissolubly combined.

[67] John Gilbert Cooper, *Letters Concerning Taste* (3rd edn., 1757), repr. in *Essays on Taste: From John Gilbert Cooper, Letters Concerning Taste, third edition (1757), & John Armstrong, Miscellanies (1770)*, ed. Ralph Cohen (Los Angeles, 1951), 5.

[68] See Christopher Ricks, *Milton's Grand Style* (Oxford, 1963), 109–17.

CHAPTER 38

MILTONIC ROMANTICISM

JOSEPH WITTREICH

Milton is, at present, the word . . .

Mary Wollstonecraft

As Christopher Caudwell coins the phrase 'Miltonic Romanticism',[1] he registers his sense of Milton's ubiquitous presence in the literature of the Romantic period, both canonical and popular, and at the same time acknowledges an influence *through the Romantics* that Milton continues to exert on later writers. '[G]etting beyond Milton's vision'[2] is part of the story, which at times entails repudiation and other times modification and elaboration of Milton's writings. One after another, Romantic writings loop back to the ending of *Paradise Lost*: 'The world was all before them,

---

[1] *Romance and Realism: A Study of English Bourgeois Literature*, ed. Samuel Hynes (Princeton, 1970), 66. The epigraph is from Mary Wollstonecraft, 'To William Roscoe', 6 Oct. 1791, in *Collected Letters of Mary Wollstonecraft*, ed. Ralph M. Wardle (Ithaca, N.Y., 1979), 203. On Milton and the Romantics, see especially *The Romantics on Milton: Formal Essays and Critical Asides*, ed. Joseph Wittreich (Cleveland, Ohio, 1970); Joseph Wittreich (ed.), *Milton and the Line of Vision* (Madison, Wis., 1975), esp. 97–230; and ibid., ' "The Illustrious Dead": Milton's Legacy and Romantic Prophecy', *Milton and the Romantics*, 4 (1980), 17–32, and ' "The Work of Man's Redemption": Prophecy and Apocalypse in Romantic Poetry', in Kenneth R. Johnston and Gene W. Ruoff (eds.), *The Age of William Wordsworth: Critical Essays on the Romantic Tradition* (New Brunswick, N.J., 1987), 39–61, as well as Lucy Newlyn, *'Paradise Lost' and the Romantic Reader* (Oxford, 1995); Lisa Low and John Harding (eds.), *Milton, the Metaphysicals, and Romanticism* (Cambridge, 1994); Jonathan Shears, *The Romantic Legacy of 'Paradise Lost': Reading against the Grain* (London, 2009); and Luisa Calè, *Fuseli's Milton Gallery: 'Turning Readers into Spectators'* (Oxford, 2006).

[2] Marlon B. Ross, *The Contours of Masculine Desire: Romanticism and the Rise of Women's Poetry* (New York and Oxford, 1989), 90.

where to choose' (*PL*, xii. 646). Thus Wollstonecraft's *Maria*: 'Whither I should go'; thus Wordsworth's *The Prelude*: 'The earth is all before me', even if 'the chosen guide / Be nothing better than a wandering cloud' (i. 14, 16–17).[3] If here Wordsworth deploys the topos of the earth or the world before him, in *Home at Grasmere* he inverts it: 'With paradise before him' (l. 14)—a topos that, in *Mary*, Wollstonecraft had already inverted in order to subvert it so that the world remains in 'darkness' (p. 38), 'in ruins' (p. 39), as visions of paradise are now dismissed as 'dear delusions, gay deceits' (p. 38).

Indeed, among the Romantics, it is William Godwin in particular who gives definition and inflection to the distinctive character of their representations of Milton. With Falkland in the role of author and Caleb Williams acting as his amanuensis, we are told of the latter's project, which encompasses the transcription of literary compositions, consisting of 'an analytical survey of the plans of different authors' and, perhaps more important, of 'conjectural speculations upon hints they afforded, tending either to the detection of their errors, or the carrying forward their discoveries'.[4] Wrestling Milton down, reconstituting his vision, is one aspect of a story that, as we shall see, includes adopting Milton's literary strategies and furthering his revelations. In Wordsworth's formulation from *The Prelude*: 'Poets . . . as Prophets' are 'each with each / Connected in a mighty scheme of truth' (xiii. 301–2).

FORGING THE ROMANTIC MYTH

Romanticism has been described as 'a new mythology'[5] with an inward turn, an interiorizing and psychologizing impulse, which, as it shifts the inflection from the loss to the recovery of paradise, projects its redemption myth from God back to man. In the process, Northrop Frye explains, artists in their creative capacity achieve God-like status in their new role as the central figure in awakening and shaping civilization. As a journeyman, Frye continues, the artist's turn is 'downward and inward', with the 'inner and hidden parts of the mind' and the depths of the soul becoming the sites of sometimes anguished illumination and with the artist simultaneously emerging, even when his or her soul is in ruin or the world is in ruins, as the hero of this quest. The central event in both individual and cultural transformation is thus situated in the consciousness of the artist and can be described as 'the attaining of an

---

[3] Wollstonecraft, *Mary/Maria*, ed. Janet Todd (1991), 84. All quotations of Wordsworth's poetry are from *The Poetical Works of Wordsworth*, ed. Paul D. Sheats (Boston, 1982) and are given parenthetically within the text.

[4] William Godwin, *Caleb Williams*, ed. Gary Handwerk and A. A. Markley (Peterborough, Ont., 2000).

[5] Northrop Frye, *A Study of English Romanticism* (New York, 1968), [16].

expanded consciousness', 'the attaining of an apocalyptic vision by the fallen but potentially regenerate mind'.[6]

If the triumph of Romanticism is to be found in this expansion of human consciousness, in such movements of the mind, in such a collision of perspectives, its tragedy resides in an insufficiency of human consciousness, in the blurring and maiming of it, in minds shackled and their eventual closing down. The inaugurating figure of Romanticism, thus construed, is John Milton. Its harbingers are his epics of consciousness with their stories of 'more and more perceiving' (to borrow a phrase from the Argument to Book 10 of *Paradise Lost*) and his *Samson Agonistes*, or tragedy of the cinching of human consciousness, its impairment before it is eventually freed again. '[T]heir eyes how opened, and their minds / How darkened', writes Milton in *Paradise Lost* as he elides the fallen Adam and Samson: 'innocence . . . / . . . was gone' (ix. 1053–5; see also ix. 1059–62). Romanticism, in alliance with Milton, worries over the prospects for recovering the lost paradise, for breaking through the cycles of history.

No less than the Romantics, Milton was gripped by the idea that only God and the poet are creators[7] and its corollary that, in the words of Gordon Teskey, 'poems . . . are extensions of the original Creation' and always 'referred back to an original Creator'—for, as Teskey suggests, Milton 'cannot accept this subordination of creativity to Creation'.[8] Teskey does not trace this idea of poetic creation back to Tasso, by whom it is popularized, nor to the biblical poetics from which it derives, though he does document Milton's embrace of an analogy between his own creation and God's even as he details Milton's transitional status as 'the last major poet in the European literary tradition for whom the act of creation is centered in God and the first in whom the act of creation begins to find its center in the human'. *Paradise Lost*, from Teskey's point of view, is about 'the underlying hum of its production', while gathering into focus the dialectics of creation through which it also exhibits the rifts at the centre of Milton's consciousness, those divisions within that are an aspect of Milton's poetics of indeterminacy and that yield his poetry of contradictions.[9] With the artist thus emerging as a microcosm of his culture, an epitome of its stresses and conflicts, but also now acknowledged as its legislator, he is then heroized, in important respects at Milton's prompting.

Henry Fuseli, responsible for the greatly acclaimed Milton Gallery of 1799, states as much when he remarks that Milton says some praise the work, some its author, indicating that at least some regard the work and its creator as indistinguishable from one another; that reading any one of Milton's works is 'reading' Milton.[10] Nor is this way of thinking particularly masculinist; for Fuseli's intimate friend Mary

---

[6] Ibid. 33 (see also 47), 37 (see also 42, 46, 37–8).

[7] See Torquato Tasso, *Discourses on the Heroic Poem*, trans. Mariella Cavalchini and Irene Samuel (Oxford, 1973), 77–8. On the poem as heterocosm, see M. H. Abrams, *The Mirror and the Lamp: Romantic Theory and the Critical Tradition* (1953; repr. New York, 1958), 272–85, and Joseph Wittreich, *Visionary Poetics: Milton's Tradition and his Legacy* (San Marino, Calif., 1979), 9–26.

[8] *Delirious Milton: The Fate of the Poet in Modernity* (Cambridge, Mass., 2006), 11, 18.

[9] Ibid. 5–6 (cf. 29), 19.

[10] See 'Lectures', in *The Life and Writings of Henry Fuseli, Esq.*, ed. John Knowles, 3 vols. (1831), iii. 124.

Wollstonecraft, in her very first novel, *Mary*, declared that the only compositions with a power to delight are those in which 'the soul of the author is exhibited, and animates the hidden springs' of a work (p. [3]), with one character now echoing the mind and another the soul of the author who, himself or herself a composite of his or her characters, may thus assume the role of hero in the tale. The hero is thus a composite figure, an imaginative construction out of the shattered fragments of characters that people a work.

In Wollstonecraft's novel, the heroine, rambling in a paradise of her own making, takes her early lessons from *Paradise Lost*, which is to say from Milton, and which is then to acknowledge that Wollstonecraft, like another of her contemporaries, William Blake, sees in Milton's last poems what we might call the Foucauldian moment when 'stories of heroes' give way to the 'author's biography', the founding moment for 'the fundamental critical category of "the man and his work"'.[11] Very likely, it is from Milton that Wollstonecraft came to distinguish between visual/iconic and verbal portraits. She may send on a painted portrait to William Roscoe, though if he wants 'a more faithful sketch', he will find it in 'a book that I am now writing [*A Vindication of the Rights of Woman*], in which "I myself... shall certainly appear, head and heart—but this is between ourselves—pay respect a woman's secret!"'[12] Milton's secret becomes woman's/her secret.

From a Romantic perspective, Milton is everywhere in his writings, hence the plethora of Romantic biographies; but he is also everywhere manifest in his characters. In the words of Samuel Taylor Coleridge:

John Milton himself is in every line of the Paradise Lost.... There is a subjectivity of the poet, as of Milton, who is himself before himself in every thing he writes.... In the Paradise Lost—indeed in every one of his poems—it is Milton himself whom you see; his Satan, his Adam, his Raphael, almost his Eve—are all John Milton; and it is a sense of this intense egotism that gives me the greatest pleasure in reading Milton's works. The egotism of such a man is a revelation of spirit.[13]

And Milton is there not just in *Paradise Lost*, but in 'Lycidas', *Paradise Regained*, and *Samson Agonistes* most notably. He is there, within the purview of Romanticism, as subject for both celebration and critique but, even more, as founder of the Romantic mythology and an author of its inward turn; as the poet, according to John Keats in his annotations to *Paradise Lost*, whose métier is 'one Mind's imagining [itself] into another'.[14]

Indeed, *turns inward* afford a framing device in *Paradise Lost*, where early on Satan famously proclaims that 'The mind is its own place, and in it self / Can make a heaven

---

[11] For these quotations, and for further discussion of them, see Joseph Wittreich, *Why Milton Matters: A New Preface to his Writings* (New York and Basingstoke, 2006), 2.

[12] Wollstonecraft, 'To William Roscoe', 6 Oct. 1791, in *Letters*, 203.

[13] Samuel Taylor Coleridge, *Table Talk*, quoted from *Romantics on Milton*, ed. Wittreich, 270, 277. For discussion of Milton's Romantic biographers, see Jerome Alan Kramer, 'Milton Biography in the Romantic Era' (Ph.D. diss., Ohio State University, 1966).

[14] John Keats, 'Annotations to *Paradise Lost*', quoted from *Romantics on Milton*, ed. Wittreich, 554.

of hell, a hell of heaven' (i. 254–5), and where, in its concluding book, Michael promises Adam that, upon leaving Eden, he will 'possess / A paradise within... [himself], happier far' (xii. 586–7), all in anticipation of *Paradise Regained*, where the entire poem is emplotted within the mind of the Son who, as he enters the desert, '[i]nto himself descended' (ii. 111). And in anticipation of *Samson Agonistes*, where Milton continues to invent what the Romantics will adopt as their own distinctive genre of mental theatre. It is not so much heroic virtue as the heroic mind that Romantic literature, under the tutelage of Milton, enshrines. Moreover, it is a mind less influenced than exercised and then, through exercise, transformed.

'[N]o poet, outside the Bible', writes Northrop Frye, 'was accorded the kind of authority that was given to a theologian.'[15] With the exception of Milton, we should add, and then say: no theologian rivals Milton, even comes close to him, in terms of the impact he has registered on how the scriptural myths of Creation, Fall, Recovery, and Apocalypse in their Miltonic modifications were perceived during the Romantic period. If the Romantics discovered Milton's heterodoxy, they were also able to document it with the uncovery of *De Doctrina Christiana* in 1823 and its publication in the Charles Sumner translation of 1826. Here was proof of what Shelley had avowed: that orthodoxy is 'merely the mask and the mantle in which these great poets [like Milton] walk through eternity enveloped and disguised'. *Paradise Lost* 'contains within itself', according to *A Defence of Poetry*, 'a philosophical refutation of that system of which, by a strange and natural antithesis, it has been a chief popular support'.[16] Not one who invites indolent, acquiescent reading, Milton in his writings affords a counter-paradigm to such books, as described by Mary Wollstonecraft, 'which support our favorite opinions,... our minds placidly... reflect[ing] the images which illustrate the tenets we have embraced. We indolently acquiesce in the conclusion.'[17] Milton fosters a resistant readership, one whose collective mind, breaking free of what in *Mary* is called its 'mouldering tenement' (p. 35), is then put on the stretch.

Paradise Lost, *Paradise Regained*, and *Samson Agonistes* form a trilogy of poems, each wrapped around a different myth and each transforming, as well as reinterpreting, the myth it appropriates. It is Milton's version of these stories that persists and prevails in the cultural consciousness of the Romantic period, each of these poems pressing towards a heightened understanding of the myth it inscribes. An abiding presence in his poems, Milton also teases us into vaulting him into the role of hero in any one of them. Certainly Blake took the hint, titling his first completed epic-prophecy *Milton*, with Northrop Frye once quipping in conversation that *Milton* should also carry as its subtitle: *Paradise Regained* by John Milton (without a comma). No poem better illustrates the salient features of 'Miltonic Romanticism',

[15] *A Study of English Romanticism*, 16.

[16] Percy Bysshe Shelley, 'A Defence of Poetry', in *Shelley's Poetry and Prose*, ed. Donald H. Reiman and Neil Fraistat (New York and London, 2002), 526. All quotations of Shelley's poetry and prose, unless otherwise indicated, are from this edition.

[17] Wollstonecraft, 'On Poetry', in *Posthumous Works: Mary Wollstonecraft*, ed. William Godwin, 4 vols. (New York, 1974), iv. 193–4.

whether we are thinking of its secularizing and humanizing impulses; of its creation of internal spaces, or mental forms and landscapes, its heavens and hells within; or of its mapping of the human mind and its movements, or its psychological explorations thereof; or its freeing of the human mind and setting of its faculties in just relation again. The poet 'ought him selfe to bee a true Poem, that is, a composition, and patterne of the best and honourablest things', Milton writes in *An Apology for a Pamphlet* (*CPW*, i. 890). Man, not God, *man or woman as artist*, is the hero of this new age, its animating spirit, its energizing force. It is his (or her) consciousness fully expanded, his (or her) senses newly awakened, his (or her) judgement quickened that effect a renovated society and a regenerated world.

It is Milton's impact on Romanticism that gives currency to an understanding of the wilderness story, which, especially in Milton's rendering of it in *Paradise Regained*, is a prophetic poem about the evolution of human consciousness and the building up of the human spirit. *Paradise Regained* is a prelude to the defining poems of British Romanticism, not only *Milton* but *The Prelude* and *Prometheus Unbound*: the delineation of a mental progress, involving self-definition and self-discovery and engaging its readership in acts of thinking about thinking that eventuate in the creation of a paradise 'in the very world', according to *The Prelude*, 'which is the world / Of all of us,—the place where, in the end, / We find our happiness or not at all' (xi. 142–4). 'A fairer Paradise is founded *now*' (iv. 613; my italics), says Milton in *Paradise Regained*, just as the Shelley of *Prometheus Unbound* invests in 'hope, till Hope creates / From its own wreck the thing it contemplates' (iv. 573–4).

Like *The Prelude*, as well as Blake's *Milton*, *Paradise Regained* and Shelley's *Prometheus Unbound* map a course of 'more and more perceiving'. All these poems are about the formation of the prophetic character, the *agon* experienced as each protagonist moves unremittingly towards (or in the case of *Samson Agonistes* falls short of) 'a moment of illumination in which the whole of reality is absorbed within the perceiving mind of the poet'.[18] Regaining paradise is provocation for the condition for which both Milton and *Milton* pray: Milton in *Areopagitica* for 'a Nation of Prophets' and a time Moses's wish is fulfilled when 'all the Lords people are become Prophets' (*CPW*, ii. 554, 556); and Blake in *Milton* praying (with Moses), 'Would to God that all the Lord's people were Prophets'.[19] As poets transform myths, they wring from them higher truths and, simultaneously, reconstitute (sometimes radically) the genres in which those myths are about to be newly emplotted. *Paradise Regained* is a poem whose transformation from epic into prophecy may be gauged by the way in which its myth of discovery morphs into a myth of deliverance. Discovery is prologue to deliverance just as an apocalypse of mind forecasts an apocalypse in history.

At least Milton leaves open this prospect, amid much equivocation in his last poems. The imminent apocalypse of the early prose works, of *Areopagitica*, for example—'Methinks I see in my mind a noble and puissant Nation rousing herself like a strong man after sleep, and shaking her invincible locks' (*CPW*, ii. 558)—has

---

[18] I am quoting Northrop Frye, *Fearful Symmetry: A Study of William Blake* (1947; Boston, 1967), 316.

[19] See William Blake, 'Milton', in *Romantics on Milton*, ed. Wittreich, 39.

gone into deferral in *Paradise Lost*, where the poet is waiting for an apocalypse he now glimpses far down the corridors of history. On the other hand, in *Paradise Regained* Milton envisages a paradise founded *now*, although the new Jerusalem of history promised in this poem becomes a question mark in *Samson Agonistes*, where the cycles of history, instead of being escaped, keep repeating themselves; where paradise again seems irrevocably lost. Signs of dis-ease with Milton's vision are evident, however muted, in Blake and Wordsworth: in the former's juxtaposition of the 'paradise' of Beulah with the heavenly city of Jerusalem, with his recasting of the Garden as a City; and in the latter's *Home at Grasmere* and his dismissal of 'all Arcadian dreams, / All golden fancies of the golden age, / The bright array of shadowy thoughts from times / That were before all time, or are to be / Ere time expire' (ll. 625–9). The veiled critiques of Blake and Wordsworth become full-blown in the writings of Mary Wollstonecraft, William Godwin, and the Shelleys.

The Romantic Critique of Milton

It is not just the character of Eve, as represented by Henry Fuseli in his Milton Gallery, that troubles Wollstonecraft. '[L]ike Milton', she writes, Fuseli 'seems quite at home in hell—his Devil will be the hero of the poetic series'. At the same time, however, Wollstonecraft admits to 'rather doubt[ing] whether . . . [Fuseli] will produce an Eve to please me in any of the situations, which he has selected, unless it be after the fall'.[20] It is then, according to Wollstonecraft, that Satan has some bearing on the human condition, now emblematizing the plight of women in the fallen world, her status in *Mary* and *Maria*, as a 'Poor solitary wretch' and 'monster' (pp. 36, 89; cf. 49, 67, 69, 73, 89, 103), as well as her Promethean stature as 'the champion for suffering humanity' (p. 91) who, in Maria's words, extends 'my thoughts beyond myself, and [makes me] grieve for human misery' (p. 83). It is woman, more so than man, who best illustrates the Blakean adage that 'The most sublime act is to put another before you'.[21]

In any case, Wollstonecraft's complaint reaches beyond Fuseli to other masculinist critics of the time, including Edmund Burke and perhaps even William Blake—'I am sick of hearing of the sublimity of Milton'[22]—and, indeed, extends to Milton himself:

---

[20] 'To William Roscoe', 3 Jan. 1792, in *Letters*, 206. For more on Eve, see 'A Vindication of the Rights of Woman', in *The Works of Mary Wollstonecraft*, ed. Janet Todd and Marilyn Butler (1989), v. 88–90, 102, 103, 114, 121, 128–9, 143.

[21] 'The Marriage of Heaven and Hell', in *Complete Poetry and Prose*, 36.

[22] Wollstonecraft, 'Thoughts on the Education of Daughters', in *Works*, iv. 21. For Fuseli on *Paradise Lost* as 'That sublime book', see *The Collected English Letters of Henry Fuseli*, ed. David W. Weinglass (Millwood, N.Y., 1982), 115. On poetry as 'sublime allegory', cf. Wollstonecraft, 'Hints', in *Posthumous Works*, v. 274, 275, and Blake, 'To Thomas Butts', Felpham, 6 July 1803, in *Complete Poetry and Prose*, 730.

both to his representation of what is called in *Mary* the 'inscrutable' and destructive 'ways of Heaven' (p. 34) and to his 'description of paradise' (long before Toni Morrison, demoted to lower casing), which 'fills . . . [her] with benevolent satisfaction', even if she 'cannot help viewing them, I mean the first pair—as if they were inferiors—inferiors because they could find happiness in a world like this'.[23] *It is a world in which she is inferior to him* and is thus represented 'as only created to see through a gross medium, and to take things on trust'.[24] He sees visions. She has dreams. He finds a Paradise within himself. She finds her paradise in him—yet another indication that she is 'the toy of man, his rattle', some 'fanciful kind of *half being*' ('Vindication of the Rights of Woman', 102, 108), and yet another reminder that for women anyway, as evidenced in *Mary*, 'happiness was not to be found on earth' (p. 31). For women to give way to such a fancy is 'madness', as we also learn from *Mary*; women are prone to building terrestrial paradises liable 'to be destroyed by the first serious thought' (ibid.), as becomes powerfully evident in *Maria* in the overlapping narratives of Maria and Jemima.

At times, as in his dialogue with God where Adam asks for an equal, Milton has him request more than a subordinate or mere satellite. Other times, as when Milton represents Adam and Eve 'Imparadised in one another's arms' (iv. 506) and, later, Eve as eventually discovering her paradise in Adam, Milton, like Rousseau, implies that paradise is not a condition of every soul but rather a circumstance in which the souls of man and woman are perfectly united. He can find Paradise without her. She finds paradise only in him:

> Thy going is not lonely, with thee goes
> Thy husband, him to follow thou art bound;
> Where he abides, think there thy native soil. (xi. 290–2)

>   . . . now lead on;
> In me is no delay; with thee to go,
> Is to stay here; without thee here to stay,
> Is to go hence unwilling; thou to me
> Art all things under heaven, all places thou . . . (xii. 614–18)

In the significantly altering eye of women's critique of Milton, equally evident in Mary Shelley's *Mathilda*, woman is not only another Satan, 'another Cain', but also another Eve wrecked by the sin of Adam. Mathilda lives in a 'Paradisaical bliss' until dislodged from it: 'I disobeyed no command, I ate no apple, and yet I was ruthlessly driven from it.'[25]

Yet, like Rousseau, Milton also gets it right when he depicts mankind, both man and woman, in *A Maske* and *Samson Agonistes*, as born free but everywhere in chains, always looking for assurances, as in *Maria*, that 'the world was not a desert' (l. 133) only to find 'pathless desert[s]' everywhere (l. 141); only to find that mankind's abode

---

[23] Wollstonecraft, 'To Everina Wollstonecraft', 10 Sept. 1790, in *Letters*, 195; see also 'Letter on the Present Character of the French Nation', in *Posthumous Works*, iv. 44–5.

[24] 'Vindication of the Rights of Woman', in *Works*, v. 122.

[25] Mary Shelley, *Mathilda*, ed. Elizabeth Nitchie (Chapel Hill, N.C., 1959), 71, 16, also 10, 11.

is a world of hissing serpents. Whereas others saw in the French Revolution a time with a tomorrow, Wollstonecraft sees 'the evils of the moment', the night before a new day of tyranny, and the world as a 'dark prison-house'.[26] The paradise women 'ramble in, must be of their own creating', says Wollstonecraft in *Mary*, only then to align such paradises wittily with Milton's 'Paradise of Fools, etc.' (p. [3]) and then only by way of suggesting that these paradises are among the sublime ideas that women must cast away; that even if as in *Maria* women almost scent 'the fresh green of spring', it is the scent of something that 'never returns' to them (p. 96).

In *Mary*, such an awareness is part of the progress of woman's understanding, as well as evidence of 'her mind expanded' by degrees (p. 16). Hence (in echoes of 'Lycidas' and its distinction between the author's former and his new self) not Mary the character but Mary the book's author holds all the trump cards. Mary the character announces approvingly that 'Milton has asserted, That earthly love is the scale by which to heavenly love we may ascend' (p. 33)—a point that Mary the author will address mockingly as she insists 'that Plato and Milton were grossly mistaken in asserting that human love led to heavenly, and was only an exaltation of the same affection'.[27] In the company of the new woman, then, we are made to wonder whether heaven was actually peopled with spirits masculine as the whole idea of women as pretty playthings is abandoned. If only because they do not do so adequately, or do so consistently, Milton's epics prompt female writers to map the minds of women, their movements of mind, their struggles, and, in the process, to portray thinking women. As much as 'Lycidas', *Paradise Lost* presents a twin consciousness, the poet's former and his new self, the poet as character/narrator in the poem and the poet as author of the poem. Evident in Adam's and Eve's different versions of *her*story, in Uriel's, Raphael's, and Adam's vying accounts of Creation, in Adam's, Raphael's, and Satan's competing speculations concerning cosmology, as well as a deft device in the Romantics' critique of Milton, that double consciousness is an increasingly prominent feature in their writings, an analytic tool.

The 'Two consciousnesses', even before *The Prelude* (ii. 32), is a core concept in Romantic poetry and fiction: in Romantic fiction especially, where (as we learn from *Mary*, for example) woman herself perceives, all too plainly, that she sees 'through a glass darkly' (p. 12); that understanding her condition of mind forged manacles is part of the learning experience in her 'probationary state' (p. 12) and eventuates in her understanding that woman's mind is a sepulchre, a moving grave, and (as reported in *Maria*) 'confined in hell itself' (p. 105) so long as she searches for paradise in another man (or woman) or invests in any existing promises of a terrestrial paradise. Yet there also remains the hope, enunciated in *Mary*, that eventually women will no longer see through a glass darkly (at which time she will cease reasoning about and finally feel happiness in a world where currently happiness is

---

[26] Wollstonecraft, 'Letter on the Present Character of the French Nation', in *Posthumous Works*, iv. 50; and 'Extract of The Cave of Fancy. A Tale', in *Works*, iv. 104.

[27] 'A Vindication of the Rights of Men', in *Works*, v. 46 (see also v. 143); cf. 'Extract', in *Posthumous Works*, iv. 154–5.

but a moment in a general drama of pain; that the time will come, as *Maria* suggests, when women will eventually escape their 'tomb of living death' (p. 79).

Complicated—and compelling—versions of these truths emerge in *Maria*, where initially Jemima, Maria, and Danford all seem to find happiness in one another:

So much heaven did they enjoy, that paradise bloomed around them.... Love, the grand enchanter, 'lapt them in Elysium' [*A Maske*, l. 257], and every sense was harmonized to joy and social extacy. So animated, indeed, were their accents of tenderness...that Jemima felt, with surprise, a tear of pleasure trickling down her ragged cheeks. She wiped it away...

...—now the sun broke forth, the rainbow appeared, and every prospect was fair...the world contained not three happier beings. (p. 79)

And then there is that paradise of the mind's—of Maria's—own making: 'Was I, indeed, free?'—Yes, free I termed myself.... How had I panted for liberty...— I rose, and shook myself; opened the window, and methought the air never smelled so sweet. The face of heaven grew fairer.... I was all soul' (p. 121). Yet it is a lustre that fades, a smell that never returns, a paradise imagined only to be irretrievably lost to women who spend their time in adversity 'brood[ing] over visions of unattainable bliss' (p. 141)—visions that, if they fence out sorrows, also exclude to her own detriment the lurking dangers, the hissing serpents in the pathless desert; visions that invariably reveal marriage to be but another bastille.

With Wordsworth, all the Romantics experience intimations of a better day and a fairer world. All of them want to dwell in a world of possibility, yet also express, in different degrees, concern over how to achieve a *fairer world*, even over the possibility of ever achieving such a world. 'If there be such a thing as truth', says Godwin, 'it must infallibly be struck out by the collision of mind with mind'[28]—a collision staged within their own writings by duelling narratives, which sometimes interact with one another's writings, often times while engaging Milton himself and even casting a dubious eye, with Milton, on apocalyptic hopes and pastoral dreams. Godwin's *Caleb Williams*, for example, begins with 'golden visions' (p. 61) that, in the course of the novel, repeatedly shatter into ruins. As *Paradise Regained* hints, people are never more in hell than when they think they are in heaven.

Wollstonecraft and Godwin share the Romantic preoccupation with Miltonic heroism, which turns around the paradox of heroes who are villains and of villains who assume heroic characteristics; of heroes who are builders as well as destroyers, providers of love and civilization even if also marked by madness. The greatest such hero, according to *Caleb Williams*, 'owes the propriety of his conduct to the habit of encountering difficulties, and calling out with promptness the energies of his mind' (p. 225). Yet heroes always seem to be ambiguous in their heroism, now displaying the best qualities of mankind and now 'the basest and most odious' (p. 431), here marred by infamy and there marked by valour. Even more than Wollstonecraft's, Godwin's novel, exploring what he came to call 'the entrails of mind and motive',[29] is a

---

[28] See Handwerk and Markley, 'Introduction' in Godwin, *Caleb Williams*, 23.
[29] Ibid. 28.

meditation on and anatomy of heroism of which Milton's Satan is the archetype, with allusions to him, as in *Caleb Williams*, often shifting in their nature from hidden, to muted, to quite explicit. Milton's Satan, 'Torment[ed] within..., as from the hateful siege / Of contraries' (ix. 121–2), anticipates the Godwinian hero, with a 'mind...full of uproar like the war of contending elements' (p. 164), where 'All was confusion...[a] hurricane within' (p. 212), all chaos and uncertainty. Furthermore, Godwin's shifting of the Satan analogy from one character to another anticipates his daughter's strategy, in *Frankenstein*, of engaging all her principal characters in that analogy.

What the Satanic archetype demonstrates, according to *An Enquiry into Political Justice*, is that even erring men of talents 'are not destitute of virtue' and that 'no ingredient...so essentially contributes to a virtuous character as a sense of justice'. Speculations like these, suggests Godwin, have caused readers to attribute heroism to Milton's Satan, who 'saw no sufficient reason for that extreme inequality of rank and power which the creator assumed' and in whose mind 'a sense of reason and justice was stronger...than a sense of brute force':

> He bore his torments with fortitude, because he disdained to be subdued by despotic power. He sought revenge, because he could not think with tameness of the unexpostulating authority that assumed to dispose of him. How beneficial and illustrious might the temper from which these qualities flowed have proved with a small diversity of situation!...
>
> A man of quick resentment, of strong feelings, and who pertinaciously resists every thing that he regards as an unjust assumption, may be considered as having in him the seeds of eminence. Nor is it easily to be conceived that such a man should not proceed from a sense of justice to some degree of benevolence; as Milton's hero felt real compassion and sympathy for his partners in misfortune.[30]

The Satan analogy produces characters ambiguous in their heroism—heroes like *Milton*'s Satan, who is for a time 'Stupidly good' (ix. 465) when, for example, he observes his fallen legions ('Thrice he assayed, and thrice in spite of scorn, / Tears such as angels weep, burst forth' (i. 619–20)) and later when, observing Adam and Eve, he is described as 'abstracted stood / From his own evil, and for the time remained / ... of enmity disarmed, / Of guile, of hate, of envy, of revenge' (ix. 463–6).

Gathered into immediate and crucial focus in the Preface that Percy Bysshe Shelley initially contributed to Mary Shelley's *Frankenstein Or The Modern Prometheus* (1818) and then again in the Preface (1831) she writes to replace his, Miltonic heroism is a huge concern for both the Shelleys. Matters of heroism—'The only imaginary being resembling in any degree Prometheus, is Satan; and Prometheus is, in my judgment, a more poetical character than Satan... the Hero of *Paradise Lost*'—referred to in Shelley's Preface to *Prometheus Unbound* (pp. 206–7) come to the fore in these Prefaces as well. Indeed, questions of heroism are especially evident in Percy's concern over differences between the characters' opinions and Mary's own and with Mary's assurance that, being 'too common-place...I did not make myself the

---

[30] See Godwin, 'Enquiry Concerning Political Justice', as reproduced in *Caleb Williams*, 486–8.

heroine of my tales',[31] almost in the same breath as she cites Lord Byron's *Childe Harold's Pilgrimage*, where the poet is doing just that: heroizing himself as he craftily distinguishes between himself as author of the poem and himself as model for its protagonist. Indeed, it is the author, not one of his characters, whose opinions usually precede rather than follow those of the rest of mankind; who transcends the reigning values of a culture and its starched conformities. If there is a resemblance between the author and his or her characters, it is a resemblance in which there is a knit of identity with the author but always distinction, all characters, as in *Frankenstein*, 'similar, yet at the same time strangely unlike the beings' (p. 103) to which each is compared. *Frankenstein* becomes a case study in this proposition, where every principal character in the book is netted within a system of sliding—and always slippery—analogies involving various characters in *Paradise Lost*, none of which completely sticks.

Positioned before the Preface to *Frankenstein* is its title page, one segment of which—*The Modern Prometheus*—recalls the extent to which Mary Shelley's hero here aligns with Prometheus and perhaps even anticipates the extent to which the Promethean hero has become irrevocably allied with Satan. In the course of *Paradise Lost*, the Prometheus myth slides from character to character: from Satan the rebel in Book 1, to the Son as creator in Book 7, to Adam as sufferer in Book 10. Seemingly fixed to Victor Frankenstein in Mary Shelley's novel—'the fangs of remorse tore my bosom' (p. 64), 'For an instant I dared to shake off my chains . . . ; but the iron had eaten into my flesh' (pp. 133–4), 'chains and darkness were the only objects that pressed upon me' (p. 168)—the Prometheus myth, through the disjunctive *Or* in the book's title, teases us with the question: just *who* is the modern Prometheus within the context of this novel? To which characters (other than Clerval, perhaps) does the phrase 'his mind expanded' (p. 134) pertain? Whose *being*, whose 'feelings are for ever on the stretch' (p. 134)? Is it Frankentein the creator, *or* the monster who rebels against his creator, *or* Captain Robert Walton, who, by the book's end, quelling his crew's rebellion, takes their suffering upon himself, and, Adam-like, emblematizes the human condition?

In the moment that Adam lies 'on the ground / Outstretched . . . , on the cold ground, and oft / Cursed his creation' (x. 850–2), he achieves full consciousness of his fallen condition and takes on Promethean characteristics. This dramatic climax in the main plot, Adam's lament, echoes the comparable moment in the subplot when Satan—'So stretched out huge in length the arch-fiend lay / Chained on the burning lake' (i. 209–10)—correspondingly achieves consciousness of and laments his own fallenness. Adam's own blasphemy is captured in the lines affording the epigraph to *Frankenstein* (chosen by Mary's poet husband): 'Did I request thee, Maker, from my clay / To mould me man? did I solicit thee / From darkness to promote me? / *Paradise Lost* (x. 743–5).' This moment in *Paradise Lost*, foregrounded by the frontispiece to

---

[31] Mary Shelley, 'Author's Introduction to the Standard Novels Edition (1831)', in *Frankenstein Or The Modern Prometheus: The 1818 Text*, ed. Marilyn Butler (Oxford, 1993), 193. All quotations from *Frankenstein* are from this edition.

Blake's *Songs of Innocence and of Experience*, is the moment of passage from one mental state to another, from innocence to experience.

In their turn, Milton's lines force the question, posed variously in different Prefaces to *Frankenstein* and addressed through systematic reference of characters in the novel to those in *Paradise Lost*: who is the hero of this story? Is it Frankenstein—'Cursed be the day, abhorred evil . . . Cursed (although I curse myself) be the hands that formed you!' (p. 78)—who as the Monster's creator must now curse himself? Or is it the Monster himself as he exclaims: 'Hateful day when I received life! . . . Accursed creator! Why did you form a monster so hideous . . . solitary and detested' (p. 105)? And the Monster exclaims again: 'Cursed, cursed creator! Why did I live?' (p. 110), but then confides that 'in my dying moments, I shall not curse my maker' (p. 121). Or is it, rather, as first suggested, Frankenstein himself who continues his cursing, now on behalf of his father: 'Cursed, cursed be the fiend that brought misery on his grey hairs, and doomed him to waste in wretchedness!' (p. 168)? Or is it Robert Walton, the controlling consciousness of the narrative (like the Milton of *Paradise Lost*, vii. 24–8), who, 'compassed round by . . . thick fog' (p. 12), is also aligned through allusion with the Milton of the Prologues to that poem? Moreover, the question of heroism in *Frankenstein*, as in *Paradise Lost*, is irrevocably involved with another: not only who is their hero, but how do these authors represent heroism and direct our perception of it?

With its epigraph from *Paradise Lost* (the poem from which the Monster gets his early education) and with all its characters referred back to *Paradise Lost* in a steady stream of allusions, *Frankenstein* is, as Stuart Curran reports, 'the most pronounced imaginative recreation of *Paradise Lost* in the Romantic period'.[32] It is a novel with an array of heroic types, in which the Monster, while gendered male, is analogized with woman, with Eve, and comes to emblematize her condition: 'At first I started back, unable to believe that it was indeed I who was reflected in the mirror; and when I became fully convinced that I was in reality the monster that I am, I was filled with the bitterest sensations of despondence and mortification' (p. 90; cf. *PL*, iv. 460–91).

Yet it is also a book in which Mary asks with her mother about the efficacy of any paradise of someone's own making. Says Walton: 'I also became a poet, and for one year lived in a Paradise of my own creation' (pp. 6–7). Says the Monster: 'I resolved to reside in this hovel . . . . It was indeed a paradise, compared to the bleak forest . . . and dank earth' (p. 84). And the Monster reiterates: 'I allowed my thoughts . . . to ramble in the fields of Paradise . . . . But it was all a dream . . . I was alone' (p. 106). Then Frankenstein remarks of Clerval: 'He felt as if he had been transported to Fairy-land, and enjoyed a happiness seldom tasted by man' (p. 129). And Mary Shelley herself declares the youthful Mary 'had a dearer pleasure than this, which was the formation

---

[32] Stuart Curran, ' "The Siege of Hateful Contraries": Shelley, Mary Shelley, Byron, and "Paradise Lost" ', in Joseph Wittreich (ed.), *Milton and the Line of Vision* (Madison, Wis., 1975), 218. See also Curran, *Poetic Form and British Romanticism* (Oxford, 1986).

of castles in the air . . . . My dreams were at once more fantastic and agreeable than my writings' (p. 192). But it is a paradise lost to everyone:

Sweet and beloved Elizabeth! I read and re-read her letter, and some softened feelings stole into my heart, and dared to whisper paradisaical dreams of love and joy; but the apple was already eaten, and the angel's own arm bared to drive me from all hope. (p. 159)

I dreamt that I wandered in flowery meadows and pleasant vales with the friends of my youth; but awoke, and found myself in a dungeon. (p. 168)

For the Mary Shelley of *Frankenstein* such hopes are vain, and such dreams built on quicksand, at least until heroism is given new underpinnings through 'enlarge[d] . . . faculties and understanding' (p. 17).

Frankenstein tells Walton: 'Learn from me, if not by my precepts, at least by my example, how dangerous is the acquirement of knowledge, and how much happier that man is who believes his native town to be the world, than he who aspires to become greater than his nature will allow' (p. 35). Yet the lesson that Frankenstein would teach others, by the end of the novel he has yet to learn himself. Even as Walton's crew threatens mutiny, Frankenstein urges them on as men 'to be hailed as the benefactors of your species; your name adored, as belonging to brave men who encountered death for honour and the benefit of mankind'. 'Return as heroes' (p. 183), Frankenstein urges upon the deaf ears of Walton and his crew.

Only now does one human being, namely Captain Walton, enter into humane communion with the Monster, whereupon the Monster, in turn, contemplates his dead creator (as he had earlier promised) with 'compassion' (p. 187). If an expanded mind is the mark and end of heroism, it is achieved by the Monster as he goes off to build his own funeral pyre. It is this same process of more and more perceiving that continues to engage Walton as, acquiescing to his crew, he directs his ship to return to civilization, all these journeymen now wiser men in large part because they have abandoned the 'heroics' of the Apocalypse, its 'wandering ministers of vengeance' (p. 172), the 'vengeance, that burned . . . as the mechanical impulse of some power' beyond and not within (p. 174). The mental progress in *Frankenstein* is especially evident in the artist-hero of the book, Walton, who moves towards the prophetic consciousness of the book's author. In Mary Shelley's *The Last Man*, on the other hand, the whole ideology of prophecy, and its attendant myth of apocalypse, is brought under renewed scrutiny. The same kind of searching scrutiny, commenced by Milton in his last poems and continued by the Romantics, is completed by Percy Bysshe Shelley in *The Cenci* and *Prometheus Unbound*.[33]

---

[33] See Mary Shelley, *The Last Man*, ed. Morton D. Paley (1994; Oxford, 1998); and on the millenarian/apocalyptic elements in this novel and Shelley's poems, see Steven Goldsmith, *Unbuilding Jerusalem: Apocalypse and Romantic Representations* (Ithaca, N.Y., 1993), esp. 209–69, 261, 313. See also M. H. Abrams, *Natural Supernaturalism: Tradition and Revolt in Romantic Literature* (New York, 1971); J. C. Harrison, *The Second Coming: Popular Millenarianism 1780–1850* (1979); Tim Fulford (ed.), *Romanticism and Millenarianism* (New York and Basingstoke, 2002); and Morton D. Paley, *The Apocalyptic Sublime* (New Haven and London, 1986), and *Apocalypse and Millennium in English Romantic Poetry* (Oxford, 1999). See also Wittreich, ' "The Illustrious Dead" ' and ' "The Work of Man's Redemption" '.

THE APOCALYPSE UNDER SCRUTINY

Paradise Lost may never cease to be a subtext in Romantic poetry and fiction, but increasingly *Paradise Regained* and *Samson Agonistes* come into interplay with Milton's epic even as these poems of 1671 eventually become the defining contexts for major Romantic texts like *The Cenci* and *Prometheus Unbound*. No traditional Christian visionary Shelley. Indeed, *The Cenci* moves against the promise of and hope for an earthly redemption and a heavenly paradise and, in its inverted apocalypse, inscribes what John T. Shawcross in another context describes as 'the tragedy of hope'.[34] In the net of ruin that gathers around all the characters in this play, all hope is vain, and the visions of paradise that are its yield become but empty dreams: 'I was just dreaming', says Beatrice, 'That we were all in Paradise' (V. iii. 9–10). But here, as in *King Lear*, the promised end of the Apocalypse turns into an image of that horror: Beatrice imagines herself on the rack as a silent corpse and the rack itself as her soft grave. Her pangs 'are of the mind, and of the heart, / And of the soul; aye, of the inmost soul, / Which weeps with tears as of a burning gal' (V. iii. 65–7). Beatrice ranges against Lucretia's vain hope, 'we shall be in Paradise' (V. iv. 77), this harsh reality:

> If there should be
> No God, no Heaven, no Earth in the void world;
> The wide, grey, lampless, deep, unpeopled world!
> If in all things there should be . . . my father's spirit
> His eye, his voice, his touch surrounding me;
> The atmosphere and breath of my dead life!
> If sometimes, as a shape more like himself,
> Even the form which tortured me on earth,
> Masked in grey hairs and wrinkles, he should come
> And wind me in his hellish arms, and fix
> His eyes on mine, and drag me down, down, down!
> For was he not alone omnipotent
> On Earth, and ever present? Even though dead,
> Does not his spirit live in all that breathe,
> And work for me and mine still the same ruin,
> Scorn, pain, despair? (V. iv. 57–72)

Fronting her mother's idle wish for a papal pardon—'We may all then live / To make these woes a tale for distant years' (V. iv. 93–4)—is Beatrice's stinging rejoinder:

> O, trample out that thought! Worse than despair,
> Worse than the bitterness of death, is hope:
> It is the only ill which can find place
> Upon the giddy, sharp, and narrow hour
> Tottering beneath us

[34] John T. Shawcross, 'Irony as Tragic Effect: *Samson Agonistes* and the Tragedy of Hope', in Joseph Wittreich (ed.), *Calm of Mind: Tercentenary Essays on 'Paradise Regained' and 'Samson Agonistes'* (Cleveland, Ohio, 1971), 289.

> . . .
>
> No, Mother, we must die:
> Since such is the reward of innocent lives;
> Such the alleviation of worst wrongs
>
> . . .
>
> Come, obscure Death,
> And wind me in thine all-embracing arms!
> Like a fond mother hide me in thy bosom,
> And rock me to the sleep from which none wake. (V. iv. 98–118)

The Cenci is a play that, invoking the Apocalypse, is written against it; that, ravaging its myth, turns apocalyptic glitz into eschatological despair. It stands in the same relationship to *Prometheus Unbound* as *Samson Agonistes* does to *Paradise Regained* and, like *Paradise Lost*, is an interrogation of God's ways, not simply a justification of them.

This is not to say that for Shelley there are *no paradises*. His *Prometheus Unbound*, composed contemporaneously with *The Cenci*, suggests otherwise. It is to say that for Shelley the paradises of the Apocalypse, earthly and otherwise, are built upon insecure foundations. The Apocalypse—its theodicy, its world view—cannot be very congenial, or compelling, to a writer who says resoundingly that poets are the unacknowledged legislators of the world in the face of a scriptural book in which powerless man depends upon an all-powerful God to turn right side up the world that mankind up side downs. The last trump may seem to sound in Shelley's play, but the play's world is one in which the skyscape of the Apocalypse becomes a mindscape: not just the heavens but now the 'eyes are full of blood' (III. i. 3; cf. 13); as the world reels, the mind goes blank; the usual apocalyptic clamour is but a prelude to scalding tears and black despair. The apocalyptic stage becomes, in Shelley's play, a mental theatre. The God of the Apocalypse and his avenging angels, who come in judgement and mete out rewards and punishments, who only after crime's punishment don the face of mercy—whose rewards are for unnourished desire, whose punishments are for crimes in which God and his agents are accomplices—this God who inspires mankind with false hopes and empty (because unrealizable) dreams—this is the God *The Cenci* would tear from the firmament.

If *Prometheus Unbound* is a companion piece to *The Cenci*, a secularization of apocalypse, *The Cenci* is otherwise—a demystification, even a deconstruction of the Apocalypse and of apocalyptic thinking. If *Prometheus Unbound* witnesses to M. H. Abrams's version of Romanticism, *The Cenci*, moving oppositely, is testimony to the proposition set forth by D. H. Lawrence that 'taken superficially', as the multitudes are wont to take it, the Apocalypse is 'the most detestable' of all the scriptural books, a handbook for popular, not thoughtful religion and, as such, an altogether pernicious and repulsive book.[35] The point, of course, is to take neither John's Apocalypse nor Shelley's play superficially, in which case we may begin to read *The Cenci* rather

---

[35] See Abrams, *Natural Supernaturalism*, and D. H. Lawrence, *Apocalypse and the Writings on Revelation*, ed. Mara Kalnins (1931; London and New York, 1995), 61. For Lawrence, the Apocalypse is 'perhaps' the Bible's 'least attractive book' (p. 59).

as Vasily Rozanov reads the Apocalypse, with both works asserting (and now I am quoting Rozanov): 'It is not the heart of man that has corrupted Christianity, but Christianity that has corrupted the human heart. Hence the rage of the Apocalypse. Without that [corruption], there would have been a "new earth" and a "new Heaven". Without that [corruption], there would have been an Apocalypse.'[36] Of *that*, *Prometheus Unbound* is a forceful reminder.

And of *this*, *The Cenci* is an enduring witness: that any truly apocalyptic poem calls for, demands a new religion—in Shelley's case, a secular religion founded upon an improved ethical system. This is the essence of the Apocalypse unveiled and of Shelley's apocalyptic poem, which participates in this unveiling. History may be the record of repeated tragedy and *The Cenci* itself, a tragedy of hope. But the mere fact that this poem is written contemporaneously with *Prometheus Unbound* is indication that Shelley was capable of hosting conflicting systems of thought, much as Milton was in his 1671 poetic volume, and, in the case of *Prometheus Unbound*, a counter-reality that is neither wholly futuristic nor wholly idealistic, that is implicit in the present, at least for those who can read its signs. Prophecy may be a horror and apocalypse a deepening of despair in *The Cenci*; but in the conclusion to *Prometheus Unbound*, which pushes *The Cenci* beyond its fifth act, prophecy and apocalypse, the former beginning in the human mind and ending there—in its transformation—is also the prelude to an apocalypse in history.

In *Prometheus Unbound*, prophecy and apocalypse, both renovated and redeemed, converge on the point of hope: that mankind, born free, will again become free; that bound down by history, mankind will once again burst its bonds. The usual scenario of apocalypse—that history is in God's control, that its progress (or regress) is the work of his intermediaries—this is, for Shelley, the opposite of hope. That history is in man's control and has visionary poets as its architects—that is true hope, or at least Shelley's hope. In such hope is mankind's freedom, and out of such freedom comes mental, as well as historical, progress and renewal. In the concluding words of *Prometheus Unbound*:

> To suffer woes which Hope thinks infinite;
> To forgive wrongs darker than Death or Night
>
> . . .
>
>   To hope, til Hope creates
> From its own wreck the thing it contemplates. (iv. 570–4)

These lines epitomize the story of how paradise is regained: in Shelley's—and in some Romantics'—translations. That story is irrevocably involved with, and sometimes trampled by, a tale of how that paradise is lost, for some irretrievably so.

By the end of the eighteenth century, the sway of Milton's influence was so powerful and its extent so large that Thomas Warton would say: 'the whole of Milton's poetical

---

[36] Vasily Rozanov, *The Apocalypse of our Times and Other Writings*, ed. Robert Payne (New York, 1977), 237. In what might be construed as a Shelleyan formulation, Rozanov argues that 'The Apocalypse is not a Christian book—it is anti-Christian' (p. 236).

works' have come to participate 'in one common interest, jointly and reciprocally cooperat[ing] in diffusing and forming just ideas of a more perfect species of poetry. A visible revolution', he concludes, has 'succeeded in the general cast and character of the national composition.'[37] The Romantics were the poets and novelists who gave to this revolution significant visibility and striking evidence, and so they offer, through their writings, a means for defining more exactly the nature of the revolution that Milton is said to have precipitated. What the Bible was for Milton, Milton came to be for the Romantics: the source for the visionary poetics that they (men and women alike) accommodated to their writings. Turning to Milton, then, the Romantics, following what Lorna Sage says of Blake, isolated his 'prophetic, apocalyptic strain—and developed it until Milton begins to merge with Jesus and the Old Testament prophets of the Millennium'. This is Milton in his 'eternal lineaments'—the Romantics' Milton who is 'an embodiment of the perennial revolutionary, provoking always new visions, overturning even his own certainties'.[38]

It is no coincidence that the last great prophecy of the Romantic era, *Prometheus Unbound*, is accompanied by a preface that both invokes and celebrates Milton as a writer of 'the golden age of our literature'. With others, he is responsible, Shelley continues, for 'that fervid awakening of the public mind which shook to dust the oldest and most oppressive forms of the Christian Religion'. We especially owe to Milton the development of this same spirit in England: 'the sacred Milton', Shelley concludes, 'was...a Republican and a bold enquirer into morals and religion' (p. 208). *The sacred Milton*, then, was the archetypal prophetic poet in England, a historical embodiment of that same mythic spirit of which *Prometheus Unbound* is a celebration—a prophecy that, while it begins in Milton and is continued by the Romantics, will keep on completing itself in the tradition that together they create and, through their cooperating thoughts, extend through time, century after century. It is a tradition that simultaneously prosecutes the ideologies it promotes. If Milton provides Romanticism with some of its ideological underpinnings, Romanticism, recoiling upon itself, as well as Milton, mounts a critique not just of Milton but, through Milton, of its paradisiacal hopes and apocalyptic yearnings. As much as *Paradise Lost*, *Paradise Regained* and *Samson Agonistes* are defining poems of British Romanticism, of the three *Paradise Regained* most strikingly so.

---

[37] 'Preface', *Poems upon Several Occasions*, 2nd edn. (1785; 1791), p. xii.

[38] Lorna Sage, 'Milton in Literary History', in *John Milton: Introductions*, ed. John Broadbent (Cambridge, 1973), 324.

INDEX

Abrams, M. H. 702
Achinstein, Sharon 649, 683
Addison, Joseph 27, 427, 444–57, 672–3, 684–5
Adolphus, Gustavus 98
Aeschylus 652
Aesop 301–2
Agar, John 17
Agar, Thomas 11, 13, 16, 17, 21, 24
Agricola 422
Aikin, John 683
Alexandrinus, Dionysius 37, 222
Alfred, King 374
Alsted, Johann-Heinrich 430
Althusser, Louis 352
America, Americans 556, 565, 675–6
Ames, William 427–8, 430, 523
Anderson, Benedict 354
Andrewes, Lancelot 168–9
Anglo–Dutch War, the first 550, 564
Anglo–Dutch War, the second 45, 410, 548, 577
Anglo–Dutch War, the third 407, 580
*Answer to a Book, Intituled, The Doctrine and
    Discipline of Divorce* 38, 196–9
antinomianism 38, 180, 204–5
antitrinitarianism 37, 214, 427, 430–2, 511–12,
    595–612; *see also* Socinianism
apocalypse, apocalyptic 72–3, 123, 129–30, 347–8,
    689, 691–3, 696, 700–4
Archer, John 213, 215
Arianism, *see* antitrinitarianism
Ariosto 54, 131, 292, 378, 449, 505
Aristeas 223
Aristotle, Aristotelian 168, 171, 173, 244–5, 344,
    371–3, 387, 399, 445, 449, 451, 454, 555–8,
    565–6, 651–9, 662, 664
Arminianism 157, 172, 379, 416, 433, 504, 524
Armitage, David 671
Army, New Model 41, 242, 249, 269, 310, 312–24,
    641
Ascham, Roger 59–61, 453
Ashley-Cooper, Anthony, Earl of Shaftesbury 684
Astell, Mary 191, 559–60
Atonement, the 71–3, 512–13, 531–3
Attaway, Mrs 198–9, 213
Attridge, Derek 464–5
Aubrey, John 5, 7–8, 55, 310, 398, 427

Augustine, St 432, 510, 512, 521, 524, 530, 565
Austin, R. G. 292

Bachelor, John 205, 211
Bacon, Francis; Baconian 161, 170, 394, 404,
    554–6
Bailie, Robert 178, 182–4, 263
Bakhtin, M. M. 459–60
Baptists 523
Barbauld, Anna Letitia 676
Barberini, Cardinal Francesco 23
Baroni, Leonora 107
Barrow, Samuel 462, 494
Bastwick, John 176, 258
Bateson, F. W. 114
Beard, Thomas 119, 126
Bellarmine, Cardinal Robert 19, 25, 368
Beckett, Samuel 57
Bene, Bartolomo del 664
Benjamin, Walter 52
Bennett, J. A. W. 150
Bentley, Richard 444, 487, 497–8, 678–9
Bernard, St, of Clairvaux 303
Best, Paul 214
Beza, Theodore 428, 430, 621
Bible, the 37, 45, 158, 171, 172, 221, 254, 267, 402,
    424, 429–34, 446–8, 459, 521, 524, 533, 534–7,
    546, 594, 604, 608, 691, 704
books:
    Genesis 179, 360, 442, 446–8, 499, 503, 508,
        513, 527, 530, 535–6, 539, 544, 567, 633,
        637, 657
    Exodus 638
    Deuteronomy 333, 413–15, 591, 596
    Judges 615–30, 633, 635
    1 Samuel 637
    Kings 179, 506, 625
    Job 585, 636–7, 645
    Isaiah 127, 414
    Jeremiah 639, 641
    Ezekiel 640
    Psalms 308
    Hosea 414
    Amos 645–6
    Habbakuk 414
    Wisdom 47

Bible, the (*cont.*)
   Matthew 186
   Luke 591
   Acts 223, 333
   Romans 222, 245, 333, 617
   1 Corinthians 222, 224, 226, 538, 557, 657
   2 Corinthians 505
   Galatians 222, 225, 333
   Colossians 333
   Thessalonians 222
   Titus 222, 528
   Hebrews 130, 503, 512, 513, 529, 630
   1 Peter 246, 336, 538
   1 John 430
   Revelation 129–30, 134, 604, 702
  Geneva 535, 633
  Junius-Tremelius 428, 430
Bilson, Thomas 643
Binkes, Joseph 581
Birrell, T. A. 253
Blackford, Paul 302
Blackmore, Richard 440, 674
Blake, William 75, 462, 476, 479, 567, 675, 680, 685,
   690–3, 698–9, 704
Boadicea 422
Bodin, Jean 46
Bodleian Library 40, 54
Boileau, Nicolas 454, 457
Bonfrerius, Jacobus 619
Book of Common Prayer 156, 158, 163–4, 338
Book of Sports 30, 164
Boscán, Juan 123
Boutcher, Warren 123
Bower, Thomas 15
Bradshaw, John 41, 281, 284
Bramhall, John, Bishop 12, 415–16
Bridgewater, Earl of, *see* Egerton, John
Brinsley, John 55, 61, 128
Broadbent, John 350
Brown, Capability 683
Browne, R. C. 138–9
Brutus, Lucius Junius 359–60
Bucer, Martin 195, 619, 625, 628–30
Buchanan, George 265
Buonmattei, Benedetto 23
Burgess, Thomas, Bishop of Salisbury 427, 429
Burke, Edmund 693
Burnet, Gilbert 307, 502, 578
Burroughs, Jeremiah 178
Burton, Henry 258
Burton, Robert 224
Byron, Lord 698

Cable, Lana 162, 234
Calamy, Edward 205, 216
Callender, of Craigforth 680

Calvin, Calvinism, Calvinists 43, 156–7, 172, 351,
   379, 416, 428–9, 433, 523–4, 615–16, 619, 621–6
Cambridge University 57, 117, 120, 124, 402, 618;
   see also Milton, John, life, education
Camden, William 376
Camões, Luis de 506
Campbell, Gordon 57, 59
Cann, Christian 680–1
Canne, John 335–6
Carew, Thomas 92–3, 96–8
Carey, John 59, 118–19, 134, 139, 146–7, 634
Cartwright, Thomas 167, 430
Cassian, John 433
Castiglione 402
Catherine, of Braganza 578
Catholics, Catholicism 39, 86, 90, 112–13, 118,
   161–2, 164, 166, 175, 202, 230, 232, 260, 263–4,
   308, 334, 338–41, 347–50, 407, 501, 506–9,
   520, 535, 578–80, 630–1, 640–4, 648;
   see also Jesuits
Cato, distichs of 150–1
Cato, the younger 451–2
Caudwell, Christopher 687
Cerdogni, Camillo 112–13, 131–2
Chancery 24
Chapman, George 117, 126
Chapman, Livewell 44, 322
Chappell, William 12
Charles I 19, 27, 33, 41, 90–8, 101, 157–8, 169, 208,
   228, 241–71, 301, 309, 321, 324, 339, 344, 345,
   350, 443, 547, 575, 577, 620
Charles II 42, 44, 45, 237, 321–4, 345, 407, 420, 576,
   578–80, 649
Charles X, of Sweden 562
chastity 91, 102–6, 112–20, 128–35
Chaucer 84, 163, 292, 303, 376
Cheke, Sir John 141, 263
Chidley, Katherine 171, 537
Chimentelli, Valerio 23
Christina, Queen, of Sweden 281, 428
Christology 430–1, 510, 591–612
Cicero, Ciceronian 46, 56, 272, 274, 276, 286–7,
   292, 304, 344, 374, 429, 551, 557, 575
Clark, Donald L. 56–7, 59, 60
Clarendon Code 580
Cleland, James 386, 393
Clifford, Henry, Lord 389
Codner, David 444–5
Coffey, John 332
Coke, Sir Edward 227–9, 231, 261
Coldiron, A. E. B. 146
Coleridge, S. T. 449, 451, 457–8, 676, 678, 690
Colley, Linda 349
Collier, Thomas 330, 337
Coltellini, Agostino 23
Comenius, Jan Amos 403–4

Conniack, Madam 94
Constantine, Emperor 169, 332
Conventicle Act 580–2, 620
Cooper, John Gilbert 686
Corns, Thomas N. 204, 215, 259, 454–5, 476
Cotton, Sir Thomas 17
Council of State 41–2, 263, 273, 276–7, 313–15, 538, 549–50
Cox, Lee 143, 145
Cleaver, Robert 190
Cleveland, John 131
Creaser, John 486, 488
Cromwell, Oliver 38, 43, 46, 119, 217, 236, 248, 266, 272, 283–6, 327, 355, 358–62, 443, 547, 556–7, 559, 575–6, 641
    Humble Petition and Advice 278, 327, 332–3
    Instrument of Government 283, 284
    Protectorate 26, 44, 278–9, 283, 285–6, 305–24, 556, 559, 576
Cromwell, Richard 46, 307, 309–10, 321, 333
Crooke, Helkiah 651, 655–7, 665
Cruttwell, Patrick 264
Culpeper, Sir Cheney 404
Curran, Stuart 674–5, 699

Da Gama, Vasco 506
Daiches, David 477
Danielson, Dennis 531
Dannhauer, Johann Conrad 631
Dante 120, 292, 378, 448
Darbishire, Helen 483, 485
Dati, Carlo 23, 40–1
Davenant, William 255, 257
Davie, Donald 474
Davies, Sir John 268
Davies, Stevie 233
Davis, Miss 35
Declaration of Breda 580
Declaration of Indulgence 580
Della Casa, Giovanni 137, 454
Dennis, John 677
De Quincey, Thomas 671–4
Derby, Countess of, see Spencer, Alice
Dering, Edward 208
Derrida, Jacques 637–8
Descartes, René 651, 658–9, 661, 666
Digby, Sir Kenelm 13
Diodati, Charles 13, 20–1, 25, 35, 54, 63, 67, 113–14, 118, 121, 134–5, 190–1, 375
Diodati, Giovanni 626–7, 630
Diodorus 506, 508
Dobranski, Stephen B. 201
Dod, John 190
Donne, John 259, 496–7
Dorian, Donald C. 139, 385
Drusius, Johannes 616

Dryden, John 59, 192, 257, 281, 410–11, 440–5, 453, 670, 677–8
Du Bartas, Guillaume de Salluste 512
Du Bellay, Joachim 63
Du Moulin, Peter 274–5, 278, 281, 286
Dury, John 390, 394–7, 404–6
Dzelzainis, Martin 242, 244, 306, 357, 624

Edgehill, Battle of 35
Edward, the Confessor 374, 408
Edward VI 141, 348
Edwards, Thomas 177, 183–4, 198–9, 211–16, 260
Egerton, Alice 94, 98, 107–8
Egerton, John, first earl of Bridgewater 13, 15, 100
Egerton, Lady Katherine 94
Eikon Basilike 42, 252–71, 575, 644
Elias, Norbert 654
Eliot, T. S. 27, 453–5, 462, 479
Ellwood, Thomas 589–90
Elyot, Sir Thomas 386
Empson, William 52, 148, 497–8, 504, 530
Erasmus, Desiderius 373, 502
Erastianism 169, 327–9, 331, 340
Erskine-Hill, Howard 262
Eton College 172, 375
Euripides 187, 218–19, 237, 256–7, 303, 635, 652
Evelyn, John 391, 400
Ezekiel 345, 360–1

Fairfax, Edward 131
Fairfax, Sir Thomas 41, 281, 284
Fairfax, Mary 56
Fall, the 244–6, 414–16, 446, 513–16, 535–46, 558, 561–2, 566; see also Milton, John, works, poetry, Paradise Lost
Fallon, Robert 283
Fallon, Stephen 112, 657
Famous Tragedie of King Charles I 256
Fanshawe, Richard 506–7
Featley, Daniel 212
Fell, Margaret 535, 539–40, 543, 545
Fenner, Dudley 430
Fernández-Armesto, Felipe 461
Fichte, J. G. 363
Filmer, Robert 249, 356–8
Fire, Great, of London 29, 45, 577, 620
Firmin, Giles 333
Fish, Stanley 137, 146–7, 244, 494–5, 498–9, 548, 649
Fisher, Samuel 329
Flannagan, Roy 62, 487
Fletcher, Harris F. 59
Fletcher, John 95
Foucault, Michel 690
Fowler, Alastair 454–5, 481
Foxe, John 340, 347–8, 375
Francini, Antonio 23

free will 414–16, 520–4; *see also* Milton, John, works, poetry, *Paradise Lost*
French, Milton J. 3–4, 6, 127, 141
Frescobaldi, Pietro 23
Friedlieb, Philipp Heinrich 615, 626
Frijhoff, Willem 389–90
Frye, Northrop 688, 691
Fuller, Nicholas 227–8
Fulton, Thomas 247
Fuseli, Henry 689–90, 693

Gaddi, Jacopo 23
Gaius 225
Galen 223–4, 656–7, 662
Galileo 450
Garnet, Henry 261
Gascoigne, George 463–70, 478
Gauden, John 255
Gentili, Alberico 564
Gerbier, Sir Balthazar 396–7, 400
Gerhard, Johan 37
Gil, Alexander, the elder 8
Gil, Alexander, the younger 9, 13
Gilbert, A. H. 592
Gilbert, Humphrey 392–3, 399–400
Gillespie, George 263
Godwin, William 688, 693, 696–7
Goldberg, Jonathan 481, 483
González de Mendoza, Juan 500
Goodall, Edward 17, 18
Goodwin, John 205, 212, 215, 433, 524
Goodwin, Thomas 181
Gower, John 163, 376
Gowing, Laura 198
Grafton, Anthony 373
Graham, Sir Fredrick 368
Graham, Richard, 1st Viscount Preston 369
Graham, Sir Richard James 369
Greece, Greeks 163, 187, 219, 459
    Athens 165, 168, 202, 218–19, 234–6, 319, 323, 353, 442, 678
Green, George Smith 679
Greg, W. W. 482
Gregerson, Linda 460
Greville, Fulke Sir 13
Greville, Robert, 2nd Baron Brooke 216, 355
Griffeth, Matthew 324
Grotius, Hugo 22, 180, 189, 564, 623, 635
Guicciardini, Francesco 158
Guillory, John 257–9
Guilpin, Edward 118

Haak, Theodore 376
Hakluyt, Richard 681
Hale, John K. 55, 114–15, 334, 339, 435, 455
Hales, John 172
Hall, John, of Durham 266, 404

Hall, Joseph 160–2, 168, 636
Hanford, James Holly 18, 367
Harington, Sir John 131
Harrington, James 307, 337, 427
Harrison, Thomas 284
Hartlib, Samuel; Hartlib circle 38, 286, 353, 373, 376, 382–406
Haydn, Joseph 447
Hayes, James 582
Hayley, William 672, 674, 676
Hazlitt, William 451
Hegel, G. W. F. 459
Heimbach, Peter 342–3, 485
Helgerson, Richard 348–9, 442
Henderson, Alexander 181
Henrietta Maria 90–8, 374, 644
Henry VIII 193–4
Henry, Nathaniel 143
'Heptaplomeres', *see* Bodin, Jean
Herbert, Lord Edward of Cherbury 387–8
Herbert, Lord Philip, Earl of Pembroke 182
Herbert, Sir Thomas 253–4
heresy 170, 202–5, 211–17, 312, 424–35, 510–24
Herring, Francis 347
Hill, Christopher 143, 498, 504, 507–9
Hippocrates 656
Hobart, John 672
Hobbes, Thomas 244, 415–16, 524, 565, 656, 660–1
Hobson, Thomas 68
Holdsworth, Richard 370–1
Holinshed, Raphael 156, 376
Holste, Lukas 22–3
Home, Henry, Lord Kames 684
Homer, Homeric 115, 258, 263, 268, 441–57, 520, 670, 677
homosexuality 193
Honigmann, E. A. J. 139, 147
Hooker, Richard 167, 171, 348, 351
Horace, Horatian 30, 40, 52, 58–65, 112–13, 126, 292, 298, 304, 306, 449, 454, 456, 627, 679
Horwood, Alfred J. 368
Hotman, François 619, 621
Howard, Henry, Earl of Surrey 463
Howell, James 391
Hughes, Merritt Y. 59, 492
Hunter, William B. 427
Hyde, Edward, Earl of Clarendon 398, 551, 577–8, 580
Hume, Patrick, 443–4, 678, 680
Humfrey, John 338
Humphrey, Colonel John 397, 402
Hurdis, James 669–70, 675, 682

idolatry 254–71, 339–41, 632–48
Independents 156–7, 172, 175–85, 204, 211, 322–3, 328, 523–4
Inns of Court 21

Irish, Ireland 42, 263–71, 359, 640, 643
Israel, Israelites 169, 227, 325–41, 345, 414–17, 421, 572, 575, 585, 587, 594, 635–41, 645–6
Isocrates 234–6

Jago, Richard 670–1
James I 64, 157, 228, 264–5, 565
James, Duke of Monmouth 578
James, Duke of York, later James II 578, 580
Jefferson, Thomas 242, 675
Jekyl, John 582
Jeremiah, jeremiad 277–8, 285, 319–20, 639
Jesuits 261–2, 552–3
Jews, Judaism 222–3, 327–39, 344, 557, 586, 636, 640
Johnson, Lee 475
Johnson, Samuel 12, 27, 36, 40, 383, 439–40, 448–50, 452, 456–7, 673–4, 677
Jones, Inigo 91
Jonson, Ben 8, 80, 91, 93, 117, 255, 297, 448
Jordan, Constance 534
Joyce, James 83
Justinian 225, 376, 558, 618
Jesuits 171

Kahn, Victoria 650, 653
Kant, Immanuel 458–9, 526
Kastan, David Scott 491–4
Keats, John 679–80
Kedermister Library 19–20, 25, 375
Keeble, N. H. 328
Keightley, Thomas 147
Kelley, Maurice 369
Kidd, Colin 352
King, Edward 53, 120–1, 123–6, 129–30
    Iusta Edouardo King 53, 121, 131
King, John N. 501
Knox, H. M. 405
Korda, Natasha 190
Kynaston, Sir Francis 393–4

Lactantius 377–9
Lambert, John 313
Landor, Walter Savage 674, 681
Languet, Hubert 621–2
Lanyer, Amelia 535–6, 544
Lapide, Cornelius à 628–9
Laud, William; Laudian 14, 18, 127, 155, 157, 168, 172, 176, 180, 204, 206–9, 232, 260, 426, 433, 501, 523
Lauder, William 674
Lawes, Henry 15, 22, 93–4, 96, 100, 108, 368
Lawrence, D. H. 702
Leavis, F. R. 445, 454–5, 461, 478
Leiden, John of 434
Leigh, Sir Francis 13
Lenthall, Sir John 13
L'Estrange, Roger 338, 420, 502, 577, 587

Lewalski, Barbara 403, 406, 548, 593–4, 596, 611, 641
Lewis, C. S. 445, 526, 530, 609
Levellers 213–14, 242, 263, 411
Lieb, Michael 126, 525, 527, 634, 637
Lilburne, John 209, 213, 245
Limborch, Phillipus van 433
Lipsius, Justus 551, 553–6, 563–4
Livy 171, 554, 575
Loewenstein, David 279, 291, 358, 548
logic 527
Longinus 446, 454, 456
Lorkin, Thomas 390
Louis XIII 388
Louis XIV 407, 410, 423, 579–80
Lucan 451
Lucas, John 326
Lucretius 294, 514
Ludlow, Edmund 283
Luther, Martin 165, 225, 344, 429, 432, 642
Luxon, Thomas 190
Lyra, Nicholas of 617, 627

McLeod, Bruce 685
Machiavelli, Niccolò 158, 166, 359, 376, 551
Magna Carta 228–9
Maimonides 639
Mair, John 555, 565
Maltzahn, Nicholas von 672
Malvezzi, Virgilio 552
Manso, Giovanni Battista 22
Mantuan 52, 57–8
Marchant, John 673, 680
Marlowe, Christopher 99, 115–35, 452, 463, 473–6, 478
Marprelate, Martin 160
Marston Moor 38, 205
Marten, Henry 166
Martindale, Charles 60
Mason, William 684
Marvell, Andrew 44, 47, 56–7, 75, 85, 104, 284–5, 462, 494, 578–80, 582, 660, 664
masque, court 90–111
Marshall, Stephen 177, 329, 333
Martial 292
Masson, David 3–4, 16, 19, 141, 147, 403
materialism 119, 503–4, 510–12, 520
Maule, Jeremy 14
Maus, Katherine 297
Maxwell, J. C. 150–1
Mead, William 582
Mede, Jospeh 642–3
Medea 187–8, 197
Melancthon, Philip 128, 428
Mendle, Michael 206, 211
Mercurius Pragmaticus 262
Meres, Francis 120
Merleau-Ponty, Maurice 656

Miller, Leo 12
Milman, Henry Hart 675
Milton, Anne, sister 5–6, 9, 11–12, 15–17, 24
Milton, Anne, daughter 36, 195
Milton, Christopher, brother 5, 7, 15, 16, 21, 23–4
Milton, Deborah, daughter 36
Milton, Elizabeth, wife 5, 36
Milton, John, life
    blindness 30–1, 42–3, 46–7, 367, 442–3, 484–5, 533
    death 47
    education
        Cambridge University 5, 8–13, 28, 41, 53, 76, 114, 127–8, 131, 156, 161, 346, 353, 376–7, 642
        St. Paul's School 6, 8, 28, 55, 57, 113, 353, 377, 384
    funeral 47
    Geneva, in 112–13, 626
    imprisonment 44, 571
    Italy, in 22–3, 29, 34, 53, 107–8, 112–13, 131–2, 274, 378
    languages, knowledge of 52–65, 67, 272–304
    marriage, see Milton, Elizabeth; Milton, Katherine; Milton, Mary
    residence, places of
        Aldersgate Street 23, 27, 401
        Barbican 28
        Bread Street 5–8, 21, 29, 66
        Bunhill Fields 28
        Hammersmith 10, 14–16, 76, 120–1, 378
        Horton 14–25, 76, 120, 131, 172, 378
        Jewin Street 28
        Lincoln's Inn Fields 28
        St Bride's Churchyard 23
        Whitehall 42
    as Secretary for Foreign Tongues 41, 252–89, 305–24, 549–64, 567
Milton, John, works
    manuscripts
        Bridgewater manuscript 495
        Commonplace Book 18, 19, 25, 39, 158, 172, 179–80, 269, 367–81, 619, 629
        De Doctrina Christiana 45, 327, 368–9, 413–16, 423, 424–35, 446, 503, 510, 525, 551, 553–4, 561, 567, 594–5, 597, 604, 610–11, 647, 657, 691
        Paradise Lost, Book 1 426, 483–4
        State papers 369
        Trinity manuscript 25, 39, 45, 139, 142, 146, 265, 368–9, 442, 495
    poetry
        'Ad Joannem Rousium' 40, 54
        'Ad Patrem' 19, 67, 125
        'Apologus de Rustico et Hero' 8, 57, 59
        Arcades 15, 68, 99–100, 106–7, 122, 606
        'Canzone' 131
        'Circumcision, Upon the' 15, 69

Comus, see Maske Presented at Ludlow Castle, A
'Cyriack Skinner Upon his Blindness, To Mr' 290
'De idea Platonica' 10
'Elegia prima ad Carolum Diodatum' 64
'Elegia secunda. In Obitum Praeconis Academici Cantabrigiensis' 10
'Elegia tertia. In Obitum Praesuli Wintoniensis' 10, 157
'Elegia quinta. In adventum veris' 10, 64
'Elegia sexta' 67, 69, 75, 113–14, 118, 125–7, 134–5
'Elegia septima' 114
'Epitaph on the Marchioness of Winchester, An' 10, 68, 122
Epitaphium Damonis 25, 54, 63, 114, 134–5, 442
'Fair Infant, On the Death of' 11–12, 67, 486
'Fifth Ode of Horace, lib., The' 58–65, 67, 486
'Haec ego mente olim laeva' 40, 67, 114–15, 127
'Il Penseroso' 11, 15, 28, 68–70, 75–7, 81–7, 118
'In Obitum Praesulis Eliensis' 10, 157
'In Obitum Procancellarii Medici' 10, 11, 64
'In Proditionem Bombardicam' 10
'In Quintem Novembris' 64, 68, 346–51, 361, 564–5
'L'Allegro' 11, 15, 68–70, 73, 75–81, 118–19, 606, 686
'Lord General Cromwell, To the' 136, 305, 328
'Lord General Fairfax at the Seige of Colchester, On the' 136
'Lycidas' 16–20, 22, 25, 39, 53, 55, 67–8, 69, 73, 89, 100, 114, 120–35, 157, 249, 442, 483, 489–90, 606, 690, 695
Mansus 442
Maske Presented at Ludlow Castle, A 15, 19, 20, 39, 53, 68, 88, 89–111, 112–13, 121, 131–2, 161, 257–8, 320, 378–9, 467, 471, 482, 486, 495, 606, 694, 696
'Nativity, On the Morning of Christ's' 10, 11, 66–75, 86, 89, 92, 109, 113, 127, 483, 486
'Naturam non Pati Senium' 10, 64
'New Forcers of Conscience under the Long Parliament, On the' 33, 142, 157, 176, 260, 262, 312, 486
Paradise Lost 17, 27, 29, 31, 39, 46, 88, 105–6, 132, 159, 179, 349, 362, 374, 423, 434, 439–612, 633, 669–704
    Abdiel 323, 359, 451, 469, 548
    Adam 36, 58, 175, 349, 362, 378, 450, 452, 457–8, 460, 470, 472, 480, 496–7, 503, 509, 511–23, 526–33, 534–46, 547–8, 551, 553, 560–7, 597–603, 645, 657, 669–70, 674, 680, 682, 685, 691, 694, 698
    angels 249, 497, 503, 511–16, 520–2, 527–32, 592–609
    Chaos 496, 499–501, 514, 520, 526, 531

Creation 46, 447, 497–9, 503–4, 508,
    511–16, 519–20, 525–33, 695
date of composition 44–5, 443, 513, 516, 549
ecology 515–16
Eden 58, 64–5, 456, 498, 502, 508, 526–8,
    531, 670, 683, 686, 691
editing of 480–95
epic, as 439–61
Eve 36, 58, 65, 108, 111, 175, 188, 349, 362,
    378, 450–2, 457–8, 460, 470, 472, 480,
    496–7, 503, 509–24, 526–33, 534–46, 547,
    560–2, 566, 597–8, 644–5, 669–70, 674,
    680, 682, 685, 694, 699
Fall, the 46, 65, 170, 452, 513–17, 527–8,
    531–2, 540–6, 602–3, 610, 674
free will 379, 414, 460, 518, 520–4, 541–2
God 46, 64, 345, 350, 360–1, 378, 469, 499,
    503–7, 510–46, 567, 595–612
Heaven 496, 499, 501, 525–33
Hell 45, 447, 459, 496, 501, 507, 637, 674
heresies of 510–24
Latinity of 62, 677
Limbo of Vanity 501–2, 515
Michael 528, 532, 547–8, 562–3, 566,
    597–604, 680, 691
Nimrod 46, 548, 566–7
politics of 283, 547–67
punctuation of 483–7, 493–4
Raphael 442, 449, 460, 473, 503–4, 509, 511,
    515–17, 520–1, 564, 598–602, 605, 657,
    690, 695
Satan 25, 45, 46, 64, 140, 149–50, 160, 175,
    320, 345, 349–50, 359, 446–52, 455, 459,
    468–9, 472, 478, 498–506, 513–16, 520–4,
    526–8, 531–2, 537, 541, 543–4, 547–9,
    561–5, 568, 595–612, 633, 645, 658, 670,
    674–5, 679, 682, 690–1, 695, 697–8
second edition of 47, 482, 494
sexuality 497–8, 516–20
Sin and Death 35, 149, 195, 445, 528
Son, the 46, 359–62, 452, 472, 511–14, 522,
    525–33, 561, 595–612
vegetarianism 518
verse of 280, 452, 454–5, 462–79
world of 64, 496–509, 680–2
Paradise Regained 26, 31, 45, 46, 88, 152, 483,
    490, 522, 525, 527, 531, 571–88, 589–612,
    635, 645, 653, 660, 690–3, 701–4
'Passion, The' 11, 40, 69, 486, 489–90
'Philosophus ad Regem' 8
Poems (1645) 10, 22, 40, 54–5, 60, 63, 67, 109,
    114, 119, 131–5, 145, 211, 483, 489
Poems (1673) 11, 133, 486, 490
Psalms 41, 67
Samson Agonistes 26, 29, 31, 36, 44, 46, 88,
    157, 257, 363, 378, 470–1, 483, 490, 525,
    561, 571–88, 613–66, 689–94, 701–4

'Shakespeare, On' 10, 68, 82, 90, 121, 252–3,
    257–9
'Sir Henry Vane the Younger, To' 43–4, 550
'Solemn Music, At a' 15, 69, 107, 486
Sonnet 1 ('On May Morning') 10
Sonnet 6 ('Per certo i bei vostr'occhi') 76
Sonnet 7 ('How soon hath time') 15, 68,
    138–40, 440
Sonnet 8 ('When the assault was intended to
    the City') 486
Sonnet 9 ('Lady that in the prime') 35
Sonnet 11 ('A book was writ of late') 140–3,
    262–3
Sonnet 12 ('On the Detraction which
    followed upon my Writing Certain
    Treatises') 37, 143–5, 199, 203, 473
Sonnet 13 ('To Mr H. Lawes') 137
Sonnet 14 ('When faith and love which
    parted from thee hence') 145–6
Sonnet 15 (On the late Massacre in
    Piedmont') 136, 146
Sonnet 16 ('When I consider how my light is
    spent') 31, 46, 68, 146
Sonnet 17 ('Lawrence, of virtuous father')
    30, 137, 147–52
Sonnet 18 ('Cyriack, whose grandsire on the
    royal branch') 549–50
Sonnet 19 ('Methought I saw my late
    espoused saint') 36
'Time, On' 15, 69
'University Carrier, On the' 68
'Vacation Exercise in College, At a' 10,
    67, 486
prose
    Accidence Commenc't Grammar 45, 409
    Animadversions 28, 34, 133, 162, 169
    Apology Against a Pamphlet, An 57, 120,
        159–60, 165, 169–70, 373–4, 378, 442,
        692
    Areopagitica 37, 39, 127, 169–70, 175, 177, 185,
        188, 200–37, 242, 248, 260, 275, 287–8, 308,
        310, 353, 357, 363, 374, 379, 460, 483, 495,
        510, 521, 522, 692
    Artis Logicae 45, 409, 628
    Brief History of Muscovia 41, 451, 508
    Brief Notes 44, 324
    Character of the Long Parliament 39, 41, 176,
        247, 357, 419–20, 677
    Colasterion 37, 38, 145, 184–5, 187, 196–7
    *Considerations Touching the likeliest mean to
        remove Hirelings out of the Church* 44,
        310–12, 315, 319–20, 322, 325–40
    Declaration, or Letters Patent 362
    Defensio, see *First Defence*
    Defensio Secunda, see *Second Defence*
    'Digression' to *History of Britain*, see
        Character of the Long Parliament

Milton, John, works (*cont.*)
   Doctrine and Discipline of Divorce 37, 175–7,
     180, 183, 186, 189–99, 203, 225, 246, 260, 328,
     353, 376, 428, 482, 618, 623
   Eikonoklastes 41, 42, 252–71, 273–4, 285, 311,
     443, 482, 557, 575, 633, 644
   Epistolae Familiares 10, 20, 409
   First Defence 27, 42–3, 226, 257, 272–8, 289,
     291–304, 306, 331, 344, 355–60, 412, 420,
     428, 482, 557, 614, 623, 626, 644
   History of Britain 31, 39, 41, 45, 407–23, 439,
     442, 506
   Judgement of Martin Bucer, The 37, 187, 211,
     428, 433, 619
   'A Letter to a Friend' 312–15
   'Mane citus lectum fuge' (theme on early
     rising) 8
   Observations upon the *Articles of Peace* 42,
     263–4, 268–9, 273, 276, 285, 328, 557
   Of Education 30, 38, 142, 211, 354, 373, 375,
     382–406, 409, 454–5, 460–1, 510, 549, 554
   Of Prelaticall Episcopacy 34, 156, 159, 379–80
   Of Reformation 32–4, 156, 159, 161–3, 166–71,
     231, 346, 350–1, 380, 443, 507, 547, 567,
     642–3
   Of True Religion 27, 31, 45, 46, 308, 338–41,
     345, 603, 644
   'Postscript' to *An Answer to a Booke
     Entituled, An Humble Remonstrance* 32,
     156
   Preface to *The Cabinet Council* 306, 552–3
   'Present Means and Brief Delineation' 321–2
   Prolusiones 10
   Pro Populo Anglicano Defensio, see *First
     Defence*
   'Proposalls of Certain Expedients' 315–17
   Pro se defensio 43, 272, 275, 279, 286–9, 428,
     627
   Readie and Easie Way, The 44, 46, 144, 237,
     277, 316–24, 362
   Reason of Church-Government, The 8, 32, 34,
     40, 115, 126–7, 156–7, 159, 163, 167–70,
     244, 277, 282, 328, 350–2, 378, 400, 441–3,
     633
   Second Defence 8, 15, 22, 23, 27, 33, 42, 112, 179,
     199, 235–6, 260, 272, 278–89, 291, 306,
     328, 355, 358–60, 381, 423, 428, 443, 533,
     557–9, 567, 575, 614, 622
   Tenure of Kings and Magistrates, The 41, 42,
     144, 241–51, 260–6, 269, 273, 280–1, 285,
     309, 323, 342–4, 412, 420, 482, 548, 555,
     557, 614, 617–18, 623–5
   Tetrachordon 37, 140–2, 145, 184, 187–8, 191,
     194, 197, 330, 376, 519, 557–8, 565–6, 618
   Treatise of Civil Power, A 44, 307–8, 310–12,
     315, 325–39, 425, 428, 434, 552, 643–4
Milton, John, father 6–7, 12–13, 15, 16, 18

Milton, John, son 36, 195
Milton, Katherine, wife 36, 46
Milton, Katherine, daughter 46
Milton, Mary, wife 34, 35
Milton, Mary, daughter 36
Milton, Sara, mother 16
Minshull, Elizabeth, *see* Milton, Elizabeth, wife
Minturno, Antonio 653
Mitchell, W. J. T. 685
Molyneux, Sir Richard 13
Monck, George 315, 317–19, 321–4, 362, 576
Monmouth, Geoffrey of 346
Montague, Walter 92
More, Alexander 27, 43, 274–5, 278, 280, 286–9
More, Henry 643
More, Thomas 170
mortalism 433–4, 515
Moseley, Humphrey 40
Moss, Ann 55
Moxon, Joseph 484
Moyles, R. G. 486
Mueller, Janel 620
Mylius, Hermann 42

Nardo, Anna K. 141
nation, nationalism 63, 250, 272–90, 325–63,
   575–6, 585–6, 616–27, 637–48, 669–86
Nedham, Marchamont 42, 255–6, 262
Neoplatonism 91
Newman, Gerald 672
Newton, Thomas 131, 444, 505
Norbrook, David 188, 310, 353, 355, 359, 548, 649
Norman conquest 409, 411–13, 417
Nye, Philip 338

Ogilvie, John 675
O'Neil, Own Roe 269
Orgel, Stephen 481, 483
Orpheus 77, 81, 85, 100, 106–9, 125–6, 129, 456
Owen, John 338
Overton, Richard 204, 212–15
Overton, Robert 284
Ovid, Ovidian 40, 59, 102, 113–19, 125–35, 292, 299,
   447, 460, 514, 543
Oxford, University of 398

Pagit, Ephraim 212
Paine, Thomas 675
Palmer, Herbert 181, 203, 216–17
Pareus, David 617–18, 622, 625–9
Parker, Henry 168, 229–30
Parker, Samuel 338
Parker, William Riley 3–4, 18, 179, 403, 425
Parliament 156, 160, 193, 285–6, 411
  'Cavalier' 580
  Long 26, 37, 39, 175–85, 200–17, 219–20, 229,
    234, 247, 312–13, 317, 333, 357, 402–3, 428

Nominated 278, 283
'Rump' 36, 41, 43, 243–4, 278, 307–8, 311–24, 333,
    336, 358
Paterson, James 673, 678, 680
Patterson, Annabel 35, 548–9
Paul, St. 222, 224–6, 615, 621, 643
Peacham, Henry 386
Peckham, Sir George 13
Pell, John 394
Penn, William 582
Pepys, Samuel 317, 579
Perkins, William 430
Peter, St 157
Petrarch 120, 163, 292, 454
Petronius 303–4
Phillips, Edward, snr. 6–7, 9, 11, 13, 14
Phillips, Edward, jnr. 5, 11, 16–17, 24, 25, 28, 45, 355,
    399, 412, 427, 440, 485, 590
Philips, John (1676–1709) 682
Phillips, John (1631–1706?) 11, 15, 16–17, 24, 28, 385
Picard, Jeremie 425–6
Piscator, Johannes 430, 622, 625–6, 629
Placentinus, Julius Casserius 655–6, 659, 661, 665
Plague, Great 6, 28, 45, 343, 577, 620
Plato, Platonism 84, 87, 115, 118, 122, 165, 168, 192,
    235, 387, 554, 655, 662
Plautus 292, 299–302
Pluvinel, Antoine de 388–90, 399–402
Pocock, J. G. A. 173
Polybius 167
polygamy 203, 434
Poole, Matthew 628
Poole, William 246, 544
Pope, Alexander 442, 457, 527, 677
Popple, William 578
Powell, Mary, see Milton, Mary, wife
Powell, Vavasour 538
Pratt, Mary Louise 685
Presbyterians, Presbyterianism 32, 33, 37, 38, 41,
    42, 143–4, 156–7, 167, 172, 175–85, 201–17, 243–
    4, 249, 260–9, 276, 309–10, 317–18, 321–4, 327–
    8, 357, 507, 524, 551, 555
Prince, F. T. 137, 141
Privy Council 20, 220, 306
Propertius 445
prophecy 86–7, 132, 319–20, 537–40, 543, 546,
    691–2, 700, 703–4
Protectorate, see Cromwell, Oliver
Prynne, William 18, 90, 96, 204, 209, 216–17, 258,
    309–10, 328, 335–6, 426
Purchas, Samuel 376, 681
Putney debates 248

Quakers 329, 523, 539–40, 582, 589
Quint, David 452, 506–7, 649, 671
Quintilian 56, 141–2, 292
Quistorp, Johann 626, 631

Radzinowicz, Mary Ann 649–50
Rahe, Paul 548
Rainsborough, Colonel Thomas 248
Rainsford, Francis 581
Rajan, Balachandra 328
Raleigh, Sir Walter 306, 376, 552
Ramus, Petrus 128, 430
Raymond, Joad 207
reason of state 552–3, 563
Reid, David 451
Renan, Ernst 347
republic, republicanism 157–8, 166–8, 173, 247,
    250–1, 256, 266, 272–90, 305–24, 353–5,
    359–60, 410–11, 423, 434, 451, 547–68, 572–5,
    585–6, 704
Revard, Stella 119
Richardson, Jonathan 36, 440, 445, 455–7, 459,
    462, 678, 685
Richardson, Richard 674
Richelieu, Cardinal 390–1, 401
Rickman, T. C. 682
Ricks, Christoper 447–8, 455, 498, 504–5
Ripa, Cesare 651
Robinson, Henry 220–1
Robinson, Luke 41
Rome, Roman, neo-Roman 41, 56, 163, 167,
    169, 171, 202, 225–6, 272–3, 282–3, 287, 294–
    304, 306, 316, 319, 324, 345, 348, 353, 416–23,
    442, 449, 496–7, 551, 558, 575, 586, 618, 672,
    678, 684
Rose, Mary Beth 654
Rospigliosi, Cardinal Guilio 23
Ross, Alexander 374
Rousseau, Jean-Jacques 694
Royston, Richard 211
Rozanov, Vasily 703
Rudd, Niall 147–52
Rudierde, Edmund 119
Rutherford, Samuel 181, 263, 619

St Paul's Cathedral 66
Sadler, John 41, 635–6
Sage, Lorna 704
Sallust 575
Salmasius, Claudius 42, 273–8, 291–304, 331, 344,
    356–7
Salzilli, Giovanni 23
Sanders, Julie 297
Sandys, Edward 166
Sarpi, Paolo 166, 172, 376
Scattergood, Anthony 628
Schiller, Friedrich 440
Scholderer, V. 150–1
Schultz, Howard 141
Schwartz, Regina 592
Scipio Africanus 169

Scotland, the Scots 38, 141–2, 175–6, 205, 261–9, 285–6, 317, 359, 551
Scott, Jonathan 168, 310
Scott, Thomas 636
sects, sectarianism 143–4, 183–4, 201, 204, 211–17, 429
Secundus, Johannes 126
Selden, John 335, 355, 374, 376
Sellin, Paul 627
Seneca 256–7, 635
Servetus, Michael 433
Seward, Anna 683–4
Shakespeare, William 8, 13, 80, 90, 98, 117, 127, 139, 149, 252–71, 452, 461, 463–4, 466–7, 469–73, 482–3, 495, 678
    As You Like It 99, 252
    Julius Caesar 255, 270
    King Lear 701
    Macbeth 259–67
    Measure for Measure 464
    The Merchant of Venice 99
    A Midsummer Night's Dream 78, 252, 459
    Richard III 253, 270–1
    The Tempest 99, 259, 267–70, 464
    Twelfth Night 252, 255, 464
Shawcross, John T. 59, 485, 701
Sheldon, Gilbert 580
Shelley, Mary 693–700
Shelley, Percy Bysshe 51–2, 57, 463, 691–3, 697–704
Shirley, James 92–3, 95–6, 255
Shore, Daniel 247
Shuger, Deborah 171
Sidney, Algernon 410–12, 427
Sidney, Sir Philip 260, 270
Sikes, George 550–1
Simmons, Samuel 485, 489, 494
Sirluck, Edward 179, 234, 355, 357, 403
Skinner, Cyriack 29, 290
Skinner, Daniel 369, 426–7, 434
Skinner, Quentin 423
slavery 225–6, 254 258–60, 314, 407–23, 555–9, 565, 575–6
Smart, J. S. 141–2, 147
'Smectymnuus' 156, 160–1, 207, 329
Smith, Nigel 256
Smith, Sir Thomas 158
Sobieski, General John 362
Socinianism 170, 172, 512–13, 595, 597, 599–603, 607, 609–10; *see also* antitrinitarianism
Sophocles 303, 652
South, Robert 329–30
Southey, Robert 681
Speed, John 156, 372, 374, 376
Speght, Rachel 536–40, 546
Spelman, Henry 328, 335
Spencer, Alice 13, 15, 99–100

Spenser, Edmund; Spenserian 70, 77, 90, 98, 105, 116, 131–5, 161, 224, 259, 268–9, 346, 376, 441, 448–9, 453, 485, 606, 660, 662, 664
Stapylton, Robert 117
Star Chamber 38, 202, 210, 220
Starkey, John 583
Stationers' Company 34, 39, 184, 202, 210–12, 230–1
Statius 40, 454
Strange, Lord 13
Steele, Richard 680, 684
Stevens, Paul 671
Stevens, Wallace 36
Stewart, Adam 263
Stoicism, Stoics 170, 224, 304, 522, 656–9
Stow, John 156, 374, 376
Strafford, Earl of, *see* Wentworth, Thomas
Stubbe, Henry 337
Stubbes, Philip 113
Suckling, Sir John 13
Sumner, Charles 691
Svendsen, Kester 138
Swetnam, Joseph 535–6
Sylvester, Joshua 512

Tacitus 422–3, 552, 575
Tanselle, G. Thomas 487, 489
Tasso, Torquato 131, 137, 152, 441, 448–50, 452, 454, 459
Tate, Nahum 672
Temple, Sir Peter 13
Terence 292, 295–9, 679
Tertullian 642–3, 646
Teskey, Gordon 689
Theocritus 126
Theophrastus 292
Thirty Years War 38
Thomason, Catherine 146, 355
Thomason, George 202, 205, 355
Thorndike, Herbert 630–1
Thucydides 554
Thurloe, John 426
Thyer, Robert 674
Tillyard, E. M. W. 139
Titian 297
Togashi, Go 242, 244
Toland, John 547–8, 559, 567
toleration 183–4, 201, 203, 308, 319, 325–41, 425, 577, 580
Tomkins, Thomas 338, 584
Tonson, Jacob 443–4, 673, 677–8
Townshend, Aurelian 93–5, 106, 111
translation 51–65
Trapnel, Anna 535, 537–8, 540–1, 543
Treaty of Dover 407, 579–80
Treip, Mindele 483
Trevor-Roper, Hugh 408
Tweedie, Fiona 435

Unitarianism, *see* antitrinitarianism
Urban VIII, Pope 23
Ussher, Bishop James 32, 169

Vane, Sir Henry 43, 337, 550–2, 564, 624
Vendler, Helen 75
Venice 237, 316, 319, 324
Verity, A. W. 478
Vermigli, Peter Martyr 617, 619, 622, 628, 631
Vida, Marco Girolamo 459
Vindiciae, contra tyrannos 619, 621–2, 625
Virgil, Virgilian 114–15, 125–35, 175, 192–3, 292, 345,
    348, 350, 440–5, 449–54, 482, 606, 670–8,
    681–2, 686
Viroli, Maurizio 166
Vittoria, Francisco de 555–6
Voltaire 444, 458

Wales 110
Walker, Clement 42, 242, 248
Walker, William 548
Wall, Moses 310, 334
Wallis, John 398
Walpole, Horace 683
Walsh, Marcus 444
Walwyn, William 204–5, 209, 211–17, 220–1, 233
Waring, Thomas 276
Warton, Thomas 133, 703
Weber, Max 654
Webber, Joan 531
Webber, Thomasine 21, 23–4
Wentworth, Thomas, Earl of Strafford 206
Wesley, John 673
Westminster Assembly 38–9, 175–85, 202–5, 263,
    328, 420, 428, 618, 620, 623, 626, 628, 635
Whitelocke, Bulstrode 95–6
Whittington, Charles 581
Wight, Sara 537

Wilkins, John 374
Wilkinson, Henry 182
Williams, Arnold 188
Williams, John, Bishop of Lincoln 18
Williams, Roger 204, 329, 331
Williamson, Sir Joseph 427, 434, 581
Wilson, Hugh 548
Wilson, Thomas 181
Windsor Castle 20, 252
Winstanley, Gerrard 524
Winthrop, John 551
Wither, George 115
Wittgenstein, Ludwig 505, 646
Wittreich, Joseph 121, 630, 634
Wolleb, Johannes 413, 427–8, 430, 432
Wollstonecraft, Mary 687–91, 693, 695–6
Wood, Anthony 674
Woodcock, Katherine, *see* Milton, Katherine
Woodhouse, A. S. P. 138–9, 146–7
Woodward, Hezekiah 212
Worsley, Benjamin 395
Wotton, Sir Henry 172
Worden, Blair 173, 624
Wordsworth, William 136, 441, 461, 675, 679, 686,
    688, 693, 695–6
Wotton, Sir Henry 22
Wren, Matthew 580
Wright, B. A. 483
Wright, George T. 464
Wright, Thomas 657
Wyclif, John 165

Xenophon 169

Yeats, W. B. 75
Young, Thomas 7–8, 9, 10, 31, 114, 156–7

Zwicker, Steven N. 255–6, 260, 271